PHARMACEUTICS

PHARMACEUTICS

Basic Principles and Application to Pharmacy Practice

SECOND EDITION

Edited by

ALEKHA K. DASH
Department of Pharmacy Sciences, School of Pharmacy and Health Professions, Creighton University, Omaha, NE, United States

SOMNATH SINGH
Department of Pharmacy Sciences, School of Pharmacy and Health Professions, Creighton University, Omaha, NE, United States

ACADEMIC PRESS

An imprint of Elsevier

ELSEVIER

Academic Press is an imprint of Elsevier
125 London Wall, London EC2Y 5AS, United Kingdom
525 B Street, Suite 1650, San Diego, CA 92101, United States
50 Hampshire Street, 5th Floor, Cambridge, MA 02139, United States
The Boulevard, Langford Lane, Kidlington, Oxford OX5 1GB, United Kingdom

Notices

Knowledge and best practice in this field are constantly changing. As new research and experience broaden our understanding, changes in research methods, professional practices, or medical treatment may become necessary.

Practitioners and researchers must always rely on their own experience and knowledge in evaluating and using any information, methods, compounds, or experiments described herein. In using such information or methods they should be mindful of their own safety and the safety of others, including parties for whom they have a professional responsibility.

To the fullest extent of the law, neither the Publisher nor the authors, contributors, or editors, assume any liability for any injury and/or damage to persons or property as a matter of products liability, negligence or otherwise, or from any use or operation of any methods, products, instructions, or ideas contained in the material herein.

ISBN: 978-0-323-99796-6

For information on all Academic Press publications visit our website at https://www.elsevier.com/books-and-journals

Publisher: Andre G. Wolff
Editorial Project Manager: Zsereena Rose Mampusti
Production Project Manager: Kumar Anbazhagan
Cover Designer: Matthew Limbert

Typeset by TNQ Technologies

Working together
to grow libraries in
developing countries

www.elsevier.com • www.bookaid.org

Contents

I
Physical principles and properties applicable to pharmaceutics

1. Introduction: Terminology, Basic Mathematical Skills, and Calculations
EMAN ATEF AND SOMNATH SINGH

2. Physical States and Thermodynamic Principles in Pharmaceutics
VIVEK S. DAVE, SEON HEPBURN, AND STEPHEN W. HOAG

3. Physical Properties, Their Determination, and Importance in Pharmaceutics
SOMNATH SINGH AND ALEKHA K. DASH

4. Equilibrium Processes in Pharmaceutics
SUNIL S. JAMBHEKAR

5. Complexation and Protein Binding
SOMNATH SINGH AND E. JEFFREY NORTH

II
Practical aspects of pharmaceutics

Companion Website:

https://www.elsevier.com/books-and-journals/book-companion/9780323997966

Instructor site:

https://educate.elsevier.com/9780323997966

Contributors

Satish Agrawal Department of Pharmacy Sciences, Creighton University, Omaha, NE, United States

Eman Atef School of Pharmacy, West Coast University, Los Angeles, CA, United States

Harsh Chauhan Shattuck Labs, Durham, NC, United States

Alekha K. Dash Department of Pharmacy Sciences, School of Pharmacy and Health Professions, Creighton University, Omaha, NE, United States

Vivek S. Dave Wegmans School of Pharmacy, St. John Fisher University, Rochester, NY, United States

Megan Derba Lafayette Family Cancer Institute, Northern Light Health, Brewer, ME, United States

Hari R. Desu Department of Pharmaceutical Sciences, University of Tennessee Health Science Center, Memphis, TN, United States

Ramprakash Govindarajan University of Iowa Pharmaceuticals, College of Pharmacy, University of Iowa, Iowa City, IA, United States

Chong-Hui Gu Foghorn Therapeutics, Cambridge, MA, United States

Mandana Hasanzad Medical Genomics Research Center, Tehran Medical Sciences, Islamic Azad University, Tehran, Iran; Personalized Medicine Research Center, Endocrinology and Metabolism Clinical Sciences Institute, Tehran University of Medical Sciences, Tehran, Iran

Mohsen A. Hedaya Department of Pharmaceutics, Faculty of Pharmacy, Kuwait University, Safat, Kuwait

Seon Hepburn School of Pharmacy, University of Maryland, Baltimore, MD, United States

Stephen W. Hoag School of Pharmacy, University of Maryland, Baltimore, MD, United States

Sunil S. Jambhekar LECOM, School of Pharmacy, Bradenton, FL, United States

Anuj Kuldipkumar Syner-G BioPharm Group, Southborough, MA, United States

Virender Kumar Department of Pharmaceutical Sciences, University of Nebraska Medical Center, Omaha, NE, United States

Maria P. Lambros Department of Pharmaceutical Sciences, College of Pharmacy, Western University of Health Sciences, Pomona, CA, United States

Ram I. Mahato Department of Pharmaceutical Sciences, University of Nebraska Medical Center, Omaha, NE, United States

Babu Medi Drug Product Development, Interius BioTherapeutics Inc., Philadelphia, PA, United States

Sarat K. Mohapatra Department of Pharmacy Sciences, School of Pharmacy and Health Professions, Creighton University, Omaha, NE, United States

Ajit S. Narang Department of Pharmaceutical Sciences, ORIC Pharmaceuticals, Inc., South San Francisco, CA, United States

E. Jeffrey North Department of Pharmacy Sciences, School of Pharmacy and Health Professions, Creighton University, Omaha, NE, United States

Behnaz Sarrami Missouri Pharmacogenomics Consulting LLC, Chesterfield, MO, United States

Surabhi Shukla Department of Pharmacy Sciences, School of Pharmacy and Health Professions, Creighton University, Omaha, NE, United States

Somnath Singh Department of Pharmacy Sciences, School of Pharmacy and Health Professions, Creighton University, Omaha, NE, United States

Laura A. Thoma Department of Pharmaceutical Sciences, University of Tennessee Health Science Center, Memphis, TN, United States

Justin A. Tolman Department of Pharmacy Sciences, School of Pharmacy and Health Professions, Creighton University, Omaha, NE, United States

Preface for the second edition

After the tremendous success of the first edition of the textbook entitled *Pharmaceutics: Basic Principles and Application to Pharmacy Practice*, we are delighted to bring forth its much improved and updated second edition. The basic paradigm of the first edition—a single pharmaceutic textbook meeting the requirement of pharmacy students for fundamental physicochemical principles of drug actions, dosage form design, and biological applications with examples of clinical cases pertaining to pharmacy practice—has been kept intact. However, the rapid progresses in pharmaceutical sciences in general and specific emergence of interesting novel therapies since the publication of the first edition warranted our work on the second edition to keep our students updated with these interesting developments.

We have meticulously read each and every word of the textbook for typos, grammatical errors, and better conceptual clarity. Moreover, we have also added the following three new chapters in response to reviewers' feedback on improving the first edition:

Chapter 5: Complexation and Protein Binding
Chapter 14: Emerging Therapeutics and Delivery
Chapter 15: Quality Assurances of Dosage Forms

Students would appreciate the latest therapeutic developments (e.g., siRNA and mRNA-based therapies, immunotherapy, cell and gene therapies, and stem cell therapy) and future revolution in practice of pharmacy due to emergence of "Pharmacogenomics and Personalized Medicine" which are covered in Chapter 14. Pharmacists have an important role in educating patients on proper use of medications for maximizing therapeutic outcomes and minimizing their adverse effects. Plasma protein-drug binding, as well as drug-drug interactions due to concurrent drug administration, may change therapeutic outcomes which are exemplified under clinical cases in Chapter 5. Finally, a drug product must be safe, reliable, and effective. Importance of these quality assurance aspects of dosage forms are covered in Chapter 15.

We have added many more cases in each chapter and many review practice questions and fun videos in online students' resources. We have also provided the original figures, tables, and equations in online instructors' resources to facilitate easy adoption of this textbook. We hope this second edition will fulfill core pharmaceutics requirement of the pharmacy curriculum for students as well as instructors.

Alekha K. Dash
Somnath Singh

Acknowledgments

We are thankful to our teachers whose wisdom and guidance have shaped our ability to publish this textbook. Our students have continuously challenged and inspired us to work on this second edition of the textbook which is a major update of the first edition. We acknowledge our spouses and children for their love and support throughout this endeavor. Finally, we would also like to acknowledge following individuals who have contributed to this book or supplemental materials: Dawn Trojanowski, Pankaj Rajdeo, and Neha S. Panchabhai.

PART I

Physical principles and properties applicable to pharmaceutics

1

Introduction: Terminology, Basic Mathematical Skills, and Calculations

Eman Atef[1] and Somnath Singh[2]

[1]School of Pharmacy, West Coast University, Los Angeles, CA, United States [2]Department of Pharmacy Sciences, School of Pharmacy and Health Professions, Creighton University, Omaha, NE, United States

CHAPTER OBJECTIVES
- Review the basic mathematics applicable in pharmacy.
- Apply the concept of significant figures in pharmacy.
- Apply basic calculus, logarithms, and antilogarithms to solve pharmaceutical problems.
- Apply basic statistics (mean, mode, median, and standard deviation) to interpret pharmaceutical data.
- Interpret a graph and straight-line trend of data to derive useful information.
- Review frequently used units and dimensions in pharmacy.

1.1 Introduction

How much drug should be prescribed to a newborn baby compared to an adult? How do different pathological conditions affect the prescribed dose? How is the drug's therapeutic dose determined? How long is a drug stable and can be used without compromising its therapeutic efficacy? Why do some drugs expire within 1 month, whereas others expire after a couple of years? How to interpret data reported in the pharmaceutical literature to derive some useful and clinically significant information about the therapeutic outcomes of a drug that can be used to counsel a patient and answer some of the pertinent questions a pharmacist encounters daily? How many digits to keep after the decimal point in the final answer obtained after a mathematical operation involving experimental/measured values? To answer such questions and more, the pharmacist must have adequate mathematical and statistical skills. Therefore, this chapter provides a basic introduction to pharmaceutical calculations, units, and basic statistics terms.

1.2 Review of basic mathematical skills

1.2.1 Integers

The numbers 0, 1, 2, 3, −1, −2, −3, and so on are called integers or whole numbers, which can be either positive or negative and can be arranged in ascending order, as shown in Fig. 1.1, where they increase as one move from left to right on the line. Therefore, a negative integer such as −3 is smaller than −2.

1.2.2 Zero and infinity

The mathematical operations involving zero and infinity do not work in the usual way, which sometimes is the reason for errors in pharmaceutical calculations. The following examples and key concepts illustrate the special rules governing the role of zero and infinity in mathematical operations.

- Any number multiplied by zero equals zero, for example, $12 \times 0 = 0$. This result is unusual because generally multiplication of any number x by y results in a number that is different from either x or y, except when y is equal to 1, which results in no change in x. Otherwise, x increases if y is a positive integer (i.e., a whole number) greater than 1 and decreases if y is a fraction or an integer lower than 1. In the following examples, x is always 12:

  $12 \times 1 = 12$ (i.e., no change in the value of x if $y = 1$).
  $12 \times 3 = 36$ (i.e., the value of x increases from 12 to 36 if $y = 3$).
  $12 \times (-3) = -36$ (i.e., the value of x decreases from 12 to −36 if $y = -3$).

  $12 \times \left(-\frac{1}{3} \right) = -4$ (i.e., the value of x decreases from 12 to −4 if $y = -\frac{1}{3}$ which is a negative fraction).

  $12 \times \frac{1}{3} = 4$ (i.e., the value of x decreases from 12 to 4 if $y = \frac{1}{3}$ which is a positive fraction).

- Any number multiplied by infinity (∞) equals infinity, for example, $12 \times \infty = \infty$. This is also unusual following the discussion provided for "multiplication by zero."
- Any number divided by zero is mathematically undefined, for example, $\frac{12}{0} =$ undefined. This result is unusual because generally division of any number x by y results in a number z, which provides x when multiplied by y. For example, dividing 12 by 4 results in 3, which is correct because 3 multiplied by 4 provides the original number 12. However, 12 divided by 0 cannot result in a specific number that can provide 12 when multiplied by 0. Therefore, the outcome of 12 divided by 0 is undefined.

- Any number divided by infinity is mathematically undefined, for example, $\frac{12}{\infty} =$ undefined. This result is also unusual following the discussion provided for "division by zero" because any number multiplied by ∞ would result in ∞; it cannot ever provide the original number, 12.

1.2.3 Rule of indices

A number with a power or exponent such as 12^7 is called an index, where 12 is called the base and 7 is the exponent. Mathematical problems involving indices with a common base are solved easily by applying the following rules.

- Exponents are added when multiplying indices having a common base, for example,

$$12^7 \times 12^5 = 12^{(7+5)} = 12^{12}$$

$$12^7 \times 12^5 \times 12^{-3} = 12^{(7+5-3)} = 12^9$$

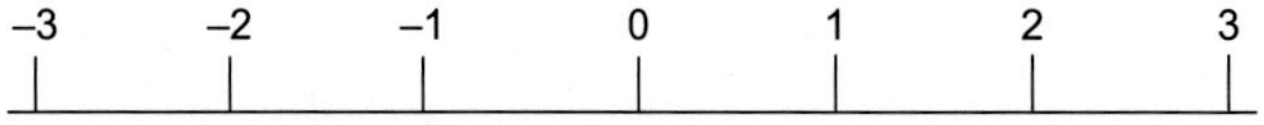

FIGURE 1.1   Ascending order of integers from left to right.

- The exponent of the divisor is subtracted from the exponent of the dividend when dividing one index by another, for example,

$$12^5 \div 12^3 = 12^{(5-3)} = 12^2$$

$$12^3 \div 12^5 = 12^{(3-5)} = 12^{-2}$$

$$(12^9 \times 12^3) \div (12^4 \times 12^2) = 12^{((9+3)-(4+2))} = 12^6$$

- Multiple exponents of a base are multiplied, for example,

$$\left(12^5\right)^3 = 12^{(5 \times 3)} = 12^{15}$$

$$\left(12^{-5}\right)^3 = 12^{(-5 \times 3)} = 12^{-15}$$

$$\sqrt{12^6} = 12^{6 \times \frac{1}{2}} = 12^3$$

$$\sqrt[3]{12^6} = 12^{6 \times \frac{1}{3}} = 12^2$$

- An index having a negative exponent is equal to its inverse with a positive exponent, for example,

$$12^{-3} = \frac{1}{12^3}$$

$$\left(\frac{5}{12}\right)^{-3} = \left(\frac{12}{5}\right)^3 = \left(\frac{12 \times 12 \times 12}{5 \times 5 \times 5}\right) = \frac{1728}{125} = 13.82$$

- An index having a fraction as its exponent is equal to its root with a power equal to the denominator of the fraction followed by an exponent equal to the numerator of the fraction, for example,

$$(64)^{\frac{2}{6}} = \left(\sqrt[6]{64}\right)^2 = \left(\sqrt[6]{2 \times 2 \times 2 \times 2 \times 2 \times 2}\right)^2 = (2)^2 = 4$$

- Any index having zero as an exponent is equal to 1, for example,

$$12^0 = 1$$

$$100^0 = 1$$

- All the rules governing mathematical operations involving indices can be summarized as shown here, assuming x as a base:

$$x^y \times x^z = x^{y+z}$$

$$\frac{x^y}{x^z} = x^{y-z}$$

$$\left(x^y\right)^z = x^{yz}$$

$$x^{-y} = \frac{1}{x^y}$$

$$x^{\frac{y}{z}} = \left(\sqrt[z]{x}\right)^y$$

$$x^0 = 1$$

1.2.4 Scientific or exponential notation

Pharmacists often encounter extremely large or small numbers, which creates a challenge when doing simple mathematical operations involving such numbers. For example, the normal range of testosterone levels in men (16–30 years old) is 72–148 pg/mL (i.e., 0.000,000,000,072–0.000,000,000,148 g/mL) [1], and the number of skin cells in human is 110,000,000,000 [2]. Therefore, scientific notation is used to handle such large or small numbers, using exponential notation or the power of 10. Thus, the testosterone level can be conveniently expressed as 7.2×10^{-11} to 1.48×10^{-10} g/mL. Similarly, the number of skin cells can be represented by 1.1×10^{11}. The number expressed by scientific notation is called the scientific number.

Generally, only one figure appears before the decimal point in the first part of scientific notation; it is called the coefficient. Numbers are expressed as 1–9.0×10^X. When multiplying or dividing two scientific numbers, the exponents are added or subtracted, respectively, as shown below:

Multiplication of scientific numbers:
$(1.1 \times 10^{-11}) \times (7.2 \times 10^{10}) = 7.92 \times 10^{-1}$; where the exponents, -11 and 10, have been added.
$(1.1 \times 10^{11}) \times (7.2 \times 10^{10}) = 7.92 \times 10^{21}$; where the exponents, 11 and 10, are added.

Division of scientific numbers:
$(1.1 \times 10^{11}) \div (7.2 \times 10^{-11}) = 0.15 \times 10^{22}$ or 1.5×10^{21}; where exponent -11 is subtracted from exponent 11.
$(1.1 \times 10^{11}) \div (7.2 \times 10^{7}) = 0.15 \times 10^{4}$ or 1.5×10^{3}; where exponent 7 is subtracted from exponent 11.

Addition or subtraction of scientific numbers can be easily carried out by following the two steps shown below:

Step 1: The exponent of each number must be the same as shown in the example below where (7.2×10^9) has been converted to (0.072×10^{11}).

Step 2: The coefficients are added or subtracted depending on the problem.

Addition of scientific numbers:
$(1.1 \times 10^{11}) + (7.2 \times 10^9) = (1.1 \times 10^{11}) + (0.072 \times 10^{11}) = (1.1 + .072) \times 10^{11}$ or 1.17×10^{11}; where the decimal point in coefficient 7.2 is moved left by two positions to make exponents in both the scientific numbers equal to 11.

Alternatively, 1.1×10^{11} can be converted to 110.0×10^9 to make the exponents in both the scientific numbers equal to 9 as shown below:

$$(1.1 \times 10^{11}) + (7.2 \times 10^9) = (110.0 \times 10^9) + (7.2 \times 10^9) = (110.0 + 7.2) \times 10^9 \text{ or } 117.2 \times 10^9 = 1.17 \times 10^{11}$$

Subtraction of scientific numbers:

$$(1.1 \times 10^{11}) - (7.2 \times 10^9) = (1.1 \times 10^{11}) - (0.072 \times 10^{11}) = (1.1 - 0.072) \times 10^{11} \text{ or } 1.028 \times 10^{11} = 1.03 \times 10^{11}$$

1.2.5 Logarithms and antilogarithms

Exponential data often are used in pharmacy calculations, for example, the acidity constant, Ka, of acetaminophen is 3.09×10^{-10} [3], which is used for developing its stable formulation. Performing mathematical calculations using such exponentials is not convenient. Furthermore, in many instances such as accelerated stability studies of drugs, it is difficult to find any correlation between exponential data. Another example is of data generated out of first-order rate kinetic studies. In such situations, using logarithms is helpful because it linearizes the data. Using logarithms makes calculations such as multiplication or division involving exponentials easy because it converts them into easy-to-handle simple addition or subtraction problems. A logarithm is the power to which a base must be raised to obtain a number. Therefore, there are two kinds of logarithms on the basis of differences in the base: the *common logarithm* (log), where the base is 10, and *natural logarithm* (ln), where the base is e (where $e = 2.7182818 \ldots$). The following examples clarify this concept.

- **Using log10 ("log to the base 10"):** $\log_{10} 1000 = 3$ (i.e., log of 1000 to the base 10 is 3) is equivalent to $10^3 = 1000$ where 10 is the base, 3 is the logarithm (i.e., the exponent or power), and 1000 is the number.
- **Using natural log(log or ln):** $\ln 100 = 4.6052$ (i.e., log of 100 to the base e is 4.6052) is equivalent to $e^{4.6052} = 100$ or $2.7183^{4.6052} = 100$ where e or 2.7183 is the base, 4.6052 is the logarithm (i.e., the exponent or power), and 100 is the number.

If a drug degrades in proportion to its concnetration (c), it can be represented by a natural logarithmic equation. Many natural phenomena such as radioactivity decay, drug degradation, drug elimination, etc. are expressed by using mathematical equations involving natural log, for example, the equation representing the first-order rate kinetics as shown below.

The first-order reaction rate is represented by $\frac{dc}{dt} = -k_1 dt$, where, c, is the concentration of the reactant at any time, t, and k_1 is the proportionality constant. Integration of this equation between concentration C_0 at time, $t = 0$ and concentration, C_t at time, $t = t$ results in the following equation using natural log:

$$\ln C_t = \ln C_0 - k_1 t$$

Therefore, it is essential to know the interconversion from a common logarithm to a natural logarithm and vice versa, which can be derived as shown next.

Assume that the ratio of a natural and common log of the same number is x, that is,

$$\frac{\ln 10}{\log 10} = x$$

Since $\ln 10 = 2.303$ and $\log 10 = 1$, the ratio $x = 2.303$.
Therefore, for any number y,

$$\ln y = 2.303 \log y$$

Sometimes the log or ln of a number is available, but one needs to find the number itself, which can be done by finding the antilogarithm (antilog) of a logarithmic number. Therefore, the antilog is also called the inverse log. The following examples illustrate this concept:

$$\log x = 2; \quad x = \text{antilog } 2 = 100$$

because $10^2 = 100$

$$\log x = -2; \quad x = \text{antilog } (-2) = 0.01$$

because $10^{-2} = 0.01$
The natural log also works in the same way:

$$\ln x = 2.303; \quad x = \text{antiln } (2.303) = 10$$

Another example:
$\ln C_2 = \ln C_1 - Kt$ which can be converted into log by dividing with 2.303 as shown below:

$$(\ln C_2)/2.303 = (\ln C_1)/2.303 - (Kt/2.303)$$

$$\log C_2 = \log C_1 - Kt/2.303$$

The rules governing log calculation are shown in Table 1.1.

TABLE 1.1 Rules for logarithmic mathematical operations.

Common logarithm	Natural logarithm
$\log xy = \log x + \log y$	$\ln xy = \ln x + \ln y$
$\log \frac{x}{y} = \log x - \log y$	$\ln \frac{x}{y} = \ln x - \ln y$
$\log x^y = y \log x$	$\ln x^y = y \ln x$
$\log \sqrt[y]{x} = \log x^{\frac{1}{y}} = \frac{1}{y} \log x$	$\ln \sqrt[y]{x} = \ln x^{\frac{1}{y}} = \frac{1}{y} \ln x$

1.2.6 Accepted errors and significant figures

All numbers can be categorized as either exact or inexact numbers.

- **Exact numbers:** Any numbers that can be determined with complete certainty, for example, there are 110 students in a class, 12 eggs in one dozen eggs, 7 days in a week, 12 months in a year, etc. All these numbers can be figured out without any doubt.
- **Inexact numbers:** Numbers associated with any measurement are not exact because accuracy depends on the sensitivity of the instrument used in the said measurement. One can increase the precision of the measurement by carefully following the standard operating procedure or by selecting a more sensitive instrument.

Let us define and differentiate these two terms that are often interchanged mistakenly: accuracy and precision. *Accuracy* refers to how closely measured values agree with the correct value, whereas *precision* refers to how closely an individual measurement agrees with another. Precision is correlated to the reproducibility of a measurement and is indicated by the standard deviation of multiple repeated measurements. A higher standard deviation indicates a lower precision of measurements. Therefore, a measurement can be of high precision but low accuracy. For example, 100 g of a drug is weighed using a balance having $+10\%$ errors due to a manufacturing defect. Thus, one can weigh out 100 g multiple times with 99.99% precision (i.e., each 100 g weighed out does not differ from another by more than 0.01 g), but the weight accuracy is 90% due to the systematic error.

In another example, if an assay method reports 495 mg of ampicillin in a 500-mg capsule of ampicillin, the measurement accuracy is 99% $[(495/500) \times 100]$, that is, a 1% error. If the assay is repeated five times for the same sample of ampicillin capsule and each time the result is 495 mg of ampicillin, the precision of the experimental method is 100%. Thus, precision indicates the repeatability of an experimental result. The result may be precise but inaccurate if the same error or mistake is repeated during each experiment.

1.2.6.1 Measurement accuracy

All measurements have a degree of uncertainty because no device can provide perfect measurement with zero error. The error can be predicted from but not limited to the process used to prepare the dosage form, the sensitivity of the utilized balance or measuring devices, or the number of significant figures.

1.2.6.1.1 Based on the official compendia

The US Pharmacopeia [6] states that unless otherwise specified when a substance is weighed for an assay, the uncertainty should not exceed 0.1% of the reading. Furthermore, according to the USP, measurement uncertainty is satisfactory if two times the standard deviation of not less than 10 replicated weighs divided by the amount to be weighed does not exceed 0.001 (0.1%). Another commonly used parameter is the relative standard deviation (RSD), which equals (*standard deviation/Mean*) $\times$ 100.

For example, if a 0.1 g of active pharmaceutical ingredient (API) is weighed 10 times ($n = 10$) and the following was recorded:

0.1001 g, 0.1002 g, 0.0999 g, 0.1003 g, 0.1003 g, 0.1002 g, 0.1001 g, 0.1001 g, 0.1003 g, 0.1003 g

one can determine the average weight, standard deviation, and relative standard deviations for these measurements as follows:

Difference from the mean	Squared differences
(0.1001−0.10018)	$(-0.00008)^2$
(0.1002−0.10018)	$(0.00002)^2$
(0.0999−0.10018)	$(-0.00028)^2$
(0.1003−0.10018)	$(0.00012)^2$
(0.1003−0.10018)	$(0.00012)^2$
(0.1002−0.10018)	$(0.00002)^2$
(0.1001−0.10018)	$(-0.00008)^2$
(0.1001−0.10018)	$(-0.00008)^2$
(0.1003−0.10018)	$(0.00012)^2$
(0.1003−0.10018)	$(0.00012)^2$

Average weight(Mean weight)

$$= \frac{0.1001\ g + 0.1002\ g + 0.0999\ g + 0.1003\ g + 0.1003\ g + 0.1002\ g + 0.1001\ g + 0.1001\ g + 0.1003\ g}{10}$$

$$= \frac{1.0018\ g}{10} = 0.10018\ g$$

Standard deviation$(SD) = \sqrt{Variance} = \sqrt{(\textit{The average of the squared differences from the mean})}$

$$\text{Average of the squared differences} = \frac{[(-0.00008)^2 + \ldots + (-0.00012)^2]}{10} = 1.56 \times 10^{-8}$$

$$\text{The standard deviation (SD)} = \sqrt{1.56 \times 10^{-8}} = 0.000125$$

Relative standard deviation (RSD) $= \frac{SD}{Mean} \times 100 = \frac{0.000125}{0.10018} \times 100 = 0.125\%$

Since, 2×0.000125 (i.e., $2 \times$ SD) $= 0.00025$ and $0.00025/0.1 = 0.0025$. Since 0.0025 is not less than 0.001, the preceding measurement uncertainty is not acceptable according to the USP 43.

1.2.6.1.2 Compounding prescriptions and industrial manufacturing

Based on the USP, a maximum error of $\pm5\%$ is acceptable in compounding prescriptions [4] which is also referred to as tolerance. Unless otherwise indicated, especially relatively potent prescriptions may require higher accuracy. On the other hand, a maximum error of $\pm1\%$ is acceptable in pharmaceutical manufacturing measurements. Examples:

1. What is the accepted tolerance of 5.56 mL based on significant figures?

   Answer:
   Tolerance = Acceptable variation/target weight
   5% is an acceptable error or variation. 5% of 5.56 mL is 0.278 mL.
   Hence, tolerance = 0.278 mL/5.56 mL = 0.05 mL.
   Therefore, the accepted tolerance based on the significant figures = **5.56 ± 0.05 mL**

2. What is the accepted tolerance (of the active ingredient and the total weight of a tablet with 20 mg active ingredient and total weight of 100 mg tablet

   Answer: **20 ± 0.05 mg and 100 ± 0.05 mg**

3. What is the accepted tolerance of 3.3×10^2 mg?

   Answer: **$3.3 \pm 0.05 \times 10^2$ mg**

4. The volume of a sample of a liquid is stated to be 30 ± 0.5 mL. What are the accepted upper and lower values limits?
   (a) **29.5–30.5**
   (b) 29–30
   (c) 28–32
5. If a powder weight is recorded as 3.6 g, what is the accepted tolerance based on the significant figures?
   (a) 3.6 ± 0.005 g
   (b) **3.6 ± 0.05 g**
   (c) 3.6 ± 0.5 g
6. A tablet is required to contain 125–175 mg of active ingredient. Express this requirement in terms of a desired weight $\pm$ maximum error?
   (a) 50 ± 10 mg
   (b) 150 ± 5 mg
   (c) **150 ± 25 mg**

7. A compounding prescription requires 0.4 mL of acetone. What is the maximum permissible error in measuring this liquid?
   (a) 0.08 mL
   (b) 0.02 mL
   (c) 0.8 mL
   (d) 0.05 mL

Answer: 5% of 0.4 mL = 0.02 mL.

1.2.6.1.3 The sensitivity of the utilized balance

The sensitivity (i.e., the lowest weight detected) of a balance is a crucial parameter that enables the pharmacist to decide on right balance to use to fulfill the needed accuracy. The following examples illustrate this concept.

Using a balance with sensitivity = 0.1 g, a powder weight of 13.2 g could actually be 13.1, 13.2, or 13.3 g In other words, one may be uncertain about that last digit; it could be a 1, 2, or 3.

On the other hand, a measurement done to the closest hundredth of a gram indicates the following: 13.21 g can be 13.22 g, 13.21 g, or 13.20 g.

Thus, the former balance should be used if the accuracy of a tenth (i.e., 10%) of a gram is required. However, if a drug is highly potent and has a narrow therapeutic window, such as digoxin or warfarin, a higher order of accuracy could be needed. Therefore, a balance with a sensitivity of a thousandth (i.e., 0.1%) of a gram should be preferred to using a balance with sensitivity only up to a tenth or hundredth of a gram.

The sensitivity is also called the resolution, which depends on the types of balances, which include the following.

- Precision top pan balances have 0.001 g (1 mg) resolution.
- Analytical balances have 0.1 mg or 0.01 mg (10–100 µg) resolution.
- Semi-micro balances have 0.001 mg or 0.002 mg (1–2 µg) resolution.
- Micro-balances have at least 0.0001 mg (0.1 µg) resolution.

1.2.6.1.4 Significant figures

The number of significant figures is the number of figures that are known with some degree of accuracy. The number 13.2 is said to have three significant figures, while 13.20 has four significant figures.

Therefore, the number of significant figures in a measurement is the number of digits that are known with certainty, plus the last one that is not absolutely certain but rather an approximate (inexact) number. For example, 13.2 g has three significant figures: 0.2 is the last and thus an inexact number; it could be 0.249 or 0.15. Both are rounded to 0.2. For simplicity, one can indicate the tolerance as 13.2 ± 0.05. A mass of 13.20 g indicates an uncertainty of 0.00 g, so the expected weight would be any value in the range of $13.20 \text{ g} \pm 0.005 \text{ g}$. Thus, any measuring instrument such as a balance with greater sensitivity would provide a measured value having a greater number of significant figures. Table 1.2 summarizes the rules helpful in deciding the number of significant figures in a measured value.

The potential ambiguity in the last rule can be avoided through the use of standard exponential, or "scientific," notation. For example, depending on whether two or three significant figures are correct, one can write 120 g as follows:

1.2×10^2 g (two significant figures).
Or
12.0×10 g (three significant figures).

1.2.6.1.5 Determining significant figures in mathematical operations

1.2.6.1.5.1 Addition and subtraction   When measured quantities are used in addition or subtraction, the uncertainty is determined by the absolute uncertainty in the least precise measurement (not by the number of significant figures). Sometimes this is considered to be the number of digits after the decimal point.

Now consider these numbers:
78,956.23 m.
11.875 m.

Addition of the preceding two numbers provides 78,968.105 m, but the sum should be reported as 78,968.11 m because there are two digits after the decimal point in 78,956.23 m, which is less precise than 11.875 m.

1.2.6.1.5.2 Multiplication and division   When experimental quantities are multiplied or divided, the number of significant figures in the result is determined by the number of digits after the decimal point in the quantity with the

TABLE 1.2 Rules for determining number of significant figures.

Measured values	Number of significant figures	Rules
12.786 g	5	All nonzero digits are significant.
12.078 g	5	Zero is significant if flanked by nonzero digits.
0.02 g	1	Zero immediately after a decimal point but before a nonzero digit is not significant where it merely indicates its position.
0.20 g	2	Zero after a decimal point is significant if preceded by a nonzero digit.
120 g	2 or 3	Zero at the end of a number and not preceded by a decimal point is not necessarily significant. If sensitivity of the balance is 10 g, the number of significant figures would be two. Similarly, the number of significant figures would be three if sensitivity of the balance is 1 g.

least number of significant figures. If, for example, a density calculation is made in which 27.124 g is divided by 2.1 mL, the density should be reported as 13.6 g/mL, not as 13.562 g/mL because the number of digits after the decimal point in the quantity with the least number significant figures is one in 2.1 mL.

1.2.6.1.5.3 Logarithmic calculations   For any log, the number to the left of the decimal point is called the *characteristic*, and the number to the right of the decimal point is called the *mantissa*. In logarithmic calculations, the same number of significant figures is retained in the mantissa as there are in the original number, for example, a 10-digit calculator would show that log 579 = 2.762,678,564. As the original number (579) contains three significant figures, the result should be reported as 2.763; that is, the mantissa should contain three significant figures. Likewise, when one is taking antilogarithms, the resulting number should have as many significant figures as the mantissa in the logarithm (so the antilog of 1.579 = 37.9 not 37.931).

Caution: The concept of the significant figure should be applied with caution while dispensing a pharmaceutical prescription. The minimum weight or volume of each ingredient in a pharmaceutical formula or prescription should be large enough that the error introduced is not greater than 5% (5 in 100); that is, pharmaceutical calculations incorporating three digits after a decimal point are of acceptable precision [4]. While applying the concept of significant figures, one should know that some of the values could never be approximate because they are exact. The question of significant figures arises only when there is an approximation in a measurement. For example, if a pharmacist combines 5 unit dose packages of a liquid that are 4.5 mL each, the total volume obtained would be (5 × 4.5 = 22.5) 22.5 mL where 5 is an exact number and 4.5 mL is a measured value having one digit after the decimal point. Therefore, the result should be reported as 22.5 mL not 23 mL.

1.2.6.1.5.4 Rules for rounding off numbers   The rules for rounding off are based on whether the digit to be dropped is equal to or greater than 5, as well as the digits flanking that digit. The following examples illustrate rules for rounding off numbers up to the required significant figures such as two.

- The last digit to be retained is increased by one if the digit to be dropped is greater than 5; for example, 17.9 is rounded up to 18 because the digit to be dropped, 9, is greater than 5.
- The last digit to be retained is left unaltered if the digit to be dropped is less than 5; for example, 17.4 is rounded down to 17 because the digit to be dropped, 4, is less than 5.
- If five is the digit to be dropped but is followed by nonzero digit(s), the last remaining digit is increased by 1, for example, 17.512 is rounded up to 18 because digits 1 and 2 follow 5 and are not zero.

1.2.7 Significant difference

Conclusions can frequently be drawn about significant differences by looking at the standard deviation or standard error bars in case of clear overlapping. But sometimes the following points should be considered.

- Clinical significance versus statistical significance
- Comparison between treatments and treatments versus control

The effect of three antipyretic drugs in Fig. 1.2 is used to clarify the preceding two points. Compared to the control group, the three tested antipyretic drugs resulted in a statistically significant drop in the patients' temperature, $P < .05$. But Antipyretic 1, although statistically significant from the control, may be insignificant because a drop of less than 1.5°C is not enough to create a clinically important effect. Although Antipyretics 2 and 3 are not significantly different, they are both statistically different from the control group, that is, both are effective medications.

1.2.8 Samples and measure of centrality

Collecting, managing, and interpreting sample data are important responsibilities for pharmacists. Samples are generally small numbers of observations or data taken from a comparatively large population with clearly defined parameters [5]. For example, all the hypertensive patients having systolic blood pressure greater than 170 mmHg are a population, but 150 such patients selected for a clinical trial study of an antihypertensive drug constitute a sample. Such a study generates a large amount of data based on the experimental design of the study. One hundred fifty patients selected for the study may be divided into different groups administering different dosages of the hypertensive drug under study. One group may be administered placebo, whereas another group may get the hypertensive drug under current clinical practice. The blood pressure change could be different between different groups or within the same group. Thus, reporting the conclusion of the study requires a summary number(s) such as mean ± SD because the original raw data would not provide useful information about the population under investigation.

One of the most useful approaches is using some sort of summary number or numbers, which are good indicators of the centrality of sampling observations or data. The three measures of central tendency used are mean, median, and mode. Calculating the mean is discussed in Section 1.2.6.1.1. The following sections describe how to calculate the median and mode using the same example used for calculating the mean.

1.2.8.1 Calculating median

The median is the middle data of observations arranged in ascending or descending order. Thus, half of the data or observation would be greater than the median, but the other half would be less than it.

If the weights of 100 mg of active pharmaceutical ingredient (API) are taken 10 times ($n = 10$) and these weightings are:

0.1001 g, 0.1002 g, 0.0999 g, 0.1003 g, 0.1003 g, 0.1002 g, 0.1001 g, 0.1001 g, 0.1003 g, 0.1003 g

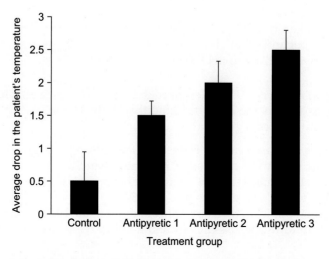

FIGURE 1.2   Average drop in the patients' body temperature following treatment with antipyretic.

one can arrange the preceding data in ascending order as follows:

0.0999 g, 0.1001 g, 0.1001 g, 0.1001 g, 0.1002 g, 0.1002 g, 0.1003 g, 0.1003 g, 0.1003 g, 0.1003 g

Therefore, the median is the mean of the fifth (i.e., 0.1002) and sixth (i.e., 0.1002) data, which is equal to 0.1002. Obviously, median is the mean of two middle data in case of an even number of observations or data, but in the case of an odd number of observations, it would be the middle datum.

It is evident that the median is not influenced by any extreme data because it would be the same in the preceding example whether the first datum is any number less than 0.0999 g or the 10th datum is greater than 0.1003. On contrast, the mean or average is significantly influenced by any extreme data.

1.2.8.2 Calculating mode

Mode is simply the data that occur most of the time and, therefore, generally is used for a large set of observations or data. In the preceding example, mode is equal to 0.1003. Sometimes, the frequency of two numbers could be equal in a data set, in which case the data are termed bimodal.

1.2.9 Dimensional analysis

Dimensional analysis is a mathematical method, also known as the unit factor method, that utilizes the units and ratios between them in calculating a desired quantity with the required unit.

To use the dimensional analysis method, one has to know the relations between different units, as in these examples: 1 kg = 2.2 lb, 1 ft = 12 inches, 1 g = 1000 mg, 1 day = 24 h.

Examples:

1. The recommended amoxicillin dose for severe infection is 25 mg/kg/day in divided doses every 12 h. How many milliliters of amoxicillin can be given to a 66 lb patient per 12 h, knowing that the oral suspension has 125 mg per 5 mL? To solve this problem using dimensional analysis, one should recognize the given parameters with the correct units and the unit required in the final answer. One needs the final answer unit to be in mL/12 h. And one has to utilize the given patient and drug information as well as knowledge of ratios between different units to solve this problem. The following relations are needed to solve the problem:1 kg = 2.2 lb; 1 day = 24 h.

$$\text{The number of mL per 12 h} = \frac{25 \text{ mg}}{\text{kg} \times \text{day}} \times \frac{1 \text{ kg}}{2.2 \text{ lb}} \times 66 \text{ lb} \times \frac{5 \text{ ml}}{125 \text{ mg}} \times \frac{1 \text{ day}}{2(12 \text{ h})} = \frac{15 \text{ mL}}{12 \text{ h}}$$

In the preceding formula, all the units that are undesired in the final answer will cancel each other, and end up with a final answer in the desired unit, that is, the number of milliliters every 12 h (The correct answer is 15 mL/12 h) It is worth mentioning that the use of dimensional analysis is not the only way to solve this problem. The problem can be solved using multiple sets of proportions and can be performed stepwise.

2. The digoxin dose of a premature baby is 20 µg/kg once a day. The available elixir is 0.05 mg/mL. How many mL should be given to a 5.5 lb baby per day? Remember that1 kg = 2.2 lb; 1 mg = 1000 µg.

$$\text{The \# of mL per day} = \frac{20 \text{ } \mu g}{\dfrac{\text{kg}}{\text{day}}} \times \frac{1 \text{ kg}}{2.2 \text{ lb}} \times 5.5 \text{ lb} \times \frac{1 \text{ mg}}{1000 \text{ } \mu g} \times \frac{1 \text{ mL}}{0.05 \text{ mg}} = 1 \text{ mL per day}$$

3. A drug provides 10,000 units/250 mg tablet. How many total units does the patient get by administering four tablets per day for 10 days? Key: The 250 mg is the total tablet weight. This is a distracting number and has nothing to do with the calculation. (The correct answer is 400,000 units/10 days.)

4. The recommended dose of a drug is 10 mg/kg/day (the drug is given every 6 h). How many mL/6 h should be prescribed to 60 lb child? The available suspension is 150 mg/tsp. The correct answer is 2.3 mL/6 h as shown below:

$$\text{The \# of mL / 6 h} = \frac{10 \text{ mg}}{\dfrac{\text{kg}}{\text{day}}} \times \frac{1 \text{ kg}}{2.2 \text{ lb}} \times 60 \text{ lb} \times \frac{5 \text{ mL}}{150 \text{ mg}} \times \frac{\text{day}}{4(6 \text{ h})} = \frac{2.3 \text{ mL}}{6 \text{ h}}$$

TABLE 1.3 Quadrants on a cartesian graph.

Quadrant II $(-x, +y)$	Quadrant I $(+x, +y)$
Quadrant III $(-x, -y)$	Quadrant IV $(+x, -y)$

1.3 Graphical representation

A graph is simply a visual representation showing the relationship between mostly two but could also be more variables. It shows how one variable (a dependent variable) changes with alteration in another variable (an independent variable). A graph consists of four quadrants in which the abscissa or ordinate is negative or positive, as shown in Table 1.3.

Looking at the theoretical and measured value changes with time in Table 1.4, one might find it difficult to observe the relationship between the two variables. However, when one looks at the graph in Fig. 1.3, the relationship becomes quite apparent. Thus, the graph is a better tool to present data in a clear, visual manner.

1.3.1 Interpreting graphs

When one attends a lecture, one's initial comprehension is high. However, as the lecture progresses, the comprehension typically decreases with time. This information may be presented graphically as a two-dimensional graph consisting of a dependent variable (comprehension) and an independent variable (time).

The magnitude of the independent variable is usually measured along the x-axis, or the horizontal scale. The dependent variable is measured along the y-axis or the vertical scale. The graph in this Fig. 1.4 enables one to see quickly that for the initial time of about 30 min, the comprehension is high at approximately 9.5, and it gradually falls to 2.0 after about 60 min, or 1 h. Graphs are useful in providing a visual representation of data.

TABLE 1.4 Theoretical and measured value changes with time.

Time (h)	Measured value	Theoretical value
0	−4.6	−5
1	−3.4	−3
2	−0.6	−1
3	0.8	1
4	3.4	3
5	4.4	5

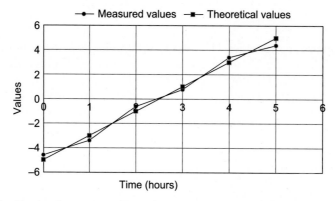

FIGURE 1.3 Graphical representation of the theoretical and measured values changes with time.

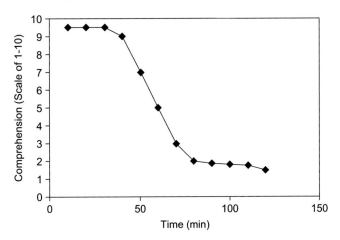

FIGURE 1.4   Graph representation of the comprehension of the students versus time.

1.3.2 Straight-line graphs (simple linear regression)

A graph is a straight line (linear) only if the equation from which it is derived has the following form:

$$y = mx + b$$

where y is the dependent variable, x is the independent variable, m is the slope of the straight line, and b is the y intercept (when $x = 0$).

Example:

The data in Table 1.5 represent the relationship between osmolality and molality of solution of nicotinamide.

1. Find the linear relationship between the molality and osmolality of nicotinamide solutions.
2. What is the predicted value of osmolality when the molality of the solution is 255 mmol/kg?
3. Calculate the correlation coefficient for the linear relationship that exists between the osmolality and molality of solutions of nicotinamide.

Answers:

1. Microsoft Excel was used to plot a graph, using the data in Table 1.5, as shown in Fig. 1.5. Using Excel functions, one can find out that the linear relationship between molality and osmolality can be described using the straight-line equation as $y = (0.9483x) + 0.8045$; that is, Osmolality $= (0.9483 \times \text{Molality}) + 0.8045$.

TABLE 1.5   Osmolality and molality of solution of nicotinamide.

Molality, mmol/kg	Osmolality, mOsmol/kg
25	23.9
50	48.2
75	71.9
100	93.2
125	122.5
150	143.7
175	168.1
200	191.2
225	215.2
250	231.1
275	262.9
300	286.9

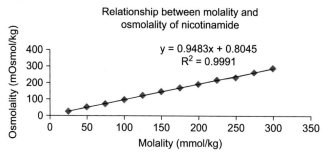

FIGURE 1.5   Graphical representation of the relationship between osmolality and the molality of solution of nicotinamide.

TABLE 1.6   General interpretation of the range of correlation coefficient.

Range of correlation coefficient	Interpretation
0.90–1.00	Very high positive correlation
0.70–0.90	High positive correlation
0.50–0.70	Moderate positive correlation
0.30–0.50	Low positive correlation
0.00–0.3	Negligible correlation

2. Substitute the molality term with 255 in the preceding equation: Osmolality = (0.9483 × 255) + 0.8045 = 242.6 mOsmol/kg.

3. The correlation coefficient, r, is the square root of R^2 shown in the plot of molality and osmolality in Fig. 1.5. So, correlation coefficient, $r = \sqrt{R^2} = \sqrt{0.99,951} = 0.9991$.

Note: The coefficient of correlation value, r, indicates the strength of the relationship between the x and y variables, which can range between −1 and +1. If the value of r is zero, this means there is no relationship between the two variables. If $r = -1$ or $+1$, there is perfect negative or positive linear correlation, respectively. In science generally, an acceptable value for r must be at least 0.70 or more. Values below 0.70 reflect weak correlation. However, a higher value such as 0.95 is considered of greater significance in clinical practice. The interpretation of various values of r is provided in Table 1.6 [7]:

The square of r is known as the coefficient of determination (represented by R^2 in Fig. 1.5), which tells how much of the variability in the dependent variable y is explained by x, the independent variable. An R^2 of 0.60 means that 60% of the variability in y is explained by x and 40% of the variability in y could be due to other factors.

1.4 Dimensions and units

To define the properties of matter—amount, composition, position in space and time, and more—one needs quantitative tools called *dimensions* and *units*. Dimensions are physical quantities that can be measured whereas units are terms used for a particular dimension to make a measurement in comparison to a standard. For example, length is a dimension that can be measured by a unit meter in comparison to a standard length assigned to it.

Why do one need to study dimensions and units? The pharmacist, being the drug expert on the healthcare team, is responsible for formulating, dispensing, and evaluating drugs and dosage forms for optimal therapeutic efficacy. A few examples in which this knowledge will help practicing pharmacists include (1) effectively formulating tablets, capsules, powders, solutions, ointments, or other dosage forms to meet therapeutic objectives; (2) performing dosage adjustments for patients based on the patients' weight, age, or body surface area; (3) determining the amount of active ingredient in a dosage form; and (4) determining the rate of infusion of a parenteral dosage form.

TABLE 1.7 Common multiples and their prefixes and symbols.

Multiple	Prefix	Symbol
10^{12}	Tera	T
10^9	Giga	G
10^6	Mega	M
10^3	Kilo	K
10^{-2}	Centi	c
10^{-3}	Milli	m
10^{-6}	Micro	μ
10^{-9}	Nano	n
10^{-12}	Pico	p

1.4.1 The three fundamental dimensions

The properties of matter are usually expressed through the use of three fundamental dimensions: length, mass, and time. Each of these properties is assigned a definite unit and a reference standard. In the metric system, these units are assigned the centimeter (cm), the gram (g), and the second (sec); accordingly, it is called the cgs system.

The International Union of Pure and Applied Chemistry (IUPAC) introduced System International, or SI, unit system to establish an internationally uniform set of units. Although physical pharmacy uses cgs units for most calculations, SI units are appearing with increasing frequency in textbooks.

1.4.2 Units based on length

Length and area: The SI unit for length is the meter. Other commonly used prefixes are listed in Table 1.7. In addition to the units here, many textbooks prefer using angstrom units (Å, equal to 10^{-10} m or 10^{-8} cm) to express microscopic distances. The prefixes shown in the table may also be used to represent other dimensions such as mass and time. For example, 10^{-9} s is termed as a nanosecond.

The units of area are cm^2 or m^2 in cgs or SI systems, respectively. Therefore, area is represented as the square of length.

Volume: Volume is also derived from units based on length, and uses unit in cm^3, also represented as cubic centimeter or cc (or m^3 in the SI system). Volume is also frequently defined in terms of the liter, with 1 L or 1 L being equal to 1000.027 cm^3. The frequently used unit for volume in physical pharmacy is the milliliter, or mL, which is roughly equal to 1 cm^3.

1.4.3 Units based on mass

Mass and weight: The SI unit of mass is the kilogram, or the kg. The cgs unit of mass is the gram, which is 1/1,000 of the kilogram. Mass is often expressed as the "weight" of a substance, which is actually a force, and is discussed under "Derived Dimensions" in Section 1.4.4.

Example:

The concentration of a drug in a patient's blood sample was reported to be 15 μg/mL. Total volume of the blood in the same patient was 5 L. Answer the following questions based on the information provided in this case study.

1. Identify the amount, volume, and concentration terms from this example.
2. What is the total amount of drug in the patient's blood?
3. Is there any relationship among concentration, volume, and amount? If so, identify it.

Answers:

1. In this example, 15 μg is an amount term, 1 mL and 5 L are volume terms, and 15 μg/mL is a concentration unit.
2. Total amount of drug in the blood = Concentration × Total Blood Volume: = 15 μg/mL × 5,000 mL = 75,000 μg = 75 mg
3. Yes, a relationship exists: Amount = Concentration × Volume.

1.4.4 Derived dimensions

Four derived dimensions are usually discussed in pharmacy calculations. They include (1) density and specific gravity; (2) force; (3) pressure; and (4) work, energy, and heat.

1.4.4.1 Density and specific gravity

The pharmacist uses the quantities density and specific gravity for interconversions between mass and volume. Density is a derived quantity and combines the units of mass and volume:

$$Density = mass/volume$$

The units of a derived quantity can be obtained by substituting the units for the individual fundamental units. This process is called dimensional analysis. For example, the units of mass and volume in the cgs system are g and cm^3. So, the units of density in the cgs system are g/cm^3.

The specific gravity of a substance is the ratio of its density to that of water, at a constant temperature. Note that, being a ratio of two similar quantities, the specific gravity is not described by a unit:

$$Specific\ gravity = density\ of\ a\ substance/density\ of\ water$$

For the same reason, any quantity expressed as a ratio is always dimensionless.

The density of the drug, excipients, and dosage form are important for the following reasons.

1. During manufacturing, mixing solids with similar densities ensures complete mixing and minimizes the solid segregation (i.e., demixing).
2. Knowing the density of a dosage form helps in predicting the final volume occupied by the prescription.
3. Knowing the density of a substance can allow the conversion of percentage (w/w) to % (w/v) and vice versa.

Example 1. Given that concentrated hydrochloric acid has 36% (w/w), (specific gravity 1.179), calculate its concentration in terms of percentage (w/v)?

Answer: Here, 36% (w/w) = 36 g in 100 g, based on the density the 100 g occupies:

$$\frac{100\ g}{1.179\ g/mL} = 84.8\ mL$$

To calculate the % (w/v), one sets a proportion:

$$\frac{36\ g}{84.8\ mL} = \frac{x\ g}{100\ mL}$$

Therefore, x = 42.5 i.e. 36% (w/w) = 42.5% (w/v)

Example 2. Calculate the volume occupied by 21.2 g of a toothpaste of the density equal to 0.94 g/mL.

Answer:

$$\frac{21.2\ g}{0.94\ \frac{g}{mL}} = 22.55\ mL$$

Example 3. Rx.
  Miconazole 2% (w/w).
  Boric acid powder qs 50 g.
  Dispense powder, DTD 50 g.
  Calculate the volume occupied by the final preparation. (The density of the powder is 1.2 g/mL).

Answer: The final volume = 50 g × 1mL/1.2 g = 41.67 mL.

Example 4. A 30 g cream with a specific gravity of 1.4 would fit in an appropriate container size of

(a) 30 mL (1 fl oz)
(b) 15 mL (1/2 fl oz)
(c) 60 mL (2 fl oz)

Answer: The powder volume = 30 g × 1mL/1.4 g = 21.42 mL. The smallest size that can hold 21.42 mL among the three available sizes is (a) 30 mL.

Example 5. A 5% (w/w) cream with a specific gravity of 1.2, will have a concentration of …. …. … % (w/v).

Answer: 5% (w/w) = 5 g/100 g cream which specific gravity is 1.2. When converting to % (w/v), the 5 g in the numerator will not change but in the denominator 100 g has to be changed into mL, that is, 100 g = 100 g/ 1.2 = 83.33 mL.
  Therefore 5 g/83.33 mL = 6 g/100 mL, that is, **6% (w/v). Ans.**

Example 6. A 150 mL of 10% (w/v) lotion with a specific gravity of 1.2, will have a concentration of …. …. … % (w/w) and a total weight of … …g.

Answer: 10% (w/v) = 10 g/100 mL lotion which specific gravity is 1.2. When converting to % (w/w), the 10 g in the numerator will not change but in the denominator 100 mL has to be changed into g, that is, 100 mL = 100 mL × 1.2 = 120 g.
  Therefore 10 g/100 mL = 10 g/120 g, that is, 8.33 g/100 g, that is, **8.33% (w/w). Ans.**
  Total volume = 150 mL = 150 mL x 1.2 (specific gravity) = **180 g = Total weight Ans.**

1.4.4.2 Force

The force exerted on a body is equal to its mass multiplied by the acceleration achieved as a result of that force:

$$\text{Force} = \text{mass} \times \text{acceleration}$$

Now can one derive the units of force in the cgs system, given that the unit of acceleration is cm/s^2 in the cgs system? Also, can one derive the units in the SI system?
  The weight of a body is equal to the force exerted on that body due to gravity. The weight of a substance with a mass of 1 g is therefore equal to

$$\text{Weight} = 1 \text{ g} \times 981 \text{ cm/s}^2 = 981 \text{ g cm/s}^2, \text{ or } 981 \text{ dyne}$$

However, it is a common practice to express weight in the units of mass (g) for convenience.
  Similarly, the weight of a substance with a mass of 1 kg is therefore equal to
  Weight = 1 kg × 9.81 m/sec^2 = 9.81 kg m/sec^2, or 9.81 N (Newton)

1.4.4.3 Pressure

Pressure is the force applied per unit area and is expressed as dynes per cm^2. Its cgs units are

$$(g \text{ cm/s}^2)/cm^2 = g/(cm \text{ s}^2)$$

1.4.4.4 Work, energy, and heat

When one applies a force on a body and move it for a certain distance, one does work. Work is defined as force × distance, and its cgs units are dynes cm, or ergs. Another commonly used unit for work is joules (J), which is equal to 10^7 ergs, and is the SI unit of work. Energy is the capacity to do work and has the same unit as work.

Heat and work are equivalent forms of energy, and their units are interchangeable. The cgs unit of heat is the calorie and is equal to 4.184 J.

1.5 Conclusions

This chapter reviewed the basic mathematical concepts frequently used in the practice of pharmacy and introduced the basic concepts of graphical data representation, interpretation, and analysis for finding linear regression. Moreover, the system of units, their interconversion, and dimensional analysis are invaluable in pharmacy calculations. We hope that the concepts presented in this chapter will help students in interpreting literature data more efficiently and that they will find it a handy tool while doing calculations for dispensing prescriptions.

Case studies

Case 1.1

The USP monograph states, "Pravastatin sodium contains not less than 90.0 percent and not more than 110.0 percent of the labeled amount of pravastatin sodium ($C_{23}H_{35}NaO_7$)." The chemical analysis of a pravastatin sodium 80 mg tablet found it to contain 71.9 mg of the chemical. Does it comply with the USP standard?

Approach: No, it does not comply with the USP standard because 71.9 mg is 89.9% of the labeled amount. The USP standard is not less than 90.0%, which means 90.1% or 90.2% is an acceptable amount, but not 89.9%.

Case 1.2

A physician in a hospital wrote a prescription for 342.45 mg of theophylline in 250 mL of 5% dextrose solution. The pharmacy department of the hospital compounded an intravenous solution containing 340 mg of theophylline per 250 mL 5% dextrose solution. The prescribing physician thought that his prescription was not accurately dispensed and returned the compounded theophylline admixture. How would one resolve this situation?

Approach: The computer program used in the calculation of dose generates data consisting of three or more digits after the decimal point, which happened in this instance. If the pharmacy department dispensed 340 mg of the drug instead of 342.45 mg, that will be acceptable. The error introduced is well below the acceptable limit of 5%. The compounding pharmacist should resolve this issue by patiently and professionally explaining the concept of significant figures and the realistic precision expected during the measurement of ingredient(s) for intravenous fluids.

Case 1.3

A prescription with a dose of 2 mg/kg was written for a 66 lb patient. The pharmacy technician calculated the dose and forgot the right conversion (1 kg = 2.2 lb). Instead, the technician used a wrong conversion factor of 1 kg = 2 lb. As the pharmacist in charge, one is supposed to inform the technician regarding her mistake and find out whether the error is within the acceptable limit of ±5%.

Approach: One knows that 66 lb should be equal to (66 lb/2.2 lb/kg = 30 kg) 30 kg.

The actual dose = 30 × 2 = 60 kg × mg/kg = 60 mg.

The wrong dose calculated by the technician = 66/2.0 = 33 kg. The calculated dose = 33 × 2 = 66 mg.

% Error = (66 − 60)/60 × 100 = (6/60) × 100 = 10%

This error is higher than 5% of the allowed limit and is *not* an acceptable calculation.

Critical reflections and practice applications

Mastering calculation is a required skill for each student of pharmacy and pharmacist, with no regard to the field they specialize in. Moreover, it is a large component of the NAPLEX test questions.

The dose calculation errors are frequently life-threatening especially if they involve unit conversions. This chapter reviews the mathematical, statistical, and dimensional concepts used in the day-to-day practice of pharmacy. Pharmacists are expected to apply concepts from diverse scientific areas to interpret clinical data because the field of pharmacy is becoming more and more complex and challenging every day. Below are some critical points about their application in clinical pharmacy practices.

 i. Calculation of dose based on the patient's age, weight, and body surface area.
 ii. Calculation of the amount of drug and inactive ingredients needed in compounding prescription and calculation of accepted errors.
 iii. Conversion of quantities within and between measuring systems.
 iv. Calculations of infusion rate and final concertation of solutions after dilution and concentration.
 v. The straight-line equation can be used in calculating the unknown concentration of a drug sample as discussed in Chapter 3.
 vi. The concept of the logarithm is used in solving problems on drug kinetic and stability (Chapter 6).

References

[1] Normal hormone level, http://www.hgh-pro.com/hormones.htm [accessed on June 03, 2022].
[2] Amazing BioNumbers, http://bionumbers.hms.harvard.edu/search.aspx?task=searchbyamaz [accessed on June 03, 2022].
[3] J.K.H. Ma, B.W. Hadzija, Basic Physical Pharmacy, Jones and Bartlett Learning, Burlington, MA, USA, 2013.
[4] J.B. Sprowls, L.W. Dittert. Sprowls' American Pharmacy: An Introduction to Pharmaceutical Techniques and Dosage Forms, 7th ed., Lippincott, Philadelphia, 2008, p. 511.
[5] S. Bolton, Pharmaceutical statistics: practical and clinical applications. [5] S. Bolton, in: Pharmaceutical Statistics: Practical and Clinical Applications2nd, 1990Marcel Dekker, Inc., New York, 1990. Marcel Dekker, Inc., New York.
[6] United States Pharmacopenia 43 General Chapter 41: Weights and Balances. https://doi.org/10.31003/USPNF_M98780_04_01.
[7] M.M. Mukaka, Statistics corner: a guide to appropriate use of correlation coefficient in medical research, Malawi Med. J. 24 (3) (2012) 69–71.

2

Physical States and Thermodynamic Principles in Pharmaceutics

Vivek S. Dave[1], Seon Hepburn[2] and Stephen W. Hoag[2]

[1]Wegmans School of Pharmacy, St. John Fisher University, Rochester, NY, United States [2]School of Pharmacy, University of Maryland, Baltimore, MD, United States

CHAPTER OBJECTIVES

- Define atoms, molecules, elements, and compounds, and discuss their roles in the composition of matter.
- Explain the binding forces between molecules.
- Define gaseous state and describe the kinetic theory of gas.
- Analyze various gas laws and interpret the liquefaction of gases.
- Discuss supercritical fluids and apply it in explaining aerosols and the implantable infusion pump.
- Define the liquid state and explain vapor pressure and boiling point of a liquid.
- Apply the Clausius—Clapeyron equation, Raoult's law, and Henry's law for explaining the behavior and properties of a liquid state.
- Define solid state and discuss amorphous and crystalline solids.
- Interpret the significance of polymorphism, dissolution, wetting, and solid dispersion in pharmacy.
- Define the basic terminology used in thermodynamics.
- Discuss laws of thermodynamics and their application in explaining protein stability and spontaneity of the transport phenomenon.

Pharmaceutics, Second Edition
https://doi.org/10.1016/B978-0-323-99796-6.00009-6

Keywords: First law of thermodynamics and second law of thermodynamics; Gas; Liquid; Physical states of matter; Solid; Thermodynamics.

2.1 Introduction

This chapter is divided into two parts: the first part deals with the nature of matter, and the second part deals with the thermodynamics of pharmaceutical systems. The goal of this chapter is to introduce the scientific principles needed to understand how and why pharmaceutical dosage forms work and what kinds of problems a dispensing pharmacist can encounter when working with pharmaceutical products and how to solve these problems.

2.2 Composition of matter

Matter can be defined as anything that has a mass and a volume. The mass of matter is generally determined by its inertia or its resistance to change in acceleration when in motion or at rest. One common way of defining this is to consider the acceleration when an external force is applied to a mass. The acceleration of matter is described by Newton's second law of motion and expressed by

$$F = ma \tag{2.1}$$

Thus, a greater mass will have a slower acceleration for the same applied force. The volume of matter is determined by the space it occupies in three dimensions. Almost all matter is composed of atoms, also called atomic matter. There are forces between the atoms and molecules that make up matter, and the nature of these forces dictates some of the important properties of matter.

One of the most important concepts is to understand the state of matter and the properties associated with each state. When dispensing tablets or capsules, the things you have to worry about are very different from that when you are dispensing a solution, emulsion, or suspension. Because every prescription should have storage conditions listed on the packaging, this knowledge will affect how you label every prescription. For example, most people know that tablets and capsules should not be stored in the same bathroom where the patient likes to take hot and steamy showers, but how about cough syrup? The goal of the following sections is to provide the scientific principles necessary to answer these questions so that one can offer better patient counseling and advise to physicians. The key concepts one need to understand are the states of matter, the properties associated with each state, and where these properties come from.

2.3 Forces of attraction and repulsion

Molecules interact with each other via the forces of *attraction* and *repulsion*. Attractive forces are of two types: *cohesive* forces and *adhesive* forces. The forces of attraction between molecules of the same substance are known as *cohesive* forces. The forces of attraction between the molecules of different substances are known as *adhesive* forces. The forces that act on molecules to push them apart are known as *repulsive* forces.

Consider two atoms that start far apart and come together. As they approach each other, a combination of attractive and repulsive forces act on the two atoms. The attractive forces act to pull the molecules closer. Attractive forces (FA) are inversely proportional to the distance separating the molecules (r), as shown by the relationship

$$F_A \propto \frac{1}{r^n} \tag{2.2}$$

where n varies with the type of atoms/molecules [1]. For example, n typically equals ≈ 6, but for some gases, such as nitrogen, $n \approx 7$. These forces arise from the Van der Waals or dispersion forces, which are described later. Using Eq. (2.2), one can represent the force of attraction between atoms/molecules as a function of the distance between them using a potential energy diagram, as shown in Fig. 2.1. As the attractive forces increase, the potential energy becomes increasingly negative. From this curve, one can see several important characteristics. First, as the atoms or molecules

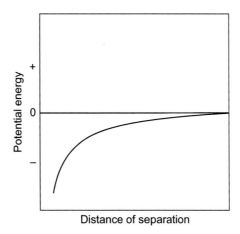

FIGURE 2.1   Potential energy diagram as a function of separation distance for attractive forces.

get close together, the attractive forces increase very rapidly; and second, the magnitude of the attractive forces act over a range of atomic distances, and it requires close proximity for the forces to affect molecular behavior.

If the overlap of the electron cloud is small, the long-range component of attractive forces is significant. Conversely, when the molecules come close enough that their electron clouds interact, the short-range component of the attractive forces dominates (see Fig. 2.2).

However, as you bring the atoms or molecules very close together, the electron clouds start to overlap, which leads to very strong repulsive forces. The repulsive forces (F_R) are proportional to an exponential relationship with the reciprocal of the distance separating the molecules (r) as follows:

$$F_R \propto e^{1/r} \tag{2.3}$$

For repulsive forces, an exponential function changes more rapidly on the potential energy diagram (see Fig. 2.3). As the repulsive forces increase, the potential energy becomes increasingly positive. Compared to repulsive forces, attractive forces act over a longer distance.

The total force on two atoms or molecules as a function of distance is given by the sum of the attractive and repulsive forces; this sum is given in Fig. 2.4. As two distant molecules approach each other, the energy changes are gradual and attractive to a point of minimum energy; this minimum in potential is the equilibrium or average bond length, which is the balance point between attractive and repulsive forces. After the minimum, as the molecules come closer together, the energy starts rising rapidly, and repulsive forces dominate. The distance where the attractive and repulsive forces balance each other is the *collision diameter*.

It is important to distinguish between *intramolecular* and *intermolecular* bonds. *Intramolecular* bonds are forces of attraction between the atoms that hold an individual molecule together (e.g., covalent or ionic bonds). *Intermolecular*

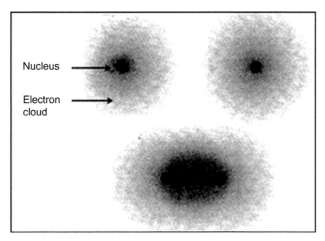

FIGURE 2.2   Overlapping electron clouds.

I. Physical principles and properties of pharmaceutics

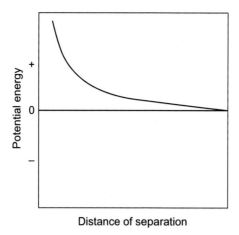

FIGURE 2.3   Potential energy diagram for repulsive forces.

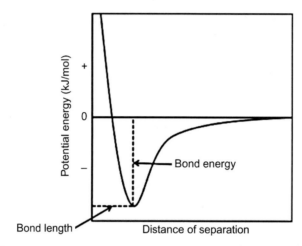

FIGURE 2.4   The total potential energy diagram of two atoms or molecules.

bonds are forces of attraction between a molecule and its neighboring molecule. All molecules exhibit intermolecular bonding to a certain degree. Most of these attractions are relatively weak in nature. The common types of intermolecular attractive forces can be divided into several classes. They include electrostatic forces, polarization forces, dispersion forces, and hydrogen bonding [2]. The sum of the electrostatic, polarization, and dispersion forces is often called the Van der Waals forces. Each of these classes is described in the following text.

Before discussing these forces, we need to introduce the concept of a dipole. A *dipole* is a charge separated over a range. For example, HCl has a permanent dipole:

$$\overset{\delta^+}{H} - \overset{\delta^-}{Cl}$$

Because H is much less electronegative than Cl, the electrons are predominantly around the Cl atom, which creates a permanent negative charge. Also, the H is electron deficient, so it has a permanent positive charge, which is separated by the bond length. Dipoles can be permanent or transient. The degree of charge separation can be quantified by calculating the dipole moment; interested readers can check out references [3,4].

2.3.1 Electrostatic forces

The class of electrostatic forces includes the interactions between charged atoms and molecules such as ion—ion, ion—permanent dipole, and permanent dipole—permanent dipole. These interaction forces can be intra- and intermolecular.

One example of electrostatic interactions is an *ionic bond*, which is a type of chemical bond formed through an electrostatic attraction between two oppositely charged ions. Ionic bonds are formed between a cation, which is usually a metal, and an anion, which is usually a nonmetal. The larger the difference in electronegativity between the two atoms involved in a bond, the more ionic (polar) the bond is. An ionic bond is formed when the atom of an element (metal), whose ionization energy is low, loses an electron(s) to become a cation, and the other atom (nonmetal), with a higher electron affinity, accepts the electron(s) and becomes an anion. An ionic bond is a relatively strong bond with a bond energy >5 kcal/mol, for example, sodium chloride.

Ion–dipole bonds are forces that originate from the electrostatic interactions between an ion and a neutral molecule containing a permanent dipole. These interactions commonly occur when solutions of ionic compounds are dissolved in polar liquids—for example, NaCl dissolving in water. The interactions occur when a positive ion attracts the partially negative end of a neutral polar molecule or vice versa. Ion–dipole attractions become stronger as either the charge on the ion increases or as the magnitude of the dipole of the polar molecule increases. Ion–dipole interactions are relatively strong and relatively insensitive to temperature and distance. When an organic base is added to an acidic medium, an ionic salt may be formed that, if dissociable, will have increased water solubility owing to ion–dipole bonding.

Dipole–dipole forces are the forces that originate from the interaction of permanent dipoles. For example, the interaction of a Cl atom with the H of an adjacent HCl molecule looks like this:

$$\overset{\delta^+}{H} — \overset{\delta^-}{Cl} \cdots\cdots \overset{\delta^+}{H} — \overset{\delta^-}{Cl}$$

These are also known as "Keesom" forces, named after Willem Hendrik Keesom. Of the Van der Waals forces, these are relatively strong forces with the energy of attraction $\sim 1–7$ kcal/mol.

2.3.2 Polarization and dispersion forces

The polarization class includes the interactions between dipoles induced in a molecule by an electric field from a nearby permanent dipole, ionized molecule, or ion. The dipole–induced dipole interaction, also known as "Debye Forces," is named after Peter J.W. Debye. Dispersion forces include the interactions between atoms and molecules, even if they are charge neutral and do not have permanent dipoles. Dispersion forces are electrodynamic in nature and occur when charge separation occurs in a molecule due to the random motion of electrons, and this transient charge induces a dipole in an adjacent molecule. These forces, called Van der Waals forces (dispersion forces), are also known as "London forces," named after a German–American physicist Fritz London, who came up with this theory.

Polarization forces originate as a result of temporary dipoles induced in a molecule by a permanent dipole in a neighboring polar or charged molecule. As a dipole approaches a molecule, the charge attracts the opposite charge and repels the same charge, which results in the polarization of the adjacent molecule, and this polarization leads to an electrostatic interaction between the two molecules:

These interactions are relatively weak with the energy of attraction $\sim 1–3$ kcal/mol.

Van der Waals forces originate from *temporary dipole fluctuations*, which affect electron distributions in adjacent molecules. The attraction between the molecules is electrical in nature. In an electrically symmetrical molecule like hydrogen, there does not seem to be any electrical distortion to produce positive or negative parts, but that is only true on average.

The preceding diagram represents a small symmetrical molecule of hydrogen (H_2). The even shading shows that, on average, there is no electrical distortion or polarization. But the electrons are mobile, and at any given moment, they might position themselves toward one end of the molecule, making that end $\delta-$. The other end will be temporarily devoid of electrons and become δ+. A moment later, the electrons may well move to the other end, reversing the polarity of the molecule, as illustrated here:

This constant motion of the electrons in the molecule results in rapidly fluctuating dipoles, even in the most symmetrical molecule. Imagine a molecule that has a temporary polarity being approached by a molecule that happens to be entirely nonpolar just at that moment:

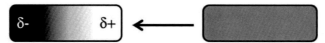

As the molecule on the right approaches, its electrons tend to be attracted by the slightly positive end of the molecule on the left. This sets up an induced dipole in the neighboring molecule, which is oriented in such a way that the δ+ end of one is attracted to the δ− end of the other:

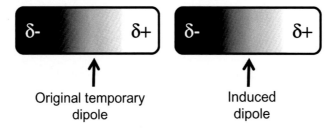

Original temporary   Induced
dipole   dipole

A moment later, the electrons in the left molecule may move up to the other end. In doing so, they repel the electrons in the molecule at the right:

For groups of molecules, these random fluctuations result in attractive forces that hold the molecules together:

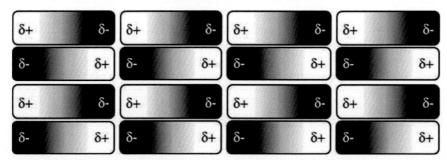

These forces between molecules are much weaker than the covalent bonds within molecules. It is difficult to give an exact value because the extent of the attraction varies considerably with the size of the molecule and its shape. Some of the main characteristics of these forces are as follows.

- Van der Waals forces are extremely weak; that is, the typical bond energies range from 0.5 to 1.0 kcal/mol for each atom involved.
- They are temperature dependent; that is, with increasing temperatures, the attractive forces diminish significantly.
- They occur at very short distances; that is, they require tight packing of molecules.
- Steric factors influence attraction; for example, branching in molecules significantly decreases attraction.
- These forces commonly occur in lipophilic materials and are relatively less significant in aqueous systems.

Despite being relatively weak in nature, Van der Waals forces may play an important role in pharmaceutical systems. An important implication of these forces is observed in the "flocculation" and "deflocculation" phenomena commonly observed in pharmaceutical suspensions [5]. The presence of Van der Waals forces between the suspended particles results in the formation of loose agglomerates, or "floccules," which rapidly settle down upon standing but are easily redispersible upon shaking. Conversely, if the repulsive forces predominate, the suspended particles do not flocculate but remain as discrete entities. These particles are slower to settle on standing; however, once settled, they form a relatively denser mass (a cake) in a process commonly known as "caking," which is difficult to redisperse.

2.3.3 Hydrogen bonds

Hydrogen bonds are stronger and an important form of dipole–dipole interactions. Hydrogen bonding originates when at least one dipole contains electropositive hydrogen. The bond exhibits an electrostatic attraction of a hydrogen atom for a strongly electronegative atom such as oxygen, nitrogen, or fluoride. Because hydrogen atoms are so small, they can get very close to the electronegative atom; and in strong hydrogen bonds, the hydrogen bond is partly covalent in nature, as the electron of the hydrogen atom is delocalized to the electronegative atom. Hydrogen bonds can be inter- or intramolecular in nature. A common example of intermolecular hydrogen bonding is that observed between water molecules, as discussed in the following paragraphs.

An example of intramolecular hydrogen bonding is a DNA molecule, where the nitrogen bases from the two strands are joined by intramolecular hydrogen bonds (see Fig. 2.5). The hydrogen bonding between nitrogen bases is critical to DNA structure and is important to DNA translation and replication.

For an example of intermolecular hydrogen bonding, consider two or more water molecules coming together:

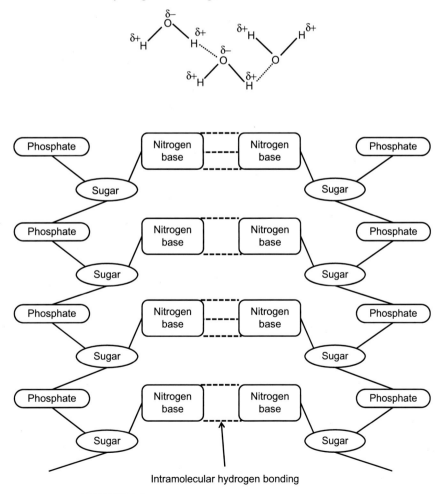

FIGURE 2.5   Hydrogen bonding between DNA standards.

The δ^+ hydrogen of one molecule is strongly attracted to the lone pair of electrons on the oxygen of other molecules. It is not a covalent bond, but the attraction is significantly stronger than a typical dipole–dipole interaction. Hydrogen bonds have about a 1/10th of the strength of an average covalent bond and are being constantly broken and reformed in water. The energy of hydrogen bonding is 1.0–10 kcal/mol for each interaction. Each water molecule can potentially form four hydrogen bonds with surrounding water molecules. This is why the boiling point of water is high for its molecular size.

2.4 States of matter

The three primary states or phases of matter are *gases*, *liquids*, and *solids* (see Fig. 2.6). In the solid state, molecules, atoms, and ions are held in close proximity by *intermolecular*, *interatomic*, and *ionic* forces. Atoms exhibit *restricted oscillations* in a fixed position within a solid. With an increase in temperature, the atoms acquire sufficient energy to overcome the forces that hold them in the solid lattice, which leads to the disruption of the ordered arrangement of the lattice as the system moves into a liquid state. This process is called *melting*, and the temperature of this transition is called the *melting point* of the substance. The further addition of energy to a liquid results in the transition into a *gaseous* state. This process is called *boiling*, and the temperature of this transition is called the *boiling point*.

Occasionally, some solids (particularly those with high vapor pressures, e.g., carbon dioxide) can pass directly from the solid to the gaseous state without melting. This process is called *sublimation*. The reverse process, that is, from gaseous to solid state, is called *deposition*. Note that a *phase* is defined as a homogeneous, physically distinct portion of a system that is separated from the other portions of the system by bounding surfaces. For example, ice in water is an example of two phases—a solid and a liquid. You can also have phases of the same state; for example, you can have an oil and water emulsion in which you have two phases—an oil phase and a water phase—both in the liquid state. These concepts are discussed in more detail later in Section 2.5 on thermodynamics.

Under certain conditions, substances can exhibit an in-between phase known as *mesophase* (Greek: *mesos* = middle), as shown in the phase diagram in Fig. 2.7. Commonly observed mesophase states include *liquid crystals* and *supercritical fluids*. *Liquid crystals* are a state of matter that has properties between those of a conventional liquid and those of a solid crystal. *Supercritical fluids* occur when a substance is at a temperature and pressure above its *critical point* or at the *triple point* because there are three phases in equilibrium at this point. When a material is in the supercritical fluid state, there is not a distinct liquid or gas phase, and the system has properties of both gas and liquid. One unique property of supercritical fluids is that gases like CO_2 can have properties similar to a solvent, and the solvent properties can be varied by changing the pressure and temperature. Because of this unique solvent property that can be varied, supercritical fluids have found significant importance in the pharmaceutical industry. For example, the selective extraction of pharmaceutical actives from biological sources is efficiently carried out using this approach.

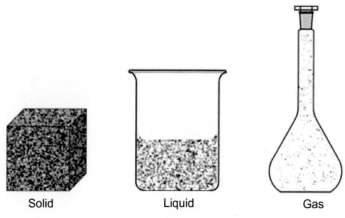

FIGURE 2.6   The different states of matter.

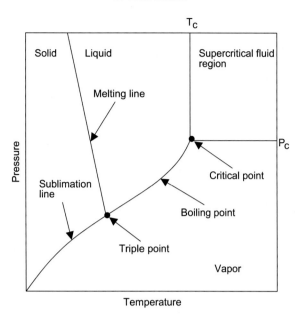

FIGURE 2.7 A typical phase diagram of a closed system in equilibrium.

2.4.1 Gaseous state

In the gaseous state, the attractive forces between the atoms or molecules are not sufficient to hold the molecules in close contact, and the molecules are free to randomly move about in three dimensions (see Fig. 2.6). Matter in a gaseous state has the following general properties.

- Molecules exhibiting rapid motion due to higher kinetic energy
- Molecules having weaker intermolecular forces
- Devoid of regular shape
- Capable of filling all the space in an enclosed system
- Compressible upon application of external pressure
- Mostly invisible to the human eye

The properties of matter in a gaseous state can be described by the ideal gas law. The *ideal gas law* describes the behavior of an ideal gas as a function of temperature, pressure, volume, and amount of gas. The ideal gas law is derived from a combination of gas laws formulated by Boyle, Charles, and Gay-Lussac. The main assumptions in the ideal gas law derivation are

- The gas molecules are hard spheres with no intermolecular interactions between the molecules.
- Collisions between the molecules are perfectly elastic; that is, there is no energy loss between the molecules of gas during collisions.

Boyle's law states that for 1 mole of an ideal gas at fixed temperature, the product of *pressure* (P) and *volume* (V) is a constant, which can be described by

$$PV = k \tag{2.4}$$

Gay-Lussac's and *Charles's laws* state that the volume and absolute *temperature* (T) of a given mass of gas at constant pressure are directly proportional, as given by the following relationship:

$$V \propto T \tag{2.5}$$

$$V = kT \tag{2.6}$$

Combining both laws gives

$$\frac{P_1 V_1}{T_1} = \frac{P_2 V_2}{T_2} \tag{2.7}$$

From the preceding equation, one can assume that PV/T is constant and can be mathematically expressed as

$$\frac{PV}{T} = R \ \ or \ \ PV = RT \tag{2.8}$$

where R is the constant value for an ideal gas. However, this equation assumes there is *only* 1 mole of gas. For n moles of an ideal gas, the equation becomes

$$PV = nRT \tag{2.9}$$

This equation is known as the *ideal gas law*. The constant R in the equation of state is also known as the *molar gas constant*; and for an ideal gas, its value is calculated to be 8.314 J/K mol, 0.08206 L atm/K mol, or 1.986 cal/K mol. As it relates the specific conditions or state (pressure, volume, and temperature of a given mass of gas), it is also called the *equation of state* of an ideal gas; see Section 2.5 on thermodynamics for more discussion about state equations. Because *real gases* do interact and exchange energy during collisions, they deviate from this law at higher pressures, that is, when the concentration of gas molecules becomes higher and the closer proximity of gas molecules increases the chances of molecules interaction increases.

The ideal gas law can be used to determine the molecular weight of a gas by expressing n in terms of mass and molecular weight (*MW*). Thus, when g/MW (gram/molecular weight) is substituted for n and the equation is rearranged, the molecular weight can be calculated as

$$M_w = \frac{g^{RT}}{PV} \tag{2.10}$$

The ideal gas law, just described, is a macroscopic law that only depends on macroscopic properties such as pressure, volume, and temperature. An alternative approach is to derive the macroscopic behavior of ideal gases from atomic/molecular properties. This theory is often called the *kinetic molecular theory*. The theory is based on postulates about the movement of atoms or molecules and uses statistical concepts to calculate the macroscopic behavior of gases and other materials. The important postulates of the theory include the following:

- A gas consists of a collection of particles that are in continuous, random motion, in straight lines, and following Newton's laws.
- In a confined space, the volume of gas molecules is negligible compared to the total volume of the space (this can happen only at low pressures and high temperatures).
- The particles of gas move with complete independence, without much interaction (only at low pressures).
- Collisions between molecules are perfectly elastic; that is, there is no exchange of energy during collisions.
- In addition to potential energy, particles have *kinetic energy*, which is responsible for their rapid, random motion.

The *kinetic molecular theory* states that the average kinetic energy of a mole of gas molecules is proportional to absolute temperature:

$$(1/2)M_wv^2 = (3/2)kT \tag{2.11}$$

where the proportionality constant k is called the Boltzmann constant and is calculated by dividing the gas constant (R) by Avogadro's constant (NA). The temperature T is the absolute temperature in K. Rearranging the equation to calculate the linear velocity (v) in m/s gives (Eq. 2.12)

$$v = \sqrt{(3RT/(M_wN_A))} \tag{2.12}$$

For a system of molecules, if you average all the individual molecular energies as given by Eq. (2.11), there is a distribution of energies. This distribution is called the Maxwell–Boltzmann distribution and is pictured in Fig. 2.8. This figure illustrates several important concepts that help you better understand pharmaceutical systems. In particular, there is a wide range of molecular energies with no molecules having zero energy, and there is no upper limit to the energy a molecule can have, but the Maxwell–Boltzmann distribution drops off exponentially as the energy increases, so there are very few molecules at the high end of the distribution. Also, as the temperature increases, the entire distribution shifts to a higher average energy level.

The Maxwell–Boltzmann distribution is at the heart of the Arrhenius equation and accelerated stability testing of active pharmaceutical ingredients (APIs) and drug products performed by virtually all pharmaceutical companies. These concepts are covered in more detail in Chapter 5. For example, when a chemical reaction occurs, that is, an API

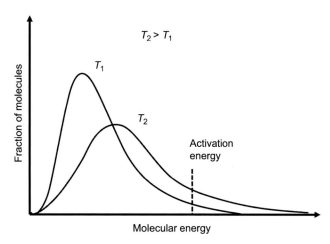

FIGURE 2.8 Maxwell–Boltzmann distribution of molecular energies.

breaks down, the molecules that are reacting must have enough energy to overcome the activation energy. As one can see in Fig. 2.8, as the temperature increases, more molecules have sufficient energy to react; thus, you can test drug products at higher temperatures and extrapolate the results to lower temperatures. Also, this helps to explain why some drugs, such as ampicillin suspensions, need to be stored in the refrigerator. At lower temperatures, far fewer molecules have enough energy to react, so the product will be more stable at cooler temperatures.

To this point, we have been describing a single pure gas, but these concepts can be extended to mixtures of gases. In a mixture of gases, each gas will contribute to the total pressure, and this individual contribution of a gas is called *partial pressure*. From these partial pressures, the total pressure can be calculated using *Dalton's law of partial pressures*, which was developed by John Dalton in 1801. Dalton's law states that "the total pressure exerted by the mixture of nonreactive gases is equal to the sum of the partial pressures of individual gases." The partial pressure is equal to the pressure a gas would exert if that gas alone occupied the whole volume of the mixture; in other words, the gases act independently of each other, and each gas contributes to the total pressure. The total pressure of a mixture of gases can be calculated by adding the partial pressures (Eq. 2.13):

$$P_{\text{total}} = P_1 + P_2 + \cdots + P_n \tag{2.13}$$

where $P_1, P_2, \cdots P_n$ are the partial pressures of each component, mathematically expressed as a summation as shown in Eq. (2.14):

$$P_{\text{total}} = \sum\nolimits_{i=l}^{n} Pi \tag{2.14}$$

2.4.1.1 Solubility of gases in liquids

Most gases are soluble in liquids to some degree. The term *solubility* is a technical term that describes how much one phase, such as a liquid, can hold of another material that is in equilibrium with a different phase. For example, to make children's cough syrup, you would dissolve a drug such as dextromethorphan into the syrup, and the solubility would be the maximum amount of dextromethorphan the liquid could hold when the dextromethorphan precipitated and formed a solid phase that was in equilibrium with the liquid. Gases also exhibit similar properties when in equilibrium with a liquid phase. The solubility of gases in a liquid can be expressed using *Henry's law* of gas solubility, formulated by William Henry in 1803. Henry's Law states that "at a constant temperature, the amount of a given gas that dissolves in a given type and volume of liquid is directly proportional to the partial pressure of that gas in equilibrium with that liquid." Henry's law can be mathematically expressed (at constant temperature) as shown in Eq. (2.15).

$$P_i = k_H C \tag{2.15}$$

where Pi is the partial pressure of the solute in the gas above the solution, C is the concentration of the solute, and k_H is a constant with the dimensions of pressure divided by concentration. The constant, known as Henry's law

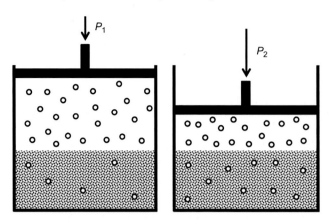

FIGURE 2.9   Illustration of Henry's law showing that as the pressure increases, the gas concentration in the liquid also increases.

constant, depends on the solute, the solvent, and the temperature. In other words, as you increase the pressure, the gas molecules move from the vapor phase into the liquid phase (see Fig. 2.9).

2.4.2 Liquid state

In the liquid state, the attractive forces between the atoms or molecules are strong enough to hold the modules in close contact, but not strong enough to hold them in a fixed position like in a solid. The molecules are free to randomly move about in three dimensions (see Fig. 2.6). Matter in a liquid state has the following general properties.

- Liquids, in general, have a defined albeit flexible volume; that is, liquids conveniently take the shape of the container in which they are held.
- Liquids differ from gases in having higher densities and viscosities and not being as compressible.
- Molecules in liquids also typically have lower kinetic energy compared to those in gases.
- Liquids respond to temperature changes and may transition to a different state, that is, solid or gas, depending on the magnitude and direction of such change.
- Liquids tend to flow readily in response to external forces, and the flow behavior is influenced by internal/external resistance, for example, friction and viscosity.

2.4.2.1 *Vapor pressure*

An important property of liquids is vapor pressure, and vapor pressure is a characteristic property of a material. *Vapor pressure* or *equilibrium vapor pressure* is defined as the pressure exerted by a vapor in equilibrium with a liquid at a given temperature in a closed system. Solids can also have vapor pressures, but they are much lower than liquids. The vapor pressure is the macroscopic expression of a molecule's tendency to escape from the liquid (or a solid), and this is related to the rate of evaporation of a liquid. Volatile substances are materials with a relatively higher vapor pressure at room temperature.

Because vapor pressure is a measure of a molecule's escaping tendency from a liquid or solid, it depends on temperature but does not depend on the amount of liquid, atmospheric pressure, or presence of other vapors. Molecules in the liquid state have a wide range of kinetic energies (see Fig. 2.8), and only the molecules with the highest energy will escape into the gaseous phase. Also, some of the molecules in the gaseous phase that collide with the liquid will remain in the liquid state; this process is called *condensation*. If a liquid is placed in a closed vacuum chamber at a constant temperature, initially, the liquid will rapidly evaporate. As the amount of vaporized liquid in the gaseous state increases, the rate of condensation will increase until the rate of condensation and vaporization are equal; that is, they are in a state of equilibrium. This equilibrium vapor pressure is known as the *saturation vapor pressure* above a liquid. The vapor pressure of a liquid is proportional to the temperature of the system, and one way it can be measured is with a mercury manometer. In this case, the units are mm Hg.

The relationship between vapor pressure and the absolute temperature of a liquid is expressed by the *Clausius–Clapeyron equation* (Eq. 2.16):

$$\ln\left(\frac{VP_2}{VP_1}\right) = \frac{\Delta H_v(T_2 - T_1)}{RT_1T_2} \qquad \text{or}$$

$$\log\left(\frac{VP_2}{VP_1}\right) = \frac{\Delta H_v(T_2 - T_1)}{2.303RT_1T_2} \tag{2.16}$$

where VP_1 and VP_2 are the equilibrium vapor pressures of a liquid at temperatures T_1 and T_2, respectively, and ΔHv is the heat of vaporization. The heat, or enthalpy, is discussed in more detail in Section 2.5 on thermodynamics. This equation can also be expressed as shown in Eq. (2.17).

$$VP_2 = VP_1 e^{\frac{\Delta H_v(T_2 - T_1)}{RT_1T_2}} \tag{2.17}$$

Fig. 2.10 shows the relationship between the vapor pressure of a liquid and its temperature for several different liquids. As you can see in Fig. 2.10 and Eq. (2.17), this relationship is exponential, and the vapor pressure increases much faster than the temperature. Note that in the equation and graphs, we assume that ΔHv is independent of temperature. The Clausius–Clapeyron equation is useful to scientists because you can calculate the enthalpy of vaporization from a plot of the log of VP versus T. (Recall that with logs if you get rid of the negative sign in Eq. (2.16), the T moves to the numerator). For example, if the vapor pressure of water at room temperature is ~20 mm Hg, when heated to 100°C the vapor pressure increases to 760 mm Hg and water vaporizes. The heat of vaporization (ΔHv) of water at 100 degrees is 9720 cal/mol. The Clausius–Clapeyron equation is also useful because it can help you to understand the behavior of liquids. For liquids with a positive enthalpy of vaporization (which is true for virtually all liquids), as the temperature increases, the vapor pressure will increase exponentially until the boiling point is reached.

The *boiling point* is the temperature at which the vapor pressure of a liquid equals the atmospheric pressure. At this point, the molecules in the liquid have enough energy to escape into the vapor phase, and because these molecules have the same pressure as the external vapor phase, when they escape, the gas bubbles that are formed

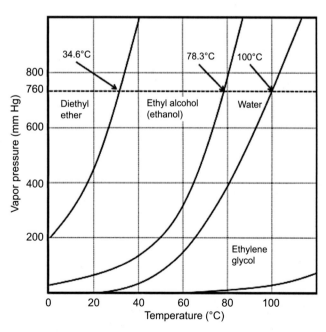

FIGURE 2.10 Interrelationship between the temperature and vapor pressure of common liquids.

do not collapse because they have the same pressure as the external pressure. From a molecular point of view, the gas molecules escape into the vapor phase because they have enough energy to overcome the attractive forces of the liquid. One consequence of this process is the lower the external pressure above a liquid, the lower the boiling point.

The vapor pressure of a system in equilibrium with a multicomponent solution is an important parameter that can be predicted from the composition of the liquid phase. The method for these calculations was developed in 1882 by François-Marie Raoult and is known as *Raoult's law,* which states that "at equilibrium, the vapor pressure of an ideal solution is dependent on the vapor pressure of each chemical component and the mole fraction of the component present in the solution." It can be mathematically expressed as (Eq. 2.18)

$$P = P_A^* x_A + P_B^* x_B + \cdots + P_i^* x_i \tag{2.18}$$

The individual vapor pressure of each component can be given as shown in Eq. (2.19)

$$P_i = P_i^* x_i \tag{2.19}$$

Where Pi is the partial pressure of the ith component, $P*_i$ is the vapor pressure of the pure component i, and x_i is the mole fraction of component i. This law assumes an ideal solution in which the intermolecular forces are the same for all molecules.

Vapor pressure is an important colligative property in pharmaceutical products. A classic example is that of nitroglycerine, which has a vapor pressure of $\sim 0.00,025$ mm at 20 degrees and ~ 0.30 mm at 93 degrees. Because of the high vapor pressure, nitroglycerine has a tendency to diffuse out of tablets and vaporize. This results in a significant loss of the drug and, consequently, the potency of the product. To lower the vapor pressure and volatility, nitroglycerin is commonly formulated along with macromolecules such as polyethylene glycol (PEG), polyvinylpyrrolidone (PVP), and microcrystalline cellulose (MCC); also, nitroglycerine tablets are stored in air-tight packaging. Because of the high volatility of nitroglycerine, it is important to counsel patients not to remove the tablets from the packaging until they actually use the tablets.

2.4.3 Phase equilibria and the phase rule

The three phases (solids, liquids, and gaseous) are generally considered individually. However, in most systems, the phases coexist, for example, a glass of ice water. The amount of each phase present depends on several variables such as temperature, pressure, type of system (e.g., enclosed), and composition. Changes in any of these variables may influence the equilibrium of all the phases. To understand and describe the state of each phase, and its relationship to the other phases, one can use the phase rule. The *phase rule* was developed by J. Willard Gibbs in 1870. The rule can be used to determine the least number of *intensive variables* (see the thermodynamic section for a definition) that can be changed without changing the equilibrium state of the system. This critical number of variables that can be varied is called the *degrees of freedom F*; the Gibbs phase rule is given by Eq. (2.20).

$$F = C - P + 2 \tag{2.20}$$

where C is the number of components and P is the number of phases. At first glance, this equation seems very odd, but a few examples should illustrate the equation and the insights it can give to pharmaceutical systems. For example, a system containing water and its vapor is a two-phase system. A mixture of ice, water, and water vapor is a three-phase system. The term *component* is defined as a distinct chemical substance in the system. For example, a mixture of ice, water, and water vapor is a one-component system, that is, H_2O. A mixture of ethanol and water is a two-component system.

To illustrate the phase rule, consider a closed gaseous system of pure water vapor. For this system, you can calculate the degrees of freedom, $F = 1-1+2 = 2$. This answer makes sense if one looks at the ideal gas law (Eq. 2.9); one can see that if any two variables T, P, or V are known, one can find the third variable and can completely describe the state of the system. Recall a closed system means that there is no mass exchange with the environment and n cannot change; however, according to the phase rule, no need to assume that n is constant, but then the argument becomes more complex and beyond the scope of this discussion. The 2 degrees of freedom means two variables are needed to describe this system; that is, one must fix two variables, such as T and P, to know the state of the system. Also, you know that two variables can change, and the equilibrium will be still of the same character as long as another phase does not form.

Another example would be ice and water in equilibrium. The degrees of freedom would be $F = 1-2+2 = 1$. When there are two phases present, you have a more constrained system, and you need only one variable, such as T or P, to be able to describe the state of the system. At the triple point of water (see Fig. 2.7), three phases are present, hence $F = 0$ (from Fig. 2.7). This makes sense because there is only one triple point for a substance; that is, at the triple point of a single component system, there is only one T and P where all phases can coexist in equilibrium.

An example of a two-component system is an ointment that can be applied to the skin. If a small amount of beta-methasone is incorporated into an ointment base such as petrolatum, initially there would be a single phase system, but as the amount of betamethasone increased, eventually its solubility would be reached, and it would precipitate in the petrolatum, forming two phases. The degrees of freedom would be as follows:

$$1 \text{ Phase: } F = 2 - 1 + 2 = 3$$

$$2 \text{ Phase: } F = 2 - 2 + 2 = 2$$

Thus, for the single-phase ointment, the system could be completely described by T, P, and composition; and for the two-phase ointment, you would need only two variables such as T and P. In a clinical setting, the patient's skin is a constant temperature, and the atmospheric pressure does not vary much. Therefore, in the single-phase ointment base, the betamethasone concentration could vary; whereas in the two-phase system, there are zero degrees of freedom, and the betamethasone concentration cannot vary as long as two phases are present. When it comes to diffusion, the release rate of a system with a fixed API concentration is very different from a system in which the API concentration can vary. See Chapter 5 for details.

2.4.4 Solid state

In a solid state, the attractive forces between atoms or molecules are sufficient to hold the molecules in close contact and often in a particular location within a crystal lattice (see Fig. 2.6). As a consequence of these interactions, matter in solid state has the following general properties.

- When a force is applied to a solid, it has a fixed shape; that is, it will not deform or flow without limit like a liquid or gas that can flow without limit.
- They are nearly incompressible.
- They have strong intermolecular forces and very little kinetic energy.
- Atoms in a solid vibrate about a fixed position and have very little translational motion.
- They are characterized by shape, size, and melting point, and a few have sublimation points.
- Pharmaceutically relevant characteristics include surface energy, hardness, elastic properties, and compactability.

Organic solids can be broadly classified by the system; see Fig. 2.11.

2.4.4.1 Crystalline solids

Crystalline solids are substances whose constituent atoms, molecules, or ions are arranged in an ordered three-dimensional pattern. A key aspect of the ordered structure of a crystalline solid is the *unit cell*, which is the basic repeating structure of the crystal. The unit cell is the smallest group of atoms that form the basic building blocks

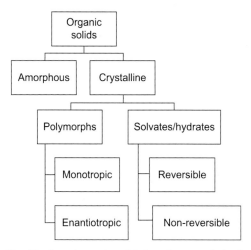

FIGURE 2.11   Classification of organic solids based on atomic/molecular morphology.

of the crystal, and this building block is repeated to build up the crystal into a macroscopic structure. The nature of the unit cell is very important because different unit cells have different properties, such as solubility, stability, and compressibility; these properties are very important for drug delivery and pharmaceutical manufacturing. In addition, macroscopic crystals can have different geometric shapes such as plates, needles, blades (like a sword blade), prisms, and blocks. These different external shapes are called the *crystal habit*.

The unit cells of a crystal can be composed of atoms (e.g., diamond, graphite), molecules (e.g., solid carbon dioxide), or ions (sodium chloride). An important property of crystalline solids is that they have fixed melting points. For organic compounds, the molecules are often held together by Van Der Waal's forces and hydrogen bonding. These compounds exhibit relatively weak binding and low melting points. Ionic and atomic crystals, in general, are hard and brittle and have higher melting points.

Based on the symmetry of the atomic, molecular, or ionic arrangements in the unit cell, these arrangements can be divided into seven major categories; see Fig. 2.12. The key differences between the different categories are whether the unit cell is cubic or rectangular and whether the angles are 90 degrees, acute, or obtuse (see Fig. 2.12). In addition, the unit cells can be primitive (do not contain any internal atoms); body centered (contain an internal atom/molecule in the middle of the cell); face centered (contain one atom/molecule in the middle of each face); or side centered, also called base centered, (contain one atom/molecule in the center of two opposite faces) (refer to Fig. 2.12).

Cubic (isometric) crystalline solids are those containing a unit cell in the shape of a cube. This is one of the most common and simplest shapes found in nature. The key dimensional characteristics are $a = b = c$ and $\alpha = \beta = \gamma = 90$ degrees. A common example of a cubic crystalline solid is sodium chloride (common table salt).

Trigonal (rhombohedral) crystals have the key dimensional characteristics $a = b = c$ and $\alpha = \beta \neq \gamma \neq 90$ degrees.

Tetragonal crystal systems can be thought of as cubic crystals stretched in one direction. The key characteristics are $a = b \neq c$ and $\alpha = \beta = \gamma = 90$ degrees. These tetragonal crystals can be either primitive or body centered. A common example of a tetragonal crystalline solid is urea.

Orthorhombic crystals do not have equal sides. The key dimensional characteristics are $a \neq b \neq c$ and $\alpha = \beta = \gamma = 90$ degrees. Orthorhombic crystals can be primitive, body centered, face centered, or side centered.

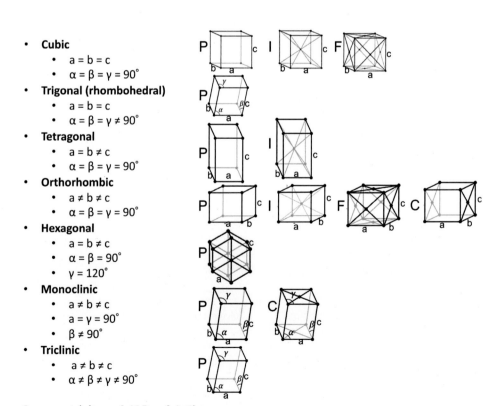

- **Cubic**
  - a = b = c
  - α = β = γ = 90°
- **Trigonal (rhombohedral)**
  - a = b = c
  - α = β = γ ≠ 90°
- **Tetragonal**
  - a = b ≠ c
  - α = β = γ = 90°
- **Orthorhombic**
  - a ≠ b ≠ c
  - α = β = γ = 90°
- **Hexagonal**
  - a = b ≠ c
  - α = β = 90°
  - γ = 120°
- **Monoclinic**
  - a ≠ b ≠ c
  - a = γ = 90°
  - β ≠ 90°
- **Triclinic**
  - a ≠ b ≠ c
  - α ≠ β ≠ γ ≠ 90°

Seven crystal classes → 14 Bravais Lattices
Four types of unit cells → P = Primitive, I = Body Centered, F = Face Centered, C = Side Centered

FIGURE 2.12   The possible unit cell arrangements.

Hexagonal crystals, as the name suggests, have a hexagonal crystal lattice, and their component atoms, ions, or molecules are arranged in the shape of a hexagon. Iodoform, a disinfectant, is an example of a solid that exists in hexagonal crystalline form.

Monoclinic crystals have the component atoms, molecules, or ions form a rectangular prism with a parallelogram as its base. The key dimensional characteristics are $a \neq b \neq c$ and $\alpha = \beta = 90$ degrees and $\gamma \neq 90$ degrees. They exist in two forms: primitive and base centered. Sucrose, a sugar, exists in monoclinic crystalline form.

Triclinic crystals are arranged so that the length and the angles formed in the lattice are unequal, and it comes only in the primitive form. The key dimensional characteristics are $a \neq b \neq c$ and $\alpha \neq \beta \neq \gamma \neq 90$ degrees. A common example of a solid existing as a triclinic crystal is boric acid.

2.4.4.2 Polymorphism and pseudopolymorphism

Polymorphism is the ability of a solid material to exist in more than one form or crystal structure; that is, one molecule can exist in two or more different unit cell types. Some elements may exist in more than one crystalline form, and these elements are said to be *allotropic*. For example, carbon exists in two allotropic forms: diamond and graphite. When polymorphism exists as a result of difference in crystal packing, it is called *packing polymorphism*. Polymorphism resulting from different conformers of the same molecule is called *conformational polymorphism*. Typical characteristics observed in different polymorphic forms of a compound include the following:

- Polymorphs have different thermodynamic stabilities and often different chemical stabilities.
- They can have different hygroscopicities, that is, different propensities to absorb moisture from the atmosphere, which can indirectly affect stability.
- They may spontaneously convert from a metastable form to a more stable form.
- They generally exhibit different melting points and different enthalpies of melting; see Section 2.5 on thermodynamics for a discussion of enthalpy.
- They exhibit different X-ray diffraction patterns.
- Although they are chemically identical, they may have significantly different solubilities.
- The crystals can have different mechanical properties, which can result in different manufacturing properties such as compactability when making tablets, different propensities for particle milling, and different propensities to stick to metal machine parts.

During API production, one of the main reasons that different polymorphic forms are created is changes in the conditions used during the crystallization process. The following factors are known to cause polymorphic changes during crystallization:

- Solvent types (the packing of crystal may be different in polar and nonpolar solvents)
- Some impurities that inhibit the growth of certain polymorphic forms, which can favor the growth of a metastable polymorph
- The rate of crystallization, which can be affected by the degree of supersaturation from which a material is crystallized (generally, the higher a concentration is above the solubility, the more likely it is to create a metastable polymorph)
- Temperature at which crystallization is carried out
- Change in stirring hydrodynamics

Polymorphs can be categorized into two types, monotropes and enantiotropes, depending on their stability over a range of temperatures and pressures below the melting point. Because most pharmaceutical systems are studied at atmospheric pressure, for this discussion, we will assume the pressure is constant. If one of the polymorphs is the most stable over a certain temperature range, while the other polymorph is the most stable over a different temperature range below the melting point, then the substance is said to be *enantiotropic*. On the other hand, if one polymorph form is always the most stable for all temperatures below the melting point, with all the other polymorphs being less stable, then this substance is said to be *monotropic*. Knowing if a substance is enantiotropic or monotropic is very important to drug companies; if manufacturers have to heat the material during tablet coating, for example, they want to make sure that it does not undergo a phase transformation that will result in a less stable polymorphic form at room temperature.

Regarding *pseudopolymorphs*, during the production of pharmaceutical ingredients, they are often crystallized out of different types of solvents. During this process, occasionally, solvent molecules are incorporated into the crystal lattice in a fixed stoichiometric ratio. This creates a *cocrystal*, which is termed a *solvate*, and when the solvent is water, this is termed a *hydrate*. For example, lamivudine methanol solvate (anti-HIV-1) is a solid compound containing

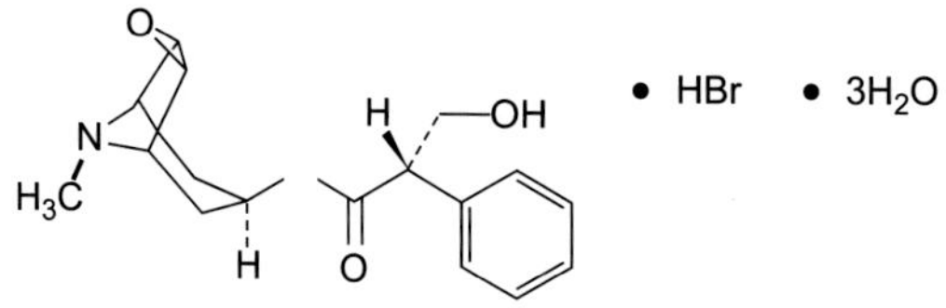

FIGURE 2.13 Structure of scopolamine HBr trihydrate.

methanol and water molecules combined in a definite ratio as an integral part of the crystal structure. However, because of concerns with toxicity of many organic solvents, generally solvates are not preferred. An example of a hydrate is scopolamine HBr trihydrate USP, which has one HBr and three molecules of water associated with each scopolamine molecule (see Fig. 2.13). All the previous discussion about polymorphs, such as different melting points, solubilities, and hygroscopicities, directly applies to solvates and hydrates, thus the term *pseudopolymorph*. When you are working with an API, it is very important to know if it will form a hydrate. For example, during the process of granulation used to make granules that can be compressed into tablets, you have to add water and then remove the water. If the API forms a hydrate during granulation or loses a hydrate during drying, the properties of the API can completely change, and this could affect the drug release rate via changes in solubility and stability. Plus, many other important properties of the API could change, which could lead to product failure.

2.4.4.3 Polymorphism in pharmaceutical drugs

Most commercially available drugs are developed in the crystalline form. However, many of the drug molecules can exist in different crystal polymorphic forms. Thus, the study of polymorphism and crystallization of pharmaceutical compounds is highly important. Nowadays, research on polymorphism (polymorph screening and characterization) and material properties of active drug compounds and excipients is an integral part of the preformulation phase of drug development. The knowledge of solid-state properties in an early stage of drug development helps avoid manufacturing problems and optimize a drug's clinical performance. Drugs that were previously known to exist only in a single form are now shown to have various polymorphic forms. This has prompted pharmaceutical companies to more extensively investigate crystal polymorphism to optimize the physical properties of a pharmaceutical solid early in drug development. Since most drugs can exist in more than one polymorphic or pseudopolymorphic form, the importance of polymorphism in the drug development paradigm is well known and well established. To illustrate this, some classic examples are discussed here.

Acetaminophen is a widely used antipyretic (fever suppressant) and analgesic (pain killer). This drug has been shown to exist in two polymorphic forms: monoclinic Form-I (P21/n), which is marketed, and orthorhombic Form-II (Pbca) [6]. Similarly, Famotidine, a histamine H_2 receptor antagonist, is also found to exist in two different polymorphic forms: metastable polymorph B and stable polymorph A [7–10]. Piroxicam, a nonsteroidal anti-inflammatory drug (NSAID), exists in three forms: I, II, and III [11,12].

Another important example is Ritonavir. It is a novel protease inhibitor for the human immunodeficiency virus (HIV). This drug was launched in 1996 and distributed for about 18 months without issues. Later batches of the drug revealed unacceptable dissolution profiles and precipitation issues. After detailed investigations, it was found that the problem was due to the conversion of the drug to a new thermodynamically more stable and less soluble polymorph Form-II. Surprisingly, multiple attempts to formulate Form-I thereafter turned out very difficult (perhaps the exact conditions could not be reproduced). The drug is now often quoted as a prime example in pharmaceutical industries to highlight the importance of polymorphism [13].

Norfloxacin is a synthetic broad-spectrum antibacterial drug for the treatment of prostate and urinary tract infections. This drug exists in two anhydrous polymorphs (A and B), an amorphous form, and several hydrate forms [14,15]. Of the two anhydrous polymorphs, Form B is the most stable at room temperature. However, the commercially used norfloxacin is Form A, which is metastable at room temperature.

As polymorphs exhibit different solubilities, for slightly soluble drugs, this may significantly influence the rate of dissolution. A classic example is that of chloramphenicol palmitate. Chloramphenicol exists as two major polymorphs (polymorph A and polymorph B) [16,17]. Fig. 2.14 shows a hypothetical plasma profile of polymorphs of chloramphenicol from oral solid formulations. As a result of polymorphism, one polymorph may show better therapeutic efficacy than another polymorph of the same drug.

All these examples clearly show the importance of selecting a desired polymorphic form of a drug early on to prevent any undesired effects in the later stages of development. Usually, the most thermodynamically stable

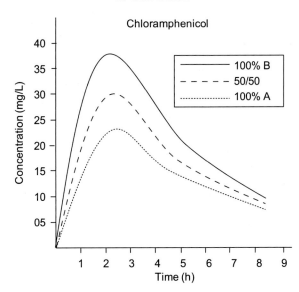

FIGURE 2.14 Hypothetical plasma profiles of polymorphs A and B of chloramphenicol from oral solid formulations. *Used with permission from Ref. [16].*

form of a drug is preferred in commercial formulations, as the metastable form may transform into other more stable forms. However, it is universally known that the metastable form has a higher solubility than the stable form and that the metastable form converts into the stable form, the rate of which depends on the activation energy required for the transition (see Fig. 2.8). Thus, whenever possible, metastable forms that have a higher solubility and can survive for years without changing to a more stable form are selected for formulation development. Such selection process requires careful evaluation of both thermodynamic parameters (tendency toward formation of stable polymorphs) and kinetic parameters (the rate of transformation) during product development.

2.4.4.4 Amorphous solids

Amorphous (Greek: *a* = without, *morphé* = shape) or noncrystalline solids are solids that lack the long-range order characteristic of a crystal; that is, they have no unit cells. They may also be considered to behave like supercooled liquids in which the molecules are arranged in a random manner as in the liquid state. They tend to flow over time, when subjected to sufficient pressure. They do not have definite melting points. Amorphous solids, as well as cubic crystals, are usually *isotropic*; that is, they exhibit similar properties in all directions. Crystalline solids other than cubic are *anisotropic*; that is, they have different properties (conductance, refractive index, etc.) in various directions along the crystal lattice. Visual differentiation between amorphous and crystalline solids is difficult. Some substances may be partially crystalline—for example, petrolatum and beeswax. The amorphous or crystalline characteristics of a solid pharmaceutical agent can influence therapeutic activity. For example, Novobiocin acid (antibiotic against *staphylococcus*) exists in both crystalline and amorphous forms. The crystalline form is poorly absorbed and exhibits no pharmacological activity, whereas the amorphous form is readily absorbed and therapeutically active.

Although amorphous solids do not have a long-range order, they are not completely random at the molecular level. At the molecular level, they may contain a short-range order and partial crystallinity. Due to their thermodynamic instability relative to crystalline solids, they may undergo partial or complete, spontaneous, or gradual conversion into a crystalline form and may even exhibit polymorphism. Many pharmaceutical materials, particularly pharmaceutical excipients, exist as multicomponent systems; that is, they contain a ratio of amorphous and crystalline forms.

Solid-state characterization of pharmaceutical materials is an important preformulation activity and is routinely carried out during the drug-development process. Common analytical techniques used for solid-state characterization of drugs and excipients are briefly summarized here.

- Powder X-ray diffractometry (PXRD) is the most widely used technique and is considered a "gold" standard for phase identification.
- Single crystal X-ray diffraction (XRD) is used to understand in-depth the structure of the crystal.

- Differential scanning calorimetry (DSC) is used to understand phase transitions and multicomponent interactions.
- Thermo gravimetric analysis (TGA) is used to analyze the stoichiometry of solvates/hydrates quantitatively.
- Infrared spectroscopy (IR) is used as a complementary tool for the identification of phases, including types of water in crystals.
- Near-infrared (NIR), Raman, and solid-state NMR are other techniques used to complement the characterization of pharmaceutical solids.

Using the preceding techniques, pharmaceutical solids undergoing the following phase transitions can be studied.

1. Polymorphic transitions—Interconversion between various polymorphic forms
2. Hydration/dehydration—Interconversion between hydrates and anhydrous forms of crystals
3. Vitrification and amorphous crystallization—Interconversion between the amorphous phase and crystalline polymorphs

2.4.5 The supercritical fluid state

A *supercritical fluid* is a mesophase formed from the gaseous state in which the gas is held under a combination of temperatures and pressures that exceed the critical point of a substance (see Fig. 2.15). A gas that is brought above its *critical temperature Tc* will still behave as a gas irrespective of the applied pressure. The *critical pressure Pc* is the minimum pressure required to liquefy a gas at a given temperature.

As the pressure is raised higher, the density of the gas can increase without a significant increase in the viscosity, and the ability of the supercritical fluid to dissolve compounds increases. Gases have little or no ability to dissolve a compound under ambient conditions, but in the supercritical range, they can completely dissolve the compound. For example, CO_2 held at the same temperature can dissolve different chemical classes from a natural product source when pressure is increased. The addition of a particular gas or a solvent can improve the solubilization process. Thus, supercritical fluids have found use in botanical extraction, crystallization, and the preparation of micro- and nanoparticle formulations. The following are some of the advantages of supercritical fluids for extraction over traditional methods:

- Supercritical fluids allow for lower-temperature extractions and purifications of compounds. This can significantly improve the stability profiles of compounds by preventing thermal degradation.
- Volatility under ambient conditions presents its own set of issues with the use of traditional solvents, for example, solvent leakage. Such issues are non-problematic with supercritical fluid extractions.

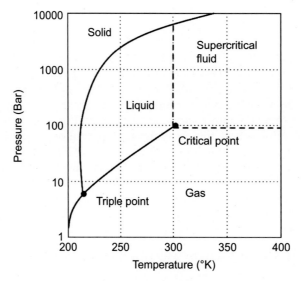

FIGURE 2.15   Carbon dioxide pressure-temperature phase diagram.

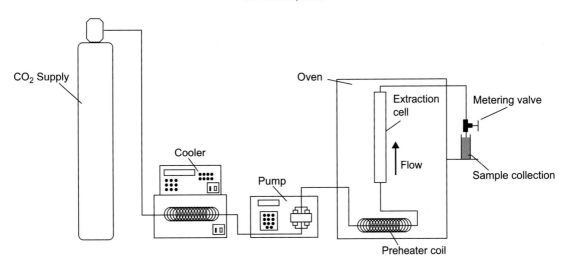

FIGURE 2.16 Schematic diagram of the supercritical fluid extraction (SFE). *Figure adapted from http://en.wikipedia.org/wiki/File:SFEschematic.jpg.*

- Supercritical fluid extraction exhibits relatively higher selectivity of extracted compounds. This avoids multiple purification steps.
- There is usually a lower long-term consumption of energy, thus reducing overhead costs.
- The viscosity of supercritical fluids is typically lower than conventional solvents. This significantly eases the handling, processing, and equipment requirements.
- There is a reduced need for hazardous solvents for extraction. This helps avoid expensive and risky waste disposal. For example, CO_2 can be released directly into the atmosphere.

As shown in Fig. 2.16, the supercritical fluid extraction process consists of the following general steps.

1. The system contains a pump for the carbon dioxide, a pressure cell to contain the sample, a pressure chamber, and a collecting vessel.
2. The carbon dioxide gas is converted to liquid and pumped to a heating zone, where it is heated to supercritical conditions.
3. It is then passed through the extraction vessel, where it rapidly diffuses into the solid matrix and dissolves the material to be extracted.
4. The dissolved material is carried from the extraction cell into a separator at lower pressure.
5. The extracted material is collected.
6. The carbon dioxide is then cooled, recompressed, or discharged into the atmosphere.

2.5 Thermodynamics

Thermodynamics is the study of energy and how energy is converted between different forms. Based on postulates or laws, the theory of thermodynamics can tell which transformations are permissible and the final equilibrium state of many different types of systems important to the pharmacy. Perhaps these aspects can best be illustrated by a simple example [18]. Fig. 2.17 shows what would happen if a ball that was resting on the edge of a bowl, with a defined amount of gravitational potential energy, was pushed into the bowl. When the ball is pushed, it will roll down the sides of the bowl and oscillate back and forth, conserving both potential and kinetic energy, but eventually, the ball will come to rest on the bottom of the bowl. In this simple example, when the ball is resting on the edge, it is in an unstable equilibrium position, and with a slight perturbation of the system, the ball rolls into the bowl. At this point, the gravitational potential energy of the ball is converted to kinetic energy (the energy of motion). Eventually, the ball will stop at the bottom of the bowl in a stable equilibrium position. What happened to the potential and kinetic energy of the ball? It was converted to heat through friction with the bowl and air. Thus, in going from an unstable equilibrium to a stable equilibrium, the ball has converted its gravitational potential energy first to kinetic energy and finally to heat. This simple example illustrates many of the attributes of thermodynamics. In other words, thermodynamics seeks to answer questions such as the following: What is the final equilibrium state of a system? Is that state stable

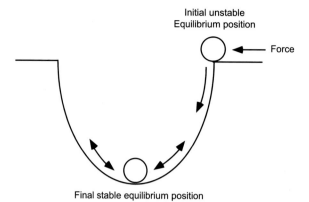

FIGURE 2.17   Energy well showing energy conversion.

or unstable? In what manner is heat converted to work and vice versa? What restrictions are placed on the conversion of energy from one form to another? Thermodynamics tries to answer these questions and much more.

While the preceding example may not be relevant to pharmacy, there are many examples in which thermodynamics is very important. For example, consider the process of life itself, in which sunlight hits a plant and through photosynthesis is converted to stored chemical energy in the plant carbohydrates. A cow can eat these plant carbohydrates and convert them into milk lactose, which you finally eat in a bowl of breakfast cereal (for some readers, the photon may have impinged on a coffee plant, giving it the energy necessary to synthesize caffeine). Finally, this gives you the energy needed to read this chapter. In this example, the energy of nuclear fusion in the sun is converted to a photon, which is converted into stored chemical energy and then converted into lactose by a cow, and finally burned up through the process of respiration. All of these energy transfers are governed by the laws of thermodynamics. Other examples in which thermodynamics are important to the understanding of pharmacy include drug—receptor interactions; active, passive, and facilitated drug transport (i.e., drug absorption); phase equilibrium; emulsion stability; and the temperature dependence of chemical reactions and drug solubility phenomena. In short, every process involves the exchange of energy, and hence, all processes are dictated by the laws of thermodynamics. Thermodynamics is a universal theory of wide applicability. By understanding this material, you can conceptually use thermodynamic principles to understand factors important to drug delivery and drug product stability.

2.5.1 Macroscopic versus microscopic thermodynamics

All matter is made up of atoms that are constantly undergoing complex motions. The actual description of all these complex motions is done in the field of statistical mechanics. Thanks to the work of Gibbs, Boltzmann, and Maxwell [24], the theory of statistical mechanics has been able to derive satisfactory descriptions of these atomic-level motions for simple systems. They have shown that these hidden modes of atomic motion act as a repository for energy and help to define temperature, the transformation of energy, and other macroscopic properties such as heat capacity, solubility, volume, and length. However, the utilization of these microscopic theories requires a molecular description, which adds a layer of complexity and is not always available. With thermodynamics, however, you can summarize much of this information with simpler macroscopic observations. Often, these descriptions are material independent. For example, recall that 12 g of carbon consists of Avogadro's number N_A of atoms ($N_A = 6.02{,}217 \times 10^{23}$ atoms), which in thermodynamics is designated as 12 g of the isotope ^{12}C. Because there are so many molecules, the average properties of these molecules are very reproducible and can be quantitated in such a manner that the macroscopic descriptions work very well. However, it is worthwhile to remember the atomic-level foundation of these macroscopic observations.

2.6 Basic concepts and definitions

Before beginning a discussion of thermodynamics, we need to describe some of the vocabulary and concepts commonly used in the study of thermodynamics.

2.6.1 Thermodynamic systems and equations of state

A *thermodynamic system* is a set of objects that are being studied or described. By definition, this set of objects is typically separated from the rest of the environment by boundary, and the *environment* is usually defined as everything else in the universe. In this system, if there is no exchange of matter with the environment, the system is *closed*; and if there is exchange of matter and/or energy with the environment, the system is *open*. The condition or mode of being of a system is known as the *thermodynamic state* of the system. The state of the system can be described by an *equation of state* (not to be confused with things that are a function of state or a state function; see the following text), which is a mathematical equation that describes the condition of the system in terms of *measurable* properties of that system [19]. One implication of this definition is that the selection of measurable properties or variables by which the system can be adequately described is a key element of thermodynamics. For example, n moles of a pure gas in a piston (in this case, the gas in the piston is the thermodynamic system; see Fig. 2.9) can be described by a mathematical function of pressure (P), volume (V), and temperature (T) as shown in Eq. (2.21):

$$f(n, P, T) = V \tag{2.21}$$

For an ideal gas, the state equation is the well-known ideal gas law, discussed previously; thus, for a given amount of an ideal gas, the state variables are temperature, pressure, and volume (Eq. 2.22):

$$V = \frac{nRT}{P} \tag{2.22}$$

The variables or properties that are used in the state equations can be divided into two categories. First, *intensive* properties are those that are independent of the amount of material present—for example, temperature, pressure, and density. The second, *extensive* properties are those that are dependent on the amount of material present—for example, volume, energy, and mass or number of moles. Some people like to think of intensive and extensive properties as intensity and capacity factors, respectively. The reason is that often the multiplication of an intensity times a capacity factor leads to a type of energy; for example, pressure times a change in volume is related to the mechanical work done (see following text) [20].

Another example of a system is a chemically defined *homogenous* liquid such as Scotch (Scotch is an alcoholic drink that contains approximately 40%–50% ethyl alcohol by volume). In this system, the state equation must include pressure, volume, temperature, and additional variables to account for the composition of the system. For example, how much water was added to the drink? If the system is *Scotch on the rocks* (a term referring to the serving of scotch with ice), the state equation must include pressure, volume, temperature, composition, and more variables necessary to account for the multiple phases present. In this example, we have two phases (Scotch and ice), which create an *inhomogeneous system*, where a *phase* is defined as a homogenous, physically distinct portion of a system that is separated from other portions of the system by bounding surfaces.

One of the most important states of matter is the *state of equilibrium*, which is when the system is left to its own, none of its measurable properties will change. In other words, the macroscopic state of the system is time invariant and will not change unless perturbed by a rise in temperature or a change in pressure, for example. The equilibrium can be a *stable equilibrium*, which means that if the system is perturbed, it has a natural tendency to return to the original equilibrium position. In the previous example, this corresponds to the ball resting on the bottom of the bowl. The equilibrium state could also be an *unstable equilibrium*, which means that if the system is perturbed, the system will try to seek a new, more stable equilibrium position. In the previous example, this corresponds to the ball resting on the top of the bowl. As you can imagine, the type of equilibrium is very important to the drug product stability, and determining thermodynamic stability is a major component of drug development research.

2.6.2 Thermodynamic processes

When the state of a system undergoes a macroscopic change from one time to another, the system undergoes a *thermodynamic process* or just a *process* during that time period. For example, if the piston in Fig. 2.18 increases in temperature or pressure, a thermodynamic process has occurred to cause this change. There are many different types of processes; the differences have primarily to do with the manner in which the process was conducted and the boundary between the system and the environment. If the boundary of a system is perfectly insulating and there is no heat exchange with the environment, a process occurring under these conditions is said to be *adiabatic*. An *isothermal process* is one in which the boundary can conduct heat, and the process is done in such a manner that the environment and system are always at the same temperature. *Isobaric* and *isochoric* processes are carried out under constant pressure and volume, respectively.

2.6.3 Reversible and irreversible processes

A *reversible process* is one that is always at equilibrium during the entire process. In theory, a reversible process can be achieved by making each step an infinitesimal step (see Appendix 2.1), which gives the system time to adjust to its new equilibrium state. For example, if the gas in the piston shown in Fig. 2.18 were expanded reversibly, then the piston would move at a rate slow enough so that no air currents or other dissipative or irreversible processes occurred. By always being in equilibrium, no temperature or pressure gradients occur within the system, and consequently, the process can be truly reversed by infinitesimally changing the forces. For example, instead of allowing the cylinder to expand, an infinitesimal change in the force would cause the gas to compress. If the cylinder is allowed to expand rapidly, then not every step is at equilibrium, and the process is said to be *irreversible*. During an irreversible process, air currents and other irreversible events can occur in the piston, which prevents the true reversal of the process. Because reversible processes occur in such a manner that each step is at equilibrium, the process is uniquely defined, and for most substances, the state of equilibrium is a unique state for a given set of conditions. Therefore, equilibrium processes provide a unique standard by which all other processes can be compared.

2.6.4 Functions of state and exact differentials

If a property or function of a system depends only on the initial and final states of the system, that property is called a *function of state* or *state function*. In other words, the change in a property depends only on the state of the system and not on the process by which it got to that state or the path it took to get to that point. For example, the gravitational potential energy of a ball dropped from the second story of a pharmacy school would depend only on the height from which it was dropped and not on how it got to the second floor. If the ball were carried to the seventh floor and then down to the second floor and dropped, it would have the same energy when it hit the ground as if it were carried directly to the second floor and dropped. Even though the amount of work done to the ball to get it to the second floor was very different for each case, the ball would still have the same gravitational potential energy and hence the same energy when it hit the ground.

Consequently, the change in a state function only depends on the difference between the initial and the final state. For example, the difference in pressure P of an ideal gas going from an initial state A to a final state B, the change can be given by

$$\Delta P = P_B - P_A$$

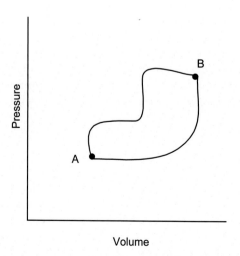

FIGURE 2.18 Cyclic path of an ideal gas undergoing a thermodynamic process.

No matter how the system goes from A to B, the difference is always the same (see Fig. 2.18). This change can be computed by the total derivative, as shown in Eq. (2.23). See Appendix 2.1 for an explanation:

$$dp = \left(\frac{\partial p}{\partial V}\right)_T dV + \left(\frac{\partial p}{\partial T}\right)_V dT \tag{2.23}$$

If the derivatives $\partial P / \partial V$ and $\partial P / \partial T$ have the property

$$\frac{\partial}{\partial T}\left(\frac{\partial p}{\partial V}\right)_T = \frac{\partial}{\partial V}\left(\frac{\partial p}{\partial T}\right)_V \tag{2.24}$$

then P is said to be an *exact differential*. If a state function is an exact differential, then the change depends only on the initial and final states of the system (see Appendix 2.1).

Another property of state functions that meet the condition given by Eq. (2.24) is that the change in the property for a closed cyclic path is zero (shown in Eq. 2.25), which can be written as:

$$\oint dP = 0 \tag{2.25}$$

where the loop around the integral sign indicates that the integral is taken over a closed cyclic path (see Fig. 2.18).

2.7 The first law of thermodynamics

2.7.1 Conservation of energy

The first law of thermodynamics is a statement of the conservation of energy. When you are trying to understand the principles involved with the conservation of energy, it is hard to understand where the law came from and why the law is formulated in this manner. In a way, the first law makes sense, but the only real justification for the first law is that no one has ever found a contrary example; that is, for some reason unknown to humanity, this is the way nature appears to behave. For a fascinating historical review of how the first law came into being, see Moore [21]. While we don't know why, the first law gives a description for how nature behaves, and the application of the principles of conservation of energy gives us a powerful tool for understanding pharmaceutical systems. As with any conservation law, it tells us that the total amount of stuff is constant; therefore, the application of a conservation law entails keeping track of where the stuff ends up. The following explanation was taken from a lecture given by Richard Feynman in 1963 and is an excellent description of the formulation of the first law [22]. Additional thoughts were also taken from Ref. [3].

Imagine a child perhaps, "Dennis the Menace," who has blocks that are absolutely indestructible and cannot be divided into pieces. Each is the same as the other. Let us suppose that he has 28 blocks. His mother puts him with his 28 blocks into a room at the beginning of the day. At the end of the day, being curious, she counts the blocks very carefully and discovers a phenomenal law—no matter what he does with the blocks, there are always 28 remaining! This continues for a number of days, until 1 day there are only 27 blocks, but a little investigating show that there is one under the rug—she must look everywhere to be sure that the number of blocks has not changed. One day, however, the number appears to change—there are only 26 blocks. Careful investigation indicates that the window was open, and upon looking outside, the other two blocks are found. Another day, careful count indicates that there are 30 blocks! This causes considerable consternation, until it is realized that Bruce came to visit, bringing his blocks with him, and he left a few at Dennis' house. After she has disposed of the extra blocks, she closed the window, does not let Bruce in, and then everything is going along all right, until one time she counts and finds only 25 blocks. However, there is a box in the room, a toy box, and the mother goes to open the toy box, but the boy says "NO, do not open my toy box," and screams. Mother is not allowed to open the toy box. Being extremely curious, and somewhat ingenious, she invents a scheme! She knows that a block weighs three ounces, so she weighs the box at a time when she sees 28 blocks, and it weighs 16 ounces. The next time she wishes to check, she weighs the box again, she subtracts 16 ounces and divides by three. She discovers the following:

$$(\text{number of blocks seen}) + \frac{\text{weight of box} - 16\ \text{ounces}}{3\ \text{ounces}} = \text{constant} \tag{2.26}$$

There then appear to be some new deviations, but the careful study indicates that the dirty water in the bathtub is changing its level. The child is throwing blocks into the water, and she cannot see them because it is so dirty, but she can find out how many blocks are in the water by adding another term to her formula. Since the original height of the water was 6 in. and each block raises the water a quarter of an inch, this new formula would be:

$$(\text{number of blocks seen}) + \frac{\text{weight of box} - 16 \text{ ounces}}{3 \text{ ounces}} + \frac{(\text{height of water}) - 6 \text{ inches}}{1/4 \text{ inch}} = \text{constant} \qquad (2.27)$$

In the gradual increase in the complexity of her world, she finds a whole series of terms representing ways of calculating how many blocks are in places where she is not allowed to look. As a result, she finds a complex formula, a quantity that *has to be computed*, which always stays the same in her situation.

Now let us examine the analogies between the preceding example and the conservation of energy. This example illustrates that you must carefully keep track of all these transformations when energy enters or leaves a system. With energy, there are many different forms; they include heat energy, radiant energy, kinetic energy, chemical energy, surface energy, gravitational energy, electrical energy, elastic energy, nuclear energy, and mass energy. Thermodynamic processes can convert energy between these different forms, and a separate accounting or equation is needed for each type of conversion. While there is a lot known about how energy behaves, to be honest, no one really knows what energy is, so it is important to keep in mind that a description, no matter how complex or detailed, is not an explanation. Fortunately, accurate descriptions are enough to gain great insight into the behavior of the pharmaceutical system and pass examinations on this subject.

Unfortunately, unlike Dennis's mother who counted the 28 blocks, you have no way to determine the total amount of energy present. However, when a thermodynamic process occurs, the total amount of heat and work transferred between the system and environment can be measured. For example, if heat energy is added or removed from a system (i.e., heating or cooling), the result is either a rise or fall in temperature, which can be measured and used to calculate the heat energy exchanged. When a rubber band is stretched, the force applied and the displacement of the rubber band can be measured and used to calculate the work done to the rubber band. In summary, the question becomes this: How is the first law of thermodynamics formulated when the total amount of energy present is unknown, but the amount of heat and work exchange between the system and environment can be measured?

If you return to the story of Dennis, because the number of blocks is conserved (i.e., the number of blocks always equals 28 and this never changes), the summation of all the changes that can occur will always equal zero. For example, if you do not know the total number of blocks and want to account for the exchange of blocks between the room and the toy box, you can measure the change in weight of the toy box and Eq. (2.26) therefore becomes

$$(\text{Change in number of blocks seen}) + \frac{\text{weight of box before} - \text{weight of box after}}{3 \text{ ounces}} = 0 \qquad (2.28)$$

In addition, because an infinite number of things could happen to the blocks when they leave the system, it is not practical for Dennis's mother to search the environment for the blocks every time the number of blocks that she sees changes. Thus, as a practical necessity, you can only keep track of the blocks as they enter or leave the room, in effect ignoring what happens to the blocks when they enter the environment. Therefore, when you focus only on the system and changes within Eq. (2.28), becomes

$$(\text{Change in number of blocks seen}) \qquad + \frac{\text{weight of box before} - \text{weight of box after}}{3 \text{ ounces}}$$
$$\pm \text{ No. going through window} \pm \text{ No. Bruce brings} = 0 \qquad (2.29)$$

Notice the change in the system is expressed in terms of the number that enters or leaves the system and *not* changes in the number going through the window or brought over by Bruce. Because the total number of blocks is conserved, the law of conservation should account for the system and environment; however, the environment is so immensely complicated that, in reality, this is impossible. Hence, the analysis can be simplified by focusing only on the system and what crosses its boundaries. In effect, the last two terms in Eq. (2.29) can account for changes in the environment that affect the number of blocks in the room.

Now let us apply the preceding principles to the conservation of energy. The change in the energy of a system can be calculated by summing the total work and heat added or removed from the system. In other words, the change in energy can be expressed as shown in Eq. (2.30):

$$\Delta U = Q + W \qquad (2.30)$$

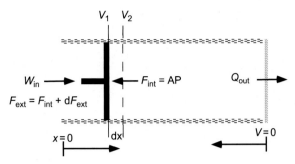

FIGURE 2.19 A friction-less piston of cross-sectional area A being compressed.

where the symbol Δ stands for "the change in," Q is the amount of heat exchanged, and W is the amount of work done. The term ΔU is the change in energy of the system, and the energy associated with changes in work and heat is called the *internal energy* (see Fig. 2.19).

2.7.2 Work

Work is defined as the transfer of energy from one physical system to another. This transfer can be done by many different mechanisms such as mechanical, chemical, electrical, but for this chapter, only mechanical work is considered. For a more complete discussion, see Ref. [18]. *Mechanical work* is the transfer of energy via the application of mechanical force to a system; in other words, mechanical work is force times distance. In calculus notation, which is used to calculate the work for a thermodynamic process such as the Carnot cycle, you use the integral of force with respect to distance as in

$$W = F \times dx \text{ for a thermodynamic process } W = \int_{x_1}^{x_2} F dx \tag{2.31}$$

where work has units of ergs or Joules, F is the force in units of dynes or Newtons, and x is distance. When you are working with gases (see Fig. 2.19), it is useful to calculate the work done in terms of pressure and volume. For the gas in the piston to be compressed, the external pressure must be greater than the internal pressure. However, for the compression to be reversible, the system must always be in a state of equilibrium, which can occur only if there is an infinitesimal difference between the inside and outside pressures. Therefore, when calculating the work, you can assume the infinitesimal pressure difference is zero $dF_{ext} \cong 0$ (see Fig. 2.19), which implies the external force equals the internal force. Because the pressure (P) is force per unit area ($P=F/A$), the work to move the cylinder a distance dx is given by Eq. (2.32):

$$W = F(x_2 - x_1) = Fdx = PAdx \tag{2.32}$$

As an arbitrary convention, work done on a system is defined as positive. In Eq. (2.32), P is positive, and because $x_2 > x_1$, dx is positive; however, when a gas is compressed, it takes up less volume, that is, $V_2 < V_1$, which makes dV negative. Therefore, to maintain this arbitrary sign convention, pressure-volume work is defined with a negative sign outside the integral (note that $V = A\,x$) as shown in Eq. (2.33):

$$W = \int_{x_1}^{x_2} PAdx = -\int_{V_1}^{V_2} PdV \tag{2.33}$$

2.7.3 Heat

Heat is a form of energy associated with the microscopic or hidden modes of atomic motion. In other words, when heat is added to a system, its internal energy increases, which, on the atomic level, results in increased molecular motion. Heat can be transferred by conduction in solids and liquids, convection in fluids, and radiation in empty space. Heat is an extensive property that is dependent on the amount of material present—not to be confused with temperature, which is an intensive property independent of the amount of material present. Again, as an arbitrary sign convention, heat absorbed by a system is considered positive.

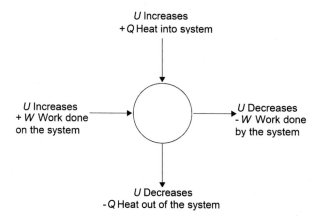

FIGURE 2.20   Sign convention from the point of view of a thermodynamics system.

2.7.4 Sign convention

The sign convention used in Eq. (2.30) was chosen arbitrarily; however, the choice needs to be standardized; otherwise, great confusion can result. All the sign conventions indicate which way the energy is going, that is, either into or out of the system. From the point of view of the system, this sign convention considers all energy going into the system positive and all energy leaving the system as negative (see Fig. 2.20). Also, for consistency with this convention, pressure-volume work adds a negative sign to the equation (see Eq. 2.33). While this convention is widely used, especially in more recent texts, many books define work with the opposite sign. This convention is based on the historic roots of thermodynamics in which steam/heat engines took in heat and gave out work; hence, both the input of heat and the output of work were positive.

2.8 Enthalpy and heat capacity

In pharmacy, processes such as the melting of a suppository base, the dissolution of a solid in a liquid, the mixing of two miscible liquids, and chemical reactions are carried out at room pressure, which is virtually constant. For this important case, the first law shown in Eq. (2.30) at constant pressure can be used to calculate the heat evolved or absorbed by a process using Eq. (2.34):

$$\Delta U = U_2 - U_1 = Q_p + W = Q_p - P(V_2 - V_2) \tag{2.34}$$

Eq. (2.34) can be rewritten as follows (Eq. 2.35):

$$Q_p = (U_2 + PV_2) - (U_1 + PV_1) \tag{2.35}$$

The P subscript is written to indicate that the expression assumes P is constant; this notation is used throughout the chapter. The expression $U + PV$ is given the special name *enthalpy*, or *heat content*. In this new notation, Eq. (2.35) becomes Eq. (2.36) as shown below:

$$Q_p = (H_2 - H_1)_p = \Delta H_p \tag{2.36}$$

The enthalpy is an extensive property that gives the amount of heat exchanged for a process occurring at constant pressure (note this definition excludes non-PdV forms of work). In addition, the enthalpy is a state function because U, P, and V are all state functions. For processes that do not occur at constant pressure, the enthalpy may not equal the heat absorbed or evolved for that process. A process that absorbs energy is *endothermic*—for example, ice melting. If the process gives off energy, it is *exothermic*, such as the freezing of water or combustion reactions.

As mentioned previously, the amount of heat exchanged cannot be directly measured, but changes in a system, such as temperature along with the heat capacity, can be used to determine the amount of heat transferred.

Assuming no phase transitions, the *heat capacity* is defined as the proportionality constant between change in temperature that occurs when a body undergoes heat exchange with the environment (Eq. 2.37):

$$Q = C(T_2 - T_1) \tag{2.37}$$

The heat capacity is an extensive property, that is, dependent on the amount of material present. The *specific heat* or *specific heat capacity* is defined as the heat capacity per unit gram of material, and the *molar heat capacity* is the heat capacity per mole of material. Because the heat capacity can change with temperature, more exact definitions determine the heat capacity for infinitesimal changes in temperature (Eq. 2.38):

$$C = \frac{\partial Q}{\partial T} \tag{2.38}$$

If you are not familiar with the symbol ∂, refer to Appendix 2.1. For a constant pressure, the change in enthalpy for a change in temperature can be given by inserting Eq. (2.36) into Eq. (2.38) to give

$$\left(\frac{\partial H}{\partial T}\right)_P = C_P \tag{2.39}$$

Thus, the enthalpy can also be calculated by integrating Eq. (2.39) as follows and shown in Eq. (2.40):

$$\Delta H = H_2 - H_1 = \int_{T_1}^{T_2} C_p dT \tag{2.40}$$

2.8.1 Phase changes

Phase changes are very important to pharmacy; for example, the vaporization of a liquid propellant in a metered-dose inhaler (MDI) is critical to particle size generation and hence therapeutic efficacy. In addition, phase changes can drastically affect dosage form stability, and understanding when a phase change can occur and how they affect stability is very important to drug development. A phase change is typically accompanied by an abrupt change in the properties of a material—for example, the melting of ice to form water.

Eq. (2.40) gives the enthalpy change over a temperature range in which no phase transitions are occurring. However, when there is a phase change, such as going from a solid to a liquid or a liquid to a gas, the system absorbs or emits heat energy during the transition. If the process is done reversibly, that is, at equilibrium, the temperature and pressure are constant during the transition. The thermodynamic process for the melting of ice in the Scotch and water example can be written as shown in Eq. (2.41).

$$\text{Phase(ice)} \Leftrightarrow \text{Phase(liquid)} \tag{2.41}$$

where the change in enthalpy for the melting or freezing of ice at a transition temperature T^* is given by Eq. (2.42).

$$H_{T*}(\text{liquid}) - H_{T*}(\text{ice}) = H_{T*}(\text{ice}) - H_{T*}(\text{liquid})$$
$$= \Delta H_{T*}(\text{ice} \rightarrow \text{liquid}) = Q_{P.T*} \tag{2.42}$$

By analogy to Eq. (2.39), the enthalpy in the differential form is as follows:

$$\left(\frac{\partial \Delta H_{T*}}{\partial T}\right)_P = C_P(\textit{liquid}) - C_p(\textit{ice}) \tag{2.43}$$

Eq. (2.43) can be integrated to yield the following (Eq. 2.44):

$$\Delta H_\gamma - \Delta H_{\gamma*} = \int_{T*}^{T} Cp(\textit{liquid}) - Cp(\textit{ice})dT \tag{2.44}$$

The heat given off or absorbed in a phase change that occurs at constant temperature and pressure is sometimes called the *latent heat*, which is the amount of energy required to reorder the atoms when they change state.

2.8.2 Hess's law

A unique property of the enthalpy is that it's a state function, which means that the change in enthalpy is path independent and depends only on the initial and final states of the system. Understanding this property can be very useful when you are trying to determine hard-to-measure changes. For example, the enthalpy of sublimation would be difficult to measure because the rate of sublimation is very slow. Therefore, one can use the fact that the enthalpy is a state function and calculate the enthalpy of sublimation by adding the enthalpies of vaporization and fusion (melting), which are more easily measured. However, there is only one difficulty with this approach: the enthalpies of fusion and vaporization are measured at their transition temperatures, which, for standard conditions, are 0°C and 100°C, respectively for water. Thus, Eq. (2.40) can be used to determine the heat that must be added or removed from the system due to a change in temperature.

To illustrate the calculation of ΔH_{sub} for water, one can use the scheme shown in Fig. 2.21. Literature values for the enthalpy of fusion at 0°C (273 K) $\Delta H_{fus} = 6.01$ kJ/mol and vaporization at 100°C (373 K) $\Delta H_{vap} = 40.7$ kJ/mol and the heat capacities for liquid $Cp = 75.5$ TJ/K mol and gaseous $Cp = 30.5$ TJ/K mol+10.3 TJ/K mol water are given in Ref. [4]. Based on Fig. 2.21, the calculation of ΔH_{sub} at 0°C is given by

$$\Delta H_{sub} = \Delta H_{fus}^{273} + \int_{273}^{373} C_P^{liq} dT + \Delta H_{vap}^{373} + \int_{373}^{273} C_P^{gas} dT$$

$$\Delta H_{sub} = 6.01 \frac{kJ}{mol} + 0.0755 \frac{kJ}{K\,mol} \times (373 - 273)K + 40.7 \frac{kJ}{mol} + 0.0305 \frac{kJ}{K\,mol} \times (273 - 373)K + 0.0103 \frac{kJ}{K\,mol} (273 - 373)K$$

$$\Delta H_{sub} = 50.2 \frac{kJ}{mol} \tag{2.45}$$

This method of determining the enthalpy of a process by adding the enthalpies of different possible paths is called *Hess's law* of heat summation. Hess's law can also be applied to chemical reactions. Using Hess's law, one can calculate the heat of a reaction from the measurement of other reactions. As the preceding example shows, when comparing the heats of reaction, it is important to have well-defined standard states so that all comparisons are done at comparable pressures and temperatures. Because phase transitions are dictated by material properties, they occur at well-defined points that can be used as a standard state for comparison. However, with chemical reactions,

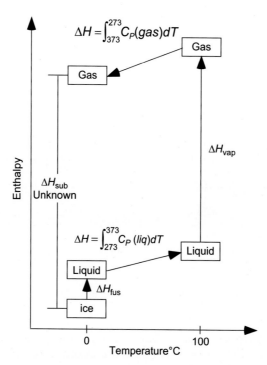

FIGURE 2.21   Schematic for calculating the enthalpy of sublimation at 0°C.

these easily defined standard states often do not exist. One convenient standard state is room temperature and pressure, which have been defined as 298.15 K and 1 atm, respectively. Under these conditions, the standard enthalpy of formation (ΔH°_f) can be calculated. The standard enthalpy of formation is defined as the ΔH of the reaction by which a compound is formed from its elements—for example, the formation of water

$$H_2 + 1/2\ O_2 \rightarrow H_2O\ (l)\quad \Delta H^\circ_{298} = 285.8\ kJ/mol$$

By summing standard heats of formation for products and reactants, one can calculate the heat of a reaction by taking the difference of these sums as shown in Eq. (2.46):

$$\Delta H_{reaction} = \sum \Delta H_{products} - \sum \Delta H_{reactants} \tag{2.46}$$

2.9 The second law of thermodynamics

The first law of thermodynamics states that energy is conserved and, for any thermodynamic process that converts energy from one form to another, the total energy in the universe remains constant. The second law of thermodynamics tells what types of conversions are possible. For example, in the previous example of the ball oscillating in the bowl, it was concluded that frictional forces between the air and bowl converted the kinetic and gravitational potential energy of the ball into heat. You could reasonably ask whether it would be possible to somehow convert this heat energy back into kinetic energy. Based on the first law, you know that the energy is there as heat, but can this heat be converted back into kinetic energy? While intuition may lead you to believe that this would not be possible, how do you know it is not a lack of intuition that prevents you from converting this energy back into kinetic? In other words, the second law specifies what is possible and puts stipulations on how heat can be removed from one source to another. The second law states that energy in the form of heat or work cannot be extracted from a system unless there is a lower temperature heat reservoir available. Thus, for the ball example that was done at room temperature, the system can be considered approximately isothermal; hence, the second law states that the heat energy can't be removed from an isothermal system without putting energy into the system, that is, doing a lot of work on the system. Along with the statement of the second law comes the definition of entropy.

These concepts are abstract and difficult to grasp; therefore, the goal of this chapter is to introduce these ideas. To really understand them, you need to consult more extensive references such as [3,21].

2.9.1 Carnot cycle and reversable heat engine efficiency

The second law of thermodynamics can be stated as follows: "It is impossible to devise an engine which, working in a cycle, shall produce no change other than the extraction of heat from a reservoir and the performance of an equal amount of work" [21]. To understand this statement, let us look at the Carnot cycle. The Carnot cycle is based on an ideal heat engine operating reversibly between hot and cold heat reservoirs at temperatures T_2 and T_1 with $T_2 > T_1$ (see Figs. 2.22 and 2.23). A *heat engine* is an engine that converts heat into mechanical work, and the material undergoing the cyclic process is called the *working substance*, which for the Carnot cycle is typically an ideal gas.

The Carnot cycle, which consists of four reversible processes, is shown in Figs. 2.22 and 2.23. Starting at point 1, the working substance, which has a state of P_1, V_1, and T_2, expands isothermally until it reaches point 2. During this expansion, Q_2 units of heat are transferred from the hot reservoir to the working substance. Starting at point 2, the engine then expands adiabatically until the temperature reaches T_1 at point 3. At this point, the working substance is isothermally compressed, returning Q_1 units of heat to the low-temperature reservoir at temperature T_1. At point 4, the working substance is adiabatically compressed until it reaches the starting point 1, thus completing a full cycle, and the working substance is returned to its initial state of P_1, V_1, and T_2.

The change in internal energy for the working substance, which goes from state 1 to 3, is given by Eq. (2.47):

$$\int_1^3 dU = U_3 - U_1 = Q_2 + \int_1^2 dW + \int_1^3 dW = Q_2 - \int_{V_1}^{V_2} PdV - \int_{V_1}^{V_3} PdV \tag{2.47}$$

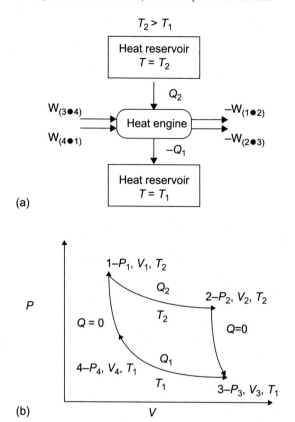

(a)

(b)

FIGURE 2.22 Diagram of a heat engine as that used in the Carnot cycle. *Adapted from Ref. [26].*

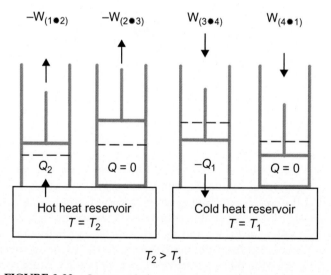

FIGURE 2.23 Carnot cycle for an ideal gas. *Adapted from Ref. [26].*

and the change in internal energy for the compression of the gas is given by Eq. (2.48)

$$\int_3^1 dU = U_1 - U_3 = Q_1 + \int_3^4 dW + \int_4^1 dW = Q_1 + \int_{V_3}^{V_4} PdV + \int_{V_4}^{V_1} PdV \qquad (2.48)$$

The change in internal energy is zero because the internal energy is a state function independent of path and only dependent on the initial and final state of the system. Thus, using the first law Eq. (2.30), one can add Eq. (2.47) and Eq. (2.48) to yield (Eq. 2.49).

$$Q_2 + Q_1 = -W = \int_{V_1}^{V_2} P\,dV + \int_{V_2}^{V_3} P\,dV + \int_{V_3}^{V_4} P\,dV + \int_{V_4}^{V_1} P\,dV \tag{2.49}$$

When you are working with reversible heat engines operating in a cycle, which absorb heat from a reservoir at one temperature and then return heat back to lower temperature reservoir and do work, it is often useful to express the work done in terms of heat and temperatures.

For an ideal gas, you can compute the preceding integrals; again, we do not refer to any particular substance, but for brevity we will demonstrate using an ideal gas (for more details, see Ref. [22]). As would be expected for heat engines, it is convenient to express the work, etc., in terms of temperature and the amount of heat absorbed or emitted. For an ideal gas, the internal energy is dependent only on the temperature and the number of molecules. As such for the isothermal steps, the change in internal energy is zero, and the work done is equal to the heat absorbed (Eq. 2.50). Thus,

$$Q_2 = \int_1^2 p\,dV = \int_{V_1}^{V_2} \frac{nRT_2}{V}\,dV = nRT_2 \ln \frac{V_2}{V_1} \tag{2.50}$$

and by analogy, the heat transfer for the isothermal compression can be given by Eq. (2.51).

$$Q_1 = nRT_2 \ln \frac{V_3}{V_4} \tag{2.51}$$

The work and heat transferred for the individual paths are summarized in Table 2.1. To eliminate the V's, one needs to express them in terms of the T's. To do this, one can use the results from the kinetic theory of gases (Eq. 2.52).

$$TV^{\gamma-1} = \text{Constant} \tag{2.52}$$

where γ is the ratio of heat capacities (the explanation is beyond the scope of this chapter, but one can see Ref. [23]). Thus, one can apply this to the system to have (Eq. 2.53)

$$T_2 V_2^{\gamma-1} = T_1 V_3^{\gamma-1} \tag{2.53}$$

And for the other compression path, one can have (Eq. 2.54)

$$T_2 V_1^{\gamma-1} = T_1 V_4^{\gamma-1} \tag{2.54}$$

If one divides Eq. (2.53) by Eq. (2.54), one can find that $V_2/V_1 = V_3/V_4$. If this is the case, then the ln in Eq. (2.50) must equal the ln in Eq. (2.51), and this yields Eq. (2.55)

$$\frac{Q_1}{T_1} = \frac{Q_2}{T_2} \tag{2.55}$$

This is the relationship that relates temperature to heat transferred in the Carnot cycle. While the results are based on an ideal gas here, it can be shown that this is a general equation that can be applied to any substance [22]. This equation can be used to define a temperature scale and the entropy, which are discussed in the next section.

TABLE 2.1 Carnot cycle of 1 mole of an ideal gas.

Path	Work	Heat
$1 \to 2$	$-RT_2 \ln \dfrac{V_2}{V_1}$	$Q_2 = RT_2 \ln \dfrac{V_2}{V_1}$
$2 \to 3$	$C_v \times (T_1 - T_2)$	0
$3 \to 4$	$-RT_1 \ln \dfrac{V_4}{V_3}$	$Q_1 = RT_1 \ln \dfrac{V_4}{V_3}$
$4 \to 1$	$C_v \times (T_2 - T_1)$	0

2.9.2 Entropy and temperature

As shown in the preceding section, the term dQ/T is a state function of special importance; in fact, it is called the entropy. This state function was first introduced by Clausius in 1850, and he named it the *entropy* (Eq. 2.56).

$$dS = \frac{dQ}{T} \tag{2.56}$$

This expression was derived for the Carnot cycle, but it can be shown that for any reversible cyclic process, this expression is valid, and because it is a state function for any cyclic process, the total of all the steps must equal zero (see Eq. 2.25).

$$\sum_i \frac{dQi}{T} = \oint \frac{dQ_{rev}}{T} = 0 \tag{2.57}$$

Note dQ_{rev} is used to indicate this is true for a reversible process only. In addition, it can be shown that for any reversible process, the entropy change is zero, and for an irreversible process, the entropy change must be greater than zero [3], that is, $dS > 0$. Also, the change in entropy for any process can be calculated by using Eq. (2.58).

$$S_2 - S_1 = \int_1^2 \frac{dQ}{T} \tag{2.58}$$

The entropy is very important because it tells whether a system will spontaneously change. Consider the case of a heat reservoir at temperature T_2 that is slowly losing heat to the environment at temperature T_1, where $T_2 > T_1$. If the temperature difference is infinitesimally small, then the process is reversible. The entropy changes in the reservoir and environment are, respectively (Eq. 2.59),

$$dS_2 = -\frac{dQ_{rev}}{T_2} \quad \text{and} \quad dS_1 = \frac{dQ_{rev}}{T_1} \tag{2.59}$$

The total change in entropy is the sum of the entropy changes (Eq. 2.60):

$$dS = dS_t + dS_2 = -\frac{dQ_{rev}}{T_2} + \frac{dQ_{rev}}{T_1} = dQ_{rev}\left(\frac{1}{T_1} - \frac{1}{T_2}\right) \tag{2.60}$$

Because $T_2 > T_1$, dS is positive. In other words, spontaneous processes occur only if the entropy change is positive. While the preceding example is very specific, this statement has been proven with general applicability [22]. In summary, the entropy change of a reversible process is zero, and for an irreversible process, the entropy change is always positive (Eq. 2.61):

$$dS = dS_{sys} + dS_{env} \geq 0 \tag{2.61}$$

This statement is one of the more profound statements in science, and much research has been done on the subject and its implications are far reaching. On a molecular level, the entropy is related to the degree of molecular randomness. Based on statistical mechanics, it has been shown that the entropy is directly correlated with the degree of randomness the molecules in a system have. For example, in a gas, the molecules are not as restricted as in a solid or liquid, and thus have a higher degree of entropy. In another example using drug diffusion, the second law would predict that drugs diffuse throughout the body because the degree of randomness of the drug molecule increases as they spread out. Hence, the second law predicts that diffusion occurs spontaneously because the entropy increases as the drug molecules go from high concentration to low concentration.

2.10 The third law of thermodynamics

One of the most popular statements of the third law of thermodynamics was given by Lewis and Randall in 1923:

If the entropy of each element in some crystalline state be taken as zero at the absolute zero of temperature, every substance has a finite positive entropy; but at the absolute zero of temperature the entropy may become zero, and does so become in the case of perfect crystalline substances [21].

The consequences of the third law are that an absolute value for the entropy can be calculated, based on absolute zero as a reference point. Given this definition, the absolute entropy can be written as shown in Eq. (2.62).

$$S^{\text{Poly}} = S_0^{\text{Poly}} + \int_0^T \frac{C_p}{T} dT \tag{2.62}$$

where S^{Poly} is the entropy of the polymorphic/crystalline form at absolute zero. If the substance is a perfect crystal, then $S^{\text{Poly}} = 0$; however, most materials do not have perfect crystalline forms. The imperfect crystals have some disorder and, hence, entropy associated with their crystalline structure even at absolute zero. The one liquid that has a zero entropy at absolute zero is liquid He, which becomes a perfect superfluid at this temperature. For a more detailed discussion of the third law, see Ref. [21].

2.11 Free energy and thermodynamic functions

Often when doing thermodynamic calculations, it is useful to define certain thermodynamic functions that have useful properties, summarize complex data, contain variables that are measurable, and can be controlled through experiments. As shown by Eq. (2.61), the entropy must increase for a process to be spontaneous. To express this in terms useful to pharmacy, the first and second laws (Eqs. 2.30, 2.56, and 2.61) can be equated as follows (Eq. 2.63):

$$TdS \geq dQ = dU - dW \tag{2.63}$$

Eq. (2.63) can be simplified for the special cases of constant temperature because $TdS = d(TS)$. Recall the product rule from calculus: $d(TS) = dTS + TdS = TdS$ and $dT = 0$ (see Appendix 2.1).

$$-d(U - TS) \geq -dW \tag{2.64}$$

Because U, T, and S are state functions,

$$A = U - TS \tag{2.65}$$

defines a new state function called the *Helmholtz free energy*, which, for constant temperature, gives the maximum work that can be done by a system during a reversible isothermal process. In other words (recall that multiplication by -1 flips $>$ to $<$):

$$dA_T \leq dW \tag{2.66}$$

Therefore, the Helmholtz free energy is less than or equal to the maximum work that can be done by a system. The equal sign applies if the process is reversible, and the less than sign applies if the process is irreversible. If the only work considered is pressure-volume work and if this work is zero, then Eq. (2.66) reduces to $dA_T \leq 0$, which gives the condition for a constant T and V process to be spontaneous, and the Helmholtz free energy equals zero at equilibrium.

Now let's look at the case of constant temperature and pressure, which is very important for pharmacy. If no-pressure volume work is included, Eq. (2.63) can be written in the form

$$TdS \geq dQ = dU - dW'' + PdV \tag{2.67}$$

where dW'' is the no-pressure volume work. At constant pressure, $PdV = d(PV)$ [see Appendix 2.1], and at constant temperature, $TdS = d(TS)$ yields an expression that contains the enthalpy.

$$-d(U + PV - TS) = d(H - TS) \geq -dW'' \tag{2.68}$$

Again, because H, T, and S are state functions $H - TS$ is also a state function called the *Gibbs free energy:*

$$G = H - TS \tag{2.69}$$

Thus, at constant temperature and pressure (recall that multiplication by -1 flips $>$ to $<$),

$$dG_{T,P} \leq dW'' \tag{2.70}$$

and if only pressure volume work is considered, $dG_{T,P} \leq 0$, where the equal sign applies for reversible processes, the less than sign applies for irreversible processes, and the Gibbs free energy equals zero at equilibrium. Any process in

TABLE 2.2   Summary of thermodynamic functions and their differential forms.

Function	State variables	Definition	Differential form
Internal energy	S, V	$U = Q + W$	$dU = TdS - PdV$
Enthalpy	S, P	$H = U + PV$	$dH = VdP + TdS$
Helmholtz free energy	T, V	$A = U + TS$	$dA = -PdV - SdT$
Gibbs free energy	T, P	$G = H + TS$	$dG = VdP - SdT$
Entropy	T, V	$S = Q/T$	

which $dG_{T,P}$ is negative will proceed spontaneously. In summary, A and G are criteria for the spontaneity of a process, which sets them apart from U and H.

2.11.1 Total differentials of free energy functions

As one can see later in the chapter, sometimes it can be useful to express thermodynamic functions as total differentials; therefore, these forms are derived. For example, to determine dG (the definition of enthalpy), Eq. (2.36) can be inserted into Eq. (2.69) and apply the chain rule of calculus (see Appendix 2.1); consequently, one can write dG as shown in Eq. (2.71) as follows:

$$dG = dU + PdV + VdP - TdS - SdT \tag{2.71}$$

By substituting in the first law (Eq. 2.30) for the internal energy, one can get Eq. (2.72)

$$dG = dQ + dW + PdV + VdP - TdS - SdT \tag{2.72}$$

If the thermodynamic process is reversible, $dQ = TdS$, and if the only work is pressure-volume work, $dW = -PdV$. One can substitute these conditions into Eq. (2.72), which, after one cancel terms, yields the following (Eq. 2.73):

$$dG = VdP - SdT \tag{2.73}$$

By analogy, the same type of relationship can be found for the Helmholtz free energy, enthalpy, and internal energy. The results are given in Table 2.2.

From the differential forms, many useful relationships can be derived. For example, the total derivative (Eq. 2.23, see also Appendix 2.1) of the Gibbs free energy (Eq. 2.69) with respect to temperature and pressure has the following form (Eq. 2.74):

$$dG = \left(\frac{\partial G}{\partial P}\right)_T dP + \left(\frac{\partial G}{\partial T}\right)_P dT \tag{2.74}$$

By comparison with Table 2.1, the values of the partial derivatives of G can be found as shown in Eq. (2.75a):

$$\left(\frac{\partial G}{\partial P}\right)_T = V \left(\frac{\partial G}{\partial T}\right)_P = -s \tag{2.75a}$$

By analogy, the other derivatives can be found by comparison with Table 2.1 as follows:

$$\left(\frac{\partial U}{\partial V}\right)_s = -P \quad \left(\frac{\partial U}{\partial S}\right)_v = T \tag{2.75b}$$

$$\left(\frac{\partial H}{\partial P}\right)_S = V \left(\frac{\partial H}{\partial S}\right)_P = T \tag{2.75c}$$

$$\left(\frac{\partial A}{\partial V}\right)_T = -P \left(\frac{\partial A}{\partial T}\right)_V = -s \tag{2.75d}$$

Because U, H, A, and G are all state functions, their differential form must satisfy Eq. (2.24) (see Appendix 2.1) by applying this relationship to functions listed in Table 2.1. Useful relationships between the partial derivative can be found; they are known as Maxwell's equations:

$$\left(\frac{\partial T}{\partial V}\right)_s = -\left(\frac{\partial P}{\partial S}\right)_V \tag{2.76a}$$

$$\left(\frac{\partial T}{\partial P}\right)_s = \left(\frac{\partial V}{\partial S}\right)_P \tag{2.76b}$$

$$\left(\frac{\partial P}{\partial T}\right)_V = \left(\frac{\partial S}{\partial V}\right)_T \tag{2.76c}$$

$$\left(\frac{\partial V}{\partial T}\right)_P = -\left(\frac{\partial S}{\partial P}\right)_T \tag{2.76d}$$

2.11.2 Gibbs free energy

To understand how pressure influences the Gibbs free energy, one can use Eq. (2.75a) to better understand this important property and how it changes. First, look at pressure:

$$\Delta G = G_2 - G_1 = \int_1^2 V dp \tag{2.77}$$

To use this equation, one needs to know how P and V are interrelated, that is, how V varies with P. For an ideal gas, this can be easily done using the $PV = nRT$ relationship. This equation then can be inserted into Eq. (2.77) to yield the following as shown in Eq. (2.78):

$$\Delta G = G_2 - G_1 = \int_1^2 nRT \frac{dP}{P} = nRT \ln \frac{P_2}{P_1} \tag{2.78}$$

Using the Eq. (2.78), one can determine many useful relationships.

2.12 Chemical equilibrium

Previously, we discussed the properties of the free energy functions and gave some information on how they relate to conditions of equilibrium. By knowing the sign and magnitude of ΔG, you know whether a process will occur spontaneously and if it is at equilibrium. Now let's examine how they relate to chemical equilibrium.

A chemical reaction in a closed system can be represented by

$$v_a A + v_b B \leftrightarrow v_c C + v_d D \tag{2.79}$$

where v_a, v_b, v_c, and v_d are the stoichiometric coefficients of the chemical reactants A and B and products C and D, respectively. For this reaction or any similar type of reaction, the total Gibbs free energy is the sum of the individual Gibbs free energies times their stoichiometric coefficients:

$$\Delta G = (v_c G_c + v_d G_D) - (v_a G_A + v_b G_B) \tag{2.80}$$

As discussed earlier, the Gibbs free energies for the reactants or products can be expressed by/ $G_i = G_i^o + RT \ln a_i$ or $G_i = G_i^o + RT \ln f_i$ for liquids or solids, respectively. Depending on the system, Eq. (2.78) can be substituted into Eq. (2.80), yielding

$$\Delta G = v_c\left(G_c^o + RT \ln a_c\right) + v_d\left(G_d^o + RT \ln a_d\right) - v_a\left(G_a^o + RT \ln a_a\right) - v_b\left(G_b^o + RT \ln a_b\right) \tag{2.81}$$

By separating the terms, you can write Eq. (2.81) as

$$\Delta G = \Delta G^o + RT \ln \frac{a_c^{vc} a_d^{vd}}{a_a^{va} a_b^{vb}} \tag{2.82}$$

where $\Delta G^o = v_c G_c^o + v_d G_d^o - v_a G_a^o - v_b G_b^o$. It is interesting to note that if the reaction has run to equilibrium, then $\Delta G = 0$ and Eq. (2.82) equals 0:

$$0 = \Delta G^o + RT \ln \left(\frac{a_c^{vc} a_d^{vd}}{a_a^{va} a_b^{vb}}\right)_{eq} \tag{2.83}$$

The logarithm is equal to the equilibrium constant if the whole system is at standard temperature and pressure (i.e., are at the same conditions as ΔG^o was determined):

$$K_{eq} = \frac{a_c^{vc} a_d^{vd}}{a_a^{va} a_b^{vb}} \tag{2.84}$$

At these conditions, you can get the following well-known equation:

$$\Delta G^o = -RT \ln K_{eq} \tag{2.85}$$

2.12.1 Temperature dependence

What happens if you or your patients leave a product in the car on a hot summer day? How will the heat affect physical and chemical stability of that product? To analyze this issue, you can look at how temperature influences chemical equilibrium. To begin, you can rewrite Eq. (2.85) as follows:

$$\ln K_{eq} = -\frac{\Delta G^o}{RT} \tag{2.86}$$

By taking the derivative with respect to time of each side, you can rewrite Eq. (2.86) as follows:

$$\frac{\partial \ln K_{eq}}{\partial T} = -\frac{1}{R}\frac{\partial(\Delta G^o/T)}{\partial T} \tag{2.87}$$

Using the quotient rule (see Appendix 2.1), taking the deviation of the right side yields the following:

$$\frac{\partial \ln K_{eq}}{\partial T} = -\frac{1}{RT^2}\left(T\frac{\partial \Delta G^o}{\partial T} - \Delta G^o\right) \tag{2.88}$$

At this point, it is useful to recall $\partial \Delta G^o/\partial T = -S$ and $\Delta G^o = H^o - TS$. As such,

$$\frac{\partial \ln K_{eq}}{\partial T} = \frac{\Delta H^o}{RT^2} \tag{2.89}$$

This is the van't Hoff equation, which can be used to assess the effect of temperature.

2.13 Open systems

The preceding analyses have been restricted to closed systems, but it would be useful to know how the addition of a material affects the thermodynamics of a system. For example, what happens when salt is added to an IV bag? There are many other important examples where understanding how the exchange of mass affects a system. This subject is very broad, so this discussion is restricted to analysis of Gibbs free energy, which is the most important case.

To begin, you can ask how the basic equation of change for Gibbs free energy (Eq. 2.74) can be modified to account for the change of mass with the environment (in this case Eq. 2.74) to take the form

$$dG = \left(\frac{\partial G}{\partial P}\right)_{T,n_1,n_2} dP + \left(\frac{\partial G}{\partial T}\right)_{P,n_1,n_2} dT + \left(\frac{\partial G}{\partial n_1}\right)_{P,T,n_2} dn_1 + \left(\frac{\partial G}{\partial n_2}\right)_{P,T,n_1} dn_2 + \cdots \tag{2.90}$$

where the term

$$\left(\frac{\partial G}{\partial n_1}\right)_{P,T,n_2} = \mu_1 \tag{2.91}$$

is given the name *chemical potential* or *partial molar free energy* and is used to assess how the addition of mass to a system affects Gibbs free energy. Also, the differential form of Gibbs free energy (Eq. 2.73) can also be modified to include the exchange of mass; in this case, it becomes

$$dG = VdP - SdT + \mu_1 dn_1 + \mu_2 dn_2 \tag{2.92}$$

If temperature and pressure are held constant, then Eq. (2.92) can be rewritten as follows:

$$dG_{TP} = \mu_1 dn_1 + \mu_2 dn_2 \tag{2.93}$$

It can be shown that the chemical potential or partial molar free energy has conditions for equilibrium of $dG = 0$. These relationships are very useful when you are analyzing pharmaceutical systems.

2.14 Conclusions

This chapter describes the various states of matter and laws governing their behavior, which are useful in designing drug, dosage form, and drug delivery systems; selecting proper storage conditions for drugs; as well as selecting their optimum formulation and administration strategies. Thermodynamics is based on three laws, and these laws have never been proved directly. However, various inferences have been deduced in the form of different mathematical equations from these laws, and the results have been found to be in close agreement with the observations. The concepts of thermodynamics help in appreciating the energy changes associated with various active biological processes and their applications in developing stable, effective, and reliable dosage forms.

Case studies

Case 2.1

There are some combination products for insulin for better management of diabetes because their onset of action, peak glycemic effect, and duration of effect are better than rapid-acting or short-acting or intermediate-acting insulin.

Question: Why do combination insulins behave differently than other insulin products?

Approach: The following three combination insulin products are listed in Lexicomp 2013 [25].

1. Insulin aspartate porotamine suspension and insulin aspartate solution (70:30)
2. Insulin lispro protamine suspension and insulin lispro solution (75:25)
3. Insulin NPH suspension and insulin regular solution (70:30)

Human insulin is able to exist in a solid-state as both amorphous and crystalline forms. The amorphous form of insulin dissolves quickly, becomes biologically available faster than the crystalline form, and thereby exhibits rapid action. In the preceding example of insulin combination products, the solid state form of it in solution is amorphous.

In contrast, the crystalline form of insulin goes into solution at a slower rate than its amorphous counterpart and hence becomes bioavailable later and exhibits effects for a longer duration of time. The solid state of insulin in suspension in the preceding examples is in crystalline form.

Thus, the mixture of insulin in amorphous and crystalline forms explains the unique efficacy profile of combination insulin products rather than other insulin products. The amorphous portion provides a quick release and absorption, followed by the slow release of the crystalline form.

Case study 2.2

It is essential not to overheat cocoa butter, which is used as a suppository base during the preparation of the suppository by fusion method. Such suppositories must be stored in the refrigerator. Why?

Theobroma oil, or cocoa butter, melts to a large degree over a narrow temperature range of 34°C–36°C. It exists in four polymorphic forms: the unstable gamma form melting at 18°C, the alpha form melting at 22°C, the beta prime form melting at 28°C, and the stable beta form melting at 34.5°C. If theobroma oil is heated to the point at which it is completely liquefied (about 35°C), the nuclei of the stable beta crystals are destroyed, and the mass does not crystallize until it is supercooled to about 15°C. Otherwise, the crystals that form are the metastable gamma, alpha, and beta prime forms, and the suppositories melt at 23–24°C or at ordinary room temperature.

Therefore, the proper method of preparation involves melting cocoa butter at the lowest possible temperature, about 34°C. The mass is sufficiently fluid to pour, yet the crystal nuclei of the stable form are not lost. When the mass is chilled in a mold, a stable suppository—consisting of beta crystals and melting at 34.5°C—is produced. These suppositories are stored in a refrigerator to preserve their stable beta polymorphic state.

Case study 2.3

Question: The concentration of urea in plasma and urine are 0.006 and 0.345 M, respectively. Calculate the free energy in transporting 0.01 mol of urea from plasma to urine. Is this transport process spontaneous, that is, would it happen on its own? How many ATP molecules would be consumed in providing energy for this transport process?

Approach: Thermodynamic principles can be used to answer this question. The Gibbs free energy equation, shown here, is the major deciding factor of spontaneous or nonspontaneous process:

$$\text{Free energy, } \Delta G = nRT \times \ln \frac{c_2}{c_1}$$

where c is the concentration.

From the question, let's see what we have already.

n = The number of moles to be transported = 0.01 mol
R = Gas constant = 1.987 cal/mol/K
T = Here, the transport of urea is inside the body, where the temperature = 37°C = 273 + 37 = 310 K
C_2 = 0.345 M
C_1 = 0.006 M (Always consider the concentration C_1 from where the transport is being initiated).

Therefore, free energy

$$\Delta G = 0.01 \text{ mole} \times 1.987 \, \frac{Cal}{mole \times K} \times 310 \, K \times \ln \frac{0.345 \, M}{0.006 \, M} = 24.96 \text{ Cal}$$

Since the value of free energy change is positive, the transport of urea from plasma or blood to urine would not be automatic but would require expenditure of energy equivalent to 24.96 calories, which most probably would be provided by hydrolysis of ATP. The hydrolysis of ATP releases 7.3 Kcals of energy in addition to producing ADP and inorganic phosphate as shown here:

$$\text{ATP} \rightarrow \text{ADP} + (P)_i + 7.3 \text{ Kcals}$$

There are 6.023×10^{23} (Avogadro's number) ATP molecules in 1 mole of ATP.

Therefore, 7300 cals (i.e., 7.3 Kcals) energy is produced by 6.023×10^{23} ATP molecules. Hence, 24.96 cals would be produced by

$$\frac{6.023 \times 10^{23} \text{ molecules}}{7300 \text{ cals}} \times 24.96 \text{ cal} = 2.059 \times 10^{21} \text{ ATP molecules}$$

Case study 2.4

The enthalpy, $\Delta H°$ and entropy, ΔS at 25°C are respectively for the following reaction:

$$\text{NH}_4\text{NO}_3(s) + \text{H}_2\text{O}(l) \rightarrow \text{NH}_4^+(aq) + \text{NO}_3^-(aq)$$

Calculate the value of ΔG° for the above reaction at 25°C and explain why ammonium nitrate spontaneously dissolves in water at room temperature.

Approach: $\Delta G^{\circ} = \Delta H^{\circ} - T\Delta S = 28.05 \text{ kJ} - (25 + 273.17)\text{K} \times 108.7 \text{ J/K}.$
$= 28.05 \times 10^{3} \text{ J} - 298.17\text{K} \times 108.7 \text{ J/K} = 28.05 \times 10^{3} \text{ J} - 32{,}411.079 \text{ J} = -4361.079 \text{ J} = -4.36 \text{ kJ}.$
A negative ΔG° value of a reaction/phenomenon indicates that it will happen spontaneously.

Critical reflections and practice applications

This chapters discussed forces responsible for existence of drug substances in various states of matter and their relationship with thermodynamic principles. These can provide some critical concepts applicable to pharmacy practices as mentioned below:

1. The solubility of a drug is influenced by intermolecular forces which can be applied for explaining why alcohol is soluble in water in all proportion although it is an organic solvent.
2. The concept of supercritical fluid is exploited for the development of nasal and pulmonary drug delivery systems, as well as extraction of essential oils from natural sources.
3. A mixture of crystalline and amorphous forms of insulin is used for developing an efficient injectable insulin cable of taking care of fluctuating blood glucose levels over longer period of time.
4. A specific polymorph of a drug is active while another polymorph is inactive.
5. Gibb's free energy concept can be used for predicting spontaneity of a chemical reactions as well as physiological process.

Appendix 2.1 calculus review

Partial derivatives

A derivative is the instantaneous rate of change of a function, given by the slope of a tangent line to a curve described by the function of interest. When you have functions of more than one variable, the symbol ∂ is used to indicate partial derivatives. When you are computing a partial derivative, all of the other variables are treated like constants, and then rules of differentiation are applied to the variable of interest. For example, let $f(x, y)$ be a function of x and y; then by the definitions of a partial derivative, the rate of change of $f(x, y)$, with respect to x and y are given by Eqs. (2.94) and (2.95), respectively:

$$\left(\frac{\partial f}{\partial x}\right)_{y} = \lim_{\Delta x \to 0} \frac{f(x + \Delta x, y) - f(x, y)}{\Delta x} \tag{2.94}$$

$$\left(\frac{\partial f}{\partial y}\right)_{x} = \lim_{\Delta y \to 0} \frac{f(x, y + \Delta y) - f(x, y)}{\Delta y} \tag{2.95}$$

However, the definition of a derivative based on limits is primarily used for theoretical investigation (see the following text). When you are computing derivatives, the standard rules of differentiation given in any calculus textbook are used. For example, the equation for an ideal gas is $PV = nRT$. To know how pressure varies with temperature and volume change, you can solve the equation for P; in functional notation, it can be written as $P = f(V, T) = nRT/V$. The partial derivatives can be represented as:

$$\frac{\partial P}{\partial T} = \frac{\partial f}{\partial T} = \frac{\partial}{\partial T}\left(\frac{nRT}{V}\right) = \frac{nR}{V} \tag{2.96}$$

$$\frac{\partial P}{\partial V} = \frac{\partial f}{\partial V} = \frac{\partial}{\partial V}\left(\frac{nRT}{V}\right) = -\frac{nRT}{V^{2}} \tag{2.97}$$

Product rule

The product rule is used to calculate the derivative for the product of two functions, where the $'$ is standard calculus notation for the derivative with respect to the variable of interest:

$$(fg)' = f'g + g'f \tag{2.98}$$

Chain rule

The chain rule is used to compute the derivative of a function of a function:

$$f(g(x))' = \frac{df}{dg} \cdot \frac{dg}{dx} \tag{2.99}$$

Quotient rule

The quotient rule for derivatives follows, and it can be derived by applying the chain rule and the product rule to a quotient:

$$\left(\frac{f}{g}\right)' = \frac{f'g - g'f}{g^2} \tag{2.100}$$

Total derivatives

Often in thermodynamics, you need to calculate change Δf of the function $f(x, y)$ when both x and y are varying. For infinitesimally small changes, the total derivative is given by

$$\Delta f = f(x + \Delta x, y + \Delta y) - f(x, y) \tag{2.101}$$

$$\Delta f = \underbrace{f(x + \Delta x, y + \Delta y) - f(x, y + \Delta y)}_{\Delta x \left(\frac{\partial f}{\partial x}\right)_y} + \underbrace{f(x, y + \Delta y) - f(x, y)}_{\Delta y \left(\frac{\partial f}{\partial y}\right)_x} \tag{2.102}$$

For example, the total derivative of P, written as dP, is given by the following equation:

$$dP = \left(\frac{\partial P}{\partial V}\right)_T dV + \left(\frac{\partial P}{\partial T}\right)_V dT \tag{2.103}$$

The total derivative has a lot of significance in thermodynamics because it gives information about exact differentials, which are path independent.

Abbreviations

a acceleration
A Helmholtz free energy
API active pharmaceutical ingredient
c concentration
C Heat capacity; Cp and Cv are the heat capacities at constant pressure and volume, respectively
C (phase equilibria) Number of components in a system
F Force [units: dyne (dyn) $= g\ cm\ s^{-2}$ or Newton (N) $= kg\ m\ s^{-2}$]
F (phase equilibria) degrees of freedom
FA attractive forces
FR repulsive forces
g weight in grams of gas
G Gibbs free energy
H enthalpy
KE kinetic energy

m mass
MW molecular weight of gas
n number of moles
P pressure (units Pascal (Pa)=N m^2)
P (phase equilibria) number of phases
Pc critical pressure
Pi partial pressure
Q heat
r distance separating the molecules
R gas constant values in different unit systems: 8.3143 J/K mol, 8.3143 × 10^{-7} erg/K mol, 1.98,762 cal/K mol, and 0.0821 L atm/K mol
S entropy (J/°K)
T temperature
T* temperature of a phase transition
T$_C$ critical temperature
U internal energy (Joule = N *m* or erg = dyne cm)
V volume
VP equilibrium vapor pressure
W Work [units: erg = dyne cm or Joule (J) = N m]
X mole fraction
x distance
δ+ positive partial charge
Δ*Hv* heat of vaporization
Δ*H*°$_f$ standard enthalpy of formation
δ− negative partial charge

References

[1] B.J. Sandmann, M.M. Amiji, B.J. Sandmann, Intermolecular forces and states of matterApplied physical pharmacy, in: M.M. Amiji, B.J. Sandmann (Eds.), Applied Physical Pharmacy, McGraw Hill, New York, 2003, pp. 27–45.

[2] J.N. Israelachvili, Intermolecular and Surface Forces, Academic Press, San Diego, 2011.

[3] H. Van Ness, Understanding Thermodynamics, McGraw-Hill, New York, 1969.

[4] G.K. Vemulapalli, Physical Chemistry, Prentice Hall, Englewood Cliffs, NJ, 1993.

[5] U.B. Hadkar, Physical Pharmacy, Nirali Prakashan, Pune India, 2007.

[6] G.L. Perlovich, T. Volkova, A. Bauer-Brandl, Polymorphism of paracetamol, J. Therm. Anal. Calorim. 89 (3) (2007) 767–774.

[7] J. Lu, X.-J. Wang, X. Yang, C.-B. Ching, Characterization and selective crystallization of famotidine polymorphs, J. Pharmaceut. Sci. 96 (9) (2007) 2457–2468.

[8] J. Lu, X.-J. Wang, X. Yang, C.-B. Ching, Polymorphism and crystallization of famotidine, Cryst. Growth Des. 7 (9) (2007) 1590–1598.

[9] R. Nagaraju, A.P. Prathusha, P.S. Chandra-Bose, R. Kaza, K. Bharathi, Preparation and evaluation of famotidine polymorphs, Curr. Drug Discov. Technol. 7 (2) (2010) 106–116.

[10] Z. Német, G.C. Kis, G. Pokol, Á. Demeter, Quantitative determination of famotidine polymorphs: X-ray powder diffractometric and Raman spectrometric study, J. Pharm. Biomed. Anal. 49 (2) (2009) 338–346.

[11] A.R. Sheth, S. Bates, F.X. Muller, D.J.W. Grant, Polymorphism in piroxicam, Cryst. Growth Des. 4 (6) (2004) 1091–1098.

[12] F. Vrečer, S. Srčič, J. Šmid-Korbar, Investigation of piroxicam polymorphism, Int. J. Pharm. 68 (1–3) (1991) 35–41.

[13] J. Bauer, S. Spanton, R. Henry, J. Quick, W. Dziki, W. Porter, Ritonavir: an extraordinary example of conformational polymorphism, Pharm. Res. (N. Y.) 18 (6) (2001) 859–866.

[14] R. Barbas, F. Martí, R. Prohens, C. Puigjaner, Polymorphism of norfloxacin: evidence of the enantiotropic relationship between polymorphs A and B, Cryst. Growth Des. 6 (6) (2006) 1463–1467.

[15] B. Šuštar, N. Bukovec, P. Bukovec, Polymorphism and stability of norfloxacin, (1-ethyl-6-fluoro-1,4-dihydro-4-oxo-7-(1-piperazinil)-3-quinolinocarboxylic acid, J. Therm. Anal. Calorim. 40 (2) (1993) 475–481.

[16] A.J. Aguiar, J. Krc, A.W. Kinkel, J.C. Samyn, Effect of polymorphism on the absorption of chloramphenicol from chloramphenicol palmitate, J. Pharmaceut. Sci. 56 (7) (1967) 847–853.

[17] A.J. Aguiar, J.E. Zelmer, Dissolution behavior of polymorphs of chloramphenicol palmitate and mefenamic acid, J. Pharmaceut. Sci. 58 (8) (1969) 983–987.

[18] H.B. Callen, Thermodynamics and an Introduction to Thermostatics, John Wiley & Sons, New York, 1985.

[19] E. Fermi, Thermodynamics, Dover, New York, 1936.

[20] P.J. Sinko, Y. Singh, Martin's Physical Pharmacy and Pharmaceutical Sciences: Physical Chemical and Biopharmaceutical Principles in the Pharmaceutical Sciences, Lippincott Williams & Wilkins, Philadelphia, 2011.

[21] W.J. Moore, Physical Chemistry, Prentice-Hall Inc, Englewood Cliffs, NJ, 1972.

[22] R.P. Feynman, R.B. Leighton, M. Sands, The Feynman Lectures on Physics, Addison-Wesley Publishing Co., Reading MA, 1963.

[23] S. Glasstone, Physical Chemistry, D. Van Nostrand Co. Inc, Princeton, NJ, 1946.

[24] P.W. Atkins, Physical Chemistry, W.H. Freeman and Co., San Francisco, 1982.

[25] Creighton University Health Sciences Online, Available from: http://online.lexi.com.cuhsl.creighton.edu/lco/action/search?q=Insulin&t=name.

[26] Carnot Cycle. https://chem.libretexts.org/Bookshelves/Physical_and_Theoretical_Chemistry_Textbook_Maps/Supplemental_Modules_(Physical_and_Theoretical_Chemistry)/Thermodynamics/Thermodynamic_Cycles/Carnot_Cycle. (Accessed 15 December 2022).

3

Physical Properties, Their Determination, and Importance in Pharmaceutics

Somnath Singh and Alekha K. Dash

Department of Pharmacy Sciences, School of Pharmacy and Health Professions, Creighton University, Omaha, NE, United States

CHAPTER OBJECTIVES

- Define surface and interfacial tension, adsorption and absorption, and surfactant working at the interface.
- Explain the working principles behind the measurement of surface tension and the extent of adsorption at the interface.
- Describe the properties of liquid interfaces and compare the forces of molecular attraction at interfaces with the bulk liquid.
- Discuss the types of surfactants and their pharmaceutical and clinical applications.
- Define and discuss various colligative properties.
- Define viscosity, fluidity, and kinematic viscosity, as well as mathematical expressions for these terms.
- Compare and contrast Newtonian and non-Newtonian liquids, and their flow characteristics.
- Explain the methods used to measure viscosity of liquids and semisolids.
- Describe the application of rheology in pharmacy.
- Define spectroscopy and the electromagnetic radiation spectrum in terms of wavelength, wavenumber, frequency, and energy.
- Compare and contrast the energy requirement for vibrational, translational, and rotational transition.
- Discuss the working principles behind ultraviolet, visible, infrared, fluorescence, nuclear magnetic resonance, and mass spectroscopy and their applications.

Pharmaceutics, Second Edition
https://doi.org/10.1016/B978-0-323-99796-6.00002-3

Keywords: Adsorption; Colligative properties; Interfacial tension; Physical properties; Rheology; Spectroscopy; Surface tension; Surfactant.

3.1 Introduction

Successful development of any dosage forms or drug delivery systems for a new drug requires that some fundamental physical and chemical properties of the drug molecule are known before proceeding to formulation development. To arrive at the target site in the appropriate form, the drug molecule has to travel from the site of administration and overcome many hurdles and barriers. As an example, for an orally administered drug, the molecule has to overcome many hurdles that include dissolving in gastrointestinal (GI) fluid, surviving a range of gastric pH (1.5—8.0), surviving intestinal enzymes, crossing many membranes, surviving liver metabolism, avoiding excretion by kidneys, partitioning into the targeted organ, and avoiding partition into undesired sites.

Some of the properties or tests that are necessary in the early stage of formulation development may include simple UV spectroscopy or high pressure liquid chromatography (HPLC) assays for the drug molecules, aqueous solubility, pKa, partition coefficient, moisture adsorption properties, dissolution, melting point, solution and solid-state stability, microscopic properties, bulk density, flow property, and compression properties. In a dosage form, besides the active pharmaceutical ingredient (API), many more inactive materials are present, which can greatly affect the overall property of the dosage form. It is also equally important to have a rational formulation. One must have a good understanding of the physicochemical properties of excipients and their influence on the overall formulation. Some of the physical properties just outlined are described in other chapters.

This chapter focuses on some of surface properties, flow properties, colligative properties, as well as some of the fundamentals of spectroscopy essential for dosage form design. Identity, purity, quality, and quality assurance are the four important aspects of dosage form design to ensure a product is safe, effective, and reliable. Various analytical tests are necessary for identification of drugs; they include FTIR, NMR, TLC, DSC, X-ray, and UV spectroscopy. To confirm purity, it is essential to determine the melting point by DSC; moisture content by Karl—Fisher titrimetry; and organic, inorganic, and heavy metal impurities. Finally, for quality assurance, various assay procedures including spectroscopy, HPLC, and other analytical methods are beneficial.

3.2 Surface and interfacial tension

3.2.1 Interfaces

When two phases exist together, the boundary between the two phases is called an interface. For example, the surface of a tablet is the interface between a solid phase (tablet) and a gaseous phase (air). Similarly, if we mix two immiscible liquids such as olive oil and water, a boundary exists between the oil and water, and it may also be called the oil—water interface. Then the following question arises: Why is the study of interfaces important in pharmacy? The study of interfaces between solids and liquids is important in the formulation of pharmaceutical suspensions. The study of interfaces between two immiscible liquids also is important in formulating pharmaceutical emulsions. In addition to their importance in the formulation and stability of suspensions and emulsions, the interfacial phenomenon plays an important role in drug absorption and penetration through biological membranes.

3.2.2 Liquid interfaces

In a beaker containing some water, the surface of the water is truly an air—water interface. Let us consider the forces that act on liquid molecules in the bulk region and compare them with the forces at the surface (see Fig. 3.1).

Consider a water molecule that is present in the bulk. It is surrounded by water molecules in all directions. The intermolecular forces of attraction are therefore, the same in all directions. In contrast, however, a water molecule at the surface is surrounded by water molecules on the sides and below, but by air molecules on the top. As the attractive forces between water—water molecules are greater than that of water—air molecules, water molecules at the surface experience a net inward pull. These molecules are therefore constantly under "tension." Because nobody, including liquids, likes to be under constant tension, liquids tend to minimize their total "tension" by minimizing their total surface area. Since a sphere has a minimum surface area—to—volume ratio, drops of most liquids, including water, assume a spherical shape. Although raindrops should also ideally assume a spherical shape, they are distorted due to the influence of wind and gravity.

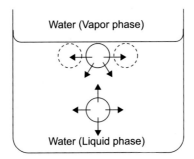

FIGURE 3.1   Schematic representation of molecular mechanism of surface tension.

One may recall that the force of attraction between like molecules (e.g., water—water) is called the force of cohesion. Similarly, the force of attraction between unlike molecules (e.g., water—air, water—glass, or water—olive oil) is called the force of adhesion. The term surface tension is used when one of the surfaces in contact is air. However, the interfacial tension term is used when any two surfaces are in contact. As the adhesive forces between two immiscible liquid phases forming the interface are greater than that of between liquid and air interface, the surface tension is generally higher than the interfacial tension. There is no interfacial tension between two completely miscible liquids.

3.2.3 The definition of surface and interfacial tension

The surface tension at any temperature is the force per unit length (dynes/cm) that has to be applied parallel to the surface to counterbalance the net inward pull of a liquid at the liquid—air interface. Similarly, interfacial tension is the tension at the interface of two immiscible liquids.

3.2.4 Effect of temperature

The surface tension of any liquid or the interfacial tension of any liquid—liquid system has to be reported at a particular temperature. The tension in both cases varies significantly with temperature as shown for water in Table 3.1. This decrease in surface tension with increase of temperature is due to the increase in the kinretic energy of water molecules that decreases their intermolecular forces.

3.2.5 Measurement of surface tension

Numerous methods are used to measure surface and interfacial tension. However, a simple method of practical importance is the capillary rise method.

When a capillary tube is placed in water in a beaker, the water rises in the capillary tube to a level higher than the liquid surface (see Fig. 3.2). Water rises in the capillary tube because the forces of adhesion between water and the wall of the glass capillary (glass) are greater than the cohesive forces between the water—water molecules. This may not be the case for all liquids. For example, in the case of mercury, placing a capillary tube at the surface will show a fall in the level of the liquid because the cohesive forces between mercury—mercury molecules are stronger than the adhesive forces between mercury—glass. However, most liquids behave similar to water, which is considered for the rest of this discussion.

TABLE 3.1   Surface tension of water at various temperatures.

Temperature (°C)	Surface tension (dynes/cm)
0	76.5
20	72.8
30	71.2
75	63.5
100	58.0

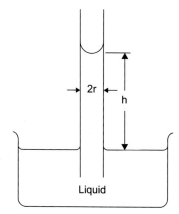

FIGURE 3.2 Determination of surface tension by the capillary rise method.

If a capillary tube of radius, *r*, is placed in a liquid, the liquid rises to a height, *h*, in the capillary tube. The surface tension of the liquid at the temperature of the measurement is given by Eq. (3.1).

$$\gamma = \frac{1}{2} r h \rho g \tag{3.1}$$

where γ is the surface tension, *r* is the inner radius of the capillary tube, *h* is the height to which the liquid rises in the capillary tube, ρ is the density of the liquid, and *g* is the acceleration due to gravity (981 cm/s^2).

3.2.6 Measurement of interfacial tension

In the DuNoüy ring method, the DuNoüy tensiometer (see Fig. 3.3) is used to measure surface and interfacial tensions. The principle behind this method is based on the fact that the force required to detach a platinum–iridium ring immersed at the surface or interface is proportional to the surface or interfacial tension. The force required to detach the ring in this manner is provided by a torsion wire and recorded in dynes on a calibrated dial.

3.3 Adsorption

3.3.1 Adsorption and absorption

Adsorption is primarily a surface phenomenon, whereas absorption occurs through the entire bulk of a substance. In the following sections, we are concerned primarily with the adsorption in liquids and solids. Adsorption of a

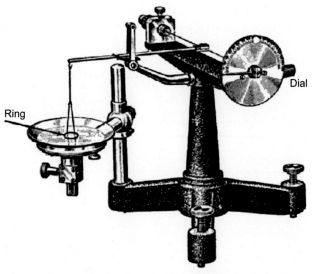

FIGURE 3.3 Tensiometer operating on DuNoüy ring method [1].

I. Physical principles and properties of pharmaceutics

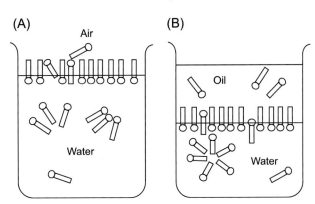

FIGURE 3.4 (A) Diagrammatic representation of accumulation of surfactants at the air—water interface and (B) formation of micelles in an aqueous medium.

poison onto an activated charcoal surface is an example of a surface phenomenon, whereas passive diffusion of a drug molecule from an oral tablet via the GI tract membrane is called an absorption phenomenon.

3.3.2 Adsorption at liquid interfaces

3.3.2.1 Surface active molecules or surfactants

Molecules or ions that are adsorbed at surfaces or interfaces and dramatically reduce the surface tension of the liquid in which they are dispersed are called surface active agents, surfactants, or amphiphiles. For a surface activity to be present in a molecule, the molecule must contain both a hydrophilic (water-loving) group and also a lipophilic (oil-loving) group on the same molecule. When such molecule is added to a beaker of water, it orients itself at the surface of the water in such a manner that the hydrophilic group faces the bulk of water and the lipophilic group faces the air (see Fig. 3.4A).

3.3.2.2 The critical micelle concentration

Surfactants are preferentially adsorbed at the water—air interface as shown in Fig. 3.4A. If we keep adding more and more surfactants to the water, there comes a time when the surface becomes completely saturated with the surfactant molecules. There is no space available on the surface to occupy that position. The surfactant molecules then start entering the bulk water, but to minimize interfacial energy, they orient themselves in a manner so that all the hydrophilic groups face the bulk water, whereas the lipophilic groups face each other (see Fig. 3.4B). These regular structures in the bulk liquid consisting of groups of molecules in a specific orientation are called micelles, whereas the individual molecules present at the surface are called monomers. Micelles may have a hydrophilic surface and a lipophilic core that can be used to entrap and solubilize lipophilic substances. The diameter of the micelles is generally of the order of 50 Å. The size may vary with the size of the individual monomers and the solvent used.

The concentration above which the monomers of surfactant start associating to form micelles is called the critical micelle concentration (CMC). Until the CMC is reached, the surface properties of the liquid, such as the surface and interfacial tension and the vapor pressure, are affected. However, at concentrations above the CMC, the bulk properties of the liquid, such as density and conductivity, are affected.

3.3.3 Surface active agents in pharmacy

This lipophilic core of micelles can be used to solubilize drug molecules in solutions and suspensions. The core can also be used to solubilize droplets of oil that are ordinarily immiscible in water. It is, therefore, evident that surfactants have a variety of uses in the manufacture of pharmaceutical solutions, suspensions, and emulsions. They are discussed in detail in the next section devoted to surfactants.

3.3.4 The hydrophilic—lipophilic-balance scale

The surface activity of surfactants can be measured by their hydrophilic—lipophilic-balance (HLB) scale. The HLB value ranges from 0 to 20 on an arbitrary scale, as shown in Fig. 3.5.

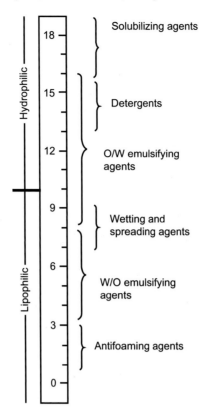

FIGURE 3.5   Hydrophilic–lipophilic-balance (HLB) scale.

The higher the HLB value of a surface active agent, the more hydrophilic it is, which determines its usefulness for a specific purpose. For example, spans or sorbitan esters have low HLB values of 1.8–8.6 and therefore are useful for preparing water-in-oil (w/o) emulsions, whereas Tweens, or polyoxyethylene derivatives of spans, have high HLB values of 9.6–16.7 and are therefore useful for making oil-in-water (o/w) emulsions. However, a mixture of surfactants (with different HLB values) can be selected and preferred over a single surfactant with the required HLB value. The following example clarifies this concept.

Example

The required HLB (RHLB) value for making an (o/w) emulsion is 10.9. Calculate the amounts of Tween 20 (HLB value = 16.7) and Span 80 (HLB value = 4.3) for making 2 g of the required emulsifiers.

Solution:

The formula for calculating the weight fraction of Tween 20 (surfactant with the higher HLB value) is as follows:

$$\text{The weight fraction of Tween 20} = \frac{\text{RHLB} - \text{HLB low}}{\text{HLB high} - \text{HLB low}}$$

$$\text{The weight fraction of Tween 20} = \frac{10.9 - 4.3}{16.7 - 4.3} = 0.53$$

Obviously, the weight fraction of Span 80 = 1 − 0.53 = 0.47. Therefore, the amount of Tween 20 = 2 g × 0.53 = 1.06 g, and the amount of Span 80 = 2 − 1.06 = 0.94 g or 2 g × 0.47 = 0.94 g.

3.3.5 Adsorption at solid interfaces

Adsorption onto solid surfaces can occur from gases or liquids. The principles of solid–gas adsorption are used in the removal of objectionable odors from rooms or food, operation of gas masks, and measurement of dimensions of particles in a powder. The principles of solid–liquid adsorption are used in decolourizing solutions, adsorption chromatography, detergency, and wetting. The clinical application of adsorption is described in Section 3.3.8.

3.3.6 The solid—gas interface

The adsorption of a gas by a solid depends on the physical and chemical nature of both the adsorbent (the material used to adsorb the gas) and the adsorbate (the substance being adsorbed). On this basis, the solid—gas adsorption may be classified as physical or chemical adsorption.

- **Physical adsorption:** This adsorption occurs due to Van der Waal's forces of attraction and can be reversed by increasing temperature or reducing pressure. The process by which a physically adsorbed gas is removed is called desorption.
- **Chemical adsorption:** This adsorption occurs due to the attachment of the adsorbate to the adsorbent by chemical bonds. Typically, only one layer (monolayer) of adsorbate is attached. This process is irreversible.

3.3.7 Quantitative measurement of physical adsorption

Physical adsorption can be measured by using the Freundlich adsorption isotherms or Langmuir adsorption isotherms.

3.3.7.1 Freundlich adsorption isotherms

The measurement of physical adsorption consists of a balance contained within a vacuum. A known amount of solid, previously degassed, is placed into the pan, and known amounts of gas are introduced into the vacuum chamber. If the weight of the solid used at the beginning of the experiment is W_s grams, then the increase in weight of the solid on introducing gas occurs due to the adsorption of the gas on the solid surface. The relation between the amount of gas adsorbed and the pressure of the gas was given by Freundlich, as shown in Eq. (3.2):

$$\frac{W_g}{W_s} = kp^{1/n} \tag{3.2}$$

where W_g is the amount of gas adsorbed, p is the partial pressure of the gas, and k and $1/n$ are empirical constants. Converting Eq. (3.2) to logarithmic form, one can obtain Eq. (3.3):

$$\log \frac{W_g}{W_s} = \log k + \frac{1}{n} \log p \tag{3.3}$$

If $\log (W_g / W_s)$ is plotted as a function of $\log p$, the slope of the straight line is $1/n$, and the antilog of the y-intercept is the constant, k.

3.3.7.2 Langmuir adsorption isotherms

Langmuir adsorption isotherms are based on the hypothesis that adsorption occurs as a monolayer. According to Langmuir, adsorption can be quantitated using Eq. (3.4):

$$\frac{p}{m_g} = \frac{1}{bm_{gs}} + \frac{p}{m_{gs}} \tag{3.4}$$

where m_g is the mass of gas adsorbed per g of adsorbent at pressure, p, and constant temperature, m_{gs} is the mass of gas adsorbed by 1 g of adsorbent when monolayer is complete, and b is a constant. In the case of adsorption of the drug from its aqueous solution onto a solid surface, the term p in Eq. (3.4) could be substituted with c, that is, the equilibrium concentration of drug. Both Freundlich and Langmuir adsorption isotherms have been used in characterizing the adsorption properties of solids; however, the former provides better results at a lower concentration of adsorbate, whereas the latter one provides better results with a higher concentration.

3.3.8 The solid—liquid interface

Numerous drugs such as dyes, alkaloids, fatty acids, and even inorganic acids and bases may be adsorbed from solution onto solids such as charcoal and alumina. The adsorption of solute molecules from solution may be treated in a manner analogous to the adsorption of molecules at the solid—gas interface. For example, the adsorption of strychnine, atropine, and quinine from aqueous solutions by many clays may be expressed by using the Langmuir adsorption isotherm as discussed earlier.

Activated charcoal is commonly employed as an antidote for poisoning by sulfonylureas (tolbutamide, acetohexamide), acetaminophen, and acetylcysteine. The adsorption by activated charcoal not only prevents bioabsorption by the gastrointestinal tract but also causes the elimination of drugs from the tissues into the GI tract by a process known as gastrointestinal dialysis. In this process, the adsorbing charcoal sets up a concentration gradient that favors the diffusion of drugs from the systemic circulation into the GI tract onto the active charcoal surface.

3.3.9 Surface active agents

Surfactants or surface active agents or amphiphiles are chemical compounds that tend to accumulate at the boundary (i.e., interface) between two phases. Therefore, they are adsorbed at the various interfaces existing between solids and/or liquids, resulting in changing the nature of interfaces. This has huge significance in pharmacy, such as in the formulation of emulsions or suspensions and solubilization of poorly soluble drugs via entrapment in the micelles.

3.3.9.1 Classification

On the basis of their charge, surfactants may be classified as anionic, cationic, amphoteric, or nonionic:

- *Anionic surfactants:* These surfactants contain carboxylate, sulfonate, or sulfate groups. Examples include sodium stearate, sodium dodecyl sulfate, and sodium lauryl sulfate.
- *Cationic surfactants:* These surfactants contain amine salts or quaternary ammonium salts. One such example is cetrimonium bromide.
- *Amphoteric surfactants:* These surfactants contain carboxylate or phosphate groups as the anion and amino or quaternary ammonium groups as the cation. The former group, consisting of carboxylate anions and amine cations, are called polypeptides or proteins, and the latter group, consisting of phosphate anions and quaternary ammonium cations, are called natural phospholipids such as lecithins and cephalins.
- *Nonionic surfactants:* These surfactants do not have any charge. Examples include sorbitan esters (Spans), polysorbates (Tweens), and poloxamer (Pluronics). Spans are mixtures of partial esters of sorbitol and its mono- and dianhydrides with oleic acid. They are generally insoluble in water and have low HLB values. Therefore, they are used for making water-in-oil emulsions and wetting a substance. Tweens differ from Spans in the sense that they are condensed with varying moles of ethylene oxide instead of oleic acid; hence, they have high HLB values, are soluble in water, and are used for making oil-in-water emulsions.

Pluronics are block copolymers of hydrophilic poly(oxyethylene) (POE) and hydrophobic poly(oxypropylene) (POP) represented by the general formula $POE_n-POP_m-POE_n$, where n and m represent the number of OE and OP, respectively. Table 3.2 shows the structures and the hydrophilic and hydrophobic components of some of the most frequently used surfactants in pharmacy.

3.3.10 Surface activity of drugs

Some drugs that are amphipathic in nature show surface activity that may influence their therapeutic activity. They differ from a surfactant in the sense that their hydrophobic groups are much more complex. Generally, the surface activity is increased due to the nature of the functional groups present on the hydrophobic moiety of these drugs. The decrease in CMC and increase in surface activity is found for the Br^- functional group containing antihistaminic drug brompheniramine in comparison to those in pheniramine [2]. Fig. 3.6 shows the structures of some drugs whose pharmacological properties can be explained by their surface activity.

3.3.10.1 Formation of film at the interface and its application

Surfactants are localized as monolayer films at the interface of water–air due to their amphiphilic nature. If the surfactant added is soluble or partially soluble in water, it forms a soluble layer at the interface, which is in equilibrium with surfactant molecules in bulk; otherwise, it forms an insoluble layer that is obviously not in equilibrium with those in the bulk region. An insoluble film or monolayer on the water surface can be conveniently obtained by adding a solution of a surfactant such as stearic acid in an organic solvent. An organic solvent would evaporate into the air due to its volatile nature, thereby leaving surfactant on the water surface as an insoluble monolayer film.

Monolayers are useful models that could be used for investigating the properties of polymers used as packaging materials. The permeability of packaging material to gas or liquid contained therein or its adsorption onto packaging

TABLE 3.2 Classification of surfactants.

Types and examples	Structures	Hydrophobic moiety	Hydrophilic moiety
Anionic surfactants			
Sodium dodecyl sulfate			
Sodium stearate			
Sodium palmitate			
Sodium cholate			
Cationic surfactants			
Cetyl trimethyl ammonium bromide (CETAB) or hexadecyl trimethyl ammonium bromide (HTAB)			
Benzalkonium or dodecyl dimethyl benzylammonium chloride			
Amphoteric surfactants			
Lecithin			

Continued

I. Physical principles and properties of pharmaceutics

TABLE 3.2 Classification of surfactants.—cont'd

Types and examples	Structures		
		Hydrophobic moiety	Hydrophilic moiety
Nonionic surfactants			
Spans			
Tween 20	$w+x+y+z=20$		
Pluronic F127 ($n=100, m=65$)			

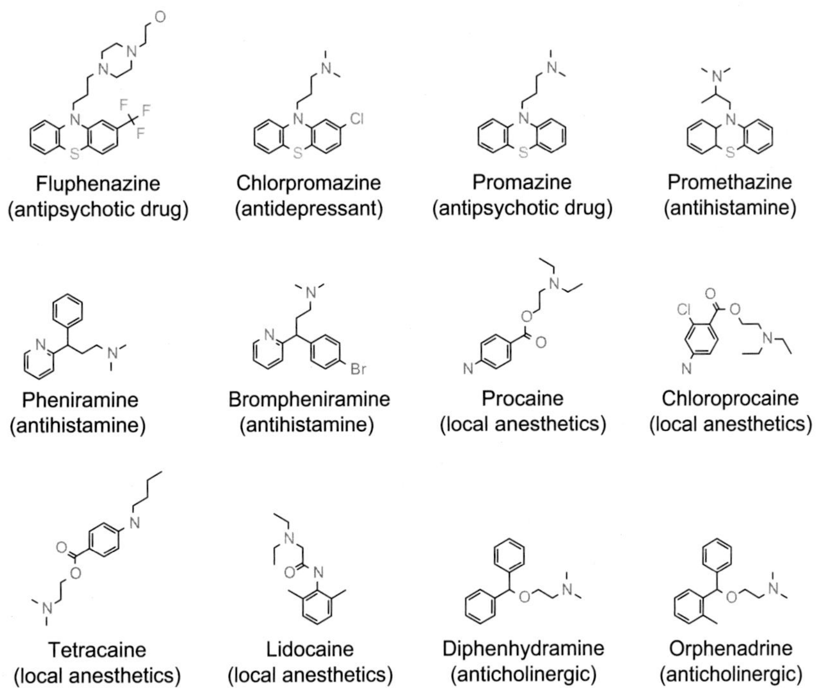

FIGURE 3.6 Structures of some of the drugs owing their activity to their surface activity.

material is important for protecting drug quality. The permeability of the packaging material or the rate of evaporation of the drug through it can be easily determined from the increase in mass of a desiccant suspended over the monolayer of the packaging material or from the decrease in weight of a Petri dish containing the drug solution over which the monolayer of packaging material is spread.

Monolayer models can also be used for screening polymers or their blends for their potential use as enteric and film-coating materials for solid dosage forms. Monolayers of cellulose acetate butyrate or stearate are not affected by pH changes from 3 to 6.5 due to the formation of highly compact condensed films that cannot be degraded either in the stomach or intestine; therefore, they are not suitable for enteric coating. However, cellulose acetate phthalate forms a condensed monolayer film at pH 3 but not at pH 6.5 and therefore is a suitable material for enteric coating purposes.

Example

When 1 mL of a 0.009% (w/v) solution of stearic acid (mol. wt. 284.3) dissolved in a volatile organic solvent is placed on the surface of water in a container, the solvent evaporates, leaving the stearic acid spread over the surface as an insoluble monolayer film. If the surface area occupied by the film is 420 cm^2, calculate the area occupied by each molecule of stearic acid in the film.

Solution:

One mole of a substance contains 6.022×10^{23} (Avogadro's number of) molecules. The number of **moles** present in 1 mL of 0.009% (w/v) of stearic acid, which occupies an area equal to 420 cm^2 is calculated first. The next step is to calculate the number of **molecules** of stearic acid present. The question asks for the area occupied by 1 molecule, which you can calculate by dividing 420 cm^2 by the number of molecules in 1 mL of 0.009% (w/v) stearic acid, as follows:

$$1 \text{ mL of } 0.009\% \text{ (w/v) stearic acid} = 0.00009 \text{ g stearic acid}$$

Therefore, # of moles in 1 mL of 0.009% (w/v) stearic acid $= \left(\dfrac{0.00009 \text{ g}}{284.3 \text{ g/moles}} \right) = 3.16 \times 10^{-7} \text{ moles}$

Therefore, the number of molecules in 1 mL of 0.009% (w/v) stearic acid $= 3.16 \times 10^{-7}$ mole $\times 6.022 \times 10^{23}$ molecules/mole $= 1.91 \times 10^{17}$ molecules. Consequently, the area occupied by one molecule $= 420$ cm^2/1.91×10^{17} molecules $= 219.89 \times 10^{-17}$ cm^2/molecule.

3.3.11 Factors affecting adsorption at monolayer surface film

3.3.11.1 Solubility of the adsorbate

The solubility of the solute (i.e., adsorbate) is inversely related to its adsorption. The bond between the adsorbate and the solvent must be broken for adsorption to happen. Greater solubility means a stronger bond between the adsorbate and the solvent. Therefore, the greater solubility of adsorbate in a solvent results in less adsorption. As an example, when iodine (an adsorbate) is dissolved in three solvents like carbon tetrachloride, chloroform, and carbon disulfide and further exposed to activated charcoal (adsorbent), the adsorption of iodine to adsorbent is higher from the carbon disulfide solution as compared to the other two solutions because iodine is less soluble in carbon disulfide than in chloroform or carbon tetrachloride.

3.3.11.2 pH of the solvent

The pH of an aqueous solution of weak acids or weak bases can affect its solubility. The pH favoring unionization decreases the aqueous solubility of a drug, which in turn increases its adsorption. The adsorption efficiency (i.e., the ratio of the amount of sulfa drug adsorbed onto zeolites to the initial amount of sulfa drug) of different sulfa drugs (see Fig. 3.7) is maximum at a pH range from pK_1 through pK_2 when they exist as unionized neutral molecules, which are the least soluble in comparison to their ionized forms.

3.3.11.3 Nature of the adsorbent

The adsorbent is the material on which adsorption occurs. The greater the surface area of the adsorbent, the greater would be the adsorption. Therefore, adsorbents having pores and fine particles would adsorb more. Adsorbent clays such as bentonite, attapulgite, and kaoline have charged sites too, which also facilitate the adsorption of oppositely charged particles. This is the basis of how bentonite detox works in its application of treating diarrhea. Some adsorbents, such as magnesium trisilicate, which is used as an antacid, adsorb digoxin. Therefore, a

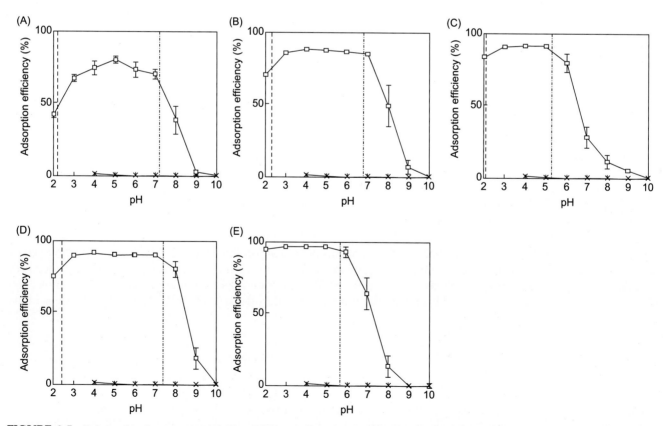

FIGURE 3.7 Relationship between pH and the adsorption efficiency of sulfa drugs on HSZ-385 (squares), and A-type zeolite (crosses): (A) sulfathiazole, (B) sulfamerazine, (C) sulfamethizole, (D) sulfadimidine, and (E) sulfamethoxazole. The $pK_{a,1}$ and $pK_{a,2}$ values for each sulfa drug are displayed as dashed and dash-dotted lines, respectively [3].

simultaneous administration of digoxin and antacid should be avoided. The use of activated charcoal in the detoxication of some orally ingested poison is another application of adsorption in clinical practice.

3.3.11.4 Temperature

Adsorption is generally an exothermic process, so an increase in temperature favors the opposite phenomenon: desorption. This technique is used to prepare activated charcoal from charcoal at a high temperature (600°C–900°C).

3.4 Solubilization

Surfactants form micelles when their concentration is greater than the CMC. Solubilization is the process of increasing the aqueous solubility of a drug through the presence of a surfactant at or above its CMC. The formation of micelles helps in solubilizing a water-insoluble substance (solubilisate) by incorporation into micelles. It is affected by many factors as described in the following sections.

3.4.1 Nature of the surfactant

Generally, the longer the hydrophobic chain of a surfactant, the larger would be the micelles' size, resulting in greater solubilization. The solubility of phenobarbital increases more in Tween 80 than in Tween 20, which contains 12 carbon chain long hydrophobic moiety versus 18 carbon chain length in Tween 80. Although the increased chain length of hydrophilic moiety results in an overall increase in solubility, the mechanism involved is different from the size of the hydrophobic chain length. An increase in the chain length of hydrophilic moiety results in a decrease in micellar size, but the number of micelles per unit volume of the liquid increases. Therefore, even if drug molecules solubilized per micelle decrease due to a decrease in size, overall solubility increases due to an increase in number of micelles formed. For example, the solubility of dexamethasone increases in n-alkyl polyoxyethylene with an increase in oxyethylene number while keeping the alkyl length constant at 16 carbons.

3.4.2 Nature of the solubilisate

There is no simple correlation between the physical properties of the solubilisate and solubilization. As a general rule, a decrease in alkyl chain length, unsaturation in comparison to saturation, and cyclization of solubilisate can affect solubilization. There could be specific rules for a particular category of drug; for example, the solubility of steroidal hormones increases with the presence of more polar groups at the 17th carbon, and the reported order of solubility is progesterone < testosterone < deoxycorticosterone, where the C_{17} substituents are $COCH_3$, OH, and $COCH_2OH$, respectively.

3.4.3 Effect of temperature

Generally, an increase in temperature increases micellar size and thus increases solubilization. This increase is particularly pronounced with nonionic surfactants. However, this situation becomes more complicated when the aqueous solubility of the solubilisate increases with an increase in temperature in the surfactant solution.

3.4.4 Application of solubilization

Micellar solubilization has been used extensively for the formulation and delivery of insoluble drugs. Following are some examples.

- Phenolic compounds (cresol, chlorocresol, chloroxylenol, and thymol) are solubilized in water with help of soap, which makes it possible to use them as disinfectants. Iodine is solubilized in Iodophor (Povidone-Iodine) by using polyvinylpyrrolidone, which releases iodine when diluted with water. Iodophor is superior to an iodine–iodide solution because less of it is lost through the sublimation process.
- Many steroidal ophthalmic solutions (e.g., dexamethasone, fluocinolone, fluorometholone, difluprednate, loteprednol, prednisolone, and triamcinolone) are prepared using the surfactants polysorbate or polyoxyethylene sorbitan esters (Tween) of fatty acids. These water-insoluble steroidal drugs can be solubilized in oily solvents but are not acceptable for ophthalmic use due to their cloudy nature.

- Water-insoluble vitamins such as vitamins A, D, E, and K are solubilized by adding polysorbate 20 or 80 for preparing parenteral formulations.
- The nonionic surfactant Cremophor EL has been used in the solubilization of a wide variety of hydrophobic drugs. They include anesthetics, photosensitizers, sedatives, immunosuppressive agents, and anticancer drugs such as paclitaxel, for which development was suspended for many years due to its solubilization problem.
- In addition to solubilization, micelles are also useful in developing a long-circulating drug delivery system. Polymeric micelles formed from polyethylene oxide (PEO)—polypropylene oxide (PPO) diblock copolymer have been found to prevent opsonization and subsequent recognition by the macrophages of the reticuloendothelial system, thereby allowing the micelles to circulate longer and deliver drugs in a sustained manner at the desired site.

Students interested in a greater understanding of the process of solubilization and its application should refer to Ref. [4], which provides comprehensive mechanistic details of its various uses.

3.5 Rheology

The term *rheology* is derived from two Greek words *rheo* (flow) and *logos* (science). Rheology is the science that studies the flow of fluids and deformation of solids. Rheology is involved in the mixing and flow of materials, their packaging into containers, and their removal prior to use, whether this is achieved by pouring from a bottle, extrusion from a tube, or passage through a syringe needle. The rheology of a particular product, which can range in consistency from a fluid to a semisolid to a solid, can affect its patient acceptability, physical stability, and even biological availability.

3.5.1 Viscosity and fluidity

Viscosity is the resistance offered by a liquid or a fluid to flow. The greater the resistance, the higher is the viscosity. For example, the viscosity of a toothpaste is significantly higher than a mouthwash. Viscosity is denoted by the symbol η. Another term also commonly used in rheology is *fluidity*. Fluidity is the ease with which a liquid or a fluid flows and is defined as the reciprocal of viscosity. Fluidity is denoted by the symbol Φ and expressed by Eq. (3.5):

$$\varphi = \frac{1}{\eta}$$

(3.5)

3.5.2 Newtonian versus non-Newtonian fluid

Fluids that flow according to Newton's law of flow are called Newtonian systems, whereas those that do not comply are called non-Newtonian systems. Water for injection is a Newtonian fluid, but zinc oxide paste and ointment are examples of non-Newtonian fluids.

For Newtonian fluids, let us consider a cube of fluid with the surface area of each side equal to A, as shown in Fig. 3.8. For convenience, let us imagine this cube to consist of parallel plates of liquid stacked on one another. If

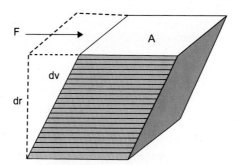

FIGURE 3.8 Diagrammatic representation of the shearing force required to produce a definite velocity gradient between the parallel planes of a block of materials.

we apply a force equal to F on the top plate, it starts moving with a velocity v. The plate below this top plate, however, does not move as fast as the top plate, and its velocity is lower than v.

The velocity of the plates decreases further with distance from the top plate, and the plate on the base does not move at all. We, therefore, see that the velocity of flow is a function of distance, and mathematically, we represent this as dv/dr, as shown in Fig. 3.8. The term dv/dr is the velocity gradient, or the rate of shear, and is often represented by V_g.

For Newtonian fluids, the force, F, applied per unit area, A (shearing stress, or P), is proportional to V_g, which is represented by Eq. (3.6):

$$\frac{F}{A} \propto \frac{dv}{dr}$$

$$\frac{F}{A} = \eta \frac{dv}{dr} \text{ or } p = \eta V_g$$

(3.6)

η is the coefficient of viscosity, or simply the viscosity. For Newtonian liquids, as the P is directly proportional to V_g, a plot of V_g versus P gives a straight line that passes through the origin, as shown in Fig. 3.9A.

3.5.3 Common units of viscosity

The unit of viscosity is the poise (p), and its CGS unit is g/cm s (1 p = 1 g/cm s).

The p is sometimes considered large for many fluids, and it is more common to represent viscosity by the centipoises, or cp, which is equal to 0.01 p.

Another commonly used term to represent the viscosity of liquids is kinematic viscosity, which is equal to the viscosity normalized to its density (ρ) at a particular temperature, as shown in Eq. (3.7):

$$\text{Kinematic viscosity} = \frac{\eta}{\rho}$$

(3.7)

The units of kinematic viscosity are stoke (s) and centistokes (cs).

3.5.4 Effect of temperature on the viscosity of a fluid

The viscosity of fluids is affected by temperature. Therefore, whenever the viscosity of a fluid is reported, the temperature at which it was determined should be provided. While the viscosity of a gas increases with temperature, for

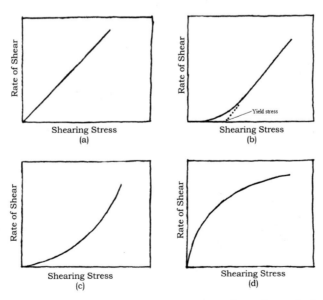

FIGURE 3.9 Various kinds of flow patterns: (A) Newtonian flow, (B) plastic flow, (C) pseudoplastic flow, and (D) dilatant flow.

liquids, it decreases with temperature. The dependence of viscosity on temperature is given by the Arrhenius equation, as shown in Eq. (3.8):

$$\eta = Ae^{E_v/RT} \tag{3.8}$$

where A is a constant depending on the molecular weight and molar volume of the liquid, E_v is the activation energy required to initiate flow, R is the gas constant, and T is the absolute temperature.

Non-Newtonian liquids do not follow Newton's equation of flow. Liquid and solid heterogeneous dispersions such as colloidal solutions, emulsions, liquid suspensions, ointments, and similar products are some examples of this class. The main types of non-Newtonian flow, as shown in Fig. 3.9, are plastic flow, simple pseudoplastic, dilatant, and thixotropic.

- *Plastic flow (shear thinning)*: A liquid that exhibits plastic flow does not flow until the applied shearing stress exceeds a minimum value (called yield value or yield stress of the plastic material). Below the yield stress, the material behaves as an elastic solid; and above the yield stress, as a Newtonian fluid (Fig. 3.9B). Plastic flow is generally exhibited by concentrated suspensions.
- *Pseudoplastic flow (shear thinning)*: A liquid that flows more readily with increased shearing stress exhibits pseudoplastic flow (Fig. 3.9C). Such liquids become thinner on the application of stress. Polymers in solution generally exhibit pseudoplastic flow. No yield value is exhibited by these systems.
- *Dilatant flow (shear thickening)*: The flow pattern exhibited by dilatant liquids is opposite to that of the pseudoplastic liquids. In this case, the liquids become thicker or flow with increased resistance with the application of stress (Fig. 3.9D). This property is generally exhibited by concentrated suspensions (more than 50% w/v).
- *Thixotropic*: Thixotropy is a special characteristic that is exhibited by shear thinning systems, such as pseudoplastic and plastic liquids. When shear is applied to these materials, the resistance to flow progressively decreases. If the shear is removed, one would expect the liquids to regain their original viscosity. Thixotropic substances, however, remain in their "thinned" state, even after the shear is removed, for an extended period of time, which is represented by the area demarked by upward and downward curve, often called hysteresis loop as shown in Fig. 3.10.

Thixotropic behavior is useful for many pharmaceutical preparations. For example, during the formulation of a drug suspension, a suspending agent is added to make the suspension more viscous to avoid the settling of drug particles. However, if the suspension is too viscous, it may not flow from the bottle containing the suspension. However, if the suspension is thixotropic, it would remain viscous in the bottle, thereby minimizing sedimentation. However, if the bottle is shaken vigorously, the shear resulting from the shaking will cause the suspension to thin down and remain in that state for long enough to facilitate pouring and dispensing from the bottle.

3.5.5 Measurement of viscosity

The measurement of viscosity is called viscometry, and numerous viscometers are available for measuring the viscosity of Newtonian and non-Newtonian liquids. The viscometers can be divided into two categories.

1. Those that operate at a single rate of shear. These viscometers are useful for determining the viscosity of Newtonian liquids because the viscosity is a constant function of the rate of shear. Examples include capillary viscometers such as the Ostwald viscometer (Fig. 3.11). These viscometers may be used for liquids that flow relatively easily because the measurement is based on the flow of the liquid through a capillary tube.

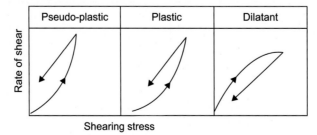

FIGURE 3.10   Thixotropic flow pattern.

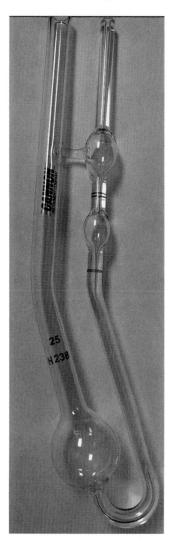

FIGURE 3.11   A diagrammatic representation of an Ostwald viscometer.

2. Those that operate at multiple rates of shear. These viscometers are useful for non-Newtonian fluids and may also be used for semisolid substances such as gels and pastes. Examples include the cup and bob viscometer and the cone and plate viscometer. A cone and plate viscometer is shown in Fig. 3.12.

3.5.6 Applications of rheology in pharmacy

Rheology affects many significant pharmaceutical issues such as mixing and preparation of dosage forms, particle-size reduction of a drug through the use of shear, removal of medicines before use by pouring from a bottle or extruding from tubes or passaging through hypodermic needles, physical stability of a drug in a dispersed system, flow of powders from hoppers to die during tablet manufacturing, and release of a drug from its dosage form, etc.

3.5.7 Clinical rheology

3.5.7.1 Plasma viscosity and blood viscoelasticity

Blood is not a fluid in the ordinary sense. It is a fluidized suspension of elastic cells whose flow profile is regulated by its viscoelastic properties. Many blood parameters, such as plasma viscosity, red blood cell deformability, aggregation, and hematocrit, influence the viscoelastic characteristics of blood. Major shifts in the viscoelasticity of blood

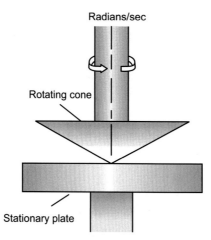

FIGURE 3.12   Constant shear rate condition in a cone and plate viscometer.

have been found to be associated with pathological conditions such as myocardial infarction, peripheral vascular disease, cancer, and diabetes.

3.5.7.2 Viscosity and viscoelasticity

If the flow is constant with time, the ratio of shear stress to shear rate is viscosity. When flows change with time, such as blood flow in human circulation, the liquid generally demonstrates both a viscous and an elastic effect, both of which determine the stress-to-strain rate relationship. Such liquids are called viscoelastic. Blood plasma normally shows viscosity only, whereas whole blood is both viscous and elastic.

3.5.7.3 Origin of blood viscoelasticity

Red blood cells (RBCs) are not rigid but elastic, which provides viscoelasticity to blood. When red cells are at rest, they tend to aggregate and stack together in a space-efficient manner, as shown in Fig. 3.13 marked by region 1. In order for blood to flow freely, these aggregates are required to be disaggregated and deformed elastically. As blood flow further proceeds, RBCs slide over each other continuously and elastically. Thus, blood flow is better characterized by both viscosity and elasticity than viscosity alone. The failure of RBCs either to disaggregate or deform (or

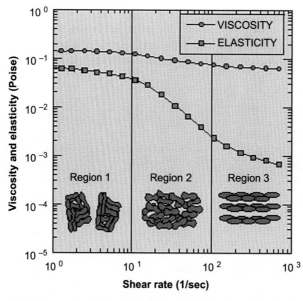

FIGURE 3.13   The dependence of normal human blood viscoelasticity at 2 Hz (i.e., about human pulse rate) and 22°C on shear rate. *Adapted from Ref. [5].*

both) results in impaired perfusion of the capillary beds and in turn surrounding tissues. As the viscoelasticity of blood is mainly determined by the disaggregation and deformability of RBCs, any factor or condition influencing the viscoelasticity of blood would eventually affect its flow pattern too.

Fig. 3.13 shows that as the shear rate increases in region 1, the viscoelasticity gradually decreases due to the expected decrease in aggregate size. As the shear rate increases further in region 2, the applied forces deform the cells even further, resulting in some sort of orientation. Finally, the increased shear rate in region 3 orients the cells in a parallel laminar sheet most suitable for easy flow of the blood, which is indicated by a decrease in both viscosity and elasticity; however, the decrease in elasticity is much more pronounced. Therefore, any condition causing a decrease in the deformability of RBCs would produce dilatant viscoelasticity marked by elevated viscosity and elasticity in the high shear rate of region 3.

Any alteration in plasma composition brought about by changes in osmotic pressure, pH, concentration of fibrinogen and other plasma proteins, clinically introduced blood volume expanders, and any pathological condition causing a change in hematocrit value can have major effects on blood viscoelasticity [5].

3.6 Colligative properties

The physical properties of solutions may be classified as additive, constitutive, or colligative.

- *Additive properties:* These properties depend on the sum of properties of constituents in a solution. For example, the mass of a solute in a solution is an additive property because it is the sum of the mass of constituent molecules.
- *Constitutive properties:* These properties depend on the arrangement of the atoms within a molecule and also the number and kinds of atoms within a molecule. Examples include refraction of light, electrical properties, surface and interfacial characteristics, and solubility. The solubility of the same substance existing in different crystalline forms could be different although all the forms represent the same substance chemically.
- *Colligative properties*: These properties depend mainly on the number of particles in a solution and are not affected by the nature of the chemical species. The colligative properties of solutions are osmotic pressure, vapor pressure lowering, freezing point depression, and boiling point elevation. For example, the osmotic pressure generated by 1 million molecules of urea in 100 mL of water is the same as that generated by 1 million molecules of sucrose or naphthalene in the same volume.

When a nonvolatile component, for example, salt, is combined with a volatile solvent, such as water, the vapor pressure above the solution is provided solely by the solvent. However, the nonvolatile solute decreases the vapor pressure of the solvent, and the decrease in vapor pressure is proportional to the number of molecules of the solute and not on the identity of the solute. As a result, the solution properties that are affected include lowering of vapor pressure, depression of freezing point, elevation of boiling point, and osmotic pressure. These properties are called colligative properties (from the Greek word, meaning "collected together") as they depend on the number rather than the nature of the constituents.

3.6.1 Vapor pressure lowering and elevation of boiling point

The normal boiling point of a solvent is the temperature at which its vapor pressure equals the external pressure or atmospheric pressure, which is equal to 760 mm of Hg. As the addition of a nonvolatile solute lowers the vapor pressure, the vapor pressure of such a solution at the normal boiling temperature is less than 760 mm of Hg. Therefore, more heat is required so that the vapor pressure can approach the value of the external pressure. In other words, an elevation of the boiling point is observed. It has also been observed that the ratio of the elevation in boiling point, $T_{solu} - T_{solv}$, or ΔT_b, to the vapor pressure lowering, $p_{solv} - p_{solu}$, or Δp is approximately a constant; that is,

$$\frac{\Delta T_b}{\Delta p} = k \qquad (3.9)$$

or

$$\Delta T_b = k\Delta p \qquad (3.10)$$

where k is a constant; T_{solu} and T_{solv} are the boiling points of solution and pure solvent, respectively; and p_{solu} and p_{solv} are vapor pressures of solution and pure solvent, respectively. As the pure vapor pressure, p_{solv}, for any solvent is a constant, we can consider elevation in the boiling point, ΔT_b, to be proportional to $\Delta p/p_{solv}$, the relative lowering of vapor pressure. By Raoult's law, the relative lowering of vapor pressure is equal to the mole fraction of the solute, X_{solute}. Therefore,

$$\Delta T_b = k' X_{solute} \tag{3.11}$$

where k' is another constant. In dilute solutions, the mole fraction is proportional to the molality, m, of the solution. As a result, Eq. (3.11) reduces to

$$\Delta T_b = k_b m \tag{3.12}$$

where k_b is known as the molal elevation constant or the *ebullioscopic* constant, which has a characteristic value for each solvent.

3.6.2 Depression of freezing point

The addition of a nonvolatile solute also causes depression of the freezing point of the pure solvent. Therefore, the freezing point of a solution is always lower than that of the pure solvent. This is the principle used to manufacture antifreeze solutions for winter or even the use of salt on icy roads in the winter. The antifreeze solutions do not freeze at 0°C due to the presence of salt, but freeze at significantly lower temperatures than the pure solvent, thus preventing freezing of the antifreeze solution at 0°C . An equation similar to that shown previously is used to quantitate this decrease in freezing point, as shown in Eq. (3.13):

$$\Delta T_f = k_f m \tag{3.13}$$

Here, ΔT_f is the depression in the freezing point, k_f, is called the molal depression constant or the *cryoscopic constant*, and m is the molality of the solution. This concept is used for adjusting the tonicity of parenterals.

3.6.3 Osmosis and osmotic pressure

If a volume of pure solvent and solution containing a nonvolatile solute, for example, sucrose solution, is separated by a semipermeable membrane, there occurs a flow of the solvent from the pure solvent to the solution, as indicated by an increase in the level of solution in the right compartment in Fig. 3.14A, called osmosis. The pressure applied by the increased level of the liquid column in the right compartment (Fig. 3.14A) is called osmotic pressure, which is a pressure just sufficient to stop the process of osmosis. Obviously, water would move in the opposite

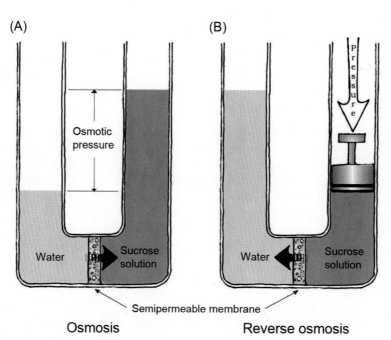

FIGURE 3.14   A diagrammatic representation of osmosis and reverse osmosis.

direction if pressure were applied over the solution (Fig. 3.14B), a process called reverse osmosis, which is used in purifying water or desalinating sea water.

The phenomenon of osmosis can be explained at a molecular level, assuming the dissolved solute (e.g., sucrose) molecules are interacting with the solvent (e.g., water) molecules. The water molecules in the left compartment containing fewer solute molecules are more mobile than those in the more concentrated right compartment. These two compartments are separated by a semipermeable membrane that permits only water to pass through itself. Consequently, the solute molecules cannot redistribute themselves between the compartments because their movement is restricted by the semipermeable membrane. However, solvent molecules can pass through the membrane; and consequently, they would flow predominantly from the compartment containing less solute to the one containing more solute, resulting in an increase in the level of solution. The increase in the level of solution over that of solvent (water) would create a pressure termed as osmotic pressure.

In fact, no membrane is perfectly semipermeable, for example, the membrane surrounding mammalian red blood cells does allow the passage of some solute particles. Thus, when two solutions are separated by a semipermeable membrane and there is no net movement of solvent across the membrane, the two solutions are said to be *isotonic* with respect to that membrane.

- Hypotonic solutions have a lower concentration of ions and undissociated molecules than blood serum. When in contact with red blood cells, liquid passes into the cells, causing them to swell and burst (hemolysis).
- Hypertonic solutions have a higher concentration of ions and undissociated molecules than blood serum. When in contact with red blood cells, liquid passes out of the cells, causing them to shrink and become crenated.

Two solutions are said to be isoosmotic if they have the same osmotic pressure. Solutions that are iso-osmotic with blood serum or tissue fluids are not always isotonic. This happens when the cell membrane is permeable to one or more solutes as well as to the solvent. Cell membranes are not perfectly semipermeable because otherwise no nutrients or waste products would diffuse through them and the cell would die.

The distinction between osmotic pressure and tonicity is illustrated in Fig. 3.15, in which a hypothetical cell membrane is assumed to be permeable to a solvent, water, and urea, but impermeable to glycogen and a neutral protein. The solutes are assumed to be present at equal and low concentration (10 mmol/L) so that their solutions are isoosmotic. The solutions inside and outside the cell are therefore initially iso-osmotic in examples A, B, and C.

In Fig. 3.15A, the solutes cannot pass through the cell membrane; therefore, the external solution is always isotonic as well as isoosmotic with the internal solution. In Fig. 3.15B, urea passes freely through the cell membrane into the cell; water also diffuses into the cell in an attempt to equalize the total concentration of solute molecules on both sides of the membrane. The external solution is, therefore, hypotonic with respect to the internal solution. Fig. 3.15C is the reverse of Fig. 3.15B. In C, both urea and water diffuse out of the cell so that the external solution is hypertonic relative to the internal solution. In both B and C, the external and internal solutions will cease to be isoosmotic when some urea has diffused through the cell membrane. In Fig. 3.15D, the total concentration of solute molecules inside the cell is initially twice that outside, so the solutions are not initially isoosmotic. Urea diffuses out of the cell, and water diffuses in; therefore, the solutions are not initially isotonic. Eventually, urea and water distribute themselves so that their concentrations are equalized on both sides of the membrane. Consequently, at equilibrium, the external and internal solutions will be both isoosmotic and isotonic too.

Pharmaceutical preparations, which on administration come into contact with blood cells or other unprotected tissue cells, need to be made isotonic to prevent tissue damage or pain. Ophthalmic and otic preparations

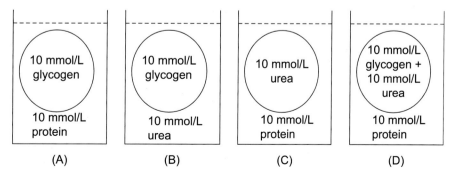

FIGURE 3.15 Isoosmoticity versus isotonicity. (A) Isoosmotic and isotonic, (B) initially isoosmotic and hypotonic, (C) initially isoosmotic and hypertonic, and (D) initially neither isoosmotic nor isotonic but at equilibrium isoosmotic and isotonic.

intended for installation into the eye or nose should be approximately isotonic to avoid irritation. Parenteral solutions for intravenous or intramuscular injection can cause tissue irritation, pain on injection, and electrolyte shifts if the solutions deviate from isotonicity with the blood. Solutions that are hypotonic with respect to blood and lacrimal secretions may be adjusted to isotonicity through the addition of suitable substances such as sodium chloride or dextrose. Hypertonic solutions cannot be adjusted; when given parenterally, they are usually administered slowly in small volumes or into a large vein such as the subclavian, where dilution and distribution occur rapidly.

The effects of hypotonic and hypertonic solutions on living cells are a function of (1) the volume of the solution added, (2) the concentration of the solute, and (3) the nature of the solute. While both hypertonic and hypotonic solutions may cause pain and damage to cells, the effects of hypotonic solutions are more easily seen because they result in the lysis of the cell, an irreversible process. Hypertonic solutions result in crenation or shrinking of the cells, which is often reversible and can be viewed with a suitable microscope only.

3.6.4 Van't Hoff equation for osmotic pressure

The osmotic pressure caused by nondissociating solute in a solution is given by

$$\pi V = nRT \tag{3.14}$$

where π is the osmotic pressure, V is the volume of the solution in liters, n is the number of moles of the solute, R the gas constant equal to 0.082 L atm/mol deg, and T is the absolute temperature. Since osmotic pressure is a colligative property, there is a correction in the preceding equation for calculating the osmotic pressure of solutions containing electrolytes, that is, dissociating solutes. Van't Hoff introduced a correction factor, i, which approaches a number equal to the number of ions, ν, produced by a solute upon complete dissociation. The ratio i/ν is called osmotic coefficient, Φ, which has been used in the following equation applicable for calculating osmotic pressure of a solution containing electrolytes:

$$\pi V = \varphi nRT \tag{3.15}$$

Calculating the osmotic coefficient is not easy; therefore, a concept of "dissociation factor" is used. This is a good approximation for "osmotic coefficient" and could be readily and easily calculated as follows:
Nonelectrolytes: 1
Substances dissociating into 2 ions: 1.8
Substances dissociating into 3 ions: 2.6
Substances dissociating into 4 ions: 3.4
Substances dissociating into 5 ions: 4.2
Tip: Contribution of 0.8 by each additional ion.
The concept of dissociation factor is based on assuming 80% dissociation if no % dissociation is given.

Example

Calculate the dissociation factor for zinc sulfate, $ZnSO_4$, if it is 40% ionized in solutions.
Solution:
If we have 100 particles of $ZnSO_4$
40 Zn ions.
40 SO_4 ions.
60 $ZnSO_4$ undissociated.
140 Total particles = 1.4 times as many particles as there were before dissociation; thus, the dissociation factor is 1.4. (*Here particles mean any ion, molecule, free radical, or any thing which can contribute to osmotic pressure—a colligative property.*)

Example

One gram of sucrose, molecular weight 342 g/mol, is dissolved in 100 mL of solution at 25°C. What is the osmotic pressure (π) of the solution?
Solution:
The # of moles of sucrose in one gram/100 mL = (10 g/L)/342 g/mol = 0.029 mol/L
Hence, π = (0.029 mol/L) × (0.0821 L atm/K) × 298 K = 0.71 atm [N.B. 25°C = 273 +25 = 298 K]

3.7 Osmolarity and osmolality

Osmotic pressure is expressed as osmolarity or osmolality. These terms can be conceptualized by comparing them with molarity and molality, respectively. Osmolarity is the mass of a solute which produces the osmotic pressure equal to that produced by 1 mol of an ideal unionized (i.e., nonelectrolyte) when dissolved in sufficient quantity of solvent (e.g., water) to produce 1 L (i.e., 1000 cm^3) of solution. Osmolality differs from osmolarity in the sense that the amount of solvent is always 1 kg instead of a quantity sufficient to produce 1 L of solution.

To make an isoosmotic, that is, physiologically stable, solution for *in vivo* use, one needs 0.155 M NaCl, or 0.1033 M CaCl$_2$ or 0.31 M sucrose. Not one of these compounds is able to freely pass through the RBC plasma membrane. Here, NaCl, CaCl$_2$, and sucrose are all equivalent osmotically because each of them would have the same osmotic pressure since each solution contains approximately the same number of dissolved particles. Sucrose, a nondissociating substance, has 0.31 mol of particles in a 0.31 M solution. As CaCl$_2$ dissociates into three separate ions (1 Ca^{2+} and 2 Cl$^-$), there are 0.31 mol of particles in a 0.1033 M solution (3 × 0.1033 or ~0.31 mol of particles). Thus, the important concept is the total concentration of dissolved solute particles, which is expressed by osmolarity. The unit of osmolarity (osmole/L) indicates the number of moles of dissolved particles per liter. Thus, in the preceding example, 0.155 M NaCl is a 0.31 osM solution (0.155 M Na$^+$ + 0.155 M Cl$^-$). One liter of water weighs differently at different temperatures; for example, at 25°C, 1 L of water weighs 997 g. Therefore, osmolality is generally greater than osmolarity and expressed by osmolality = (1000/997) × osmolarity at 25°C.

The mass of a solvent remains the same regardless of any changes in pressure or temperature; therefore, osmolality is the common method of measurement in osmometry and is used to determine medical conditions such as diabetes, shock, and dehydration, whereas osmolarity is used for the detection of the concentration of dissolved particles in urine.

Example

A 0.9% (w/w) solution of sodium chloride has an osmotic coefficient 0.928. What is its osmolality?
Solution:
Osmolality is the number of moles of total ions in 1 kg of solvent. Therefore,

$$\text{Osmolality} = \text{\# of ions} \times \text{\# of moles of solute in 1 kg of solvent} \times \text{osmotic coefficient}$$

$$0.9\% \text{ (w/w) solution of NaCl} = \frac{9 \text{ g of NaCl}}{1 \text{ kg of solvent}} = \frac{9 \text{ g NaCl}}{58.5 \text{ g NaCl per mole}} = 0.154 \text{ mole NaCl}$$

Therefore,
Osmolality = 2 × 0.154 × 0.928 = 0.286 osmol/kg or 286 mosmol/kg

3.7.1 Adjusting tonicity

Due to the presence of numerous salts and osmotic ingredients, body fluids such as blood and lachrymal fluid exert a certain osmotic pressure. As a result, the tonicity or osmotic pressure of pharmaceutical solutions that are meant to be applied to delicate membranes of the body should be adjusted so that they are isotonic with body fluids. Isotonic solutions cause no swelling or contraction of the tissues with which they come in contact and produce no discomfort when instilled in the eye, nasal tract, blood, or other body tissues. Isotonic sodium chloride is a familiar example of such a preparation and consists of 0.9 g NaCl per 100 mL of water.

The tonicity of a hypotonic pharmaceutical solution can be adjusted by adding a sufficient amount of sodium chloride, which would increase the tonicity of the solution to isotonic levels. The amount of sodium chloride to be added can be measured by the cryoscopic method or the sodium chloride equivalent method. In the opposite case of hypertonic solution, isotonicity may be achieved by adding water calculated by the White–Vincent method or Sprowl method.

3.7.2 Adjusting tonicity of hypotonic drug solution

In the cryoscopic method, the freezing point depression is calculated for a drug concentration using the $\Delta T_f^{1\,\%}$ values available in the reference books [6,7]. For the remaining freezing point depression, the required NaCl is calculated using L_{iso} equal to 3.4 or ΔT_f of 1% solution equal to 0.58.

3.7.3 L_{iso} values

The freezing point of human blood and lachrymal fluid is $-0.52°C$. Therefore, any drug solution having a freezing point depression, ΔT_f, equal to $-0.52°C$ would be isotonic. Therefore the freezing point depression, $\Delta T_f = k_f m = ik_f M = L_{iso} M$. Since 0.9% NaCl is isotonic and equal to 0.154 M [i.e., (9 g/L)/(58.5 g/mol) = 0.154 M], its L_{iso} value can be calculated as shown below.

$$L_{iso} \text{ of } 0.9\% \ NaCl = \frac{\Delta Tf}{M} = \frac{0.52}{0.154} = 3.4 \tag{3.16}$$

Therefore, L_{iso} is the decrease in freezing point brought about by 1 M drug solution which depends on the number of ions produced on dissociation (see Table 3.3).

Example

How much NaCl is required to render 150 mL of a 1.1% solution of apomorphine hydrochloride isotonic with blood serum?

Solution:

In this problem, first, one should calculate the amount that 100 mL of a 1.1% solution of apomorphine hydrochloride will decrease the freezing point. One will find the $\Delta T_f^{1\%}$ value for apomorphine hydrochloride equal to 0.08. Therefore, the decrease in freezing point by 1.1% solution = 0.08 × 1.1 = 0.088 degrees.

Therefore, one needs to add NaCl to decrease the freezing point by (0.52−0.088) 0.43 degrees, which can be calculated as follows:

Since 0.52 degrees decrease in freezing point happens due to 0.9% NaCl, 0.43 degrees decrease in freezing point would happen with [(0.9%/0.52) × 0.43 = 0.74%] 0.74% NaCl. Therefore, the amount of sodium chloride required to make 150 mL 1.1% apomorphine solution isotonic will be equal to [(0.74 g/100 mL) × 150 mL = 1.11g] 1.11 g. So, one would have to dissolve 1.65 g of apomorphine hydrochloride (1.65 g is needed to make 1.1% 150 mL) and 1.11 g of NaCl in sufficient water to make 150 mL solution which will be isotonic with blood serum.

Sodium chloride equivalent method: In this method, the quantity of the drug is multiplied by a factor, E, whose product is equal to the quantity of NaCl having similar osmotic pressure as that of the drug [7]. This quantity is subtracted from the quantity of NaCl isotonic with blood (i.e., 0.9%) to obtain the quantity of NaCl required to be added to the drug solution to make it isotonic.

TABLE 3.3 L_{iso} values for various types of electrolytes.

Electrolytes	L_{iso}	Examples[a]
Nonelectrolytes	1.9	Sucrose, dextrose
Weak electrolytes	2.0	Cocaine, ephedrine, atropine
Di-divalent electrolytes	2.0	Zinc sulfate
Uni-univalent electrolytes	3.4	Sodium chloride, oxycodone hydrochloride
Uni-divalent electrolytes	4.3	Sodium sulfate, ephedrine sulfate, atropine sulfate
Di-univalent electrolytes	4.8	Calcium chloride, zinc chloride
Uni-trivalent electrolytes	5.2	Sodium citrate
Tri-univalent electrolytes	6.0	Ferric chloride
Tetraborate electrolytes	7.6	Sodium borate

[a]Tabulated on the basis of various editions of the Merck Index, literature, and online searches [6].

If the NaCl equivalent, E, is not available in any reference book, it can be calculated for 1 g of such drug as follows.

Here, the concept is that 1 g of the drug and its equivalent amount of NaCl, E, will decrease the freezing point by the same amount. Therefore,

$$\Delta T_f^{1\ \%} = L_{iso} \times 1 g/M_w = 3.4 \times E/58.5,$$

where 3.4 is L_{iso} value for sodium chloride.

$$\text{Therefore}, E = 17 \times \frac{L_{iso}}{M_w}$$

Example

A 150 mL aqueous solution contains 1.2% apomorphine hydrochloride . What quantity of sodium chloride must be added to make the solution isotonic?

Solution:

The amount of apomorphine hydrochloride required for preparing 150 mL solution containing 1.2% apomorphine hydrochloride = (1.2 g/100 mL) × 150 mL = 1.8 g. The E value for apomorphine hydrochloride is 0.14. So, 1.8 g of apomorphine hydrochloride = 1.8 g × 0.14 = 0.252 g of NaCl.

To make a 150 mL aqueous solution isotonic, one needs [0.9 g /100 mL × 150 mL= 1.35 g] 1.35 g NaCl; however, apomorphine hydrochloride available is equivalent to 0.252 g of NaCl. Therefore, one needs to add 1.35−0.252 g = 1.098 g NaCl and 1.8 g apomorphine hydrochloride in sufficient water to make 150 mL solution.

3.7.4 Adjusting tonicity of hypertonic drug solution

The White−Vincent method involves adding water to drugs to make an isotonic solution, followed by the addition of an isotonic or isotonic-buffered diluting vehicle to bring the solution to the final volume.

Example

Make the following solution isotonic with respect to plasma.
Dibucaine hydrochloride: 0.08 g.
Sodium borate: 0.40 g.
Sterilized isotonic solution q.s.: 150.0 mL.

Solution:

Find E values from a reference book [7]; they are 0.13 and 0.42 for dibucaine hydrochloride and sodium borate, respectively:

NaCl equivalents of 0.08 g Dibucaine hydrochloride and 0.40 g Sodium borate = (0.08 g × 0.13) + (0.40 g × 0.42)

= 0.178 g NaCl

Because 0.9 g NaCl is isotonic in 100 mL solution, 0.178 g NaCl would be isotonic in (100 mL/0.9 g) × 0.178 g = 19.78 mL. Therefore, 0.08 g dibucaine hydrochloride and 0.40 g of sodium borate will be dissolved in sterilized water sufficient to make 19.78 mL, to which sufficient diluting isotonic solution will be added to make 150 mL.

The Sprowls method uses the V value, which gives volumes in milliliters for 0.3 g of a drug whose solution will be isotonic. Sufficient diluting isotonic solution can be added to obtain the desired volume.

The preceding problem can be solved using this method as follows.

The V values for dibucaine hydrochloride and sodium borate are 4.3 and 14 mL, respectively. This means that for 0.3 g of dibucaine hydrochloride, one needs 4.3 mL water. Hence, for 0.08 g dibucaine hydrochloride, (4.3 mL/ 0.3 g) × 0.08 g = 1.15 mL water would be needed. Likewise, for 0.3 g of sodium borate, one needs 14 mL water. Hence, for 0.40 g sodium borate, (14 mL/0.3 g) × 0.40 g = 18.67 mL water would be needed. Thus, the total volume of water required = 1.15 mL + 18.67 mL = 19.82 mL. Therefore, 0.08 g of dibucaine hydrochloride and 0.40 g of sodium borate should be dissolved in sterilized water sufficient to make 19.82 mL, to which a sufficient diluting isotonic solution will be added to make 150 mL.

For a list of constants used for adjusting the tonicity of drug solutions, see Table 3.4.

TABLE 3.4   List of constants used for adjusting tonicity of drug solutions.

Drugs	E value	V Value	ΔT_f^1 %
Apomorphine hydrochloride	0.14	4.7	0.08
Atropine sulfate	0.13	4.3	0.07
Boric acid	0.52	16.7	0.29
Calcium lactate	0.23	7.7	0.14
Dextrose monohydrate	0.16	5.3	0.09
Dibucaine hydrochloride	0.13	4.3	0.08
Ephedrine hydrochloride	0.30	10.0	0.18
Ephedrine sulfate	0.23	7.7	0.14
Homatropine hydrobromide	0.17	5.7	0.10
Lactose	0.17	5.7	0.10
Morphine hydrochloride	0.15	5.0	0.09
Morphine sulfate	0.14	4.8	0.08
Phenylephrine hydrochloride	0.32	9.7	0.18
Pilocarpine nitrate	0.23	7.7	0.14
Sucrose	0.08	2.7	0.05
Tetracaine hydrochloride	0.18	6.0	0.11
Urea	0.59	19.7	0.35

E value = 1 g of drug would have osmotic pressure equal to E g of NaCl. v value = 0.3 g of drug when dissolved in V mL of water would be isotonic. ΔT_f^1 % = Decrease in freezing point of water by 1% solution of the drug. Tabulated on the basis of various editions of Merck Index, literature, and online searches [6].

3.7.5   Clinical significance of osmosis

Existence of equal osmotic pressure inside and outside of living cells is required for their viability and maintenance of homeostasis. The osmotic imbalances can lead to many pathological conditions, such as diarrhea. Oral rehydration therapy (i.e., administration of a mixture of glucose and salts in a physiological amount) is required to replenish and stop the water loss during diarrhea. *E. coli* and other diarrhea-causing microorganisms either increase the secretion of Cl^- ions into the intestinal lumen or decrease the absorption of Na^+ ions into the blood. Consequently, the ionic concentration in the intestine becomes more than in the blood, which creates an osmotic gradient in favor of the intestine. Hence, there is a net flow of water from the systemic circulation to the intestine.

Fortunately, in addition to absorption by intestinal villus cells, Na^+ ions are also actively transported from the intestine to blood via transporters that are not impaired in diarrhea. However, these transporters require the presence of glucose molecules to transport Na^+ ions. Therefore, oral rehydration therapy (ORT) includes a mixture of glucose and other electrolytes that do not do anything about the severity of diarrhea but replace the lost fluids, thereby minimizing the risk of dehydration.

A higher concentration of glucose would not speed up the activity of the cotransport system; rather, an osmotic pressure would be built up, which would induce the flow of water from the systemic circulation to the intestinal lumen. However, substituting glucose in ORT with starch is a better choice because it releases hundreds of glucose molecules on being broken down by the normal, gradual digestive process, and they are immediately taken up by the cotransport systems and removed from the intestinal lumen. The presence of starch does not cause any generation of osmotic gradients because osmotic pressure is a colligative property. A similar useful effect can also be obtained by using proteins instead of starch because there is a cotransport system for amino acids, too. This forms the basis of food-based ORT, which can be prepared at home from inexpensive materials.

3.8 Solubility and solutions of nonelectrolytes

Nonelectrolytes are substances that do not yield ions when dissolved in water.

Example: Solution of glucose in water.

Electrolytes are substances that form ions in solution and conduct electric current.

Examples: Hydrochloric acid, sodium chloride, etc.

Depending on the particle size of the dispersed phase in a dispersed medium, three different types of dispersions can be formed (molecular dispersion, colloidal dispersion, and coarse dispersion). A true solution is a mixture of two or more components that form a homogeneous molecular dispersion. Particle size of the dispersed phase in solution (molecular dispersion) is less than 1.0 nm.

A coarse dispersion represents a system in which the diameter of the dispersed particles is larger than 0.5 μm.

Examples: Emulsions, suspensions.

In the case of a colloidal dispersion, the particle size of the dispersed medium is in between true solutions and coarse dispersions.

Examples: Colloidal silver sols and polymeric solutions.

A solution consists of two substances: a solute and a solvent. A substance that is dissolved is generally referred to as a solute, and the substance in which it is dissolved is called the solvent.

Example: Sodium chloride solution in water.

Sodium chloride is the solute, and water is the solvent.

3.8.1 Saturated solution

A solution that contains as much solute as the solvent can hold in the presence of a dissolving substance (solute) at a stated temperature is called a saturated solution. Any solution that contains less than this amount is called unsaturated, and if it contains more than that amount, it is called a supersaturated solution.

Solubility is the extent to which the solute dissolves in a saturated solution at a specified temperature.

The United States Pharmacopeia (USP) describes solubility in descriptive terms rather than exact solubility (see Table 3.5).

3.8.2 Concentration expressions

The concentration of a solution can be expressed in a variety of ways:

Molarity (M, C): Gram molecular weights (moles) of solute in 1 L of solution.

Normality (N): Gram equivalent weights of solute in 1 L of solution.

Molality (m): Gram molecular weights (moles) of solute in 1000 g of solvent.

Mole fraction (X, N): Ratio of the moles of the solute to the total moles of all constituents (solute + solvent) in the solution.

Percent by weight (% w/w): Grams of solute in 100 g of solution.

Percent by volume (% v/v): Milliliters of solute in 100 mL of solution.

TABLE 3.5 Descriptive solubility terms.

Descriptive terms	Parts of solvent per one part of solute
Very soluble	Less than 1
Freely soluble	1—10
Soluble	10—30
Sparingly soluble	30—100
Slightly soluble	100—1000
Very slightly soluble	1000—10,000
Practically insoluble	More than 10,000

Example

A solution of sodium chloride is prepared by dissolving 317.1 g of sodium chloride in enough water to make 1000 mL (i.e. 1 L) solution at 25°C. The density of the solution is 1.198 g/cc. The molecular weight of sodium chloride is 58.45.

Calculate the (1) molarity, (2) molality, (3) mole fraction of sodium chloride and water, and (4) percentage by weight of sodium chloride.

1. Molarity

$$\text{Moles of NaCl} = \frac{\text{g NaCl}}{\text{Molecular weight of NaCl}} = \frac{317.1\ \text{g}}{58.45\ \frac{\text{g}}{\text{mol}}} = 5.43\ \text{moles}$$

$$\text{Molarity, } M = \frac{\text{moles of NaCl}}{\text{L of solution}} = \frac{5.43\ \text{moles}}{1\ \text{L}} = 5.43\ \text{M}$$

2. Molality

$$\text{Mass of solution (g)} = \text{Volume} \times \text{density} = 1000\ \text{mL} \times 1.198\ \frac{\text{g}}{\text{mL}} = 1198\ \text{g}$$

$$\text{Mass of solvent (g)} = \text{Mass of solution} - \text{Mass of solute} = 1198\ \text{g} - 317.1\ \text{g} = 880.9\ \text{g} = 0.8809\ \text{kg}$$

$$\text{Molality, } m = \frac{\text{moles of NaCl}}{\text{kg of solvent}} = \frac{5.43\ \text{moles}}{0.8809\ \text{kg}} = 6.16\ \text{m}$$

3. Mole fraction of sodium chloride and water

$$\text{Moles of water} = \frac{\text{g of water}}{\text{Mol. wt. of water}} = \frac{880.9\ \text{g}}{18.02\ \frac{\text{g}}{\text{mole}}} = 48.88\ \text{moles}$$

$$\text{Mole fraction of NaCl} = \frac{\text{Moles of NaCl}}{\text{Moles of NaCl} + \text{Moles of water}} = \frac{5.43\ \text{moles}}{5.43\ \text{moles} + 48.88\ \text{moles}} = 0.0999$$

$$\text{Mole fraction of water} = \frac{\text{Moles of water}}{\text{Moles of water} + \text{Moles of NaCl}} = \frac{48.88\ \text{moles}}{48.88\ \text{moles} + 5.43\ \text{moles}} = 0.9001$$

or

$$\text{Mole fraction of water} = 1 - \text{Mole fraction of NaCl} = 1 - 0.0999 = 0.9001$$

∗ Note mole fraction does not have an unit since it is a ratio

4. Percentage by weight of sodium chloride.

$$\% \text{ weight of NaCl} = \frac{\text{Weight of NaCl}}{\text{Weight of solution}} \times 100 = \frac{317.1\ \text{g}}{1198\ \text{g}} \times 100 = 26.47\% \left(\frac{\text{w}}{\text{w}}\right)$$

$$\text{NB: Equivalent weight} = \frac{\text{Atomic weight}}{\text{\# of equivalent per atomic weight (valence)}}$$

Example

Magnesium has a valence of 2, and its atomic weight is 24.

Therefore, the equivalent weight $= \dfrac{24}{2} = 12$ g/equivalent

Furthermore, equivalent weight (g/Eq) $= \dfrac{\text{molecular weight (g/mole)}}{\text{equivalent/mole}}$

Equivalent weight of Nacl $= \dfrac{58.5 \text{ g/mole}}{1 \text{ equivalent/mole}} = 58.5$ g/equivalent

3.8.3 Ideal and real solutions

An ideal solution is defined as a solution in which there is no change in the properties of the components other than dilution when they are mixed to form the solution. There is no absorption or evolution of heat during the solution process. The final volume of the solution also shows an additive property of the individual components. Ideality in gas implies the complete absence of attractive forces, whereas ideality in solution denotes the complete uniformity of attractive forces. Furthermore, ideal solutions must strictly obey Raoult's law of vapor pressure throughout the complete range of temperature.

Raoult's law states that in an ideal solution, the partial vapor pressure of a component of a solution is equal to the vapor pressure of the pure constituent multiplied by its mole fraction in the solution.

If a solution of two volatile and miscible liquids is represented by A and B, then the partial vapor pressures of the two substituents above the solution are as follows:

$$P_A = P_A^\circ X_A$$

$$P_B = P_B^\circ X_B$$

where P_A and P_B are the partial vapor pressures of the constituents over the solution; X_A and X_B are the mole fractions of A and B in the solution, respectively; and P_{AA}° and P_{BB}° are the vapor pressures of the pure A and pure B, respectively. The total vapor pressure can be expressed graphically, as shown in Fig. 3.16.

Example

What is the partial vapor pressure of ethylene chloride (A) and benzene (B) in solution at a mole fraction of benzene of 0.7. The vapor pressures of pure benzene and pure ethylene chloride are 268 and 236 mm at 50°C, respectively. Calculate the total pressure at this temperature.

Solution:

$$P_B = 268 \text{ mm} \times 0.7 = 187.6 \text{ mm}$$

$$X_A = 1 - X_B = 0.3$$

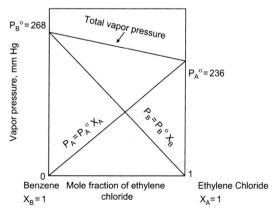

FIGURE 3.16 Vapor pressure-composition curve for an ideal binary system.

$$P_A = 235 \text{ mm} \times 0.3 = 70.5 \text{ mm}$$

$$\text{Total pressure} = 235 \text{ mm} + 70.5 \text{ mm} = 258.1 \text{ mm}$$

3.8.4 Real solutions

In a real solution, complete uniformity of attractive forces does not exist, and it does not obey Raoult's law throughout the entire range of composition. Two types of deviation are generally recognized.

- Negative deviation
- Positive deviation

3.8.4.1 Negative deviation

When the force of attraction between unlike molecules (adhesive force) exceeds the force of attraction between like molecules (cohesive force), the total vapor pressure of the system is less than that expected from Raoult's law, as shown in Fig. 3.17.
    Examples:
    Chloroform and acetone which manifest greater adhesive forces via the formation of hydrogen bond as shown in Fig. 3.17.

3.8.4.2 Positive deviation

When the adhesive forces are less than the cohesive forces, a positive deviation from Raoult's law is generally noticed. The total vapor pressure of the system is higher than that expected from Raoult's law, as shown in Fig. 3.18.

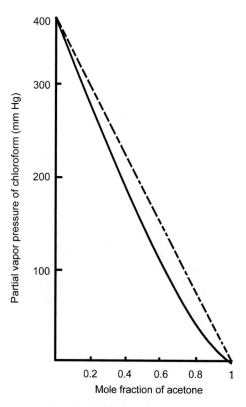

FIGURE 3.17   Decrease in partial vapor pressure of chloroform with increase in mole fraction of acetone. Key (——) vapor pressure calculated by using Raoult's law; (___) experimental data. *Adapted from Ref. [24].*

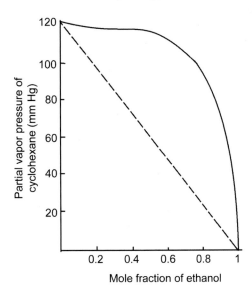

FIGURE 3.18 Increase in partial vapor pressure of cyclohexane with increase in mole fraction of ethanol. Key (——) vapor pressure calculated by using Raoult's law; (___) experimental data. *Adapted from Ref. [24].*

Examples:

Cyclohexane and ethanol
Benzene and ethyl alcohol
Carbon disulfide and acetone

3.9 Spectroscopy

The word *spectroscopy* is derived from *spectrum*, which means a blend of different colors formed when light (visible electromagnetic radiation, or EMR) passes through matter such as a prism, due to a difference in wavelength, and *skopin*, which means examination or evaluation. Thus, spectroscopy is the branch of science that deals with the interaction between EMR and matter.

EMR is the energy emitted in the form of photons by matter possessing either kinetic or potential energy or both. EMR has dual characteristics of both waves and particles. An EMR waveform consists of mutually perpendicular oscillating electric and magnetic fields and travels at the speed of light, c, which is given by

$$c = f\gamma \tag{3.17}$$

where f is frequency, which is the number of peaks passing a given point in 1 s; and γ is a wavelength of the radiation, which is the distance between two successive peaks, as shown in Fig. 3.19.

Electromagnetic radiation is absorbed or emitted when the molecule, atom, or ion of the sample moves from a lower to higher or from a higher to lower energy state, resulting in changes in rotational, vibrational, and/or electronic energies that are measured by spectroscopic methods. Absorption spectroscopy, such as UV−visible and infrared spectroscopy, measures the absorption, whereas emission spectroscopy, such as fluorescence spectroscopy, measures the emission of radiation.

The full EMR spectrum is continuous, and each region merges partially into the neighboring regions. However, for convenience of reference, the Joint Committee on Nomenclature in Applied Spectroscopy has assigned wavelengths for various spectral regions, as shown in Table 3.6.

3.9.1 UV−visible spectroscopy

The wavelength range of UV and visible radiation is in the range of 200−380 nm and 380−780 nm, respectively, which are expressed in nanometers or in angstroms, but their absorption is expressed in terms of wave number

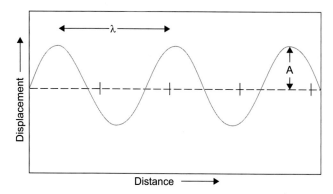

FIGURE 3.19   Diagrammatic representation of a wave.

TABLE 3.6   Spectral regions and their wavelength.

Spectral regions	Wavelength (nm)
Gamma rays	0.2–10
Far ultraviolet	10–200
Near ultraviolet	200–380
Visible	380–780
Near infrared	780–3000
Middle infrared	3000–30,000
Far infrared	30,000–300,000
Microwave	300,000–1,000,000,000
Radiowave	>1,000,000,000

(cm^{-1}), which is the inverse of wavelength. Radiation in this region is of sufficient energy to cause the electronic transition of outer valence electrons.

Electronic transitions are associated with vibrational as well as rotational transitions. A compound appears colored if it selectively absorbs light in the visible region. The main function of absorbed energy is to raise the molecule from a ground energy state (E_0) to a higher excited energy state (E_1), the difference of which is given by

$$\Delta E = E_1 - E_0 = hf = h\frac{c}{\lambda} \tag{3.18}$$

where h is Plank's constant, f is the frequency of radiation absorbed, c is the velocity of light, and λ is the wavelength of radiation absorbed.

ΔE depends on bond strength, that is, how tightly the electrons are held in the bonds, and accordingly, absorption will occur in the UV or visible range. For example, if the electrons of a molecule are held by sigma bonds (e.g., in saturated compounds), no visible range of radiation will be absorbed because the energy requirement for transitioning such electrons to the next higher energy level is so high that it cannot be provided by absorbing radiation in the visible range. The absorption of radiation in the UV region may provide energy sufficient for exciting sigma bond-held electrons, and hence such compounds appear colorless. Some sigma bond-held electrons, such as those found in alkanes, require such a large amount of energy for their excitation that only absorption of gamma radiation can provide sufficient excitation energy; hence, they are used as solvents in UV–visible spectroscopy. On the other hand, electrons held by π bonds or nonbonding electrons (located principally in the atomic orbital of N, O, S, and halogens [X] as a lone pair of electrons) can be excited by the absorption of UV radiation. Thus, the energy required for such transitions can be represented by

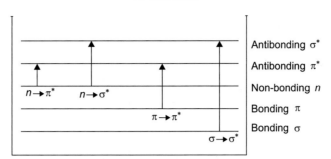

FIGURE 3.20   Energy levels of electronic transitions.

$$n \rightarrow \pi^* < \pi \rightarrow \pi^* < n \rightarrow \sigma^* < \sigma \rightarrow \sigma^* \qquad (3.19)$$

where the $n \rightarrow \pi^*$ transition requires the lowest energy, and $\sigma \rightarrow \sigma^*$ requires the highest amount of energy, as shown in Fig. 3.20.

3.9.2 Correlation of molecular structure and spectra conjugation

Conjugation of unsaturated groups in a molecule increases the absorption intensity in comparison to the $n \rightarrow \pi^*$ transition occurring in an isolated group in a molecule. Consequently, the wavelength of maximum absorption shifts to a longer wavelength (i.e., bathochromic or red shift). Some examples are provided in Fig. 3.21.

A similar effect happens when a group containing n electrons is conjugated with a group containing π electrons, as shown in the following, where oxygen contains n and the methylene group contains π electrons:

Aromatic systems that also contain π electrons strongly absorb UV radiation where hypsochromic or blue shift (i.e., a shift toward a lower wavelength) occurs, as shown in the following, where the order of electronegativity is $C < S < N < O$:

Thus, it appears that as the length of a conjugated system in a molecule increases, the λ max moves toward the visible region. Moreover, the absorption of radiation of a particular wavelength is characteristic of a group of atoms rather than the electrons themselves. Two types of groups—chromophores and auxochromes—can influence the absorption of energy required for the transition of electrons.

3.9.2.1 Chromophores

The term *chromophore* literally means "color-bearing," which is a functional group not conjugated with any other group and has a characteristic UV or visible absorption spectrum. Table 3.7 shows some typical chromophores.

The conjugation of chromophores leads to absorption at longer wavelengths with an increase in absorptivity.

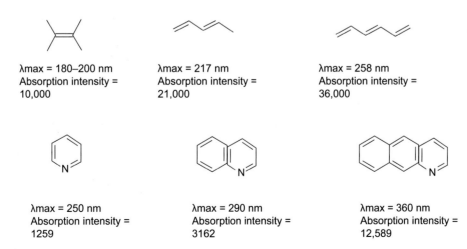

FIGURE 3.21   The effect of increasing conjugation on spectral properties.

TABLE 3.7 Some important chromophores and their characteristic absorption bands.

Chromophores	Formula	Wavelength (nm)
Nitrile	CN	<180
Nitro	NO_2	210
Nitrite	ONO	225
Nitrate	ONO_2	270
Azo	NN	>290
Nitroso	NO	300
Ethene	CC	190
Thiol	SH	195
Benzene	PhH	184
Conjugated chromophores		
Nitroethene	$CCNO_2$	230
Enamine	CCCN	220
Phenol	ArOH	280

3.9.2.2 Auxochromes

Auxochromes do not absorb significantly on their own but rather increase the absorption of a chromophore to which it is attached. Their effect is related to polarity. For example, auxochromes such as CH_3^-, $CH_3CH_2^-$, and Cl^- have very little effect, usually in the range of 5–10 nm, whereas chromophores such as NH_2 and NO_2 completely alter the spectra of a molecule; for example, benzene does not display color because it does not have a chromophore, but nitrobenzene is pale yellow color because of the presence of a chromophore nitro group. Para-hydroxynitrobenzene exhibits a deep yellow color where an auxochrome (OH) is conjugated with the chromophore NO_2. Similar behavior occurs in azobenzene (red color), but para-hydroxy azobenzene is a dark red color.

3.9.3 Visible spectra

Generally, a compound absorbs in the visible range if it contains at least five conjugated chromophoric and auxochromic groups; for example, methylene blue absorbs at 660 nm, and its chemical structure is shown in Fig. 3.22.

3.9.4 The Beer–Lambert law

The Beer–Lambert law states that the concentration of a substance in solution is directly proportional to the "absorbance," A, of the solution, which can be written mathematically as

$$A = k \times c \times l \tag{3.20}$$

where c and l are the concentration of the solution and path length of sample cuvette, respectively, and k is a constant that is called the molar absorption coefficient if c and l are expressed as moles per liter and cm, respectively, or the specific absorption coefficient if c and l are g per liter and cm, respectively.

The law is true only for monochromatic light, which is light of a single wavelength or narrow band of wavelengths, provided that the physical or chemical state of the substance does not change with concentration.

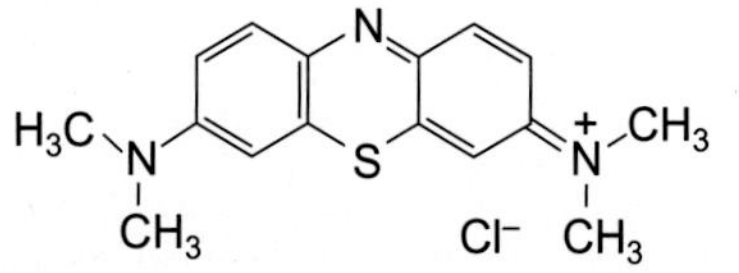

FIGURE 3.22 Methylene blue bearing conjugated chromophores and auxochromes.

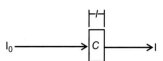

FIGURE 3.23 Diagrammatic representation of the change in intensity of radiation passing through a sample cuvette.

When monochromatic radiation passes through a homogeneous solution in a cuvette, the intensity of the emitted radiation depends on l and c of the solution. I_0 is the intensity of the incident radiation, and I is the intensity of the transmitted radiation. The ratio I/I_0 is called transmittance, which is sometimes expressed as a percentage and referred to as %transmittance, %T. Fig. 3.23 schematically represents such phenomena.

Absorbance is equal to the inverse of T or %T, which is expressed by Eq. (3.21):

$$A = \log\left(\frac{I_0}{I}\right) = \log\left(\frac{1}{T}\right) = \log\left(\frac{1}{\%T}\right) = \log\left(\frac{100}{T}\right) = kcl \tag{3.21}$$

According to the Beer–Lambert law, A is proportional to c, which is valid for drugs/substances in low concentration range. Therefore, in all quantitative UV–visible spectroscopy, A is used instead of T.

3.9.5 Applications of absorption spectroscopy (UV, visible)

3.9.5.1 Detection of impurity present in a compound

UV absorption spectroscopy is one of the best methods for the determination of impurities in organic molecules. Additional peaks may be observed in the UV spectrum due to impurities in the sample, and they can be compared with that of standard raw material. Impurities can also be detected by measuring the absorbance at specific wavelengths; for example, benzene appears as a common impurity in cyclohexane and can be detected by its absorption at 255 nm because cyclohexane absorbs at 200 nm.

3.9.5.2 Quantitative analysis

UV–visible absorption spectroscopy can be used for the quantitative determination of compounds by applying the Beer–Lambert law.

3.9.5.3 Qualitative analysis

UV–visible spectroscopy can be used for identification by comparing the absorption spectrum with the spectra of known compounds; for example, aromatic compounds and aromatic olefins are generally characterized by using UV–visible spectroscopy.

3.9.5.4 Determination of dissociation constants of acids and bases

To determine the dissociation constants of acids and bases, the Henderson–Hasselbalch (H–H) equation (see Chapter 4 for details about this equation) can be used; for example, Eq. (3.22) is the H–H equation for an acid where [A$^-$] and [HA] indicates concentrations of the ionized and unionized form of acid, respectively:

$$pH = pK_a + \log\frac{[A^-]}{HA} \tag{3.22}$$

pK_a of an acid can be calculated from Eq. (3.22) if the ratio [A$^-$]/[HA] is known at different pH, which can be easily determined spectrophotometrically. A plot of pH versus log[A$^-$]/[HA] will result in a straight line. The y intercept of this plot will provide the pK_a value.

3.9.5.5 Quantitative analysis of pharmaceutical substances

Many drugs can be assayed by making a suitable solution of the drug in a solvent and measuring the absorbance at a specific wavelength; for example, diazepam tablets can be analyzed by making the solution in acidic methanol and measuring the absorbance at 284 nm.

3.9.5.6 *Quantification of nucleic acid samples*

The polymeric nucleic acid absorbs at 260 nm, which can be used for their quantification. For example, it has been generally observed that an absorbance of 1.0 equals 50, 40, and 33 µg/mL for DNA, RNA, and short oligonucleotides, respectively.

3.9.5.7 *Detection of impurity in nucleic acid samples*

There is a probability of the presence of proteins/peptides in nucleic acid samples, which can be easily determined by using their absorbance at 280 nm because nucleic acid absorbs at 260 nm. It has been found that pure DNA samples have a ratio of absorbance at 260 and 280 nm equal to 1.8. A ratio less than 1.8 indicates contamination of DNA samples with proteins and/or peptides. Similarly, the ratio is equal to 2 for a pure RNA sample.

3.9.5.8 *Quantification of protein and peptide solutions*

Generally, proteins with no prosthetic group absorb at 280 nm, which is mainly contributed by tryptophan and tyrosine amino acid residues. Tryptophan and tyrosine have molar absorptivity of about 5700 and $1300\ M^{-1}\ cm^{-1}$ at 280 nm, respectively. Therefore, the molar absorptivity of a protein can be estimated by using Eq. (3.23) because no other amino acid residues contribute to the absorbance at 280 nm:

$$\text{The absorbance of } 1\frac{mg}{mL} \text{ protein solution in a sample}$$

$$\text{cuvette of } 1\ cm = \frac{(5700 \times \#\text{of Trp} + 1300 \times \#\text{of Tyr})}{M} \tag{3.23}$$

where M is molecular weight of the protein. It has been found that an absorbance of 1.0 at 280 nm indicates 1 mg/mL for protein but 0.33 mg/mL for a peptide sample solution.

3.9.6 Infrared spectroscopy

A molecule is always vibrating as its bonds stretch, contract, or bend with respect to one another. Absorption of radiation in the infrared (IR) region causes changes in the vibrational pattern of a molecule. This vibration is recorded in infrared spectroscopy, which is a plot of the frequency of radiation absorbed/transmitted in terms of wavenumber versus absorbance/transmittance.

An infrared spectrum is a characteristic property of a drug molecule (see Fig. 3.24), which can be used for both establishing the identity of a compound and revealing the structure of a new compound. An IR spectrum from $1450-600\ cm^{-1}$ is called the fingerprint region, which can be used for the identification of a compound due to its uniqueness. The rest of the region from 4000 to $1450\ cm^{-1}$ is due to various types of molecular vibration and hence appropriately called the group frequency region.

The IR spectrum provides information about the functional groups present in a compound. This information, in turn, can be used for elucidating its structure in conjunction with other analytical techniques. A particular functional

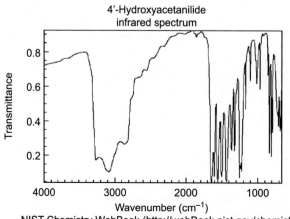

FIGURE 3.24   The IR spectrum of solid-state acetaminophen powder.

group absorbs radiation of certain frequencies that are almost the same irrespective of in which compound they are present. For example, the CO group of ketone absorbs strongly at 1710 cm^{-1} and the CH$_3$ group absorbs strongly at 1450 and 1375 cm^{-1}. However, the OH group of alcohols absorbs strongly at 3200–3600 cm^{-1}; but the OH group of carboxylic acid absorbs strongly at 2500–3000 cm^{-1} whose peak shape is broad due to its interaction with other groups via hydrogen bonds.

3.9.6.1 Applications

IR spectroscopy has been applied in pharmacy to solve many problems, such as investigating identity, purity, and crystalline structure of a drug and their interaction with excipients either as a stand-alone method or in combination with other analytical methods. Following are some of the important applications of IR spectroscopy in pharmacy.

- *Verification of drug identity*: IR spectroscopy was first introduced to identify drugs in USP XVI. The USP 35 NF 30 lists 1321 monographs that use the IR spectrum to identify drugs, which is based on a comparison of the IR spectrum of a drug with that of a reference standard. However, precautions should be taken because sometimes two drugs might have exactly identical overlapping spectra, such as in the case of the homologs of the long-chain fatty acids and esters and drugs exhibiting polymorphism or pseudopolymorphism.
- *Testing purity of a drug:* The manufacturing process of a drug may introduce tiny amounts of some unwanted materials that might cause some adverse reactions or modify therapeutic outcomes, which could be identified by IR spectroscopy. For example, the presence of dichloroacetic acid in chloramphenicol is detected by the appearance of a band at 1765 cm^{-1} in the IR spectrum of chloramphenicol. Therefore, the peak at 1765 cm^{-1} is defined as an analytical band of impurity in chloramphenicol samples.
- *Investigation of drug structure*: At one time, there were three proposed structural formulas for penicillin. This issue was resolved by the presence of a strong band at 1780 cm^{-1}, indicating a CO group related with the presence of a cyclic β-lactam ring. Therefore, the structural formula containing the β-lactam ring was accepted as the correct formula for penicillin.
- *Elucidation of crystalline structures*: IR spectroscopy has been reported to have an advantage over X-ray powder diffraction for obtaining information about conformational characteristics of polymorphs of a drug containing types of H-bonds that affect vibrations of OH, NH, or CO groups. For example, α and β forms of chloramphenicol palmitate are characterized by peaks at 858 and 843 cm^{-1}, respectively; forms I, II, IV, and the solvates of indomethacin by means of their markedly different IR spectra at 1700 cm^{-1}; forms I and II of rotenone in 800–850 cm^{-1}; a quantitative analysis of a mixture of acetylsalicylic acid (aspirin) and salicylic acid by bands at 920 and 760 cm^{-1}, respectively, etc.
- *Investigation of drug–excipient interaction*: The interaction of a drug with excipients involving complexation, hydrogen bonding, etc., modifies its physicochemical properties, resulting in changes in pharmacological actions and pharmacokinetic behaviors. Interactions are identified by the appearance of a new IR absorption peak indicating formation of a new compound, disappearance of a peak, shifting of a characteristic peak, broadening of a peak, or alteration in intensity of a particular peak.

3.9.7 Fluorescence spectroscopy

In UV–visible spectroscopy, the absorption of electromagnetic radiation in the UV and visible region leads to the transition of a molecule from the ground state to the excited state. Because the excited state possesses higher energy than the ground state, ultimately these excited electrons come back to the ground state by emitting absorbed energy as well as losing it in some other way. The emission of absorbed energy is broadly termed luminescence.

The electrons at the ground state (which contains the lowest energy) are paired in such a way that their spin is antiparallel to each other, which cancels the energy associated with both paired electrons, resulting in zero energy for the ground state. This is termed a singlet state of electrons. However, excited electrons can orient either parallel (triplet state, $S = 1$) or antiparallel (singlet state, $S = 0$). When electrons return to the ground state by emitting energy from the triplet state, the phenomenon is termed phosphorescence. Fluorescence is the phenomenon that occurs when excited electrons come back to the ground state from the singlet state. Phosphorescence has a long lifetime (10^{-2} to 100 s), and its rate is slow. In contrast, fluorescence has a short lifetime (10^{-8} s), and emission of energy is fast enough to be comparable with other processes, such as collisional deactivation and intersystem crossing. The overall energy balance for the fluorescence process can be written as

$$E_{fluor} = E_{abs} - E_{vib} - E_{solv.relax.} \tag{3.24}$$

where E_{fluor} is the energy of the emitted radiation, E_{abs} is the energy of the radiation absorbed by the molecule during excitation, and E_{vib} is the energy lost by the molecule during vibrational relaxation. The term $E_{solv.relax.}$ indicates the energy lost to the solvent cage where the excited electrons reorient themselves or relax to the ground state. As is obvious from Eq. (3.24), the energy of fluorescence is always less than the energy absorbed during excitation. Therefore, the wavelength of emitted radiation during fluorescence is always greater than that of the absorbed radiation.

3.9.7.1 Applications

All the applications of fluorescence spectroscopy are based on comparisons of wavelengths of radiation required for the excitation of an electron and wavelengths of radiation emitted during the relaxation of the excited electron to the ground state. The difference between excitation and emission wavelengths is much less in comparison to wavelengths of incident and transmitted radiation involved in UV—visible spectroscopy. Thus, fluorescence intensity is measured above a low background, where a very low absorbance is measured by comparing two very large signals that are slightly different. In contrast, in UV—visible spectroscopy, a very high absorbance is measured by comparing one similarly high signal with another very low signal. Therefore, fluorescence spectroscopy is a very sensitive technique, up to 1000 times more sensitive than UV—visible spectrophotometry. Moreover, recent advances in instrumentation have made it possible to detect the fluorescence of even a single molecule.

Not all drugs are suitable for investigation by fluorescence spectrometry because they have to absorb radiation of a particular wavelength to get their electrons excited and must come back to the ground state by emitting radiation of different wavelengths. Generally, the molecules capable of displaying fluorescence or phosphorescence contain a rigid conjugated structure, for example, aromatic hydrocarbons, rhodamines, coumarins, oxines, polyenes, etc. Many drugs (e.g., morphine, riboflavin, bumetanide, chlorophyllin copper complex sodium, copovidone, digoxin, ergotamine, estradiol, fluorescein sodium, hydroxyprogesterone, quinine sulfate, stanozolol, thiamine hydrochloride, triamterene, etc.), some natural amino acids and cofactors (e.g., tyrosine, tryptophan, nicotinamide adenine dinucleotide, flavin adenine dinucleotide, etc.) fluoresce and hence can be investigated using fluorometer for qualitative and quantitative characterization.

Manipulation of biopolymers such as nucleic acid and proteins and the imaging of biological membranes and living organisms are emerging areas utilizing extensively fluorescence-based detection and analysis. As amino acids such as tyrosine and tryptophan fluoresce, fluorometry can differentiate proteins and peptides from biological matrices; this is not possible with UV—visible spectrometry due to an overlap of absorbance by proteins and peptides around 190 nm with other substances present in the cellular matrices. The recent development of dyes and fluorophores for biological applications is further expanding the applications of fluorescence spectroscopy.

3.9.8 Nuclear magnetic resonance spectroscopy

The nuclei of certain atoms spin just like electrons do. Hydrogen is one such atom whose nucleus contains only one proton. As a circulating charge creates a magnetic field along the axis of spin, a hydrogen atom or a proton placed in an external magnetic field would orient either parallel or antiparallel to its magnetic moment of it. A parallel arrangement or alignment along with the external magnetic field is more stable; therefore, energy must be absorbed by the proton to change its alignment against the field. Consequently, if a magnetic field is continuously changed over a proton placed in a constant radiation energy, at a certain magnetic field strength value, the energy required to flip the orientation of the proton matches with the applied radiation energy when energy is absorbed, which will appear as a peak on a plot between magnetic field versus absorption of energy.

3.9.8.1 Nuclear magnetic resonance spectrum

Different protons exist in different environments and thereby possess different magnetic field strengths. This would require different external magnetic fields to flip over their alignment, provided the applied radiation energy is constant. Therefore, a plot of the magnetic field and energy absorbed would have various peaks corresponding to various protons present in the sample, which would differ in intensity as well as their location. Such a plot is called the nuclear magnetic resonance (NMR) spectrum.

Thus, while one is interpreting an NMR spectrum, attention is focused on the following aspects:

Number of peaks: This provides information about the number of different kinds of protons in the sample molecule because protons with the same environment absorb at the same applied magnetic field. For example, ethyl chloride (CH_3—CH_2—Cl) would have two NMR peaks because the protons represented by methyl (CH_3) and methylene (CH_2) groups are surrounded by different groups. Similarly, isopropyl chloride [(CH_3)$_2$—CH—Cl] also would have two

NMR peaks not three because both the methyl groups are equivalent because they are surrounded by similar neighboring groups. The methyl groups in both would appear upfield of methylene group. However, the methyl group would be split in three in ethyl chloride but two in isopropyl chloride. Interestingly, methylene groups in both are deshielded by electronegative chloride ions, which would split into 4 in ethyl chloride but into 7 in isopropyl chloride.

Locations of peaks: This provides information about the electronic environment of each peak, that is, whether the protons representing a peak are aromatic, aliphatic, primary, secondary, tertiary, benzylic, vinylic, acetylenic, or adjacent to halogen or to other atoms or groups.

In addition to protons, an atom/molecule also contains electrons, in which spinning can also generate a magnetic field in an NMR experiment called the secondary or induced magnetic field. The induced magnetic field either can oppose or reinforce the applied magnetic field depending on the relative location of protons. As a result, the field experienced by protons is diminished or reinforced, and the protons are called either shielded or deshielded, respectively, from the influence of the externally applied magnetic field.

Obviously, shielding means that a greater external magnetic field strength is required to change the orientation of the spinning proton, which results in an upfield shift in the NMR absorption peak. In contrast, deshielding causes a downfield shift of the NMR absorption peak. Benzene causes deshielding of aromatic protons, but acetylene causes shielding of acetylenic protons. Such down- or upfield shifts in NMR peaks due to electrons are called chemical shifts (see Table 3.8), in which the units are parts per million (ppm) of the total applied external magnetic field. The reference point for measuring chemical shifts is not a single proton but the compound tetramethylsilane, $(CH_3)_4Si$, where silicone is a very low electronegative compound. Therefore, the shielding of protons in silane is greater than in most of the other molecules. Consequently, the NMR signals from most of the other organic molecules appear downfield compared to silane.

TABLE 3.8 Characteristic proton NMR chemical shifts.

Type of proton	Type of compound	Chemical shift range (ppm, δ)
RCH_3	1 degrees aliphatic	0.9
R_2CH_2	2 degrees aliphatic	1.3
R_3CH	3 degrees aliphatic	1.5
CCH	Vinylic	4.6—5.9
CCH	Vinylic, conjugated	5.5—7.5
CCH	Acetylenic	2—3
ArH	Aromatic	6—8.5
ArCH	Benzylic	2.2—3
$CCCH_3$	Allelic	1.7
HCF	Fluorides	4—4.5
HCCl	Chlorides	3—4
HCBr	Bromides	2.5—4
HCI	Iodides	2—4
HCOH	Alcohols	3.4—4
HCOR	Ethers	3.3—4
RCOOCH	Esters	3.7—4.1
HCCOOR	Esters	2—2.2
HCCOOH	Acids	2—2.6
HCCO	Carbonyl compounds	2—2.7
RCHO	Aldehydic	9—10

Continued

TABLE 3.8   Characteristic proton NMR chemical shifts.—cont'd

Type of proton	Type of compound	Chemical shift range
ROH	Hydroxylic	2—4
ArOH	Phenolic	4—12
CCOH	Enolic	15—17
RCOOH	Carboxylic	10.0—13.2
RNH_2	Amino	1—5

There are two commonly used scales for measuring chemical shift values: δ (delta) and τ (tau). The position of tetramethylsilane in the δ scale is taken as 0.0 ppm, whereas most other chemicals have chemical shift values of 0—10 ppm. In the τ scale, the position of tetramethylsilane is taken as 10.0 ppm. Thus, the two scales are related by the equation $\tau = 10 - \delta$. The electron-withdrawing groups such as halogens cause deshielding by lowering the electron density in the vicinity of the proton.

Intensities of peaks: This provides information about the number of protons in each kind; this number is proportional to the area under the peak. This intensity is due to the absorption of a quantum of energy required by a proton for flipping over in a magnetic field. As the field strength is the same, the greater absorption of energy could be due only to the proportionally greater number of protons.

Splitting of a peak: A chemical shift is caused by shielding and/or deshielding effects of electrons, but the splitting of a peak appearing at a particular position is due to the effect of neighboring protons, which is called spin—spin coupling. For example, the NMR spectrum of dichloroethane (see Fig. 3.25) shows two peaks: one is a doublet and another is a quartet. The doublet is due to the coupling of three CH_3 protons with a single CH proton whose spin aligns either along or opposite to the external applied magnetic field. On the contrary, the quartet is due to the coupling of a single CH proton with three CH_3 protons, which can spin four different ways, as shown in Fig. 3.26. It should be noted that peak intensity, that is, the area under the peak, is proportional to the number of protons represented by them; and the separation between two peaks, termed a coupling constant, is the same in both doublet and quartet peaks.

3.9.8.2 Applications

NMR has been widely used for the analysis of body fluids to assess drug toxicity and therapeutic effects. Although it has intrinsically low sensitivity, it is a nondestructive technique, allows the simultaneous detection of many compounds usually present in samples of drug metabolites and generally does not require sample preparations, or if any, they are minimal. Following are some of the specific applications of nuclear magnetic resonance.

- *Anticancer drugs:* Tumors have numerous metabolic pathways that are altered in comparison to healthy normal tissue, which can be detected by ^1H NMR spectroscopy. Thus, changes in the spectral patterns of samples with

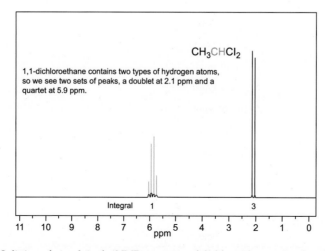

FIGURE 3.25   Splitting of a peak in the NMR spectrum of dichloroethane using δ scale of chemical shift.

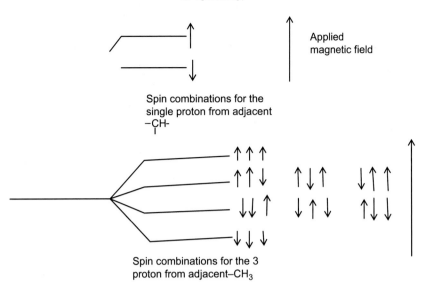

Spin combinations for the single proton from adjacent –CH–

Applied magnetic field

Spin combinations for the 3 proton from adjacent–CH₃

FIGURE 3.26 Spin–spin coupling in dichloroethane.

respect to the control are used to diagnose or predict the progression of malignant diseases. A number of spectroscopic markers such as choline-containing compounds have been proposed to assess proliferative rates in the spectra of tumors. Fatty acid synthase (FAS) is overexpressed in tumors, which need *de novo* synthesis of fatty acids to accelerate membrane production for highly proliferative cancerous cells. Therefore, the treatment targets inhibiting FAS activity, which results in a decrease of phosphatidylcholine and its precursor phosphocholine levels that can be measured by NMR spectroscopy.

- *Drugs for infectious diseases:* The ability of NMR spectroscopy to detect metabolic changes in cells has been exploited to obtain information about the mechanism of action of antimicrobial agents. For example, it has been reported that 8-azaxanthine inhibits *Aspergillus nidulans* hyphal growth by *in vivo* inactivation of urate oxidase by using a mutant strain *A. nidulansuaZ14* mutant and comparative NMR metabolomics data.
- *Antidiabetic drugs:* Rosiglitazone is an antidiabetic drug that works by enhancing insulin sensitivity. In a small clinical study, NMR was used to obtain biomarkers in plasma and urine, indicating treatment outcomes of rosiglitazone. The multivariate analysis of NMR data showed that the rosiglitazone treatment led to a reduction in urine hippurate and aromatic amino acids, as well as an increase in plasma branched-chain amino acids, alanine, and glutamine/glutamate, which were linked to an increase in hepatic insulin sensitivity in diabetic patients.
- *Drug-induced toxicity:* The ability of NMR spectroscopy to provide information on changes in the metabolite concentration has been used for figuring out drug-induced toxicities. Cyclosporine is an immunosuppressant drug widely used in organ transplants to reduce the activity of the patient's immune system and, thereby, the risk of organ rejection. However, its clinical use is limited by its nephrotoxicity, which is enhanced when combined with the immunosuppressive inhibitor sirolimus. The NMR spectroscopy analysis of urine metabolites after 6 days of cyclosporine treatment showed changes of 2-oxoglutarate, citrate, and succinate concentrations, together with increased urine isoprostane concentrations, that were indicative of oxidative stress. After 28 days of treatment, increased lactate and glucose concentrations in urine and decreased concentrations of Krebs cycle intermediates were detected, indicating proximal tubular damage. Thus, the urine NMR metabolic patterns indicated that cyclosporine and/or sirolimus induced damage of the renal tubular system, which is reported to be more sensitive than currently used clinical kidney function markers such as creatinine concentrations in serum.

3.9.9 Mass spectroscopy

Mass spectroscopy is an analytical technique used to separate electrically charged particles on the basis of their masses. It involves the bombardment of the sample molecules with a beam of extremely energetic electrons. Consequently, molecules become charged and fragmented, some of which are positively charged ions. Each ion has a particular value for ratio of mass and charge (*m/z* ratio). As the value of charge is generally 1; the *m/*

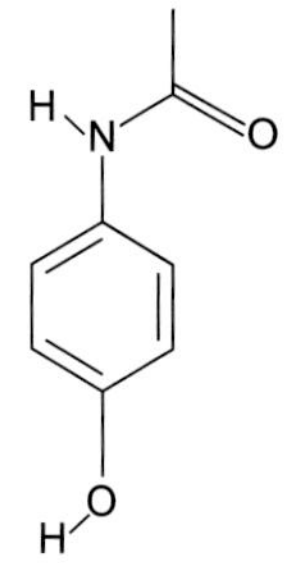

FIGURE 3.27   Structure of acetaminophen.

z ratio is simply the mass of the ion. A mass spectrum is the plot of signals representing m/z ratios of all the ions produced due to fragmentation and their intensities, indicating relative abundance. Fig. 3.27 shows the structure of acetaminophen, and Fig. 3.28 shows its mass spectrum ($C_8H_9NO_2$; mol. wt 151.16), where the prominent signals are numbered and their m/z ratios are shown in parentheses. Signal # 1 at 151 is called the molecular ion or parent ion and is generally represented by M^+. A molecular ion is produced when high-energy electrons bombarding on the sample (here, e.g., acetaminophen) knock off one electron; hence, M^+ represents the molecular weight of the sample.

The molecular ions are highly unstable; therefore, some of them would further fragment into smaller pieces whose relative intensities or abundances are controlled by their relative stability. The tallest signal in the spectrum (signal # 2 in Fig. 3.28) is called the base peak, whose intensity is arbitrarily assigned a height of 100 and the rest of the peak heights are assigned relative to it. The signal # 2 (mol. wt. 109) is due to knocking off CH_3CO moiety (mol. wt. 43) from acetaminophen. Signal # 4 represents CH_3CO moiety because it corresponds to mol. wt. of 43. The appearance of tiny peaks around ±1 or 2 m/z ratio units in both molecular as well as base peaks are due to their corresponding isotopes.

3.9.9.1 Applications

Mass spectra are useful in proving the identity of a compound as well as helping in establishing the structure of a new compound. Generally, we accept two compounds as the same if their physicochemical properties are the same. Because a single mass spectrum provides the relative abundances of a number of fragments that are involved in many of the physicochemical properties, if the mass spectrum of an unknown compound is identical with the mass spectrum of a previously reported compound, the two compounds are the same without any doubt. Moreover, the mass spectrum provides an exact molecular weight of a compound and also its molecular formula, which can be of immense help in establishing the structure of the new compound or at least confirming the presence of certain structural units.

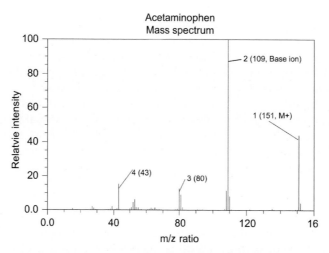

FIGURE 3.28   Mass spectrum of acetaminophen. *Retrieved from http://webbook.nist.gov/cgi/cbook.cgi?ID=C103902&Units=SI&Mask=200#Mass-Spec [Accessed on Feb. 26, 2022].*

Mass spectrometry-based techniques using electrospray and matrix-assisted laser desorption ionization have found use in the area of nucleic acid; for example, they include sequencing techniques for oligonucleotides, approaches to mixture analysis, microscale sample handling, and targeted DNA assays. Mass spectrometry coupled with liquid chromatography is of immense help in unraveling column-outlet multicompound bands, where it is universally applicable yet has excellent sensitivity. Tandem mass spectrometry has been used in studies with S-(N-methylcarbamoyl)glutathione, a metabolite of the antineoplastic agent N-methylformamide for characterizing derivatized glutathione conjugates.

3.10 Conclusions

This chapter discussed some of the physical properties of drug molecules that are of immense importance during the development of safe, effective, and reliable dosage forms. Some of the surface properties, such as surface tension, interfacial tension, and adsorption, and electrical properties play a very important role in various aspects of pharmaceutics and their application in dosage form design. The flow properties of different fluids encountered in pharmacy practice and their applications are discussed in the rheology section. Different colligative properties and their application in various aspects of pharmacy are also discussed. Some of the spectroscopic techniques and their basic principles and applications in evaluating quality products are critically evaluated. The concepts developed in this chapter would be useful in the overall quality assessment of the drugs and dosage forms influencing their therapeutic outcomes.

Case studies

Case 3.1

A patient suffering with osteoarthritis was administered a full course (one injection containing 20 mg of sodium hyaluronate in 2 mL phosphate buffered saline for 5 weeks) of Hyalgan (sodium hyaluronate injection) intra-articularly in the knee joint, but the symptoms did not improve significantly. What option or options would you suggest?

Approach: One reason for pain in osteoarthritis is the decrease in lubrication between two bony joint surfaces provided by synovial fluid. Therefore, sodium hyaluronate is injected into the joint. Because it is antithixotropic in nature, the sodium hyaluronate supplements the loss in the viscoelastic property of the synovial fluid. The viscoelasticity of sodium hyaluronate is mainly dependent on the molecular weight of the hyaluronic acid used. The different brands of sodium hyaluronate vary in the molecular weight of hyaluronic acid used, as shown in Table 3.9.

Thus, the next logical viable option could be using Orthovisc or Euflexxa. Synvisc should be tried last because it consists of the highest-molecular-weight hyaluronic acid. There are some reports indicating lower to middle-molecular-weight hyaluronans exhibit better clinical efficacy than ones with higher molecular weight [8]. Here, one should note that although a higher apparent viscosity is expected with an increased molecular weight of hyaluronic acid, which could be expected to provide better cushioning and lubrication to joints, there could be limit because activity provided by hyaluronic acid is not only mechanical, but also could be biological. In fact, the lubricating and cushioning activity provided by the synovial fluid is highly complex.

TABLE 3.9 Commercially hyaluronans [8].

Brand name	Generic name	Manufacturer	Mol. Wt. (K Da)
Hyalgan	Sodium hyaluronate	Sanofi-aventis	500—730
Supartz	Sodium hyaluronate	Smith and Nephew	620—1170
Synvisc	Hylan G-F 20	Genzyme Corporation	80% hylan A (6,000)+Hylan B (>6000)
Orthovisc	High-molecular-weight hyaluronan	DePuy Mitek	1000—2900
Euflexxa	Sodium hyaluronate	Ferring pharmaceutical	2400—3600

Case 3.2

You are the drug information pharmacist in your state, and a few pharmacy interns are working under your supervision. You receive a phone call from the local hospital emergency center regarding a case of acetaminophen poisoning. The patient has ingested 20 Tylenol caplets. What information do you need to collect to provide a better understanding of the dose of activated charcoal needed for this patient?

Approach: You have to look for a source for any review or meta-analysis on activated charcoal (AC) in acute poisoning. For one excellent source, see the review article in Ref. [9].

Understand the time of ingestion, the time of treatment with other decontamination modalities before activated charcoal administration, and what type of activated charcoal to use. AC is produced by heating sawdust or coconut shells at 600°C–900°C followed by activation using a stream of hot air and a vacuum to create a more adsorptive surface area in them by degassing the surfaces. The typical surface area of AC is 800–1200 m^2/g. A 50 g dose of AC has an adsorptive surface area equivalent to the surface area of seven football fields. Super-activated charcoal may have a surface area of 2800–3500 m^2/g. Activated charcoal acts as an adsorbent because of its high surface area. The usual dose to be administered is a 10:1 ratio (dose of AC: weight of drug ingested). For 1 g of drug, you need 10 g of AC. In this case, 20 Tylenol caplets contain 10 g of active drug. Therefore, you need at least 100 g of AC for this patient.

Case 3.3

A study reported in the *British Journal of Dermatology* [10] suggests that ointment is evenly spread on the skin as compared to creams and solutions. Ointment showed an even spread to the applied areas. Cream, low-viscosity cream, and solution showed poor spreading, resulting in an uneven distribution of dose (lower dose in the periphery). Can you explain the reasons?

Approach: This was a study for comparing the spreadability resulting in even distribution of active principle of four topical formulations—ointment, cream, low viscosity cream, and solution. A fixed quantity (0.1 g) of each of the four formulations was applied to the abdominal skin of human volunteers. To explain the differences in spreadability, one has to know the composition and surfactants used in each formulation. Creams and solutions have some disadvantages in getting spread rapidly as well as evenly due to rapid evaporation of alcohol/water used in their formulation, resulting an uneven distribution of drug on the applied surface. Ointments, on the other hand, distribute and spread well to the applied area. The presence of surfactants also helps in spreading because they reduce the contact angle. Therefore, patients should be recommended to apply creams and solutions to multiple sites and to spread them quickly.

Case 3.4

A community pharmacist engaged in compounding is preparing some Nystatin popsicles using the same recipe for drug, water, coloring agent, flavoring agent, and sugar as a sweetener as used previously. To his utter surprise, when he opens the freezer, he finds the batch he made last night has not solidified. Rechecking the calculation also reveals that all the weights of materials and volumes of solvents used were correct. Can you establish a cause of this problem?

Approach: The first issue you have to think about is why the solution is not freezing. Since the solvent is water, it should freeze at 0° or less than that temperature. Checking the freezer to see whether it is in workable condition is the next issue. From the colligative properties, it is known that the presence of salt decreases the freezing point of water. Because the pharmacist used the right amount and previously had success in making Nystatin popsicles, it could be some extra salt that might be causing this problem. That can be easily tested by using organoleptic methods. In this case, possibly the pharmacist used mistakenly crystalline NaCl instead of crystalline sugar, which may have been stored in identical plastic containers. A pharmacist must read labels carefully before selecting an active or inactive pharmaceutical ingredient.

Case 3.5

A 20% salicylic acid ointment was prepared for a patient to use as a wart treatment. After 1 week of treatment, the patient did not see a keratolytic effect of this particular batch of ointment. The patient reported this failure to the pharmacist who compounded the prescription. How should the pharmacist respond to this situation?

Approach: The first and foremost thing the pharmacist should do is report the complaint in the pharmacy's book. If possible, the pharmacist may request some of the prepared ointment from the patient. The lot number of the salicylic acid used and the ointment base should be retrieved from the batch and preparation records. If the pharmacy has a spectrophotometer, the concentration of salicylic acid in the used ointment should be measured at that time. If the pharmacy has an infrared spectrometer, the pharmacist should get an IR spectrum of the salicylic acid used in the preparation. This IR spectrum should be compared to the library data that already exists for salicylic acid. If the spectra are different, then the salicylic acid used in the preparation is not really salicylic acid. Therefore, the patient was not getting any keratolytic effect with its use.

Case 3.6

A higher frequency of occurrence of necrotizing enterocolitis (NEC) has been observed in premature infants in intensive care units fed enterally undiluted calcium lactate than those fed no calcium lactate or calcium lactate diluted with water or formula. Can you figure out why?

Approach: The tonicities of oral medications such as calcium lactate commonly used to feed premature infants kept in intensive care are very high, and this may lead to necrotizing enterocolitis if administered undiluted. Furthermore, orally administered calcium lactate or gluconate can have many additives, for example, ethyl alcohol, sorbitol, and propylene glycol, in a significantly greater amount than generally found in parenterals, leading to unusually higher osmolalities in oral medications. The high osmolalities of orally fed nutritional supplements are the reason for the development of NEC in premature infants. Therefore, extreme precautions should be taken while feeding premature babies in intensive care units.

Case 3.7

A baby was fed formula milk regularly bought from your pharmacy. The mother of the baby came to your store and reported that the baby has a high fever with swelling around the eyes, face, feet, and ankles. Moreover, the baby was crying severely while peeing which frequency had also got increased. She also observed some blood/cloudiness in the baby's urine. What would you suggest to her?

Approach: The baby's symptoms reported by the mom indicate acute kidney failure and nephrolithiasis which may be due to imported infant formula milk. There are reports of the presence of melamine in some imported formula milk [11] or if its ingredients were imported. Some unscrupulous manufacturers may add melamime, a nonnutritive synthetic compound containing nitrogen (Fig. 3.29), to falsely increase the protein content to pass the quality testing based on determining nitrogen content as an indicative of protein contents [12]. However, melamine is a toxic substance reported to cause many types of toxicities including kidney diseases [13–15].

Therefore, you should check the source of formula milk and enquire whether baby was taking the same brand of formula milk earlier. The baby should stop taking the current brand of formula milk and its sample should be tested for the presence of melamine which can be done by using UV spectrophotometer [16]. If the presence of melamine is confirmed, you must notify FDA officially. You should advise patient's mom to go to an urologist immediately.

Case 3.8

A woman diagnosed with breast cancer came to your pharmacy to get her refill for the over-the-counter (OTC) medicine Zantac for her heartburn. She has been using zantac for many years. Would you refill Zantac or recommend some other OTC medicines for heartburn?

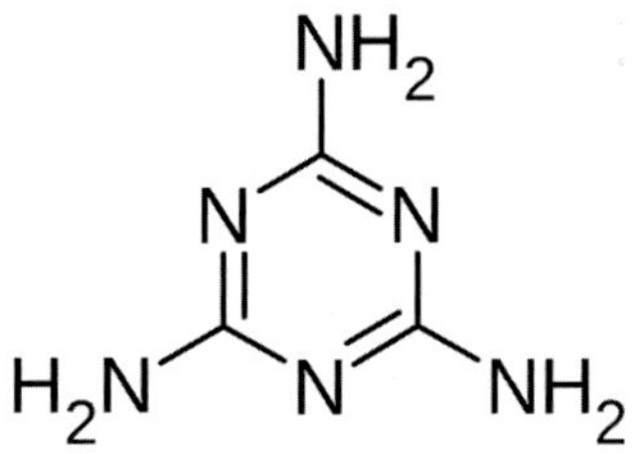

FIGURE 3.29 Structure of melamine.

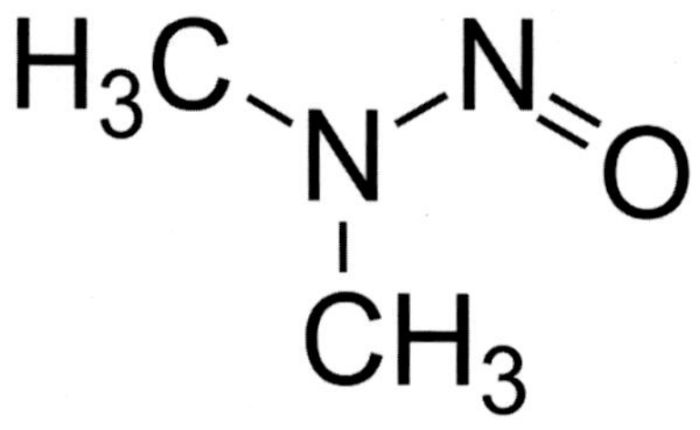

$$H_3C-N-N=O$$
$$|$$
$$CH_3$$

FIGURE 3.30   Structure of N-nitrosodimethylamine.

Approach: The online pharmacy Valisure identified a high level of a likely carcinogen, N-nitrosodimethylamine (NDMA) (Fig. 3.30), in Zantac, and its generic versions in 2019 [17]. On further investigation using mass spectroscopy, it was found that ranitidine (an active ingredient of Zantac) is unstable under physiological conditions and, in fact, produces NDMA [18]. There are various studies reporting the association between the high risk of occurrence of cancers and ingestion of NDMA present in food and medicines as contaminants [19–21], resulting in the FDA directive of withdrawal of all products containing ranitidine [22]. Therefore, you should recommend another heartburn medicine not contra-indicated to her current breast cancer medicines.

Critical reflections and practice applications

This chapter emphasizes some of the properties related to the surface, flow, and colligation, along with some of the common spectroscopic methods used in the analysis of some of these physicochemical properties of drug molecules. These concepts can be used in the following practice applications.

i. The surface activity described at the beginning of the chapter is applicable for solubilizing a drug used in compounding pharmacy and optimizing the dose of charcoal powder in a clinical setting for the emergency treatment of certain kinds of poisoning such as food poisoning [23].

ii. The concept of mixing two surfactants to obtain specific HLB values can be helpful in optimizing the use of surfactants for preparing a stable emulsion or suspension.

iii. Rheometer can be used in evaluating the thixotropic flow pattern of suspensions, ointments, lotions, and creams for ensuring uniformity of each dose and patient compliance.

iv. The concept of depression of freezing points and L_{iso} values are useful for adjusting the tonicity of a parenteral dosage form of a new drug for which commonly used approaches, based on NaCl equivalents (E value) or White Vincent (v value) methods, may not be available in literatures.

vi. The negative or positive deviations in total vapor pressures of a mixture of solvents would be helpful in figuring out an optimal combination of solvents used for preparing an aerosol formulation.

vii. Spectroscopic methods can be used for controlling the quality of medications and determining the presence of impurities linked to reported adverse effects.

References

[1] H.N. Holmes, Laboratory Manual of Colloid Chemistry, Wiley, New York, 1922.
[2] D. Attwood, O.K. Udeala, The surface activity of some antihistamines at the air-solution interface, J. Pharm. Pharmacol. 27 (10) (1975) 754–758.
[3] S. Fukahoria, T. Fujiwaraa, R. Itob, N. Funamizu, pH-dependent adsorption of sulfa drugs on high silica zeolite: modeling and kinetic study, Desalination 275 (1–3) (2011) 237–242.
[4] C.O. Rangel-Yagui, A. Pessoa Jr., L.C. Tavares, Micellar solubilization of drugs, J. Pharm. Pharmaceut. Sci. 8 (2) (July 8, 2005) 147–165. PMID: 16124926.
[5] Plasma viscosity and blood viscoelasticity. <http://www.vilastic.com/tech10.html> [Accessed 05.06.2013].
[6] The Merck Index, thirteenth ed., Merck and Co., Inc., Whitehouse Station, NJ, 2001, pp. MISC 32–MISC42.
[7] E.R. Hammarlund, Sodium chloride equivalents, cryoscopic properties, and hemolytic effects of certain medicinals in aqueous solution IV: supplemental values, J. Pharmaceut. Sci. 70 (1981) 1161–1163.
[8] P.C. Vitanzo Jr., B.J. Sennett, Hyaluronans: is clinical effectiveness dependent on molecular weight? Am. J. Orthoped. 35 (9) (September 2006) 421–428. PMID: 17036778.
[9] K.R. Olson, Activated charcoal for acute poisoning: one toxicologist's journey, J. Med. Toxicol. 6 (2) (2010) 190–198.
[10] U.I. Ivens, Ointment is evenly spread on the skin, in contrast to creams and solutions, Br. J. Dermatol. 145 (2001) 264–267.

[11] China's Tainted Milk Caused Kidney Damage, Feb. 23, 2010, 11:57 AM CST/Source: The Associated Press, https://www.nbcnews.com/health/health-news/chinas-tainted-milk-caused-kidney-damage-flna1c9442765.

[12] C.B. Langman, U. Alon, J. Ingelfinger, et al., A position statement on kidney disease from powdered infant formula-based melamine exposure in Chinese infants, Pediatr. Nephrol. 24 (2009) 1263–1266, https://doi.org/10.1007/s00467-009-1129-6.

[13] C.G. Skinner, J.D. Thomas, J.D. Osterloh, Melamine toxicity, J. Med. Toxicol. 6 (1) (March 2010) 50–55, https://doi.org/10.1007/s13181-010-0038-1. PMID: 20195812; PMCID: PMC3550444.

[14] A.K. Hau, T.H. Kwan, P.K. Li, Melamine toxicity and the kidney, J. Am. Soc. Nephrol. 20 (2) (February 2009) 245–250, https://doi.org/10.1681/ASN.2008101065. Epub 2009 Feb 4. PMID: 19193777.

[15] R.P. Dalal, D.S. Goldfarb, Melamine-related kidney stones and renal toxicity, Nat. Rev. Nephrol. 7 (5) (May 2011) 267–274, https://doi.org/10.1038/nrneph.2011.24. Epub 2011 Mar 22. PMID: 21423252.

[16] R. Bakain ZA, S.A. Degs, Y.H. El-Sheikh, S. H Arar H, Spectrophotometric determination of melamine in liquid milk by multivariate second order calibration, Curr. Anal. Chem. 12 (1) (2016) 74–84.

[17] Valisure links 'unstable' Zantac and its ilk to carcinogen buildup, cancer risk. https://www.fiercepharma.com/pharma/valisure-links-unstable-zantac-and-its-ilk-to-carcinogen-build-up-cancer-risk [Accessed Jan. 18, 2022].

[18] L.Z. Braunstein, E.D. Kantor, K. O'Connell, A.J. Hudspeth, Q. Wu, N. Zenzola, D.Y. Light, Analysis of ranitidine-associated N-nitrosodimethylamine production under simulated physiologic conditions, JAMA Netw. Open 4 (1) (January 4, 2021) e2034766, https://doi.org/10.1001/jamanetworkopen.2020.34766. PMID: 33512515; PMCID: PMC7846938.

[19] H.J. Yoon, J.H. Kim, G.H. Seo, H. Park, Risk of cancer following the use of N-nitrosodimethylamine (NDMA) contaminated ranitidine products: a nationwide cohort study in South Korea, J. Clin. Med. 10 (1) (2021) 153.

[20] W. Gomm, C. Röthlein, K. Schüssel, G. Brückner, H. Schröder, S. Heß, R. Frötschl, K. Broich, B. Haenisch, N-Nitrosodimethylamine-contaminated valsartan and the risk of cancer—a longitudinal cohort study based on German health insurance data, Dtsch. Arztebl. Int. 118 (21) (May 28, 2021) 357–362, https://doi.org/10.3238/arztebl.m2021.0129. PMID: 34247699; PMCID: PMC8372009.

[21] N.A. Chikan, N. Shabir, S. Shaff, M.R. Mir, T.N. Patel, N-nitrosodimethylamine in the Kashmiri diet and possible roles in the high incidence of gastrointestinal cancers, Asian Pac. J. Cancer Prev. APJCP 13 (3) (2012) 1077–1079, https://doi.org/10.7314/apjcp.2012.13.3.1077. PMID: 22631641.

[22] R.H. Adamson, B.A. Chabner, The finding of N-nitrosodimethylamine in common medicines, Oncol. 25 (6) (June 2020) 460–462, https://doi.org/10.1634/theoncologist.2020-0142. Epub 2020 Apr 17. PMID: 32267983; PMCID: PMC7288647.

[23] C. Ornillo, N. Harbord, Fundaments of toxicology-approach to the poisoned patient, Adv. Chron. Kidney Dis. 27 (1) (January 2020) 5–10, https://doi.org/10.1053/j.ackd.2019.12.001. PMID: 32147001.

[24] Z. Liron, S. Srebrenik, A. Martin, S. Cohen, Theoretical derivation of solute-solvent interaction parameter in binary solution: case of the deviation from Raoult's law, J. Pharmaceut. Sci. 75 (1986) 463–468.

4

Equilibrium Processes in Pharmaceutics

Sunil S. Jambhekar

LECOM, School of Pharmacy, Bradenton, FL, United States

CHAPTER OBJECTIVES

- Define and exemplify equilibrium processes applicable in pharmaceutics.
- Identify and define various physicochemical properties of drugs determined under equilibrium condition.
- Define the "Rule of Five" and its importance.
- Application of Henderson–Hasselbalch equation in drug absorption.
- Illustrate the interplay among partition coefficient, lipophilicity, and permeability of a drug.
- Introduce the concept of equilibrium processes as they apply in pharmaceutics.
- Introduce concept of drug dissolution, importance of drug dissolution, and various theories used to describe drug dissolution.
- Discuss the importance of physicochemical properties of drugs in the drug discovery process, drug dissolution, drug absorption, and the bioavailability of drugs.
- Discuss the role of the gastrointestinal tract and biological membranes, diffusion and passive diffusion, and pH-partition theory in drug absorption.
- Introduce Biopharmaceutical Classification System for drugs.

Keywords: Absorption; BCS classification system; Diffusion and passive diffusion; Drug dissolution; Equilibrium condition; Gastrointestinal physiology; Ionization; pH-partition hypothesis; Rule of five; Surface activity; Viscosity.

Pharmaceutics, Second Edition
https://doi.org/10.1016/B978-0-323-99796-6.00017-5

4.1 Introduction

The term equilibrium has been defined in many ways in dictionaries. The definitions that closely apply to many processes, observed in pharmaceutics, are as follows:

A condition, at which, all acting influences are canceled by others, resulting in a stable, balanced, or unchanged system.

The state of a chemical reaction in which its forward and reverse reactions occur at equal rate so that the concentration of the reactants and products remain unchanged with time.

The state of a reversible chemical reaction in which the forward and reverse reactions occur at equal rates so that there are no further changes in the concentrations of the reactants and products.

The equilibrium process or condition is quite common in the life sciences; and pharmaceutics and biopharmaceutics, of course, are no exceptions. Following are a few examples of equilibrium processes that play an important role in pharmaceutics: ionization of weak acids and weak bases, partition coefficient and lipid solubility of a drug, equilibrium or saturation solubility, diffusion, in general and passive diffusion, in particular. It is important to note that some of these properties are very much interrelated, for example, the ionization of weak acids and weak bases and solubility, solubility and drug dissolution, and lipophilicity and membrane permeation. There are other physicochemical properties, which also play an equally important role in pharmaceutics and biopharmaceutics, and depend on the equilibrium processes mentioned earlier. They include drug dissolution, passive diffusion, drug absorption, and drug distribution.

Physicochemical properties of drugs depend on the equilibrium processes and play an important role in influencing the *in vivo* performance of a drug from a particular dosage form, as well as in the early stages of the drug discovery process. In the former, it is often reflected in the rate and extent of drug absorption following the administration of a dosage form, and, in the latter, it is frequently reflected in the extended timeline and higher cost in developing new therapeutic agents or active pharmaceutical ingredients. To reduce delays and attrition rate, most pharmaceutical companies are now evaluating their lead compounds for drug-like properties, which depend upon equilibrium processes. Early assessment of a lead compound with respect to physicochemical properties provides opportunities for an early optimization of the therapeutic agent. These physicochemical properties also play an important role in the selection of the drug delivery system or dosage form. This chapter will discuss the important physicochemical properties of a drug that depend on the equilibrium processes in the discipline of pharmaceutics and biopharmaceutics. The processes will be ionization of weak acids and base at equilibrium, partition coefficient, equilibrium solubility, drug dissolution, and passive diffusion.

The importance of the physicochemical properties of drugs in the early drug development and discovery process has been recognized for a long time. The publication of the so-called "Rule of Five" [1,2], however, has generated widespread interest and elevated interest in regard to applying calculated physicochemical properties in the drug discovery process to separate poor drug candidates before they (i.e., selected candidates) go into clinical trials. According to the Rule of Five, poor intestinal absorption is associated with and attributed to the molecule possessing any two of the following properties: molecular weight greater than 750 Da, number of hydrogen bond donors greater than five, number of hydrogen bond acceptors greater than 10, and calculated log P (partition coefficient) greater than five. These guidelines have been proven to be very useful for approximate predictions of intestinal drug absorption. The critical role of lipid solubility in drug absorption is a major guiding principle in the drug discovery and development process. Because the lipid-solubility of a drug molecule is the sum of the individual partition coefficients for each of its functional groups, the prediction of lipid solubility ($c \log P$) can be estimated.

A recent examination [2] of the relationship of molecular surface properties with the biological performance of a molecule has been revealing. Most notably, it has been demonstrated that the polar surface area (PSA) of a drug molecule has a strong correlation in predicting drug transport from the human intestine and across the biological membranes. The PSA is defined as the sum of the Van der Waals surface areas for the polar atoms, oxygen, nitrogen, and attached hydrogen atom (or the number of H-bond donors and H-bond acceptors) (see http://www.molinspiration.com for calculating the PSA). The PSA is a major determinant for oral absorption and brain penetration of drugs that are transported by the transcellular route (movement across cell membranes). This property should be considered in the early phase of drug screening. Another related parameter, dynamic PSA (PSAd), has surfaced [3] as a parameter of value in predicting membrane permeability and oral absorption in humans. Interpolation of the sigmoidal plot for 20 selected compounds suggests that when the PSAd is greater than 140 Å^2, incomplete absorption (<10%) ocurrs. However, when the PSAd value is less than 60 Å^2, drug absorption can happen in excess of 90%. Amidon and his co-workers [4−6] have contributed significantly to their seminal work by developing a biopharmaceutical classification system (BCS), which is based on physicochemical properties such as equilibrium solubility and partition coefficient, among others.

A consideration of these physicochemical properties is fundamental to discuss several important aspects of the overall effects attributed to equilibrium processes. For a given chemical entity (drug), there often would be a difference in physiological availability and, presumably, in clinical responses, primarily because drug molecules must cross various biological membranes and interact with intercellular and intracellular fluids before reaching the elusive region termed the "site of action." Under these conditions, the physicochemical properties of the drug must contribute favorably to facilitate absorption and distribution processes to augment the drug concentration at various active sites. Furthermore, equally important is the fact that these biopharmaceutical properties of a drug must ensure a specific orientation on the receptor surface so that a sequence of events is initiated that leads to the observed pharmacological effects. Drug molecules that are deficient in the required biopharmaceutical properties may, generally, display marginal pharmacological action or be totally ineffective.

Before these physicochemical properties are discussed in detail, it is, however, important to understand gastrointestinal physiology, the biological membrane, the absorption process, and how orally administered drugs reach the systemic circulation and elicit their pharmacological effects.

Biopharmaceutics may be defined as the study of the influence of formulation factors on the therapeutic activity of a drug product or dosage forms. It involves the study of the relationship between some of the physicochemical properties of a drug and the biological effects observed following the administration of a drug via various dosage forms or drug delivery systems. Almost any alteration in a drug delivery system is likely to alter the drug delivery rate and the amount of the drug delivered to the desired site of action in the body. This includes the chemical nature of the drug (e.g., ester, salts, and complexes), the particle size and surface area of the drug, the type of dosage form (e.g., solution, suspension, capsule, and tablet), and the excipients and processes used in the manufacturing of the drug delivery system.

Drugs in dosage forms most often are administered to human subjects by the oral route. Compared to other routes of drug administration, especially the intravenous route, the oral route is unusually complex with respect to the physicochemical conditions existing at the absorption site. Therefore, before we discuss the physiochemical properties and how the physicochemical properties of a drug in a dosage form may affect the availability and action of that drug, it is prudent to review gastrointestinal physiology.

4.2 Gastrointestinal physiology

Fig. 4.1 schematically represents the gastrointestinal tract and some of the problems encountered in drug absorption following oral administration of a drug [7]. The stomach can be divided into two main parts: the body of the stomach, and the pylorus. Histologically, these parts correspond to the pepsin- and HCl-secreting area and the mucus-secreting area, respectively, of the gastric mucosa. In the human, the stomach contents usually are in the pH range of 1.0−3.5, with pH 1.0−2.5 being the most common range. Furthermore, there is a diurnal cycle of gastric acidity in humans. During the night, stomach contents usually are more acidic (pH ∼1.3); during the day, because of food consumption, the pH is less acidic. The recovery of stomach acidity, however, occurs quite rapidly. The presence of protein, being amphoteric in nature, acts as an excellent buffer, and as digestion proceeds, the liberated amino acids increase the neutralizing capacity enormously.

The small intestine is divided anatomically into three sections: the duodenum, the jejunum, and the ileum. All three areas are involved in the digestion and absorption of food. The available absorbing area is increased by surface folds in the intestinal lining. The surface of these folds possesses villi and microvilli (Fig. 4.2). The duodenal contents in the human usually are in the pH range of 5−7. There is a gradual decrease in acidity along the length of the gastrointestinal tract, with the ultimate pH being 7−8 in the lower ileum. It has been estimated that approximately 8 L of fluid enter the upper intestine per day, with approximately 7 L of this arising from digestive juices and fluids and approximately 1 L arising from oral intake. Over the entire length of the large and small intestine and the stomach is the brush border, which consists of a uniform coating (thickness, 3 mm) of mucopolysaccharide. This coating layer serves to act as a mechanical barrier to bacteria or food particles.

When a dosage form containing a drug or drug molecules moves from the stomach through the pylorus into the duodenum, the dosage form encounters a rapidly changing environment with respect to pH. Furthermore, digestive juices secreted into the small bowel contain many enzymes not found in gastric juices. Digestion and absorption of

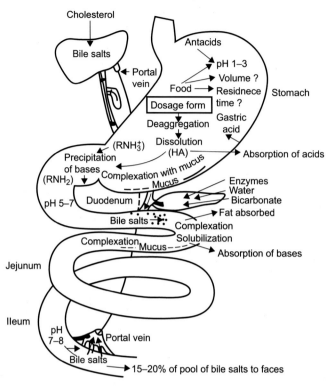

FIGURE 4.1   Processes occurring along with drug absorption when drug molecules travel down the gastrointestinal tract and the factors that affect drug absorption [7]. *From Florence A.T. Attwood, D,* Physiochemical Principles of Pharmacy, *fifth ed., Pharmaceutical Press, New York, 2011, with permission.*

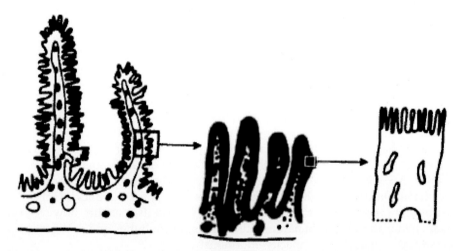

FIGURE 4.2   The epithelium of the small intestine at different levels of magnification. From left to right: The intestinal villi and microvilli that constitute the brush border.

foods occur simultaneously in the small intestine. Intestinal digestion is the terminal phase of preparing foodstuff for absorption and consists of two processes: completion of the hydrolysis of large molecules to smaller ones, which can be absorbed, and bringing the finished product of hydrolysis into an aqueous solution or emulsion.

Drug absorption, whether from the gastrointestinal tract or from other sites, requires the passage of the drug in a molecular form across the barrier membrane. Most drugs are presented to the body as solid or semi-solid dosage forms, and the drug particles must first be released from these dosage forms. These drug particles must dissolve, and if they possess the desirable biopharmaceutical properties, they will pass from a region of high concentration to a region of low concentration across the membrane into the blood or general circulation (Fig. 4.3). Knowledge

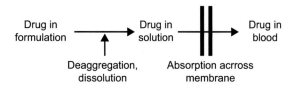

FIGURE 4.3   Sequence of events in drug absorption from formulations of solid dosage forms.

of biological membrane structure and its general properties is pivotal in understanding absorption processes and the role of the biopharmaceutical properties of drug substances.

4.2.1 Biological membrane

The prevalent view is that the gastrointestinal membrane consists of a bimolecular lipoid layer that is covered on each side by protein with the lipid molecule oriented perpendicular to the cell surface (Fig. 4.4). The lipid layer is interrupted by small, water-filled pores with a radius of approximately 4 Å. Hence, a molecule with a radius of 4 Å or less may pass through these water-filled pores. Thus, membranes have a specialized transport system to assist the passage of water-soluble material and ions through the lipid interior, a process sometimes termed as "convective absorption." The rate of permeation of such small molecules through the pore is affected not only by the relative sizes of the holes and the molecules but also by the interaction between permeating molecules and the membrane. When permeation through the membrane occurs, the permeating substance is considered to have transferred from solution in the luminal aqueous phase to the lipid membrane phase, then to the aqueous phase on the other side of the membrane. Biological membranes differ from a polymeric membrane in that they are composed of small amphipathic molecules, phospholipids, and cholesterol. The protein layer associated with membranes is hydrophilic in nature. Therefore, biological membranes have a hydrophilic exterior and a hydrophobic interior. Cholesterol is a major component of most mammalian biological membranes, and its removal will render the membrane highly permeable. The presence of a cholesterol complex with phospholipids reduces the permeability of the membrane to water, cations, glycerides, and glucose. The shape of the cholesterol molecule allows it to fit closely with the hydrocarbon chains of unsaturated fatty acids in the bilayer. It is a general opinion that cholesterol makes the membrane more rigid. The flexibility of the biological membrane to reform and adapt to the changed environment is its important feature. The details of membrane structure are still widely debated, and a more recent membrane model is shown in Fig. 4.4.

In addition to physicochemical properties, several physiological factors also may affect the rate and extent of gastrointestinal absorption. These factors are as follows: properties of epithelial cells, segmental activity of the

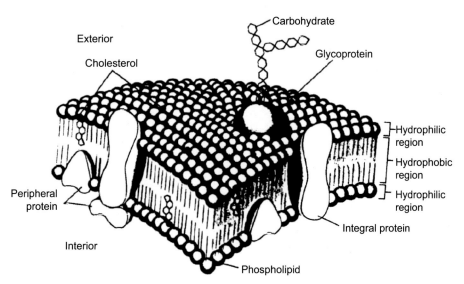

FIGURE 4.4   Basic structure of an animal cell membrane. *From C. Smith, A. Marks, M. Lieberman (Eds.), Basic Medical Biochemistry, Baltimore: Lippincott, Williams and Wilkins, 2004, 159–163, with permission.*

bowel, degree of vascularity, effective absorbing surface area per unit length of gut, surface and interfacial tensions, electrolyte content and their concentration in luminal fluid, enzymatic activity in the luminal contents, and gastric emptying rate of the drug from stomach.

4.2.2 Mechanisms of drug absorption

Drug transfer often is viewed as the movement of a drug molecule across a series of membranes and spaces (Fig. 4.5), which, in aggregate, serve as a macroscopic membrane. The cells and interstitial spaces lying between the gastric lumen and the capillary blood, or the structure between sinusoidal space and the bile canaliculi are examples. Each of the cellular membranes and spaces may impede drug transport to varying degrees; therefore, any one of them can be a rate-limiting step to the overall process of drug transport. This complexity of structure makes quantitative prediction of drug transport difficult. Therefore, a qualitative description of the processes of drug transport across functional membranes is attempted in following sections.

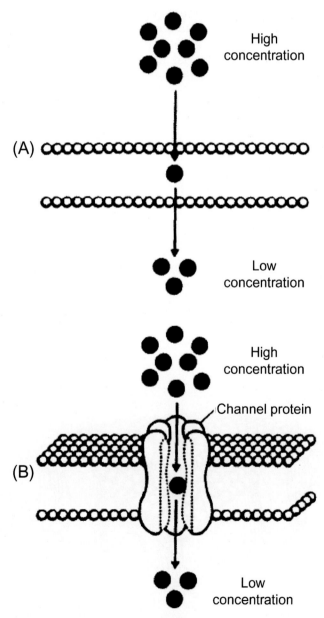

FIGURE 4.5 (A) Simple diffusion; (B) membrane channels. *From C. Smith, A. Marks, M. Lieberman (Eds.),* Basic Medical Biochemistry, *Baltimore: Lippincott, Williams and Wilkins, 2004, 159–163, with permission.*

4.2.3 The pH-partition hypothesis and drug absorption

Drug absorption is influenced by many physiological factors. Additionally, it also depends on many physico-chemical properties of the drug itself. Shore, Brodie, Hogben, Schanker, Tocco, and others [8–14] concluded from their research that most drugs are absorbed from the gastrointestinal tract by a process of passive diffusion of the unionized moiety across a lipid membrane. Furthermore, the dissociation constant, lipid solubility, and pH of the fluid at the absorption site determine the extent of drug absorption from a solution. The interrelationship among these parameters is known as the pH-partition theory. This theory provides a basic framework for the understanding of drug absorption from the gastrointestinal tract and drug transport across the biological membrane. The principal points of this theory are as follows:

- The gastrointestinal and other biological membranes act as lipid barriers.
- The unionized form of the acidic or basic drug is preferentially absorbed.
- Most drugs are absorbed by passive diffusion.
- The rate of drug absorption and amount of drug absorbed are related to its oil–water partition coefficient (i.e., the more lipophilic the drug, the faster is its absorption).
- Weak acidic and neutral drugs may be absorbed from the stomach, but basic drugs are not.

When a drug is administered intravenously, it is immediately available to body fluids for distribution to the site of action. All extravascular routes, however, can influence the overall therapeutic activity of the drug, primarily because of its dissolution rate, a step that is necessary for a drug to be available in a solution form. When a drug is administered orally in a dosage form such as a tablet, capsule, or suspension, the rate of absorption across the biological membrane frequently is controlled by the slowest step in the following sequence:

$$\underset{\text{form}}{\text{Dosage}} \xrightarrow{\text{dissolution}} \underset{\text{solution}}{\text{Drug in}} \xrightarrow{\text{absorption}} \underset{\text{circulation}}{\text{Drug in general}}$$

In many instances, the slowest, or rate-limiting, step in the sequence is the drug dissolution. When dissolution is the controlling step, any factors that affect the rate of dissolution also must influence the rate of absorption. This, in turn, affects the extent and duration of action. Several factors can influence the dissolution rate of drug from solid dosage forms and, therefore, the therapeutic activity. These factors include solubility of a drug, particle size and surface area of drug particles, crystalline and salt form of a drug, and the rate of disintegration.

4.3 Ionization

Most therapeutic agents appear to be either weakly acidic or basic in nature. For a compound containing acidic or basic functional groups, solubility at a given pH is influenced by the compound's dissociation constant (pK_a). The solubility of a compound in an aqueous medium is greater in the ionized state than in the neutral (unionized) state. Therefore, the solubility of a weakly acidic or basic drug depends on the pH of the solution. Many weakly acidic and basic drugs, therefore, are ionizable, in the gastrointestinal tract; therefore, solubility, dissolution, and absorption of a weak acidic or basic drug depend on the pH of the surrounding fluid.

Solubility, dissolution, and absorption of a weakly acidic drug can be altered by changes in the gastric pH (coadministration of antacids). While a weakly basic compound might fully dissolve in the acidic environment of the stomach and result in high exposure levels under such conditions, co-administration of drugs that raise the pH can lead to greatly decreased solubility and lower exposure. The ionization of a drug can also alter its stability and permeability. For compounds containing both acidic and basic functional groups, the formation of zwitterions may lead to the lowest solubility at an isoelectric point.

If a compound is ionizable, a salt can be formed, which may exhibit better dissolution as well as solubility. The greater solubility and faster dissolution present an advantage in formulating a solution and a solid dosage form, respectively.

4.3.1 Ionization of weakly acidic and basic drugs

The fraction of the drug that exists in its unionized form in a solution is a function of both the dissociation constant of a drug and the pH of the solution. The dissociation constant, for both weak acids and bases, often is expressed as the pK_a (the negative logarithm of a dissociation constant, K_a). The Henderson–Hasselbalch equation for the ionization of a weak acid, HA, is derived from the following equation:

$$HA + H_2O \rightleftarrows A^- + H_3O^+ \tag{4.1}$$

The equilibrium constant of the above Eq. (4.1) can be expressed as follows:

$$K_a = \frac{[_aH_3O^+][_aA^-]}{[_aHA]} \tag{4.2}$$

where K_a is the dissociation constant under the equilibrium condition and a is the activity coefficient. Assuming the activity coefficients approach unity in dilute solutions, the activity coefficients may be replaced by concentration terms, and Eq. (4.2) becomes

$$K_a = \frac{[H_3O^+][A^-]}{[HA]} \tag{4.3}$$

The negative logarithm of K_a is referred to as the pK_a. Thus,

$$pK_a = -\log K_a \tag{4.4}$$

Taking the logarithm of the expression for the dissociation constant of a weak acid in Eq. (4.3) yields

$$-\log K_a = -\log[H_3O^+] - \log[A^-] + \log[HA] \tag{4.5}$$

where A^- is the ionized form of a weak acid and HA is the unionized form.

$$pH - pK_a = \log\frac{[\text{Ionized}]}{[\text{Un-ionized}]} \tag{4.6}$$

Assuming that α is the fraction of ionized species and that $1 - \alpha$ is the fraction remaining as the unionized form, Eq. (4.6) can be written as

$$pH - pK_a = \log\frac{\alpha}{1-\alpha} \tag{4.7}$$

or

$$\frac{\alpha}{1-\alpha} = \text{antilog}(pH - pK_a) \tag{4.8}$$

From Eq. (4.8), the fraction or percentage of the absorbable and non-absorbable forms of a weak acid can be calculated if the pH condition at the site of administration is known. Analogously, the dissociation or basicity constant for a weak base is derived as follows:

$$B + H_2O \leftrightarrow BH^+ + OH^- \tag{4.9}$$

The dissociation constant, K_b, is derived as follows:

$$K_b = \frac{[_aOH][_aBH^+]}{[_aB]} = \frac{[OH^-][BH^+]}{[B]} \tag{4.10}$$

and

$$pK_b = -\log K_b \tag{4.11}$$

The pK_a and pK_b values provide a convenient means of comparing the strength of weak acids and bases. The lower the pK_a, the stronger is the acid, and the lower the pK_b, the stronger the base. The values for pK_a and pK_b of conjugate acid–base pairs are linked by the expression

$$pK_a + pK_b = pK_w \tag{4.12}$$

where pK_w is the negative logarithm of the dissociation constant of water. Taking the logarithm of Eq. (4.10) and rearranging yields

$$-\log K_b = -\log[OH^-] - \log[BH^+] + \log[B] \tag{4.13}$$

Although the dissociation constant of a weak base, under equilibrium condition, is described by the term K_b, it is conventionally expressed in terms of K_a, using the relationship expressed in Eq. (4.12).

Eq. (4.13) can then be written as

$$pH = pK_w - pK_b - \log\frac{[BH^+]}{[B]} \tag{4.14}$$

Because $pK_w - pK_b = pK_a$, Eq. (4.14) takes the following form for a weak base (where BH^+ is the ionized form, and B is the unionized form):

$$pK_a - pH = \log\frac{[Ionized]}{[Unionized]} \tag{4.15}$$

Again, assuming that α is the fraction of ionized species and that $1 - \alpha$ is the fraction of unionized species, Eq. (4.15) becomes

$$pK_a - pH = \log\frac{\alpha}{1 - \alpha} \tag{4.16}$$

or

$$\frac{\alpha}{1 - \alpha} = antilog(pK_a - pH) \tag{4.17}$$

From Eq. (4.17), one can calculate the fraction or percentage of absorbable and non-absorbable form of a weak base if the pH condition at the site of drug absorption is known. Fig. 4.6 shows the pK_a values of several drugs and the relative acid or base strength of these compounds.

The relationship between pH and pK_a and the extent of ionization is provided by Eqs. (4.8) and (4.17) for weak acids and weak bases, respectively. Accordingly, most weak acidic drugs are predominantly in the unionized form at lower pH of the gastric fluid and, therefore, may be preferentially absorbed from the stomach but also

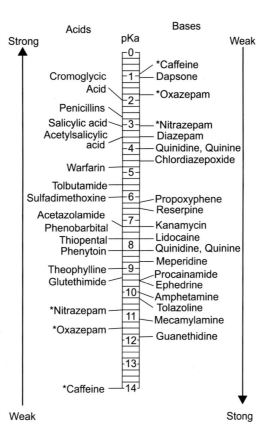

FIGURE 4.6   The pK_a values of certain acidic and basic drugs. Drugs denoted with an asterisk are amphoteric [15]. *From M. Rowland, T. Tozer, Clinical Pharmacokinetics: Concepts and Application, second ed., Lea and Febiger, Philadelphia, 1989, with permission.*

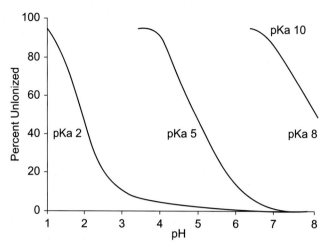

FIGURE 4.7 For very weak acids, pK_a values greater than 8.0 are predominantly unionized at all pH values between 1.0 and 8.0. Profound changes in the unionized fraction occur with pH for an acid with a pK_a value that lies within the range of 2.0–8.0. Although the fraction unionized of even strong acids increases with increase in hydrogen ion concentration (i.e., decrease in pH), the absolute value remains low at most pH values shown [15]. *From M. Rowland, T. Tozer,* Clinical Pharmacokinetics: Concepts and Application, *second ed., Lea and Febiger, Philadelphia, 1989, with permission.*

from the upper part of the intestine (duodenum) where generally pH exists in the range of 5–7. Some very weakly acidic drugs, such as phenytoin and many barbiturates, the pK_a values of which are greater than 8.0, are essentially unionized at all gastrointestinal pH values. Therefore, for these weak acidic drugs, transport is more rapid and independent of pH, provided that the unionized form is lipophilic or non-polar. Furthermore, it is important to note that the fraction unionized changes dramatically only for weak acids with pK_a values between 3 and 7. Therefore, for the weak acids, a change in the rate of transport with pH is expected, as shown in Fig. 4.7 [15]. Although the transport of weak acids with pK_a values less than 3.0 should theoretically depend on pH, the fraction unionized is so low that transport across the gut membrane may be slow even under the most acidic conditions.

Most weak bases are poorly absorbed, if at all, in the stomach, because they are present largely in the ionized form at pH 1–2. Codeine, a weak base with a pK_a of approximately eight, will have about 1 in every 1 million molecules in its unionized form at gastric pH 1.0. Weakly basic drugs with a pK_a of less than 4, such as dapsone, diazepam, and chlordiazepoxide, are essentially unionized through the intestine. Strong bases, which are those with pK_a values between 5 and 11, show pH-dependent absorption. Stronger bases, such as guanethidine ($pK_a > 11$) are ionized throughout the gastrointestinal tract and tend to be poorly absorbed.

The evidence of the importance of dissociation in drug absorption is found in the result of studies in which pH at the absorption site is changed (Tables 4.1 and 4.2). Table 4.1 clearly shows the decreased absorption of a weak acid at pH 8.0 compared to pH 1.0 [15]. On the other hand, an increase to pH 8.0 promotes the absorption of a weak base, with practically nothing absorbed at pH 1.0. The data in Table 4.2 also permits a comparison of intestinal absorption of acidic and basic drugs from buffered solutions ranging from pH 4.0 to 8.0 [16]. These results are in agreement with the pH-partition hypothesis.

The pH-partition theory provides a basic framework for the understanding of drug absorption and, sometimes, is an oversimplification of a more complex process. For example, experimentally observed pH–absorption curves are less steep (Fig. 4.8) than that expected theoretically and are shifted to higher pH values for bases and lower pH values for acids. This deviation, observed experimentally, has been attributed by several investigators to factors such as limited absorption of ionized species of drugs, the presence of an unstirred diffusion layer adjacent to the cell membrane, and a difference between luminal pH and cell membrane surface pH.

4.4 Partition coefficient and lipophilicity

This property of a solute or drug affects the solubility and permeability of a drug which, in turn, will influence other properties of a drug like dissolution, absorption, distribution, metabolism, and elimination. The partitioning of a compound between two completely immiscible phases depends on the availability of the drug in unionized form. Therefore, the ionization of a compound plays an important role in determining the lipophilicity and permeability of the compound.

TABLE 4.1 Comparison of gastric absorption of acids and bases at pH 1 and 8 in the rat [8,16].

	pK$_a$	% absorbed at pH 1	% absorbed at pH 8
Acids			
5-Sulfosalicylic acid	- 2.8	0	0
5-Nitrosalicylic acid	2.3	52	16
Salicylic acid	3.0	61	13
Thiopental	7.6	46	34
Bases			
Aniline	4.6	6	56
p-Toluidine	5.3	0	47
Quinine	8.4	0	18
Dextromethorphan	9.2	0	16

TABLE 4.2 Comparison of intestinal absorption of acids and bases at pH 4-8 in rat [8,16].

		% Absorbed from rat intestine			
Acids	pK$_a$	pH 4	pH 5	pH 7	pH 8
5-Nitrosalicylic acid	2.3	40	27	0	0
Salicylic acid	3.0	64	35	30	10
Acetylsalicylic acid	3.5	41	27	–	–
Benzoic acid	4.2	62	36	35	5
Bases					
Aniline	4.6	40	48	58	61
Aminopyrine	5.0	21	35	48	52
p-Toluidine	5.3	30	42	65	64
Quinine	8.4	9	11	41	54

Some drugs may be poorly absorbed after oral administration even though they are available predominantly in the unionized form in the gastrointestinal tract. This is attributed to the low lipid solubility of the unionized molecule. A guide to the lipid solubility or lipophilic nature of a drug is provided by a property called the partition coefficient (*P*). This parameter, therefore, influences the transport and absorption processes of drugs, and it is one of the most widely used properties in quantitative structure—activity relationships.

The movement of molecules from one phase to another is called partitioning. Drugs partition themselves between the aqueous phase and lipophilic membrane. Preservatives in emulsions partition between the water and oil phases; antibiotics partition from body fluids to microorganisms; and drugs and other adjuvants can partition into the plastic and rubber stoppers of containers. It is, therefore, important that this process is clearly understood.

If two immiscible phases are placed adjacent to each other, with one containing a solute soluble in both phases, the solute will distribute itself between two immiscible phases until equilibrium is attained; therefore, no further transfer of solute occurs. At equilibrium, the chemical potential of the solute (free energy of the solute in solvent) in one phase is equal to its chemical potential in the other phase. If we consider an aqueous (w) and an organic (o) phase, we write according to the theory:

$$\mu_w^\Theta + RT\ln a_w = \mu_o^\Theta + RT\ln a_o \tag{4.18}$$

I. Physical principles and properties of pharmaceutics

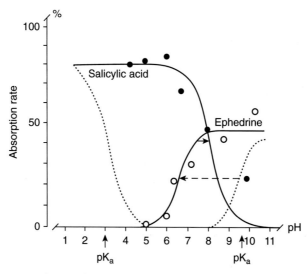

FIGURE 4.8 Relationship between absorption rates of salicylic acid and ephedrine and bulk phase pH in the rat small intestine *in vivo*. Dashed lines represent curves predicted by the pH-partition theory in the absence of an unstirred layer [18]. *From D. Winne, The influence of unstirred layers on intestinal absorption in intestinal permeation, In: M. Kramer, F. Lauterbach F (Eds.), Workshop Conference Hoechest, vol. 4, Excerpta Medica, Amsterdam, 1977, 58–64, with permission.*

where *a* represents the activity coefficient of a solute (effect of solute concentration on inter-solute interactions). Rearranging Eq. (4.18) yields

$$\frac{\mu_w^\Phi - \mu_0^\Phi}{RT} = \ln\frac{a_0}{a_w} \tag{4.19}$$

The term on the left side of Eq. (4.19) is a constant at a given temperature and pressure. Therefore,

$$\frac{a_w}{a_o} = \text{constant or } \frac{a_o}{a_w} = \text{constant} \tag{4.20}$$

These constants are the partition (*P*) or distribution coefficients (*D*). Because most drugs are ionic, their partition coefficients are pH-dependent and usually reported at pH 7.4 and are therefore appropriately called distribution coefficients. If the solute under consideration forms an ideal solution in either phases or in solvent, the activity coefficient can be replaced by the concentration term, and Eq. (4.20) becomes

$$P = \frac{C_o}{C_w} \tag{4.21}$$

Eq. (4.21) is used conventionally to calculate the partition coefficient of a drug. In Eq. 4.21, C_o, the concentration of a drug in the organic or oil phase, is divided by the concentration of a drug in the aqueous phase once the equilibrium is attained. The greater the value of *P*, the higher is the lipid solubility of the solute. It has been demonstrated for several systems that the partition coefficient can be approximated by the solubility of the solute in the organic phase divided by the solubility in the aqueous phase. Therefore, the partition coefficient is a measure of the relative affinities of the solute for an aqueous or non-aqueous or oil phase. Octanol is often used as the non-aqueous or organic phase in experiments to measure the partition coefficient of drugs. Its (Octanol) polarity suggests that water is solubilized to some extent in the octanol phase and thus partitioning is bit more complex than with an anhydrous solvent. Its usefulness, however, stems from the fact that biological membranes are also not simple anhydrous phases. While octanol is favored, other alcohols have also been used to determine the partition coefficient. Example includes isobutanol.

The effect of lipid solubility and, hence, the partition coefficient on the absorption of a series of barbituric acid derivatives is shown in Table 4.3. The term partition coefficient is more commonly expressed exponentially as log *P*. Tables 4.4 and 4.5 provide the partition coefficient values for various analogs of tetracycline and for different drugs, respectively.

The lipid solubility of four tetracyclines (Table 4.4) correlates inversely with mean antibiotic plasma concentration and with renal excretion. Only the more lipophilic minocycline and doxycycline pass through the blood–brain and

TABLE 4.3 Comparison of barbiturate absorption in rat colon and partition coefficient (chloroform/water) of undissociated drug [8,16].

Barbiturate	Partition coefficient	% absorbed
Barbital	0.7	12
Apobarbital	4.9	17
Phenobarbital	4.8	20
Allylbarbital	10.5	23
Butethal	11.7	24
Cyclobarbital	13.9	24
Pentobarbital	28.0	30
Secobarbital	50.7	40
Hexethal	>100	44

TABLE 4.4 Partition coefficients of four analogs of tetracycline [7].

Analogs of tetracycline	Partition coefficient[a]	Partition coefficient[b]
Minocycline	30.0	1.1
Doxycycline	0.48	0.60
Tetracycline	0.09	0.036
Oxytetracycline	0.007	0.025

[a]Measured by using chloroform/water system.
[b]Measured by using octanol/water system.

TABLE 4.5 Log of P Values for representative drugs*.

Drug	Log P
Acetylsalicyclic acid (aspirin)	1.19
Amiodarone	6.7
Benzocaine	1.89
Caffeine	0.01
Chlorpromazine	5.30
Ciprofloxacin	- 1.12
Indomethacin	3.1
Lidocaine	2.26
Methadone	3.9
Phenytoin	2.50
Prednisone	1.46

blood ocular barriers in measurable concentrations. It must be clearly understood that even though drugs with greater lipophilicity and, therefore, partition coefficient, are better absorbed, it is imperative that drugs exhibit some degree of aqueous solubility. This is essential because the availability of the drug molecule in a solution form is a prerequisite for drug absorption and the biological fluids at the site of absorption are aqueous in nature. Therefore, from a practical viewpoint, drugs must exhibit a balance between hydrophilicity and lipophilicity. This

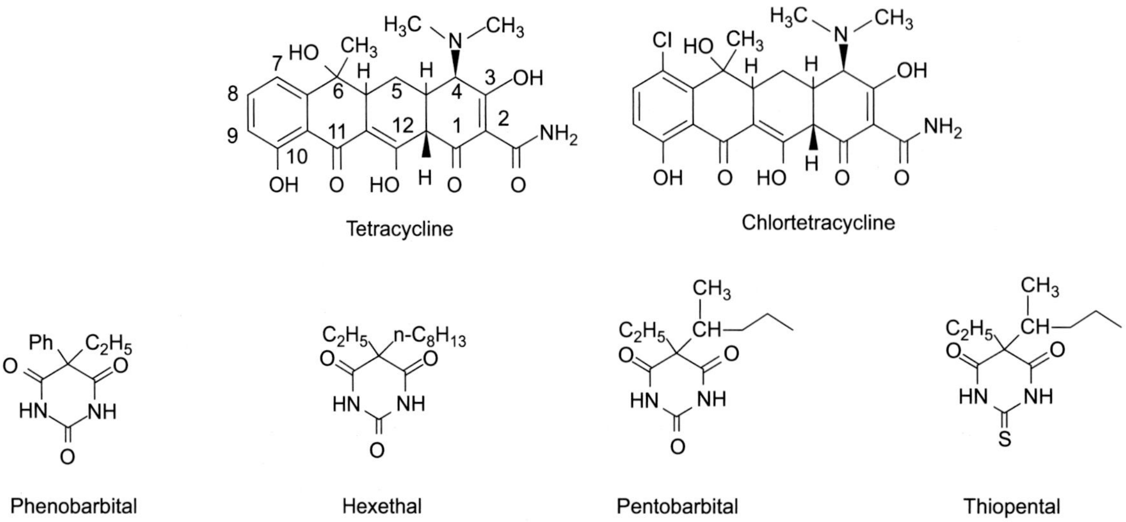

FIGURE 4.9   Drug pairs in which chemical modification enhances lipophilicity.

factor is always taken into account while a chemical modification is being considered as a way of improving the efficacy of a therapeutic agent.

Examples of polar or hydrophilic molecules that are poorly absorbed following oral administration and, therefore, must be administered parenterally include gentamicin, ceftrixine (ceftriaxone and cefotaxime), and streptokinase. Lipid-soluble drugs with favorable partition coefficients generally are well absorbed after oral administration. Very often, the selection of a compound with a higher partition coefficient from a series of research compounds provides the improved pharmacological activity. Occasionally, the structure of an existing drug is modified to develop a similar pharmacological activity with improved absorption. Chlortetracycline, which differs from tetracycline by the substitution of a chlorine at C-7, substitution of an *n*-hexyl (Hexethal) for a phenyl ring in phenobarbital, or replacement of the 2-carbonyl of pentobarbital with a 2-thio group (thiopental) are examples of enhanced lipophilicity (Fig. 4.9).

It is important to note that even a minor molecular modification of a drug may also promote the risk of altering the efficacy and safety profile of a drug due to alteration in the lipophilicity and other physicochemical properties. For this reason, medicinal chemists prefer the development of a lipid-soluble pro-drug of a drug with poor oral absorption characteristics.

4.5 Equilibrium solubility

The aqueous solubility of a drug substance is a fundamental physicochemical property and should be evaluated early in the discovery stage. Inadequate solubility can affect the results in the early screening process, may preclude the development of certain dosage forms, and may influence the drug dissolution and, therefore, the rate and extent of drug absorption.

Equilibrium or saturated solubility can be defined as the maximum amount of solute that is present in a solution form per unit volume of a solvent at a constant temperature and pressure. It can also be defined as the maximum amount of solute present in solution per unit volume of a solvent when the rate of transfer of a solute from solid into solution is the same as the rate of transfer of solute molecules from solution onto the powder particles. The attainment of equal transfer rates indicates that equilibrium condition is attained and, therefore, there will be no change in the concentration of solute in a solvent.

4.5.1 Expressions of solubility

The solubility of a solute in a solvent can be expressed quantitatively in several ways. They include grams/L; moles/L, and molal concentration. Other less-specific and less common forms of reporting solubility include parts per parts of solvent (e.g., parts per million, ppm).

Many Pharmacopoeias and other chemical and pharmaceutical compendia frequently use this form and also the expressions "insoluble," "very highly soluble," and "soluble." These are imprecise and often not very helpful; however, these terms provide the general guidance about the solubility of a drug. For quantitative work, specific concentration terms must be used.

Most substances have at least some degree of solubility in water and while they may appear to be "insoluble" by a qualitative test, their solubility can be measured and quoted precisely. In aqueous media at pH 10, chlorpromazine base has a solubility of 8×10^{-6} mol/lit, that is it is very slightly soluble, but it might be considered to be "insoluble" if judged visually by the lack of disappearance of solid placed in a test-tube of water.

There are many reasons why it is important to understand the way in which drugs dissolve in solution and the factors that maintain solubility or cause drugs to come out of solution, that is, to precipitate. These include the facts that:

- Many drugs are formulated as solutions or are added in powder or solution form to the liquids such as infusion fluids in which they must remain in solution for a given period.
- In whatever way drugs are presented to the body, they must usually be in a molecularly dispersed form (i.e., in solution) before they can be absorbed across biological membranes.
- Drugs of low aqueous solubility (e.g., Taxol) frequently present problems in relation to their formulation and bioavailability.
- Patients are frequently advised to take poorly soluble drugs with plenty of water or fluids.
- For injectable solutions, the high solubility of a drug under the conditions close to physiological pH of 7.4 is essential. For small-volume injectables such as intramuscular and subcutaneous, the solubility should be as high as possible to accommodate the dose to be administered in 0.5–2 mL for subcutaneous or up to 5 mL for intramuscular administration. The solubility requirement for intravenous injections is less stringent because volumes up to 20 mL can be administered. With low solubility drugs, one has to resort to infusions of volumes of up to 1000 mL.
- Injectable solutions of drugs require particularly high chemical stability. Ideally, a drug substance must withstand heat sterilization in solution and subsequent storage for up to 5 years. For those drug substances, lacking such optimum stability, it is possible to circumvent heat stress by sterile filtration. Naturally, for injectable, solid-state drug properties are of minor importance as long as they do not hamper processing or the dissolution of a lyophilizate.
- For solid oral dosage forms (tablets and capsules) the most critical step, after swallowing a tablet or capsule (i.e., unit dose), is the release of the drug substance. Solubility, and therefore dissolution, can control or limit, this important process. Therefore, a solubility that is reasonably high in relation to the drug dose is desirable.

Knowledge and understanding of the equilibrium solubility of a drug, therefore, is absolutely essential and plays a very critical role in the drug discovery process, drug formulation process, selection of a dosage form for a drug, drug dissolution in the gastrointestinal tract, and drug absorption. Tables 4.6 and 4.7 provide the equilibrium solubility of some commonly used drugs in water as well as other solvents.

4.5.2 Factors that affect solubility

There are number of factors that influence the solubility of a drug. They include temperature, molecule shape, and substituent groups, pH of the aqueous solution, and the solvent system.

4.5.2.1 Temperature

In general, higher the temperature greater is the solubility of a drug. This is particularly true, if the drug possesses high heat of solution, a property of a solid. If the heat of solution is very low or almost zero, temperature may not have any effect on the solubility of that solute. In other words, increasing the temperature will not alter the solubility of that compound. On the other hand, if the solute exhibits negative heat of solution, increasing the temperature will result in decrease in the solubility of that drug. Based on the influence of temperature on the solubility of a solute, solids have been classified as endothermic and exothermic. Endothermic solutes will absorb heat from the surrounding during the formation of solution, and exothermic solute will liberate heat during the formation of solution. The magnitude of the influence of temperature on the solubility, however, depends on the intrinsic solubility of a solute as well as the availability of a solute in a salt form or weak acid or weak base form. If the intrinsic solubility of a solute is very low and the solute is either a weak acid or base, temperature will exert greater influence on the

TABLE 4.6 Solubility comparison of selected drugs.

Name of drug	Solubility in water (mg/mL)	Solubility in alcohol (mg/mL)
Acetaminophen	Slightly soluble	100 mg/mL
Alprazolam	Insoluble	Soluble
Chlorpropamide	2 mg/mL	Soluble
Methocarbamol	25 mg/mL	Soluble
Terfenadine	0.01 mg/mL	38 mg/mL

TABLE 4.7 Aqueous solubility of tetracycline and erythromycin salts.

Name of drug	Solubility in water (mg/mL)
Tetracycline	1.70
Tetracycline HCL	10.90
Tetracycline phosphate	15.90
Erythromycin	2.10
Erythromycin estolate	0.16
Erythromycin stearate	0.33
Erythromycin lactobionate	20.0

Modified from Ref. [7] with permission.

solubility. Salts of weakly acidic or basic drugs are generally more soluble than the corresponding weakly acidic and basic drugs and, therefore, their solubility is less influenced by the temperature.

4.5.2.2 Shape and substituent groups

Interactions between nonpolar groups and water are important in determining its influence on solubility. The straight-chain carbon compounds exhibit solubility that is related to the length of the carbon chain. As the carbon chain gets longer, the solubility will decrease as a consequence of the molecule becoming larger, with an increase in the molecular weight. These molecules exhibit a more compact molecular arrangement. Chain branching of hydrophobic groups makes a molecule less compact and, as a result, it exhibits greater solubility. The melting point of solids is an indicator of the solubility of a compound (Table 4.8). The melting point of a compound reflects the strength of interactions between the molecules in the solid state.

The influence of substituent groups on the solubility of molecules in water can be due to molecular cohesion or to the effect of the substituent on its interaction with water molecules. It is not easy to predict the effect of a particular substituent on crystal properties; however, as a guide to the solvent interactions, substituents can be classified as either hydrophobic or hydrophilic, depending on their polarity (Table 4.9). The position of the substituent on the molecule also can influence its solubility. This can be seen in the aqueous solubilities of o-, m- and p-dihydroxybenzenes; as expected, all are much greater than that of benzene, but they are not the same, being 4, 9 and 0.6 mol/L, respectively. The relatively low solubility of the *para* compound is due to the greater stability of its crystalline state. The melting points of the derivatives o-, m- and p-dihydroxybenzenes conform with the solubility, as they are 105°C, 111°C, and 170°C, respectively. In the case of the *ortho* derivative, the possibility of intramolecular hydrogen bonding in an aqueous solution, decreasing the ability of the OH group to interact with water, may explain why its solubility is lower than that of its *meta* analog.

Information in Table 4.9 best illustrates the influence of substituents on solubility by considering the solubility of a series of substituted acetanilide, data for which are provided in Table 4.10. The strong hydrophilic characteristics of polar groups capable of hydrogen bonding with water molecules are evident. The presence of hydroxyl groups can therefore markedly change the solubility characteristics of a compound; phenol, for example, is 100 times more soluble in water than is benzene. In the case of phenol, where there is considerable hydrogen-bonding capability, the solute–solvent interaction outweighs other factors in the solution process. But, as we have discovered, the position of any substituent on the parent molecule will affect its contribution to solubility.

TABLE 4.8 Correlation between melting points of sulfonamide derivatives and aqueous solubility [7].

Compound	Melting point ($^\circ$C)	Solubility (g/L)
Sulfadiazine	253	0.077
Sulfamerazine	236	0.200
Sulfapyridine	192	0.285
Sulfathiazole	174	0.588

TABLE 4.9 Substitutent group classification [7].

Substituents	Classification
—CH_3	Hydrophobic
—CH_2—	Hydrophobic
——Cl, —Br, ——F	Hydrophobic
—$N(CH_3)2$	Hydrophobic
——$SCH3$	Hydrophobic
—$OCH_2 CH_3$	Hydrophobic
—OCH_3	Slightly hydrophilic
——NO_2	Slightly hydrophilic
—CHO	Hydrophilic
—COOH	Slightly hydrophilic
—COO	Very hydrophilic
—NH_2	Hydrophilic
——NH_3	Very hydrophilic
—OH	Very hydrophilic

TABLE 4.10 The effect of substituents on solubility of acetanilide derivatives in water [7].

Derivative	Substituents	Solubility (mg/L)
Acetanilide	H	6.38
	Methyl	1.05
	Ethoxyl	0.93
	Hydroxyl	0.93
	Nitro	15.98
	Aceto	9.87

4.5.2.3 The effect of pH

pH of a solvent is one of the primary influences on the solubility of the great majority of drugs that contain ionizable groups.

The solubility of weak acids and bases is a function of the pH of the solution and the pK_a of the drug. Therefore, differences in the dissolution rate are expected to occur in different regions of the gastrointestinal tract. The solubility of a weak acid, C_{sa}, is obtained by

$$C_{sa} = [HA] + [A^-] \qquad (4.22)$$

where [HA] is the intrinsic solubility of the unionized acid (i.e., C_{oa}) and [A$^-$] is the concentration of its anion, which can be expressed in terms of its dissociation constant, K_a, and intrinsic solubility, C_{oa}; that is,

$$C_{sa} = C_{oa} + \frac{K_a C_{oa}}{H^+}$$
(4.23)

Eq. (4.23) suggests that the higher the hydrogen ion concentration of solution (i.e., lower the pH of the solution), the lower will be the solubility of a weakly acidic drug. Therefore, weakly acidic drugs, such as non-steroidal anti-inflammatory agents, barbituric acid derivatives, aspirin, and phenytoin, are less soluble in acidic solution than in alkaline solution This can be attributed to the existence of predominant undissociated species of a weak acidic drugs in acidic solution, which being in un-hydrated form, cannot interact with water molecules to the same extent as ionized form, which are readily hydrated. Moreover, Eq. (4.23) suggests that solubility of a weakly acidic drug at any pH can be calculated from the knowledge of the dissociation constant (pK_a), and the intrinsic solubility of the drug.

Analogously, the solubility of a weak base is obtained by

$$C_{sb} = C_{ob} + \frac{C_{ob}[H^+]}{K_a}$$
(4.24)

Eq. (4.24) suggests that the higher the hydrogen ion concentration of solution (i.e., lower the pH of the solution), the higher will be the solubility of a weak basic drug. Therefore, weakly basic drugs, such as tetracycline, erythromycin, and ciprofloxacin, are more soluble in acidic solution than in alkaline solution. The predominant dissociated species of the weak basic drug in acidic medium, being in hydrated form, can interact with water molecules much readily compared to the unionized form in basic/alkaline medium, which is not readily hydrated. The Eq. (4.24), moreover, suggests that the solubility of weakly basic drugs at any pH can be calculated from the knowledge of the dissociation constant (pK_a), and the intrinsic solubility of the drug. Both equations (Eqs. 4.23 and 4.24) permit the determination of the pH required to keep the weakly acidic and basic drugs, respectively, in solution form or the pH above or below which the drug will precipitate out from the solution.

4.5.2.4 Use of co-solvents

The technique of using a co-solvent is resorted to when drug solubility in a single solvent is limited or perhaps when the stability of the drug forbids the use of a single solvent. Many pharmaceutical dosage forms are complex systems. Water-miscible solvents commonly used in liquid dosage forms include glycerol, propylene glycol, ethyl alcohol, and polyethylene glycols. The addition of another component complicates the system, and one needs to exercise prudence in balancing between the improvement of solubility and other potential adverse effects, such as less stability of a drug.

Solubility of phenobarbital in glycerol-water, ethanol-water, and ethanol-glycerol mixtures has been reported in the literature. Phenobarbital dissolves up to 0.12% (w/v) in water at 25°C. Glycerol, even when used in high concentrations, does not significantly increase the solubility of phenobarbital. Ethanol, on the other hand, is a much more efficient co-solvent than glycerol, as it is less polar. Solubility is at maximum at 90% ethanol in ethanol−water mixtures and at 80% ethanol in ethanol−glycerol mixtures. It is naïve to assume that the drug dissolves in "pockets" of the co-solvent (e.g., ethanol in ethanol-water mixtures), although obviously the affinity of co-solvent for the solute is of importance.

Additives will influence solute-solvent interfacial energies or dissociation of electrolytes through changes in the dielectric constant. A reduction in ionization through a decrease in the dielectric constant will favor decreased solubility, but this effect may be counterbalanced by the greater absorption of the undissociated species in the presence of the co-solvent (Table 4.11).

We have now addressed four physicochemical properties, mentioned in the introduction, which work on the principles of the equilibrium condition, that play vitally important roles in influencing drug's availability from the dosage form. The introduction also mentions the role of another physicochemical property, drug dissolution, which depends on the equilibrium property and plays an equally important role in influencing the drug's availability from solid dosage forms. It is, therefore, important to discuss this property to some extent in this section.

TABLE 4.11 Solubility of phenobarbital and sodium phenobarbital in various solvents.

Solvent	Free acid (mg/mL)	Sodium salt (g/mL)
Water	1.0	1.00
Alcohol	125	0.100
Chloroform	25	Practically insoluble
Ether	76.92	Practically insoluble

4.6 Drug dissolution and dissolution process

When a drug is administered orally via tablet, capsule, or suspension, the rate of absorption often is controlled by how fast the drug particles dissolve in the fluid at the site of administration. Hence, the dissolution rate often is the rate-limiting (slowest) step in the following sequence:

$$\text{Solid drug} \xrightarrow[\text{Step I}]{\text{Dissolution}} \text{Drug in solution} \xrightarrow[\text{Step II}]{\text{Absorption}} \text{Drug in systemic circulation}$$

If the dissolution of the drug (Step I) is slow or controlling the rate of absorption, then dissolution is the rate-determining step. Factors controlling dissolution, such as solubility, ionization, or surface area of a drug particle, would then control the overall dissolution process. Fig. 4.10 describes the absorption of aspirin from solution and from two different types of tablets.

It is clear from Fig. 4.10 that aspirin absorption is more rapid from solution than from tablet formulations. This rapid absorption of aspirin is an indication that the rate of absorption is dissolution rate limited.

A general relationship describing the dissolution of a drug was first reported by Noyes and Whitney [17,18]. The equation derived by those authors is as follows:

$$\frac{dm}{dt} = KS(C_s - C_t) \tag{4.25}$$

where dm/dt is the dissolution rate, K is a constant, S is the surface area of the dissolving solid, C_s is the equilibrium solubility of the drug in the solvent, and C_t is the concentration of the drug in the solvent at time t.

The constant K in Eq. (4.25) has been shown to be equal to D/h, where D is the diffusion coefficient of the dissolving material of the drug in the dissolution medium and h is the thickness of the diffusion layer surrounding the dissolving solid particles. This diffusion layer is a thin, stationary film of a solution adjacent to the surface of a solid particle (Fig. 4.11) and is saturated with drug [7]; in other words, the drug concentration in the diffusion layer is equal to C_s, the equilibrium solubility.

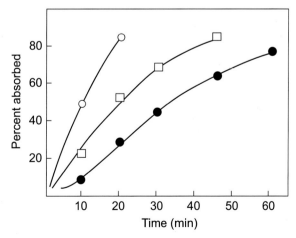

FIGURE 4.10 Absorption of aspirin after oral administration of a 650 mg dose in solution (O), in buffered tablets (□), or in regular tablets (●) [19]. *From G. Levy, J.R. Leonard, J.A. Procknal, Development of in vitro dissolution tests which correlate quantitatively with dissolution rate limited absorption, J Pharm Sci 54 (1965) 1319–25, with permission.*

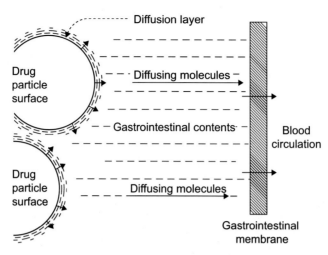

FIGURE 4.11   Dissolution from a solid surface. *Reproduced with permission from, Physiochemical Principles of Pharmacy (5e), (A.T. Florence, D. Attwood, Physiochemical Principles of Pharmacy, second ed., Chapman and Hall, New York, 1988), Pharmaceutical Press, 2011.*

The term (C_s-C_t) in Eq. (4.25) represents the concentration gradient for the drug between the diffusion layer and the bulk solution. If dissolution is the rate-limiting step in the absorption process, the term C_t in Eq. (4.25) is negligible compared to C_s. Under this condition (sink condition), Eq. (4.25) is reduced to

$$\frac{dm}{dt} = \frac{DSC_s}{h} \tag{4.26}$$

Eq. (4.26) describes a diffusion-controlled dissolution process [7]. It is visualized that when solid drug particles are introduced to the fluids at the absorption sites, the drug promptly saturates the diffusion layer (Fig. 4.11). This is followed by the diffusion of drug molecules from the diffusion layer into the bulk solution, which is instantly replaced in the diffusion layer by molecules from the solid crystal or particle. This is a continuous process. Although it oversimplifies the dynamics of the dissolution process, Eq. (4.26) is a qualitatively useful equation and clearly indicates the effects of some important factors on the dissolution and, therefore, the absorption rate of drugs. When dissolution is the rate-limiting factor in absorption, then bioavailability is affected. These factors are listed in Table 4.12.

The Noyes-Whitney equations (Eqs. 4.25 and 4.26) demonstrate that the equilibrium solubility (C_s) is one of the major factors determining the rate of dissolution. Changes in the characteristics of solvents, such as pH, which affect the solubility of the weakly acidic/basic drug, also affect its dissolution rate. Similarly, the use of a different salt or other physicochemical forms of a drug, which exhibits solubility different from the parent drug, usually affects the dissolution rate. Increasing the surface area of a drug exposed to the dissolution medium, by reducing the particle size, usually increases the dissolution rate. In the discussion to follow, some of the more important factors affecting dissolution and, therefore, absorption are presented in greater detail.

TABLE 4.12   The effect of changing parameters from the dissolution equation on the rate of solution [7].

Equation parameter	Comments	Effect on rate of solution
D (diffusion coefficient of drug)	May be decreased in the presence of substances that increase viscosity of the medium	(−)
A (area exposed to solvent)	Increased by micronization and conversion to amorphous form from crystalline form	(+)
h (thickness of diffusion layer)	Decreased by increased agitation in gut or flask	(+)
C_S (solubility in diffusion layer)	Increased/decreased by change in pH by use of appropriate drug salt or buffer ingredient	(−) (+)
C (concentration in bulk)	Decreased by intake of fluid in stomach, by removal of drug by partition or absorption	(+)

(−) = decrease and (+) = increase.

There are other equations that are also employed to describe drug dissolution under specific conditions. The Hixson and Crowell [19,20] cube-root equation for dissolution kinetics is based on the assumptions that dissolution takes place normally to the surface of the solute, there is no stagnation, agitation is identical on all exposed surfaces, and the solute particle retains its geometric shape. By appropriate substitution, the general form of the cube-root equation expresses the factors related to the solid in terms of weight; this is advantageous, as the surface is constantly changing and is difficult to experimentally evaluate.

Although the general form is cumbersome, it may be greatly simplified by imposing certain restrictions. If the concentration change is negligible, that is, (C_s-C_t) is almost constant, dw/dt, the amount dissolved per unit time, is proportional to the surface area. This special case is expressed by the equation

$$\frac{dW}{dt} = 3KS = 3KaW^{2/3} \tag{4.27}$$

where $a = \alpha_{sv}/\rho^{2/3}$ The integrated form of this equation is

$$Kt = W_0^{1/3} - W^{1/3} \tag{4.28}$$

where W_o is the initial weight, W the weight of the solid at the time t, and K the rate constant for a given set of conditions. A plot of $W_0^{1/3} - W^{1/3}$ against time is linear with a slope of rate constant K.

As dissolution is a surface phenomenon, a given weight of smaller particles of a substance dissolves in a shorter time that larger particles of the same weight by virtue of the greater surface area exposed to the dissolving medium. For example, l g of powdered alum dissolves faster than l g of lump alum in a given amount of water; however, the dissolution rate is not changed by further reduction of particle size. It should be stressed that the dissolution rate is expressed in terms of the amount of solute dissolved per unit surface, for example, $g\,hr^{-1}\,cm^{-2}$.

The special case, in which the concentration change is negligible, is applicable to pharmacy. If absorption of a dissolved substance from the gastrointestinal tract is rapid, and dissolution is the rate-limiting step in drug availability, the drug is absorbed and removed from the gastrointestinal tract as fast as it dissolves. Consequently, there is no change in concentration in the gastrointestinal lumen. Thus, the effect of various factors on the *in vitro* dissolution rate determined with negligible concentration change may be extrapolated to a similar effect of these factors on *in vivo* dissolution rate.

4.7 Factors influencing the dissolution rate

4.7.1 Un-reacting additives

When neutral electrolytes and nonionic organic compounds are additives in the solvent phase, the dissolution rate of the solid is linearly dependent upon the solubility of the additive solid in the solvent system. The dissolution rate of benzoic acid in aqueous solutions of sodium chloride or sodium sulfate decreases as its solubility decreases. The ion—dipole interaction competitively binds the water and, therefore, it is not as available for hydrogen bonding with the benzoic acid.

In examining the dissolution rates and solubility of 55 compounds, it has been found that the ratio of dissolution rate to solubility ranged from 1.5 to 3. Thus, the dissolution rate of a new chemical entity or derivative may be roughly estimated by a consideration of its solubility.

As dissolution proceeds, the concentration of a solute in the solution is increased and the concentration gradient is decreased. This results in a slowing of the dissolution rate. Constituents of the gastrointestinal tract and excipients in solid dosage forms may adsorb a drug. If an additive adsorbs the dissolved solute, the concentration gradient (C_s-C_t) remains large, and the dissolution rate remains rapid.

4.7.2 Viscosity

In most dissolution processes applicable in pharmacy, the reaction at the interface of the solid and the solvent occurs much faster than the rate of transport or diffusion of the reactants from the interface to the bulk solution. An increase in viscosity, therefore, decreases the dissolution rate of a diffusion-controlled process. Numerous equations have been proposed that show the dissolution rate to be a function of the viscosity raised to a power where the exponent ranged from -0.25 to -0.8.

4.7.3 Surface activity

In highly irregular particles with pores and crevices, the total surface area of the powder particles may be incompletely exposed to the solvent, due to occlusion by air. In the presence of surface-active agents, the surface tension between the powder particle and liquid medium is lowered and the entire surface is wetted. This increased surface contact between the solid and solvent, that is, effective surface, increases the apparent dissolution rate.

Surface-active agents in low concentrations, that is, below the critical micelle concentration, do not markedly affect the dissolution rate. It has been postulated that a slight increase in the rate at low concentrations can be attributed to the orientation of the dissolved solute between ionized surfactant molecules and the reduction of their repulsive force. When used in high concentrations, surface-active agents tend to increase the dissolution rate. This is probably a consequence of the greater total solubility resulting from the incorporation of the dissolved solute in a micellar structure.

4.7.4 Temperature

In general, solids dissolve faster if the system is warmed. If a substance absorbs heat in the dissolution process, its solubility is increased by an increase in temperature. The increase in solubility provides an increased concentration gradient which results in an increased dissolution rate. The increase in temperature increases kinetic motion and diffusion of the solute through the diffusion layer into the bulk solution which increases the dissolution rate. A flow pattern in which the velocity is variable, and the path is curved is known as curvilinear flow. In the region of curvilinear flow for each $10°$ rise in temperature, the dissolution rate increases approximately 1.3 times.

4.7.5 Agitation

As most dissolution procedures in pharmacy are accomplished by stirring, this discussion is limited to rotational agitation. The intensity of agitation is one of the most important factors in determining the dissolution rate of a solid. The thickness of the diffusion layer is inversely proportional to the agitation. This has been expressed in the empirically developed relationship.

$$K = aN^b \tag{4.29}$$

where N is the agitation in terms of revolutions per minute, K represents the dissolution rate, and a and b are constants. For a diffusion-controlled process $b \rightarrow 1$. If the dissolution is controlled by an interfacial reaction, the agitation does not influence the dissolution rate and $b \rightarrow 0$.

When a stirrer is operated in a liquid so that the only friction is from the walls and bottom of the container and the viscosity of the fluid, the type of agitation is known as free rotational agitation. In free rotational agitation, the flow of fluid may be one of three types.

At very low rpm (rotations per minute), the flow is passive. The solids do not move, and the dissolution rate depends on the manner in which the solid is scattered on the bottom of the container. The solid and solution are not transported to the top of the system, and the system has layers of different concentrations. Dissolution does not occur where the particles touch one another in the pile at the center of the tank bottom. At very high rpm the flow is turbulent. The centrifugal force of the rotating fluid tends to force the particles outward and upward. The cube-root equation does not apply to turbulent or passive flow.

Between these two extremes of flow is the useful curvilinear type of flow. In the curvilinear region, the dissolution rate is nearly linearly proportional to the rpm. In curvilinear flow, the particles move to the center and pile up and then they move around circularly to the center. The cube-root equation applies to curvilinear flow.

4.7.6 Dissolution in a reactive medium

The discussion has been concerned with the dissolution of a solid in a nonreactive medium. This is applicable to the preparation of solutions and the dissolution of drugs that do not undergo chemical reactions in body fluids. With these slightly soluble non-reacting drugs, for example, chloramphenicol and griseofulvin, an increase in the specific surface of the administered solid is a practical means of decreasing the time required for the drug to dissolve and to speed up the onset of therapeutic activity. As physiological conditions are not neutral, acidic and basic drugs react to the various pH's of the gastrointestinal tract with marked changes in solubility and dissolution rates.

The dissolution rate in the reactive medium is decreased as the viscosity is increased. The dissolution rate is slowed by the addition of other solutes, which compete for the solvent molecules and effectively decrease the solubility of the drug. Conversely, if the solubility of the drug in the diffusion layer is increased, the dissolution rate of the drug is increased. The solubility of acidic and basic drugs may be increased by modifying the pH of the diffusion layer.

The dissolution of a solid acidic drug may be increased by increasing the pH of the diffusion layer. In the administration of oral dosage forms, antacids may be administered to raise the pH of the stomach. This method has its limitations and is impractical because of the massive dose of antacid required. Certainly, it is an uninspiring and unfavorable method if one is attempting to formulate a product as a single tablet or capsule.

A second method for increasing the dissolution rate of a solid acid is to mix the acid with a solid basic substance, for example, sodium bicarbonate or sodium citrate. This mixture provides an increased pH of the immediate environment of the acid. There is an optimum ratio of the two constituents, depending on the fraction of the total surface of each and the strength of the acid.

4.8 Passive diffusion

Strictly speaking, diffusion is the tendency of gas molecules or liquid molecules or dissolved solute molecules at a constant temperature to distribute themselves uniformly over the space available. It is a spontaneous process by which molecules move from the region of high concentration to the region of low concentration and, therefore, as long as the concentration gradient is maintained, molecules will continue to move. Diffusion is the result of random molecular motion. The concentration gradient is the driving force for the diffusion of molecules from the region of high to the region of low concentration. In 1855, Fick, quantitatively, described the diffusion of molecules. It is described as Fick's first law of diffusion. It is expressed, mathematically, as

$$J = -D \times \frac{dC}{dX} \tag{4.30}$$

where J is the flux; D is the diffusion coefficient; dC/dX is the concentration gradient in the direction of X (distance in the direction). The negative sign indicates that the direction of molecular movement is opposite to the increase in the concentration.

Drug transfer often is viewed as the movement of a drug molecule across a series of membranes and spaces (Fig. 4.5), which, in aggregate, serve as a macroscopic membrane. The cells and interstitial spaces lying between the gastric lumen and the capillary blood or structure between the sinusoidal space and the bile canaliculi are examples. Each of the cellular membranes and spaces may impede drug transport to varying degrees; therefore, any one of them can be a rate-limiting step to the overall process of drug transport. This complexity of structure makes quantitative prediction of drug transport difficult. A qualitative description of the processes of drug transport across functional membranes follows.

The transfer of most drugs across a biological membrane occurs by passive diffusion, a natural tendency for molecules to move from an area of higher concentration to an area of lower concentration. This movement of drug molecules is caused by the kinetic energy of the molecules. The rate of diffusion depends on the magnitude of the concentration gradient across the membrane and can be represented by the following equation:

$$-\frac{dC}{dt} = K \cdot dC = K(C_{abs} - C_b) \tag{4.31}$$

where $-dC/dt$ is the rate of diffusion across a membrane; K is a complex proportionality constant that includes the area of membrane, the thickness of the membrane, the partition coefficient of the drug molecule between the lipophilic membrane and the aqueous phase on each side of the membrane, and the diffusion coefficient of the drug; C_{abs} is the drug concentration at the absorption site; and C_b is the drug concentration in the blood.

The gastrointestinal absorption of a drug from an aqueous solution requires transfer from the lumen to the gut wall followed by penetration of the epithelial membrane by a drug molecule to the capillaries of the systemic circulation. On entering the blood, the drug distributes itself rapidly. Because of the volume differences at absorption and distribution sites, the drug concentration in blood (C_b) will be much lower than the concentration at the absorption

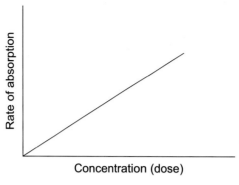

FIGURE 4.12 Effect of drug concentration on the rate of absorption when passive diffusion is operative.

site (C_{abs}). This concentration gradient is maintained throughout the absorption process that is, ($C_{abs}-C_b$). As a result, the concentration gradient, is approximately equal to C_{abs}, so Eq. (4.31) can be written as

$$-\frac{dC}{dt} = K \cdot C_{abs}$$

(4.32)

Because absorption by passive diffusion is a first-order process, the rate of absorption (dC/dt in Eq. 4.32) is directly proportional to the concentration at the site of absorption (C_{abs}). The greater the concentration of drug at the absorption site, the faster is the rate of absorption (Fig. 4.12). The percentage of dose absorbed at any time, however, remains unchanged.

A major source of variation is membrane permeability, which depends on the lipophilicity of the drug molecule. This is often characterized by its partition between oil and water. The lipid solubility of a drug, therefore, is a very important physicochemical property governing the rate of transfer through a variety of biological membrane barriers. Fig. 4.13 illustrates the role of partition coefficients in the drug absorption process from the colon, and that a good correlation exists between the percentage of drug absorption and the partition coefficient of an unionized drug.

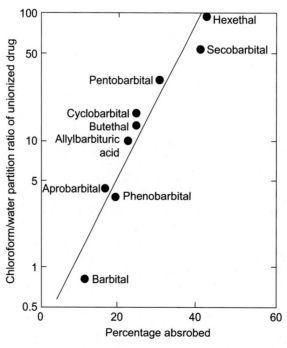

FIGURE 4.13 Comparison between colonic absorption of barbiturates in the rat and lipid-to-water partition coefficient of the unionized form of the barbiturates [9]. *From A.S. Schanker, Absorption of drugs from the colon,* J Pharmacol *Exp* Ther *126 (1959) 283–94, with permission.*

4.9 Biopharmaceutical classification system

As mentioned in the introduction of the chapter, Amidon and co-workers [4–6] in their seminal work created the biopharmaceutical classification system (BCS). It was reported [21–24] that factors that affect the rate and extent of drug absorption from the gastrointestinal (GI) tract include physiochemical factors (e.g., pK_a, solubility, stability, diffusivity, lipophilicity, polar-nonpolar surface area, presence of hydrogen bonding functionalities, particle size, and crystal form), physiological factors (e.g., GI pH, GI blood flow, gastric emptying rate, small intestinal transit time, colonic transit time and absorption mechanisms) and factors related to the dosage form (e.g., tablet, capsule, solution, suspension, emulsion, and gel).

Though all factors stated above contribute to drug absorption, the fundamental events that control oral drug absorption are the permeability of the drug through the GI membrane and the solubility/dissolution of the drug dose in the GI milieu. These key parameters are characterized in the BCS [21] by three dimensionless numbers: absorption number (A_n), dissolution number (D_n), and dose number (D_0). These numbers take into account both physiochemical and physiological parameters fundamental to the oral absorption process [5]. Based on their solubility and intestinal membrane permeability characteristics, drug substances have been classified into one of four categories according to the BCS.

4.9.1 Class I drugs (high solubility and high permeability)

These drugs provide both rapid dissolution and high membrane permeation. This class includes small molecule hydrophilic drugs that are not ionized in the gastrointestinal tract. Examples include acetaminophen, valproic acid, ketoprofen, disopyramide, verapamil, and metoprolol. Class I drugs are well absorbed and are affected by a limited set of interactions that alter drug absorption. As gastric emptying will frequently control the rate of absorption for this class of drugs, interactions that delay gastric emptying will delay drug absorption. This can be important for class I analgesic drugs where a rapid rate of absorption and quick rise in the plasma level to within the therapeutic range is needed to alleviate pain quickly.

4.9.2 Class II drugs (low solubility and high permeability)

For immediate-release formulations of many poorly water-soluble drugs, the dissolution rate limits drug absorption. Along with this limitation, a greater impact on drug absorption will be observed with high oral doses. For example, the antifungal drug griseofulvin and the cardiac glycoside drug digoxin are both poorly water-soluble and possess similar dissolution profiles which limit the rate of drug absorption. However, the extent of griseofulvin absorption is incomplete for a typical dose of 500 mg, whereas a normal 0.25 mg oral dose of digoxin usually provides a fairly complete absorption.

Any interactions that increase drug solubility and dissolution rate in the gastrointestinal tract will exert a positive effect on the gastrointestinal absorption of this class of drugs. The absorption of this class of drugs is often enhanced in proportion to the fat content of the co-administered meal. This is attributed to the increased gastrointestinal fluid volume from a co-administered meal, stimulated gastrointestinal secretions, and biliary solubilization effects that increase the dissolution rate. Furthermore, increased gastric residence time as a function of the calorie density permits greater time for drug dissolution.

4.9.3 Class III drugs (high solubility and low permeability)

For drugs possessing high water solubility, the intestinal membrane permeation rate is often the rate-limiting step in drug absorption from immediate-release dosage forms. Many drugs in this class also show region-dependent absorption with better absorption in the upper small intestine. Therefore, any interactions that compromise upper intestinal absorption may result in a significant decrease in oral bioavailability. Consequently, these drugs show a sharp decrease in absorption with a co-administered meal that is independent of fat content. Meals tend to decrease the absorption of some drugs in this category as a result of a simple physical barrier that compromises the availability of drug molecules to the upper intestinal membrane.

4.9.4 Class IV drugs (low solubility and low permeability)

Poor aqueous solubility may not necessarily impart high lipophilicity and, therefore, high membrane permeation for a drug. Class IV drugs possess both low solubility and low permeability, both of which are undesirable for good drug absorption. Drugs in this class, however, may still be administered orally if the plasma concentrations obtained are sufficient to produce the desired therapeutic effect and the drugs do not possess a narrow therapeutic index.

Although, the BCS has been recognized as one of the most significant prognostic tools created to facilitate oral drug product development in recent years; the validity and broad applicability of the BCS have been the subject of extensive research and discussion [25–28]. It has been adopted by the US Food and Drug Administration (FDA), the European Medicines Agency (EMEA) and the World Health Organization (WHO) for setting bioavailability/bioequivalence (BA/BE) standards for immediate-release (IR) oral drug product approval. Moreover, the BCS principles are extensively used by the pharmaceutical industry throughout the drug discovery and development.

Up to now, the FDA has implemented the BCS system to allow waiver of *in vivo* BA/BE testing of IR solid dosage forms for class I (high-solubility, and high-permeability) drugs. As for class III (high solubility, low-permeability) drugs, as long as the drug product does not contain agents and/or excipients that may modify intestinal membrane permeability, *in vitro* dissolution test can ensure BE. The absorption of class III is likely limited by its permeability and less dependent upon its formulation, and its bioavailability may be determined by *in vivo* patterns. If the *in vitro* dissolution of a class III drug product is rapid under all physiological pH conditions, its *in vivo* behavior will essentially be similar to that of an oral solution (i.e., controlled by gastric emptying), and as long as the drug product does not contain permeability modifying agents (this potential effect is largely mitigated by the large gastric dilution), an *in vitro* dissolution test can ensure BE. Hence, biowaivers for BCS class II drugs are scientifically justified and have been recommended [29–31].

4.10 Conclusions

From the information presented in this chapter, it is clear that a number of important physicochemical properties of a drug that play an important and influential role in drug discovery process, drug dissolution process, and drug absorption process are measured under the equilibrium conditions. They include equilibrium solubility, partition coefficient, ionization, and diffusion, particularly passive diffusion. With the acceptance of rule of five and the biopharmaceutical classification system of drugs, these properties have attained greater importance in the early drug discovery process. A number of other properties such as powder particle size, particle size distribution, intrinsic and derived powder properties, and pH of the gastrointestinal fluid is discussed here since they also play an equally important role in drug dissolution and absorption processes. The importance of these properties and other factors such as pH of the dissolution fluid, solubility of a drug in the diffusion layer, and composition of the fluid is evident when one examines the absorption process, Noyes-Whitney equation, biological membrane, and gastrointestinal physiology.

Case studies

Case 4.1

An oil-in-water (o/w) emulsion uses both methyl paraben and propyl paraben as preservatives. Recently, a compounding pharmacist found out that he did not have methyl paraben; so instead, he used butyl paraben and propyl paraben as preservatives for this emulsion. To his surprise, he found his emulsion showing some growth after few days. Explain the possible cause of this problem, accounting for the antimicrobial mechanism of parabens.

Approach: Parabens, esters of 4-hydroxybenzoic acid, are used as preservatives in liquid dosage forms. Preservation of an emulsion is an important issue because this system is composed of two immiscible phases. Some of the parabens are more water soluble than others. As the chain length of the paraben increases, its aqueous solubility decreases and oil solubility increases. They can partition more to the oil phase than to the water phase. Due to the solubility and partitioning into the oil phase, and the interaction with emulsifiers, they may not attain an effective concentration in the aqueous phase. Since bacterial contamination happens in the aqueous phase, one may expect instability in the emulsion. In this case, both propyl and butyl parabens are more hydrophobic, and one expects more partition of both of these preservatives to the oil phase, causing even a further decrease of the effective antibacterial concentration in the aqueous phase and causing an instability in this (o/w) emulsion.

The alternative way to avoid this problem is to use different preservatives or switch over to a methyl and propyl paraben combination.

Case 4.2

A 65-year-old HIV + male patient is taking Atripla (a combination of three medicines: efavirenz, tenofovir, and emtricitabine). A Foley catheter was inserted into his urinary bladder to help him pass urine. When he was also administered acyclovir (which has two pKas, 2.27 and 9.25), a white cloudy precipitate was observed in the catheter, indicating possibly crystallization of acyclovir. This was further confirmed by the appearance of needle-like structures in the urine samples. What is your advice to this patient to overcome this problem of crystalluria?

Approach: Atripla is a non-nucleoside reverse transcriptase inhibitor. Therefore, according to FDA guidelines, it is combined with a nucleoside reverse transcriptase inhibitor such as acyclovir. Obviously, the idea is that these two different mechanisms would inhibit reverse transcriptase in viruses more efficiently. The two pKas of acyclovir, an amphipathic drug, suggest its maximum solubility of 2.5 mg/mL at physiologic pH [32]. Generally, acyclovir intravenous infusion contains 50 mg of acyclovir per mL. Therefore, to prevent the formation of crystals in urine, both the infusion rate of acyclovir and the water intake should be manipulated. The former should be decreased, whereas the latter should be increased.

Case 4.3

Rifaximin a BCS class IV (low-solubility, low-permeability) drug and also known as a Pgp substrate. Rifaximin amorphous solid dispersion (ASDs) formulations using different hydrophilic polymers were prepared by Spray-dried technique [33]. Copovidone/HPC-SL (low viscosity hydroxypropylcellulse) formulation containing Rifaximin ASDs showed higher apparent solubility and intestinal permeability. How can this be explained to a pharmaceutics student?

Approach: Amorphous solid dispersion (ASD) is one of the promising approaches used to increase the apparent solubility of a hydrophobic drug. The internal free energy of the amorphous (metastable) form is higher than that of its crystalline counterpart. During the dissolution of the drug, this energy is released, resulting in increased apparent solubility. This may lead to enhanced absorption and bioavailability of an amorphous drug relative to its crystalline equivalent. This work has further shown that delivering a high supersaturation level of the BCS class IV drug rifaximin via ASD, thereby saturating the drugs' P-gp-mediated efflux transport, led to a favorable and unique win-win situation, where both the solubility and the permeability increased simultaneously.

Case 4.4

The preservative action of benzoic acid and its ionized form (benzoate ion) were compared at different pH values by Rahn and Conn (1944) [34] and found to be entirely dependent on the undissociated acid not on its dissociated form. The yeast saccharomyces ellipsoideus, which grows at a pH of 2.5–7.0 is ceased to grow in the presence of undissociated benzoic acid when the concentration of benzoic acid is around 0.25 mg/mL. How can you explain this fact on your knowledge on permeability and octanol water partition coefficient of ionized versus unionized form of antibacterial?

Approach: Benzoic acid a weak acid with pK_a of 4.2 will be present in unionized form in an acidic environment. The yeast is completely inactivated when the concentration of the undissociated benzoic acid concentration in a liquid formulation is 0.25 mg/mL. The effectiveness of undissociated acid as compared to the ineffectiveness of the benzoate ion is based on the fact that unionized (undissociated) benzoic acid molecule is easily permeable to the living membrane of the yeast. However, its ionic counterpart shows the difficulty in cellular uptake and permeability. The solubility of the undissociated form of benzoic acid in the lipoidal membrane and its high partition coefficients are responsible for its activity.

Critical reflections and practice applications

Many physicochemical properties of drugs influencing their *in vivo* actions are dependent on equilibrium processes, such as ionization of drugs, partition coefficient, equilibrium solubility, drug dissolution, passive diffusion, etc. The concepts covered in this chapter are frequently applied in pharmacy practice. Some are summarized below:

i. The Henderson–Hasselbalch equation can be used for the preparation of a buffer with the required pH needed for the stability of the drug.

ii. The absorption or elimination of a drug can be manipulated by taking acidic or basic food/drink along with the drug.

iii. Pharmacist can use the pH of a weakly acidic/basic drugs in counseling patients whether the drug should be taken with food or empty stomach or there should be time-gap between the drug and the food.

iv. Pharmacist can use the solubility-enhancing approaches discussed in this chapter while compounding a poorly soluble drug.

v. The concept of solubility can be used for determining the rate of injection of a poorly soluble drug such as diazepam.

vi. Dissolution characteristics of a brand vs. generic drug product can be used for comparing their bioavailability.

References

[1] C.A. Lipinsky, F. Lombordo, W. Dominy, et al., Experimental and computational approaches to estimate solubility and permeability in drug discovery and development settings, Adv. Drug Deliv. Rev. 23 (1997) 3–25.

[2] B. Stewart, Y. Wang, N. Surendran, *Ex. In vivo* approaches to predicting oral pharmacokinetics in humans, in: Ann Repts Med Chem., 35, 2000, pp. 299–307.

[3] P. Ertl, B. Rohde, P. Selzer, Fast calculation of molecular polar surface area as a sum of fragment-based contributions and its application to the prediction of drug transport properties, J. Med. Chem. 43 (2000) 3714–3717.

[4] G. Amidon, H. Lenncranas, V. Shah, et al., A theoretical basis for a biopharmaceutics drug classification: the correlation of *in vitro* drug product and *in vivo* bioavailability, Pharm. Res. (N. Y.) 12 (1995) 413–420.

[5] M.N. Martinez, G.L. Amidon, A mechanistic approach to understanding the factors affecting drug absorption: a review of fundamentals, J. Clin. Pharmacol. 42 (2002) 620–643.

[6] H. Lennernas, Human intestinal permeability, J. Pharm. Sci. 87 (1998) 402–410.

[7] A.T. Florence, D. Attwood, Physiochemical Principles of Pharmacy, second ed., Chapman and Hall, New York, 1988.

[8] L.S. Schanker, Absorption of drugs from the rat colon, J. Pharmacol. Exp. Therapeut. 126 (1959) 283–294.

[9] P.A. Shore, B.B. Brodie, C.A.M. Hogben, The gastric secretion of drugs: a pH partition hypothesis, J. Pharmacol. Exp. Therapeut. 119 (1957) 361–369.

[10] C.A.M. Hogben, D.J. Tocco, B.B. Brodie, et al., On the mechanism of intestinal absorption of drugs, J. Pharmacol. Exp. Therapeut. 125 (1959) 275–282.

[11] L.S. Schanker, On the mechanism of absorption of drugs from the gastrointestinal tract, J. Med. Pharmaceut. Chem. 2 (1960) 343–359.

[12] L.S. Schanker, Mechanism of drug absorption and distribution, Annu. Rev. Pharmacol. 1 (1961) 29–44.

[13] L.S. Schanker, Passage of drugs across the gastrointestinal epithelium in drugs and membrane, in: C.A.M. Hogben (Ed.), Proceedings of the First International Pharmacology Meeting, vol 4, The Macmillan Company, New York, 1963.

[14] L.S. Schanker, Physiological transport of drug, in: N.J. Harper, A.B. Simons (Eds.), Advances in Drug Research, Academic Press, London, 1966, pp. 71–106.

[15] M. Rowland, T. Tozer, Clinical Pharmacokinetics: Concepts and Application, second ed., Lea and Febiger, Philadelphia, 1989.

[16] L.S. Schanker, Absorption of drugs from the rat small intestine, J. Pharmacol. Exp. Therapeut. 128 (1958) 81–87.

[17] N.A. Noyes, W.J. Whitney, The rate of solution of solid substances in their own solution, J. Am. Chem. Soc. 19 (1897) 930–942.

[18] N.A. Noyes, W.J. Whitney, Ueber die auslosungsgesch wingdigkeit von festen stossen in ihern eigenen losungen, Z. Phys. Chem. 23 (1897) 689–692.

[19] A. Hixson, J. Crowell, Dependence of reaction velocity upon surface and agitation I: theoretical consideration, Ind. Eng. Chem. 23 (1931) 923–931.

[20] A. Hixson, J. Crowell, Dependence of reaction velocity upon surface and agitation II: theoretical consideration, Ind. Eng. Chem. 23 (1931) 1002–1009.

[21] A. Dahan, J. Miller, G. Amidon, Prediction of solubility and permeability membership: provisional BCS Classification of the world's oral drugs, AAPS J. 3 (4) (2009) 740–746.

[22] A. Dahan, G. Amidon, Gastrointestinal dissolution and absorption of class II drugs, in: H. Van de Waterbeemdand, B. Testa (Eds.), Drug Bioavailability: Estimation of Solubility, Permeability, Absorption, and Bioavailability, Wiley-VCH, Weinheim, 2008.

[23] D. Sun, L. Yu, M. Hussain, D. Wall, R. Smith, G. Amidon, In Vitro testing of drug absorption for drug 'developability' assessment: forming an interface between in Vitro preclinical data and clinical outcome, Curr. Opin. Drug Discov. Dev 7 (2004) 75–85.

[24] A. Dahan, G.L. Amidon, Small intestinal efflux mediated by MRP2 and BCRP shifts sulfasalizine intestinal permeability from high to low, enabling its colonic targeting, Am. J. Physiol. Gastrointest. Liver Physiol. 297 (2009) G371–G377.

[25] J. Polli, B. Abrahamsson, L. Yu, G. Amidon, J. Baldoni, J. Cook, et al., Summary of workshop report: bioequivalence, biopharmaceutics classification system, and beyond, AAPS J. 10 (2008) 373−379.

[26] V.E. Thiel-Demby, J.E. Humphreys, L.A. St John Williams, H.M. Ellens, N. Shah, A.D. Ayrton, et al., Biopharmaceutics classification system: validation and learning of an in vitro permeability assay, Mol. Pharm. 6 (2009) 11−18.

[27] Y. Yang, P.J. Faustino, D.A. Volpe, C.D. Ellison, R.C. Lyon, L.X. Yu, Biopharmaceutics classification of selected beta blockers; solubility and permeability class membership, Mol. Pharm. 4 (2007) 608−614.

[28] H.H. Blume, B.S. Schug, The biopharmaceutics classification system (BCS): class III drugs- better candidate for BA/BE waiver? Eur. J. Pharmaceut. Sci. 9 (1999) 117.

[29] C.L. Cheng, X.L. Yu, H.L. Lee, C.Y. Yang, C.S. Lu, C.H. Chou, Biowaiver extension potential to BCS class III high solubility low permeability drugs: bridging evidence for metformin immediate release tablet, Eur. J. Pharmaceut. Sci. 22 (2004) 297.

[30] E. Jantratid, S. Prakongpan, G.L. Amidon, J. Dressman, Feasibility of biowaiver extension to biopharmaceutics classification system class III drug products: cimetidine, Clin. Pharmacokinet. 45 (2006) 385−399.

[31] S. Stavchansky, Scientific perspective on extending the provision for waivers of *in vivo* bioavailability and bioequivalence studies for drug products containing high solubility-low permeability drugs (BCS Class 3), AAPS J. 10 (2008) 300−305.

[32] Atripla. http://online.statref.com/document/z6NEIbX604OzTQuqt7LzsD?searchid=1658515877413575630&categoryType=All [Accessed on July 22, 2022].

[33] A. Beig, N. Fine-Shamir, D. Lindley, et al., Advantageous solubility-permeability interplay when using amorphous solid dispersion (ASD) formulation for the BCS class IV P-gp substrate rifaximin: simultaneous increase of both the solubility and the permeability, AAPS J. 19 (2017) 806−813.

[34] O. Rahn, E. Jean, Conn, Effect of increase in acidity on antiseptic efficiency, Ind. Eng. Chem. 36 (2) (1944) 185−187, https://doi.org/10.1021/IE50410A020.

Further reading

[1] S. Jambhekar, in: Williams, Lemke (Eds.), In Foye's Principles of Medicinal Chemistry, seventh ed.Wolters Kluwer/Lippincott, Williams and Wilkins, 2012.

[2] S. Jambhekar, P. Breen, Basic Pharmacokinetics, second ed., Pharmaceutical Press, 2012.

[3] S. Jambhekar, in: D. Parikh (Ed.), Bioavailability and Granule Properties in Handbook of Pharmaceutical Granulation Technology, fourth ed., CRC Press, 2021.

[4] A. Florence, D. Attwood, Physiochemical Principles of Pharmacy, fourth ed., Pharmaceutical Press, 2006.

[5] P. Sinko (Ed.), Martin's Physical Pharmacy and Pharmaceutical Sciences, sixth ed., Lippincott, Williams and Wilkins, 2006.

[6] Pandit, K. Nita, Introduction to Pharmaceutical Sciences, Lippincott, Williams, and Wilkins, 2007.

[7] D. Grant, T. Higuchi, Solubility Behavior of Organic Compounds, in: Techniques of Chemistry, vol 21, Wiley Interscience, 1990.

[8] A. Avdeef, Absorption and Drug Development: Solubility, Permeability, and Charge State, Wiley-Interscience, New York, 2003.

[9] X.-Q. Chen, M. Antman, C. Greenberg, O. Gudmundsson, Discovery pharmaceutics- Challenges and opportunities, AAPS J. 8 (2) (2006) E402−E408.

[10] C. Ganellin, S. Roberts (Eds.), Medicinal Chemistry: The Role of Organic Chemistry in Drug Research, second ed., Academic Press, New York, 1993.

[11] M. Gibaldi, Biopharmaceutics and Clinical Pharmacokinetics, fourth ed., Lea and Febiger, Philadelphia, 1991.

[12] D. Horter, J.B. Dressman, Influence of physiochemical properties on dissolution of drugs in the gastrointestinal tract, Adv. Drug Deliv. Rev. 46 (2001) 75−87.

[13] M. Rowland, T. Tozer, Clinical Pharmacokinetics: Concepts and Application, third ed., Lea and Febiger, Philadelphia, 1994.

[14] J. Taylor, P. Kennewell, Modern Medicinal Chemistry: Ellis Horwood Series in Pharmaceutical Technology, Ellis Horwood, New York, 1993.

[15] C. Wermuth, N. Koga, H. Konig, et al., Medicinal Chemistry for the 21st Century, Blackwell Scientific Publications, Boston, 1992.

[16] D. Winne, The influence of unstirred layers on intestinal absorption in intestinal permeation, in: M. Kramer, F. Lauterbach (Eds.), Workshop Conference Hoechest, vol 4, Excerpta Medica, Amsterdam, 1977, pp. 58−64.

[17] G. Levy, J.R. Leonard, J.A. Procknal, Development of *in vitro* dissolution tests which correlate quantitatively with dissolution rate limited absorption, J. Pharmaceut. Sci. 54 (1965) 1319−1325.

[18] N. Phadnis, S. Raj, Polymorphism in anhydrous theophylline—implications on the dissolution rate of theophylline tablets, J. Pharmaceut. Sci. 86 (1997) 1256−1263.

5

Complexation and Protein Binding

Somnath Singh and E. Jeffrey North

Department of Pharmacy Sciences, School of Pharmacy and Health Professions, Creighton University, Omaha, NE, United States

CHAPTER OBJECTIVES

- Define complex and chelation.
- Differentiate the molecular similarities and differences between complex and chelate.
- Discuss the pharmaceutical application of complexes and chelates.
- Discuss the influences of drug action given various complex and protein binding events.
- Discuss the pharmaceutical application of plasma protein binding percentages.
- Given a drug structure, predict intermolecular binding interactions.
- Describe the role of entropy in promoting intermolecular interaction between lipophilic entities on drugs and receptors.

Keywords: Chelate; Complex; Cyclodextrin; Protein-binding.

5.1 Introduction

Complexation is the process of formation of a stable complex, which may be covalent, but is commonly formed through noncovalent interactions between two or more compounds. The molecule that interacts with a central molecule/metal ion, that is, substrate, is called a ligand. Drugs form complexes with many small as well as large macromolecules such as a polymer or protein. When a drug forms a complex with its pharmacological target, it will elicit its drug action yielding a therapeutic response. Complexation with exogenous compounds typically will alter the physical and chemical properties of the complexing molecules such as solubility, stability, and partitioning.

5.2 Complexes and chelates

As stated earlier, complexes are two (or more) compounds bound together typically through noncovalent interactions. The substrate can be an organic compound, such as a drug, or a metal ion, which is typically charged +2. Complexes and chelates are formed to enhance various physicochemical and pharmacokinetic properties; however, there are also some nonbeneficial effects as well.

Beneficial effects obtained by complexation:

1. Aminophyline obtained due to complexation between theophyline and ethylenediamine is more soluble than theophyline.
2. Inclusion complexes with cyclodextrin enhances solubility.
3. Protein-binding, that is, complex formation with protein reduces tissue distribution of the drug.

Nonbeneficial effects obtained by complexation:

1. Decrease in aqueous solubility of tetracycline due to its complexation with calcium.
2. Coadministration of some drugs orally, specifically with low solubility, with antacids decreases their absorption due to the complexation of drugs with metal cations in the antacids.
3. Complexation of a drug with a hydrophilic compound increases its elimination.
4. Complexation of a drug can alter its pharmacological activity due to alteration in its receptor-binding efficiency.

There are two types of complexes termed coordination complexes and molecular complexes.

5.2.1 Coordination complexes

A coordination complex (also called metal coordination) is a structure consisting of a central atom or ion (usually metallic) bonded to a surrounding array of molecules or anions (ligands, complexing agents) via the formation of a coordinate bond. The central metal cations are electron acceptors, functioning as a Lewis acid, and the ligands are electron donors, making it a Lewis base. Metal cations can typically bind up to six negative or partially negative groups on the ligand. If the metal cation is bound to only one anionic site on the ligand, it is considered a monodentate. If there are two anionic/partially negative ligand sites binding, then it is considered a bidentate ligand, and so on. Fig. 5.1 shows the quadradentate complex between copper II and salicylate anion, and the monodentate complex cisplatin and transplatin. Notice that copper (Cu) and platinum (Pt) are the central ions and salicylate, ammonia, or chlorine are the ligands. Ammonia or chlorine has a single pair of electrons for bonding with metal ions and thus are monodentate ligands.

The complexes in which the central metal ion is bound with two or more sites of the same ligand are called chelate, for example, hemoglobin where Fe^{+2} is bound at multiple sites of ligand porphyrin ring (Fig. 5.2). Ethylenediaminetetraacetic acid (EDTA) is a very useful chelating agent (or sequestering agent), which is used for treating poison conditions used as detoxifying agent to remove unwanted metals (in particular calcium, mercury, lead, cadmium, and arsenic) from the body's organs and cardiovascular system. EDTA is used extensively in packaged foods, pharmaceuticals, shampoos, detergents, cosmetics, mouthwash, etc. Moreover, EDTA also works as a free radical scavenger and thereby, works as an antioxidant. Following are some of its principal uses:

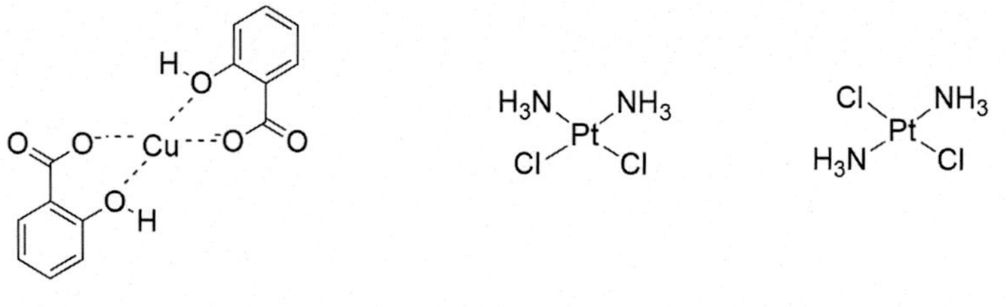

Copper II Salicylate   Ciplatin   Transplatin

FIGURE 5.1   Bidentate coordination complex of copper II salicylate.

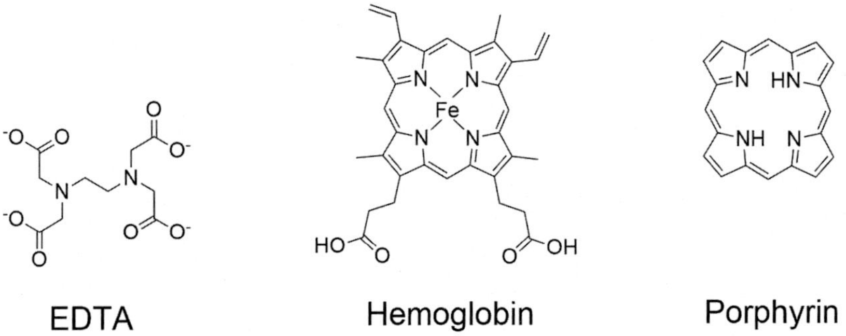

FIGURE 5.2 Chelation example ligands EDTA and porphyrin. Hemoglobin is utilizing the porphyrin ring to bind Fe^{+2}.

EDTA   Hemoglobin   Porphyrin

- Removes undesirable metals from the body
- Slows down and can improve the process of atherosclerosis
- Improves cerebrovascular arterial occlusion
- Improves memory, concentration, and vision
- Reversal of gangrene
- Supports autoimmune disorders, such as arthritis, scleroderma, and lupus
- Prevents and reverses problems of degenerative disease
- Minimizes/manages radiation toxicity, snake venom poisoning, digitalis intoxication, cardiac arrhythmia

Cisplatin's mechanism of action is shown in Fig. 5.3. Before interacting with DNA, the chloride ligands of cisplatin must be displaced through nucleophilic attack by cellular water. When water (no charge) comes in to attack, it displaces the two chloride anions ($2\,Cl^-$) leaving the Pt complex with a net +2 charge. This aquatic displacement occurs readily in the chloride-poor environment of the tumor cell (<100 mM), as the low intracellular Cl^- concentrations will drive the displacement reaction forward. The hydrated (monoaqua and diaqua) products are the active forms. Only the *cis* isomer of this Pt(II) metal complex is cytotoxic enough to be of therapeutic use. The *cis* form (which positions the chlorides in adjacent corners of the imaginary square) is preferentially taken up into cells when DNA replication is at its maximum. Once water displaces both chloride anions, the diaquo complex will have both the proper charge (+2) and the proper geometry to interact with the adjacent guanine residues and induce damage that DNA repair mechanisms cannot undo. For all of these reasons, cisplatin is approximately 14 times as cytotoxic as transplatin (which is not marketed).

Cu ion is present in a variety of important proteins and enzymes such as hemocyanin, superoxide dismutase, and cytochrome oxidase. Hemocyanin is another carrier of oxygen, other than hemoglobin which is colorless but turns blue when binds with oxygen due to the conversion of Cu (I) to Cu (II). Co is found in vitamin B_{12} (cyanocobalamine). Zn is present in many proteins including insulin where it confers structure and stability. Proteins bound

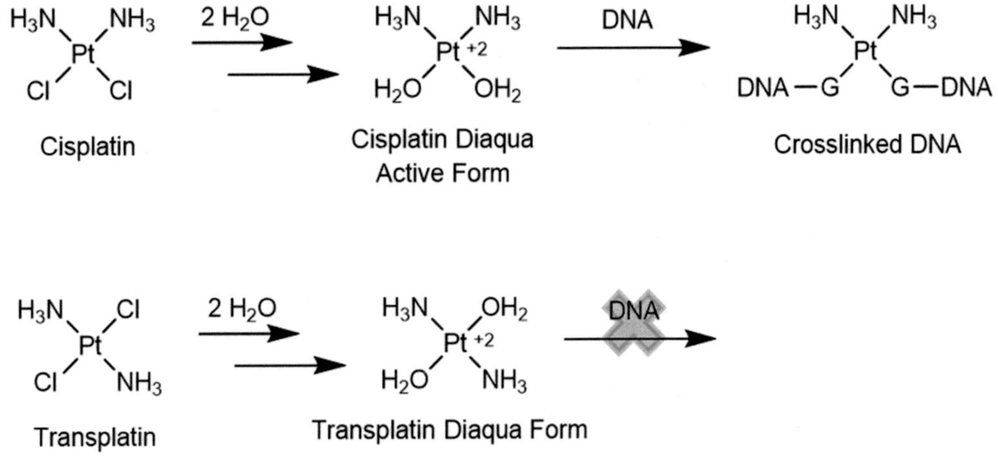

FIGURE 5.3 Mechanism of antineoplastic cytotoxicity of cisplatin leading to cross-linked DNA of two adjacent guanidine nucleotides. Transplatin does not have the proper diaqua form for DNA cross-linking.

with zinc interact with DNA at specific sequences. It binds with two histidine and two cysteine residues of the protein to form a loop called zinc finger which can fit into the major groove of DNA. It is present in enzymes too, for example, carboxypeptidase, and carbonic anhydrase.

5.3 Organic molecular complexes

5.3.1 Molecular complexes

Molecular complexes are different from coordination complexes in the sense that the binding force between the central metal cation and ligand is noncovalent intermolecular binding forces instead of covalent. These intermolecular binding forces are typically electrostatic forces, van der Waals forces, hydrogen bonds, or hydrophobic interactions.

Examples: Aminophylline formed from ethylenediamine and theophylline, Povidone formed from iodine and poly(vinylpyrrolidone), binding of drugs with proteins, self-association to form aggregates such as surfactant micelles, and inclusion complexes such as cyclodextrin complexes.

5.3.2 Types of noncovalent interactions utilized in forming molecular complexes

Ion—ion bonds (electrostatic interactions)—The ion—ion bond is the strongest noncovalent bond. Both drug and receptor must be charged, with one entity being cationic (positively charged) and the other anionic (negatively charged). Common anionic functional groups are carboxylates and sulfonamides, and common cationic functional groups are protonated amines and quaternary ammonium ions. Fig. 5.4 shows the interaction between protonated amine and carboxylate.

Ion—dipole bonds—In an ion—dipole bond, only one entity has a unit charge (either the drug or the receptor, but not both). The other entity has partial charge … what is referred to as a "dipole moment." A dipole moment is a partial separation of charge between two atoms connected by sigma bonds or conjugated through a pi system. For a functional group to be polar it must have a dipole or charge. The difference in partial charge is based on electronegativity, with the more electronegative atom assuming a partial negative charge (δ^-) and the less electronegative atom assuming a partial positive charge (δ^+). In an ion—dipole bond, if the ion is a cation (+ charge), it will bind to the δ^- end of the dipole. If the ionized functional group is an anion (− charge), it will bind to the δ^+ end of the dipole. Remember … opposite charges attract one another, while like charges repel one another (Fig. 5.5).

Dipole—dipole bonds—In a dipole—dipole bond, the interacting groups on both drug and receptor have a partial charge. Neither the drug functional group nor the receptor functional group is fully ionized in this type of binding interaction. As opposite charges attract, the δ^+ end of one dipole will interact with the δ^- end of the other dipole to form the bond. All the polar functional groups listed above can interact with one another, and almost all can be found on both a drug and a receptor. The hydrogen bond (H-bond) is a *special type of dipole—dipole interaction* where hydrogen is the δ^+ end of one of the dipoles involved in the bond. Hydrogen bonding involves hydrogen sharing between two electronegative atoms (Fig. 5.6).

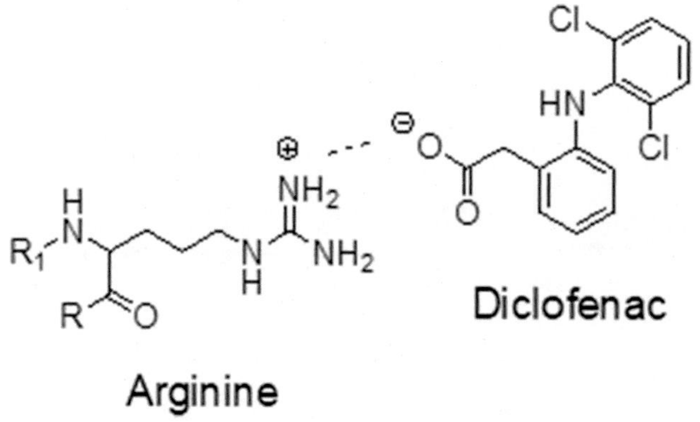

FIGURE 5.4   Example ion—ion interaction between the anionic nonsteroidal antiinflammatory drug (NSAID), diclofenac, and the cationic amino acid arginine.

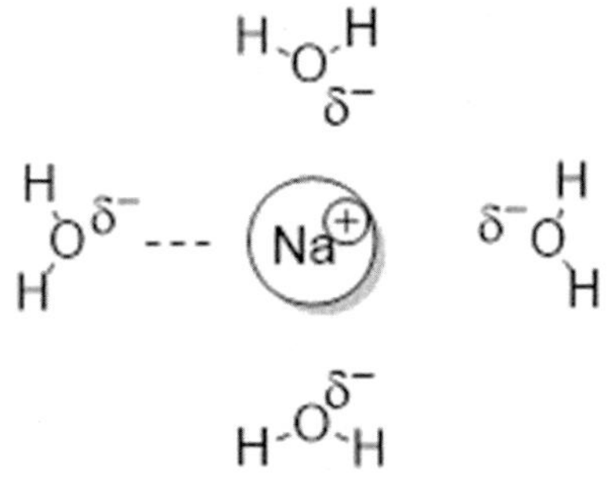

FIGURE 5.5   Example of ion–dipole interaction between water and sodium cation.

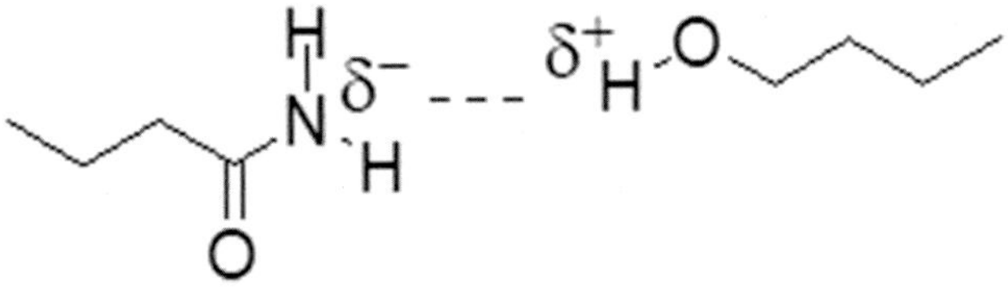

FIGURE 5.6   Example of hydrogen bond (dipole–dipole).

Van der Waals bonds—The Van der Waals bond (induced dipole-induced dipole, π stacking interaction) is involved in the binding of π electron systems, most commonly aromatic rings, to one another. Aromatic rings like benzene (phenyl group) have p orbitals that contain mobile π electrons. In an isolated phenyl ring the π electrons can be found in equal density both above and below the plane of the flat (sp^2 hybridized) ring. This means that the isolated phenyl ring is totally nonpolar … there is no partial separation of charge since the π electrons are found in equal measure on both sides of the ring system (Fig. 5.7).

When two aromatic rings (one on the drug and the other on the receptor) approach each other, things change in a hurry because these electrons are mobile, the π electrons of one ring can repel the π electrons of the other. The closer the rings approach, the more repulsion of electron density occurs, but these rings can approach each other closely since they are absolutely flat (remember that the geometry of sp^2 hybridized atoms is trigonal coplanar). The electrons of one ring move to the side of the ring away from the approaching second ring to get away from the invading π electrons. The side of the ring that takes the π electrons becomes δ^- with respect to the side of the ring that lost the electrons, which is now δ^+. A dipole is born! The δ^+ side of this ring, now being electron deficient, welcomes the invading electrons of the second ring, and the side of that ring that is closest to the first ring becomes δ^-.

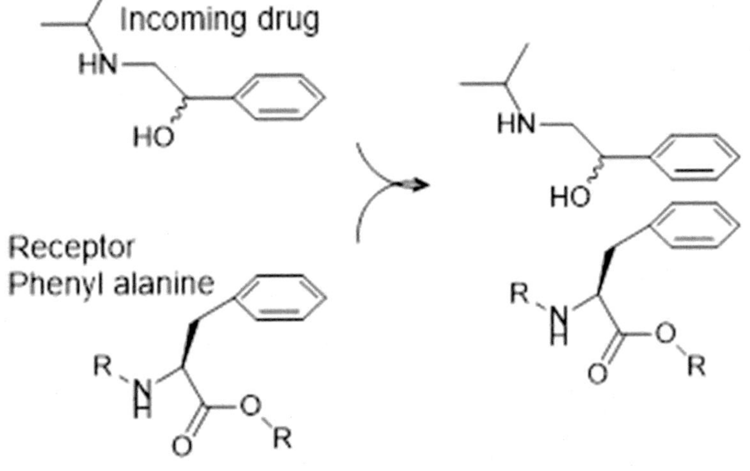

FIGURE 5.7   Example of van der Waals interaction.

I. Physical principles and properties of pharmaceutics

Hydrophobic interaction—Hydrophobic interactions take place between carbon-rich, lipophilic alkyl chains, alicyclic rings, or aromatic rings. The hydrophobic interaction is the weakest of all interactions. While it is not a bond, it is critical in binding drugs to their receptor surfaces because lipophilic groups are plentiful on drug structures. Each individual interaction is not strong, but when they are all added up they become a powerful force in promoting high-affinity binding between drug and receptor. The driving force for hydrophobic interactions is the increase in entropy of the entire system that results when water molecules are displaced from the binding site by a lipophilic drug.

5.4 Inclusion compounds

5.4.1 Cyclodextrin complexes

Cyclodextrin is a donut-shaped molecule consisting of 6—8 molecules of D-glucopyranose whose internal cavity size ranges from 5 through 8 Å. The poorly soluble drug molecules of suitable size (5—8 Å) fit into the cyclodextrin cavity via van der Waals attraction and hydrophobic interaction. The nature of the cyclodextrin cavity is hydrophobic while that of the outer surface is hydrophilic due to the presence of many hydroxyl groups capable of making hydrogen bonds with water. There are five commercially available and commonly used cyclodextrins. They are α-cyclodextrin, β-cyclodextrin, γ-cyclodextrin, 2-hydroxypropyl-β-cyclodextrin, and sulfobutylether-β-cyclodextrin (Fig. 5.8). The molecular differences among α, β, and γ are the number of glucopyranose rings, where α, β, and γ cyclodextrin have 6, 7, and 8 glucopyranose rings, respectively. There are two unique β-cyclodextrins with functionalized primary alcohols to include a 2-hydroxypropyl or sulfobutylether groups. These groups generally improve the binding of lipophilic drugs.

Cyclodextrins have been used to enhance the solubility of digoxin, steroidal hormones (progesterone, testosterone, etc.) barbiturates, paclitaxel, coumarin, etc. In the case of aspirin and other NSAIDs, cyclodextrin inclusion complexes have been found to decrease gastric toxicity (irritation or bleeding) [1].

5.5 Protein binding

5.5.1 Protein—ligand interaction

Protein—ligand interaction is important in drug—receptor interaction for pharmacological activity, enzyme—substrate interaction in catalysis, antibody—antigen recognition, and the drug—plasma protein interaction influencing tissue distribution. Protein—drug (or ligand) interaction is reversible and can be represented by:

$$[P] + [L] \rightleftharpoons [PL] \tag{5.1}$$

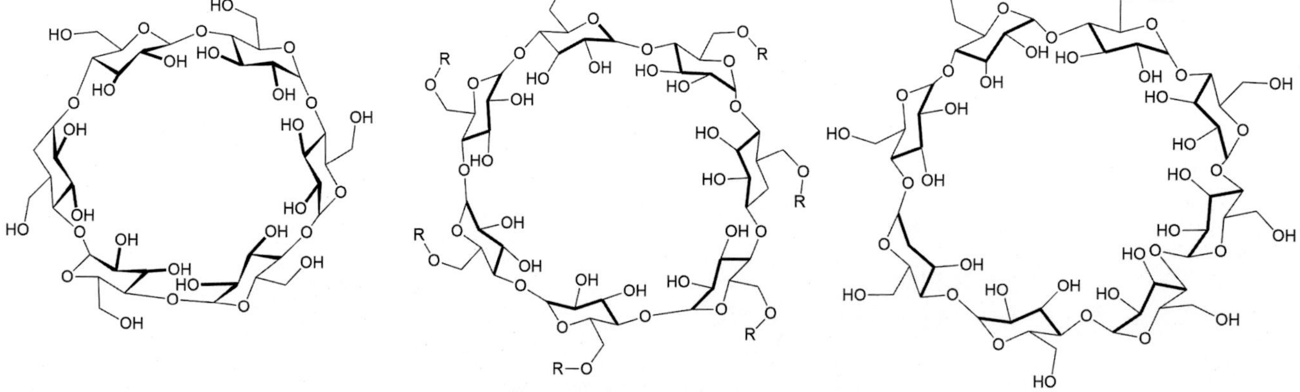

Alpha-Cyclodextrin

Beta-Cyclodextrin (R = H)
2-Hydroxypropy-Beta-Cyclodextrin (R = $CH_2CH(OH)CH_3$)
Sulfobutylether-Beta-Cyclodextrin (R = $CH_2CH_2CH_2CH_2SO_3$)

Gamma-Cyclodextrin

FIGURE 5.8 Molecular structures of five commercially available cyclodextrins.

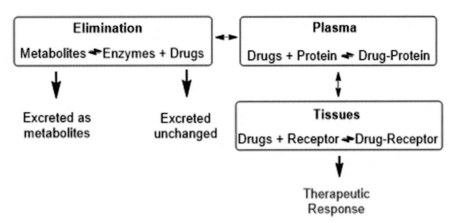

FIGURE 5.9 Effect of plasma protein binding on drug distribution into the tissues and elimination from the body.

where [P] = the molar concentration of protein, [L] = the molar concentration of ligand or drug, and [PL] = the molar concentration of protein-ligand or drug complex. The affinity between the protein and drug is indicated by the association constant, K_a, which has a unit of 1/M, that is, liters per mole.

$$K_a = \frac{[PL]}{[P][L]} \tag{5.2}$$

The association constant, K_a, is the opposite of the dissociation constant, K_d.

Ligand-binding sites on the proteins are usually depressions on the surface of the protein. The ligand must have size and shape complementary to such surface depressions for strong interaction. As a generalization, steric complementarity (i.e., the shape of the drug is mirrored in the shape of the binding site) and physicochemical complementarity must be met to allow molecular reaction between the drug and the binding sites on the protein surface.

5.5.2 Plasma protein binding

Therapeutic proteins, on being systematically administered, encounter many plasma proteins, for example, albumin, α_1 acid glycoprotein, and lipoprotein which can interact with the drug and affect its actions. The relationship between plasma protein binding, physiologic distribution, and elimination is shown in Fig. 5.9.

Marketed drugs are all associated with a nonspecific percent binding to plasma proteins. Drugs bound to plasma proteins are unable to elicit their biological action. Therefore, only the free/unbound drug is able to elicit its therapeutic response. In other words, highly bound drugs to plasma proteins are limited and will have a small fraction of free/unbound drugs available to bind to their biological target and elicit a therapeutic response. In addition, highly bound drugs have limited tissue distribution, which can have a positive impact on metabolism increasing the half-life of the drug *in vivo*. Highly protein-bound drugs tend to remain mainly in the systemic circulation contrary to binding with adipose tissue, and have a relatively lower volume of distribution and longer half-life in the body. Conversely, a drug with low plasma protein binding have a large tissue distribution, including the liver and may suffer a quick metabolic profile.

The protein binding profile of a drug is characterized by the terms—affinity and capacity. Affinity of binding, or the association constant, K_a, is a measure of the strength of the interaction between the protein and the drug molecule. A drug having larger K_a can displace another drug molecule from the same binding site. Displacement of bound drugs can lead to significant toxicity as the free drug interacts with the free active sites on the receptor to elicit pharmacological effects. Some drugs, such as warfarin, are extensively bound to plasma protein (i.e., high capacity) but with relatively weak affinity (i.e., lower K_a). Therefore, many NSAIDs can displace warfarin from its binding site and can cause serious hemorrhagic complications. Furthermore, the changes in concentrations of available proteins due to age, pathological conditions, malnutrition, and trauma are important factors to consider while investigating the effect of binding with plasma protein on the therapeutic outcome of a drug. If the protein concentration decreases in the plasma, the relative increase in the free drug concentration would cause significant toxicity at the same dose.

5.6 Factors influencing complexation and protein binding

Ligands that bind metal cations must contain a Lewis base, which is anionic or partially anionic functional groups, most commonly represented as carboxylates and hydroxyl groups. Generally, an increase in lipophilicity will increase nonspecific drug binding to plasma proteins. In addition, increased drug concentration in the blood will also typically increase drug binding to plasma proteins. Complexation to ligands or plasma proteins generally increases with a larger number of binding sites on the ligand. For example, plasma albumin, due to its large size at approximately 65 kDa, has a larger number of binding sites compared to other plasma proteins [2]. Drug—drug interactions can also affect drug binding to plasma proteins. If drug A has a high affinity for a plasm protein over drug B, then drug A will displace drug B and increase its free fraction in the blood, which could lead to significant adverse effects.

5.7 Conclusions

The majority of drugs elicit their action through forming stable drug/receptor complexes, which are typically formed through various noncovalent interactions. Complexes are formed between two compounds which can be through coordination or molecular complexes. These complexes are essential for modulating the physicochemical and pharmacokinetic action of drugs along with the homeostasis and detoxification of endogenous toxins. Additionally, molecular interactions with exogenous compounds, such as cyclodextrins, yielding molecular complexes with drugs have abilities to improve drug pharmacokinetics by increasing aqueous solubility, which is a major physicochemical property influencing absorption. Drugs are able to nonspecifically bind to plasma proteins which have a significant impact on drug action and metabolism. Thus, a significant understanding of complexes can rationalize contemporary drug action in pharmacy practice.

Case studies

Case 5.1

Coumarin (Fig. 5.10) is an eight-membered fused aromatic lactone with known metabolic liabilities, where nearly every position is known to be metabolized by various metabolic enzymes [3]. Therefore, many drugs containing coumarin have short half-lives. Warfarin is a highly prescribed blood thinner that contains the coumarin functional group with an unusually long half-life (20—60 h) [4]. How can this be explained?

Approach. Warfarin is highly bound to plasm proteins, namely albumin [5]. With this high percentage of plasma protein-bound drug, warfarin distribution to the liver is significantly reduced. Therefore, warfarin is not exposed to various metabolic enzymes and is not metabolized effectively. This leads to an increased half-life.

Case 5.2

The most common preliminary experiment to determine antibiotic efficacy is to determine the minimum inhibitory concentration (MIC) of the drug to block bacterial growth. Moxifloxacin is a fluoroquinolone with an MIC value of approximately 0.12 µg/mL against *Streptococcus pneumoniae* [6]. With the addition of 4% human albumin to the MIC determination assay, the MIC value for moxifloxacin significantly increases [7]. Rationalize this observation.

Approach. MIC values are determined typically in Mueller Hinton broth (MHB) which is recommended by the Clinical and Laboratory Standards Institute for initial susceptibility studies. This broth does not contain any plasma

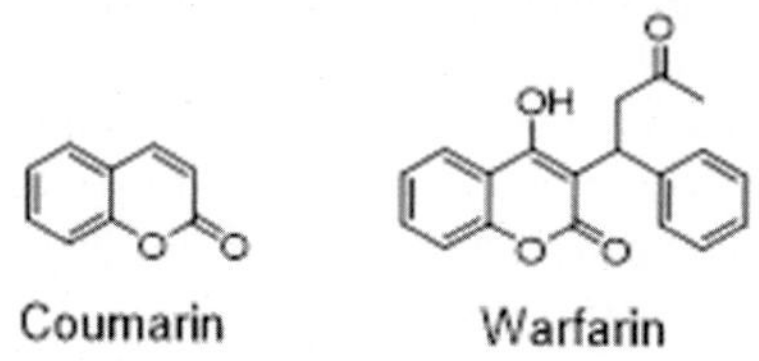

Coumarin   Warfarin

FIGURE 5.10   Structures of coumarin and warfarin know to bind with albumin.

proteins; therefore, all drug added is a free drug. Moxifloxacin is determined to be approximately 50% protein bound in plasma, therefore the addition of 4% human albumin binds up half of the free drug concentration. As there is less free drug to inhibit bacterial growth, the MIC value is increased.

Case 5.3

Warfarin is a popular blood thinner/anticoagulant that is highly bound to plasma proteins. Many NSAIDs, such as diclofenac, are also highly protein bound. What concerns should you have with the coadministration of NSAIDs and warfarin?

Approach. Diclofenac has a binding affinity for albumin of approximately $29.0 \pm 0.20 \times 10^6 \, M^{-1}$ [8]. Warfarin has a binding affinity for albumin of approximately $14.1-19.2 \times 10^4 \, M^{-1}$ [9]. Therefore, diclofenac has a higher affinity for serum albumin than warfarin and could displace warfarin from albumin and significantly increase the free drug concentration. As warfarin is an anticoagulant, life-threatening hemorrhaging could occur.

Critical reflections and practice applications

The following are the key points of complexation and plasma protein binding and their application in contemporary pharmacy practice.

1. Improve understanding on how intermolecular binding interactions can be applied to complex formation and protein binding
2. Complex formation with metal or organic (drug) substrates can improve physicochemical and pharmacokinetic profiles
3. Plasma protein binding percentages can rationalize drug dose and drug half-life

Acknowledgments

Authors are grateful for the exceptional help from Ms. Katherine M. Cunningham, Ms. Jenny N. Grissom, and Ms. Mariaelena Roman Sotelo.

References

[1] I.A. Alsarra, et al., Influence of cyclodextrin complexation with NSAIDs on NSAID/cold stress-induced gastric ulceration in rats, Int. J. Med. Sci. 7 (2010) 232–239, https://doi.org/10.7150/ijms.7.232.

[2] P. Lee, X. Wu, Review: modifications of human serum albumin and their binding effect, Curr. Pharmaceut. Des. 21 (2015) 1862–1865, https://doi.org/10.2174/1381612821666150302115025.

[3] B.G. Lake, Coumarin metabolism, toxicity and carcinogenicity: relevance for human risk assessment, Food Chem. Toxicol. 37 (1999) 423–453, https://doi.org/10.1016/s0278-6915(99)00010-1.

[4] J.D. Horton, B.M. Bushwick, Warfarin therapy: evolving strategies in anticoagulation, Am. Fam. Physician 59 (1999) 635–646.

[5] A.M. Rosengren, B.C. Karlsson, I.A. Nicholls, Monitoring the distribution of warfarin in blood plasma, ACS Med. Chem. Lett. 3 (2012) 650–652, https://doi.org/10.1021/ml300112e.

[6] M.E. Jones, et al., Benchmarking the *in vitro* activities of moxifloxacin and comparator agents against recent respiratory isolates from 377 medical centers throughout the United States, Antimicrob. Agents Chemother. 44 (2000) 2645–2652, https://doi.org/10.1128/aac.44.10.2645-2652.2000.

[7] J. Beer, C.C. Wagner, M. Zeitlinger, Protein binding of antimicrobials: methods for quantification and for investigation of its impact on bacterial killing, AAPS J. 11 (2009) 1–12, https://doi.org/10.1208/s12248-008-9072-1.

[8] M.K. Hossain, A. Khatun, M. Rahman, M.N. Akter, S.A. Chowdhury, S.M. Alam, Characterization of the effect of drug-drug interaction on protein binding in concurrent administration of sulfamethoxazol and diclofenac sodium using bovine serum albumin, Adv Pharm Bull. 4 (2016) 589–595, https://doi.org/10.15171/apb.2016.073.

[9] F.G. Larsen, C.G. Larsen, P. Jakobsen, R. Brodersen, Interaction of warfarin with human serum albumin. A stoichiometric description, Mol. Pharmacol. 27 (1985) 263–270.

6

Rate Processes in Pharmaceutics

Ramprakash Govindarajan

University of Iowa Pharmaceuticals, College of Pharmacy, University of Iowa, Iowa City, IA, United States

> ## CHAPTER OBJECTIVES
> - Understand fundamental principles of kinetic processes.
> - Recognize kinetic processes in pharmaceutics.
> - Apply principles of chemical kinetics to drug stability.
> - Identify factors influencing drug stability.
> - Understand product shelf-life and its determination.
> - Appreciate the relevance of diffusion processes in pharmaceutics.
> - Understand factors affecting (1) drug dissolution and (2) drug release from drug delivery systems.

Keywords: Chemical kinetics; Diffusion; Dissolution; Drug release; Mass transport; Permeability; Pharmaceutics; Rate process; Reaction order; Stability.

6.1 Introduction

Pharmaceutics includes the study of physical, chemical, biological, and technological processes, which influence the quality of drug products. Knowledge of these processes is applied to the development of safe, effective, commercially manufacturable, and patient-acceptable products. Each discipline of pharmaceutics, therefore, requires the understanding of such processes and the interplay between them.

A rate process may be defined as the course of change in a system as a function of time [1]. In this chapter, two broad categories of rate processes, chemical reactions and mass transport, are discussed. As in other disciplines, the ability to accelerate certain processes and slow down others enables a pharmaceutical scientist to maximize desirable outcomes.

6.1.1 Thermodynamics versus kinetics

The laws of thermodynamics dictate if a process will occur spontaneously and define the position of equilibrium states. For example, physical and chemical changes that result in a decrease in the Gibbs free energy of the system

Pharmaceutics, Second Edition
https://doi.org/10.1016/B978-0-323-99796-6.00012-6

($\Delta G < 0$, exergonic process) are thermodynamically favored and occur spontaneously. The free energy change, ΔG, represents the driving force for the conversion of reactants to products with lower free energy. For reversible processes, the system spontaneously approaches an equilibrium state, which represents a free energy minimum. At equilibrium, there is no net change in concentrations of reactants or products.

While thermodynamics deals with the direction of spontaneous changes, it does not address the time taken for the change to occur. Kinetics, on the other hand, is the study of the time course of processes. Kinetics deals with process velocities and how they are influenced by factors such as concentration, pressure, temperature, catalysis, surface area, and medium properties. This chapter discusses the kinetics of chemical reactions and mass transport processes relevant to pharmaceutics.

6.2 Chemical reaction kinetics

One of the tasks for a pharmaceutical scientist is to provide the active pharmaceutical ingredient (API) in a drug product that retains the API's chemical integrity within specified limits over shelf-life. Drug molecules can chemically degrade by hydrolysis, oxidation, isomerization, polymerization, or photochemical decomposition. Such processes can occur in the drug substance after synthesis, during drug product manufacturing, and during product storage. These chemical changes decrease intact drug content and generate degradation products. Therefore, an understanding of these processes is an important first step in the development of stable formulations.

6.2.1 Reaction rate and order

Consider a reaction (Eq. 6.1) in which reactants A and B react to form products X and Y. The stoichiometric coefficients $m, n, p,$ and q are the number of molecules of A, B, X, and Y, respectively, in the balanced chemical equation.

$$mA + nB \rightarrow pX + qY \tag{6.1}$$

The velocity of the change (consumption of A and B, generation of X and Y) is the rate of reaction. Therefore, at any given time t, the reaction rate can be expressed in terms of the rate of decrease in reactant concentration or increase in product concentration (Eq. 6.2).

$$\text{Rate} = -\left(\frac{1}{m}\frac{d[A]}{dt}\right) = -\left(\frac{1}{n}\frac{d[B]}{dt}\right) = \left(\frac{1}{p}\frac{d[X]}{dt}\right) = \left(\frac{1}{q}\frac{d[Y]}{dt}\right) \tag{6.2}$$

For a given reaction velocity, the rate of concentration change for each species is proportional to the number of molecules of the species participating in the reaction. Therefore, in Eq. (6.2), the rate of concentration change for each species is divided by the respective stoichiometric coefficient as depicted in Eq. (6.1). Since reactants are depleted with reaction progress, negative signs are included for the rate expressions in terms of reactant concentrations.

Based on the law of mass action, the rate equation [shown in Eq. (6.3) for the reaction in Eq. 6.1] relates the reaction rate at any given time to the concentration of reactant(s).

$$\text{Rate} = k[A]^{\alpha}[B]^{\beta} \tag{6.3}$$

The constant k in Eq. (6.3) is the rate constant for the reaction. The value of the rate constant will depend on factors such as temperature and reaction medium properties. The exponents α and β define the manner in which the reaction rate varies with the concentrations of reactants A and B. The reaction is of order α and β (partial orders) with respect to A and B. The overall reaction order is the sum of the exponents of the concentration terms in the rate equation, that is, $(\alpha+\beta)$. It is important to note that α and β are not always the stoichiometric coefficients m and n but have to be experimentally determined. Reaction order is defined based on the rate equation obeyed and is a kinetic property of the process. Reaction order reveals how reaction rates change as the reaction progresses and reactants are consumed.

6.2.2 Reaction order versus molecularity

Molecularity refers to the number of reactant molecules participating in a given reaction step and hence is related to the reaction mechanism. An elementary reaction is a single-step reaction, for example, A + B $\rightarrow$ products, where molecules of reactants A and B react in a single step to yield products. For such elementary reactions, the exponents in the rate equation (partial orders) are the same as the stoichiometric coefficients in the balanced chemical equation. In other words, molecularity and order are the same for elementary reactions.

A chemical change depicted by a balanced chemical equation, while defining the starting reactants and the final end-products, may involve a series of elementary reactions and intermediate species. Such reactions are termed as nonelementary or complex reactions. For example, three elementary steps A → X; X + B → Y; and Y → C, may be involved in a complex reaction, A + B → C. The *overall rate* of the complex reaction is determined by the slowest elementary step (rate-determining step). For a complex reaction, each elementary step has a reaction order. The mechanisms of elementary steps and the rate-determining step in the sequence will determine the overall rate law equation and overall reaction order.

6.2.3 Order and pseudo-order

Consider a bimolecular reaction—alkaline hydrolysis of ethyl acetate in a dilute aqueous solution to yield acetate and ethanol (Eq. 6.4).

$$(6.4)$$

The hydrolysis rate at any given time t is directly proportional to the concentrations of *both* ethyl acetate and hydroxide ions.

$$Rate = -\left(\frac{d[CH_3COOC_2H_5]}{dt}\right) = k_2 [CH_3COOC_2H_5]^1 [OH^-]^1 \tag{6.5}$$

Eq. (6.5) is a second-order rate equation, and k_2 is the second-order rate constant. If the same reaction was carried out in a buffered solution where pH is controlled, $[OH^-]$ would be unchanged as the reaction progressed. As hydrolysis proceeds, ethyl acetate concentration and the reaction rate would both decrease. The rate of loss of ethyl acetate would appear to depend *only* on the concentration of ethyl acetate and the second-order process appears to follow first-order kinetics (rate equation in Eq. 6.6). The reaction, therefore, exhibits apparent or pseudo-first-order kinetics and k_1' is the pseudo-first-order rate constant.

$$Rate = -\left(\frac{d[CH_3COOC_2H_5]}{dt}\right) = k_1'[CH_3COOC_2H_5]^1; \quad \text{where } k_1' = k_2[OH^-] \tag{6.6}$$

Consider an aqueous suspension of a poorly soluble ester drug, RCOOR'. The dispersion medium (suspending vehicle) is buffered at a pH where ester hydrolysis occurs by reaction with hydroxide ions. The suspended solid drug is in equilibrium with the drug dissolved in the dispersion medium (Eq 6.7). *Dissolved* ester undergoes alkaline hydrolysis (Eq. 6.8).

$$RCOOR'_{solid} \rightleftharpoons RCOOR'_{solution} \tag{6.7}$$

$$RCOOR'_{solution} + OH^- \longrightarrow RCOO^- + R'OH \tag{6.8}$$

As the dissolved ester is depleted by hydrolysis, the dissolution of solid ester (dispersed phase) continues to replenish ester concentration in the dispersion medium. Therefore, as long as there is undissolved solid ester present, ester concentration in the solution is maintained (and equal to its solubility in the medium). As the concentration of both reactants is maintained constant in the reaction medium, the reaction proceeds at a constant rate. The reaction rate, therefore, is independent of the *total* ester concentration in the suspension (dissolved + undissolved), which decreases with the reaction progress. The second-order process appears to follow zero-order kinetics. The constant rate of loss of ester by this hydrolytic process (Eq. 6.9) is therefore equal to k_0', the pseudo-zero-order rate constant, which is related to the second-order and pseudo-first-order rate constants as expressed in Eq. (6.10).

$$Rate = -\left(\frac{d[RCOOR']}{dt}\right) = k_0' \tag{6.9}$$

$$k_0' = k_1'[RCOOR'] = k_2[RCOOR'][OH^-] \tag{6.10}$$

The concentration terms in Eq. (6.10) are (1) the solubility of the ester in the medium, at the temperature of the experiment, and (2) the constant OH^- concentration maintained by the buffer.

This kinetic behavior would continue as long as there is undissolved ester. Once all the solid (i.e. undissolved ester) is consumed, ester concentration in solution will decrease, and the reaction will exhibit pseudo-first-order kinetics. In this example, it is assumed that the medium is adequately buffered to maintain pH, even with ester hydrolysis furnishing a carboxylic acid as a reaction product.

6.2.4 Half-life and shelf-life

The half-life of a reaction ($t_{0.5}$) is defined as the time required to decrease the reactant concentration to 50% of the initial concentration. For pharmaceutical products, shelf-life is defined as the period of time after manufacture, until which critical quality attributes of the product are within acceptable limits. Solely in terms of API content, it is the time until which the concentration of the API is above defined minimum acceptable levels (say 90% or 95% of the initial content) needed for the indended activity. It is important to note that changes in other product attributes (such as impurity levels, drug dissolution, and physical properties) may also influence the establishment of shelf-life.

6.2.5 Zero-order kinetics

A zero-order reaction proceeds at a constant rate, independent of reactant concentration. If a_0 and a represent reactant concentrations, initially and after time t, the rate equation and its integrated form for a zero-order reaction are shown in Eqs. (6.10) and (6.11).

$$\text{Rate} = -\left(\frac{da}{dt}\right) = k_0 \tag{6.10}$$

$$a = a_0 - k_0 t \tag{6.11}$$

The zero-order rate constant k_0 has units of concentration time^{-1}. Eq. (6.11) represents the linear decrease in reactant concentration with time. From Eq. (6.11), the half-life [time at which $a = (\frac{1}{2})a_0$], and the shelf-life (say when $a = 0.9\ a_0$) are expressed in Eq. (6.12).

$$t_{0.5} = \frac{a_0 - 0.5a_0}{k_0} = \frac{a_0}{2k_0}; \quad t_{0.9} = \frac{a_0 - 0.9a_0}{k_0} = \frac{a_0}{10k_0} \tag{6.12}$$

The half-life and shelf-life for a zero-order reaction, therefore, depend on the initial reactant concentration (Eq. 6.12; Case study 6.1).

A zero-order reaction can occur if the reaction rate is limited by the concentration of a catalyst. In such cases, k_0 may be proportional to the catalyst concentration. For example, in a photochemical process, k_0 may be proportional to the intensity of light.

As discussed earlier, degradation may exhibit pseudo-zero-order kinetics for drug suspensions. A suspension formulation of amiodarone hydrochloride (20 mg/mL amiodarone), an antiarrhythmic drug, was prepared by crushing Pacerone 200 mg tablets and dispersing the powder in an aqueous suspending vehicle [2]. Samples of the suspension were stored at various temperatures and analyzed for intact amiodarone over a period of 13 weeks. Given its poor aqueous solubility [3], amiodarone HCl is expected to be predominantly in the undissolved dispersed phase in the temperature range of the experiment. Fig. 6.1 is a plot of *total* amiodarone concentration in the suspension as a function of time, at 60°C. A linear decrease in total drug concentration, that is, a constant degradation rate, suggests zero-order kinetic behavior. The drug concentration versus time ("a vs. t") plot has a slope of $-k_0$ and y-intercept of a_0 (Eq 6.11). For the suspension stored at 60°C, a pseudo-zero-order rate constant (k_0) for amiodarone loss, determined from the slope, is 0.055 mg mL^{-1} day^{-1} and a half-life calculated using Eq. (6.12) is 182 days.

6.2.6 First-order kinetics

For first-order reactions, the sum of the exponential terms in the rate equation is one. For example, the rate of an elementary unimolecular reaction, such as A → products, would be directly proportional to the concentration of reactant A. As the reaction proceeds and A is consumed, the reaction rate would therefore decrease. Using similar symbols as in Eq. (6.10), the rate equation for the first-order reaction and the integrated forms are shown in Eqs. (6.14)–(6.17). Converting to common logarithm yields Eq. (6.18). The first-order rate constant k_1 has units of (time^{-1}).

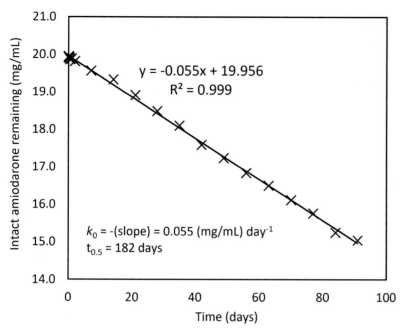

FIGURE 6.1 Plot of total amiodarone concentration versus time in suspensions (20 mg/mL of amiodarone initially) prepared from crushed Pacerone 200 mg tablets and stored at 60°C. Plot was constructed using data obtained from Ref. [2].

$$\text{Rate} = -\frac{\mathrm{d}a}{\mathrm{d}t} = k_1 a \tag{6.14}$$

$$\int_{a_0}^{a} \frac{\mathrm{d}a}{a} = -\int_{0}^{t} k_1 \mathrm{d}t \tag{6.15}$$

$$\ln a - \ln a_0 = -k_1 t \tag{6.16}$$

$$a = a_0\, e^{-k_1 t} \tag{6.17}$$

$$\log_{10}\left[\frac{a}{a_0}\right] = \frac{-k_1 t}{2.303} \tag{6.18}$$

The half-life for the reaction can be obtained by substituting a with $0.5a_0$ in Eq. (6.18):

$$t_{0.5} = \frac{2.303}{k_1}\log\left[\frac{a_0}{0.5a_0}\right] = \frac{0.693}{k_1} \tag{6.19}$$

Eq. (6.19) reveals that the half-life of a first-order reaction is *independent* of the initial reactant concentration. Fig. 6.2A is a plot of % reactant remaining versus time for a hypothetical first-order process. The time axis is scaled as multiples of the half-life. Each half-life period progressively decreases the amount of reactant by half. As the reaction progresses, and the reactant is consumed, the slope of the curve (reaction rate) decreases exponentially. A semilog plot of the same data [$\log_{10}$ (% reactant remaining) versus time] yields a straight line (Fig. 6.2B, Eq. 6.18) with a slope of $(-k_1/2.303)$.

Cefoxitin underwent rapid degradation in solution. The solution stability of cefoxitin at various solution pH values was investigated [4]. Fig. 6.3A contains plots of % remaining cefoxitin versus time at 25°C and reveals decreasing reaction rates. Plots of log (% remaining cefoxitin) versus time (Fig. 6.3B) were linear. The observed first-order rate constants (k_{obs}) at 25°C, obtained from the plots were 3.42×10^{-3}, 2.46×10^{-3}, and $7.83 \times 10^{-3}\,\text{h}^{-1}$, at pH 3, 7, and 9, respectively. The corresponding calculated half-life values were 212, 288, and 89 h. The shelf-life, $t_{0.9}$, can be calculated using Eq. (6.18) and $a = 0.9a_0$.

$$t_{0.9} = \frac{2.303}{k_1}\log\left[\frac{a_0}{0.9a_0}\right] = \frac{0.105}{k_1} \tag{6.20}$$

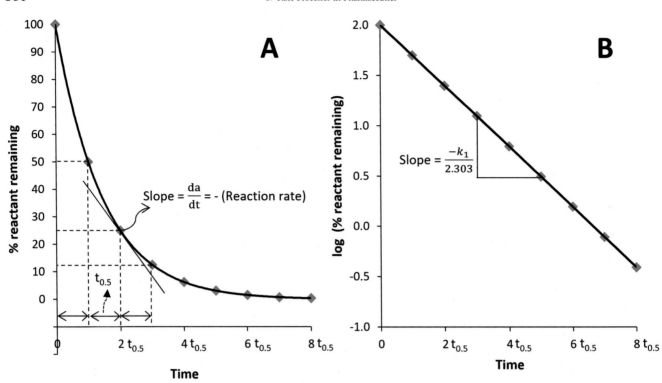

FIGURE 6.2 First-order reaction progress. The time axis has been scaled as multiples of the half-life ($t_{0.5}$). (A) On a linear scale, the reactant quantity decreases exponentially. (B) When the logarithm of the reactant quantity is plotted against time, a straight line with a slope of $-k_1/2.303$ is obtained.

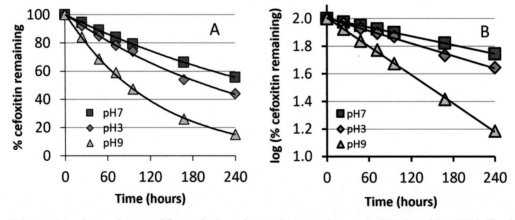

FIGURE 6.3 Cefoxitin degradation plots reveal first-order loss of intact drug, in solutions at pH 3, 7, and 9, at 25°C. The degradation rates exhibited dependence on solution pH. Figures constructed using data from Ref. [4], with permission from Elsevier.

The calculated $t_{0.9}$ values for the cefoxitin solutions at 25°C were 40, 49, and 14 h at pH 3, 7, and 9, respectively. The short half-lives preclude the formulation of aqueous parenteral solutions for cefoxitin. These studies revealed the need for cefoxitin to be provided as a sterile solid (with superior stability) to be reconstituted before administration.

6.2.7 Second-order kinetics

For a bimolecular reaction, where two reactant molecules react and yield products, the product formation rate would depend on the concentrations of both reactants. For a second-order reaction A + B → products, where A and B react with a 1:1 stoichiometry, the rate equation is shown in Eq. (6.21). k_2 is the second-order rate constant and a and b are the concentrations of reactants A and B at time t.

$$\text{Rate} = -\left(\frac{da}{dt}\right) = -\left(\frac{db}{dt}\right) = k_2 a\, b \tag{6.21}$$

If x is the concentration of A and B that has reacted at time t, then $a = (a_0 - x)$ and $b = (b_0 - x)$. The reaction rate can be expressed as Eq. (6.22). For unequal initial concentrations ($a_0 \neq b_0$), the integrated form is Eq. (6.24). The second-order rate constant k_2 has units of (concentration^{-1} time^{-1}).

$$\text{Rate} = -\left(\frac{da}{dt}\right) = -\left(\frac{db}{dt}\right) = \left(\frac{dx}{dt}\right) = k_2 (a_0 - x)(b_0 - x) \tag{6.22}$$

$$\int_0^x \frac{dx}{(a_0 - x)(b_0 - x)} = -\int_0^t k_2 dt \tag{6.23}$$

$$\left(\frac{2.303}{a_0 - b_0}\right) \log\frac{a\, b_0}{b\, a_0} = k_2 t \tag{6.24}$$

If the starting concentrations of the two reactants are not the same, their half-life values would also be different. The half-life for a given reactant, say A, can be calculated by substituting $a = \frac{1}{2} a_0$ and $b = b_0 - \frac{1}{2} a_0$ in Eq. (6.24).

$$t_{0.5,A} = \frac{1}{k_2}\left(\frac{2.303}{a_0 - b_0}\right) \log\left(\frac{0.5\, b_0}{b_0 - 0.5\, a_0}\right) \tag{6.25}$$

Eq. (6.25) would only be valid, if $b_0 \geq 0.5 a_0$, that is, if there was adequate reactant B to react with at least 50% of reactant A. When drug molecules react with formulation components that are present at lower concentrations, the maximum extent of the reaction will be limited by the concentration of these components (Case study 6.2).

BMS-204352, an investigational drug, reacted with formaldehyde (present as a trace impurity in excipients polysorbate 80 and polyethylene glycol 300) in a parenteral formulation, to form a formaldehyde adduct. The levels of formaldehyde impurity in formulations correlated well with the quantity of degradant formed. Selecting excipient lots with low formaldehyde levels provided control over degradation extent [5].

Epinephrine is susceptible to oxidation and parenteral solutions of epinephrine often include sodium bisulfite as an antioxidant. Higuchi and Schroeter studied the reaction of epinephrine with sodium bisulfite at different solution pH values [6]. Fig. 6.4 includes a kinetic plot for a phosphate-buffered solution of epinephrine and sodium bisulfite (pH 6.5), flushed with nitrogen and stored at 56°C under nitrogen atmosphere. Initial reactant concentrations were 55 mM ($-$)-epinephrine (Ep_0) and 19.2 mM bisulfite (Sul_0). Bisulfite (HSO_3^-) ionizes to yield sulfite (SO_3^{2-}) with a pK_a of ~ 6.3 at 56°C [7,8]. Optically active ($-$)-epinephrine reacts with bisulfite or sulfite ion to form a racemic sulfonate (nucleophilic substitution, Fig. 6.4). The total sulfite concentration ("Sul" = bisulfite + sulfite) in the solution was monitored by iodometric titration. As the reaction progressed, the rate of loss of optical activity due to a decrease in ($-$)-epinephrine concentration was the same as the rate of decrease of total sulfite. Fig. 6.4A is a plot of reactant concentrations versus time for both reactants and suggests a progressive decrease in the reaction rate. A plot of log $[(Sul_0)\,(Ep)/(Sul)\,(Ep_0)]$ versus time was linear (see Eq. 6.24) suggesting second-order kinetic behavior (Fig. 6.4B). The slope of the line, $(2.303\, k_2)/(Ep_0 - Sul_0)$, was used to calculate the second-order rate constant, $k_2 = 0.83$ L mol^{-1} h^{-1}.

Consider a simpler case in which the initial molar concentrations of both the reactants are the same, that is, $a_0 = b_0$, and A and B react with a 1:1 stoichiometry. At any given time, t, therefore, $a = b$. Eq. (6.21) can be simplified.

$$\text{Rate} = -\left(\frac{da}{dt}\right) = -\left(\frac{db}{dt}\right) = k_2 a^2 \tag{6.26}$$

$$\int_{a_0}^a \frac{da}{a^2} = -\int_0^t k_2 dt \tag{6.27}$$

$$\left(\frac{1}{a}\right) - \left(\frac{1}{a_0}\right) = k_2 t \tag{6.28}$$

$$\left(\frac{a_0 - a}{a\, a_0}\right) = k_2 t \tag{6.29}$$

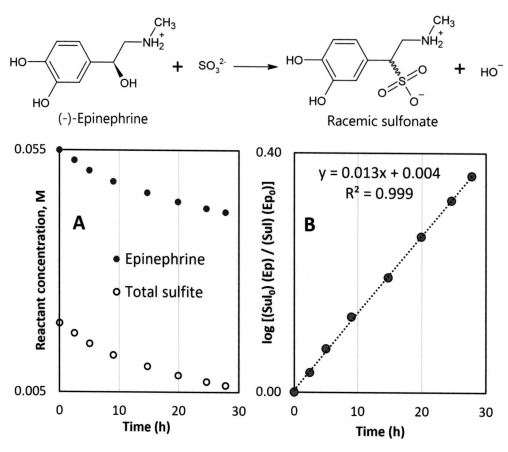

FIGURE 6.4 Second-order reaction of $(-)$-epinephrine with sulfite to form a racemic sulfonate. The starting concentrations of epinephrine and total sulfite were 55 and 19.2 mM, respectively. The solution was phosphate-buffered (pH 6.5) and reaction progress was monitored at 56°C. Additional details in the text. Graphs constructed from data in Ref. [6], with permission from Elsevier.

In this scenario, where $a = b$, a plot of $(1/a)$ versus time yields a straight line (see Eq. 6.28) with a slope of k_2 and a y-intercept of $(1/a_0)$. When the epinephrine - bisulfite reaction was carried out at pH 6.5 with equal initial concentrations of reactants ($Ep_0 = Sul_0 = 50$ mM), the reciprocal of optical rotation (a measure of intact $(-)$-epinephrine) and the reciprocal of total sulfite concentration, both increased linearly with time, indicating second-order kinetics [9].

For this simple case in which $a_0 = b_0$, the half-life of both reactants can be expressed by modifying Eq. (6.29).

$$t_{0.5} = \left(\frac{a_0 - 0.5a_0}{0.5k_2a_0^2}\right) = \left(\frac{1}{k_2\,a_0}\right) \tag{6.30}$$

The half-life of this second-order reaction, therefore, is inversely proportional to the initial reactant concentration.

6.2.8 Determination of reaction order

Experimental data on reaction progress (reactant concentration vs. time) can be substituted into rate equations (Eqs. 6.11, 6.16, 6.24, or 6.28) to calculate rate constants at each time point. The rate equation, which yields a consistent calculated value for the rate constant, represents the reaction order.

Reaction orders can also be determined graphically by plotting experimental data in the form of the rate equations (e.g., a, $\log a$, or $1/a$ versus time) and determining the equation that provides the best fit.

The *isolation method* can be employed, say for a reaction, which follows the rate equation in Eq. (6.31).

$$\text{Rate} = k[\text{A}]^\alpha[\text{B}]^\beta \tag{6.31}$$

As a first step, the reaction can be conducted with a large excess of A, say a concentration a' such that $k(a')^{\alpha}$ remains fairly constant as the reaction proceeds and B is depleted. The reaction, therefore, exhibits pseudo-β-order kinetics with a rate constant k'.

$$\text{Rate} = k'[\text{B}]^{\beta}, \text{where } k' = k(a')^{\alpha} = \text{constant} \tag{6.32}$$

By following the disappearance of B, the value of β and the apparent rate constant k' can be determined. In the second step, by holding the concentration of B at a large excess, α can be determined. The overall reaction order would then be $\alpha + \beta$.

Alternatively, in the second step, the reaction could be repeated, with a large excess of A, but at a different concentration, a''. The rate equation is similarly written in Eq. (6.33).

$$\text{Rate} = k''[\text{B}]^{\beta}, \text{where } k'' = k(a'')^{\alpha} = \text{constant} \tag{6.33}$$

With the apparent rate constants, k' and k'' corresponding to the two concentrations of A (a' and a''), the value of α can be calculated using Eq. (6.34).

$$\log \frac{k'}{k''} = \alpha \log \frac{a'}{a''} \tag{6.34}$$

The relationship between half-lives and initial reactant concentration has been discussed earlier (Eqs. 6.12, 6.19 and 6.30). In general, if the initial concentrations of all reactants (a_0, b_0, c_0 ...) are equal and expressed as a_0, the dependence of $t_{0.5}$ on initial reactant concentration is defined in Eq. (6.35), where n is the reaction order.

$$t_{0.5} \propto \frac{1}{(a_0)^{n-1}} \tag{6.35}$$

If the same reaction is conducted at two different initial concentrations (a_0' and a_0'') and the corresponding half-life values are determined to be $t_{0.5}'$ and $t_{0.5}''$, the reaction order n can be calculated using Eq. (6.36).

$$n = 1 + \frac{\log(t_{0.5}'/t_{0.5}'')}{\log(a_0''/a_0')} \tag{6.36}$$

6.2.9 Complex reactions

Chemical changes in pharmaceutical systems may involve reversible reactions, sequential multistep processes and drugs may degrade simultaneously by multiple chemical pathways. The following sections will introduce such chemical changes with pharmaceutical examples and discuss rate equations describing them.

6.2.9.1 Reversible reactions

In a reversible process, while reactants undergo a chemical change to yield products (forward reaction), products simultaneously react to yield back reactants (reverse reaction). Consider a simple reversible reaction, with first-order forward and reverse reactions with rate constants k_f and k_r, respectively.

$$\text{A} \underset{k_r}{\overset{k_f}{\rightleftharpoons}} \text{B} \tag{6.37}$$

Forward and reverse reaction rates (R_f and R_r), can be expressed as $R_f = k_f a$ and $R_r = k_r b$, where a and b are the concentrations of reactant and product at time t.

In a system starting from 100% A, for example, the forward reaction would progress at a rate $k_f a$, consuming A to produce B. As B is formed, the reverse reaction would progress at rate $k_r b$ producing A. The opposing reactions continue as the system approaches an equilibrium state. At equilibrium, forward and reverse reaction rates are equal. If a_{eq} and b_{eq} are the equilibrium concentrations of A and B, the equilibrium state is described in Eq. (6.38)

$$k_f a_{eq} = k_r b_{eq} \tag{6.38}$$

In other words, at equilibrium, the formation rate of a species (A or B) is the same as its consumption rate, and there is no net change in its concentration. The equilibrium constant (K_{eq}) is a measure of the extent to which the forward reaction is favored relative to the reverse reaction (Eq 6.39) and is related to $\Delta G°$, the standard free energy change for the forward reaction (Eq 6.40)

$$K_{eq} = \frac{k_f}{k_r} = \frac{b_{eq}}{a_{eq}} \tag{6.39}$$

$$\Delta G^0 = -RT \ln K_{eq} \tag{6.40}$$

$\Delta G°$ is the free energy change for the conversion of reactants to products in their standard states, at a given temperature. When $\Delta G° < 0$, $K_{eq} > 1$, the equilibrium favors the products. When $\Delta G° > 0$, $K_{eq} < 1$, the equilibrium favors the reactants (Eqs. 6.39 and 6.40).

The net reaction rate (rate of approach to equilibrium) is the difference between the rates of forward and reverse reactions (Eq. 6.41).

$$\text{Rate} = -\frac{da}{dt} = \frac{db}{dt} = k_f a - k_r b \tag{6.41}$$

Using the relationships, (1) $b = (a_0 - a)$, (2) $a_0 = (b_{eq} + a_{eq})$, and (3) $b_{eq} = (k_f/k_r) a_{eq}$ the rate equation can be rewritten as Eq. (6.42).

$$\text{Rate} = -\frac{da}{dt} = \left(k_f + k_r\right)\left(a - a_{eq}\right) \tag{6.42}$$

Integration and logarithmic transformation yield the expressions in Eqs. (6.43) and (6.44).

$$\frac{a - a_{eq}}{a_0 - a_{eq}} = e^{-\left(k_f + k_r\right)t} \tag{6.43}$$

$$\log_{10}\left(\frac{a - a_{eq}}{a_0 - a_{eq}}\right) = -\left(\frac{k_f + k_r}{2.303}\right)t \tag{6.44}$$

The term $(a - a_{eq})$ is the concentration change further required, at time t, to achieve equilibrium and $(a_0 - a_{eq})$ is the total concentration change from the start of the reaction to attainment of equilibrium. Eq. (6.43) therefore is the rate equation describing the approach to equilibrium. A comparison of Eq. (6.44) with Eq. (6.18) suggests that for a reversible process with first-order forward and reverse reactions, the approach to equilibrium is a first-order process with a rate constant of $(k_f + k_r)$.

When the reaction in one direction (say the forward direction) is favored *much* more than the reverse, such that the reaction *approaches* complete transformation in that direction (when $k_f \gg k_r$, such that a_{eq} approaches zero and $k_f + k_r \approx k_f$, then Eq. (6.44) approaches Eq. (6.18) (a unidirectional first order process).

Topotecan, a topoisomerase inhibitor, is used in the treatment of ovarian, cervical, and small-cell lung cancer. The active lactone form of topotecan undergoes reversible hydrolysis to the inactive ring-opened form (see Fig. 6.5). Underberg et al. studied the lactone—carboxylate equilibrium in solution, as a function of pH, at 25°C [11]. Starting from 100% lactone, solutions were analyzed over time for concentrations of closed ring (lactone) and ring-opened (ionized + unionized carboxylic acid) forms, till equilibrium was attained. The reversible reaction with forward and reverse rate constants k_1 and k_{-1}, and the observed ring-opening equilibrium constant K_{obs}, are described in Eqs. (6.45) and (6.46).

$$\underset{\text{(lactone)}}{\text{Closed E} - \text{Ring}} \underset{k_{-1}}{\overset{k_1}{\rightleftharpoons}} \underset{\text{(carboxylic acid + carboxylate)}}{\text{Ring} - \text{opened forms}} \tag{6.45}$$

$$K_{obs} = \frac{k_1}{k_{-1}} = \frac{[\text{carboxylic acid} + \text{carboxylate}]_{eq}}{[\text{lactone}]_{eq}} \tag{6.46}$$

The lactone fraction decreased with time at pH ≥ 5, with a corresponding increase in the hydrolyzed product. As shown in Fig. 6.5, at pH 5, 6, 7 and 8, the lactone remaining at equilibrium was 91%, 70%, 26%, and 11% of initial, respectively. An increase in the solution pH favors ionization of the ring-opened carboxylic acid, and this shifts the equilibrium toward the ring-opened species [10,12]. The K_{obs} values calculated from the equilibrium concentrations (using Eq. 6.46) increased from 0.1 at pH 5 to 20.2 at pH 9 [11].

At each pH value, the measured lactone concentration (L) as a function of time, and the equilibrium lactone concentration L_{eq}, allowed the kinetic data to be plotted in the form of Eqs. (6.43) and (6.44) and such plots are reconstructed in Fig. 6.6. The rate constant for approach to equilibrium, $(k_1 + k_{-1})$, can be obtained from the slopes of plots

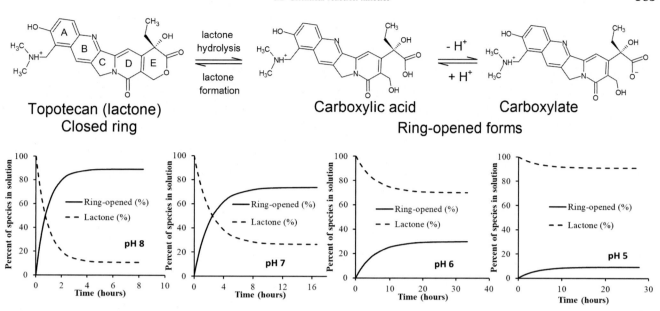

FIGURE 6.5 Top: Reversible lactone ring opening of topotecan. The molecule contains several ionizable groups—phenol ($pK_a \sim 7$) and tertiary amine ($pK_a \sim 10.5$) on ring A and the carboxylic acid in the ring-opened species ($pK_a \sim 4$) [10]. Depending on pH, the lactone and the ring-opened forms exist in multiple ionization states. For illustrative purposes, only a single ionization state for the lactone, carboxylic acid, and carboxylate is shown. Bottom panels: Attainment of equilibrium starting from 100% lactone in solutions at pH 8, 7, 6, and 5 (ionic strength 0.3 M, 0.01 M buffer, 25°C). An increase in pH progressively favors the ring-opened forms at equilibrium. Graphs constructed using rate constants reported in Ref. [11].

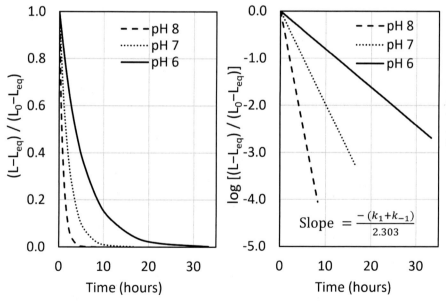

FIGURE 6.6 Graphs constructed for illustrative purposes using data obtained from Ref. [11]. Kinetic plots for approach to equilibrium starting from 100% topotecan lactone in solutions at pH, 6, 7, and 8. *Left panel*—$[(L-L_{eq})/(L_0-L_{eq})]$ versus time revealing pH-dependent kinetics. *Right panel*—$\log_{10}[(L-L_{eq})/(L_0-L_{eq})]$ versus time. The slopes of the straight lines were used to calculate $(k_1 + k_{-1})$ values: 3.11×10^{-4}, 1.27×10^{-4}, and 5.17×10^{-5} at pH 8, 7, and 6, respectively.

in Fig. 6.6 (*right panel*). The $(k_1 + k_{-1})$ values along with the calculated K_{obs} values were used by the authors to determine the rate constants for the forward (k_1) and the reverse (k_{-1}) reactions [11].

At pH 4, only the lactone form of topotecan was detected and at pH 10, conversion to the ring-opened forms was complete [11]. Topotecan injections are therefore formulated at acidic pH values <4. For example, Hycamtin (topotecan hydrochloride freeze-dried powder for injection) is prepared from a solution that is adjusted to pH 2.5—3.5 [13].

While topotecan exists as the lactone in acidic formulations, it undergoes rapid conversion after intravenous administration to the carboxylate under physiological conditions (pH 7.4), where the open-ring form predominates. After oral administration, the bioavailability of topotecan from Hycamtin capsules is ~40%. Hydrolytic degradation of the lactone in the intestine (to the poorly absorbed open-ring form), may contribute to the lower fraction of the dose being absorbed [14].

Another class of drugs which exhibit lactone—hydroxy acid equilibria are HMG CoA reductase inhibitors. Atorvastatin and Rosuvastatin, for example, are administered as the active hydroxy-acid forms. Simvastatin and lovastatin are prodrugs, administered as the inactive lactone, but converted to the active form *in vivo*.

6.2.9.2 Consecutive reactions

A reaction product may react further, resulting in series or consecutive reactions. Consider the two-step consecutive reaction of misoprostol, a synthetic prostaglandin (see Fig. 6.7). Misoprostol (M), in solution, undergoes dehydration to form product A, which on isomerization yields product B. Both reactions are first-order processes with rate constants k_d and k_i (Eq. 6.47).

$$\text{Misoprostol(M)} \xrightarrow{k_d} \text{Dehydration product (A)} \xrightarrow{k_i} \text{Isomer (B)} \tag{6.47}$$

If m_0 is the initial concentration of M, its rate of dehydration can be written as follows where m is its concentration at any time, t:

$$m = m_0\, e^{-k_d t} \tag{6.48}$$

The net rate of concentration change of A is determined by the rates of its formation by dehydration, and loss by isomerization where a is its concentration at any time, t

$$\frac{da}{dt} = k_d m - k_i a = k_d m_0\, e^{-k_d t} - k_i a \tag{6.49}$$

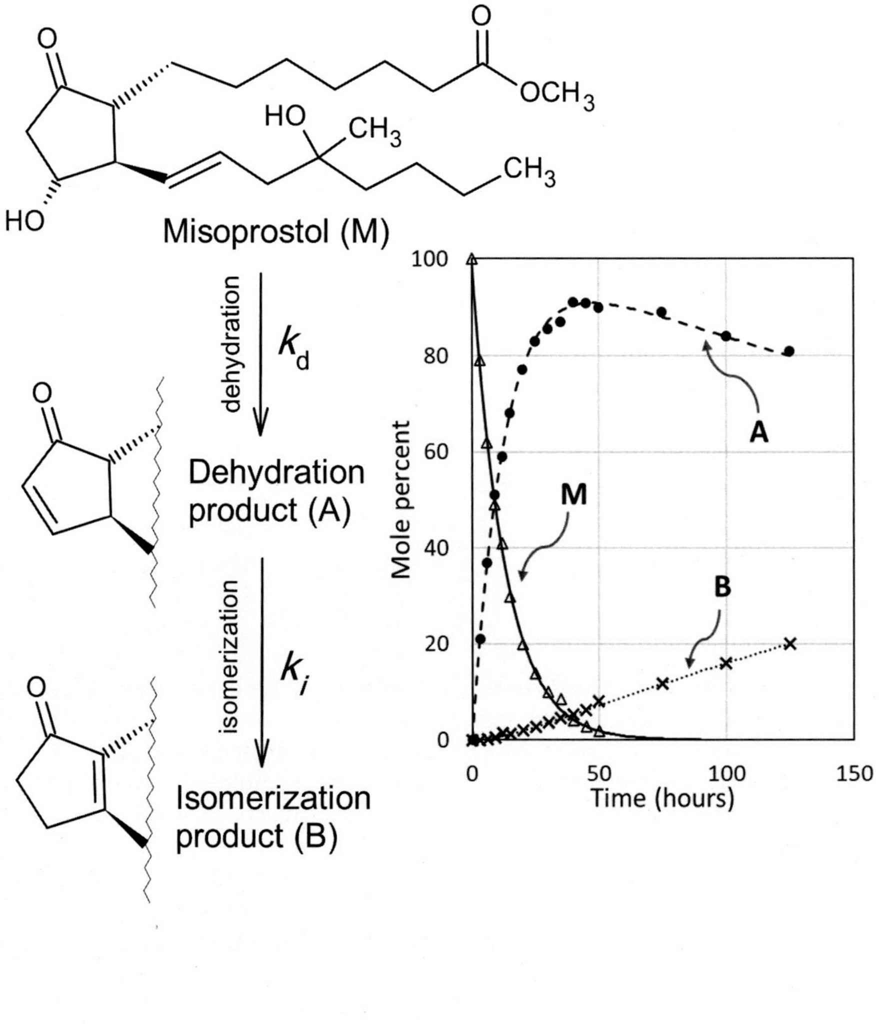

FIGURE 6.7 Consecutive dehydration and isomerization of misoprostol. The graph shows the change in concentration of reactant and product species starting from 100% misoprostol. The plot describes reaction progress starting from a 5.2×10^{-5} M misoprostol solution in a pH 7.66 citrate-phosphate buffer at 60°C. Graph reproduced from Ref. [15] with permission from Elsevier.

Integrating Eq. (6.49) yields an expression describing the change in concentration of A as a function of time.

$$a = \frac{k_d m_0}{k_i - k_d} \left[e^{-k_d t} - e^{-k_i t} \right]$$

(6.50)

The concentration of the final product B can be expressed by a mass balance equation where b is its concentration at any time, t

$$b = m_0 - m - a$$

(6.51)

Substituting expressions for m and a from Eqs. (6.48) and (6.50) yields Eq. (6.52).

$$b = m_0 \left[1 + \left(\frac{1}{k_i - k_d} \right) \left(k_d e^{-k_i t} - k_i e^{-k_d t} \right) \right]$$

(6.52)

Toledo-Velasquez et al. studied the kinetics of this two-step reaction by measuring concentrations of M, A and B over time, starting from solutions of M stored at 60°C [15]. The first-order loss of M was studied by plotting ln (m) versus time to graphically obtain the value of k_d. The value of k_i was obtained by nonlinear regression of the experimental data. As an example, the change in concentrations of M, A and B in a solution starting with 100% M, at pH 7.66, stored at 60°C is shown in Fig. 6.7. The data points in the graph are experimentally determined concentrations of the three species and the lines represent the best fit of Eqs. (6.48), (6.50) and (6.52) to the data. The k_d and k_i values determined under these experimental conditions were 0.079 and 0.002 h^{-1}, respectively. The concentration of M decreases exponentially as it degrades to A. The concentration of A increases as long as $k_d m > k_i a$ (see Eq. (6.49), Fig. 6.7). When its formation becomes slower than its degradation ($k_i a > k_d m$), the concentration of A starts to decline. Knowledge of mechanisms and kinetics of such complex reactions is therefore critical in understanding the evolution of impurity profiles in pharmaceutical compositions.

6.2.9.3 Parallel reactions

Drugs often degrade simultaneously by multiple reaction pathways. The predominant pathway may depend on the reaction conditions. These pathways could include different chemical transformations or different catalytic pathways for the same transformation.

Eq. (6.53) is the degradation scheme for a molecule A, which degrades by parallel first-order pathways, leading to products B and C.

$$B \xleftarrow{k_b} A \xrightarrow{k_c} C$$

(6.53)

The rate of loss of A would therefore be the sum of the rates along both pathways. In Eqs. 6.54, k_b and k_c are the first-order rate constants for formation of B and C, respectively, and k_{obs} is the observed first-order rate constant for overall loss of A.

$$\text{Rate of loss of A} = -\frac{da}{dt} = k_b a + k_c a = (k_b + k_c)a = (k_{obs})a$$

(6.54)

$$\text{Integration yields:} \quad a = a_0 e^{-k_{obs} t} = a_0 e^{-(k_b + k_c)t}$$

(6.55)

$$\text{Rate of formation of B} = \frac{db}{dt} = k_b a = k_b a_0 e^{-k_{obs} t}$$

(6.56)

$$\text{By integration,} \quad b = \frac{k_b a_0}{k_{obs}} \left(1 - e^{-k_{obs} t} \right)$$

(6.57)

$$\text{Similarly,} \quad c = \frac{k_c a_0}{k_{obs}} \left(1 - e^{-k_{obs} t} \right)$$

(6.58)

Eqs. (6.55), (6.57) and (6.58) describe the time course of changes in reactant and product concentrations. From these equations, the following relationships can be derived.

$$\frac{b}{c} = \frac{k_b}{k_c}; \quad \frac{c}{c + b} = \frac{k_c}{k_{obs}}; \quad \frac{b}{c + b} = \frac{k_b}{k_{obs}}$$

(6.59)

Thus, the proportion of each product formed depends on the contribution of the rate constant for that pathway to the overall observed rate constant for reactant loss. The reaction conditions for a drug in a formulation (composition,

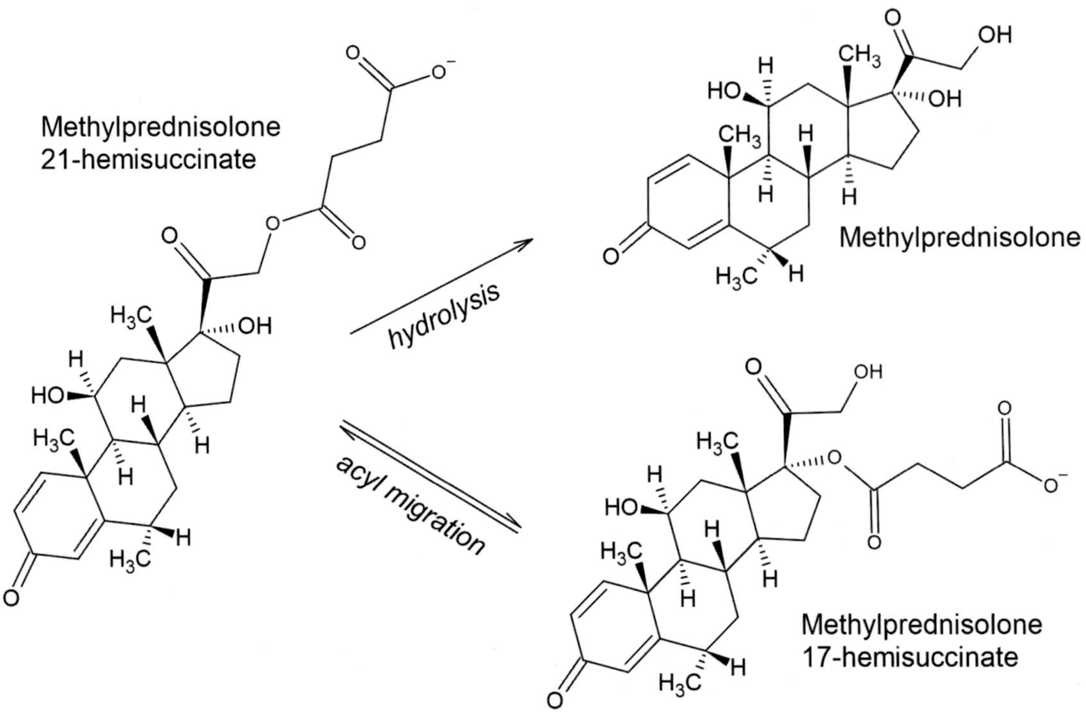

FIGURE 6.8 Parallel reaction pathways for methylprednisolone 21-hemisuccinate—(1) ester hydrolysis to form methylprednisolone and (2) acyl migration to form methylprednisolone 17-hemisuccinate [16].

packaging, and storage conditions) may influence the relative rates of such parallel pathways. During product development, it may be necessary to perform a "balancing act" either to minimize overall degradation, or to control the levels of certain degradants within specified limits.

Methylprednisolone 21-hemisuccinate (MP21S) is a soluble prodrug of methylprednisolone (MP). *In vivo*, ester hydrolysis of MP21S produces its active form, MP. In solution, in addition to hydrolysis, MP21S also underwent a parallel acyl migration reaction (Fig. 6.8). Succinate, esterified to the −OH group on C-21 migrated to the −OH group on C-17, resulting in the formation of methylprednisolone 17-hemisuccinate (MP17S). Anderson and Taphouse investigated the kinetics of these parallel reactions [16]. The authors determined that the acyl migration reaction was reversible, with MP21S being the more stable isomer. Due to rapid hydrolysis of MP21S, a true equilibrium between MP21S and MP17S is not attained. Relative to MP21S, the direct hydrolysis of MP17S (to form MP) appeared to be much slower, likely due to steric hindrance.

6.2.10 Enzyme catalysis and the Michaelis−Menten equation

Catalysts are reagents that increase chemical reaction rates without being consumed in the reaction. Enzymes are proteins that catalyze biochemical reactions, such as those responsible for drug metabolism [17]. The steps involved in an enzymatic reaction are shown in Eq. (6.60). The enzyme (E) interacts *reversibly* with the substrate (S, say a drug molecule), to first form an enzyme-substrate complex (ES) which then leads to the formation of the product (P, say a drug metabolite). In Eq. (6.60), the rate constants for formation and dissociation of ES, and for formation of P from ES, are k_i, k_{ii} and k_{iii}, respectively.

$$E + S \underset{k_{ii}}{\overset{k_i}{\rightleftharpoons}} ES \overset{k_{iii}}{\rightarrow} E + P \tag{6.60}$$

As no enzyme is consumed in the reaction, the total enzyme concentration, $[E_T]$, is the sum of concentrations of free (unbound) enzyme $[E_F]$ and substrate-bound enzyme $[ES]$.

$$[E_T] = [E_F] + [ES] \tag{6.61}$$

Eq. (6.62) is the rate equation describing the changes in ES concentration, where $[S]$ is the substrate concentration.

$$\frac{d[ES]}{dt} = k_i[E_F][S] - k_{ii}[ES] - k_{iii}[ES] \tag{6.62}$$

$$\frac{d[ES]}{dt} = k_i[E_F][S] - (k_{ii} + k_{iii})[ES] \tag{6.63}$$

In order to derive an equation describing the kinetics of the enzymatic process, a *steady-state approximation* is applied. At steady state, the rate of change in ES concentration is negligibly small and rates of formation and consumption of ES are equal. In other words, $d[ES]/dt = 0$ and the steady state concentration of ES, $[ES]_{ss}$, is constant.

Since measurement of concentrations of the ES complex may not be easy, the steady state approximation allows elimination of [ES] from the rate equation, which can then be expressed in terms of measurable quantities such as substrate and product concentrations. Applying the steady state approximation to Eq. (6.63) yields Eqs. (6.64) and (6.65)

$$\frac{d[ES]}{dt} = k_i[E_F][S] - (k_{ii} + k_{iii})[ES]_{ss} = 0 \tag{6.64}$$

$$(k_{ii} + k_{iii})[ES]_{ss} = k_i[E_F][S] \tag{6.65}$$

Substituting $[E_T]—[ES]_{ss}$ for E_F yields Eq. (6.66)

$$\frac{(k_{ii} + k_{iii})[ES]_{ss}}{k_i} = ([E_T] - [ES]_{ss})[S] \tag{6.66}$$

A constant, K_m (the Michaelis—Menten constant), is defined in terms of the three rate constants in Eq. (6.67) and hence is a measure of the tendency of the ES complex to either dissociate back to unbound enzyme and substrate (k_{ii}) or form product (k_{iii}), relative to the tendency to form the ES complex (k_i).

$$K_m = \frac{k_{ii} + k_{iii}}{k_i} \tag{6.67}$$

Combining Eqs. (6.66) and (6.67) yields Eq. (6.68).

$$K_m[ES]_{ss} = ([E_T] - [ES]_{ss})[S] \tag{6.68}$$

Under steady-state conditions, the overall velocity of the reaction (V), the product formation rate, can be expressed as follows.

$$V = \frac{d[P]}{dt} = k_{iii}[ES]_{ss} \tag{6.69}$$

Combining Eqs. (6.68) and (6.69) yields Eq. (6.70).

$$\frac{K_m V}{k_{iii}} = [E_T][S] - \frac{[S]V}{k_{iii}} \tag{6.70}$$

The enzymatic reaction proceeds at maximum velocity (V_{max}) when all the enzyme is complexed with the substrate, $[E_T] = [ES]$. This occurs when the substrate concentration is much higher than the enzyme concentration. Under such conditions, Eq. (6.69) can be written as $V_{max} = k_{iii}[E_T]$. Using this expression for V_{max}, to substitute for k_{iii} in Eq. (6.70) and simplifying provides the Michaelis—Menten equation, which relates the velocity of an enzymatic reaction to the concentration of the substrate (Eq. 6.71).

$$V = \frac{V_{max}[S]}{K_m + [S]} \tag{6.71}$$

Fig. 6.9A includes a V versus [S] plot describing Michaelis—Menten kinetics. From Eq. (6.71) and from the plot, at low substrate concentrations ($[S] \ll K_m$; $(K_m + [S]) \approx K_m$), the reaction velocity is roughly proportional to the substrate concentration and approximates first-order kinetics. At high substrate concentrations, that is, when $[S] \gg K_m$ and $(K_m + [S]) \approx [S]$, the velocity approaches V_{max} and is independent of substrate concentration (zero-order kinetics). Also from Eq. (6.71), when $K_m = [S]$, $V = \frac{1}{2} V_{max}$. Therefore, the Michaelis—Menten concentration represents the substrate concentration at which the reaction proceeds at half of the maximum velocity.

Linear transformations of the Michaelis—Menten equation are used to estimate the kinetic parameters K_m and V_{max}. The Lineweaver—Burke and the Eadie-Hofstee transformations of the Michaelis—Menten equation, derived from Eq. (6.71), are shown in Eqs. (6.72) and (6.73), respectively.

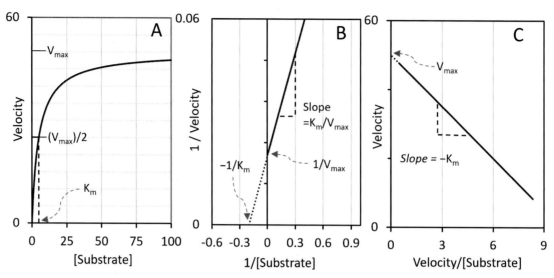

FIGURE 6.9 (A) Reaction velocity versus substrate concentration plot for an enzymatic reaction following Michaelis–Menten kinetics. Linear transformations yield the Lineweaver–Burke (B) or the Eadie–Hofstee plots (C).

$$\frac{1}{V} = \frac{1}{V_{max}} + \frac{K_m}{V_{max}} \frac{1}{[S]} \tag{6.72}$$

$$V = V_{max} - \frac{K_m V}{[S]} \tag{6.73}$$

Fig. 6.9B is the Lineweaver–Burke plot, a double reciprocal plot ($1/V$ vs. $1/[S]$), with a slope of K_m/V_{max} and a y-intercept of $1/V_{max}$. The Eadie–Hofstee plot (Fig. 6.9C; V vs. $V/[S]$) is linear with a slope of $-K_m$ and a y-intercept of V_{max}.

Quintieri et al. studied the oxidative metabolism of diclofenac (substrate), catalyzed by human liver microsomes (HLM) which contain drug metabolizing enzymes including cytochrome P450. HLM (final protein concentration 0.05 mg/mL) were incubated at 37°C, in mixtures containing 50 mM potassium phosphate buffer, pH 7.4, 0.5 mM NADPH (reduced nicotinamide adenine dinucleotide phosphate), and varying concentrations (1–50 mM) of diclofenac. The initial velocity (V) of formation of 4′-hydroxy diclofenac (metabolite) was determined. The data is plotted in Fig. 6.10 as a V versus [S] plot (*left panel*), and the linear Eadie-Hofstee plot (*right panel*). Analysis suggested that a single enzyme, following classical Michaelis–Menten kinetics, catalyzed the 4′-hydroxylation of diclofenac in the concentration range studied. V_{max} and K_m values determined were 3.04 ± 0.27 nmol min^{-1} per mg of protein and 10.07 ± 0.08, respectively [18]. Michaelis–Menten kinetics is also applied to carrier-mediated transport processes of drugs across biological membranes. For example, carried-mediated transport of cefalexin, a cephalosporin antibiotic, into placental brush border plasma membrane vesicles followed Michaelis–Menten kinetics [19].

6.2.11 Reaction kinetics in the solid state

Chemical reaction kinetics described in earlier sections were derived from kinetic behavior in homogeneous liquid and gaseous systems. However in case of solid-state reactions, reaction sites are not homogeneously distributed. In a crystalline solid, for example, the reaction occurs or is initiated at higher energy sites such as crystal defects. Therefore, the kinetic equations developed for homogeneous systems cannot be applied directly to the processes occurring in nonhomogeneous systems.

Pure solids—The kinetics of chemical reactions in pure solids can depend on the reaction mechanism. For example, models describing kinetics can be based on (1) nucleation and growth of the product phase in the solid reactant, (2) contracting geometries of reactant phases, where the reaction is initiated on particle surfaces and the reaction front moves inwards toward the center, or (3) diffusion-controlled reactions, where the reaction rate is governed by the diffusion of reactants into reaction sites. Detailed discussions can be found in Refs. [20,21].

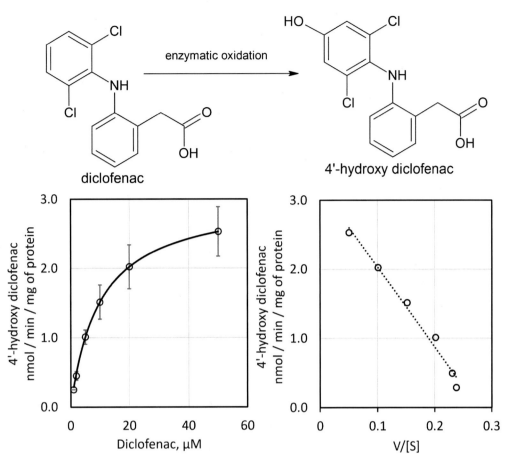

FIGURE 6.10 Enzymatic oxidation of diclofenac. *Left panel*—plot of reaction velocity (formation rate of 4'-hydroxy diclofenac) versus diclofenac concentration. Solid line represents the Michaelis–Menten model fit to the data. *Right panel*: Eadie Hofstee plot of the data. Graphs reproduced from Ref. [18] with permission from Elsevier.

One specific kinetic model, the Prout–Tompkins model, is discussed here. Mechanistically, it is based on initiation of reactions from active nuclei present throughout the solid phase. The model includes an induction time required for generation of an appropriate density of active nuclei. This is followed by reaction propagation through the solid as the reaction accelerates and finally a decay phase as the propagation terminates. This mechanism, therefore, results in reactant amount versus time plots that are sigmoidal. The model is expressed in Eq. (6.74), where a_0 represents the initial amount of reactant, a is the amount remaining at time t, k is the reaction rate constant, and the term C accounts for the induction time.

$$\ln\left[\frac{a}{(a_0 - a)}\right] = k\,t + C \tag{6.74}$$

Stanisz studied the solid-state decomposition of enalapril maleate, an inhibitor of angiotensin-converting enzyme at different temperatures and relative humidity conditions [22]. The reaction progress was followed by chemical analysis, and the Prout–Tompkins model was fit to the data. The reported model parameters (k and C, Eq 6.74) have been used to construct "a versus t" plots in Fig. 6.11. Panel A compares the loss of enalapril at 0% RH and different temperatures and reveals a decrease in induction (lag) times as well as an increase in reaction rates (slope of the propagation phase) with an increase in temperature. When the reaction was conducted at the same temperature (363 K) but at different relative humidity conditions, presence of water was found to shorten lag times and increase reaction rates (Fig. 6.11B).

Solid dosage forms are multicomponent systems containing drug in contact with several excipients. Drug-excipient interactions therefore, introduce additional stability risks. Unit operations such as granulation and tablet compression facilitate intimate contact between components, thereby increasing the likelihood of interactions. Compression may also generate disordered regions with higher free energy and reactivity at the interface of reacting

FIGURE 6.11 Solid-state decomposition of enalapril. (A) Over a temperature range of 363– 383 K and 0% RH and (B) at 363 K and either 0% RH or 76% RH. All plots have been constructed using Prout–Tompkins kinetic parameters reported in Ref. [22].

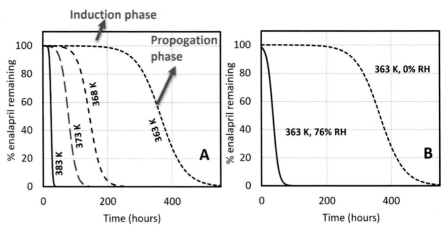

solids. Excipient selection is; therefore, based on compatibility studies, where intimate drug-excipient blends are stored under higher temperature and humidity conditions, and analyzed over time to identify compatible excipients [23]. Chemical degradation in solid dosage forms often exhibit zero- or first-order kinetics, but it may often be difficult to distinguish between the two [20].

6.2.12 Factors affecting reaction kinetics

Previous sections discussed the influence of reactant concentrations on reaction rates. This section considers additional factors such as presence and concentration of reactive or catalytic species, and environmental or medium properties, which influence rate constants.

6.2.12.1 Temperature

Collision Theory—Collisions between reacting molecules enable intermolecular interactions, potentially leading to chemical change. However, not all collisions will result in conversion of reactants to products. The activation energy (E_a) for a reaction is a measure of the minimum energy required for colliding molecules to overcome repulsive forces to interact and form high-energy intermediates (activated states). The activated state leads to product formation. The activation energy; therefore, represents an energy barrier for reacting molecules to convert to products.

The *Arrhenius equation,* relating temperature with reaction rate, is expressed in Eq. (6.75) and, after logarithmic transformation, in Eq. (6.76).

$$k = A\, e^{-E_a/RT} \tag{6.75}$$

$$\log k = \log A - \left(\frac{E_a}{2.303\,R}\right)\frac{1}{T} \tag{6.76}$$

In the Arrhenius equation, k refers to the specific reaction rate (rate constant). R is the universal gas constant ($8.31\ J\,K^{-1}\,mol^{-1}$ or $1.987\ cal\,K^{-1}\,mol^{-1}$), T is the *absolute* temperature, and E_a the activation energy.

The term A, the frequency factor, is a measure of the number of collisions that occur with the proper orientation to react. It includes a collision number Z, which is the rate of collisions and a steric factor P, which is the probability that a collision will lead to a reaction ($A = Z \times P$).

Molecules possess a distribution of velocities and, hence, a distribution of energy levels. The term $e^{(-E_a/RT)}$ in the Arrhenius equation is a measure of the fraction of molecules that possess energy greater than or equal to E_a at temperature T. With an increase in temperature, the fraction of molecules that possess adequate energy increases and; therefore, reaction rate increases.

Thus, reacting species that come together in the right orientation, with adequate energy to overcome the energy barrier, will undergo reaction to yield products. Activation energy determines the impact of temperature change on reaction rate (Eq. 6.76).

Garrett evaluated the stability of active ingredients in multivitamin preparations [24]. The degradation of thiamine HCl in the formulation was monitored at storage temperatures of 40°C–70°C. Fig. 6.12 contains a plot of

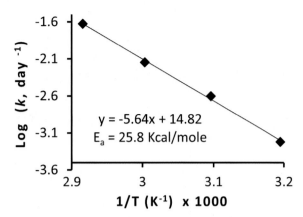

FIGURE 6.12 Log k versus $1/T$ plots for loss of thiamine HCl in a multivitamin preparation. The linear relationship is described by the Arrhenius equation (Eq. 6.76). Graph generated using data reported in Ref. [24].

log k for thiamine HCl degradation versus $1/T$, revealing an increase in reaction rates with temperature (Eq. 6.76). The energy of activation (E_a = 25.8 kcal/mol) was calculated from the slope of the plot (E_a = slope × 2.303R). The value of the frequency factor A obtained from the y-intercept is 6.61×10^{14} day^{-1}. Based on activation energies determined for 166 drug-like molecules with a variety of chemical structures and for a variety of transformations in solution, MacFaul et al. reported a mean E_a value of 23.6 kcal/mol (range of 11.9−47.2 kcal/mol) [25].

Transition state theory—Reacting molecules must interact and first achieve an activated higher-energy state (transition state) before product formation (Fig. 6.13). The reaction scheme for a bimolecular reaction is shown in Eq. (6.77).

$$\underset{\text{Reactants}}{A + B} \rightleftharpoons \underset{\substack{\text{Activated} \\ \text{complex}}}{[A.....B]^{\ddagger}} \rightarrow \underset{\text{Product}}{P} \tag{6.77}$$

If the equilibrium constant for formation of the activated complex is $K^{\ddagger}$, it can be expressed as follows

$$K^{\ddagger} = \frac{[A....B]^{\ddagger}}{[A][B]} \tag{6.78}$$

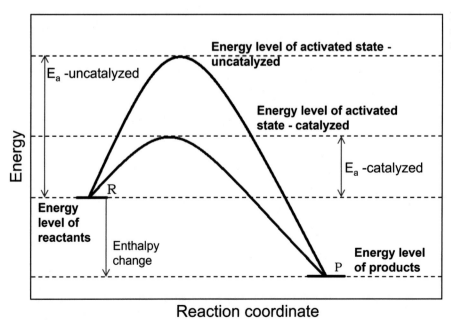

FIGURE 6.13 Reaction coordinate diagram illustrating the energy barrier for conversion of reactants to products and the effect of a catalyst.

The equilibrium constant $K^{\ddagger}$ can also be expressed in terms of the standard free energy of activation ($\Delta G^{\ddagger}$).

$$\Delta G^{\ddagger} = -RT \ln K^{\ddagger} \tag{6.79}$$

$\Delta G^{\ddagger}$ is related to the standard enthalpy ($\Delta H^{\ddagger}$) and entropy ($\Delta S^{\ddagger}$) changes for formation of the activated complex from the reactants, by the relationship $\Delta G^{\ddagger} = \Delta H^{\ddagger} - T\Delta S^{\ddagger}$. Therefore, the equilibrium constant can be expressed as in Eq. (6.80).

$$K^{\ddagger} = e^{-\Delta G^{\ddagger}/RT} = \left(e^{-[\Delta H^{\ddagger} - T\,\Delta S^{\ddagger}]/RT}\right) = \left(e^{-\Delta H^{\ddagger}/RT}\right)\left(e^{\Delta S^{\ddagger}/R}\right) \tag{6.80}$$

Reaction progress is determined by the rate of activated complex breakdown to form product. The reaction rate is expressed in Eq. (6.81), where v is the vibrational frequency of breakdown of the transition state. The term $v = (k_B T/h)$, where k_B and h are the Boltzmann constant and Planck constant, respectively.

$$\text{Reaction rate} = v\,[\text{A....B}]^{\ddagger} = \frac{k_B T}{h}[\text{A....B}]^{\ddagger} \tag{6.81}$$

From Eqs. (6.78), (6.80), and (6.81):

$$\text{Reaction rate} = \frac{k_B T}{h}\left(e^{-\Delta H^{\ddagger}/RT}\right)\left(e^{\Delta S^{\ddagger}/R}\right)[\text{A}][\text{B}] \tag{6.82}$$

Since reaction rate is also equal to $k[\text{A}][\text{B}]$ for the bimolecular reaction, the rate constant k can be expressed as the Eyring equation.

$$k = \left(\frac{k_B T}{h}\,e^{\Delta S^{\ddagger}/R}\right)\left(e^{-\Delta H^{\ddagger}/RT}\right) \tag{6.83}$$

Both Arrhenius and Eyring equations relate reaction rate constant to the absolute temperature. A comparison between the Eyring and Arrhenius equations (Eqs. 6.75 and 6.83), reveals similarity between E_a and $\Delta H^{\ddagger}$ (standard enthalpy of activation). The frequency factor in the Arrhenius equation is analogous to the term $(k_B T/h)\,e^{(\Delta S^{\ddagger}/R)}$. For example, the more ordered the activated complex is, less conformational freedom it would have compared to the reactants and remain uncatalyzed. Similarly, the more negative the entropy change ($\Delta S^{\ddagger}$) is, lower would be the probability of formation of the transition state resulting in lower reaction rate constant.

Catalysis is a phenomenon in which a reagent, the catalyst, interacts with a reactant and reduces the activation energy for the reaction. Consequently, in the presence of a catalyst at a given temperature, a larger fraction of reactant molecules is energetic enough to overcome the reduced energy barrier. This leads to a faster reaction rate. The concentration of the catalyst remains constant since it itself does not undergo any change. Fig. 6.13 contains a reaction coordinate diagram illustrating the energy barrier (E_a) for conversion of reactants to products, which is related to the energy level of the activated state. The figure also illustrates the decrease in E_a in the presence of a catalyst.

6.2.12.2 Solution pH

The influence of solution pH on chemical reactivity in drug solutions has been extensively studied. In particular, hydrolytic reaction rates can exhibit dependence on solution pH, due to catalytic effects of H^+ ions, OH^- ions, and buffer species. The effect of solution pH on reaction kinetics can be complex and is discussed in a stepwise fashion. The term *specific acid/base catalysis* describes the catalytic effect of protons and hydroxide ions. Catalysis by other acidic or basic components, such as buffer salts, is termed as *general acid/base catalysis*.

6.2.12.2.1 Specific acid and base catalysis

If degradation of a drug E occurs along water-catalyzed and specific acid- and base-catalyzed pathways, they can be treated as three parallel reactions (section 6.2.9.3). If the overall loss of drug E in a dilute aqueous solution is described by the first-order rate equation in Eq. (6.84), the observed rate constant, k_{pH}, can be expressed as the sum of contributions from the three pathways, as shown in Eq. (6.85).

$$\text{Rate} = -\frac{d[\text{E}]}{dt} = k_{pH}[\text{E}] \tag{6.84}$$

$$k_{pH} = k_{H_2O} + k_{acid}\left[H^+\right] + k_{base}[OH^-] \tag{6.85}$$

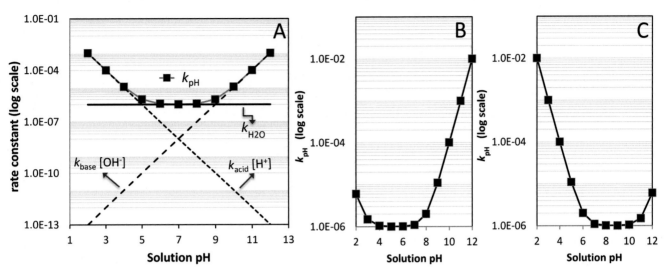

FIGURE 6.14 pH-rate constant profile for a hypothetical reaction exhibiting specific acid and base catalysis. Logarithmic scaling is used for the y-axis. The unit of k_{pH} and k_{H2O} is (time^{-1}) and the unit of k_{acid} and k_{base} is (concentration^{-1} time^{-1}). In all panels, the rate constant for the water-catalyzed pathway, $k_{H2O} = 10^{-6}$. (A) Second-order specific acid- and base-catalyzed rate constants are equal ($k_{acid} = k_{base} = 0.1$). The figure includes contributions of the water-, H$^+$-, and OH$^-$-catalyzed pathways over the pH range of 2–12. The overall rate constant, k_{pH} (Eq. (6.85)), is also plotted. (B) Plot of k_{pH} versus pH; $k_{acid} = 0.0005$; $k_{base} = 1.0$. (C) Plot of k_{pH} versus pH; $k_{acid} = 1.0$; $k_{base} = 0.0005$.

$$\text{Rate} = -\frac{d[E]}{dt} = \left(k_{H_2O} + k_{acid}[H^+] + k_{base}[OH^-]\right)[E] \tag{6.86}$$

The specific acid- and base-catalyzed pathways are second-order processes. The rates of these catalyzed pathways will depend on the concentration of the respective catalysts, that is, H$^+$ or OH$^-$ ions, and hence are *pH-dependent*. The terms k_{acid} and k_{base} are the second-order specific acid- and base-catalyzed rate constants. In buffered systems at constant pH, the terms $k_{acid}[H^+]$ and $k_{base}[OH^-]$ can be considered as the pseudo first-order rate constants for the respective pathways. The term k_{H2O} describes the rate constant associated with the *pH-independent* water-catalyzed pathway. It also represents a pseudo first-order process as the term includes the concentration of water, which is in large excess in a dilute aqueous solution.

Fig. 6.14A contains plots of k_{H2O}, $k_{acid}[H^+]$, and $k_{base}[OH^-]$ as a function of solution pH for a hypothetical reaction with values of $k_{H2O} = 10^{-6}$, $k_{acid} = k_{base} = 0.1$. The unit of k_{pH} and k_{H2O} is (time^{-1}) and the unit of k_{acid} and k_{base} is (concentration^{-1} time^{-1}). Note that a logarithmic scale is used for the y-axis. As seen in Fig. 6.14A, the pH-independent k_{H2O} stays constant, while the values of $k_{acid}[H^+]$ and $k_{base}[OH^-]$ decrease and increase with increasing solution pH. The graph also contains a plot of k_{pH} versus solution pH, calculated using Eq. (6.84). The acid- and base-catalyzed pathways predominate at lower and higher pH values, respectively, and at intermediate pH values (pH 6–8), the water-catalyzed reaction predominates. As seen in Fig. 6.14A, a U-shaped curve results with a flat region of lower overall reaction rates at pH 6–8. The shape of the pH-rate profile and the width of the flat region would depend on the rate of the water-catalyzed process relative to the acid/base-catalyzed pathways. For example, if the water-catalyzed pathway is much slower than acid/base-catalyzed pathways *over the entire pH range* (k_{H2O} is negligible in Eq. 6.84), a V-shaped profile would result.

When the catalytic effects of H$^+$ and OH$^-$ are not of equal magnitude (i.e., $k_{acid} \neq k_{base}$), the pH of maximum stability (i.e. minimum degradation) will shift. In Fig. 6.14B, when $k_{acid} = 5 \times 10^{-4}$ and $k_{base} = 1.0$ ($k_{H2O} = 10^{-6}$), the pH of maximum stability (pH ~ 5–6) is shifted to the acidic side. Similarly, when $k_{acid} >> k_{base}$, the pH of maximum stability is shifted to the alkaline side (see Fig. 6.14 C). For example, the pH-rate constant profile for the hydrolysis of atropine at 20°C revealed maximum stability at pH 4 ($k_{base} > k_{acid}$) [26].

6.2.12.2.2 General acid and base catalysis

The solution pH of pharmaceutical formulations is often controlled with buffers to achieve minimum degradation rates. While the buffer may maintain the desired solution pH, the choice of buffer can be critical since the reaction can be catalyzed by the buffer itself. For example, while the components of phosphate, acetate and borate buffers catalyzed the degradation of ertapenem, a carbapenem antibiotic, bicarbonate buffer did not [27].

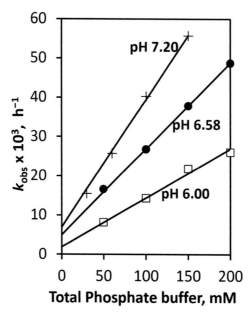

FIGURE 6.15 Effect of phosphate buffer concentration on the pseudo-first-order rate constant (k_{obs}) for degradation of cefadroxil at three solution pH values. Graph reproduced from Ref. [28] with permission from Elsevier.

If a buffer system comprising a monoprotic weak acid HX and its conjugate base X^- is utilized, Eq. (6.86) can be expanded to include terms for buffer catalysis, where k_{HX} and k_{X-} are the general acid- and base-catalyzed rate constants, respectively.

$$k_{obs} = k_{H_2O} + k_{acid}[H^+] + k_{base}[OH^-] + k_{HX}[HX] + k_{X-}[X^-] \tag{6.87}$$

$$k_{obs} = k_{pH} + k_{HX}[HX] + k_{X-}[X^-] \tag{6.88}$$

For a given total buffer concentration (B_T), the concentrations of the conjugate acid and base forms of the buffer depend on the dissociation constant and the solution pH.

$$[HX] = \frac{B_T[H^+]}{[H^+] + K_a^{HX}} \text{ and } [X^-] = \frac{B_T K_a^{HX}}{[H^+] + K_a^{HX}}; \ K_a^{HX} = \text{dissociation constant of HX} \tag{6.89}$$

Combining Eqs. (6.88) and (6.89) gives Eq. (6.90).

$$k_{obs} = k_{pH} + B_T\left(\frac{k_{HX}[H^+] + K_a^{HX} k_{X-}}{[H^+] + K_a^{HX}}\right) \tag{6.90}$$

$$k_{obs} = k_{pH} + k_{Buff} B_T \tag{6.91}$$

The term within brackets in Eq. (6.90) has been replaced by k_{Buff} in Eq. (6.91), which is a measure of the combined catalytic effects of both the buffer species. The rate constant k_{Buff} is a *pH-dependent* constant (see Eq. 6.90), which accounts for the general catalytic rate constants of both the buffer species as well as the ionization extent of the buffer.

Cefadroxil, a cephalosporin antibiotic, undergoes specific and general acid/base catalyzed degradation [28]. Cefadroxil degradation was studied at 35°C, in phosphate-buffered solutions with increasing buffer molarity, at three pH values. The ionic strength was adjusted to 0.5 M and the initial cefadroxil concentration was 5 mM. Each data set in Fig. 6.15 represents, at a given pH, the effect of phosphate buffer concentration (B_T, x-axis) on the observed degradation rate constant (k_{obs}, y-axis). At each pH, the buffer-independent rate constant (k_{pH}) was obtained by extrapolation of the straight-line relationship to zero buffer concentration (y-intercept, Eq. 6.91). The k_{pH} values were 1.5×10^{-3}, 4.5×10^{-3}, and 7.5×10^{-3} h^{-1} at pH 6.00, 6.58 and 7.20, respectively [28].

The k_{obs} value for each data point can be expressed as Eq. (6.92).

$$k_{obs} = k_{pH} + k_{H_2PO_4^-}[H_2PO_4^-] + k_{HPO_4^{2-}}[HPO_4^{2-}] \tag{6.92}$$

The authors determined the values of the phosphate buffer-catalyzed second-order rate constants.

$$k_{H_2PO_4^-} = 6.8 \times 10^{-2} \text{ lit mol}^{-1} \text{ h}^{-1} \tag{6.93}$$

$$k_{HPO_4^{2-}} = 37.8 \times 10^{-2} \text{ lit mol}^{-1} \text{h}^{-1} \tag{6.94}$$

In Fig. 6.15, the slopes of the lines (k_{Buff}, Eq. 6.91) increased with solution pH. With an increase in pH, buffer ionization increases, and the buffer component HPO_4^{2-}, which has the higher catalytic rate constant, is present as a greater fraction of the buffer. Therefore, the influence of phosphate buffer concentration on overall reaction rates is greater at higher pH values.

6.2.12.2.3 Ionization states of the degradant

The effect of solution pH on drug degradation kinetics, due to specific and general acid/base catalysis, has been discussed. Solution pH, by affecting reactant ionization, may further influence reaction rates, if ionized and unionized forms differ in reactivity. At a given solution pH, depending on the catalytic pathways that are relevant, and the reactant forms present, multiple reaction pathways would contribute to the overall rate.

Consider a basic drug D. If $DH^+ \rightleftharpoons D + H^+$ is the dissociation equilibrium, the fractions of deprotonated and protonated forms (f_D and f_{DH+}) in solution are expressed in Eq. (6.95).

$$f_D = \frac{K_a^D}{[H^+] + K_a^D}; \quad f_{DH^+} = \frac{[H^+]}{[H^+] + K_a^D}; \quad K_a^D = \text{Dissociation constant} \tag{6.95}$$

If k_D and k_{DH+} are the first order rate constants for degradation due to reaction of D and DH^+, respectively, the observed first order rate constant for overall drug loss (k_{obs}), is expressed in Eq. (6.96).

$$k_{obs} = k_{DH^+}f_{DH^+} + k_D f_D \tag{6.96}$$

In a buffered solution of D containing a ($HX + X^-$) buffer, if all degradation pathways such as water-, specific, and general acid- and base-catalyzed, are considered, the rate constants can be expressed as follows:

$$k_{DH^+} = k_{H_2O}^{DH^+} + k_{acid}^{DH^+}[H^+] + k_{base}^{DH^+}[OH^-] + k_{HX}^{DH^+}[HX] + k_{X^-}^{DH^+}[X^-] \tag{6.97}$$

$$k_D = k_{H_2O}^D + k_{acid}^D[H^+] + k_{base}^D[OH^-] + k_{HX}^D[HX] + k_{X^-}^D[X^-] \tag{6.98}$$

However, not all the terms in Eqs. (6.97) and (6.98) may be relevant. For example, at a pH where the drug is almost completely protonated, the rate constant terms for the deprotonated form would not be relevant. Similarly, in the absence of buffer catalysis, all buffer terms can be ignored. It is likely that ionization in one part of a molecule may not influence reactivity in another part. In such instances, the reaction of unionized and ionized forms may proceed at the same rate. When there are measurable differences in the reactivity of the unionized and ionized forms, it may be seen as an inflection in the pH-rate constant profile at the corresponding pK_a.

Cefadroxil is amphoteric and can exist in four different ionization states, a cation (AH_3^+), a zwitterion ($AH_2^{\pm}$), an anion (AH^-), and a dianion (A^{2-}). Since buffer catalysis was observed, the authors determined the buffer-independent rate constants (k_{pH}) across the pH range [28]. The overall buffer-independent, pH- rate constant profile could be described using terms corresponding to (1) water-catalyzed degradation of AH_3^+ and $AH_2^{\pm}$, (2) water-catalyzed degradation of AH^- and A^{2-}, and (3) specific base-catalyzed degradation of AH^- and A^{2-} [28].

For solution formulations, the knowledge of the pH range of maximum drug stability and compatible buffers, helps in defining critical formulation variables. In solid dosage forms, acidic or basic excipients have been used to enhance stability. It is suggested that these excipients influence the pH of sorbed water on solid surfaces, thereby providing environments conducive to chemical stability [29].

6.2.12.3 Ionic strength

Our discussions so far have assumed dilute aqueous solutions and ideal behavior, where activity coefficients are assumed to be equal to one. Properties of systems and processes, such as pH, reaction rates and equilibrium constants, have been expressed in terms of *concentrations* of components. However, most systems of practical interest are nonideal and rate equations and equilibrium expressions need to be written in terms of *activities*. Activity is related to concentration by the activity coefficient which is a measure of deviation from ideality.

$$\text{Activity } (a) = \text{concentration } (c) \times \text{activity coefficient } (\gamma) \tag{6.99}$$

Activity accounts not only for the quantity of the species but also for intermolecular interactions and hence is a measure of the "effective concentration." Medium properties that affect the activity coefficients of reacting species will therefore influence reaction kinetics.

Electrolytes are often added to solution formulations, as buffers to maintain solution pH or as salts to adjust osmolality. In addition, ionizable drugs can furnish ions in solution. The ionic strength of a solution, μ, can be calculated using Eq. (6.100), where m is the molar concentration and Z is the charge of each ionic species.

$$\mu = 0.5 \sum \left(mZ^2\right) = 0.5 \left(m_A Z_A^2 + m_B Z_B^2 \ldots \ldots \ldots \right) \tag{6.100}$$

Due to electrostatic effects, ionic strength influences the activity coefficients of ions. An expression describing this effect for *aqueous* solutions is the modified Debye-Hückel equation (Eq 6.101), where γ_i and Z_i are the activity coefficient and charge of the ion.

$$\log \gamma_i = -\left(\frac{0.509\, Z_i^2 \sqrt{\mu}}{1 + \sqrt{\mu}}\right) \tag{6.101}$$

At zero ionic strength, the ionic activity coefficient is one, and it decreases with an increase in ionic strength. Ionic strength affects reaction rates by influencing activity coefficients of reacting ions. This influence, called the primary kinetic salt effect, is described by the modified Brønsted–Bjerrum equation, valid up to an ionic strength of ~ 0.1 M (Eq. 6.102).

$$\log k_\mu = \log k_0 + A\, Z_1 Z_2 \left(\frac{\sqrt{\mu}}{1 + \sqrt{\mu}}\right) \tag{6.102}$$

Z_1 and Z_2 are the charges on the two interacting species, k_μ is the rate constant at an ionic strength of μ, and k_0 is the rate constant at zero ionic strength (in an infinitely dilute solution). In Eq. (6.102), the constant A depends on the dielectric constant, density, and temperature of the medium and is equal to 1.018 for dilute aqueous solutions at 298 K.

If the reacting ions have the same charge, $Z_1 Z_2$ is positive, and the reaction rate increases with μ. When at least one reacting species is neutral, $Z_1 Z_2 = 0$ and the reaction rate is independent of μ. If the reaction occurs between oppositely charged ions, $Z_1 Z_2$ is negative, and the reaction rate decreases with increase in μ.

Although Eq. (6.102), as such, is strictly valid at $\mu \leq 0.1$ M, studies have demonstrated its applicability even at $\mu > 0.5$ M [30]. The degradation rate for cefotaxime was studied in 0.2 M borate buffer at pH 9.5. At this pH, the anionic form of the drug predominated and specific base catalysis and catalysis by the borate anion $H_2BO_3^-$ were the primary reaction pathways (reactions between similarly charged ions). The reaction rates increased with an increase in ionic strength (Fig. 6.16). At pH 2.2 and 6.0, however, where the water-catalyzed reaction predominated (neutral reactant), ionic strength did not influence reaction rate [31].

By influencing ionic activity coefficients, ionic strength affects dissociation constants of weak acids and bases. At ionic strengths of up to 0.3 M, the influence of μ on dissociation constants in *aqueous solution* can be expressed by a generalized equation.

$$pK_a^\mu = pK_a^0 + \left(\frac{0.51\,(2Z - 1)\,\sqrt{\mu}}{1 + \sqrt{\mu}}\right) \tag{6.103}$$

In Eq. (6.103), K_a^μ is the *apparent dissociation constant* at an ionic strength of μ, K_a^0 is the thermodynamic dissociation constant at $\mu = 0$, and Z is the charge on the *conjugate acid*. For example, for a weak acid HA, where $Z = 0$, $pK_a^\mu < pK_a^0$. In general, an increase in ionic strength will favor the formation of ionized species.

If ionized and unionized forms of a drug exhibit different reactivities, ionic strength can thus affect overall degradation rates. Similarly, by influencing the apparent pK_a values of buffers, ionic strength changes can affect pH and hence rates of acid/base-catalyzed reactions. This influence of electrolytes on reaction rates by changing concentrations of reactive species is the secondary kinetic salt effect (Case study 6.3).

6.2.12.4 Dielectric constant

Nonaqueous cosolvents are often used to enhance drug solubility. While the presence of the drug in solution itself may be detrimental to chemical stability (relative to solid drug), the solvent used will also alter medium properties. The ability of a medium to facilitate interaction of reactants and formation of transition states will influence reaction rates. For example, (1) reactions that involve formation of a charged transition state from neutral molecules and (2)

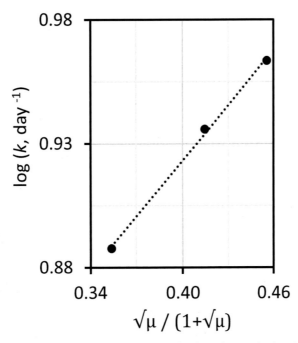

FIGURE 6.16 The effect of ionic strength on the first order rate constant for degradation of cefotaxime in 0.2 M borate buffer, pH 9.5 (ionic strength of 0.3, 0.5, and 0.7 M). Graph plotted using data in Ref. [31].

reactions between similarly charged species, are favored in media with higher dielectric constants. On the other hand, reactions between oppositely charged ions are faster in media with lower dielectric constants.

The rate of ampicillin degradation in 0.08N HCl in water-ethanol mixtures was evaluated as a function of ethanol concentration. In the acidic solution, the reaction mechanism was proposed to involve specific acid catalysis of protonated ampicillin. The cation−cation reaction forming a di-cation activated complex is favored in media of higher dielectric constant. Therefore, the reaction rate decreased with an increase in the ethanol content of the medium [32].

The degradation kinetics of lomustine, an antineoplastic agent, was studied in formate buffer (pH 2.52) in water-dioxane mixtures [33]. The degradation proceeds via an uncatalyzed unimolecular step forming a charged intermediate. A decrease in dielectric constant with increase in dioxane content decreased reaction rates (Fig. 6.17).

6.2.12.5 Water

Water is a major component of liquid and semisolid preparations. For drugs sensitive to water (such as those susceptible to hydrolysis), formulation design requires an understanding of the effect of pH, buffers, ionic strength, and cosolvents, among other factors, on degradation rates. For drugs that are highly unstable in presence of water, nonaqueous formulations or freeze-dried products can be viable design approaches.

Solid dosage forms, due to their lower water content, may be less susceptible to degradation mediated by water. Water is introduced into solid formulations through raw materials, during manufacturing, or from the environment. Hygroscopic components increase water uptake by the formulation. Water can influence chemical reactivity as a reactant or as a reaction medium. When the amount of water adsorbed on solid surfaces is adequate for dissolution of surface molecules, chemical reactions can occur in the solution phase. Water can also plasticize amorphous phases in solid formulations, increasing molecular mobility and reactivity [34].

For water-sensitive drugs, manufacturing operations that avoid water may be preferred. Approaches such as protective tablet coatings, protective packaging, and use of desiccants may be employed to enhance stability.

6.2.12.6 Light

Photolabile compounds, when exposed to light, absorb certain frequencies and sufficient energy to get activated. Activation may lead to photochemical reactions. Photochemical oxidation and reduction reactions are common and reaction mechanisms are often multistep and complex. Protection of photo-labile drugs from light may be required during manufacturing and product storage.

FIGURE 6.17 *Left*: Proposed mechanism of lomustine degradation. *Right*: Effect of medium dielectric constant on the observed first-order rate constant at 50°C. The medium contained lomustine at an initial concentration of 8.6×10^{-5} M in water-dioxane mixtures with formate buffer (0%–30% dioxane; dielectric constant 69.6–45.3, 50°C). Graph plotted using data obtained from Ref. [33]. Note. Dioxane was employed to understand the reaction mechanism and it is not an excipient used in pharmaceutical formulations.

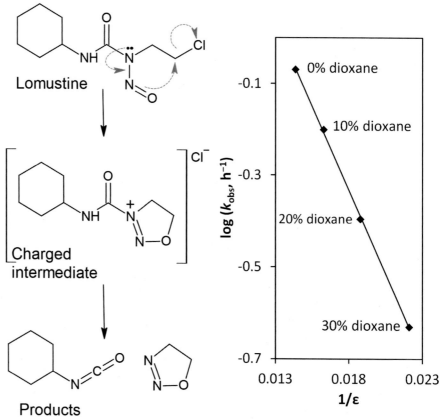

The degradation of β-lapachone, an antineoplastic agent, was studied in solution at 40°C either (1) protected from light or (2) exposed to light from white fluorescent and UV lamps. The drug showed different degradation pathways—primarily hydrolysis when protected from light and photolysis when exposed to light. The rate of drug loss and the main degradation products are compared in Fig. 6.18 [35]. Both pathways exhibited pseudo-first-order kinetics. Under the conditions employed, photolysis was rapid ($k = 0.28$ day^{-1}) with the orange-colored drug solution turning colorless. When protected from light, hydrolysis proceeded with formation of a red-colored solution ($k = 2.1 \times 10^{-3}$ day^{-1}).

6.2.12.7 Oxidizing agents

For drugs susceptible to oxidation, access for atmospheric oxygen to the product is detrimental to stability. Minimizing dissolved oxygen during solution manufacturing, reducing headspace oxygen levels in the packed product and protective packaging can be employed as strategies to enhance stability.

Oxidation reactions can occur by (1) uncatalyzed auto-oxidation with molecular oxygen, or (2) by free radical-initiated chain reactions with initiation, propagation, and termination steps [36]. Free radicals generated by the action of light, heat, or transition metal impurities, can initiate the chain process. Stabilization strategies may include (1) initiation inhibitors such as chelating agents to sequester metal-ion initiators (example—EDTA and citric acid); (2) protection against a part of the UV–visible spectrum by using amber-colored containers; (3) chain-breakers such as butylated hydroxy toluene and alpha-tocopherol, which react with free radicals to form less-reactive species; and (4) reducing agents or oxygen scavengers such as sodium metabisulfite and ascorbic acid [36].

The oxidation kinetics of ethyl eicosapentaenoate (EPA ethyl ester), an omega-3 polyunsaturated fatty acid ester, was studied [37]. The reaction progress was described by consecutive reaction kinetics with an initial induction period (Eq. 6.104). During the induction step, the concentration of initiator radicals reaches a minimum required concentration. This is followed by the formation of peroxides which further degrade to yield secondary products. Lovaza capsules (omega-3-acid ethyl esters) include α—tocopherol as an antioxidant, which inhibits propagation of free radical intermediates [38].

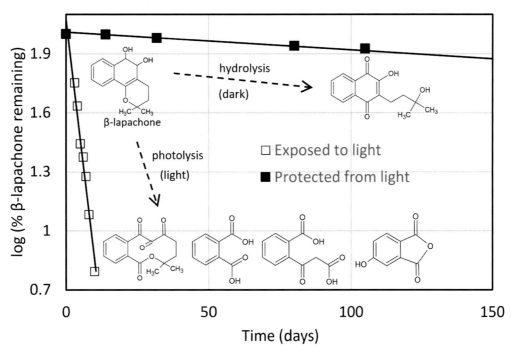

FIGURE 6.18 First-order degradation of β-lapachone in an aqueous solution (30 μg/mL) at 40°C, either (1) protected from light or (2) exposed to light from white fluorescent and UV lamps (370 nm). The degradation rate was faster in samples exposed to light and the degradation products were different. Graph plotted using data tabulated in Ref. [35].

$$\begin{bmatrix} \text{EPA} \xrightarrow[\text{formation}]{\text{Initiator radical}} \text{EPA}^* \end{bmatrix} \xrightarrow{k'} \text{Peroxide} \xrightarrow{k''} \begin{array}{l} \text{Secondary products} \\ (\text{Acids, aldehydes}) \end{array} \tag{6.104}$$

6.2.13 Stability evaluation and assignment of shelf-life

Pharmaceutical products are assigned a shelf-life, during which they retain their identity, safety, and efficacy by staying within established quality specifications. During early product development stage, *stress testing* of drug substances or drug products is conducted under harsh conditions to forcibly cause degradation. This enables identification of degradation pathways and products, and validation of stability-indicating analytical methods. Stability studies are routinely conducted for drug products to guide formulation development. When carried out under normal storage conditions, these studies can often take a long time to provide meaningful and useful data. To expedite the process of defining stable compositions and manufacturing processes, accelerated stability studies are employed. The drug product is exposed to "exaggerated" conditions of temperature and humidity to accelerate physical and chemical changes. For example, for a proposed shelf-life storage at controlled room temperature, 40°C/75% RH (accelerated), 30°C/65% RH (intermediate) and 25°C/60% RH (long term) conditions may be employed.

Drug degradation data, collected over time, can be used to assess reaction order, and determine rate constants. If data is generated at multiple temperatures, a plot of log k versus $1/T$ (Arrhenius plot, Eq. (6.105)) enables calculation of activation energy (Fig. 6.12).

$$\log k = \log A - \left(\frac{E_a}{2.303\,R}\right)\frac{1}{T} \tag{6.105}$$

Using the Arrhenius equation and a known activation energy allows prediction of rate constants at lower temperatures, using data from higher temperature experiments (Eq. 6.106, where k' and k'' are rate constants at temperatures T' and T'', respectively, see Case study 6.4).

$$\log \frac{k''}{k'} = \frac{E_a \left(T'' - T' \right)}{2.303 \ R \ T'' T'} \tag{6.106}$$

For a first-order reaction, $k = 0.105/t_{0.9}$ (Eq. 6.20). Substituting this relationship in Eq. (6.106), provides a relationship between shelf-life and temperature, where $t_{0.9}'$ and $t_{0.9}''$ are shelf-lives at temperatures T' and T'', respectively (Eq. 6.107, Case study 6.4).

$$\log \frac{(t_{0.9})'}{(t_{0.9})''} = \frac{E_a \left(T'' - T' \right)}{2.303 \ R \ T'' T'} \tag{6.107}$$

In early drug development process, it is useful to determine the factor ($Q_{\Delta T}$), by which the shelf life would change with a given change in temperature (say from T to T-ΔT). An expression for $Q_{\Delta T}$ can be derived from Eq. (6.107).

$$Q_{\Delta T} = \frac{(t_{0.9})_{T-\Delta T}}{(t_{0.9})_T} = 10^{\left(\frac{E_a (\Delta T)}{2.303R \ T \ (T-\Delta T)} \right)} \tag{6.108}$$

Knowing the activation energy thus, allows prediction of shelf-life (Eq 6.108) at a lower temperature ($T-\Delta T$), using shelf life determined under an accelerated condition (T). For example, for $E_a = 10$ kcal/mol, the shelf life of a drug solution at 25°C would be 2.25 times longer than that determined at 40°C. It would be 5.05 times longer if $E_a = 20$ kcal/mol.

Although rates of chemical reactions decrease with decreasing temperatures, storage at lower temperatures may not always be an option. For example, a solution product stored at lower temperature may result in drug precipitation, if the solubility at that temperature is exceeded in the formulation. Suspension and emulsion products may be physically destabilized on freezing. When protein solutions are frozen, solutes are concentrated due to ice crystallization, ice-solution interfaces are formed, and pH shifts can occur due to buffer salt crystallization. These changes can result in freezing-induced denaturation and aggregation of proteins [39]. Guidance on stability considerations in dispensing practice is included in USP Chapter 1191 [40].

Accelerated stability studies may have limited predictive utility for formulations that exhibit physical transitions under accelerated conditions (for example, melting, glass transitions, crystallization, and polymorphic transformations). In such cases, there might be a discontinuity in the Arrhenius relationship between reaction rate and temperature. In addition, higher temperature can (1) decrease solubility of reactive species like oxygen, (2) affect solution pH and (3) influence relatively humidity in the headspace of sealed containers. These factors can influence reaction rates at elevated temperatures and result in non-Arrhenius behavior [42].

Higher temperature data should therefore be used with a thorough understanding of additional factors that might influence reaction rates. For example, in drug suspensions, higher temperature storage can result in increased drug concentration in the continuous phase. For a pseudo-zero-order reaction in the suspension, and a first-order reaction in the solution phase, the rate equation is expressed in Eq. (6.109), where C_s is the concentration of the drug in the continuous phase (equal to its saturation solubility).

$$\frac{da}{dt} = k_0 t = k_1 C_s t; \quad k_0 = k_1 C_s \tag{6.109}$$

The effect of temperature on reaction rate would therefore include effects on the first-order rate constant k_1 and on solubility, C_s. If the value of k_0 at different temperatures is available from suspension stability studies and the drug solubility in the vehicle is also known at the same temperatures, values of k_1 can be calculated using Eq. (6.110). E_a for the reaction can be determined from $\log k_1$ versus $1/T$ plots and used for stability predictions at temperatures of interest.

Product shelf-life is defined for a prescribed storage condition. A drug product may experience excursions in temperature outside the prescribed ranges, for example during shipping, storage and in pharmacies and hospitals. A mean kinetic temperature (MKT) can be calculated with the knowledge of a product's time-temperature history. It is a single calculated "effective" temperature, at which the extent of degradation over a given time period would be the same as the sum of the degradation extents due to a given thermal history, over that time period. If the temperature is recorded for a product at "n" *equal* intervals as T_1, T_2 .... T_n, MKT can be expressed as in Eq. (6.110).

$$\text{MKT} = \cfrac{E_a/R}{-\ln\left[\cfrac{e^{(-E_a/RT_1)} + e^{(-E_a/RT_2)} + \ldots\ldots\ldots + e^{(-E_a/RT_n)}}{n}\right]} \tag{6.110}$$

For example, the USP defines controlled room temperature as the temperature maintained at 20°C−25°C, with excursions permitted between 15°C and 30°C and transient spikes up to 40°C (only if the manufacturer instructs and as long as they do not exceed 24 h), all provided the MKT does not exceed 25°C [41].

6.3 Mass transport processes

In the previous section, chemical-change processes were discussed, focusing mostly on degradation in pharmaceuticals. These chemical changes were classified based on reaction mechanisms and kinetics, and factors influencing process rates were examined. "Speeding up" of such changes to facilitate drug product development (accelerated stability testing) and approaches to slow down undesirable changes (stabilization of drug products) were discussed.

This section deals with mass transport including molecular diffusion across membranes, drug dissolution, and release of drug from controlled-release formulations.

6.3.1 Diffusion

Diffusion is the transport of individual molecules on a microscopic scale, as a result of random molecular motions. Diffusion is related to a *driving force*, such as differences in activity (concentration), pressure or electrical potential, which determines the direction of transport. Examples of diffusion processes relevant to pharmaceutics include (1) transport of drug molecules across biological membranes during absorption and disposition processes, (2) diffusion of reactive gaseous molecules such as oxygen and water vapor through packaging components, (3) dissolution of solid drug (4) drug release from delivery systems and (5) pharmaceutical unit operations such as drying.

6.3.1.1 Fick's first law of diffusion

Fig. 6.19A is a schematic representation of a barrier of thickness *x*, separating compartments with different concentrations of a molecule (the diffusant), which provides the driving force for diffusion. Fick's first law of diffusion describes the relationship between the driving force and the resulting mass transfer rate across a barrier. Flux (*J*) is

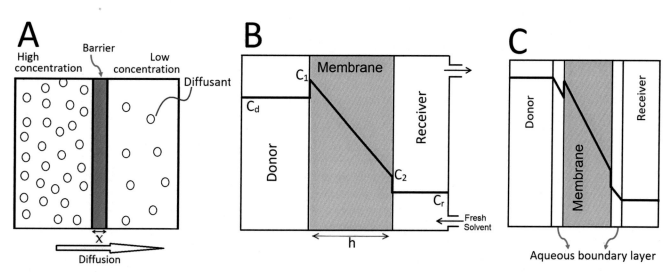

FIGURE 6.19 A) Schematic of diffusional transport across a barrier membrane. (B) Diffusion across a membrane (thickness *h*) from donor to receiver compartments with diffusant concentrations of C_d and C_r, respectively ($C_d > C_r$). The concentrations *in* the membrane at the donor interface and the receiver interface are C_1 and C_2, respectively. (C) Schematic representation of aqueous boundary layers at the membrane-medium interfaces, depicting concentration gradients in the unstirred diffusion layers and in the barrier membrane.

defined as the mass of material (M) moving across unit cross-sectional area of a barrier in unit time, that is, the mass transfer rate (dM/dt), normalized to barrier surface area S. Flux has units of (mass area^{-1} time^{-1}).

$$\text{Flux} = J = \frac{1}{S}\frac{dM}{dt} \tag{6.111}$$

Flux is proportional to the driving force (concentration gradient, dC/dx), which is responsible for transport. The expression for Fick's first law is given in Eq. (6.112).

$$J = -D\frac{dC}{dx} \tag{6.112}$$

D is the *diffusion coefficient* or *diffusivity* of the molecules undergoing transport through the barrier and has units of (area time^{-1}). The diffusion coefficient is directly proportional to absolute temperature and inversely related to the diffusant size and barrier medium viscosity. The negative sign in Eq. (6.112) signifies that the mass transfer occurs down the concentration gradient. When the concentrations are equalized by diffusion, the gradient disappears, and there is no further net transport.

6.3.1.2 Fick's second law of diffusion

Fick's second law deals with changes in concentration of the diffusant, in a given region of the barrier during the diffusion process, as a function of time. Consider a particular volume unit of the barrier. The change in *concentration* (C) of the diffusant in that region *with time* is related to the rate of mass transport into and out of the region, that is, the change in flux (J) of the material as a *function of distance* (x), along the direction of diffusion. Since both concentration and flux are functions of time and distance, this relationship is expressed using partial derivatives.

$$\frac{\partial C}{\partial t} = -\frac{\partial J}{\partial x} \tag{6.113}$$

Differentiating the first law equation (Eq. 6.112) with respect to x (distance), gives Eq. (6.114).

$$\frac{\partial J}{\partial x} = -D\frac{\partial[\partial C/\partial x]}{\partial x} = -D\frac{\partial^2 C}{\partial x^2} \tag{6.114}$$

Eqs. (6.113) and (6.114) provide the expression for Fick's second law of diffusion (Eq. 6.115).

$$\frac{\partial C}{\partial t} = D\frac{\partial^2 C}{\partial x^2} \tag{6.115}$$

In a given region of the barrier, the rate of concentration change due to diffusion is directly proportional to the change in the concentration gradient as a function of distance (second derivative of concentration with distance). The proportionality constant is the diffusion coefficient, D.

6.3.1.3 Diffusion across membranes—permeability and resistance

Consider a thin membrane of thickness h separating (1) a donor compartment containing a solution with a higher diffusant concentration (C_d) from (2) a receiver compartment initially containing pure solvent (Fig. 6.19B). The concentration difference will drive diffusion across the membrane. In the receiver compartment, there is a constant inflow of fresh solvent and outflow of the receiver compartment fluid, which keeps the diffusant concentration (C_r) low. This is referred to as a sink condition.

With time, the membrane equilibrates with the donor and receiver media. Let us assume a quasi-stationary state where the concentration gradient *within the membrane* from the donor side (concentration C_1) to the receiver side (concentration C_2) is constant. This state assumes a constant concentration in the donor and the receiver compartments. Under these conditions, (1) the concentration of diffusant *at a given location* in the membrane is constant ($\partial C/\partial t = 0$), (2) by Fick's second law the concentration gradient is constant through the thickness of the film ($\partial^2 C/\partial x^2 = 0$; $\partial C/\partial x$ = constant) and (3) the concentration of the diffusant (C) within the membrane increases linearly with distance from the receiver side to the donor side (Fig. 6.19B). Under these conditions, the concentration gradient can be approximated as [$C_2 - C_1/h$]. Therefore, the first law of diffusion can be written as follows.

$$J = -D\frac{dC}{dx} = -D\frac{(C_2 - C_1)}{h} = D\frac{(C_1 - C_2)}{h} \tag{6.116}$$

In Fig. 6.15, concentrations C_1 and C_2 have been shown as being higher than C_d and C_r, respectively. This is accounted for by the membrane/medium partition coefficient K having a value greater than unity, implying that the diffusant has higher affinity for the membrane compared to the solvent.

$$K = \frac{C_1}{C_d} = \frac{C_2}{C_r}; \quad KC_d = C_1 \text{ and } KC_r = C_2 \tag{6.117}$$

From Eqs. (6.111), (6.116) and (6.117):

$$J = \frac{1}{S}\frac{dM}{dt} = \frac{DK}{h}(C_d - C_r) \tag{6.118}$$

The term DK/h is the *permeability* (P) of the barrier for the diffusant. Permeability is a measure of the ability of the diffusant to partition into the membrane and diffuse through it. The reciprocal of the permeability (h/DK) is the diffusional resistance. Permeability has units of (distance time^{-1}). Eq. (6.118) can be written as follows.

$$\frac{dM}{dt} = \frac{DSK}{h}(C_d - C_r) = PS(C_d - C_r); \quad \text{where } P = \frac{DK}{h} \tag{6.119}$$

If the receiver compartment can be maintained as a perfect sink, $C_r \approx 0$, diffusional transport rate can be expressed as in Eq. (6.120).

$$\frac{dM}{dt} = \frac{DSKC_d}{h} = P(S\,C_d) \tag{6.120}$$

The permeability of biological membranes to drug molecules determines the ability of the drug to reach target sites and exert pharmacological effects. Therefore, permeability characterization of drug candidates is critical in assessing challenges and determining strategies for drug delivery. Permeability assays for drug molecules may utilize cell monolayers separating donor and receiver chambers. Drug transport is assessed by adding drug to the donor and analyzing the rate of its appearance in the receiver.

Intestinal permeability. Permeability of the intestinal barrier to a drug molecule determines drug absorption after oral administration. As per the Biopharmaceutics Classification System, high intestinal permeability can be concluded when >85% of the administered dose is absorbed [43]. Permeability assays employing cultured Caco-2 epithelial cell monolayers derived from a human colon adenocarcinoma cell line are widely used to estimate intestinal drug absorption in humans. These cells have characteristics that resemble intestinal epithelial cells and form polarized monolayers with well-defined brush border on the apical surface, intercellular tight junctions, and active transporters, as in the small intestine. For example, permeability values of 3, 21 and 338 mm/s were measured across a Caco-2 monolayer for doxorubicin, ranitidine and naproxen which exhibit oral absorption in humans of ~5%, 50% and 100% respectively [44]. Additional controls, and careful interpretation of *in-vitro* data is required to account for different transport mechanisms and experimental variables.

Similarly, *in vitro* skin permeation testing for topical and transdermal products may use human skin in a diffusion cell apparatus to assess (1) delivery of drug to various layers of skin and (2) percutaneous absorption of topically administered drug [45].

6.3.1.4 Multilayer diffusion

A membrane, in contact with aqueous fluids has a static (unstirred) aqueous layer at the interface called the aqueous boundary layer (ABL). The previous section, as a first step to describe diffusion through a membrane, ignored these static layers (Fig. 6.19B). The membrane, sandwiched between these ABLs on both sides, represents a multi-layered barrier to diffusional transport (Fig. 6.19C). *Net* transport of molecules would involve (1) diffusion across the ABL on the donor side, (2) partition into and diffusion across the membrane, (3) partition into and diffusion across the ABL on the receiver side, into the bulk receiver medium. Such multilayer diffusion can be encountered in several systems, for example, (1) drug molecules sequentially diffusing through lipophilic (stratum corneum) and hydrophilic layers in skin, and (2) water vapor diffusing through multiple layers of laminated packaging materials. (3) diffusion of drug molecules across the ABL on the intestinal membrane, prior to permeation through the intestinal barrier.

For multiple layers in series, the permeability across *each* layer i (P_i), can be represented as $P_i = D_i K_i/h_i$, where K_i is the partition coefficient of a barrier phase relative to the initial external phase; h_i is the thickness of the barrier layer; and D_i is the diffusivity in the layer. The resistance of each layer to diffusion, R_i, is the reciprocal of the permeability of that layer. The total resistance of multiple layers in series is the sum of the resistance of each layer [46].

$$R_i = \frac{1}{P_i} = \frac{h_i}{D_i K_i} \tag{6.121}$$

$$R \text{ (n layers)} = \frac{h_1}{D_1 K_1} + \frac{h_2}{D_2 K_2} \text{................} \frac{h_n}{D_n K_n} \tag{6.122}$$

If one of the layers introduces a much higher resistance to permeation than all other layers, it acts as the "flux-determining" layer.

For a two-layer diffusion system, the overall permeability, for example, can be described by Eq. (6.123).

$$P = \frac{D_1 K_1 D_2 K_2}{h_1 D_2 K_2 + h_2 D_1 K_1} \tag{6.123}$$

6.3.1.5 Gas diffusion

Gas diffusion involves random molecular movement of gaseous molecules, causing net transport from areas of high partial pressure to areas of low partial pressure. For example, water vapor can diffuse from the external environment at higher relative humidity into product containers through packaging materials. This can adversely affect the stability of products susceptible to hydrolytic degradation or to water-induced physical changes.

Moisture Vapor Transmission Rate (MVTR): The steady-state water permeation rate through a packaging system under specified conditions of temperature and humidity is termed as the MVTR. Determination of MVTR can employ (1) sealed desiccant-filled containers (bottles or blister cavities, internal RH = 0%) stored at 40°C/75% RH and weighed at intervals to measure rate of net water ingress or (2) sealed water-filled containers (internal RH = 100%), stored at 40°C/25% RH, and weighed at intervals to measure net water loss from the container. In both methods, the driving force for diffusion is a ΔRH of 75% at 40°C [47].

The MVTR values determined for blister packs are expressed as the water transmission rate per blister cavity, which in the final product, would contain a single dosage unit (tablet or capsule). Based on MVTR values, blister packs are classified as (1) low barrier blister, MVTR >1.0 mg/cavity per day, example - thermoformed PVC blisters sealed with foil, (2) high barrier blisters, MVTR <1.0 mg/cavity per day, example -thermoformed PCTFE (polychlorotrifluoroethylene) blister, sealed with foil and (3) ultra-high barrier blister, MVTR <0.01 mg/cavity per day, example-cold-formed foil blister, sealed with foil.

Similarly, MVTR determined for multi-unit packaging systems, (say, high density polyethylene, HDPE, bottles) can be normalized for the number of dosage units in the container. This allows comparison of the moisture protection provided in different packaging configurations (Case Study 6.5).

MVTR, the water transport rate, normalized for the barrier surface S and barrier thickness h, can be expressed as a function of the driving force, ΔRH, using a proportionality constant P (permeability).

$$(\text{MVTR})\left(\frac{h}{S}\right) = P\,(\Delta\text{RH}) \tag{6.124}$$

External conditions and permeability of the packaging system to water vapor determine the rate of water entry into a drug product container. The affinity of the drug product for water and presence of a desiccant in the container, for example, will influence the distribution of water between the container contents and the headspace.

Hom et al. determined that an increase in the glycerin (plasticizer) content of a soft-gelatin capsule shell wall, and higher relative humidity, increased the water content of the shell. Higher water content correlated with an increase in the shell wall permeability to oxygen [48].

6.3.2 Dissolution

Dissolution is a process by which molecules of a solid (in contact with a solvent), leave the solid phase, and form a homogeneous, molecular mixture with the solvent. For example, an orally administered solid drug undergoes dissolution in the gastrointestinal (GI) fluids to provide drug molecules in solution at sites of absorption. Dissolved drug may then be transported across biological membranes by passive diffusion or active transport, and eventually into the blood circulation. Rapid dissolution therefore, facilitates higher rate and extent of drug absorption.

USP Chapter 711 describes *in-vitro* dissolution testing for solid oral dosage forms. The drug dissolution rate is evaluated by placing the dosage form in a dissolution medium at 37°C under defined experimental conditions (medium type, volume, apparatus type, agitation speed). Dissolved drug concentrations in the medium are analyzed over time [49].

This section discusses mechanisms and kinetics of the drug dissolution process. Consider a drug particle being mixed in a dissolution medium. The rate at which the solid particle dissolves when in contact with the medium is described by the Noyes–Whitney equation (Eq 6.125).

$$-\frac{dM_{solid}}{dt} = \frac{DS}{h}(C_s - C_{bulk}) \tag{6.125}$$

M_{solid} is the mass of solid (undissolved) drug at any time t, and dM_{solid}/dt is the rate of disappearance of solid drug due to dissolution (negative sign indicates a decrease in M_{solid} as dissolution proceeds). S is the surface area of the solid available to interact with the medium (solid-liquid interfacial area). This solid-liquid interface has an unstirred liquid film (diffusion layer) of thickness h (Fig. 6.20). Molecules of the solute leave the solid phase, dissolve in the liquid film, and achieve a saturation concentration (C_s) close to the interface. C_s is the saturation solubility of the solute *in the diffusion layer*, at the temperature of the experiment. C_{bulk} is the concentration of the dissolved drug in the bulk medium at time t. Since ($C_{bulk} < C_s$), a concentration gradient results across the diffusion layer. Transport of drug to the bulk medium continues by diffusion of molecules from the solid surface across the static diffusion layer. D is the diffusion coefficient of the solute molecules in the diffusion layer.

Beyond the unstirred diffusion layer, in the bulk solution, mixing of contents occurs and solute concentrations are uniform. If C_{bulk} is substantially lower than C_s (say $C_{bulk} < 0.1\ C_s$, and $C_s - C_{bulk} \approx C_s$), then sink conditions apply and Noyes–Whitney equation for sink conditions is expressed in Eq. (6.126).

$$-\frac{dM_{solid}}{dt} = \frac{DSC_s}{h} \tag{6.126}$$

When drug powder is dispersed in a particular volume of medium, the dissolution process occurs from particle surfaces. If the solubility of the drug in the medium is insufficient to completely dissolve all the added solid, the bulk medium approaches saturation. When $C_{bulk} = C_s$, the concentration gradient disappears, and solubility equilibrium is attained. In the following subsections, we consider factors that influence dissolution rates.

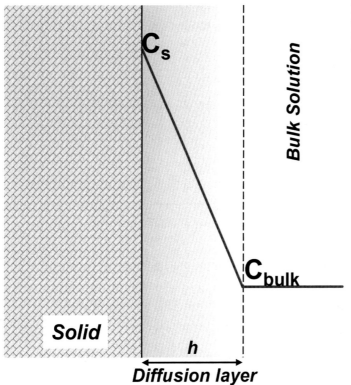

FIGURE 6.20 Schematic representation of the dissolution process from a particle surface. The Noyes–Whitney equation describes the rate of diffusional transport of the solute molecules from the solid surface to the bulk solution.

6.3.2.1 Surface area and particle size

From Eq. (6.125), the dissolution rate of a solid is directly proportional to the solid surface available for interaction with the medium. As a particle dissolves and becomes smaller, its surface area decreases, and dissolution rate from that particle decreases. For example, for a dissolving spherical particle suspended in a medium under sink conditions, the particle diameter decreases linearly with time. The square root of the particle surface and the cube root of the particle volume (or mass) would decrease at a constant rate. Therefore, particle dissolution kinetics can be expressed as the modified Hixson—Crowell equation (Eq. 6.127), where M_0 is the initial mass of the particle, M_t is mass of the undissolved particle at time t and the coefficient κ includes the effects of solubility, diffusivity, diffusion layer thickness and particle density. The mass of drug dissolved at any time t is $M_0—M_t$.

$$\sqrt[3]{M_0} - \sqrt[3]{M_t} = \kappa t \qquad (6.127)$$

For a given dose of drug provided as a powder, the overall dissolution rate when stirred in a medium is the sum of dissolution rates from each individual particle, as described by Eq. (6.127). Fig. 6.21 is a simulated graph containing dissolution profiles for the same dose of a drug. Each curve represents dissolution from the dose provided as *spherical particles, all of the same diameter*. The different curves represent different particle diameters. The dissolution profiles following the kinetics in Eq. (6.127), were calculated assuming a constant value of κ. Fig. 6.21 demonstrates the effect of particle size on drug dissolution rates. The specific surface area (surface area per unit mass) of the powder increases with a decrease in particle size. Therefore, the same dose provided as smaller particles dissolves faster.

API powders, however, are polydisperse. Fig. 6.22 reveals the reduction in particle size distribution of a drug substance due to a milling operation. Milled drug due to its smaller particle size distribution would have a higher specific surface area. When capsules were prepared using the same formula, but with either milled or unmilled API, faster dissolution was observed from capsules prepared using milled drug [50].

Most tablets designed for immediate drug release, when in contact with GI fluids, break apart by *disintegration* into smaller aggregates (granules) and then by granule *de-aggregation* to yield the individual particles. These breakdown processes increase the solid drug-medium interfacial area and accelerate dissolution (Fig. 6.23).

Intrinsic dissolution rates. Dissolution rate is affected by the available solid surface area and hence particle size distribution. Dissolution rates from powders also decrease as dissolution proceeds, due to decreasing surface area. Determination of an intrinsic dissolution rate (IDR) involves compression of the powder to be evaluated into a flat disc holder, such that a single face of the compact with a defined area is exposed to the dissolution medium. The dissolution test is carried out under defined conditions of medium composition, temperature and stirring. As the dissolving surface area is fixed, a constant initial dissolution rate is achieved, which is used to calculate IDR, expressed as mass dissolved per unit time per unit area.

$$IDR = \left(\frac{1}{S}\frac{dM}{dt}\right) = \left(\frac{DC_s}{h}\right) \qquad (6.128)$$

Determination of IDR enables comparison of dissolution behavior of different solid forms of an API, independent of particle size and surface area effects.

FIGURE 6.21 Simulated drug dissolution plots for the same dose of drug, provided as monodisperse spherical particles, for particle diameters of 10, 20, 50, and 100 μm. The dissolution curves were calculated using the modified Hixson—Crowell cube-root equation (Eq. 6.127), assuming a fixed value of κ.

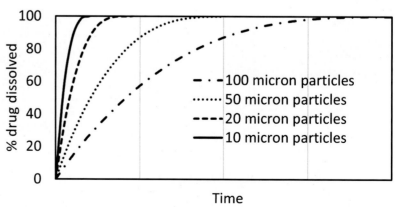

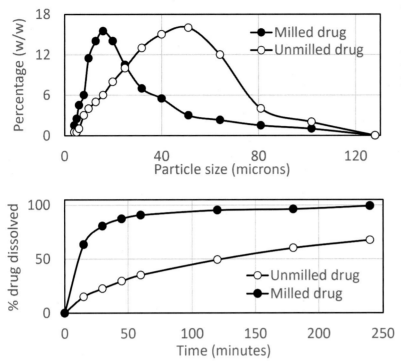

FIGURE 6.22 Top panel—Particle size distribution for a drug substance powder before and after a milling operation. Bottom panel—Drug dissolution profiles from capsules made with the same formula but with either the unmilled or milled drug substance. Graphs were prepared using data obtained from Ref. [50], with permission from Elsevier.

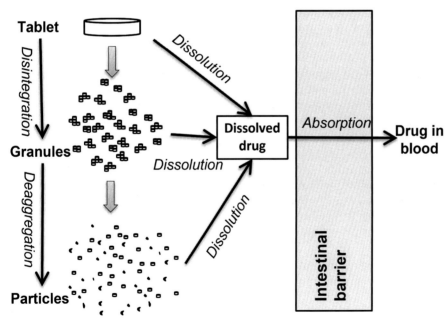

FIGURE 6.23 Schematic representation of the breakdown of a tablet formulation after oral administration by disintegration and deaggregation.

6.3.2.2 Drug solubility

Drug dissolution rate is directly influenced by the saturation solubility, C_s, which determines the driving force for diffusion. Saturation solubility of a stable crystalline solid in a specified solvent, at a given temperature, is a thermodynamic property. However, when a metastable solid form of the same compound, possessing higher free energy is used (for example, amorphous drug), higher concentrations achieved in the diffusion layer result in increased dissolution rates. Concentrations achieved in excess of the stable crystal solubility (supersaturation), may cause crystallization of the stable solid form. Crystallization may negate the advantage of higher dissolution rates achieved from metastable forms. *In vivo*, if supersaturation can be sustained (by inhibition of crystallization), higher rate and extent of drug absorption may be realized. Use of stabilized amorphous forms of drugs is a widely reported approach for improving bioavailability of poorly water-soluble drugs [51].

The pH of dissolution media (or GI contents *in vivo*) can influence solubility and dissolution rates for ionizable drugs. For example, the pH dependence of total solubility for weak acids and bases is described in Eq. (6.129), where S_0 is the intrinsic solubility of the weak acid or base and S_T is the total solubility due to ionization.

$$\text{For weak acids, } S_T = S_0 \left(1 + \frac{K_a}{[H^+]} \right); \text{ For weak bases, } S_T = S_0 \left(1 + \frac{[H^+]}{K_a} \right) \tag{6.129}$$

Therefore, solubility and dissolution rates will increase for weak acids as medium pH approaches and increases above pK_a and for weak bases as pH approaches and decreases below pK_a.

Ionizable drugs can influence diffusion layer pH, which can affect solubility in the diffusion layer, and hence dissolution rates. For example, salt forms of drugs may alter diffusion layer pH (relative to medium pH), depending on the medium buffer capacity, drug solubility, drug pK_a, and the salt counterion. By altering the diffusion layer pH in a direction that increases total solubility (Eq. 6.129) salt forms may enhance dissolution rates compared to the free acid or base forms [52].

6.3.2.3 *Diffusion layer thickness*

Diffusion layer thickness (h, Eq. 6.125) affects diffusion path length. In laboratory tests, the stirring speed and the hydrodynamics in the medium can influence the diffusion layer thickness and hence the dissolution profiles. *In vivo*, peristaltic movements of the GI tract and the composition of GI contents can influence diffusion layer thickness on particle surfaces.

6.3.3 Drug release kinetics

Our discussions in the previous section relate to drug dissolution from solid particle surfaces, rapidly made available by disintegration of immediate-release dosage forms. Controlled-release formulations on the other hand are designed to prolong drug release, extend duration of pharmacological effect, and thereby decrease dosing frequency. Different approaches to prolong drug release, employed successfully for various routes of administration, have been enabled by a variety of functional excipients. The mechanism of release control will dictate the kinetics of drug availability for absorption. The most common types of oral controlled release systems include matrix- or membrane-controlled formulations and osmotic pumps. These systems are discussed briefly in subsequent subsections.

Long-acting parenteral products are administered intramuscularly or subcutaneously and may employ, for example (1) oily drug solutions, from which the drug is released by partitioning into aqueous tissue fluids, (2) suspension formulations where drug dissolution in tissue fluids controls its availability for absorption, (3) complexed or self-associated forms of the drug, where dissociation of the free/monomeric drug molecules controls drug release, and (4) polymeric systems (microspheres, implants or *in-situ* gelling systems). For example, biodegradable poly (DL-lactide-co-glycolide) polymer (PLGA) is used in long-acting parenteral formulations (Case study 6.6). The drug embedded in the PLGA matrix can be released by diffusion, polymer erosion and osmotic pumping mechanisms [53].

Transdermal drug delivery systems (patches), depending on their design, release drug by diffusion of drug molecules through polymer matrices, or across release controlling membranes, to deliver drug to the skin surface. The drug then permeates through the stratum corneum (the primary barrier to drug delivery into the skin) and the viable epidermis before absorption.

6.3.3.1 *Matrix systems*

Porous insoluble matrices—The drug is dispersed in a matrix of an inert, insoluble polymer such as ethyl cellulose or polyvinyl acetate. Ingress of dissolution medium into the surface pores of an insoluble matrix tablet causes dissolution of drug, and other soluble components. This creates channels which allow further medium access into the matrix. Drug and soluble excipients continue to dissolve in the medium and diffuse out through the channels. The drug release kinetics from such systems is described by the Higuchi model (Eq. 6.130).

$$M_t = \sqrt{\left(\frac{D \, \varepsilon \, C_s}{\tau} \right).(2A - \varepsilon \, C_s) \, t} \tag{6.130}$$

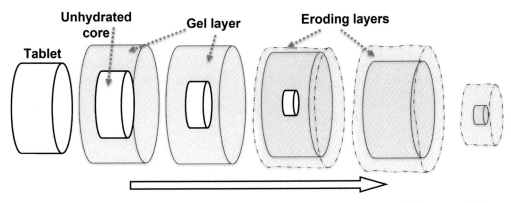

FIGURE 6.24 Schematic representation of drug release mechanism from hydrophilic matrix tablets.

In Eq. 6.130, A is the initial quantity of drug per unit volume of the matrix, M_t is the mass of drug *released* from unit surface area of the matrix at time t, D is the diffusion coefficient of the drug, and C_s is the saturation solubility of drug in the medium, The term ε is the total porosity of the matrix after all the drug and soluble components have been released and τ is the tortuosity of the matrix channels. Drug release is proportional to the square root of time.

An increase in the porosity of the matrix increases the rate and extent of water influx, facilitating faster drug dissolution and release. An increase in tortuosity (a measure of the bends and turns in the matrix channels), decreases release rate by increasing diffusion path lengths. Tortuosity and porosity of the matrix can be modified by the formulation composition. For example, inclusion of soluble excipients that dissolve in the medium and diffuse out of the system will increase porosity, decrease tortuosity, and thereby increase release rates.

Hydrophilic swellable matrices—Hydrophilic matrices are commonly employed in oral controlled-release formulations. These matrices utilize high molecular weight hydrophilic polymers such as hypromellose or polyethylene oxide. On exposure to the dissolution medium, these polymers absorb water, swell, and form a viscous gel layer, which controls drug release. Polymer hydration and gel formation proceed toward the tablet core (Fig. 6.24). The drug dispersed in the matrix dissolves and is released by diffusion through the swollen polymer and the water-filled pores in the gel. Simultaneously, the outer layers of the swollen matrix continue to hydrate, the polymer chains disentangle and erode off the surface. Drug release is by a combination of dissolution, diffusion, and erosion mechanisms (Fig. 6.24). Especially for highly water-soluble drugs, rapid dissolution from the tablet surface layers occurs before the gel layer is formed, causing an initial "burst-release" effect.

Formulation factors influence polymer hydration, gel viscosity and gel erosion rates and thereby affect drug release. For example, higher viscosity-grade polymer, higher polymer concentrations, and polymer blends that yield stronger gels, result in higher gel viscosity, which decreases rates of diffusional transport (slower water ingress and slower rates of drug diffusion) as well as rates of matrix erosion. On the other hand, lower viscosity-grade polymers, lower polymer levels and water-soluble excipients, result in weaker gels and faster drug release. Matrix properties, release mechanisms and hence drug release kinetics can be tailored by careful choice of formulation variables [54].

The power law equation by Korsmeyer et al. (Eq. 6.130) describes release kinetics from swellable matrices [55].

$$f_r = kt^n \tag{6.130}$$

$$\log f_r = \log k + n \log t \tag{6.131}$$

In Eq. (6.130), f_r is the fraction of drug released from the matrix at time t, and k is a system-dependent kinetic constant. The exponent n provides information on the mechanism of release. Depending on the geometry of the dosage form, values of n close to 0.5 are seen for release that is predominantly by diffusion (release proportional to $t^{1/2}$). When release is predominantly due to polymer swelling and erosion, values of n close to 1 are obtained (zero-order release). A value of n between 0.5 and 1.0 is seen when both release mechanisms are involved.

Fig. 6.25 is an example of the influence of drug solubility and matrix composition on drug release rates. Verapamil HCl matrix tablets (120 mg verapamil HCl/tablet) were prepared using hypromellose K4M (average molecular weight 500 kDa) as the matrix-forming polymer. The levels of two components (polymer and succinic acid), were varied while the total tablet weight was maintained at 500 mg with an insoluble diluent, dibasic calcium phosphate. The solubility of verapamil, a basic drug, decreases from ~ 80 mg/mL at pH 2 to ~ 0.44 mg/mL at pH 7.3 [57]. The release of drug from the matrix tablets was evaluated in 900 mL of phosphate buffer, pH 7.5, in a USP Type 2 dissolution test apparatus with paddles at 50 rpm [49]. Due to the low solubility of the drug in the dissolution medium,

FIGURE 6.25 Release of verapamil from hydrophilic matrix tablets (120 mg verapamil HCl/tablet) containing different levels of polymer (hypromellose K4M, HPMC) and succinic acid. Tablets contained either 10% w/w or 30% w/w of HPMC and 0% w/w or 40% w/w of succinic acid. The dissolution study was carried out in 900 mL of phosphate buffer, pH 7.5 at 37°C in a USP dissolution testing apparatus with paddles at 50 rpm [56].

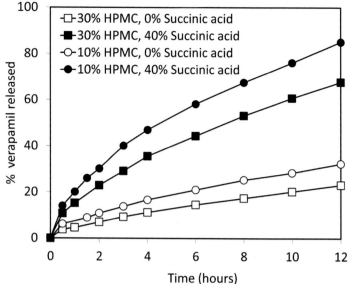

drug release in the absence of succinic acid was slow, even at low polymer concentrations (10% w/w), where a strong coherent gel is not formed. Inclusion of succinic acid in the matrix resulted in an acidic environment within the gel. Higher drug solubility in this environment increased drug diffusion rates out of the matrix (Fig. 6.25). Dissolution of succinic acid and its release from the matrix would also contribute to faster drug release due to an increase in matrix porosity [56].

6.3.3.2 Membrane-controlled release

Membrane-controlled systems have a drug-containing core (tablets or pellets), coated with an insoluble release-controlling polymeric film. Water from the dissolution medium enters the core through the film, the drug in the core dissolves, and diffuses out through the film (Fig. 6.26). The film controls water entry and drug release. The release mechanism can be described by Fick's law. Drug release rate can be expressed using the terms S (diffusional surface area), D (diffusion coefficient of the drug through the membrane), ΔC (concentration gradient across the film), h (film thickness), and K (partition coefficient of the drug between the film and the medium).

$$\frac{dM}{dt} = \frac{S\,D\,K\,\Delta C}{h} \tag{6.132}$$

For a given drug and dosage unit, S, D, K, and h are constant. If sink conditions are assumed (low external drug concentrations compared to the concentrations inside the coating), then ΔC is maintained constant as long as solid drug remains in the core. Therefore, the drug release rate is constant (zero-order). The permeability of the barrier film can be controlled by incorporating pore-formers (soluble components that dissolve when exposed to the dissolution medium to generate pores). In such systems, drug release would then be predominantly through the aqueous pores in the film. A change in the film thickness (diffusion path length) would also alter release rates.

FIGURE 6.26 Schematic representation of drug release from membrane-controlled extended-release tablet.

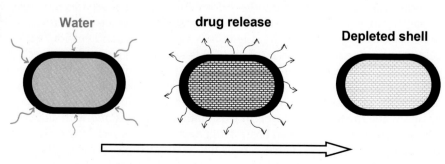

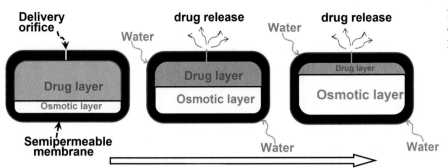

FIGURE 6.27 Schematic representation of drug release from a push–pull type osmotic pump tablet.

Delayed-release oral formulations, referred to as enteric-coated formulations, are membrane-controlled systems where the membrane has pH-dependent solubility. As an example, coatings based on methacrylic acid—ethyl acrylate copolymer dissolve at pH values >5.5. The dosage unit coated with these polymers remains intact at lower pH values and dissolves to rapidly release drug in the upper intestine. These coatings (known as enteric coatings) are commonly employed for protection of acid-sensitive drugs from the lower pH environments in the stomach (example-omeprazole) or to minimize side effects such as gastric irritation and nausea produced by the drug (example-aspirin).

6.3.3.3 Osmotic pumps

Osmotic pumps are delivery systems that rely on water entry into an osmotically active tablet core through a semipermeable membrane/coat. The resulting volume changes inside the core causes drug transport out of the tablet through (1) predrilled apertures in the coat or (2) pores created by pore-formers in the coating. The push-pull type osmotic pump is discussed and shown in Fig. 6.27.

The core of the push-pull system is a bilayer tablet, with one osmotically active, expandable, pushing layer, containing an osmogen (such as sodium chloride) to maintain osmotic pressure, and a swellable polymer (such as polyethylene oxide). The other layer contains the drug, along with other excipients including an osmogen. The tablet is coated with a semipermeable membrane (e.g., cellulose acetate) with an aperture laser-drilled on the side of the drug layer. When the tablet is exposed to GI fluids, water uptake occurs by osmosis into both layers through the coat. The drug layer is converted to a homogeneous drug suspension, while the osmotic layer expands to pump the drug suspension out through the orifice. Unlike diffusion-controlled systems, drug dissolution is not a prerequisite for release from osmotic pumps. This is an advantage for poorly water-soluble drugs.

Drug release is controlled by water entry into the tablet. The rate of water imbibition into the tablet (dV/dt) through the membrane is determined by the osmotic pressure gradient across the membrane ($\Delta \pi$) and the hydraulic permeability (k), thickness (h), and surface area (S) of the membrane.

$$\frac{dV}{dt} = \frac{Sk}{h} \Delta \pi \tag{6.133}$$

For the push-pull type osmotic system, the rate of water entry into each layer and the consequent volume change is governed by the corresponding parameters in Eq. (6.133) for that layer. The total water uptake rate into the tablet is the sum of water imbibition rates into the osmotic (O) and drug (D) layers (Eq. 6.134).

$$\left[\frac{dV}{dt}\right]_O + \left[\frac{dV}{dt}\right]_D = \left[\frac{dV}{dt}\right]_{total} \tag{6.134}$$

When the semipermeable coating is rigid (volume inside the coat stays constant), the rate at which drug suspension is pumped out is equal to the rate of total volume change caused by water imbibition. Drug release rate (dM/dt) is thus expressed in Eq. (6.135), where ($C_{D, susp}$) is the concentration of the drug in the suspension pumped out.

$$\frac{dM}{dt} = \left[\frac{dV}{dt}\right]_{total} C_{D,susp} \tag{6.135}$$

Zero-order release, independent of drug properties, medium pH, ionic strength, and other physiological variables, can be achieved [58]. An example of a push-pull type osmotic tablet is Procardia XL, an oral controlled release formulation for nifedipine [59,60].

Different controlled-release systems may prolong drug release over similar durations. However, release kinetics will dictate the availability of drug for absorption, over time. These differences coupled with physiological factors such as GI transit times and regional absorption characteristics, can result in differences in pharmacokinetics.

6.4 Conclusions

Physical, chemical, and biological rate processes are important in all fields of pharmaceutics including formulation, manufacturing, product stability, drug delivery, pharmacokinetics, and drug action. An understanding of relevant processes and of factors affecting them forms the basis of rational design of drug products.

Thermodynamics defines the direction of spontaneous processes, but kinetic factors dictate the rates at which they occur. For example, solubility of an API in a given medium, at a given temperature and pressure, is a thermodynamic property, defined by the solubility equilibrium. However, when a tablet containing the solid API is administered orally and comes in contact with GI fluids, the solubility equilibrium is not attained instantaneously. The process of drug dissolution involves transport of drug *molecules,* from the solid drug phase to a dissolved state in the GI fluids. In addition to solubility, factors such as drug—medium interfacial area, medium viscosity, and mixing dynamics influence the rate at which drug molecules enter the solution phase.

Dissolution rate will dictate drug concentrations achieved in the intestinal lumen over time. *Dissolved* drug from the intestinal lumen is transported by absorption through the intestinal wall, into the bloodstream. Gastric emptying and intestinal transit of the drug will also define the time during which dissolved drug can be absorbed [61]. Thus, the rates of *kinetic* processes (drug dissolution, absorption, GI transit) influence transport of an orally administered drug into the blood circulation.

Stability is a critical quality attribute for pharmaceutical products. A deteriorative change may be thermodynamically favored. An understanding of the mechanisms of change and the kinetic factors affecting the rates of change forms the basis of stabilization strategies.

Case studies

Case 6.1

An experimental drug is available as a capsule but requires dispensing as a suspension. A 40 mg/mL formulation, pure drug suspended in a commercially available suspending vehicle, was evaluated earlier. Stability studies at 25°C, for the 40 mg/mL suspension, revealed good physical stability, and pseudo-zero-order degradation with a rate constant of 0.066 mg mL^{-1} day^{-1}. At 25°C, drug solubility in the vehicle is reported as 0.10 mg/mL. A new clinical requirement is for a 20 mg/mL suspension. A similar formulation in the same suspending vehicle has been prepared at the lower concentration. Studies have been initiated to assess stability. Based on available data, predict the time period at 25°C, over which you expect not more than 10% degradation for both formulations. Calculate the first order rate constant for degradation of the drug dissolved in the vehicle.

Approach:

The pseudo zero-order rate constant, $k_0 = 0.066$ mg mL^{-1} day^{-1}, at 25°C

(i) For Formulation A—40 mg/mL suspension:

$$\text{Time required for 10\% drug loss (Eq. 6.12)} = t_{0.9,A} = \frac{40 \text{ mg/mL}}{10 \left(0.066 \text{ mg mL}^{-1}\text{day}^{-1}\right)}$$

$t_{0.9,A} = 60.6$ days, at 25°C

(ii) For Formulation B—20 mg/mL suspension in the same vehicle:

$$\text{Time required for 10\% drug loss (Eq. 6.12)} = t_{0.9,B} = \frac{20 \text{ mg/mL}}{10 \left(0.066 \text{ mg mL}^{-1}\text{day}^{-1}\right)}$$

$t_{0.9,B} = 30.3$ days, at 25°C

(iii) In the continuous phase, the first-order rate constant for the loss of drug can be expressed as

$k_1 = k_0/C_s$, where C_s is the solubility of the drug in the vehicle at 25°C.

$$k_1 = \frac{k_0}{C_s} = \frac{0.066 \text{ mg mL}^{-1}\text{day}^{-1}}{0.10 \text{ mg mL}^{-1}} = 0.66 \text{ day}^{-1}$$

A decrease in the total suspension concentration, therefore, decreases product shelf-life. The continuous phase of the suspension would have the same concentration of the drug in both formulations. As long as there is undissolved solid drug, degradation would continue at a rate equal to $k_0 = k_1C_s$, in both formulations. In Formulation B (20 mg/mL), the degradation extent would be a larger fraction of the total concentration and therefore the shelf-life would be lower.

Case 6.2

During the development of low-strength Avapro tablets (irbesartan 18.75 and 37.5 mg/tablet), stability studies revealed formation of a previously unknown impurity. This impurity was identified as a hydroxymethyl derivative of irbesartan formed by the reaction of the drug with formaldehyde. Can you develop a plan to investigate the reason for the formation of the impurity? How can you prevent it?

Approach: When each excipient present in the formulation was individually mixed with the drug and stressed at a higher temperature, the impurity was formed only when mixed with the film-coating excipient Opadry II White. The plasticizer polyethylene glycol in the film-coating composition was identified as a source of formaldehyde. When kinetic studies were conducted in an aqueous solution, the rate of impurity formation increased linearly (1) with formaldehyde concentration when irbesartan concentration was kept constant and (2) with irbesartan concentration when formaldehyde concentration was kept constant. Thus, the reaction exhibited partial order of one with respect to each reactant and an overall order of two. The second-order rate constant in solution was determined to be $2.6 \times 10^{-4} \text{ M}^{-1} \text{ min}^{-1}$ at 25°C. The impurity formation was controlled by eliminating polyethylene glycol from the film coat composition [62].

Case 6.3

A freeze-dried drug product contains a nonionizable drug along with lactate buffer. The lactic acid: sodium lactate molar ratio in the buffer is 2: 3. The reconstitution procedure calls for the addition of 5 mL of 5% dextrose injection (diluent) to the solid to obtain a solution for injection. The reconstituted solution is a 5 mM lactate-buffered drug solution in the diluent. The reconstituted solution pH specification is 4.0 ± 0.5 to ensure adequate drug stability.

You wish to evaluate the suitability of 5 mL of 0.9% sodium chloride (normal saline) as the reconstitution fluid. Calculate the effect of normal saline on the ionic strength, apparent pK_a of lactic acid and the reconstituted solution pH. Thermodynamic K_a of lactic acid (monoprotic acid) at 25°C ($\mu = 0$) = 1.39×10^{-4}. The ionic strength contribution of the buffer salt in the reconstituted fluid (~ 0.003M) is small relative to the contribution of the added sodium chloride, and for the purposes of this exercise is ignored.

Approach:

(i) pK_a of lactic acid ($\mu = 0$), $pK_a^0 = -\log_{10}(1.39 \times 10^{-4}) = 3.86$

(ii) Molarity of normal saline (0.9% w/v NaCl; molecular weight- 58.44) = 0.154 M

(iii) If the contribution of the buffer salt is ignored, the ionic strength due to 0.154 M Na^+ ions and 0.154 M Cl^- ions can be calculated.

$$\text{Ionic strength} = \frac{1}{2}\left[0.154 \ (1)^2 + 0.154 \ (1)^2\right] = 0.154 \text{ M}$$

(iv) The apparent pK_a of lactic acid at $\mu = 0.154$ M can be calculated using Eq. (6.103)

$$pK_a^\mu = 3.86 + \left(\frac{0.51 \ (2(0) - 1) \ \sqrt{0.154}}{1 + \sqrt{0.154}}\right) = 3.72$$

The thermodynamic dissociation constant expression for lactic acid can be written in terms of the activity of lactic acid (LH) and lactate (L$^-$) and activity can be expressed as a product of concentration and activity coefficients

$$K_a^0 = \frac{(a_{L^-})(a_{H^+})}{a_{LH}} = \frac{(c_{L^-})}{(c_{LH})} \frac{(\gamma_{L^-})}{(\gamma_{LH})} (a_{H^+}) \tag{6.135}$$

The activity coefficient of the neutral undissociated lactic acid γ_{LH} in dilute solution is one. A logarithmic transformation of the equation yields

$$pK_a^0 = \left[pH - \log \frac{(c_{L^-})}{(c_{LH})} \right] - \log(\gamma_{L^-}) \tag{6.136}$$

Expressing the activity coefficient of the lactate ion using Eq. (6.101), Eq (6.136) can be rearranged to yield expressions for the apparent pK_a

$$\left[pH - \log \frac{(c_{L^-})}{(c_{LH})} \right] = pK_a^0 + \left(\frac{0.509 \, (1)^2 \sqrt{\mu}}{1 + \sqrt{\mu}} \right) = pK_a^\mu \tag{6.137}$$

The solution pH at the higher ionic strength can be calculated using the apparent pK_a and the molar concentration ratio of salt: acid.

$$pH = pK_a^\mu + \log \frac{(c_{L^-})}{(c_{LH})} = 3.72 + \log \frac{3}{2} = 3.90$$

The predicted pH of the reconstituted solution is within the pH limits specified by the manufacturer. Stability studies will confirm the acceptability of the alternate diluent.

Case 6.4

An unstable antibiotic, provided as a freeze-dried solid, is reconstituted with saline before preparation of IV infusions. The shelf-life specification for the reconstituted solution includes a requirement of not more than 5% degradation after reconstitution. Stability studies conducted on the reconstituted solutions, at 25, 35 and 45°C (298, 308 and 318 K), yielded first-order degradation rate constants (k) of 0.011, 0.027 and 0.059 h^{-1} and corresponding shelf-life values ($t_{0.95}$) of 4.7, 1.9 and 0.87 h, respectively. To increase the shelf life of the reconstituted solution, determine the impact of refrigerated storage at 5°C on degradation rate constant and shelf-life.

Approach:

(i) A plot of log k versus $1/T$ (in Kelvin) yields a straight line with a slope of −3458 K (see Eq. 6.76).

$$E_a = - (\text{slope} \times 2.303 \times 1.987) \, \text{cal/mole} = 15,824 \, \text{cal/mole} = 15.8 \, \text{kcal/mole}$$

(ii) The rate constant at 5°C (278 K) is calculated using the value of k at 25°C and Eq. (6.106).

$$\log k_{5°C} = \left[\log 0.011 - \frac{15824 \, (298 - 278)}{2.303 \times 1.987 \times 298 \times 278} \right] = -2.79$$

$$k_{5°C} = 10^{-2.79} \, \text{h}^{-1} = 1.62 \times 10^{-3} \, \text{h}^{-1}$$

(iii) The time required for 5% degradation ($t_{0.95}$) is calculated (see Eq. 6.19)

$$t_{0.95 \, (5°C)} = \frac{2.303}{k_{5°C}} \log \left[\frac{a_0}{0.95 a_0} \right] = \frac{0.0513}{1.62 \times 10^{-3} \, \text{h}^{-1}} = 31.9 \, \text{h}$$

Thus, the shelf life may increase by a factor of 6.79 for a temperature decrease from 25°C to 5°C.

Case 6.5

Stability data generated on a drug product suggested that water uptake by the tablet led to physical changes and a consequent decrease in the drug dissolution rate. A scientific approach to selection of protective packaging is described below.

TABLE 6.1 MVTR values for three packaging configurations for a tablet formulation. Dissolution test results, in a stability study, for tablets packed in the three configurations.

Packaging configuration	Experimental MVTR (40°C/75% RH)	MVTR per tablet (40°C/75% RH)	Drug dissolution performance
Tablets in PVDC coated PVC blisters, 250-micron PVC blister pack with 40 g/m^2 PVDC	0.82 mg cavity^{-1} day^{-1}	0.82 mg tablet^{-1} day^{-1}	Fail
Tablets in blister containing poly (chlorotrifluoroethylene) (PCTFE) barrier film, Aclar^{TM} UltRx 2000 (51 microns)	0.142 mg cavity^{-1} day^{-1}	0.142 mg tablet^{-1} day^{-1}	Pass
60 cc HDPE bottle, heat induction sealed, containing 30 tablets/bottle	1.42 mg bottle^{-1} day^{-1}	0.047 mg tablet^{-1} day^{-1}	Pass

Adapted from example provided in Ref. [63].

TABLE 6.2 Proposed new packaging configurations and the calculated MVTR/tablet.

	Packaging configuration	Known MVTR (40°C/75% RH)	MVTR per tablet (40°C/75% RH)
A	45 cc bottle, heat induction sealed, 14 tablets/bottle	1.00 mg bottle^{-1} day^{-1}	0.071 mg tablet^{-1} day^{-1}
B	100 cc bottle, heat induction sealed, 90 tablets/bottle	1.95 mg bottle^{-1} day^{-1}	0.022 mg tablet^{-1} day^{-1}

Adapted from example provided in Ref. [63].

Approach: Protective packaging was the primary strategy for drug stabilization. Tablets stored in PVDC-coated PVC blisters (MVTR = 0.82 mg/tablet per day) failed to meet dissolution specifications at the end of the stability study. However, tablets packed in blisters with 51 μm PCTFE barrier films, and those in heat induction-sealed HDPE bottles (MVTR values—0.142 and 0.047 mg/tablet per day, respectively) met the dissolution performance specification (Table 6.1). Results, therefore, suggested the need for protection from water vapor. The highest MVTR/tablet at which acceptable product stability was demonstrated was 0.142 mg/tablet/day. It is recognized that container-closure systems that have the same water vapor transmission rate per dosage unit (irrespective of package type and configuration) may be considered equivalent for moisture protection. For a subsequent clinical study, two packaging configurations were identified which had MVTR/tablet values lower than the maximum level identified (Table 6.2).

Case 6.6

Eligard injection is a matrix formulation of leuprolide acetate (a nonapeptide). The formulation and drug delivery approach for a long-acting product is described below.

Approach: The product is provided as two separate syringes—one containing the peptide and another containing the biodegradable poly (DL-lactide-co-glycolide) polymer (Atrigel drug delivery system, Atrix Laboratories, Inc.) dissolved in N-methyl-2-pyrrolidone (solvent). The two syringes are mixed before administration and the mixture, a suspension, is injected subcutaneously. The polymer precipitates in the subcutaneous tissue to rapidly form a solid drug depot entrapping the drug within the matrix. The polymer erodes by hydrolytic cleavage of the ester bonds in the polymer backbone and leuprolide is released from the depot.

Four product strengths correspond to leuprolide acetate doses of 7.5, 22.5, 30, and 45 mg, designed for controlled drug release over 1, 3, 4, and 6-month periods, respectively. In these different strengths, in addition to varying the amounts of drug, polymer, and solvent, polymer chemistry is varied. Specifically, the lowest strength uses uncapped copolymer with carboxylic acid end-groups and the other products employ copolymer end-capped with hexanediol. The lactide:glycolide ratio in the copolymer is also varied (50:50, 75:25, 75:25, and 85:15 for the 7.5, 22.5, 30, and 45 mg formulations, respectively) [64]. Lower lactide:glycolide ratio and uncapped polymer end groups decrease hydrophobicity and increase rates of water absorption, hydrolysis, and erosion. Thus, the *in vivo* erosion rates of the depot have been tailored to extend drug release over the desired time periods, for the different strengths.

Case 6.7

An implantable drug pump underwent clinical trials as a drug delivery system for antibiotics, in your hospital. A separate study evaluated the stability of vancomycin solutions (1 mg/mL in water, pH 3.6) incubated at 37°C for 4 weeks in the pump. Bioassay and high-pressure liquid chromatography data demonstrated a loss of up to 50% activity over 4 weeks and colloidal precipitation of vancomycin in the pump was observed at the end of the experiment.

As the lead pharmacist on your team, explain your recommendation to the company.

Approach: Literature review reveals instability of aqueous vancomycin solutions. Vancomycin undergoes acid- and base-catalyzed degradation with maximum stability in the pH range of ~ 5 − 8. In this pH range, at 37°C, a half-life of 20-30 days is reported [68], similar to the chemical stability data in the implantable drug pumps. You conclude that simple vancomycin solutions may not have adequate stability. You recommend formulation development work aimed at enhancing physical and chemical stability of vancomycin solutions, before evaluation of compatibility with the infusion pumps.

Case 6.8

You are a third-year pharmacy student in a reputed school of pharmacy. You receive a call from a friend who is a final-year chemistry student regarding an OTC medication. He usually stores all his medicine in a medicine cabinet in his apartment bathroom. Recently, while removing aspirin tablets from the bottle, he discovered something unusual. There was white crystal-like solid on the tablet surface, and he also noticed the smell of vinegar from the bottle. He wants to know whether it is safe to use this medicine. If not, then why?

Approach: Aspirin, or acetylsalicylic acid, can undergo a hydrolytic degradation in the presence of moisture to form salicylic acid and acetic acid (see Fig. 6.28). The vinegar-like smell is possibly due to formation of acetic acid. The white crystal-like material is possibly salicylic acid, the other degradation product. The recommendation is to not take this medication anymore. Doing so may cause gastric irritation and ulcers.

Case 6.9

Protein drug products are stored frozen or freeze-dried to enhance stability. Is this always true? Can low temperature processes be detrimental to protein stability?

Approach: During cooling and freezing, low temperature, ice crystallization and freeze concentration of solutes, are the key stresses that influence protein stability. Freeze concentration could also facilitate second-order reactions, crystallization of solutes including buffer salts, and phase separation. For a given protein, an understanding of the relevant stresses is critical to formulate a stable product [65].

Case 6.10

Phadnis and Suryanarayanan [66] prepared metastable anhydrous theophylline (form I*) by dehydration of theophylline monohydrate. Tablets were prepared using both the metastable anhydrous theophylline (form I*) as well as stable anhydrous theophylline (form I). Tablets were exposed to two different humidity conditions (33% and 52% RH) and subjected to the USP dissolution test. Form I* in tablets was completely converted to form I in less than 10 days when stored at both RH conditions. Tablets made using form I* failed the USP dissolution test after storage at 52% RH. The approach to investigate this finding is described below.

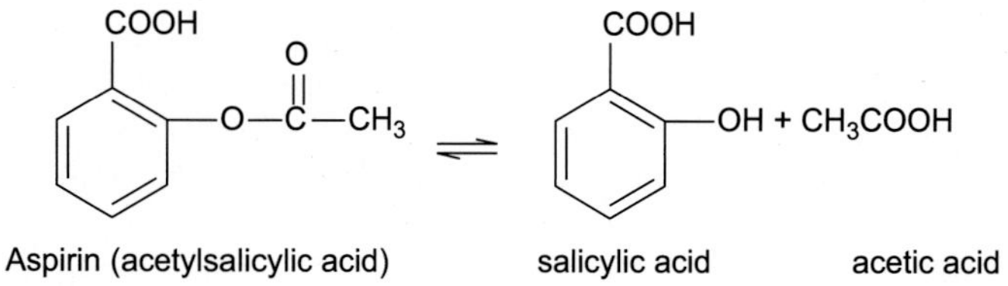

FIGURE 6.28 The degradation of acetylsalicylic acid into salicylic acid and acetic acid in presence of moisture.

Approach: Scanning electron microscopy clearly showed the crystallization of form I (stable anhydrous theophylline) in stored form I* tablets. This *in situ* solid-state transition appeared to be responsible for the decrease in dissolution. However, tablets made using form I, stored under both RH conditions did not show any phase changes or change in dissolution performance. Two potential risks of using metastable forms in formulations are (1) metastable forms, having higher free energy than the stable form, can exhibit increased reactivity and inferior chemical stability; (2) conversion from metastable to stable form can have undesirable consequences on product performance.

Case 6.11

Rifaximin is a BCS class IV (low-solubility, low-permeability) drug and is also a known P-glycoprotein (P-gp) substrate. Rifaximin amorphous solid dispersion (ASD) formulations using different hydrophilic polymers were prepared by the spray-drying technique [67]. A Copovidone/HPC-SL (low viscosity hydroxypropylcellulose) ASD formulation containing Rifaximin exhibited higher apparent drug solubility and intestinal permeability. How can this be explained?

Approach: ASD is a promising approach used to increase the apparent solubility of hydrophobic drugs. The free energy of the amorphous (metastable) form is higher than that of its crystalline counterpart resulting in an increased apparent solubility. This may lead to enhanced absorption and bioavailability of an amorphous drug relative to the crystalline form. This work has further shown that delivering a high supersaturation level of rifaximin (250-times the crystalline solubility) using ASD, saturated the drug's P-gp-mediated efflux transport, and the absorption rate coefficient was doubled. This led to a favorable outcome where both the solubility and the permeability increased simultaneously [68].

Critical reflections and practice applications

- Chemical reaction kinetics are described by rate equations which define the dependence of reaction velocity on reactant concentrations and reveal reaction order. Rate constants are proportionality constants relating reaction rate to reactant concentrations.
- Reaction rates are independent of reactant concentration for zero-order reactions. For example, for first- and second-order reactions, rates may be directly proportional to the concentration of a single reactant and to the product of concentrations of two reactants, respectively.
- Pseudo-orders are encountered if a reactant concentration is maintained constant in the reaction phase (degradation in the continuous phase of suspensions), or when a reactant is in large excess (e.g., water in aqueous solutions).
- Catalyzed reactions may proceed via enzymatic (e.g., drug metabolism) or nonenzymatic (e.g., acid/base catalysis) pathways.
- For complex reactions, rate constants for overall drug loss may be a function of rate constants for different processes and pathways.
- Reaction rates are influenced by a variety of factors including concentrations, temperature, presence of reactive species or reaction facilitators (incompatible components, water, oxygen), catalysts (acids, bases, metal ions, light), and medium properties (ionic strength, dielectric constant, viscosity).
- Knowledge of reaction order and rate constants allows prediction of product shelf-life. Knowledge of factors influencing reaction rates enables the selection of stabilization approaches.
- Reaction rates for drug products are accelerated by storage under higher temperature (and humidity) conditions to obtain useful stability data in shorter time periods. Kinetic parameters (rate constants, energy of activation) determined at higher temperatures can be used to predict reaction rates and shelf-life at lower temperatures, using the Arrhenius equation.
- Molecular diffusion describes the mass transport of drug molecules during (1) dissolution of solid drug, (2) permeation across biological membranes, and (3) permeation across rate-controlling membranes in drug delivery systems. The driving force (concentration gradient) and barrier characteristics (permeability) dictate mass transport rates.
- Diffusion of water and oxygen through packaging components may influence drug product stability. Characterizing the kinetics of water vapor permeation through packaging (MVTR), provides a measure of the protection conferred by the packaging components to water-sensitive drug products.

- Dissolution of the solid drug is a critical step that furnishes drug molecules in solution before absorption. Particle size reduction to increase specific surface area (micronized or nano-milled drug) or drug forms with higher metastable solubility (amorphous forms, nanocrystals, salt forms) have been employed to enhance dissolution rates and oral bioavailability.
- Characterization of solubility and permeability of drug molecules reveals challenges for drug delivery and aids the selection of formulation strategies.
- Modified release formulations employ a variety of release mechanisms, enabled by functional excipients, to control drug release, reduce dosing frequency, and facilitate better disease-state management.

References

[1] M.S. Paterson, Rate processes, in: M.S. Paterson (Ed.), Materials Science for Structural Geology, Springer Netherlands, Dordrecht, 2013, pp. 31–69.

[2] K.S. Alexander, N. Thyagarajapuram, Formulation and accelerated stability studies for an extemporaneous suspension of amiodarone hydrochloride, Int. J. Pharm. Compd. 7 (5) (2003) 389–393.

[3] S.H. Eghrary, R. Zarghami, F. Martinez, A. Jouyban, Solubility of 2-butyl-3-benzofuranyl 4-(2-(diethylamino)ethoxy)-3,5-diiodophenyl ketone hydrochloride (amiodarone HCl) in ethanol + water and N-methyl-2-pyrrolidone + water mixtures at various temperatures, J. Chem. Eng. Data 57 (5) (2012) 1544–1550.

[4] E.R. Oberholtzer, G.S. Brenner, Cefoxitin sodium: solution and solid–state chemical stability studies, J. Pharm. Sci. 68 (7) (1979) 863–866.

[5] M.N. Nassar, V.N. Nesarikar, R. Lozano, W.L. Parker, Y. Huang, V. Palaniswamy, W. Xu, N. Khaselev, Influence of formaldehyde impurity in polysorbate 80 and PEG-300 on the stability of a parenteral formulation of BMS-204352: identification and control of the degradation product, Pharm. Dev. Technol. 9 (2) (2004) 189–195.

[6] T. Higuchi, L.C. Schroeter, Reactivity of bisulfite with a number of pharmaceuticals, J. Am. Pharmaceut. Assoc. (Scientific Ed.) 48 (9) (1959) 535–540.

[7] L.C. Schroeter, Kinetics and mechanism of the salicyl alcohol-bisulfite reaction, J. Pharm. Sci. 51 (3) (1962) 258–260.

[8] J.W. Munson, A. Hussain, R. Bilous, Precautionary note for use of bisulfite in pharmaceutical formulations, J. Pharm. Sci. 66 (12) (1977) 1775–1776.

[9] T. Higuchi, L.C. Schroeter, Kinetics and mechanism of formation of sulfonate from epinephrine and bisulfite, J. Am. Chem. Soc. 82 (8) (1960) 1904–1907.

[10] J. Fassberg, V.J. Stella, A kinetic and mechanistic study of the hydrolysis of camptothecin and some analogues, J. Pharm. Sci. 81 (7) (1992) 676–684.

[11] W.J.M. Underberg, R.M.J. Goossen, B.R. Smith, J.H. Beijnen, Equilibrium kinetics of the new experimental anti-tumour compound SK&F 104864-A in aqueous solution, J. Pharm. Biomed. Anal. 8 (8) (1990) 681–683.

[12] K.D. Fugit, B.D. Anderson, The role of pH and ring-opening hydrolysis kinetics on liposomal release of topotecan, J. Control. Release 174 (2014) 88–97.

[13] Hycamtin® Package Insert, Hycamtin-Topotecan Hydrochloride Injection, Lyophilized Powder for Solution, Novartis Pharmaceuticals Corporation. Updated July 7, 2022; Available from: https://dailymed.nlm.nih.gov/dailymed/drugInfo.cfm?setid=eeee060c-a9ec-423e-a374-8484009f8524, accessed on 30-Sep-2022.

[14] V.M.M. Herben, W.W. ten Bokkel Huinink, J.H. Beijnen, Clinical pharmacokinetics of topotecan, Clin. Pharmacokinet. 31 (2) (1996) 85–102.

[15] D. Toledo-Velasquez, H.T. Gaud, K.A. Connors, Misoprostol dehydration kinetics in aqueous solution in the presence of hydroxypropyl methylcellulose, J. Pharm. Sci. 81 (2) (1992) 145–148.

[16] B.D. Anderson, V. Taphouse, Initial rate studies of hydrolysis and acyl migration in methylprednisolone 21-hemisuccinate and 17-hemisuccinate, J. Pharm. Sci. 70 (2) (1981) 181–186.

[17] E. Seibert and T.S. Tracy, Fundamentals of enzyme kinetics: michaelis-menten and non-michaelis–type (atypical) enzyme kinetics, in: S. Nagar, U.A. Argikar, and D. Tweedie (Eds.), Enzyme Kinetics in Drug Metabolism: Fundamentals and Applications, 2021, Springer US, New York, NY, pp. 3-27.

[18] L. Quintieri, S. Bortolozzo, S. Stragliotto, S. Moro, M. Pavanetto, A. Nassi, P. Palatini, M. Floreani, Flavonoids diosmetin and hesperetin are potent inhibitors of cytochrome P450 2C9-mediated drug metabolism in vitro, Drug Metabol. Pharmacokinet. 25 (5) (2010) 466–476.

[19] Y. Kudo, T. Urabe, A. Fujiwara, K. Yamada, T. Kawasaki, Carrier-mediated transport system for cephalexin in human placental brush-border membrane vesicles, Biochim. Biophys. Acta Biomembr. 978 (2) (1989) 313–318.

[20] J. Carstensen, Stability of solids and solid dosage forms, J. Pharm. Sci. 63 (1) (1974) 1–14.

[21] A. Khawam, D.R. Flanagan, Solid-state kinetic models: basics and mathematical fundamentals, J. Phys. Chem. B 110 (35) (2006) 17315–17328.

[22] B. Stanisz, Evaluation of stability of enalapril maleate in solid phase, J. Pharm. Biomed. Anal. 31 (2) (2003) 375–380.

[23] A. Serajuddin, A.B. Thakur, R.N. Ghoshal, M.G. Fakes, S.A. Ranadive, K.R. Morris, S.A. Varia, Selection of solid dosage form composition through drug-excipient compatibility testing, J. Pharm. Sci. 88 (7) (1999) 696–704.

[24] E.R. Garrett, Prediction of stability in pharmaceutical preparations III. Comparison of vitamin stabilities in different multivitamin preparations, J. Am. Pharmaceut. Assoc. (Scientific Ed.) 45 (7) (1956) 470–473.

[25] P.A. MacFaul, L. Ruston, J.M. Wood, Activation energies for the decomposition of pharmaceuticals and their application to predicting hydrolytic stability in drug discovery, MedChemComm 2 (2) (2011) 140–142.

[26] A.A. Kondritzer, P. Zvirblis, Stability of atropine in aqueous solution, J. Am. Pharmaceut. Assoc. (Scientific Ed.) 46 (9) (1957) 531–535.

[27] M. Zając, J. Cielecka-Piontek, A. Jelińska, Stability of ertapenem in aqueous solutions, J. Pharm. Biomed. Anal. 43 (2) (2007) 445–449.

[28] A. Tsuji, E. Nakashima, Y. Deguchi, K. Nishide, T. Shimizu, S. Horiuchi, K. Ishikawa, T. Yamana, Degradation kinetics and mechanism of aminocephalosporins in aqueous solution: cefadroxil, J. Pharm. Sci. 70 (10) (1981) 1120–1128.

[29] S.I.F. Badawy, M.A. Hussain, Microenvironmental pH modulation in solid dosage forms, J. Pharm. Sci. 96 (5) (2007) 948−959.

[30] J.T. Carstensen, Kinetic salt effect in pharmaceutical investigations, J. Pharm. Sci. 59 (8) (1970) 1140−1143.

[31] H. Fabre, N.H. Eddine, G. Berge, Degradation kinetics in aqueous solution of cefotaxime sodium, a third-generation cephalosporin, J. Pharm. Sci. 73 (5) (1984) 611−618.

[32] J.P. Hou, J.W. Poole, Kinetics and mechanism of degradation of ampicillin in solution, J. Pharm. Sci. 58 (4) (1969) 447−454.

[33] T. Loftsson, H. Fridriksdóttir, Degradation of lomustine (CCNU) in aqueous solutions, Int. J. Pharm. 62 (2) (1990) 243−247.

[34] S.R. Byrn, W. Xu, A.W. Newman, Chemical reactivity in solid-state pharmaceuticals: formulation implications, Adv. Drug Deliv. Rev. 48 (1) (2001) 115−136.

[35] M.S. Cunha-Filho, A. Estévez-Braun, E. Pérez-Sacau, M.M. Echezarreta-López, R. Martínez-Pacheco, M. Landín, Light effect on the stability of β-lapachone in solution: pathways and kinetics of degradation, J. Pharm. Pharmacol. 63 (9) (2011) 1156−1160.

[36] S.W. Hovorka, C. Schöneich, Oxidative degradation of pharmaceuticals: theory, mechanisms and inhibition, J. Pharm. Sci. 90 (3) (2001) 253−269.

[37] R. Teraoka, M. Otsuka, Y. Matsuda, Chemical stability of ethyl icosapentate against autoxidation. I. Effect of temperature on oxidation kinetics, Pharm. Res. 9 (12) (1992) 1673−1676.

[38] Lovaza® Package Insert, Lovaza-Omega-3-Acid Ethyl Esters Capsule, Liquid Filled, Woodward Pharma Services LLC. Updated February 24, 2021; Available from: https://dailymed.nlm.nih.gov/dailymed/drugInfo.cfm?setid=c1920576-1b04-4b20-bb00-061f09032574, accessed 30-Sep-2022.

[39] H.-C. Mahler, W. Friess, U. Grauschopf, S. Kiese, Protein aggregation: pathways, induction factors and analysis, J. Pharm. Sci. 98 (9) (2009) 2909−2934.

[40] USP, Chapter 1191, Stability considerations in dispensing practice, in: USP-NF Online, USPC Committee of Revision, United States Pharmacopeial Convention, 2022. DocId: GUID-564A3F58-D2DB-4DF8-92D8-92A21DB36D02_3_en-US.

[41] USP, Chapter 1079.2, Mean kinetic temperature in the evaluation of temperature excursions during storage and transportation of drug products, in: USP-NF Online, USPC Committee of Revision, United States Pharmacopeial Convention, 2022. DocId: GUID-C65501B2-4215-49ED-8563-BBCE2760D93E_2_en-US.

[42] K.C. Waterman, R.C. Adami, Accelerated aging: prediction of chemical stability of pharmaceuticals, Int. J. Pharm. 293 (1) (2005) 101−125.

[43] ICH-M9, ICH Guideline M9—Biopharmaceutics Classification System-Based Biowaivers, The International Council for Harmonisation of Technical Requirements for Pharmaceuticals for Human Use, Geneva, Switzerland, 2019.

[44] C. Li, T. Liu, X. Cui, A.S. Uss, K.C. Cheng, Development of in vitro pharmacokinetic screens using Caco-2, human hepatocyte, and Caco-2/human hepatocyte hybrid systems for the prediction of oral bioavailability in humans, J. Biomol. Screen 12 (8) (2007) 1084−1091.

[45] C. Günther, K. Kowal, T. Schmidt, A. Jambrecina, F. Toner, R. Nave, Comparison of in vitro and in vivo percutaneous absorption across human skin using BAY1003803 formulated as ointment and cream, Clin. Pharmacol. Drug Dev. 9 (5) (2020) 582−592.

[46] G.L. Flynn, S.H. Yalkowsky, T.J. Roseman, Mass transport phenomena and models: theoretical concepts, J. Pharm. Sci. 63 (4) (1974) 479−510.

[47] USP, Chapter 671, Containers—performance testing, in: USP-NF Online, USPC Committee of Revision, United States Pharmacopeial Convention, 2022. DocId: GUID-99FB391E-ADC7-4247-B254-094C4DC7486C_3_en-US.

[48] F.S. Hom, S.A. Veresh, W.R. Ebert, Soft gelatin capsules II: oxygen permeability study of capsule shells, J. Pharm. Sci. 64 (5) (1975) 851−857.

[49] USP, Chapter 711, Dissolution, in: USP-NF Online, USPC Committee of Revision, United States Pharmacopeial Convention, 2022. DocId: GUID-AC788D41-90A2-4F36-A6E7-769954A9ED09_2_en-US.

[50] R.J. Hintz, K.C. Johnson, The effect of particle size distribution on dissolution rate and oral absorption, Int. J. Pharm. 51 (1) (1989) 9−17.

[51] N. Shah, H. Sandhu, D.S. Choi, H. Chokshi, A.W. Malick, Amorphous Solid Dispersions, Theory and Practice, Springer, Berlin, Germany, 2014.

[52] A.T.M. Serajuddin, Salt formation to improve drug solubility, Adv. Drug Deliv. Rev. 59 (7) (2007) 603−616.

[53] S. Fredenberg, M. Wahlgren, M. Reslow, A. Axelsson, The mechanisms of drug release in poly(lactic-co-glycolic acid)-based drug delivery systems–a review, Int. J. Pharm. 415 (1−2) (2011) 34−52.

[54] C. Maderuelo, A. Zarzuelo, J.M. Lanao, Critical factors in the release of drugs from sustained release hydrophilic matrices, J. Control. Release 154 (1) (2011) 2−19.

[55] R.W. Korsmeyer, R. Gurny, E. Doelker, P. Buri, N.A. Peppas, Mechanisms of solute release from porous hydrophilic polymers, Int. J. Pharm. 15 (1) (1983) 25−35.

[56] R. Govindarajan, Solubility Enhancement for Improved and Modified Oral Drug Delivery, PhD Thesis, University of Mumbai, 2001.

[57] H. Vogelpoel, J. Welink, G.L. Amidon, H.E. Junginger, K.K. Midha, H. Möller, M. Olling, V.P. Shah, D.M. Barends, Biowaiver monographs for immediate release solid oral dosage forms based on biopharmaceutics classification system (BCS) literature data: verapamil hydrochloride, propranolol hydrochloride, and atenolol, J. Pharm. Sci. 93 (8) (2004) 1945−1956.

[58] V. Malaterre, J. Ogorka, N. Loggia, R. Gurny, Oral osmotically driven systems: 30 years of development and clinical use, Eur. J. Pharm. Biopharm. 73 (3) (2009) 311−323.

[59] D.R. Swanson, B.L. Barclay, P.S. Wong, F. Theeuwes, Nifedipine gastrointestinal therapeutic system, Am. J. Med. 83 (6) (1987) 3−9.

[60] Procardia XL® Package Insert, Procardia XL-Nifedipine Tablet, Film Coated, Extended Release, Pfizer Laboratories. Updated April 28, 2021; Available from: https://dailymed.nlm.nih.gov/dailymed/drugInfo.cfm?setid=8ebcb33c-f43b-4b36-9f94-9774b2a59e06, accessed 30-Sep-2022.

[61] W. Huang, S.L. Lee, L.X. Yu, Mechanistic approaches to predicting oral drug absorption, AAPS J. 11 (2) (2009) 217−224.

[62] G. Wang, J.D. Fiske, S.P. Jennings, F.P. Tomasella, V.A. Palaniswamy, K.L. Ray, Identification and control of a degradation product in Avapro™ film-coated tablet: low dose formulation, Pharm. Dev. Technol. 13 (5) (2008) 393−399.

[63] USP, Chapter 1671, Application of moisture vapor transmission rates for solid oral dosage forms in plastic packaging systems, in: USP-NF Online, USPC Committee of Revision, United States Pharmacopeial Convention, 2022. DocId: GUID-52690118-4600-4C92-B755-8E9CFFAE5-B46_3_en-US.

[64] Eligard® Package Insert, Eligard-Leuprolide Acetate Kit, Tolmar Pharmaceuticals Inc. Updated April 29, 2019; Available from: https://dailymed.nlm.nih.gov/dailymed/drugInfo.cfm?setid=b78d1919-9dee-44fa-90f9-e0a26d32481d, accessed 30-Sep-2022.

[65] B. Bhatnagar, R.H. Bogner, M.J. Pikal, Protein stability during freezing: separation of stresses and mechanisms of protein stabilization. Pharm. Dev. Technol. 12 (5) (2007) 505–523.

[66] N.V. Phadnis, R. Suryanarayanan, Polymorphism in anhydrous theophylline–implications on the dissolution rate of theophylline tablets, J. Pharm. Sci. 86 (11) (1997) 1256–1263, https://doi.org/10.1021/js9701418. PMID: 9383736.

[67] A. Beig, N. Fine-Shamir, D. Lindley, et al., Advantageous solubility-permeability interplay when using amorphous solid dispersion (ASD) formulation for the BCS class IV P-gp substrate rifaximin: simultaneous increase of both the solubility and the permeability, AAPS J. 19 (2017) 806–813, https://doi.org/10.1208/s12248-017-0052-1.

[68] J.S. Claudius, S.H. Neau, The solution stability of vancomycin in the presence and absence of sodium carboxymethyl starch, Int. J. Pharm. 168 (1998) 41–48, https://doi.org/10.1016/S0378-5173(98)00080-5.

PART II

Practical aspects of pharmaceutics

7

Biopolymers

Somnath Singh and Alekha K. Dash

Department of Pharmacy Sciences, School of Pharmacy and Health Professions, Creighton University, Omaha, NE, United States

CHAPTER OBJECTIVES

- Define and differentiate polymer, protein, and oligonucleotide.
- Discuss the structural properties that distinguish polymers from other molecules.
- Describe some polymers and their uses that are commonly used as excipients in the pharmaceutical industry.
- Discuss the important physical properties of pharmaceutical polymers.
- Discuss briefly the properties of polymers in solution.
- Discuss briefly the solid-state properties of polymeric materials.
- Discuss pharmaceutical applications of polymers.
- Introduce protein and peptide and discuss their unique structure, stability, and applications.
- Introduce oligonucleotides and discuss their applications with examples.

Keywords: Oligonucleotides; Oligonucleotides Therapeutics; Peptides and Proteins; Peptides/Proteins Therapeutics; Polymers; Polymer Properties; Polymers as Excipients.

7.1 Introduction to polymers

Polymers are natural or synthetic compounds made up of numerous repeated monomer units. Chemical properties of a polymer depend on the monomer units and the way they have been arranged. Polymers can be either linear or branched. Branched polymers are then categorized as isotactic (similar side chains), atactic (random pattern of side chains), and syndiotactic (a regular pattern of alteration inside chains). Linear or branched chains can be covalently bonded together using cross-linking agents. Polymers with only one type of monomer unit are called

Pharmaceutics, Second Edition
https://doi.org/10.1016/B978-0-323-99796-6.00008-4

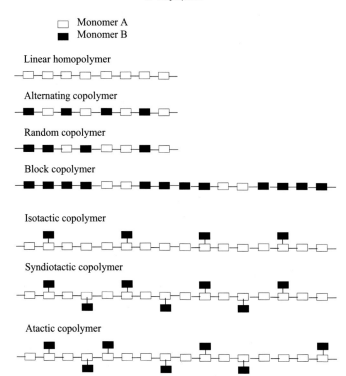

FIGURE 7.1 Various polymer structures attained due to alteration in polymerization pattern of two different monomers diagrammatically represented by ☐ and ■.

homopolymers. Polymers with different monomer units are referred to as copolymers. Various copolymers can be prepared in which monomers may repeat in a specific regular pattern, termed alternating polymers, or arranged in no pattern at all, referred to as random copolymers, respectively (Fig. 7.1).

7.1.1 Properties of polymers

7.1.1.1 Polydispersity

Almost all naturally and synthetically produced polymers exist as a mixture of molecules with varying molecular weights and chain lengths. Therefore, the molecular weight of polymer is expressed as average calculated on the basis of either number or weight of each monodispersed fraction. The number average molecular weight (M_n) of a polymer containing n_1, n_2, $n_{3,...}$ molecules with molecular weights M_1, M_2, M_3, ... is calculated using the formula shown in Eq. (7.1) whereas the weight average molecular weight (M_w) is calculated using Eq. (7.2):

$$M_n = \frac{n_1 M_1 + n_2 M_2 + n_3 M_3 + \cdots}{n_1 + n_2 + n_3 + \cdots} = \frac{\sum n_i M_i}{\sum n_i} \tag{7.1}$$

$$M_w = \frac{n_1 M_1^2 + n_2 M_2^2 + n_3 M_3^2 + \ldots}{n_1 M_1 + n_2 M_2 + n_3 M_3 + \ldots} = \frac{\sum n_i M_i^2}{\sum n_i M_i} \tag{7.2}$$

The ratio of M_w and M_n provides polydispersity index (PDI) which influences polymer properties in addition to its molecular weight. PDI values <0.05 are indicative of monodisperse polymer samples while values >0.7 indicate a broad size distribution (polydisperse) of the polymer sample as per international standards organizations (ISOs) standards ISO 22412:2017 and ISO 22412:2017. PDI values less than 0.7 is clinically much useful because they indicate greater stability for nanodrug delivery systems [1]. If the PDI value is a little greater than 0.7, it can be reduced by purifying polymers or isolating unacceptable polymer fractions.

7.1.1.2 Solubility

After the addition of polymer to a solvent, the polymer undergoes wetting followed by swelling. Solvent takes a longer time to diffuse into high-molecular-weight polymers because more energy is required to break the intramolecular bonds, which are more prevalent than those in polymers of low molecular weight. If the solubility parameter of a polymer is the same as or close to the solubility parameter [2] of the solvent, the solvent is considered a good solvent and can dissolve the polymer to yield a polymer solution. Water-soluble polymers increase the solution viscosity at low concentrations due to swelling. These water-soluble polymers have numerous pharmaceutical applications, including functioning as suspending agents in pharmaceutical suspensions by slowing the settling of solid insoluble particles in suspension. Some pharmaceutically utilized water-soluble polymers include hydroxyethyl cellulose, alginates, and chitosan. Hydrophilic polymers are a separate group of polymers that will absorb water and swell but do not completely dissolve. Some hydrophilic polymers are used pharmaceutically to control the release rate of drugs. Furthermore, there are some polymers which have high melting point due to strong internal bonds. This high internal stability might cause the polymer to take a longer time to dissolve or not dissolve at all. Such poorly or insoluble polymers are also used in pharmaceutical preparations to form thin films, film-coating materials, surgical dressings, etc.

7.1.2 General properties of polymer in solutions

7.1.2.1 Viscosity

Polymers increase the viscosity of solutions and suspensions due to strong internal friction between the randomly coiled swollen polymers and the surrounding solvent. This increase in viscosity is one of the key properties for pharmaceutical polymer use. Numerous terms are used to describe the influence of polymers on solution viscosities. Note that η_0 is the viscosity of pure solvent and η is the viscosity of the polymer solution.

1. **Relative viscosity**, η_r: this is the viscosity of a polymer solution relative to the normal viscosity of the solvent as given in Eq. (7.3):

$$\eta_r = \frac{\eta}{\eta_0} \tag{7.3}$$

2. **Specific viscosity**, η_{sp}: specific viscosity describes the difference of viscosities of a solvent and polymer solution relative to viscosity of the polymer solution as shown in Eq. (7.4). It is the fractional increase in viscosity, due to the addition of the polymer, relative to the solvent viscosity:

$$\eta_{sp} = \frac{\eta - \eta_0}{\eta_0} = \eta_r - 1 \tag{7.4}$$

3. **Inherent viscosity**, η_i: the inherent viscosity is another way to describe the relative increase in viscosity due to the polymer concentration in the solution. It is calculated by taking the natural log of relative viscosity of a polymer solution divided by its concentration (c), as shown in Eq. (7.5):

$$\eta_i = \frac{\ln \eta_r}{c} \tag{7.5}$$

4. **Intrinsic viscosity** $[\eta]$: the intrinsic viscosity is not a true viscosity measurement but it provides size of the molecular mass of the polymer in a solution. It describes the polymer's ability to increase the viscosity of a given solution. It is defined as the limit of the ratio of specific viscosity to polymer concentration (referred to as reduced viscosity) as polymer concentration approaches zero and is represented by Eq. (7.6):

$$[\eta] = \lim_{c \to 0} \frac{\eta_{sp}}{c} \tag{7.6}$$

The intrinsic viscosity of solutions of linear high-molecular-weight polymers is proportional to the molecular weight, M, of the polymer as given by the Mark−Houwink equation (Eq. 7.6):

$$[\eta] = KM^a \tag{7.7}$$

where a is a constant in the range $0-2$ (most high-molecular-weight polymers have a value between 0.6 and 0.8), and K is a constant for a given polymer-solvent system.

7.1.2.2 Gelling

The association or cross-linking of long polymer chains in a concentrated polymer solution induces a three-dimensional continuous network that traps and immobilizes the liquid within it to form a rigid structure called gel. Thus, a gel contains a three-dimensional network of stable physical or chemical bonds characterized by high viscosity and rubber-like appearance. There are two main types of gels.

- **Type I:** irreversible gel system made of covalent bonds
- **Type II:** heat-reversible gels held together by weak hydrogen bonds

Polymer solutions can have a gel point that defines the state at which sufficient polymer bonding has occurred to create a coextensive polymer phase (i.e., the solution turns into a dense semisolid). Gel points can be temperature dependent, with some polymer solutions forming gels with a decrease in temperature, whereas others with an increase in temperature. Type I gels are more prevalent in pharmacy because of their superior stability.

Some copolymers have different solubility characteristics due to varied monomer units in the polymer. Copolymers can also form gels when dissolved in high concentration and can be referred to as heterogels. A common pharmaceutical example of a gel-forming block copolymer is polyoxyethylene—polyoxypropylene—polyoxyethylene, also known as Pluronic or poloxamer; which is found in a wide variety of pharmaceutical preparations.

7.1.2.3 Cross-linking

Cross-linking is the formation of covalent bonds between polymer chains to form networks of varying densities based on the degree of cross-linking. Water-soluble polymers can form gels when they are cross-linked. Several pharmaceutical polymers are cross-linked to affect solution or gel viscosities and drug release characteristics. One example is drug-containing hydrophilic contact lenses made from cross-linked poly(2-hydroxyethyl methacrylates) [3]. Other ophthalmologic solutions and gels are prepared with cross-linked polymers to increase the contact time of the drug with the cornea by increasing the viscosity of the formulation [4].

7.1.3 Application of water-soluble polymers in pharmacy and medicine

Water-soluble or hydrophilic polymers are widely used in pharmaceutical preparations and drug products as suspending agents, surfactants, emulsifying agents, binding agents in tablets, thickening or viscosity-enhancing agents in liquid dosage forms, film-coating agents, etc. Some of the most common water-soluble polymers and their applications in pharmaceutical preparations can be found in Table 7.1. Other polymers that are not included in Table 7.1 have specific functions for uses such as coatings, enteric coatings, film formation, and hot melt extrusion.

7.1.4 Application of water-insoluble polymers in pharmacy and medicine

Water-insoluble polymers are often used in pharmaceutical preparations of controlled drug release formulations, membranes, containers, and tubing material. Permeability of drugs and their adsorption are two important parameters deciding the suitability of these polymers for use in pharmacy. Some drug solutions that come in contact with insoluble polymers can be adsorbed onto the polymer surface depending on drug-polymer affinity. Some slow-molecular weight drugs as well as many biological medications (therapeutic proteins, peptides, antibodies, and oligonucleotides) may bind to insoluble polymers, especially in intravenous syringes, bags, and tubing. Special precautions and practices are warranted to avoid or minimize drug product binding to insoluble polymers used in the packaging of the drug product. In addition to surface adsorption, some small drug molecules can permeate into and possibly diffuse through insoluble polymers. The intercalation of small drug molecules into insoluble polymers such as plastics can affect polymer strength and integrity as well as interfere with the patient receiving the desired medication dose.

7.2 Introduction to peptides and proteins

The tremendous advances in biotechnology and the sequencing of the human genome have made it possible to develop and produce an increasingly diverse number of therapeutically active proteins and peptides. Some examples

TABLE 7.1 Examples of water-soluble or hydrophilic polymers and their pharmaceutical applications.

Polymers	Description	Applications
Carboxymethylcellulose sodium	This polymer is the sodium salt of substituted polycarboxymethyl cellulose. It is hygroscopic and soluble in water at all temperatures. Once hydrated or solubilized, it has acidic characteristics (pKa ~4.3).	It is used in oral and topical formulations as a coating agent, stabilizer, suspending agent, tablet binder, tablet disintegrant, and viscosity-increasing agent.
Carboxypolymethylene or Polyacrylic acid (Carbomer®, Carbopol®)	These high-molecular-weight polymers of acrylic acid that contain carboxylic acid groups (pKa ~6). These polymers form viscous gels in neutralized water due to repulsion between ionized functional groups.	They are used as controlled drug release agents, emulsifiers, emulsion stabilizers, viscosity enhancing agents, gelling agents, suspending agents, and tablet binders.
Methylcellulose	These methyl ether substituted long-chain cellulosic polymers are poorly soluble in cold water. Physical properties are influenced by the degree of substitution.	Low-viscosity grades are used as tablet binders, sustained release agents, emulsifiers, suspending agents, and thickeners. High-viscosity grades are used as tablet disintegrants and topical thickening agents.
Hydroxyethylcellulose (HEC)	HEC is a partially substituted poly(hydroxyethyl) ether of cellulose. This is soluble in both hot and cold water; it does not form gel.	It is used as a thickening agent in ophthalmic and topical preparations.
Hypromellose (Hydroxypropylmethylcellulose, HPMC)	This is a partially substituted cellulose derivative of methoxy and hydroxyl propanoyl groups. The degree and composition of substitutions affect polymer properties. It forms a viscous colloidal solution.	Hypromellose is widely used in a wide variety of pharmaceutical preparations including oral, ophthalmic, otic, nasal, and topical preparations. It is used as a film-coating agent, tablet binder, controlled drug release modifier, dispersing and suspending agent, emulsifier and emulsion stabilizer, thickener, and gelling agent.
Povidone (polyvinylpyrrolidone, Kollidon®)	This is a variable-length linear polymer of 1-vinyl-2-pyrrolidone groups. The polymer viscosity is used to categorize molecular weight grades described by "K-values."	Povidone has a variety of uses but is principally used in oral dosage forms as a tablet binder and disintegrant. It can also be used as a suspending and viscosity-enhancing agent. Povidone also increases the solubility of numerous poorly soluble drugs.
Polyoxyethylene glycol (PEG, Macrogols)	PEG is a linear polymer of oxyethylene groups of varying lengths. Low-molecular-weight PEGs (PEGs 200–700) are liquid at room temperature, whereas higher-molecular-weight PEGs are solid.	PEG is a widely used polymer in oral, rectal, topical ophthalmic/otic, and parenteral products. It is a solvent, diluent, viscosity-enhancing agent, suspending agent, ointment base, suppository base, tablet binder, plasticizer, lubricant, controlled drug release agent, etc.
Acacia (Arabic gum)	This natural polymer is a complex and branched loose aggregate of cellulosic compounds and sugars that is soluble in water up to 30%. The viscosity of its aqueous solution is pH-dependent.	Acacia is principally used in topical formulations as a stabilizing, suspending, and viscosity-enhancing agent. It has also been used in controlled-release tablets.
Alginate salts (sodium salt, potassium salt, calcium salt, etc.)	These are salts of natural alginic acid polymer, which is a block mixture of polyuronic acids (D-mannuronic and L-glucoronic acid residues).	Alginate salts have a variety of pharmaceutical uses, such as tablet binder and disintegrant, suspending agent, viscosity-increasing agent, and sustained drug release agent.
Chitosan	This natural polymer is partially deacetylated and depolymerized from chitin. Polymer properties are based in part on the degree of acetylation. It is soluble at acidic pH values and gels at neutral pH values due to the presence of amine groups (pKa 5.5–6.5.)	Chitosan is used as a coating and film-forming agent, disintegrant, tablet binder, and viscosity-enhancing agent.

Continued

TABLE 7.1   Examples of water-soluble or hydrophilic polymers and their pharmaceutical applications.—cont'd

Polymers	Description	Applications
Pectin	Pectin is a high-molecular-weight complex polysaccharide obtained from the rind of citrus fruit. It consists of partially methoxylated polygalacturonic acid. Gelation is affected by the extent of esterification.	It is used as an adsorbent, thickening, emulsifying, gelling, and stabilizing agent.
Tragacanth (tragacanth gum)	This natural polymer composed of insoluble and soluble polysaccharides. It dissolves partially in water to produce highly viscous suspensions.	It is used topically as a suspending and viscosity-enhancing agent.

of biotechnology-enabled pharmaceutical products include hemophiliac globulins, growth hormones, erythropoietin, colony-stimulating factors, interferon, natural proteins or "first-generation recombinant proteins," viral or bacterial proteins (as vaccines), monoclonal antibodies, and older products such as insulin and immunoglobulins. Despite this expansion in therapeutic proteins and peptides, they possess unique physical and chemical properties that present substantial difficulties in formulation and delivery.

Unlike conventional small-molecular-weight compounds, therapeutic proteins and peptides are biological macromolecules that are polypeptides and consist of polymerized amino acids. The linear polymers are composed of covalently linked amino acid monomers. Short peptide polymers are often referred to as polypeptides, whereas longer-chain-length molecules are considered proteins. Proteins and polymers are characterized by a regularly repeating backbone with distinctive functionalized amino acid side chains that interact with each other to promote the formation of a therapeutically essential three-dimensional conformational structure. This structure has four principal different levels of organization—namely, a primary structure, secondary structure, tertiary structure, and a quaternary structure—that determine the therapeutically active or functional three-dimensional structure [5].

7.2.1 Primary structure

The primary structure of a protein consists of the protein's linear amino acid sequence. The primary structure is held in a fixed sequence by covalently linked amino acids through peptide (amide) bonds that provide flexibility and allow rotational movement. The primary structure also has a definitive orientation due to the carboxyl-terminal and amino-terminal functional groups that make up the two ends of the amino acid chain. Ultimately, the structure and function of therapeutic proteins and peptides depend on the unique primary structure of a protein.

7.2.2 Secondary structure

Secondary structures are composed of localized patterns of orientation due to hydrogen bonds between the amino acid backbone and side-chain amide or the carboxyl groups. Generally, the amino acid backbone N—H residues form hydrogen bonds with C=O groups on a separate residue. Secondary structures are classified based on their localized geometries with common structures described as α-helices and β-pleated sheets. The α-helix is a structurally ridged single-stranded right-handed spiral where hydrogen bonding occurs between amino acid residues that are spaced approximately four residues apart based on the primary structure sequence. Fibrous structural proteins, such as keratins, are mainly made up of α-helical structures. The β-pleated sheet is a weaker structural unit formed as a twisted and pleated sheet of amino acid strands. The hydrogen bonds might or might not form between residues that are in proximity to each other based on the primary structure sequence. Proteins can contain numerous secondary structural regions of both α-helix and β-pleated sheets in the same polypeptide chain. It is important to note that the hydrogen bonding potential in secondary structures depends on the relative orientation, spacing, and sequence of amino acids as well as the spatial proximity of amino acid residues based on the tertiary structures.

7.2.3 Tertiary structure

The tertiary structure is the actual three-dimensional spatial structure of the protein. It is often composed of secondary structures packed into compact globular units known as domains. Domains are precisely folded, bent, and arranged in secondary structures. Tertiary structures are principally folded and formed based on the properties of side-chain functional groups. Domains form in part to minimize hydrophobic side-chain exposure to aqueous environments, promote hydrogen bonding, stabilize polar or ionized functional groups, form disulfide bonding, and ensure the protein is conformed in such a manner to be in an energy state minimum.

7.2.4 Quaternary structure

Quaternary structures are composed of multiple separate polypeptide chains, known as subunits, arranged into complex three-dimensional structures. These subunits may be connected to each other through disulfide bonds and are stabilized by ionic bonds, hydrogen bonds, and Van der Waals interactions. While common for many biological proteins, not all therapeutic proteins exhibit quaternary structures. Fig. 7.2 depicts the four different levels of protein structure [6].

7.2.5 Protein stability

Many therapeutic proteins are chemically and structurally unstable and have the potential to lose their conformational stability and biological activity. Much of this instability is due to normal physiologic processes for protein digestion, cleavage, and processing throughout the body due to wide range in biological pH, biological conditions, enzymatic cleavage and modifications, and antigen processing and preparation. Moreover, most proteins are impermeable across biological membranes and have short elimination half-lives in biological conditions. Therefore, the development of effective and efficient delivery systems for peptides and proteins is a substantial pharmaceutical challenge.

Protein and peptide delivery systems must be able to supply conformationally active molecules to the site of drug action. These systems should also include (1) the ability to control the release rate and/or location of drug release to ensure the therapeutic drug concentration is maintained at the site of action for the intended duration of time, (2) mechanisms to protect the stability and biological activity of the protein/peptide in the body, and (3) mechanisms to maintain drug product stability during shipping and long-term storage. In-depth knowledge about protein structure, product stability, and handling requirements is essential for healthcare providers to educate and communicate appropriately with patients and other healthcare professionals.

Protein stability refers to the maintenance of the primary, secondary, tertiary, and quaternary structures. Various interactions between charged groups, hydrophobic interactions, and hydrogen bonds help in protecting the stability of the native protein structures. Peptidyl—prolyl isomerization, disulfide bridges methylation, phosphorylation, or glycosylation provides covalent contributions to protein stability. Non-covalent factors that contribute to protein stability are hydrophobic interactions, hydrogen bonds, Van der Waals forces, aromatic interactions, and ion pairs/salt bridges. Hydrophobic polypeptide segments are buried in the interior of protein molecules, normally out of contact with water. If these interactions are not optimized, an increase in entropy can occur and may lead to a disruption of protein stability.

Protein instability occurs when the structure is disrupted by the conversion of the native protein (i.e., therapeutically active and folded) to non-native or denatured states (i.e., unfolded, cleaved, or inactivated proteins). Typically, these instabilities ultimately result in an alteration to pharmacologic effects or the complete loss of the protein's biological activity.

Many therapeutic proteins have fragile three-dimensional structures and are susceptible to various degradation pathways categorized as physical and chemical instability. Physical instability refers to an alteration in secondary or higher degrees of structures, whereas chemical instability refers to any changes leading to the formation of a new chemical entity such as the formation or deletion of an amide bond between any two amino acids or alterations to the side chain functional groups.

7.2.6 Physical instability

7.2.6.1 Aggregation

Aggregation is typically the reversible association of materials to form small, loose composite particles. For therapeutic proteins, this association can result in the loss of a protein's native structure due to the disruption of tertiary or quaternary structural bonds or associations which can potentially lead to irreversible protein instability. Aggregation can occur in the presence of thermal, chemical, or physical stress. Furthermore, aggregates can form due to the

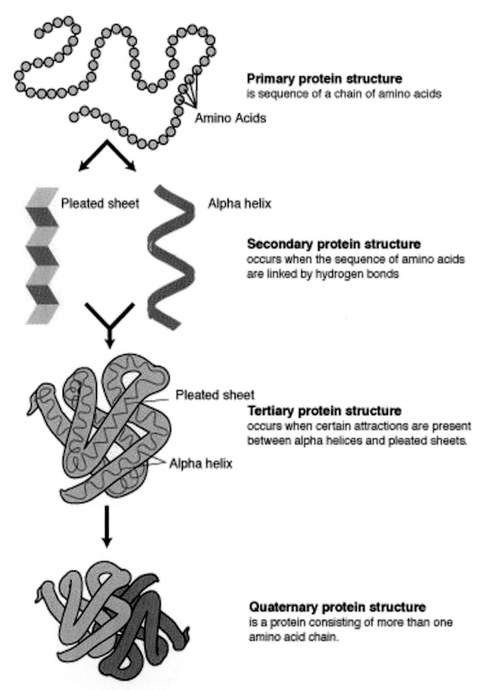

Primary protein structure
is sequence of a chain of amino acids

Amino Acids

Pleated sheet

Alpha helix

Secondary protein structure
occurs when the sequence of amino acids
are linked by hydrogen bonds

Pleated sheet

Tertiary protein structure
occurs when certain attractions are present
between alpha helices and pleated sheets.

Alpha helix

Quaternary protein structure
is a protein consisting of more than one
amino acid chain.

FIGURE 7.2   Primary, secondary, tertiary, and quaternary structure of proteins. *Courtsey of the National Human Genome Institute.*

creation of non-native β-sheet structures. Some factors that contribute to protein aggregation include elevated temperature, altered solution pH values, changes in salt concentration, and the presence of co-solutes including preservatives and surfactants.

7.2.6.2 *Adsorption*

Adsorption is the physical association of particles to an encountered surface. It is related to the adhesion of the proteins to various surfaces due to favorable interactions to coat or form a monolayer. Many therapeutic proteins have a high likelihood to adsorb onto the surfaces of water-insoluble polymers used in drug administration devices, for example, syringe bodies, IV fluid bags, tubing, seals, and plungers. Adsorption to these surfaces can alter the physicochemical properties of the protein causing conformational instability, leading to loss of activity and in some cases even adverse effects. Protein adsorption to plastics/polymers can also lead to a reduction in administered drug dose resulting in suboptimal pharmacologic responses. Although some adsorbed proteins can be disassociated, most are irreversibly adsorbed, unable to be recovered under normal clinical conditions.

7.2.6.3 Precipitation

Precipitation is similar to aggregation but occurs at a macroscopic level when irreversible particle flocculation occurs. Precipitated protein particles have lost important structural elements and are unable to be resuspended. Precipitation can be caused due to the presence of salts, the addition of organic solvent or other additives, and a change in the pH of the protein solution. Insulin frosting is a type of protein precipitation, where finely divided insulin precipitation occurs on the walls of a container. This occurs due to the denaturation of insulin at the air—water interface. Proteins are known to be less soluble at their isoelectric point (the pH at which a protein molecule carries no net electric charge).

7.2.6.4 Denaturation

Denaturation is described as the disruption of the secondary and tertiary structures of proteins. A schematic representation of normal and denatured protein is depicted in Fig. 7.3 [7]. It can occur due to various physical factors such as temperature, pH, and the addition of organic solvents or other denaturants. Protein denaturation is often irreversible but might be reversible in specific circumstances. For example, elevated temperature can cause an increase in the energy of the system to promote bond rotation, which could lead to unfavorable interactions that could then disrupt protein structure and cause the unfolding of the protein. Sometimes, lowering the temperature can reverse the effect and allow the favorable interactions to reform to promote the proper folding of the therapeutic protein in a phenomenon called reversible denaturation. In cases of irreversible denaturation, the unfolding or misfolding occurs, but the process is not reversible; hence, the protein does not regain its native state [7].

7.2.7 Chemical instability

7.2.7.1 Deamidation

Deamidation of the hydrolysis of the side chain amide linkage in asparagine or glutamine residues occurs, resulting in the formation of free carboxylic acid. The rate of deamidation is affected by temperature, pH, ionic strength, and the presence of buffer ions in the solution. In a neutral pH solution, deamidation causes the introduction of a negative charge and results in isomerization, which then affects the biochemical properties of peptides and proteins.

7.2.7.2 Racemization

Racemization of amino acids can occur in all amino acids except glycine because of a chiral center at the carbon bearing a side chain. Racemization generally occurs via the removal of α-methine hydrogen by the base to form a carbanion ion. The rate of racemization is controlled by the stabilization of the carbanion ion, typically by the close association of electronegative functional groups or molecules. Racemization can result in the formation of

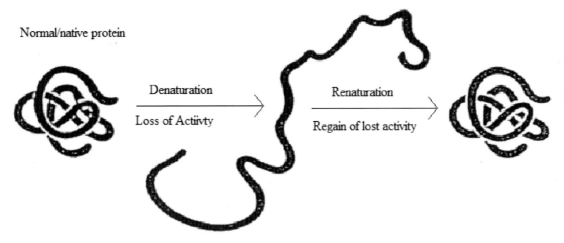

FIGURE 7.3 Schematic representation of normal and denatured protein [7].

nonmetabolizable forms of amino acids or it can form peptide bonds that are accessible to proteolytic enzymes. Racemization of therapeutic proteins and peptides has the potential to disrupt protein structure via chemical destabilizing interactions.

7.2.7.3 Oxidation

The side chains of methionine, histidine, cysteine, tryptophan, and tyrosine residues in proteins are sites that are susceptible to oxidation. Methionine residues can be oxidized even by atmospheric oxygen. The thio-ether group of methionine is a weak nucleophile and is not protonated at a low pH, which can allow oxidation under acidic conditions. The rate of oxidative degradation will increase in the presence of visible light and is thought to be related to the formation of free radicals. The solution pH is also found to affect the rate of oxidation with slow histidine oxidation, that is, protonation occurring at low pH values.

7.2.7.4 Disulfide exchange

The interchanging of disulfide bonds in proteins can cause incorrect pairing and distort protein structure and loss of pharmacologic activity. Thiol ions cause a nucleophilic attack on the sulfur ion of the disulfide in neutral and alkaline conditions. Thiol scavengers such as p-mercuribenzoate and copper ions can be used to prevent disulfide exchange as they catalyze the oxidation of thiols.

7.2.7.5 Hydrolysis

Hydrolysis of amide bonds in the peptide backbone can occur under a variety of circumstances. Enzymatic cleavage, pH-dependent hydrolysis, and intramolecular catalysis at the N-terminal or C-terminal end at a residue adjacent to an aspartic acid residue via the ionized carboxyl group can cause protein hydrolysis. Often, cleavage of peptide linkages and chemical hydrolysis can cause a complete loss of pharmacologic activity and protein denaturation.

7.2.8 Protein and peptide-based drugs

The number of marketed therapeutic proteins and peptides continues to expand. The clinical utility of these agents is also expanding to diverse groups of therapeutic applications such as replacing a deficient or an abnormal endogenous protein or peptide, providing some novel function or activity, augmenting an existing physiological pathway or process, binding with a molecule or receptor, delivering other compounds, eliciting an immune response for the purpose of vaccination, or diagnosis. Table 7.2 gives brief descriptions of select marketed drug products with clinically relevant approaches to the pharmaceutical principles of therapeutic proteins and peptides.

7.3 Introduction to oligonucleotides

Oligonucleotides are short linear nucleic acid polymers that typically have 50 or fewer nucleotide bases. Although some oligonucleotides have been approved as therapeutic agents, a great deal of research is being devoted to the development of these drug products. Oligonucleotides typically exert their pharmacologic activity as antisense oligonucleotides by interfering with normal DNA replication to silence a gene expression. Therefore, oligonucleotides therapeutics include antisense oligonucleotides and siRNA that bind to RNA, antigene oligonucleotides that bind to DNA, and aptamers, decoys, and CpG oligonucleotides that bind to proteins. As natural polymers, oligonucleotides present substantial barriers to drug product development, absorption, formulation, and delivery.

7.3.1 Antisense oligonucleotides

Therapeutic oligonucleotides (oligo) typically have very specific nucleotide sequences that target specific sequences of DNA or RNA that are exposed during normal cellular processes. The therapeutic oligo is complementary to a chosen sequence with which it can bind with very high affinity. Antisense oligonucleotides containing complementary nucleotide sequences target mRNA or DNA but with modifications to promote cellular degradation of the complex into nucleotide residues as shown in Fig. 7.4 [8]. The oligo-DNA/RNA hybrid duplex is then enzymatically degraded and results in the inhibition of the expression of the chosen gene sequence.

TABLE 7.2 Protein and peptide-based drugs.

Proteins/peptides	Trade name	Description
Angiotensin receptor	Angiotensin II	Use for increasing blood pressure in shock
	Losartan	Angiotensin receptor blocker; decreases blood pressure
L-asparaginase	Elspar	Asparaginase inhibits protein synthesis by hydrolyzing asparagine to aspartic acid and ammonia. It is used in acute lymphocytic leukemia, which requires exogenous asparagine for proliferation.
Bevacizumab	Avastin	It is a recombinant, humanized monoclonal antibody that binds to all isoforms of vascular endothelial growth factor (VEGF), preventing its association with endothelial receptors, Flt-1, and KDR required for angiogenesis; therefore, it is used in the treatment of colorectal cancer and non–small-cell lung cancer.
Blood clotting factor VIII	Advate	It is used to treat hemophilia A.
Blood clotting factor IX	BeneFIX	This factor IX of recombinant DNA origin is used in the prevention and control of hemorrhagic episodes in patients with a deficiency of coagulation factor IX associated with hemophilia B (Christmas disease).
Botulinum toxin type A	Botox	This is a neurotoxin produced by *Clostridium botulinum*, which appears to affect only the presynaptic membrane of the neuromuscular junction in humans, where it prevents calcium-dependent release of acetylcholine and produces a state of denervation. Muscle inactivation persists until new fibrils grow from the nerve and form junction plates on new areas of the muscle-cell walls. This is used to treat cervical dystonia and minimize the appearance of glabellar lines.
β-Gluco-cerebrosidase	Cerezyme	It hydrolyzes glucocerebroside to glucose and ceramide. Therefore, it is used in Gaucher's disease, in which the patient is genetically deficient of enzyme β-Gluco-cerebrosidase, resulting in an accumulation of the harmful fatty acid substance glucocerebroside in the liver, spleen, lungs, and bone marrow.
Calcitonin	Fortical, Miacalcin	This is a peptide hormone that is used in osteoporosis. Salmon calcitonin (SCT) is more potent than human calcitonin (HCT) because it is not fibrillated in physiological solution. The pK_a values of SCT and HCT are 10.4 and 8.7, respectively; therefore, SCT remains charged at pH 7.4, which repels each other, thereby inhibiting fibrillation.
Denileukin diftitox	Ontak	It is a fusion protein (a combination of amino acid sequences from diphtheria toxin and interleukin-2) that directs the cytocidal action of diphtheria toxin to cells expressing the IL2 receptor. Therefore, it is used in the treatment of T-cell lymphoma, whose malignant cells overexpress the IL2 receptor.
Erythropoietin	Procrit	It stimulates erythropoiesis and therefore is used in anemia due to some chronic diseases, renal failure, or chemotherapy.
Growth hormone, somatotropin	Genotropin, Nutropin	This anabolic and anticatabolic effector is used in growth failure due to growth hormone deficiency or chronic renal insufficiency, Prader–Willi syndrome, Turner syndrome, and AIDS wasting (or cachexia) with antiviral therapy.
Guanylate cyclase C receptor	Plecanatide	Indicated for the treatment of chronic idiopathic constipation
Human papillomavirus (HPV) vaccine	Gardasil	It contains major capsid proteins from four HPV strains and is used as a vaccine for the prevention of HPV infection.
Hepatitis B surface antigen (HBsAg)	Engerix	This is derived from the hepatitis B surface antigen (HBsAg) produced through recombinant DNA techniques from yeast cells and is used for immunization against infection caused by all known subtypes of the hepatitis B virus.

Continued

TABLE 7.2   Protein and peptide-based drugs.—cont'd

Proteins/peptides	Trade name	Description
Insulin NPH (isophane suspension)	(HumuLIN N, NovoLIN N)	This is an intermediate-acting insulin (onset, peak glycemic effect, and duration are 1–2, 4–12, and 14–24 h, respectively).
Insulin NPH suspension and insulin regular solution	NovoLIN 70/30	This is a combination of two types of insulin for which onset, peak glycemic effect, and duration are 0.5, 2–12, and 8–24 h, respectively.
Insulin zinc	Lente	Insulin zinc, like insulin NPH, is an intermediate-acting insulin that consists of a mixture of crystalline and amorphous insulin in a ratio of approximately 7:3.
Insulin glargine	Lantus	This is a long-acting insulin (onset and duration are 3–4 and >24 h, respectively) that does not have any pronounced peak glycemic effect.
Interferon-α2b (IFN- α2b)	Intron A	It works as an immunoregulator although the exact mechanism is not known. It is used in hepatitis B and C, melanoma, Kaposi's sarcoma, follicular lymphoma, etc.
Lactase	Lactaid	This is able to digest lactose; hence, it is used in gas, bloating, cramps, and diarrhea due to the patient's inability to digest lactose.
Lutropin-α	Luveris	It is a recombinant human luteinizing hormone that increases estradiol secretion and therefore is used in treating infertility due to luteinizing hormone deficiency.
Melanocortin-4 receptor	Setmelanotide	Indicated for chronic weight management of obesity
Natriuretic peptide receptor	Nesiritide	Indicated for acute decompensated heart failure
Peginterferon-α2b	Peg-Intron	This is IF Nα2b conjugated with polyethylene glycol to increase its half-life.
Trastuzumab	Herceptin	Trastuzumab is a monoclonal antibody that binds to the extracellular domain of the human epidermal growth factor receptor 2 protein (HER-2) and controls cancer cell growth. Therefore, it is used in the treatment of breast cancer, which overexpresses HER-2 receptors.
Somatostatin receptors	Lutetium-177 dotatate	Indicated for the treatment of somatostatin receptor–positive gastroenteropancreatic neuroendocrine tumors
	Edotreotide gallium	Indicated for diagnosing somatostatin receptor–positive neuroendocrine tumors

7.3.2 Therapeutic oligonucleotides [9,10]

The drug delivery challenges for therapeutic oligonucleotides are substantial. They are not capable of permeating through biological membranes, are sensitive to widespread nuclease activity throughout the body, and are susceptible to chemical degradation and nonspecific adsorption to surfaces. Various chemical modifications and formulations have been investigated to overcome these barriers. Currently, there are some FDA-approved oligonucleotide-based drug products available. However, future scientific advancements will likely lead to more marketed oligonucleotides. Examples of currently marketed products are described in the following sections.

7.3.2.1 Pegaptanib sodium (Macugen)

Pegaptanib is a modified oligonucleotide that is conjugated to PEG and is selective to inhibit vascular endothelial growth factor (VEGF). It is approved for the treatment of age-related macular degeneration as an intravitreal injection directly into the vitreous humor of the eye. This invasive intraocular injection bypasses biological membranes and eliminates the need for membrane permeation. Pegaptanib is available as a prefilled, single-dose, glass syringe with an attached needle that is all enclosed in a sterile foil pouch. The drug solution is preservative-free and contains only sodium chloride and phosphate salts to ensure the solution is isotonic and has a neutral pH.

7.3.2.2 Fomivirsen (Vitravene)

Fomivirsen is an antisense oligonucleotide that inhibits human cytomegalovirus (CMV) replication. It is approved for injection into the vitreous humor of the eye and is active against strains of CMV resistant to ganciclovir, foscarnet,

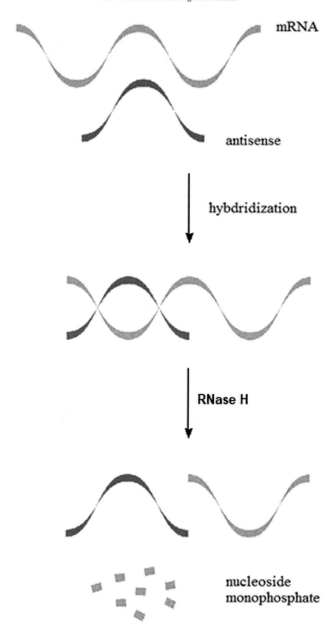

FIGURE 7.4 Diagrammatic representation of RNase H mediated destruction of mRNA bound to an antisense oligonucleotide. *Modified and adapted from Ref. [8].*

and cidofovir. It is a sterile, preservative-free, buffered solution in a single-use glass vial. A sterile filter needle should be used to withdraw the solution and injected intravitreally using a new small gauge (30G) needle.

7.3.2.3 Mipomersen (Kynamro)

Mipomersen is an antisense oligonucleotide that inhibits the synthesis of apo B-100 involved in the production of low-density lipoprotein and very low-density lipoprotein associated with familial hypercholesterolemia. It is injected subcutaneously into the abdomen, thigh, or upper and outer part of the arm and binds extensively to plasma proteins. Mipomersen is available as a sterile, preservative-free, single-dose, prefilled glass syringe. The drug solution contains only pH adjustment ingredients.

7.3.2.4 Inotersen (Tegsedi)

Inotersen was approved by the FDA and EMA in 2018 for the treatment of patients with hereditary amyloid trans-thyretin (ATTR) amyloidosis, a rare systemic disorder that is characterized by progressive peripheral polyneuropathy, cardiomyopathy, nephropathy, and gastrointestinal dysfunction. The disorder is caused by dominant-negative mutations in the *TTR* gene that lead to the destabilization of the tetrameric TTR protein complex, causing aggregation of monomers into extracellular amyloid deposits. *Inotersen is* designed to bind and elicit RNase H-mediated degradation of mutant and wild-type *TTR* transcripts, resulting in decreased mutant and wild-type TTR proteins in plasma and targeted organs.

7.3.2.5 Volanesorsen *(Waylivra)*

Volanesorsen was authorized in by the European Medicines Agency (EMA) in 2019 for the treatment of familial chylomicronemia syndrome (FCS). The levels of triglyceride are about 10—100 times more in FCS patients than in normal healthy individuals. FCS patients carry recessive mutations in the *LPL* gene, which causes reduced or lack of lipoprotein lipase enzyme activity resulting in an increase in triglyceride levels. Volanesorsen reduces the levels of apolipoprotein C *(APOC3)* mRNA and thereby APOC3 protein, which is a known inhibitor of lipoprotein lipase — an enzyme causing the degradation of circulating triglycerides in the bloodstream.

7.3.2.6 Nusinersen *(Spinraza)*

Nusinersen was approved by the FDA in December 2016 and the EMA in 2017 for the treatment of spinal muscular atrophy (SMA) caused by mutations in chromosome 5q that lead to survival motor neuron (SMN) protein deficiency. SMN protein deficiency is associated with recessive mutations in the survival motor neuron 1 (*SMN1*) gene. Its copy gene SMN2 mitigates the disease symptoms, although, it produces a low level of SMN proteins. A single nucleotide change in *SMN2* exon 7, decreases its inclusion in the final mRNA, leading to an unstable SMN protein. Nusinersen works by binding to a specific sequence in the intron downstream of exon seven of the *SMN2* messenger ribonucleic acid (mRNA) leading to increased production of full-length normal stable SMN protein.

7.3.2.7 Eteplirsen *(Exondys)*

Eteplirsen was approved by the FDA in 2016 for the treatment of Duchenne muscular dystrophy (DMD) caused by complete loss-of-function mutations in the X-linked *DMD* gene, which produces dystrophin protein. Eteplirsen (a 30-mer phosphorodiamidate morpholino oligomer) binds with exon 51 of the DMD gene resulting in a partially functional dystrophin protein with less severe DMD. This works in about 15% of DMD patients who are amenable to escaping exon 15.

7.3.2.8 Olodirsen *(Vyondys)* and viltolarsen *(Viltepso)*

Golodirsen and viltolarsen were approved by the FDA in 2019 and 2020, respectively, for the treatments of DMD where exon 53 escaping is associated with the production of truncated DMD protein. They are useful for about 8% of DMD patients where exon 53 is amenable.

7.3.2.9 Milasen

Milasen is a custom antisense oligonucleotide drug that was developed for a single person named Mila for a fatal neurodegenerative condition called Batten disease caused by a single mutation in both copies of the *CLN7* gene. However, the single mutation was missing from another copy of *CLN7* gene which instead was having retrotransposon (a piece of viral DNA) inserted into the middle of the noncoding region. This glitch appeared to prematurely halt the process of RNA splicing which is responsible for stitching together genes of coding region needed for the production of normal native proteins. An antisense oligomer, Milasen, was capable of blocking the inserted retrotransposon in the *CLN7* gene and restored normal RNA splicing resulting in significant improvement in disease symptoms such as multiple epileptic seizures per day.

7.3.2.10 Defibrotide *(Defitelio)*

Defibrotide is a polydisperse mixture of all the single-stranded phosphodiester oligodeoxyribonucleotides obtained from the controlled depolymerization of porcine intestinal mucosal genomic DNA [11]. It is indicated for the treatment of hepatic sinusoidal obstruction syndrome for patients with renal or pulmonary dysfunction following a hematopoietic stem cell transplant. It reduces endothelial cell (EC) activation and increases EC-mediated fibrinolysis by increasing tissue plasminogen activator and thrombomodulin expression, as well as by decreasing von Willebrand factor and plasminogen activator inhibitor-1 expression.

7.4 Conclusions

The pharmaceutical utilization of polymers provides key functions in formulations and pharmacologically active drugs. However, polymers are unlike many other active pharmaceutical ingredients and excipients in numerous ways. Many polymers used as pharmaceutical excipients have formulation-specific functions that are dependent on their chemical structure and molecular weight. Many polymers are used for the enhancement of viscosity, gelation, tablet binding of other ingredients, film formation, coatings, etc. Other polymers are therapeutically active proteins, peptides, and oligonucleotides. Scientific advances in pharmaceutical biotechnology will further expand the clinical utility and availability of these therapeutic biopolymers.

Case studies

Case 7.1

Lyophilization is generally used to provide long-term storage stability to protein and peptide-based therapeutics. Explain how does lyophilization provide stability? What important considerations should a pharmacist provide to enhance such therapeutics' stability during storage?

Approach: Lyophilized proteins exist in highly viscous amorphous glassy states with low molecular mobility and low reactivity and are very stable under this condition. According to the "vitrification hypothesis," stability is highly dependent on storage temperature. If the same material is stored at a temperature higher than its glass transition temperature (Tg), the viscous glass will be transformed to a less viscous "rubbery" state with increased heat capacity, molecular mobility, and decreased stability. Crystallization of the glass-forming excipients can occur above the Tg value, further decreasing its stability. Excipients such as sugars are reported to link with the protein via hydrogen bond in the same manner as water, conserving its native structure by replacing water lost during drying and stabilizing the formulation during storage. Many studies have shown that optimal stabilization is provided by glass-forming excipients that bind with the protein molecule through hydrogen bond, thus preserving its native structure during lyophilization and storage. Storage temperature and moisture are the two important considerations pharmacists have to consider for stability. Moisture can act as a plasticizer and affect Tg and thereby stability.

Case 7.2

As a manufacturing pharmacist, one is supposed to determine the drug load of a silicone rubber implantable delivery of a steroidal drug. The pharmacist has no information available regarding how to proceed on this issue. What information will help the pharmacist to address this issue? Is this particular implant is a biodegradable or nonbiodegradable polymeric implant?

Approach: A silicone implant is not biodegradable. To determine the drug load, the pharmacist has to use an analytical method for the quantitation of the drug in the implant. There is also a need to know a good solvent system for dissolving the polymer and to extract the drug from the polymeric solution. A good solvent is one for which the solubility parameter of the solvent is similar/close to that of the polymer. All this information can be obtained from the literature or a polymer handbook. In the case of silicone rubber, hexane is a good solvent to dissolve the implant. The pharmacist can find an assay method for the drug in the literature and use it to determine the concentration in the implant after dissolving it in hexane. Extraction of the drug from the organic solvent followed by its analysis using a robust analytical technique will determine the drug concentraion in the implant.

Case 7.3

The major component of hard and soft gel capsules is gelatin. Knowing some of the properties of the polymer, explain why such differences occur between those two.

Also, one of your patients refuses to take such capsules because of his religious beliefs. What alternatives do you have for this patient?

Approach: The difference between hard and soft gel capsules is the amount of plasticizer used. The use of a plasticizer in a polymer decreases the glass transition temperature (Tg) of a polymer. It can exist as a rubbery polymer at room temperature, but not as a glass. Glycerol or sorbitol is used as a plasticizer for gelatin.

To provide other alternatives for your patient, you can do the following.

- Dispense the same drug in a different dosage form (suspension) if its physicochemical properties allow.
- Dispense capsules from which alternative sources besides animals are used to create the gelatin. Some hard shell capsules are made from materials other than gelatin. For alternatives to gelatin that will be of interest to those who, for religious, cultural, or other reasons, wish to avoid capsules manufactured from animal sources, consider offering starch hydrolyzate (Capill is the commercial product) or Hydroxypropyl methylcellulose (Vegicaps, or V-caps, is the commercial product in the market).

Case 7.4

A familial chylomicronemia syndrome (FCS) patient is taking volanesorsen but his symptoms are not improving. You are a member of the patient's healthcare team. What alternative therapy will you suggest?

Approach: FCS is a disease in which triglyceride level is extremely high. This disease is due to reduced production or lack of lipoprotein lipase enzyme which degrades triglycerides in plasma. Volanesorsen works by reducing the production of *APOC3* protein which is a known inhibitor of lipoprotein lipase enzyme. Patient's symptoms are not improving which may be due to the complete loss of lipoprotein lipase enzyme because even its reduced level generally keeps the symptoms mild. Therefore, volanesorsen may not be a good fit for this patient, and it should be either replaced or combined with other medicines such as statins known to reduce triglyceride levels via another mechanism.

Critical reflections and practice applications

Biopolymers discussed in this chapter have played indispensable roles in the preparation of various pharmaceutical dosage forms as well as many have been used to provide some unique therapeutic benefits. Below are some salient points about their application in clinical pharmacy practices.

- **i.** A general understanding of the unique physicochemical properties of polymers, proteins, and oligonucleotides in contrast to smaller molecular weight drugs would help pharmacists in their proper handling and patient counseling.
- **ii.** Compounding pharmacists can use various polymers for preparing efficient dosage forms. For example, viscosity-enhancing polymers for preparing a stable suspension.
- **iii.** Pharmacists can manipulate transdermal gels for preparing veterinary patches for which there is no commercially available product.
- **iv.** Special handling and storage are needed to preserve the structural integrity of protein/peptide-based therapeutics to achieve desired biological effects.
- **v.** A pharmacist working in a healthcare team can provide patient-specific recommendations about oligonucleotide-based therapeutics.

References

[1] M. Danaei, M. Dehghankhold, S. Ataei, F. Hasanzadeh Davarani, R. Javanmard, A. Dokhani, S. Khorasani, M.R. Mozafari, Impact of particle size and polydispersity index on the clinical applications of lipidic nanocarrier systems, Pharmaceutics 10 (2) (May 18, 2018) 57, https://doi.org/10.3390/pharmaceutics10020057. PMID: 29783687; PMCID: PMC6027495.

[2] S. Jankovic, G. Tsakiridou, F. Ditzinger, N.J. Koehl, D.J. Price, A.R. Ilie, L. Kalantzi, K. Kimpe, R. Holm, A. Nair, B. Griffin, C. Saal, M. Kuentz, Application of the solubility parameter concept to assist with oral delivery of poorly water-soluble drugs - a PEARRL review, J. Pharm. Pharmacol. 71 (4) (April 2019) 441–463, https://doi.org/10.1111/jphp.12948. Epub 2018 Jul 5. PMID: 29978475.

[3] L.D. Wuchte, S.A. DiPasquale, M.E. Byrne, *In vivo* drug delivery via contact lenses: the current state of the field from origins to present, J. Drug Deliv. Sci. Technol. 63 (June 2021) 102413, https://doi.org/10.1016/j.jddst.2021.102413. Epub 2021 Feb 18. PMID: 34122626; PMCID: PMC8192067.

[4] F. Rohde, M. Walther, J. Wächter, N. Knetzger, C. Lotz, M. Windbergs, In-situ tear fluid dissolving nanofibers enable prolonged viscosity-enhanced dual drug delivery to the eye, Int. J. Pharm. 616 (January 24, 2022) 121513, https://doi.org/10.1016/j.ijpharm.2022.121513. Epub ahead of print. PMID: 35085733.

[5] KauzmannW, The three dimensional structures of proteins, Biophys. J. 4 (1 Pt 2) (1964) SUPPL43–SUPPL58, https://doi.org/10.1016/s0006-3495(64)86925-3.

[6] Three Dimensional Protein Structure available at: https://www.genome.gov/genetics-glossary/Protein [Accessed on Feb. 20, 2022].

[7] M.C. Lai, E.M. Topp, Solid-state chemical stability of proteins and peptides, J. Pharmaceut. Sci. 88 (1999) 489–500.

[8] Oligonucleotides as drugs. Available at: http://www.atdbio.com/content/13/Oligonucleotides-as-drugs>[Accessed on Feb. 22, 2022].

[9] T.C. Roberts, R. Langer, M.J.A. Wood, Advances in oligonucleotide drug delivery, Nat. Rev. Drug Discov. 19 (10) (October 2020) 673–694, https://doi.org/10.1038/s41573-020-0075-7. Epub 2020 Aug 11. PMID: 32782413; PMCID: PMC7419031.

[10] J. Kim, C. Hu, C. Moufawad El Achkar, L.E. Black, J. Douville, A. Larson, M.K. Pendergast, S.F. Goldkind, E.A. Lee, A. Kuniholm, A. Soucy, J. Vaze, N.R. Belur, K. Fredriksen, I. Stojkovska, A. Tsytsykova, M. Armant, R.L. DiDonato, J. Choi, L. Cornelissen, L.M. Pereira, E.F. Augustine, C.A. Genetti, K. Dies, B. Barton, L. Williams, B.D. Goodlett, B.L. Riley, A. Pasternak, E.R. Berry, K.A. Pflock, S. Chu, C. Reed, K. Tyndall, P.B. Agrawal, A.H. Beggs, P.E. Grant, D.K. Urion, R.O. Snyder, S.E. Waisbren, A. Poduri, P.J. Park, A. Patterson, A. Biffi, J.R. Mazzulli, O. Bodamer, C.B. Berde, T.W. Yu, Patient-customized oligonucleotide therapy for a rare genetic disease, N. Engl. J. Med. 381 (17) (October 24, 2019) 1644–1652, https://doi.org/10.1056/NEJMoa1813279. Epub 2019 Oct 9. PMID: 31597037; PMCID: PMC6961983.

[11] N. Kornblum, K. Ayyanar, L. Benimetskaya, P. Richardson, M. Iacobelli, C.A. Stein, Defibrotide, a polydisperse mixture of single-stranded phosphodiester oligonucleotides with lifesaving activity in severe hepatic veno-occlusive disease: clinical outcomes and potential mechanisms of action, Oligonucleotides 16 (1) (2006) 105–114, https://doi.org/10.1089/oli.2006.16.105. Spring PMID: 16584299.

Suggested readings

[1] T. Avdeef Yamamoto, M. Nakatani, K. Narukawa, S. Obika, Antisense drug discovery and development, Future Med. Chem. 3 (2011) 339–365.

[2] D.J. Florence Labarre, G. Ponchel, C. Vauthier, Biomedical and Pharmaceutical Polymers, Pharmaceutical Press, London, UK, 2011.

[3] R.C. Ganellin Rowe, P.J. Sheskey, M.E. Quinn, A.P. Association, Handbook of Pharmaceutical Excipients, sixth ed., Pharmaceutical Press, London, UK, 2009.

[4] P.J. Gibaldi Sinko, Colloidal Dispersions. Martin's Physical Pharmacy and Pharmaceutical Sciences: Physical Chemical and Biopharmaceutical Principles in the Pharmaceutical Sciences, Lippincott Williams, New York, USA, 2006, pp. 386–409.

8

Drug, Dosage Form, and Drug Delivery Systems

Alekha K. Dash

Department of Pharmacy Sciences, School of Pharmacy and Health Professions, Creighton University, Omaha, NE, United States

---

CHAPTER OBJECTIVES

- Recognize the difference between drug, dosage forms, and drug delivery systems.
- Appreciate the need for various dosage forms and drug delivery systems.
- Identify the role of active and inactive pharmaceutical ingredients (excipients) in a dosage form.
- Recognize the importance of preformulation studies in dosage form design.
- Understand some of the important preformulation strategies commonly used in dosage form development.
- Understand various chemical and physical properties determined during the preformulation process.
- Appreciate the working principles involved in the characterization techniques used in preformulation.

Keywords: Active pharmaceutical ingredient; Dosage form; Dosage form design; Excipients; Pharmaceuticals ingredients; Preformulation.

8.1 Introduction

Drug substances are rarely administered alone. They are administered either as dosage forms or as drug delivery systems. Acetaminophen is the drug or, more precisely, the active pharmaceutical ingredient (API) in a Tylenol tablet. This tablet, irrespective of its strength, does not contain only acetaminophen but numerous inactive ingredients also called excipients or inactive pharmaceutical ingredients.

Pharmaceutics, Second Edition
https://doi.org/10.1016/B978-0-323-99796-6.00020-5

Dosage form is a physical form of a pharmaceutical formulation containing the drug and some inactive ingredients necessary to prepare it. In the preceding example of the Tylenol tablet, acetaminophen is the drug, and the tablet is the dosage form. Cellulose, pregelatinized starch, and magnesium stearate are some of the inactive materials also present in this tablet formulation. Other dosage forms may include capsules, powders, emulsions, solutions, suspensions, syrups, lotions, elixirs, parenteral, suppositories, ointments, creams, and pastes.

Drug delivery systems, on the other hand, are specialized dosage forms where one can predict the release of the drug from such systems. The nicotine transdermal patch and Procardia XL are two examples of drug delivery systems. Procardia XL is a tablet and should be initially interpreted as a dosage form. However, a thorough understanding of this specialized tablet dosage form reveals its mechanism of drug release, which is based on an osmotic drug delivery system. More importantly, one can predict the rate of nifedipine (API in Procardia XL tablet) release from such tablets. Therefore, this specialized dosage form is more appropriately called a drug delivery system. Dosage forms as well as drug delivery systems contain various inactive ingredients besides the active pharmaceutical ingredient (drug). Various inactive pharmaceutical ingredients or excipients that are incorporated into the dosage form to accomplish one or more of the needed functions are outlined in Table 8.1.

Pharmaceutics is the science of dosage form design and belongs to a branch of pharmacy that deals with the general area of study concerned with the formulation, manufacture, stability, and evaluation of the effectiveness of various pharmaceutical dosage forms and drug delivery systems.

Various dosage forms are necessary to accomplish many important functions associated with the drugs, which are listed below.

- Provide safe and convenient delivery of an accurate dose of a drug.
- Protect the drug from the destructive influences of atmospheric oxygen, light, microbial contamination, and humidity (e.g., coated tablets, sealed ampoules, amber colored glass container, incorporation of antibacterial agents, incorporation of antioxidants).
- Protect tablets from the destructive effect of gastric acid during oral administration (e.g., enteric-coated tablets).
- Protect drugs from their irritative effect in the GI tract during oral administration (e.g., enteric-coated tablets and film-coated tablets).
- Mask the unpleasant taste or odor of the drug substance (e.g., flavored syrup, sugar-coated tablet, or capsule).
- Administer a high dose of an insoluble drug in a liquid dosage form (e.g., suspension).
- Provide clear liquid dosage forms for a drug substance (e.g., syrups, solutions, elixirs).
- Provide an optimal drug action from topical administration sites (e.g., ointments; creams; transdermal patches; ophthalmic, otic, and nasal routes).

TABLE 8.1   Functions of pharmaceutical ingredients.

Functions to be accomplished	Inactive pharmaceutical ingredient (excipient)	Examples
Solubilize	Surfactants	Tween 20
Suspend	Suspending agent	Methylcellulose
Thicken	Thickening agent	Gum acacia
Dilute	Solvent	Water
Emulsify	Emulsifying agent	Tween 20, Span 80
Preserve	Preservatives	Methyl and propyl paraben
Color	Coloring agent	FD&C yellow color
Flavor	Flavoring agent	Peppermint oil
Disintegrate	Disintegrating agent	Starch
Bind	Binders	Starch

- Provide delivery of drugs by insertion into one of the body cavities (e.g., suppositories).
- Administer a drug directly into the body tissues (e.g., parenteral dosage form, implantable delivery systems).
- Provide optimal drug action through inhalation therapy (e.g., aerosols).
- Provide time-controlled drug action (e.g., controlled-release tablets, capsules, and suspensions).

8.2 Inactive pharmaceutical ingredients (Excipients)

Excipients generally establish the primary features of the dosage form and contribute to the physical form, texture, stability, taste, and overall appearance of the dosage form.

In the preparation of liquid dosage forms, the following excipients may be used.

- Solvents and co-solvents are used for the formulation of solutions
- Preservatives are used to prevent microbial growth in aqueous solutions
- Stabilizers are used to prevent drug decomposition and maintain drug stability in formulation
- Flavoring agents are added to enhance palatability
- Coloring agents are used to enhance product appeal and identification.

In the formulation of tablet dosage forms, the following excipients are commonly used.

- Diluents or fillers are used to increase the bulk of the formulation
- Binders are used to adhere the powdered drug and excipients to form granules
- Disintegrants are used to promote tablet disintegration (break-up) in the gastrointestinal tract
- Lubricants are used to assist proper powder flow during tablet manufacturing
- Coatings are applied to improve stability and enhance appearance.

In the preparation of semisolid dosage forms.

- For the preparation of ointments and pastes, the major inactive pharmaceutical ingredient used is the ointment base
- For suppository, the major excipient used is the suppository base.

8.3 Preformulation studies

Preformulation is the process of optimizing a drug through the determination of its physical and chemical properties considered important in the formulation of a stable, effective, and safe dosage form. This also includes the determination of any possible interactions with various ingredients in the final formulation. The overall objective of preformulation is to collect useful information of a drug and excipients needed for developing a stable and bioavailable dosage form that can be scaled up for mass production. A thorough preformulation study helps in understanding the physicochemical properties of the drug molecule in development. It also provides the foundation for the development of a robust dosage form that can withstand rigorous processing challenges.

Pharmaceutical preformulation work is generally initiated when a compound shows sufficiently impressive results during biological screening. The preformulation flow sheet is shown in Fig. 8.1 and illustrates the various steps involved in the preformulation process [1,2].

Preformulation study involves three areas of information gathering that include chemical, physical, and biological properties of the API as described below.

8.3.1 Chemical properties

- Structure, form, purity, and reactivity

Chemical property characterization includes attributes like identity, purity, assays, and quality. The tests involved to characterize these attributes are outlined in Table 8.2.

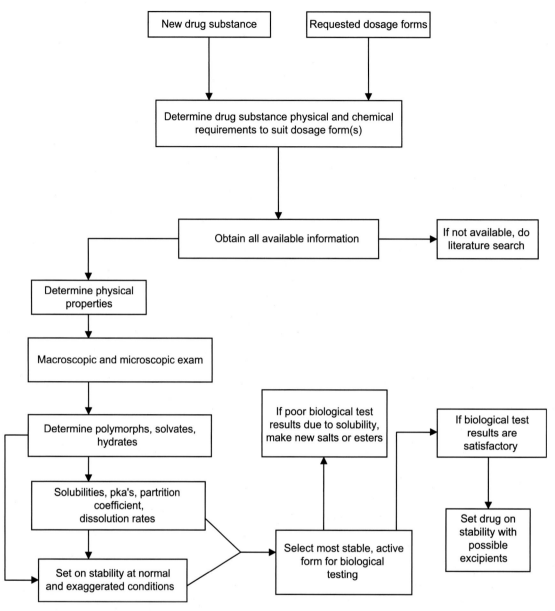

FIGURE 8.1   The preformulation process flow sheet.

8.3.2 Physical properties

- Macroscopic and microscopic properties
- Partition coefficient
- pKa
- Solubility
- Dissolution
- Polymorphism
- Melting point
- Membrane permeability
- Drug and drug product stability

8.3.3 Biological properties

- Ability to get to the site of action and elicit a biologic response.

TABLE 8.2 Chemical property characterization.

S. No.	Attribute	Tests
1	Identity (structure and form)	Nuclear magnetic resonance (NMR)
		Infrared spectroscopy (IR)
		Ultraviolet spectroscopy (UV)
		Differential scanning calorimetry (DSC)
		Optical rotation
2	Purity (purity and reactivity)	Moisture/solvate (water and solvents)
		Inorganic elements
		Heavy metals
		Organic impurities and DSC
3	Assays (form, purity, and reactivity)	Titration, UV, HPLC, UPLC
4	Quality (form, purity, and reactivity)	Appearance, odor
		Solution color and pH of slurry (saturated solution)
		Melting point

8.4 Physical description

Most drug substances in use today occur as solids. However, they may be available as a liquid or even less frequently as a gas. This physical form plays an important role in determining the ultimate dosage form. If the drug is available as a liquid, and the requested dosage form is a solid, the preformulation scientist does not have enough options available to fulfill this request. In such cases, more preferred options are:

- providing different salt forms of the product
- or even rethinking of a different dosage form

8.5 Liquid dosage forms

Examples of some liquid drugs and their clinical use in parentheses are listed below.

- Amyl nitrite (vasodilator)
- Nitroglycerin (antianginal)
- Ethchlorvynol (hypnotic)
- Clofibrate (antihyperlipidemic)
- Paraldehyde (sedative-hypnotic)
- Undecylenic acid (antifungal)

Some of the challenges encountered during the formulation of liquid dosage forms are as follows:

1. Many liquids are volatile and flammable. Therefore, they should be physically sealed in ampoules (e.g., amyl nitrate).
2. Liquids cannot be formulated into tablet forms intended for oral administration. An exception to this is nitroglycerin tablet triturates, which disintegrate within seconds when placed under the tongue. Two approaches are generally used to deliver liquid orally as a solid formulation:

a. Liquid drug delivered in soft gelatin capsules (e.g., Paramethadione and Ethchlorvynol)
b. Liquid drug converted to a solid salt or ester (e.g., liquid scopolamine is converted to a scopolamine hydrobromide solid).

3. Stability problems arise more frequently with liquid dosage forms. Drug is more stable in a solid dosage form as compared to the same drug in a liquid formulation.

Besides the preceding disadvantages, liquid drugs also pose certain advantages, as follows.

1. Large doses can be administered orally (e.g., l5 mL dose of mineral oil).
2. Topical application becomes easy and effective (e.g., undecylenic acid in the local treatment of a fungal infection).
3. Liquid doses are convenient for administration to pediatric and geriatric patients.

8.6 Solid dosage forms

Tablets and capsules comprise the dosage forms dispensed more than 70% of the time by community pharmacists, with tablets dispensed twice as frequently as capsules [3].

8.6.1 Solid-state properties

Some of the properties of solids that need to be thoroughly investigated during a preformulation study are listed below.

Macroscopic properties: Appearance, color, and odor of a drug substance should be recorded. Bulk density and true density of the material need to be determined at this stage if not available to a preformulation scientist.

Density: Density is a derived property that is based on the relationship between two important attributes of the material, which include its mass and volume. It is not measured directly but rather calculated or derived. Many such density terms are used in pharmacy and are listed below.

True density: This is the density of the actual solid material, and it is an inherent physical property of the material. For nonporous material, density is measured by displacement in an insoluble liquid. For porous solids, a helium densitometer is generally used to determine density. True density measurement considers the true volume that is occupied by the particles themselves, *excluding any potential interior voids, cracks, or pores at the surface of particles.*

Bulk density: Bulk density is defined by the mass of the powder divided by its bulk volume. About 100 cc (cc = cm^3) of powder passed through a US standard sieve #18 is weighed with 0.1% accuracy (mass = M) and placed in a 250 cc volumetric cylinder without any compact. The unsettled apparent volume (volume = V_0) is measured. The bulk density is calculated using Eq. (8.1).

$$\text{Bulk Density} \left(\frac{\text{gram}}{\text{mL}}\right) = \frac{M}{V_0} \tag{8.1}$$

Tapped Density: The tapped density is an increased bulk density attained after mechanically tapping a graduated measuring cylinder containing a known mass of a powder sample. The apparatus consists of a 250-mL graduated cylinder (readable to 2 mL) with a settling apparatus capable of producing in 1 min, either nominally 250 ± 15 taps from a height of 3 ± 0.2, mm, or nominally 300 ± 15 taps from a height of 14 ± 2 mm. Volume of the powder after 10 (V_{10}), 500 (V_{500}), and 1250 (V_{1250}) taps on the same powder was determined. If the differences between V_{500} and V_{1250} are less than or equal to 2 mL then V_{1250} is the tapped volume (V_f). If the volume difference is more than 2 mL, then the determination is repeated. The tapped density is determined using Eq. (8.2).

$$\text{Tapped Density} \left(\frac{\text{gram}}{\text{mL}}\right) = \frac{M}{V_f} \tag{8.2}$$

Flow properties: Angle of repose is a measure of the flow properties of a powder or a granule. Powders are allowed to pass through a funnel until the angle of inclination is large enough to balance the frictional forces and form a heap. The *angle of repose* or, more precisely, the *critical angle of repose* is the steepest angle of dip of the slope relative to the horizontal plane when a material on the slope face is on the verge of sliding and is shown in Fig. 8.2. This angle is given by the number (0—90 degrees). The tangent of the angle of repose is a measure of the internal friction of the powder bed as shown in Eq. (8.3):

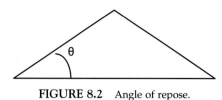

FIGURE 8.2 Angle of repose.

TABLE 8.3 Flow properties and the corresponding angle of repose [4].

Flow properties	Angle of repose (degrees)
Excellent	25–30
Good	31–35
Fair—aid not needed	36–40
Passable—may hang up	41–45
Poor—must agitate, vibrate	46–55
Very poor	56–65
Very, very poor	>66

$$\tan(\theta) = \mu_s = \frac{height}{0.5\ base} \tag{8.3}$$

where μ_s is the coefficient of static friction, and θ is the angle of repose. The flow properties of powder and their corresponding angle of repose as specified by USP are shown in Table 8.3.

Angle of repose is not an intrinsic property of the powder. It depends on the method used to form a cone of the powder.

Flow properties of a powder can also be determined from tapped and bulk density determinations using compressibility index and Hausner ratio as shown in Eqs. (8.4) and (8.5).

$$Compressibility\ Index = 100 \times \left(\frac{V_0 - V_f}{V_0}\right) \tag{8.4}$$

$$Hausner\ Ratio = \frac{V_0}{V_f} \tag{8.5}$$

Alternatively, they can also be determined using Eqs. (8.6) and (8.7).

$$Compressibility\ index = 100 \times \left(\frac{Tapped\ Density - Bulk\ Density}{Tapped\ Density}\right) \tag{8.6}$$

$$Hausner\ Ratio = \frac{Tapped\ Density}{Bulk\ Density} \tag{8.7}$$

As per USP, Table 8.4 describes 3 different flow properties of powders using both compressibility index and Hausner ratio.

8.6.2 Microscopic examination

A microscopic examination provides information on particle size, size distribution, and crystal habit (shape) of a drug. These properties can be best identified through the use of a *polarizing* microscope. Crystal shape may be of prime importance and a deciding factor for certain formulations. Needle-like crystals, for example, are not suitable for parenteral formulations. A microscope attached to a hot stage (Hot stage microscopy or Thermo-microscopy) may be utilized to determine.

- The purity of a drug sample semi-quantitatively (the melting point)
- The presence of any hydrates or solvates in the crystal
- Physical changes that may occur during heating

TABLE 8.4   Flow properties of powders using compressibility index and hausner ratio [4].

Compressibility index (%)	Flow character	Hausner ratio
≤10	Excellent	1.00—1.11
11—15	Good	1.12—1.18
16—20	Fair	1.19—1.25
21—25	Passable	1.26—1.34
26—31	Poor	1.35—1.45
32—37	Very poor	1.46—1.59
>38	Very, very poor	>1.60

8.6.3 Particle size

Particle size and size distribution can affect various important properties of drug substances. It may affect dissolution, absorption, solubility, content uniformity, taste, texture, color, and stability. The following methods can be used to determine the particle size of powders during preformulation studies:

Sieving: Sieving and screening are generally used for particle size analysis when the particles are approximately 44 µm and greater. The only disadvantage of this method is that a relatively large sample size is required. This method is very simple both in technique and equipment requirements that use various standardized sieves.

Microscopy: The optical microscopy can be utilized to determine the particle size, size distribution, and shape of new drug substances. This method is tedious, time consuming, and suitable for particle size determination within the ranges of 0.2—100 µm.

Sedimentation: The sedimentation technique utilizes the relationship between the rate of sedimentation of particles and their size as described by Stoke's equation (Eq. 8.8). This method is generally used for particles within a range of 3—250 µm. The following precautions must be observed with this method: proper particle dispersion, good temperature control of the settling medium, and appropriate particle concentration.

$$v = \frac{d^2 \, (\rho_s - \rho_0) \, g}{18\eta} \qquad (8.8)$$

where v = the velocity of sedimentation (cm/s)

d = the diameter of the particle (cm)
ρ_s = the density of the particle (g/cc)
ρ_0 = the density of the medium (g/cc)
g = the acceleration due to gravity (cm/s^2)
η = the viscosity of the medium (poise)

Stream scanning: This technique utilizes a fluid suspension of particles that pass the sensing zone where individual particles are electronically sized, counted, and tabulated (e.g., a Coulter counter). Coulter counter method determines the volume distribution of particles suspended in an electrolyte solution. When a particle paces through an orifice, it replaces the equal volume of electrolyte solution, and this volume is used to calculate particle size assuming a spherical shape of the particle. The main advantage of this method is that a large volume of data can be generated in a relatively short period of time. However, it has the shortcoming of not providing information relative to particle shape.

Laser diffraction is used to measure the size of particles in a sample. This technique is based on the principles of light diffraction. When a laser beam falls on a sample containing particles, the particles will scatter the light in different directions. The amount of scattering will depend on the size of the particles. Large particles scatter light at small angles relative to the laser beam and small particles scatter light at large angles. By measuring the amount of scattering, it is possible to determine the size of the particles in the sample in the particle size range of 0.02—2000 µm.

8.7 Partition coefficient and pKa

To produce a biological response, a drug molecule must cross the biological membrane. Biological membranes are made up of lipid and protein material and act as a lipophilic barrier to the passage of many drugs. The oil/water (octanol/water, chloroform/water) partition coefficient is a measure of a molecule's lipophilic nature. It has been demonstrated that the hypnotic activity of a series of barbiturates is closely related to their octanol/water partition coefficient [5]. The octanol–water partition coefficient (P) of a drug can be determined as follows Eqs. (8.9) and (8.10):

$$P = \frac{(\text{Concentration of drug in octanol})}{(\text{Concentration of drug in water})} \tag{8.9}$$

For an ionizable drug:

$$P = \frac{(\text{Concentration of drug in octanol})}{(1 - \alpha)(\text{Concentration of drug in water})} \tag{8.10}$$

where α is the degree of ionization.

From the preceding equation (Eq. 8.10), the determination of the dissociation constant in preformulation work is important because it may be an indicator of a drug substance's absorption characteristics. Since many drugs are either weakly acidic or basic compounds, depending on the pH of the solution, these compounds can exist in ionized and unionized species. The unionized forms are more lipid soluble and are readily absorbed through the lipid membrane. The opposite is true for the ionized species. Factors that affect the absorption of weakly acidic or basic drug include the pH at the site of absorption, the lipid solubility of the unionized form, and ionization constant of the drug. The ratio of the unionized to ionized species of the drug at a particular pH can be determined by using Henderson–Hasselbalch Equations as shown in Eqs. (8.11) and (8.12).

$$\text{For weakly acidic drugs}: pH = pK_a + \log\frac{[\textit{ionized form}]}{[\textit{unionized form}]} \tag{8.11}$$

$$\text{For weakly basic drugs}: pH = pK_a + \log\frac{[\textit{unionized form}]}{[\textit{ionized form}]} \tag{8.12}$$

The ionization constant is usually determined by potentiometric pH titration. Besides titration method, other methods listed below can also be used to determine the pKa of a drug.

- Spectrophotometric pKa determination
- pKa determination from partition data
- pKa determination from solubility data

8.8 Solubility

Solubility of an API is an important parameter determined during preformulation study. For determining this important property, enough drug substance is required at hand. This may pose a further challenge for highly soluble drugs. Relatively insoluble compounds (in water) sometimes exhibit either incomplete or erratic absorption. In such situations, preformulation work for increasing solubility may include.

- Preparation of more soluble salts or esters of the drug
- Solubilization by the use of a surfactant
- Complexation
- Micronization, and
- Amorphous solid dispersion

8.8.1 Equilibrium solubility versus kinetic solubility [6,7]

Equilibrium solubility (the concentration of compound in a saturated solution when an excess solid is present, that is, solution and solid are at equilibrium) can be measured by the classical shake-flask method. This method is accurate when performed to a high standard, but this determination method is slow. Although kinetic solubility (the solubility at the time when an induced precipitate first appears in a solution) is much faster than shake-flask, it is often much higher than measured equilibrium solubilities. This happens because certain circumstances, associated with either the dissolving substance or the dissolution medium, lead to the formation of a supersaturated solution, where an excess amount of solute exceeding the equilibrium solubility of the compound will be able to be dissolved in the medium. Supersaturated solutions are thermodynamically metastable, and any such concentration value represents a kinetic solubility rather than an equilibrium solubility value that is intrinsic to the drug substance.

As described earlier, equilibrium solubility is determined by dispersing the excess of a drug into a solvent (0.9% NaCl solution, water, 0.1 N HCl, or pH 7.4 buffer) in a suitable container and agitating it in a constant temperature bath (37°C or any temperature of interest) till equilibrium. Samples are withdrawn from the supernatant, filtered, and assayed until the concentration is constant in the supernatant. One must consider the common ion effect (e.g., hydrochloride salts are less soluble in 0.9% NaCl and 0.1 N HCl as compared to water). The solubility of the API is expressed in one of the concentration units (mg/mL, g/L, etc) at the specified temperature.

pH solubility profile: Many APIs are either weakly acidic or weakly basic compound and have a higher or lower pKa value, respectively. Their solubility depends on the pH of the solution. Weakly acidic drugs are less soluble in an acidic medium, and their solubility is much higher in basic pH. Molecules having polybasic functional groups (e.g., triamterene) may form complex salts at varying pH values. pH solubility profiles of two salts of a new drug are shown in Fig. 8.3.

8.9 Dissolution

Dissolution rate of a drug substance, when combined with the solubility, partition coefficient, and pKa results, provides some insight into the potential *in vivo* absorption characteristics. The dissolution of a solid in solution is described by Noyes—Whitney equation (Eq. 8.13).

$$\frac{dc}{dt} = \frac{DA}{hV}(C_s - C) \quad or \quad \frac{dm}{dt} = \frac{DA}{h}(C_s - C) \tag{8.13}$$

where $dm/dt = (dc/dt) \times V$ = dissolution rate; A = surface area of the dissolving sold; D = diffusion coefficient of the solid in the release medium; C = concentration of the drug in the bulk medium at any time; h = diffusion layer thickness; V = volume of the dissolution medium; C_S = saturated solubility of the solid in the dissolution medium.

When A is kept constant and during the early phase of the dissolution $C_s \gg C$ (under sink condition). Sink condition is a specific situation during the dissolution process when the concentration of the drug in the release medium is below 15% of the saturated solubility of the drug. In such a situation, Eq. (8.13) reduces to Eq. (8.14).

$$\frac{dc}{dt} = \frac{DA}{hV}(C_s) = K C_s \tag{8.14}$$

K = intrinsic dissolution rate constant.

Compounds with intrinsic dissolution rates greater than 1 mg min^{-1} cm^{-2} are not likely to have dissolution rate-limited absorption. However, rates below 0.1 mg min^{-1} cm^{-2} would have dissolution-limited absorption. Intrinsic dissolution rate can be determined using Wood's apparatus [8]. The dissolution rate of an API may be affected by many factors that may include the chemical form, crystal form, particle size, and surface properties of a drug.

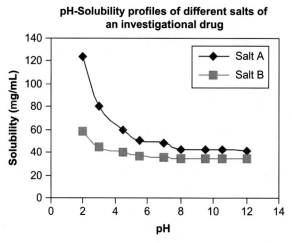

FIGURE 8.3   pH solubility profiles.

- **Chemical form:** Acid, base, and salt forms have significant differences in dissolution rate. For example, the dissolution rate of sodium sulfathiazole (salt) in 0.1 N HCI is 5,500 times faster than sulfathiazole (free acid).
- **Crystal form:** The metastable form has a greater dissolution rate compared to the stable form (e.g., metastable sulfathiazole II has a higher dissolution rate than stable sulfathiazole I).
- **Particle size:** A reduction in particle size increases the surface area of the particles and the dissolution rate.
- **Surface properties of drug:** High surface energy of micronized powder may result in poor wettability and agglomeration. In this case, the dissolution rate decreases because the total surface area of the material is unavailable to the fluid.

8.10 Polymorphism

Polymorphism is the existence of at least two different crystal structures, known as polymorphs of the same chemical substance. Different polymorphs are different in their crystal structures but identical in the liquid and vapor states. They have differences in their physical properties, such as solubility, melting point, density, hardness, crystal shape, optical properties, electrical properties, and vapor pressure. The occurrence of polymorphism in pharmaceutics is important because of differences in the rate and extent of absorption of a compound by the body. Different polymorphs of the same compound might give entirely different therapeutic responses. Some drugs and excipients showing polymorphism include progesterone, warfarin sodium, enalapril maleate, ranitidine HCl, nicotinamide, and Theobroma oil.

In addition to the polymorphic forms in which compounds exist, they also can occur in noncrystalline or amorphous forms. The amorphous form of a compound is always more soluble than the corresponding crystal forms.

Evaluation of crystal structure, polymorphism, and solvate form is an important preformulation activity. The most widely used methods to characterize these properties are.

- Thermal analyses: Differential Scanning Calorimetry (DSC); Thermogravimetric Analysis (TGA), and hot-stage microscopy
- Spectroscopy (infrared, Raman, solid-state NMR)
- X-ray powder diffraction (XRPD).

8.11 Stability

The stability of a new drug (both physical and chemical) must be evaluated during the preformulation process. Validated stability indicating assay is commonly used for such evaluation processes. Thin-layer chromatography, thermal analyses, and diffuse reflectance spectroscopy have also been used in preformulation development. During preformulation studies, more attention is provided to address factors such as light, heat, oxygen, moisture, pH, and excipients that can affect drug quality rather than the degradation mechanisms and pathways. Since drug stability and factors affecting it are described in detail in a separate chapter, we suggest the reader refer to Chapter 6.

8.12 Preformulation: physical characterization and analytical methods used [9]

Some of the important organoleptic, fundamental, and derived properties needed to be evaluated during preformulation work are listed in Tables 8.5 and 8.6.

8.13 Characterization techniques used in preformulation studies

Characterization techniques used in preformulation studies can be classified into three categories.

- Spectroscopic methods: Ultraviolet/visible, infrared, Raman, near-infrared, X-ray, nuclear magnetic resonance, and atomic absorption
- Separation methods: Thin layer chromatography, high-pressure liquid chromatography, ultra-pressure liquid chromatography, capillary electrophoresis, and liquid chromatography/mass spectrometry

TABLE 8.5 Physical characterization (organoleptic properties).

Color	Odor	Taste
Off-white	Pungent	Acidic
Cream yellow	Sulfurous	Bitter
Tan	Fruity	Bland
Shiny	Aromatic	Intense
	Odorless	Sweet
		Tasteless

TABLE 8.6 Physical characterization (fundamental and derived properties).

S. No.	Test	Method/function characterization
Fundamental		
1	Spectroscopy	UV method for assay
2	Solubility	Phase solubility/purity
	a. Aqueous	Intrinsic and pH effect
	b. pKa	Ionization, solubility control, and salt formation
	c. Salt	Solubility, hygroscopicity, and stability
	d. Solvents	Vehicles and extractability
	e. Partition coefficient (octanol/water)	Lipophilicity, permeability, and structure activity
	f. Dissolution	*In vitro* surrogate marker for bioavailability
3	Melting point	DSC—polymorphism, hydrate, and solvates (pseudopolymorphs)
4	Assay method development	UV, HPLC, UPLC, TLC
5	Stability	
	a. Solution	Thermal, hydrolysis, pH, light
	b. Solid	Oxidation, proteolysis by metal ion
Derived		
6	Microscopy	Particle size and morphology
7	Bulk density	Tablet and capsule formation
	Flow properties	Tablet and capsule formation
	Compression properties	Excipient selection
	Excipient compatibility	Preliminary screening by DSC and confirmation by TLC

- Thermal analyses methods: Differential Scanning Calorimetry (DSC), Hot Stage Microscopy, Thermogravimetric Analysis (TGA).

Some of the characterization methods used routinely during preformulation studies are listed in Table 8.7.

TABLE 8.7 Analytical methods commonly used in preformulation studies.

Analytical technique	Output	Properties
X-ray diffraction (single crystal, X-ray powder diffraction (XRPD), variable temperature X-ray diffraction (VTXRD)	Diffractograms	Crystallographic properties
Infrared (IR) spectroscopy	IR spectrum	Chemical functional group information
Raman spectroscopy	Raman spectrum	Chemical information complimentary to IR
Differential scanning calorimetry (DSC)	Heat flow versus temperature	Thermal events
Thermogravimetric analysis (TGAs)	Change of mass with temperature	Solvate/hydrate identification, degradation
Microscopy: polarized light microscopy, scanning electron microscopy (SEM)	Microscopy under the influence of light or electron radiation	Morphology, surface topography

8.14 Conclusions

Drugs are not administered as pure chemical drug substances; rather, they are administered as a dosage form. A dosage form, sometimes known as a drug product, contains many more inactive materials, called excipients, besides the active drug. Selecting the right dosage form with the right excipients to make a drug product safe, reliable, and effective starts at an early stage of the dosage form design, and this process is called preformulation. Therefore, preformulation is an important first step in the dosage form design process. Its overall importance is underscored when one sees a successful dosage form in the market for a long time without any formulation challenges. Preformulation helps in identifying the best salt with ideal solubility and stability for a drug substance. Based on the knowledge gained from understanding all the physicochemical properties of drugs in a therapeutic group, the preformulation process can help the chemist identify ideal candidates with the best biological activity and select the best salt forms of the API with the needed particle size, compression properties, etc., to minimize processing problems during scale-up and future manufacturing. This chapter focuses on the dosage form design during the preformulation process.

Case studies

Case 8.1

The label of a pharmaceutical liquid formulation contains the following information:
Formulation Name: Chloraseptic Sore Throat Spray.
Phenol 1.4%, Blue #1, Flavor, Glycerin, Purified Water, Saccharin Sodium.
Answer the following questions:

1. Identify the active pharmaceutical ingredients (APIs) in this preparation.
2. Identify the dosage form and a drug from this example.
3. Name at least two inactive pharmaceutical ingredients and the purpose of their inclusion in this formulation.

Approach:

1. The active pharmaceutical ingredient in this preparation is phenol 1.4% (drug).
2. The dosage form is a liquid spray that contains phenol 1.4% as the drug and many more inactive ingredients such as water, coloring agent, and flavor.
3. Saccharin sodium is a sweetener used to enhance the sweetness of the product, and purified water is used as a solvent for this solution dosage form which are at least the two excipients used in this formulation.

Case 8.2

If one assumes the pH of the stomach to be 1–3 and that of the small intestine to be 5–8, in most cases a drug substance with a p*Ka* of 3 (salicylic acid) will be more rapidly absorbed in the stomach. On the other hand, a drug with p*Ka* of 8 (quinine) will be absorbed more rapidly in the intestine. Can you explain this to a healthcare colleague of yours without a pharmacy background?

Approach: This can be explained if one has a better understanding of pH partition theory and ionization of acids and bases and p*Ka*.

- Absorption of the drug via GI membrane requires that the drug should be lipophilic, which has a better membrane permeability and absorption as compared to a drug that is more water-soluble.
- Ionization of the drug can be affected by both pH and p*Ka*.
- Ionized drugs are more water soluble as compared to the unionized portion. The unionized drugs are more lipophilic.

Once these three concepts are well understood, one can explain the scenarios presented in this case without any difficulty. As p*Ka* of salicylic acid is 3, in acidic pH conditions like the first scenario, the drug will be in the unionized state and will be more lipid soluble and will have a better membrane permeability. As the surface area of the stomach is much less than the intestine, that may limit some of the drug absorptions. In the case of quinine, the basic drug with a p*Ka* of 8, more of the drug will be present in the unionized state in the intestine; therefore, it is more lipophilic and has higher permeability and will have a better absorption from the intestine.

Case 8.3

Abbott laboratory stopped sales of Norvir, an approved novel protease inhibitor for HIV [10]. Norvir contained Ritonavir as the API, discovered by Abbott in 1992. In December 1995, Abbott filed a New Drug Application (NDA) for it. In January 1996, the commercial start-up of the drug began operation. In March 1996, the US FDA approved Norvir as a semisolid capsule and as a liquid formulation. In early 1998, final product lots failed the dissolution test and were seen to be precipitated out from the semisolid formulated product. As a pharmacovigilance person, how can one explain these facts?

Approach: One must identify the precipitate by IR and powder XRD, etc. In this case, the precipitate was identified as a new polymorph of ritonavir (Form II). Form II was thermodynamically more stable and much less soluble than Form I. After 2 years of intensive research, the Abbott scientists found a way to control the formation of either Form I or Form II polymorphs. Abbott received FDA approval on the reformulated Norvir soft gelatin capsule in June 1999. This is a classic case in which a pharmaceutical company took a serious look at the polymorphism of solids in 1998.

Case 8.4

A hypertensive patient on Procardia XL once-a-day therapy called your pharmacy and wished to talk to the pharmacist in charge. He explained to the pharmacist that from a Google search, he found two extended-release preparations of nifedipine, Procardia XL (Pfizer, Inc., New York, NY) and Adalat CC (Miles Inc., West Haven, CT) that are available for once-daily dosing with a big price difference. His question was with the current budgetary constraints, can he substitute Procardia XL with Adalat CC?

Approach: The pharmacist must explain to the patient all the facts available to date clearly and concisely. Nifedipine, a calcium channel antagonist with arterial vasodilatory properties is a first-line agent for the treatment of hypertension. Due to the nifedipine's relatively short half-life of 2.5 h, several doses are required to control blood pressure throughout 24 h. Two extended-release preparations of nifedipine, Procardia XL and Adalat CC, are available for once-daily dosing. However, both dosage forms act on a distinctly different mechanism. Procardia XL delivers nifedipine from an osmotically driven process. Adalat CC consists of a slow-release coat surrounded by a fast-release core and after oral intake under fasting conditions plasma concentration peaks at 2.5–5 h with a small secondary peak occurring around 6–12 h.

According to the FDA, Adalat CC carries an FDA rating of BC, which means it is subject to bioavailability differences with Procardia XL because of their differences in the extended-release mechanism. The FDA does not consider different extended-release forms of the same ingredient in equal strength to be therapeutically equivalent unless equivalence is demonstrated in both rate and extent. Therefore, pharmacies are reluctant to interchange Adalat

CC for Procardia XL. However, a recent study by Granbery et al. (1996) has shown in limited patients (15) that blood pressure reduction obtained with Adalat CC was comparable with that obtained with Procardia XL [11]. Their recommendation was to substitute Adalat CC for Procardia XL when hypertension is the sole indication. This study further recommends monitoring the adverse effect in patients with Adalat CC in addition to heart rate and blood pressure.

Case 8.5

Chloramphenicol palmitate, a prodrug of chloramphenicol with antibiotic properties was developed with the objective of obtaining a more flavored derivative of the highly bitter chloramphenicol for oral use. Some of the commercial products showed very low serum levels of the drug in patients taking this oral preparation. As a clinical pharmacist, how can you explain this to your healthcare team members?

Approach: A review of the literature suggests that chloramphenicol palmitate exists in three polymorphic forms: the stable form α is a biologically inactive form, the metastable form β is the active modification, and the unstable form γ. Polymorph α is the thermodynamically stable one, but its absorption in humans is significantly lower than that of polymorph β, because Form β dissolves faster than Form α, and has much higher solubility [12]. These solubility differences could contribute to the difference in ester hydrolysis rates of the prodrug, and thus in the difference in oral absorption if one considers that chloramphenicol palmitate must be hydrolyzed by intestinal esterases before it can be absorbed. This poor oral absorption will show low serum levels reached by the stable polymorph α, whereas the metastable polymorph will produce much higher serum levels when the same dose is administered.

Case 8.6

A first-year pharmacy student is working on their IPPE rotation in a community pharmacy setting and had a question for their preceptor on the difference between drug, dosage form, and drug delivery system. The student asked the pharmacist to provide some practical examples of products in a pharmacy to clarify these terms and concepts.

Approach: The pharmacist must provide the student with some examples of products available commercially to explain the differences. One such example is the Procardia capsule, Procardia XL tablet, and the drug (Nifedipine) in both the Procardia products as shown in Fig. 8.4.

The drug nifedipine is a calcium channel antagonist used for the treatment of hypertension. This drug is present in both Procardia capsules and Procardia XL extended-release tablets. Procardia XL Extended-Release Tablet consists of a semipermeable membrane surrounding an osmotically active drug (Nifedipine) core. The core itself is divided into two layers: an "active" layer containing the drug, and a "push" layer containing pharmacologically inert (but osmotically active) components. As water from the gastrointestinal tract enters the tablet through the semipermeable membrane, pressure increases in the osmotic layer and "pushes" against the drug layer, releasing the drug through the precision laser-drilled tablet orifice in the active layer. Three dose strengths are available (30, 60, and 90 mg). However, the Procardia soft gelatin capsule contains 10 mg of the drug (Nifedipine). In this example, Nifedipine is the drug, the Procardia soft gelatin capsule is a dosage form, and Procardia XL is a drug delivery system because it is a specialized dosage form where the drug can be released at a predetermined rate over an extended period.

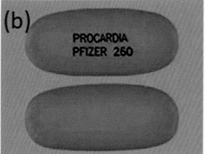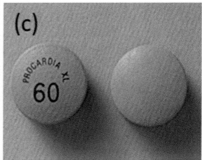

FIGURE 8.4   Comparing (a) drug, (b) dosage form, and (c) delivery system.

Drug: Nifedipine.
Dosage Form: Procardia 10 mg soft gelatin capsule.
Drug Delivery System: Procardia XL tablet.

Case 8.7

In a community pharmacy, you noticed brown color development in tablets in a bottle of a drug product containing a primary amine group. On further investigation, it was confirmed that this batch of drug products was seating in the warehouse with high temperature and humidity for a long time due to a supply chain delivery issue. What could be a possible reason for this color change?

Approach: This could be a case of Maillard's reaction. Maillard reaction is a reaction between an amine and a reduced sugar. As most of the tablets contain reduced sugar in higher amount (lactose) as excipients, they can react with amine to form a colored product. However, non-reducing sugars like mannitol, sucrose, and trehalose are not subjected to the Maillard reaction. This reaction is further aggravated by high temperature and moisture.

Critical reflections and practice applications

- Drugs are rarely used alone in patients. Instead, dosage forms (drug products) or drug delivery systems containing the drug are used.
- Dosage forms can be available in many physical forms, for example, solid, liquid, semisolid, or gas.
- Besides the active pharmaceutical ingredient (API), many other inactive pharmaceutical ingredients (excipients) are needed and used in formulating dosage forms and drug delivery systems
- The primary goal of a formulation pharmacist/scientist is to prepare a dosage form that is safe, effective, and reliable.
- Preformulation studies is the first step in the rational design of a dosage form.
- During the early development of a new chemical entity (NCE), preformulation plays an important role in the drug development process.

References

[1] F.I. Wells, M.E. Aulton, Aulton M.E., Preformulations Pharmaceuticals, the science of dosage form design. In: Aulton M.E., Pharmaceuticals, the Science of Dosage Form Design. Churchill and Livingstone, 1994223–1994253.

[2] E.F. Fiese, T.A. Hagen, L. Lachman, H.A. Lieberman, J.L. Kanig, Preformulation. The theory and practice of industrial pharmacy. In: L. Lachman, H.A. Lieberman, J.L. Kanig, The Theory and Practice of Industrial Pharmacy. Lea & Febiger, 1986171–196.

[3] L.V. Allen, N. Popovich, H.C. Ansel, Ansel's Pharmaceutical Dosage Forms and Drug Delivery Systems, Wolters Kluwer/Lippincott Williams & Wilkins, 2011.

[4] USP General Chapters: <1174> POWDER FLOW (uspbpep.com), Accessed on July 26, 2022.

[5] L.S. Schanker LS, Absorption of drugs from the rat colon, J. Pharmacol. Exp. Therapeut. 126 (1959) 283–290.

[6] https://www.americanpharmaceuticalreview.com/Featured-Articles/160452-Thermodynamic-vs-Kinetic-Solubility-Knowing-Which-is-Which/, Accessed July 27, 2022.

[7] K.J. Box, G. Völgyi, E. Baka, M. Stuart, K. Takács-Novák, J.E. Comer, Equilibrium versus kinetic measurements of aqueous solubility, and the ability of compounds to supersaturate in solution–a validation study, J. Pharmaceut. Sci. 95 (2006) 1298–1307.

[8] J.H. Wood, J.E. Syarto, H. Letterman, Improved holder for intrinsic dissolution rate studies, J. Pharmaceut. Sci. 54 (1965) 1068.

[9] P.T. Sankeerth, N. Bhavana, P.V. Suresh, N. Ramarao, Preformulation analytical techniques during drug development, Int. J. Pharm. Pharmaceut. Res. 8 (2017) 107–125.

[10] G. Saurabh, C. Kaushal, Pharmaceutical solid polymorphism in abbreviated new drug application (ANDA)-A regulatory perspective, J. Chem. Pharmaceut. Res. 3 (2011) 6–17.

[11] M. Granberry, S. Gardner, E. Schneider, I. Carter, Comparison of two formulations of nifedipine during 24-hour ambulatory blood pressure monitoring, Pharmacotherapy 16 (1996) 932–936.

[12] A.J. Aguiar, J. Krc Jr., A.W. Kinkel, J.C. Samyn, Effect of polymorphism on the absorption of chloramphenicol from chloramphenicol palmitate, J. Pharmaceut. Sci. 56 (1967) 847–853.

9

Solid Dosage Forms

Alekha K. Dash

Department of Pharmacy Sciences, School of Pharmacy and Health Professions, Creighton University, Omaha, NE, United States

CHAPTER OBJECTIVES

- Define and describe the various solid dosage forms commonly used in pharmacy practice.
- Explain and understand the application of basic pharmaceutics principles necessary to prepare these dosage forms.
- Identify the applications of these dosage forms in practice, including powder, tablet, and capsule dosage forms.
- Identify the methods used for the manufacture of solid dosage forms including powder, tablet, and capsule dosage forms.
- Describe the various methods used to evaluate the quality of these solid dosage forms including powder, tablet, and capsule dosage forms.

Keywords: Effervescent powder; Granules; Hard gelatin capsule; Powder; Soft gelatin capsule and tablet.

9.1 Introduction

Pharmacists are regarded as the experts on drugs in a healthcare team. They deal with these drug products every day in their professional practice. Drugs, irrespective of their sources, are available in three possible physical forms of matter, including solid, liquid, and gases. These physical forms can be used as such, or in formulations with many other inactive pharmaceutical ingredients. Such formulations are also known as drug products or dosage forms that contain a drug or drugs and inactive ingredients called excipients. Many drugs and dosage forms that are used today in practice are solid. The solid dosage form is the preferred dosage form in the United States. Approximately one-third of the dosage forms dispensed by community pharmacists are solid dosage forms, usually tablets or capsules [1]. The solid dosage form encompasses the largest group of dosage forms used in clinical practice. This high acceptance is probably due to many factors, including the convenience of handling and self-administration, chemical and physical stability, high-throughput production in a nonsterile environment, relatively inexpensive to manufacture, and a long history of the understanding of their manufacturing processes. Some of the solid dosage forms that are

Pharmaceutics, Second Edition
https://doi.org/10.1016/B978-0-323-99796-6.00014-X

most used in practice are powders, tablets, and capsules. Other solid dosage forms that are less frequently used are implants, lozenges, suppositories, and plasters.

9.2 Powders

Powders are intimate mixtures of dry, finely divided drug/s with or without excipients and can be used either internally or externally. Powders consist of particles ranging from about 10,000 to 0.1 μM. The USP describes powder in descriptive terms such as *coarse, moderately coarse, fine*, and *very fine* depending on their passage through standard sieves and is presented in Table 9.1. Antacids (sodium bicarbonate powder USP), laxatives (Miralax (PEG 3350 powder)), dietary supplements (creatine monohydrate powder), dentifrices (Colgate tooth powder), dusting (Gold bond medicated powder), and douche powders (Massengill vaginal douche powder) are some examples of commonly used powders. Medicated powders are intended either for oral use or for external application.

9.2.1 Powder versus granule

Pharmaceutical powder is a mixture of finely divided drug particles (primary particles) alone or mixed with other powdered excipients in a dry form. Granules on the other hand are agglomerates (secondary particles) of powder particles that are larger in size than the primary particles. Granulation is the process in which dry *primary powder particles* (single, discrete powder particles) adhere to form larger multiparticle entities called *granules*. Pharmaceutical granules typically have a size range between 0.2 and 4.0 mm. As an example, calcium carbonate powder and calcium carbonate granules are shown in Fig. 9.1. Granulation of drug particles is necessary to achieve the following tasks:

- To improve the flow properties of powders
- To prevent segregation of particles during processing
- To improve the compaction properties of the powders

Many oral powder dosage forms are available as fine powders or as granules, usually administered orally with a glass of water or juice. As granules have less surface area compared to fine powder, their dissolution in water or juice is much less as compared to primary powder particles.

Powders used for internal use:

- Sodium bicarbonate powder (antacid)
- Psyllium (Metamucil) powder (laxative)
- Massengill powder (vaginal douche powders)

Powders used for external use:

- Bacitracin zinc and polymyxin B sulfate (anti-infective)
- Tolnaftate powder (antifungal)
- Gold bond dusting powder (medicated body powder)

TABLE 9.1 Classification of powders by fineness.

Classification of powder	d_{50} Sieve opening (μm)[a]
Very coarse	> 1000
Coarse	355−1000
Moderately fine	180−355
Fine	125−180
Very fine	90−125

[a]d_{50} = smallest sieve opening through which 50% or more of the material passes.

FIGURE 9.1 (A) Calcium carbonate powder, and (B) calcium carbonate granules.

9.2.2 Advantages of powders

- Wide choice of ingredients, and doses can easily be achieved for patient administration
- Powders have increased stability as compared to solutions
- A large dose that cannot be administered in other forms (tablets and capsules) can be administered as powder
- Rapid onset of action as compared to a tablet since disintegration is not required
- Powder can be dispersed in water or another liquid and more easily swallowed

9.2.3 Limitations

Some of the disadvantages of powder dosage form are:

- Powder dosage form is not the dosage form of choice for drugs with an unpleasant taste
- Drugs that deteriorate rapidly with exposure to the atmosphere or acidic pH should not be dispensed as powders. Ferrous iron salts are easily oxidized and should not be administered as powders
- Powders are bulky and inconvenient to carry

9.2.4 Mixing of powders

A good powder formulation requires a narrow particle size distribution. If the particle size distribution is wide, the powder can segregate and would have an un-uniform dissolution rate. Reducing the particle size of a powder is called comminution and results in a narrow distribution of powder particles. Powders do not mix spontaneously; therefore, effective mixing requires a thorough understanding of the materials to be mixed, as well as the science of mixing. Effective mixing of powders poses the greatest challenge when the amount of one of the components of the mix is relatively small compared to the other components. There are four main methods used for mixing of powders in small-scale operations [2].

- Trituration
- Spatulation
- Sifting
- Tumbling

9.2.4.1 Trituration

The trituration process involves direct rubbing or grinding of hard powder in a mortar and pestle. The trituration method is used for both pulverization and mixing. Two different types of mortar and pestle are commonly used in extemporaneous compounding.

FIGURE 9.2   A wedgewood pestle and mortar.

- A Wedgewood mortar (Fig. 9.2) is used for pulverization and grinding because of its rough inner surface.
- A glass mortar (Fig. 9.3) is used for simple mixing and for mixing of colored materials and dyes.

9.2.4.2 Spatulation

A powder spatula is used in the spatulation method, and the powders are mixed on a pill tile (ointment slabs: Fig. 9.4A and B) or in a mortar. This method is adequate for mixing small amounts of powders and combinations of powders having the same densities. The possible loss during transfer is minimal in this method, and mixing does not reduce the particle size. This method is used when there is a possibility of liquefaction during the mixing of two solid powders (eutectic compounds).

9.2.4.3 Sifting

The sifting method is helpful for powders that resist mixing by trituration. Very light powders, such as magnesium oxide and charcoal, can be completely mixed by shaking them through a sieve. Standard-size prescription sieves are available, but an ordinary household flour sifter can be used effectively for this purpose as shown in Fig. 9.5. This process allows the removal of any large foreign bodies and agglomerates from the powder mix.

9.2.4.4 Tumbling

Tumbling is a process of mixing powders by shaking or rotating them in a closed container. This method is used when two or more powders have considerable density differences. This mode of mixing does not yield particle size reduction and compaction. Wide-mouthed closed containers or zip-locked bags can be used when the powder volume should be within one-third to one-half field. The powder mixture should flow freely in the air and avoid sliding the powder through the side of the container.

FIGURE 9.3   A glass pestle and mortar.

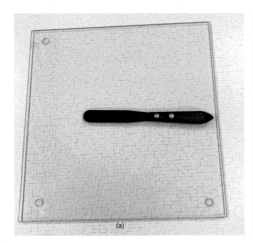

FIGURE 9.4   (a) A glass ointment slab with a stainless-steel spatula, and (b) porcelain ointment slab with plastic spatula.

FIGURE 9.5   Powder mixing by the process of sifting.

Homogeneity in large-scale mixing is achieved through the use of an appropriate mixer, which ensures the correct speed and sufficient time for mixing. Homogenous mixing is ascertained in a mixture when the concentration of each component in any region of the mixture is identical.

The mixing of pharmaceutical powders generally requires low shear rates; the mixers used for this purpose are planetary bowl mixers, high speed mixers, V blenders, ribbon/trough mixers, and rotating drum mixers (Fig. 9.6).

9.2.4.5 Problems encountered during mixing

Most of the problems encountered during mixing of pharmaceutical powders can be minimized using special techniques, assuming that the cause of the problem is clearly understood.

9.2.4.6 Problems encountered during trituration

Crystalline salts are mixed well by trituration in a mortar. The inner surface of Wedgewood mortars grows smooth with long-term use. When this happens, powders do not mix well. In such instances, the surface of a mortar can be made rough by triturating with a little powdered pumice or pharmaceutical grade sand.

9.2.4.6.1 Electrification

Electrification is a phenomenon in which some substances repel each other during mixing. This might be due to simple resistance to admixture, or it may be due to electrical charges. This problem can be eliminated by moistening the powders very slightly with a few drops of alcohol or mineral oil.

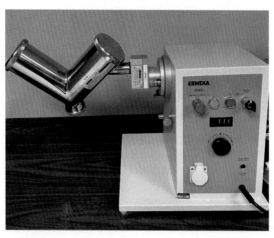

FIGURE 9.6 Rotating V-blender for powder mixing.

9.2.4.6.2 Packing

A packing problem may be encountered when powders are pressed heavily during trituration. This problem can be avoided by triturating lightly and scraping the sides of the mortar frequently with a spatula.

9.2.4.6.3 Physical immiscibility

The phenomenon of physical immiscibility may occasionally present minor problems. Mixing resinous materials with granular salts and mixing heavy powder (starch) with a light one (zinc stearate) may lead to this incompatibility issue. This problem can be minimized by triturating each substance separately to a fine state and then mixing by sifting or tumbling.

9.2.4.6.4 Dampening or liquefaction

Dampening, or liquefaction, is the most troublesome problem in powder mixing and can happen for three different reasons.

- *Absorption of moisture from the air* (*deliquescent/hygroscopic*): A substance that absorbs moisture from the air is termed *hygroscopic* (e.g., ephedrine sulfate, lithium bromide, ammonium chloride). A hygroscopic material that absorbs the moisture from the air to such an extent that it liquefies partially or fully is termed *deliquescent* (*e.g., sodium hydroxide, calcium chloride*). Hygroscopic materials should not be ground finer than is necessary and should be wrapped in close containers.
- *Giving up moisture to the air and liquefying during the process* (*efflorescent*): Some examples of efflorescent materials include atropine sulfate, quinine HCl, and scopolamine hydrobromide.
- *Lowering the melting point of the mixture* (*eutectic mixture*): Eutectic mixtures result when certain organic compounds (phenol, aldehydes, and ketones) are mixed in varying proportions. The melting point of a fixed composition of a mixture is considerably below that of any of the individual ingredients and forms a damp mass or even liquefies when mixed. When mixed in a definite composition from the following ingredients, some of these compounds may form a eutectic mixture and liquefy:
  Acetylsalicylic acid, aminopyrine, camphor, menthol, phenol, salol, thymol, and chloral hydrate.

There are three ways to handle eutectic powder mixtures as outlined below:

- Separately dispense the individual components
- Mix each component with an equal amount of inert diluents (lactose, starch, talc) and finally combine the diluted powders with light trituration
- Mix the materials together and allow them to liquefy, followed by the addition of enough adsorbents to adsorb the eutectic liquid mixture and remain as a free-flowing powder

9.2.4.6.5 Three basic rules for mixing of powders

- When mixing powders with different particle sizes (granular salt and fine powders), reduce each powder separately to fine particles before mixing.

- When mixing powders with different densities, put the light powder first and then put the heavier one on top of it.
- When mixing small amounts of a drug to a large volume of bulk powder, use the principle of geometric dilution as explained in the next section.

9.2.4.6.6 Geometric dilution

In this technique, the quantity of powder with the least weight of the formulation is placed either in a mortar or on an ointment slab. The other powder that constitutes the major portion of the powder formulation is sequentially added with an equal portion and mixed thoroughly either with a pestle or a spatula. This process is repeated until all the powders are intimately mixed to ensure equal distribution (homogenity).

Example:

One gram of a potent drug to be mixed with 20 g of the diluent lactose.

- First dilution: Mix 1 g drug with ~1 g lactose (~2 g mixture)
- Second dilution: Mix 2 g of the first dilution with ~2 g of lactose with trituration (~4 g mixture)
- Third dilution: Mix ~4 g of the second dilution with ~4 g of lactose with trituration (~8 g mixture)
- Fourth dilution: Mix ~8 g of the third dilution with ~8 g of lactose with trituration (~16 g mixture)

This process continues until all the required amount of lactose is fully mixed with the blend.

9.2.4.7 Classification of powders

Powders can be classified by the way they are presented to the user. This may be given as bulk or divided powders.

9.2.4.7.1 Bulk powders

Doses of bulk powders are measured out by the patient; they are limited to nonpotent drugs. The patient should be educated regarding the appropriate handling, storage, and solvent to be used if needed for reconstitution, etc. Pasteboard boxes or wide-mouth glass jars with screw-caps containers are used for dispensing bulk powders.

Examples:

- Dusting powder (Johnson's white baby powder with cornstarch)
- Powders used internally, a teaspoonful at a time (laxatives (e.g., psyllium [Metamucil])
- Powders used for making solution (cloxacillin sodium, and penicillin V potassium)
- Powders used for inhalation (Symbicort inhaler)

9.2.4.7.2 Divided powders

Divided powders, or chartulae, refer to single doses of powdered drug mixtures individually enclosed in paper, cellophane, or metallic foil wrappers or packets. *Chartula*, which is abbreviated as *chart*, is the Latin word for powder paper. Some divided powders are commercially available in folded papers or packets. The divided powders are a more accurate dosage form as compared to bulk powders as the patient is not involved in the measurement of the dose.

Example: Cholestyramine resin powder as shown in Fig. 9.7.

9.2.4.8 Special powders

- Effervescent salt
- Dusting powders
- Dentifrices
- Insufflations
- Powder aerosols

9.2.4.8.1 Effervescent salts

Powders or granules containing sodium bicarbonate, a suitable organic acid (citric or tartaric), or inorganic (sodium biphosphate) acid and medicinal agents are known as effervescent salts. When mixed with water, the acid and the base react to form carbon dioxide, which produces effervescence. One such example is E-Z Gas II oral effervescent granules.

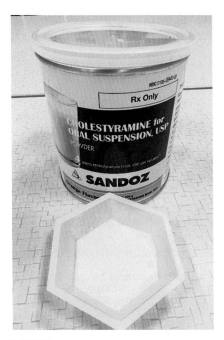

FIGURE 9.7   Cholestyramine resin powder.

9.2.4.8.1.1 Advantages

- Effervescent salts mask the unpleasant taste of many drugs.
- Carbon dioxide stimulates the flow of gastric fluid and accelerates the absorption of many drugs.
- Effervescent salts have a favorable psychological effect on the patient.
- They have enhanced stability since they are stored in low moisture-content packages.

A representative formula for an effervescent salt formulation:

Sodium bicarbonate (dry powder)	477 g
Tartaric acid (dry powder)	252 g
Citric acid crystals	162 g

9.2.4.8.1.2 Preparation   Effervescent salts can be prepared using two methods:

- *Heat method*: This method requires blending of all the components, with 15%—20% of the acid ingredients as citric acid monohydrate, and heating in a bath (about 100°C). The mole of water released from citric acid during heating moistens the powder, and granules are formed from this moistened powder mass.
- *Wet method*: The citric acid is moistened and added to sodium bicarbonate. Granules are then formed from this partially fused mass, using a suitable granulator.

9.2.4.8.2 Dusting powders

Dusting powders are used for external use only and should have the following properties:

- Homogenous
- Free from local irritation
- Free flowing
- Uniform spreading and covering capability
- Good adsorptive and absorptive capability

Medicated dusting powders are applied onto intact skin, open wounds, or even mucous membranes. Highly absorptive dusting powders should be avoided in areas with high liquid exudates because a hard crust may form. Starch and talc are commonly used as excipients for dusting powder formulations. Being organic, starch may support bacterial growth. On the other hand, talc is inert but can easily be contaminated and may be a potential source of infection. Therefore, sterilized talc is commonly used in medicated dusting powder formulations.

9.2.4.8.3 Dentifrices

Fine powders that are used to clean teeth are called dentifrices. The cleaning properties of these powders are achieved through the incorporation of detergents. Aside from the detergent, a small amount of mild abrasive (precipitated calcium carbonate or hydrous dibasic calcium phosphate) is also included. Dentists usually use dentifrices with high abrasive properties that are not suitable for daily use. In such instances, dentists use pumice powder. Example of a dentifrice is Colgate tooth powder.

9.2.4.8.4 Insufflations

Insufflations are finely divided powders intended for application into body cavities, such as tooth sockets, ears, nose, vagina, and throat. An applicator known as an insufflator is used to deliver a stream of finely divided powder to the target organ. Intranasal insufflation is preferred over oral route if the therapeutic efficacy of the drug is lost upon oral use. It can be utilized for both local application and systemic absorption. The powder is placed in an insufflator and when the bulb is pressed, the powder is discharged with the air current through the nozzle. Some of the disadvantages of an insufflator are the difficulty of obtaining uniform dosage delivery each time and agglomeration of particles inside the device. However, the newer generation powder aerosols have minimized these problems. The norisodrine sulfate aerohaler cartridge is an example.

9.2.4.8.5 Powder aerosols

Powders can be dispensed as aerosols from pressurized containers that have a push-button actuator. They are easy to apply, can be evenly applied to a larger surface, and provide protection against harmful external exposure. The major disadvantages of powder aerosols include valve clogging, agglomerative sedimentation, and leakage.
Examples:
Antiperspirants and deodorants as powder aerosols.
Tinactin powder aerosol.

9.3 Capsules

Capsules are solid dosage forms designed to contain drug(s) for administration. Two types of capsules are commonly used in pharmacy: hard (two-piece) gelatin capsules and soft (one-piece) gelatin capsules [3]. Capsules are administered orally but can also be used rectally or vaginally.

9.3.1 Hard gelatin capsules

Hard-shell gelatin capsules are solid dosage forms in which one or more medicinal agents and/or inert materials are enclosed within a small shell. Hard gelatin capsules consist of two parts: the body designed to contain the drug and the diluent, and the cap that is approximately half as long as the body. Hard capsules are available in a variety of standard sizes and are designated by numbers from 000 to 5. The size of the 000 capsule is the highest and that of the number 5 capsule is the smallest, as shown in Table 9.2.

The large range of weights of powders that can be filled into different-sized capsules depends on their bulk densities and compressibility. Mixtures of dry powdered materials may be incorporated in capsules as loose powders, granules, slightly compressed plugs, or tablets.

9.3.1.1 Advantages of capsules

- There are fewer steps involved as compared to the wet granulation method of tablet manufacturing
- Certain bioavailability problems encountered in the case of tablet formulations may be avoided by capsule formulation
- Completely mask unpleasant taste and odor
- Easier to swallow than tablets
- Can be made opaque and offer advantages for photosensitive drugs
- Do not deposit powder or small fragments into the containers in which they are stored
- Tamper resistant

TABLE 9.2 Various sizes of hard gelatin capsules.

Capsule size designation	Usual range of powder size
5	60–130 mg
4	95–260 mg
3	130–390 mg
2	195–520 mg
1	225–650 mg
0	325–920 mg
00	390–1300 mg
000	650–2000 mg

9.3.1.2 Disadvantages of capsules

- Extremely water-soluble materials cannot be administered
- Not suitable for efflorescent or deliquescent materials.
- Require specialized manufacturing equipment and are expensive.
- May contain animal products

9.3.1.3 Capsule shell components

The major component of a capsule shell is gelatin. Other than gelatin, it may contain 10%–15% moisture, dyes, plasticizer, and opacifying agents. Starch and hydroxypropylmethyl cellulose are being investigated as possible capsule shell materials. Gelatin is a mixture of proteins derived from animal collagen by irreversible hydrolytic extraction. Depending on the method of extraction, two types of gelatins can be produced. Type A gelatin is prepared by treating pig skin with acid and has an isoelectric point between 7 and 9. Type B gelatin is prepared by base-treating bovine bones and has isoelectric points between 4.7 and 5.3. Because of this difference in isoelectric points, both gelatins show solubility differences at different pH values. Gelatin grade is further specified by bloom strength. This is defined as the weight in grams that is required to depress a cylindrical plunger of 12.7 mm diameter and a depth of 4 mm with an aged gelatin gel of 6.6% (w/w) in water. Gelatin with higher bloom values results in firmer gels, and high-bloom gelatin has a much higher molecular weight than low-bloom gelatin.

9.3.1.4 Capsule filling

In a compounding pharmacy, capsules are generally filled by hand by placing the powder to be filled on paper or on a pill tile and pressing the open end of the capsule downward until it is filled. The cap is then placed to close the capsule.

Semiautomatic and fully automated filling machines are available for large-scale operations.

9.3.1.5 Storage conditions

Capsule shells contain 10%–15% (w/w) moisture. Under high humidity conditions, capsules absorb moisture. Above 16% moisture, they lose their mechanical strength and may become sticky. Storage under extremely dry conditions will result in brittle capsules due to moisture loss. The best storage and process conditions for capsules are within a temperature range of 10–25°C and a relative humidity of 35%–45%.

9.3.1.6 Filling of hard gelatin capsules

The powders to be filled in hard gelatin capsule shells should be homogeneous and have excellent flow property. Flow property of a powder mix can be determined by the angle of repose, which is the angle the powder makes with the horizontal plane when it flows from a funnel onto a flat surface. The tangent of this angle is a measure of the internal friction of the powder bed. If the measured angle is around 25 degrees, the flow is excellent; if it is 50 degrees or more, the flow is considered to be poor. In such instances, the use of a glidant will enhance powder flow by reducing particle–particle cohesion. During the filling of hard gelatin capsules, the following problems may be encountered.

- *Improper flow of the powder mixture during the filling operation*: This problem can be overcome by the incorporation of a suitable amount of glidants or lubricants into the powder mixture.
- *Segregation and homogeneity*: This problem is generally encountered when semiautomatic or automatic machines are used for filling the capsules. The vibration during the operation of these heavy-duty machines can cause the segregation of particles and inhomogeneity. This segregation can be minimized by keeping particle sizes and densities of the powders as uniform as possible.
- *Incompatibility*: In some instances, incompatibility between formulation ingredients, formulation components, and the capsule shell may create problems. A proper understanding of the physicochemical properties of each ingredient may avoid such incompatibility issues.

Some of the excipients commonly used in the filling of hard gelatin capsules may include the following:

- Diluents to increase the overall working mass of the powder for easy and accurate handling during filling operations. These diluents include lactose, corn starch, and microcrystalline cellulose.
- Disintegrants to break up the powder mass when exposed to a liquid medium. Corn starch, microcrystalline cellulose, sodium starch glycolate, and croscarmellose are disintegrants used in hard gelatin capsules.
- Glidants to lower the interparticle attraction and thereby reduce agglomeration and enhance the flow of powder. Colloidal silicon and talc are commonly used for this purpose.
- Lubricants to reduce the interaction between powders and components of the filling machine handling the powder. Magnesium and other metallic stearates are generally used as lubricants.
- When hydrophobic components are present in higher amounts in the formulation, surface-active agents are incorporated into the powder mix to decrease surface tension and enhance the wetting of the powder with the release medium. Sodium lauryl sulfate is commonly used for this purpose.

9.3.1.7 Finishing

Filled capsules may have small amounts of powder formulation adhering to the outside of the capsule during the filling operation. Therefore, the filled capsules require dusting and polishing to remove powder from the surface of these capsules. For small-scale operations, clean clothes or scientific cleaning wipes (e.g., Kimwipes) may be used to de-dust the capsules. However, in large-scale operations, the following methods are generally used.

- *Pan polishing*: Accela-Cota pan coating machines lined with polyurethane or cheese cloth are used.
- *Cloth dusting*: Capsules are rubbed with a cloth that may be impregnated with an inert oil.
- *Brushing*: Capsules are fed under rotating soft brushes that remove the dust from the capsule surface, followed by using a vacuum system for dust removal.

9.3.2 Soft gelatin capsules

Soft gelatin capsules are made from shells of gelatin to which plasticizers such as glycerol and polyols (sorbitol, propylene glycol) have been added. The distinctive feature of this capsule is its one-piece construction. The feeding and sealing are achieved by only one machine. Hard gelatin capsules are manufactured in a two-step process, in which shells are manufactured by one type of machine and the filling is achieved by a different machine. Soft gelatin capsules are usually produced from two thin sheets of gelatin suitably molded and sealed together after the amount of drug to be encapsulated is inserted between them, as shown in Fig. 9.8. Soft gelatin capsules are available in various sizes, shapes, and colors. Soft gelatin capsules have grown in popularity in recent years because they enable the administration of a liquid in a solid dosage form with a bioavailability advantage over other commonly used solid dosage forms (e.g., tablets).

9.3.2.1 Advantages of soft gelatin capsules

- Soft gelatin capsules permit liquid medication to be easily transportable and administered in a solid dosage form.
- They provide accuracy and uniformity of the dose to be administered.
- They provide better drug bioavailability than tablets and hard gelatin capsules.

9.3.2.2 Pharmaceutical applications of soft gelatin capsules

- Soft gelatin capsules are generally used as an oral dosage form
- They are also available as a suppository dosage form

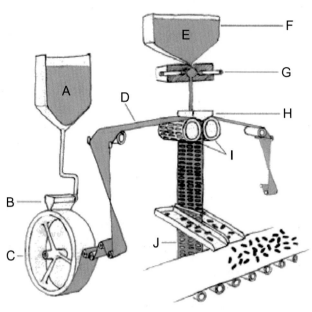

FIGURE 9.8 Schematic drawing of a rotary die process of making soft gelatin capsules. (A) Gelatin mix, (B) spreader, (C) cooling drum, (D) gelatin ribbon, (E) fill material, (F) fill tank, (G) fill pumps, (H) injection wedge, (I) die, and (J) gelatin net.

- They can be used as a single-dose application of topical and ophthalmic preparations.
- They are extensively used in the cosmetic industry to dispense bath oil, perfume, topical creams, breath fresheners, etc.

9.3.2.3 Basic components of a soft gelatin capsule

The major components of soft gelatin capsule shells are gelatin, plasticizer (Glycerin USP, Sorbitol USP), and water. Besides these three components, they may contain other ingredients such as preservatives, coloring, flavoring, opacifiers, and sweetening agents. Type B gelatin is commonly used in the preparation of soft gelatin capsules; however, Type A gelatin can also be used. The presence and the amount of plasticizer used in the preparation of the capsule shell determines its flexibility. In general, 20%–30% (w/w) of plasticizer is recommended. If the plasticizer concentration is less than 20%, the shell becomes very brittle. When the amount is above 30%, it becomes very tacky. The ratio of plasticizer and gelatin determines the overall hardness of the finished product. The plasticizer-to-gelatin ratio of 0.4:1.0 produces extremely hard-shell capsules; when this ratio is 0.8:1.0, the capsules become very flexible. The ratio of water (on weight basis) to dry gelatin varies from 0.7 to 1.3 (water) to 1.0 (dry gelatin). Commonly, a 1:1 (water:gelatin) ratio is used. Since water is lost during the drying and manufacturing process, the final water content of the capsule shell lies in between the range of 5%–8%. Some of the other additives used in soft gelatin capsules are listed in Table 9.3.

TABLE 9.3   Other ingredients added to soft gelatin capsule shells.

Ingredients	Concentration	Used as
Methylparaben and propylparaben (4:1 ratio)	0.2%	Preservative
Titanium dioxide	0.2%–1.2%	Opacifier
Sugar (sucrose)	Up to 5%	Sweetener
Ethyl vanillin	0.1%	Flavoring agent
Cellulose acetate phthalate (CAP)	4%	Enteric coating agent
Fumaric acid	Up to 1%	Solubility enhancer and reduce aldehydic tanning of gelatin

9.3.2.4 Capsule content in a soft gelatin capsule

The fill material for soft gelatin capsules is mostly liquids, but solids and semisolid materials can be dispensed in this dosage form. Solutions of solids in liquid and suspensions of solids in liquid are also filled in soft gelatin capsules.

9.3.2.5 Liquids

Several categories of liquids can be used as fill material. This includes lipophilic liquids, self-emulsifying liquids, and water-miscible liquids. Some water-miscible and volatile liquids, such as ethyl alcohol, cannot be incorporated as major constituents since they can migrate to the capsule shell and volatilize from the surface. A high proportion of plasticizers such as glycerol and propylene glycol cannot be incorporated due to their softening effects on the shell. Lipophilic materials such as vegetable oil and esters of fatty acids are mostly used. Since these solvents have limited solubility to many solutes, other pharmaceutics techniques, such as co-solvent and solubilization using a surfactant, are commonly used. Self-emulsifying systems consist of lipophilic liquids containing nonionic surfactants. When these liquids come into contact with the GI fluid, instantaneously from emulsions with high surface areas, they aid in the rapid dissolution and absorption of hydrophobic drugs. Water-miscible liquids, such as high-molecular-weight alcohols like polyethylene glycols (PEG 400 and 600), nonionic surfactants like Tweens, and polyoxyethylene-polyoxypropylene block co-polymers (Pluronics), could be used as fill materials in soft gelatin capsules. The formulation of the capsule content is individually selected according to the product specification and end use of the product.

Examples of liquids used as filling material in soft gelatin capsules for human use:

- Oily active ingredients (clofibrate)
- Vegetable oils (soybean oil)
- Mineral oil
- Nonionic surface-active agents (polysorbate 80)
- Oil-soluble vitamins

9.3.2.6 Liquid solutions and suspensions as fill material

Before being filled into soft gelatin capsules, these fill materials should be homogenous, free of air, and flow freely under gravity at room temperature but not at the sealing temperature, which is around 37—40°C for soft gelatin capsules. The pH of the liquid fill should be in the range of 2.5—7.5. Highly acidic solution may cause hydrolysis of gelatin and leakage of the gelatin shell. Highly alkaline pH may lead to the tanning of gelatin, which can affect its solubility.

Examples of commercially available drugs prepared as soft gelatin capsules include the following.

- Ethchlorvynol (Placidyl, Abbott)
- Chlorohydrate (Noctec, Squibb)
- Vitamin A, vitamin E, etc.

9.3.2.7 Soft gelatin capsule manufacturing

The original patent for the manufacture of soft gelatin capsules was granted to R.P. Scherer in 1933. A schematic representation of the manufacturing process is shown in Fig. 9.8. The first step is the preparation of the gelatin ribbons. The wet mass containing gelatin, water, plasticizer, and other needed ingredients is prepared. This gelatin solution is spread over two drums using a spreader box. The formed gelatin ribbons with controlled thickness are fed through a mineral oil lubricating bath, over guide rolls, and fed in between two rotary dies that are lubricated with mineral oil. The pump accurately meters the filled material through the leads and the wedge and into the gelatin ribbons between the die rolls. The two halves of the capsule containing the fill material are sealed by temperature (37—40°C) and pressure. The capsules are removed from the ribbon, subjected to a naphtha wash unit to remove the mineral oil, and exposed to an infrared drying unit to remove 60%—70% of the water. Capsules are equilibrated with forced air conditions of 20%—30% RH at 21—24°C, and the water content of the shell is within 6%—10%.

9.3.2.8 Quality control of capsules

Quality control and inspection for both hard and soft capsules are almost the same as for other solid dosage forms and must follow good manufacturing practices. Some of the additional steps needed for capsules are outlined here:

- *Empty capsules*: For hard gelatin capsules, care should be taken to evaluate and control the physical dimensions, wall thickness, length, and overall join length. Visual inspections for air bubbles, dents, cracks, loose caps, etc. are essential in the quality assurance protocols.
- *Filled capsules*: In the case of filled capsules, content uniformity, moisture content, fill weight, disintegration, dissolution, and stability evaluation are essential to maintain quality capsules and compare batch-to-batch variation and control. However, in the case of soft gelatin capsules, some additional quality control measures are used, including evaluation of seal thickness, total or shell moisture content tests, and the effect of freezing and high temperature on the capsule shell. In the case of capsules containing liquids, leaking and other defects need to be determined.

9.3.2.9 *Recent advancements in capsule technology*

For the capsule dosage forms two areas have shown rapid advancements that include innovations in capsule systems and capsule shells.

- Innovation in capsule system:
  o Programable oral release technology (PORT) capsules. This is a specialized capsule dosage form. This system consists of a hard gelatin capsule coated with a semipermeable polymeric membrane. Inside the coated capsule both the osmotic agent and the drug were present. When taken orally, the capsule dissolves and the initial dose is released followed by activation of GI fluid on the osmotic agents to push the second dose.
  o Hydrophilic sandwich (HS) capsule. Consists of a capsule in a capsule where the inner space of the capsule is filled with a swellable hydrophilic polymer like HPMC. With oral ingestion, the outer gelatin layer dissolves and the HPMC layer swells which control the release of the drug from the inner capsule.
  o Chewable soft gelatin capsule. Comprised of different bloom strength (low and medium bloom) gelatin, plasticizer, and water.
  o Innercap technology. This technology allows the administration of two or more drug components in a capsule. Using this technology compatible and incompatible APIs can be co-administered in different physical forms.
  o Capsule camera. Capsule containing a video camera can be used for GI endoscopy. This technology can photograph the bowel for 8 hours after oral ingestion.
- Innovation in capsule shells
  o Advancements in material science and chemistry have developed a vegan hydroxypropyl methylcellulose (HPMC) capsule shell material as compared to the conventional animal source gelatin. HPMC capsule shells are not only vegan but also have a lower moisture content. Greater performance consistency and product stability are their major advantages as compared to gelatin capsule shells. Pullulan is a water-soluble polysaccharide. PVA and starch have been used to make vegan capsule shells as an alternative substitute for gelatin capsule shell. Enteric capsules are currently under development and will be a great benefit to a formulator and patients in the future. Dry powder inhalation drug delivery using a hard capsule has been explored and will see many advances in the future.

9.4 Tablets

Tablets are solid dosage forms containing medicinal agents, with or without any diluents. Based on the method of manufacture, tablets can be classified into two groups [3].

- Molded tablets or tablets triturates
- Compressed tablets

Compressed tablets are solid dosage forms prepared by compaction of a formulation containing a drug and certain excipients selected to aid in processing and to improve product properties.

9.4.1 Advantages of tablets as a dosage form

- Tablets are convenient and easy to use.
- Tablets are less expensive to manufacture than other oral dosage forms.
- Tablets are physically and chemically stable.
- Special release profiles, such as enteric or sustained release, can be achieved.

- Tablets are of high patient acceptance because of their portability and compact form.
- Tablets are the most tamper-proof of all oral dosage forms.
- They provide economy and convenience of production, storage, and transportation.

9.4.2 Disadvantages

- Some individuals experience psychological difficulties in swallowing tablets.
- Preparing tablets extemporaneously is impractical.

9.4.3 Essential properties of a good tablet

- Tablets must be sufficiently strong to maintain their shape during manufacture, packing, shipping, and use.
- The drug in tablets should be bioavailable and released in a reproducible and predictable manner.
- Tablets should be accurate and uniform in weight.
- They should be elegant in appearance and easily identifiable.
- They should have reasonable physical and chemical stability during average storage conditions.
- They should be free of cracks, chipped edges, discoloration, and contamination.
- They should provide ease of manufacture and economy of production.

9.4.4 Types of tablets

Tablets are generally classified according to their method of manufacturing (molded vs. compressed) and their intended use.

9.4.4.1 Conventional compressed tablets

Most tablets used today in clinical practice are conventional compressed tablets. They are manufactured by a single compression cycle using powders or granules of both active and inactive agents. Disintegration and dissolution of the tablet after oral administration in the GI tract aid in the absorption of the drug via the gastric mucosa.

Examples: Tylenol tablet, metformin tablet.

9.4.4.2 Molded tablets

Molded tablets are not manufactured by compression. They are prepared by molding and are very soft and disintegrate quickly. One example of molded tablets is tablet triturates. Tablet triturates are administered sublingually, or by placing them on the tongue followed by swallowing with a small volume of water. Lactose and sucrose are the common diluents used for tablet triturates.

Examples: Nitroglycerin tablet triturates.

9.4.4.3 Buccal tablets

Buccal tablets are designed to dissolve slowly in the mouth between the cheek and the gingiva. These tablets are manufactured so that the release of the drug happens slowly in the mouth without disintegration. The drug is absorbed into the blood circulation directly through the oral mucosa. Direct absorption through oral mucosa avoids first-pass metabolism.

Example: Fentanyl buccal tablet.

9.4.4.4 Sublingual tablets

Sublingual tablets are placed beneath the tongue and dissolve rapidly. This mode of administration also avoids first-pass metabolism.

Example: Glyceryl trinitrate sublingual tablet.

9.4.4.5 Chewable tablets

Chewable tablets are chewed in the mouth before swallowing. They are not intended to be swallowed intact. These tablets are intended for children, the elderly, and patients who have difficulty in swallowing. Mannitol is commonly used as an excipient in chewing tablets because of its cooling effect during dissolution in the mouth.

Examples: Pepcid chewable tablet, chewable aspirin tablet.

9.4.4.6 Effervescent tablets

Effervescent tablets are produced from the compression of effervescence granules that contain an organic acid (citric) and sodium bicarbonate. When such tablets are placed in water, the chemical reaction of acid with the base produces carbon dioxide in the form of gas bubbles in the water. Quick disintegration of these tablets helps in quick dissolution and absorption.

Example: Alka-Seltzer tablet.

9.4.4.7 Lozenges and troches

Lozenges and troches are intended to be sucked and held in the mouth, where they exert a local effect in the mouth or throat. These dosage forms are most used in sore throat and cough remedies for common colds. Lozenges are made by fusion, compression, or a candy-molding process. Troches are made by a compression process. These dosage forms do not disintegrate in the mouth but slowly dissolve or erode with time.

Examples: Clotrimazole troches, Chloraseptic lozenges, Nicorette lozenges.

9.4.4.8 Multiple compressed tablets

Multiple compressed tablets are designed to enable the separation of incompatible ingredients or make sustained-release products, or they are merely designed for appearance. There are two classes of multiple compressed tablets: layered tablets and compression-coated tablets.

Examples: Phenylephedrine HCL, ascorbic acid with acetaminophen.

9.4.4.9 Sugar-coated tablets

Conventional compressed tablets are coated with successive coats of sugar solution with or without a color to produce elegant, glossy, and easy-to-swallow tablets for oral use.

Example: Perphenazine tablet, sugar-coated.

9.4.4.10 Enteric-coated tablets

Enteric-coated tablets are conventionally compressed tablets coated with a polymer that does not dissolve in the acidic condition of the stomach but readily dissolves in the alkaline pH of the small intestine. Such a coating can protect drugs from the degradative effects of gastric acidity. They also protect the gastric mucosa from irritation from certain drugs. Polymers that have enteric-coating ability include cellulose acetate phthalate (CAP), cellulose acetate butyrate (CAB), hydroxypropylmethylcellulose succinate, and methacrylic acid co-polymers (Eudragit).

Examples: Enteric-coated aspirin tablet, naproxen enteric-coated tablet.

9.4.4.11 Film-coated tablets

Film-coated tablets are compressed tablets coated with a colored polymeric coating that forms a thin skin-like film around the tablet core. The film coating is more durable than sugar coating and can be formed quickly. Polymers used in film coatings include hydroxy propyl methyl cellulose, hydroxy propyl cellulose, and Eudragit E100, etc.

Example: Glyburide/metformin (5 mg/500 mg) film-coated tablets.

9.4.4.12 Sustained-release tablets

Sustained-release tablets are designed to release an initial therapeutically effective amount of a drug followed by maintaining this effective level over an extended period of time. This is achieved by design approaches. The advantages of sustained-release tablets include the maintenance of therapeutic effect for a longer time, reduced frequency of administration, and enhanced patient compliance.

Example: Wellbutrin SR (bupropion hydrochloride) tablet.

9.4.4.13 Vaginal tablets

Vaginal tablets are ovoid- or pear-shaped conventional compressed tablets that are inserted into the vagina using a plastic inserter. Antibacterial drugs, antifungal drugs, and steroids are generally administered using this dosage form. Lactose and sodium bicarbonate are used as diluents for vaginal tablets. After insertion, the drug is released by slow dissolution. Disintegration of these tablets must be avoided for proper retention inside the vagina. Both systemic and local delivery of drugs can be achieved by using this dosage form.

Examples: Vagifem (estradiol vaginal tablets), nystatin vaginal tablets, USP.

9.4.4.14 Orally disintegrating tablets

Orally disintegrating tablets (ODTs) are a solid dosage form containing medicinal substances that disintegrate rapidly, usually within a matter of seconds, when placed on the tongue. They are produced by dry granulation and compression, have a hardness of 40 N or more, a disintegration time of 30 seconds or shorter, a friability of 0.1% or less, and an excellent feeling upon ingestion that is capable of disintegrating with a small amount of water.

Example: Zofran ODT (Ondansetron ODT); Imodium Instant Melts (Loperamide HCI ODT).

9.5 Manufacture of compressed tablets

Tablets are manufactured by compression using a tablet press. A compressed tablet is composed of two basic groups of ingredients: the medicaments, also known as the active pharmaceutical ingredients (APIs; always present except when it is a placebo tablet for investigational use), and excipients (all other materials needed to make the tablet except the medicament), which may or may not be present. Therefore, a tablet excipient is an inert substance used to give a preparation a suitable form or consistency and, in some instances, is present in higher amounts than the API. The choice of excipients depends on the process used for the manufacturing of compressed tablets. Some common excipients used in tablet formulations include diluents or fillers, binders, disintegrants, lubricants, glidants, coloring agents, and flavoring agents. Each of these excipients serves a unique function and, in some instances, may serve more than one functions [3].

9.5.1 Diluents

Diluents are needed in all methods of tablet manufacturing when the active mass per each tablet is not sufficient for processing. Diluents can be categorized into two groups: insoluble and soluble. Some commonly used soluble diluents include lactose, sucrose, dextrose, and mannitol. However, calcium sulfate dihydrate, dibasic and tribasic calcium phosphate, starch, and microcrystalline cellulose (MCC) are some examples of insoluble diluents that are used as fillers in the tablet dosage form.

9.5.2 Binders

Binders (binding agents) are adhesive materials used to hold powders together to form granules and assist in holding the tablet together after compression with adequate hardness (see Table 9.4). Binders can be used as dry powder (as in the case of direct compression) or as a liquid mixture (wet granulation). Binder is essential to maintain the integrity of a tablet during its self-life. Binder and disintegrant serve opposite function in a tablet formulation. Disintegrants enhance the disintegration of a tablet, but binders decrease the disintegration.

- Dry tablet binders: Dry tablet binders are used in direct compression or added to dry granules prepared by wet granulation process. Some examples of this category include polyvinyl pyrrolidone (PVP), hydroxy propyl methyl cellulose (HPMC), sodium carboxy methyl cellulose, polyethylene glycol (PEG), and methyl cellulose.

TABLE 9.4 Examples of binders.

Binder	Usual concentration (% w/v)
Corn starch USP	5%—10% aqueous paste
Starch 1500	5%—10% aqueous paste
Gelatin	2%—10% aqueous solution
Acacia	5%—20% aqueous solution
PVP	5%—20% aqueous, alcoholic, or hydroalcoholic
Methyl cellulose	2%—10% aqueous solution
Sodium carboxymethyl-cellulose	2%—10% aqueous solution

TABLE 9.5 Examples of disintegrating agents.

Disintegrants	Concentration (% w/w) in granulation
Starch USP	5–20
Starch 1500	5–15
Microcrystalline cellulose (Avicel)	5–15
Alginic acid	5–15
Guar gum	2–8
Methylcellulose, sodium carboxymethylcellulose	5–10

- Tablet binders in liquid form: These binders are used in wet granulation processes. These binders are dissolved/dispersed in different solvents such as water or alcohol. Examples of such tablet binders include gelatin, cellulose derivatives, polyvinyl pyrrolidone, starch, sucrose, mannitol, and polyethylene glycol.

9.5.3 Disintegrating agents

Disintegrating agent (disintegrant) is an important component of tablet dosage forms. They are added to a tablet formulation to break apart (disintegrate) the compressed tablet when placed in aqueous environments. Disintegration of conventional compressed tablets must occur within 15 minutes. Disintegrants may work by one of the following mechanisms (see Table 9.5).

- Disintegrants can increase the porosity and wettability of compressed tablets. In doing so, they enhance the penetration and uptake of GI fluids into the tablet matrix and disintegrate. Starch and microcrystalline cellulose act by this mechanism.
- Disintegration can happen due to the effervescence properties of granules, which can break the tablets very quickly when in contact with water.
- Swelling of the disintegrant in the presence of water can increase the internal pressure of the tablet matrix and cause the eventual disintegration of the tablet. Sodium starch glycolate, croscarmellose, and pregelatinized starch work according to this mechanism.

Disintegrants can be added to tablet formulations before compression by three different methods:

- *Internal addition*: In this method, the disintegrant is mixed with other powders before granulation.
- *External addition*: The disintegrant is added to the granules before compression (mixing before compression).
- *Combination method*: Both internal and external additions of disintegrants are used. This combination method is the most efficient way of adding a disintegrant to a tablet formulation *before* compression. These agents swell when exposed to gastric fluids and exert sufficient mechanical pressure from within the tablet to cause it to break apart into small fragments. The disintentegrants present in the granules (added by internal addiotion method) then disintegrate into the release medium.

Chemically modified disintegrants termed as superdisintegrants have been developed to improve the disintegration processes. Superdisintegrants are used at a low level (1%–10%) by weight basis as compared to a conventional disintegrant in the solid dosage form. Some of the commonly used superdisintegrants include sodium starch glycolate (Explotab, Primogel), cross-linked polyvinyl-pyrrolidone (crospovidone, PolyplasdoneXL, PolyplasdoneXL10), croscarmellose sodium (Ac-Di-Sol), and magnesium aluminum silicate (Veegum HV).

9.5.4 Lubricants and glidants

Lubricants are added to granules before compression to achieve many functions. They enhance the flow of granules, reduce adhesion to punches and dies, facilitate ejection through the die wall, and reduce die and punch wire. Two types of lubricants are commonly used, depending on their aqueous solubility. The amount of lubricant used may adversely affect the disintegration and dissolution of tablets and should be carefully monitored. Some of the insoluble lubricants used in tablet formulations include magnesium stearate (0.25%−0.5% w/w), stearic acid (1%−3% w/w), and glycerylpalmitostearate (1%−3% w/w). Soluble lubricants are used to minimize the adverse effect of insoluble lubricants on tablet disintegration and dissolution. However, the lubricative powers of soluble lubricants are inferior to their insoluble counterparts. Some soluble lubricants include polyethylene glycol (PEG) 4000, 6000, and 8000; polyoxyethylene stearate (1%−2% w/w); and sodium or magnesium lauryl sulfate (1%−2% w/w).

Glidants are added to enhance the flow properties of powders in the hopper and the feed frame into the die in the tablet press. Glidants act in between the particle and the surface of the hopper or die to reduce the friction and aid in enhanced flow. Since glidants are hydrophobic, they can adversely affect disintegration and dissolution. Therefore, their amount in the tablet should be carefully monitored. Talc and silicon dioxide are commonly used as glidants in tablet formulations.

9.5.5 Flavoring agents, coloring agents, and sweetening agents

Flavoring agents are mostly used in chewable tablets. Flavors can be available as oils and spray-dried beadlets. Oils can be sprayed onto dry granules as an alcoholic solution or incorporated in the lubricant. FD&C color is normally used to add appropriate color to a tablet. Color can be added to a binding solution or can be sprayed onto the granules. Dye can also be mixed with the dry powder blend before the wet granulation process. Sweetening Agents (sweeteners) are used to mask the unpleasant taste of oral medications. They are used mostly in chewable tablets and pediatric preparations. Pharmaceutical sweeteners can be classified as bulk sweeteners, which include dextrose, fructose, maltitol, sorbitol, sucrose, trehalose, and xylitol and intense sweeteners, into two major groups that include aspartame (NutraSweet), sodium saccharin (Syncal), stevia (Rebaten), and Sucralose (Splenda).

9.6 Methods used for manufacture of compressed tablets

A tablet granulation must be prepared first in a form suitable for compression on a tablet press. Such a procedure is called *granulation*. The granules used for tablet compression must have good flow properties, be compressible to form the compact, and have lubricant properties for the ejection of the tablet from the die [3]. Three processes are used for making tablets by compression.

- Wet granulation
- Dry granulation (slugging)
- Direct compression

The wet and dry granulation processes are designed to improve the flow and compressibility of powders that would otherwise be unsuitable for compression. When the formulation has a satisfactory flow and compressibility, the ingredients can be mixed and directly compressed.

9.6.1 Wet granulation

Wet granulation is the process in which a liquid is added to a powder with agitation to produce agglomeration or granules. Wet granules are prepared using oscillating granulators, high-speed mixers, or even fluidized-bed granulators. The wet granules are properly dried and mixed with other essential excipients and finally pressed in a tablet press. This is the oldest and most conventional method of making tablets. It is also the method of choice when large-dose drugs are to be compressed into a tablet.

9.6.1.1 Advantages of wet granulation

Wet granulation modifies the properties of formulation components to overcome their tableting deficiencies. Granules are relatively more spherical than the powders and have better flow properties. During compaction, granules are fractured, exposing new surfaces, which improves compressibility. Improved compressibility allows lower pressure to be used during tablet compaction, which improves the life of the machine.

- This process ensures better content uniformity, especially for soluble low-dose drugs
- It prevents the segregation of components
- It may improve the dissolution rate of an insoluble drug by proper choice of solvent and binder

9.6.1.2 Limitations

- The cost of wet granulation is higher because of the space, time, and equipment involved
- This process is not suitable for moisture and heat-sensitive materials
- Migration of soluble materials, including dyes, in the solvent to the surface of the granules may occur during the drying process
- Incompatibilities between formulation components can be aggravated by the granulating solvent, bringing them into close contact
- There is a possibility of material loss during processing due to the transfer of material from one unit operation to the other

9.6.2 Dry Granulation

Dry granulation involves compacting the components of a tablet formulation by means of a tablet press and then milling the compact to obtain the granules. Compaction for the dry granulation process is generally achieved either by slugging or roller compaction. No water or heat is needed for this granulation process. In the slugging process, large tablets are compressed in a heavy-duty tablet press. These tablets are then broken into granules in a conventional mill. In the case of a roller compacter, the powders are pressed in a roller mill, and the thin sheet of compacted materials is further broken into granules with a conventional mill.

9.6.2.1 Advantages of dry granulation

- Dry granulation eliminates the use of binder solutions and can be used for moisture-sensitive materials (e.g., aspirin, effervescent tablets)
- No drying step is involved, so this process can be used for heat-sensitive materials
- This process improves solubility
- It improves blending since there is no migration

9.6.2.2 Disadvantages of dry granulation

- Dry granulation requires a heavy-duty press
- It does not permit uniform color distribution

9.6.3 Direct compression

The direct compression process involves the compression of mixed powder components into tablets without an intermediate granulation step. Recently, there has been a great deal of research to develop diluents for direct compression. With advances in material science and engineering, many available direct compression diluents are currently available that include lactose, spray-dried lactose, microcrystalline cellulose, calcium sulfate, dibasic calcium phosphate, and starch 1500.

9.6.3.1 Advantages of direct compression

- Direct compression is less expensive (labor, time, equipment, space, fewer steps involved in the process)
- This process eliminates heat and moisture
- It increases surface area for rapid drug dissolution once the tablet disintegrates
- It creates more stable tablets

9.6.3.2 Limitations of direct compression

- Differences in particle size and density in direct compression may lead to segregation in the hopper
- Low-dose drugs may not be uniformly blended
- High-dose drugs that have both poor flow and compressibility characteristics cannot be used for direct compression

TABLE 9.6 Comparison of various steps used in different methods of tablet manufacturing processes.

Wet granulation	Dry granulation	Direct compression
1. Milling of all solid ingredients	1. Milling of all solid ingredients	1. Milling of all solid ingredients
2. Mixing of powders	2. Mixing of powders	2. Mixing of powders
3. Preparation of binder solution	3. Primary compression to make slugs	3. Tablet compression
4. Mixing of binder solution to powder mixture to form wet mass	4. Screening of slugs 5. Mixing with lubricant and disintegrating agent 6. Tablet compression	
5. Screening of wet mass through 6–12-mesh screen to form granules		
6. Drying of moist granules		
7. Screening of dry granules through 14–20-mesh screen		
8. Mixing of screened granules with lubricant and disintegrant		
9. Tablet compression		

9.6.4 Comparison of methods used for manufacture of tablets

It is evident from Table 9.6 that direct compression has the least number of steps, as compared to the other two methods. Therefore, direct compression is more economical and is currently the preferred method of preparation for compressed tablets.

9.7 Tablet compression and basic functional units of a tablet press

The final step in the manufacture of a conventional compressed tablet is the compression step. Powders and granules are compressed in a tablet press, and two types of presses are used: single-punch presses and rotary presses. A schematic diagram of a single tablet press with its essential parts is shown in Fig. 9.9.

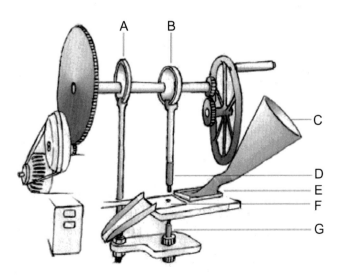

FIGURE 9.9 Schematic drawing of a single punch tablet press. (A) Lower lifting cam, (B) upper lifting cam, (C) hopper, (D) upper punch, (E) feed shoe, (F) die, and (G) lower punch.

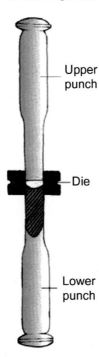

FIGURE 9.10 Schematic representation of punch and die assembly.

The basic functional units of these presses are outlined below:

- *Hopper*: for storing material to be compressed
- *Feed frame*: for distributing the materials into dies
- *Dies*: for controlling the size and shape of the tablet (as shown in Fig. 9.10)
- *Punches*: for compacting the materials within dies (as shown in Fig. 9.10)
- *Cams*: for guiding the punches for tablet ejection from the dies

9.7.1 Common processing problems encountered during tablet compression [3]

9.7.1.1 Capping and lamination

Capping is the partial or complete separation of the top or bottom layer of a tablet from the main body. Lamination is the separation of a tablet into two or more layers.

9.7.1.1.1 Causes

- Entrapped air in the granules
- Improper setting of the tablet press
- Plastic deformation to produce die wall pressures greater than that can be relieved by elastic recovery on removal of the punch

9.7.1.1.2 Remedies

- Change granulation procedures
- Increase binder concentration
- Increase or change the lubricant in the formulation
- Add dry binder to the formulation
- Use tapered dies

9.7.1.2 Picking and sticking

Sticking refers to tablet surface to stick to punch faces during a compression process. Sticking happens due to slight dampness of the granulation. Picking is a form of sticking in which a small portion of granules sticks to the punch face and the problem worsens with time. Picking may result from compressing granules that are not properly dried or when scratched punches are used in the compression of tablets. Both picking and sticking result in defective tablets.

9.7.1.2.1 Remedies

- Decrease the moisture content of the granules
- Add an adsorbent (microcrystalline cellulose)
- Polish the punch face
- Clean and coat the punch face with light mineral oil or plate the punch faces with chromium
- Reduce the fraction of low-melting tablet components

9.7.1.3 Mottling

Mottling is defined as an unequal distribution of color on a tablet with light and dark areas.

9.7.1.3.1 Causes

- Drug color different from other components
- Migration of colors during drying
- Uneven distribution of color when using a colored adhesive gel solution

9.7.1.3.2 Remedies

- Reduce drying temperature
- Grind to smaller particle size
- Change the binder system
- Change the solvent system

9.7.1.4 Weight variation

Variations in the ratio of small to large granules and differences in granule size may lead to filling dies with the same volume but different weight of filling materials. Sporadic flow by granules may also lead to unequal filling and weight variations. Segregation due to vibration of a tablet press may lead to weight variation in tablets.

9.7.1.5 Hardness

The same causes responsible for weight variation may cause hardness variation. Besides the concentration of binders used and the compression force, the hardness of a tablet depends on the weight of the material to be compressed and the space between the upper and lower punches at the time of compression. If the volume of the material to be compressed and the distance between punches varies, this will lead to variation in tablet hardness.

9.7.1.6 Double impression

A double impression involves only lower punches that have a monogram or other engraving on them. The punch can make double impressions on a tablet surface during the ejection process. This can be avoided by incorporating antiturning devices for the punches.

9.8 Quality control of tablet dosage form

During the manufacturing of tablet dosage forms, routine quality control tests are performed to maintain product quality. Some of these tests include thickness, hardness, disintegration, tablet weight, and elegance.

9.8.1 Thickness

Factors that can affect tablet thickness at a constant compression load include changes in die fill, particle size distribution, and packing of the particle mix during compression. Tablet thickness becomes very important in packing operations. Use of micrometer calipers to measure the thickness of tablets is common in practice. Variations in tablet thickness should not be more than $\pm5\%$.

9.8.2 Hardness and friability

Although hardness is not an official test, diametral crushing is most frequently used in process control because of its simplicity. Hardness is generally expressed as the force required to break a tablet in a diametric compression test; it is often called breaking strength or tablet crushing strength. Various instruments are used to measure the breaking strength of tablets, including the Monsanto Tester, Strong—Cobb Tester, Pfizer Tester, Erweka Tester, and Herberlein Tester. Tablet hardness depends on compression load. Hardness increases with an increase in pressure, as this causes the tablet to laminate or cap.

Friability is a measure of the tendency of a tablet to powder, chip, and fragment during handling and is another measure of tablet strength. A Roche friabilator is used to measure the friability of a tablet. A preweighed tablet sample is placed in the friabilator and dropped over a distance of 6 inches height during each revolution and operated for 4 minutes (100 revolutions). The tablets are dusted and reweighed. Accepted tablets are those that do not lose more than 0.5%—1.0% of their weight. The friability of tablets may be influenced by moisture content. Chewable tablets show a high friability weight loss as compared to conventional compressed tablets.

9.8.3 Disintegration

When taken orally, the first thing that happens to a compressed oral tablet before absorption is disintegration or breaking down of the tablets to granules and powders before dissolving in the gastric fluid. The time it takes to disintegrate is called disintegration time and is measured by a USP disintegration apparatus, as described in the USP NF. The USP disintegration apparatus uses six tubes (3 in. long) open at both ends with a 10-mesh screen at the bottom of the tube. Baskets are reciprocated up and down through a distance of 5—6 cm at a frequency of 28—32 cycles per minute. The medium can be water or simulated gastric or intestinal fluid, and the volume of the medium is 1000 mL. The temperature is maintained at $37 \pm 2°C$.

The tablet must disintegrate, and all particles pass through to 10-mesh screen in the specified time. For ordinary compressed tablets, the disintegration time should be within 5—30 minutes. For enteric-coated tablets, no disintegration should occur within 1 hour in simulated gastric fluid, but the same tablets must disintegrate in 2 hours plus the time stated in the USP monograph when they are placed in simulated intestinal fluid. Many factors can affect the disintegration time of compressed tablets. Some of the major factors include media and the temperature of the disintegration test media, the nature of the drug, the diluent used in the formulation, the type and amount of binder and disintegrant used, and the compression load.

9.8.3.1 Dissolution

When a tablet is administered, disintegration results in the breaking down of the tablets into granules and primary particles (see Fig. 9.11). For absorption to take place, dissolution of the drug in the gastrointestinal fluid has to occur, since only the drug in solution is absorbed.

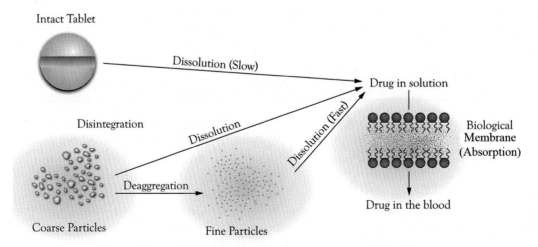

FIGURE 9.11   Absorption of a drug from an intact tablet.

9.8.3.2 Objectives of a dissolution study

The objectives of a dissolution study are to ensure that the drug is completely released or close to 100% release from the tablet, and that the rate of drug release is uniform from batch to batch and is the same as the release rate from batches proven to be bioavailable and clinically effective.

The rate at which a solid dissolve in a solvent is given by the Noyes and Whitney (1897) equation:

$$\frac{dc}{dt} = \frac{DA}{Vh}(C_s - C)$$

$$\frac{dc}{dt} \times V = \frac{DA}{h}(C_s - C)$$

$$\frac{dm}{dt} = \frac{DA}{h}(C_s - C)$$

where dm/dt is the dissolution rate, D is the diffusion coefficient of the solute in the dissolution medium, A is the surface area of the exposed solid, h is the thickness of the diffusion layer, C_s is the solubility of the solid in the dissolution medium, C is the concentration of the solute at any time t, and V is the volume of the release medium.

9.8.3.3 Factors affecting dissolution rate

Various factors can affect the dissolution of a drug; they are classified under three categories as follows.

1. Physiochemical properties of the drug
   - *Polymorphic form*: A metastable form of a solid has higher solubility and dissolution compared to its stable counterpart.
   - *Particle size*: The smaller the particle size of a solid, the larger the particle surface area and the higher the dissolution.
   - *Salt form*: A salt form of a drug has a higher aqueous solubility compared to its conjugate acid or base, as well as higher dissolution.
   - *Hydrates* versus *anhydrates*: The anhydrous form shows higher dissolution than hydrates due to their solubility differences.
2. Factors related to tablet manufacturing
   - The amount and type of binder can affect the hardness, disintegration, and dissolution of tablets.
   - The method of granulation, granule size, and size distribution can affect tablet dissolution. The amount and type of disintegrants used, as well as the method of their addition, can affect disintegration and dissolution. Compression load can influence density, porosity, hardness, disintegration, and dissolution of tablets.
3. Factors related to method of dissolution study
   - Composition of the dissolution medium, pH, ionic strength, and viscosity.
   - Temperature of the medium.
   - Intensity of agitation.
   - Volume of the dissolution medium.
   - Sink or nonsink conditions (under a sink condition, the concentration of the drug should not exceed 10%–15% of its saurated solubility in the dissolution medium in use).
   - Type of dissolution equipment.
   - Sensitivity of analytical method used to determine drug concentration in the release medium.

9.8.3.4 Dissolution testing methods

According to USP, there are many dissolution apparatuses used to determine the dissolution profiles of drugs from different dosage forms. Some of them are outlined in Table 9.7.

USP dissolution conditions are maintained as close as possible to the *in vivo* situation.

Temperature:	$37° \pm 0.5°C$
Medium:	1.1 N HCl, pH 7.4 buffer Simulated gastric fluid, Simulated intestinal fluid, water
Agitation:	Mild
Volume of the medium:	Enough to maintain sink condition (1000 mL)

TABLE 9.7 Comparison of different USP dissolution apparatuses.

USP apparatus	Description of the apparatus	Rotation speed	Dosage forms to be tested
I	Basket	50–120 rpm	Immediate-release tablets
			Delayed-release tablets
			Extended-release tablets
II	Paddle	25–50 rpm	Immediate-release tablets
			Delayed-release tablets
			Extended-release tablets
III	Reciprocating cylinder	6–35 dpm (dips per minute)	Immediate-release tablets Extended-release tablets
IV	Flow-through cells	N/A	Extended-release tablets Poorly soluble drug
V	Paddle over disk	25–50 rpm	Transdermal
VI	Cylinder	N/A	Transdermal
VII	Reciprocating disk	30 rpm	Extended-release tablets

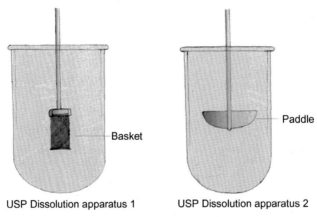

USP Dissolution apparatus 1   USP Dissolution apparatus 2

FIGURE 9.12 USP dissolution apparatus one and two.

USP Apparatus #1 (rotating basket) and USP Apparatus #2 (paddle method) are commonly used to evaluate the dissolution profile of solid dosage forms (see Fig. 9.12). The dissolution testing may be repeated three times for a batch if necessary. First, the dissolution of six tablets is tested and accepted if all six tablets are not less than the USP monograph tolerance limit plus 5%. If they fail, another six tablets will be tested. The tablets will be acceptable if the average of the 12 tablets is greater than or equal to the USP monograph tolerance limit and no unit is less than this limit minus 15%. If this fails, an additional 12 tablets will be tested. The tablets will be acceptable if the average of the 24 tablets is greater than or equal to the USP monograph tolerance limit and not more than two tablets are less than the USP monograph limit minus 15%. Dissolution results are plotted as concentration versus time, and values such as $t_{50\%}$ and $t_{90\%}$ or the percentage dissolved in 30 minutes are used for comparison purposes. A value of $t_{90\%}$ in 30 minutes is considered satisfactory during a dissolution study.

9.8.4 Weight variation

Tablets generally are manufactured to contain a certain amount of active ingredients in a certain weight of tablet. A weight variation test is essential to ensure that this is satisfied. In this test, samples of 10 tablets are removed from a batch from time to time during compression and are weighed to determine whether they conform to the required weight criteria. There still may be a difference in the individual weights even when 10 tablets show the expected total weight.

TABLE 9.8 USP weight variation test.

Average weight of tablet (mg)	Maximum (%) weight difference allowed
130 or less	10
130–324	7.5
More than 324	5.0

9.8.4.1 USP weight variation test

Twenty tablets are weighed individually. Individual weights are compared with the average weight. If no more than two tablets are outside the percentage limit, and if no tablet differs by more than two times the percentage limit, the tablets pass the USP weight variation tests (see Table 9.8).

9.8.4.2 USP potency and content uniformity test

For tablets in which the active ingredients make up about 90% of the tablet weight, the weight variation test will give a good measure of content uniformity. The acceptable potency range for low-dose, highly potent drugs is 90% –110%. For large-dose drugs, the range is 95%–105% of the labeled amount.

9.8.4.3 Method of determining content uniformity

Thirty tablets are selected randomly from a batch. Ten tablets are assayed individually. Nine of them must contain not less than 85% or more than 115% of the labeled drug content. The 10th tablet may not contain less than 75% or more than 125% of the labeled drug content. If the preceding conditions are not met, the 30 remaining tablets are assayed individually, and none may fall outside the 85%–115% range. Various factors are responsible for the variable content uniformity in tablets. This may include nonuniform distribution of the drug in the powder or granules, segregation of the powder mixture or granulation during manufacturing processes, and tablet weight variation.

9.9 Tablet coating

Tablet coatings are essential to achieve certain tasks, as follows.

- An enteric coating is used to protect the drug from GI irritation and from acidic degradation in the stomach
- Film and sugar coatings are used to mask the unpleasant taste and improve the pharmaceutical elegance of the tablet
- A film coating can be used to protect the drug from environmental degradation and to provide sustained release dosage forms
- Special tablet coatings may help in targeting the drug to a certain area of the GI tract (e.g., colon delivery).

Four different coatings are commonly used in tablets: sugar coating, film coating, compaction coating, and air suspension coating [4].

9.9.1 Sugar coating

Sugar is one of the oldest forms of tablet coatings. In this process, successive layers of sugar coatings are applied by spraying sugar solution into pans in which tablets are rotated and tumbled. Coating pans are supplied with air blowers to admit cold or hot air as needed during the coating operation. Exhaust ducts are attached to these pans to remove dust and moisture. For this type of coating, a convex surface tablet is preferred because flat tablets are difficult to coat. The following steps are commonly used in sugar-coating operations.

- Dusting of tablets to remove excess dust
- Application of a waterproofing seal (shellac, ethyl cellulose, silicones)
- Subcoating to fill the edge (heavy sugar solutions containing acacia with occasional dusting with starch and powder sugar)
- Smoothing (addition of heavy syrup followed by drying with warm air)

- Application of color coat
- Polishing

9.9.2 Film coating

Sugar coatings are time consuming. To avoid the extra time required for sugar coatings, formulation scientists introduced film coatings. A polymer solution is sprayed on the tablet surface with constant rotation and tumbling. Film coatings avoid the need for the subcoating and smoothing operations needed for sugar coating. Similar coating pans that are used for sugar coating are used for film coating. The polymers used for this coating operation include carboxymethylcellulose, ethyl cellulose, hydroxyl propyl methyl cellulose, cellulose acetate phthalate, povidone, and acrylate polymers.

9.9.3 Compression coating

Compression coating is also termed as dry coating. In this process, very fine coating materials are compressed over the tablet surface by compression in a die with the aid of punches. This coating process is beneficial for those drugs that cannot withstand heat and moisture during the coating operation. Multiple-layer tablets can also be produced by this compression coating to separate two incompatible drugs. Repeat action and sustained action tablets are produced by this coating method.

9.9.4 Air suspension technique

The air suspension technique is a very rapid and efficient method of coating tablets or granules. The tablets to be coated are suspended in a vertical chamber with an upward stream of warm air. A coating solution is spread from the bottom of the fluidized-bed coating chambers. This process is repeated until a uniform coating is achieved. In this coating, operation efficiency and quality are controlled by fluidized air volume, specific humidity of the warm air chamber, solvent evaporation rate, and the coating spray rate and duration.

9.9.5 Enteric coating

Enteric coating of tablets starts with a waterproof coating with shellac in a coating pan, followed by several coats with the enteric-coated material. In some instances, a sugar coat is applied over the enteric coating. Materials that are used in enteric coating include shellac, cellulose acetate phthalate (CAP), cellulose acetate butyrate, lipids (mixture of myristic acid, hydrogenated castor oil, castor oil, cholesterol, and sodium taurocholate), hydroxy propyl methyl cellulose succinate, and methacrylic acid co-polymers (Eudragit).

Problems associated with the coating of tablet formulations may include poor adhesion of coating material to the tablet surface, blistering, color variation, cracking, abrasion, roughness, and filling of tablet markings.

Quality control of coated tablets must include testing of their appearance and performance. Checking for color, size, appearance, and physical defects in a coating that can affect the release or stability of the drug in the dosage form is essential for quality assurance. The *in vitro* disintegration and dissolution methods of the coated tablets in appropriate media need careful evaluation. Other tests such as the evaluation of mechanical strength and resistance to chipping and cracking during handling need careful evaluation.

9.10 Innovation in tablet technology

Three-dimensional (3D) printing or additive manufacturing is an emerging field that creates solid objects layer-by-layer using computer-aided-design (CAD). In 3D printing technology, digital object representation is used to construct the desired object using modeling software. One of the most used modeling software is CAD. The modeling software can define the dimensions, surface shape of the object, color, internal structure, texture, etc. Once the object has been constructed, the 3D printer must understand the input from modeling software. For this purpose, a language or file type like Standard tessellation language (STL), Object file (OBJ), Additive manufacturing file format (AMF), and 3D manufacturing format (3 MF) are employed. After the 3D printer understands the input from CAD, a digital representation is converted into the actual object. The first FDA-approved tablet prepared using 3D technology Spritam was introduced in 2015. Spritam (levetiracetam) is a fast-dissolving tablet used in the treatment of epilepsy. This tablet was prepared based on powder bed liquid 3D printing technology (ZipDose) [5,6]. Complex tablet geometries could be achieved by 3D technology, not otherwise possible by conventional methods. However, the major challenges of 3D printing technology include the limited availability of 3D printable biomaterials and the need for improvement for the resolution, reproducibility, printing accuracy, and durability of the 3D printing process.

9.11 Conclusions

The solid dosage form, the most established and most preferred route of administration, still offers many opportunities and challenges for a future formulation scientist. Some of the recent innovations in solid dosage form development include the use of novel pharmaceutical excipients obtained from innovative material science research, more efficient ways of manufacturing, and the advancement of oral sustained-release formulations. The availability of quick disintegrants and taste-masking technology has made orally disintegrating tablets (ODT) more cost effective and an attractive alternative. Although the solid dosage form still has a promising future, it is not free from many challenges and hurdles. Some of these challenges may include improving the oral bioavailability of poorly soluble drugs, oral delivery of biologics, and size limitation of oral dose via a tablet or a capsule and controlling the release characteristics of the active drug from the dosage form and site-specific delivery of the drug to a definite part of the GI tract. Some of these challenges will be overcome in the future by innovative drug delivery approaches, which may require an interdisciplinary collaborations of many fields, including material science, molecular biology, biochemistry, physiology, computer technology, and pharmaceutics.

Case studies

Case 9.1 (Capsules)

In a rural community pharmacy, you receive a prescription for an older patient for 0.2 mL of peppermint oil to be dispensed as a solid dosage form. What do you do, as the only pharmacist in the pharmacy, for this prescription?

Approach: Peppermint oil is available in the pharmacy as a viscous oily liquid. To dispense an oil as a solid dosage form, you need to dispense it in a soft gelatin capsule. This approach is not feasible in a community pharmacy. The other possible alternative is dispensing 0.2 mL of oil via a syringe into the body of an appropriately sized hard gelatin capsule, followed by sealing and locking the cap of the capsule carefully with a thin band of water near the outer rim of the body and replacing the cap for sealing.

You must address the following concerns regarding quality assurance.

1. The weight of oil dispensed in the capsule should be carefully determined and documented.
2. Leakage of oil, if any, from the filled capsule should be evaluated by placing the filled capsules on a Kimwipe.

Case 9.2 (Powder)

An herbal resinous product is supposed to be diluted with an appropriate filler and dispensed as divided powder for a patient who is lactose intolerant. What do you do?

Approach: Since the patient is lactose intolerant, one cannot use lactose as a diluent. The other alternatives are microcrystalline cellulose (MCC) or calcium phosphate. As calcium phosphate is too granular, one may have a problem mixing it with resinous material in a pestle and mortar. Therefore, MCC may be a better choice. If the patient is not diabetic, dextrose or mannitol can be the other alternatives.

Case 9.3 (Tablets)

As the director of the clinical pharmacy, you are discussing with a pharmacy intern the reported *in vitro* dissolution profile of an investigational drug from the pharmaceutical literature. Following is some of the information available for this new drug:

In vitro dissolution data:

Solubility of the drug in a simulated gastric fluid is 100 μg/mL.

Concentration of the drug in the dissolution medium at the end of 4 hours = 34 mg/mL.

In vivo data:

Concentration of drug in the blood after 4 hours of oral administration = 6 µg/mL.

Total volume of blood in the patient = 4.8 L.

Solubility of the drug in the plasma at body temperature = 100 µg/mL.

At the end of 4 hours, does the dissolution follow the sink condition? At the end of 4 hours, does the oral absorption follow the sink condition?

Approach: To answer the first question, one must understand the concept of the sink condition. At the sink condition, the concentration of the drug in the release medium at any time during dissolution should not exceed 10%−15% of the solubility of that drug in the release medium. As the concentration at 4 hours of the dissolution study is 34 mg/mL, which is 34% of the solubility (100 mg/mL), the concentration exceeds 15% of the solubility limit; therefore, it does not maintain the sink condition.

The second part of the *in vivo* question can be answered similarly. The solubility of the drug in the plasma is 100 µg/mL and the drug concentration is 6 µg/mL = (6/100) × 100 = 6%. The concentration of the drug in the plasma is below 10%−15% of the solubility limit; therefore, absorption happens under the sink condition.

Case 9.4 (Tablet)

Carbamazepine, a drug used in the treatment of epilepsy and trigeminal neuralgia can exist in many different polymorphic forms. Several clinical failures were reported with generic carbamazepine tablets. More recently, it was confirmed that the initial dissolution rate of carbamazepine was in the order of form III > form I > dihydrate, while the order of AUC values was form I > form III > dihydrate. How can you explain this failure and discrepancy of this dosage form to a rotation student working under your supervision?

Approach: As this drug has poor solubility and exists in many polymorphic forms, this discrepancy may be attributed to the rapid transformation of form III to a dihydrate in the GI fluids. As the dissolution, as well as the AUC of the dihydrate carbamazepine, is very low as compared to other polymorphic forms, one can expect such failure and discrepancies in different polymorphic forms of the drug [7].

Case 9.5 (Capsule)

What is the justification for a two-tier dissolution test for gelatin capsule dosage forms that were introduced in the 25th edition of USP?

Approach: A major issue with gelatin-based formulations is a decrease in dissolution upon aging. This is attributed to the cross-linking of stressed gelatin (exposure of gelatin to formaldehyde). The crosslinking causes the formation of a swollen, thin but tough, water-insoluble membrane called a pellicle. This pellicle acts as a barrier and restricts the release of the drug from the crosslinked capsules. The pellicle does not disappear on gentle agitation, dissolution values drop and often rejected [8,9]. To identify and avoid this, a two-tier test that includes the initial dissolution study in the plain medium (without enzymes) as specified in the individual monograph and a second dissolution is conducted in the medium that contains enzymes for the aged, stored capsules. The reactivity of the gelatin arises from the trifunctional amino acid lysine. The lysine is oxidatively deaminated to yield terminal aldehyde groups. One of these terminal aldehyde groups is attacked by a free -amino group of a neighboring lysine to yield an imine, which subsequently undergoes a series of aldol-type condensation reactions to produce a cross-linked product. Gelatin crosslinking can be inhibited by using Type B gelatin, using inhibitors (semicarbazide hydrochloride, hydroxylamine hydrochloride, piperazide hydrate, pyridine, piperidine, glycerin, and p-aminobenzoic acid), controlling humidity and photo stabilization.

Critical reflection and practice applications

- Oral solid dosage forms are the leading dosage forms in practice in the pharmaceutical market today
- The three most used solid dosage forms are powders, capsules, and tablets
- Approximately one-third of the dosage forms dispensed by community pharmacists are solid dosage forms, usually tablets and capsules

- Oral route of drug administration is still the preferred route in humans because of its many advantages compared to other routes of administration
- Oral solid dosage forms have seen many innovations like programable, time-controlled delivery approaches using instrumentation, computer modeling, and 3D printing technology

References

[1] L.V. Allen, N. Popovich, H.C. Ansel, Ansel's Pharmaceutical Dosage Forms and Drug Delivery Systems, Walters Kluwer/Lippincott Williams and Wilkins, 2011.

[2] J.E. Hoover, Dispensing of medication, in: J.E. Hoover (Ed.), Dispensing of Medication, Mack Publishing Company, 1976.

[3] L. Lachman, H.A. Lieberman, J.L. Kanig, in: The Theory and Practice of Industrial Pharmacy3rd, Lea and Febiger, 1986, pp. 293–429, 1986 Lea and Febiger.

[4] D. Jones, Pharmaceutics Dosage Forms and Design, Pharmaceutical Press, 2008.

[5] A. Goyanes, J. Wang, A. Buanz, et al., 3D printing of Medicines: engineering noveloral devices with unique design and drug release characteristics, Mol. Pharm. 12 (2015a) 4077–4084.

[6] A. Goyanes, H. Chang, D. Sedough, et al., Fabrication of controlled-release budesonide tablets via desktop (FDM) 3D printing, Int. J. Pharm. 496 (2015b) 414–420.

[7] Y. Kobayashi, S. Ito, S. Itai, K. Yamamoto, Physicochemical properties and bioavailability of carbamazepine polymorphs and dihydrate, Int. J. Pharm. 193 (2000) 137–146.

[8] G.A. Digenis, T.B. Gold, V.P. Shah, Cross-linking of gelatin capsules and its relevance to their *in vitro*–*in vivo* performance, J. Pharmaceut. Sci. 83 (7) (1994) 915–921.

[9] J.T. Carstensen, C.T. Rhodes, Pellicule Formation in gelatin capsules, Drug Dev. Ind. Pharm. 19 (20) (1993) 2709–2712.

10

Liquid Dosage Forms

Hari R. Desu[1], Ajit S. Narang[2], Virender Kumar[3],
Laura A. Thoma[1] and Ram I. Mahato[3]

[1]Department of Pharmaceutical Sciences, University of Tennessee Health Science Center, Memphis, TN, United States
[2]Department of Pharmaceutical Sciences, ORIC Pharmaceuticals, Inc., South San Francisco, CA, United States
[3]Department of Pharmaceutical Sciences, University of Nebraska Medical Center, Omaha, NE, United States

CHAPTER OBJECTIVES

- Identify and classify various liquid dosage forms.
- Describe factors that can affect drug solubility in liquids.
- Explain various formulation aspects of liquid dosage forms.
- Recognize various solution dosage forms, additives used, and their formulation aspects.
- Recognize various suspension dosage forms, additives used, and their formulation aspects.
- Recognize various emulsion dosage forms, additives used, and their formulation aspects.
- Appraise the manufacturing, packaging, and storage of liquid dosage forms.
- Recognize the importance of quality assurance and regulatory considerations for liquid dosage forms.

Keywords: Cosolvent; Elixir; Emulsion; Liquid dosage forms; Self-emulsifying drug delivery; Solubilization; Solution; Suspension and syrup.

List of abbreviations

Abbreviations	Full form
BA	bioavailability
BCS	Biopharmaceutics Classification System
BE	bioequivalence
CFCs	chlorofluorocarbons
CGMP	current good manufacturing practices

DMF   drug master file
EDTA   ethylene diamine tetra-acetic acid
FDA   Food and Drug Administration
HLB   hydrophilic—lipophilic balance
ICH   International Conference on Harmonization
NDA   new drug application
NF   national formulary
OTC   over the counter
RES   reticular endothelial system
TPN   total parenteral nutrition
USP   United States Pharmacopeia
WFI   water for injection

10.1 Introduction

A dosage form is a combination of drug substances and excipients to facilitate dosing, administration, and delivery of medicines to patients. The design of a dosage form is determined by the physical, chemical, and pharmacological properties of the drug substance, as well as the administration route. Dosage forms can be classified as solid, semisolid, liquid, and gaseous forms at room temperature. Liquids are pourable dosage forms and can be solutions or dispersions. Pharmaceutical solutions are clear, homogeneous, and single-phase systems containing one or more drug substances dissolved in one or more solvents, while liquid dispersions can be two-phase or multiphase systems composed of one phase dispersed through another phase(s). The dispersed phase can be composed of solid particles (suspensions), oil droplets (emulsions), micelles (surfactant solutions), and lipid vesicles (liposomes). For convenience, dispersions can be classified as molecular (e.g., solutions), colloidal (micelles, nanoemulsions, and nanosuspensions), and coarse dispersions (suspensions), whose particle sizes are in the range of <1 nm, 1—500 nm, and >500 nm, respectively.

Liquid dosage forms can be administered by oral and parenteral (injectable, inhalation, ophthalmic, otic, nasal, and topical) routes. Oral liquids are nonsterile, whereas liquids administered by the parenteral route are available as sterile and nonsterile formulations. The liquid formulations can be supplied as ready-to-use liquids or reconstitutable powders. This chapter details physicochemical factors that determine formulation aspects of liquid formulations, manufacturing processes, quality control assurance, and regulatory guidelines for manufacturing both sterile and nonsterile liquid dosage forms.

10.2 Selection of liquid dosage forms

The solubility in gastrointestinal (GI) fluids, coupled with biologic membrane permeability, plays a critical role in eliciting a biological response when administering a dosage form [1]. Both these parameters formed the basis for the Biopharmaceutics Classification System (BCS) [2,3]. According to BCS, drugs whose highest administered dose strength dissolves in ≤250 mL of water between pH 1 and 7.5 are considered highly soluble drugs; those not meeting this criterion are considered poorly soluble. Permeability is measured using bioavailability with a "high-permeability" drug, defined as ≥90% absorption of the administered dose; those compounds not meeting this specification are considered low-permeability compounds. Fig. 10.1 illustrates four classes of BCS classification [1]. The low-water solubility compounds (class II and IV) and low-permeability compounds (class III and IV) often suffer from limited oral bioavailability. A challenge for pharmaceutical scientists is formulating these drug molecules into oral dosage forms with sufficient bioavailability. A wide variety of solubility-enabling formulation approaches have been developed (e.g., the use of surfactants, buffer compositions, cyclodextrins, and cosolvents). However, an apparent solubility increase often decreases intestinal membrane permeability. This trade-off goes back to the definition of permeability (i.e., intestinal permeability is equal to the diffusion coefficient of a drug through an intestinal membrane times the partition coefficient (membrane/aqueous) of a drug divided by membrane thickness). Accordingly, increasing the apparent solubility of a drug in the aqueous medium via formulation will decrease the drug's membrane/aqueous partition coefficient, leading to decreased apparent intestinal permeability. The opposing effects of apparent solubility and permeability must be considered to fully understand the impact on the overall fraction of drug absorbed when solubility enhancement approaches are employed to increase the oral exposure of poorly soluble drugs. The interplay between increased solubility and decreased permeability is applicable to drugs with low aqueous solubility and high membrane permeability (i.e., BCS class II drugs). Indeed, solubility

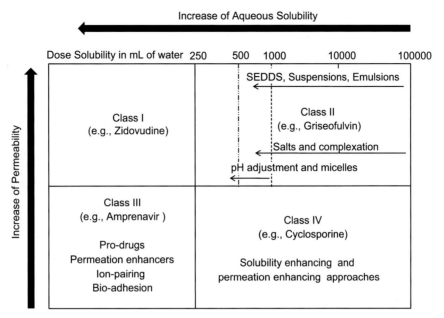

FIGURE 10.1 Possible formulation approaches for BCS-classified drugs. Formulation approaches are applied to overcome solubility and permeability limitations. Based on solubility and permeability parameters, orally administered drugs are classified into four classes (I, II, III, and IV). With a decrease in the solubility of drugs (class II and IV), drug delivery approaches, such as dispersions (suspensions, emulsions, nanoparticles, SEDDS) and chemical modification (salts) are viable, while approaches such as pH adjustments and surfactant micelles are deemed to be suitable for drugs with solubility limits approaching class I levels (i.e., highest dose strength solubilized in ≤250 mL of water). For permeability-limited drugs (class III and IV), inclusion of absorption enhancers and drug efflux transporters increases drug absorption. Drug solubility is expressed as "parts of solvent needed to dissolve one part of solute, i.e., grams of solute in milliliters of water." Some of the examples of formulation approaches for drugs include BCS class II (griseofulvin (suspension), sodium valproate (salt-form); risperidone (pH adjustment)); BCS class III (valacyclovir (prodrug), amprenavir (permeation enhancer)); BCS class IV (Cyclosporin (SEDDS formulations)).

enhancement approaches, such as cosolvents/surfactant micelles, may increase the membrane permeability of drugs with poor intrinsic intestinal membrane permeability (e.g., BCS class III and IV drugs). This may occur through inhibition of efflux transporters or membrane disruption to increase paracellular transport (e.g., tight junction opening) of drugs.

With many drug compounds, the solubility–permeability relationship may be an overwhelming barrier to achieving bioavailable concentrations, otherwise possible with injectable routes. Various solubility enhancement approaches are used for administering drug substances through injectable routes. Particulate approaches, such as emulsions, liposomes, and lipid complexes, can be developed to achieve specific objectives, such as sustained drug release, reduced drug toxicity, minimized drug degradation, or even provision of calories. The injectable route is still the only viable for large molecules, such as proteins and polysaccharides, which are permeability limited.

10.3 Types of liquid dosage forms

10.3.1 Solutions

Solutions are defined as a mixture of two or more components that form a homogeneous molecular dispersion (i.e., a one-phase system). The components of a solution are referred to as the *solute* and the *solvent*. For example, when a solid is dissolved in a liquid, the liquid is usually considered solvent and the solid as a solute, irrespective of their relative proportions. Solutes are classified as nonelectrolytes and electrolytes, with the latter producing ions when dissolved in water. Electrolytic substances are strong or weak electrolytes, depending on whether the substance is completely or partially ionized in water. For example, hydrochloric acid and sodium hydroxide are strong electrolytes, whereas ephedrine and phenobarbital are weak electrolytes. Nonelectrolytes (e.g., docetaxel) are less polar and exhibit poor solubility in water than electrolytes. In addition to the polarity of drug substances, molecular weight and functional groups play an important role in their solubility.

TABLE 10.1 Representative examples of solubility enhancement approaches for solutions administered by oral route [4].

Approach	Examples	Ingredients
Chemical modification	Hydromorphone HCl (Dilaudid®), Atropine sulfate (Atropine care®)	Hydrochloride salt form, Sulfate salt form
pH adjustment	Risperidone (Risperdal®), Hyoscyamine sulfate (Hyoscine)	Tartaric acid, sodium hydroxide
Cosolvents	Digoxin (Lanoxin®) Phenobarbital	20% Ethanol and rest water 40% glycerin, 22% ethanol, and rest water
Cosolvent/surfactant micelle	Cetylpyridinium chloride (Colgate mouthwash) Fluphenazine HCl (Prolixin®)	Propylene glycol, polysorbate 2014% v/v alcohol, polysorbate 40
Complexation	Itraconazole (Sporanox®)	Hydroxypropyl-β-cyclodextrin (HPβCD)TPGS, poly(ethylene glycol) (PEG) 400, PG
SMEDDS	Amprenavir (Agenerase®) Calcitriol Cyclosporin (Sandimmune®) Cyclosporin (Neoral®) Saquinavir	Medium chain triglycerides (MCTs) Alcohol, olive oil, labrafil 1944 CS Cremophor EL, alcohol Medium chain mono- and di-triglycerides dl-tocopherol
Syrups	Amantadine HCl (Symmetrel®) Docusate sodium (Docqlace®)	Sorbitol solution Sucrose solution

10.3.1.1 Approaches to enhance solubility

The aqueous solubility of a drug substance may not always be sufficient for its pharmacological purpose. In such cases, solubility can be altered in a number of ways, including chemical modification, complexation, cosolvency, micelle solubilization, and self-emulsifying drug delivery systems (SEDDS). In the majority of cases, the goal is to enhance solubility, thereby increasing the bioavailability of a drug substance. Table 10.1 lists representative examples of solubility-enhancing approaches to form solutions.

10.3.1.1.1 Chemical modification

The physicochemical properties of a drug substance may be improved by the chemical modification of parent drug moieties. Ester formation, salt form, and drug-adduct formation are some of the common chemical modifications employed to improve stability, solubility, and depot action and to avoid formulation difficulties. *In vivo*, the modified drug (prodrug) transforms back to the active parent drug moiety. Prodrugs can be prepared by chemical reaction of amine/alcohol and carboxylic acid functional moieties [5]. Examples of ester prodrugs include benzathine penicillin, procaine penicillin, triptorelin pamoate, fluphenazine decanoate, and olanzapine pamoate. For instance, the amine functional group of procaine reacts with the carboxylic acid group of penicillin to yield procaine penicillin. In recent years, prodrug derivatization-targeting transporters (e.g., amino acid, peptide, nucleoside and nucleobase, bile acid, and monocarboxylic acid) and receptors have been developed to enhance bioavailability.

A number of drug substances exist in a range of salt forms, each form exhibiting different aqueous solubility [6]. The phenomenon of salting-in may be used to increase the solubility of a drug substance through the formation of ion pairs. The nature of functionality dictates the appropriate choice of counter-ion, so acidic solutes will require the use of a cation, whereas basic solutes will require an anion. The pharmaceutical salt form with adequate solubility and stability that meets dose requirements is incorporated into the dosage form. Some of the representative examples of salt-form approaches include methylprednisolone sodium succinate, dexamethasone phosphate, and chloramphenicol acetate.

10.3.1.1.2 Cosolvents

Cosolvents are liquid components incorporated to enhance the solubility of poorly soluble drugs [7]. Common cosolvents in liquid formulations include glycerol, propylene glycol, ethanol, and polyethylene glycols. Cosolvents are partially polar due to the presence of hydrogen bond donors and/or acceptors, thus ensuring miscibility with water. Cosolvents improve the solubility of nonpolar drugs because small hydrocarbon regions of cosolvents reduce the ability of water to squeeze out nonpolar solutes. High drug solubilities can be achieved by cosolvents or cosolvent mixtures with similar polarity to the drug substance. Yalkowsky has shown that the solubility of a drug substance in a cosolvent mixture (Sm) can be estimated through the log-linear solubility relationship, as shown in Eq. (10.1) [7]:

$$\log \frac{Sm}{Sw} = f\sigma \tag{10.1}$$

where Sw is the solubility of a drug substance in water, f is the volume fraction of cosolvent, and σ is the slope of f versus $\log(Sm/Sw)$ plot, which indicates an enhanced solubility effect of the cosolvent for ionized and unionized forms. The selection of a cosolvent depends on a number of factors, including the solubility and stability of the drug substance in the vehicle and toxicity of the vehicle. Each cosolvent is characterized by an acceptable concentration range, which cannot be exceeded without incurring biological damage [8]. In parenterals, uncontrolled precipitation of the drug substance upon dilution in aqueous/biological media/cosolvents results in embolism or necrosis at the injection site. The toxicity of cosolvents and uncontrolled precipitation of the drug substance upon injection has limited this approach in parenteral formulations. *In vitro* and *in vivo* models are available to evaluate the safety of cosolvent excipients [9].

10.3.1.1.3 Micellar solubilization by surfactants

Surfactants possess both hydrophilic and hydrophobic groups that may associate with aqueous media to form dynamic aggregates, known as micelles [10]. According to the nature of the hydrophilic group, surfactants can be anionic (negative charge), cationic (positive charge), zwitter-ionic (positive and negative charges), or nonionic. Table 10.2 lists typical examples of surfactants in pharmaceutical liquid dosage forms. Due to hydrophilic functional groups, micelles can enhance the solubility of poorly water-soluble drug compounds [13]. As surfactant concentration in aqueous medium increases, surface tension decreases and reaches a constant value. The concentration at which such inflections occur is the critical micelle concentration (CMC), which is attributed to the self-association of surfactant molecules into small aggregates called micelles (Fig. 10.2A). At CMC, there is a change from a solution containing single surfactant molecules or ions (monomers) to one containing monomers and micelles. Above CMC, surfactant molecules orient themselves with polar ends facing the aqueous solution and nonpolar ends facing the interior. A hydrophobic core is formed at the center of the micelle, with hydrophobic solute molecules residing in the core (Fig. 10.2B). Solubilization in surfactant micelle solutions can be regarded as a partition phenomenon. The nonionized form of compounds can partition and reside in the hydrophobic core of micelles. Buffer selection is made to achieve the nonionized form of drug substances, thus enabling partitioning into micelles. Normal micelles can be spherical, cylindrical, or lamellar in shape depending on surfactant concentration. Nonionic surfactants, rather than ionic surfactants, are generally considered to be more suitable for pharmaceutical applications, not

TABLE 10.2 Examples of surfactants used in liquid dosage forms [11,12].

Range of HLB value	Surfactant category	Examples	Applications
1—3	Antifoaming agents	Dimethicone, simethicone ethylene glycol distearate, sorbitan tristearate	Creams, lotions
3—6	W/O emulsifier	Propylene glycol monostearate, glyceryl monostearate, propylene glycol monolaurate, sorbitan stearate (Span 60), diethylene glycol monostearate, sorbitan monooleate (Span 80)	Creams, lotions, W/O emulsions
6—8	Wetting agent	Diethylene glycol monolaurate, sorbitan monopalmitate, sucrose dioleate	Suspensions
8—13	O/W emulsifier	Polyethylene glycol monooleate, sorbitan monolaurate (Span 20), polyoxyethylene sorbitan monostearate, polyoxyethylene sorbitan tristearate	O/W emulsions
13—14	Detergent	Polyethylene glycol (400) monolaurate, polyoxyethylene sorbitan monolaurate, triethanolamine oleate, PEG-8 laurate	Lotions
15—18	Solubilizer	Polyoxyethylene sorbitan monooleate (Tween 80), polyoxyethylene sorbitan monopalmitate (Tween 60), sodium oleate, polyoxyethylene stearate, potassium oleate	Solutions, O/W emulsions, lotions

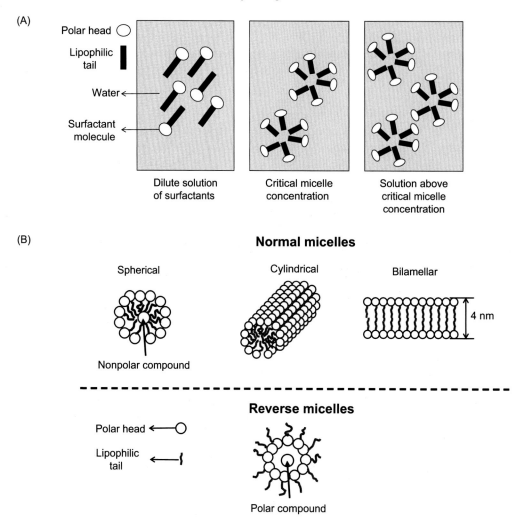

FIGURE 10.2 (A) Formation of normal micelles. The concentration at which amphiphilic surfactants start to self-associate into small aggregates, called micelles, is termed as critical micelle concentration (CMC). In general, surfactant molecules exist as monomers and do not associate themselves below CMC or in very dilute solution. On the other hand, concentrations of surfactants above CMC yield strong (in terms of micelle number) micelle solutions. (B) Types of micelles depending on the assembly of surfactant molecules. In normal micelles, polar head groups face the external aqueous phase, and lipophilic tails face the nonpolar interior. Normal micelles can assemble in spherical, cylindrical, and bilamellar forms depending on water content in the external phase. In reverse micelles, polar head groups face the interior polar phase, and lipophilic tails face the nonpolar solvent phase. Normal micelles are capable of loading nonpolar drug compounds into their lipophilic core, while reverse micelles can incorporate hydrophilic drugs into their aqueous core.

only because of their lower toxicity but also because the surfactant's shell can confer stealth properties to the micelle, avoiding uptake by macrophages of the reticular endothelial system (RES), prolonging their lifetime in blood circulation [14]. Docetaxel and paclitaxel formulations are two examples of surfactant-based formulations.

10.3.1.1.4 Complexation

Complexation refers to the interaction of a poorly soluble compound with an organic molecule (e.g., surface-active agents, hydrophilic polymers) to generate a soluble intermolecular complex [15]. Cyclodextrins are torus-shaped, cyclic oligosaccharides consisting of either six (α-cyclodextrin), seven (β-cyclodextrin), or eight (γ-cyclodextrin) D-glucose units. Due to their hydrophobic interior, various cyclodextrins can include various solutes in their interior cavity. The predominant forces responsible for the formation of host-guest complexes are hydrogen bonding and Van der Waals forces. A derivative of β-cyclodextrin, 2-hydroxypropyl-β-cyclodextrin (HPβCD) has been found to enhance the solubility of the antifungal compound, itraconazole (Sporanox). Another β-cyclodextrin derivative, sulfobutylether-β-cyclodextrin (Captisol), has been used to enhance the solubility of the insoluble drug voriconazole (Vfend). The application of another class of complexing agents, the drug-polymer resin complex, has been identified as extended-release oral suspensions [16]. β-cyclodextrin alone is not always very helpful in increasing the solubility of a drug. In those situations, additional agent (s) along with β-cyclodextrin, such as L-arginine and polyvinyl pyrrolidone-K30 are used.

10.3.1.1.5 Self-emulsifying drug delivery systems

Self-emulsifying drug delivery systems (SEDDS) have attracted attention after the commercial success of HIV protease inhibitors, ritonavir (Norvir) and saquinavir (Fortovase), and cyclosporin (Neoral or Sandimmune) formulations. SEDDS encompass lipidic excipients to improve the solubility and permeability of drug substances. When exposed to GI fluids, these excipients emulsify to form oil-in-water emulsions or microemulsions [17,18]. Based on the droplet size, SEDDS can be termed self-microemulsifying drug delivery systems (SMEDDS) or self-nanoemulsifying drug delivery systems (SNEDDS). SMEDDS are transparent microemulsions with droplet sizes ranging between 100 and 250 nm, while the droplet size of SNEDDS is less than 100 nm [19].

Pouton et al. introduced the lipid formulation classification system (LFCS) on the basis of composition and the possible effect of dilution on drug precipitation [17,20]. Table 10.3 shows four classes of lipid formulations. Type I formulations comprise drugs that exhibit poor aqueous solubility but are soluble in triglycerides and mixed glycerides. These formulations require digestion by pancreatic lipase/colipase in GI fluids to produce oil-in-water dispersion and promote drug absorption [21]. For example, valproic acid is solubilized in corn oil. Type II formulations are isotropic mixtures of lipids [e.g., lipophilic surfactants (hydrophilic—lipophilic balance, HLB<12) or cosurfactants] and drug substances. In GI fluids, these mixtures form oil-in-water emulsions under mild agitation. Self-emulsification is obtained at surfactant concentrations above 25% (w/w). Type III formulations, referred to as SEDDS, comprise oils, hydrophilic surfactants (HLB>12), and cosolvents (e.g., ethanol, propylene glycol, and polyethylene glycol). For example, Neoral consists of corn oil glycerides, cremophor RH40, glycerol, propylene glycol, and ethanol. Type IV formulations are hydrophilic formulations that are devoid of oils. These formulations produce fine dispersions with aqueous media. Amprenavir (Agenarase) is an example of a type IV lipid formulation.

Lipidic excipients include vegetable oils and their derivatives [22,23]. Vegetable oils contain mixtures of triglycerides, fatty acids, phospholipids, and nonsaponifiable matter, such as pigments and sterols. According to carbon chain length, triglycerides are classified as short-chain (<5 carbons), medium (6—12 carbons), and long-chain (>12 carbons) compounds. Some of the vegetable oils include castor oil, coconut oil, corn oil, olive oil, and sesame oil. Vegetable oil derivatives are used as solubilizers or bioavailability enhancers. Some of the classes of vegetable oil derivatives include the following.

a. Hydrogenated vegetable oils are produced by partial or complete hydrogenation of long-chain triglycerides. Examples are hydrogenated castor oil (Lubritab, Akofine, and Cutina HM) and soybean oil (Hydrocote).
b. Partial glycerides are products of glycerolysis and are produced by partial esterification of fatty acids and glycerol, yielding mono- or diglycerides. Examples include glyceryl monocaprylocaprate (Capmul MCM), glyceryl monostearate (Imwitor 191), and glyceryl monooleate (Peceol).

TABLE 10.3 Lipid formulation classification system (LFCS) of lipid-based formulations [20].

Typical composition	Type I	Type II	Type IIIA	Type IIIB	Type IV
Triglycerides/mixed triglycerides	100	40—80	40—80	0	—
Surfactants (%w/w)	—	0—20 (HLB<12)	20—40 (HLB>12)	20—50 (HLB>12)	0—20 (HLB<12) or 30—80 (HLB>12)
Cosolvents (%w/w)	—	—	0—40	20—50	40—60
Particle size (μm)	>250	100—250	100—250	50—100	<50
Significance of dilution	Limited importance	Solvent capacity unaffected	Some loss of solvent capacity	Significant phase changes	High risk of precipitation
Significance of digestion	Crucial requirement	Not crucial but likely to occur	Not crucial but may be inhibited	Not required	Not required

c. Polyoxylglycerides (macrogolglycerides) are produced by polyglycolysis of vegetable oils with polyethylene glycols. These are derivatives of unsaturated fatty acids (Labrafil M1944CS and Labrafil M2125CS), saturated medium-chain fatty acid esters (Labrosol), Gelucire 44/14), or long-chain fatty acids (Gelucire 50/13).

d. Ethoxylated glycerides are castor oil derivatives. Classic examples include ethoxylated castor oil (Cremophor EL) and ethoxylated hydrogenated castor oil (Cremophor RH40 and Cremophor RH60).

e. Esters of fatty acids and alcohols are the most prominent family of vegetable oil derivatives. Some of the examples include

- Polyglycerol derivatives—for example, polyglycerol oleate (Plurol)
- Propylene glycol derivatives—for example, propylene glycol monocaprylate (Capryol 90)
- Polyoxyethylene glycol derivatives—for example, PEG-8 stearate (Mrij 45), PEG-40 stearate (Mrij 52), PEG-12 hydroxystearate (Solutol HS 15)
- Sorbitol derivatives—for example, sorbitan monooleate (Span 80), polyoxyethylene-20 sorbitan monooleate (Tween 80)

As discussed earlier, type III formulations contain cosolvents. Common cosolvents used in SEDDS include ethanol, propylene glycol, polyethylene glycol, glycerol, and sorbitol. In addition, SEDDS include preservatives and stabilizers to prolong the shelf-life of formulations. SEDDS are formulated in hard gelatin or soft gelatin capsules. Design and optimization of SEDDS formulations involve solubility and stability screening using phase diagrams. These diagrams are necessary to determine the concentration of excipients required for drug loading.

Advantages of SEDDS include.

- The improved oral bioavailability of drug substances belonging to BCS class II and IV drug substances
- The increased drug-loading capacity of formulations to deliver appropriate drug dose
- Reduced intersubject and intrasubject variability and negated food effects on drug absorption
- Inhibition of enzymatic hydrolysis of drug substances

10.3.1.2 Formulation considerations

Solutions can be classified by route of administration as inhalation, injectable, oral, ophthalmic, otic, mouthwashes and gargles, nasal, topical, enemas, and douches. Based on composition, solutions can be aqueous or nonaqueous. Aqueous solutions include simple solutions, syrups, dilute acids, aromatic waters, and dry powder mixtures for reconstitution. Nonaqueous solutions may include hydro-alcoholic solutions, such as mouthwashes, gargles, elixirs, and oily preparations (e.g., oil-soluble vitamins).

10.3.1.2.1 Oral solutions

Oral solutions are liquid preparations intended for oral administration. Oral solutions contain one or more active substances and inactive excipients, such as solubilizers, stabilizers, buffers, preservatives, flavoring agents, coloring agents, and sweetening agents. Table 10.4 lists inactive ingredients and their concentration range in solutions. Purified water (USP) is a common vehicle used in the preparation of aqueous dosage forms. Solution formulations require solubilizing excipients when the active ingredient dose is large relative to its aqueous solubility. For water-insoluble drugs, solubilizing vehicles include water-miscible cosolvents, such as ethanol, glycerin, polyethylene glycol 300 or 400, and propylene glycol [25]. The maximum amount of solvent used can be up to 55% propylene glycol, 17% polyethylene glycol 400, and 42% ethanol. Among the alcohols, ethanol (USP, 94.9—96.0 %v/v), dehydrated ethanol (USP), or dilute ethanol (50:50 ethanol:water) are used. With water, ethanol forms a hydro-alcoholic mixture that dissolves alcohol and water-soluble substances.

Water-miscible surfactants are also common in the solubilization of poorly water-soluble substances. Surfactants can be used either alone or mixed with cosolvents in an aqueous solution. Nonionic surfactants are common in oral formulations. Some of the typical examples of nonionic surfactants include polyoxyl 35 castor oil (Cremophor EL), polyoxyl 40 hydrogenated castor oil (Cremophor RH40), polysorbate 20 (Tween 20), polysorbate 80 (Tween 80), tocopheryl polyethylene glycol succinate (TPGS), solutol HS 15, and sorbitan monooleate (Span 80).

The solubility of a vast number of drugs is pH-dependent and may be compromised by small changes in the pH of the solution. The pH plays a critical role in the stability (e.g., hydrolysis and oxidation) of drug substances. Buffer solutions are employed to control the pH of the solutions. The pH range for oral solutions is usually in the range of 2—10 to maximize the chemical stability of drug substances. Examples of buffer salts in pharmaceutical solutions include acetates, citrates, and phosphates.

Preservatives in solutions control the microbial bioburden of formulations. Ideally, preservatives should exhibit properties such as (1) a broad spectrum of antimicrobial activity against gram-positive and gram-negative bacteria,

TABLE 10.4 Excipients in solution and suspension formulations [24].

		Concentration (% v/v)	
Inactive ingredients	Example	Solutions	Suspensions
Solubilizers	Alcohol	0.05–35	0.1–52
	Propylene glycol	0.125–55	1–28.5
	PEG 400	1–60	1–5
	Glycerin	1–75	0.01–40
	Sorbitol	1–90	0.1–72
	Docusate sodium	na	0.01–0.1
	Polyoxyl 35 castor oil (Cremophor EL)	1–51.5	0.01–0.05
	Polyoxyl 40 castor oil (Cremophor RH 40)	1–45	na
	Polysorbate 20 (Tween 20)	na	0.01–0.5
	Polysorbate 40 (Tween 40)	0.001	0.1–0.5
Surfactants	Polysorbate 60 (Tween 60)	na	0.1–3
	Polysorbate 80 (Tween 80)	0.01–12.6	0.01–5
	D-α-tocopheryl polyethylene glycol 1000 succinate (TPGS)	1–20	na
	Sorbitan monooleate (Span 20)	1–15	0.01–0.05
	Sorbitan monostearate (Span 60)	na	0.1–2
	Tyloxapol	na	0.01–0.3
Buffers	Acetates, borates, citrates, phosphates		
	Benzalkonium chloride	0.01–2	0.01–0.02
	Benzyl alcohol	0.1–5	0.1–5
	Methyl parabens	0.1–1.5	0.1–20
Preservatives	Propyl parabens	0.02–36	0.01–0.1
	Butyl parabens	na	0.01–0.2
	Thimerosal	na	0.001–1
	Ascorbic acid	0.01–0.6	0.1–0.5
	Butylated hydroxy toluene (BHT)	0.001–0.02	na
Antioxidants	Butylated hydroxy anisole (BHA)	0.01–2.0	0.01–0.1
	Sodium bisulfite	0.01–0.1	0.001–0.05
	Sodium metabisulfite	0.1–0.2	0.01–0.30
Chelating agents	EDTA disodium	0.01–0.5	0.01–0.1
	Microcrystalline cellulose	0.1–2.0	0.1–3.0
	Carboxymethylcellulose (CMC)	0.1–3.5	0.1–40
	Hydroxyethyl cellulose (HEC)	0.1–3.5	0.1–3
	Hydroxypropyl methylcellulose (HPMC)	0.1–2	0.1–2.5

Continued

TABLE 10.4   Excipients in solution and suspension formulations [24].—cont'd

Inactive ingredients	Example	Concentration (% v/v)	
		Solutions	Suspensions
Viscosity modifiers	Carbomers	0.1–0.25	0.1–1.5
	Tragacanth	na	0.1–6.0
	Xanthan gum	0.1–4.0	0.01–19.0
	Gellan gum	0.1–0.6	na
	Guar gum	na	0.01–0.2
	Sucrose	85	1–55.5
Sweeteners	Sucralose	0.1–0.8	0.1–1
	Saccharin sodium	0.05–2	0.1–0.6
Coloring agents	FD&C colors	0.0001–2.5	0.0001–2.0

na—not available.

as well as fungi; (2) stability over the shelf-life of drug products; and (3) low toxicity. Various preservatives in oral solutions include benzoic acid and its salts, sorbic acid its and salts, and alkyl esters of parahydroxybenzoic acid (parabens). Drug substances undergo oxidation when exposed to atmospheric air. Oxidation of a drug substance in a pharmaceutical preparation can be accompanied by a change in color, odor, or precipitation of the drug substance. The oxidative process can be prevented by including antioxidants in the formulation. In an aqueous solution, antioxidants are oxidized in preference to the therapeutic agents, thereby protecting the drug substance from decomposition. Water-soluble antioxidants include sodium sulfite (Na_2SO_3, at high pH values), sodium bisulfite ($NaHSO_3$, at intermediate pH values), sodium metabisulfite ($Na_2S_2O_5$ at low pH values), and ascorbic acid; oil-miscible antioxidants include butylated hydroxytoluene (BHT), butylated hydroxyanisole (BHA), and propyl gallate. Certain pharmaceuticals require an oxygen-free atmosphere during preparation and storage. In such cases, inert gases, such as nitrogen and argon, can replace atmospheric air.

The viscosity of formulations can be controlled to ensure accurate measurement of the volume to be dispensed and to increase palatability. The viscosity of solutions may be increased by the addition of hydrophilic polymers (e.g., cellulose derivatives) and natural gums (e.g., sodium alginate, xanthan gum, and guar gum). Sweeteners, flavoring agents, and coloring agents are added to enhance the palatability and appearance of solutions. Common sweetening agents are sucrose, liquid glucose, glycerol, sorbitol, saccharin sodium, and aspartame. Artificial sweeteners replace sugars in formulations to meet the prescription requirements for children and diabetes patients. Coloring agents are added to impart the preferred color to the formulation. When used in combination with flavors, the selected color should "match" the flavor of the formulation (e.g., green for mint-flavored solutions, and red for strawberry-flavored formulations). Flavoring agents often are included in liquid formulations to mask the unpleasant taste of drug substances. In aqueous formulations, alcohol (USP) may be used in small portions to solubilize oil-based flavoring agents (e.g., orange oil). Flavor adjuncts (e.g., menthol) are also added to desensitize taste receptors. The flavor adjuncts may augment the taste-masking properties of conventional flavors.

Oral formulations are either formulated in a conveniently administered volume, 5 mL or a multiple or filled into gelatin capsules in size range of 0.19–0.5 mL. An adult full dose is contained within a reasonable upper volume, 30 mL, and the pediatric dose is contained within a measurable lower volume, 0.25–1.0 mL.

10.3.1.2.2 Syrups

Syrups are concentrated, aqueous preparations of sugar or sugar substitutes intended for the oral administration of bitter-tasting drug substances. Syrups containing flavoring agents without drug substances are called nonmedicated or flavored vehicles (syrups). These syrups serve as pleasant-tasting vehicles for drug substances to be added later, either in the extemporaneous compounding of prescriptions or in the preparation of medicated syrups. A typical nonmedicated syrup formulation contains (1) sugar (sucrose) or sugar substitute to provide sweetness and viscosity, (2) an antimicrobial preservative (e.g., benzoates and parabens), (3) a buffering agent (e.g., citrates), (4) a flavoring agent, and (5) a coloring agent (e.g., FD&C colors) [11]. In addition, syrups may contain solubilizing agents, thickeners, or stabilizers to improve the stability of formulations. Medicated syrups contain drug substances and inactive ingredients. Examples of nonmedicated syrups include cherry, corn, and orange syrups, and medicated syrups include chlorpromazine hydrochloride, perphenazine, piperazine citrate, promazine hydrochloride, sodium valproate, ritonavir, and guaifenesin.

Syrup vehicles with appropriate viscosity and sweetness mask the taste of drug substances. Both these properties conceal the taste of bitter compounds, which otherwise is not possible with dilute aqueous preparations. Most syrup solutions contain sucrose, but it may be replaced in whole or part by sugars, such as dextrose, or nonsugars, such as sorbitol. In contrast to the unstable nature of dilute sucrose solutions, syrup vehicles containing a high proportion (60%–80%) of sugar impart desirable viscosity and stability [24,26]. The aqueous sugar medium of dilute sucrose solutions serves as a source for the growth of microorganisms, particularly yeasts and molds. Concentrated sugar solutions (e.g., syrup NF) are hyperosmolar and resistant to the growth of microorganisms. Under cold storage conditions, some sucrose may crystallize from the solution, resulting in an unsaturated solution suitable for microbial growth. Many of the commercial syrups are not as saturated as syrup NF, and therefore, include preservatives to prevent microbial growth during shelf-life. In these syrup formulations, the amount of preservative required to protect syrup against microbial growth varies with the proportion of water available for growth and inherent preservative efficacy. In some instances, sugars are replaced by artificial sweeteners and viscosity modifiers, such as cellulose derivatives, which provide a syrup-like vehicle for medications intended for diabetic patients.

The majority of syrup preparations are manufactured on a big scale by boiling the ingredients to dissolve them. This method creates a syrup solution by heating purified water with sugar added. Other heat-stable components are added to the hot syrup, and the mixture is allowed to cool. The final volume is adjusted by the addition of purified water. In some instances, heat-sensitive ingredients or volatile substances are added after the solution is cooled to room temperature. Uncontrolled heating hydrolyzes sucrose into dextrose and fructose. This hydrolytic reaction is referred to as inversion, which results in a bitter taste and darkening of the vehicle. The syrup may be prepared without heat by agitation to avoid heat-induced inversion of sucrose. Solid ingredients, except sucrose, are dissolved in a small portion of purified water by agitation, and the resulting solution is incorporated into the syrup. Preparation of syrup solutions by agitation is time-consuming but yields a stable syrup formulation.

Another method is the addition of sucrose to vehicles containing fluid extracts or tinctures. However, the direct addition of the aqueous phase (containing sucrose) to alcohol-containing fluid extracts or tinctures precipitates resinous material dissolved in alcohol. An alternative approach is to allow the mixture (fluid extract or tincture and water) to stand for a few hours. The mixture is then filtered to remove suspended resinous material and produce a clear solution. Sucrose is then added to the medicated vehicle to produce medicated syrup. This method is not preferable if the precipitated materials are expensive. Aromatic eriodictyon syrup (USP) is prepared using this method. The percolation method is used to prepare ipecac syrup and syrup (USP) commercially. In this method, purified water or the aqueous phase percolates through a crystalline sucrose bed. A flow-meter (stopcock) can regulate the aqueous phase flow, thereby regulating the aqueous phase flow and improving contact of the aqueous phase with the sugar bed. Precautions include the use of a cylindrical or conical percolator to hold and direct the flow of the aqueous phase; the use of coarse sugar to provide adequate porosity for the aqueous phase flow; and careful insertion of a cotton plug into the neck of the percolator to avoid hindering (a tight plug) the flow or allowing turbid solution (a loose plug) to pass through. If the percolation process is adopted for preparing medicated syrups, plant parts, such as leaves or bark, are percolated with water; then, the percolate is collected into a vessel containing sucrose. The vessel is agitated to dissolve the sucrose and other ingredients and facilitate the mixing operation to prepare the final syrup formulation.

Dry syrups are prepared to improve the stability of ingredients and minimize contamination. Dry syrups can be prepared as powders, whole granules, or partial granules. For dry powders, process and instrumentation requirements are minimal. However, powders exhibit segregation of ingredients, resulting in nonuniform syrup. Whole granules contain all the ingredients, and the granules are sieved or screened to obtain particular particle-size distributions. Whole granules offer advantages, such as better flow and minimal segregation properties. Partial granules are prepared to take advantage of granules and powders. In partial granules, stable ingredients are prepared as granules, while thermolabile ingredients (e.g., flavors) are added to dried granules. Before they are dispensed to patients, dry syrup powders or granules are mixed with purified water and shaken well to prepare the liquid syrup.

10.3.1.2.3 Mouthwashes and gargles

Mouthwashes are concentrated hydroalcoholic solutions containing one or more active ingredients and excipients. Mouthwashes can be used for therapeutic, diagnostic, and cosmetic purposes. Examples of therapeutic mouthwashes include allopurinol for treating stomatitis [27], pilocarpine for xerostomia (dry mouth) [28], and nystatin for oral candidiasis [29]. Toluidine blue mouth rinse is used for the detection of oral cancer and lesions [30]. Cosmetic mouthwashes (e.g., phenol and mint mouthwashes) may be used for refreshing purposes. Other topical mouthwashes include antiplaque (e.g., cetylpyridinium chloride) and fluorinated mouthwashes (Oral-B rinse, Colgate Phos-Flur, and Fluoride dental rinse). In general, mouthwashes contain alcohol as a flavor, enhancing taste and mask active ingredients' unpleasant taste. Alcohol may serve as a solubilizer for active and inactive ingredients. Common active ingredients in mouthwashes include thymol, eucalyptol, hexetidine, methyl salicylate, menthol, and chlorhexidine gluconate. Preservatives in mouthwashes and gargles include benzalkonium chloride, parabens, benzoates, and sorbates. Various surfactants are included as solubilizers for active and inactive ingredients. Humectants (e.g., glycerin and sorbitol) are used to improve the viscosity of mouthwash solutions. Other inactive ingredients include antioxidants, chelating, flavoring, and coloring agents.

Gargles are aqueous solutions containing antiseptics, antibiotics, or anesthetics intended to relieve or treat sore throats. Gargles contain high concentrations of active ingredients and are diluted with warm water before use. Medicated gargles may be taken inside the mouth, swished around as long as possible, and then gargled and swallowed. Betadine (7.5% (w/v) povidone-iodine) and chlorhexidine gluconate are examples of gargles. Betadine aids in the treatment of sore throats caused by bacteria and viruses, and chlorhexidine gluconate reduces swelling, redness, and bleeding of the gums.

10.3.1.2.4 Elixirs

Elixirs are clear, sweetened, hydroalcoholic (5%—40% (v/v)) solutions for oral use. Nonmedicated elixirs are employed as vehicles for medicated elixirs. Advantages of elixirs are (1) insoluble drug compounds can be incorporated into the hydroalcoholic vehicle; (2) drug concentrates can be prepared in high-alcohol-containing elixirs; (3) hydroalcoholic vehicles can be self-preserving, and (4) elixirs are less viscous and contain a lower proportion of sugar. Some of the disadvantages of elixirs are (1) they cannot be administered to pediatric patients and patients on antidepressant medication; (2) the concentration of active and inactive ingredients may vary if not preserved in cool places, and (3) water-insoluble drug compounds may precipitate due to alcohol evaporation.

Hydroalcoholic vehicles enhance the solubility of both water-soluble and -insoluble ingredients. The proportion of alcohol in elixirs can be varied with the solubility requirements of active ingredients. In addition to alcohol and water, glycerin and propylene glycol can be used as adjunct solvents. Elixirs are sweetened with sweeteners, such as sucrose, sucrose syrup, sorbitol, glycerin, and saccharin. Elixirs with a high alcohol content use artificial sweeteners, such as saccharin. All elixirs contain flavoring agents to increase their palatability and coloring agents to enhance their appearance. Elixirs are stored in cool, tight, and light-resistant containers due to the presence of alcohol and volatile oils in their formulations. Nonmedicated elixirs are useful as vehicles for extemporaneous filling of prescriptions and dilution of existing medicated elixirs. Common nonmedicated elixirs include aromatic and compound benzaldehyde; examples of medicated elixirs are dexamethasone, fluphenazine HCl, and hyoscyamine sulfate.

Elixirs are prepared by simple solution with agitation or by admixture of two or more liquid ingredients. Alcohol-soluble and water-soluble components are dissolved in alcohol and purified water, respectively. In general, the aqueous solution is added to the alcoholic solution to avoid changes in alcohol strength and separation of alcohol-soluble ingredients. The final volume is made with a specified solvent vehicle. Elixirs are then allowed to stand for saturation of the hydroalcoholic mixture and to permit excess flavoring agent oil globules to coalesce. These coalesced oil globules are removed by filtration using talc as a filter aid. Talc absorbs excess oils. During filtration, presoaked filters (in solvent vehicles) are used to prevent the loss of elixir ingredients.

10.3.1.2.5 Injectable solutions

The United States Pharmacopeia (USP) and The National Formulary (NF) published public standards for formulating sterile preparations. The procedures outlined in USP chapter <797> are intended to prevent patient harm from ingredient errors and microbial contamination. The advantages of injectable sterile products include rapid onset of action, complete bioavailability, the negation of variable drug absorption, and ease of administration for ill patients. Large-volume parenterals include intravenous admixtures, intravenous fluids, electrolyte solutions, irrigation solutions, and dialysis solutions. Some examples of small-volume parenterals include injectable antibiotics and antineoplastic agents, available as solutions or reconstitutable powders. An increasing number of biotechnology drugs and critical nutritional mixtures are available for administration through various parenteral routes.

10.3.1.2.6 Ophthalmic solutions

Ophthalmic liquid products are sterile preparations for application to the conjunctiva, conjunctival sac, or eyelids. Common categories of ophthalmic liquids are eye drops and irrigation solutions. Ophthalmic drops can be formulated as aqueous solutions, suspensions, emulsions, or reconstitutable powders. Irrigating solutions (e.g., intraocular and periocular solutions) maintain hydration and clarity of the cornea, providing a clear view of the surgical area.

A majority of instilled eye drops drain into the nasolacrimal duct due to the tendency of the eye to maintain precorneal fluid volume at 7–10 µL [31]. Various factors influencing drainage include instilled volume, viscosity, pH, and tonicity. Pharmaceutical excipients are added to ophthalmic solutions to maintain the stability and sterility of the formulation, as well as prolong solution precorneal residence time. A typical ophthalmic solution is composed of the ingredients described elsewhere [31].

10.3.1.2.6.1 Vehicles Water for injection (WFI) is the most widely used solvent for ophthalmic and parenteral preparations. WFI is obtained by distillation of deionized water or a reverse osmosis procedure. Inorganic metal traces are removed by distillation, reverse osmosis, deionization, or a combination of these processes. Membrane filters are used to remove particulate contaminants, and charcoal beds may be used to remove organic materials. Filtration and autoclaving procedures reduce microbial growth and prevent pyrogen formation. The USP also lists sterile WFI and bacteriostatic WFI for use in sterile preparations. Sterile water for injection (USP) is sterilized and packaged in single-dose containers not exceeding 1000 mL. Bacteriostatic WFI (USP) must not be placed in containers larger than 30 mL to prevent the administration of large quantities of bacteriostatic agents (phenol) that could become toxic. Aqueous isotonic vehicles are often used in sterile preparations. A common vehicle is sodium chloride solution, 0.9% (w/v) solution (also known as normal saline), which is sterilized and packaged in single-dose containers no larger than 1000 mL. Sodium chloride irrigation also is a 0.9% (w/v) solution; however, it has no preservatives. Other vehicles include boric acid solution (pH 5.0), which serves as a vehicle for active ingredients, such as cocaine, neostigmine, procaine, tetracaine, atropine, homatropine, and pilocarpine. The boric acid vehicle contains benzalkonium chloride as the preservative.

10.3.1.2.6.2 Buffering agents The physiological pH range of tears is 7.0–7.7 and is governed by substances present in the tear fluids, including salts and proteins. Due to the low buffer capacity of tear fluids, acidic or basic pH solutions cause excessive secretion of tears and may cause damage to corneal epithelial cells. Hence, pH adjustments are made close to the pH of tears. Furthermore, pH adjustments are made to maintain drug compounds in unionized form, which enables rapid penetration across the corneal epithelial barrier. The pH values of ophthalmic solutions are adjusted to a range in which an acceptable shelf-life of at least 2 years can be achieved. If buffers are required, their capacity is controlled to be as low as possible, enabling tears to bring the pH of the eye to the physiological range. Common buffering agents in ophthalmic preparations are acetates, borates, citrates, and phosphates. The pH adjustments of ophthalmic solutions are usually made with hydrochloric acid, sulfuric acid, or sodium hydroxide.

10.3.1.2.6.3 Preservatives Antimicrobial preservatives are added in multidose ophthalmic solutions to inhibit the growth of microorganisms, but this is not intended to prepare a sterile solution. US Food and Drug Administration (FDA) regulations also allow unpreserved ophthalmic solutions to be packaged in multidose containers only if they are packaged and labeled in a manner that affords adequate protection and minimizes microbial contamination. This can be accomplished by using a reclosable container with a minimum number of doses that is to be discarded 12 h after initial opening. Unit-dose ophthalmic preparations do not contain preservatives.

Common preservatives in ophthalmic preparations include quaternary ammonium compounds (benzalkonium chloride), substituted alcohols and phenols (chlorobutanol), organic mercurials (phenyl mercuric acetate; thimerosal), esters of para hydroxybenzoic acid (methyl and propyl parabens), poly quad, chlorhexidine, and polyaminopropyl biguanide. Benzalkonium chloride is a typical preservative in more than 65% of ophthalmic products and is usually combined with disodium ethylene diamine tetra-acetic acid (EDTA). Benzalkonium chloride is cationic and is therefore incompatible with anionic drug compounds or inactive excipients. Despite its compatibility limitations, it has shown to be a most effective and rapid-acting preservative. Benzalkonium chloride is stable over a wide pH range and does not degrade even under high-temperature storage conditions. Chlorobutanol, aromatic alcohol, is considered to be a safe preservative but has slow antimicrobial action and packaging and formulation limitations. Chlorobutanol indicates the use of glass containers since it permeates polyolefin plastic ophthalmic containers. Methyl and propyl parabens have been used primarily to prevent mold growth. Paraben use is limited by its low aqueous solubility, ability to cause ocular irritation, and nonspecific binding to surfactants and polymer components.

10.3.1.2.6.4 Tonicity agents

The osmolarity of lacrimal fluid is between 280 and 320 mOsm/kg, which is dependent on the number of ions dissolved in the aqueous layer of the tear film. Ophthalmic solutions need to be isotonic with tear secretions. A hypotonic solution results in excessive secretion of tears and causes irritation of the corneal epithelium. An osmotic pressure corresponding to the normal saline solution is considered to be isotonic. Tonicity-adjusting agents employed in ophthalmic solutions include sodium chloride, dextrose, mannitol, and buffering salts.

10.3.1.2.6.5 Viscosity modifiers

Ophthalmic solutions may contain viscosity-imparting polymers to prolong the retention time of drug solution in the precorneal area and decrease the lachrymal drainage of drug substances. Polymers, such as methylcellulose, hydroxymethyl cellulose, hydroxypropyl methylcellulose, polyvinyl alcohol, and carbomers are used in the concentration range of 0.2%−2.5% to produce viscosities in the range of 5−30,000 cP. These polymers are also used as viscoelastic agents in artificial tear solutions for their lubrication and moistening properties in dry-eye therapy. The major commercial viscous vehicles are hydroxypropyl methylcellulose (Isopto) and polyvinyl alcohol (Liquifilm).

10.3.1.2.6.6 Surfactants

Surfactants are used to solubilize or disperse drugs in solutions and dispersions. However, the use of surfactants is limited due to irritation and toxicity issues. Several nonionic surfactants are used in small concentrations to reduce irritation to eye tissues. Surfactants are also used to prevent drug loss to adsorption on the container walls. For example, polyoxyl hydrogenated castor oil (HCO-40) has been used to stabilize Travoprost, indicated for the reduction of elevated intraocular pressure in patients with glaucoma or ocular hypertension.

10.3.1.2.6.7 Stabilizers

Trace metal sources in drug materials, excipients, solvents, containers, or closures are a constant source of oxidation. The trace metals can be eliminated in free-form from labile preparations through chelation (complexation). Chelating agents are added to complex and inactivate metals, such as copper, iron, and zinc, that catalyze the oxidation of drug substances. In some instances, chelating agents (e.g., metal complexing agents) and antioxidants are added together to stabilize ophthalmic solutions. Common chelating agents include edetate disodium, citric acid, and tartaric acid. Sulfur salts, such as bisulfate, metabisulfite, and sulfite, are the most common antioxidants in ophthalmic solutions. These antioxidants stabilize the products by acting as oxidizable substrates for free radicals and reactive oxygen species.

10.3.1.2.7 Otic solutions

Otic solutions, also called ear or aural solutions, are administered in small volumes to treat ear ailments. Most otic solutions are nonsterile, while a few are sterile preparations (e.g., Floxacin, Cortisporin). The middle ear and tympanic membrane are commonly infected with pathogens such as *Streptococcus pneumonia*, *Hemophilus influenza*, *Moraxella catarrhalis*, and less commonly with *Streptococcus pyrogens*, *Pseudomonas aeruginosa*, and *Staphylococcus aureus*, causing otitis media (inflammation of the middle ear) and otic discharge. These ear infections can be treated by topical antibiotics, such as chloramphenicol, colistin sulfate, neomycin, polymyxin B sulfate, ofloxacin, gentamicin, and antifungal agents, such as nystatin.

Otic solutions contain vehicles, such as glycerol, propylene glycol, and polyethylene glycol 300 or 400. Propylene glycol in otic solutions also lowers surface tension and improves drug substance contact time with infected tissues. Some anti-infective otic solutions (e.g., acetic acid otic solution, USP) contain surfactants, such as benzethonium chloride, to promote contact with the solution with tissues. Dehumidifying agents, such as isopropyl alcohol, lower the moisture content needed for bacteria to survive, thus limiting the spread of infection. Solutions containing analgesics (e.g., antipyrine) and local anesthetics (e.g., benzocaine) are formulated in vehicles containing anhydrous glycerin or propylene glycol. Antipyrine and benzocaine solution combines the hygroscopic property of anhydrous glycerin and the analgesic action of antipyrine and benzocaine to relieve pressure, reduce inflammation and congestion, and alleviate pain and discomfort in acute otitis media. Multiuse otic solutions contain preservatives, such as benzyl alcohol and benzalkonium chloride. The pH of otic solutions was kept between 2.0 and 7.5 and adjusted using buffers, hydrochloric acid, or sodium hydroxide.

Over-the-counter otic solutions, such as cerumen cleansing solutions (e.g., carbamide peroxide, Debrox), cleanse accumulated cerumen. Otic solutions containing surfactants, such as triethanolamine oleate, emulsify cerumen and aid in its removal. Light mineral oils, vegetable oils, and hydrogen peroxide have been used for cerumen removal.

These cerumen-cleansing solutions are placed in the patient's ear canal and retained for a while; then, they are flushed with a fine stream of warm water using applicators.

Commercial otic solutions available for relieving otic pain and infections include acetic acid; antipyrine, and benzocaine; benzocaine (Americaine); ciprofloxacin and dexamethasone (Ciprodex); gentamicin sulfate, and betamethasone valerate; hydrocortisone and acetic acid; and neomycin, polymyxin B sulfate, and hydrocortisone.

10.3.1.2.8 Nasal solutions

Most nasal solutions are administered as nasal drops or sprays for local and systemic purposes. Rapid absorption and onset of action are major advantages of nasal administration. The nasal route may also be useful for administering biologics (e.g., proteins and peptides) to avoid first-pass metabolism and GI degradation, thus contributing to a rapid increase in therapeutic concentrations [32]. For example, 1-deamino-8-D-arginine-vasopressin (DDVP; Desmospray) is used to treat pituitary diabetes insipidus. Nasal solutions are formulated to be isotonic to nasal secretions (equivalent to 0.9% (w/v) sodium chloride) and are buffered to the normal pH range of nasal fluids (pH 5.5–6.5) to prevent damage to ciliary transport in the nose [33]. The normal dose volume of nasal formulations is in the range of 25–200 μL.

Nasal solutions are usually formulated in water and cosolvents, such as ethanol, propylene glycol, and polyethylene glycol 400. Nasal solutions may contain excipients, such as preservatives (e.g., benzalkonium chloride, benzyl alcohol, parabens, phenylethylalcohol, and potassium sorbate), buffering agents (e.g., citrate and phosphate), antioxidants (e.g., sodium metabisulfite, sodium bisulfite, butylated hydroxytoluene, tocopherol, and disodium EDTA), isotonic adjusting agents (e.g., sodium chloride), viscosity enhancers (e.g., cellulose derivatives), absorption enhancers, flavoring agents (e.g., menthol, eucalyptol, camphor, and methylsalicyate), and sweetening agents (e.g., saccharin). Since nasal formulations are administered in small volumes, nasal secretions may alter the pH of the administrated dose. This can affect the concentration of the unionized drug available for absorption. Therefore, buffers with high buffer capacity (phosphates or citrates) are employed to maintain pH *in situ*. Nasal formulations without buffering agents are pH adjusted with hydrochloric acid or sodium hydroxide. The FDA requires that all nasal drug products be manufactured as sterile (e.g., unit-dose) or preserved (multidose) products [34]. Depending on the drug and formulation characteristics, sterility may be accomplished via aseptic filling processes, terminal sterilization, or both.

Numerous delivery devices are available for intranasal administration. Currently, nonpressurized metered-dose pumps provide dose accuracy and reproducibility. Delivery devices are important for delivering medication and protection from microbial contamination and chemical degradation. For most pumps, dispensed volume per actuation is set between 50 and 140 μL. Standard spray pumps will deposit most of the sprayed dose into the anterior region of the nasal cavity. The surface tension of the droplets and mucus layer will cause an immediate spread of the spray. Afterward, mucociliary clearance will distribute the liquid layer within the nasal cavity.

Commercial nasal sprays include butorphanol tartrate (Stadol) for relieving migraine pain; calcitonin salmon (Miacalcin) for treating osteoporosis; cromolyn sodium (NasalCrom) for relieving nasal allergy and eustachian tube congestion; tetrahydrozoline hydrochloride (Tyzine) for relieving nasal congestion; and xylometazoline hydrochloride (Sinosil) for relieving nasal congestion and respiratory allergies.

10.3.1.2.9 Enemas

Enemas are oily or aqueous solutions that are administered rectally. Examples include arachis oil and magnesium sulfate. Retention enemas are administered for local action (e.g., prednisolone), systemic absorption (e.g., diazepam), or topical irrigation purpose (e.g., sodium phosphate, sodium citrate, or docusate sodium). Enemas are packaged in plastic containers with a nozzle for insertion into the rectum. Large-volume enemas should be warmed to body temperature before administration. Extemporaneous enemas are packaged in amber, fluted-glass bottles, whereas manufactured enemas are packaged in disposable polyethylene or polyvinyl chloride bags. Patients are advised on how to use the enema if it is intended for self-administration. Enemas available for relieving constipation are saline laxative (Equaline), mineral oil (GENT-L-TIP), and bisacodyl (FLEET). Mesalamine enema is available for treating ulcerative colitis and proctitis.

10.3.1.2.10 Dry mixtures for solution

A number of pharmaceutical compounds are unstable in aqueous solution over shelf-life. The commercial manufacturers of these products provide them in dry powder or granule form for reconstitution with a prescribed volume of diluent or reconstitution fluid. Dry powders are available either as simple powders containing only the active pharmaceutical ingredient or manufactured by processes such as lyophilization, crystallization, and spray drying. These processed dry powders may contain formulation ingredients, stabilizers, and buffer salts. Once reconstituted, the resulting solutions are either administered or further diluted according to packaging instructions. Some dry mixtures for reconstitution are alteplase (Activase), azacytidine (Vidaza), bortezomib (Velcade), etoposide phosphate (Etopophos), gemcitabine (Gemzar), and temozolomide (Temodar).

10.3.2 Suspensions

Suspension is a liquid dosage form of poorly water-soluble drug(s) dispersed in a liquid medium. In an ideal suspension, particles are uniformly dispersed, free from aggregation. Even if sedimentation occurs, particles should be resuspended upon mild agitation. Aqueous suspensions are intended for oral, ophthalmic, inhalation, and topical applications, while oil-based suspensions have parenteral applications (e.g., sustained-release depot formulations). Oral and topical suspensions contain a high concentration of solids in the range of 5%–50% solid particles, while parenteral suspensions incorporate 0.5%–25% solid particles. Based on particle size, suspensions are classified as coarse or colloidal dispersions, with the former containing particles of mean diameter in the range of 1–25 μM and the latter containing particles with a mean diameter less than 1 μM [35].

Suspensions offer advantages, such as (1) water-insoluble drug compounds can be formulated as suspensions; (2) they prolong drug release rates; (3) they slow down the degradation rate of hydrolytic drug compounds; and (4) for patients with swallowing difficulties, suspensions can be formulated as palatable formulations. Some of the disadvantages include (1) aggregation of particles, (2) complex manufacturing processes, and (3) pourability and syringeability issues (e.g., injectable suspensions).

10.3.2.1 Applications

Suspensions have a number of therapeutic applications across different routes of administration. Most suspensions are available in ready-to-use form from the manufacturer. In physical or chemical incompatibility cases, the pharmacist will have to reformulate a tablet or capsule into a suspension (e.g., oral suspension). Table 10.5 lists representative examples of pharmaceutical suspensions and their therapeutic indications. Some of the specific applications of pharmaceutical suspensions administered through various routes are detailed below.

TABLE 10.5   Examples of suspension products administered by various routes [4].

Active ingredient (brand name)	Suspending agents	Indication
Oral suspensions		
Acyclovir (Zovirax®)	Carboxymethylcellulose sodium (CMC sodium) and microcrystalline cellulose	Herpes simplex virus infections
Indomethacin (Indocin®)	Tragacanth	Moderate to severe arthritis and spondylitis
Megestrol acetate (Megace®)	Xanthan gum	Anorexia, cachexia, significant weight loss in patients with AIDS
Megestrol acetate (Megace ES)	Hydroxypropyl methylcellulose	Anorexia, cachexia, significant weight loss in patients with AIDS
Cefpodoxime proxetil (Vantin®)	Carboxymethylcellulose sodium, microcrystalline cellulose, carrageenan, croscarmellose sodium, hydroxypropylcellulose, and propylene glycol alginate	Bacterial infections
Pantoprazole sodium (Protonix®)	Crospovidone, hypromellose, methacrylic acid copolymer, microcrystalline cellulose, and povidone	Short-term treatment of erosive esophagitis associated with gastroesophageal reflux disease (GERD)
Oxcarbazepine (Trileptal®)	Cellulose	Epilepsy
Ampicillin for oral suspension (Principen®)	Lecithin	Bacterial infections

TABLE 10.5 Examples of suspension products administered by various routes [4].—cont'd

Active ingredient (brand name)	Suspending agents	Indication
Griseofulvin (Grifulvin V)	Sodium alginate	Fungal infections
Otic suspensions		
Ciprofloxacin and dexamethasone (Ciprodex®)	Hydroxyethyl cellulose	Acute otitis media/externa
Neomycin sulfate and hydrocortisone (Cortisporin®)	Cetyl alcohol	Acute otitis externa
Ophthalmic suspensions		
Brinzolamide (Azopt®)	Carbomer 974P	Elevated intraocular pressure
Loteprednol etabonate (Lotemax®)	Povidone	Allergic conjunctivitis
NASAL suspensions		
Budesonide (Rhinocort® Aqua)	Microcrystalline cellulose and CMC sodium	Seasonal and perennial allergic/nonallergic rhinitis
Triamcinolone acetonide (Nasacort® AQ)	Microcrystalline cellulose and CMC sodium	Seasonal and perennial allergic rhinitis
Beclomethasone dipropionate (Beconase® AQ)	Microcrystalline cellulose and CMC sodium	Seasonal allergic rhinitis
Topical suspensions		
Sulfacetamide topical suspension (Plexion®)	Xanthan gum NF	Topical treatment of acne vulgaris

10.3.2.1.1 Oral suspensions

- Drugs with poor solubility and poor bioavailability are formulated as fine colloidal suspensions to increase their bioavailability (e.g., megestrol acetate oral suspension, Megace ER).
- Drugs for patients with difficulties in swallowing solid dosage forms can be formulated as palatable suspensions (e.g., megestrol acetate oral suspension, Megace).
- Drugs unstable in aqueous media are prepared as powder granules and reconstituted in water to form suspension before administration to patients (e.g., ampicillin suspension).

10.3.2.1.2 Ophthalmic/otic/nasal suspensions

- Drug substances can be formulated as suspensions to prolong therapeutic action (e.g., brinzolamide suspension (Azopt), ciprofloxacin (Ciprodex)).
- Despite poor aqueous solubility, drug substances administered to nasal mucosa are suspended in aqueous vehicles to avoid mucosa irritation (Rhinocort Aqua).
- Drugs unstable in aqueous media are prepared in nonaqueous media to overcome stability issues (e.g., tetracycline hydrochloride in coconut oil for ophthalmic use).

10.3.2.1.3 Parenteral suspensions

- Drug substances which show poor oral absorption or extensive first-pass metabolism can be formulated as parenteral suspensions to improve bioavailability.
- Drug substances can be formulated as parenteral suspensions to prolong drug release rates (e.g., naltrexone extended-release injectable suspension, Vivitrol).

10.3.2.1.4 Pulmonary suspensions

Antiasthmatic drugs (e.g., steroids and antibiotics), which have poor solubility in water, are delivered as suspensions to treat pulmonary diseases. Most pharmaceutical aerosol suspensions have been propelled with chlorofluorocarbons, but current global regulations require pharmaceutical aerosols to be reformulated to contain nonozone-depleting propellants [36]. Alternatives to chlorofluorocarbon propellants are hydrofluorocarbon (HFC) 134a [also known as hydrofluoroalkane (HFA) 134a or 1,1,1,2-tetrafluoroethane] and HFC-227ea (HFA-

227ea or 1,1,1,2,3,3,3-heptafluoropropane) [37,38]. However, eliminating chlorine from HFCs has added a significant solvency challenge. The lower solvency of HFC fluids has turned attention from solution-based aerosols to suspension-based metered-dose inhalers (MDIs) [39].

10.3.2.1.5 Topical suspensions (lotions)

Many topical suspensions (lotions) are available for treating acne, and fungal and viral infections. Cosmetic applications of lotions are numerous, ranging from sun protectors to antiperspirants. Examples include calamine lotion, ciclopirox lotion, and sodium sulfacetamide lotion. Calamine lotion contains 8% each of zinc oxide and calamine, the latter composed of zinc oxide and a small amount of ferric oxide. In the preparation of a lotion, powders are levigated with a small portion of glycerin (levigating agent); the mixture is diluted with a combination of bentonite magma and calcium hydroxide solution. The product is made to volume with an additional calcium hydroxide solution. The bentonite magma can be used to suspend zinc oxide and calamine; however, the powders do settle on standing. Calamine lotion relieves itching, pain, and skin irritation.

10.3.2.2 Flocculated and deflocculated suspensions

Particle interactions and their settling properties in a suspension vehicle determine the suspension's rheological behavior and render them into deflocculated or flocculated suspensions. In flocculated suspensions, particles tend to agglomerate to form loose structures (floccules). In contrast, a deflocculated suspension consists of drug particles that do not agglomerate into floccules. Given that flocculated and deflocculated suspensions have the same drug particle-size distribution, drug crystal habit, drug particle density, and vehicle viscosity, drug particles in deflocculated suspensions exhibit more rapid sedimentation than in flocculated suspension. Sedimented flocculated drug particles can be redispersed upon mild agitation, whereas sediments in deflocculated suspensions are difficult to redisperse. No clear boundary between the sedimented cake and the supernatant liquid is formed in deflocculated suspensions. The supernatant remains turbid for an extended period of time due to varied sedimentation rates by different particle sizes. The formation of a clear supernatant liquid or a turbid layer during settling, is a good indication of flocculated and deflocculated suspensions, respectively.

The selection of a suspension (flocculated versus deflocculated) is dependent on the physicochemical properties of drug substances and their compatibility with excipients. Therefore, the selection of a suspension should be treated as specific to drug substances. Sedimentation can be minimized with structured vehicles (viscous) instead of unstructured vehicles, where rapid sedimentation occurs. Structured vehicles exhibit pseudoplastic and plastic flow behavior. These vehicles reduce particle settling by entrapping particles. It is preferred that thixotropy be associated with these two types of flows. At a steady state, thixotropic vehicles are physically stable and readily pourable upon mild agitation. The shear thinning property of these vehicles facilitates uniform dispersion and pourable characteristics when shear is applied.

In many instances, deflocculated suspensions in structured vehicles are also desirable. For example, in a structured vehicle in which large particles (floccules) sediment faster than smaller particles, a deflocculated suspension in which drug particles exist as separate entities (as opposed to floccules) is desirable. Another aspect is that deflocculated suspensions are devoid of flocculating agents, which can catalyze the chemical degradation of drug compounds and excipients. On the contrary, physical and chemical incompatibility of drug substances with excipients could result in rapid sedimentation and hard cake formation. It is for these reasons that flocculated suspensions are preferred over deflocculated suspensions.

Flocculated suspensions can fulfill the requisites of an ideal pharmaceutical suspension (i.e., sedimentation volume being equal to one as shown in Fig. 10.3B). In practice, some sedimentation occurs; therefore, suspending agents are added to retard the sedimentation of floccules. For example, a dispersion of positively charged drug particles can be flocculated by the addition of an anionic electrolyte. The physical stability of the suspension can be increased further by the addition of anionic protective colloids, which are compatible with anionic flocculating agents. However, if a negatively charged suspension is flocculated with positively charged electrolytes, the subsequent addition of anionic colloids may result in strong ionic interactions between oppositely charged ions, forming a mass with little or no suspending action. Therefore, to preclude ionic interactions, it is necessary to include a protective colloid with the same charge (i.e., positively charged) as flocculating agents.

10.3.2.3 Stability aspects

10.3.2.3.1 Physical stability

Often, rapid sedimentation and hard cake formation in suspensions are a result of the physical characteristics of drug particles. Some of the key particle features that determine the stability of suspensions include size distribution, hydrophobicity, crystal habit, and density. Solids are milled to reduce particle size before dispersing in a vehicle. Reduction in particle size leads to an increase in both surface area and surface free energy, resulting in an unstable thermodynamic system. In an energy compensation phenomenon, particles tend to regroup/flocculate to decrease surface area and, thus, surface-free energy. The formation of aggregates/floccules is considered a suspension's tendency to form a stable thermodynamic system. Surface free energy and total surface area can be correlated by Eq. (10.2):

$$\Delta F = \gamma_{SL} \times \Delta A \tag{10.2}$$

where γ_{SL} is the interfacial tension between solid particles and the liquid vehicle in dyne/cm, F is the surface free energy in dyne×cm (erg), and A is the surface area in cm^2. Since the suspension of solid particles in a liquid vehicle is an interfacial phenomenon, intermolecular forces at the particle surface affect the degree of flocculation and agglomeration in a suspension. In particular, weak Van der Waals attractive forces and repulsive forces arising from the interaction of electric double layers surrounding each particle influence the degree of flocculation [40,41]. In a flocculated suspension, the energy barrier between approaching particles is high enough (when distance between particles >1,000 Å) to be surmounted. However, when the approaching distance between particles is less than 1,000 Å, attractive forces become dominant, leading to sedimentation.

Although it is not possible to prevent settling completely, it is necessary to consider factors that influence sedimentation and adopt formulation strategies to minimize it. The velocity of sedimentation can be expressed by Stoke's law as shown in Eq. (10.3):

$$v = d^2(\rho_s - \rho_o)g/18\eta_o \tag{10.3}$$

Where v is the terminal velocity in cm/sec; d is the diameter of the particle in cm; ρ_s and ρ_o are densities of the dispersed phase and dispersion medium, respectively; g is the acceleration due to gravity in cm/sec^2, and η_o is the viscosity of dispersion medium in poise (1 ·g.cm^{-1}.sec^{-1}). From the equation, it can be concluded that the rate of fall of a suspended particle in a vehicle of a given density is greater for larger particles than for smaller particles. Also, the greater the density difference between particles and vehicles, the greater the sedimentation rate. An increase in the viscosity of the dispersion medium can reduce the sedimentation rate. Thus, a decrease in the sedimentation rate in a suspension could be achieved by reducing the size of particles and by increasing the density and viscosity of the dispersed phase.

Stoke's equation can be applied only in conditions such as (1) suspensions contain spherical particles in a very dilute suspension (0.5%–2% suspension); (2) particles do not collide with each other, and (3) free settling of particles may occur. However, in most pharmaceutical suspensions, the concentration of suspended particles is >5%, and they exhibit slow settling. Even a corrected Stoke's equation could not represent the mass rate of settling of irregular particles in concentrated suspensions. However, two parameters that are useful to measure sedimentation velocity are sedimentation volume and degree of flocculation [42]. The sedimentation volume, F, is defined as the ratio of the final volume, V_i, of the sedimented suspension to the original volume of the suspension, V_o, as shown in Eq. (10.4):

$$F = V_i/V_o \tag{10.4}$$

Fig. 10.3 demonstrates that sedimentation volume can have values ranging from less than 1 to greater than 1. In a settled deflocculated suspension, $F < 1$, where the final volume of sediment is smaller than the original volume of the suspension. In a stable suspension, $F = 1$, where the final volume of sediment in a flocculated suspension equals the original volume of the suspension. It is possible that $F > 1$, when the final volume of the suspension is greater than the original suspension volume. This increase in volume could be due to an expanded structure formed due to the slow swelling of excipient polymers.

Another parameter is the degree of sedimentation (β), which is more of a quantitative estimate of sedimentation. The degree of sedimentation is defined as the ratio of the final sedimentation volume of a flocculated suspension (V_f) to the final sedimentation volume (V_d) of a deflocculated suspension, as shown in Eq. (10.5):

$$\beta = \left(V_f / V_o\right) / (V_d / V_o) \tag{10.5}$$

10.3.2.3.2 Interfacial phenomenon and electrochemical stability

In a suspension medium, particles become charged due to ion adsorption onto the particle surface or ionization of functional groups at the particle surface. Selective adsorption of ions could be due to ions from excipients (e.g., electrolytes), hydronium, and hydroxyl ions of water. The overall charge is dependent on the pH of the liquid medium.

10. Liquid Dosage Forms

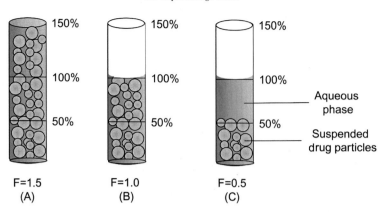

F=1.5   F=1.0   F=0.5
(A)   (B)   (C)

FIGURE 10.3 Three cases of sedimentation volumes: (A) swollen suspension, (B) flocculated suspension, and (C) deflocculated suspension. In a settled deflocculated suspension, $F < 1$, where the final volume of the sediment is smaller than the original volume of the suspension. In a stable suspension, $F = 1$, that is, final volume of the sediment in a flocculated suspension equals the original volume (100%) of the suspension. It is possible that $F > 1$, where the final volume of the suspension is greater than the original suspension volume. This increase in volume could be due to an expanded loose structure. For example, excessive concentrations of polymer swell over a period of standing, resulting in expansion of suspension volume. *Adapted with permission from ref. [20].*

For a description of an electric double layer, consider suspended particles in contact with a liquid polar medium (Fig. 10.4) [12]. Some cations (hydronium or cations from ionic excipients), which are adsorbed onto the surface, are assumed to have an inherent negative charge on the solid surface. The adsorbed ions that imparted cationic charge are referred to as potential-determining ions ($\alpha\alpha'$ layer). This cationic layer attracts anions (counter-ions) of the suspension medium and repels cations (vice versa, if the potential determining ion is negative, positive counter-ions may present in the layer). The limit of this region is termed line $\beta\beta'$, whose potential is still positive due to fewer anions than cations bound to the solid surface. In the region $\beta\beta'-\gamma\gamma'$, the concentration of anions is higher; at $\gamma\gamma'$, anion concentration becomes equal to cations (i.e., the system becomes electroneutral); and beyond $\gamma\gamma'$, anion concentration decreases. Despite the uneven distribution of charged regions, the system as a whole is considered neutral.

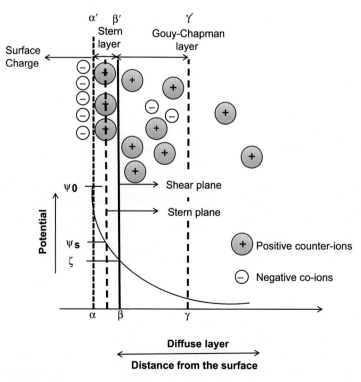

FIGURE 10.4 Changes in potentials with distance from the particle surface.

Due to formulation composition (e.g., high concentration of ionic excipients, such as flocculating agents, and suspending agents) changes in the electroneutral region occur. For example, if the total charge of counter-ions in the region αα′−ββ′ exceeds potential determining ions, then the net charge at ββ′ will be negative rather than positive. Instead of electric neutrality at the γγ′ boundary, an excess of positive ions must be present in the region ββ′−γγ′. Also, electrical neutrality may occur at the ββ′ boundary itself if the concentration of counter-ions equals potential determining ions.

Fig. 10.4 represents changes in potential with distance from the solid surface. The electric distribution at the interface is equivalent to the charge of the first double layer, αα′−ββ′, which is termed the stern layer or Helmholtz layer. The diffused double layer ββ′−γγ′ is termed the Gouy−Chapman layer. The potential at the solid surface (αα′) due to potential determining ions is termed the Nernst potential (ψ_0), defined as the potential difference between the solid surface and neutral region (γγ′) of the dispersion medium. The potential at the shear plane (where counter-ions diffuse away) is considered the zeta potential (ζ), which can be defined as the potential difference between the shear plane and neutral region (γγ′) of the dispersion medium.

When a suspended particle moves (e.g., gravity or Brownian motion), Stern and Gouy−Chapman layers move along, and ions beyond the Gouy−Chapman layer boundary remain in the bulk dispersion medium. While moving, particles undergo attractive and electrical double-layer repulsive forces. The repulsive forces between particles prevent them from approaching each other and getting adhered. However, particle collisions could overcome the repulsive force energy barrier, resulting in the adherence of particles. Often, zeta potential measurements are made to determine the magnitude of interactions between colloidal particles and assess the stability of colloidal systems. If the suspended particles have a large negative or positive zeta potential, then particles tend to repel each other. However, if the particles have low zeta potential values, then attractive forces exceed repulsive forces, and the particles come together, triggering the settling of particles. In general, stable and unstable suspensions are on either side of +25 or −25 mV (i.e., particles with zeta potentials more positive than +25 mV or more negative than −25 mV are considered stable). It is important to remember that particles whose density is different from the dispersion medium will also undergo sedimentation, forming a hard cake.

Various factors, such as pH, ionic strength, and concentration of formulation components, influence the zeta potential value of suspended particles. Imagine a weak acid drug being suspended in a dispersion medium (pH > pKa). Drug particles undergo ionization and exhibit negative zeta potential. If more alkali is added to this suspension, particles tend to acquire a more negative charge. If acid is added to this suspension, neutralization occurs at a certain pH of the medium. Further addition of acid will result in positive zeta potential. For a weak acid, a zeta potential versus pH plot exhibits a negative potential at high pH and a positive potential at low pH of the dispersion medium. The point of zero potential is termed the isoelectric point, at which the suspension is unstable. The concentration of ions in suspension determines the thickness of the double layer. The higher the ionic strength, the more compressed the double layer and the greater the magnitude of interactions on the particle surface. Also, the high valence of ions causes the compression of double layers.

10.3.2.3.3 Chemical stability

In suspensions, a kinetic equilibrium exists between the suspended insoluble drug and soluble forms. At a particular temperature, the drug concentration of the soluble form remains constant with time; therefore, the rate of formation of the soluble form in suspensions follows zero-order kinetics. Although insoluble, the suspended drug substances have intrinsic solubility, which triggers chemical reactions, such as hydrolysis, leading to degradation. From these observations, it is assumed that the decomposition of drug substances in suspensions is due to the amount of drug dissolved in the aqueous phase. Despite decomposition, the concentration of the drug solution remains constant with time (i.e., zero-order kinetics).

The kinetics of the formation of a soluble drug concentration in a suspension is also referred to as apparent zero-order because the soluble form follows zero-order only as a result of the suspended drug reservoir. If the suspended particles are converted into a drug solution, the entire system changes from zero-order to first-order, and degradation then depends on solution concentration. However, most suspension dosage forms are stable (shelf-life period) enough for the soluble drug fraction to exhibit zero-order kinetics. It is also uncommon to design and manufacture suspension dosage forms in which the soluble fraction undergoes rapid degradation, triggering first-order kinetics. In such a case, there is the potential to produce degradants at greater than acceptable thresholds.

10.3.2.4 Formulation considerations

Drugs are formulated as suspensions due to their low aqueous-soluble nature. Different categories of inactive ingredients are required for suspending drug particles in aqueous vehicles. To produce stable suspension, inactive ingredients are intended to alter physicochemical characteristics of drug, such as particle-size distribution, surface tension, and surface charge. Some excipients are added to modulate suspensions' rheological behavior and minimize particles' irreversible sedimentation. Table 10.4 lists common inactive ingredients and their concentration ranges in pharmaceutical suspensions, which include wetting agents (surfactants), viscosity modifiers, buffers, taste-masking agents, flavoring agents, and coloring agents.

10.3.2.4.1 Vehicles

Deionized water is a common suspending medium in pharmaceutical suspensions. In a few instances, viscous nonaqueous solvents, such as propylene glycol and polyethylene glycols, are used to provide stability to suspended drug particles.

10.3.2.4.2 Wetting agents

The foremost requirement to produce a pharmaceutical suspension is to achieve adequate wetting of solid particles by the liquid vehicle. Wetting of solids is related to a phenomenon in which the solid—air interface is instantly replaced by a solid—liquid interface when the drug is suspended in a vehicle. The wetting phenomenon (spreading) can be expressed in terms of surface tension, W_s, given by Eq. (10.6):

$$W_s = \gamma_S - \gamma_L - \gamma_{SL} \tag{10.6}$$

where γ_S is the surface tension of the solid, γ_L is the surface tension of the liquid, and γ_{SL} is the solid—liquid interfacial tension. The surface tension of liquids is readily measured by well-established methods, such as the Wilhelmy plate or du Nuoy ring [43]. In the case of solids, only indirect methods are available to estimate γ_L and γ_{SL} based on Young's equation (Eq. 10.7) [43]:

$$\gamma_L \cos(\theta) = \gamma_S - \gamma_{SL} \tag{10.7}$$

where θ is the contact angle between the solid surface and tangent to the liquid phase. The wettability of hydrophobic drugs can be achieved by reducing the contact angle of water on solid surfaces. Surfactants are added to wet the solid surfaces. The adsorption of surfactants can increase the stability of particles against aggregation. The solid—liquid interfacial interactions of adsorbed surfactants can be one of the following [44]: (1) ion-exchange (i.e., the substitution of previously adsorbed ions on the solid by surfactant ions of identical charge); (2) ion-pairing (i.e., adsorption of surfactant ions on the surface sites of opposite charge not occupied by counter-ions); (3) acid—base interactions, mainly hydrogen bonds; (4) adsorption by the polarization of π electrons; (5) adsorption by dispersion forces occurs via Van der Waals forces between solid surface and liquid; and (6) hydrogen bonding.

Typical examples of surfactants in pharmaceutical suspensions include docusate sodium, sodium dodecyl sulfate, and ammonium lauryl ether sulfate (anionic); benzalkonium chloride, benzethonium chloride, and cetyltrimethylammonium bromide (cationic); and polyoxyethylene alkylphenylethers (e.g., nonoxynol 9 and nonoxynol 10), poloxamers, polyoxyethylene fatty acid glycerides (e.g., Labrasol), polyoxyethylene (35) castor oil, polyoxyethylene (40) hydrogenated castor oil, polyoxyethylene sorbitan esters (e.g., polysorbate 20 and polysorbate 80), propylene glycol fatty acid esters (e.g., propylene glycol laurate), glyceryl fatty acid esters (e.g., glyceryl monostearate), and sorbitan esters (e.g., sorbitan monolaurate, sorbitan monooleate, sorbitan monopalmitate, and sorbitan monostearate) (nonionic). Nonionic surfactants whose HLB is in the range of 6—9 are often used in low concentrations to wet solid surfaces [45]. Nonionic surfactants minimize sedimentation through the steric hindrance of particle interactions. Polysorbate 80 is the most widely used nonionic surfactant in parenteral and oral suspensions [46].

An adequate concentration of surfactants should be used for wetting insoluble powder. Excessive surfactant concentration in suspensions leads to the undesirable dissolution of drugs. As the dissolved fraction of a drug is susceptible to chemical degradation and interaction with other ingredients, suspensions comprising free drugs can be chemically unstable. Also, high free-surfactant concentration could result in more rapid sedimentation of flocculated particles than deflocculated particles. High surfactant concentration could result in air entrainment inside the particles, leading to lowered wetting and non-uniform doses. In addition to surfactants, hygroscopic substances can be used as wetting aids. For example, glycerin flows into voids between particles to displace air and during the mixing operation so that water can penetrate individual wet particles.

10.3.2.4.3 Flocculating agents

In suspensions, agents are added to produce controlled flocculation of wetted particles to prevent the formation of compact sediments that are difficult to redisperse. Substances such as salts, surfactants, and polymers act as flocculating agents. Salts reduce the electric barrier between particles to link them to form floccules. One example of an electrolyte is monobasic potassium phosphate. Surfactants, such as docusate sodium, sodium dodecyl sulfate, benzalkonium chloride, and cetyltrimethylammonium bromide, have been used as flocculating agents. However, it is critical to maintain low surfactant concentration, which otherwise may hinder flocculation. Polymers (e.g., xanthan gum, carbopols, and cellulose derivatives) also function as flocculating agents because part of the chain is adsorbed onto the particle surface, with the remaining parts projecting out into the dispersion medium. Bridging between these portions leads to the formation of floccules. Hydrophilic polymers (e.g., clays) act as protective colloids, and particles coated with polymers are less prone to caking than uncoated particles. These polymers exhibit pseudoplastic flow, which serves to promote the physical stability of suspensions.

10.3.2.4.4 Viscosity modifiers

According to flow behavior, liquids are classified as Newtonian and non-Newtonian. Simple liquids follow Newtonian flow behavior, in which stress is proportional to shear. Emulsions and suspensions follow non-Newtonian (e.g., plastic, pseudoplastic, dilatant) flow behaviors [47,48]. In concentrated suspensions, it is challenging to control particle—particle collisions, which affect the flow properties of suspensions. An increase in the dispersion medium's viscosity will reduce collisions' frequency while hindering particle sedimentation. Viscosity modifiers are added to impart physical stability to suspensions. These viscosity modifiers should be associated with thixotropic features (i.e., physically stable at the steady state and pourable upon mild agitation). Viscosity modifiers must have the following properties: (1) water-soluble or swell in aqueous media; (2) stable; and (3) compatible with other suspension components. Common viscosity modifiers are cellulose derivatives (e.g., methylcellulose, microcrystalline cellulose, and hydroxypropyl methylcellulose), clays (e.g., bentonite and kaolinite), natural gums (e.g., acacia, guar gum, tragacanth, and xanthan gum), synthetic polymers (e.g., polyvinylpyrrolidone), and miscellaneous compounds (e.g., colloidal silicon dioxide and silicates). Each of the viscosity modifiers has its own mechanism of action. It is common to use more than one category of viscosity modifier to exert a synergistic effect on rheological behavior and improve the stability of suspensions. For example, magnesium aluminum silicate and xanthan gum are used in nystatin oral suspension. The silicate exerts a synergistic effect with xanthan gum, enhancing the thixotropic characteristic of the suspension.

10.3.2.4.5 Buffers

In an ideal situation, pharmaceutical suspensions should be stable in a wide pH range. Citrates and phosphates are commonly used buffers in pharmaceutical suspensions. Citrate buffers are used to stabilize suspensions in the pH range of 3—5, while phosphate buffers are used in the pH range of 7—8.

10.3.2.4.6 Tonicity-adjusting agents

Tonicity-adjusting agents are added to produce osmotic pressure comparable to biological fluids when the suspension is intended for ophthalmic or parenteral purposes. Common tonicity-adjusting agents for ophthalmic suspensions are dextrose, mannitol, and sorbitol, while tonicity-adjusting agents used in parenteral suspensions are sodium chloride, sodium sulfate, dextrose, mannitol, and glycerol.

10.3.2.4.7 Other additives

A number of additives are needed for the preparation of an elegant and stable suspension. A few of them include preservatives, complexing agents, colorants, and flavoring agents. In colloidal formulations, trace metals may trigger aggregation and an oxidation reaction. Complexing agents hinder the formation of large aggregates responsible for the caking phenomenon. Flavoring agents, cellulose derivatives, and natural gums (viscosity modifiers) are a source of microbial growth. Preservatives are added to prevent microbial growth in suspensions. Common preservatives in suspensions are parabens, alcohol, glycerin, propylene glycol, and sorbates. Preservatives lose antimicrobial action due to one of several factors, such as oxidation, solubility in oils, incompatibility with ions or containers, and closures. In general, ionic preservatives are active in the unionized form; therefore, suitable buffers are chosen to maintain preservatives in the unionized form and exert antimicrobial action. In a few instances, a combination of two or more preservatives is used to exert a wide spectrum of antimicrobial action.

10.3.3 Emulsions

Emulsions are liquid disperse systems consisting of two immiscible phases, one of which is dispersed as globules in the other liquid phase [49]. The presence of an emulsifier stabilizes the two phases of emulsions. The droplet diameter of the dispersed phase extends from about 0.1 to 10 μM, although particle diameters as small as

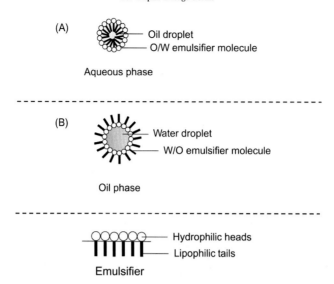

FIGURE 10.5　(A) Oil-in-water dispersion, where (o/w) emulsifier disperses the oil phase in a continuous aqueous phase; (B) water-in-oil emulsion, where (w/o) emulsifier disperses water in a continuous oil phase.

0.01 μM and as large as 100 μM are not uncommon [50]. The consistency of emulsions ranges from that of a liquid (e.g., fat emulsions) to a semisolid (e.g., ointments and creams).

As illustrated in Fig. 10.5, one liquid phase of an emulsion is polar (e.g., aqueous), and the other is relatively nonpolar (e.g., oil). When an oil phase is dispersed as globules through a continuous aqueous phase, the system is referred to as an oil-in-water (o/w) emulsion. When an oil phase serves as the continuous phase, the emulsion is referred to as a water-in-oil (w/o) emulsion. Pharmaceutical emulsions are usually the (o/w) type and require the use of an (o/w) emulsifier. Topical emulsions may be (o/w) or (w/o) emulsions; the latter is currently popular. Other special classes of emulsions include multiple and microemulsions. Multiple emulsions may be water-oil-water, in which the oil phase is between two aqueous phases, or oil-water-oil, in which an aqueous phase separates the internal and external oil phases. Multiple emulsions are being investigated to prolong drug release rates by incorporating drug substances in the inner aqueous or oil phase of an emulsion [51]. Microemulsions are another class of emulsions that consist of large or swollen micelles in the internal phase, much like that of a solubilized solution [52]. Microemulsions appear as clear transparent solutions or translucent disperion depending on droplet size and are thermodynamically stable. Microemulsions contain droplet diameters of about 0.1–0.4 μM.

10.3.3.1 Applications

In general, oil-in-water emulsions are designed for oral (e.g., cod liver emulsion), injectable, ophthalmic, and topical purposes. Table 10.6 lists representative examples of pharmaceutical emulsions. Intravenous fat emulsions employed for total parenteral nutrition (TPN) are formulated using vegetable oils as the dispersed phase and phospholipids as the emulsifier, with an objective to provide calories and essential fatty acids. Fat emulsions are particularly indicated in cases of GI tract traumas, cancer, infections, burns, radiation exposures, and psychological disorders (e.g., bulimia). Fat emulsions are oil-in-water emulsions with mean droplet diameters in the range of 0.2–0.5 μM [53,54]. For intravenous applications, there must be no droplets larger than the diameter of blood capillaries (~5 μM) to avoid blockage [55]. Intravenous fat emulsions can be used as drug carriers. Emulsions containing hypnotics, such as diazepam, etomidate, or propofol, are available. A number of drug-containing emulsions are in preclinical and clinical trials. Advantages that favor the use of fat emulsions as drug carriers [56] are (1) poor solubility of drugs in water but excellent solubility in oil; (2) stabilization of drugs that are sensitive to hydrolysis; (3) reduction of side effects associated with drugs; and (4) drug targeting. Although injectable emulsions present several potential advantages, the number of approved products is relatively low. Some of the major issues preventing a broader application of injectable emulsions are (1) oil phase compositions (e.g., long- and medium-chain triglycerides) approved by the regulatory agencies are not necessarily good solvents for lipophilic drugs; (2) the oil phase should not exceed 20–30% of the emulsion, which possibly limits the required solubility of drug substances; an increase of the oil phase over 20% poses challenges to concentration limits of the emulsifier and processing conditions to obtain a droplet diameter less than 5 μM; and (3) drug crystallization out of emulsions.

TABLE 10.6 Examples of marketed emulsion products [4].

Approved marketed product	Composition	Indication
Liposyn® (USA)	10%/20% soy oil/safflower oil, egg phospholipid, water for injection	Total parenteral nutrition
Intralipid® (USA)	10%/20%/30% soy oil/egg phospholipid/water for injection	Total parenteral nutrition
Lipofundin® (USA)	10%/20% soy oil/egg phospholipid, water for injection	Total parenteral nutrition
Cleviprex® (USA)	Clevidipine butyrate, soy oil, egg phospholipid, glycerol, water for injection	Reduction of blood pressure
Diazemuls® (USA)	Diazepam, acetylated glycerides, egg phospholipid, glycerol, sodium hydroxide	Anxiolytic or sedative
Disoprivan® (Worldwide)	Propofol, soybean oil, egg lecithin, disodium edetate, glycerol, sodium hydroxide, water for injection	Induction and maintenance of anesthesia, conscious sedation for surgical procedure
Etomidate-Lipuro® (Germany)	Etomidate, soy oil, MCT, egg lecithin, glycerol, sodium oleate	Induction of anesthesia
Fluosol-DA® (Worldwide)	Perfluorodecalin, perfluorotripropylamine, egg phospholipid, glycerol, pluronic F68, potassium oleate	Blood substitute
Restasis® (USA)	Cyclosporine, glycerin; castor oil; polysorbate 80; pemulens, sodium hydroxide, and purified water	Keratoconjunctivitis sicca (dry eye syndrome)
Durezol® (USA)	Difluprednate, boric acid, castor oil, glycerin, polysorbate 80, sodium acetate, sodium EDTA, sodium hydroxide, sorbic acid, and purified water.	Postoperative inflammation

Emulsions have applications for ophthalmic purposes; they transfer drug substances in an effective concentration to ocular disease sites and prolong drug release. Cyclosporin (Restasis) and Difluprednate (Durezol) are the available topical ophthalmic emulsions. Cyclosporin, an immunosuppressant, is indicated for treating keratoconjunctivitis sicca (dry-eye syndrome), while difluprednate is indicated for treating postoperative inflammation and pain associated with ocular surgery. Because both cyclosporin and difluprednate have such a low solubility in water, it is difficult to prepare ophthalmic drops in a concentration effective to produce therapeutic efficacy. Cyclosporin and difluprednate exhibit better solubility in oils than in the aqueous phase and therefore are administered as oil-in-water emulsions.

The use of emulsions for oral application is limited since other alternatives, such as SEDDS, are popular. Emulsions containing contrast agents have been used in computed tomography, magnetic resonance imaging, and radionuclide imaging. Perfluorochemical emulsions serve as vehicles for respiratory gas (e.g., oxygen). Fluosol-DA (Green Cross and Alpha Therapeutics, Japan), which consists of perfluorodecalin and perfluorotripropylamine, has been marketed as an artificial blood substitute for tissue oxygenation. Topical emulsion formulations include creams and lotions.

10.3.3.2 Theories of emulsions

Several theories have been proposed to explain the stability of emulsions. Some theories related to the functional role of emulsifiers and others to processing conditions. The most important theories are surface tension, oriented-wedge, and interfacial film theories. According to surface-tension theory, emulsifiers lower interfacial tension between two immiscible liquids, thus allowing the miscibility of phases [57]. The oriented-wedge theory assumes the formation of a monomolecular layer of emulsifier around the droplet of the internal phase of an emulsion [58]. Certain emulsifiers orient themselves around a liquid droplet in a manner reflective of their solubility in a particular phase. The interfacial theory describes that the emulsifier is located at the interface between oil and water phases, forming a thin film by being adsorbed onto the surface of internal phase droplets [59]. The surfactant film must be sufficiently rigid to stabilize the interface but it also needs to be flexible enough that the collision of emulsion droplets does not lead to the rupture of the film, resulting in coalescence. None of the theories of emulsification is of universal application, and though each may cover a particular class of emulsifiers, different classes of emulsifiers exert a slightly different mechanism of action from one another. Emulsifiers may be divided into three groups as follows.

a. Surface-active agents, are adsorbed at the oil-in-water interface to form monomolecular films and reduce interfacial tension

b. Hydrophilic colloids, which form a multimolecular film around the dispersed droplets of oil-in-water emulsion

c. Finely divided solid particles, which are adsorbed around dispersed globules

An essential property of emulsifiers that determines their type is their hydrophilic—lipophilic-balance (HLB) value [60]. Emulsifiers with HLB values between 9 and 12 typically create oil-in-water emulsions, while those with HLB values between 3 and 6 typically create water-in-oil emulsions. The emulsion type is also a function of the relative solubility of surfactants (i.e., the phase in which it is more soluble is the continuous phase). This sometimes is referred to as the Bancroft rule. Thus, an emulsifier with a high HLB value is preferentially soluble in water and forms an oil-in-water emulsion. The reverse is true with surfactants of low HLB, which tend to form water-in-oil emulsions.

Emulsions may undergo a wide variety of shear stresses during preparation or use. In many of these processes, the flow properties will be vital for the proper performance of an emulsion [48,61]. For example, the flow of a parenteral emulsion through a hypodermic needle, removal of an emulsion from a bottle or tube, and flow behavior of an emulsion in various milling operations employed in manufacturing require correct flow characteristics. Flow properties of emulsions are influenced by factors such as phase volume ratio, droplet-size distribution, and viscosity of the internal phase. Most emulsions, except dilute ones, exhibit non-Newtonian flow. When the phase volume of the dispersed phase is low (less than 0.05 or 5%), the system is Newtonian. As the volume is increased, the system becomes more resistant to flow and exhibits pseudoplastic flow. When the phase volume approaches 0.74 or 74%, phase inversion may occur with marked viscosity changes. Droplet-size distribution is another factor that affects the viscosity of emulsions. Reduction in mean droplet size increases viscosity; however, polydisperse emulsions exhibit lower viscosity compared to monodisperse systems (i.e., narrower particle-size distribution). Another factor is the emulsifier and its concentration. The higher the concentration of an emulsifier, the greater the viscosity of an emulsion.

10.3.3.3 *Stability aspects*

The stability of pharmaceutical emulsions can be characterized by the absence of the aggregation of emulsion droplets, separation of phases, and maintenance of elegance with respect to appearance, color, and odor. As shown in Fig. 10.6, the stability of emulsions is governed by different mechanisms (i.e., flocculation, creaming, and coalescence), which may lead to irreversible destabilization (cracking).

10.3.3.3.1 Flocculation

Flocculation may be subdivided into two general categories: sedimentation aggregation and Brownian motion aggregation. In sedimentation aggregation, droplet paths are vertically linear. High-density droplets (e.g., water droplets of water-in-oil emulsions) settle at the bottom, leading to aggregation. In Brownian aggregation, emulsions consisting of droplets of different sizes cream (negative to settling) at different rates, with large droplets moving faster and colliding with slow-moving small droplets. These collisions lead to the aggregation of droplets. Flocculation is a precursor phenomenon to creaming. An estimate of the relative rates of each type of flocculation can be made from Eq. (10.8) [62]:

$$\tau_{max} = \frac{2\pi(\rho - \rho_0)gr4}{3K_bT} \tag{10.8}$$

where ρ is the density of the droplet, ρ_0 is the density of the dispersion medium, r is the droplet radius, K_b is the Boltzmann constant, and T is the absolute temperature. When $\tau_{max} > 10$, Brownian aggregation is negligible; when $\tau_{max} < 0.1$, sedimentation aggregation is negligible.

10.3.3.3.2 Creaming

Creaming is a process by which the disperse phase separates from an emulsion and is typically the precursor of coalescence. The creaming rate can be estimated from Stoke's equation. According to Stoke's law, if the dispersed phase is less dense than the continuous phase, which is the case of oil-in-water emulsions, the velocity of sedimentation becomes negative (i.e., upward creaming results). If the internal phase is heavier than the external phase (e.g., water-in-oil emulsions), the globules settle, which is referred to as creaming in the downward direction. The greater the difference between the densities of the phases, the greater the creaming rate. The size of the globules is also a determining factor in the creaming rate. As per Stoke's law, doubling the diameter of oil globules increases the

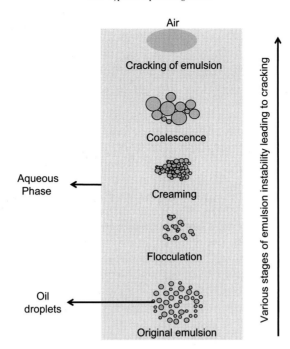

FIGURE 10.6 Schematic representation of various mechanisms leading to cracking of oil-in-water emulsion. Primary mechanisms of an unstable emulsion are flocculation, creaming, and coalescence. In some instances (e.g., unoptimized formulation composition or processing conditions), emulsion exhibits the cracking phenomenon without showing signs of flocculation, creaming, and coalescence.

creaming rate by a factor of four. The rate of creaming can be reduced by adding viscosity enhancers, such as methylcellulose, and droplet-size reduction.

10.3.3.3.3 Coalescence and breaking

Creaming is a reversible process, whereas breaking is irreversible. The cream floccules may be redispersed, and a uniform mixture can be obtained by agitation. When breaking occurs, the emulsifier film surrounding the globules will be destroyed, and the oil droplets tend to coalesce. In such a case, simple mixing fails to resuspend globules. The coalescence phenomenon could result from numerous factors, such as inappropriate emulsifier selection, inadequate emulsifier concentration, errors in the manufacturing process, phase volume ratio, the viscosity of emulsion, and droplet size. Viscosity alone does not produce stable emulsions; however, viscous emulsions may be more stable than dilute ones by virtue of retardation of flocculation and coalescence. The phase volume ratio, which refers to the relative volume of the internal phase to the external phase in an emulsion, also influences the stability of the emulsion. Incorporation of more than 74% of oil in oil-in-water emulsion results in the coalescence of oil globules [63]. This value, known as the critical point, is defined as the concentration of the internal phase above which the emulsifier cannot produce a stable emulsion.

10.3.3.4 Formulation considerations

Emulsion formulation contains a number of inactive ingredients, such as oil phase-soluble lipids, emulsifiers, preservatives, pH-adjusting agents, and antioxidants. The selection of inactive ingredients depends on their approved use, route of administration, concentration limits, stability, and nontoxic nature. Lipids (e.g., triglycerides) approved by regulatory agencies, alone or in combination, are generally the first choice for developing emulsions [64]. Long-chain triglycerides include soybean oil, safflower oil, sesame oil, and castor oil, while medium-chain triglycerides include Miglyol 810 and 812. The solubility and stability of active ingredients govern the selection of the lipid phase. The oil phase must be of high purity and free of undesirable components, such as peroxides, pigments, degradation products, and unsaponifiable matter (e.g., sterols). Lipid peroxides of the oil phase can act as oxidation initiators and destabilize compounds susceptible to oxidation. The oxidation of oil can be minimized by the addition of antioxidants.

Emulsifiers are a class of emulsion stabilizers that reduce the interfacial tension between oil and aqueous phases to produce a stable colloidal dispersion. Egg and soy lecithins have been used extensively as emulsifiers in injectable emulsions. These emulsifiers are biocompatible and nontoxic [65]. However, hydrolysis of lecithin during emulsification, sterilization, and storage leads to the formation of lysophospholipids with detergent-like properties and causes hemolysis. Process optimization (e.g., cold homogenization) and storage conditions (e.g., mild temperatures) could reduce the hydrolysis of emulsions. Other potential emulsifiers in injectable emulsions include PEGylated phospholipids (e.g., polyethylene glycol phosphatidylethanolamine) and nonionic surfactants (e.g., Pluronic F68).

The aqueous phase includes additives such as antioxidants, preservatives, tonicity modifiers, and pH-adjusting agents. Antioxidants that impart protection in the aqueous phase include sodium metabisulfite, ascorbic acid, thioglycerol, and cysteine. Oil-soluble antioxidants include α-tocopherol, propyl gallate, ascorbyl palmitate, and butylated hydroxytoluene. Microbial organisms degrade emulsifiers and glycerin, with a substantial deterioration of emulsion, and therefore require adequate concentration of preservatives to resist microbial growth. Due to emulsions' heterogeneous nature, preservatives will be partitioned between oil and water phases. In general, bacteria grow in the aqueous phase of emulsions, and preservatives with a tendency to partition into the oil phase may be ineffective because of the low concentration remaining in the aqueous phase. In addition, the preservative must be in an unionized state to penetrate the bacterial membrane. Finally, preservative molecules must not bind to other components of the emulsion since the complexes are ineffective as preservatives. Antimicrobial agents, such as benzalkonium chloride, benzyl alcohol, EDTA, parabens, and sodium benzoate, are added to the aqueous phase to prevent microbial growth. Tonicity can be achieved with glycerol and sorbitol. Buffering agents, which consist of weak or strong electrolytes, interact with phospholipids and cause catalysis of lipids, leading to the destabilization of the emulsion. Instead, small amounts of sodium hydroxide are used to adjust the pH of the emulsion to around 8.0 before sterilization.

Ophthalmic emulsion compositions differ from injectable emulsions, specifically surfactants and thickening agents. Water-soluble and oil-soluble ingredients are solubilized in the aqueous and oil phases, respectively. Different oils used in ophthalmic emulsions include castor oil, soybean oil, safflower oil, olive oil, arachis oil, and mineral oil. In ophthalmic emulsions, emulsifiers, such as polysorbates, glyceryl esters, and acrylate crosspolymers are used to form stable dispersion [66]. Acrylate polymers include carbomers and pemulens, which also act as viscosity agents. The pH of emulsions can be adjusted using sodium hydroxide to a near ocular pH level (7.2–7.8). In general, buffering agents are not required; if they are required, suitable buffers may include phosphates, citrates, acetates, and borates.

Emulsion-based topical lotions are low-to medium-medicated or nonmedicated topical preparations. Most lotions are oil-in-water emulsions; these are preferred due to their water washable and nonabsorptive nature. It is not uncommon for the same active pharmaceutical ingredient to be formulated into lotion, cream, and/or ointment dosage forms. Lotions are less viscous than creams and may be readily spread to affected regions. Some of the emulsion-based lotions are lindane, metronidazole (Metrolotion), clotrimazole and betamethasone dipropionate (Lotrisone), and ivermectin (Sklace).

Typically, lotions include one or more of the following: a surfactant, thickener, emulsifier, emollient, perfuming agent, coloring agent, preservative, or buffer. Due to functional requirements, excipients used in topical lotions are extensive, and their concentration limits are higher than those administered through other routes. Emulsifiers used in lotions are derived from natural or synthetic sources. Natural emulsifiers in lotions are egg or soy lecithins and gelatin. Among the synthetic emulsifiers are anionic, cationic, and nonionic surfactants. Predominantly, nonionic surfactants contain the following classes: polyoxyethylene sorbitan fatty ester derivatives (e.g., polysorbate 80); glycerin fatty acid ester derivatives (e.g., glyceryl monocaprylate); polyethylene fatty acid ester derivatives (e.g., polyoxyethylene 40 monostearate); and fatty acid mono- or diglycerides (e.g., caprylic acid diglyceride); they may be used alone or in combination. Emulsifier concentration ranges from about 0.01% to 2.5% (w/w). Auxiliary emulsifiers are added to improve the emulsifying capacity of primary emulsifiers. Examples of auxiliary emulsifiers are agar, pectin, and cholesterol. Some of the primary emulsifiers are also used as auxiliary emulsifiers.

Emollients or skin conditioning agents can be included in lotions to provide a softening or soothing effect on the skin. Emollients also help control the rate of evaporation and the tackiness of the lotion. Emollients are used in concentrations of 0.1%–10% (w/w). Suitable emollients include hydrocarbons, such as petrolatum and mineral oil, and fatty acid alcohols or their esters, such as myristyl alcohol, cetyl alcohol, stearyl alcohol, cetostearyl alcohol, glyceryl monostearate, glyceryl monooleate, isopropyl myristate, isopropyl palmitate, cholesterol, lanolin alcohols, and glycerin. Among the preceding examples, oleaginous hydrocarbons are widely used for occlusive properties. Fatty acids, fatty acid alcohols, or their esters are used for multifunctional roles, such as primary or auxiliary emulsifiers, emollients, and thickening agents. Thickening agents or viscosity enhancing agents in lotions aid in the attainment of the desired texture and spreadability. Thickeners from natural, semisynthetic, and synthetic sources can be used. Natural thickeners include acacia, tragacanth, carrageenan, clay, and magnesium aluminum silicate. One or more fatty acids, fatty acid alcohols, or their esters of the series $C_{14}-C_{20}$ may be used in combination to obtain a particular consistency of lotion. For example, in sufficient concentration, stearyl alcohol produces a firm consistency, which can be softened with cetyl alcohol. Suitable preservatives include phenoxyethanol, parabens, benzyl alcohol, chlorhexidine gluconate, imidurea, and hydantoin derivatives. Preservative concentrations range from 0.01% to 5% (w/w). Antifoaming and antiwhitening agents may be included in lotions to increase elegance and inhibit the formation of a white soapy appearance upon rubbing the lotion onto the skin. Antifoaming agents are used in the concentration range 0.2%–3% (w/w) of the total weight of lotions. Some examples include silicone fluid, dimethicone, and simethicone.

Typical antioxidants in lotion formulations are butylated hydroxytoluene, butylated hydroxy anisole, sulfite salts, sodium ascorbate, and propyl gallate. Optionally, chelating agents may be included in the continuous phase of lotion to inactivate metals during processing, thereby, increasing the formulation's stability. Suitable chelating agents include dipotassium ethylene diamine tetraacetate (EDTA), diethylenetriamine (DETA), and aminoethylethanolamine (AEEA). Chelating agents are used in the concentration range 0.25%–1% (w/w). Perfume agents may sometimes be included in lotions to impart a soothing olfactory sensation. Common perfume agents are cocoa butter and floral oil fragrances, such as rose oil, lilac, jasmine, wisteria, and apple blossom. Coloring agents improve the aesthetic appearance of lotions. Colorants suitable for lotions may be derived from water-soluble synthetic organic food additives (FD&C colors), water-insoluble lake dyes (e.g., aluminum salts of water-soluble dyes), and natural pigments (e.g., beta-carotene). Approximately 0.0075%–1% (w/w) of colorant is included in lotions. Common buffer salts are gluconate, lactate, acetate, oleate, citrate, phosphate, and/or carbonate salts, as well as triethanolamine or 2-amino-2-methyl-1-propanol. The liquid media used as the continuous phase in lotions are water, lower alcohols (e.g., ethanol, isopropyl alcohol), glycols (e.g., ethylene glycol and propylene glycol), glycerin, and mixtures thereof. Liquid medium ranges from about 50% to 95% (w/w) of the total weight of lotions.

10.4 General aspects of liquid dosage forms

In general, ease of swallowing, palatability, and convenience of administration constitute the advantages of liquid dosage forms. However, liquid dosage forms may deteriorate and lose potency more quickly than solid and semi-solid dosage forms if not designed and tested during product development studies. A testing protocol must consider not only physical and chemical but also biological properties of the dosage form. Table 10.7 summarizes general aspects, including physicochemical stability, antimicrobial stability, taste masking, and bioavailability considerations, that may be required to meet some of the target product quality features of liquid dosage forms.

10.4.1 Physicochemical stability

The stability of a drug substance may be the major criterion in determining the suitability of dosage forms. Drug substances undergo chemical and physical degradation, leading to loss of potency, production of toxic degradation products, and a decrease in bioavailability. These degradation reactions may result in substantial changes in the physical appearance of dosage forms (e.g., discoloration or precipitation). Different degradation pathways could be triggered by incompatibility between ingredients of the dosage form, incompatibility with primary packaging material (container and closure), vehicles, and storage conditions (temperature, humidity, light, and headspace).

Common chemical degradation reactions manifested in dosage forms include solvolysis, oxidation, photolysis, dehydration, and racemization. Drug substances with functional groups, such as esters (e.g., aspirin), lactones (e.g., spironolactone), amides (e.g., chloramphenicol acetate), lactams (e.g., penicillins), oximes, imides, and nitrogen mustards, are prone to hydrolysis. Oxidation is one of the most prominent degradation pathways for many drug substances. Mechanisms of oxidation reactions are complex and involve multiple pathways for initiation, propagation, branching, and termination steps. Many oxidation reactions are initiated by trace amounts of impurities, such as metal ions or free radicals. Oxidation reactions are manifested as changes in the appearance of the dosage form. Drug substances with functional groups, such as phenols, catechols, ethers, thiols, and carboxylic acids, are prone to oxidation. Photolytic reactions may be mediated by normal sunlight, which causes an increase in the energy of absorbed molecules sufficient to achieve activation. Photolysis is often associated with oxidation and is a common reaction in steroids. Racemic mixtures of drug substances would result in different absorption, distribution, metabolism, and elimination profiles. These racemization reactions can be catalyzed by either acid or base.

TABLE 10.7   Summary of general considerations for oral liquid dosage forms.

Dosage form	Taste-masking approaches	Stability considerations	Antimicrobial stability	Factors affecting bioavailability
Solutions	1. Sweeteners and flavors are added 2. In general, flavors that match colors are added	1. Oxidation: antioxidants and packing under inert gas or vacuum 2. Hydrolysis: buffers 3. Photolysis: amber-colored primary packages	Preservatives added to control bioburden	1. Solubility and permeability of drugs 2. Inclusion of permeability affecting excipients
Mouthwashes, gargles, and elixirs	1. Sweeteners and flavor adjuncts added to mask the unpleasant tastes 2. Flavor adjuncts augment taste-masking properties of conventional flavors	1. Vapourization of volatile ingredients: store in cool place and tight packaging containers 2. Chemical degradations (oxidation, hydrolysis, and photolysis): as listed under solutions	1. Alcohol components of the formulation are self-preservative 2. Additional preservatives may be added	na[c]
Syrups	1. Syrup vehicle acts as sweetener 2. Artificial sweetener may be added to nonsugar vehicles	1. Inversion of sugars: thermal control and processing under nonthermal mixing conditions 2. Crystallization of ingredients: store in controlled thermal conditions	1. High concentration of solids impede growth of microbes 2. Preservatives may also be included	1. Solubility and permeability of drugs 2. Palatability 3. Viscosity
Suspensions[a]	1. Sweeteners are added to mask the taste of actives and high concentration inactive solids 2. Flavors added to reduce cloying taste of inorganic solids	1. Flocculation 2. Sedimentation 3. Caking	Preservatives added to 1. Protect stabilizers, suspending agents, and thickening agents 2. Control bioburden	1. Particle size 2. Particle size distribution 3. Particle shape 4. Viscosity
Emulsions[b]	1. Nonreducing sugars (sucrose, trehalose) as sweeteners 2. Lecithins and fruit flavors are added	1. Flocculation 2. Creaming 3. Coalescence 4. Cracking	Preservatives added to 1. Protect oil phase, stabilizer/emulsifier, and thickening agents 2. Control bioburden	1. Droplet size 2. Oil phase content 3. Emulsification 4. Viscosity

[a]*Similar particle size distribution, good wetting properties of solids, minimal density difference between the suspended drug particles and vehicle, and viscosity form a stable suspension formulation.*
[b]*Similar droplet size distribution, low oil phase content, good emulsification with GI fluids, viscous, and wide range of pH stability impart stability to emulsions.*
[c]*na, not applicable (localized actions).*

Physical degradation reactions of drug substances in solutions include polymorphic transition, vaporization of actives or vehicles, and adsorption to containers. Due to differences in physicochemical characteristics, polymorphs exhibit different bioavailability profiles. Volatile actives and inactives (e.g., flavors) with high vapor pressures at room temperature permeate through the container and result in the loss of desirable characteristics of drug products. Similar to solutions, drug molecules in dispersed systems exhibit similar physical degradation processes. For more details on the degradation of drug substances in disperse systems, readers are suggested to refer to the literature [67]. Suspensions manifest agglomeration of particles, sedimentation, and caking phenomena, while emulsions exhibit flocculation, creaming, and coalescence.

During drug product development studies, experimental designs include a thorough study of factors affecting the stability of drugs. These study conditions include pH, humidity, temperature, container, and compatibility studies with potential inactive ingredients (buffers, surfactants, complexing agents, antioxidants) to be included in formulations. International Conference on Harmonization (ICH) guidelines (Q1A(R)) provide guidance for conducting the stability testing of a drug substance or drug product under a variety of environmental factors, such as temperature, humidity, and light, and establish a retest period for the drug substance or a shelf-life period for the drug products.

10.4.2 Antimicrobial stability

The presence of microorganisms in nonsterile preparations may have the potential to reduce or even inactivate the therapeutic activity of drug products. Therefore, manufacturers need to ensure a low bioburden of finished dosage forms by implementing cGMP during manufacturing, storing, and distributing pharmaceutical preparations. Antimicrobial preservatives are added to nonsterile dosage forms to protect drug products from microbiological growth or microorganisms that may be introduced during or subsequent to the manufacturing process. In the case of sterile products packaged in multidose containers, antimicrobial agents are added to inhibit the growth of microorganisms that may be introduced during repeated withdrawal of doses.

The efficacy of antimicrobial agents varies with the physicochemical characteristics of the preservative, concentration, spectrum of activity against microbes, and temperature. Antimicrobial agents are toxic substances, and the concentration of preservatives shown to be effective in the final packaged product should be below a level that may be toxic to human beings. Antimicrobial preservative efficacy must be demonstrated in products packaged in multidose containers. In all cases, antimicrobial agents must not be used as a substitute for good manufacturing practices of sterile products. USP general chapter <51> enumerates criteria and methods for the determination of antimicrobial preservative effectiveness.

10.4.3 Bioavailability considerations

The definition of bioavailability focuses on processes by which active ingredients or moieties are released from an oral dosage form and moved to the site of action. From a pharmacokinetics perspective, bioavailability data provide an estimate of the relative fraction of an administered dose (e.g., oral solution or suspension) that is absorbed into systemic circulation when compared to bioavailability data for an intravenous dosage form. In addition, bioavailability studies provide information related to absorption, distribution, and elimination. Bioavailability data can also indirectly provide information about a drug substance's properties before entry into the systemic circulation, such as permeability, the influence of presystemic enzymes, and transporters (e.g., p-glycoprotein).

The absorption of drugs from liquid dosage forms is governed by various physicochemical properties (pH, solubility, permeability, stability, and absorption potential) of drug substances. Drug movement from an oral dosage form into blood circulation is a multistep process (i.e., disintegration, dissolution, permeation via GI membranes, and absorption into blood circulation). The slowest of these steps, termed as the rate-limiting step, will determine the rate and extent of drug absorption. Among oral dosage forms, the solution form should have the maximum bioavailability, but the drug substance may precipitate from the solution owing to changes in the pH of GI fluids.

For drugs in suspension, the rate-limiting step could be the disintegration of aggregates, if any; dissolution of fine particles into drug solution; and then absorption across GI membranes. Factors influencing the aggregation phenomenon of suspensions could be particle size, particle surface area, particle-size distribution, wetting properties of solid particles, the density difference between suspended particles and suspension medium, and viscosity of the suspending medium. The aggregation phenomenon could be a rate-limiting step for disintegration, which in turn could become a rate-limiting step for the dissolution of drug substances.

In comparison to solutions and suspensions, oral administration of emulsions is not popular due to the unpalatability of the oil phase and unpredictable drug release profiles. Emulsions also pose challenges to drug release due to complex solubility and partitioning phenomena. In oil-in-water emulsions, the drug may partition from the internal oil phase to its continuous aqueous phase or emulsify directly with GI fluids. This equilibrium is dependent on oil phase composition and partitioning equilibrium between the oil and aqueous phases, emulsification with GI fluids, and external emulsifier concentration. Emulsification with GI fluids may increase drug absorption across GI membranes.

The bioavailability of oral liquid dosage forms can be optimized by developing a systemic exposure profile. A profile can be obtained by measuring the concentration of drug substances and its active metabolites over time in samples collected from systemic circulation. Systemic exposure patterns reflect the release of a drug substance from the dosage form and a series of possible presystemic/systemic actions on the drug substance after its release from the dosage form. The systemic exposure profiles of clinical trial batches can be used as a benchmark for subsequent formulation changes and can be useful as a reference for future bioequivalence studies.

10.4.4 Taste masking

Taste is one of the most important parameters governing patient compliance. Oral administration of bitter drugs with an acceptable degree of palatability is a key issue for healthcare providers, especially for pediatric patients. Several oral liquid dosage forms and bulking agents have unpleasant and bitter-tasting components. In particular, oral liquid dosage forms have the drug in solubilized form, which may further enhance the unpleasant taste of drug substances. Improved palatability in these products has prompted the development of numerous palatable formulations. Inactive excipients available for taste-making include aromatic flavors, sweeteners, amino acids, ion-exchange resins, gelatin, gelatinized starch, lecithin, surfactants, salts, and polymers. Taste masking is achieved using techniques such as polymer coating, conventional granulation, spray congealing, cyclodextrin complexation, freeze-drying process, and emulsification (e.g., multiple emulsions).

Taste masking with flavors, sweeteners, and amino acids is the most straightforward approach, especially in the case of pediatric liquid formulations. The flavor adjuncts may augment the taste-masking properties of conventional flavors. For example, the unpleasant taste of mouthwashes containing medicinal and bitter-tasting substances, such as eucalyptus oil, can be masked by adding flavor adjuncts (e.g., fenchone, borneol, or isoborneol), which suppress unpleasant organoleptic sensations of volatile oils. Clove oil has been found to mask the bitter taste of a number of drugs, particularly analgesics, expectorants, antitussives, and decongestants.

For suspensions, taste-masking agents are added to mask the bitterness of the solubilized fraction of drug substances and other unpleasant sensations of inactive ingredients. Several of the sweeteners used in oral suspensions are ionic and have the potential to interact with other components of suspensions. Some of the sweeteners in suspensions include acesulfame, aspartame, sodium cyclamate, dextrose, fructose, galactose, sorbitol, xylitol, sucrose, and trehalose. Oral suspensions produce a cloying sensation in the mouth due to high levels of inorganic excipients. Flavors reduce the cloying taste and improve the palatability of oral suspensions. One problem with flavors in oral suspensions is adsorption onto finely divided suspending agents, thus reducing their effectiveness. Flavor preferences vary with age, but citrus flavors are acceptable to most age groups.

Coating with hydrophilic polymers is one of the standard methods to achieve taste masking. The polymeric coating acts as a physical barrier to drug particles, thereby minimizing interaction between the drug substance and taste buds. A specialized technique (i.e., microemulsification) has been used for the taste masking of powders and liquid suspensions. Ion-exchange resins (IERs) are another class of polymers (high molecular-weight polymers with cationic and anionic functional groups) used in liquid suspensions. The most widely used resin in liquid dosage forms is a copolymer of styrene and divinylbenzene. Quinolones and their derivatives are formulated using ion exchange resins, such as methacrylic acid polymer crosslinked with divinylbenzene as a carrier. The formation of the quinolone-resin complex (resinate) eliminates the extreme bitterness of quinolones to make liquid orals palatable.

10.4.5 Over-the-counter agents

Drugs that do not require a physician's prescription and are bought off the shelf in stores are termed as over-the-counter (OTC) medications. The FDA regulates all OTC medications through OTC monographs. Products conforming to the monographs may be marketed without further FDA clearance, while those that do not conform must undergo review and approval through the new drug approval system. Due to convenience and cost-effectiveness, many patients prefer OTC medications to avoid physician's appointments. As OTC treatment options can be overwhelming, it is important that physicians, manufacturers, and regulatory agencies provide appropriate information about treatment regimens and potential drug interactions, which enable patients to select the correct medication and its dose. Some of the important considerations for OTC medication for consumers include

- Always follow the printed directions and warnings. It is essential to talk to your physician before starting a new OTC drug. Administration procedures should be strictly followed. For example, nasal sprays should be administered through the nasal route.
- Check the expiration date before administration.
- Women should consult their physicians before taking OTC medication while pregnant or breastfeeding. Any medicine may have a different effect on children. People who are in these age groups should take special care when taking OTC products.

OTC medications comprise solids, semisolids, and liquid dosage forms. Liquid dosage forms administered for otic, ophthalmic, dental, cough, allergic rhinitis, diarrhea, and heartburn include solutions, syrups, elixirs, enemas, douches, sprays, lotions, and suspensions. As per FDA guidance, orally administered liquid products should be provided with appropriate devices marked with calibrated liquid measurement units. These markings should be clearly visible when the liquid product is added to the device to avoid dosing errors. Table 10.8 lists some of the examples of OTC medications administered for different medical conditions.

TABLE 10.8 List of over-the-counter (OTC) medications [4].

Therapeutic class	Medical use	Dosage form	Marketed products
Otic agents			
Earwax-softening agents	Removes excess cerumen	Solution	Carbamide peroxide, 6.5% (Murine, Debrox), hydrogen peroxide, olive oil, mineral oil, and docusate sodium
Water-clog removal solutions	Avoids otitis owing to tissue maceration	Solution	95% isopropyl alcohol and 5% anhydrous glycerin
Dental agents			
Dental irrigation	Cleans gum and dental infection areas	Solution	Interplak Water Jet, Hydro-Pik, and Waterpik
Mouthwash	Debris removal	Solution	Biotene, Sensodyne, Rembrandt Natural
	Anti-plaque removal	Solution	Cepacol, Scope, Oral-B rinse, Crest Pro-Health rinse, Colgate PerioGard, Fluorigard
	Gingivitis treatments	Solution	Listerine, 1.5% peroxide solution
Artificial saliva	Relieves xerostomia (dry mouth)	Solution	Moi-Stir and Xero-Lube
Wound-cleansing agents	Cleans oral wounds	Solution	Carbamide peroxide, 10%—15%; hydrogen peroxide, 3%
Cosmetic whitener	Teeth whitener	Solution	Carbamide peroxide, 10% (Gly-Oxide)
Ophthalmic agents			
Artificial tears	Relieves dry eye	Solution	Advanced Eye Relief, Bion tears, Murine tears, Viva-Drops
Antihistamines	Relieves itching from allergic conjunctivitis	Solution	Zaditor
Vasoconstrictor and antihistamines	Allergic conjunctivitis	Solution	Naphcon A, Opcon A, Visine-A
Contact lens solution	Maintains moisture for contact between contact lenses and eyes	Solution	Opti-Free, Opti-Free Express
Dermatological agents			
Retinoids	Acne	Solution	Differin, Retin-A
Antibiotics	Acne	Solution	Clindamycin, Erythromycin
Others	Acne	Lotion	Sulfacetamide (Klaron)
Antihistamines	Relieves itching from contact dermatitis	Spray solution	Benadryl
Inorganic salts	Relieves itching	Solution	Domeboro
Corticosteroids	Relieves eczema	Lotion	Cortizone

Continued

TABLE 10.8 List of over-the-counter (OTC) medications [4].—cont'd

Therapeutic class	Medical use	Dosage form	Marketed products
Analgesics, antipyretics, and decongestants			
Oxymetazoline	Relieves nasal discomfort caused by cold, allergies, and hay fever	Spray solution	Afrin
Naphazoline HCl	Nasal decongestion	Spray solution	Privine
Xylometazoline	Nasal decongestion	Spray solution	Otrivin
Phenylephrine	Nasal decongestion	Spray solution	Neo-Synephrine
Local anesthetics	Oral decongestant (relieves sore throat)	Spray solution	Chloraseptic, Cepacol
Gastrointestinal agents			
Saline laxative	Relieves constipation	Solution	Fleet Phospho-Soda
Osmotic laxative (glycerin, lactulose)	Relieves constipation	Solution, syrup	Fleet Babylax, Chronulac Syrup
Emollient laxative (docusate salts)	Relieves constipation	Solution, syrup	Colace, Kaopectate Suspension
Antidiarrheal agents	Relieves upset stomach	Suspension	Pepto-Bismol
Others			
Astringents	Lessens mucous secretions and protects underlying tissue	Solution	Witch hazel
Antacids	Relieves heartburn and acid indigestion	Suspension	Mylanta

10.5 Manufacturing processes and conditions

As per good manufacturing practice (GMP) requirements, the manufacturing of solutions includes the procurement of raw materials, compounding, filling, and packing [68]. Each stage of the process is critical in ensuring the safety and stability of dosage forms. In general, raw materials, semifinished drug products (bulk solutions), and finished drug products are handled in batches. Batch management of production simplifies the process and makes it easier to control the status of transformation between starting materials and final products. For scale-up, it is necessary to divide the process into stages, batches, and unit operations. These unit operations are coordinated together in the manufacturing of final dosage forms.

10.5.1 Solutions

Flow properties of liquids rarely vary due to their constant density at a constant temperature. Solutions are formulated on a weight basis (gravimetric) to measure the final volume by weight before filling and packaging [69]. The importance of selecting the gravimetric method instead of the volumetric method to measure liquids is illustrated by the volume contraction of water–ethanol liquid mixtures. The National Formulary diluted alcohol is a typical example of volume contraction of liquid mixtures [70]. This solution is prepared by mixing equal volumes of alcohol and purified water (USP). The final volume of this solution is about 3% less than the sum of the individual volumes because of contraction during mixing.

Temperature control during compounding is important because heat supports mixing and filling operations. Uncontrolled thermal operations may cause chemical and physical instabilities, such as potency loss of drugs in solutions, oxidation of components, and activation of microbiological growth after degradation of preservatives. Oxidation-prone materials are protected from oxygen by methods such as nitrogen purging through solution stored in sealed tanks or overlaying the headspace of tanks with a nitrogen atmosphere.

The low-solubility drugs or preservatives in the "dead leg" at the bottom of the tank result in a loss of potency [69]. When there is inadequate solubility of a drug in the chosen vehicle, the dose will not contain the correct amount of the drug substance. Therefore, processing parameters should be optimized to obtain a uniform and accurate dosage form. Whenever possible, ingredients should be added together, and an impeller mixer should often be located near the bottom of the vessel for an efficient mixing process. The mixing of high-viscosity materials requires higher velocity gradients in the mixing zone than in regular mixing operations. During the filling and sampling process, constant mixing of the bulk solution to ensure solution homogeneity is indispensable to ensure an acceptable quality level for finished products.

The preparation of sterile products requires a number of manufacturing processes and classified environments intended to control bioburden and reduce particle levels. All these activities are conducted in controlled environments and are subject to qualification. Materials and components must be transferred from a warehouse environment into a classified area. Material containers are disinfected and passed through airlocks into different zones of operation within the aseptic area. Raw materials may be weighed in ISO 7 areas, while sterile ingredients are opened only in aseptic environments. The majority of parenteral formulations are solutions that require tanks, stirrers, filtration-related equipment and accessories, transfer tubings, washing accessories for containers, and closures. Process equipment and accessories are subjected to washing/rinsing to remove particles and reduce bioburden and endotoxin levels. Following cleaning, items for sterilization are dried, wrapped, and staged for steam sterilization. Washed containers are placed in trays or boxes for depyrogenation in ovens or tunnels. It is a common practice to protect all washed items with ISO 5 air, from completion of washing through wrapping and placing into a sterilizer.

The scale of manufacturing varies from more than 5000 L (LVPs) down to less than 50 mL (e.g., for radiopharmaceuticals). The majority of the equipment is composed of 300-grade stainless steel lined with tantalum or glass. The vessels can be equipped with an external jacket for controlling thermal operations. Compounded formulations are subjected to sterilization procedures depending on the stability requirements of formulation ingredients. The USP recognizes six methods of sterilization: (1) steam sterilization, (2) dry heat sterilization, (3) gas sterilization, (4) sterilization by ionizing radiation, (5) sterilization by filtration, and (6) aseptic processing. Sterile product holding and filling operations are generally conducted in ISO 5 areas. The holding vessels are often steam sterilized along with product transfer tubings before use. A number of times, the filling is performed from the compounding vessel using in-line filtration, eliminating the intermediate vessel. When this approach is used, a small moist heat-sterilized surge tank or reservoir tank may be required for pressure-assisted filling. An inert gas (nitrogen/argon) is overlaid into the headspace of the container or purged into an empty container to protect oxygen-sensitive formulations.

10.5.2 Suspensions

Pharmaceutical suspensions have a characteristic particle-size distribution, which is dependent on mean particle size, particle size distribution, drug crystal habit, dissolution characteristics, and temperature. Particle size reduction can be accomplished by using a ball mill, jet mill, or hammer mill. Ball milling is used at the preformulation stage to reduce the particle size of small amounts of a drug substance through a combined process of impact and attrition. Ball-milled micronized particles are typically less than 10 µM in diameter. The efficiency of the milling process is affected by the rotation speed, the number of balls, mill size, wet or dry milling, amount of powder, and milling time. On a large scale, the hammer mill is preferable. The powder is bled into the mill house via the hopper, and rotating hammers impact the powder. The minimum particle size is about 50 µM. Heavy-duty hammer mills may give 20 µM-size particles. For particles less than 10 µM, micronizers are preferred [12].

For injectable nanosuspensions, particles in the size range of 0.1—5 µM are required to avoid thrombophlebitis. A popular approach producing nanosuspensions is a combination of micronization and high-pressure homogenization [71]. The drug powder can be micronized using a jet mill or colloid mill and dispersed in a surfactant-added buffer solution. The micronized drug suspension (<25 µM) is passed through a homogenizer. High-pressure homogenizers are available with different capacities ranging from 40 mL (lab scale) to a few thousand liters (large-scale production). The drug suspension is subjected to cavitation and high-shear forces in the homogenization gap during the homogenization process to achieve nano-size. Both homogenizer pressure and the number of homogenization cycles play a critical role in the reduction of the particle size of hard drug substances. A high-pressure homogenizer can handle pressures ranging from 1,000 to 20,000 pounds per square inch (psi). Typically, multiple cycles are required to achieve the desired particle size. If nanosuspensions are intended for oral administration, two homogenization cycles often are necessary to obtain a product of sufficient quality for oral administration. If nanosuspensions are intended for the parenteral route, 5—10 homogenization cycles are anticipated to obtain a fine particle size.

Sterile suspensions need to be sterile, which can be accomplished by approaches such as termination sterilization (autoclaving, sterile filtration, and gamma irradiation) of finished products or aseptic processing [12,72]. In a number of cases, termination sterilization procedures are not possible due to drug chemical instability, surfactant aggregation (e.g., autoclaving), and physical incompatibility (e.g., sterile filtration) of the suspension. Along with sterilization validation concerns, gamma irradiation may generate impurities. Therefore, the aseptic processing of suspensions is of high importance. In some cases, a combination of one of the terminal sterilization procedures and aseptic processing is employed to produce a sterile suspension. For example, brinzolamide (Azopt) suspension preparation involves autoclaving and aseptic processing. A milling slurry comprising brinzolamide (active ingredient), milling beads, and surfactant is autoclaved, followed by ball milling in aseptic conditions to obtain the desired particle size range. Filling, capping, and sealing operations are carried out in ISO 5 rooms to obtain a sterile suspension.

10.5.3 Emulsions

Emulsions may be prepared by using different methods, depending on the nature of the emulsion components and instrumentation available for use. On a small scale, as in the laboratory or pharmacy, emulsions may be prepared using equipment such as a porcelain mortar and pestle, mechanical blenders, and homogenizers. In small-scale extemporaneous preparation of emulsions, four methods may be used: the (1) continental, or dry gum, method; (2) English, or wet gum, method; (3) in situ soap method; and (4) mechanical method. The dry gum method is also called the "4:2:1" method because, for every four parts (volumes) of oil, two parts of water and one part of gum are added to prepare the primary emulsion. About 1 min of trituration is required to produce a creamy white primary emulsion, during which the oil phase is converted into oil droplets, producing a cracking sound. In the wet gum method, the proportions of oil, water, and emulsifier are the same (4:2:1), but the order and techniques of mixing are different. Emulsifier (one part) is triturated with two parts water to form a viscous mass; then four parts of oil are added slowly in portions while triturating. After all the oil is added, the mixture is triturated for several minutes to form the primary emulsion.

On a large scale, injectable and ophthalmic emulsions are manufactured using the mechanical method. Water- and oil-soluble ingredients are dissolved in the aqueous and oil phases, respectively. With the aid of cosolvents, water-insoluble drugs can be incorporated into the oil phase of emulsions prior to emulsification (de novo method) or added to prepared emulsions (extemporaneous addition). For drugs that are highly oil-soluble, the de novo method is popular. Alternatively, oil-soluble drugs that are liquid at room temperatures, such as halothane and propofol, can be extemporaneously added to preformed emulsions in which the drug substance preferentially partitions into the oil phase. Another approach involves dissolving drugs and phospholipids in organic solvents, followed by evaporation of the organic phase under a vacuum. Emulsifiers, such as lecithins, can be dispersed in the oil or aqueous phase. However, solubilizing in the aqueous phase is preferred due to ease of dispersion, while heating may be required for dispersing in the oil phase. The oil phase is added to the aqueous phase under controlled temperature and agitation (using high-shear mixers) to form a homogeneous coarse emulsion with droplet size in the range of 20–30 µM. The coarse emulsion is then homogenized using a high-shear homogenizer or microfluidizer at optimized pressure, temperature, and cycles to reduce droplet size. The pH of the fine emulsion can be adjusted to a designated value and filtered through 1–5 µM filters. Sterilization of emulsions can be achieved by terminal heat sterilization (e.g., steam sterilization) or aseptic filtration. For heat-labile emulsions, sterile filtration can be used. However, sterile filtration requires droplet (>95% of droplet population) diameters less than 0.2 µM. Alternatively, aseptic processing may be adopted for heat-labile emulsions whose droplet diameters are greater than 0.2 µM.

Ophthalmic emulsions are produced on a large scale in aseptic conditions. Due to the heat-labile and viscous nature of ophthalmic emulsions, heat sterilization and sterile filtration methods may not be employed to obtain a sterile formulation. Drugs incorporating the oil and aqueous phases (emulsifiers and tonicity-adjusting agents) are subjected to aseptic homogenization (with or without heating aid) to produce a fine emulsion. The fine emulsion is then subjected to pH adjustment using sodium hydroxide. The final emulsion can be clarified before filling. Ophthalmic emulsions whose mean droplet diameters are less than 0.2 µM and whose viscosity is close to water (~1 cP) can be subjected to sterile filtration.

Lotions are manufactured using homogenizers. The oil phase, consisting of preservatives, emulsifiers, auxiliary emulsifiers, antioxidants, emollients, antifoaming agents, and fatty acid-derived thickeners, is maintained at a temperature of 65°C–70°C. Similarly, water-soluble ingredients, such as preservatives, buffers, antioxidants, and thickeners, are dissolved in the aqueous phase and maintained at a temperature of 65°C–70°C. The oil phase is added to the aqueous phase slowly and homogenized until the desired droplet-size distribution and consistency are obtained. Drug suspension is added during homogenization. The product is cooled under slow stirring, and water is adjusted as necessary.

10.6 Packaging

Pharmaceutical packaging is a combination of components necessary to contain, preserve, protect, and deliver safe and efficacious drug products. From the contemporary definition, primary packaging is composed of packaging components and subcomponents that come into contact with the product or those that may have a direct effect on product shelf-life. Typical primary packaging components are containers (e.g., ampoules, vials, bottles), closures (e.g., screw caps, stoppers), closure liners, stoppers overseas, container inner seals, administration ports (e.g., on large-volume parenterals), overwraps, and administration accessories. The outer packaging components are referred to as secondary and tertiary packaging including outer labels, wrappers, cartons, corrugated shipments, and pallets. cGMP regulations titled "Drug Product Containers and Closures" provide the statements most relevant to packaging [73].

Each component must have adequate prior testing to ensure the appropriateness of the chosen packaging system. Subsequently, shelf-life tests (to ensure expiration date) and specifications (to ensure the quality of components) are required for the packaging systems in which the product will be marketed. The package evaluation is performed for the characterization of the packaging material and is performed together with the drug product system. Characterization procedures include physicochemical and biological procedures to evaluate glass and plastic bottles, metal closures, elastomeric closures, and syringe components. For example, USP tests (<661> for containers; <381> for elastomeric closures for injections; <87> for biological reactivity *in vitro*, and <88> for biological reactivity *in vivo*) are generally required for containers and closures to address protection. Testing for properties other than those described in USP (e.g., gas transmission) may also be necessary. A comprehensive study is appropriate for drug products, such as injection, inhalation, and ophthalmics. This involves leachable and extractable studies on packaging components to determine the migration of chemical species into the dosage form from container and closure and toxicological evaluation of substances extracted to determine the safety level of exposure.

The evaluation studies include the effect of packaging components on finished products during accelerated, intermediate, and long-term stability studies. Stability study protocols also include photo-stability studies. Light can act as a catalyst for oxidation reactions, transferring its energy (photons) to drug molecules, making the latter more reactive. Most photo-degradation reactions occur in UV (190–280 nm) and visible (320–380 nm) light ranges. As a precaution against the acceleration of oxidation, sensitive drug formulations are packaged in light-resistant containers (e.g., amber glass and aluminum foil wraps).

It is a common practice to store liquid dosage forms inverted and upright to assess the effect of long-term contact with the closure. Such studies provide detailed information on absorption or adsorption of the drug substance or degradation of the drug substance induced by a chemical entity leached from packaging material, reduction in the concentration of excipients, precipitation, pH changes, discoloration of the dosage form or packaging components, or increase in the brittleness/softening of packaging components. Package evaluation studies result in setting up specifications for each packaging component. The specifications serve as a guideline for the qualification of containers and closures.

10.6.1 Oral liquids

The primary packaging components for oral liquids (solutions, syrups, elixirs, emulsions, and suspensions) include pouches, cups, and bottles. Bottles are usually made of glass or plastic, often with a screw cap and liner, and possibly with a tamper-resistant seal. Glass offers the following advantages: they (1) are inert to most medicine, (2) are impervious to air and moisture, (3) can be amber-colored to protect light-sensitive medicine contents, and (4) provide ease of inspection of the contents. Disadvantages include the following: they (1) are fragile, (2) release alkali into container contents, and (3) is heavy, resulting in increased transportation costs. Plastics made of resin have been used as primary and secondary packaging materials. Bottles made of low-density polyethylene (LDPE), high-density polyethylene (HDPE), PVC, or polypropylene (PP) are used as primary packaging materials. Plastic bottles are available as plain or amber-colored bottles to protect photosensitive contents. Advantages of plastic packaging include these: they (1) release minimal particles into the container, (2) are flexible and lightweight for transportation, and (3) can be heat sealed and molded into various shapes.

Along with the container, it is essential to assess the interactions of closures with formulation components. Loss of moisture (leakage or permeation losses) is another important factor to be considered when a closure is applied to a container. Closures are made of aluminum, polypropylene, or high-density polyethylene. For the pediatric population, several designs of child-resistant containers are used for pharmaceutical packaging under the assumption that children cannot coordinate containers' opening. These designs include cap-bottle alignment systems, push-down-and-turn caps, and squeeze-and-turn caps. The closures in common use with dispensed medicines are the Snap-safe alignment and Clic-loc closures. Various tamper-evident closure designs are also available to avoid unlawful access to containers. These closures cannot be opened until the tamper-evident band connecting the cap to the skirt of the container is torn away.

10.6.2 Injectables and ophthalmics

Packaging parenteral and ophthalmic dosage forms presents a major challenge because package, product, and package-product interactions must all be more detailed than nonsterile liquid dosage forms. For each major type of parenteral product, the investigator should consider the effect of the drug manufacturing process on the integrity of packaging materials. For example, if the product is subjected to terminal sterilization, the effect of the sterilization method must be evaluated. Various packaging materials are available for parenteral containers; thus, the range of potential interactions has multiplied, requiring advanced analytical methods for characterizing interactions.

For parenterals, glass containers made by blowing and tubing methods are common packaging materials. Blown containers have a seam line running from the top finish to the bottom of the sidewall. The tubing container has smooth, seamless sidewalls and no bottom markings. Blown glass is used for making vials and bottles, while tubing glass is used for packaging forms such as ampoules, vials, and prefilled syringes. USP/NF has primarily classified the glass used for pharmaceutical packaging into four types based on the capacity of hydrolytic resistance to aqueous solutions: type I (highly resistant borosilicate glass), type II (treated soda-lime glass), type III (soda-lime glass), and type IV (general-purpose soda-lime glass). Because of the chemical differences in glass, it is important to consider these compositional factors when choosing containers. Although glass is considered to be an inert material, leaching and corrosion of glass surfaces in contact with water or buffered solutions are common phenomena. As a result, glass containers are surface-treated (e.g., ammonium sulfate) to avoid reactions with formulation compositions. These treatments enhance three things: the durability of glass during handling, resistance to chemical corrosion of filled products, and the lubricity of glass on production lines. Some of the treatments are temporary and removable before product filling. Advanced test methods are available to discriminate among glass types and find the best suitable glass for a particular application.

Injectable solutions, suspensions, and fine emulsions are packaged in type I glass containers. Siliconized glass containers may be used to prevent droplet-size growth (e.g., emulsions) or particle aggregation (e.g., suspensions). Lyophilized powders for reconstitution are packaged in type II glass containers. LDPE and HDPE are also widely used as packaging materials for small-volume and large-volume parenterals, such as plastic infusion bags (LDPE), vials (LDPE or HDPE), form-fill-seal containers (LDPE), plastic syringes (HDPE), and tubing for infusions (LDPE). Intralipid emulsions are supplied in PVC bags. However, it is advisable to observe any oiling out on the surface of the emulsion bag and discoloration of the emulsion formulation. With the exception of ampoules, all glass and plastic parenteral containers require a closure made of rubber elastomeric material. Typically, the stopper consists of ingredients such as an elastomer, vulcanizer, plasticizer, filler, emulsifier, and coloring agents. Teflon-coated stoppers may be used to prevent oxygen permeation and to soften on contact with the oil phase (e.g., emulsions). Stoppers used for lyophilization are designed to facilitate lyophilization (i.e., vacuum evaporation of solvents).

Ophthalmic drops (solutions and suspensions) are frequently packaged in multidose containers ranging from 4 to 60 mL. Ophthalmic drops are marketed in LDPE bottles with a dropper built into the neck (sometimes referred to as DROP-TAINER). The main advantages of DROP-TAINER and similar designs are ease of use, decreased contamination potential, low weight, and low costs. The patient removes the cap, turns the bottle upside down, and then squeezes gently to form a single drop that falls into the eye. The dispensing tip can deliver a single drop or a stream of fluid for irrigation. When the plastic bottle is squeezed, the solution or suspension is minimally exposed to airborne contaminants; thus, it will maintain very low to nonexistent microbial content as compared to glass bottles with a separate dropper assembly. The caps of primary packaging components are made of hard plastic materials, such as HDPE or polypropylene. The major disadvantage of plastic containers is the permeation of formulation components through the container. Volatile ingredients, such as preservatives (e.g., chlorobutanol and phenyl ethyl alcohol), can migrate into plastic and permeate through the walls of the container. In such cases, a safe and reasonable excess of the permeable component may be added to balance the loss over shelf-life. Another means of overcoming permeation effects is to employ a secondary package, such as a peel-apart blister or pouch composed of nonpermeable materials (e.g., aluminum foil or vinyl). The plastic bottles are also permeable to water and contribute to weight loss by water vapor transmission. The consequences of water vapor transmission must be taken into consideration during the analysis of components.

A few ophthalmic solution products use glass containers due to stability (e.g., oxidation) and permeation concerns of plastic packaging components. Powders for reconstitution also use glass containers due to heat-transfer characteristics necessary during lyophilization. Ophthalmic glass containers are usually made with type I glass materials and are sterilized by dry heat or steam. The dropper assembly is made of glass or plastic and is usually gas sterilized in a blister composed of a vinyl and Tyvek package. Large-volume intraocular solution (for irrigation) may be packaged in a glass or polyolefin (polyethylene and/or polypropylene) container. Some of the heat-labile and nonfilterable ophthalmic products use the blow-fill-seal process, whereas plastic containers are blow-molded, filled, and sealed in one continuous aseptic operation. The blow-fill-seal process is applied to packaging unit-dose ophthalmic products in the volume range of 0.3—1 mL or multidose products in the range of 5—15 mL.

10.6.3 Nasal, otic, and topicals

Otic solutions and suspensions are supplied in type II glass bottles with a dropper built into the neck. Droppers made of glass or plastic are used to pull out medication from the bottles. Nasal formulations are filled into bottles made of type II glass or plastic materials (e.g., HDPE), which are closed by attaching a spray pump, including a dip tube. The pump may be fixed by a screw closure, crimped on, or simply snapped onto the bottle. Safety clips are included in pump units to prevent accidental discharge of the spray. Due to convenience and cost-effectiveness, multidose dispensers are widely used for the administration of nasal formulations. Bottles made of hydrolytic glass types I and II are used for sterile nasal drops, while bottles made of plastic material are necessary because a bottle squeeze is needed to dispense spray solutions. Topical liquids, including solutions, suspensions, and lotions, are packaged in type III glass containers or HDPE plastic bottles.

10.7 Labeling

All the finished dosage forms are labeled to serve the following functions: (1) identify the contents of the container, (2) ensure patients have clear and concise information on how to use the medicine, and (3) satisfy legal requirements. The details that appear on the label of a finished dosage form include (1) the name of the preparation, strength, and form; (2) quantity; (3) instructions for use; (4) precautions on handling and usage of the product; (5) warning or advisory labels; (6) batch number or lot number; (7) storage conditions; (8) manufacturing and expiration date; and (9) manufacturer or distributor. In the case of extemporaneously dispensed medicines, identification information of patients for whom the medicine is dispensed, name and address of the pharmacy, and beyond use date (BUD) indicating the shortened shelf-life should be included.

In general, solutions are stored at the temperature range of 2°C—25°C. Photosensitive medications are usually labeled with the instruction "protect from light or store in tight and light-resistant containers." Oral suspensions are labeled with the instruction "shake well before use," as some sedimentation is expected. Shaking the bottle will redisperse contents and ensure an accurate dose. In addition, suspensions are labeled with instructions such as "store in a cool place" to slow down degradation reactions. The stability of suspensions is affected by extreme variations in temperature. Extemporaneously prepared and reconstituted suspensions will have a relatively short shelf-life (7—14 days). The manufacturer's packaging inserts literature for reconstituted products will provide recommended storage conditions. Intralipid emulsions are labeled with the instruction "should not be stored above 25°C/77°F to avoid creaming and breaking phenomena." Ophthalmic emulsions are stored in the temperature range of 15°C—25°C. If refrigerated products are frozen, they need to be discarded.

10.8 Quality assurance and quality control

10.8.1 Quality assurance

The terms *quality assurance* and *quality control* are sometimes used interchangeably, but quality assurance is a broader term that includes quality control, written operating procedures, personnel training, record keeping, facility design, and monitoring. The objective of quality assurance is to build quality into products, rather than relying on final product testing to identify defective products.

10.8.2 Quality control

The capacity of drug products to remain within specifications to ensure their identity, strength, quality, and purity is referred to as stable drug products. The manufacturing and storage conditions pose challenges to the stability of drug products, resulting in the degradation of drug substances and excipients. Therefore, it is important to assess the quality of products. Quality control testing is performed in two stages to evaluate the actual performance of final products against product and process specifications. The two stages include (1) in-process quality control and (2) final product quality control.

10.8.2.1 In-process quality control

In-process quality control involves monitoring critical variables during the manufacturing process to assess the quality of final products and give necessary instructions if any deviations are observed. The process manufacturing controls are established and documented by quality control and production personnel to ensure that a predictable amount of each cycle's output falls within the acceptable standard range. Common product characteristics that are evaluated in-process include the assay and degradation products' profile of drug substances, pH, and appearance. In-process controls during the production of sterile preparations may also include monitoring environmental conditions (especially concerning particulate and microbial contamination) and pyrogens (e.g., limulus amebocyte lysate, or LAL, test).

10.8.2.2 Finished products testing

In addition to in-process testing parameters, finished products require additional tests, such as antimicrobial preservative efficacy and particulate matter. Testing specifications change with drug formulation, intended use, and device characteristics. For example, drop size and plume geometry (spray pattern) are critical for ophthalmic and nasal products, respectively. Both drop size and spray pattern determine the dose delivered to respective tissues/organs; any changes in these respective parameters will likely result in a change of dose. The USP recommends sterility testing for all sterile products.

For suspensions and emulsions, parameters such as rheological properties, electrical properties, and particle-size distribution play a critical role. Suspensions are observed for color, air globules, and separation of phases. The color changes could result from oxidative degradation of active or inactive ingredients. Caution should be exercised for the presence of air bubbles during the sampling of suspensions because these bubbles may lower the assay of drug compounds and even produce erroneous particle-size distribution results. Photon correlation spectroscopy or dynamic laser diffraction particle-sizing measurements can be made to assess the particle-size distribution of suspensions. Any deviation in particle-size distribution from specifications may lead to the physical instability of suspensions. The quantitative procedures for particle-size distribution testing should be appropriately validated in terms of sensitivity and ability to detect shifts that may occur in size distribution. In case of technologies that cannot be validated, qualitative and semiquantitative methods (e.g., microscopy) for particle-size distribution can be used.

Electrophoretic mobility or zeta potential measurements of suspensions indicate changes in the adsorption or desorption of chemical species from the particle surface. During zeta potential measurements, the electric field strength is applied to obtain the electrophoretic mobility parameter, which is converted to zeta potential in millivolts (mV) using the Helmholtz—Smoluchowski equation. As a rule of thumb, suspensions with a zeta potential on either side of −30 mV and +30 mV are physically stable. Suspensions with a zeta potential close to the isoelectric point undergo pronounced aggregation [74].

The stability of a suspension is dependent on the sedimentation rate of the dispersed phase, which is dependent on the viscosity of the dispersion medium. The viscosity measurements can be made with the Brooke field viscometer. Sedimentation volume is also a good measure of the rate of settling of suspended particles in a dispersion medium. An increase in the sedimentation volume may indicate the formation of particle aggregates. Syringeability and pourability of suspensions also characterize the flow properties of suspensions. In the case of flocculated suspensions, syringeability may become difficult due to large floccule sizes. Pourability is performed to determine whether the final preparation is pourable.

Release studies of suspensions can be performed using type II or IV USP dissolution apparatus to determine the release rates of a drug substance. Release rates are modeled to describe the behavior of suspensions. According to the Nernst—Brunner and Levich modification of the Noyes—Whitney dissolution model, the rate of dissolution of nanosuspensions is described as Eq. (10.9) [75—77].

$$\frac{dX}{dt} = \left(\frac{DA(C_s - C)}{Vh} \right) \tag{10.9}$$

where dX/dt is the rate of dissolution, D is the diffusion coefficient, A is the particle surface area, h is the diffusion distance, Cs is the saturation solubility of the drug substance, C is the concentration of the drug substance in the surrounding liquid, and V is the volume of the dissolution medium. For a suspension consisting of monodisperse spherical particles, the rate of dissolution is given by the Hixon–Cromwell cube root Eq. (10.10) [77]:

$$\sqrt[3]{Mo} - \sqrt[3]{M} = kt \tag{10.10}$$

where Mo is the original mass of drug particles, M is the mass of drug particles at time t, and k is the dissolution rate constant.

Emulsions exhibit creaming, flocculation, and coalescence before phase separation becomes visible. The phase separation processes are dependent on electrical, rheological, and droplet-size distribution. The USP specifies light-scattering and light-obscuration methods for determining mean droplet diameter. On the other hand, for the determination of the number of fat globules comprising larger diameters of size $\geq 5\ \mu M$, the use of the light-obscuration or light-extinction method is recommended.

Any variation in droplet-size distribution, degree of flocculation, or phase separation results in viscosity changes. Flocculation of emulsions will increase viscosity during storage and is important for assessing stability and shelf-life. Since most emulsions are non-Newtonian, a cone-plate type viscometer can be used to determine viscosity changes. The surface charge and zeta potential of emulsified droplets can be a useful indicator of the stability of emulsions because electrostatic repulsion can contribute to the avoidance of flocculation and coalescence. A number of factors, such as pH, ionic strength, type and concentration of emulsifiers, and presence of electrolytes, can affect the zeta potential of emulsions.

Characterizing *in vitro* drug release from emulsions is a challenging task because of the submicron size of droplets and the difficulty in separating the dispersed and continuous phases. A number of experimental techniques, such as the dialysis bag method, diffusion cell method, and centrifugal ultrafiltration technique, have been investigated to measure drug release from colloidal emulsions [78]. However, caution should be exercised because the surface area of emulsion droplets available for the diffusion of drug substance from submicron emulsion droplets is considerably larger than the surface area of the dialysis membrane available for the diffusion of the drug substance. Drug released from oil droplets accumulates and leads to high concentration inside the dialysis bag, rather than maintaining equilibrium between drug release from oil droplets and drug diffusion across the dialysis membrane.

For emulsions, water washability tests can be performed to distinguish oil-in-water and water-in-oil emulsions. Water-in-oil emulsions are immiscible with water; therefore, they are not washable with water, occlusive, and greasy due to an external oil phase. Oil-in-water emulsions are washable with water, nonocclusive, and nongreasy due to an external water phase.

10.9 Regulatory considerations

The manufacture and sale of dosage forms are regulated by federal and state laws, as well as the USP. The USP provides specifications, test procedures, standards, and training programs. In addition to individual monographs, the USP and the FDA limit the dose administered to patient populations, the use of excipients, and the size of multi-dose containers. The chemistry, manufacturing, and controls (CMCs) guidance documents prepared by the FDA recommend the inclusion of information regarding drug product components, manufacturing processes, and associated controls, and labeling. The guidance only suggests approaches that are appropriate for submitting CMC-related regulatory information. Also, CMC recommendations may vary depending on specific drug products (e.g., sterility requirements for sterile drug products).

A new drug application or abbreviated new drug application should include a statement of the quantitative composition of the unit formula of the drug product and the names and amounts of active and inactive ingredients. The amounts are expressed in concentration (i.e., amount per unit volume or weight) and the amount per container. Similarly, a production batch formula representative of the one to be employed in the manufacture of the drug product is included. Any intended change in the formulation of the commercial product from that used in the submitted batches (e.g., critical clinical, biobatch, primary stability, production) is indicated in the CMC documentation.

10.9.1 Drug substance

Comprehensive characterization of the physical and chemical properties of the drug substance must be included in the CMC documentation. Appropriate acceptance criteria and routine control tests (i.e., release, stability, and retests) are adopted for evaluating key physicochemical properties of the drug substance. Any impurity found in the drug substance at a concentration of 0.10% or 1.0 mg (mg) per day intake (whichever is lower) relative to the drug substance should be identified. The justification of acceptance criteria for drug substance impurities should be based on toxicological considerations. For suspension formulations, drug substance specifications include controls for particle-size distribution, surface area, and drug crystal morphology.

10.9.2 Excipients

Depending on the route of administration and the sensitive nature of various patient populations, a thorough characterization of excipients used in drug products is considered to ensure safety and effectiveness. Critical excipients are those that can affect the quality, stability, and performance of drug products. The source of excipients is assessed, and materials supplied should meet appropriate acceptance criteria based on test results from a minimum of one batch used to prepare submitted batches of drug products (e.g., critical clinical, biobatch, primary stability, production). For noncompendial excipients, a drug master file is prepared by the excipients' manufacturer. The drug master file information includes analytical procedures, acceptance criteria, and a brief description of manufacturing controls. When a USP or NF monograph material is used, associated specifications may not always provide adequate assurance regarding the assay, quality, or purity of the material or its performance in drug products. In these cases, monograph specifications are supplemented with appropriate controls (e.g., particle-size distribution, crystal forms, amorphous content, foreign particulates) to ensure batch-to-batch reproducibility of the components.

10.9.3 Manufacturers

The name, street address, and, if available, registration number of each facility involved in the manufacture of a drug substance is listed, along with a statement of each manufacturer's specific operations and responsibilities. The same information is provided for each facility involved in the manufacturing, processing, packaging, controls, stability testing, or labeling of drug products, including all contractors (e.g., testing laboratories).

10.9.4 Manufacturing process and controls

A detailed description of drug product manufacturing, processing, and packaging procedures is included. A copy of the actual (executed) batch record containing process controls is submitted, as appropriate, for representative batches (e.g., critical clinical, biobatch, primary stability). A schematic diagram of the proposed production process, a list of process controls, and a master batch production and controls record also are submitted. The manufacturing directions include control procedures on process variables (mixing time, mixing speeds, and temperature) to reduce batch-batch variability of drug products. These controls are performed at specified production steps and can include assay, osmolarity, and pH.

10.9.5 Drug product description

Comprehensive and well-defined *in vitro* performance characteristics should be established before initiating critical clinical or bioequivalence studies. Appropriate, validated test procedures and corresponding acceptance criteria that are reflective of the test results for submitted batches (e.g., critical clinical, biobatch, primary stability, and production) are critical to define and control these characteristics.

10.9.6 Containers and closures

The composition and quality of materials used in the manufacture of containers and closures are carefully selected. For safety considerations, materials are chosen that minimize or eliminate leachables without compromising the integrity or performance of drug products. The identity and concentration of recurring leachables in drug products or placebo formulations (i.e., drug product formulation without drug substance) are determined through the end of the drug product's shelf-life. The following information is included in the application so that the applicant can ensure continued product quality with respect to the container closure system.

- Manufacturers of container, closure, and the assembled pump, if any
- Engineering drawings of container and closure
- Composition and quality of materials of container and closure and pump components
- Control extraction methods and data for elastomeric and plastic components
- Toxicological evaluation of extractable
- Acceptance criteria, test procedures, and analytical sampling plans
- Qualitative and quantitative extractable profiles from container and closures

10.9.7 Stability data

Stability studies provide a means for evaluating the physical and chemical stability of drug products at various storage conditions, including the compatibility of the formulation device and the performance of drug products. The application should contain a complete, detailed stability protocol; stability report and data; and information regarding the suitability of employed test procedures. The protocol includes drug product specifications and acceptance criteria, test time points, container storage orientations (upright and inverted, upright and horizontal), and test storage conditions (accelerated, intermediate, long-term, and photo-stability studies) for protective packaged products, semipermeable containers without protective packaging (e.g., ophthalmics), and refrigerated products.

10.9.8 Patient population

10.9.8.1 Pediatrics

In a continuing effort to improve the safety and efficacy of drugs in the pediatric population, the FDA has defined five subgroups of this population by age. Each subgroup has similar characteristics that are considered milestones in the growth and development of children. Accurate pediatric doses are determined by both weight and age. Age affects the capacity of physiological functions, such as drug absorption, distribution, metabolism, and elimination, resulting in differences in drug responses. Because of immature metabolic pathways, infants and children may have metabolic patterns different from those of adults.

When one is selecting excipients for drug products intended for use in the pediatric population, additional cautions must be taken. Several subgroups of the pediatric population have been identified as being susceptible to excipient reactions. Many of these reactions are related to the number of excipients found in the dosage form. Benzyl alcohol, propylene glycol, and polysorbates are associated with dose-related toxic reactions, which are of concern in infants because of immature hepatic and renal functions. Sucrose is a popular sweetener in oral liquid formulations. The sucrose content of oral liquids may cause significant problems (asthma, seizure control, recurrent infections) when these products are administered long-term in infants. Oral liquid preparations containing sucrose can pose a substantial carbohydrate load to children with juvenile diabetes. In another example, ethanol is employed as a solubilizer, preservative, and flavoring agent in pharmaceuticals. Young children have a limited ability to metabolize and detoxify ethanol. The American Academy of Pediatrics Committee on Drugs recommended that pharmaceutical formulations intended for use in children should not produce ethanol blood levels >25 mg/dL after a single dose. Another major problem in pediatrics is dosing errors in intravenous administration. Due to the unavailability of stock solutions for pediatric doses, errors in dilution have resulted in errors in administered doses.

Parents have to be educated about package insert instructions to improve compliance with prescribed dosing regimens for pediatric patients. The FDA issued guidelines recommending that pediatric safety and efficacy studies be completed before marketing a new drug [79] for use in children.

10.9.8.2 Geriatrics

Elderly patients constitute the largest segment of consumers of drug products. In older patients, the aging process contributes to a significantly larger interindividual variation in drug responses than is observed in younger populations. Aside from the alteration of pharmacokinetic and pharmacodynamic processes, elderly patients tend to suffer from a number of chronic conditions, which may result in complex dosing regimens. Geriatric individuals are advised to take liquid dosage forms to combat the decreased rate of drug absorption brought on by

GI-related issues (a increase in stomach pH and a decrease in gastric emptying rate). They may also require dose adjustment.

Liquid dosage forms may not be packaged in unit dosage forms and therefore, require the withdrawal of the required amount of medication from the container. Visual impairments and neurologic disorders may impair the accuracy of withdrawal of dosage, resulting in dosing errors. Errors in the dispensed amount of suspension medications may occur when a patient cannot see or disregards labeling instructions (e.g., "shake well before use"). This may result in either under- or overdosing. These errors may precipitate with concentrated solutions because small errors represent large dosing errors. The compliance issues can be mitigated to some extent by using alternative drug delivery systems or using packaging and labeling designs that enable accuracy in dosing administration.

10.10 Conclusions

Liquid dosage forms encompass numerous dosage forms for treating a variety of diseases. Special techniques are required to solubilize or disperse poorly soluble drugs. Drug-delivery technologies, such as micelles, suspensions, emulsions, and liposomes, have been developed to meet therapeutic challenges. These dosage forms pose formulation challenges to manufacturing scientists and extemporaneous compounding challenges to compounding pharmacists. A greater degree of understanding of formulation composition, processes, and regulatory guidance is essential for manufacturing stable liquid dosage forms.

Case studies

Case 10.1

The stability of a drug in a solid dosage form and the stability of the same drug in a solution dosage form of the same strength were compared. Stability data at room temperature revealed that the drug in solution degrades much faster than in the solid dosage form. How can one explain this fact? If the same drug solution is kept in a refrigerator, the degradation is shown to be slower as compared to keeping it at room temperature.

Approach: Chemical degradations are due to collision between two reactants to give products. The collision theory shows that the rate of a chemical reaction depends on the rate of collision between reactant molecules [80]. In a solid state, the rate of collision between reactants is much slower as compared to the solution. This explains that the rate of degradation in a solid is much slower as compared to the same drug in solution.

The rate of a reaction increases about 2—3-fold for every 10°C rise in temperature. Since the temperature difference between a refrigerator (2°C—8°C) and room temperature (23°C—25°C) is at least 20°C, one can expect a 4—6 fold increase or decrease in the rate of degradation depending on the storage condition. It is one of the reasons that refrigerated products have a better shelf-life.

Case 10.2

The bioavailability of griseofulvin from three different oral dosage forms was compared and shown in Fig. 10.7. Explain why the emulsion dosage form has a larger area under the curve (AUC) than the other dosage forms?

Approach: The same dose of the drug in corn oil emulsion showed the highest AUC as compared to the suspensions. High bioavailability of griseofulvin from emulsion dosage form could be due to greater partitioning of the hydrophobic oil phase containing griseofulvin and higher surfactant content.

Case 10.3

Clopidogrel is an antithrombotic drug with low aqueous solubility and poor chemical stability. Clopidogrel is indicated for a suspected coronary event. Oral clopidogrel tablets have poor bioavailability and delayed onset of action, thus not ideal for administration in an emergency setting. Poor stability of the molecule restricts the use of the majority of excipients used for solubility enhancement approaches. As a pharmacist, what formulation would you suggest for this drug?

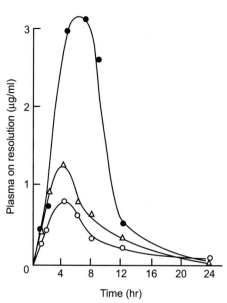

FIGURE 10.7 Administration of griseofulvin in different dosage forms (30 mg/kg of micronized griseofulvin in rats). (o) Aqueous suspension; (Δ), corn oil suspension; and (●), corn-oil-in-water emulsion containing suspended griseofulvin. *Adapted with permission from ref. [81].*

Approach: The barriers to developing clopidogrel's fast-acting liquid formulations are its unfavorable properties, low water solubility, physical form, and poor chemical stability. Clopidogrel is a weak base with a pKa of 4.5, and it is practically insoluble at neutral pH. Its bisulfate salt form is soluble at low pH but unsuitable for injection. Clopidogrel is a semisolid, viscous, oily substance, thus not suitable for storage, dispensing, and processing. Further, the free-base form is chemically unstable and undergoes hydrolysis, oxidation, and chiral conversion in liquid formulations. An adequate method for making clopidogrel injection formulation is its oil-in-water nano-emulsion formulation. Nano-emulsions are advantageous formulations for poorly water-soluble drugs intended to be administered via injection. Nanoemulsions have acceptable chemical and physical stability and require a low quantity of surfactants, significantly reducing the risk of injection site pain. Although the free base is not very soluble at plasma pH, when it is incorporated into the oil phase of the nano-emulsion, the drug becomes significantly more soluble and is immediately available for pharmacological activity following injection.

Case 10.4

Anna is a 5-year-old girl who weighs 30 pounds and was prescribed clindamycin 30 mg/kg/day, taken three times per day for 5 days for an acute otitis media infection.

Her prescription says "clindamycin oral solution 2.5 mL po tid" with food. She was dispensed a reconstituted 100-mL bottle of clindamycin 75 mg/mL oral suspension. Instructions on the bottle indicate to keep the clindamycin suspension at room temperature (i.e., do not refrigerate) and discard it after 14 days. Due to the bad taste of the medication, an additional grape flavor was added. After 5 days, Anna's symptoms of otitis media were not fully resolved because she only took the dose once as it tasted terrible and caused Anna to have an upset stomach. Further, the clindamycin bottle was inadvertently kept in the refrigerator for a few hours on the fourth day of treatment. As a pharmacist, how will you improve the outcomes of the treatment?

Approach: Oral liquid drugs offer greater dosing flexibility and are simpler for children to consume since they are easier to swallow. Palatability may be enhanced by adding sweetener (e.g., sucrose) and more robust flavors (e.g., chocolate). Dispensing oral liquid medications with a higher concentration will necessitate lower dose volumes that can be tolerated better. Providing medication syringes for dose measurements instead of household spoons, simplifying the frequency (e.g., once-daily dosing, if possible), minimizing incorrect handling, and discussing educational materials with the parents can all help improve adherence and decrease administration errors in pediatric patients.

Case 10.5

Nebulized amoxicillin and the clavulanic acid formulation were prescribed for a cystic fibrosis patient to prevent new lung infections, exacerbations or to reduce the strength of long-term infection. However, after a set amount of time since the start of the therapy, the patient's condition appeared to have worsened due to a lung infection. What are the likely causes of these effects, and how may they be resolved?

Approach: Certain gram-negative bacteria such as *Pseudomonas aeruginosa* and *Burkholderia cepacia* are well-known contaminants in liquid formulations. These microorganisms typically form biofilms that cause lung infection and exaggerate the symptoms of cystic fibrosis. Pharmacies must employ an aseptic approach to produce a low microorganism-contaminated formulation. Microbes not only cause patient infection but can modify chemical, physical, and organoleptic qualities of formulations' active drugs. Furthermore, to ensure the shelf life of multiple dosage formulations, specified preservative levels must be present and effective. The selection of the preservative system is based on different considerations, such as the site of use, interactions, spectrum, stability, toxicity, cost, taste, odor, solubility, pH, and comfort. Alcohols, acids, esters, and quaternary ammonium compounds are commonly used preservatives in pharmaceutical formulations.

Critical reflections and practice applications

Liquid dosage forms are an indispensable component of pharmaceutical preparations that are intended to deliver the maximum therapeutic response in patients with difficulties swallowing solid dosage forms and provide immediate therapeutic benefits. Essential considerations for using them in clinical pharmacy settings are outlined below.

i. Antimicrobial preservatives may not be used in small-volume injectables for single-dose administration, but they are frequently used in multidose vials to maintain sterility throughout multiple uses.

ii. For physical and chemical stability, the pharmacist should select a container that must neither physically or chemically interact with the liquid dosage forms to affect its strength, quality, or purity.

iii. Formulations containing light-sensitive drugs should be dispensed in light-resistant containers.

iv. Because these products are more likely to be misdosed, pharmacists may need to provide instructions, warnings, and precautions.

v. In oral solutions, unpalatable tastes are difficult to swallow; pharmacists may use taste masking methods to dispense formulations.

vi. A careful selection of flavoring agents is needed for the emulsion formulations. Flavors may denature or separate upon storage because they partition into the oil base and causes the emulsion to separate.

References

[1] G.L. Amidon, H. Lennernas, V.P. Shah, J.R. Crison, A theoretical basis for a biopharmaceutic drug classification: the correlation of *in vitro* drug product dissolution and *in vivo* bioavailability, Pharm. Res. (N. Y.) 12 (1995) 413—420.

[2] A. Dahan, J.M. Miller, G.L. Amidon, Prediction of solubility and permeability class membership: provisional BCS classification of the world's top oral drugs, AAPS J. 11 (2009) 740—746.

[3] M. Martinez, G.L. Amidon, A mechanistic approach to understanding the factors affecting drug absorption: a review of fundamentals, J. Clin. Pharmacol. 42 (2002) 620—643.

[4] The Internet drug Index, Accessed at, www.rxlist.com, 2012.

[5] J. Rautio, H. Kumpulainen, T. Heimbach, Prodrugs: design and clinical applications, Nat. Rev. Drug Discov. 7 (2008) 255—270.

[6] S.M. Berge, L.D. Bighley, D.C. Monkhouse, Pharmaceutical salts, J. Pharm. Sci. 66 (1977) 1—19.

[7] W. Jeffrey, J.W. Millard, F.A. Alvarez-Núñez, S.H. Yalkowsky, Solubilization by cosolvents: establishing useful constants for the log—linear model, Int. J. Pharm. 245 (2002) 153—166.

[8] J.S. Trivedi, Solubilization using cosolvent approach, in: J.S. Trivedi (Ed.), Solubilization Using Cosolvent Approach, CRC Press, Boca Raton, FL, 2008.

[9] R.C. Fu, D.M. Lidgate, J.L. Whatley, T. McCullough, The biocompatibility of parenteral vehicles—*in vitro/in vivo* screening comparison and the effect of excipients on hemolysis, J. Parenter. Sci. Technol. 41 (1987) 164—168.

[10] M.J. Rosen, Micelle formation by surfactants, in: M.J. Rosen (Ed.), Micelle Formation by Surfactants, John Wiley and Sons, Inc., Hoboken, NJ, 2004.

[11] R.C. Rowe, P.J. Sheskey, S.C. Owen, Handbook of pharmaceutical excipients, in: R.C. Rowe, P.J. Sheskey, S.C. Owen (Eds.), Handbook of Pharmaceutical Excipients, American Pharmacists Association and Pharmaceutical Press, Washington, DC, 2006.

[12] F. Gonzalez-Caballero, J.D.G. Lopez-Duran, Suspension formulation, in: F. Gonzalez-Caballero, J.D.G. Lopez-Duran (Eds.), Suspension Formulation, Marcel Dekker, New York, 2000.

[13] C.O. Rangel-Yagui, A. Pessoa, L.C. Tavares, Micellar solubilization of drugs, J. Pharm. Pharmaceut. Sci. 8 (2005) 147—165.

[14] J.H. Lee, H.B. Lee, J.D. Andrade, Blood compatibility of polyethylene oxide surfaces, Prog. Polym. Sci. 20 (1995) 1043–1079.

[15] M.E. Brewster, T. Loftsson, Cyclodextrins as pharmaceutical solubilizers, Adv. Drug Deliv. Rev. 59 (2007) 645–666.

[16] inventors, assignee K. Mehta, T. Yu-Hsing, Tris Pharma, Modified Release Formulations Containing Drug-Ion Exchange Resin Complexes, U.S.A. Patent 20100166858, 2010.

[17] C.W. Pouton, Formulation of poorly water-soluble drugs for oral administration: physicochemical and physiological issues and the lipid formulation classification system, Eur. J. Pharmaceut. Sci. 29 (2006) 278–287.

[18] P.P. Constantinides, Lipid microemulsions for improving drug dissolution and oral absorption: physical and biopharmaceutical aspects, Pharm. Res. (N. Y.) 12 (1995) 1561–1572.

[19] S. Chakraborty, D. Shukla, B. Mishra, S. Singh, Lipid—an emerging platform for oral delivery of drugs with poor bioavailability, Eur. J. Pharm. Biopharm. 73 (2009) 1–15.

[20] C.W. Pouton, Lipid formulations for oral administration of drugs: non-emulsifying, self-emulsifying and 'self-microemulsifying' drug delivery systems, Eur. J. Pharmaceut. Sci. 11 (2000) S93–S98.

[21] C.J. Porter, C.W. Pouton, J.F. Cuine, W.N. Chapman, Enhancing intestinal drug solubilisation using lipid-based delivery systems, Adv. Drug Deliv. Rev. 60 (2008) 673–691.

[22] V. Jannin, J. Musakhanian, D. Marchaud, Approaches for the development of solid and semi-solid lipid-based formulations, Adv. Drug Deliv. Rev. 60 (2008) 734–746.

[23] A. Mullertz, A. Ogbonna, S. Ren, T. Rades, New perspectives on lipid and surfactant based drug delivery systems for oral delivery of poorly soluble drugs, J. Pharm. Pharmacol. 62 (2010) 1622–1636.

[24] Inactive Ingredients Guide, 2012. Accessed at, www.accessdata.fda.gov/scripts/cder/iig/index.cfm.

[25] PDR Network L, Physician's Desk Reference, Medical Economics Company, Inc., Montvale, NJ, 2003.

[26] U.S.P-N.F., in: USP (Ed.), The United States Pharmacopeia and National Formulary USP 32-NF 27, 2009. Rockville, MD.

[27] T. Hanawa, N. Masuda, K. Mohri, K. Kawata, M. Suzuki, S. Nakajima, Development of patient-friendly preparations: preparation of a new allopurinol mouthwash containing polyethylene(oxide) and carrageenan, Drug Dev. Ind. Pharm. 30 (2004) 151–161.

[28] A.V. Nieuw Amerongen, E.C. Veerman, Current therapies for xerostomia and salivary gland hypofunction associated with cancer therapies, Support. Care Cancer 11 (2003) 226–231.

[29] M.E. Ellis, H. Clink, P. Ernst, Controlled study of fluconazole in the prevention of fungal infections in neutropenic patients with haematological malignancies and bone marrow transplant recipients, Eur. J. Clin. Microbiol. Infect. Dis. 13 (1994) 3–11.

[30] B.K. Joseph, Oral cancer: prevention and detection, Med. Princ. Pract. 11 (Suppl. 1) (2002) 32–35.

[31] J. Lang, Ocular drug delivery conventional ocular formulations, Adv. Drug Deliv. Rev. 16 (1995) 39–43.

[32] L. Illum, Nasal drug delivery—possibilities, problems and solutions, J. Contr. Release 87 (2003) 187–198.

[33] J. Arora, Development of nasal delivery systems: a review, Drug Deliv. Technol. 2 (2002) 70–73.

[34] FDA, Nasal Spray and Inhalation Solution, Suspension, and Spray Drug Products—Chemistry, Manufacturing, and Controls Documentation, CBER, FDA, Rockville, MD, 2002, pp. 1–45.

[35] A. Zimmer, J. Kreuter, Microspheres and nanoparticles used in ocular delivery systems, Adv. Drug Deliv. Rev. 16 (1995) 61–73.

[36] M.J. Molina, F.S. Rowlands, Stratospheric sink for chlorofluoromethanes: chlorine atomcatalysed destruction of ozone, Nature 249 (1974) 810–812.

[37] M.R. Partridge, A.A. Woodcock, in: M.R. Partridge, A.A. Woodcock, Propellants (Eds.), Propellants, Marcel Dekker, New York, 2002.

[38] K.J. McDonald, G.P. Martin, Transition to CFC-free metered dose inhalers: into the new millennium, Int. J. Pharm. 201 (2000) 89–107.

[39] S.P. Newman, Principles of metered-dose inhaler design, Respir. Care 50 (2005) 1177–1190.

[40] B.A. Haines, A.N. Martin, Interfacial properties of powdered material; caking in liquid dispersions. II. Electrokinetic phenomena, J. Pharm. Sci. 50 (1961) 753–756.

[41] A.N. Martin, Physical chemical approach to the formulation of pharmaceutical suspensions, J. Pharm. Sci. 50 (1961) 513–517.

[42] E.N. Hiestand, Theory of coarse suspension formulation, J. Pharm. Sci. 53 (1964) 1–18.

[43] A. Couper, Surface tension and its measurement, in: A. Couper (Ed.), Surface Tension and its Measurement, John Wiley and Sons, New York, 1993.

[44] M.J. Rosen, J.T. Kunjappu, Adsorption of surface-active agents at interfaces: the electrical double layer, in: M.J. Rosen, J.T. Kunjappu (Eds.), Adsorption of Surface-Active Agents at Interfaces: The Electrical Double Layer, John Wiley and Sons, Inc., Hoboken, N.J, 2012.

[45] M.M. Rieger, in: M.M. Rieger (Ed.), Surfactants, Surfactants. Marcel Dekker, New York, 1988.

[46] R. Duro, J.L. Gómez-Amoza, R. Martínez-Pacheco, C. Souto, A. Concheiro, Adsorption of polysorbate 80 on pyrantel pamoate: effects on suspension stability, Int. J. Pharm. 165 (1998) 211–216.

[47] S. Shijie Liu, J.H. Masliyah, Rheology of suspensions, in: S. Shijie Liu, J.H. Masliyah (Eds.), Rheology of Suspensions, American Chemical Society (ACS), Washington, DC, 1996.

[48] S.R. Derkach, Rheology of emulsions, Adv. Colloid Interface Sci. 151 (2009) 1–23.

[49] D.H. Everett, Definitions, Terminology and Symbols in Colloid and Surface Chemistry, International Union of Pure and Applied Chemistry, Washington DC, 1972.

[50] A. Martin, J. Swarbrick, A. Cammarata, A.H.C. Chun, Physical pharmacy: physical chemical principles in the pharmaceutical sciences, in: A. Martin, J. Swarbrick, A. Cammarata, A.H.C. Chun (Eds.), Physical Pharmacy: Physical Chemical Principles in the Pharmaceutical Sciences, Lea and Febiger, Malvern, PA, 1983.

[51] A. Vaziri, B. Warburton, Slow release of chloroquine phosphate from multiple taste-masked W/O/W multiple emulsions, J. Microencapsul. 11 (1994) 641–648.

[52] M.J. Lawrence, G.D. Rees, Microemulsion-based media as novel drug delivery systems, Adv. Drug Deliv. Rev. 45 (2000) 89–121.

[53] R.H. Müller, S. Heinemann, Fat emulsions for parenteral nutrition II: characterisation and physical long-term stability of Lipofundin MCT LCT, Clin. Nutr. 12 (1993) 298–309.

[54] L.C. Collins-Gold, R.T. Lyons, L.C. Bartholow, Parenteral emulsions for drug delivery, Adv. Drug Deliv. Rev. 5 (1990) 189–208.

[55] V.S. Koster, P.F.M. Kuksa, R. Langea, H. Talsmab, Particle size in parenteral fat emulsions, what are the true limitations? Int. J. Pharm. 134 (1996) 235–238.

[56] R.J. Prankerd, V.J. Stella, The use of oil-in-water emulsions as a vehicle for parenteral drug administration, J. Parenter. Sci. Technol. 44 (1990) 139–149.

[57] L. Roon, The physical significance of emulsions, J. Am. Pharm. Assoc. 5 (1916) 496–505.

[58] W.D. Harkins, N. Beeman, The oriented wedge theory of emulsions, Proc. Natl. Acad. Sci. U. S. A. 11 (1925) 631–637.

[59] J.A. Serrallach, G. Jones, R.J. Owen, Strength of emulsifier films at liquid-liquid interfaces, Ind. Eng. Chem. 25 (1933) 816–819.

[60] W.C. Griffin, Calculation of HLB values of non-ionic surfactants, J. Soc. Cosmet. Chem. 5 (1954) 259.

[61] R. Pal, Effect of droplet size on the rheology of emulsions, AIChE J. 42 (1996) 3181–3190.

[62] S.R. Reddy, H.S. Fogler, Emulsion stability—experimental studies on simultaneous flocculation and creaming, J. Colloid Interface Sci. 82 (1981) 128–135.

[63] P. Taylor, Ostwald ripening in emulsions, Adv. Colloid Interface Sci. 75 (1998) 107–163.

[64] D.F. Driscoll, Lipid injectable emulsions: 2006, Nutr. Clin. Pract. 21 (2006) 381–386.

[65] A.G. Floyd, Top ten considerations in the development of parenteral emulsions, Pharmaceut. Sci. Technol. Today 4 (1999) 134–143.

[66] inventor, assignee D. Shulin, C.A. Allergan, Nonirritating Emulsions for Sensitive Tissue, U.S.A. Patent US5474979, 1995.

[67] J.T. Carstensen, C.T. Rhodes, Drug stability: principles and practices, in: J.T. Carstensen, C.T. Rhodes (Eds.), Drug Stability: Principles and Practices, Marcel Dekker Inc, New York, NY, 2000.

[68] FDA, in: HHS (Ed.), Pharmaceutical cGMPs for the 21st Century—A Risk-Based Approach, US FDA, Rockville, MD, 2004.

[69] FDA, in: HHS (Ed.), Guide to Inspections Oral Solutions and Suspensions, US FDA, Rockville, MD, 1994.

[70] M.M. Crowley, Solutions, emulsions, suspensions, and extracts, in: M.M. Crowley (Ed.), Solutions, Emulsions, Suspensions, and Extracts, Lippincott, Williams and Wilkins, Philadelphia, PA, 2005.

[71] K. Krause, R.H. Muller, Production and characterisation of highly concentrated nanosuspensions by high pressure homogenization, Int. J. Pharm. 214 (2001) 21–24.

[72] FDA, in: HHS (Ed.), Sterile Drug Products Produced by Aseptic Processing—Current Good Manufacturing Practice, CBER, FDA, Rockville, MD, 2004, pp. 1–59.

[73] FDA, in: HHS (Ed.), Guidance for Industry—Container and Closure Systems for Packaging Human Drugs and Biologics. Chemistry, Manufacturing, and Controls Documentation, CBER and CDER, FDA, Rockville, MD, 1999, pp. 1–56.

[74] R.H. Muller, Zetapotential and partikelladung in der laborpraxis—einfuhrung in der theorie, praktische mebdurchfuhrung dateninterpretation, Wissenschaftliche Verlagsgesellschaft, 1996.

[75] E. Brunner, Reaktionsgeschwindigkeit in heterogenen systemen, Z. Phys. Chem. 43 (1904) 56–102.

[76] W. Nernst, Theorie der Reaktionsgeschwindigkeit in heterogenen systemen, Z. Phys. Chem. 47 (1904) 52–55.

[77] V. Levich, Physicochemical hydrodynamics, in: V. Levich (Ed.), Physicochemical Hydrodynamics, Prentice-Hall, Eagle Cliffs, NY, 1962.

[78] C. Washington, Drug release from microdisperse systems: a critical review, Int. J. Pharm. 58 (1990) 1–12.

[79] FDA, in: HHS (Ed.), Guidance for Industry—Qualifying for Pediatric Exclusivity under Section 505A of the Federal Food, Drug, and Cosmetic Act, CBER and CDER, FDA, Rockville, MD, 1999, pp. 1–26.

[80] A.W. Hixson, J.H. Crowell, Dependence of reaction velocity upon surface and agitation (I) theoretical consideration, Ind. Eng. Chem. 23 (1931) 923–931.

[81] Gastrointestinal absorption of griseofulvin from liquid organic acids and esters in rats. Int. J. Pharmaceut. Volume 33, (1986) 235–242.

11

Aerosol Dosage Forms

Justin A. Tolman[1] and Megan Derba[2]

[1]Department of Pharmacy Sciences, School of Pharmacy and Health Professions, Creighton University, Omaha, NE, United States [2]Lafayette Family Cancer Institute, Northern Light Health, Brewer, ME, United States

CHAPTER OBJECTIVES

- Describe lung anatomical and physiological barriers to pulmonary drug delivery.
- Relate physiological lung volumes with breathing patterns for appropriate patient counseling on proper pulmonary drug administration.
- Describe the factors that affect pulmonary drug deposition in the lungs.
- Explain the role, mechanisms of aerosol generation, and parts/components of devices used for pulmonary drug delivery.
- Compare and contrast the properties of inhaled gases, nebulizers, pressurized metered-dose inhalers, dry powder inhalers, and soft mist inhalers.
- Anatomical and physiological considerations for pulmonary drug delivery.
- Formulation requirements and factors that affect gas inhalation or aerosol production.
- Device design and relationship to inhaled formulations.

Keywords: Aerosols; Dry powder inhaler; Lung anatomy; Lung physiology; Metered-dose inhaler; Nebulizer and pulmonary drug deposition.

11.1 Introduction

The inhalation of substances for pharmacologic effects has been reported throughout history [1]. Substances have been inhaled for localized effects in the treatment of pulmonary disorders or conditions. Systemic effects are also possible due to the extremely large absorptive surfaces and capillary networks present in the lungs. However, substances were principally inhaled either as suspended particulates in smoke or fumes from burning or heating

Pharmaceutics, Second Edition
https://doi.org/10.1016/B978-0-323-99796-6.00005-9

materials. Few substances were able to retain pharmacological activity following incineration to exert localized or systemic action.

Scientific advances in the 1700 and 1800s saw the development of the first medicinal uses of inhaled anesthetic gases and vapors, including nitrous oxide, chloroform, and ether—the forerunners to modern anesthesia. Specialized medical devices were also developed from the 1600s through the 1800s to facilitate the delivery of vapors and dispersions which have been categorized as inhalers. These early inhalers ranged from simple pots that passed inspiratory airflow through moistened and heated medicinal solutions to devices that atomized medicinal liquids or powders. In 1867, the British Pharmacopeia included several inhaled medications as formal recognition of therapeutic drug delivery to the lungs [2]. Since that time, pulmonary drug administration has advanced for the rational delivery of gases and vapors, solid particles, and liquid droplets by a variety of devices. Inhaled drug delivery devices include vaporizers, nebulizers, pressurized metered dose inhalers (pMDIs), dry powder inhalers (DPIs), and soft mist inhalers (SMIs). However, pulmonary drug delivery is predicated on the mechanisms by which a device interacts with the lung anatomy and physiology.

11.2 Lung anatomy

The pulmonary system is principally designed to support the process of respiration—the exchange of gases between a cell with functioning metabolic processes and the external environment [3]. In humans, respiration first occurs through air movement and gas exchange in the lungs, followed by the distribution of dissolved gases through systemic circulation, concluding with the utilization of dissolved gases for biological processes in cells and tissues. The first stage of respiration, focused on air movement and gas exchange, is dependent on anatomical structures of the nose, nasal cavity, mouth, and throat; the trachea and conducting airways; and the lungs composed of alveoli and the pulmonary vasculature (Fig. 11.1).

The nose and nasal cavity warms, moistens, and serves as a coarse particle filter for inhaled air. The mouth also serves as a separate airway for inhaled air but has less efficient warming, moistening, or filtering capacity than the nose/nasal cavity. The throat, or pharynx, is the anatomical structure that unifies airflow from the nasal and mouth airways. The pharynx redirects the inhaled air down into the thorax through the trachea by way of a sharp angle change of approximately 90 degrees. The back of the throat also serves as a principal impaction surface for inhaled particles and reduces large particle deposition deeper in the conducting airways. These deposited particles are then ingested or expectorated.

The trachea is the first generation airway, or principal conducting airway, in the lungs [4]. At the base of the trachea, the airway then asymmetrically bifurcates into the left or right main bronchi. The right bronchus is slightly larger in diameter and shorter in length compared to the left. This initial point of bifurcation changes airflow direction as inhaled air encounters the second generation of airways and is drawn deeper into the lungs. The bronchi further subdivide into conducting airways of narrowing diameters through successive generations of bifurcations. Conducting airway generations 3 through approximately 16 are classified as bronchioles. These airways are covered with a pseudostratified epithelium composed of ciliated or mucous-producing cells. The specialized epithelial linings of conducting airways form a mucociliary escalator to entrap and then physically translocate particles up to the throat for eventual ingestion or expectoration for particles that deposit on conducting airway surfaces.

Starting in approximately airway generation 17, terminal bronchioles begin and contain a small number of alveolar structures. At approximately airway generation 20, alveolar structures become more prevalent, and respiratory bronchioles can be found. Final airway generations occur at approximately generation 23 and terminate in porous alveolar sacs where principal gas exchange can occur. Collateral ventilation throughout alveolar regions is facilitated by holes or pores between adjacent alveoli. Alveoli are specialized pulmonary structures designed for efficient gas exchange. They are composed mainly of very thin Type I cells with membrane thicknesses of $0.1-0.2$ μm with some larger surfactant-producing Type II cells that help maintain alveolar integrity. Alveoli are surrounded by a vast network of pulmonary capillaries to facilitate gas diffusion into and out of the blood. The alveolar—capillary interface is then the principal site of gas exchange and respiration. Ventilation and respiration as well as pulmonary drug deposition are dependent on pulmonary epithelial surfaces.

Airway and alveolar epithelial membranes are sensitive to potential irritation and inflammation caused by inhaled drugs. Pulmonary inflammatory processes are often immune-mediated if inhaled substances have antigenic potential. Additional inflammatory processes can be triggered by airway irritation caused by the drug chemical structure, functional groups, and reactivity as well as the drug product tonicity, ion content (e.g., chloride ion concentration), and pH. Additionally, the lungs do not have significant levels of biometabolism, which require that inhaled drugs, drug products, and degradation by-products be biodegradable, bioabsorbable, and/or biocompatible

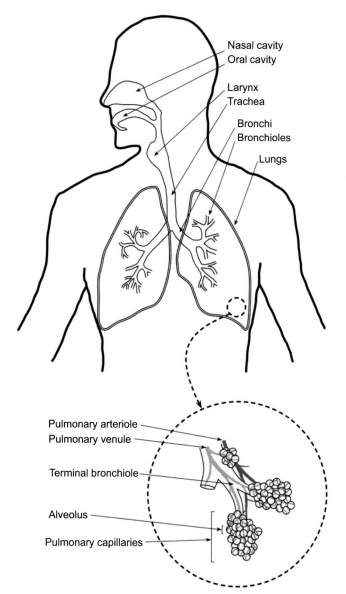

FIGURE 11.1 Schematic representations of the lungs. (A) The respiratory system, (B) the alveolar region of the lungs.

with the lung epithelia. The FDA has approved only a limited number of excipients for use in the lungs and inhaled drug products (Table 11.1).

Often, airway irritation and inflammation produce bronchospasms or coughing in attempts to eliminate or expel the cause of irritation. Bronchospasms are involuntary responses and substantially interfere with normal breathing and drug delivery to the lungs.

11.3 Lung physiology

Breathing is defined as the physiological process that facilitates gas exchange [5]. Specifically, breathing is composed of two different actions that cause air movement in the lungs. Inspiration or inhalation is the movement of air into the lungs, whereas expiration or exhalation is the expulsion of air from the lungs. A breath is then a single set of paired air movements: inspiration and expiration. Breathing is highly variable between patients based on numerous factors (e.g., age, gender, activity level, body position, pathological processes, etc.). However, comparisons between physiologic or pathologic differences can be made based on a standardized set of lung volumes and lung capacities (Fig. 11.2) [6].

TABLE 11.1 Physicochemical properties of inhaled anesthetic agents.

Inhaled anesthetic	Molecular weight (g/mol)	Specific gravity	Boiling point (°C)	Vapor pressure (mm Hg)	MAC[a] (%)	Partition coefficient at 37°C		
						Blood: gas	Brain: blood	Fat: blood
Desflurane	168.04	1.47	23	669	6.0	0.42	1.3	27
Enflurane	184.49	1.52	56	175	1.6	1.8	1.4	36
Isoflurane	184.49	1.50	48	250	1.2	1.4	2.6	45
Halothane	197.38	1.87	50	243	0.75	2.5	2.9	51
Sevoflurane	200.05	1.52	58	160	2.0	0.65	1.7	48

[a]MAC: minimum alveolar concentration.

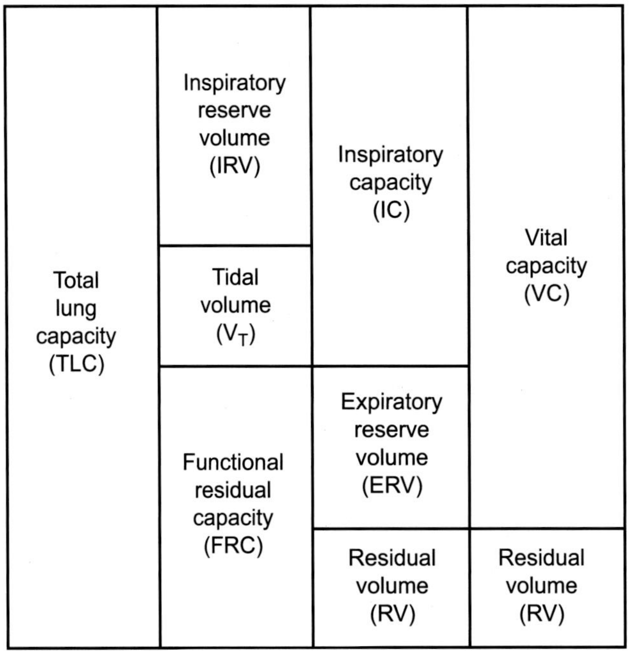

FIGURE 11.2 Standardized lung air volumes and lung capacities.

Normal breathing causes a volume of air referred to as the tidal volume (V_T) to be exchanged per breath. Under resting conditions, patients do typically have conscious control over the tidal volume. This air volume represents the baseline levels for passive inspiration and expiration. Patients have an additional inspiratory reserve volume (IRV) of air that can be inhaled into the lungs during maximal forced inspiration. The inspiratory capacity (IC) is then the V_T plus the IRV. A separate air volume that can be forcibly expired from the lungs following maximal inspiration is the vital capacity (VC) of the lungs. This vital capacity represents the maximal air volume that can be exchanged per breath. An expiratory reserve volume (ERV) represents the air volume that is not normally exhaled but can be forcibly exhaled and is represented by the VC minus the V_T and the IRV. A residual volume (RV) represents the dead air space that cannot be exhaled and is necessary to prevent the lungs from collapsing under low air volumes. A functional residual capacity (FRC) represents air volumes that are present in the lungs during normal breathing (breaths that only utilize tidal volume) and not exhaled. The FRC is equal to the ERV plus the RV. The total lung capacity (TLC) then represents the maximal air volume a patient can contain within the lungs following the greatest inspiratory effort possible and is equal to the sum of the IRV, V_T, ERV, and RV.

With an understanding of various lung volumes and capacities, one can use objective measures to both evaluate lung function and train patients on proper breathing techniques for optimal drug delivery. A patient's respiration rate is defined as the number of breaths, usually tidal breaths, which an individual takes per unit time. Basal respiration rates for healthy adults are typically 8−12 breaths per minute but highly variable based on physiologic and pathologic factors. Assessment of a patient's vital capacity is also possible through a forced vital capacity (FVC) test where maximal expiratory effort is made following maximal inspiratory effort. During this test, the forced expiratory volume in the first second (FEV_1) represents the maximal volume of air the body is able to initially forcefully exhale. It is often used as a measure of lung inflammation because FEV_1 is particularly sensitive to impaired airflow resulting from altered airway epithelial pathologies that impair air movement out of the lungs. Patients with sufficient cognition can therefore affect the respiration rate, breath volume (to some degree), breath holding, force of inspiration and expiration, and position and posture to influence pulmonary drug deposition and delivery.

11.4 Pulmonary drug targets

The majority of inhaled medications are used in modern medicine for their therapeutic use in localized lung conditions (e.g., asthma, emphysema, pneumonias, etc.) [7]. Targeted lung delivery via inhalation of active pharmaceutical ingredients (APIs) continues to be investigated for cancers, gene therapy, and other therapeutic applications. These uses of pulmonary drug delivery are essentially topical and use patients' inspiration or breathing only to get the drug to the site of action. Dependent on the clinical application, it could be therapeutically optimal for the drug to be delivered to the upper airways, conducting airways, and/or alveoli.

The pulmonary route of administration can also be utilized for systemic drug delivery if drugs are delivered to the highly vascularized alveolar regions of the lungs [8]. To reach the alveoli, inhaled APIs must be able to avoid deposition in the upper airways or conducting airways but then deposit on the alveolar epithelium. Once a drug is deposited, it can potentially be absorbed across the very thin alveolar cell membrane and into systemic circulation. Clinical decisions and patient counseling points are then informed through an understanding of the physics that govern drug deposition in the lungs.

11.5 Pulmonary drug deposition

Drugs administered to the lungs can be inhaled as drug molecules mixed in a gas or as dispersions, coarse or colloidal, of drug or particles containing drug in a gaseous continuous phase [9]. Drug deposition in the lungs is principally influenced by three mechanisms: inertial impaction, gravimetric sedimentation, and diffusion (Fig. 11.3) [10,11]. Additional deposition mechanisms include interception for fibrous particles and electrostatic deposition for charged particles [12].

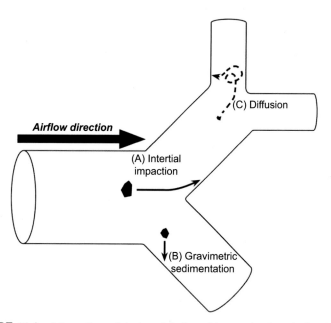

FIGURE 11.3 Schematic model of particle deposition mechanisms in the airways.

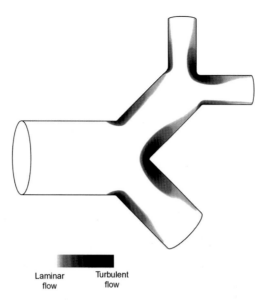

Laminar   Turbulent
flow   flow

FIGURE 11.4 Schematic diagram that represents airflow patterns in simulated airway bifurcations.

The principal deposition mechanism for many inhaled particles is inertial impaction and can be illustrated using a simplified model of bifurcating tubes to represent the conducting airways (Fig. 11.2) [13]. Air movement in the conducting airways is a complex physiologic process that is affected by numerous physiologic and pathologic factors [14]. In this simplified system, the air is assumed to have a laminar flow through the start of the conducting airways. Laminar flow is the smooth ordered movement of parallel layers of air and can occur in this model due to the circular tube, smooth walled sides, unidirectional airflow, and constant air velocity. When moving layers of air encounter an airway bifurcation, turbulence is induced as airflow is redirected into new airflow paths (Fig. 11.4).

This airflow redirection causes chaotic air subcurrents while retaining overall unidirectional flow through the airways. Turbulent airflow becomes predominant in lung regions where bifurcations become more prevalent (especially in airway generations through 16), in airways that are not smooth, when air velocity is not constant throughout the airways, and when air direction changes due to breathing [15]. Laminar flow can be reinstated in airway generations greater than 16 as ordered airflow is imposed by small-diameter airways. Modeling drug deposition by impaction, sedimentation, and diffusion in the lungs is a complex process and is described by each component process.

Inertial impaction occurs when a drug particle suspended in an airstream resists a change in air direction induced by airway bifurcations and collides with the airway walls. Stoke's number (S_t) (Eqn. 11.1) is a dimensionless parameter that a particle's likelihood to follow an initial trajectory due to high inertial energy or change trajectory based on redirected airflow:

$$S_t = \frac{v_a \rho_p d^2}{18R\eta} \tag{11.1}$$

where v_a is the air velocity, ρ_p is the particle density, d is the particle diameter, R is the airway radius, and η is the viscosity of air. Systems that have large Stoke's numbers will likely have substantial particle deposition by impaction. Impaction can also occur due to chaotic airflow patterns in regions of turbulence that induce particle collisions with airway surfaces. The magnitude of a particle's inertia is directly proportional to the force imparted by the air velocity. Particles with large sizes and/or densities will have more inertial energy in an airstream and have higher probabilities of collisions with pulmonary surfaces. Particle impaction is much more probable in the tortuous air pathways of the central lungs or conducting airways. However, inhaled particles can also impact in alveolar regions if their size and density are small enough to avoid impaction in the central airways.

Gravimetric sedimentation is another deposition mechanism by which particles settle in the lungs [16]. Spherical particle sedimentation in airflow is described by Stoke's Law. This law states that the particle velocity (v_p) is defined by Eq. (11.2):

$$v_p = \frac{d^2 \left(\rho_p - \rho_a\right) g}{18\eta} \tag{11.2}$$

where d is the particle diameter, ρ_p is the particle density, ρ_a is air density, g is the force of gravity, and η is the viscosity of air. The sedimentation velocity is proportional to the size and density of the particle. The residence time of inhaled particles represents the average time a suspended particle is retained within the respiratory system before either deposition or expiration. Eventually, inhaled particles will settle and come in contact with the lung epithelium if particles are unperturbed by air movement. Deposition by sedimentation is then more probable if inhaled particles have long residence times in a space unperturbed by air movement.

Diffusion is another deposition mechanism by which inhaled particles can collide with epithelial linings in the lungs. Particle diffusion in air is due to the random and chaotic collision of particles with gas molecules. Diffusion is governed by the Stokes–Einstein Equation. The diffusivity of a particle (D) is described by Eq. (11.3):

$$D = \frac{k_B T}{3\pi\eta d} \tag{11.3}$$

where k_B is Boltzmann's constant, T is the temperature (in Kelvin), η is the viscosity of air, and d is the particle diameter. Diffusion is inversely proportional to particle size. Particle diffusion will be more pronounced under physiological conditions (e.g., 37°C, standard air viscosity, and normal breath-holding times) for particles with diameters <100 nm. Drug deposition by diffusion is also more probable when the diffusional distance is short or the particle residence time in the lungs is long.

These three main mechanisms for drug deposition in the lungs are all influenced by the size of an inhaled particle. Particle density also is significant for deposition by impaction and sedimentation. The nominal particle size does not adequately describe how an inhaled particle behaves in the airstream. An aerodynamic particle size is used to describe and relate the size and density of a suspended particle intended for pulmonary delivery with its behavior in moving air. The mass median aerodynamic diameter (MMAD) is the average diameter of a sample of particles that have the same aerodynamic behavior as spheres of a known size (Fig. 11.5).

The MMAD is not necessarily a "true" diameter but suggests that large non-dense particles can behave aerodynamically like smaller but denser particles. Specifically, a particle's aerodynamic diameter (da) is described by Eq. (11.4):

$$d_a = d\sqrt{\frac{\rho_p}{\rho_0}} \tag{11.4}$$

where d is the true diameter, and $\sqrt{\frac{\rho_p}{\rho_0}}$ is the particle-specific gravity. MMAD values have been associated with region-specific drug deposition (Fig. 11.5) [7]. For therapeutic purposes, inhaled particles with MMAD values of >5 μm tend to be deposited in the conducting airways while particles <5 μm tend to be deposited in the alveolar regions. This 5 μm "cutoff" diameter is also used to describe the dose fraction below this size and is referred to as either the fine particle dose (FPD) with mass units or the fine particle fraction (FPF) expressed as a percentage of the delivered dose below this diameter.

Ultimately, pulmonary drug deposition patterns of inhaled medications are influenced by impaction, sedimentation, and diffusion to varying degrees [17]. Many patients can be trained to have breathing parameters conducive to

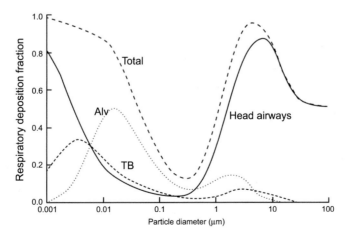

FIGURE 11.5 Average predicted total and regional lung deposition based on International Commission on Radiological Protection (ICRP) deposition model for nose-breathing males and females engaged in light exercise. *Alv*, alveolar region; *TB*, tracheobronchial region. *Reproduced with permission from Danish EPA, Report No. 12352008 [33].*

optimal drug deposition for varying clinical needs based on patient and formulation factors. For example, patients can alter the rate and extent of inspiration to induce fast airflow velocities to promote particle deposition in the conducting airways by inertial impaction. This could be beneficial for drugs used to treat central airway conditions (e.g., asthma). Conversely, slow airflow rates can be induced through slow inspiration to minimize the energy imparted to particles and thereby minimize inertial impaction. Patients can refrain from breathing for short periods of time through breath-holding to promote sedimentation and diffusion of smaller particles. The "depth" of a breath can also be varied to recruit alveolar regions during maximum ventilation and utilization of the total lung capacity. "Shallow" breathing can also be used to reduce alveolar availability if breathing is restricted to the tidal volume or less. These breathing techniques can be used to alter the drug deposition patterns and are important considerations for achieving optimal drug therapy outcomes for inhaled medications.

While particle size may not have a direct effect on drug deposition in the lungs, it does have clinical implications. Controlling particle size, both on the large (5–30 μm, to avoid macrophage clearance) and small (nanoparticles, to avoid detection) can potentially aid in controlling the clearance of these drug particles from lung tissues and fluids. Most of the drugs available on the market today are for the treatment of respiratory illnesses such as asthma and COPD. Due to this, the technologies and devices that are used to deliver these drugs are suited for the potency of bronchodilators and glucocorticoids, typically in the range of 10–500 μg. If higher doses of the drug need to be delivered, typically jet nebulizers are utilized with more frequent dosing schedules to accommodate the need for higher drug delivery. Higher treatment burden means more frequent dosing, longer nebulization times, and then an associated increase in the need to clean the equipment for the next use. Additional work is being done in this area to decrease the treatment burden for drugs that require large doses to be clinically efficacious [18].

11.6 Therapeutic gases

A relatively small portion of inhaled pulmonary drugs are delivered as gases or vapors. This is due to the limited number of drug molecules that are physically in a gaseous state at standard temperature and pressure or which have very low vapor pressures. Therapeutic gases typically have low molecular weights, very weak intermolecular interactions, and are nonpolar and highly lipophilic (Table 11.1, Fig. 11.6).

However, once inhaled, therapeutic gases utilize normal lung physiology for rapid therapeutic effects and efficient systemic drug delivery.

Systemic delivery is possible following inhalation due to the physiologic structure of the lungs as per Fick's Law of Diffusion as shown below by Eq. (11.5):

$$-\frac{dC}{dt} = \frac{DAK(C_L - C_B)}{h} \tag{11.5}$$

where $\frac{dC}{dt}$ is the rate of concentration change with respect to time, D is the diffusion coefficient, A is the surface area across which diffusion is occurring, K is the partition coefficient, C_L is the drug concentration in the lung, C_B is the

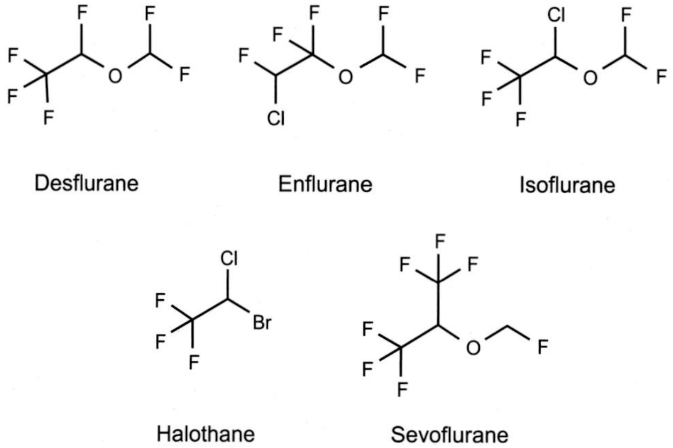

FIGURE 11.6   Chemical structures of inhaled anesthetic agents.

drug concentration in the blood, and h is the membrane thickness. Drug diffusion across the alveolar–capillary interface is then highly likely due to the enormous alveolar surface area, a very thin alveolar membrane thickness, and good molecular diffusivity due to the nonpolar or mildly polar nature of these APIs. Additionally, the concentration gradient ($C_L - C_B$) of gas across the diffusional membrane can usually be regulated to ensure sufficient therapeutic effects are obtained while also allowing for the exhalation of the drug. Inhaled gases are almost always administered as gaseous mixtures, often with varying concentrations of oxygen. Assuming these gaseous mixtures have minimal intermolecular interactions, the fractional pressure of each component in these mixtures can be described by Dalton's Law shown below by Eq. (11.6):

$$p_T = p_1 + p_2 + \ldots p_n \tag{11.6}$$

where p_T is the total pressure of the system and is equal to the summation of each individual component's partial pressure (p_n) in the mixture. The partial pressure for each gas in the mixture is determined by the mole fraction of each component, and the Ideal Gas Law states that

$$PV = nRT \tag{11.7}$$

where P is pressure, V is volume, n is the number of particles, R is Avogadro's number, and T is the temperature. The partial pressure of mixtures is also applicable to dissolved gases in liquids (e.g., blood) and can be used with Fick's Law of Diffusion to describe the process of gaseous drug distribution across a membrane. Once absorbed, dissolved gases distribute thoroughly into tissues in the body. Distribution equilibrium is reached when the partial pressure of the gas is equal in all tissues in the body. The concentration of inhaled gas in different regions of the body will not be equal during equilibrium due to tissue-specific API solubility in different tissues. Partition coefficients are used to describe the relative concentrations of gases in tissues (e.g., blood: gas, brain: blood, and fat: blood) (Table 11.1).

A class of drugs that are administered as gases is inhaled anesthetics, which induce general anesthesia (Table 11.1) [19]. These drugs often have very narrow therapeutic indices and must be used with extreme caution. The pharmacologic effects of these drugs are generally independent of patient breathing parameters but instead are affected by drug physicochemical properties and by the devices used for their administration.

Many but not all inhaled anesthetic drugs are short-chain halogenated ethers that are structural mimics of diethyl ether. These agents are mildly polar compounds with high hydrogen bonding potential. Halogen substitution alters drug solubility, boiling point, vapor pressure, flammability, and potency to varying degrees. Most inhaled anesthetics are commercially available as liquids that typically have low molecular weights and very low vapor pressures. These liquid APIs are used in drug-specific, specialized, and calibrated vaporizers that convert the drug liquid to a drug vapor. These anesthetic vapors are then mixed with varying concentrations of oxygen and possibly other agents based on clinical need before delivery to the patient. Anesthetic gas mixtures are then delivered directly to the lungs through equipment such as a complete face mask, an endotracheal tube, or a laryngeal mask airway (a specialized airway tube).

A key clinical mechanism to evaluate anesthetic gas potency is through the minimum alveolar concentration (MAC). The MAC is the gas concentration in the alveoli, as measured by the drug concentration during expiration that causes no pain response in 50% of patients. It is a relative pharmacodynamic measure and can be affected by numerous physiological or pathological conditions (e.g., age, temperature, pregnancy, and co-administration of drugs). Drug potency is inversely related to the MAC value for inhaled anesthetic agents because the relationship between the MAC and the anesthetic blood concentration is directly related to the concentration gradient across the alveolar–capillary interface. This concentration gradient is proportional to the partial pressure of the gas and inversely proportional to the concentration of the dissolved gas in the blood. Once dissolved, the drug will distribute throughout the body as determined by tissue: gas partition coefficients. The rate of anesthesia induction is controlled by the rate at which drug concentrations in the brain equal the MAC. This rate is also approximately equal to the rate at which the alveolar partial pressure reached the MAC value. Therefore, the rate of anesthesia induction is inversely proportional to the solubility of gas in the blood but directly proportional to the partial pressure of gas administered to the patient.

Desflurane is one example of an inhaled anesthetic that has special considerations for drug delivery. It is a moderately polar compound that readily diffuses across the alveolar–capillary interface. Desflurane has a blood: gas partition coefficient of 0.42 and a brain: blood coefficient of 1.3, indicating low relative blood solubility and rapid induction of anesthesia. It also has a relatively high vapor pressure but a low boiling point. This necessitates a specialized vaporizer for desflurane that utilizes heat to regulate vapor concentrations in gaseous mixtures administered to patients.

11.7 Inhaled aerosols

The majority of drugs delivered to the lungs are administered as disperse systems of solid particles or liquid droplets suspended in air [20,21]. These disperse systems are referred to as aerosols (aero—air and sol—solution) in the broadest sense of the term. "Aerosol" also has an official and more restrictive definition by the United States Pharmacopeia: a system under pressure. This definition is appropriate for inhaled medications formulated as pressurized systems that produce fine drug dispersions in the air due to the rapid vapourization of volatile propellants from a metered volume of drug/propellant mixture (more information about these systems later). However, the broadest definition of an aerosol as solid or liquid particles dispersed in a gas will be used to describe inhaled aerosols.

All currently available aerosolized drug products are drug—device combinations or are drug products that require a separate device for proper therapeutic utilization. The reason is that aerosol creation is a device-specific process that is influenced by both patient and formulation factors. A discussion of inhaled aerosols then is typically centered around broad device categories of nebulizers, pMDIs, DPIs, and SMIs. Recent advances in inhaler technology have also led to breath-assisted devices that adapt drug delivery to the patient's inspiratory patterns. In each of these device categories, the aerosol is created at the time of inspiration. The aerosol's aerodynamic particle size distribution as measured by the MMAD and FPF (or FPD) in conjunction with the patient's breathing parameters will significantly affect how the aerosol particles navigate the anatomical and physiologic barriers of the lungs to reach their intended targets. Therefore, these broad categories do not supersede the device-specific aerosol creation processes or patient-handling requirements for proper therapeutic use.

11.7.1 Nebulizers

Nebulizers are devices that continuously produce a dispersed cloud of liquid droplets in an air stream [22]. The aerosol cloud is then inspired and expired through normal tidal breathing. Most patients do not need to be compliant with breathing regulations or have the dexterity to manipulate the device. Indeed, nebulizers are often used to deliver inhaled medications to pediatric patients and intubated or mechanically ventilated patients. Nebulized aerosols are often delivered to patients through a face mask or mouthpiece and can often be delivered to mechanically ventilated patients through in-line junctions.

There are three principal types of nebulizers currently used for drug delivery: air-jet, ultrasonic, and vibrating-mesh nebulizers. All three produce an aerosol of drug-containing droplets from solutions or suspensions. However, the aerosol generation mechanisms differ between devices and result in varied clinical utility based on comparative advantages and disadvantages.

11.7.1.1 Air-jet nebulizers

Air-jet nebulizers are the oldest type of nebulizer and consist of a diverse group of devices produced by a variety of manufacturers. All air-jet nebulizers produce an aerosol through the Bernoulli effect. That is, a reduction in pressure occurs as air velocity increases in a given space. When compressed air is passed through the air-jet nebulizer, a volume of liquid is drawn up from a liquid reservoir into a region of high-shear forces. This liquid is then forcefully dispersed into droplets that are then carried out of the nebulizer on a gentle stream of carrier air, usually produced by the patient's breathing (Fig. 11.7).

Generally, these nebulizers consist of a drug-containing fluid reservoir or cup that is connected by a tube to a region through which a high-velocity airstream is directed. An external air source, often a compressor, is the source of the high-velocity airstream. As the air moves across the mouth of the tube connected to the reservoir, a low-pressure region is created by the Bernoulli principle that draws fluid up into the high-velocity airstream. Droplet shear, air turbulence, and a series of impaction baffles then create a gentle aerosol cloud with a polydisperse particle size distribution. Some droplets coalesce and return to the fluid reservoir while other particles form an aerosol cloud above the drug reservoir. This aerosol can then be suspended in the inspired airstream and be inhaled by the patient.

A minimum volume within the reservoir cup is required for the Bernoulli effect to be effective. This often results in residual volumes that are retained within the nebulizer and cannot be nebulized through these devices. The chaotic environment of aerosol generation is also potentially wasteful because much of the dose fails to be nebulized initially. Aerosolized droplets often impact within the device and are further subjected to repeated shear stresses. Long nebulization times are often necessary due to these aerosolization inefficiencies. This turbulent aerosol generation mechanism is also potentially damaging to sensitive drug product formulations. Special considerations should be given to drug products that have possible sensitivity to repeated physical stresses (e.g., some suspensions or

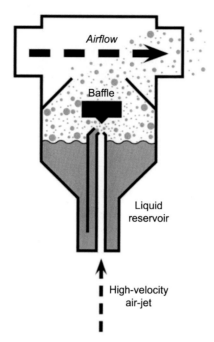

FIGURE 11.7 Schematic representation of an air-jet nebulizer.

emulsions). Additionally, environmental exposure to exhaled drug aerosol is possible, especially for caregivers and healthcare workers, and could be cause for concern based on possible drug effects.

Most air-jet nebulizers have a very broad aerodynamic particle size distribution due to the chaotic system of liquid shearing forces and droplet impaction before inspiration of the aerosol cloud. This broad distribution can lead to low FPF values for these nebulizers and inefficient drug delivery to the alveolar region of the lungs. Formulation factors such as surface tension, viscosity, osmolality, fluid reservoir volume, and temperature can affect the fluid dynamics within the nebulizer and ultimately droplet creation. Typically, those formulation factors that impede or inhibit droplet formation (e.g., increasing viscosity or increasing surface tension) would tend to create larger-sized droplets. Conversely, smaller droplets would be more prevalent for formulations that stabilize or induce droplet formation (e.g., surfactants or co-solvents that reduce surface tension). The air velocity, air composition, temperature, and humidity can also affect droplet creation and aerodynamic particle size distribution changes of the aerosol cloud. Typically, commercial products for nebulization are approved for use with specific air-jet nebulizers due to the variability in drug product aerosolization between different systems.

Despite the small nebulizer size, air-jet nebulizers are not typically very portable due to the need for a large external compressor. Some newer models integrate a small compressor with the nebulizer and are substantially smaller and quieter than older models. However, the compressor needed for the proper functioning of air-jet nebulizers is a limitation for these systems because they are typically loud and bulky. Some compressors have variable pressure regulation, whereas others lack any regulation ability. Familiarity with the air compressor is a key requirement for the patient or caregiver for proper medication inhalation using air-jet nebulizers.

11.7.1.2 Ultrasonic nebulizers

Ultrasonic nebulizers were developed much later than air-jet nebulizers and were designed to be more portable. These nebulizers incorporate a piezoelectric crystal at the bottom of the drug reservoir or cup. This crystal mechanically vibrates at a high frequency when subjected to an electric field. Crystal vibrations send shockwaves through the liquid-filled reservoir and cause droplet formation at the liquid surface through turbulence on the liquid surface and by cavitation in the liquid. Cavitation is the creation and implosion of voids in the liquid caused by crystal vibrations. The resulting droplets form a gentle aerosol cloud above the liquid reservoir. The aerodynamic particle size distribution of aerosols is also polydisperse due to the chaotic liquid surface environment but is generally less disperse than for air-jet systems. The aerosol cloud can then be mixed with inspiratory airflow for pulmonary drug delivery (Fig. 11.8).

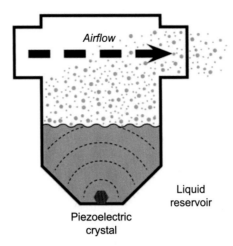

FIGURE 11.8   Schematic representation of an ultrasonic nebulizer.

Ultrasonic nebulizers do not have a minimum volume for operation as do air-jet nebulizers and can indeed operate with relatively small volumes. These devices are often more efficient and require shorter nebulization times. The lack of a compressor allows hand-held ultrasonic nebulizers to be much more portable, quiet, and user-friendly. An electric source is required for operation and can often be supplied by battery power. The crystal vibrations can induce large temperature elevations in the liquid. Heat-labile drugs should be used with caution in ultrasonic nebulizers. As with air-jet nebulizers, formulation factors such as viscosity and surface tension can influence aerosol generation in ultrasonic nebulizers. Sensitive drug formulations have varied responses in ultrasonic nebulizers but are typically more stable through the aerosolization process than air-jet nebulizers.

11.7.1.3 *Vibrating-mesh nebulizers*

The vibrating-mesh nebulizer is a relatively new nebulizer system that was designed to have more consistent aerosol particle size distributions and operate with a wider variety of formulations. These nebulizer systems attach a piezoelectric crystal to a laser-drilled metal mesh at the bottom of a drug reservoir or cup. When the crystal is subjected to an electric field, the metal mesh rapidly oscillates and forces the drug liquid through the holes in the mesh. A gentle aerosol is then produced with a uniform aerodynamic particle size distribution due to the uniform nature of the laser-drilled holes in the metal membrane. This aerosol is generated below or to the side of the liquid reservoir and can be delivered to a patient through a mouthpiece, face mask, or in-line junction for mechanically ventilated patients (Fig. 11.9).

Vibrating-mesh nebulizers are relatively compact and portable systems that require a small nebulizer unit and a companion controller unit that houses the system electronics. These nebulizers are operationally silent and do not produce fluid heating as do ultrasonic nebulizers. They can aerosolize a wide range of liquid drug formulations. Specifically, low-stability formulations and sensitive drug products have been reported to be well aerosolized

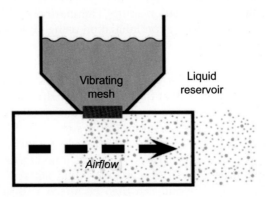

FIGURE 11.9   Schematic representation of a vibrating mesh nebulizer.

with these systems. Vibrating-mesh nebulizers have generated inhalable aerosols with formulations of higher viscosities and surface tensions than other nebulizers. However, the cost for vibrating mesh nebulizers is typically high.

11.7.1.4 Nebulizer use and respiratory infection transmission

Traditionally when discussing nebulizers, emphasis was placed on the advantages and disadvantages from a drug delivery to the patient standpoint. However, with the Covid-19 Pandemic, consideration surrounding nebulization as a potential source of viral transmission has been a focus as of late. As noted in an article by Cazzola et al., published in 2021, "it has not yet been established whether SARS-CoV-2 might spread through aerosols from respiratory droplets" [23]. The 2020 version of the Global Initiative for Asthma (GINA) recommends, when possible to avoid use of nebulizers due to the potential risk of SARS-CoV-2 transmission, instead, a pMDI and spacer should be used. Other organizations, such as the Australian National Asthma Council and the American College of Allergy, Asthma and Immunology, all recommend the same, noting that SARS-CoV-2 particles have the potential of remaining suspended in the air via droplets for 30 min or more post-nebulization treatment. It is important to note that this is a controversial topic, having other organizations, such as the British National Institute for Health and Care Excellence (NICE) state that nebulizer treatment is not a viral droplet-generating procedure. Due to the fact that it is unclear whether using a nebulizer can indeed suspend SARS-CoV-2 particles in the air increasing risk of contamination, many hospitals and hospital systems have chosen to institute strict infection prevention strategies, opting to use pMDIs where feasible.

Implementing these safety guidelines may be operationally feasible, but it should also be noted the financial impact that switching from nebulizers to pMDIs has on the healthcare system. Most hospitals traditionally have opted to use nebulized drugs in all hospitalized patients, regardless of patient respiratory status, due to the fact that nebulized drugs come in unit-dose packaging. These unit-dosed medications are typically more cost effective and decrease the potential for waste in a pMDI that contains many doses that may go unused if a patient remains in the hospital setting for 3—5 days. Institutional size pMDIs are available, but do still have the potential to have waste due to varying lengths of admission per patient, potential for device to be lost or needing to be replaced upon transfer to different units, shifts in nursing staff, etc. To minimize this wastage, before the COVID-19 pandemic, many hospitals preferred to use nebulizer treatments. However, as noted above, due to the risk of viral transmission through aerosol-generating procedures, most hospitals have switched back to pMDIs, drastically increasing the financial bottom line in a healthcare system already stretched due to the pandemic.

11.7.2 Pressurized metered-dose inhalers

A pMDI is a self-contained aerosol device that is composed of (1) a drug-containing canister; (2) a valve assembly and metering chamber; and (3) an actuator that activates and directs drug formulation aerosolization and serves as a mouthpiece for aerosol inhalation (Fig. 11.10) [24—26]. The canister is pressurized with a liquefied compressed gas, termed a propellant, which is metered by the actuator. The propellant is rapidly volatilized when exposed to atmospheric pressure following actuation, which leaves behind a liquid or solid aerosol cloud that is then inspired by the patient.

pMDIs are compact and portable inhalation devices that have gained wide acceptance for pulmonary drug delivery in the treatment of a variety of conditions, most notably asthma. Despite wide clinical acceptance, a substantial degree of coordination is needed between physically manipulating the pMDI device and patient breathing for optimal inhaled aerosol delivery. Each component in pMDI systems affects aerosol generation and inhaled aerosol delivery.

11.7.2.1 Canister and drug formulation

The canisters used for pMDIs must be able to withstand high pressures and be compatible with the drug formulation. Aluminum, stainless steel, and glass have all been used for the creation of canisters, with aluminum being the most common. Occasionally, inert coatings are applied to the canister interior to ensure compatibility with the formulation, prevent drug adhesion to the container, and ensure the formulation is able to be metered appropriately. The canister must be able to contain the pMDI formulation as well as headspace to compensate for formulation pressurization and allow for propellant vapor equilibrium.

pMDI formulations contain a propellant, the API, and excipients with varied functions (e.g., surfactants, solubilizers, stabilizers, lubricants, pH/tonicity adjustment agents). Based on API properties and excipient use, these formulations could be drug solubilized in propellant, drug solution mixed with propellant, drug suspended in

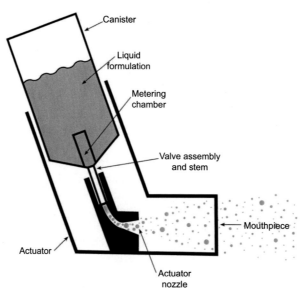

FIGURE 11.10   Schematic representation of a pressurized metered-dose inhaler (pMDI).

TABLE 11.2   Physicochemical properties of some hydrofluoroalkane (HFA) propellants.

Property	HFA134	HFA227
Molecular formula	$C_2H_2F_4$	C_3HF_7
Molecular weight (g/mol)	102.0	170.0
Boiling point (°C)	−26.3	−16.5
Vapor pressure (psig at 20°C)	68.4	56.0
Liquid density (g/cm³)	1.21	1.41
Solubility in water (%w/w)	0.193	0.058

propellant, and drug suspensions mixed with propellants. The resulting aerosol following pMDI actuation could then be liquid droplets or solid particles suspended in air. This versatility for the inhaled aerosol formulation is an additional reason pMDI use is so prevalent for inhaled aerosol systems. Key formulation limitations then are based on the propellant properties and excipient acceptability. Currently formulated propellants include hydrofluoroalkane compounds (HFA) (Table 11.2) [27].

Only a limited number of excipients have been approved for use in inhaled delivery systems (Table 11.3). The FDA has expressed concerns for the pulmonary biocompatibility and clearance of inhaled excipients. Additionally, many excipients that are generally regarded as safe (GRAS) are not approved for pulmonary systems due to the potential for safety, toxicity, and irritation concerns when inhaled. Therefore, pharmaceutical companies must complete additional exhaustive toxicological and safety studies on any unapproved excipients that are formulated in new drug approval applications. Despite these limitations, several excipients have been approved as co-solvents, surfactants, lubricants, antioxidants, flavoring agents, and agents to adjust pH and tonicity.

11.7.2.2 Valve assembly

All pMDI valves contain a metering chamber and a valve stem despite numerous valve assembly designs. The valve assembly in pMDI devices is the key mechanical determinant for drug dosing because the metering chamber volume capacity and drug concentration within the formulation limit the potential dose a patient can receive. Most metering chambers have 25–100 μL volume capacities and are surrounded by a reservoir of liquid drug formulation to promote complete chamber filling. Some devices require priming of the metering chamber before patient dosing can begin.

TABLE 11.3 FDA-approved excipients for inhaled drug products.

FDA-approved function in inhaled formulations	Excipient
Co-solvents	Water
	Ethanol
	Glycerin
	Propylene glycol
	PEG 1000
Surfactants/Lubricants	Sorbitan trioleate
	Soya lecithin
	Lecithin
	Oleic acid
	Magnesium stearate
	Sodium lauryl sulfate
Carrier particles	Lactose
	Mannitol
	Dextrose
Preservatives/Antioxidants	Methylparaben, propylparaben
	Chlorobutanol
	Benzalkonium chloride
	Cetylpyridinium chloride
	Thymol
	Ascorbic acid
	Sodium bisulfite, sodium metabisulfite, sodium bisulfate
	EDTA
Buffers, pH adjustment, or tonicity adjustment	NaOH, tromethamine, ammonia
	HCl, H_2SO_4, HNO_3, citric acid
	$CaCl_2$
	$CaCO_3$
	Sodium citrate
	Sodium chloride
	Disodium EDTA
Flavoring	Saccharin
	Menthol
	Ascorbic acid
Others	Glycine
	Lysine
	Gelatin
	Povidone K25

Continued

TABLE 11.3   FDA-approved excipients for inhaled drug products.—cont'd

FDA-approved function in inhaled formulations	Excipient
	Silicone dioxide
	Titanium dioxide
	Zinc oxide

Some products might have multiple functions in a given formulation.

Valve assemblies mechanically operate based on the actuation of the device by depressing the canister so that the valve stem is depressed against the actuator. When the valve stem is depressed, a valve opens to connect the metering chamber to the channel in the valve stem. The pressurized metered dose expands through a channel in the valve stem. This channel directs the pressurized formulation into the actuator where rapid propellant vapourization produces a high-velocity aerosol cloud. Actuation then allows the formulation to refill the metering chamber in preparation for the next dose.

11.7.2.3 Actuator

The actuator is a molded or formed plastic component that performs several functions for proper pMDI use. It holds the canister in the proper orientation for device use, serves as a surface against which the valve stem can depress, provides a space for principal propellant vaporization, redirects the high-velocity aerosol cloud toward the patient, and has a mouthpiece for patient use. Canisters are typically operated in an inverted position where the valve assembly is in contact with the pressurized liquid formulation to allow for proper metering. The valve stem is in contact with a specialized plastic component that contains an expansion chamber and the actuator nozzle. The expansion chamber receives the metered dose and acts as a space for the propellant to vaporize and induce droplet shear. The actuator nozzle restricts formulation movement out of the expansion chamber to form a spray cone and induces substantial particle turbulence. The actuator nozzle hole diameter is a key determinant for aerosol particle size distribution.

11.7.2.4 Patient use of pMDI devices

The high-velocity aerosol cloud produced by most pMDI devices imparts a substantial amount of momentum to aerosolized particles. This tends to produce high levels of inertial impaction in the back of the throat unless an optimal breathing technique is employed, or particles decelerate before inhalation. A spacer is often a static air-volume particle deceleration chamber that allows particles to lose velocity before inhalation. Many spacers fit on the actuator mouthpiece adapter and facilitate better drug deposition in the lungs than can be achieved following typical inhaler use. Another option some healthcare providers recommend to promote aerosol deceleration is for the patient to hold the pMDI close to and in front of the mouth for actuation.

Proper pMDI use requires a substantial degree of patient cognition and physical coordination. The patient must be able to physically handle and actuate the device while controlling breathing and timing inspiration with device actuation. Typical patient counseling for pMDI devices could contain the following steps: (1) take a few deep cleansing breaths and expel the breaths fully; (2) while holding the device in the proper orientation, slowly and deeply inspire; (3) during this inspiration, actuate the device and continue to inspire a full breath even after the device has been actuated; (4) hold your breath for a short period of time; (5) slowly expel the held breath; and (6) repeat steps 1—5 for the prescribed dose as instructed by the healthcare provider.

Thoroughly mixing the formulation before device actuation will promote inter-dose uniformity and homogenous metered doses. Mixing can be promoted by the patient before each dose by vigorously shaking the pMDI device. Dose uniformity can then be impaired by improper formulation mixing and over the life span of the device as the formulation is exhausted. Dose uniformity is also improved by consistent device priming but is unlikely in clinical settings due to dose wasting. It is critical that patients clean and maintain pMDI devices. Patients should not mechanically disturb the nozzle but instead, use gentle cleaning procedures if the nozzle becomes obstructed.

11.7.3 Dry powder inhalers

DPIs are a very diverse group of often portable inhaler devices that create an aerosol of solid particles suspended in the air [28]. These devices generally have an air-inlet channel, a dose metering and holding chamber, and a mouthpiece adapter. Substantial differences exist between the various aerosolization mechanisms used by these inhalers for drug powder dispersion. DPIs can be single-dose devices where the drug dose is loaded into the machine before each use and multidose devices that contain either a drug reservoir or multiple unit doses. Once a dose is loaded into the holding chamber and before inspiration, all DPIs require a proper orientation to prevent the prepared and primed dose from leaking or spilling out of the device. A key limitation for these devices is the requirement of both physical dexterity and cognitive ability to manipulate the device to load, meter, prime, prepare, and/or actuate the dose.

11.7.3.1 Passive DPI devices

The aerosolization mechanisms vary substantially between DPIs. Some devices use the patient's inspiratory airflow to disperse the dose. These mechanisms direct air from inlet channels in various device-specific pathways to inducing airflow turbulence, vibrations, and/or powder motion in the dose-holding chamber. A mesh or screen is also often placed in between the dose-holding chamber and the mouthpiece adapter to assist in aerosol dispersion and prevent the inhalation of large dose fragments or particles. These aerosolization mechanisms are generally passive and require very rapid and full patient inspirations to adequately aerosolize the dose. As a result, inter- and intra-patient pulmonary drug deposition can vary substantially based on inspiratory inconsistencies. Additionally, many patients are incapable of producing inspiratory airflows of sufficient velocity to adequately aerosolize the drug dose. Dose retention in the inhaler can be a significant problem in passive devices based on patient use and might require training and device cleaning.

11.7.3.2 Active DPI devices

Other DPI devices utilize active aerosolization mechanisms by using external energy sources. Active devices can use compressed gases, induced pressure differences, and electronic or piezoelectric mechanisms to disperse the powder drug dose. For example, some DPI systems use pressurized air or vacuums to induce airflow through the device for drug powder aerosolization. Other devices induce vibrations or acoustic waves to aerosolize drug powders. Active aerosolization mechanisms separate inspiration from aerosol generation and can avoid the drug deposition variability of passive systems. Patients are then instructed to inspire slowly and deeply, often with breath-holding for active DPI use.

11.7.3.3 DPI formulations

Drug powder formulations differ substantially from those used in nebulizers and pMDIs [29]. It is common for particle engineering technologies to be used to prepare DPI formulations. These technologies can involve: (1) milling, grinding, and other forms of physical particle size reduction; (2) thermogenic or cryogenic powder preparation such as spray drying or lyophilization; (3) supercritical fluid processing; (4) powder mixing or blending; or (5) new and emerging areas of science to produce powders with specified properties. Often, inhaled formulations have been prepared for maximum pulmonary particle deposition by having powder MMAD values between 1 and 5 μm. Significant efforts are expended to rationally engineer and prepare dry powder drug particles in this optimal aerodynamic size range. However, these fine particle sizes often have poor flowability and dispersibility in air. Some products are formulated as small-particle loose aggregates that will readily disperse under the DPI aerosolization mechanisms. Other systems employ small drug particles adhered to the surface of large, inert carrier particles that have improved aerosolization properties. Once adhered particles are dispersed in the airstream, the smaller particles can be inhaled deeper into the lungs.

11.7.4 Soft mist inhalers

A relatively new category of inhalers also delivers liquid formulations but does so without an external aerosol generation mechanism of nebulizers or a propellant as in pMDI devices [30]. Instead, soft mist inhalers are self-contained aerosol devices that use mechanical energy to force a volume of metered formulation through a special

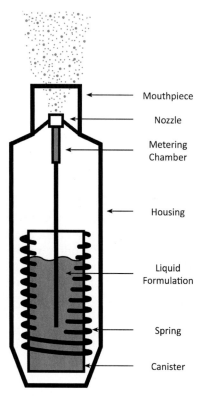

FIGURE 11.11   Schematic representation of a soft-mist inhaler (SMI).

nozzle to produce a fine jet of droplets. Approved drug—device combinations refer to the device as an "inhalation spray" or "nonpressurized metered dose inhaler". Currently, the only approved SMI in the United States is Respimat (Boehringer-Ingelheim, Germany). It is likely other SMI devices will receive approval in the coming years with several devices in early to late stage development.

11.7.4.1 SMI devices

Key components of SMI devices include a mouthpiece, nozzle, metering chamber, the canister containing the liquid formulation, and a source of mechanical energy (Fig. 11.11). The currently approved device uses a spring to store mechanical energy produced when the patient turns a portion of the device. This motion also primes the liquid formulation into the metering chamber. When the patient actuates the device, mechanical energy forces the metered dose through a microfluidic nozzle that produces a gentle aerosol plume. The mouthpiece allows airflow to carry the generated aerosol into the lungs with the patient's inspiration. SMI formulations and canisters are often similar to those used for pMDI devices without the need for a propellant. The nozzle is a critical component for SMI devices in development and could use piezoelectric vibrations (similar to ultrasonic nebulizers), pumping of liquid droplets through an oscillating mesh (similar to vibrating mesh nebulizers), or another system to produce a mechanical force for the generation of a soft mist aerosol.

11.7.4.2 Patient use of SMI devices

SMI devices overcome many of the limitations of pMDI and DPI devices. SMI devices retain a metering chamber, similar to pMDI devices, for accurate patient dosing. However, SMI devices are not reliant of propellants or patient inspiration for aerosol generation. Similarly, SMI devices are less dependent on the patient's inspiratory patterns with manipulation of the device compared to pMDI and DPI devices for drug deposition to the lung. Finally, SMI drug formulations are potentially less affected by environmental conditions such as humidity, temperature, elevation, and patient posture.

SMI devices do not require the same level of patient awareness and dexterity as pMDI and DPI devices and are less influenced by patient inspiration. Typical patient counseling for the daily use of the approved SMI device could contain the following steps: (1) turn the base of the device until it clicks; (2) open the cap that protects the mouthpiece; (3) take a cleansing breath and expel the breath fully; (4) close your lips around the mouthpiece and aim the device toward the back of the throat; (5) while taking a slow, deep breath, actuate the device by pressing the button and continue to inspire a full breath; (6) hold your breath for a short period of time; and (7) repeat steps 1–6 for the prescribed dose as instructed by the healthcare provider. The currently approved SMI device requires the inhaler to be primed before the first use. Patients should not obstruct air vents on the mouthpiece when using the SMI device. Additionally, patients should not mechanically disturb the nozzle.

11.7.5 Breath-assisted inhalers

Newly developed technology has been incorporated into inhaler devices to better optimize drug delivery to the lungs. This technology synchronizes the device function with the patient's breathing for superior drug delivery compared to typical devices. Improved drug delivery can be achieved by avoiding drug retention within the device, minimizing drug waste by expiration, and ensuring appropriate inspiratory airflow will carry aerosols into the lung. These devices monitor the patient for changes in breathing patterns (e.g., respiration rate, peak flow, tidal volume) and only generate an aerosol timed for the beginning of inspiration. Breath-assisted inhalers can also assist and train patients in proper breathing techniques for optimized pulmonary drug delivery. Studies have demonstrated the drug delivery efficiency and benefit of these devices. However, a major disadvantage for these systems is a very high cost.

11.8 Conclusions

Aerosol dosage forms are becoming increasingly common as drug products are designed and developed for the pulmonary route of drug administration. However, lung anatomy and physiology impose challenges for the formulation, aerosol generation methods, and delivery of aerosols and gases to the lungs. Patient breathing and device manipulation and coordination can also impact pulmonary drug delivery. Current and future drug development has allowed the rational delivery of gases and vapors, solid particles, and liquid droplets through several devices. The most common aerosol dosage forms include liquid formulations delivered by air-jet, ultrasonic, or vibrating mesh nebulizers; solid or liquid propellant-based formulations delivered through pressurized metered-dose inhalers; and solid powders delivered through dry powder inhalers.

Case studies

Case 11.1

The vapor pressure of pure propellant 11 (MW = 137.4 g/mol) is 13.4 pounds per square inch (psi), and the vapor pressure of propellant 12 (MW = 120.9 g/mol) is 84.9. A mixture of 50:50 g weight of two propellants was added to prepare an aerosol in a glass container. You, as a fourth-year pharmacy student, are asked to find out the total pressure of this propellant mixture and advise the manufacturer whether he can use a glass container for this aerosol packaging.

Approach: Both Raoult's law and Dalton's law of partial pressure are used to calculate the total pressure:

Moles of Prop-11 = 50 g/137.4 g/mol = 0.364 mol, Moles of Prop-12 = 50 g/120.9 g/mol = 0.414 mol.

Mole fraction of Prop-11 = 0.364 mol/(0.364 mol + 0.414 mol) = 0.468, Mole fraction of Prop-12 = 1−0.468 = 0.532.

Partial pressure of Prop-11 = 0.468 × 13.4 psi = 6.27 psi.

Partial press of Prop-12 = 0.532 × 84.9 psi = 45.2 psi.

Total pressure = 6.27 psi + 45.2 psi = 51.5 psi.

The second question is whether this mixture can be packaged in a glass container. The total pressure is more than 25 psi, which is the maximum pressure a glass container can withstand. Advise the manufacturer to use aluminum or plastic containers instead.

Case 11.2

One of the advantages of a pulmonary delivery system is that it is a noninvasive alternative for parenteral injection. Then why was Exubera, the first FDA-approved inhaled insulin, pulled from the market?

Approach: Inhaled insulin (brand name Exubera) was approved in January 2006. Upon its approval, Pfizer and market analysts predicted that Exubera would be a blockbuster drug since it was the first inhaled option on the market for people who needed to take insulin. However, Exubera's high price and bulky inhaler, as well as concerns about its effects on lung function, led to much lower sales than had been expected. The journal *Diabetes Care* reported a study in which 582 adults with Type 1 diabetes were tested for participants' lung function; the study found that both test groups experienced small declines within the first 3 months [31]. The decline observed in the inhaled insulin group was larger than that of the parenteral insulin users. However, neither group experienced a drop in lung function of more than 2%, and deterioration did not progress in either group for the rest of the study period (2 years). The inhaled insulin group also experienced more coughing than the injected insulin group (38% vs. 13%). Rates of other side effects were similar between the two groups.

In a statement on the Exubera product website (www.exubera.com), Pfizer emphasizes that Exubera was a safe and effective dosage form and was not discontinued because of any concerns in those areas. Rather, it says, "Pfizer has made this decision because too few patients are taking Exubera."

Case 11.3

There are multiple pulmonary drug delivery devices available. What would be the best device to use in a 3-year-old asthma patient to delivery albuterol, a rescue medication, used during an asthma attack?

Approach: A few key patient-specific components to take into consideration when determining the best device for the patient would be: patient age, urgency of drug delivery to lungs, patient/caregiver competency in using the device, and need for repeat doses. Given the described patient in the case is a pediatric patient, a device should be used that has a focus on ease of use. Secondly, due to the fact that the drug delivered needs to be given in an emergent scenario with a quick onset of action, it would be preferred to use a device that already contains the drug, rather than requiring the patient/caregiver to load the drug into the device itself. Secondly, due to the fact that the drug needs to emergently be given to the patient ensuring the patient inhales the drug into the lungs, it is important that the device is used properly. This scenario is perfectly set up for a pediatric patient to use a pMDI with a spacer. The addition of the spacer ensures proper use of the pMDI which ensures that the drug is deposited into the lungs in the proper location for it to be effective in mitigating the emergent asthma attack.

Critical reflections and practice applications

Drug delivery to the lungs is a complicated route of administration, especially compared to other routes. The inhaled active pharmaceutical ingredient can be a solid, liquid, or gas and is directly influenced by the formulation and device used to deliver the drug to the lung. Furthermore, the patient's lung physiology and breathing patterns can affect drug deposition in the lungs that would ultimately influence the success or failure of therapy. A pharmacist must understand the relationships between a drug, the formulation, the inhaled device, pulmonary physiology, and patient breathing when evaluating drug therapy to the lungs. A pharmacist must give special consideration based on the drug-device formulation such as (1) a therapeutic gas or vapor, (2) a nebulized solution or suspension, (3) a pressurized metered dose inhaler, (4) a dry powder inhaler, (5) a soft mist inhaler, or (6) a breath assisted device. The pharmacist must then match those considerations with an evaluation of the goal of therapy and patient's disease state, lung function and respiratory patterns, physical dexterity, and ability to follow device use instructions. Additionally, information related to aerosol drug delivery and devices may be included in the North American Pharmacist Licensure Examination (NAPLEX) in following areas related to Ref. [32].

- Area 1—Obtain, Interpret, or Assess Data, Medical, or Patient Information
- Area 2—Identify Drug Characteristics
- Area 3—Develop or Manage Treatment Plans
- Area 4—Perform Calculations
- Area 5—Compound, Dispense, or Administer Drugs, or Manage Delivery Systems

Acknowledgments

The authors wish to thank G. Scott Oldroyd, MD, for technical guidance regarding inhaled anesthetics.

References

[1] P.J. Anderson, History of aerosol therapy: liquid nebulization to MDIs to DPIs, Respir. Care 50 (9) (2005) 1139–1150.

[2] M. Sanders, Inhalation therapy: an historical review, Primary Care Respir J 16 (2) (2007) 71–81.

[3] N.S. Wang, E.E. Bittar, Anatomy and ultrastructure of the lungPulmonary biology in health and disease, in: E.E. Bittar (Ed.), Pulmonary Biology in Health and Disease, Springer, New York, 2004, pp. 1–19.

[4] K.P. O'Donnell, H.D.C. Smyth, H.D.C. Smyth, A.J. Hickey, Macro- and microstructure of the airways for drug deliveryControlled pulmonary drug delivery, in: H.D.C. Smyth, A.J. Hickey (Eds.), Controlled Pulmonary Drug Delivery, Springer, 2011, pp. 1–20.

[5] M.G. Levitzky, Pulmonary Physiology [9] M.G. Levitzky, Pulmonary physiology, seventh ed., McGraw Hill, Chicago, IL, 2007, p. 280. McGraw Hill, Chicago, IL 2007.

[6] J.I. Peters, S.M. Levine, J.T. DiPiro, Introduction to pulmonary function testingPharmacotherapy: a pathophysiologic approach, in: J.T. DiPiro (Ed.), Pharmacotherapy: A Pathophysiologic Approach, McGraw Hill, Chicago, IL, 2011.

[7] A. Henning, M. Schäfer-Korting, Pulmonary drug delivery: medicines for inhalationDrug delivery, in: M. Schäfer-Korting (Ed.), Drug Delivery, Springer, 2010, pp. 171–192.

[8] J.S. Patton, P.R. Byron, Inhaling medicines: delivering drugs to the body through the lungs, Nat. Rev. Drug Discov. 6 (1) (2007) 67–74.

[9] H.C. Yeh, R.F. Phalen, O.G. Raabe, Factors influencing the deposition of inhaled particles, Environ. Health Perspect. 15 (1976) 147–156.

[10] R.O. McClellan, P. Gehr, J. Heyder, Particle interactions with the respiratory tractParticle-lung interactions. In: P. Gehr, J. Heyder, Particle-lung Interactions. Marcel Dekker, Inc., New York, NY20003–N20063.

[11] H. Schulz, P. Brand, J. Heyder, P. Gehr, J. Heyder, Particle deposition in the respiratory tractParticle-lung interactions, in: P. Gehr, J. Heyder (Eds.), Particle-lung Interactions, Marcel Dekker, Inc., New York, NY, 2000, pp. 229–290.

[12] Z. Xu, A.J. Hickey, H.D.C. Smyth, A.J. Hickey, The physics of aerosol droplet and particle generation from inhalers Controlled pulmonary drug delivery, in: H.D.C. Smyth, A.J. Hickey (Eds.), Controlled Pulmonary Drug Delivery, Springer, 2011, pp. 75–100.

[13] C. Kleinstreuer, Z. Zhang, Z. Li, Modeling airflow and particle transport/deposition in pulmonary airways, Respir. Physiol. Neurobiol. 163 (1–3) (2008) 128–138.

[14] E.R. Weibel, What makes a good lung? Swiss Med. Wkly. 139 (27–28) (2009) 375–386.

[15] Z. Zhang, C. Kleinstreuer, Airflow structures and nano-particle deposition in a human upper airway model, J. Comput. Phys. 198 (1) (2004) 178–210.

[16] P.J. Sinko, ColloidsMartin's Physical Pharmacy and Pharmaceutical Sciences, Lippincott Williams & Wilkins, New York, NY, 2006.

[17] T.C. Carvalho, J.I. Peters, R.O. Williams, Influence of particle size on regional lung deposition—what evidence is there? Int. J. Pharm. 406 (1–2) (2011) 1–10.

[18] D.E. Geller, J. Weers, S. Heuerding, Development of an inhaled dry-powder formulation of tobramycin using PulmoSphere technology, J. Aerosol Med. Pulm. Drug Deliv. 24 (2011) 175–182.

[19] P.M. Patel, H.H. Patel, D.M. Roth, L.L. Brunton, General anesthetics and therapeutic gasesThe pharmacological basis of therapeutics, in: L.L. Brunton (Ed.), The Pharmacological Basis of Therapeutics, McGraw Hill, Chicago, IL, 2011.

[20] G. Pilcer, K. Amighi, Formulation strategy and use of excipients in pulmonary drug delivery, Int. J. Pharm. 392 (1–2) (2010) 1–19.

[21] J.J. Sciarra, C.J. Sciarra, L.V. Allen, AerosolsThe science and practice of pharmacy, in: L.V. Allen (Ed.), The Science and Practice of Pharmacy, Pharmaceutical Press, 2013, pp. 999–1016.

[22] A. Gibbons, H.D.C. Smyth, H.D.C. Smyth, A.J. Hickey, Science and technology of nebulizers and liquid-based aerosol generators Controlled pulmonary drug delivery, in: H.D.C. Smyth, A.J. Hickey (Eds.), Controlled Pulmonary Drug Delivery, Springer, 2011, pp. 223–2011236.

[23] M. Cazzola, J. Ora, A. Bianco, P. Rogliani, M.G. Matera, Guidance on nebulization during the current COVID-19 pandemic, Respir. Med. 176 (2021) 1–4.

[24] S.R.P. da Rocha, B. Bharatwaj, S. Saiprasad, H.D.C. Smyth, A.J. Hickey, Science and technology of pressurized metered-dose inhalers Controlled pulmonary drug delivery, in: H.D.C. Smyth, A.J. Hickey (Eds.), Controlled Pulmonary Drug Delivery, Springer, 2011, pp. 165–202.

[25] S.P. Newman, Principles of metered-dose inhaler design, Respir. Care 50 (9) (2005) 1177–1190.

[26] B.K. Rubin, J.B. Fink, Optimizing aerosol delivery by pressurized metered-dose inhalers, Respir. Care 50 (9) (2005) 1191–1200.

[27] C.L. Leach, The CFC to HFA transition and its impact on pulmonary drug development, Respir. Care 50 (9) (2005) 1201–1208.

[28] T.M. Crowder, M.J. Donovan, H.D.C. Smyth, A.J. Hickey, Science and technology of dry powder inhalers Controlled pulmonary drug delivery, in: H.D.C. Smyth, A.J. Hickey (Eds.), Controlled Pulmonary Drug Delivery, Springer, 2011, pp. 2011203–2011222.

[29] M.J. Telko, A.J. Hickey, Dry powder inhaler formulation, Respir. Care 50 (9) (2005) 1209–1227.

[30] P.J. Anderson, Use of Respimat® soft Mist™ inhaler in COPD patients, Int. J. Chronic Obstr. Pulm. Dis. 1 (3) (2006) 251–259.

[31] J.S. Skyler, L. Jovanovic, S. Klioze, J. Reis, W. Duggan, Two-year safety and efficacy of inhaled human insulin (Exubera) in adult patients with type 1 diabetes, Diabet. Care 30 (2007) 579–585.

[32] National Association of Boards of Pharmacy, NAPLEX Competency Statements, 2021.

[33] Danish EPA, Report No. 12352008, Regional deposition of particles within the lung. Depending on the particle size and the overall inhalation maneuver, particles deposit within different regions of the lung. https://eng.mst.dk/.

12

Semisolid Dosage Forms

Somnath Singh[1], Alekha K. Dash[1] and Satish Agrawal[2]

[1]Department of Pharmacy Sciences, School of Pharmacy and Health Professions, Creighton University, Omaha, NE, United States [2]Department of Pharmacy Sciences, Creighton University, Omaha, NE, United States

CHAPTER OBJECTIVES

- Identify and classify the various types of semisolid dosage forms.
- Discuss the theory involved in the preparation of ointments, creams, pastes, and transdermal patches.
- Describe the clinical applications of semisolid dosage forms.
- Define percutaneous absorption.
- Discuss the methods of enhancement of percutaneous absorption.
- Explain the quality evaluations for ointments, creams, pastes, and transdermal patches.
- Discuss the mechanism of drug release from the transdermal system.

Keywords: Cream; Ointment; Paste; Percutaneous absorption; Suppository; Transdermal patch.

12.1 Introduction

Semisolid dosage forms represent pharmaceutical preparations that have properties in between the solids and liquids. They possess rheological properties that are suitable for easy application to the skin or accessible to mucous membranes. They tend to remain on the site of application for a prolonged time. Additionally, they can alleviate or treat a pathological condition or offer protection to the skin against harmful environmental conditions.

Semisolid dosage forms may contain one or more active pharmaceutical ingredients (APIs) in a suitable excipient. These dosage forms are applied topically to the skin or on to the surface of the eye, nasal cavity, vagina, rectum, or any other mucosal membranes for the local and/or systemic effects [1–3]. The semi-solid dosage forms accounted for the largest revenue share of 78.3% in 2019 and is anticipated to maintain its lead over the forecast period of 2020–27 [2]. Commercially, they constitute about 8%–10% of all dosage forms in the pharmaceutical marketplace [4].

The ideal physical and physiological properties of semisolid dosage forms are listed below:
Ideal physical properties [5].

- Easy to apply
- Smooth texture
- Non-gritty
- Elegant in appearance
- Non-dehydrating
- Non-hygroscopic
- Non-greasy
- Non-staining to both skin and cloth

Ideal physiological properties [5].

- Non-irritating
- Non-sensitive to skin
- Non-affecting membrane/skin functions
- Miscible with skin secretion

If the API is insoluble in the vehicle, the potency of the semisolid dosage forms depends on its particle size in addition to the uniformity of its distribution in the vehicle. An increase in the particle size causes a reduction in the surface area resulting in decreased percutaneous absorption but increased grittiness leading to skin irritation [6,7].

The semisolids can be divided into different types of formulations based on their traditional usages such as creams, gels, ointments, pastes, suppositories, and transdermal drug delivery systems. Creams are semisolid emulsions containing an emulsifying base approved for use in dermatology and cosmetology. Creams are of two types: (1) oil-in-water (o/w) (aqueous cream) and (2) water-in-oil (w/o) (oily cream) type emulsion systems. In the case of (o/w) creams, oil is dispersed in water whereas the reverse is true for (w/o) creams. The (o/w) creams are hydrophilic by nature, whereas (w/o) creams are hydrophobic resulting in a greasy appearance, but they moisturize the skin very effectively.

Examples:

- Hydrocortisone cream USP, 2.5% (used in the treatment of inflammatory dermatoses) (Fig. 12.1).
- Miconazole nitrate cream USP, 2% (used in the treatment of fungal infection) (Fig. 12.2).

Gels are semisolid systems in which a liquid phase is immobilized by a three-dimensional network, composed of a self-assembled, intertwined, net-like structure cross-linked by a suitable gelling agent. Despite their liquid composition, these systems demonstrate the appearance and rheological behavior of solids [8]. They are coherent masses

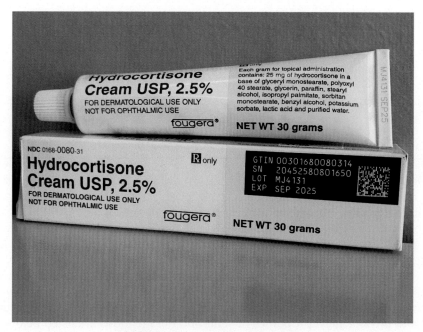

FIGURE 12.1 Hydrocortisone cream.

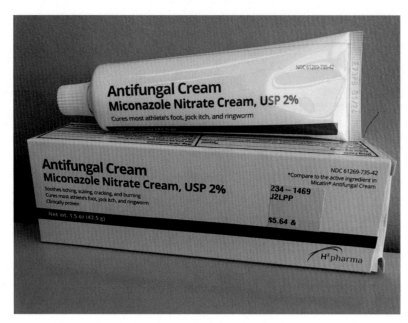

FIGURE 12.2   Miconazole nitrate cream.

generally composed of one phase (oil or water) or two phases (oil and water) such as emulsion. The intermolecular forces provide gels their characteristic stability and structural rigidity which are manifested as their decreased mobility and increased viscosity [9].

Examples:

- Benadryl® gel (used as anti-itching gel) (Fig. 12.3).
- Lidocaine hydrochloride (2%) gel (Lidogel, used to relieve local pain) (Fig. 12.4).

Pastes are semisolid, stiff preparations containing a higher proportion (more than 20%) of finely divided solids into a conventional ointment base. Powders such as zinc oxide, titanium dioxide, starch, kaolin, and talc are incorporated in high concentrations into a preferably lipophilic, greasy vehicle. A clinically distinctive feature of pastes is its ability to absorb exudates due to physiochemical properties of the powder or other absorptive materials used in its preparation [11]. Because of their stiffness, pastes are not suitable for application to hairy parts of the body. Pastes

FIGURE 12.3   Benadryl® gel.

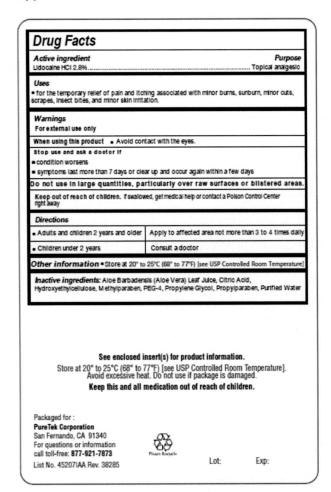

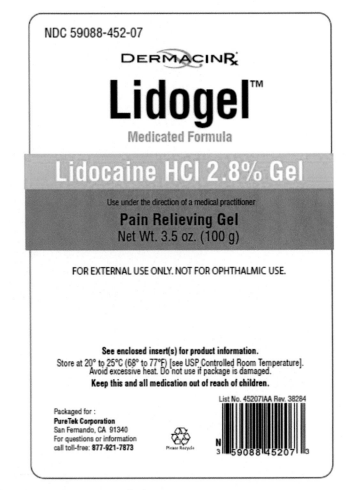

FIGURE 12.4   Lidogel information in an FDA report [10].

are prepared either using fatty bases, such as petrolatum and hydrophilic petrolatum, or aqueous gels, such as celluloses.

Examples:

- Toothpaste (Pronamel, used for sensitive teeth) (Fig. 12.5).
- Zinc oxide paste (Desitin Paste used for mitigating diaper rash) (Fig. 12.6).

Ointments are viscous semisolid preparations used topically on body surfaces such as skin and the mucous membranes of the eye, vagina, anus, and nose which may or may not be medicated. Medicated ointments contain an API dissolved, suspended, or emulsified in the base whereas a non-medicated ointment does not contain any API. Ointments are used topically for several purposes such as protectants, antiseptics, emollients, antipruritics, keratolytics, or astringents.

Examples:

- Lidocaine ointment USP, 5% (used for relief of pain) (Fig. 12.7).
- Mupirocin ointment USP, 2% (used for the treatment of skin infection) (Fig. 12.8).

Suppositories are solid bodies of various weights, sizes, and shapes suitable for insertion into a body cavity, which includes the rectum, vagina, or urethra, for both local as well as systemic effects. They usually melt, soften, or dissolve at body temperature.

Examples:

- Hemmorex-HC™ suppository (Hydrocortisone acetate, 10 mg, used as anti-inflammatory and anti-itching) (Fig. 12.9).

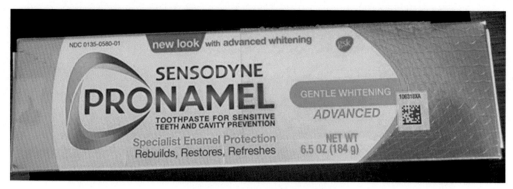

FIGURE 12.5   Pronamel toothpaste.

FIGURE 12.6   Desitin diaper rash paste.

- Acetaminophen suppository (Acetaminophen 120 mg, used as pain-reliever and fever reducer) (Fig. 12.10).

A chemically synthesized material or a plant extract can be used as a drug in semisolid formulations. The formulation of the dosage form is a combination of the drug and different types of inactive components called additives or excipients. The additives, such as emulsifiers, thickening agents, antimicrobial agents, antioxidants, or stabilizing agents, are added to the formulation to provide specific functions. A suitable antimicrobial agent should be added in an appropriate concentration if the formulation is prone to the growth of microorganisms unless the preparations themselves may have adequate antimicrobial properties. Assurance must be provided from the preformulation studies that APIs are compatible with the excipient used in the formulation.

12.1.1 Advantages of semisolid dosage forms [12−15]

- Direct application to the affected area providing site-specific delivery
- Requiring less amount of drug due to direct local application
- Better surface adherence with rapid onset and longer duration of action
- Improved patient compliance and convenience of application in specialized patient groups such as unconscious patients, children, and geriatric patients

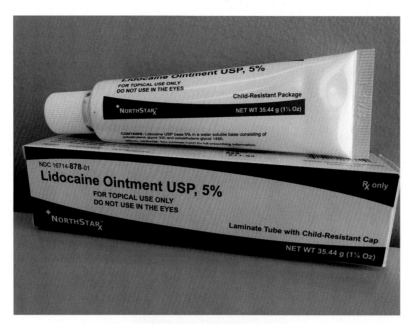

FIGURE 12.7   Lidocaine ointment.

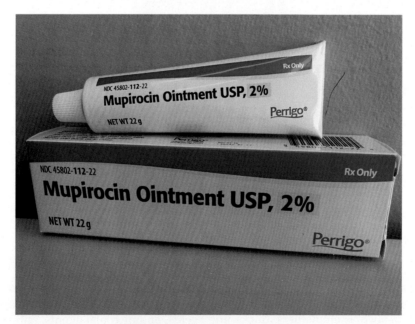

FIGURE 12.8   Mupirocin ointment.

- Avoiding risks and inconveniences of intravenous therapy
- Easy way of combining drugs in a single dosage form
- Reduced risk of side effects because of external and local application
- Avoids first pass metabolism since not taken orally
- Higher stability as compared to liquid dosage forms
- Suitable for API with a bitter taste

12.1.2 Disadvantages of semisolid dosage forms [12–17]

- Inaccuracy of doses delivered
- Greasy texture and sometimes difficult to clean

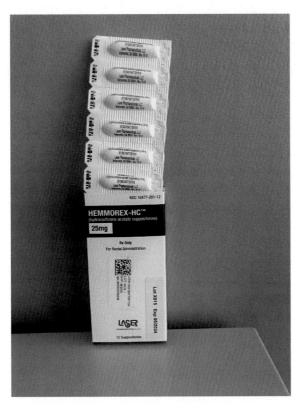

FIGURE 12.9 Hemmorex-HC™ suppository.

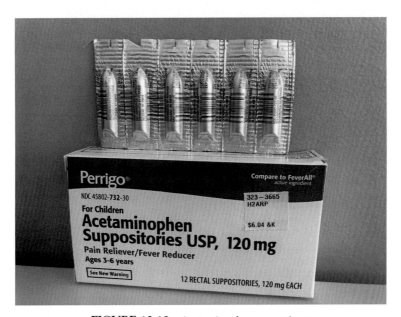

FIGURE 12.10 Acetaminophen suppository.

- Less stable as compared to solid dosage forms
- Rancidity due to oxidation of lipid bases used
- Contamination of dosage forms due to use of fingers for application
- Some allergic reaction or irritation after application is possible
- Expensive due to complex manufacturing process
- Can stain cloth and skin

12.2 Classification of semisolid dosage forms

Physicochemical properties such as loss on drying; specific gravity, rheology; and composition of the formulation are important parameters that are used by a decision tree (Fig. 12.11) to design a new semisolid dosage form [18] which are classified as shown in Fig. 12.12.

12.2.1 Ointments

Ointments are homogenous semisolid dosage forms applied onto the skin intended for the topical or transdermal delivery of APIs. These semisolid preparations are intended to adhere to the skin or certain mucous membranes and are usually solutions or dispersions of one or more medicaments in nonaqueous bases. Ointment bases are often anhydrous and include fats, oils, and waxes of animal, vegetable, or mineral origin. It may also include nonoleaginous and synthetic substances.

The rate of drug-diffusion from the ointment bases has been observed to be pH-dependent [19]. The amount of drug released depends on the composition of the vehicle and the concentration of the drug incorporated in it [20]. The use of ointments as an ocular drug vehicle adds an important dimension to topical therapy. Ointments are well tolerated and fairly safe; they also provide an excellent means for enhanced ocular contact time. In the case of certain antibiotics, this improved contact time yields increased ocular drug levels. Corticosteroid ointments as well as suspensions do not penetrate the eye, which may be related to the binding of the drug to the ointment base and also to the physicochemical property of the particular drug. Like other ophthalmic preparations, ointments may become contaminated. Ophthalmic ointments should not be instilled into eyes with open wounds. Instillation of ointments into postoperative eyes where wound closure is secure appears to be safe and effective.

There are two main types of ointments.

- *Water-soluble ointments* include mixtures of polyethylene glycol 400 (a liquid) and propylene glycols 3350 (a solid) in which their consistency can be easily controlled. They are easily washed off and are used in burn dressings, as lubricants, and as vehicles that readily allow passage of drugs into the skin, for example, Cortizone-10 ointment (hydrocortisone ointment USP) (Fig. 12.13).
- *Water-insoluble ointments* are further divided into two classes:
- *Emulsifying ointments* are made from emulsifying wax (cetostearyl alcohol and sodium lauryl sulfate) and paraffin oils. They are used to moisturize very dry skin such as in eczema or dermatitis. Examples: Aquaphor Healing Ointment (Fig. 12.14). CeraVe Healing ointment (Fig. 12.15).
- *Nonemulsifying ointments* do not mix with water. They adhere to the skin to prevent evaporation and heat loss, that is, they can be considered a form of occlusive dressing, with increased systemic absorption where skin maceration may occur. Nonemulsifying ointments are helpful as vehicles in chronic dry and scaly conditions, such as atopic eczema; they are not appropriate where there is significant exudation. They are difficult to remove except with oil or detergent and are messy and inconvenient, especially on hairy skin. Paraffin ointment contains beeswax, paraffin, and cetostearyl alcohol, is an example of a nonemulsifying ointment [21].

12.2.1.1 Classification of ointment bases

i. Hydrocarbon (oleaginous) bases: These anhydrous bases contain oils/fats. They are insoluble in water, not water-washable, and cannot absorb water [22]. **Examples:**
   - Petrolatum USP is a mixture of semisolid hydrocarbons. Melting point 38°C–60°C. Commercial Product: Vaseline.
   - Yellow ointment, USP, 95% (w/w) petrolatum and 5% (w/w) yellow wax.
   - White ointment, 95% (w/w) petrolatum and 5% (w/w) white wax.
   - Paraffin NF: It is a purified mixture of solid hydrocarbons obtained from petroleum. It is used to stiffen oleaginous semisolid ointment bases.
   - Mineral oil, USP: It is a mixture of liquid hydrocarbons obtained from petroleum. It is used as a levigating agent. Commonly known as liquid petrolatum.
ii. Absorption bases: These bases are called absorption bases because they can absorb water. They should not be confused with the absorption of these bases through the skin [22]. There are two types of absorption bases:
   a. Anhydrous bases:

Those that permit the incorporation of aqueous solutions to become (w/o) emulsions.

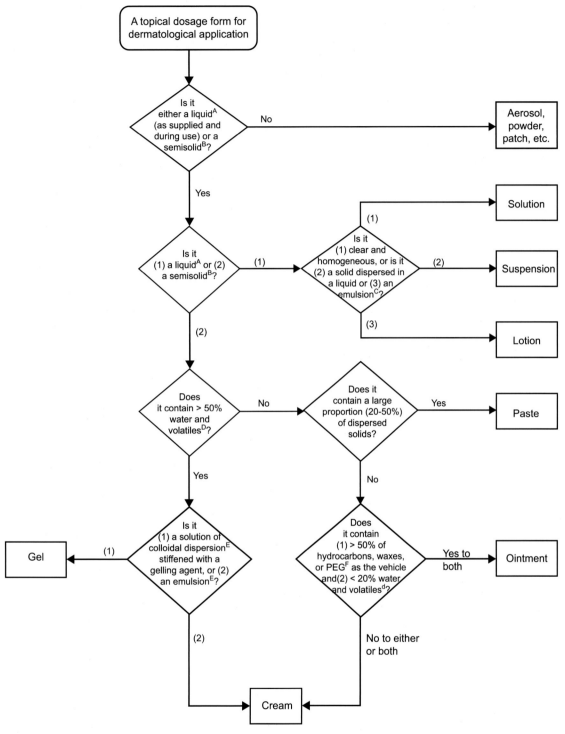

FIGURE 12.11 Decision tree on topical dosage form nomenclature. (A) A liquid is pourable; it flows and conforms to its container at room temperature. A liquid displays Newtonian or pseudoplastic flow behavior. (B) A semisolid is not pourable; it does not flow or conform to its container at room temperature. It does not flow at low shear stress and generally exhibits plastic flow behavior. (C) An emulsion is a two-phase system consisting of at least two immiscible liquids, one of which is dispersed as globules (internal or dispersed phase) within the other liquid phase (external or continuous phase), generally stabilized by an emulsifying agent. (D) Water and volatiles as measured by a loss on drying (LOD) test by heating at 105°C until constant weight is achieved. (E) A colloidal dispersion is a system in which particles of colloidal dimension are distributed uniformly throughout a liquid. (F) Polyethylene glycol, a vehicle for semisolid dosage forms.

FIGURE 12.12 Classification of various semisolid dosage form.

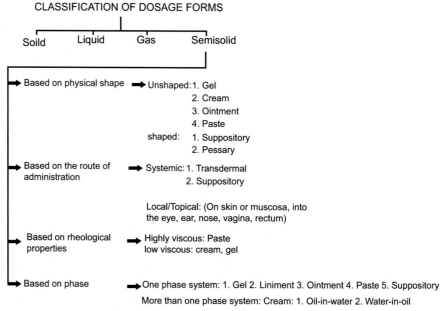

FIGURE 12.13 Cortizone-10 ointment.

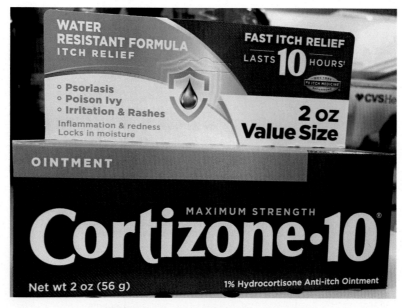

Examples:

- Hydrophilic petrolatum, USP (3% cholesterol in white petrolatum)
- Anhydrous lanolin USP
- Aquaphor (6 parts wool-wax alcohol and 99 parts of aliphatic hydrocarbons)

b. Hydrous bases: They consist of hydrous water-in-oil emulsion which permits the incorporation of the additional quantity of water.

Example: Cold cream USP, Lanolin USP

iii. Water-removable bases: These bases are (o/w) emulsions and can be washed from skin or clothing with water. These bases are nonocclusive, nongreasy, and cannot absorb water [22]. These bases can be diluted with water or

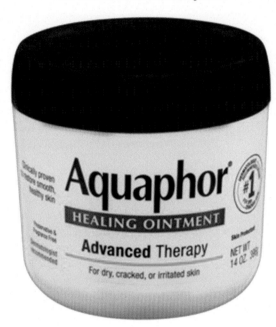

FIGURE 12.14 Aquaphor healing ointment.

FIGURE 12.15 CeraVe healing ointment.

with an aqueous solution because their external phase is water. The water-removable bases consist of three parts: an oil phase, a water phase, and emulsifiers. Many cosmetic preparations such as vanishing creams and foundation creams are (o/w) emulsion bases. **Example:** Clobetasol propionate Cream (Fig. 12.16) and Cetaphil cream (Fig. 12.17).

iv. Water-soluble bases: Water-soluble bases consist of only water-soluble substances like polyethylene glycol. They are water-removable, greaseless, spread readily without rubbing, and form a protective film on the skin surfaces.

Example: Polyethylene glycol ointment, USP.

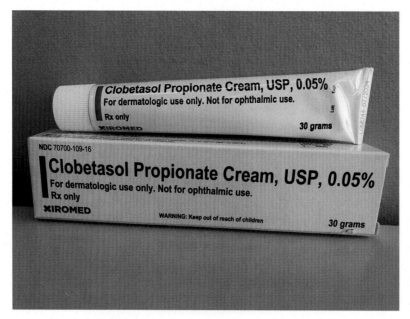

FIGURE 12.16   Clobetasol propionate cream.

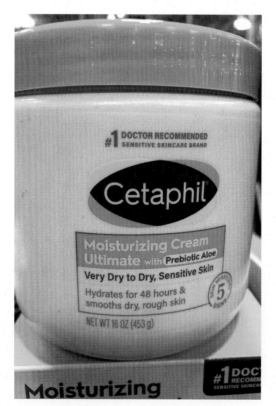

FIGURE 12.17   Cetaphil cream.

12.2.1.2 *Selection of the appropriate base*

The following factors should be considered before selecting an ointment base:

- The release rate of the drug from the ointment base
- Extent of percutaneous absorption
- Drug stability and incompatibility in the ointment base

- Physical changes (change in consistency) if any due to the presence of the drug

12.2.1.3 Ideal properties of an ointment base

- Nonirritating, nondehydrating, and nongreasy
- Compatible with common medicaments
- Chemically stable
- Easily removable with water
- Good absorptive properties (water and other aqueous liquids)
- Good release properties of the drug from the base
- Partition of the drug from ointment base to the skin
- Non-staining to the skin and garments

12.2.1.4 Preparation of ointments

Ointments can be prepared by two methods.

- Mechanical incorporation
- Fusion

The choice of method depends on the drug used and the physical properties of the constituents of the base.

12.2.1.4.1 Preparation by mechanical incorporation

Mechanical incorporation involves mixing a drug into the ointment base which can be achieved by using either a mortar and pestle or a glass slab and a pair of spatulas if amount to be prepared is small. When ointments are to be prepared in large amounts (5 pounds or more), mechanical mixers are generally used.

Examples of large-scale mixing equipments.

- Roller mill
- Hobart mixer

When solid ingredients are incorporated, their particle size must be kept as small as possible. The best result is obtained by mixing small amounts of the base with the powder to form a very smooth nucleus, which is eventually mixed with the remainder of the base in a geometric dilution. The ingredient(s) can also be levigated with a levigating agent (mineral oil for oleaginous base or glycerol for oil-in-water bases) to form a smooth paste which is eventually mixed with the remainder of the base. Use of levigating agent is specifically important for preparing salicylic acid ointment.

12.2.1.4.2 Fusion method

In the fusion method, all the ointment base components are melted together in the order of decreasing melting points, that is, the component with the highest melting point is melted first followed by the component with second highest melting point, and so on. In this way, the component with lowest melting point is protected from overheating which otherwise may lead to degradation and other physicochemical changes. Usually, heating is achieved by using a water bath to avoid excessive temperatures. The solid to be incorporated is also added to this melted base in the order of decreasing melting point and stirred until it congeals to ensure a homogeneous product. If the ointment contains any volatile material, it should be added last during congealing process.

12.2.1.5 Containers

Two different types of containers are most commonly used for the packaging of ointments: ointment jars and tubes as shown in Fig. 12.18. The label of an ointment must indicate "For External Use Only."

12.2.2 Creams

Creams are viscous semisolid emulsion systems that have an opaque appearance in contrast to translucent ointments [5]. This dosage form can penetrate the outer layer (keratinized layer) of the skin and provide emollience. Creams are widely used in cosmetics as they are an essential part of daily make-up used to moisturize skin. The consistency and rheological characteristics of creams depend on the types of emulsion [(w/o) or (o/w)]. Creams can be classified into two categories based on the presence/absence of API: medicated and nonmedicated.

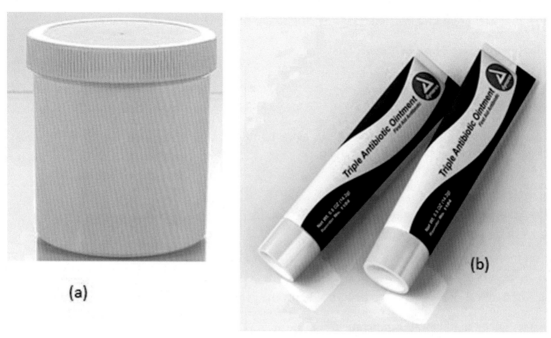

FIGURE 12.18   (a) Ointment jar and (b) tube.

Medicated creams have APIs with a particular pharmacological activity such as antibacterial [e.g., Clindamycin (cleomycin) for bacterial vaginosis], antifungal [e.g., Tinactin (tolnaftate) topical cream for tinea, ringworm infection], or antipruritic [e.g., Taclonex (a combination product containing betamethasone and calcipotriene) for psoiasis]. Whereas nonmedicated creams [e.g., CeraVe (Fig. 12.19), Nivea etc., Moisturizing Cream] are used for cosmetic purposes to moisturize, beautify, and nourish the skin. Skin cream reduces surface roughness and increases the hydrophilic properties of the skin. Application of cream can reduce charge build-up on the skin surface [23].

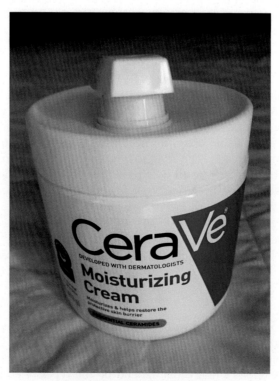

FIGURE 12.19   CeraVe cream.

Creams, being semisolid emulsions, are also classified as (o/w) and (w/o) types depending on whether the continuous/external phase is water or oil, respectively. The emulsion type also significantly influences the consistency and rheological characteristics of a cream. Properly designed (o/w) creams are an elegant drug delivery system, pleasing in both appearances and feel after application. Furthermore, the (o/w) creams are nongreasy and can be easily removed by rinsing with water due to the aqueous makeup of the external phase. They are good for most topical purposes and are considered particularly suitable for application to oozing wounds because they can absorb water easily. Conversely, the (w/o) creams are composed of small droplets of water dispersed in a continuous oily phase. Therefore, such creams are more difficult to handle and are not water washable because oil is used as an external phase. However, these creams release the incorporated hydrophobic drugs less readily than the (o/w) creams [24]. Moreover, the (w/o) creams are also more moisturizing because they provide an oily barrier that reduces water loss from the stratum corneum, the outermost layer of the skin. Hence, they are widely used as cold creams where the oil phase forms a protective covering and prevents excessive loss of moisture from the skin during the winter season when the atmospheric moisture content is severely low. Below are some examples of creams:

- The (o/w) creams
  - Foundation creams
  - Hand creams
  - Shaving creams
- The (w/o) creams
  - Cold creams
  - Emollient creams

12.2.3 Pastes [24,25]

Pastes are basically ointments into which a high percentage (20–50) of an insoluble solid has been added. This higher amount of particulate matter stiffens the system through direct interactions of the dispersed particulates and by adsorption of the liquid hydrocarbon fraction of the vehicle on the particle surface.

Pastes are usually prepared by incorporating solids directly into a congealed system by levigation, with a portion of the base to form a paste-like mass. The remainders of the base are added with continued levigation until the solids are uniformly dispersed in the vehicle.

Pastes are less penetrating and less macerating than ointments and make a particularly good protective barrier when placed on the skin. Pastes are less greasy because of the absorption of the fluid hydrocarbon fraction into the particulates. In addition to forming an unbroken film, they can absorb serous secretions and thereby neutralize certain noxious chemicals before they ever reach the skin. Like ointments, pastes form an unbroken relatively water-impermeable film that is opaque; therefore, zinc oxide paste is an effective sun barrier. Skiers apply the paste around the nose and lips to gain dual protection.

There are two types of pastes.

- Fatty pastes (e.g., zinc oxide paste).
- Non-greasy pastes (e.g., bassorin paste, which is also named tragacanth jelly since the hydrophilic component of the base i.e., tragacanth gels in water).

12.2.4 Gels (jellies)

Gels are a semisolid system in which a liquid phase is constrained within a three-dimensional polymeric matrix having a high degree of physical or chemical cross-linking. They are aqueous colloidal suspensions of the hydrated forms of an insoluble gelling agent along with medicament, for example, Aluminum Hydroxide Gel, USP. Gels may be a single-phase system or two-phase system based on the existence of an apparent boundary between the macromolecules (gelling agent) and the liquid. Two-phase systems contain floccules of small, distinct particles with higher viscosity and are referred to as magma. Jellies are transparent or translucent nongreasy semisolid gels. Some are as transparent as water; others are turbid due to dispersion of light by the colloidal aggregates. Gels are used for medication, lubrication, and some miscellaneous applications such as carriers for spermicidal agents to be used intravaginally with diaphragms as an adjunctive means of contraception. For example, VCF® vaginal contraceptive gel (Fig. 12.20) which contains nonoxynol-9 (4%), and diclofenac sodium topical gel (Voltaren) (Fig. 12.21) are few examples of marketed gels.

FIGURE 12.20   VCF® vaginal contraceptive gel.

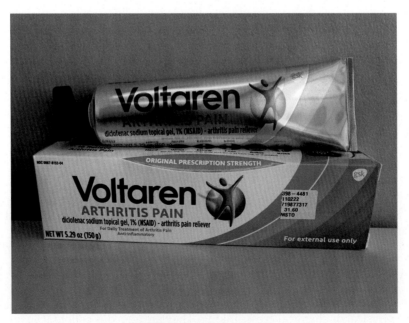

FIGURE 12.21   Voltaren gel.

12.2.5 Poultices

Poultices are soft, viscous wet masses of solid substances applied to the skin for relieving pain or inflammation. For example, Kaolin poultice (BPC), which is applied to the affected part of the body after heating it in a China dish with occasional stirring. Its temperature must be tested for tolerable heat before applying on the affected area. The melted poultice is spread as a thick film on a dressing material which is applied on to the affected area.

FIGURE 12.22   BSN Gypsona Plaster of Paris bandage.

12.2.6 Plasters

Plasters are solid or semisolid masses that adhere to skin when spread upon cotton, felt, linen, or muslin as a backing material; they are mainly used to provide protection and mechanical support. They may provide an occlusive and macerating action and bring medication into close contact with the surface of the skin, for example, Plaster of Paris Bandage BP (Fig. 12.22).

12.2.7 Foams

Foams are a dispersion of gas in a liquid or a semisolid continuous phase that contains drug substance and suitable excipients. Excipients are generally consisted of aqueous or nonaqueous carriers, foam structuring agents, surfactants, and propellants (in the case of pressurized aerosol-based foams). Foams dispensed from non-pressurized containers such as shaving creams use mechanical forces for mixing of the formulation (drug and excipients) and air for generating foam. In case of pressurized containers, such as whipped creams, aerosolized shaving creams, liquefied propellants are used in the container to increase the inside pressure. When the nozzle of the actuator is depressed, the liquid phase containing a dispersed vapor or gas is emitted resulting in the formation of a foam. Foams are convenient to apply drug substances topically to areas where physical application is painful and inconvenient (e.g., third degree burn patient). They are a convenient form of API delivery to certain areas like ear canal or to mucosal sites such as the rectum, vagina, or oropharynx.

12.2.8 Suppositories

Suppositories are solid dosage forms containing medicinal agents intended for insertion into body cavities, including the rectum, vaginal cavity, or urethral tract but not through the oral cavity. While suppositories are frequently used for local action, they can also be used to achieve an adequate systemic concentration of a drug. This dosage form is specifically useful for drugs that are degraded or converted into inactive forms by hepatic first-pass metabolism. Drug absorption from rectal suppositories can be affected by the following factors.

- Anorectal physiology
- Solubility of the drug
- Particle size and concentration of the drug
- Physiochemical properties of the suppository base used
- Melting point of the base
- Solubility of the drug in the base
- Polymorphism of the base as well as of the drug

The major inactive component of a suppository dosage form is the suppository base which should have the following properties:

- Melting at rectal temperature 37.5°C
- Nontoxic and nonirritating to sensitive and inflamed tissues
- Physically stable and compatible with a variety of drugs
- Convenient for the patient to handle and not breaking or melting during administration
- No leakage from the rectum
- Stable on storage and no change in color, odor, and drug release pattern

Suppository bases can be classified into three categories according to their physicochemical properties.

- Oleaginous
  - Cocoa butter (Theobroma oil)
  - Cocoa butter substitutes
- Water-soluble
  - Glycerinated gelatin
  - Polyethylene glycol mixtures
- Water-dispersible
  - Polyethylene glycol derivatives
  - Cocoa butter substituted with surfactants

Cocoa butter is the most widely used suppository base for rectal use. This is the base of choice when no suppository base is specified because it satisfies many of the requirements for an ideal base.

12.2.8.1 Manufacture of suppositories

Earlier suppositories were prepared by using the rolling method, but at present, they are prepared either by using the fusion or cold compression method [26]. In the fusion method, the molten mass of base and drug is poured into a lubricated mold kept over ice. The mold is made up of plastic/stainless steel, containing two halves that are fixed firmly by a screw. The mold, filled with molten base and drug, is then cooled at room temperature for 10–15 min. The suppositories, when set, are removed, wiped off with a clean cloth, and wrapped individually in wax paper.

The cold compression method is used for thermolabile and insoluble drugs. It makes use of a mold and cylinder. The medicament, incorporated into theobroma oil, is placed into the mold and then is passed into the cylinder through a narrow opening, where it is compressed until it forms a homogenous fused mass. Before the suppository achieves its final form, the compression cylinder of the machine is chilled to prevent the heating of suppositories. They are stored in a cool place to retain their shape at room temperature.

In a large-scale manufacturing, automatic molding is commonly used. The suppositories can be poured, cooled, and removed from the mold by rotary automatic molding machines. The output of a typical rotary machine is from 3500 to 6000 suppositories per hour.

Disposable molds are more frequently used now, with some additional advantages over conventional metal molds:

- Costly molds and wrapping materials are not required
- Mold shapes can be changed with less expense
- The costly and time-consuming wrapping process with aging and precooling is eliminated
- Disposable plastic molds may not require lubrication before filling

12.2.8.2 Calculation of base replacement

When calculating the amount of suppository base needed to completely fill a particular mold, one needs to subtract the volume occupied by the drug from the total volume of the mold.

However, if the amount of the drug is very small, for example, 100 mg or less, it becomes insignificant in comparison to the volume of a typical mold requiring 2 g of a base such as coca butter and need not be subtracted. But if the amount of the drug is significant (i.e., more than 100 mg for a 2 g suppository), the amount of base replaced by it can be calculated by using the following method where each weight is an average of 10 suppositories.

i. Dose replacement factor (DRF) method: The DRF is the weight in a gram of the drug replacing 1 g of the base which is calculated by the following formula:

$$DRF = \frac{100\ (W_{sb} - W_{sbd})}{(W_{sbd})(X\%)} + 1 \tag{12.1}$$

where W_{sb} = Weight of the suppository filled with base only

W_{sbd} = Weight of the suppository filled with the base containing $X\%$ of a drug

Cocoa butter is a standard base that is arbitrarily assigned a DRF value of 1. The DRF values of other bases are shown in Table 12.1. If the DRF value of a drug is not available in the literature, it can be calculated by using Eq. (12.1). The W_{sb} and W_{sbd} value should be the average of 10 suppositories filled with same volume of base and base mixed with a known % of the drug, respectively.

Example:

Calculate the weight of a suppository containing 650 mg of acetaminophen whose DRF value is 0.65. The weight of the suppository containing only the base is 2 g.

Solution:

$$X\% = \frac{0.650\ g}{2\ g} \times 100 = 32.5$$

W_{sb} = Weight of the suppository filled with base only = 2 g given

$DRF = 0.65$.

$X\% = 32.5$ calculated above for 650 mg acetaminophen.

W_{sbd} = Weight of the suppository filled with the base containing $X\%$ of a drug? W_{sbd} can be calculated using Eq. (12.1):

$$DRF = \frac{100\ (W_{sb} - W_{sbd})}{(W_{sbd})(X\%)} + 1$$

$$0.65 = \frac{100\ (2\ g - W_{sbd})}{(W_{sbd})(32.5)} + 1$$

Therefore, $W_{sbd} = 2.257$ g Answer

ii. Density factor (DF) method: This is the amount of the drug replacing 1 g of the base which is calculated by using the following formula:

$$DF = \frac{W_d}{W_{sb} - W_{sbd} - W_d} \tag{12.2}$$

where W_d = Weight of the drug in each suppository

The DF of cocoa butter is 0.9. If DF of a base is not known, it can be calculated as the ratio of the weight of the suppository filled with the base to one filled with cocoa butter as shown below:

$$DF\ of\ a\ base = \frac{weight\ of\ suppository\ filled\ with\ the\ base}{weight\ of\ suppository\ filled\ with\ cocoa\ butter}$$

Table 12.2 shows the DF of some drugs.

Example:

Calculate the amount of each ingredient to prepare 10 suppositories and the weight of each suppository containing 100 mg phenobarbital whose density factor, DF, is equal to 1.2. Two gram of cocoa butter is needed to completely fill the suppository mold.

Solution: This can be solved using the formula (Eq. 12.2):

TABLE 12.1 Dose replacement factors (DRFs) of some drugs and bases.

Drugs/bases	DRF values
Acetaminophen	0.67
Acetylsalicylic acid	0.65
Atropine sulfate	0.65
Balsam Peru	0.83
Bisacodyl	0.30
Bismuth subgallate	0.37
Bismuth subnitrate	0.33
Caffeine	0.60
Camphor	1.49
Castor oil	1.00
Chloral hydrate	0.67
Chlorpromazine hydrochloride	0.65
Codeine phosphate	0.65
Cyclizine hydrochloride	0.70
Ergotamine tartarate	0.65
Ichthammol	0.91
Lactose monohydrate	0.60
Lidocaine	1.0
Mesalazine	0.55
Morphine hydrochloride	0.65
Pethidine hydrochloride	0.65
Phenobarbital	0.81
Phenol	0.90
Procaine hydrochloride	0.80
Progesterone	0.85
Quinine hydrochloride	0.83
Rsorcin	0.71
Silica colloidal anhydrous	0.65
Silver protein mild	0.61
Soy lecithin	0.9
Spermaceti	1.0
Tartaric acid	0.65
Valproic acid	1.0
White/yellow wax	1.0
Zinc oxide	0.25

TABLE 12.2 Density factors (DFs) of some drugs and bases for cocoa butter suppository.

Drugs/bases	DF values
Alum	1.7
Aminophyline	1.1
Aminopyrin	1.3
Aspirin	1.3
Balsam Peruvian	1.1
Barbital	1.2
Belladona extract	1.2
Benzoic acid	1.5
Bismuth carbonate	4.5
Bismuth salicylate	4.5
Bismuth subgallate	2.7
Bismuth subnitate	6.0
Boric acid	1.5
Castor oil	1.0
Chloral hydrate	1.3
Cocaine hydrochloride	1.3
Cocoa butter	0.9
Codeine phosphate	1.1
Digitalis leaf	1.6
Diphenhydramine hydrochloride	1.3
Gallic acid	2.0
Glycerin	1.6
Ichthammol	1.1
Iodoform	4.0
Menthol	0.7
Morphine hydrochloride	1.6
Paraffin	1.0
Phenobarbital	1.2
Phenol	0.9
Potassium bromide	2.2
Potassium iodide	4.5
Procaine	1.2
Quinine hydrochloride	1.2
Resorcinol	1.4
Secobarbital sodium	1.2
Sodium bromide	2.3
Spermaceti	1.0
Sulfathiazole	1.6

Continued

TABLE 12.2   Density factors (DFs) of some drugs and bases for cocoa butter suppository.—cont'd

Drugs/bases	DF values
Tannic acid	1.6
White wax	1.0
White hazel fluid extract	1.1
Zinc oxide	4.0
Zinc sulfate	2.8

$$\text{Density Factor}, DF = \frac{W_d}{W_{sb} - W_{sbd} - W_d}$$

$DF = 1.2$ as provided in the problem.

1.2 g of phenobarbital would replace 1 g of cocoa butter.

Therefore, 0. 1 g of phenobarbital would replace 0.08 g of cocoa butter.

$W_{sb} = 2$ g cocoa butter given

$W_{sbd} = $ Needs to be calculated which can be done using Eq. (12.2) as shown below:

$$1.2 = \frac{0.1}{2 - W_{sbd} - 0.1}$$

Therefore, $W_{sbd} = 1.82$ g

Therefore, the amount of base needed for 10 suppositories = 10 (1.82−0.1) = 17.2 g.

$W_d = 100$ mg $= 0.1$ g; so for 10 suppositories, 10×0.1 g = **1.0 g phenobarbital needed**

So, 1 g of phenobarbital will be added to 17.2 g of molten cocoa butter based to prepare 10 suppositories.

iii. **Volume factor (VF) method:** This indicates that 1 g of base will be replaced by VF g of the drug. The VF value of a drug is the ratio of the densities of the drug and the base (density of cocoa butter is 0.9) as shown below by Eq. (12.3):

$$VF = \frac{\rho_D}{\rho_B} \tag{12.3}$$

where $\rho_D = $ density of the drug

$\rho_D = $ density of the base

Amount of each ingredient can be determined by following the steps shown below:

a. Determine W_{sb} which is generally 2 g per suppository.

b. Determine VF using Eq. (12.3).

c. Determine base displaced by the drug which is obtained by dividing the amount of drug with VF.

d. Amount of base needed $= a - b$ per suppository

Example:

Calculated the amount of each ingredient needed for preparing 10 suppositories containing 300 mg of acetaminophen per suppository using VF method. Given that density of acetaminophen and cocoa butter are 1.26 and 0.9 g/cm³, and $W_{sb} = 2$ g

Solution:

a. $W_{sb} = 2$ g

b. $VF = \frac{\rho_D}{\rho_B} = \frac{1.26}{0.9} = 1.4$

c. Amount of the drug, acetaminophen per suppository = 300 mg = 0.3 g. So, the amount of base displaced by 0. 3 g of drug = 0.3 g/1.4 = 0.21 g

d. Amount of base needed per suppository = 2−0.21 g = 1.79 g base per suppository

Therefore, amount of cocoa butter needed for 10 suppositories = 1.79 g × 10 = **17. 9 g cocoa butter**, and Amount of acetaminophen needed for 10 suppositories +0. 3 g × 10 = **3 g acetaminophen.**

Note: While compounding suppositories in a pharmacy practice setting, it is a good practice to calculate for some extra-suppositories such as 20% to account for the loss of materials during handling and preparation.

12.2.8.3 *Characterization and evaluation of suppositories*

12.2.8.3.1 Measurement of hardness

This test provides the mechanical force required to break the suppositories which are useful for ensuring suppository stability and integrity during transportation from manufacturing/compounding facilities to retail community pharmacy. Moreover, optimal mechanical strength is also needed during the administration of suppositories. The hardness test is also called the crushing test because it measures the mass (in kilograms) that a suppository can bear without breaking. A value of 1.8–2 kg is considered acceptable optimal mechanical strength for a suppository [27]. Fig. 12.23 [27] shows the laboratory set-up for measuring hardness of a suppository. The suppository is held in an upright position over which increasing weights are placed until it loses its integrity and collapses.

12.2.8.3.2 Measurement of the melting point

A suppository consists of various ingredients with different melting points. Therefore, it melts completely in a range of melting temperatures, often called melting zone. A differential scanning calorimeter (DSC) can be used to measure the melting point of a base at a heating rate of 3–10°C/min where the peak of the endotherm is indicative of its melting point [28]. In an another approach, a small-diameter wire is placed into the mold containing the suppository melt and it is left to solidify. After solidification, the suppository held by wire is immersed in water. The temperature of water is raised slowly (about 1°C every 2–3 min) until the suppository slips off the wire which indicates the melting point of the suppository.

12.2.8.3.3 Determination of drug release

It is essential to know the drug release rate from suppositories to study the absorption of the drug within a given period. *In vitro* drug release studies can be performed by using the rotating dialysis cell method. In this method, the

FIGURE 12.23   Determination of mechanical strength of a suppository (*Used with permission from reference* 27).

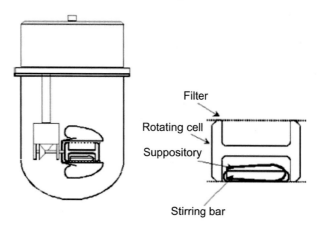

FIGURE 12.24 Schematic representation of *in vitro* release testing apparatus: PTSW-type rotating dialysis cell method with a stirring bar [29].

rotating cell assembly is placed in a cylindrical vessel containing 900 mL dissolution media. It requires the placement of suppositories in a rotating cell that is continuously stirred by a Teflon-coated stirring bar at 25 rpm (Fig. 12.24). A constant temperature is maintained through the dissolution process using a thermostat. The drug samples are withdrawn at a predetermined time interval and are replaced with equal volume of fresh release medium. The drug concentration can be determined by using a suitable analytical technique [29].

12.2.9 Transdermal drug delivery systems

Transdermal drug delivery systems (TDDS) are used to facilitate the transportation of drugs through the skin for a systemic effect. This noninvasive method of delivery is ideal for drugs with a short biological half-life, susceptible to first-pass metabolism, or with unpredictability gastrointestinal absorption.

The TDDS are broadly classified as matrix systems, reservoir systems, or drug-in-adhesive systems. These are usually prepared by various approaches such as the form-fill-seal method, the solvent cast method, or the extrusion method. With the advent of newer penetration enhancers, the scope of such delivery systems has widened, and now high-molecular-weight drugs and drugs with a varying degree of hydrophilicity or lipophilicity can be incorporated into such systems.

12.3 Percutaneous absorption

Despite the complex structure of the skin, chemical agents and medicinal substances that are lipophilic in nature permeate through the skin. When a substance comes into contact with the skin, it penetrates the keratinized *stratum corneum* containing lipid keratinocytes. The stratum corneum behaves as a permeability barrier membrane because it contains extracellular lipids composed of 50% ceramides, 25% cholesterol, and 15% free fatty acids [30], whereas viable epidermis is permeable to highly lipophilic compounds.

The lipids are delivered to the extracellular space by the secretion of lamellar bodies, which contain phospholipids, glucosylceramides, sphingomyelin, cholesterol, and enzymes. In the extracellular space, the lamellar body lipids are metabolized by enzymes to the lipids that form the lamellar membranes. The lipids contained in the lamellar bodies are derived from both epidermal lipid synthesis and extracutaneous sources. Inhibition of cholesterol, fatty acid, ceramide, or glucosylceramide synthesis adversely affects lamellar body formation, thereby impairing barrier homeostasis.

12.3.1 Structure of skin

Skin is a flexible, self-repairing barrier that separates the internal environment of the body from the external environment. In adult humans, skin covers an area of about 2 square meters and is about 16% of total body weight. It ranges in thickness from 0.5 mm on the eyelids to 4.0 mm on the heels; however, it is 1—2 mm thick in other body parts. Skin is composed of two layers, the epidermis and the dermis, separated by a basement membrane zone. Beneath the dermis, there is a layer of adipose tissue and sweat glands [31].

12.3.1.1 Epidermis

Keratinocytes, which are part of the epidermis (50−100 μm thick), migrate outward from the basal cell into highly differentiated non-dividing cells and forms 90% of epidermal cells. During proliferation, keratinocytes transition from polygonal cells to spinous cells, flattened granular cells, and finally to flattened polyhedral dead corneocytes full of the protein keratin. The epidermis can be divided into (1) stratum basale, (2) stratum spinosum, (3) stratum granulosum, and (4) stratum corneum, which are interconnected by desmosomes [31].

The *stratum basale* is a thick layer made up of polygonal cells superficially, and columnar or cuboidal epithelial cells in the deeper parts. Here, new cells are formed continuously by mitotic division and move regularly upward the stratum corneum as well as some projection extends downward to the dermis [32].

The *prickle cell* layer is composed of several layers of polygonal prickle cells or squamous cells. The layers become flat as they near the surface so that their long axis appears parallel to the skin surface. These cells possess intracellular bridges called tonofilaments that contain material that is a precursor of keratin.

The *granular cell* layer consists of one to three layers of flat cells containing keratohyaline basophilic granules which are PAS-negative. The granular cell layer is much thicker in the palms and soles.

The *stratum lucidum* is present exclusively in the palms and soles as a thin homogenous, eosinophilic, and non-nucleate zone. The *horny layer* (stratum corneum) is also normally devoid of nuclei and consisted of eosinophilic layers of keratin. Intraepidermal nerve endings are present in the form of Merkel cells, which act as touch receptors [33].

12.3.1.2 Dermis

The dermis is formed from connective tissue and a matrix containing collagen fibers interlaced with elastic fibers, making it tough and elastic. Rupture of the elastic fiber occurs when the skin is overstretched, resulting in permanent striae, which are generally observed in pregnancy and obesity. A collagen fiber binds with water and gives the skin its tensile strength, but as this ability declines with age, wrinkles develop.

The dermis consists of two parts: the superficial *pars papillaris* or *papillary dermis*, and the deeper *pars reticularis* or *reticular dermis*. The dermis is composed of fibrocollagenic tissue containing blood vessels, lymphatics, and nerves. In the skin of fingers, arteriovenous shunts or *glomera* are normally present. The specialized nerve endings present at some sites perform specific functions shown below.

- *Pacinian corpuscles* concerned with pressure are present in deep layers of skin.
- *Meissner corpuscles* are touch receptors, located in the papillae of skin on palms, soles, tips of fingers, and toes.
- *Ruffini corpuscles* and *End-bulbs of Krause* are cold receptors found in the external genitalia.

Besides these structures, the dermis contains cutaneous appendages or adnexal structures which include the following [31,34].

- *Sweat glands:* These are of two types: eccrine and apocrine.
- *Eccrine glands:* These glands are present all over the skin but are more abundant on the palms, soles, and axillae. They are coiled tubular glands lying deep inside the dermis. Their ducts pass through the epidermis on the surface of the skin as pores through which they empty their secretions, that is, sweat. The glands are lined by secretory cells and are surrounded by myoepithelial cells.
- *Apocrine glands:* These glands are located only in a few areas such as the anogenital region, the external ear as modified glands called ceruminous glands, the eyelid as Moll's glands, and the breast as mammary glands. Apocrine glands are also tubular glands but have larger lumina. Apocrine glands have a single layer of secretory cells that contain acidophilic, PAS-positive, prominent granular cytoplasm. The type of secretion in the apocrine glands is called decapitation secretion as if the cytoplasm of the secretory cells is pinched off.
- *Sebaceous (holocrine) glands:* Sebaceous glands are found everywhere on the skin except on the palms and soles. They are often found in association with hair but can be seen in a few areas devoid of hair as modified sebaceous glands such as the external auditory meatus, nipple, and areola of the male and female breast; labia minora; prepuce; and meibomian glands of the eyelids. Sebaceous glands are composed of lobules of sebaceous cells containing small, round nuclei and abundant fatty, network-like cytoplasm.

- *Hair:* The hair grows from the bottom of the follicle, hence it, has an intracutaneous portion present in the hair follicle and the shaft. The hair follicles consist of epithelial and connective tissue components whereas the hair shaft is made up of an outer sheath, pigmented cortex, and inner medulla.
- *Arrectores pilorum:* These small bundles of smooth muscles are attached to each hair follicle. When the muscle contracts, the hair becomes more erect, and the follicle is dragged upward to become prominent on the surface of the skin, producing what is known as "goose skin" or "goosebumps."
- *Nails:* The nails are thickenings of the deeper part of the stratum corneum that develop at a specially modified portion of the skin called the nail bed. The nail is composed of clear horny cells, resembling stratum lucidum, but are much more keratinized [32].

12.3.2 Integrity of the barrier

The stratum corneum layer of the epidermis is a major barrier to percutaneous absorption. Anything that alters the structure or function of the stratum corneum will affect epidermal absorption. The integrity of this barrier is reduced by inflammation of the skin, such as any form of dermatitis or psoriasis, which may result in increased percutaneous absorption. Similarly, gradual removal of the stratum corneum by stripping or damage by alkalis, etc., will increase absorption.

12.3.3 Factors influencing dermal absorption

Percutaneous absorption is influenced by many physicochemical and biological factors that can be manipulated for developing a safe and an effective topical medication [35].

12.3.3.1 Skin-related

- Occluded or diseased
- Area and site of application
- Differences in races and sex
- Age of the patient
- Temperature and moisture

12.3.3.2 Drug related

- Physicochemical properties of the drug
- The concentration of drug at the site of action
- Molecular weight
- Partition coefficient
- Molecular volume
- Metabolism
- Melting point

12.3.3.3 Formulation related

- The vehicle in the formulation
- Partition coefficient
- Degree of hydration
- Drug–excipients interaction
- Viscosity of vehicle

12.3.4 Condition of the skin

The diffusion of some drugs in semisolids may be increased by more than 10% by skin occlusion due to associated changes in temperature, surface area, blood flow, microbial flora, and water content in the stratum corneum [35]. Occlusion usually means the skin is covered directly or indirectly by impermeable films or substances such as diapers, tape, chambers, gloves, textile garments, wound dressings, or transdermal devices, but certain topical vehicles that contain fats and/or mineral oils (petrolatum, paraffin, etc.) may also generate occlusive effects [36]. Thus, permeability of topical hydrocortisone may be increased by more than 10-fold after occlusion when applied on the forearm [37]. Occlusion not only increases the permeability but also decreases the mean residence time of drugs [38].

Permeability of skin varies from one part to another part, and it largely depends on the thickness of the stratum corneum. According to the findings of one study, the highest total absorption of hydrocortisone is from the scrotum, followed in order from forehead, scalp, back, forearms, palm, and plantar surface [39]. Another study reports that ketoprofen's 3% absorption is similar in all body parts except the knee [40,41]. Topical application of hydrocortisone in a vehicle containing ethanol would penetrate faster through leg skin from the lower leg when compared with the thorax or groin, which, depending on cutaneous blood flow, may result in higher systemic drug concentrations or greater efficiency in treating local inflamed tissue [42]. An increase in skin temperature enhances the rate of permeation due to increased blood flows associated with increased skin temperature [43].

The greatest toxicological response to topical administration has been seen in infants. Preterm infants do not have an intact barrier function and are susceptible to systemic toxicity from topically applied drugs. Normal full-term infants probably have a fully developed stratum corneum barrier with a complete barrier function. However, topical application of the same amount of compound to both adults and newborns reveals greater systemic availability in newborns. The skin contains both Phase-1 and Phase-2 metabolic enzymes that are capable of metabolizing a wide range of xenobiotics, although their effects are relatively low when compared to their equivalent hepatic forms [44].

12.3.5 Physicochemical properties of the penetrant

Percutaneous absorption of a drug is affected by its intrinsic hydrophilicity and lipophilicity, as well as solubility in the formulation vehicle(s), compared with solubility in the stratum corneum. For a chemical to penetrate through the skin into the systemic circulation, it requires both a degree of lipophilicity (to facilitate its entry into the stratum corneum) and hydrophilicity (to aid its passage through the viable epidermis and dermis). Percutaneous absorption of the penetrant depends on the lipid content, appendageal density, and imperfection (pores and correction) of the site of application. Other factors such as molecular weight, molecular volume, and melting point of the drug also affect diffusion across the skin [45].

It has been observed that the stratum corneum is a major diffusional barrier as permeation through viable skin without the stratum corneum is more than 100 times greater than through intact skin [45]. Additionally, the diffusion coefficients of the drug across viable skin are dependent on the molecular weight, size, and shape of the penetrant.

Melting point also has an important effect on drug permeability, which is inversely proportional to the melting point of a drug. It has been reported that the lower the melting point, the higher the solubility and free energy, and the greater is the absorption through the stratum corneum [46].

The partition coefficient of drugs also affects their permeation through the skin. A balance between lipophilicity and hydrophilicity is a prerequisite for drug absorption through the skin. The amount and concentration of a drug in a vehicle also affects the solubility and flux of the drug due to increased thermodynamic activity. It has been observed that a higher partition coefficient favors permeation through the skin.

12.3.6 Vehicle used in formulation

The selection of a vehicle is an important parameter in the formulation of a new percutaneous product due to its unique influence on the integrity of the stratum corneum [47]. Some vehicles, such as polyethylene glycol, produce occlusions on the stratum corneum and increase the skin permeability of the drug. These vehicles increase the penetration of hydrophilic drugs to a certain extent but are not applicable for all drugs.

The partition coefficient of a vehicle is also an important factor in percutaneous absorption. A lipophilic drug easily enters the stratum corneum due to its high lipid content, but a viable epidermis restricts the entry of a highly lipophilic drug. Ointments can enhance the percutaneous absorption of a topical product by providing an occlusive barrier. Creams, lotions, and gels have lower oil content and therefore are less absorptive.

Permeation of hydrocortisone improves in the presence of ethanol in the vehicle, although significant regional differences (i.e., among the thorax, neck, and groin areas) have been observed [48].

From the equation of diffusion coefficient, it is clear that the diffusion coefficient is inversely proportional to the viscosity of a vehicle. Generally, the more viscous the vehicle, the less percutaneous absorption of the drug. However, some contradictory results too are reported in the literature. In one study, thickening agents promoted penetration, probably due to enhanced hydration caused by the thicker formulations resulting in greater stratum corneum diffusivity [49]. In another study, there was no effect of a vehicle's viscosity on drug absorption through the skin [50].

TABLE 12.3 Function of skin [51].

Function	Structure/Cell involved
Protect against:	Stratum corneum
Chemical, particle, desiccation	Melanin is produced by melanocytes and transferred to keratinocytes
UV radiation	Langerhans cells, lymphocytes, mast cells, and mononuclear phagocytes
Antigen, haptens	Stratum corneum, langerhans cells, mast cells, and mononuclear phagocytes
Microbes	
Preserve a balanced internal environment, prevent loss of water, electrolytes, and macromolecules	Stratum corneum
Shock absorber. Strong yet elastic and compliant covering	Dermis and subcutaneous fat
Sensation	Specialist nerve-ending pain, leading to withdrawal; itch leading to scratch; and hence the removal of the parasite
Vitamin D synthesis	Keratinocytes
Temperature regulation	Eccrine sweat gland and blood vessel
Protection and fine manipulation of small objects	Nails
Hormonal Testosterone synthesis and conversion to other androgenic steroids	The hair follicle and sebaceous gland

12.3.7 Mechanism of percutaneous absorption

The penetration of a drug through the stratum corneum involves partition phenomena of applied molecules between lipophilic and hydrophilic compartments. For many substances, the penetration takes place through an intercellular way, more than transcellular, diffusing around the keratinocytes. The functions of different parts of the skin are shown in Table 12.3 [51]. The rate of diffusion in creams, ointments, gels, and other semisolids may be determined by the following:

Transcellular movement: Intracellular components of the stratum corneum lack a functional lipid matrix around keratin and keratohyalin, resulting in low permeability of corneocytes [52]. Degradation of the corneodesmosomes causes the formation of a continuous lacunar Dominio ("aqueous pore"), allowing intracellular penetration. Such lacunae formed are scattered and can also form as a result of occlusion, ionophoresis, and ultrasound waves. They may become larger and get connected forming a net ("pore-way") though which drugs can permeate easily [53].

Intercellular movement: The lipid lamellae of the intercellular spaces (each one including two or three bilayers and made mainly of ceramides, cholesterol, and free fatty acids) are the intercellular structure of the horny layer having the main role in providing barrier function. Most solute substances, nonpolar or polar, penetrate across intercellular lipid avenues. The permeability of very polar solutes is constant and similar to the transport of ions (e.g., potassium ions).

Transfollicular movement: Such movement includes hair follicles, pilosebaceous units, and eccrine glands via which the permeability of a drug is limited. The orifices of the pilosebaceous units represent about 10% in areas where their density is high (face and scalp) and only 0.1% in areas where their density is low. This is a possible selective way of permeation for some drugs. Follicular penetration may be influenced by sebaceous secretion that favors the absorption of substances soluble in lipids. The penetration through the pilosebaceous units is dependent on the property of the substance and the type of preparation.

12.4 Methods of enhancement of percutaneous absorption

Generally, percutaneous absorption of a drug is very low and limited due to the excellent barrier properties of stratum corneum as discussed in previous sections. Various methods and approaches have been adopted to increase the percutaneous absorption of drugs as discussed in the following sections.

12.4.1 Chemical method

A chemical permeation enhancer enters into the stratum corneum, interferes with its lipid content, and disrupts the barrier function of the skin. Some examples of chemical penetration enhancers are water, sulfoxides (e.g., dimethylsulfoxide (DMSO)), azones [31] (e.g., laurocapram), pyrrolidones (e.g., 2-pyrrolidone, 2P), alcohols and alkanols (ethanol or decanol), glycols (e.g., propylene glycol, PG), surfactants, fatty acids, and terpenes [54].

A chemical penetration enhancer should have the following properties:

- It should be nontoxic to the skin
- It should be inert and not show any pharmacological activity
- It should be effective at a very low concentration
- It does not have any incompatibility with other substances (APIs or excipients)
- It should have a rapid and reversible onset of action

12.4.1.1 Water

Water is a well-recognized solvent used in many pharmaceutical preparations. This is physiologically innocuous but chemically reactive. Due to its innocuous nature, water is also used as a penetration enhancer to promote the permeation of several drugs (e.g., steroids). Water causes the occlusion or hydration of the stratum corneum but does not affect the lipid bilayer. However, the presence of numerous inorganic ions in it may interfere with the action of surfactants reducing its penetration-enhancing effect. Additionally, water can also promote microbial growth which can contaminate and degrade the formulation.

12.4.1.2 Sulfoxides

Dimethyl sulfoxide (DMSO) has been the most frequently used chemical penetration enhancer in a concentration of 5%—10% [55]. It is a clear, colorless to yellowish liquid with a characteristic bitter odor and taste. This is a highly polar and stable compound that can easily absorb moisture and dissolve polar, nonpolar, and lipophilic drugs. DMSO is well-absorbed in the skin and oral mucosa. When DMSO is applied topically, a taste of this solvent comes into the mouth within 5 min, which indicates its high skin permeability. It alters the protein structure and lipid content of the stratum corneum. Moreover, it also alters the partition coefficient of the drug. The most frequent adverse effect associated with DMSO is dry skin [56]. Despite its many beneficial effects, it should be used with caution.

12.4.1.3 Azone

Azone (1-Dodecylazacyloheptan-2-one) is a smooth, oily, hydrophobic liquid that has been reported to be nonirritating to human skin and capable of enhancing the percutaneous penetration of many compounds. Topical formulations of the antiviral compound trifluorothymidine (TFT) were prepared with different proportions of azone, propylene glycol (PG), polyethylene glycol (PEG-300), and/or water and evaluated by measuring in vitro diffusion of TFT through excised guinea pig skin. Azone was found to increase its flux dramatically which was further increased in presence of PG [57]. Similarly, 1% azone along with 18% propylene glycol dramatically enhanced the permeability of metronidazole through human skin as compared to 1% azone or 1% azone with 18% PEG 400 [58].

Azone is a good candidate for the enhancement of percutaneous absorption but an ophthalmic formulation containing azone showed ocular toxicity when applied to rat eyes on the basis of the conjunctivae and iris discharge, and corneal edema. This toxicity can occur due to the direct penetration of an azone in the stratum corneum or the increased permeation of benzalkonium chloride used as a preservative in the formulation.

12.4.1.4 Pyrrolidone

Pyrrolidone is a colorless liquid used in industrial settings as a high-boiling noncorrosive polar solvent for many applications. It is miscible with a wide variety of other solvents, including water, ethanol, diethyl ether, chloroform, benzene, ethyl acetate, and carbon disulfide. It has been reported that pyrrolidone increases the penetration of various drugs such as sulfaguanidine, aminopyrine, flurbiprofen, and Sudan III.

Pyrrolidone is a very good penetration enhancer but it also shows a hypersensitive reaction on rabbit skin. So, there should always be a balance between the penetration-enhancing effects and other adverse effects. Methyl pyrrolidone and azone have been observed to be good penetration enhancers for the improvement of percutaneous absorption of heparin sodium salt through human skin [59].

12.4.1.5 Alkanol

Among alkanols, ethanol has been an attractive and most frequently used candidate as a penetration enhancer for percutaneous absorption. Ethanol is a semipolar solvent that is miscible with water and other organic solvents. Ethanol shows less irritation as compared to other penetration enhancers. In addition, it leaves a cooling sensation upon evaporation. The migration of 1-alkanol in the lipid bilayer is very rapid. A bond is assembled between the hydroxyl group of 1-alkanol and the carbonyl group of the lipid, and a hydrocarbon chain is formed, which resides in the hydrophobic core of the lipid bilayer. Ethanol diffuses easily in the lipid bilayer as compared to other long-chain alkanols [60].

12.4.1.6 Propylene glycol

Propylene glycol is a water-miscible, colorless, highly flammable liquid substance. It is a type of alcohol made from fermented yeast and carbohydrates and is commonly used in a wide variety of pharmaceutical preparations. Even though there are warnings against skin contact with propylene glycol, it is still used in skin-care products. Propylene glycol has been used in many semisolid formulations as humectants, antibacterial agents, and antifungal agents. Propylene glycol interferes with the lamellar lipid in corneocytes and improves the partition of the drug and acts as a penetration enhancer. For the delivery of drugs from topical formulations of 5-fluorouracil and haloperidol, having an appropriate propylene glycol content in the vehicle is reported to be useful [61]. Despite its various uses in semisolid dosage forms, propylene glycol at higher doses may result in reversible acute renal failure caused by proximal renal tubular cell injury [62].

12.4.1.7 Surfactants

Surfactants have a lipophilic alkyl or aryl chain together with a hydrophilic moiety in their structure. According to the number and nature of a group, surfactants may be classified as predominantly hydrophilic or lipophilic. Solubilizing agents, detergents, and (o/w) emulsifying agents come under the hydrophilic category due to their value of hydrophilic—lipophilic balance (HLB), whereas wetting, antifoaming, and (w/o) emulsifying agents come under the lipophilic category. Surfactants such as Span are lipophilic and have low HLB (1.8—8.6), whereas Tween is hydrophilic and has a higher HLB value. These substances are absorbed at the interface and exhibit a self-association at a specific concentration. Nonionic surfactants like polyoxyethylene-2-oleyl ether (Poloxamer) show higher percutaneous transportation of drugs as compared to other nonionic surfactants. Thermal analysis of skin suggests that the stratum corneum is fluidized to form a loosely layered structure and thus, the intercellular space becomes broad in the presence of poloxamer. Sodium lauryl sulfate causes increase in transepidermal water loss and should be avoided in daily-applied cosmetics [62]. It has been observed that glyceryl monocaprylate/caprate increased 5-FU flux up to 10-fold which can be attributed to its optimum alkyl chain length [63].

12.4.1.8 Fatty acids

Natural oils, obtained directly from plant and vegetable sources, are the main sources of fatty acids containing the carbon—carbon double bond and hydroxyl bond. Viscosity of fatty acids depends on their molecular weight and hydroxyl content. Natural vegetable oil is safe and less irritating but undergoes rancidity very easily. Percutaneous absorption of drugs is enhanced with an increase in the carbon chain length of fatty acids [64]. Various fatty acids such as corn oil and cod liver oil are considered to be safe and inert ingredients for use in topical formulations. The fatty acids enhance the partitioning of drugs into the lipid core in the stratum corneum [65]. A greater piroxicam flux was observed from its gel containing oleic acid resulting in 2-fold increase in its percutaneous absorption [66].

12.4.1.9 Terpenes

Terpenes are natural penetration enhancers that are classified as generally regarded as safe (GRAS) and less irritating as recognized by the Food and Drug Administration [67]. Terpenes interfere with lipid bilayers in the keratinocytes of the stratum corneum and do not affect the highly ordered structure of keratins [61]. Terpenes increase the penetration of hydrophilic drugs by partitioning the drugs from aqueous solutions to the stratum corneum. Terpenes showed a significant synergistic effect when used with other penetration enhancers. For example, the flux of 5-fluorouracil increases when propylene glycol is used along with terpene which is attributed to disruption and phase separation of lipid in stratum corneum [67].

12.4.2 Physical penetration enhancers

Skin penetration of a topical product can be enhanced via physical means such as using adhesive tape stripping, microneedles, jet propulsion, electric current, and ultrasonic or photomechanical waves.

12.4.2.1 Electroporation

Electroporation is a very effective technique used in the enhancement of penetration through the skin. This technique utilizes a controlled electric field of high voltage for milliseconds to a few seconds to disturb the lipid bilayer of the stratum corneum for a temporary period to allow the entry of aqueous substances. This technique involves many applications, including the transfer of DNA, large-molecular-weight drugs, and also lipophilic as well as hydrophilic molecules. This technique reduces the pain or discomfort of injection and quickly passes the drug through the skin barrier. The rate of diffusion of a drug depends on its electrical and physical properties. The application of electroporation has many advantages but may cause cell death and muscle contraction due to improper pulse [68].

12.4.2.2 Iontophoresis

Iontophoresis is a technique used to enhance percutaneous absorption of drugs in topical and transdermal drug delivery through the application of a constant electric current of about $0.5 \, mA/cm^2$. This technique is based on the general concept of coulombic force in which two anions experience a mutual repulsive force, as do two cations. When a positively charged molecule is transported through the barrier, it is placed under the anode electrode, which repels the ion toward skin that behaves like a cathode (human skin and rat skin both are negatively charged at a pH more than 4) and attracts a positive-charged ion to it by removing other positive ions from its inner surface. Similarly, cathode electrode is used for a negatively charged drug molecule [69]. It provides sustained drug delivery, increased patient compliance, and easy termination of therapy at any stage; it also reduces inter and intrasubject variability because this therapy is based directly on applied current.

Many drugs have been delivered through skin using this approach including small molecules such as apomorphine [70], sumatriptan [71], 5-fluorouracil [72], rotigotine [73], and buspirone hydrochloride [74] and large molecules having a high molecular weight (heparin and hormones), insulin, etc. [75–78]. Some of the disadvantages of this approach include the need for an ionic form of the drug, relatively expensive, etc.

12.4.2.3 Sonophoresis

Sonophoresis is a process that utilizes microwaves or ultrasound waves of frequency (20 kHz–3 MHz) which enhance the absorption of drugs through the skin by the formation of cavitation, streaming, and heating. Acoustic streaming occurs at low-intensity waves whereas heating and acoustic cavitation will predominate on high levels. Low-frequency sonophoresis is said to be more significant than high-frequency waves [79]. The highly ordered structure of the stratum corneum is disrupted by low-frequency waves and enhances percutaneous absorption. The examination of the permeation pathway of lanthanum nitrate tracer suggests that microwaves interfere with the diffusion of stratum granulosum (SG) or the upper SG layer. Additionally, lanthanum nitrate also diffuses into the viable epidermis through the intercellular pathway. It shows a synergistic effect with other chemical penetration enhancers such as oleic acid [80]. This technique can be applied to several therapeutic agents that can be delivered through the skin.

12.4.2.4 Photomechanical waves

Compressed photomechanical waves contain high-amplitude pressure waves of 100 atm for a few seconds which interact with cells and tissues. The influence of such interaction depends on the pressure, duration, and time. Photomechanical waves can be high-power pulse or low-power pulse used for medical purposes, but low-power waves have more advantages in drug delivery and gene therapy. Stress or compressed waves can enhance the diffusion of macromolecules (40 kDa dextran and 20 nm latex particles) by increasing the permeability of cell membranes of the stratum corneum by forming a cavity and increasing permeability, thereby increasing the diffusion rate of drug molecules into the viable epidermis and dermis. This approach causes the transport of the drug to the innermost skin layer resulting in systemic effect, for example, an insulin transdermal delivery system using photomechanical waves reduced the blood sugar level for many hours [81].

12.4.2.5 Microneedle

Many patients panic when they learn that they are going to be injected with a needle, although the treatment is meant for their benefit. One advanced technique uses microneedles that do not induce any pain; these needles vary in size. This alternative method to deliver drugs does not affect the blood vessels and nerve endings in the hypodermis layer. There is also less risk of infection and contamination from the device used for drug administration. Shape and size of the microneedle affect the magnitude of pain and discomfort. Pyramidal wet-etch microneedles can cause less pain and discomfort because the microchannel created by these needles is quickly repaired. Enhanced skin permeability has been observed with microneedles that have a size greater than 600 μm [82].

Researchers have developed biodegradable microneedles made from polymers such as poly-N-isopropyl acrylamide and poly-lactic-co-glycolic acid. These microneedles swell in presence of biological fluids and thereby degrade and release the drug content [83]. Applications with microneedles include the delivery of cosmetics, vaccines based on oligonucleotides, insulin, and antibody for the induction of immune responses.

12.4.2.6 Jet propulsion

The jet propulsion technique is a needle-free injection that uses a high-velocity stream of drugs to penetrate the skin to access the systemic circulatory system. Jet diameter and velocity are the two main parameters for the penetration of drugs into the skin. Jet streams that flow through a gauge diameter of 152 μm have a threshold velocity in the range of 80−100 m/s. Jet propulsion has not yet gained commercial success because of the pain induced on injection by this approach. The drug is delivered from a traditional jet injector that penetrates near the pain receptors located in the deep layers of the skin. Recently, conventional jet injectors were replaced with micro-jet injectors that deliver the drug on the superficial layer or above the pain receptors [84].

12.4.3 Formulations-based enhancers

12.4.3.1 Liposomes

Liposomes are lipid vesicles where the aqueous compartment is enclosed by a bimolecular phospholipid membrane. The release rate of a drug depends on the composition and morphology of the lipid vesicle. Generally, phospholipids are amphiphilic molecules containing a polar head and hydrophilic (phosphoric acid bound to water-soluble molecules) and hydrophobic tail, composed of two fatty acid chains containing 10−24 carbon atoms and 0−6 double bonds in each chain.

The structure of intracellular lipids in the skin resembles the composition of liposomes; hence, liposomes have been tested for better skin penetration with faster diffusion. Many investigations have been performed using reconstructed human skin to determine the exact mechanism of permeation of drugs through topical liposomes. Two distinctive mechanisms are responsible for enhanced topical localization: the transepidermal pathway and the transfollicular pathway.

Liposomes have proved to be useful carriers for several drugs, including peptides, proteins, plasmid DNA, antisense oligonucleotides, and ribozymes for pharmaceutical, cosmetic, and biochemical purposes [85].

The enormous versatility in particle size and the physical parameters of the lipids affords an attractive potential for constructing tailor-made liposomes for a wide range of applications, including drug targeting. One proprietary product currently being marketed is Celadrin topical liposome lotion although it is not approved by the FDA [86].

12.4.3.2 Niosomes

Niosomes are also a carrier-type vesicular drug delivery system like liposomes where the lipid bilayer is replaced with a nonionic surfactant. They are used as an alternative to liposomes due to their stable character and cost-effectiveness [87]. A wide variety of nonionic surfactants are useful in the fabrication of noisome. However, they can also be prepared using ionic amphiphiles such as negatively charged diacetyl phosphate and positively charged stearyl amine. Niosomes have been used in topical and transdermal dosage forms containing hydrophilic and/or hydrophobic drugs, including biotechnological products such as vaccines [88].

12.4.3.3 Nanoparticles

Nanoparticles are solid colloidal drug carriers ranging from 10 to 1000 nm in diameter and are composed of synthetic, natural, or semisynthetic polymers encapsulating the drug molecule [89]. Many hydrophilic (gelatin, albumin, casein, polysaccharide lectin, etc.) and hydrophobic polymers (polycaprolactone, polyesters, polyanhydrides, polycyanoacrylate) are used in the formation of nanoparticles. The biomedical applications include efficient and controlled drug delivery targeting skin and skin appendages, transcutaneous vaccination, and transdermal gene therapy. The nanoformulations have modernized conventional transdermal drug delivery for the treatment of various skin diseases as well as cosmetic usages, but there is a need for their safety assurance and toxicity evaluation before application on the skin [90].

Solid lipid nanoparticles (SLNs) are composed of a solid and lipid particle-matrix that proves to be an alternative carrier system to liposomes and emulsions. SLNs exhibit a wide application in the field of cosmetics and pharmaceuticals due to an increase in the rate of permeation, occlusion, and hydration of the skin. Lipid nanoparticles are formed from biodegradable lipids that are safe carriers with excellent tolerability. Cosmetic companies rank high among nanotechnology patent holders in the United States, for example, L'Oreal is the industry leader on nano patents [91].

12.4.3.4 Transferosomes

Transferosomes are elastic and deformable vesicles due to the use of edge modifiers (e.g., non-ionic surfactant) that replace a portion of cholesterol used in its preparation. The vesicles contain soy phosphatidylcholine encapsulating sodium cholate where ethanol is added in small concentrations as an accelerant. The drug can penetrate through the skin into the systemic circulation by hydration and osmotic force without affecting the occlusion process. Many small molecules, peptides, steroids, proteins, and vaccines including products for gene therapy have been delivered transdermally encapsulated in transferosome [92].

12.5 Theory of semisolid dosage forms

12.5.1 Hydrophilic properties

The water-absorbing capacity of oleaginous and water-in-oil bases may be expressed in terms of the water number which is defined as the maximum quantity of water that is held (partly emulsified) by 100 g of a base at 20°C. The test consists of adding increments of water to the melted base and triturating until the mixture has cooled. When no more water is absorbed, the product is placed in a refrigerator for several hours, removed, and allowed to come to room temperature. The material is then rubbed on a slab until water does not exude, and finally, the amount of water remaining in the base is determined.

12.5.2 Rheological properties

Semisolid dosage forms differ widely in their rheological properties. They do not flow at low shear stresses but undergo reversible deformation like elastic solids. When characteristic shear stress, called the yield value or yield stress, is exceeded, they may flow like liquids. Yield stresses usually are caused by structural networks extending throughout an entire system. To break such a network requires stress that produces no flow but only elastic deformation. When the yield stress is exceeded, the network is partly ruptured, and flow occurs.

Gels or jellies are characterized by a comparatively high degree of elasticity. They undergo rather large elastic deformation at shear stresses below the yield value, from which they recover their shape when the stresses are removed. Recoverable deformations of 10%–30% are not unusual, especially for polymer gels. Clay gels are less elastic, and their rheological properties resemble a paste.

Pastes possess little elasticity and cannot recover their shape except for very small deformations. At stresses above their yield values, pastes behave like free-flowing liquids. This type of rheological behavior is called plasticity. The Brownian motion builds up the networks in gels and pastes and restores them when they have been ruptured by stress higher than the yield value. Examples of plastic materials are ointments and pastes, creams, butter and margarine, dough, putties, and modeling clay.

Semisolids with high yield values are described as "hard." When their plastic viscosity is high, they are described as "stiff." For example, in Fig. 12.25 [93] hydrophilic petrolatum has a higher yield value as compared to hydrophilic petrolatum containing water and may be termed hard petrolatum. The best instrument for determining the rheologic properties of pharmaceutical semisolids is some form of a rotational viscometer. The cone-plate viscometer is particularly well adapted for the analysis of semisolid emulsions and suspensions. The Stormer viscometer, consisting of a stationary cup and rotating bob, is also satisfactory for semisolids.

Consistency curves for the emulsifiable bases, hydrophilic petrolatum, and hydrophilic petrolatum incorporated with water are shown in Fig. 12.25 [93]. The addition of water to hydrophilic petrolatum lowers the yield-point (the intersection of the x-axis and extrapolated down curve). The plastic viscosity (the reciprocal of the slope of the down curve) and the thixotropy (the area between the upcurve and down curve generally termed the hysteresis loop) are increased by the addition of water to the hydrophilic petrolatum.

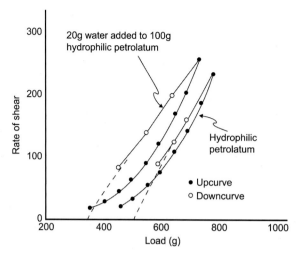

FIGURE 12.25   Flow curves obtained for hydrophilic petrolatum and hydrophilic petrolatum containing water [93,94].

Fig. 12.26 [91] shows the change in plastic viscosity, and Fig. 12.27 [94] shows the thixotropic behavior of petrolatum and plastibase as a function of temperature. The modified Stormer viscometer was used to obtain such curves. As observed in Fig. 12.26, both of the bases show about the same temperature coefficient of plastic viscosity which accounts for their similar degree of softness.

The mechanical properties of gels are characterized by two separate parameters, rigidity and viscosity, which are affected by temperature. The rigidity index, f, of a gel is the force required for depressing its surface to a fixed distance. To measure rigidity, one subjects a sample of gel mass to penetrative compression using a flat-ended cylindrical plunger that operates at a constant speed when the strain (rate of deformation of gel) is constant and independent of stress (force applied). The thermal degradation of a gel with respect to rigidity follows second-order kinetics, as shown in Eq. (12.3a):

$$-\frac{df}{dt} = k_f f^2 \tag{12.3a}$$

The preceding equation can be integrated into Eq. (12.3b):

$$\frac{1}{f} - \frac{1}{f_0} = k_f t \tag{12.3b}$$

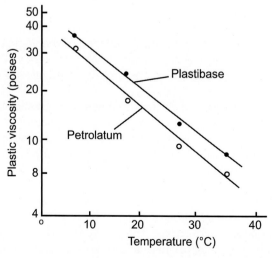

FIGURE 12.26   Plastic viscosity of petrolatum and plastibase as a function of temperature [93,94].

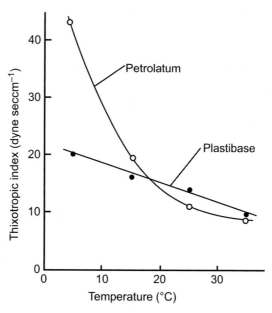

FIGURE 12.27   Thixotropic behavior of petrolatum and plastibase as a function of temperature [93,94].

where f is the rigidity index of the gel at time t, f_0 is the rigidity index at time zero, k_f is the rate constant $(g^{-1} h^{-1})$, and t is the heating time in hours. Eq. (12.3b) conforms to a straight-line equation; therefore, f_0 and k_f can be calculated from its intercept and slope, respectively, at a given temperature.

The effect of temperature on the rate constant, k_f, can be expressed using the Arrhenius equation (Eq. 12.3c):

$$k_f = Ae^{-E_a/RT} \tag{12.3c}$$

The preceding equation can be represented also by Eq. (12.4):

$$ln\, k_f = ln\, A - \frac{E_a}{RT} \tag{12.4}$$

Thus, a plot of $ln\, k_f$ versus $1/T$ would result in a straight line with slope and intercept equal to $-\frac{E_a}{R}$ and $ln\, A$, respectively, which in turn can be used to measure the Arrhenius constant A and the energy of activation E_a.

12.5.3 Rheological changes

Homogenization frequently increases the consistency of a semisolid emulsion because it increases the number of emulsified particles. However, it can also have the opposite effect of decreasing the viscosity of the product owing to the electrolyte effect. Some creams are sensitive to agitation and stress. The continuous rotation of an auger in the hopper of the filling machine may cause the cream to liquefy. Such creams may be made more resistant to agitation by manipulating their formulation parameters.

12.6 Characterization and evaluation of semisolid dosage forms

Many significant factors such as particle size and shape, texture, rheological properties, mucoadhesive properties, and surface pH can influence the complex structure of semisolid dosage forms. These properties directly affect the percutaneous absorption and therapeutic efficacy of drugs in this dosage form. Some of the properties that are important in this respect are discussed below.

12.6.1 Particle size

Particle size is an important property for the pharmaceutical and cosmetic industry because it directly affects drug bioavailability. A decrease in particle size results in increased surface area, leading to enhanced dissolution and finally the absorption of the drug. Particle size and size distribution in dispersion play important roles in the safety and efficacy of dosage forms. Content and dose uniformity, rheological properties, grittiness, and irritability are directly related to the size and shape of particles [95]. One study conducted on porcine skin suggested that nanoparticles with a smaller particle size favor follicular localization [93]. Particle size significantly affects the skin penetration of drugs. Drugs with a particle size less than 3 nm may penetrate both in the stratum corneum and hair follicle whereas drugs with a particle size greater than 10 nm usually do not cross the epidermal layer. Drugs with a particle size between 3 and 10 nm may get concentrated on the hair follicles. Therefore, accurate determination of particle size and distribution is a critical parameter in the performance evaluation of topical dosage forms that can be achieved by the following methods.

12.6.1.1 Laser diffraction

Any particle that passes through a laser beam scatters light in proportion to its size depending on the angle through which it travels. The intensity of scattered light depends on particle size and volume. The wider the angle, the higher the particle scattering intensity, and vice versa. Laser diffraction can be used to determine the particle size of API during the manufacturing of the semisolid dosage form so that sedimentation and other physical attributes can be avoided or optimized. The laser diffraction equipment can measure the particles in the size range of 0.5–3500 µm with good precision [96].

12.6.1.2 Dynamic light scattering

The dynamic light scattering technique involves an optical procedure that measures the fluctuation of scattered light intensities as defined through the Brownian motion of particles in the submicron range (5 nm–5 µm). The upper limit of the range is decided by the weight of the scattered particles. Dynamic light scattering can be used as an analytical technique to determine particle size, polydispersity, and the size distribution of highly complex samples of proteins, nanoparticles, cosmetics, etc [97].

12.6.1.3 Disc centrifuge

A disc centrifuge works on the principle of centrifugal sedimentation in a liquid medium where centrifugal force is generated by a rotating disc. The sedimentation is stabilized by a slight density gradient within the liquid. This procedure is used for particle size determination where the sedimentation of particles depends on the viscosity of the dispersion, the density gradient, and the centrifugal force used by the disc centrifuge.

12.6.1.4 Optical microscopy

The optical microscopy method uses a large number of photomicrographs to capture particle size distribution. It was a technology-intensive method that automatically analyzes particle size through an optical microscope, that is fitted with a dedicated digital camera that can handle the collective analysis of images. This analysis helps in measuring the length, width, area, and circle diameter of particles and their surface topography. The upper limits of the particles under observation can be increased up to several millimeters at low magnification while the lower limits can be decreased close to a micrometer through the use of white light illumination [98].

12.6.1.5 Raman chemical imaging

The Raman chemical imaging technique is a combination of optical microscopy and Raman spectroscopy used to generate hyperspectral images that contain a high-resolution power that separates the individual spectrum. It can detect droplets of different chemical agents and is used to analyze the morphology, composition, and spatial distribution of particles in semisolid preparations. It yields better results as compared to conventional microscopy in terms of speed, image clarity, the droplet size distribution of oil and emulsion, and simultaneous detection of droplets of different compositions. Raman chemical imaging has been utilized successfully to determine the particle size, chemical identity, and particle size distribution of API in topical formulations [99].

12.6.2 Rheological properties

Semisolid dosage forms represent a wide range of formulations that include creams, ointments, gels, pastes, and suppositories. These formulations have different flow properties due to their viscoelastic nature. Viscosity has a considerable effect on the percutaneous absorption of the drug from a semisolid formulation. It is generally considered that the higher the viscosity of the dosage form, the lesser is the rate of diffusion of medicament. Evaluation of rheological parameters is important not only for assessing the rate of diffusion of a drug but also for evaluating the consistency of dosage form, which has a significant effect on the spreadability, flow property from containers, and duration of action of the API.

Characterization of rheological properties is essential for ensuring batch-to-batch uniformity, which is required for maintaining a quality product during manufacturing. The rheological behavior of semisolids can be classified into various non-Newtonian flow patterns that may include pseudoplastic, plastic, shear-thinning (thixotropic), and shear-thickening (dilatant) [100]. These differences in flow properties are due to the inherent physical structure of the product. The temperature has a significant effect on the rheology of semisolid dosage forms. As the temperature is increased, semisolid products show a decrease in viscosity. The molecular weight and concentration of the polymer used influences significantly viscosity and flow properties. For example, the concentration of propylene glycol in a ternary solvent mixture with water and ethanol increases the elasticity of gel and hence makes it highly viscoelastic in nature. Spreadability, stickiness, and fluidity of the formulation after application depend on rheological characteristics and significantly affect patient acceptability of semisolid dosage forms [101].

12.6.2.1 Measurement of rheological property of semisolid dosage forms

12.6.2.1.1 Viscometer/rheometer

Various viscometers and rheometers are used to characterize the shear rate and viscoelastic properties of semisolid dosage forms. A rheometer can be classified as concentric cylinder, cone and plate, parallel plate, and rectangular torsion based on geometry as shown in Fig. 12.28.

12.6.2.1.2 Concentric cylinder viscometer

The concentric cylinder viscometer functions on a moderate shear rate, making this a good choice for the measurement of the rheological properties of various pharmaceutical products. This type of instrument consists of two co-axial cylinders: the outer cylinder forms the cup, and the inner cylinder forms a bob. Two types of instruments exist depending on whether the cup or bob rotates. One is a Couette-type system, in which the cup rotates, and the bob is stationary; this type can be used to calculate the shear rate of low viscous substances. In another type known as the Searle type, the bob is rotated, and the cup is stationary. The Brookfield viscometer, which comes under the second category, is widely used in the viscosity measurement of diverse topical formulations.

12.6.2.1.3 Cone and plate viscometer

The instrument essentially consists of a flat, circular plate with a wide-angle cone placed centrally above it. It contains a moderate shear rate device that is appropriate for semisolids containing smaller particles because the cone angle is small.

12.6.2.1.4 Parallel plate and rectangular torsional rheometer

In a parallel plate and rectangular torsional rheometer, shear stress is determined from the torque response of the instrument, which is evaluated by constructing a force-balance equation on the disk and integrating it over the radius. Thus, this rheometer is comparatively complicated in comparison to a cone plate viscometer where the shear

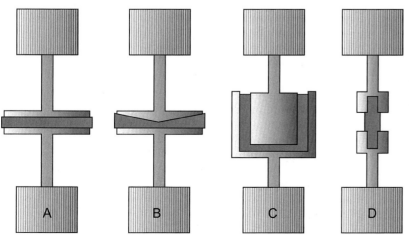

FIGURE 12.28 Schematic diagrams for dynamic rheometers: (A) parallel plates, (B) cone and plate, (C) concentric cylinder (Couette), and (D) solid or torsion rectangular. The appropriate geometry is dictated primarily by the properties of sample material, but may also be dictated by the desire to simulate a process or *in situ* application. *Adapted from http://www.ceramicindustry.com/articles/print/using-rheology-to-improve-manufacturing.*

stress is constant and can be directly and easily evaluated. Samples are applied on the lower plate in parallel and to the inside of the stator in the concentric plate. The stress is directly proportional to the strain in the viscoelastic region and modulus. The frequency sweep analysis is performed in a frequency range of 0.1−10 Hz with constant stress and is used to calculate the modulus and dynamic viscosity [102].

12.6.3 Consistency

Batch-to-batch uniformity in consistency (i.e., thickness or firmness) of semisolid dosage forms is important for quality control. A cone penetration test is used to measure the consistency of various substances, such as petroleum products, food, cosmetics, and other semisolid materials with the help of a penetrometer [103]. This is based on the principle that a standard penetrant, such as a cone or a needle, penetrates the depth of the semisolid substance under defined conditions of sample size, penetrant weight, geometry, and time, where a higher penetration depth indicates a greater softness and lesser stiffness of the sample.

12.6.4 Surface pH

Semisolid dosage forms contain very limited quantities of a liquid or aqueous phase. The surface pH of semisolids should be tested during manufacturing for monitoring batch-to-batch uniformity and quality control of dosage forms. Surface pH can be measured by using a simple pH meter or by using a probe-type pH meter. If the formulation is thick, the pH can be measured by diluting it with distilled water. Because the skin has a neutral pH, the formulation should also have nearly the same pH; otherwise, it may cause local irritation and can affect drug release.

12.6.5 Drug content and content uniformity

The drug content in topical dosage forms can be evaluated by adding a fixed quantity of a formulation to a solvent in sealed ampoules. The mixture is stirred in a constant temperature bath at 37°C for a defined time, and the samples are withdrawn at the time of separation of the aqueous and oily phases. The samples are filtered and then analyzed using a suitable analytical technique such as spectrophotometry or chromatographic technique such as HPLC. The uniformity of content of cyclosporine in the formulation containing poly (lactide-co-glycolide), for example, can be determined by radio immune assay (RIA). Conformational stability can be predicted by spectroscopic methods such as FTIR and circular dichroism (CD) spectroscopy [104]. In a study of controlled-release insulin gel, the content of insulin in the formulation was evaluated by enzyme-linked immunosorbent assay (ELISA), and conformational stability was confirmed by electrophoresis, FTIR, and CD spectroscopy [105].

12.6.6 Spreadability

A semisolid formulation spreads well if the force of adhesion (attractive forces between formulation and the application surface) is greater than cohesive forces (attractive forces between formulation molecules). This is used to determine the spreading coefficient (S) as shown below:

$$S = W_a - W_c$$

where, W_a = Work of adhesion; W_c = Work of cohesion

A positive value of S indicates ease of spreading whereas a negative value represents difficulty in spreading at the application site. Spreading is an important property in the effectiveness of a dosage form to the target site, extrusion from the container, ease of application, and consumer preference. The use of surfactants in a formulation improves spreadability.

Several methods such as the parallel plate method, subject assessment (use of human volunteers), master curve (subject assessment plus the instrumental method), and *in vivo* studies on animals and humans are used to measure the spreading of semisolid dosage forms. A master curve derived by plotting rate of shear and the consistency of spreading can be used to measure the spreadability of creams and ointments using a Ferranti—Shirley cone and plate viscometer at 25°C and 34°C [106].

12.6.7 Texture analysis

The texture is the feel of a substance which can be quantified through properties such as silkiness, roughness, and stiffness. All the mechanical properties including texture, hardness, compressibility, adhesiveness, and cohesiveness of a vaginal gel containing clomiphene citrate, for example, can be analyzed using the TA-XT Plus Texture analyzer (Stable Micro Systems, UK) containing controlled penetrometer software at a temperature of $37 \pm 0.5°C$. The assembly contains a universal bottle at a fixed height of 8 cm, which is kept in an ultrasonic water bath to remove air bubbles. It also contains a Perspex probe with a 10 mm diameter that is twice compressed into each formulation at a particular depth and time, and the compression property is evaluated with the help of software in the instrument [107].

12.6.8 Mucoadhesive properties

Mucoadhesive strength is the force required to detach a hydrated formulation from the mucous membrane. In semisolid dosage forms, for example, ointments, pastes, gels, etc, may contain bioadhesive polymers incorporated into the hydrophobic base. The mechanism of mucoadhesion gives an idea about the retention time of formulation on the mucosa, which depends on the surface energy, along with the viscoelastic properties of liquid [108].

The mucoadhesive properties of a formulation may be evaluated by using a texture analyzer in which mucin discs are attached horizontally with double-sided adhesive tape to the lower end of a probe. Samples of each formulation are packed into a shallow cylindrical vessel. The mucin disc in the analytical probe is lowered to the surface of each formulation with a particular force and time to ensure intimate contact between the mucin disc and sample; then the probe is moved upward at a constant speed. The force required to detach the mucin disc from the surface of the formulation can be measured from a force-time plot. At least four readings should be taken for the accuracy of the result. However, a modified physical balance can also be used to measure the mucoadhesive strength of formulations, where the force required to detach the film is measured [109].

12.6.9 Evaluation of drug release and permeation

The stratum corneum of the skin acts as a barrier for most of the drugs applied topically. A lipophilic drug, however, can more easily cross through this barrier. Therefore, an *in vitro* and/or *in vivo* evaluation of dosage form is required to determine the route of penetration and the amount of drug permeated through the skin so that an effective formulation can be developed that can easily cross the skin barrier and provide safe and efficacious drug delivery. Drug permeation up to stratum corneum/epidermis is ideal for a desired local effect whereas permeation to dermis region is required for systemic absorption. The drug release from semisolid dosage form is predominantly diffusion controlled. Therefore, characterizing the diffusion provides insight for optimizing drug action.

12.7 Procedure and apparatus for diffusion experiment

Diffusion is a process of mass transfer of molecules via random molecular motion due to a concentration gradient across a barrier that offers resistance to the diffusant. Generally, a membrane consisting of a sheet of solid or semisolid material is used as a barrier to separate the phases and materials passing through it.

Examples of diffusion.

- Transport of drugs through a polymeric membrane
- Percutaneous absorption of drugs
- Passive diffusion of drugs in the GI tract

12.7.1 Mathematics of diffusion

Mathematics of the diffusion process is described in detail in Chapter 6.3 which readers are requested to refer.

12.7.2 Diffusion apparatus

The apparatus used for measuring the diffusion coefficients of substances are called diffusion cells. These cells consist of two chambers (donor and receiver chambers) separated by a membrane and differ widely in shape and size [110]. Fig. 12.29 shows a schematic representation of a horizontal side-by-side diffusion cell. To measure the diffusion coefficients of a substance, one adds the drug to the donor chamber, and the amount of drug that penetrates the receiver chamber is measured as a function of time as shown in Fig. 12.30. The concentration of the drug in the

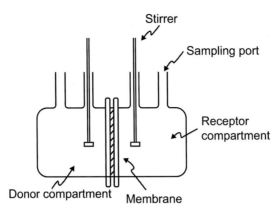

FIGURE 12.29 Schematic representation of a horizontal diffusion cell.

donor chamber should be kept constant. In other words, it should contain a saturated solution of the drug. However, in real practice, sometimes it is very difficult to maintain a saturated solution of the drug due to its solubility in the release media. Samples are collected from the receiver chamber at pre-determined time intervals and replaced with an equal volume of fresh medium. The concentration of the drug in the sample is determined by a suitable analytical method. A plot is constructed by using concentration versus time data as shown below in Fig. 12.30: All diffusion experiments should be carried out under sink conditions. The sink condition means that the concentration of the drug in the receiver chamber at any time should not exceed 10%–15% of the saturated solubility of the drug in the release media.

Flux can be determined from the slope of the steady-state portion of the plot. The lag time (t_L) can be determined by extrapolating the steady-state portion of the curve to the abscissa (x axis). The diffusion coefficient (D) of the drug can be determined from the lag time (t_L) using Eq. (12.5):

$$t_L = \frac{h^2}{6D} \tag{12.5}$$

where h is the thickness of the membrane used.

12.7.2.1 Determination of release of drugs from semisolid formulations

The release of drugs suspended in ointment bases can be calculated by using the Higuchi equation, Eq. (12.6) [107] as shown below:

$$Q = 2C_0(Dt/\pi)^{1/2} \tag{12.6}$$

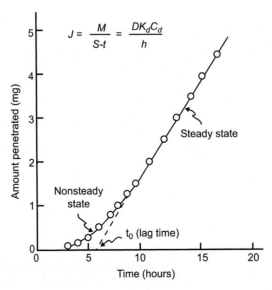

FIGURE 12.30 Graphical plot of a typical diffusion data.

where Q is the amount of drug released into the receptor phase per unit area (mg/cm^2), C_0 is the initial drug concentration in the dosage form (mg/mL), D is the apparent diffusion coefficient of the drug (cm^2/s), t is the time after application, and π is a constant.

Many apparatus and diffusion cells have been used to determine the release kinetics of drugs from semisolid formulations. The following sections provide details on diffusion apparatus/cells described in the USP.

12.7.2.2 Modified USP apparatus with enhancer cell

The Enhancer Cell assembly contains an enhancer cell (Fig. 12.31) placed in the USP apparatus. The Enhancer Cell (VanKel, NJ), made of Teflon, consisting of a cap, an o-ring, a washer, and a drug reservoir used for *in vitro* release studies of semisolid dosage forms by placing a membrane on the top of the reservoir. The diameter of the body, cap, and the solid ring is kept identical, which helps in keeping the membrane in its position while tightening the cell. The cell is placed in the USP dissolution tester that is a modified form of the USP apparatus 2 with a 200 mL capacity flask instead of a 900 mL flask.

During the experiment, one must ensure that no air is trapped in the interface of the formulation and the membrane. Thus, the equipment is degassed using a sonicator to remove air bubbles. The enhancer cell is then placed in a modified USP apparatus (Fig. 12.32). The receptor medium is stirred constantly with a magnetic stirrer. Samples are collected using an automatic sampler and are replaced with fresh samples. This simple method ensures batch-to-batch consistency of semisolid dosage forms and can detect products of different strengths. It reduces costs by requiring fewer accessories and apparatus that give reliable and reproducible results as compared to data obtained from other diffusion cells used as screening devices in preformulation and product development [111].

12.7.2.3 USP apparatus 4 with dialysis adapter

In 1957, a flow-through cell was developed by the FDA to evaluate the release rate of dosage forms. Bhardwaj et al. later modified the USP apparatus 4 with a dialysis adapter (Fig. 12.33). The dialysis adapter is made of a hollow cylinder containing a circular Teflon fabricated base at top, supported by metallic wire to provide a framework for the adapter. A dialysis membrane is placed over the teflon top and sealed with an o-ring at the top and bottom. The whole assembly is then placed in the USP apparatus in an upright position. The base of a sample cell is filled with ruby beads or glass beads at the bottom of the cell. The dosage form is applied to the adapter and sealed with a screw on the top. The sample is withdrawn from the media reservoir container of the apparatus and replaced with a fresh solvent. Sink condition is maintained during the experiment.

This method provides better simulation for *in vivo* conditions. Additionally, it can provide biorelevant conditions such as the addition of serum or enzymes, change in temperature or pH, and addition of a surfactant to trigger release and does not alter the mechanism of drug release. It is used mainly for liposome, microemulsion, suspension, etc., but now it can also be used to study semisolid dosage forms where microdialysis is recommended.

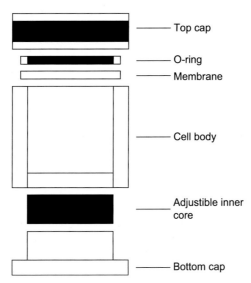

FIGURE 12.31 The enhancer cell assembly.

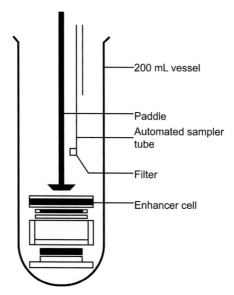

FIGURE 12.32   Modified USP apparatus with enhancer cell.

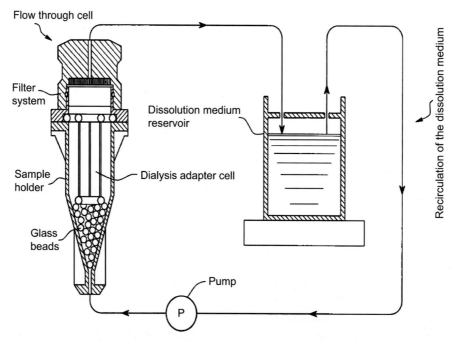

FIGURE 12.33   USP apparatus 4 with dialysis adapter.

Several other *in vitro* release methods can be used to evaluate semisolid dosage forms. These methods can provide simple, reproducible quality control tests that can be used to test the quality and stability of semisolid dosage forms containing hydrophilic and lipophilic drugs but not applied for bioequivalence studies of dosage forms. None of these methods can be used as official methods in Pharmacopeia. Regulatory agencies are continuously trying to search for more stringent methods comparable to dissolution testing of oral dosage forms.

12.7.3 Method of preparation of semisolid dosage form

The required mixing of semisolids depends on the type of dosage form, the quantity of product, and the types of bases used in the formulation of the product [113] (Tables 12.4 and 12.5). The ointments, pastes, and gels can be prepared either by trituration or fusion. The trituration method, performed on a laboratory scale, involves mixing the

TABLE 12.4 Summary chart: properties of ointment bases.

	Oleaginous ointment bases	Absorption ointment bases	Water/oil emulsion ointment bases	Oil/water emulsion ointment bases	Water-miscible ointment bases
Composition	Oleaginous compounds	Oleaginous base+(w/o) surfactant	Oleaginous base + water (<45% w/w)+(w/o) surfactant (HLB <8)	Oleaginous base + water (>45% w/w)+(o/w) surfactant (HLB >9)	Polyethylene glycols (PEGs)
Water content	Anhydrous	Anhydrous	Hydrous	Hydrous	Anhydrous, hydrous
Affinity for water	Hydrophobic	Hydrophilic	Hydrophilic	Hydrophilic	Hydrophilic
Spreadability	Difficult	Difficult	Moderate to easy	Easy	Moderate to easy
Washability	Nonwashable	Nonwashable	Non- or poorly washable	Washable	Washable
Stability	Oils poor; hydrocarbons better	Oils poor; hydrocarbons better	Unstable, especially alkali soaps and natural colloids	Unstable, especially alkali soaps and natural colloids; nonionic better	Stable
Drug incorporation potential	Solids or oils (oil solubles only)	Solids, oils, and aqueous solutions (small amounts)	Solids, oils, and aqueous solutions (small amounts)	Solid and aqueous solutions (small amounts)	Solid and aqueous solutions
Drug release potential	Poor	Poor, but > oleaginous	Fair to good	Fair to good	Good
Occlusiveness	Yes	Yes	Sometimes	No	No
Uses	Protectants, emollients (+/−), vehicles for hydrolyzable drugs	Protectants, emollients (+/−), vehicles for aqueous solutions, solids, and non-hydrolyzable drugs	Emollients, cleansing creams, vehicles for solid, liquid, or non-hydrolyzable drugs	Emollients, vehicles for solid, liquid, or non-hydrolyzable drugs	Drug vehicles
Examples	White petrolatum, white ointment	Hydrophilic petrolatum, anhydrous lanolin, Aquabase™, Aquaphor®, Polysorb®	Cold cream type, hydrous lanolin, rose water ointment, Hydrocream™, Eucerin®, Nivea®	Hydrophilic ointment, Dermabase™, Velvachol®, Unibase®	PEG ointment

TABLE 12.5 Formulation and component of semisolid dosage form.

Component	Properties	Example
BASES		
Ointment bases		
Oleaginous bases	Occlusive, hydrophobic, greasy, non-washable	White petrolatum, white ointment
Absorption bases	Occlusive, water-absorbent, anhydrous, greasy	Anhydrous lanolin, hydrophilic petrolatum
(W/O) type emulsion bases	Occlusive, hydrous, greasy, hydrophilic, non-washable	Lanolin, cold cream
(O/W) type emulsion bases	Washable, non-greasy, can be diluted with water, non-occlusive	Hydrophilic ointment
Water-soluble bases	Water-soluble and washable, non-greasy, non-occlusive, lipid-free	Polyethylene glycol ointment
Suppository bases		
Oily bases	Low absorption of water, hydrophobic, immiscible with mucus	Theobroma oil, hydrogenated oil
Water-soluble/Water-miscible	Hydrophilic, some are hygroscopic	Glycerol gelatin, polyethylene glycol
Emulsifying bases	Water-dispersible, contain non-ionic surfactant with oils or waxy solids	Witespol, massupol, massa esterinum
Vehicle		
Aqueous vehicle	Hydrophilic, non-reactant, and nontoxic	Ethanol and water
Non-aqueous vehicle	Hydrophobic, oily	Mineral oil and volatile oil
Emulsifying agents		
Anionic	Contain a negative charge, produce (o/w) emulsions, high pH	Soaps, sulfated alcohols, dioctyl sodium sulphosuccinate
Cationic	Bear a positive charge, used in creams and lotions	Benzalkonium chloride, cetrimide
Non-ionic	Stable, used in both o/w and (w/o) emulsion	Sorbitan monostearate, macrogol ethers
Gelling agents/thickening agents	Form gel by increasing viscosity may be natural, semisynthetic, and synthetic	Silicates, bentonites, carbomers, cellulose derivatives, gelatins
Antioxidants	Prevent or reduce the rate of oxidation, the chelating agent acts as a catalyst for the oxidation process	BHA, BHT, ascorbic acid, citric acid, tartaric acid,
Buffers	Control pH and provide stability by preventing drug ionization	Citrate, phosphate, and acetate buffer
Humectants	Minimize water loss and prevent drying out	Glycerol, propylene glycol, sorbitol
Preservatives	Kill or inhibit the growth of microorganisms	Benzoic acid, hydroxyl benzoates, benzalkonium compounds

drug with a base and other excipients using a metal spatula. The fusion method, used for large-scale manufacturing, involves heating waxes and solids according to the descending order of melting points with continuous mixing in a mixer or homogenizers to produce the desired homogeneity of products. One problem involved in the process of mixing semisolids is dead-spot formation which can be prevented by using the blade of proper shape. The mixing process includes low-speed shear, smearing, wiping, folding, stretching, and compressing. Low-speed shear is required due to changes in rheological properties with the changes in shear stress applied to semisolids.

Two types of mixers are used for mixing semisolids: double-kneading machines and Banbury mixers. For very stiff masses, the kneading machine is commonly used. It consists of an open trough with an approximately semi-cylindrical bottom. Within this trough, two horizontal Z-shaped knives, called sigma blade, rotate so that the material turned up by one knife is immediately turned under by the adjacent one. These machines are built in large sizes which can consume a very large amount of energy. They may also be jacketed for heating or cooling and closed to retain volatile solvents. They always operate on the batch principle and are therefore mounted so that they can be dumped by power-operated jacks. The Banbury mixer is an exceedingly heavy machine with two pear-shaped knives or blades, each rotating in a cylindrical shell, but these cylinders partly intersect each other. The projection is spiral along the axis, and the two spirals interlock. Because heat may be produced during mixing in the cylinder, the walls are cooled by a water spray.

Creams can be prepared by simultaneously heating both the aqueous phase and oily phase at the same temperature, 70°C, and mixing. After mixing, the congealed mass is cooled, and volatile ingredients are added after cooling to 25−30°C. To avoid grittiness, particle size reduction can be achieved by using a colloidal mill or triple-roller mill. According to the USP, dilution should not be preferred in creams and ointments until and unless it is required because excessive dilution can affect the stability of the emulsion-based formulation. The dilution should be performed in hygienic conditions to avoid any microbial contamination. Any unsuitable diluents, excessive dilution, or heating during mixing can cause incompatibility or instability. The preparations should be used within 2 weeks after the dilution.

12.7.4 Packaging, storage, and labeling

Packaging for semisolid preparations is often dictated by the nature of the medicament and the base. It is also dependent on how the semisolid is applied or the shipment of the product is done, depending on the quantity involved in the packaging. Stainless steel, tin plate drums, and collapsible aluminum tubes [112] are used where the semisolids are devoid of reactive ingredients with the metals, that is, they do not cause any corrosion or rusting. Glass packaging is used mostly in products that are not affected by light and mainly used for medium bulk quantities up to 2 kg in weight. Most bulk packaging is done in high-density polyethylene containers because they are light, moldable, and they regain their original shape, causing no wastage. They, therefore, are more suitable for semisolids in which sensitive applications are involved, such as ointments used for ocular or oral treatments. The most extensively used packing material these days is collapsible plastic tubes, but they do have the disadvantage of possibly causing oxidation. Metal tubes provide good protection from oxidation and do not let aqueous solutions dry out because they retain the volatile ingredients of the medicaments; however, these tubes may not be cost-effective [110,114].

Semisolids must be stored very carefully at a suitable temperature for a given period of time depending on the nature of the products to be stored. Aluminum-collapsible tubes containing an epoxy-resin coating are used for products that must be stored for a longer period of time because they are known for their good mechanical properties and chemical resistance. These tubes are good for semisolid dosages that are sterile in nature and are stored in air-tight, tamper-proof containers at less than 25°C.

12.7.5 Packaging, storage, and labeling of suppositories

The suppositories are packaged in glass and plastic screw-top jars due to their hygroscopic nature and stored at low temperature. The label must contain the "use for" instructions, that is, "for rectal use only," "for vaginal use only." It also should mention the temperature at which they are to be stored, such as "store in a cool place."

The next step before launching a drug requires marketing surveillance, ensuring the labeling of the drug is in compliance with drug regulatory authority and pharmacopeial guidelines. The label on the container should state "For external/internal use"; the strength of API as a percentage or volume; the "best before" date/date of expiry/manufacturing date; name and amount of added antimicrobial preservatives; storage condition; batch number; dilution required, if any; and/or sterility of preparation, as the case may be.

12.8 Conclusions

Semisolid dosage forms are available in a wide range of products with unique characteristics and applications in humans as well as animals. They are used both in pharmaceutical and cosmetic products. Semisolid drug products are usually intended for localized drug delivery (topical dosage forms). However, over the last few decades, these dosage forms have also been used for the systemic delivery of drugs (e.g., transdermal patches, suppositories, etc.). With increased number of geriatric patient population, their use will be extremely beneficial in the future. The other two areas where these dosage forms will find increased use are in the animal health and cosmetic industry. The use of nanotechnology in semisolid-based cosmetic products has shown tremendous growth over the years. The projected global topical drug delivery market is around $318 billion by 2027 from its market value of $207 billion in 2022. This projected market growth is attributed to the high incidence of burn injuries due to increased global conflicts and wars, increased numbers of smokers globally, growing prevalence of diabetes, and advancements in transdermal drug delivery systems [115]. Similarly, the transdermal delivery and device market are projected to grow at a rate of about 6% during 2021–28 [116].

Case studies

Case 12.1

Mrs. Turner needs to purchase a prescription of 0.25% (w/w) steroid cream to treat eczema on her infant son's cheeks. She asks the pharmacist about a prescription she got from her doctor 2 weeks ago for the same steroid in an ointment but at a higher concentration (1%). As the cost of this topical formulation is very high, she wants to know why she needs to purchase the 0.25% cream for her son when she could use the leftover 1% ointment instead. How should the pharmacist respond to Mrs. Turner?

Approach: This is an interesting case because it deals with multiple factors.

1. The cream formulation is not the same as an ointment.
2. An infant's skin is very different from that of an adult, with different barrier properties. One has to consider the percutaneous absorption properties of the topical formulation which is quite different from that for adults.
3. The strength of the ointment is four times more concentrated than the prescription for the cream. **Therefore, caution should be taken not to substitute the ointment for the cream.**
4. The release of the same steroids from both formulations (cream and ointment) will be different (concentration and formulation differences).

Case 12.2

A family of three is planning a long trip to Europe. Both parents and their teenage son suffer from travel sickness during long-term air travel. Unfortunately, the trip was so quickly arranged that the teenage son does not have a scopolamine patch to prevent his motion sickness during this travel. His mother calls the pharmacist for a consultation, explaining that her son's age is exactly half of her age. She wants to know why she cannot cut one of her transdermal patches in half and use that half patch for her son. What should be the attending pharmacist's response to the mother in this situation?

Approach: The attending pharmacist should explicitly say no to this query. Explain to the mother that by cutting her patch into two, she will destroy the rate-controlling membrane of the patch. The patch will lose its controlled release mechanism and dumping of drug will happen that may cause toxic and adverse effects.

Case 12.3

A 5% (w/w) salicylic acid ointment was prepared for a local and topical delivery for a skin disease. The rate of release of the drug from the ointment base is the major factor in the treatment of this condition. The compounding pharmacist prepared this ointment using two different bases: white petrolatum and an oil-in-water emulsion base. Which ointment base is more preferred in this situation?

Approach: Salicylic acid is known to be approximately five times more soluble in the oils and fat as compared to water (salicylic acid is hydrophobic). The solubility of salicylic acid in petrolatum is higher than oil-in-water emulsion base. The release rate from the oil-in-water emulsion base will be much higher than the petrolatum base. As petrolatum will be showing a slow release, the oil-in-water base is the more preferred base to be used in this situation.

Case 12.4

A community pharmacist prepared some rectal suppositories using Theobroma (cocoa butter) as the suppository base for a patient who has used such suppository in the past. After a few days of use, the patient reported that these suppositories are not as stiff as the previous batches. Therefore, not easy to insert as they become malleable just by holding between fingers. How this pharmacist, with his pharmaceutics knowledge, will find out an answer for this cause?

Approach: Theobroma oil base is a fatty suppository base. Polymorphism in a fatty suppository base is well-known. This may lead to different melting points of these polymorphs ranging from 18 to 34.5°C. The melting points of different polymorphic forms of cocoa butter are: γ form 18°C, α form 22°C, β' 28°C, and β 34.5°C. The way heat was added and the extent the base was heated can influence the polymorphic transition. Therefore, the possible cause could be a polymorphic change in the fatty acid base with a lower melting point (α, β', and γ) resulting in decrease in mechanical stiffness needed for convenient insertion of the suppository. This can be confirmed if there is a left-over suppository available from this batch. A melting behavior evaluation by a DSC will be necessary to confirm this. On further review, it was noted that since the hot water bath of the pharmacy was out of service, the pharmacist has used the microwave to melt this base without any optimization. This might have contributed to this polymorphic transition and have affected the quality of the finished product.

Case 12.5

A high concentration of a keratolytic agent (salicylic acid) ointment was prepared in petrolatum. This ointment was prepared in a hurry by the pharmacist and the patient reported local irritation and blister after the application of this formulation. What can the possible cause of this incidence.

Approach: Salicylic acid is a crystalline material. Incorporation of this highly crystalline material into a viscous petrolatum base needs careful levigation and spatulation. The pharmacist must use some levigating agent like the light mineral oil to dissolve all the crystals followed by thorough mixing by spatulation. Missing these important steps may cause the crystal to be present in the ointment which will be irritant and can cause blisters in sensitive skin areas when applied directly. To confirm this, a pharmacist can visually observe the presence of crystals in the ointment, which can further be confirmed by microscopic observation.

Case 12.6

A patient with two over-the-counter (OTC) products asks a pharmacist a question for a suggestion. Her daughter has some severe diaper rash with oozing surfaces. She had a petrolatum ointment and the other one is a paste. Which product should be advised to the patient and why? If the pharmacy intern asks the question to the pharmacist, why did he recommend the paste even though the API was zinc oxide in both?

Approach: Paste contains a higher amount of solid (around 40%), which can have both protective and liquid-absorbing property. It will help in absorbing the liquid exudates from the oozing wound and act as a protective barrier so that urine and other materials will not be coming in direct contact with the abrasive skin surfaces. Whereas the petrolatum ointment lacks this absorptive property and cannot help in absorbing the exudates from the rashes but can have the protective property only. Therefore, the pharmacist should recommend the paste over the ointment.

Critical reflections and practice applications

Semisolid dosage forms comprise many pharmaceutical preparations (e.g., ointments, creams, pastes, suppositories, transdermal patches, etc.), which can be easily prepared in a compounding pharmacy. Thus, a unique prescription optimal for a specific patient can be dispensed for which a manufactured dosage form may not be easily available. For example, a specialty veterinary pharmacy can dispense antidepressant or antiemetic transdermal patches for pets which can be customized according to their body weight and/or surface. Below are some important points about semisolid dosage forms.

- Topical formulations are applied on the skin surface or mucus membrane.
- The USP defines a topical medication as any route of administration characterized by application to the outer surface of the body.
- These preparations can be divided into two major categories: dosage forms and devices.
- Dosage forms may include liquid (solution, suspension, liniment), Semisolid (creams, ointment, gels, pastes, and lotions) and solid (powders, sprays, and suppositories).
- Transdermal patches and other transdermal devices fall in the device category.

- Non-invasive nature of its application, high prevalence of dermal and eye diseases, diabetes burn injuries, and increase in the number of geriatric populations have seen steady growth in this market.
- The topical drug delivery market is projected to reach USD 129.8 billion by 2025 from USD 95.2 billion in 2020.
- The future growth will be around the delivery of biologics through transdermal route and topical formulation for animals.

Acknowledgments

We thank the late Dr. Shailendra Kumar Singh, and Dr. Kalpana Nagpal from Amity University Noida, India, and Dr. Sangita Saini⸴ PDM College of Pharmacy, Sarai Aurangabad, Bahadurgarh, Haryana, India, who contributed in the 1st edition of this book.

References

[1] S.N. Murthy, H.N. Shivakumar, Topical and transdermal drug delivery, in: V.S. Kulkarni, pub (Eds.), Handbook of Non-invasive Drug Delivery Systems, William Andrew Publishing, Boston, USA, 2010, pp. 1—36.

[2] J.M. Durgin, Z.I. Hanan, M. Bellegarde, Pharmaceutical dosage forms. Pharmacy practice for technicians, in: M. Bellegarde (Ed.), Pharmacy Practice for Technicians, Cengage Learning, New York, USA, 2010.

[3] S. Niazi, Handbook of Pharmaceutical Manufacturing Formulations: Semisolid Products, CRC Press, Boca Raton, Florida, USA, 2004.

[4] Topical Dispenser Market Size, Share & Trends Analysis Report By Type (Metered, Swab), By Dosage Form (Solid, Semi-solid, Liquid), By Region, And Segment Forecasts, 2020 − 2027. Available at: https://www.grandviewresearch.com/industry-analysis/topical-dispenser-market [Accessed on Aug. 4, 2022].

[5] G.K. Jani, Dispensing Pharmacy, third ed., B.S. Shah Publication, 2003-04, 201 -203,222.

[6] I. Eros, J.A. Ehab, A. Cserne, I. Csoka, E. Csanyi, Factors influencing liberation of drug from semisolid dosage forms, Acta Pharm. Hung. 70 (2000) 29—34.

[7] E. Petró, A. Balogh, G. Blazsó, I. Erös, I. Csóka, In vitro and in vivo evaluation of drug release from semisolid dosage forms, Pharmazie 66 (12) (2011) 936—941. PMID: 22312698.

[8] A. Vintiloiu, J.C. Leroux, Organogels and their use in drug delivery—a review, J. Contr. Release 125 (3) (2008) 179—192.

[9] L. Lu, S. Yuan, J. Wang, Y. Shen, S. Deng, L. Xie, Q. Yang, The Formation mechanism of hydrogels, Curr. Stem Cell Res. Ther. 13 (7) (2018) 490—496, https://doi.org/10.2174/1574888X12666170612102706. PMID: 28606044.

[10] Lidogel® information in a FDA report available at: https://fda.report/DailyMed/c2e13ea2-7d2b-ebf8-e053-2995a90a474a [Accessed on Aug. 4, 2022].

[11] R.D. Juch, T. Rufli, C. Surber, Pastes: what do they contain? How do they work? Dermatology 189 (4) (1994) 373—377.

[12] A. Maqbool, M.K. Mishra, S. Pathak, A. Kesharwani, A. Kesharwani, Semisolid dosage forms manufacturing: Tools, critical process parameters, strategies, optimization, and recent advances, Indo Am. J. Pharmaceut. Res. 7 (11) (2017) 882—893.

[13] P. Bharat, M. Paresh, R.K. Sharma, B.W. Tekade, V.M. Thakre, V.R. Patil, A review: novel advances in semisolid dosage forms & patented technology in semisolid dosage forms, Int. J. PharmTech Res. 3 (2011) 420—430.

[14] A. Mishra, R. Panola, B. Vyas, D. Marothia, H. Kansara, Topical antibiotics and semisolid dosage forms, Int. J. Pharm. Erud. 4 (2014) 33—54.

[15] A. Bora, S. Deshmukh, K. Swain, Recent advances in semisolid dosage form, Int. J. Pharmaceut. Sci. Res. 5 (9) (2014) 3596.

[16] R. Parhi, Recent Advances in the Development of Semisolid Dosage Forms. Pharmaceutical Drug Product Development and Process Optimization: Effective Use of Quality by Design, 2020, pp. 125—189.

[17] R. Mehta, Topical and Transdermal Drug Delivery: What a Pharmacist Needs to Know, Inet Continuing education, InetCE. com, 2004, 1-0.

[18] L. Buhse, R. Kolinski, B. Westenberger, A. Wokovich, J. Spencer, C.W. Chen, S. Turujman, M. Gautam-Basak, G.J. Kang, A. Kibbe, B. Heintzelman, E. Wolfgang, Topical drug classification, Int. J. Pharm. 295 (1—2) (2005) 101—112, https://doi.org/10.1016/j.ijpharm.2005.01.032. PMID: 15847995.

[19] F.W. Ezzedeen, F.A. Shihab, S.J. Stohs, Release of sorbic acid from ointment bases, Int. J. Pharm. (Amst.) 28 (1986) 113—117.

[20] A.S. Velissaratou, G. Papaioannou, In vitro release of chlorpheniramine maleate from ointment bases, Int. J. Pharm. (Amst.) 52 (1989) 83—86.

[21] P.N. Bennett, M.J. Brown, Clinical Pharmacology, 9 edit, Churchill Livingstone/Elsevier, UK, 2008.

[22] M. De Villiers, Ointment bases, Pract Guide Contemp Pharm Pract 3 (2009) 277—290.

[23] B. Bharat, Nanotribological and nanomechanical properties of skin with and without cream treatment using atomic force microscopy and nanoindentation, J. Colloid Interface Sci. 367 (1) (2011) 1—33.

[24] L. Lachman, H.A. Lieberman, J.L. Kanig, Theory and Practice of Industrial Pharmacy, 4th Indian Edition, Verghese Publishing House, 1991, pp. 534—563.

[25] G.S. Banker, C.T. Rhodes, Modern Pharmaceutics, vol 7, Marcel Deckker Inc, 1979, pp. 272—276.

[26] L.J. Coben, Modern suppository manufacturing, Drug Dev. Ind. Pharm. 3 (6) (1977) 523—546, https://doi.org/10.3109/03639047709055631.

[27] Allen Jr., V. Loyd, Quality Control of Suppositories, Chapter 9, Suppositories, Pharm Press, 2007, ISBN 978 0 85711 093 0, pp. 139—158.

[28] R. Yahagi, H. Onishi, Y. Machida, Preparation and evaluation of double-phased mucoadhesive suppositories of lidocaine utilizing Carbopol and white beeswax, J. Contr. Release 61 (1—2) (1999) 1—8, https://doi.org/10.1016/s0168-3659(99)00111-x. PMID: 10469898.

[29] T. Takatori, N. Shimono, K. Higaki, T. Kimura, Evaluation of sustained release suppositories prepared with fatty base including solid fats with high melting points, Int. J. Pharm. 278 (2) (2004) 275—282, https://doi.org/10.1016/j.ijpharm.2004.03.030. PMID: 15196632.

[30] K.R. Feingold, Thematic review series: skin lipids. The role of epidermal lipids in cutaneous permeability barrier homeostasis, J. Lipid Res. 48 (2007) 2531—2546.

[31] K. Sembulingam, P. Sembulingam, Structure of skin. Essentials of medical physiology, in: Essentials of Medical Physiology, Jaypee Brothers, Medical Publishers, New Delhi, 2012.

[32] H. Yousef, M. Alhajj, S. Sharma, Anatomy, skin (Integument), epidermis, in: StatPearls [Internet]. Treasure Island (FL), StatPearls Publishing, 2021, 2022 Jan–. PMID: 29262154.

[33] The Human Body: Skin Biology and Structure, The Derm Review, Available at: https://thedermreview.com/the-human-body-skin-biology-and-structure/?nbt=nb%3Aadwords%3Ax%3A17689790824%3A%3A&nb_adtype=&nb_kwd=&nb_ti=&nb_mi=&nb_pc=&nb_pi=&nb_ppi=&nb_placement=&nb_si={sourceid}&nb_li_ms=&nb_lp_ms=&nb_fii=&nb_ap=&nb_mt=&gclid=Cj0KCQjw_7KXBhCoARIsAPdPTfjF8Uw4lPt3Up5q9iFoEX4kOgZLmwcR9-WOvuRitCfkRSCXXRnxDugaAs5YEALw_wcB [Accessed on Aug. 5, 2022].

[34] B. Ravara, C. Hofer, H. Kern, D. Guidolin, A. Porzionato, R. De Caro, G. Albertin, Dermal papillae flattening of thigh skin in *Conus Cauda* Syndrome, Eur J Transl Myol 28 (4) (2018) 7914.

[35] S.J. Newton, J.M. Cook, Considerations for percutaneous absorption, Int. J. Pharm. Compd. 14 (4) (2010) 301–304. PMID: 23965536.

[36] H. Matsumura, K. Oka, K. Umekage, H. Akita, J. Kawai, Y. Kitazawa, S. Suda, K. Tsubota, Y. Ninomiya, H. Hirai, et al., Effect of occlusion on human skin, Contact Dermatitis 33 (4) (1995) 231–235, https://doi.org/10.1111/j.1600-0536.1995.tb00472.x. PMID: 8654072.

[37] Y.H. Leow, H.I. Maibach HI, Effect of occlusion on skin, J. Dermatol. Treat. 8 (1997) 139–142.

[38] H. Zhai, H.I. Maibach, Effects of occlusion (II): wound healing, Cosmet. Toilet. (2004) 36–39.

[39] G.L. Qiao, J.E. Riviere, Significant effects of application site and occlusion on the pharmacokinetics of cutaneous penetration and biotrans-formation of parathion *in vivo* in swine, J. Pharmaceut. Sci. 84 (4) (1995) 425–432, https://doi.org/10.1002/jps.2600840408. PMID: 7629731.

[40] J.L. Bormann, H.I. Maibach, Effects of anatomical location on *in vivo* percutaneous penetration in man, Cutan. Ocul. Toxicol. 39 (3) (2020) 213–222, https://doi.org/10.1080/15569527.2020.1787434. Epub 2020 Jul 9. PMID: 32643443.

[41] A.K. Shah, G. Wei, R.C. Lanman, V.O. Bhargava, S.J. Weir, Percutaneous absorption of ketoprofen from different anatomical sites in man, Pharm. Res. (N. Y.) 13 (1) (1996) 168–172, https://doi.org/10.1023/a:1016014308638. PMID: 8668669.

[42] P.C. Mills, S.E. Cross, Regional differences in the in vitro penetration of hydrocortisone through equine skin, J. Vet. Pharmacol. Therapeut. 29 (1) (2006) 25–30, https://doi.org/10.1111/j.1365-2885.2006.00705.x. PMID: 16420298.

[43] F. Akomeah, T. Nazir, G.P. Martin, M.B. Brown, Effect of heat on the percutaneous absorption and skin retention of three model penetrants, Eur. J. Pharmaceut. Sci. 21 (2–3) (2004) 337–345, https://doi.org/10.1016/j.ejps.2003.10.025. PMID: 14757507.

[44] P. Hewitt, H.I. Maibach, L. Kanerva, Systemic toxicity. Handbook of occupational dermatology, In: L. Kanerva, Handbook of Occupational Dermatology, Springer, New York2000044–54.

[45] F.K. Akomeah, G.P. Martin, M.B. Brown, Variability in human skin permeability in vitro: comparing penetrants with different physicochem-ical properties, J. Pharmaceut. Sci. 96 (4) (2007) 824–834, https://doi.org/10.1002/jps.20773. PMID: 17177207.

[46] T. Miyagi, T. Hikima, K. Tojo, Effect of molecular weight of penetrants on iontophoretic transdermal delivery in vitro, J. Chem. Eng. Jpn. 39 (2006) 360–365.

[47] K.M. Mackay, A.C. Williams, B.W. Barry, Effect of melting point of chiral terpenes on human stratum corneum uptake, Int. J. Pharm. 228 (1–2) (2001) 89–97, https://doi.org/10.1016/s0378-5173(01)00808-0. PMID: 11576771.

[48] A. Williams, P. Augustijns, M. Brewster, Pharmaceutical solvents as vehicles for topical dosage forms Solvent systems and their selection in pharmaceutics and biopharmaceutics, In: P. Augustijns, M. Brewster, Solvent Systems and Their Selection in Pharmaceutics and Bio-pharmaceutics, Springer, 2007403–2007426.

[49] P.C. Mills, B.M. Magnusson, S.E. Cross, Effects of vehicle and region of application on absorption of hydrocortisone through canine skin, Am. J. Vet. Res. 66 (1) (2005) 43–47, https://doi.org/10.2460/ajvr.2005.66.43. PMID: 15691034.

[50] L. Binder, J. Mazál, R. Petz, V. Klang, C. Valenta, The role of viscosity on skin penetration from cellulose ether-based hydrogels, Skin Res. Technol. 25 (5) (2019) 725–734, https://doi.org/10.1111/srt.12709. Epub 2019 May 6. PMID: 31062432; PMCID: PMC6850716.

[51] J.J. Ashley, G. Levy, Effect of vehicle viscosity and an anticholinergic agent on bioavailability of a poorly absorbed drug (phenolsulfonph-thalein) in man, J. Pharmaceut. Sci. 62 (4) (1973) 688–690, https://doi.org/10.1002/jps.2600620436. PMID: 4698998.

[52] O.M.V. Schofield, J.L. Rees, N.A. Boon, S. Davidson, Skin disease Davidson's principles and practice of medicine, In: N.A. Boon, S. Davidson, Davidson's Principles and Practice of Medicine, Elsevier/Churchill Livingstone, Edinburgh 20061257–20061316.

[53] M.S. Roberts, S.E. Cross, M.A. Pellett, Skin Transport, Marcel Dekker, Inc., New York, 2002.

[54] G.K. Menon, P.M. Elias, Morphologic basis for a pore-pathway in mammalian stratum corneum, Skin Pharmacol. 10 (5–6) (1997) 235–246, https://doi.org/10.1159/000211511. PMID: 9449162.

[55] A.C. Williams, B.W. Barry, Penetration enhancers, Adv. Drug Deliv. Rev. 56 (5) (2004) 603–618, https://doi.org/10.1016/j.addr.2003.10.025. PMID: 15019749.

[56] S. Zafar, A. Ali, M. Aqil, A. Ahad, Transdermal drug delivery of labetalol hydrochloride: feasibility and effect of penetration enhancers, J. Pharm. BioAllied Sci. 2 (4) (2010) 321–324, https://doi.org/10.4103/0975-7406.72132. PMID: 21180464; PMCID: PMC2996075.

[57] P. Fuller, S. Roth, Diclofenac sodium topical solution with dimethyl sulfoxide, a viable alternative to oral nonsteroidal anti-inflammatories in osteoarthritis: review of current evidence, J. Multidiscip. Healthc. 4 (2011) 223–231, https://doi.org/10.2147/JMDH.S23209. Epub 2011 Jul 11. PMID: 21811389; PMCID: PMC3141840.

[58] S.L. Spruance, M. McKeough, K. Sugibayashi, F. Robertson, P. Gaede, D.S. Clark, Effect of azone and propylene glycol on penetration of trifluorothymidine through skin and efficacy of different topical formulations against cutaneous herpes simplex virus infections in guinea pigs, Antimicrob. Agents Chemother. 26 (6) (1984) 819–823, https://doi.org/10.1128/AAC.26.6.819. PMID: 6441511; PMCID: PMC180031.

[59] P.K. Wotton, B. Møllgaard, J. Hadgraft, A. Hoelgaard, Vehicle effect on topical drug delivery. III. Effect of azone on the cutaneous permeation of metronidazole and propylene glycol, Int. J. Pharm. (Amst.) 24 (1985) 19–26.

[60] F.P. Bonina, L. Montenegro, Penetration enhancer effects on in vitro percutaneous absorption of heparin sodium salt, Int. J. Pharm. 8 (1992) 171–177.

[61] B. Griepernau, S. Leis, M.F. Schneider, M. Sikor, D. Steppich, R.A. Böckmann, 1-Alkanols and membranes: a story of attraction, Biochim. Biophys. Acta 1768 (11) (2007) 2899–2913, https://doi.org/10.1016/j.bbamem.2007.08.002. Epub 2007 Aug 24. PMID: 17916322.

[62] H.K. Vaddi, P.C. Ho, S.Y. Chan, Terpenes in propylene glycol as skin-penetration enhancers: permeation and partition of haloperidol, fourier transform infrared spectroscopy, and differential scanning calorimetry, J. Pharmaceut. Sci. 91 (7) (2002) 1639–1651, https://doi.org/10.1002/jps.10160. PMID: 12115825.

[63] P.D. Yorgin, A.A. Theodorou, A. Al-Uzri, K. Davenport, L.V. Boyer-Hassen, M.I. Johnson, Propylene glycol-induced proximal renal tubular cell injury, Am. J. Kidney Dis. 30 (1) (1997) 134–139, https://doi.org/10.1016/s0272-6386(97)90577-1. PMID: 9214414.

[64] R.A. Tupker, J. Pinnagoda, J.P. Nater, The transient and cumulative effect of sodium lauryl sulphate on the epidermal barrier assessed by transepidermal water loss: inter-individual variation, Acta Derm. Venereol. 70 (1) (1990) 1—5. PMID: 1967864.

[65] P.A. Cornwell, J. Tubek, van Gompel, P. HAH, C.J. Little, J.W. Wiechers, Glyceryl monocaprylate/caprate as a moderate skin penetration enhancer, Int. J. Pharm. (Amst.) 171 (1998) 243—255.

[66] J. Choi, M.K. Choi, S. Chong, S.J. Chung, C.K. Shim, D.D. Kim, Effect of fatty acids on the transdermal delivery of donepezil: in vitro and in vivo evaluation, Int. J. Pharm. (Amst.) 422 (1—2) (2012) 83—90.

[67] S.A. Ibrahim, S.K. Li, Efficiency of fatty acids as chemical penetration enhancers: mechanisms and structure enhancement relationship, Pharm. Res. (N. Y.) 27 (1) (2010) 115—125, https://doi.org/10.1007/s11095-009-9985-0. Epub 2009 Nov 13. PMID: 19911256; PMCID: PMC2898574.

[68] S. Santoyo, A. Arellano, P. Ygartua, C. Martin, Penetration enhancer effects on the in vitro percutaneous absorption of piroxicam through rat skin, Int. J. Pharm. 117 (1995) 219—224.

[69] M. Aqil, A. Ahad, Y. Sultana, A. Ali, Status of terpenes as skin penetration enhancers, Drug Discov. Today 12 (23—24) (2007) 1061—1067, https://doi.org/10.1016/j.drudis.2007.09.001. Epub 2007 Oct 17. PMID: 18061886.

[70] J. Jampilek, K. Brychtova, Azone analogues: classification, design, and transdermal penetration principles, Med. Res. Rev. 32 (5) (2012) 907—947, https://doi.org/10.1002/med.20227. Epub 2010 Nov 9. PMID: 22886628.

[71] J.J. Escobar-Chávez, D. Bonilla-Martínez, M.A. Villegas-González, A.L. Revilla-Vázquez, Electroporation as an efficient physical enhancer for skin drug delivery, J. Clin. Pharmacol. 49 (11) (2009) 1262—1283, https://doi.org/10.1177/0091270009344984. Epub 2009 Aug 28. PMID: 19717723.

[72] K. Ita, Transdermal iontophoretic drug delivery: advances and challenges, J. Drug Target. 24 (5) (2016) 386—391, https://doi.org/10.3109/1061186X.2015.1090442. Epub 2015 Sep 25. PMID: 26406291.

[73] G.L. Li, J.J. de Vries, T.J. van Steeg, H. van den Bussche, H.J. Maas, H.J. Reeuwijk, M. Danhof, J.A. Bouwstra, T. van Laar, Transdermal iontophoretic delivery of apomorphine in patients improved by surfactant formulation pretreatment, J. Contr. Release 101 (1—3) (2005) 199—208, https://doi.org/10.1016/j.jconrel.2004.09.011. PMID: 15588905.

[74] M. Vikelis, D.D. Mitsikostas, A.M. Rapoport, Sumatriptan iontophoretic transdermal system for the acute treatment of migraine, Pain Manag. 4 (2) (2014) 123—128, https://doi.org/10.2217/pmt.13.71. PMID: 24641436.

[75] C.H. Lin, I.A. Aljuffali, J.Y. Fang, Lasers as an approach for promoting drug delivery via skin, Expet Opin. Drug Deliv. 11 (4) (2014) 599—614, https://doi.org/10.1517/17425247.2014.885501. Epub 2014 Feb 3. Erratum in: Expert Opin Drug Deliv. 2014 Dec;11(12):1979. PMID: 24490743.

[76] A.K. Nugroho, G. Li, A. Grossklaus, M. Danhof, J.A. Bouwstra, Transdermal iontophoresis of rotigotine: influence of concentration, temperature and current density in human skin in vitro, J. Contr. Release 96 (1) (2004) 159—167, https://doi.org/10.1016/j.jconrel.2004.01.012. PMID: 15063038.

[77] V.M. Meidan, M. Al-Khalili, B.B. Michniak, Enhanced iontophoretic delivery of buspirone hydrochloride across human skin using chemical enhancers, Int. J. Pharm. 264 (1—2) (2003) 73—83, https://doi.org/10.1016/s0378-5173(03)00390-9. PMID: 12972337.

[78] O. Pillai, N. Kumar, C.S. Dey, S.N. Borkute, R. Panchagnula, Transdermal iontophoresis of insulin: III. Influence of electronic parameters, Methods Find Exp Clin Pharmacol 26 (6) (2004) 399—408. PMID: 15349135.

[79] M. Ogura, S. Paliwal, S. Mitragotri, Low-frequency sonophoresis: current status and future prospects, Adv. Drug Deliv. Rev. 60 (10) (2008) 1218—1223, https://doi.org/10.1016/j.addr.2008.03.006. Epub 2008 Apr 3. PMID: 18450318.

[80] S.E. Lee, K.J. Choi, G.K. Menon, H.J. Kim, E.H. Choi, S.K. Ahn, S.H. Lee, Penetration pathways induced by low-frequency sonophoresis with physical and chemical enhancers: iron oxide nanoparticles versus lanthanum nitrates, J. Invest. Dermatol. 130 (4) (2010) 1063—1072, https://doi.org/10.1038/jid.2009.361. Epub 2009 Nov 26. Erratum in: J Invest Dermatol. 2010 Jun;130(6):1750. PMID: 19940858.

[81] A.G. Doukas, N. Kollias, Transdermal drug delivery with a pressure wave, Adv. Drug Deliv. Rev. 56 (5) (2004) 559—579, https://doi.org/10.1016/j.addr.2003.10.031. PMID: 15019746.

[82] G. Yan, K.S. Warner, J. Zhang, S. Sharma, B.K. Gale, Evaluation needle length and density of microneedle arrays in the pretreatment of skin for transdermal drug delivery, Int. J. Pharm. 391 (1—2) (2010) 7—12, https://doi.org/10.1016/j.ijpharm.2010.02.007. Epub 2010 Feb 25. PMID: 20188808.

[83] M. Kim, B. Jung, J.H. Park, Hydrogel swelling as a trigger to release biodegradable polymer microneedles in skin, Biomaterials 33 (2) (2012) 668—678, https://doi.org/10.1016/j.biomaterials.2011.09.074. Epub 2011 Oct 13. PMID: 22000788.

[84] K. Cu, R. Bansal, S. Mitragotri, D. Fernandez Rivas, Delivery strategies for skin: comparison of nanoliter jets, needles and topical solutions, Ann. Biomed. Eng. 48 (7) (2020) 2028—2039, https://doi.org/10.1007/s10439-019-02383-1. Epub 2019 Oct 15. PMID: 31617044; PMCID: PMC7329764.

[85] A.S. Ulrich, Biophysical aspects of using liposomes as delivery vehicle, Biosci. Rep. 2 (2002) 129—150.

[86] NOW Solutions, Celadrin Topical Liposome Lotion, Available at: https://www.ubuy.vn/en/product/21KLU64O-now-solutions-celadrin-topical-liposome-lotion-advanced-joint-cream-with-clinically-tested-celadrin Accessed on Aug. 09, 2022.

[87] S. Chen, S. Hanning, J. Falconer, M. Locke, J. Wen, Recent advances in non-ionic surfactant vesicles (niosomes): fabrication, characterization, pharmaceutical and cosmetic applications, Eur. J. Pharm. Biopharm. 144 (2019) 18—39, https://doi.org/10.1016/j.ejpb.2019.08.015. Epub 2019 Aug 22. PMID: 31446046.

[88] A. Azeem, M.K. Anwer, S. Talegaonkar, Niosomes in sustained and targeted drug delivery: some recent advances, J. Drug Target. 17 (9) (2009) 671—689, https://doi.org/10.3109/10611860903079454. PMID: 19845484.

[89] K. Nagpal, S.K. Singh, D.N. Mishra, Chitosan nanoparticles: a promising system in novel drug delivery, Chem. Pharm. Bull. (Tokyo) 58 (11) (2010) 1423—1430, https://doi.org/10.1248/cpb.58.1423. PMID: 21048331.

[90] D. Papakostas, F. Rancan, W. Sterry, U. Blume-Peytavi, A. Vogt, Nanoparticles in dermatology, Arch. Dermatol. Res. 303 (8) (2011) 533—550, https://doi.org/10.1007/s00403-011-1163-7. Epub 2011 Aug 12. PMID: 21837474.

[91] I.P. Kaur, R. Agrawal, Nanotechnology: a new paradigm in cosmeceuticals, Recent Pat. Drug Deliv. Formulation 1 (2) (2007) 171—182, https://doi.org/10.2174/187221107780831888. PMID: 19075884.

[92] K. Rai, Y. Gupta, A. Jain, S.K. Jain, Transfersomes: self-optimizing carriers for bioactives, PDA J. Pharm. Sci. Technol. 62 (5) (2008) 362—379. PMID: 19055232.

[93] H.B. Kostenbauder, A.N. Martin, A rheological study of some pharmaceutical semisolids, J Am Pharm Assoc Am Pharm Assoc 43 (7) (1954) 401−407, https://doi.org/10.1002/jps.3030430706. PMID: 13183835.

[94] A.H.C. Chun, The Measurement of Hydrophile-Lipophile Balance of Surface Active Agents, MS Thesis, Purdue University, 1959.

[95] B.Y. Shekunov, P. Chattopadhyay, H.H. Tong, A.H. Chow, Particle size analysis in pharmaceutics: principles, methods and applications, Pharm. Res. (N. Y.) 24 (2) (2007) 203−227, https://doi.org/10.1007/s11095-006-9146-7. Epub 2006 Dec 27. PMID: 17191094.

[96] Malvern Instruments, Laser Diffraction, Available from: http://www.malvern.com/labeng/technology/laser_diffraction/laser_diffraction.htm accessed 07.11.2022.

[97] J. Moore, E. Cerasoli, L. John, Particle light scattering methods and applications. Encyclopedia of spectroscopy and spectrometry. In: L. John, Encyclopedia of Spectroscopy and Spectrometry, Academic Press, Oxford20102077−2088.

[98] A.L. Philo Morse, Light microscopic determination of particle size distribution in an aqueous gel, Drug Delivery Technol. 9 (2009). Available from, http://www.particlesciences.com/docs/DDT-Particle_Size_Dist-May_09.pdf. (Accessed 7 June 2022).

[99] A. Paudel, D. Raijada, J. Rantanen, Raman spectroscopy in pharmaceutical product design, Adv. Drug Deliv. Rev. 89 (2015) 3−20, https://doi.org/10.1016/j.addr.2015.04.003. Epub 2015 Apr 11. PMID: 25868453.

[100] C.T. Ueda, V.P. Shah, K. Derdzinski, G. Ewing, G. Flynn, H. Maibach, M. Marques, Topical and transdermal drug products, Pharmacopeial Forum 35 (2009) 750−764.

[101] J.P. Marty, C. Lafforgue, J.L. Grossiord, P. Soto, Rheological properties of three different vitamin D ointments and their clinical perception by patients with mild to moderate psoriasis, J. Eur. Acad. Dermatol. Venereol. 19 (Suppl. 3) (2005) 7−10, https://doi.org/10.1111/j.1468-3083.2005.01330.x. PMID: 16274405.

[102] D.S. Jones, M.L. Bruschi, O. de Freitas, M.P. Gremião, E.H. Lara, G.P. Andrews, Rheological, mechanical and mucoadhesive properties of thermoresponsive, bioadhesive binary mixtures composed of poloxamer 407 and carbopol 974P designed as platforms for implantable drug delivery systems for use in the oral cavity, Int. J. Pharm. 372 (1−2) (2009) 49−58, https://doi.org/10.1016/j.ijpharm.2009.01.006. Epub 2009 Jan 18. PMID: 19429268.

[103] W.S. Goldenberg, R. Shah, A Useful Tool for the Determination of Consistency in Semi-Solid Substances, 2007. Available from, http://www.koehlerinstruments.com/literature/applications/Penetration-Paper.pdf. (Accessed 7 May 2022).

[104] S. Dhawan, R. Kapil, D.N. Kapoor, M. Kumar, Development and evaluation of in situ gel forming system for sustained delivery of cyclosporine, Curr. Drug Deliv. 6 (5) (2009) 495−504, https://doi.org/10.2174/156720109789941669. PMID: 19863490.

[105] S. Dhawan, R. Kapil, D.N. Kapoor, Development and evaluation of in situ gel-forming system for sustained delivery of insulin, J. Biomater. Appl. 25 (7) (2011) 699−720, https://doi.org/10.1177/0885328209359959. Epub 2010 Mar 5. PMID: 20207780.

[106] B.W. Barry, A.J. Grace, Sensory testing of spreadability: investigation of rheological conditions operative during application of topical preparations, J. Pharmaceut. Sci. 61 (3) (1972) 335−341, https://doi.org/10.1002/jps.2600610303. PMID: 5013364.

[107] E. Cevher, D. Sensoy, M.A. Taha, A. Araman, Effect of thiolated polymers to textural and mucoadhesive properties of vaginal gel formulations prepared with polycarbophil and chitosan, AAPS PharmSciTech 9 (3) (2008) 953−965, https://doi.org/10.1208/s12249-008-9132-y. Epub 2008 Aug 16. PMID: 18709556; PMCID: PMC2977016.

[108] J.D. Smart, The basics and underlying mechanisms of mucoadhesion, Adv. Drug Deliv. Rev. 57 (2005) 1556−1568.

[109] K. Bansal, M.K. Rawat, A. Jain, A. Rajput, T.P. Chaturvedi, S. Singh, Development of satranidazole mucoadhesive gel for the treatment of periodontitis, AAPS PharmSciTech 10 (3) (2009) 716−723, https://doi.org/10.1208/s12249-009-9260-z. Epub 2009 May 29. PMID: 19479385; PMCID: PMC2802163.

[110] T.J. Franz, Percutaneous absorption on the relevance of in vitro data, J. Invest. Dermatol. 4 (1975) 190−195.

[111] P.R. Rege, V.D. Vilivalam, C.C. Collins, Development in release testing of topical dosage forms: use of the Enhancer Cell with automated sampling, J. Pharm. Biomed. Anal. 17 (8) (1998) 1226−1233, https://doi.org/10.1016/s0731-7085(97)00184-2. PMID: 9800641.

[112] J.B. Haverkamp, U. Lipke, T. Zapf, R. Galensa, C. Lipperheide, Contamination of semi-solid dosage forms by leachables from aluminium tubes, Eur. J. Pharm. Biopharm. 70 (3) (2008) 921−928.

[113] Topical Drug Delivery Market by Type (Semi-solids (Creams, Gels, Lotions), Solids (Suppositories), Liquids (Solutions), Transdermal products), Route(Dermal, Ophthalmic), Facility of Use (Homecare setting, Hospitals, Burn Centres) - Global Forecast to 2027. Available at: https://www.marketsandmarkets.com/Market-Reports/topical-drug-delivery-market-124871717.html [Accessed on Aug. 14, 2022].

[114] H. Lockhart, F.A. Paine, Packaging of Pharmaceuticals and Healthcare Products, 1 edit, Blackie Academic and Professional, Madras, India, 1996.

[115] Global Semi-solid Dosage Form Market 2022 Size Estimation, Trend Analysis, and Competitive Landscape Forecast to 2028, The Market-Watch, 2012. Available at: https://www.marketwatch.com/press-release/global-semi-solid-dosage-form-market-2022-size-estimation-trend-analysis-and-competitive-landscape-forecast-to-2028-2022-07-12. (Accessed 4 August 2022).

[116] Market Analysis and Insights : Global Transdermal Patches Market. Available at: https://www.databridgemarketresearch.com/reports/global-transdermal-patches-market [Accessed on Aug. 14, 2022].

13

Special Dosage Forms and Drug Delivery Systems

Sarat K. Mohapatra and Alekha K. Dash

Department of Pharmacy Sciences, School of Pharmacy and Health Professions, Creighton University, Omaha, NE, United States

CHAPTER OBJECTIVES

- Distinguish the difference between a drug, a conventional dosage form, and a specialized dosage form.
- Recognize innovations in technology and their impact on special dosage forms of the future.
- Understand the various parenteral technologies in practice.
- Appraise the various osmotic drug delivery systems.
- Recognize the growing field of nanotechnology in drug delivery.
- Understand the use of liposomes as special dosage forms.
- Understand the application of magnetic drug delivery and its challenges.
- Describe the various implantable dosage forms in pharmacy practice and their future prospects.
- Recognize the application of prodrugs as special dosage forms.

Keywords: Conventional dosage form; Implantable drug delivery; Liposomal delivery; Magnetic delivery; Nano-delivery; Osmotic delivery; Parenteral delivery; Prodrug and Specialized dosage form.

13.1 Introduction

A dosage form is a combination of both active and inactive drug ingredients, also known as excipients, in any of the three physical forms of matter. The addition of excipients is essential to deliver sometimes a very small quantity

Pharmaceutics, Second Edition
https://doi.org/10.1016/B978-0-323-99796-6.00018-7

of the drug that will have therapeutic value without causing toxicity. For example, a therapeutically significant dose of 10 mg of Clotrimazole, an antifungal drug, or even 0.05 mg of ethinyl estradiol, an estrogen drug, is too small to weigh and dispense to patients. Excipients are needed in such instances as inactive fillers to create a safe and accurate bulk dose that can be easily weighed and administered to patients more reliably. Conventional dosage forms are available in different physical forms depending on the route of delivery. Tablets, capsules, thin films (e.g., Listerine pocketpaks), liquid solutions (syrup and elixir), suspension, powder, and granules are dosage forms administered through the oral route. Aerosol, inhalers, and nebulizers are used for pulmonary drug delivery. Intradermal, intramuscular, intraperitoneal, intravenous, subcutaneous, and intrathecal injections are examples of parenteral drug delivery methods. Creams, gels, balms, lotions, ointments, ear drops, eye drops, and skin patches are delivered topically. Suppositories are used for rectal, urethral, and vaginal routes. Even today, these conventional dosage forms are the primary pharmaceutical products available and used.

Note that dosage forms are designed for specific routes based on their chemical stability and pharmacokinetic properties. For example, insulin cannot be delivered orally because it will be metabolized in the gastrointestinal (GI) tract before entering the bloodstream. Similarly, to avoid first-pass metabolism in the liver, intravenous or intramuscular drug delivery may be among the preferred choices. Details on various conventional dosage forms used in pharmacy practice are covered in a number of chapters in this book. The objective of this chapter is to make readers aware of a number of special dosage forms and drug delivery approaches either currently in practice or on the horizon. Numerous tables provide information on various dosage forms currently available on the market.

An ideal drug delivery system has two prerequisites [1]. First, it should be a single dosage form to last the duration of the treatment. Second, it should be directed to the site of interest. This is not possible with conventional dosage forms. In fact, conventional dosage forms have a number of drawbacks:

- Drugs may be released rapidly, requiring frequent administration of the dosage form
- Such forms are difficult to monitor
- Careful calculation may be necessary to prevent overdosing
- There is an increased chance of missing a dose
- Fluctuations in the plasma concentration may lead to overshooting or undershooting the therapeutic window. This fluctuation causes adverse effects for drugs with a small therapeutic index
- Drugs can distribute to non-target cells and therefore be ineffective
- Such dosage forms can be expensive because of the need to use more drugs than may be necessary to achieve therapeutic concentration

In the past 3-4 decades, many new techniques and drug delivery systems that were not realized through conventional dosage forms have been developed to improve the drug delivery process. These techniques can be divided into three main categories:

- Controlled-release drug delivery
- Sustained-release drug delivery
- Site-specific or targeted drug delivery

The aforementioned techniques are capable of controlling the rate of drug delivery, extending the duration of drug delivery, or delivering the drug at the appropriate location in the human body. Fig. 13.1 shows a hypothetical plasma concentration-time profile of the drug versus time for conventional, controlled, and sustained drug delivery

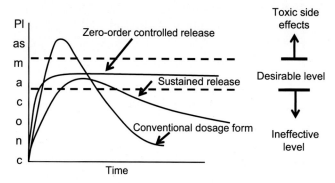

FIGURE 13.1   Plasma drug concentration versus time for zero-order controlled release, sustained release, and release from conventional dosage forms.

techniques. Note that the conventional dosage form requires frequent delivery of doses. It can overshoot or undershoot the therapeutic window, reducing not only the effectiveness of the drug but also easily creating a toxic effect. An ideal sustained drug delivery system should be able to maintain an effective plasma concentration of the drug over an extended period of time. Sustained-release systems developed so far mimic zero-order release through a slow first-order release kinetics. On the other hand, a controlled-release system delivers an agent at a controlled rate for an extended period of time. Properly designed, it will provide steady-state drug delivery within the therapeutic window. Normally, it follows zero-order kinetics. It may also target drug action by delivering the drug at the site of action. Thus, controlled-release drug delivery has the following advantages:

- The rate is reproducible, resulting in prolonged delivery
- Zero-order kinetics is feasible
- Less frequent administration is necessary, which results in increased convenience and better patient compliance
- Site-specific targeting is possible, which eliminates damage to nonspecific organs
- Less drug is used, resulting in reduced cost
- Re-patenting of the delivery system is possible without the need for new drug development

In the following sections, numerous special dosage forms and drug delivery systems, their operating principles, and their current status will be presented in detail.

13.2 Special dosage forms

Five primary areas are covered in this chapter: (1) parenteral drug delivery, (2) osmotic drug delivery, (3) nanotechnology, (4) implantable drug delivery, and (5) prodrug approaches. These areas were chosen because of current marketed products. The nanotechnology area is fairly extensive. Different nanotechnology areas, with the exception of liposomes and super paramagnetic iron oxide nanoparticles (SPIONs), are briefly covered. Marketable products using SPIONS are very limited at this time. It is expected that they will have a large impact on different facets of medicine in the future.

13.3 Parenteral drug delivery

The term "parenteral" is derived from two Greek words: *para* (besides) and *nteron* (the gut). This means the administration of drugs other than the gastrointestinal tract. A parenteral drug is defined as a sterile product that is suitable for administration by injection, internal irrigation, or for use in dialysis procedures.

13.3.1 Routes of parenteral administration

Parenterals are administered through various routes. Common parenteral routes of administration, as shown in Fig. 13.2, include intravenous (IV), intramuscular (IM), subcutaneous (SC), and intradermal (ID). Each parenteral route of administration is described in detail in Chapter 19.

13.3.1.1 *Intravenous*

Intravenous injections are introduced directly into the bloodstream. The IV route is used when an immediate systemic response is desired. These solutions are generally administered slowly so that they are diluted by the blood flowing past the needle point. The intravenous route is indicated when a drug is poorly absorbed via the oral route or is destroyed by digestive enzymes. This route is helpful when the patient is uncooperative, unconscious, and therefore unable to take medications by the oral route. Much greater volumes of the drug can be administered via this route. Adverse effects of this mode of administration include thrombosis, phlebitis, embolism, particulate material, infection, and need for trained personnel for administration.

13.3.1.2 *Intramuscular*

IM injections are administered into the striated muscle fibers under the subcutaneous skin layer. Limited sites are available for administration, such as the deltoid, gluteus medius, and vastus lateralis muscles. The usual needle length for this administration is from 1 to 1½ inch. Volume limitations are 2 mL for deltoid and thigh and 5 mL for gluteus medius. The IM route is less hazardous and easier to use than IV. However, the IM route is more painful than IV, and the onset of action is longer than that of IV but shorter than that of SC.

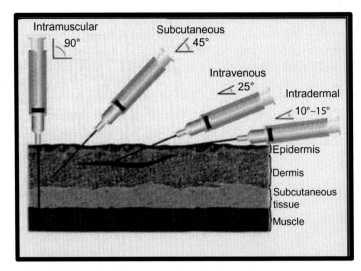

FIGURE 13.2   Various common routes for parenteral drug delivery.

13.3.1.3 *Subcutaneous*

SC injections are introduced into the loose interstitial tissues under the skin surface. A drug may be injected directly into the SC space or released into SC tissues via an implanted device. This route of administration is useful for short-term and long-term therapies. There are many sites available, such as the upper arm, anterior thigh, lower abdomen, and upper back. The usual needle length for this administration is around 3/8 to 1 inch. Volume limitation is about 2 mL. SC absorption is slower than that of IM but faster and more predictable than the oral route. Solutions, suspensions, and emulsions are appropriate for this route. Commonly used medications include heparin, enoxaparin, insulin, and some vaccines. Drugs that are irritating or highly viscous can produce induration, tissue sloughing, and abscess formation or can be painful to the patient.

13.3.1.4 *Intradermal*

The ID route is otherwise known as intracutaneous (IC). Injection is introduced directly into the more vascular layers of the skin just under the epidermis. Usual sites are the volar surface (inside) of the forearm, upper chest, and back. Usual needle length for this route is 3/8 inch. with a volume limitation of about 0.1 mL. This route of administration is used for diagnosis, desensitization, and immunization. Solutions, suspensions, and emulsions are appropriate for this route.

A few special administration sites for parenteral injections are provided in Table 13.1.

13.3.2 Advantages and limitations of parenteral administration

13.3.2.1 *Advantages*

- Drug action is quick
- The whole drug is administered, and bioavailability can be fast if the drug is given by the IV route
- Administration of intravenous fluids in case of dehydration or shock will save the life of the patient
- Some drugs, such as insulin and heparin, are destroyed if given orally. However, they can be effective when given by parenteral routes

13.3.2.2 *Limitations*

- The dosage form must be administered by trained personnel
- The effect of overdose or hypersensitive reaction to the drug is difficult to reverse
- There is a need for strict adherence to aseptic procedures
- Contamination of dosage form before injection is possible
- Due to strict requirements in manufacturing and packaging, the dosage form is more expensive than preparations given by other routes

TABLE 13.1 Special administration sites for parenteral injections.

Sites	Description
Intrathecal	Solution is injected directly into the subarachnoid space. Volumes of 1–2 mL are usually administered.
Intra-articular	Therapeutic agents are injected into the joint spaces.
Intracardial	Solutions are directly injected into the heart.
Intraperitoneal	The solutions are injected directly into the peritoneal cavity (for example, the rabies vaccine).
Intravesical	Solution is injected into the bladder.
Intraosseous	Solution is injected into the bone marrow. It's, in effect, an indirect IV access route because bone marrow drains directly into the venous system.

13.3.3 Parenteral containers

13.3.3.1 *Small volume parenteral*

Small volume parenteral (SVP) solutions are usually 100 mL or less and are packaged in different ways depending on the intended use. If the SVP is a liquid that is used primarily to deliver medications, it is packaged in a small plastic bag called a minibag of 50–100 mL. SVPs can also be packaged as ampules, vials, and prefilled syringes. Liquid drugs are supplied in prefilled syringes, heat-sealed ampules, or in vials sealed with a rubber closure. Powdered drugs supplied in vials must be reconstituted (dissolved in a suitable liquid).

13.3.3.2 *Large volume parenteral*

Large volume parenteral (LVP) solutions are single-dose injections intended for intravenous use and packaged in containers labeled as containing more than 100 mL. LVPs are packaged in glass bottles or in large-volume flexible containers. LVPs may contain greater than 100 mL to greater than 1–2 L of solution, and must be sterile, pyrogen-free, and essentially free of particulate matter. LVPs should not have any antimicrobial agents and should be isotonic. LVPs can consist of electrolytes, carbohydrates, nutritional solutions (proteins and lipid emulsions), peritoneal dialysis, and irrigating solutions.

13.3.4 Drug administration

Parenteral administration is accomplished by the use of syringes and needles.

13.3.4.1 *Syringes and needles*

The word "syringe" is derived from the Greek word *syrinx*, meaning "tube." A syringe is a simple pump consisting of a plunger that fits inside a tube. The pump can be pulled and pushed inside the pump to intake or expel a liquid or gas through an orifice at the open end of the tube. The open end of the syringe can be fitted with a hypodermic needle, a nozzle, or tubing.

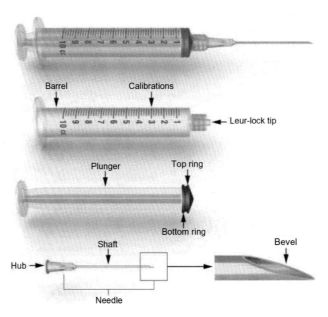

FIGURE 13.3   Parts of a 10 mL Luer–Lock hypodermic syringe.

The barrel of the syringe is made of plastic or glass and usually has graduated marks indicating the volume of fluid inside the syringe. The glass syringes can be sterilized in an autoclave. However, most modern syringes are made of plastic with a rubber piston for a better seal inside the tube. These are cheap and can be disposed of after each use.

Various parts of a 10 mL Luer–Lock hypodermic syringe with a needle are shown in Fig. 13.3.

13.3.4.2 Types of syringes

The two major types of syringes are hypodermic and oral.

13.3.4.2.1 Hypodermic syringe

In 1853, Drs. Charles Pravaz and Alexander Wood were the first to develop a syringe with a needle that was fine enough to pierce the skin. This is known as a hypodermic syringe. These syringes are calibrated in cubic centimeters (cc) or milliliters (mL). The smaller capacity syringes (1, 2, 2½, and 3 mL) are used most often for subcutaneous or intramuscular injections of medication. The larger sizes (5, 6, 10, and 12 mL) are commonly used to draw blood or prepare medications for intravenous administration. Syringes that are 20 mL and larger in volume are used to inject large volumes of sterile solutions. The 1 mL syringe is also known as a tuberculin syringe and is calibrated in a hundredth of a milliliter. Insulin syringes are used for the subcutaneous injection of insulin and calibrated in "units" rather than milliliters. The most prepared concentration of insulin is 100 units per mL, which is referred to as "units 100 insulin." A 50-unit Lo-Dose insulin syringe is shown in Fig. 13.4.

13.3.4.2.2 Oral syringe

An oral syringe is a measuring device used to accurately measure the dosage of liquid medicine expressed in milliliters. Oral syringes are available in sizes 1–10 mL and larger. The most used sizes for oral syringes are 1, 2.5, and 5 mL.

FIGURE 13.4   Insulin syringe with 50-unit capacity.

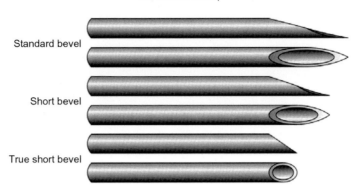

FIGURE 13.5 Various cannula designs used in needles.

13.3.4.3 Types of needles

A needle is composed of two parts: a hub, which locks to the tip of the syringe, and the canula, the pointed hollow tube, as shown in Fig. 13.3.

Needles have three dimensions:

1. The length of the needle (from the hub to the tip) usually ranges from ¼ to 1½ in.
2. The outside diameter (gauge) usually ranges from 13 to 27 gauge, according to the English Wire Gauge System. For example, an 18-gauge needle is larger than a 22-gauge needle.
3. Canula wall thickness is either a regular or thin wall.

Various canula designs are shown in Fig. 13.5.

13.4 Osmotic delivery

In the osmotic drug delivery system, the driving force is the osmotic pressure, and the operating principle is osmosis. Osmosis is the passive net movement of solvent molecules through a semipermeable membrane from a region of lower concentration of solute to a region of higher solute concentration.

Abbé Nollet discovered the Osmotic effect in 1748. In 1877, Pfeffer used a semipermeable membrane to separate sugar solution from pure water and found that osmotic pressure is proportional to the solute concentration and temperature. It was Van't Hoff who identified the proportionality between osmotic pressure, solute concentration, and temperature. Van't Hoff osmotic pressure equation is shown in Eq. (13.1):

$$\Pi = iCRT \tag{13.1}$$

where Π is the osmotic pressure, i is the Van't Hoff factor (the number of ions produced due to dissociation of one molecule of a solute), C is the concentration in molarity, R is the gas constant, and T is the absolute temperature. Osmotic pressure is the pressure that, if applied, will prevent the movement of a solvent through the semipermeable membrane to the region of higher solute concentration.

Osmosis has played a very important role in the osmotic pump first pioneered by the Alza Corporation. Note that a constant osmotic pressure implies a constant drug release rate and, therefore, a controlled drug delivery. Significant osmotic pressure can be developed by a number of compounds or mixtures of compounds. They are listed in Table 13.2.

13.4.1 Osmotic pump

The Alza Corporation pioneered the development of the first osmotic pump for drug delivery. It was called an elementary osmotic pump (EOP) [2,3]. Fig. 13.6 shows a cross-section of an EOP. It consists of an osmotic core containing the drug, surrounded by a semipermeable membrane and a delivery orifice. When exposed to water, the drug in the core imbibes water osmotically at a controlled rate determined by the permeability of the membrane and osmotic pressure of the core formulation. If the internal volume is constant, the osmotic pump delivers a volume of the saturated solution at a controlled rate. Delivery of the system is constant as long as excess solid is present in the core.

TABLE 13.2   Osmotic pressure of saturated solutions of common pharmaceutical solutes.

Compound or mixture	Osmotic pressure (atm)	Compound or mixture	Osmotic pressure (atm)
Lactose-fructose	500	Mannitol-sucrose	170
Dextrose-fructose	450	Sucrose	150
Sucrose-fructose	430	Mannitol-lactose	130
Mannitol-fructose	415	Dextrose	82
Sodium chloride	356	Potassium sulfate	39
Fructose	335	Mannitol	38
Lactose-sucrose	250	Sodium phosphate tribasic 12H$_2$O	36
Potassium chloride	245	Sodium phosphate dibasic 7H$_2$O	31
Lactose-dextrose	225	Sodium phosphate dibasic 12H$_2$O	31
Mannitol-dextrose	225	Sodium phosphate dibasic anhydrous	29
Dextrose-sucrose	190	Sodium phosphate monobasic H$_2$O	28

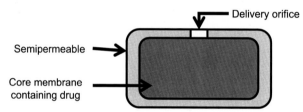

FIGURE 13.6   Cross-section of an elementary osmotic pump.

The rate of drug release, dm/dt, can be expressed by Eq. (13.2):

$$\mathrm{d}m/\mathrm{d}t = (A\,/\,h)\,L_p\,(\sigma\Delta\varPi - \Delta P)C \tag{13.2}$$

where $\Delta\varPi$ and ΔP are the osmotic and hydrostatic pressure differences, respectively, between the inside and outside of the system; L_p is the mechanical permeability of the membrane; σ is the reflection coefficient; A is the membrane area; h is the membrane thickness; and C is the concentration of the compound in the dispensed fluid. Normally, $\Delta\varPi \gg \Delta P$ with the appropriate selection of the size of the orifice. Also, when osmotic pressure, $\varPi$, of the formulation is large compared to the hydrostatic pressure difference, Eq. (13.2) simplifies to

$$\mathrm{d}m/\mathrm{d}t = (A\,/\,h)\,L_p\,\sigma\,\varPi\,C \tag{13.3}$$

Eq. (13.3) gives zero-order kinetics with a constant value of C. As the formulation gets saturated and no excess solid is present, the release rate follows non-zero order release kinetics. A single chamber osmotic pump such as the EOP just discussed is useful for delivering a moderately soluble active pharmaceutical ingredient (API).

13.4.2 Advantages and limitations of osmotic drug delivery

13.4.2.1 *Advantages of the osmotic drug delivery system*

- Zero-order release is achievable
- Delivery can be designed for delayed or pulsed delivery
- Drug delivery is independent of pH variations
- Delivery can be predictable based on mathematical calculations
- Agitation outside the pump does not have any effect on drug delivery
- Greater latitude in the size of the opening orifice is possible

- This delivery system is relatively simple to fabricate using conventional pharmaceutical manufacturing equipment
- Implantable systems can deliver a drug for a very long time (≥ 6 months)

13.4.2.2 Limitations of the osmotic drug delivery system

- Special equipment is needed to fabricate these systems
- The manufacturing process is more complicated than that of conventional dosage forms
- Osmotic pump residence time in the body varies with gastric motility and food intake
- This delivery system may cause irritation or ulcer due to release of saturated drug solution from the reservoir
- The drug release rate is fixed by the manufacturer

13.4.2.3 Key parameters influencing the design of the osmotic pump

- Solubility of the solute inside the drug delivery system affects the drug release rate. Some general strategies can be employed to increase the solubility of low soluble compounds such as swellable polymers, use of wicking agents to increase the surface area of the drug with the incoming aqueous fluids (colloidal silicon dioxide, sodium lauryl sulfate, etc.), use of effervescent mixtures (a mixture of citric acid and sodium bicarbonate), and use of cyclodextrin derivatives that increase the solubility of poorly soluble drugs.
- The osmotic pressure gradient inside the compartment and outer environment it is exposed to be optimized. The simplest way to control the osmotic pressure is to maintain a saturated solution of appropriate osmotic agent inside the device. Table 13.2 shows the osmotic pressure of commonly used solutes in formulations [4].
- Osmotic agents maintain a concentration gradient across the membrane. Osmotic compounds usually are ionic compounds such as the chlorides of Li, Na, K, Mg, sodium, or potassium hydrogen phosphate; and water-soluble salts of organic acids such as sodium and potassium acetate, sodium benzoate, citrate, and ascorbate. They generate a driving force for the uptake of water through the semipermeable membrane.
- A semipermeable membrane is one of the most important components of the osmotic system. It helps in the unidirectional movement of water from the body fluid into the osmotic chamber. It should possess certain performance criteria, such as sufficient wet strength, water permeability, and good biocompatibility. It should be rigid and non-swelling and should be thick enough to withstand the pressure in the device. Good permeability to water and impermeability to solute are important requirements for a good semipermeable membrane. Some examples are cellulose esters such as cellulose acetate, cellulose acetate butyrate, cellulose triacetate, ethyl cellulose, and Eudragits.
- Plasticizers can change the viscoelastic behavior of polymers, and these changes may affect the permeability of the polymeric films. Some of the plasticizers used include polyethylene glycols, ethylene glycol monoacetate and diacetate, triethyl citrate, diethyl tartrate, or diacetin for more permeable films.
- The size of the orifice is critical to obtain zero-order kinetics in osmotic drug delivery. It must be smaller than the maximum size to minimize drug delivery by diffusion. The orifice area should be larger than the minimum to minimize hydrodynamic pressure build-up in the system. Typical orifice size in osmotic pumps is between 600 μm and 1 mm. Although the orifice can be mechanically drilled, it is normally laser-drilled by a CO_2 laser for large-scale manufacturing.

13.4.3 Variations in osmotic pumps

Since the introduction of the EOP, a number of variations of osmotic pumps have been designed and developed. Some important variations are described in the following sections.

13.4.3.1 Push–pull osmotic pump

The push–pull osmotic pump (PPOP) is used for the delivery of APIs having extremes of water solubility (poorly water-soluble to highly water-soluble drugs). This consists of two separate chambers: one containing the drug and the other containing the osmotic agents that are surrounded by a semipermeable membrane. Water can enter both chambers. The osmotic agent swells after water absorption through the semipermeable membrane and pushes the drug through the orifice. A cross-section of the PPOP before and during operation is shown in Fig. 13.7.

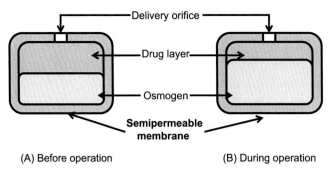

FIGURE 13.7   Schematic of a push—pull osmotic pump (A) before and (B) during operation.

13.4.3.2 *Osmotic controlled drug delivery in colon targeting*

Osmotic controlled drug delivery in the colon (OROS-CT) was developed by Alza Corporation to target the delivery of the drug locally to the colon for the treatment of colon-specific diseases or for systemic absorption that is otherwise unattainable. This can consist of a single osmotic unit or multiple units (5—6 push—pull units), each 4 mm in diameter. Each unit is surrounded by an enteric coating to prevent fluid entry into the highly acidic environment of the stomach. Note that enteric polymer coatings are primarily weak acids containing acidic functional groups, which are capable of ionization at elevated pH. However, in low stomach pH, these polymers are insoluble. The entire capsule is surrounded by a gelatin layer. Immediately after the capsule is swallowed, the gelatin layer dissolves. These individual POP units escape the stomach because of the enteric coating. The enteric coating dissolves in the higher pH of the small intestine. Each push—pull unit is designed with a 3—4-hour gastric delay to prevent drug release in the small intestine. Drug release starts in the colon. A schematic cross-section of OROS-CT is shown in Fig. 13.8.

OROS-CT is also used as one of the approaches for the pulsatile drug delivery system (PDDS) in which a delay time from the administration of the drug is required for maximum benefit. This is due to the fact that certain pathological conditions require drug release to have a time lag after the administration of the drug. For example, airway restrictions in asthma patients increase in the nighttime. Chemotherapy drugs may be more effective and less toxic if given at proper tumor cell cycles. Pain in rheumatoid arthritis patients peaks in the morning and decreases throughout the day.

13.4.3.3 *Liquid oral osmotic system pump*

The liquid oral osmotic system, abbreviated (L-OROS), is targeted to deliver liquid drug formulations. A schematic cross-sectional view of the L-OROS system is shown in Fig. 13.9 before ingestion and during release. The liquid drug formulation is surrounded consecutively by a soft gelatin layer, an osmotic layer, and a rate-controlling membrane, the semipermeable membrane. The delivery orifice is formed through the three outer layers but not through the gelatin layer. As the osmotic engine expands, hydrostatic pressure inside the system increases, thereby breaking the gelatin layer at the orifice, and starts releasing the drug. The inner barrier layer isolates the gelatin wall of the drug solution chamber from hydration.

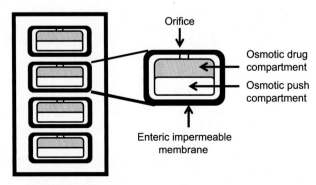

FIGURE 13.8   Schematic of an OROS-CT osmotic pump.

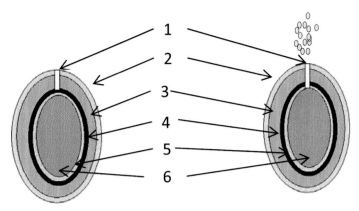

FIGURE 13.9 Schematic cross-sectional view of the L-OROS drug delivery system before and after drug release. 1 = Delivery orifice, 2 = semipermeable membrane, 3 = osmotic layer, 4 = inner layer, 5 = gelatin layer, and 6 = liquid drug formulation.

The L-OROS system comes in soft cap, hard cap, and delayed liquid bolus configurations. The delayed liquid bolus configuration has an additional placebo delay layer. The acetaminophen soft gelatin capsule is an over-the-counter product by Leiner Health Products, Inc.

There are numerous proposed configurations of osmotic drug delivery systems [4–6]. In addition to the osmotic pump tablets for oral drug delivery, there are numerous implantable osmotic pumps such as ALZET and DUROS implantable systems currently available. They are manufactured by the Alza Corporation. The implantable osmotic pumps are discussed in detail in Section 13.6 on implantable drug delivery.

Numerous osmotic pump systems are currently available in the market, and Table 13.3 provides a summary of many of these systems.

13.5 Nanotechnology for drug delivery

Nanotechnology deals with submicron particles and systems. "Nano" is a Greek word meaning "dwarf." One nanometer is the same as one billionth of a meter (10^{-9} m). There are various size definitions of nanoparticles. It suffices to say that nanoparticles range in size from 1 nm to 1000 nm. For more practical applications in biology, nanoparticles in the 3–300 nm range are preferred. Table 13.4 shows the size of some biological species in nanometers.

Liposomes, polymer conjugates, polymeric micelles, nanospheres, nanocapsules, dendrimers, etc. can be prepared as nanoparticulate (NP) systems. A number of these nanoparticle systems that have potential uses in pharmacy and medicine are schematically shown in Fig. 13.10. Polymer conjugates, polymer micelles, dendrimers, liposomes, nanospheres, nanocapsules, and nanosuspensions (not shown in Fig. 13.10) belong to polymer therapeutics. Solid lipid nanoparticles (SLNs) and variants thereof, such as nanostructured lipid carriers (NLCs) and lipid drug conjugates (LDCs), belong to the lipidic systems. Super-paramagnetic iron oxide NPs can be categorized as ceramic systems. Another area not represented in Fig. 13.10 is nanoemulsion, which may act as a precursor for the preparation of some of the nanoparticulate systems described here.

13.5.1 Advantages of nanotechnology

Nanotechnology offers some unique advantages for drug delivery applications. Some of them are listed as follows.

- Nanoparticles can encapsulate both hydrophobic and hydrophilic agents and thereby protect the encapsulated drug from harmful external conditions.
- Because of small size of the nanoparticles, they provide a high dissolution rate, improve aqueous solubility, and thereby improve bioavailability. Note that roughly 40% of all investigational compounds fail at the developmental stage because of their poor bioavailability, often associated with their poor aqueous solubility [8].
- Because of their small size, nanoparticles can be passively targeted at the leaky vasculature of a tumor. Active targeting is possible by attaching ligands/antibodies to the nanoparticles, which helps in preferential anchoring

TABLE 13.3 Osmotically controlled drug delivery systems in the market [7].

Product name	Drug	Formulation	Dose(mg)	Use	Manufacturer
Acutrim	Phenylpropanolamine	EM	75	Congestion associated with allergies, hay fever, sinus infection	Alza/Heritage
Adalat OROS	Nifedipine	OOP	30, 60	Hypertension	Bayer
Alpress LP	Prazosin	PP	2.5, 5	Hypertension	Alza/Pfizer
Cardura XL	Doxazosin	PP	4, 8	Hypertension	Alza/Pfizer
Concerta	Methyl phenidate	Imp	18, 27, 36, 54	Psychostimulant drug approved for ADHD	Alza
Coverta HS	Verapamil	PP	180, 240	Hypertension, angina	Alza/GD Searle
Ditropan XL	Oxybutynin chloride	PP	5, 10	Overactive bladder	Alza/UCB Pharma
Dynacirc CR	Isradipine	PP	5, 10	Hypertension	Alza/Novatris
Sudafed 24	Pseudoephedrine	EP	240	Stuffy nose and sinus pressure	Alza/Novatris
Efidac 24	Chlorpheniramine maleate	EP	4, 12	Sneezing, runny nose	Alza/Novatris
Glucotrol XL	Glipizide	PP	5, 10	Hyperglycemia	Alza/Pfizer
Minipress XL	Prazosin	EP	2.5, 5	Antihypertensive agent	Alza/Pfizer
Procardia XL	Nifedipine	PP	30, 60, 90	Calcium channel blocker	Alza/Pfizer
Teczem	Enalapril maleate and diltiazem maleate	EP	280 and 5	Hypertension	Merck/Aventis
Tiamate	Diltiazem HCl	PP	120, 240	Cardiovascular disorder	Merck/Aventis
Volmax	Albuterol	EP	4,8	Bronchospasm	Alza/Muro Pharma
Tegretol XR	Carbamazepine	EP	100, 200, 400	Anticonvulsant drug	Alza/Novatris
Viadur	Leuprolide acetate	Imp	18, 27, 37 and 54		
Chronogesic	Sufentanil	Imp		Anesthetics, IV narcotics	
Invega	Palperidone	OOP	1.5, 3, 6, 9	Scizophernia	Jansen
Exalgo	Hydromorphone	OOP	32	Management of pain	Mallinckrodt

EP, elementary pump; *Imp*, implantable pump; *OOP*, oral osmotic pump; *PP*, push—pull pump.

TABLE 13.4 Examples of particle size from atoms to protozoa.

Specie	Size (nm)
Protozoa	100,000
Cells	10,000
Bacteria	1000
Viruses	100
Macromolecules	10
Width of DNA	2.5
Atoms	0.1

of the drug-loaded nanoparticles at the tumor site. Targeted nanodrug carriers reduce drug toxicity and provide more efficient drug distribution.

• Nanoparticles are taken up by cells more efficiently than large-sized microparticles [9].
• Nano delivery system can be used for various routes of administration, such as oral, nasal, parenteral, and intraocular.

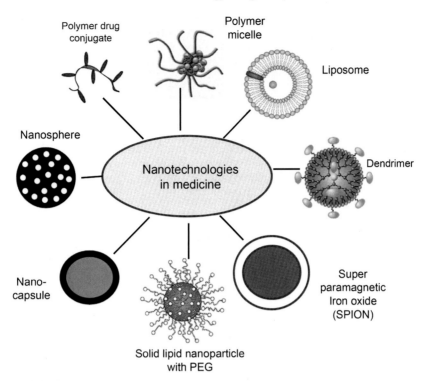

FIGURE 13.10 Schematic representation of various nanotechnologies in medicine.

13.5.2 Nanoparticle systems

Currently, more than 50 nanoparticulate formulations have been approved by US FDA or the European union [10]. These formulations include dendrimers, polymer micelles, liposomes, solid-lipid nanoparticles, and metal nanoparticles. These nanoformulations can be categorized into four groups. Polymeric, non-polymeric, nanocrystalline, and lipid-based nanoparticles. The percent distribution of these nanoformulation categories at the present time in the global market is as follows.

- Polymeric (35%)
- Non-polymeric (10%)
- Nanocrystals (26%)
- Lipid-based (29%)

13.5.2.1 Dendrimers

The term dendrimer comes from the Greek word, "dendri" meaning "tree-like" and "meros" meaning "part off." Dendrimers are three-dimensional, highly branched macromolecules. They consist of an initiator core and multiple layers of repeating groups. Each layer is called a generation, with the core denoted as generation zero. Fig. 13.11 shows a three-generation (G3) dendrimer structure. Precise control over size can be achieved by the extent of polymerization. Dendrimers are made up of different types of polymers, such as polyamidoamine (PAMAM), poly(L-glutamic acid), polyethylene imine, polypropylene imine, and polyethylene glycol (PEG). Drugs can be loaded into the dendrimers using cavities in their cores through hydrophobic interaction, hydrogen bonds, or chemical linkage. Drugs can also be adsorbed or attached to surface groups. An excellent review on dendrimers was published by Sonke and Tomalia [11].

Dendrimer-based nanomedical product was first introduced in late 1990. During the last 30 years, a number of dendrimer-based products have been introduced and marketed. A list of the products is given in Table 13.5.

The advantages of dendrimers as a delivery system are as follows:

- Low polydispersity index indicating a tight control of the molecular distribution
- Small size of the dendrimers with anticancer drugs will have easy permeation through the leaky vasculature and also higher permeability through blood—brain barrier

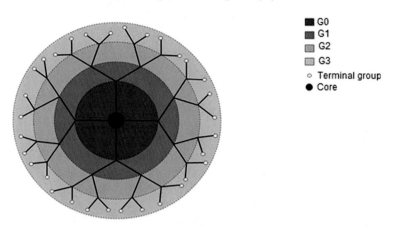

FIGURE 13.11   Schematic representation of a three-generation dendrimer.

TABLE 13.5   Dendrimer Based Product in the Market.

Name of the product	Dendrimer type	Use	Manufacturer	Status
Priostar	PEHAM/PEA	Therapeutic	Starpharma	Marketed
Starbust	PMPAMAM	Therapeutic	Starpharma	Marketed
Vivagel	Polt-L-lysine	HIV & STD	Starpharma	Marketed
Stratus CS	PAMAM	Cardiac Assay Diagnosis	Dade Behring	Marketed
Superfect	PAMAM	Transfection agent	Qiagen	Marketed
Priofect	PAMAM	Transfection agent	Starpharma	Marketed
Alert Ticket	PAMAM	Anthrax detection agent	US Army Lab	Marketed

HIV, human immunodeficiency virus; *PAMAM*, poly(amidoamine); *PEA*, poly(esteramine); *PEHAM*, poly(-etherhydroxylamine); *STDs*, sexually transmitted diseases.

- Sustained drug delivery with slower release of drugs and higher accumulations can be achieved
- Controlled multivalency of dendrimers is helpful in attaching several different drug molecules at the periphery of the dendrimers
- Hydrophobic drugs can be incorporated in the interior cavity, whereas hydrophilic drugs can be attached to the exterior of the dendrimer
- Dendrimer with its three-dimensional molecular framework can be used as scaffold for various biomedical applications

13.5.2.2 Nanospheres and nanocapsules

Nanospheres are nanosized spherical particles consisting of synthetic or natural polymers such as collagen and albumin. The drug of interest is either dissolved/dispersed or entrapped inside the polymer matrix. These matrices range in size from 100 to 200 nm. Depending on the nature of the preparation and the polymer matrix, the release characteristics can be tailored. The surface of these particles is hydrophobic and is more susceptible to opsonization. Therefore, their surfaces need to be modified with hydrophilic materials to avoid opsonization.

Polymeric nanocapsules are colloidal-sized vesicular systems in which the active drug is confined within a cavity surrounded by a membrane or coating. The outer shell prevents direct interaction of the drug. The core is usually an oily liquid with the surrounding shell as a single polymer layer. Polymers typically used in nanocapsule preparation are biodegradable, such as polylactic acid (PLA), polylactic-co-glycolic acid (PLGA), and polycaprolactone (PCL). PEG and PLA prevent opsonization and help in long plasma circulation time. Nanocapsules have a higher drug-loading efficiency compared to nanospheres. In drug loaded nanocapsules, the drug-to-polymer ratio can be as high as 5:1 when the core consists of pure drugs. This ratio is about 1:10 for nanospheres [12].

TABLE 13.6 Polymeric micellar products in the market or in clinical trial.

Product	Application	Company
Genexol PM	Non-small cell lung cancer, breast cancer	Samyang
Estrasorb	Topical estrogen therapy	Novavax
NK 105 (Paclitaxel micelle)	Stomach and breast cancer	NanoCarrier
Flucide	Anti-influenza	NanoViricides
Basulin	Long-acting insulin	Flamel Technologies
DO/NDR/02	Paclitaxel delivery	Dabur Research Foundation

13.5.2.3 Polymeric micelles

Amphiphilic molecules have both hydrophobic and hydrophilic ends. When put in an aqueous solution, the hydrophilic end orients toward water and the hydrophobic block is removed from the aqueous environment to assume minimum free energy. At a certain critical amphiphilic concentration (termed critical micellar concentration or CMC), several amphiphiles will self-assemble to create colloidal-size particles called micelles. These are 10–100 nm in size. These micellar colloids form a cargo space for lipophilic drugs. The core of the micelles can entrap hydrophobic drugs. Above the CMC, the micelles will be thermally stabilized against disassembly. The core region of these micelles is surrounded by a corona of the hydrophilic portion of the amphiphilic polymer. The corona provides steric stabilization of the micelles, resists phagocytosis by macrophages, and increases the plasma circulation time of the micelles. Polymeric micelles for drug delivery have been the subject of intense research over the past decades. However, the number of products approved by FDA is limited. Estrasorb by Novavax is a polymeric micellar product approved by the FDA for the topical application of estradiol as an emulsion. A micellar formulation of cyclosporine for ocular application was approved by FDA in 2018. A number of other products are at different stages of clinical trial and are listed in Table 13.6.

13.5.2.4 Solid-lipid nanoparticles

Lipids are known to improve oral absorption of drugs [13]. Vitamins such as A and E and antifungal agent Griseofulvin are better absorbed orally in the presence of fats. An excellent model drug such as Cyclosporin A in the form of microemulsion reduces the bioavailability variation of the drug. In the early 1960s, the first parenteral administration (Intralipid) began the administration of lipophilic drugs. In the early 1990s, various groups focused attention on solid lipid nanoparticles. As the name suggests, these nanocarriers contain solid lipids. They have the advantages of physical stability, controlled release, and low toxicity; they also help in protecting labile drugs from degradation from the external environment. They are generally prepared with physiological lipids or molecules that have a history of safe use and are better tolerated than polymeric carriers. Additionally, avoidance of organic solvents makes them better candidates compared to many of the polymeric systems. There are three important variations of lipid nanoparticles tested in the pharmaceutical literature: solid-lipid nanoparticles (SLNs), nanostructured lipid carriers (NLCs), and lipid–drug conjugates (LDCs).

13.5.2.4.1 Solid-lipid nanoparticles

SLNs are nanoparticles that are solid at room temperature and at body temperature. The starting material is a solid lipid such as triglycerides (e.g., Triacaprin), partial glycerides (e.g., glyceryl monostearate), fatty acids (e.g., stearic acid), steroids (e.g., cholesterol), and waxes (e.g., cetyl palmitate). Additionally, emulsifiers or mixtures of emulsifiers are used to stabilize the lipid emulsion [14]. The choice of the emulsifier depends on the administration route. High-pressure homogenization [15], breaking of (o/w) microemulsion [16], solvent emulsification-evaporation [17], and high-shear homogenization [16] are some of the techniques used in the manufacturing of these nanocarriers. Despite many advantages of the SLNs, the drug-loading capacity of conventional SLNs is limited by the solubility of the drug in the lipid matrix. Drugs are normally incorporated between the fatty acid chains of lipids. Highly purified lipids crystallize in a more ordered state and leave little room for drug incorporation and thereby reduce the drug-loading capacity of the SLNs. SLNs can encapsulate hydrophobic, hydrophilic drugs and nucleic acids. They are considered as one of the most versatile nano drug delivery vehicles.

Drug expulsion during storage is another factor in reducing the drug-loading capacity of the SLNs. After production, drugs crystallize in a highly ordered state. During storage, the lipids show a slow transition to a low energy and stable ordered state. This contributes to drug expulsion.

13.5.2.4.2 NLCs

NLCs were developed to improve the drug payload or drug-loading capacity of SLNs. Three different approaches are followed in the manufacturing process. (1) NLC I is produced by mixing spatially different lipids, that is, glycerides composed of different fatty acids, to create more space in the fatty acid chains. This creates imperfect lipid nanoparticle structure to create more space for drug molecules. (2) When liquid lipid (oil) is added to the lipid (e.g., isopropyl myristate with hydroxy octacosanyl hydroxystearate), the lipid solidifies in the amorphous state. Increased disorder of the lipid increases drug loading and reduces drug expulsion. This is known as NLC II structure. (3) NLC III is produced by increasing the amount of oil such that there is a phase separation of oil droplets. More of the drug is partitioned in the liquid droplets than the solid lipid. For example, when Compritol is mixed with Miglyol 812 (>30%) and the mixture is subjected to hot homogenization, Miglyol droplets are formed inside the Compritol lipid matrix after cooling [18,19].

13.5.2.4.3 LDCs

SLNs and NLCs are useful for the incorporation of lipophilic drugs. Lipid drug conjugates, or LDCs, help in the incorporation of hydrophilic drugs. In this process, an insoluble drug-lipid conjugate is formed either through salt formation (e.g., conjugation through fatty acid) or through covalent linking of the drug with the lipid [20].

13.5.3 Nanoemulsions

Emulsion is a heterogeneous system consisting of two immiscible liquid phases dispersed in one another in the presence of a surface active agent (emulsifying agent). In an emulsion, one immiscible liquid (the dispersed phase) is dispersed in another liquid (the continuous phase). Nanoemulsions are submicron-sized droplets in the continuous phase with approximate droplet size of 100–500 nm. The droplets can be oil (oil-in-water or o/w) or water (water-in-oil or w/o). Multiple emulsions such as (o/w/o) or (w/o/w) can also exist. These nanoemulsions act as carriers for hydrophobic (o/w) or hydrophilic (w/o) drugs.

Some advantages of nanoemulsions include.

- Very small particles are less susceptible to gravitational settling. Brownian motion can negate the gravitational settling
- The rate of absorption can be increased
- They can provide an aqueous dosage form for water-insoluble drugs (o/w emulsion)
- The drug is protected from hydrolysis and oxidation because it is in the oil phase (o/w emulsion).
- They can be formulated into a variety of dosage forms such as foams, creams, liquids, and sprays.
- The ingredients are safe and therefore are nontoxic and nonirritating and can be easily applied to skin and mucous membranes.
- They provide better uptake of oil-soluble supplements (o/w emulsion) for cell culture technologies.

Nanoemulsions or emulsions, in general, do not form spontaneously. If oil is added to water, it will separate immediately. However, when a surface active agent, that is, surfactant, is added to this mixture with high mechanical agitation, a stable emulsion may form. Small droplets can be formed by applying extra-energy or shear force to the two phases system. This is schematically shown in Fig. 13.12.

Application of high shear can be achieved through high-pressure homogenization, microfluidization, ultrasonication, and high-shear stirring techniques [21,22]. The fundamental relationship governing the rupture of an isolated liquid droplet in another immiscible and continuous liquid phase was developed by Taylor [23]. This can be expressed as shown in Eq. (13.4):

$$a \sim (\sigma) / (\eta_c\, \gamma) \tag{13.4}$$

where a is the size of the liquid droplet, σ is the interfacial tension, η_c is the viscosity of the continuous phase, and γ is the shear rate applied. Using the preceding equation one can be able to get an estimate of the shear rate needed to create a 100 nm droplet. Using a surface tension value of 10 dyn/cm and viscosity of 10^{-2} P (o/w emulsion with

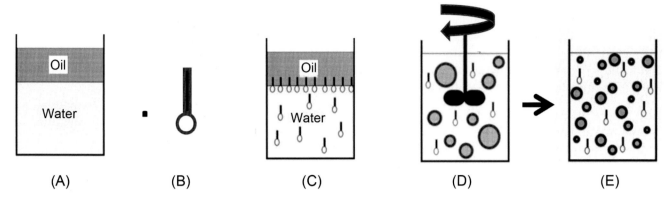

FIGURE 13.12 Steps in the formation of nanoemulsion. (A) Oil added to water; (B) surfactant added; (C) surfactant primarily at the oil—water interface; (D) high shear applied; (E) nanoemulsion formed.

water as the continuous phase), the calculated shear rate of $10^8\,\mathrm{s}^{-1}$ is needed. These shear rates are feasible with high-frequency ultrasonic devices and microfluidic systems.

13.5.3.1 Components of nanoemulsion

The major components of a nanoemulsion are oil, surfactants and cosurfactants, an aqueous phase, and other additives. Some excipients used for (o/w) emulsion are listed in Table 13.7. Oils should be appropriately chosen for enhanced solubility and stability of the lipophilic drug. Sometimes, a mixture of oils may be employed to improve solubility. Additionally, oils should be compatible with other excipients. Since oils are triglycerides, care should be taken to prevent oxidation by adding antioxidants such as α-Tocopherol. Sometimes, components such as lecithin and oils with high caloric potential may promote microbial growth. Preservatives such as parabens and Ethylenediaminetetraacetic acid (EDTA) are used to prevent microbial growth. Glycerol, sorbitol, and xylitol are used as tonicity modifiers, and NaOH and HCl can be used for adjusting the pH.

13.5.3.2 Stability of nanoemulsions

Nanoemulsions are thermodynamically unstable, exhibiting flocculation, creaming, and coalescence. Instability comes from the positive free energy change in the process where the generally higher interfacial term combined with the large surface area of the small particles dominate over the entropy term. Flocculation is a process by which the dispersed phase comes out of the formulation in flocs. Coalescence is a process in which small droplets bump into each other and combine to make bigger droplets. Emulsions can also undergo creaming such that one of the phases rises to the top or sedimentation settles to the bottom depending on the relative densities of the two phases (oil or water). Degradation can also be due to Ostwald ripening, wherein small particles can slowly dissolve and migrate toward larger particles and thereby promote the growth of larger particles. Note that this process does not require proximity of the small particle with the larger particles, as in coalescence.

Thermodynamic instability of a nanoemulsion can be minimized through the appropriate additions of surfactants into the formulation. Surfactants reduce the interfacial tension between oil and water and help in the formation of

TABLE 13.7 Formulation Additives for nanoemulsion.

Oil	Surfactant	Other additives
Sesame oil	Natural lecithins	α-Tocopherol
Castor oil	Phospholipids	Glycerol
Soya oil	Polysorbate 80	Xylitol
Paraffin oil	Poloxamer 407	Sorbitol
Lanolin	Poloxamer 188	EDTA
Glyceryl monostearate	Miranol C2M	Methyl and propyl paraben
Linseed oil	Tyloxapol	NaOH, HCl

the nanoemulsion. At the same time, they help in the stability of the nanoemulsion against flocculation, coalescence, and creaming. Van der Waals—London attractive forces induce particle flocculation or agglomeration. To overcome the attractive forces, one can put electric charges on the surface of the nanoparticles or provide steric hindrance between particles. Based on the surfactant or combination of surfactants to produce submicron droplets, anionic surfactants produce a negative charge on the surface. Cationic surfactants yield a positive surface charge, and nonionic surfactants such as poloxamers like Tyloxapol stabilize emulsion through steric hindrance.

There have been attempts to rationalize surfactant behavior in terms of their hydrophilic-lipophilic balance (HLB). The HLB takes into account the relative magnitudes of the hydrophilic and lipophilic fragments of the molecules. The approach is highly empirical but provides a guide to surfactant selection. It is generally accepted that a low HLB value (3—6) is more suitable for (w/o) emulsions, whereas surfactants with a high HLB value (8—18) are suitable for (o/w) emulsions. A required HLB value can be obtained through an appropriate combination of surfactants.

13.5.3.3 *Applications of nanoemulsions*

Nanoemulsions have been used in numerous pharmaceutical applications in cosmetics, prophylactics, bioterrorism attacks, mucosal vaccines, nontoxic disinfectant cleaners, oral delivery of poorly soluble drugs, vehicles for transdermal drug delivery, cancer therapy, targeted drug delivery, and parenteral and pulmonary drug delivery [22,24]. Some nanoemulsion products available in the market are listed in Table 13.8 [24].

13.5.4 Nanosuspensions

In nanosuspensions, the particle sizes of the dispersed particles in the suspensions are in the nano range. These systems have the advantage of higher mass-to-volume loading. Therefore, nanosuspensions are useful when there is a higher dosing requirement. For intramuscular or ophthalmic delivery in which there is a need for low administration volume, a nanosuspension is a better choice because of the high drug loading in the nanosuspension. In many conventional approaches, excessive amounts of co-solvents are used to solubilize the drug, that is, Cremophore EL in paclitaxel delivery. However, high dosages of co-solvents have toxic side effects.

A number of drugs using the nanosuspension technique are in the market as well as in clinical trials. The drugs marketed as nanosuspension dosage forms are summarized in Table 13.9.

13.5.5 Polymer conjugates

Polymer conjugates are a rapidly growing drug delivery area. Today, the vast majority of clinically approved drugs have a low molecular weight (typically under 500 g mol^{-1}) [28]. They typically have a short half-life in the blood plasma and a high overall clearance. An important requirement for drug delivery is to improve the pharmacological and pharmacokinetic profiles of therapeutic molecules. Two possible routes to improve drug delivery are through chemical conjugation and physical encapsulation. The encapsulation approach originated from the seminal work by Folkman and Long [29] and later by Langer and Folkman [30]. In these systems, drugs are physically incorporated in the nanoparticulate systems, such as emulsions, liposomes, polymeric micelles, and lipid nanoparticles, described earlier.

The covalent conjugation approach was first introduced by Ringdorf in 1975 [31]. A schematic representation of this approach is shown in Fig. 13.13.

TABLE 13.8 Commercial therapeutic nanoemulsion products.

Drug	Brand name	Manufacturer	Indications
Propofol	Diprivan	AstraZeneca	Anesthetic
Propofol	Troypofol	Troikaa	Anesthetic
Dexamethasone	Limehason	Mitsubishi Pharmaceutical	Steroidal anti-inflammatory
Alprostadil palmitate	Liple	Mitsubishi Pharmaceutical	Vasodilator platelet inhibitor
Flurbiprofen axetil	Ropion	Kaken Pharmaceuticals	Nonsteroidal analgesic
Vitamin A, D, E, K	Vitalipid	Fresenius Kabi	Parenteral nutrition

TABLE 13.9 Nanosuspension drug products in the market [25–27].

Product	Drug	Indication	Manufacturer	Route of administration
Abraxane	Paclitaxel	Anticancer	American Pharmaceutical Partners/American Bioscience	Intravenous
Rapamune	Sirolimus	Immunosuppressant	Wyeth/Elan Nanosystems	Oral
EMEND	Aprepitant	Anti-emetic	Merck/Elan Nanosystems	Oral
Triglide	Fenofibrate	Lipid lowering	First Horizon Pharma/SkyPharma	Oral
MEGACEES	Megestrol acetate	Steroid hormone	Par Pharma/Elan Nanosystems	Oral
Tricor	Fenofibrate	Lipid lowering	Abbott/Elan Nanosystems	Oral

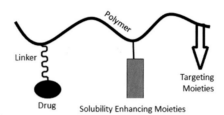

FIGURE 13.13 Schematic of drug–polymer conjugate model proposed by Ringdorf [31].

It's important to know the mechanism of drug action, that is, whether the conjugated drug is the active moiety or the released free drug. In most cases, the covalent bond between the drug and the linker or spacer breaks and makes the drug active. A covalent link formed between the hydrophilic polymer to protein to form polymer–protein conjugates has been the preferred strategy. Targeting moieties to the polymer backbone can help in the active targeting of the conjugated drug. Significant progress in the protein–polymer conjugate was possible after the introduction of PEGylation of the protein molecules with PEG. PEG is a linear chain polymer that is flexible, highly water soluble, nondegradable, nontoxic, and nonimmunogenic. Conjugation increases hydrodynamic volume of the macromolecular carrier, decreasing renal filtration. Additionally, PEGylation helps in shielding the protein from the reticuloendothelial system, thereby improving stability, increasing half-life, and improving the enhanced permeability and retention (EPR) effect. Protein PEGylation has been responsible for the introduction of numerous drugs, which are listed in Table 13.10. A large number of polymer-drug conjugates are in various clinical trials. Xyotax [Polyglutamic acid (PGA)-Paclitaxel] by Cell Therapeutics, which is undergoing a Phase III clinical trial, may be the first polymer–drug conjugate to be available in the market [32,33].

13.5.6 Liposomes

Liposomes were discovered in the early 1960s by British scientist Alec Bangham during electron microscopic observation of lecithin suspensions [34]. He observed that hydration of dry lipids would form closed-shell structures encapsulating part of the liquid medium core. The closed-shell structure has a lipid bilayer similar to a biological membrane. Since this discovery by Bangham, significant progress has been made by scientists in utilizing these closed structures for drug delivery applications. The first liposomal drug delivery system to be marketed was a formulation of Amphotericin B (AmBisome, NeXstar Pharmaceuticals Inc, San Dimas, CA, USA). This formulation received approval for sale in Ireland in late 1990, followed by other European countries. Other Amphotericin B formulations (Amphotec) in 1994 and Abelcet in 1995 followed.

13.5.6.1 Constituents and configurations

The primary constituents of a liposome are phospholipids. Some of the phospholipids used in the preparation of liposomes are dimyristoyl phosphatidylcholine (DMPC), dipalmitoyl phosphatidylcholine (DPPC), distearoyl phosphatidylcholine, dioleyl phosphatidylcholine (DOPC), dimyristoyl phosphatidyl ethanolamine (DMPE), distearoyl

TABLE 13.10 Polymer conjugate products in the market [32,33].

Compound and name	Year to market	Indication	Manufacturer
SMANCS (Zinostatin Stimalmer)	1993	Hepatocellular carcinoma	Yamanouchi Pharmaceuticals
Oncaspar (PEG-asparaginase)	1994	Acute lymphoblastic leukemia	Enzon
Adagen (PEG-adenosine deaminase)	1990	SCID syndrome	Enzon
PEG-Intron (Linear PEG-interferon α 2b)	2000	Hepatitis C, clinical evaluation on cancer, multiple sclerosis, and HIV/AIDS	Schering—Plough/Enzon
Pegasys (Branched PEG-interferon α 2a)	2002	Hepatitis C	Roche
Pegvisomant (PEG-growth hormone receptor antagonist)	2002	Acromegaly	Pfizer
Neulasta (PEG-G-CSF)	2002	Prevention of neutropenia associated with cancer chemotherapy	Amgen
Macugen (Branched PEG-anti-VEGF aptamer	2004	Age-related macular degeneration	OSI Pharmaceuticals/Pfizer
Cimzia (PEG-anti-TNF Fab)	2008	Rheumatoid arthritis and Crohn's disease	UCB
Krystexxa (PEG-Uricase)	2010	Chronic gout	Horizon Pharma
Plegridy (PEG-Interferon β1a)	2014	Relapsing multiple sclerosis	Biogen
Movantik (PEG-Naloxone)	2014	Opioid-induced constipation	AstraZeneca
Adynovate (PEG-Factor VIII)	2015	Hemophilia A	Baxalta
Palynziq (PEG-Phenylalanine ammonia lyase)	2018	Phenylketonuria	BioMarin
Jivi (PEG Factor VIII)	2018	Hemophilia A	Bayer

phosphatidyl ethanolamine (DSPE), dilauryl phosphatidylcholine (DLPC), dilauryl phosphatidyl ethanolamine (DLPE), dioleoyl phosphatidyl ethanolamine (DOPE), and distearoyl phosphatidyl serine (DSPS). Cholesterol can be added to the bilayer mixtures to act as a fluidity buffer and as an intercalator with the phospholipid molecules. All these lipids have a hydrophilic head group and a hydrophobic tail group. In general, a hydrophobic tail with a single chain (tail) forms micelles and a double chain forms a bilayer. The hydrophobic tails are composed of 10—24 carbon atoms. The hydrophilic head group will point toward the water in the core and outside the membrane. The transformation of the lipid to the bilayer structure is shown in Fig. 13.14.

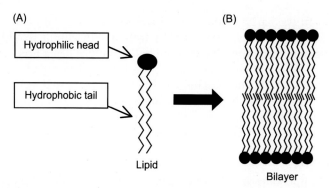

FIGURE 13.14 (A) An amphiphilic lipid molecule showing a double chain hydrophobic tail and a hydrophilic head. (B) Formation of a bilayer membrane from the amphiphilic lipid film under hydration.

Conventional

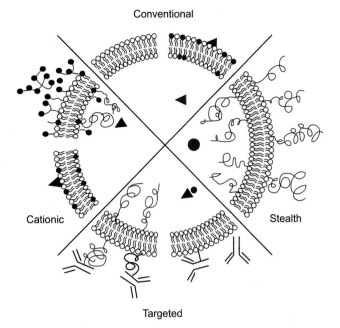

Cationic

Stealth

Targeted

FIGURE 13.15 Schematic representation of liposomes that are either neutral or negatively charged. Stealth liposomes have polymer coatings such as polyethylene glycol (PEG) to improve circulation. Immunoliposomes or targeted liposomes carry antibody for selective targeting. Cationic liposomes have a net positive charge through mono or multivalent cations. Hydrophobic drug molecules are embedded in the lipid bilayer, and hydrophilic drug molecules are entrapped inside the core [35] of different configurations of conventional and modified liposomes.

A liposome bilayer can have a surface charge. It can be associated with an antibody for active targeted delivery. Hydrophilic polymers such as polyethylene glycol can be attached to the bilayer membrane surface to improve the systemic circulation time. This is schematically shown in Fig. 13.15.

The vesicular structure of liposomes can have different configurations. They can be unilamellar, or a single bilayer enclosure; multilamellar with many layers separated by a water layer in between; or multivesicular, where a large vesicle encapsulates a number of small vesicles. Table 13.11 shows these configurations along with their approximate size ranges.

Unilamellar vesicles are used in research applications because of their well-characterized membrane properties. Oligolamellar vesicles cannot be reproducibly prepared and are rarely used. Multilamellar vesicles are frequently used in drug delivery and cosmetic applications. Multivesicular vesicles are used in nanoreactor assemblies and drug delivery tools.

13.5.6.2 Advantages and challenges of liposomes

13.5.6.2.1 Advantages of liposomes

- Liposomes are biocompatible, biodegradable, and nontoxic because they are composed of natural lipids.
- They can encapsulate both hydrophilic (in the core) and hydrophobic drugs (in the bilayer membrane).
- By encapsulating the drugs, liposomes can protect the drugs from the external environment and help in the extended release of the drugs.
- By encapsulating the drugs, liposomes reduce the drug toxicity to the tissues.
- Through passive and active targeting, site-specific drug delivery can be achieved.
- Size, charge, and surface properties can be modified by appropriate addition of chemicals to the lipid mixture before or after liposome preparation.
- Liposomes can be formulated into various dosage forms such as aerosol and semisolid forms such as gel, creams, and lotions. These forms can be lyophilized for subsequent reconstitution and administration through various routes, such as intravenous, ocular, nasal, subcutaneous, and intramuscular.

13.5.6.2.2 Challenges of liposomes

- Production costs are high.
- Hydrophobic drug solubility needs to be increased.

TABLE 13.11 Liposome structures [36].

Liposome structure	Size (μm)	Structure (schematic)
Unilamellar vesicles (UV)	~0.02–0.2	
Large unilamellar vesicles (LUV)	~0.2–1.0	
Giant unilamellar vesicles (GUV)	>1.0	
Oligolamellar vesicles (OLV)	~0.1–1.0	
Multilamellar vesicles, (MLV)	>0.5	
Multivesicular vesicles (MVV)	>1.0	

- Liposomes suffer from leakage and fusion of encapsulated drug molecules.
- An effective sterilization process is needed for parenteral application.

13.5.6.3 Liposome preparation

Thin film hydration is widely used in the preparation of multilamellar vesicles (MLVs). In this approach, lipid solution is dried by evaporation, spray drying, or lyophilization. The dried film is hydrolyzed in the presence of a buffer and agitated to form multilamellar vesicles. Liposomes of different sizes require different preparation techniques. An abbreviated description of various techniques is given in Table 13.12. Details of the techniques can be found in numerous references [35–42].

13.5.6.4 Factors affecting liposome performance

A number of factors are responsible for the stability of liposomes during storage as well as *in vivo* performance which are outlined below [43].

13.5.6.4.1 Surface charge

Based on the head group of the lipid and the pH, the surface charge of the liposome can be positive, negative, or neutral. The nature of the surface charge can affect stability, site-specific drug delivery, and biodistribution. Neutral surface charge will have lower suspension stability. These also have a lower tendency to be cleared by

TABLE 13.12 Liposome preparation techniques.

MLV	UV	LUV	GUV
Thin film hydration of lipids prepared by evaporation, spray drying, or lyophilization process	• Bath or probe sonication • Extrusion • High-pressure homogenization • Ink-Jet injection into an aqueous phase	• Freeze-thaw cycling • Swelling in non-electrolytes • Dehydration/Rehydration • Extrusion • Detergent dialysis • Reverse evaporation	• Dehydration/Rehydration • Electroformation • Solid film hydration • Detergent dialysis

reticuloendothelial system (RES). Liposomes with negative surface charge can be endocytosed faster than the neutral liposomes. Positively charged liposomes can have an enhanced uptake by the RES. Positively charged liposomes are often used for intracellular gene delivery.

13.5.6.4.2 Surface hydration and steric effect

The surface of the liposome can be modified to reduce aggregation and with appropriate attachment of hydrophilic polymers to be recognized by RES. This is often achieved by conjugating polyethylene glycol to the terminal amine of the phospholipid material. The resulting liposomes cannot be recognized by macrophages and RES as foreign particles. The optimum PEG molecular weight is @ 2000, and the PEG should be at a level of 5%–10% of the total lipid composition of the liposome.

13.5.6.4.3 Fluidity of the lipid bilayer

Liposomes and the lipid bilayer exhibit a well-ordered gel phase below a critical transition temperature (T_c). At and above this critical temperature, liposomes show leaky behavior. This will give rise to enhanced permeability, protein binding, aggregation, and fusion. The addition of cholesterol (>30 mol%) can eliminate phase transition and reduce leakage and permeability. The addition of cholesterol enhances particle stability by modulating membrane integrity and rigidity.

13.5.6.4.4 Liposome size

An increase in liposome size can enhance the uptake by RES. Unilamellar vesicles (50–100 nm) in size help in drug delivery by increasing systemic circulation time. This small size also applies to the PEG-treated liposomes (pegylated liposomes). Note that antifungal medication such as Ambisome is formulated to the size specification of 45–80 nm to reduce RES uptake.

13.5.6.4.5 Liposome applications

Over the past 3 decades, liposomal drug delivery has made a lot of progress and gained a lot of attention. Based on the information from multiple sources, we have come across more than 20 clinically approved products in the United States and a number of products at various stages of clinical trials. The marketed liposomal products are listed in Table 13.13. Note that these products operate in wide-ranging applications, as shown in the table.

13.5.7 Polymerosomes

Amphiphilic polymer, which has both hydrophobic and hydrophilic groups, can self-assemble in an aqueous solution to form vesicles known as polymerosomes. Amphiphilic polymers are block copolymers such as polybutadiene-block-polyethylene oxide (PB-b-PEO), poly(ethyl ethylene)-block-polyethylene oxide (PEE-b-PEO), polydimethylsiloxane-block-poly-2-methyl-2-oxazoline (PDMS-b-PMOXA), and polyethylene oxide-b-polypropylene oxide (PEO-b-PPO). Copolymers consisting of an inner hydrophobic block with two outer hydrophilic blocks called triblock copolymers can also be used for polymerosome formation. Triblock copolymers such as PEO-b-PPO-b-PEO have been used for gene delivery [44]. A review on the application of polymerosomes for drug delivery and other biomedical applications is provided elsewhere [45].

Preparation of self-assembly of amphiphilic block copolymers to form polymerosomes can be achieved by two distinct processes as described below.

TABLE 13.13 Liposome products currently available in the market.

Product name	Active drug	Routes of administration	Indications	Manufacturer
DaunoXome	Daunorubicin Citrate	IV	Kaposi sarcoma in AIDS	NeXstar
Daunoxome	Daunorubicin Citrate	IV	Kaposi sarcoma in AIDS	Galen
Myocet	Doxorubicin	IV	Breast cancer	Zeneus
Doxil	Doxorubicin in PEG liposome	IM	Kaposi sarcoma in AIDS	Sequus
AmBisome	Amphotericin B	IV	Serious fungal infections	NeXstar
Abelcet	Amphotericin B	IV	Serious fungal infections	Leadiant Biosciences
Funzizone	Amphotericin B	IV	Serious fungal infections	Bristol–Myers–Squibb
Amphotec	Amphotericin B	IV	Fungal infections leishmaniasis	Gilead Sciences
Amphocil	Amphotericin B	IV	Serious fungal infections	Zeneca
ALEC	Dry protein-free powder of DPPC-PG	Aerosol	Expanding lung diseases in infants	Britannia Pharm
DepoCyt	Cytarabine	IT	Lymphomatous meningitis	Pacira
Onco-TCS	Vincristine sulfate	IV	Non-Hodgkin's lymphoma	Elan
VincaXome	Vincristine	IV	Solid tumors	NeXstar
Nyotran	Nystatin	IV	Systemic fungal infections	Aronex
Lipoplatin	Cisplatin	IV	Solid tumors	Regulon
Evacet	Doxorubicin	IV	Ovarian cancer, metastatic breast cancer	Sanofi Pasteur
Epaxal Berna vaccine	Inactivated hepatitis- A vaccine	IM	Hepatitis-A	Swiss serum and vaccine institute, Switzerland
Inflexal V	IRIV vaccine	IM	Influenza	Crucell
DepoDur	Morphine sulfate	Epidural	Post-surgical analgesia	Sequus Pharmaceutical
Visudyne	Verteporfin	IV	Macular degeneration	Baush and Lomb
Estrasorb	Micellular estradiol	Topical	Menopausal therapy	Novavax
Topex Br	Terbutaline Sulfate	Oral	Asthma	Ozone
Arikayce	Amikacin	Amikacin liposome inhalation suspension	Bacterial lung disease	Insmed
Mikasome	Amikacin	IV	Bacterial infections	NeXstar
SPIKEVAX	mRNA-1273	IM	SARS-CoV-2 vaccine[a]	Moderna
Tozinameran/ BTN162b2	mRNA-BTN162b	IM	SARS-CoV-2 vaccine[a]	Pfizer-BioTech

[a]*Lipid nanoparticles (ionizable cationic lipid nanoparticles).*
IM, Intramuscular; *IV*, Intravenous.

- Solvent-switching techniques where block copolymers are dissolved in a good organic solvent for all the blocks present, followed by hydration of the solution. The hydration can be done by either slowly adding water to the organic polymer solution or by injecting organic solution into water.
- Polymer rehydration where the polymers are first dissolved in an organic solvent and then evaporated to form a thin film. Subsequently, the film is hydrated by the addition of water.

Advantages of polymerosomes

- Polymerosomes have a thicker membrane wall and are, therefore, more rugged than liposomes

TABLE 13.14 Stimuli-responsive block copolymer vesicles and their payloads [44].

Polymer	Encapsulated drug	Stimuli/Release mechanism	References
PMPC-PDPA	Doxorubicin	pH sensitive	Du et al. [46]
PEO-PNIPAm	Doxorubicin	Temperature responsive	Quin et al. [47]
PEG-PLA + PEG-PDB	Doxorubicin + Paclitaxel	Hydrolysis	Ahmed et al. [48]
PMPC-PDPA	pDNA	pH sensitive	Lomas et al. [49]

- Similar to liposomes, polymerosomes can be pegylated and, therefore, will have a long circulation time
- Polymerosomes can be surface functionalized to help in targeted drug delivery
- Polymerosomes can carry both hydrophobic drugs in the membrane and hydrophilic drugs in the lumen

Stimuli-responsive polymerosome research has seen many advancements over the last 2 decades. These external stimuli can be pH, temperature, or redox systems. Several stimuli-responsive block copolymer vesicles tested for polymerosome drug delivery are provided in Table 13.14.

13.5.8 Magnetic nanoparticle delivery

Magnetic nanoparticles offer some attractive possibilities both in the areas of therapeutics and diagnostics in medicine. Because of their small size (few nanometers to tens of nanometers), they are smaller than or comparable to cells (10−100 μm), viruses (20−50 nm), proteins (5−50 nm), or a gene (2 nm wide to 20−450 nm long) and can bind to a biological entity of interest [50].

13.5.8.1 Magnetic nanoparticles

Magnetic nanoparticles (MNPs) can be formed from various metals such as iron, cobalt, or nickel. A significant amount of research and development has gone into magnetic iron oxide, that is, Fe_3O_4 (magnetite) and γ-Fe_2O_3 (hematite). Magnetite nanoparticles are by far the most employed iron oxide nanoparticles in biomedical applications because of their biocompatibility, high magnetic susceptibility, high saturation magnetization, chemical stability, and inexpensiveness [51,52]. The magnetic properties of these particles have size-dependent behavior. Nanoparticle of magnetite with a size up to ~80 nm has single-domain characteristics. Below ~25 nm, it shows superparamagnetic behavior [53]. The superparamagnetic iron oxide nanoparticles (SPION) show neither remanence nor coercivity (Figs. 13−15). The residual magnetization (M) at zero magnetic fields is called remanence. Magnetic field at zero magnetization is called coercivity. This is the magnetic field to be overcome to increase magnetization. The Fe_3O_4 nanoparticle, above a particle size of 25 nm, shows hysteresis in the magnetization behavior.

There are many different approaches used in synthesizing magnetic nanoparticles. The most used approach is through coprecipitation of bivalent and trivalent iron chlorides [54]. In the aqueous media, iron oxide nanoparticles have a tendency to aggregate and precipitate without appropriate surface coatings. For *in vivo* applications, these nanoparticles need to be coated with a variety of moieties to prevent aggregation and attack by macrophages. Amphiphilic polymeric surfactants such as poloxamers, poloxamines, and polyethylene glycol are generally used. Antibody attachment to these moieties can improve the active targeting of these nanoparticles.

Magnetization behavior (change in magnetization with magnetic field) of these materials dictates the range of applications of these materials. Magnetization characteristics of superparamagnetic, paramagnetic, and ferromagnetic particles are shown in Fig. 13.16.

13.5.8.2 Applications of superparamagnetic iron oxide nanoparticles

Because of their magnetic properties, superparamagnetic particles can be used for several important applications.

- Magnetic contrast agents in MRI imaging
- Hyperthermia agents in which the magnetic particles are heated by the application of a high-frequency magnetic field
- Targeted drug delivery by an external magnetic field gradient. This is otherwise known as magnetic targeting
- Cell labeling and magnetic separation

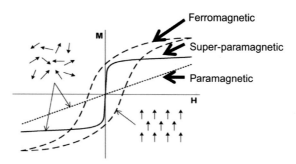

FIGURE 13.16   Magnetization characteristics of ferromagnetic, paramagnetic, and superparamagnetic nanoparticles.

13.5.8.2.1 Magnetic contrast agents in MRI imaging

MRI contrast agents are important to improve the visibility of internal body parts especially soft tissue. Iodinated contrast media improves contrast in X-ray imaging because of increased absorption through iodine. But, in MRI, increased contrast comes from the paramagnetic ions, which enhance the proton relaxation by reducing T_1 (Spin—lattice relaxation time) and T_2 (Spin—spin relaxation time). Spin—lattice (or longitudinal) relaxation time, T_1 refers to the rate of transfer of energy from the nuclear spin system to the neighboring molecules. Spin—spin (or transverse) relaxation time T_2 refers to the rate of magnetization decay in the $X-Y$ plane. Most current contrast agents are either simple paramagnetic metal ion ligand complexes or superparamagnetic particles. The first paramagnetic contrast agent (CA) approved in 1987 was gadolinium (III) diethylenetetraamine pentaacetic acid (GdDTPA). The free and unchelated Gd^{3+} is toxic in most biological systems and is not used. However, toxicity of Gd^{3+} is greatly reduced by forming Gd^{3+} complexes such as Gd^{3+} chelates. Gadolinium contrast agents are still the largest Gadolinium CAs used today. About 1 in three MRI scans use Gadolinium contrast agents. It is given by intravenous injection, that is, through a small needle into a vein in the arm, either by manual injection or by an automated injector. There are numerous Gadolinium-based contrast agents. Some of these agents include gadodiamide (Omniscan), gadopentetate dimeglumine (Magnevist), gadoversetamide (OptiMARK), gadobenate dimeglumine (MultiHance), gadobutrol (Gadovist, Gadavist), gadoterate meglumine (Dotarem, Clariscan), gadoteridol (ProHance), and gadoxetate disodium (Eovist, Primovist).

Because of concerns about nephrogenic sclerosis and gadolinium deposition in the brain, medical practitioners are actively seeking alternative materials such as SPIONs. SPIONs >50 nm are rapidly phagocytosed by Kupffer cells in the liver. SPIONs< 50 nm are known as USPION or ultra-small SPIONs have a longer blood half-life and, therefore, can be used for a wider spectrum of imaging applications such as MR angiography, tumor perfusion imaging, liver imaging, lymph node imaging, bone marrow imaging, atherosclerotic plaque imaging, and imaging of various types of inflammation. As shown in Fig. 13.15, these SPIONs are single-domain nanoparticles and show no hysteresis in their magnetization behavior. These also have no remanence in their magnetization characteristics which is a desirable property. Some of the SPIONs approved for use as MRI contrast agents include Feridex, Ferumoxytrol (Ferahem), Ferumoxtran-10, and NanoTherm.

13.5.8.2.2 Hyperthermia

Hyperthermia is a promising approach for cancer therapy aside from the traditional approach to surgery. In 1957, Gilchrist et al. [55] heated various tissue samples with 20—100 nm size particles of γ-Fe$_2$O$_3$ with a 1.2 MHz magnetic field. A temperature increase of 14°C was observed. No control experiments were used. Because of the high frequency used, there remains the possibility that the temperature rise is because of the induced electric field rather than due to nanoparticle heating.

There are two different regimens of hyperthermia. A temperature change between 41°C and 46°C stimulates the immune response in cancer cells. This is considered as mild hyperthermia. A temperature rise from 46°C to 56°C is a region of thermo-ablation. This causes tumor destruction by cell necrosis, coagulation, and carbonization.

There are three mechanisms of heating, that is, Eddy current heating, heating through hysteretic effect, and heating through superparamagnetic nanoparticles.

The power density for eddy current (P_E) heating is given by Eq. (13.5). P_E is the amount of heat generated per unit volume by eddy current [55].

$$P_E = Ef^2H_{max}^2d^2 \tag{13.5}$$

where E is the eddy current coefficient, f, the frequency, H_{max}, the maximum field strength, and d is the particle diameter.

Since P_E increases as d^2, eddy current heating becomes negligible in the nanoscale. The above equation also suggests that P_E increases as f^2 increases. Increasing the frequency beyond a few hundred kHz is not an attractive option because it will also increase tissue heating.

Ferromagnetic particles (FM) possess hysteretic properties between magnetization (M) and magnetic field (H), as shown in Fig. 13.15. In general, these are multimagnetic domain particles. Alternating magnetic fields induce heating of these particles. The amount of heat generated per unit volume is given by the frequency multiplied by the area of the hysteretic loop, as shown in Eq. (13.6):

$$P_{FM} = \mu_0 f \int H \, dM \tag{13.6}$$

where μ_0 is the permeability of free space and f is the frequency. As frequency is not part of the integral in the preceding equation, P_{FM} can be evaluated from quasistatic measurements. Even though substantial hysteretic heating can be achieved by the FM particles, the amplitude of H required will be high. Also, when the field is turned off, there will be some remnant magnetization which may be unacceptable. In principle, substantial hysteresis heating of the ferromagnetic particles could be achieved using strongly anisotropic magnets such as Nd—Fe—B or Sm—Co.

Magnetic particle hyperthermia has been revitalized by the advent of magnetic fluid hyperthermia (MFH), in which the magnetic particles are superparamagnetic. Note that (Fig. 13.15) these are single-domain nanoparticles with a diameter of 10—50 nm. They do not have any hysteresis in their magnetization behavior. These particles (SPIONs) don't have any remanence or coercivity. The physical basis of the heating of SPIONs has been reviewed by Rosensweig [56]. Based on the model, heat generation can be given by

$$P_{SPM} = \mu_0 \, \pi f \, \chi'' \, H^2 \tag{13.7}$$

where μ_0 is the permeability, f the frequency, χ'' is the complex part of susceptibility, and H is the magnetic field strength.

This simple theory compares favorably with the experimental results. SPIONS are capable of generating impressive levels of heating at lower fields compared to the ferromagnetic materials.

It should be noted that magnetic particle hyperthermia is still under experimental investigation.

There are two ways to administer magnetic nanoparticles to induce hyperthermia. The first is to directly inject SPIONS into the tumor, and the second is to infuse them into the veins. The first approach was successfully applied to the treatment of glioblastoma in 2011 [57,58]. One of the challenges in magnetic particle hyperthermia is off-target accumulation and heating. The magnetic nanoparticles can accumulate in off-target organs, for example, liver, kidneys, bladder, spleen, etc. [59]. This will lead to unintended heating of off-target tissues. A new technique, magnetic particle imaging has been developed to pinpoint spatially localized magnetic nanoparticles to help in the hyperthermia treatment [60].

Despite the slow development of direct magnetic particle hyperthermia, there has been a number of adjuvant therapy developments. Hyperthermia can be used to stimulate an anticancer response. It can serve as a trigger for drug administration in diseases of the gastrointestinal tract. Magnetic hyperthermia can also be used in the therapy of people infected with HIV.

13.5.8.2.3 Cell labeling and magnetic separation

Magnetic separation deals with separating specific biological entities from their native environment. This helps in preparing concentrated samples for analysis or subsequent use. For example, the production of recombinant pharmaceuticals and isolation of proteins and nucleic acids from natural samples require that the macromolecules be separated from the complex samples and should be highly purified. These can be achieved through magnetically controlled particles [61].

This is a two-step process. First, the biological entities need to be tagged with the magnetic material. In the second step, the tagged material needs to be separated out from the fluid-based magnetic separation device. This is schematically shown in Fig. 13.17 [52]. Tagging is done by coating the magnetic nanoparticles with dextran, polyvinyl alcohol, etc. The biomolecule of interest needs to have a linker, which will attach to the iron oxide nanoparticle. The magnet on the container wall attracts the tagged biomolecule to the magnet on the outside of the container wall. The unwanted supernatant solution can be removed, leaving the purified biomolecule material.

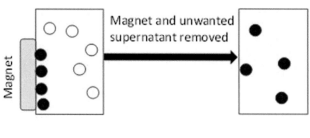

● Magnetically tagged bimolecule
○ Unwanted biomaterial

FIGURE 13.17   Schematic of magnetic separation of biomolecule in a solution.

13.5.8.3 *Magnetic nanoparticle targeting drug delivery*

Chemotherapeutic agents are mostly nonspecific, and when administered intravenously, they are available for general systemic distribution and cannot distinguish healthy cells from tumor cells. Therefore, specific targeting is a real delivery challenge. However, a number of approaches are being developed to have site-specific delivery. Some of these approaches use drug-loaded solid lipid nanoparticles, liposomes, magnetic, micro-, and nanoparticle carrier systems, etc. Application of a magnetic field attracts the magnetic nanoparticles to the target site. This is known as magnetic targeting, which is shown schematically in Fig. 13.18 [62].

The geometry of the magnetic field is very important to direct the drug-loaded magnetic nanoparticles to the tumor and not to the peripheral tissues. As the magnetic gradient decreases with distance, for effective tumor treatment, the tumor location should be within 10−15 cm from the surface of the body.

Targeted drug delivery through magnetic nanoparticles holds a lot of promise but has to overcome a number of challenges for clinical practice. A number of companies currently manufacture and supply coated and uncoated magnetic nanoparticles for drug delivery research and magnetic particle hyperthermia application. A list of these companies is given in Table 13.15.

13.6 Implantable drug delivery

Oral delivery is a preferred approach to drug delivery. However, the bioavailability of many therapeutic drugs dictates alternative approaches such as parenteral dosage forms, polymer depots, osmotic pumps, and implantable drug delivery. In 1861, Lafarge pioneered the concept of the implantable drug delivery system (IDDS) [63] for long-term continuous administration of crystalline hormone in the form of a solid steroidal pellet. In the late 1930s, Danckwerts et al. [64] began research on sustained-release implantable drug delivery systems administered through subcutaneous routes. Research and product commercialization have steadily increased, and IDDS has grown to a market size greater than $6 billion annually.

The implantable therapeutic systems are used for long-term, continuous, and sustained-release applications of drugs. The IDDS systems are surgically placed below the skin or cornea (for intraocular drug delivery). Ideal requirements of an IDDS system are environmental stability, biocompatibility, sterility, improvement in patient compliance by reducing the frequency of drug administration through the entire cycle of drug administration,

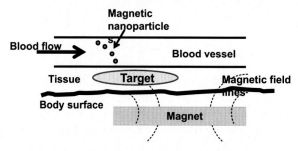

FIGURE 13.18   Schematic representation of magnetic nanoparticle targeting with external magnetic field.

TABLE 13.15 Companies involved in the development and production of magnetic particles for drug delivery.

Company	Application	Contact
Micromod Partikelttechnologie GMBH	Drug Delivery, biomagnetic separation	Micromod.de
NanoparTZ	Coated nanoparticles	Nanopartz.com
Amag Pharmaceuticals	Treatment of anemia	Amagpharma.com
MSI Automation	Instrumentation for hyperthermia	dave@msiautomation.com
NN Crystals US corporation	Nanoparticles of magnetic and semiconductor nanoparticles	contact@nn-labs.com
Nanoscale Biomagnetics	Magnetic nanoheating instrumentation	contact@nbnanoscale.com

controlled drug release, easy termination, and manufacturability. It is also important that the implanted system should be readily recoverable (surgical removal) by trained personnel or should be biodegradable. There are three classes of implantable drug delivery systems in use today: drug implants, drug-coated implants, and implantable pumps containing the drug. The first category uses various types of polymers and polymeric membranes to control the release kinetics of drugs from the delivery system. Polymeric systems can further be classified as nondegradable and biodegradable systems [65,66].

13.6.1 Nondegradable systems

Two types of nondegradable implants are shown in Fig. 13.19. In the reservoir type system, a central compact core contains the drug, surrounded by a permeable nondegradable outer membrane. Drug release is governed by diffusion through the outer polymeric membrane. For this system, a potential complication may arise from a rupture of the outer membrane. This may result in "drug dumping." Depending on the nature of the drug, this will cause potential toxic side effects. The "drug dumping" has made the system less popular. The most widely used reservoir-type implant system is Norplant. This was available as a set of six small (2.4 × 34 mm) silicone capsules, each filled with 36 mg of Levonorgestrel for birth control. It is implanted intradermally on the inside of the upper arm and usually effective for 5 years. Norplant was approved by the FDA in 1990 and was phased out in 2002. Norplant II (Jadelle) is a two-capsule system containing 75 mg levonorgestrel, each approved by the FDA in 1996.

In the past, anticancer drugs such as doxorubicin were studied as nondegradable microcapsule-based reservoir systems. However, the biodegradable matrix system containing doxorubicin had fewer toxic side effects compared to the nondegradable reservoir system.

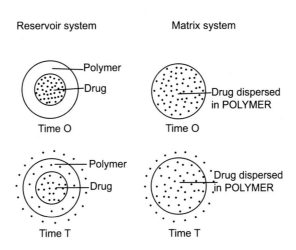

FIGURE 13.19 Cross-sectional view of idealized nonerodible reservoir and matrix systems, showing diffusion of the drug across the polymer.

Matrix systems are also used as nondegradable implants. Note that it is generally easier to fabricate a matrix-type implant than a reservoir-based system. Matrix systems consist of uniformly distributed drugs throughout a solid nondegradable polymer matrix (Fig. 13.19). Like reservoir systems, these systems also rely on the diffusion of drugs through the polymer matrix network. Kinetics of drug release from the matrix system is not constant and depends on the volume fraction of the drug in the polymer.

The major drawback of the nondegradable polymeric implant system is the need for surgical removal of the implant after the completion of the intended drug delivery cycle. One of the major uses of nondegradable polymer matrix systems is the sustained release of hormones in animals. Compudose is a matrix-type implant in which microcrystalline estradiol is dispersed in a silicone rubber matrix, which is then used to coat a biocompatible inert core of silicone rubber without any drug particles. Depending on the structure of the implant, estradiol in Compudose gets released in 200–400 days.

Another nondegradable carrier system that has found wide use in the treatment of osteomyelitis is polymethyl methacrylate (PMMA). Gentamicin (as a sulfate salt) incorporated into PMMA beads is commercially available under the trade name Septopal in Europe. It is implanted close to the site of surgery to prevent infection. Other antibiotics incorporated into PMMA are Tobramycin, Kanamycin, and Ceftriaxone.

A reservoir/matrix hybrid approach has also been approved for a number of nondegradable implants. One such implant is Implanon, which is fabricated by dispersing the drug, 3-ketodesogestrel, in an ethylene vinyl acetate (EVA) copolymer matrix. This polymer matrix is then coated with another layer of EVA copolymer without the drug. Diffusion through the membrane is the rate-limiting step in the release process. Implanon, made by Organon International, is a single-rod long-acting hormonal contraceptive implanted under the skin of a woman's upper arm. It lasts for 3 years. The reasoning behind the hybrid approach is to improve the drug release kinetics from a $t^{0.5}$ dependence (square root of time release) as observed in the matrix-type implant to close to zero-order kinetics.

13.6.2 Biodegradable systems

Two types of biodegradable implant systems are currently used: solid and injectable. In a solid biodegradable implant, the implant is inserted during surgery. It does not require a second surgical process for its removal, as in the case of nondegradable implants discussed in the preceding section. This improves patient compliance. Developing biodegradable systems is more complicated compared to developing nondegradable systems because many variables need to be controlled. Drug-release kinetics from a degradable polymeric system depends on both diffusion and polymer erosion. Alteration in body pH or temperature can cause a change in the degradation rate of the polymer. The surface area of the polymer also changes with polymer erosion. To obtain a more uniform and constant release, one needs to use geometric shapes whose surface area doesn't change as a function of time.

Polymers used in biodegradable implants must be water soluble and/or degradable in water. Some examples of synthetic polymers used in the fabrication of biodegradable implants are given in Table 13.16.

Lupron Depot (Tap Pharmaceuticals, USA) is used for the treatment of prostate cancer in male patients and treatment of endometriosis and anemia in female patients. It is composed of a PLA/PLG microsphere delivery system with leuprolide. It is supplied in a single-dose vial containing lyophilized microspheres and an ampule containing a diluent. Before the intramuscular injection, the diluent is mixed with the lyophilized microspheres. Depending on the polymer ratio (PLA/PLG), the release rate can last from 1 to 4 months.

Gliadel is a biodegradable polyanhydride implant composed of poly[bis(p-carboxyphenoxy) propane: sebacic acid] in a 20:80 monomer ratio for the delivery of carmustine. The implant is indicated in the treatment of recurrent glioblastoma multiforme, a common and fatal type of brain cancer. Up to eight Gliadel wafers are implanted in the cavity formed after the removal of the brain tumor, providing a highly localized dosage of anticancer agent for a long time.

TABLE 13.16   Synthetic polymers used in the fabrication of biodegradable implants [66].

Water-soluble polymers	Degradable polymers
Poly(acrylic acid), or PAC	Poly(hydroxyl butyrate), or PHB
Poly(ethylene glycol), or PEG	Poly(lactide-co-glycolide), or PLG
Poly(vinyl pyrrolidone), or PVP	Polyanhydrides, or PA

Atrigel (Atrix Laboratories) is an injectable implant. It can be used for parenteral and site-specific drug delivery. It consists of biodegradable polymers in a biocompatible carrier. When injected, it solidifies in the body at body temperature and releases the active drug over a prolonged time.

The FDA has approved a few products using Atrigel technology; they include Atridox, for periodontal treatment; Atrisorb, a free-flow polymer that, when injected at a bone graft site, helps in cell regeneration; and Atrisorb D, which provides a controlled release of Doxycycline for a period of 7 days and prevents bacterial colonization at the barrier.

Regel is a proprietary drug delivery system from MacroMed. It employs 23% (w/w) copolymer of PLGA–PEG-PLGA in phosphate buffer saline. It's a thermally reversible polymer developed for parenteral delivery. The thermal characteristics of Regel can be modified as a function of molecular weight, hydrophobicity, and polymer concentration to help in programmed delivery of the active agent.

The synthetic process involves additions of Poly(ethylene glycol), lactide, and glycolide monomers along with stannous octoate catalyst, which results in 95% yield and 99% purity. Sterilization of the product is done by filtration and gas sterilization. Before injection, the product is reconstituted, yielding aqueous Regel as a free-flowing liquid with a viscosity of less than 1 P. After injection, the polymer undergoes a phase change and becomes a water-insoluble biodegradable implant.

MacroMed's first product, OncoGel, is supplied as a frozen formulation of Paclitaxel in Regel in clinical trials. This unique drug therapy delivers a highly concentrated dose of the chemotherapy gel injected directly onto hard-to-reach tumors in the esophagus non-surgically.

The Alazamer Depot technology (Alza Corporation, Mountain View, CA, USA) was designed to offer sustained delivery of therapeutic agents, including proteins, other biomolecules, and small-molecular-weight compounds. The technology consists of a biodegradable polymer, suitable solvent, and formulated drug particles. The formulation is injected subcutaneously, with the drug released by diffusion from the system, while water and other biological fluids diffuse in. At later stages, the polymer degrades and further contributes to drug release.

Delivering proteins is often a challenging task because of their large size, stability issues, and fragile three-dimensional structure, which must be maintained for their therapeutic activity. The development of an effective system would require overcoming some key obstacles such as (1) protein's fragile conformation, which is maintained in the processing and formulation process, (2) controlling the release to maintain the therapeutic levels for the required time and (3) developing a sterile product to produce quantities of materials for clinical trial and commercialization.

Alkermes, a global company headquartered in Dublin, Ireland, developed a microencapsulation process to achieve high encapsulation efficiency while maintaining protein integrity. The process involves preparing freeze-dried proteins by atomization into liquid nitrogen. The lyophilized protein powder is added to the polymer solution and dispersed through sonication or high-pressure homogenization to reduce the drug particle size. Frozen drug/polymer microspheres are produced by atomization into liquid nitrogen. Filtration and vacuum drying are done to produce the final protein product inside the polymer microspheres. The polymer most commonly used is poly(lactide-co-glycolide), or PLG.

The microsphere may be administered by subcutaneous or intramuscular injection after dispersion in viscous aqueous diluents and delivery through a hypodermic needle. The first approved long-acting formulation of a therapeutic protein, Neutropin Depot (Genetech Inc., San Francisco, CA, USA), a human growth hormone (hGH) product, is manufactured by the ProLease process.

13.6.3 Pump systems

13.6.3.1 Diaphragm pumps

Many different drugs require external control of delivery rate and volume over a prolonged period. Such control is not achievable by nondegradable or biodegradable delivery. Pump systems provide the required control needed in such situations. The first such implantable infusion pump was invented at the University of Minnesota [67,68] and developed in a combined effort with the Metal Bellows Corporation of Sharon, Massachusetts, USA, which was spun out to form Infusaid Corporation; the implantable pump was called the Infusaid pump. A schematic of the pump is shown in Fig. 13.20.

Briefly, the pump is a hollow titanium disc divided into two chambers by flexible titanium bellows. A volatile charging fluid is sealed in the outer chamber, and the inner chamber is filled with the appropriate drug. Vapor pressure from the volatile fluid at the physiological temperature displaces the bellows, causing the drug to be pushed out through a bacterial filter. The flow is controlled by a capillary flow control mechanism. The inner chamber of the

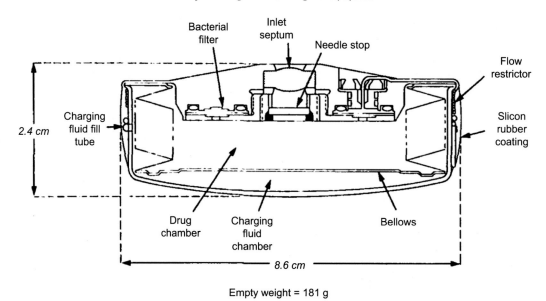

FIGURE 13.20   Schematic diagram of diaphragm pump.

pump can be filled by a needle injection through a self-sealing septum, simultaneously compressing and condensing the vapor in the outer chamber. This first pump had a single flow rate. The pump was placed in the peritoneal cavity through surgery.

Since the invention of the Infusaid implantable pump, there have been numerous developments on the design, controlled drug delivery, and remote programmability of implantable pumps. A cross-sectional view of Medtronic's programmable, implantable MiniMed pump is shown in Fig. 13.21. This type of pump is used for delivering insulin to Type 1 diabetic patients.

The pump in Fig. 13.21 is completely encased in a biocompatible titanium case. It operates in an open-loop configuration. A closed-loop configuration for insulin delivery is now available. This has a two-chamber configuration like the Infusaid pump. The pumping mechanism is a solenoid operated in a hermetically sealed pulsatile pump (Peristaltic pump). The pump electronics has a microprocessor designed to receive telemetry signals, store programming information, control the pulsing of the pump, and send information from stored memory. The battery life is 3—5 years. The future of insulin delivery is in closed-loop control where the blood glucose is continuously measured and fed back to the electronic module of the pump for controlling insulin delivery. The Medtronic MiniMed uses a needle-type glucose sensor that has been approved by FDA. The sensor is implanted in the subcutaneous tissue using a specifically designed indwelling tool to prevent tissue trauma. It is connected by wire to a portable page-

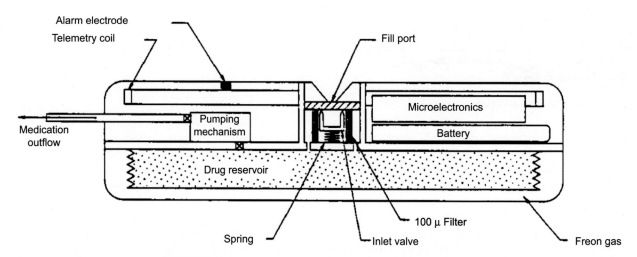

FIGURE 13.21   Schematic of a programmable implanted pump.

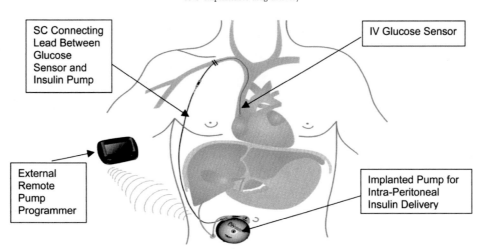

FIGURE 13.22 An artistic rendering of the closed-loop glucose control system.

size external monitoring unit that monitors the glucose level in the patient and sends appropriate signals to the implanted pump in the peritoneal cavity. Frequent calibration and inter-sensor variability are some of the issues in this approach. Additionally, stopping the glucose infusion shows a persistently lower sensor signal. In the near future, it may be possible to use closed-loop glucose sensing by IV glucose sensor. Such an effort is currently in clinical trials. An artistic rendering of such a system is shown in Fig. 13.22 [69].

13.6.3.2 Micro-electromechanical pumps

There has been a surge of interest in miniaturizing implanted drug delivery systems, reducing cost, improving performance, and integrating features. Micro- and nanoelectromechanical systems (MEMS and NEMS) for drug delivery will provide some unique opportunities in the future for advanced drug delivery techniques. Some additional benefits of these techniques are that they are fast acting; deliver drugs in a pulsatile or continuous mode; deliver multiple drugs at their optimum therapeutic level; are stable; provide hermetic storage of therapeutic drugs in solid, liquid, or gel form; and provide wireless communication with an external controller for device monitoring and therapy modification. Some but not all these benefits are met in the implantable pumps discussed earlier. MEMS and NEMS are based on well-established technologies in microelectronic industries.

Microelectromechanical systems, or MEMS, is a technology that, in its most general form, can be defined as miniaturized mechanical and electrical elements (i.e., devices and structures) that are made using the techniques of microfabrication (see Fig. 13.23). The critical physical dimension can vary from less than a micron to several millimeters. Also, MEMS can have simple structures with no moving parts to more complex electromechanical systems with multiple moving parts with integrated microelectronics. MEMS technology borrows a lot of microfabrication technologies from the silicon microelectronic industries and therefore has seen rapid growth in many areas, including biology and drug delivery devices.

When the devices get small, the usual question is whether they will be practical. Let's consider a few examples [70]. Fentanyl, a powerful narcotic drug widely used for anesthesia and analgesia, has a dosage regimen of $\sim$25 µg for a typical 50 kg adult. Adult dosages for antibiotics, such as penicillin and amoxicillin, are typically 1 g/day. If we scale down the size as in MEMS, we reduce available volume. Let us consider a drug reservoir size of 10 µm×10 µm ×1 mm. Volume of this drug reservoir is around 100 pL. A Synchromed 8637-20 pump comes with a volume of 20 mL. This is some eight orders of magnitude greater than the small MEMS reservoir. This volume can be circumvented by using these small structures in conjunction with a large reservoir attached to it or using an array of small reservoirs. Also, note that many of the drugs come with many excipients. These may be unnecessary for the MEMS drug delivery systems.

Currently, no MEMS micropumps are available for implanted drug delivery. Many of the technologies are in clinical or preclinical trials or under development. If we look at the time horizon, they may take 5–15 years before FDA approval. Let us consider a few examples that have undergone several clinical trials. Fig. 13.22 shows a device with cross-sections of several drug reservoirs. Some of the early prototypes were made with a 10×10 matrix array of drug reservoirs. Each of these can be individually addressed. Each microchip was $15 \times 15 \times 1$ mm^3 with a reservoir

(A)

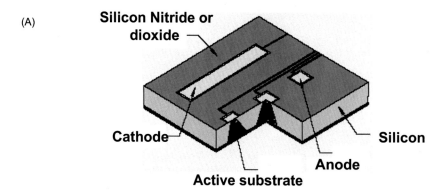

(B)

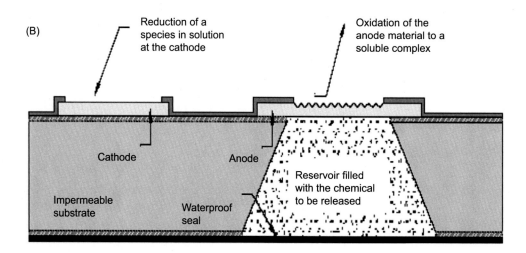

(C)

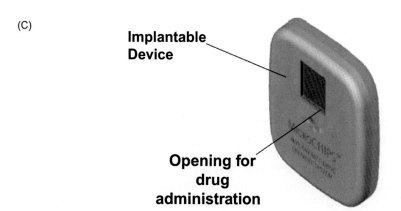

FIGURE 13.23 An implantable MEMS structure on silicon substrate. (A) Fabricated device with micro-reservoir and the electrode structure; (B) cross-section of the device showing a single reservoir with cathode, anode, drug, and partial oxidation of the anode material; and (C) a completed device with enclosure.

capacity of 300 nL [71]. Application of a voltage between the gold cathode and anode causes electrochemical dissolution of the gold thin film protecting the drug based on the following chemical reactions:

$$Au + 4\,Cl^- \rightarrow [AuCl_4]^- + 3\,e^-$$

$$Au + m\,H_2O \rightarrow [Au(H_2O)m]3^+ + 3\,e^-$$

$$2\,Au + 3\,H_2O \rightarrow Au_2O_3 + 6\,H^+ + 3\,e^-$$

$$2\,Cl^- \rightarrow Cl_2 + 2\,e^-$$

$$Au_2O_3 + 8\,Cl^- + 6\,H^+ \rightarrow 2[AuCl_4]^- + 3\,H_2O$$

The body naturally contains an aqueous solution containing sodium (Na^+) and chloride (Cl^-) ions, which help in the gold dissolution process under the application of a voltage between the gold cathode and anode. This device by Microchips Inc. is undergoing clinical trial.

Intraocular diseases such as retinitis pigmentosa, age-related macular degeneration, diabetic retinopathy, and glaucoma are presently incurable and affect many people worldwide. Innovative drug therapy is the most effective way of treating these diseases. Oral and topical drugs require large doses to reach therapeutic levels in the intraocular space. Implantable pumps haven't been successful because of their large size. A small, active MEMS device has been designed, fabricated, and tested in porcine eyes. The intraocular device and surgical implantation are shown in Fig. 13.24A and B, respectively.

The drug delivery device consists of an electrolysis pump, drug reservoir, and a transscleral cannula. The electrolysis pump consists of an interdigitated platinum electrode immersed in an electrolyte. Application of a current gives rise to electrolysis of water. The gas bubbles thus formed apply the pressure to inject the drug into the eye through the cannula.

13.6.4 Osmotic pumps

13.6.4.1 ALZET osmotic pumps

Similar to the other osmotic pumps, the ALZET osmotic pump operates because of an osmotic pressure difference between the osmotic agent chamber or the salt chamber and the drug chamber. The basic principle of this drug delivery is outlined in Section 13.4 on osmotic drug delivery.

The ALZET osmotic pump consists of three concentric cylinders. The outermost layer is a semipermeable membrane constructed from cellulose materials. A supersaturated salt solution is kept in this layer. This outer cylinder surrounds the impermeable drug reservoir. A 25- or 27-gauge filling tube is used to fill the drug in this cylinder. A schematic of the ALZET pump is shown in Fig. 13.25.

When this pump is implanted, the interstitial fluid enters the semipermeable membrane and creates an osmotic pressure in the salt chamber. This compresses the drug reservoir and forces the drug solution out of the delivery portal.

These pumps can be implanted subcutaneously or intraperitoneally or used with a catheter to infuse a vein or artery or target tissues such as the brain. Implanting the pump subcutaneously is much quicker and less stressful than using intravenous catheterization.

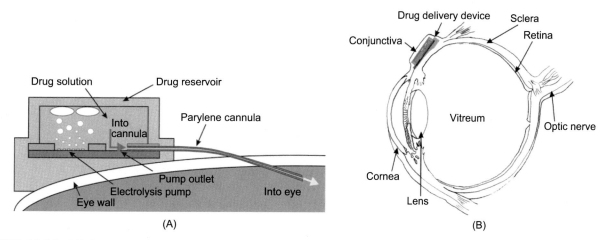

FIGURE 13.24   (A) Cross-section of the ocular drug delivery device showing the electrochemical pumping of the drug into the eye; (B) conceptual illustration of the implanted ocular drug delivery device [72].

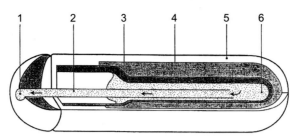

FIGURE 13.25　Schematic of the implantable ALZET osmotic pump showing (1) delivery portal, (2) flow moderator, (3) impermeable reservoir wall, (4) osmotic agent, (5) semipermeable membrane, and (6) drug reservoir [3].

Three sizes of ALZET pumps are available. These pumps can deliver drugs from 3 days to 6 weeks depending on the size of the pump. The drug delivery rates can vary from 0.11 μL/h to 10 μL/h. The delivery profiles of these pumps are independent of the drug formulation to be dispensed. Note that each pump configuration is fixed at the factory for one delivery rate. The drug delivery follows zero-order kinetics. These pumps have been used successfully with a wide range of drugs, largely for animal studies.

13.6.4.2 DUROS osmotic pumps

The success of the ALZET osmotic pump showed the breadth of applicability of osmosis for parenteral drug delivery by the osmotic process. This gave rise to the DUROS platform technology. A schematic of the implant is shown in Fig. 13.26.

The DUROS device consists of a cylindrical titanium alloy reservoir capped at one end by a semipermeable membrane made of polyurethane polymer and capped at the other end by a diffusion moderator. Positioned next to the membrane is the osmotic engine, which contains primarily NaCl along with other pharmaceutical excipients in tablet form. Next to the osmotic engine is a piston made from elastomeric materials; it serves to separate the osmotic engine from the drug reservoir.

All DUROS components are biocompatible. Radiation (gamma radiation) sterilization of the device may be used to sterilize the final drug product. If the drug formulation cannot withstand the sterilizing radiation, the device is radiation sterilized with the drug sterilized by appropriate aseptic techniques.

The device comes in two different sizes (4 mm OD×44 mm length or 10 mm OD×44 mm length) and can last from 3 months to a year. For many applications, the preferred site for implantation is subcutaneous placement in the inside of the upper arm. An implanter is used in the implantation process. Targeted delivery of the drug is possible through a catheter integrated at the exit port. The catheter can give rise to more effective drug delivery at targeted sites.

Viadur by Alza Corporation using the DUROS technology platform was the first such product approved by the FDA in 2000. Viadur (leuprolide acetate implant) is a sterile, nonbiodegradable, osmotically driven miniaturized implant designed to deliver leuprolide acetate for 12 months at a controlled rate. To address the needs of chronic pain sufferers, the DUROS technology platform has been applied to the delivery of the drug Sufentanil. This DUROS system has the trade name Chronogesic and is designed to deliver the drug for 3 months. Because Sufentanil is 500× more potent than morphine, a 1-month therapy can be contained in a 155 μL drug reservoir. Chronogesic is undergoing clinical trials.

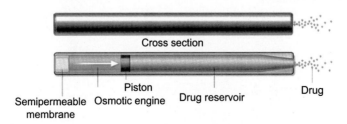

FIGURE 13.26　A schematic of the DUROS osmotic pump.

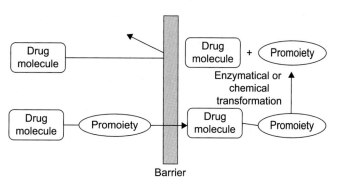

FIGURE 13.27   A simplified representation of the prodrug concept.

13.7 Prodrugs

Almost all drugs have some undesirable characteristics in their physicochemical and biological properties. These undesirable characteristics and therapeutic efficiency can be improved by suitable modification through biological, physical, or chemical means. The biological approach is to alter the route of administration. The physical approach is to modify the dosage form. The third approach is to enhance drug selectivity while minimizing toxicity [73]. This third approach leads to the design of prodrugs. The concept of prodrugs is not new. Adrian Albert [74] was the first to introduce the concept of prodrugs and suggested that the technique can be used to temporarily alter and therefore optimize the physicochemical properties and thus the pharmacological and toxicological profiles of an agent.

According to International Union of Pure and Applied Chemistry (IUPAC), a prodrug is defined as any compound that undergoes biotransformation before exhibiting pharmacological effects. Prodrugs are considered to be inactive or at least less significantly active than the released drugs. Once inside the body, these prodrugs undergo an enzymatic or chemical reaction to show drug-like properties (i.e., absorption, distribution, metabolism, and excretion). The transformation of a prodrug to actual drug behavior is schematically shown in Fig. 13.27.

Note the "barrier" shown in Fig. 13.27. Prodrugs provide possibilities to overcome various barriers to drug formulation and delivery, such as aqueous solubility, chemical instability, insufficient oral absorption, rapid pre-systemic metabolism, insufficient penetration into the brain, toxicity, local irritation, and patient compliance such as odor and taste [75].

The design of the prodrug structure is considered in the early phase of clinical development. This will include the appropriate functional groups (promoiety) for derivatization. Promoiety should be safe and rapidly excreted from the body. The choice of promoiety should be appropriate for the disease state. Some of the common functional groups used in prodrug design are carboxylic, hydroxyl, amine, phosphates, and carbonyl groups. They are shown in Table 13.17.

Esters are the most common prodrugs used and account for ∼49% of the marketed products. Following are some examples of prodrugs and their principles of action.

Dipivefrin is a prodrug that gives rise to epinephrine used as an intraocular drug to reduce pressure in the eye (see Fig. 13.28). The addition of pivaloyl groups to the epinephrine molecule improves the lipophilic character of the drug and thereby increases penetration into the anterior chamber of the eye. Once inside the anterior chamber, Dipivefrin is converted to epinephrine through hydrolysis. Epinephrine reduces intraocular pressure by reducing humor production.

Parkinson's disease is known to be due to a deficiency in dopamine. Because of its polar characteristic, dopamine cannot cross the blood—brain barrier. Levodopa (L-3,4-dihydroxy-phenylalanine), an amino acid, is recognized by the amino acid carrier proteins and is carried across the cell membrane (see Fig. 13.29). It is a prodrug for dopamine. When Levodopa is inside the cell, the enzyme decarboxylase removes the acid group to produce dopamine.

Most drugs administered orally or intravenously go through the bloodstream to the site where they are required. During this process of transport, they can cause other toxic effects. Anticancer chemotherapeutic drugs are cytotoxic because they also affect normal growing cells. A site-specific prodrug can alleviate the toxicity to normal cells. Diethylstilbestrol diphosphate is a prodrug designed for breast cancer; this prodrug can be activated through an enzyme in the breast tissue, as shown in Fig. 13.30.

TABLE 13.17 Functional groups and their derivatives used in the design and synthesis of prodrugs.

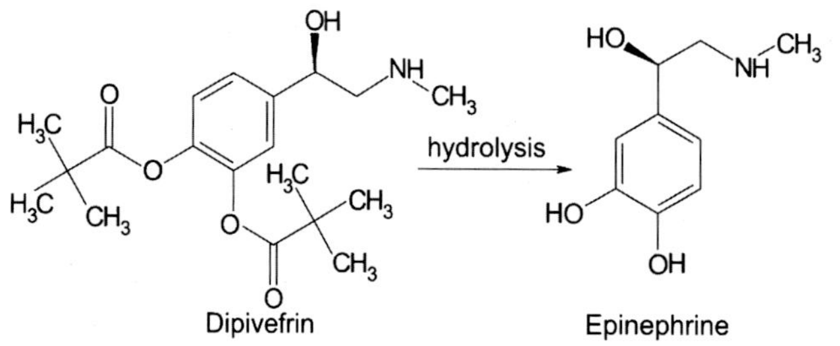

FIGURE 13.28 Hydrolysis of the prodrug dipivefrin to functional epinephrine inside the anterior chamber of the eye.

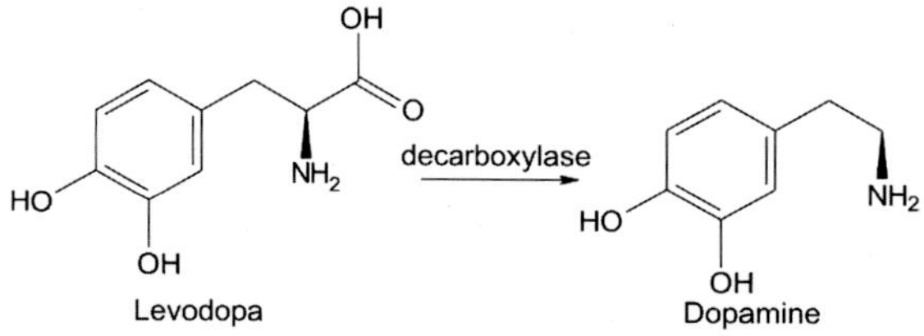

FIGURE 13.29 Enzymatic conversion of the prodrug levodopa to functional dopamine inside the cell.

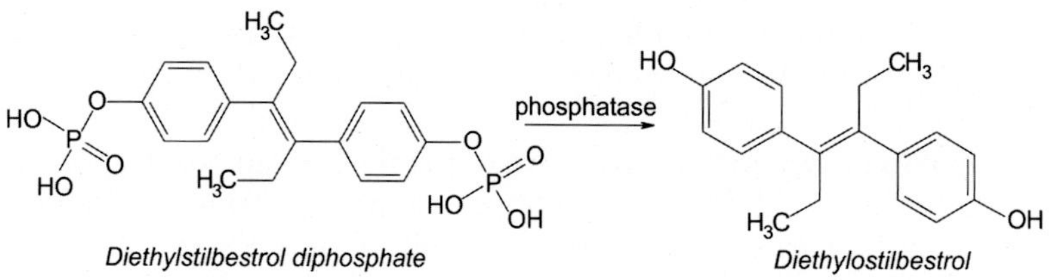

FIGURE 13.30 Breast cancer prodrug diethylstilbestrol diphosphate converts to diethylstilbestrol in the breast tissue in the presence of an enzyme phosphatase.

Fosphenytoin sodium salt is a prodrug for phenytoin used as an antiepileptic agent (see Fig. 13.31). This prodrug is used to reduce drug precipitation and consequent local irritation by phenytoin at the injection site. The prodrug has an aqueous solubility of more than 7000 times greater than phenytoin. The prodrug has a short half-life (<15 min) in blood and is rapidly converted to phenytoin in blood. The enzymatic action initially releases an unstable intermediate, which is rapidly converted to phenytoin.

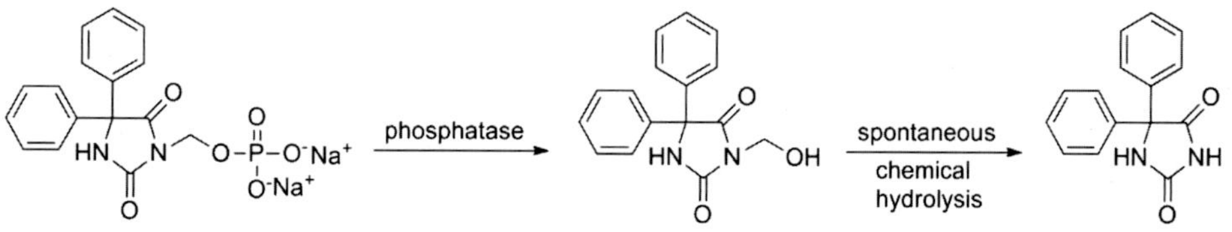

FIGURE 13.31 A two-step conversion of the prodrug fosphenytoin sodium to phenytoin in the blood.

TABLE 13.18 Prodrugs currently available in the market.

Therapeutic area	Prodrug name (Trade name)
Proton pump inhibitors	Esomeprazole (Nexium)
	Lansoprazole (Prevacid)
	Pantoprazole (Protonix)
	Rabeprazole (Sciphex)
Antiplatelet agent	Clopidogrel (Plavix)
Antiviral agent	Valacyclovir (Valtrex)
Hypercholesterolemia	Fenofibrate (Tricor)
Antiviral agent	Tenofovir disoproxil (Atripla)
Psychostimulant	Lisdexamfetamine (Vyvanse)
Influenza	Oseltamivir (Tamiflu)
Hypertension	Olmesartan medoxomil (Benicar)
Immunosuppressant	Mycophenolate mofetil (CellCept)
Glaucoma	Latanoprost (Xalatan)

Some of the prodrugs currently available in the market are shown in Table 13.18.

13.8 Conclusions

Development of new chemical entities (NCEs) is expensive. Additionally, more than 60% of the NCEs in the pipeline have poor aqueous solubility, and most of them have some bioavailability issues. This chapter describes some of the special dosage forms and drug delivery systems that have emerged over the past few decades to address some of the deficiencies of conventional dosage forms. For example, osmotic drug delivery provides a means of controlled and site-specific drug delivery without significant effect of pH variation in the gastrointestinal tract. Liposomes are biocompatible and can deliver both hydrophilic and hydrophobic drugs. Liposomes provide versatility in the formulation of various dosage forms such as aerosols, gels, creams, and lotions and deliver the drugs through various routes such as intravenous, ocular, nasal, and subcutaneous. Dosage forms incorporating solid lipid nanoparticles, nanoemulsions, and nanosuspensions improve the apparent solubility of the drugs. Parenteral formulations using nanotechnologies can result in long systemic circulation as well as site-specific drug delivery. Magnetic nanoparticles can provide a multifunctional approach with site-specific drug delivery at the tumor site with the added benefit of hyperthermia, leading to tumor cell death. Implantable drug delivery is an approach used to prolong the delivery of a drug from weeks to months to years, resulting in improved patient compliance. Pharmacological effectiveness of a drug can be improved by the formulation of prodrugs.

This chapter also lists many of the products currently available in the market using special dosage forms. Amorphous solid dispersions, co-crystals, etc., are some of the emerging technologies that are not described in this chapter. All these technologies will harness the benefits of the existing drugs and enhance the therapeutic effects of the new ones.

Case studies

Case 13.1

Mr. Smith, a cardiac patient, recently visited his physician and was put on Procardia XL 60 mg tablet per day. His physician advised him to reduce the nifedipine dose from 60 to 30 mg/day. He still had 24 tablets left from his previous prescription, so he decided to cut the 60 mg tablet in half to meet his dosage need. When he brought this decision to the attention of his pharmacist, the pharmacist immediately called Mr. Smith and wanted to talk to him before he used the remaining 60 mg tablets. Is there any concern with the approach to cut tablets in half? If so, what type of counseling to the patient is needed for this case?

Approach: One should first understand the specialized dosage form of Procardia XL. This is not a conventional oral tablet. Even though, this extended release tablet is similar in appearance to a conventional tablet, it consists of a semipermeable membrane surrounding an osmotically active drug core. The core itself is divided into two layers: an "active" layer containing the drug nifedipine and a "push" layer containing pharmacologically inert (but osmotically active) components. As water from the gastrointestinal tract enters the tablet via the semipermeable membrane, pressure increases in the osmotic layer and "pushes" against the drug layer, releasing the drug through the precision laser-drilled tablet orifice in the active layer in a zero-order manner. The Procardia XL extended-release tablet is designed to provide nifedipine at an approximately constant rate over 24 h as long as the osmotic gradient remains constant, and then it gradually falls to zero. When the patient swallows the tablet, the biologically inert components of the tablet remain intact during gastrointestinal transit and are eliminated in the feces as an insoluble shell. This controlled rate of drug delivery into the gastrointestinal lumen is independent of pH or gastrointestinal motility. Procardia XL depends on the existence of an osmotic gradient between the contents of the bilayer core and fluid in the gastrointestinal tract for its action. Cutting this tablet into two halves will destroy the membrane and will dump the entire drug content at one time, and no constant release will be achieved.

Therefore, the pharmacist's advice is not to use the 60 mg tablet anymore. Instead, the patient should use 30 mg Procardia XL extended-release tablets.

Case 13.2

A healthy man is admitted to an emergency room for a hernia repair due to a suspected obstruction. The patient's medical history reveals an uneventful anesthesia for orthopedic surgery in the past year. It is decided to use a modified rapid sequence induction with rocuronium (40 mg) and thiopental sodium (375 mg) through a 20 G cannula connected to a 1000 mL Hartmann's solution. It is noted that the patient, upon intubation, is not fully relaxed despite an appropriate dose of relaxant. It is noticed that Hartmann's infusion stopped, and there is a 10 cm long column of fluid containing a flaky precipitate in the IV line, which was unsuccessfully flushed with 10 mL of saline through the injection port. Explain the possible cause of this problem to the attending surgeon and the nursing staff based on your knowledge of pharmaceutics.

Approach: This problem was possibly caused by drug incompatibility due to acid–base properties, pH, and solubility. Rocuronium given through a poorly flowing cannula may have led to crystallize thiopental and subsequent obstruction of the cannula. Literature data [76] reveal the pH of thiopentone is 11–12, and for the muscle relaxant, rocuronium, is 4.0. In a highly acidic pH, the basic drug will precipitate to thiopentone acid, which has a very low solubility <0.1 mg/mL as compared to sodium salt (700 mg/mL). A combination of a free-flowing drip as well as fluids running through the drip can minimize this precipitation. Another alternative is to change the drugs. Use of propofol or any of the muscle relaxants instead may be an alternative and better choice.

Case 13.3

As a working pharmacist in a community pharmacy setting, you received a question from a parent of a child suffering from attention deficit hyperactivity disorder (ADHD) and on osmotic-controlled release oral delivery system (OROS) methylphenidate ER (Concerta) therapy. The parent requested to switch to a generic product available for his child. How this request will be handled by the practicing pharmacist?

Approach: The pharmacist must perform a literature search on this subject using some key words in Google Scholar or Pubmed). An article in clinical pediatrics by Lally et al. [77] describes that all generic versions of Concerta are not equal in their therapeutic outcomes for the treatment of ADHD. In this study, authors have compared the brand drug product with three available generic products. The brand product (Concerta is an OROS of methylphenidate hydrochloride extended-release tablet. Out of these three generics, one of them is manufactured as an OROS time-release technology. However, the other two use non-OROS technology. According to the FDA, drugs are considered to be therapeutic equivalents and thus suitable for generic substitution if they are both pharmaceutical equivalents and bioequivalent. Pharmaceutical equivalents contain the same active ingredients, same dosage and form, and same route of administration and are identical in strength or concentration. Drugs are bioequivalent if the rate and extent of absorption do not show a significant difference. This study supports the US FDA's concerns regarding the therapeutic equivalence of non-OROS versus OROS for the treatment of ADHD. Therefore, the pharmacist should advise the parent that Methylphenidate HCl oral formulation based on OROS technology (brand) should not be substituted with non-OROS generic products. However, they can be substituted with generic Methylphenidate HCl oral formulation manufactured based on OROS technology.

Case 13.4

A clinical pharmacist is working in an academic institution and has the responsibility to improve common drug therapy problems, provide active and ongoing outreach to educate practitioners on problems associated with medication therapy with the goals of improving prescribing or dispensing practices so that patients' medication compliance and overall health can be improved significantly. The practicing oncologist and the medical intern working in the same academic hospital wish to know the pros and cons of the two formulations, Taxol and Abraxane, commonly used in breast cancer treatment. What approach will the Clinical Pharmacist take to educate these practicing physicians?

Approach: The most important consideration is to collect enough literature data and information on these two formulations. One of such manuscripts published by Wang et al. [78] would help to address these issues related with comparative benefits of these two formulations. Since the information available are massive, it may be advisable to have few PowerPoint slides or tables to explain the informations shown below:

- Taxol and Abraxane are the two paclitaxel (PTX) based chemotherapies approved by the FDA
- PTX has a very poor aqueous solubility
- Both formulations (Taxol and Abraxane) are administered via the iv route but have different excipients
- Taxol, marketed by Bristol–Myers–Squibb since 1992, contains 6 mg of PTX per mL solubilized by 527 mg Cremophor EL (polyoxyethylated castor oil) and ethanol (49.7%, v/v. which is typically administrated through three- or 24-h infusion after dilution with a balanced fluid
- It has been approved for the treatment of primary and metastatic breast cancer, ovarian cancer, non-small cell lung cancer, and AIDS-related Kaposi's sarcoma
- One major shortcoming in the clinical application of Taxol is its **nonlinear pharmacokinetics** and **hypersensitivity** believed to be due to Cremophor EL, in addition to the nephrotoxicity and neurotoxicity induced by PTX
- To minimize hypersensitivity reactions, patients should be pretreated with corticosteroids, diphenhydramine, and H2 antagonist
- Abraxane received approval by FDA in 2005 initially for the treatment of metastatic breast cancer
- In Abraxane, PTX is formulated with human serum albumin (HSA). It is a nanoformulation (albumin nanoparticles containing PTX) with many advantages as compared to Taxol
- In comparison with Taxol, the maximum tolerated dose of Abraxane can be increased to 300 mg/m^2, which also involves a much-shortened administration time (30 min for Abraxane vs. 3 or 24 h for Taxol)
- Abraxane has a predictable, linear pharmacokinetic profile and increases intratumor PTX concentration by 33% when compared to an equal dose injection of Taxol
- Absence of Cremophor EL eliminates solvent-related hypersensitivity reactions, as well as the medical needs for premedication and special IV tubing needed for administrating Taxol
- Abraxane showed improved pharmacokinetic profiles, improved tolerance, and an increase in overall response rate (ORR)
- Phase III clinical trial of Abraxane directly compared its anti-tumor activity and tolerability to those of Taxol in women with measurable metastatic breast cancer. In this trial, patients received three-week cycles of either Abraxane 260 mg/m^2 i.v. over 30 min or Taxol 175 mg/m^2 i.v. over 3 h. The ORR for Abraxane was almost twice that of Taxol
- Despite the 49% higher PTX dose in the Abraxane group, the incidence of Grade 4 neutropenia was significantly lower for patients treated with Abraxane

Critical reflections and practice applications

Special dosage forms and drug delivery systems are some of the important tools in the toolbox of a practicing pharmacist to address the challenges and shortcomings of current-day therapy. With the advances in science and technology, their numbers are increasing year after year. These innovative dosage forms and drug delivery may include but not limited to parenteral delivery; osmotic drug delivery systems; nanotechnology in drug delivery such as nanocrystals, lipid nanoparticles, dendrimers, liposomes, polymerosomes, pegylated polymeric nanoparticles, protein-based nanoparticles, and metal-based nanoparticles; implantable drug delivery and prodrug approaches. The entire world has seen the benefit of liposomal nanoparticles that have been used in both the Pfizer/BioNTech and Moderna vaccines to control the deadly COVID-19 pandemic.

References

[1] G.M. Jantzen, J.R. Robinson, Sustained and controlled release drug delivery systems, in: 3rdModern Pharmaceutics, vol 5751995, Marcel Dekker, New York, Marcel Dekker, New York, 1995.

[2] F. Theeuwes, The elementary osmotic pump, J. Pharmaceut. Sci. 64 (12) (1975) 1987–1991.

[3] F. Theeuwes, S.I. Yum, Principles of the design and operation of generic osmotic pumps for the delivery of semisolid or liquid drug formulations, Ann. Biomed. Eng. 4 (1976) 343–353.

[4] G.M. Zentner, G.S. Rork, K.J. Himmelstein, Controlled Porosity Osmotic Pump, U.S. Patent 4968507, 1990.

[5] R.K. Verma, D.M. Krishna, S. Garg, Formulation aspects in the development of osmotically controlled oral drug delivery systems, J. Contr. Release 79 (2002) 7–27.

[6] G. Santus, P. Baker, Osmotic drug delivery: a review of the patent literature, J. Contr. Release 35 (1995) 1–21.

[7] B.P. Gupta, N. Thakur, N.P. Jain, Osmotically controlled drug delivery system with associated drugs, J. Pharm. Pharmaceut. Sci. 13 (2010) 571–588.

[8] R.A. Prentis, Y. Lis, S.R. Walker, Pharmaceutical innovation by the seven UK owned pharmaceutical companies (1964–1984), Br. J. Clin. Pharmacol. 25 (1998) 387–396.

[9] J. Panyam, V. Labhasetwar, Biodegradable nanoparticles for drug and gene delivery to cells and tissues, Adv. Drug Deliv. Rev. 55 (2003) 329–347.

[10] A.A.H. Abdellatif, A.F. Alsowinea, Approved and marketed nanoparticles for disease targeting and applications in COVID-19, Nanotechnol. Rev. 10 (2021) 1941–1977, https://doi.org/10.1515/ntrev-2021-0115.

[11] S. Sonke, D.A. Tomalia, Dendrimers in biomedical applications—reflections on the field, Adv. Drug Deliv. Rev. 57 (2005) 2106–2129.

[12] P. Courveur, G. Couarraze, J.P. Devissaguet, F. Puisieux, S. Benita, Nanoparticles: preparation and characterization, in: S. Benita (Ed.), Microencapsulation Methods and Industrial Applications, Marcel Dekker, New York, 1996, pp. 183–211.

[13] W.N. Charman, Lipids, lipophilic drugs and oral drug delivery—some emerging concepts, J. Pharmaceut. Sci. 89 (2000) 967–978.

[14] W. Mehnert, K. Mader, Solid lipid nanoparticles: production, characterization, and applications, Adv. Drug Deliv. Rev. 47 (2001) 165–196.

[15] R.H. Muller, S.A. Runge, Solid lipid nanoparticles for controlled drug delivery Submicron emulsion in drug targeting and delivery, in: S. Benita (Ed.), Submicron Emulsion in Drug Targeting and Delivery, Harwood Academic Publishers, Netherlands, 1998, pp. P219–P234.

[16] M.R. Gasco, Method of Producing Solid Lipid Microspheres Having a Narrow Size Distribution, U.S. Patent 5250236, 1991.

[17] B. Sjostrom, B. Bergenstahl, Preparation of submicron drug particles in lecithin-stabilized O/W emulsions I. Model studies of the precipitation of cholesterylacetate, Int. J. Pharm. 88 (1992) 53–62.

[18] S.A. Wissing, O. Kayser, R.H. Muller, Solid lipid nanoparticles for potential drug delivery, Adv. Drug Deliv. Rev. 56 (2004) 1257–1272.

[19] R.H. Muller, M. Radtke, S.A. Wissing, Nanostructured lipid matrices for improved microencapsulation of drugs, Int. J. Pharm. 242 (2002) 121–128.

[20] C. Olbrich, A. Gessner, O. Kayser, R.H. Muller, Lipid-Drug-Conjugate (LDC) nanoparticles as novel carrier system for the hydrophilic antitrypanosomal drug diminazediaceturate, J. Drug Target. 10 (5) (2002) 387–396.

[21] M.Y. Koroleva, E.V. Yurtov, Nanoemulsions: the properties, methods of preparation and promising applications, Russ. Chem. Rev. 81 (2012) 21–43.

[22] C. Lovelyn, A.A. Attama, Current state of nanoemulsions in drug delivery, J. Biomaterials Nanobiotechnol. 2 (2011) 626–639.

[23] G. Taylor, The formation of emulsions in definable fields of flow, Proc Royal Soc A 146 (1934) 501.

[24] S.S. Abolmaali, A.M. Tamaddon, F.S. Farvadi, S. Daneshamuz, H. Moghimi, Pharmaceutical nanoemulsions and their potential topical and transdermal applications, Iran. J. Pharm. Sci. 7 (2011) 139–150.

[25] B.E. Rabinow, Nanosuspensions in drug delivery, Nat. Rev. Drug Discov. 3 (2004) 785–796.

[26] X. Pu, J. Sun, M. Li, Z. He, Formulation of nanosuspensions as a new approach for the delivery of poorly soluble drugs, Curr. Nanosci. 5 (2009) 417–427.

[27] J. Chingunpituk, Nanosuspension technology for drug delivery, Walailak, J. Sci. Technol. (Peshawar) 4 (2007) 139–153.

[28] R. Haag, F. Kratz, Polymer therapeutics: concepts and applications, Angew. Chem. Int. Ed. 45 (2006) 1198–1215.

[29] J. Folkman, D.M. Long, The use of silicone rubber as a carrier for prolonged drug delivery, J. Surg. Res. 4 (1964) 139–142.

[30] R. Langer, J. Folkman, Polymers for sustained release of proteins and other macromolecules, Nature 263 (1976) 797–800.

[31] H. Ringdorf, Structure and properties of pharmacologically active polymers, J. Polym. Sci., Polym. Symp. (1975) 135–153.

[32] G. Pasut, F.M. Veronese, Polymer-drug conjugation, recent achievements and general strategies, Prog. Polym. Sci. 32 (2007) 933–967.

[33] I. Ekladious, Y.L. Colson, M.W. Grinstaff, Polymer–drug conjugate therapeutics: advances, insights and prospects, Nat. Rev. Drug Discov. 18 (2019) 273–294.

[34] A.D. Bangham, M.M. Stondish, J.C. Watkins, Diffusion of univalent ions across the lamellae of swollen phospholipids, J. Mol. Biol. 13 (1965) 238–252.

[35] G. Storm, D.J.A. Crommelin, Liposomes: quo vadis? PSTT 1 (1998) 29–31.

[36] A. Jesorka, O. Owe Orwar, Liposomes: technologies and analytical applications, Annu. Rev. Anal. Chem. 1 (2008) 801–832.

[37] F. Szoka, D. Papahadjopoulos, Procedure for preparation of liposomes with large internal aqueous space and high capture by reverse-phase evaporation, Proc. Natl. Acad. Sci. USA 75 (1978) 4194–4198.

[38] D.J. Woodbury, E.S. Richardson, A.W. Grigg, R.D. Welling, B.H. Knudson, Reducing liposome size with ultrasound: biomedical size distribution, J. Liposome Res. 16 (2006) 57–80.

[39] S. Hauschild, U. Lipprandt, A. Rumplecker, U. Borchert, A. Rank, R. Schubert, Direct preparation and loading of lipid and polymer vesicles using inkjets, Small 1 (2005) 1170–1180.

[40] D.J. Estes, M. Mayer, Giant liposomes in physiological buffer using electroformation in a flow chamber, Biochim. Biophys. Acta 1712 (2005) 152–160.

[41] D.D. Lasic, Liposomes, Sci Med. May/June (1996) 34–43.

[42] M.R. Mozafari, K. Khosravi-Darani, An overview of liposome-derived nanocarrier technologies, in: M.R. Mozafari (Ed.), Nanomaterials and Nanosystems for Biomedical Applications, 2005, pp. 113–123.

[43] T. Lian, R.J.Y. Ho, Trends and developments in liposome drug delivery systems, J. Pharmaceut. Sci. 90 (6) (2000) 667–680.

[44] O. Onaca, R. Enea, D.W. Hughes, W. Meier, Stimuli-Responsive Polymerosomes as nanocarriers for drug and gene delivery, Macromol. Biosci. 9 (2009) 129–139.

[45] I. Meerovich, A. Dash, Polymersomes for drug delivery and other biomedical applications, in: H. Alina-Maria, M.G. Alexandru (Eds.), Materials for Biomedical Engineering: Organic Micro and Nanostructures, Elsevier, MA, USA, 2019, ISBN 978-0-12-818433-2, pp. 269–310.

[46] J. Du, Y. Tang, A.L. Lewis, S.P. Armes, pH-sensitive vesicles based on a biocompatible zwitterionic diblock copolymer, J. Am. Chem. Soc. 27 (2005) 17982–17983.

[47] S. Qin, Y. Geng, D.E. Discher, S. Yang, Temperature-controlled assembly and release from polymer vesicles of poly(ethylene oxide)-block-poly(N-isopropylacrylamide), Adv. Mater. 18 (2008) 2905.

[48] F. Ahmed, R.I. Pakunlu, A. Brannan, F. Bates, T. Minko, D.E. Discher, Biodegradable polymersomes loaded with both paclitaxel and doxorubicin permeate and shrink tumors, inducing apoptosis in proportion to accumulated drug, J. Contr. Release 116 (2006) 150.

[49] H. Lomas, M. Massignani, K.A. Abdullah, I. Canton, S. Lo Presti, S. MacNeil, J. Du, A. Blanajas, J. Madsen, S.P. Armes, A.L. Lewis, G. Bataglia, Non-cytotoxic polymer vesicles for rapid and efficient intracellular delivery, Faraday Discuss. Chem. Soc. 139 (2008) 143.

[50] Q.A. Pankhurst, J. Connolly, S.K. Jones, J. Dobson, Applications of magnetic nanoparticles in biomedicine, J. Phys. D Appl. Phys. 36 (2003) R167–R181.

[51] C.C. Sun, J.S.H. Lee, M.M. Zhang, Magnetic nanoparticles in MR imaging and drug delivery, Adv. Drug Deliv. Rev. 60 (2008) 1252–1265.

[52] J.L. Corchero, A. Villaverde, Biomedical applications of distally controlled magnetic nanoparticles, Trends Biotechnol. 27 (2009) 468–476.

[53] Q. Li, C.W. Kartkowati, S. Horie, T. Ogi, T. Iwaki, K. Okuyama, Correlation between particle size/domain structure and magnetic properties of highly crystalline Fe3O4 nanoparticles, Sci. Rep. (2017) 1–7.

[54] T.K. Jain, M.M. Torres, S.K. Sahoo, D. Leslie-Pelecky, V. Labhasetwar, Iron oxide nanoparticles for sustained delivery of anticancer agents, Mol. Pharm. 2 (2005) 194–205.

[55] R.K. Gilchrist, R. Medal, W.D. Sorey, R.C. Hanselman, J.V. Parrott, C.B. Taylor, Selective inductive heating of lymph nodes, Ann. Surg. 146 (1957) 596–606.

[56] R.E. Rosensweig, Heating magnetic fluid with alternating magnetic field, J. Magn. Magn Mater. 252 (2002) 370–374.

[57] T. Kobayashi, Cancer hyperthermia using magnetic nanoparticles, J. Biotechnol. 6 (2011) 1342–1347.

[58] O. Sandre, C. Genevois, E. Garaio, L. Adumeau, S. Mornet, F. Couillaud, In vivo imaging of local gene expression induced by magnetic hyperthermia, Genes 8 (2017) (2017) 61.

[59] S. Wilhelm, A.j. Tavares, Q. Dai, et al., Analysis of nanoparticle delivery to tumors, Nat. Rev. Mater. 1 (2016) 1–12.

[60] B. Gleich, J. Weizenecker, Tomographic imaging using the nonlinear response of magnetic particles, Nature 435 (2005) 1214–1217.

[61] M. Zborowski, J.J. Chalmers, Rare cell separation and analysis by magnetic sorting, Anal. Chem. 83 (2011) 8050–8056.

[62] V.V. Mody, A. Cox, S. Shah, et al., Magnetic nanoparticle drug delivery systems for targeting tumor, Appl. Nanosci. 4 (2014) 385–392.

[63] P.K. Bharodiya, A.B. Solanski, Approaches to the Development of Implantable Drug Delivery System, 2010. http://www.slideshare.net/pareshbharodiya/implantable-drug-delivery-system.

[64] M. Danckenwerts, A. Fassini, Implantable controlled release drug delivery systems: a review, Drug Dev. Ind. Pharm. 17 (1991) 1465–1502.

[65] A.K. Dash, G.C. Cudworth, Therapeutic applications of implantable drug delivery systems, J. Pharmacol. Toxicol. Methods 40 (1998) 1–12.

[66] H. Sah, Y.W. Chien, A.M. Hilery, A.W. Lloyd, A. Swarbrick, Rate control in drug delivery and targeting: fundamentals and applications to implantable systems. In: A.M. Hilery, A.W. Lloyd, A. Swarbrick, Drug Delivery and Targeting for Pharmacists and Pharmaceutical Scientists, Taylor Francis, 2001, pp. 73–103.

[67] P.J. Blackshear, F.D. Dorman, P.L. Blackshear, R.L. Varco, H. Buchwald, A permanently implantable self-recycling low flow constant rate multipurpose infusion pump of simple design, Surg. Forum 21 (1970) 136.

[68] P.J. Blackshear, F.D. Dorman, P.L. Blackshear Jr., R.L. Varco, H.A. Buchwald, Implantable infusion pump, U.S. Patent 3,731,681 (1973) 1–7.

[69] E. Renard, Implantable closed-loop glucose-sensing and insulin delivery: the future of insulin pump therapy, Curr. Opin. Pharmacol. 2 (2002) 708–716.

[70] D.A. LaVan, T. McGuire, R. Langer, Small scale systems for in vivo drug delivery, Nat. Biotechnol. 21 (2003) 1184–1191.

[71] J.H. Prescott, S. Lipka, S. Baldwin, N.F. Sheppard, J.M. Maloney, J. Coppeta, Chronic programmed polypeptide delivery from an implanted, multireservoir microchip device, Nat. Biotechnol. 24 (2006) 437–438.

[72] P.Y. Li, J. Shih, R. Lo, S. Saati, R. Agrawal, M.S. Humayun, An electrochemical intraocular drug delivery device, Sens. Actuators, A 143 (2008) 41–48.

[73] A. Verma, B. Verma, S.K. Prajapati, K. Tripathi, Prodrugs as a chemical delivery system: a review, Asian J. Res. Chem. 2 (2009) 100–103.

[74] A. Albert, Chemical aspects of selective toxicity, Nature 182 (1958) 421–423.

[75] J. Rautio, H. Kumpulainen, T. Heimbach, R. Oliyai, D. Oh, T. Jarvinen, Prodrugs: design and clinical applications, Nat. Rev. Drug Discov. 7 (2008) 255—270.

[76] S. Khan, N. Stannard, J. Greign, Precipitation of thiopental with muscle relaxant: a potential hazard, J R Soc MedSh Rep 2 (2011) 58.

[77] M.D. Lally, M.C. Kral, A.D. Boan, Not all generic concerta is created equal: comparison of OROS versus non-OROS for the treatment of ADHD, Clin. Pediatr. 55 (2016) 1197—1201.

[78] F. Wanga, M. Portera, A. Konstantopoulosb, P. Zhanga, H. Cui, Preclinical development of drug delivery systems for paclitaxel-based cancer chemotherapy, J. Contr. Release 267 (2017) 100—118.

CHAPTER

14

Emerging Therapeutics and Delivery

Alekha K. Dash[1], Babu Medi[2], Behnaz Sarrami[3], Mandana Hasanzad[4,5], Somnath Singh[1] and Surabhi Shukla[1]

[1]Department of Pharmacy Sciences, School of Pharmacy and Health Professions, Creighton University, Omaha, NE, United States [2]Drug Product Development, Interius BioTherapeutics Inc., Philadelphia, PA, United States [3]Missouri Pharmacogenomics Consulting LLC, Chesterfield, MO, United States [4]Medical Genomics Research Center, Tehran Medical Sciences, Islamic Azad University, Tehran, Iran [5]Personalized Medicine Research Center, Endocrinology and Metabolism Clinical Sciences Institute, Tehran University of Medical Sciences, Tehran, Iran

Keywords: Adult stem cells; Embryonic stem cells; Multipotent stem cells; Perinatal stem cells; PGx; Pharmacodynamics; Pharmacogenetics; Pharmacogenomics; Pharmacokinetics; Pluripotent stem cells; Precision medicine; Psychiatry; Stem cell.

14.1 Introduction

There are many complex diseases for which either there is no cure or the current medicines have limited utility such as neurodegenerative diseases (e.g., glaucoma), diabetes, and obesity. There are many emerging therapies on the horizon that can bring a paradigm shift in the treatment and management of such diseases. Many decades of research and development in the area of mRNA-based therapeutics resulted in the successful development of the mRNA COVID-19 vaccine within 1 year in comparison to at many years involved in the development of past many vaccines using the traditional inoculation-based approach. Many more such vaccines for other diseases including cancer and Alzheimer are at various stages of development.

Tremendous progress in discovering many facets of immunopharmacology and mechanisms involved in disease-relevant target recognition by antibodies have led to the recent development of CAR-T (chimeric antigen receptor) cell therapy for hematological cancers. The potential of CAR-T cell-based therapies is further boosted by the significant progress in cell therapies, gene therapies in combination with CRISPER (clustered regularly interspaced short palindromic repeats) gene editing tool applied as per patient's unique pharmacogenomic profile. Similarly, stem cell therapies have the potential to treat autoimmune, inflammatory, neurological, orthopedic conditions, and traumatic injuries, and currently intensive researches are going on for investigating stem cell therapy potential for many complicated diseases such as Crohn's disease, Multiple Sclerosis, Amyotrophic Lateral Sclerosis (ALS), Lupus, and Parkinson's disease. This chapter provides a basic understanding of foundational sciences underlying some of such emerging therapeutics.

14.2 siRNA, mRNA, and immunotherapy

OBJECTIVES

- Describe siRNA-based therapies and discuss some of the siRNA-based drugs either approved by FDA or in late-stage clinical trials.

- Describe the siRNA mechanism of action.
- Discuss challenges and barriers associated with siRNA-based therapeutics.
- Describe some of the drug delivery strategies for siRNA-based therapeutics and delivery.
- Introduce mRNA-based therapeutics and describe the process of development of mRNA-based drugs.
- Discuss the delivery system for mRNA-based drugs and provide some examples.
- Describe immunotherapy, its principle of action, and types of immunotherapies used in cancer treatment.

14.2.1 siRNA-based therapies

Ribonucleic acid interference (RNAi) is a biological gene regulatory mechanism in eukaryotes. The natural RNAi mechanism involves short strands of double-strand RNA such as small interfering RNA that bind sequence specifically to mRNA leading to gene suppression. Over 2 decades, it has become a significant tool and has incredible applications in the field of functional genomics and therapeutics. Small interfering ribonucleic acid (siRNA)-based therapies have seen tremendous development in the last 20 years [1]. In 2018, the US Food and drug administration (FDA) approved the first siRNA agent patisiran for the treatment of hereditary amyloidogenic transthyretin (hATTR) amyloidosis with polyneuropathy in adults [2]. Since then, there are four FDA-approved siRNA-based drugs available: patisiran, givosiran, lumasiran, and inclisiran and there are many other siRNA-based products in clinical trials (Table 14.1).

14.2.1.1 siRNA and its mechanism of action

siRNAs are short double-stranded RNAs (20–30 nucleotide long) that regulate genes and genomes. siRNAs produce their effect through a biological mechanism called RNAi interference by which double-stranded RNAs target complementary mRNA sequences and result in gene silencing or suppression. For siRNA to bind to target mRNA, dissociation of double-stranded RNA occurs that results in single strands. The released single strands bind specifically to target messenger RNA (mRNA). The binding of a single strand to target mRNA leads to cleavage and degradation of target mRNA, which in turn results in the prevention of translation and gene expression and affects the function of the protein [3]. The detailed process of RNAi involves cleavage of long dsRNA or short hair RNA by an endonuclease Dicer to produce siRNA (21–23 base long) in the cytoplasm (Fig. 14.1).

14.2.1.2 Challenges in siRNA drug delivery

The siRNA-based drugs have great therapeutic potential; however, their delivery has some challenges [5]. Major challenges associated with siRNA delivery to patients are their intracellular delivery, stability, and off-target effect that may lead to unintentional suppression of other genes. For siRNA drug to exert its effect, they should be delivered and effectively taken by the target site. Some of the problems associated with siRNA drugs are as follows:

- Low bioavailability: siRNA drugs owing to their large size and being anionic in nature have low bioavailability.
- Systemic elimination: Inefficient delivery to target sites with systemic administration due to rapid clearance by the kidney.
- Poor stability: Unlike DNA and protein, siRNA undergoes rapid degradation by nucleases present in cytoplasm, tissue, and plasma. Therefore, they are highly unstable having a short half-life (~5 min).
- Destruction by reticuloendothelial system: Nanocarrier encapsulated siRNAs' uptake is subject to adsorption by serum protein. Which leads to opsonization and uptake by the reticuloendothelial system and phagocytosis leading to their clearance.

TABLE 14.1 siRNA-based drugs in clinical trials [1].

Drug name/other names	Disease targeted	Approval status	Company name
Patisiran (ONPATTRO)	Hereditary transthyretin-mediated amyloidosis	FDA approved on October 82,018	Alnylam Pharmaceuticals
Givosiran (GIVLAARI)	Acute hepatic porphyria	FDA approved on November 20, 2019	Alnylam Pharmaceuticals
Lumasiran (ALN-GO1)	Primary hyperoxaluria type 1 (PH1)	FDA approved on November 23, 2020	Alnylam Pharmaceuticals
Inclisiran (ALN-PCSSC)	Heterozygous familial hypercholesterolemia (HeFH) and hypercholesterolemia	FDA approved on December 22, 2021	Novartis
Tivanisiran (SYL-1001)	Dry eyes ocular pain	Phase 3 trial NCT05310422	Sylentis
SYL040012	Glaucoma Ocular hypertension	Phase 1 and 2 NCT01227291	Sylentis
Vutrisiran	Hereditary transthyretin-mediated amyloidosis	FDA approved on June 13, 2022	Alnylam Pharmaceuticals
Fitusiran (ALN-AT3sc, ALN-APC, SAR439774)	Hemophilia A and B	Phase 3 trials ATLAS-(NCT03417102) ATLAS-PPX (NCT03549871) A/B (NCT03417245) ATLASs-INH ATLAS-PEDS (NCT03974113) ATLAS-OLE (NCT03754790)	Alnylam Pharmaceutical Sanofi Genzyme
Cosdosiran QPI-1007	Non-arteritic anterior ischemic optic neuropathy (NAION)	Phase 2/3 trial NCT02341560	Quark
Teprasiran (AKIi-5, DGFi, I−5NP, QPI-1002)	Acute kidney injury and delayed graft function	Phase 3 trial ReGIFT (NCT02610296)	Quark Novartis
Nedosiran (DCR-PHXC)	Primary hyperoxaluria	Phase 3 trial PHYOX 3 (NCT04042402)	Dicerna Alnylam Pharmaceuticals
Stratum II PF655	Age-related macular degeneration/diabetic macular degeneration AMD/DME	Phase 2 NCT01445899	Qurark
QPI-1007	Chronic optic nerve neurotrophy	Phase 1 NCT01064505	Qurark

- Immune response: siRNA can induce undesired immune response. Immunoreceptors like TLRs (Toll-like receptors) and protein kinase receptors can recognize siRNA falsely as viral RNA and induce an immune response by secreting certain cytokines and interferons that lead to adverse reactions.
- Off-target effect: siRNAs are not very target specific. Administration of siRNA can sometimes lead to an off-target effect by binding to a sequence other than the target sequence. This may lead to the suppression of genes other than the target or desired gene. Off-target effects may result in gene mutations and undesirable effects.

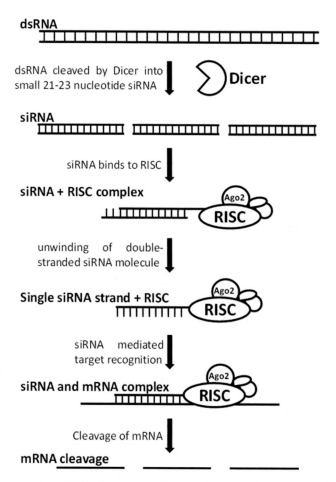

FIGURE 14.1 After the formation of mature siRNA, they are bound to a multiple proteins complex called RNA-induced silencing complex (RISC) that also includes Dicer and Ago-2. The RISC complex leads separation of siRNA into sense and antisense strands. The sense strand incorporates into RISC while the antisense strand acts as the guide and assists in binding of complex to target mRNA sequence. This complementary binding of guide activates cleavage of target mRNA by Ago-2 protein, which further leads to inhibition of translation [4].

- Cellular barriers penetration through cell membranes: siRNA being large in size and hydrophilic in nature face difficulty in moving across the cell membrane. siRNA drugs also have poor diffusion through the extracellular matrix. They have poor tissue penetration that leads to poor extravasation of siRNA molecules [5–7].

14.2.1.3 Strategies to overcome barriers associated with siRNA drug delivery

The strategies employed to overcome these barriers are chemical modifications to siRNA and loading the siRNA drugs in viral vectors, liposomes, nanoparticles, and other drug delivery systems.

14.2.1.3.1 Chemical modification

The aim of the chemical modification is to increase the stability of siRNA. The siRNA can be chemically modified at the sugar phosphate backbones of RNA and at pyrimidine and purine bases.

Sugar phosphate backbones modification: It is one of the widely used modifications. In this modification, highly charged unstable phosphodiester backbone is replaced with a phosphorothioate (PS) backbone [8]. Substitution of one of the non-bridge oxygen atoms on the phosphate group with a sulfur atom leads to protection from phosphodiesterase and nuclease activity. Also, it causes an increase in molecular hydrophobicity that helps in binding to plasma protein albumin, which in turn increases its circulation time and slows the degradation process leading to an improved pharmacokinetic profiles.

Sugar modification: Occurs at 2′-OH position, due to the nonessential role of siRNA's silencing effect [9]. The 2′-OH plays a role in nuclease-mediated cleavage, hence substituting the OH with other functional groups helps in protection through endonuclease enzyme degradation and improves stability. The most common group to replace the OH is 2′-O-methyl (2′-OMe), 2′-fluoro (2′-F), or a 2′-O-methoxyethyl (2′-MOE).

14.2.1.3.2 Delivery system

siRNA drugs being hydrophilic and large (13—14 kD) face difficulty crossing lipophilic cell membranes by passive diffusion to the target site. This problem can be overcome by designing a delivery system that can carry the drug to the target site. Also, conjugating them with a ligand targeting to receptor present at the target organ.

There are various formulation-based approaches developed or currently in development for the effective delivery of siRNA therapeutics to the target site. Some of the delivery methods include polymeric nanoparticles, micelles, niosomes, dendrimers, metal nanoparticles, liposomes, complexes with cationic transfection agents, oligonucleotide nanoparticles, human serum albumin-based nanoparticles, and oligonucleotide. However, these formulation strategies are not free of limitations and challenges and need thorough research before they can be utilized for pharmaceutical uses [10].

14.2.1.3.3 Lipid nanoparticles

These are the most used and successful delivery methods for siRNA-based drugs. Lipid nanoparticles (LNPs) are 100 nm in size. They are composed of cationic lipids such as cholesterol, 1,2-dimyristoyl-rac-glycero-3-methoxypolyethylene glycol-200, 1,2-distearoyl-sn-glycero-3-phosphocholine (DSPC), and D-Lin-MC3-DMA. LNPs have been used as a delivery vehicle for patisiran, the first FDA-approved siRNA drug.

- Advantage: Having cationic and ionizable lipids helps in the packaging of RNA and in providing stability. This overcomes the problem associated with transport of RNA drugs across the lipophilic layer.
- Encapsulation of siRNA drug in LNPs also provides protection against degradation. Surface of LNPs is pegylated, which further prevents RNA drugs from reticuloendothelial system clearance by reducing aggregation and opsonization. Overall, this improves the bioavailability and pharmacokinetics of the siRNA drugs and facilitates low-dose requirements.
- LNPs being small in size (~100 nm) can pass through fenestrated epithelium in the liver and therefore aid in targeting the drug to the liver. They can also be used to target liver tumors as they have the capacity to pass through leaky vasculature in liver tumor.

Disadvantage of LNPs: LNPs possess tremendous clinical utility owing to some of the advantages mentioned earlier. However, there are some limitations associated with their use.

Toxicity associated with LNPs: Excipients used in the formulation of LNP exhibit inflammation associated with the administration of the drug. This requires pre-treating patients with a mixture of anti-inflammatory drugs.

IV infusion of LNPs: IV infusion of LNPs requires trained medical professionals for the administration of drugs to patients. Also, this method is invasive, time consuming, and is not patient-friendly.

Liver targeting: Due to the large size of LNPs, they can easily be used to target the liver with large fenestration. However, the utility of these drugs to other tissue and organs becomes extremely limited.

Formulation scientists are working to overcome these challenges to improve the future application of LNPs. One approach to improve targeting is to bioconjugate with unique targeting ligands. The nanocarriers or siRNA drugs are covalently conjugated with a ligand or molecule. The strategy of bioconjugation helps in improving the uptake and delivery of siRNA drug molecules. The conjugate molecules could be a targeting ligand or peptide and antibodies against specific cell receptors in target cells. The advantage of bioconjugation is that it allows for target-specific drug delivery. Also, increases the concentration of siRNA at the target sites and therefore increases bioavailability and efficacy of siRNA molecules. It decreases off-target effect associated with siRNA molecules. Bioconjugates, owing to their small size, are less toxic and immunogenic as compared to LNPs.

Examples of a few ligands receptor pairs that are used for targeting include glycoproteins terminating with N-acetylgalactosamine (GalNAc) sugars and its receptor glycoprotein (ASGPR) in hepatocytes. GalNAc conjugates find wide application in siRNA-based therapeutics and have been successfully used in some of the FDA-approved and late-stage clinical trial siRNA drugs such as givosiran, fitusiran, vutrisiran, inclisiran, and nedosiran (Setten et al.). Some of the advantages of GALNAC conjugates over LNPs include easy synthesis, low toxicity profile, specific targeting to the liver, and ease of self-administration via subcutaneous injection; also, they do not require pre-treatment with anti-inflammatory drugs [11,12].

Other receptor ligand includes transferrin and its receptor protein 1 in cardiac and skeletal muscle, glucagon-like peptide-1 and its receptor in pancreatic beta cells, folate and folate receptor in cancer cells, and cyclic arginyl-glycyl-aspartic acid and integrins on cancer cells. Other antibodies against specific cell receptors and cationic peptides moieties like endoporter and penetratin can also be used for conjugation to improve penetration of drugs across the cell membrane barrier. Conjugation to lipophilic molecules such as cholesterol are utilized to improve pharmacokinetic characteristics and serum stability. These recent developments in drug delivery methods and chemical modification have led to the FDA approval of numerous siRNA drugs in the pharmaceutical market (Table 14.1).

14.2.1.4 FDA-approved siRNA-based therapies

14.2.1.4.1 Patisiran

It was the first siRNA therapeutics approved by FDA in August 2018. It is indicated for the treatment of the polyneuropathy of hereditary transthyretin-mediated amyloidosis in adults. It is a double-strand RNA formulated as a lipid nanoparticle that is taken up by liver cells by binding to the Apo lipoprotein E (ApoE) receptor. Patisiran exerts its therapeutic effect by breaking down both wild-type and mutant transthyretin (TTR) mRNA resulting in decreased production, circulation, and deposition of TTR protein in tissues and organs. It is a lipid complex injection and is administered as an intravenous infusion to patients [1,13].

14.2.1.4.2 Givosiran

The second siRNA therapeutics was approved by FDA after Patisiran in the year 2019. It is used for the treatment of acute hepatic porphyria in adults. Givosiran is a double-stranded RNA conjugated with N-acetylgalactosamine (GalNAc) ligand for uptake in the liver. It exerts its effect through the RNA I mechanism by targeting aminolevulinate synthase 1 (ALAS1) mRNA present in the liver resulting in the breakdown and cleavage of ALAS1 and leading to a reduction in aminolevulinic acid (ALA) and porphobilinogen (PBG) levels in the blood. It is administered subcutaneously at a dose of 2.5 mg/kg once in a month [1,13].

14.2.1.4.3 Lumasiran

This is the third siRNA therapeutics drug approved by FDA in November 2020. It is indicated for the treatment of primary hyperoxaluria type 1 (PH1) and reduced urinary oxalate levels in pediatric and adult patients. It is a double-stranded siRNA that is conjugated with GalNAc ligand for effective uptake to the liver. It targets hydroxy acid oxidase 1 (HAO1) mRNA and leads to cleavage and breakdown of HAO1. HAO1 is responsible for the production of an enzyme glycolate oxidase (GO) that leads to the production of glyoxylate. Glyoxylate is a substrate for the synthesis of oxalate. The inhibition of the GO enzyme leads to reduced oxalate that further leads to a decrease in the alanine glyoxylate aminotransferase (AGT) enzyme that is mutated in PH1. It is administered via subcutaneous injections as a loading dose followed by a maintenance dose [1,13].

14.2.1.4.4 Inclisiran

This siRNA therapeutics agent was approved by FDA in December 2021. This agent is used for lowering the level of low-density lipoprotein cholesterol (LDL-C). It is indicated for heterozygous familial hypercholesterolemia (HeFH) or clinical atherosclerotic cardiovascular disease (ASCVD) in adult subjects. The mechanism of action of inclisiran is through RNAi interference in the liver. The siRNA agent is attached to the GalNAc ligand for efficient delivery to the liver. In the liver, it targets the degradation of proprotein convertase subtilisin/kexin type 9 (PCSK9). PCSK9 functions to internalize and breakdown the LDL receptor. Inclisiran inhibits PCK9, thereby leading to an increase in the expression of LDL-C receptor and helps in recycling of the receptor to the cell surface. The binding of LDL-C receptor to cell surface leads to lysosomal degradation of LDL-C. This leads to an increase in the uptake of receptors and therefore reduces the level of LDL-C in the blood. Inclisiran is subcutaneously administered to subjects with heterozygous familial hypercholesterolemia [1,13].

14.2.2 Introduction to messenger RNA-based therapeutics

Messenger RNA (mRNA) is a single-strand RNA that plays a vital role in the process of protein synthesis in cells (Fig. 14.2). For over 50 years, a tremendous amount of basic and applied research has been devoted to the field of mRNA. However, very recently mRNA-based therapeutics have come up as a new class of drugs that find vast applications in regenerative medicine, cancer therapy, prophylactic and therapeutic vaccines for infectious disease, and

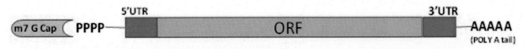

FIGURE 14.2 Structure of mRNA. An mRNA to have high translational efficiency must have these five structural and functional components in it. (1) 5′ caps, (2) 3′ poly A tail, (3) open reading frame (ORF), (4) 3′ untranslated regions (UTRs), and (5) 5′ UTR (untranslated regions).

in vivo delivery of mRNA to replace or supplement protein [14]. Recent development has made it possible to produce any protein and peptide in the human body by delivering mRNA as a vaccine or therapeutic protein. Messenger RNA delivery has some advantages over traditional gene delivery using DNA. The mRNA delivery can introduce mRNA in the cytoplasm of any cell (dividing or non-dividing for producing protein, while in DNA delivery, the DNA must enter the nucleus from the cytoplasm. There is also no risk associated with random integration of the genome in mRNA delivery in comparison to DNA delivery. The other advantage of mRNA delivery over DNA delivery is that the optimization of the promoter is not required as once mRNA enters the cell it instantly leads to the translation of protein. However, some of the limitation and insufficient knowledge about mRNA instability and immunogenicity has impeded mRNA delivery progress as new therapeutics. RNA is a negatively charged macromolecule and is prone to degradation by ubiquitous RNase. It can stimulate an immune response that leads to toxicity. Cellular barriers such as impermeability to anionic cell membrane also exist as mRNA is negatively charged, which may lead to low translational efficiency. However, recent developments in overcoming these barriers to mRNA delivery are evident from the development of the COVID-19 vaccine, which is an mRNA vaccine for the severe acute respiratory syndrome coronavirus 2 (SARS-CoV-2) pandemic. Most of these problems or limitations could be overcome by chemically modifying the nucleotide sequence that makes mRNA. The development of the COVID-19 vaccine has also led to speeding up more research in developing mRNA therapeutics with increased stability, reduced immunogenicity, and increased translational efficiency [15].

14.2.2.1 *Process of development of mRNA-based therapeutics*

Development of mRNA-based therapeutics involves several steps such as the design of mRNA, *in vitro* synthesis of mRNA, loading of mRNA drug into delivery carriers, safety evaluation, pharmacokinetics and pharmacodynamic studies manufacturing and clinical trial (Fig. 14.3). The most important process in the synthesis of the mRNA-based medicine is the design of mRNA drugs as it is a crucial step in maintaining the key features of mRNA (Fig. 14.2).

The five prime caps (m7 G ppp) are present at 5 prime terminus of mRNA contain a 7-methylguanosine (m7 G) attached to a triphosphate linkage and plays a significant role in providing the stability to mRNA by preventing its degradation by RNAase enzyme. The 3′ poly A is made up of 10—250 adenine ribonucleotides. The length of Poly(A) tails is important in determining mRNA translation efficacy and expression of protein. 5 prime and 3 prime UTRs play key roles in translation by recruiting RNA-binding proteins thereby playing a crucial role in regulating translational efficiency and playing a significant part in maintaining mRNA stability. The ORF are regulators of translation and modifying the codon also helps with mRNA stability. Recent advances in research focus on modifying these

1. **Identification of target gene sequence for a protein/antigen and designing target gene**

2. **Inserting target gene sequence into plasmid DNA**

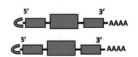

3. ***In-vitro* transcription of mRNA**

4. **Purification to obtain pure mRNA**

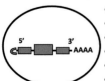

- Lipid nanoparticles
- Cationic liposomes
- Cationic polymer liposomes
- Polymer micelle
- Polymer lipid hybrid nanoparticles
- Modified dendrimer particle

5. **Formulation of mRNA drug into suitable drug delivery vehicle**

6. **Safety evaluation (*In-vitro* and *In-vivo*) and pharmacodynamics**

7. **Manufacturing of mRNA therapeutics**

FIGURE 14.3 Steps in process of mRNA drug production. Various steps involved in the development of mRNA-based therapeutics.

structural and functional elements of mRNA i.e., noncoding (5′cap, 5′ and 3′UTR and poly A tail) and coding region of mRNA (ORF) to increase the translational efficiency and intracellular stability of mRNA. These research efforts have led to the emergence of synthetic mRNA as a drug that leads to the production of proteins in the cell [15].

14.2.2.2 Delivery system for mRNA therapeutics

An ideal drug delivery system for mRNA drugs having high translational efficiency should be able to provide efficient cellular uptake (transfection) and permit endosomal escape, protect mRNA from degradation, and have low toxicity and low immunogenicity. Delivery of mRNA drugs is difficult due to a negative charge and large size (~1 kb) of mRNA that makes the cellular uptake challenging; drugs get accumulated in endosomes and are not able to enter the cytoplasm, and they have a very short half-life [16,17].

14.2.2.2.1 Lipid nanoparticles

Lipid nanoparticles (LNPs) are the most utilized drug delivery vehicles for mRNA therapeutics and are clinically approved. Various advantages associated with lipid nanoparticles had made this a suitable delivery system for mRNA vaccines and mRNA drugs. Encapsulation of mRNA drugs in LNPs prevents it from degradation and provides stability. Also, these particles can be tailored to target specific tissue by optimizing size, surface charge, and lipid composition. LNPs provide high transfection efficiency, safety, and efficacy. Additionally, the cost involved in manufacturing LNPs is low. Some of the lipid nanoparticles that are used are cationic lipid particles and ionizable lipid nanoparticles.

Other drug delivery methods that are currently being studied and utilized include polymeric nanoparticles, cationic nanoemulsions, and other mRNA delivery vectors, which are under development and trial including exosomes, extracellular vesicles, and protamine-condensed mRNA [139].

14.2.2.3 Application of mRNA-based therapeutics

mRNA-based drugs are emerging as powerful therapeutics and are becoming one of the most attractive areas for drug development that are continuing to expand. mRNA finds application as a vaccine and as therapeutics. mRNA as a vaccine encodes for viral protein and thereby induces immune response and protection against virus. The development of mRNA vaccine is rapidly growing after the emergency use authorization of two mRNA-based coronavirus vaccine. That has further demonstrated the effectiveness of mRNA-based technology. mRNA as therapeutics encodes a dysfunctional or absent protein in patients leading to functional expression of a protein. Due to the key role of mRNA in protein expression, mRNA finds broad clinical utility in the treatment or prevention of various diseases such as cardiovascular disease, infectious disease, cancer, genetic disease, rare disease, autoimmune disease, and others. mRNA replacement therapy for the genetic disease of the lungs and liver is also in development [18,19]. Table 14.2 gives a brief description of selected mRNA-based drugs and vaccines developed, under development, or in clinical trials.

14.2.3 Immunotherapy

Immunotherapy is a biological therapy used primarily for treating cancer. Biological therapy utilizes substances produced from living organisms to treat cancer. Immunotherapy makes use of the body's immune system to fight against cancer cells. Cancer is a complicated disease that is marked by an uncontrolled division of cells that may grow abnormally leading to a malignant tumor. The treatment modalities include surgery, which is the first line of treatment. Other treatment methods include radiotherapy and chemotherapy or combination therapy. However, progress in cancer treatment remains limited due to some of the adverse effects associated with chemotherapy such as systemic toxicity and the killing of healthy cells along with abnormal cells. Recently, immunotherapy has gained importance in cancer treatment owing to less side effects associated with it in comparison to conventional chemotherapy [20].

14.2.3.1 Principle of immunotherapy in cancer

Naturally, our body has a defense mechanism, the immune system of our body detects and destroys abnormal cells and may lead to the prevention of cancer cells. The immune system is composed of innate immunity and adaptive immunity. Innate immunity is a first line of defense and is responsible for generating sudden and short-lived responses against the antigen with the help of components of the innate immune system such as natural killer cells (NK cells), macrophages, mast cells, dendritic cells (DC), phagocytes, neutrophil, basophils, and the complement system. Adaptive immunity produces long-term response and generates long-term memory against antigens,

TABLE 14.2 mRNA-based drugs and vaccines developed, under development or in clinical trials.

Name	Diseases	Encoded protein	Delivery vehicle	Manufacturer
Infectious disease—mRNA vaccines				
BNT162b2 mRNA-1273	Covid 19	S—2P Full-length S protein with 2 proline mutation	Lipid nanoparticles encapsulated mRNA	BioNtech Pfizer
CV7201	Rabies	Rabies virus glycoprotein (RABV-G)	RNactive protamine	Cure vac
MRNA-1325	Zika virus	Zika virus antigen	LNP encapsulated mRNA	Moderna
VAL-50644	Influenza	Hemaglutinin glycoprotein	Lipid nanoparticles encapsulated mRNA	Moderna
NA	HIV infection	HIV gag and Nef	Dendritic cell-loaded mRNA	Massachusetts General Hospital
mRNA-1647/1443	Cytomegalovirus infection (CMV)	CMV glycoprotein H (gH) pentamer complex	Lipid nanoparticle encapsulated mRNA	Moderna,
Cancer—mRNA vaccines				
mRNA-4157	Solid tumor	Neo Ag	Lipid nanoparticles encapsulated mRNA	Moderna
Lipo-MERIT	Melanoma	Tyrosinase, tumor-associated antigen (TAA), putative tyrosine protein- phosphatase (TPTE)	Lipoplex DOTMA(DOTAP)/DOPE lipoplex	BioNtech
Protein replacement—other disorder				
AZD8601	**Metabolic disorder** Type II diabetes	Vascular endothelial growth factor A (VEGFA)	Naked mRNA	Moderna
AZD8601	**Cardiovascular disease** Heart failure	VEGFA	Naked mRNA	Moderna
MRT5005	**Genetic disorder** Cystic fibrosis	Cystic fibrosis transmembrane conductance regulator (CFTCR)	Unknown	Translate Bio, Inc
mRNA-3927	Propionic acidemia	Propionyl-Co A carboxylase	Unknown	Moderna
MRT5201	Ornithine transcarbomylase deficiency (OTD)	Orninthine transcarbomylase	Lipid nanoparticles	Translate Bio, Inc.

pathogens, or abnormal cells so that if our body encounters the same antigen, pathogen, or abnormal cells they will be marked for destruction. The component of the innate immune system with the help of a receptor can also recognize the tumor cells or abnormal cells, microorganisms, antigens, and present them to adaptive immune system constituents so that destruction of tumor cells or microorganisms can take place, and long-term memory response is generated. Adaptive immunity is composed of B lymphocytes and T lymphocytes (CD4+ helper T lymphocytes, and CD8+ cytotoxic T lymphocytes (CTLs)). These B cells or T cells proliferate and destroy the antigen by different mechanistic pathways [20].

Even though the immune system can delay and slow the progression of cancer development or growth by destroying the abnormal cells, the cancer cells have developed a mechanism to evade the immune system's mechanism of destruction of cells. Some of the mechanisms by which they can escape the immune system are by changing some of the cell surface proteins that can be identified by the immune system, or the cancerous cells undergo some genetic mutation that makes them less likely to be recognized by the immune system. Also, they may change normal cells surrounding the tumor cell and by doing that they interrupt how the immune system will respond to tumor cells. In a way, the cancer cells develop an immunosuppression mechanism against the immune system and thereby escape killing by immune cells. Thus, immunotherapy helps in activating the body's own immune system so that the abnormal, damaged, or cancer cells can be recognized by the immune cells for destruction [20,21].

TABLE 14.3   List of selected drugs used for immunotherapy.

Types of immunotherapies	Drugs name (target)	Indication
Monoclonal antibodies	Bevasizumab (VEGF) Rituximab (CD 20) Blinatumomab (CD19 and CD3) Trastuzumab (HER2) Cetuximab (EGFR) Isatuximab (CD38)	Renal cancer, glioblastoma, non-small cell lung cancer, colorectal cancer, and ovarian cancer Non-hodgkin's lymphoma Acute lymphoblastic leukemia Breast cancer Head and neck squamous cell carcinoma Multiple myeloma
Adaptive cell therapy	**CAR-T therapy** Tecartus Abecma Carvycti Kymriah Yescarta Breyanzi	Mantle B cell lymphoma and precursor B lymphocytic lymphoma Multiple myeloma Multiple myeloma B-cell acute lymphoblastic leukemia and B-cell non-hodgkin lymphoma B-cell non-hodgkin lymphoma B-cell non-hodgkin lymphoma
Immunomodulating agents	Aldesleukin (Proleukin®) Interferon alpha- 2b Pomalidomide (Pomalyst) Lenalidomide (Revlimid) Thalidomide (Thalomid)	Melanoma and kidney cancer cells Melanoma, leukemia Multiple Kaposi Sarcoma Multiple myeloma, mantle cell lymphoma, follicular lymphoma and marginal zone lymphoma Multiple myeloma
Cancer vaccine	Sipuleucel-T (provegene) Talimogene laherparepvec (T-VEC)	Hormone refractory prostate cancer Melanoma

14.2.3.2 Types of immunotherapies

Immunotherapy treatments can be grouped into four major categories: targeted antibodies, immunomodulating agents, adoptive cell therapy, and cancer vaccine [22]. A few FDA-approved drugs, belonging to these categories, for the treatment of cancer are listed in Table 14.3.

14.2.3.2.1 Targeted antibodies

Monoclonal antibodies, which are specific antibodies against a specific antigen, are used to target specific receptors on cancer cells. The high specificity of monoclonal antibodies has been widely utilized in the specific targeting of cancer cells and there are many monoclonal antibody drugs in the pharmaceutical market. The major advantage of using monoclonal antibodies for treatment is protection from systemic toxicity. Some monoclonal antibodies mark the cell so that it can be recognized by immune cells and can be killed. One such example is Rituximab, which was the first monoclonal antibody approved for the treatment of non-Hodgkin's lymphoma. Rituximab binds to the CD20 receptor on the B cells and on some cancer, cells leading to the destruction of cancer cells by the immune cells. These monoclonal antibodies can be combined with anticancer drugs. This form of drug and antibody conjugate can increase the specificity of targeting cancer cells and also therapeutic efficiency is increased. Adcetris is approved by FDA for the treatment of Hodgkin lymphoma. It is a conjugation of the anticancer drug monomethyl auristatin E and a chimeric IgG1 that targets CD30 receptors on the cancer cell surface [22].

14.2.3.2.2 Immunomodulating agents

These are agents that can activate and enhance the body's immune response against cancer. Immunomodulating agents commonly used in cancer are cytokines. Cytokines are proteins or growth factors produced by immune cells and that play an important role in the growth of other cells. Interferons, interleukins, and some growth factors are examples of cytokines. Many immunomodulating agents are approved for the treatment of cancer. For example, Interferons alpha 2b, which is produced by recombinant DNA technology, is used for the treatment of lymphoma, leukemia, and melanoma. Interferon alpha 2b works in increasing the immune response by promoting the growth of natural killer and dendritic cells and slows the growth of cancer cells. Another immunomodulator is Aldesleukin (Proleukin), which is Interleuckin-2, a protein produced by recombinant technology. Proleukin is used for the treatment of melanoma and kidney cancer. IL-2 induces the immune response to cancer by promoting the growth of a number of white blood cells such as natural killer cells, killer T cells, and B cells. These white blood cells can damage the cancer cells and generate an immune response [22].

14.2.3.2.3 Adoptive cell therapy

A type of immunotherapy that makes our own immune cells combat cancer by boosting the ability of T cells to respond to attack cancer cells. T-cell therapy can be done in two ways: (1) tumor-infiltrating lymphocytes (TIL infiltrating therapy) and (2) chimeric antigen receptor T-cell immunotherapy (CAR T-cell therapy) [23].

14.2.3.2.3.1 *TIL immunotherapy*   In this therapy, tumor-infiltrating lymphocytes that are a type of T cells are collected from the tumor of the patient and grown outside in large numbers and then these T-cells are reinfused back into the patients in sufficient numbers. This therapy works on the principle that the lymphocytes around the tumors have capability to recognize the tumor cells; however, they are not enough to kill the tumor cells, so reinfusing the patient with a large number of cells may lead to the advantage of killing the tumor cells. TIL therapy is utilized for the treatment of melanoma in some patients. The main disadvantage of this therapy is that despite the outside production of a large number of TILs, sometimes it is difficult to achieve enough lymphocytes in cancer patients [22,23].

14.2.3.2.3.2 *CAR-T cell therapy*   This therapy overcomes some of the limitations of TIL therapy by genetic engineering of the T cells. T cells are taken from patients and are modified outside to have chimeric antigen receptors that can specifically bind to tumor cells. After that, they are grown in large numbers and given back to cancer patients. Yescarta, Kymriah are CAR-T drugs that have been approved by FDA and EMA for the treatment of lymphoma [22,23].

14.2.3.3 *Cancer vaccines*

These cancer treatment vaccine uses specific antigen present in tumor cell as a vaccine to induce an immune response in the cancer patient. This tumor-specific antigen when introduced in the patient can help recognize the tumor-containing specific antigen and can kill the cancer cells and prevent the relapse of cancer. Other cancer vaccines known as dendritic cell cancer vaccines are developed from a kind of immune cells known as dendritic cells. These vaccines induce an immune response toward antigens present in tumor cells. Example: sipuleucel-T (provegene), FDA approved in the year 2010 for treatment of hormone-refractory prostate cancer. Another category of cancer treatment vaccine is oncolytic virus therapy. This uses an oncolytic virus that can infect, break down or damage the tumor cells without affecting the healthy cells [22,24]. Also, they can produce proteins like Granulocytes-macrophage-colony-stimulating factor (GM-CSF) Example: Talimogene laherparepvec (T-VEC) and FDA-approved oncolytic virus vaccine made using genetically modified Herpes simplex virus type1. T-VEC is used for the treatment of melanoma.

14.3 Cell and gene therapies

OBJECTIVES

- Introduce and define cell and gene therapy products
- Discuss how cell and gene therapy products are different from other biopharma products
- Discuss FDA-approved cell and gene therapy products
- Discuss handling requirements and pharmacists' role in ensuring therapeutic success
- Example case studies with cell and gene therapy (CGT) product products

14.3.1 Introduction

The ability to sequence the human genome and rapid advances in the fields of biology, biotechnology, and medicine has led to the development of novel and highly innovative medicinal products, including Cell and gene therapy (CGT) products. CGT products belong to a diverse class of biopharmaceuticals, and regulatory agencies consider these products as complex biological products. These therapies are regulated in the United States by the Center for Biologics Evaluation and Research, a division of the US FDA and in Europe by the European Medicines Agency (EMA). The EMA refers to cell and gene therapies as Advanced Therapy Medicinal Products (ATMPs). Cell and gene therapies involve modifying the genetic material of cells, either *ex vivo* or *in vivo* to manipulate the patient's own cells (autologous) or introduce new cells (allogeneic) for the treatment of inherited or acquired diseases [25]. Cell and gene therapies both use cells and genetic information to fight disease but do so in different ways. While gene therapy involves altering cellular genes inside the body, cell therapy involves infusion or transplantation of cells and in some cases cells that may be genetically modified *ex vivo*, to treat or stop disease [26]. Cell and gene therapy products are rather complex compared to traditional products but are a growing class of medications that has the potential to treat serious conditions, particularly in patients with unmet medical needs. The full potential of CGT products is only just beginning to emerge and may offer permanent or longer-lasting effects compared to traditional medicines [27]. While the initial focus has been primarily on oncology and monogenetic disorders, CGT products are being tested for other areas including neurodegenerative diseases, diabetes, cardiovascular diseases, infectious diseases, and ophthalmology.

Cell and gene therapy-related research and product development in the United States continue to grow at a fast rate, with a few US FDA-approved products and several products advancing through clinical development. With more than 1000 clinical trials ongoing for CGT products, FDA expects to approve 10−20 cell and gene therapy products a year by 2025 [28]. The clinical success of cell and gene therapy products requires close collaboration of Physicians, Pharmacists, and other healthcare professionals to meet specific handling and administration requirements for these products [29]. Thus, it is critical for pharmacists, especially health system pharmacists, to understand the complexity of CGT products and other unique product-specific requirements to ensure therapeutic success and safety of patients and healthcare professionals involved. While the CGT products are promising and have the potential to treat and cure serious unmet medical conditions, there are several challenges for these products to be widely available as these products are complex to develop, manufacture, and use, leading to high prices and their commercial success may require novel reimbursement models [30].

14.3.2 Cell and gene therapies versus traditional biopharma products

While traditional small molecule and protein-based biological drugs are relatively short lived within the body and thereby need chronic administration, CGTs are being designed as potentially one-time treatments that offer long-lasting effects and have the potential to address complex and rare disorders for which there are no effective treatments available [31]. Manufacturing of cell and gene therapies is a complex process requiring several critical starting materials and specialized equipment [32]. Testing these products for potency and safety is different and challenging due to the complexity of their modes of action, which are not always fully understood and often involve multiple pathways [33]. Regulatory review and approval of these novel products can be daunting with limited and evolving regulatory guidance. There is also a need for long-term follow-ups and safety evaluations due to the long-acting nature of these products. Long-term follow-up studies for 15 years are being required for these products as a post-marketing commitment to monitor subjects for delayed adverse events [34].

14.3.3 Cell therapy

Cell therapy is the introduction of new cells into a patient's body to grow, replace, or repair damaged tissue to treat a disease [25]. Cell therapy products fall under regenerative medicine therapies (RMTs). A variety of different types of cells can be used in cell therapy, including stem cells, lymphocytes, dendritic cells, and pancreatic islet cells. In some cases, such as chimeric antigen receptor-T cells (CAR-T), the cells are genetically modified *ex vivo* before being (re) introduced into the patient. The cells may originate from the patient (autologous cells) or a donor (allogeneic cells).

The most common cell therapy is blood transfusion, and the transfusion of red blood cells, white blood cells, and platelets from a donor [25]. Another common cell therapy is hematopoietic stem cell transplantation (HSCT) from bone marrow. It is used to treat patients with a variety of blood cancers and hematological conditions using either autologous or donor-matched allogeneic transplants [35]. Hematopoietic stem cells (HSCs) are present in the blood, bone marrow, and cord blood. Cord blood is approved for HSCT to treat disorders of the hematopoietic system including blood cancers, and other conditions such as inherited and acquired blood and immune system disorders [36]. When cord blood is transplanted, it can serve as a graft source to restore the body's ability to produce blood cells.

Another type of cell therapy that has shown great promise recently for blood cancer indications is chimeric antigen receptor (CAR) T cell therapy. CAR T cell therapy may be considered a type of cell-based gene therapy that involves adding genes to T cells enabling them to express a receptor on their surface that recognizes and attack cancer cells. CARs are engineered receptors that redirect CAR-positive lymphocytes, most commonly T cells, to recognize and eliminate cells expressing a specific target antigen [37]. The manufacturing process involves modifying T cells collected from the patient using a viral vector encoding the desired CAR and then culturing the cells to expand the number of cells before reinfusing the CAR T cells back into the patient [38]. The CAR T cell therapies rapidly advanced from a promising form of immuno-oncology in preclinical models to multiple commercially approved products to treat leukemia and lymphoma [39]. Autologous CAR T cell therapy involves removing patient's own cells and takes a few days to weeks before the patient can receive the treatment as illustrated in Fig. 14.4. While the CAR T cell therapy products approved so far are autologous therapies, there is a push to bring allogeneic CAR T cell therapies that can be manufactured using donor derived cells used in an "off-the-shelf" manner for any patient eligible for the CAR T treatment [40].

Table 14.4 shows the list of US FDA-approved cell therapy products with their indications, dosage, and route of administration. All the cell therapy products are supplied frozen in the vapor phase of liquid nitrogen and require to be stored in the vapor phase of liquid nitrogen.

14.3.4 Gene therapy

American Society of Gene and Cell Therapy (ASGCT) defines gene therapy as the introduction, removal, or modification of genetic material of patient's cell to alter gene expression and thereby the biological function with the objective of achieving a therapeutic benefit and potentially preventing or curing a disease (Fig. 14.5) [25]. Examples of gene therapy approaches include replacing a mutated gene that causes disease with a healthy copy or introducing a new or modified gene into the body. Transfer of genetic material into cells may be accomplished through viral vector-based or nonviral vector-based delivery systems [41].

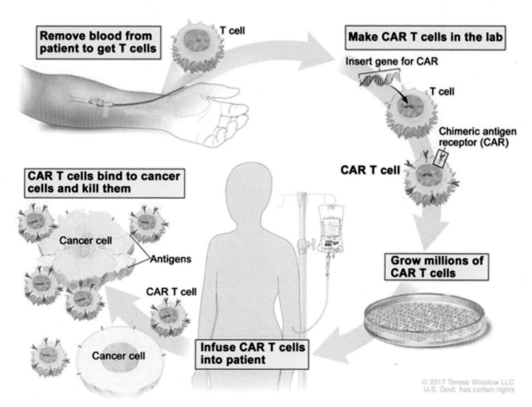

FIGURE 14.4 Illustration of different steps in CAR T cell therapy. *Used with permission from Ref. [138]. https://visualsonline.cancer.gov/details.cfm? imageid=11776.*

TABLE 14.4 Approved CAR T cell therapy products in the United States.

Product name (proper name)	Company	Indication[a]	Dosage and route of administration[a]
ABECMA® (idecabtagene vicleucel)	Celgene Corporation, a Bristol-Myers Squibb Company	ABECMA is a B-cell maturation antigen (BCMA)-directed genetically modified autologous T-cell immunotherapy indicated for the treatment of adult patients with relapsed or refractory multiple myeloma after four or more prior lines of therapy.	$300-460 \times 10^6$ CAR-positive T cells administered by intravenous infusion
BREYANZI® (lisocabtagene maraleucel)	Juno Therapeutics, Inc., a Bristol-Myers Squibb Company	BREYANZI is a CD19-directed genetically modified autologous T-cell immunotherapy indicated for adult patients with large B-cell lymphoma (LBCL), including diffuse large B-cell lymphoma (DLBCL), high-grade B-cell lymphoma, primary mediastinal large B-cell lymphoma, and follicular lymphoma grade 3B.	$50-110 \times 10^6$ CAR-positive viable T cells (consisting of 1:1 CAR-positive viable T cells of the CD8 and CD4 components) administered by intravenous infusion
CARVYKTI™ (ciltacabtagene autoleucel)	Janssen Biotech, Inc.	CARVYKTI is a B-cell maturation antigen (BCMA)-directed genetically modified autologous T-cell immunotherapy indicated for the treatment of adult patients with relapsed or refractory multiple myeloma after four or more prior lines of therapy.	$0.5-1.0 \times 10^6$ CAR-positive viable T cells per kg of body weight, with a maximum dose of 1×10^8 CAR-positive viable T cells per single infusion
KYMRIAH® (tisagenlecleucel)	Novartis	KYMRIAH is a CD19-directed genetically modified autologous T-cell immunotherapy indicated for the treatment of acute lymphoblastic leukemia, chronic lymphoid leukemia and diffuse large B-cell lymphoma in patients up to 25 years old, and the treatment of adult patients with relapse/refractory (r/r) large B-cell lymphoma.	$0.2-5.0 \times 10^6$ CAR-positive viable T cells per kg body weight for patients 50 kg or less. 0.1 to 2.5×10^8 CAR-positive viable T cells for patients above 50 kg. The product is administered by intravenous infusion
SKYSONA® (elivaldogene autotemcel)	Bluebird Bio, Inc	SKYSONA is genetically modified autologous hematopoietic stem cells (HSCs) enriched for CD34+ cells and transduced *ex vivo* with lentiviral vector encoding ABCD1 complementary deoxyribonucleic acid (cDNA) for human adrenoleukodystrophy protein (ALDP). SKYSONA is indicated to slow the progression of neurologic dysfunction in boys 4–17 years old with early, active cerebral adrenoleukodystrophy (CALD).	The minimum recommended dose is 5.0×10^6 CD34+ cells/kg. SKYSONA is provided as a single dose for infusion containing a suspension of CD34+ cells in one or two bags for intravenous infusion.
TECARTUS® (brexucabtagene autoleucel)	Kite Pharma, Inc.	TECARTUS is a CD19-directed genetically modified autologous T cell immunotherapy indicated for the treatment of adult patients with relapsed or refractory mantle	Target dose for MCL is 2×10^6 CAR-positive viable T cells per kg body weight, with a maximum of 2×10^8 CAR positive viable T cells. Target dose for ALL is

TABLE 14.4 Approved CAR T cell therapy products in the United States.—cont'd

Product name (proper name)	Company	Indication[a]	Dosage and route of administration[a]
		cell lymphoma (MCL) and adult patients with relapsed or refractory B-cell precursor acute lymphoblastic leukemia (ALL).	1×10^6 CAR-positive viable T cells per kg body weight, with a maximum of 1×10^8 CAR-positive viable T cells. The product is administered by intravenous infusion
YESCARTA® (axicabtagene ciloleucel)	Kite Pharma, Inc.	YESCARTA is a CD19-directed genetically modified autologous T-cell immunotherapy indicated for the treatment of B-cell malignancies such as non-hodgkin lymphoma, acute lymphoblastic leukemia, mantle cell lymphoma, chronic lymphoid leukemia and diffuse large B-cell lymphoma and follicular lymphoma.	The target dose is 2×10^6 CAR-positive viable T cells per kg body weight, with a maximum of 2×10^8 CAR-positive viable T cells administered by intravenous infusion.
ZYNTEGLO® (betibeglogene autotemcel)	Bluebird Bio, Inc.	ZYNTEGLO is a β^{A-T87Q}-globin gene therapy consisting of autologous CD34+ cells, containing hematopoietic stem cells (HSCs), transduced *ex vivo* with lentiviral vector encoding β^{A-T87Q}-globin. ZYNTEGLO is indicated for the treatment of adult and pediatric patients with β-thalassemia who require regular red blood cell (RBC) transfusions.	A single dose of ZYNTEGLO contains a minimum of 5.0×10^6 CD34+ cells/kg of body weight, in one or more bags for intravenous infusion.

[a]Refer to the corresponding package insert for more details.

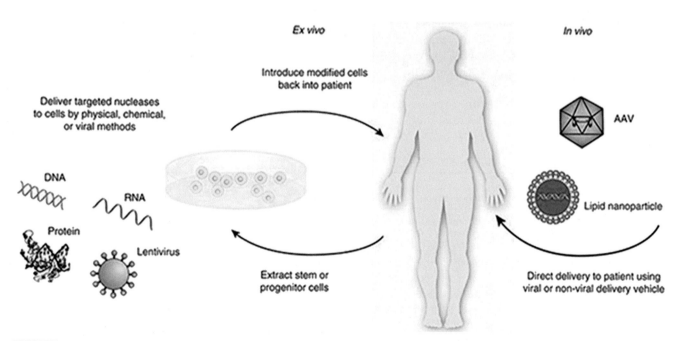

FIGURE 14.5 Illustration of *in vivo* and *ex vivo* gene therapy. *Source: https://www.fda.gov/vaccines-blood-biologics/cellular-gene-therapy-products/what-gene-therapy; accessed on Aug. 06, 2022.*

Gene editing is considered a type of gene therapy by which DNA sequences are added, deleted, altered, or replaced at specified location(s) in the genome of human somatic cells, *ex vivo* or *in vivo*, using either nuclease-dependent or nuclease-independent technologies. Gene editing offers the ability to precisely manipulate and edit the sequence of DNA in human cells to treat a specific disease. This approach requires the ability to deliver gene editing agents to target organs and tissues safely and efficiently. Several different delivery methods are being developed including viral vectors and non-viral delivery systems.

Viral vectors have been shown to be efficient for gene delivery to target cells, which is critical to achieving a therapeutic effect. Although a large number of viral vectors exist with diverse properties, several of them also pose safety risks including oncogenesis and immunogenicity. Viral vectors that are currently being used for *in vivo* gene therapy products belong to retroviruses (primarily lentivirus), adenoviruses (Ads), or adeno-associated viruses (AAVs) [41]. Alternatively, a therapeutic transgene can be delivered *ex vivo*, whereby cells of a patient are removed to culture and genetically modify by inserting a therapeutic transgene and cells are reintroduced into the patient. Although several products using Adenovirus, Lentivirus and AAV vectors are in development, only two AAV-based *in vivo* gene therapy products are currently approved in the United States [42]. Table 14.5 shows the list of approved gene therapy products in the United States. Although viral vectors represent a promising platform for *in vivo* gene therapy, major challenges still remain including safety, cost of treatment, and manufacturing.

Non-viral delivery systems did not gain traction due to their poor efficiency of gene transfer and manufacturing challenges. The major advantage of using non-viral vectors is its biosafety as compared to viral vectors [43]. Non-viral delivery systems include lipid-based and polymer-based encapsulation systems that have the potential to address many of the limitations of viral vectors, particularly with respect to safety [44]. Non-viral delivery, especially using LNPs is gaining lot of interest for gene editing applications [45].

14.3.5 Handling of cell and gene therapy products

CGT products are relatively new, and their handling is different from other drugs, and the guidance from the regulatory agencies and professional associations regarding their pharmaceutical application is still being developed. These products require ultra-cold chain depending on the product, -20 to $-80°C$ for gene therapy products and -150 to $-190°C$ (vapor phase liquid nitrogen) compared to traditional biological therapies requiring refrigerated temperature control. The products are sensitive to temperature after taking them out of ultra-cold storage temperature and need to be administered within minutes to hours after thawing. The use of cell and gene therapy products requires close collaboration of the Physicians and Pharmacists to meet specific handling, dose preparation, and administration requirements for these products to ensure therapeutic success and safety of patient and healthcare professionals involved [46]. Pharmacists have a key role to play to ensure successful outcomes with these new, complex products that require training, infrastructure, policies, and protocols for the handling and transport of gene therapies. Developing standard operating procedures specific for cell and gene therapy products detailing procurement, receipt, storage, handling, transport of the finished product, and waste disposal will help [47]. Particular attention needs to be paid to the training of healthcare professions involved, to ensure maximum compliance with the procedures at all stages of the treatment process including dose preparation and delivery to the patient [29]. Because gene therapies may utilize viral vectors, they are considered biohazardous materials and must be handled using

TABLE 14.5 Approved gene therapy products in the United States.

Product name (proper name)	Company	Product type	Indication	Dosage and route of administration[a]
Luxturna (voretigene neparvovec-rzyl)	Spark Therapeutics	Adeno-associated virus type 2 (AAV2) vector-based gene therapy	For the treatment of patients with confirmed biallelicRPE65mutation-associated retinal dystrophy Patients must have viable retinal cells as determined by the treating physician(s)	1.5×10^{11} vector genomes (vg) for each, administered by subretinal injection in a total volume of 0.3 mL
ZOLGENSMA (onasemnogene abeparvovec-xioi)	Novartis Gene Therapies, Inc.	Adeno-associated virus type 9 (AAV9) vector-based gene therapy	For the treatment of pediatric patients less than 2 years of age with spinal muscular atrophy (SMA) with biallelic mutations in the survival motor neuron 1 (SMN1) gene.	1.1×10^{14} vector genomes (vg) per kg of body weight, administered as an intravenous infusion over 60 min

[a]*Refer to the corresponding package insert for more details.*

proper procedures. In addition, it is essential for the Pharmacists to work with the manufacturers and professional associations along with regulatory agencies to help the field, especially with the expected increase in the number of approved cell and gene therapy products in the future.

14.4 Stem cell therapy: basics and clinical application

> **OBJECTIVES**
> - Introduce stem cells and compare them with other somatic cells
> - Describe source of stem cells
> - Compare and contrast various stem cells
> - Discuss potentials of stem cell therapy
> - Describe routes and delivery strategies being explored
> - Discuss challenges and barriers of stem cell therapy

14.4.1 Introduction

As cells mature, they differentiate into specialized cells performing specific tissue function. Stem cells are undifferentiated cells not yet committed to a specific function but have the potential to differentiate to do a specific function. That is why stem cells are also called precursor cells or pluripotent cells. According to Mayo clinic "Stem cells are the body's raw materials—cells from which all other cells with specialized functions are generated. Under the right conditions in the body or a laboratory, stem cells divide to form more cells called daughter cells (Fig. 14.6A) [Mayo Clinic link]. These daughter cells become either new stem cells or specialized cells (differentiation) with a more specific function, such as blood cells, brain cells, heart muscle cells or bone cells (Fig. 14.6) [48]. No other cell in the body has the natural ability to generate new cell types."

14.4.2 Source of stem cells

There are several sources of stem cells.

a. **Embryonic stem cells**: These stem cells come from the blastocyst, which is a 3—5 days-old embryo containing about 150 cells. These stem cells are having the ability to differentiate into any type of cell. Therefore, they are also called pluripotent stem cells, which can be used to regenerate or repair diseased tissue and organs.

b. **Adult stem cells**: There is intense research going on to find non-embryonic stem cells due to ethical issues surrounding embryonic stem cells. A smaller number of stems cells are found in many adult tissues, such as bone marrow or fat. However, they have limited ability to give rise to various cells of the body. For example, stem cells residing in the bone marrow mainly produce blood cells only. However, emerging evidence suggests bone marrow stem cells may be able to create bone or heart muscle cells [49].

c. **Induced pluripotent stem cells**: These are in fact adult stem cells such as skin and blood, which have been transformed into multipotent stem cells using genetic reprogramming. They act similarly to embryonic stem cells and prevent immune system rejection of the new stem cells, often observed with non-autologous stem cells.

d. **Perinatal stem cells**: These are multipotent stem cells derived from amniotic fluid as well as umbilical cord blood. Multipotent stem cells can differentiate into many cells whereas pluripotent into any cells.

14.4.3 Potentials of stem cells

There is massive interest in stem cell research due to its following potential.

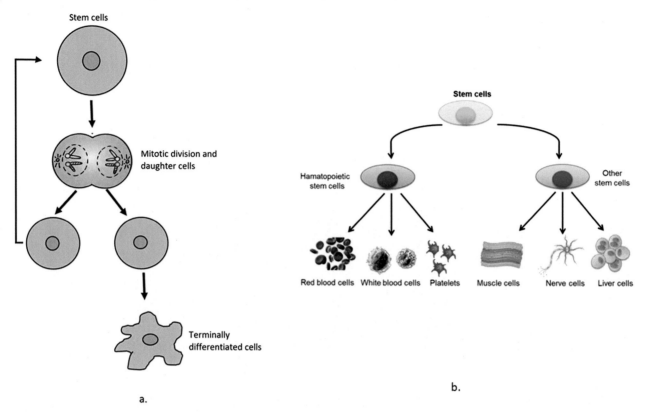

FIGURE 14.6   (a) Differentiation of a stem cell showing mitotic division of one stem cell into two daughter cells. Each daughter cell either remain a stem cell or become terminally differentiated. (b) Stem cells differentiated into various specialized cells. *Used with permission from Ref. [49].*

 i. **Understanding of disease pathogenesis**: As stem cells mature into cells forming various tissues and organs such as bones, heart, and nerves, researchers may better understand how diseases and conditions develop by a comparative understanding of the development of healthy normal organs versus ones having the disease.
 ii. **Regenerative medicine**: Theoretically stem cells can be induced to differentiate into specific cells that can be used in patients to regenerate and repair or transplant organs/tissues damaged or affected by the disease, for example, spinal cord injuries [50], type 1 diabetes [51], Parkinson's disease [52], amyotrophic lateral sclerosis [53], Alzheimer's disease [54], heart disease [55], stroke [56], burns [57], cancer [58], and osteoarthritis [59].
iii. **Drug discovery and development**: Stem cells have been used in all stages of the drug discovery pathway such as target identification, high throughput screening, disease modeling, regenerative drugs, and toxicology studies [60,61]. Stem cells can be directed to differentiate into a specific lineage containing a particular genomic profile associated with a disease. The treatment of such stem cells with drug candidates can provide information about gene expression profile and a molecular mechanism helpful in finding potential drug targets and further development of the existing drugs. Therefore, researchers can use some types of stem cells to test the investigational drugs for safety and quality, before using them in human subjects in clinical trials.

14.4.4 Barriers and challenges

Stem cell research encounters unique challenges in comparison to other new therapeutic strategies as shown below [62].

1. Need of human embryo to establish new embryonic stem cell lines. In many countries including the United States using human embryo is not permitted, thereby, sources of stem cells needed for preclinical and clinical research are limited.
2. Safety issues of stem cell therapy application to humans are not completely understood.
3. Regulatory compliances are cumbersome for stem cell-based drug development with regard to risk evaluation, clinical outcomes determination and management, and recruiting human subjects for early clinical phase trials.

4. It is a challenge to develop standard protocols to ensure the objectivity and safety of patients and research investigators due to: (1) illegality of the destruction of a human embryo to isolate embryonic stem cells, (2) investigators' biases about the highly positive outcomes of such study, and (3) desire of the participating patient to get a miracle cure [63].

14.4.5 Clinical application

The hematopoietic system consists of organs and tissues, primarily the bone marrow, spleen, tonsils, and lymph nodes involved in the production of blood. Bone marrow is found inside the large bones of our skeleton, such as the thigh bone and the pelvis (hip bone). These bone marrow stem cells in humans are capable of producing 200 billion red cells, 10 billion white cells, and 400 billion platelets per day [64]. Blood-forming stem cells (hematopoietic progenitor cells) derived from cord blood are the only stem cell-based product approved by FDA for use in the United States [65]. This is indicated for use in "unrelated donor hematopoietic progenitor cell transplantation procedures in conjunction with an appropriate preparative regimen for hematopoietic and immunologic reconstitution in patients with disorders affecting the hematopoietic system that are inherited, acquired, or result from myeloablative treatment." Thus, HPC derived from cord blood is useful in patients with disorders (such as rare genetic disorders, anemia, conditions related to HIV, sickle cell disease, and complications from chemotherapy or transfusions) affecting the hematopoietic system responsible for the production of blood. They are available as an injectable suspension for intravenous administration. Table 14.6 indicates some of the FDA-approved suppliers of cord blood-derived stem cells and vehicles needed for its administration by transfusion.

14.4.6 Administration routes and delivery systems for stem cells

Promising results have been achieved by using stem cells in many diseases including ischemia-associated cardiovascular diseases (CVD) [74]. However, there are many barriers and challenges needed to be overcome, such as identifying the most appropriate mode of delivery suitable for survival, retention, and integration of stem cells to the site of ischemia with the enhancement of revascularization and angiogenesis. Stem cells have been transplanted or administered in CVD through various routes. However, each route is associated with some advantages and limitations (Table 14.7).

Generally, the intravascularly administered stem cells exhibit poor efficiency of the migration and colonization of damaged organs. Still, researchers have not been able to understand completely the mechanisms regulating the migration and colonization of stem cells in the targeted organs. The success of SC therapy depends on its increased influx and implantation within the damaged organs for which many approaches are used [79]. The pretransplant

TABLE 14.6 Suppliers of HPC, cord blood and other ingredients needed for its administration.

Trade name	Manufacturer	FDA approval
Clevecord [66]	Cleveland Cord Blood Center	STN: BL 125594
ALLOCORD [67]	SSM Cardinal Glennon Children's Medical Center	STN: BL 125413
Ducord [68]	Duke University School of Medicine	STN: BL 125407
Hemacord [69]	New York Blood Center, Inc.	STN: BL 125397
HPC, Cord Blood No trade name	Clinimmune Labs, University of Colorado Cord Blood Bank [70]	STN: BL 125391
HPC, Cord Blood No trade name	MD Anderson Cord Blood Bank [71]	STN: BL 125657
HPC, Cord Blood No trade name	LifeSouth, Community Blood Centers, Inc. [72]	STN: BL 125432/0
HPC, Cord Blood No trade name	Bloodworks, Cord Blood Services [73]	STN: BL 125585

TABLE 14.7   Advantages and limitations of stem cells route of delivery in CVD.

Delivery route	Advantages	Limitations	References
Intracoronary artery infusion	Homogenous administration of a maximum number of cells to the damaged site	Cells do not reach to non-perfused/occluded artery, embolism might occur during infusion	[75]
Surgical intramyocardial Injection	Most preferred approach specifically in case of chronic heart failure, smaller number of stem cells needed	Increased risk of morbidity and mortality. Potential induction of arrhythmia. Need for a surgical approach	[76]
Trans-endocardial injection	Stem cells access occluded areas easily	Possibility of occurrence of myocardial perforation, cardiac tamponade, and ventricular arrhythmia	[77]
Transvenous infusion	Non-invasive simple delivery	Possible micro-embolism, low cellular migration and differentiation, homing to non-cardiac organs	[78]

conditions, such as oxygen content, cell density, and culture medium composition, of stem cells have been optimized to simulate that of the targeted organ. In another approach, the viral expression vectors are introduced into the stem cells that encode a specific protein useful for enhanced transfection. For example, increased colonization of bone marrow-derived SCs was observed if they were transduced with a retroviral vector containing the CXCR4 receptor coding sequence [80]. Similarly, the stem cell membrane is attached to some molecules (e.g., selectin family protein) helpful in binding or conjugating with the target site [81]. On the other hand, the target organ properties also have been manipulated to enhance colonization. An example of this approach is target-tissue irradiation, which causes increased influx and implantation of systemically administered stem cells in muscle, skin, intestine, and bone marrow exposed to gamma rays [82]. These approaches have been combined with formulation approaches as well.

Hydrogels based on biomaterials, such as chitosan, polylactide, polyglycolide, poly lactide-co-glycolide, and polysaccharide [83], have been used to encapsulate stem cells such as human placental-derived mesenchymal stem cells (MSCs). They are reported to exhibit sustained release of encapsulated cells with good regeneration ability [84,85]. Microencapsulation of cells generates a porous polymeric matrix that can localize the stem cells in a protected environment and enable the exchange of nutrients and waste products between the encapsulated cells and the surrounding tissue to maintain stem cells viability [86].

14.5 Emerging role of pharmacogenomics in precision medicine

> **OBJECTIVES**
> - Define personalized (precision) medicine.
> - Describe pharmacogenomics (PGx) approach
> - Discuss pharmacokinetic (PK) and pharmacodynamics (PD)
> - Discuss briefly epigenetics and phenoconversion
> - Introduce PGx resources

14.5.1 Introduction

Medication selection has always been influenced by various factors such as the age of a patient, kidney function, ethnicity, and body weight to name a few. In 2015, when President Barack Obama launched the Precision Medicine

Initiative, an added factor of genetics turned out to play a big role in further personalizing patients' medications [89]. The healthcare system is moving away from the "one size fits all" approach or the trial-and-error process especially when it comes to mental health prescribing.

STAR*D Trial was one of the largest depression studies conducted with $35-million-dollar funding by the National Institute of Health (NIH) with over 4000 patients enrolled. Below is a summary of the findings of the study [90].

- There is no one medication that is best to treat depression
- About half of the patients did not respond the first time in the first trial
- The remission rate dropped with each consecutive treatment option

Why does this matter? Because depression is one of the most common mental health disorders in the United States. It is estimated that 19.4 million adults have at least one depressive episode. The Covid-19 pandemic has further exacerbated mental health for millions of people [91]. Depression is treatable yet less than 50% of the population receive treatment. Some barriers to treatment are lack of access, low response or remission rates, and non-adherence due to adverse events [92].

The current mental health prescribing is a trial-and-error process where an antidepressant is selected based on its side effect profile combined with the clinical judgment and experience of a prescriber. Antidepressants take about 4–6 weeks for their full effect to be shown. After that "trial" period of 4–6 weeks, the patient is either switched to a different medication, augmented with another, or the dosage of the same medication is changed. The patient is expected to wait for another 4–6 weeks to see if the medication regimen is effective. This continues till the right medications are selected. This trial-and-error process can take months to get a patient to stable mental status [93,94].

Not every patient has mild depression and can afford to wait months before feeling better. Some may be suicidal, or on the verge of losing their job or their relationships. The longer it takes a patient to start feeling better, the less adherent they can become to the medication [95] as seen in the STAR*D Trial. The key is trying to find ways to select the *right* medication at the *start* of the treatment and avoid the months of trial that the patient has to go through.

14.5.2 Factors affecting metabolism

The PGx combines the science of pharmacology and genomics to personalize patients' medications. Based on a person's genomic makeup, we can predict which medication can be more effective or potentially cause more adverse effects. Precision medicine is the umbrella that PGx falls under. There are many factors that go into personalizing patient's medications. Let us look at some of the main elements of precision medicine.

- **Age**—A 6-month-old would not be given the same drug or dose as a 66-year-old [96].
- **Kidney function**—The dose of the drug would need to be altered depending on the kidney function [97].
- **Timing of a medication**—knowing when to properly take a medication can be the difference in the increase, decrease, or lack in efficacy [98].
- **Drug–drug interaction**—Taking multiple medications that interact with each other may cause more harm than benefit [99].
- PGx—At the center of precision medicine [100].
- **Epigenetics**—Various environmental factors or social behaviors can affect the way our genes work which can alter drug metabolism [101].
- **Phenoconversion**—A mismatch between a patient's expected phenotype based on genotype and the actual phenotype. This is further discussed in the later sections of this chapter [102].

14.5.3 Pharmacogenomics in personalized medicine

Personalized medicine refers to a shift away from a "one size fits all" approach to treating and caring for patients with a specific disorder in favor of one that employs new techniques to better manage patients' health and target therapies to ensure the best possible outcome in managing a patient's disease or propensity for disease. The basis for personalized medicine can really be traced back to Hippocrates (460–370 BCE), who stated, "It is much more important to know what individual the disease has than what disease the individual has," integrating the patient-centric definition [103].

Precision Medicine is a novel approach that uses the genetic variability found in individuals, the effects of the environment, and lifestyle factors to tailor the prevention of disease and drug therapy treatment [104]. Precision medicine uses the information attained from specific gene mutations to look at an individual from a more holistic viewpoint [105].

Precision, personalized, stratified, and individualized medicine are terms that are frequently used interchangeably [106]. Precision medicine has the potential to significantly decrease the global burden of non-communicable diseases [107]. It is better considered as an evolution rather than a revolution in medicine because it is unlikely to replace conventional therapy and may significantly improve it. Over the past 50 years, the field of PGx has developed with the goal of defining the genetic/genomic basis of drug actions. In terms of host toxicity and treatment efficacy, there is a lot of variation in how different people react to drugs [108]. Significant inter-individual heterogeneity in drug response is largely due to genetic variations in an individual's ability to respond to drugs.

There are at least seven key "pillars" of precision medicine: diagnostics, prediction (of the primary disease), prevention (of the primary disease), prognostics (prediction of secondary disease), personalized treatment (PGx, and targeted therapy in the case of cancer), monitoring (of behavior, risk exposure, treatment response, and disease progression), participatory (of patients, citizens, and healthcare professionals) [109]. PGx is one of the most important pillars of Precision Medicine that can predict the response of a medication based on the likelihood of creating less side effects and better efficacy [110].

PGx is currently suggested for a small number of drugs that cover multiple specialties including cardiology, allergy and immunology, dermatology, endocrinology, gastroenterology, infectious diseases, nephrology, neurology, oncology, pediatrics, psychiatry, anesthetics, respiratory medicine, and rheumatology. The use of medications is increasing as people live longer lives and have multiple long-term conditions. For example, in England alone, the National Health Service (NHS) delivered well over a billion prescription drugs in 2015, a figure that was 50% higher than in 2005 [111]. Pharmacogenetics and pharmacogenomics are terms that are frequently used interchangeably [112]. There have been substantial breakthroughs in our understanding of the significance of genetic variants in pharmacokinetics and pharmacodynamics to variation in medication response over the last decade.

There are roughly 21,000 protein-coding genes in the human genome [113]. The single-nucleotide polymorphism (SNP), which is described as single-base changes across individuals, is now the most frequent variation. Polymorphisms are commonly seen in genes encoding drug metabolism, drug transporter, and drug-target proteins [114]. Scientists can now use the DNA to do more robust research, thanks to the Human Genome Project which sequenced over 20,000 human genes.

The genes associated with the PGx response to medications are divided into five categories: Genes involved in disease pathogenesis; Drug action mechanisms (enzymes, receptors, transporters, messengers); Drug metabolism (phase I—II reaction enzymes); Drug transporters; and Pleiotropic genes engaged in complex cascades and metabolic responses [115,116]. Some of those genes work through the PK and PD pathways [117]. Since then, over 120 drugs have been mentioned with a PGx indication in their package inserts, and newer drugs currently in development are incorporating genetics testing to be included as part of the phases [118]. An example of this is the common antidepressant, Citalopram, a Selective Serotonin Reuptake Inhibitor (SSRI) with a boxed warning of reduction in dose for patients who cannot metabolize as efficiently based on a liver enzyme CYP2C19 and avoiding a higher dose than 20 mg/day in those individuals due to QT prolongation [119]. Warfarin is an example of PK and PD, which are influenced by both the *CYP2C9* and *VKORC1* genotypes.

To understand how PGx helps with clinical decisions and medication selection, we need to know to go back to the structure of DNA. As one may recall DNA is made up of nucleic acids Adenine (A), Guanine (G), Cytosine (C), and Thymine (T) that pair together. A sequence of these base pairs creates a gene that can code for a certain protein. Any mispairing within the gene, called Single Nucleotide Polymorphism (SNPs), can cause a downstream effect by creating a *different* set of proteins. PGX is focused on germline and mitochondrial DNA variation. It excludes somatic genetic mutations, which are changes that occur after conception or arise in a clonal manner in a cancer. In targeted therapies of cancer, somatic gene driver mutations, information is successfully used [120,121].

Each individual carries two alleles inherited from each parent [120]. The genotype can be named based on the allele naming system or the base pairing such as *2/*3 or C/T, respectively. These "symbols" are giving a scoring system that translated into four different phenotypes: Normal Metabolizer or Extensive Metabolizer (NM or EM), Intermediate Metabolizer (IM), Poor Metabolizer (PM), or Ultra-rapid Metabolizer (UM) [122]. PGx uses a star nomenclature (e.g., CYP2C19*2) to designate gene variations as a way to identify PGx biomarkers and effectively communicate patient's genotype and predicated phenotype [123].

One can start to see and appreciate the value of personalized medicine and how it can play a part in every aspect of an individual's life. There is tremendous value in the use of PGx when it comes to a clinical setting. However, it is vital to understand that PGx is just a piece of the entire picture of precision medicine and not the sole answer. It is used to guide therapy. Imagine one goes to a doctor's office with complain of feeling lethargic. The doctor would need bits and pieces of information to be able to detect the underlying issue. After asking various types of questions such as how long the patient has felt this way or if anything new going on in his/her life, the provider may order some blood work. The provider would want to check patient's B_{12} levels, total complete blood count (CBC) count, vitamin D level, and thyroid levels. All those pieces are needed to paint a better and bigger picture to be able to make a comprehensive clinical decision and treat accordingly.

Consider precision medicine as part of the bigger picture and PGx as a part of that entire clinical decision-making process. This is why when a PGx test is done and the test reports are looked at, it cannot be taken at face value and used solely to make a comprehensive decision. It must be used in conjunction with knowing the patient and personalizing the patient's medication. If used appropriately, precision medicine can provide valuable information that can be used in any clinical setting such as oncology, cardiovascular, and more. Mental health has been mentioned in this section as it has gained momentum due to increased incidence and therefore, needs an urgent attention to treat this complex disease.

14.5.4 Drug metabolism

Defining metabolism is important before moving forward. The biotransformation of a drug is called metabolism. Most medications pass through the liver to be metabolized or converted to a more water-soluble or smaller compound to be excreted out of the body easier. Most medications are in their active form, meaning when ingested they cause their therapeutic effect. On the other hand, an inactive form of a drug needs to get activated in the liver to show its effect followed by getting metabolized at the end. The primary factors that metabolize medications in the liver are the group of Cytochrome P450 (CYP) class of enzymes [124,125]. These CYP450 enzymes fall under the PK pathways that define the movement of a drug in the body from the time of absorption or ingestion to its excretion. In simpler terms, what the *body* does to a drug. The term that defines this process is called ADME.

ADME stands for.

Absorption: from site of administration to site of action
Distribution: transfer from one location to another
Metabolism: chemical reactions to facilitate removal
Excretion: removal of a drug from the body

Both the pharmacokinetics (drug absorption, metabolism, distribution, and excretion) and the pharmacodynamic (drug targets such as receptors, enzymes, and ion channels) aspects of a drug can be influenced by genetic variability.

The Food and Drug Administration (FDA) published a table containing over 50 gene-drug interactions that it claims are supported by scientific evidence, as well as an announcement that it is considering novel strategies to test pharmacogenetic associations. Patient outcomes, PK, and PD information are all included in FDA data [126]. If the CYP enzyme metabolizes a medication slowly in comparison to "normal," it is then called a PM. This can cause the drug to hang around longer in the body versus a UM that is getting rid of that drug more quickly than "normal" and not allowing the body to retain it, causing a potential decrease in the serum levels in the body. Therefore, for a PM status, a decrease in the dose of that active drug may be indicated versus a potential increase in dose for a UM status may be more appropriate to create the optimal therapeutic effect [125].

In the case of inactive medication, the scenario may be reversed. A very common pain medication, codeine as an example. Codeine by itself has no analgesic effect. It uses the CYP2D6 enzyme to get converted to morphine to cause pain relief [127]. Therefore, a PM status may not get pain relief versus a UM that might be converting too quickly, attaining higher serum concentration levels, and experiencing the toxicity or side effects profile of morphine, the active form of codeine (Fig. 14.7).

PD is also another process that needs mentioning. Simply stated, it is what the drug does to the body. For a drug to be able to produce its effect, drugs interact with biological structures such as transporters or receptors on the pre- and postsynaptic neurons, respectively [128].

FIGURE 14.7 Pharmacokinetic pathway of codeine.

14.5.5 Epigenetics and phenoconversion

Our genes do not change but sometimes environmental factors or behaviors such as stress or smoking can affect the way our genes respond *without* altering the DNA sequence. This is called "epigenetics" where epi means in addition to [129]. Another factor that can affect the way medications work is called phenoconversion. This can be considered a transient change from one phenotype to another creating a different clinical outcome. This phenomenon is usually achieved by co-administering different medications that can impact the way each of them works [100,130].

Most medications are already in their active form and are metabolized to be eliminated. There are some medications that are inactive or pro-drugs where the same CYP enzymes would activate them so they can have their therapeutic effect *before* they are eliminated. Thus, there are two different types of drugs, active versus pro-drugs [131].

Tamoxifen is metabolized by CYP2D6 to active metabolites. The clinical PGx implementation consortium (CPIC) guidelines recommend considering aromatase inhibitors rather than tamoxifen in patients who carry two no function alleles due to the reduced effectiveness of tamoxifen in these patients. As described earlier, the CYP2D6 enzyme converts codeine to its active metabolite morphine using CYP2D6 enzyme. If an individual's CYP2D6 status is an NM, the conversion from codeine to morphine can be achieved. If, however, a drug is added that *inhibits* the activity of CYP2D6, the ability of codeine to convert can be diminished changing NM to PM. A classic inhibitor of CYP2D6 enzyme is fluoxetine. Fluoxetine uses CYP2D6 as its main enzyme to metabolize but it also inhibits its own metabolism (Fig. 14.8). This creates a loop of metabolism, inhibition, metabolism, inhibition and that is why fluoxetine has a long half-life, staying in the body for a long time [132].

There are other factors that can influence the change in a phenotype such as environmental factors like smoking [133] or other supplements such as classic grapefruit juice [134], to name a few. It is vital to understand that drug-drug interaction is more than just two medications with the same mechanism of action but can diminish or amplify the effects of the other in many ways.

There are also non-metabolizing enzymes that influence drug pharmacodynamics. CYP450s such as the *CYP2D6* mentioned earlier are part of the PK genes. Serotonin transporters and receptors, as examples, are considered PD genes. The serotonin transporter gene called *SLC6A4* has been the most studied as a potential factor in the efficacy of SSRIs. It's important to understand how SSRIs work at a molecular level to understand what it means when there is a variation in the transporter gene [135].

Neurons communicate with each other through chemicals. A presynaptic neuron is where the production or storage of neurotransmitters (NT) occurs and postsynaptic is where the NT is received to cause an action [136]. In the presynaptic neuron, serotonin is stored in the vesicles (shown below) and when triggered, they are released into the synaptic space, when they move to attach to the serotonin receptors on the post-synaptic cell or the receiving end. To recycle the serotonin, it is picked back up by the serotonin transporter, demonstrated by the two bolded parallel lines, and put back into their vesicles for when they are needed [137] (Fig. 14.9).

The mechanism by which SSRIs function, is to block the reuptake transporter to prevent the recycling of serotonin leaving more of this neurotransmitter in the synaptic space between the two neurons. The gene, *SLC6A4*, is thought to regulate how many transporters are produced. A genetic variation in this gene can cause lower production of these transporters causing less transporters that the SSRI would block, which may lead to a decrease in the efficacy of SSRIs [138]. This transporter is just one example of how variations in PK and PD genes can be used to predict clinical outcomes by gaining a better insight into the efficacy or incidence of adverse events of a drug.

14.5.6 Role of pharmacists and the future perspective

Pharmacists are well equipped and should be part of an interdisciplinary team of providers that can guide clinicians. All pharmacists should learn the basics of PGx so they are able to use it as another added piece to medication

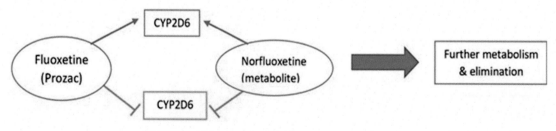

FIGURE 14.8 Pharmacokinetic pathway of fluoxetine.

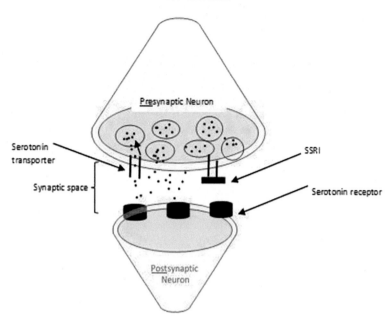

FIGURE 14.9 Neuronal communication.

therapy management (MTM) to optimize their patient outcomes. Pharmacists should be able to educate healthcare professionals, patients, and organizations that treat patients about PGx. Education is key to a lot of the barriers to the adoption of PGx. Some of the barriers for both patients and clinicians can be the cost, lack of integration into the electronic health records (EHR), time to spend with patients interpreting the results, and lack of PGx experts to educate various healthcare professionals.

14.5.7 Resources

Just as there are guidelines to each chronic condition such as diabetes or hypertension, there are guidelines for PGx as well. For example, if a patient is a PM for a particular CYP450 enzyme, there are guidelines on how a medication may be dosed. Below are the top two most commonly used resources to learn more:

1. CPIC

An online knowledge-based site that was started in the year 2000 by volunteers that are dedicated to facilitating the adoption and implementation of PGx. It holds multiple peer-reviewed, evidence-based guidelines along with published journals to support it which is funded by NIH (http://cpicpgx.org).

2. PGx knowledgebase (PhamGKB)

An online knowledge-based searchable database is full of literature that works in conjunction with CPIC but also provides the pathways of many PK and PD genes in a nice graphic layout. It is also funded by NIH but managed by Stanford University since its start in the year 2000 (http://pharmgkb.org).

14.6 Conclusions

In the post-genomic era, these emerging therapeutics such as siRNA, mRNA-based drugs, gene-based therapies, and immunotherapy are rapidly growing and becoming part of the pharmaceutical market. These drugs have demonstrated their utilization in personalized medicine and other rare diseases, cancer, autoimmune disease, and genetic disease. There are some challenges associated with delivery and stability of these emerging therapeutics. However advances in novel drug delivery methods and strategies of improving their stability, will lead to tremendous growth of these emerging therapeutics. These therapeutics in coming decades will provide prevention and treatment for many diseases that are incurable now.

The cell and gene therapies represent advanced approaches that offer a potential one-time treatment and their effects could last long term or permanently for treating many chronic conditions. The full potential of CGT products is only just beginning to be realized and has the potential to offer longer-lasting or permanent cure to diseases. Although, there are still several challenges to be addressed including the high prices, long-term safety, and efficacy. However, cell and gene therapy-related research and product development in the United States continue to draw a lot of interest and the field is growing at a fast rate that could lead to multiple commercial products in the next 5—10 years [30]. The clinical success of cell and gene therapy products require close collaboration of physicians, pharmacists, and other healthcare professionals. Thus, it is essential to train Pharmacists and other healthcare professionals involved to handle this new class of medical products to ensure therapeutic success and safety of patients and healthcare professionals involved.

Stem cell therapies may offer the potential to treat diseases or conditions for which few treatments exist. Sometimes called the body's "master cells," stem cells are the cells that develop into blood, brain, bones, and all of the body's organs. They have the potential to repair, restore, replace, and regenerate cells, and could possibly be used to treat many medical conditions and diseases. However, there are many fraudulent and unscrupulous claims about curing many diseases by using stem cells. Hence, anyone planning to use any service provided by a stem cell clinic should verify whether it is FDA-approved or being studied under an Investigational New Drug Application (IND).

PGx is a key component on the path to precision medicine. The pharmacogenetic components include pathogenic, mechanistic, transporter, and metabolic genes that encode for effectors (enzymes, proteins) involved in drug metabolism. The field of PGx has explained common gene variants with large impact sizes. Genetic variations in pharmacokinetics and pharmacodynamics pathways frequently impact drug efficacy, adverse drug reaction (ADR), and dose adjustment like warfarin, which are influenced by both the *CYP2C9* and *VKORC1* genotypes. Variability in drug response, especially in toxicity risk, is a near unavoidable feature of the therapeutic approach which has an outstanding genetic component.

The first step in the implementation and adoption of any new knowledge is education. Healthcare professionals such as pharmacists, general practitioners, and nurses need to be educated on precision medicine for more individualized clinical decision-making.

Case studies

Case 14.1

A patient who took the COVID-19 vaccination and had a lab test done for checking protective antibodies against the COVID virus. From the patient's history, you came to know that the patient has taken Ibuprofen before taking the vaccination. The lab results indicate low serum antibodies. What could be the reason for less antibodies generation and immune response.

Approach: Taking non-steroidal anti-inflammatory drug such as Ibuprofen may compromise the immune response against the virus and the production of protective antibodies may be minimized (https://www.verywellhealth.com/pain-reliever-covid-19-vaccine-5111319). The patient took Ibuprofen before getting the shot of COVID-19 which may be the reason for less immunity. A study on mice indicates (https://pubmed.ncbi.nlm.nih.gov/33441348/) that the use of NSAID drugs such as ibuprofen before COVID-19 exposure reduces the production of protective antibodies and inflammatory response.

Case 14.2

What are some of the considerations as a hospital pharmacist you will take if a patient will be having IV infusions of siRNA drug patrisan and undergoing preinfusion of anti-inflammatory medicines? Why is the pre-infusion of anti-inflammatory drugs with siRNA drug administration?

Approach: The drug patrisan is a unique drug belonging to siRNA drug. As it is an RNA drug which is prone to degradation by ubiquitous RNase enzymes, it is enclosed in lipid nanoparticles (LNPs) to prevent its degradation. However, the excipient used in the LNPs can trigger their own immune response and induce inflammation. Therefore, the patient must be started with pre-infusion of anti-inflammatory drugs such as steroid, acetaminophen, antihistamine to reduce the probability of having inflammation and immune response.

Case 14.3

A 57-year-old woman with follicular lymphoma developed profound fatigue and hypercalcemia. A PET scan and a bone marrow biopsy found that she now has diffuse large B-cell lymphoma (DLBCL). Over the following 18 months, she was treated with three different chemotherapy regimens, all with a mixed response but ultimately progressive disease. Can CAR T-cell therapy be useful in this cae? How can you explain it?

Approach: Due to the relapsed or refractory disease, she is not eligible for an autologous stem cell transplant, and she had been started on rituximab and lenalidomide. She was also eligible for an anti-CD19 chimeric antigen receptor (CAR) T-cell therapy. She received Yescarta CAR T-cell infusion that she tolerated remarkably well. Within a month, her PET scan showed that she had achieved a complete response, and by 6 weeks she was back to normal activity. She is now 1 year from her treatment and her scans show an ongoing remission and she feels better and is back to work and doing regular activities.

Case 14.4

A newborn boy presented at his 3-month-old check-up with significant weight loss (30th percentile) despite no feeding difficulties or intercurrent illness. On examination, he was noted to have poor head control and was referred to the neurologist for evaluation. His parents reported no developmental regression but did confirm delayed milestone acquisition. Can gene therapy work in this case?

Approach: Upon neurologic evaluation, the patient was found to have significant generalized hypotonia with diaphragmatic respiration and absent reflexes. He was admitted to the hospital for further neurologic workup with suspected Spinal Muscular Atrophy (SMA). Genetic testing confirmed SMA with a mutated survival motor neuron 1 (SMN1) gene. He was started on Nusinersen (Spinraza) within 2 weeks of diagnosis.

Following the initiation of Nusinersen, he was slowly acquiring new milestones with an improved tone. He required no respiratory support at that time. At 9 months old, he developed acute respiratory failure and biphasic noninvasive ventilatory support (NIV) was initiated. He was discharged with the home ventilator to be used noninvasively during sleep. With intercurrent respiratory illnesses, he would require NIV continuously for a few days. No further hospitalizations occurred. He received gene therapy with Zolgensma at 12 months old and continued with his quarterly Nusinersen treatment.

The patient is now almost 3 years old and has not been hospitalized since 7 months old. He continues to display significant improvements in his overall motor function. He can independently propel his wheelchair and can stand using a stander. His bulbar muscle strength has improved to the point where he is now safely tolerating small oral feeds with gastrostomy tube supplementation. Furthermore, his most recent polysomnogram showed no evidence of sleep-disordered breathing or alveolar hypoventilation.

Case 14.5

Mr. Gass suffered stroke couple of years ago. He visits the clinic of Dr. John Chi, the director of Neurosurgical Spine Cancer at Brigham and Women's Hospital in Boston. His current symptoms include severe pain at the lower back area radiating to other lower parts of the body, the pain was becoming worse at night. When Dr. Chi surgically opened the lower spine, he was aghast to find it entirely filled with a huge mass of tissues that he had never seen before [87]. What could be the rationale for it.

Approach: The tissue samples were sent for testing whether it consisted of tumor cells. The test reports showed that the mass was made up of abnormal, primitive cells that were growing very aggressively. On further investigation, it was a shock to find these cells did not come from Mr. Gass but they were someone else's cells.

A closer look at patient's profile and further discussion with him indicated that he traveled to Mexico, China, and Argentina to get stem cell injections in a desperate attempt to recover from a stroke he had a couple of years ago. There are a growing number of unregulated clinics in many foreign countries claiming that they can treat, even cure, diseases such as strokes, muscular dystrophy, and spinal cord injury by injecting patients with stem cells. Theoretically stem cells can develop into a missing nerve, a muscle, or other cells and repair damage from an illness or an injury. However, such claims have not been verified with rigorous scientific studies and clinical trials. As stem cells divide very rapidly, there are reports that can quickly accumulate cancerous mutations forming tumors in laboratory animals.

Case 14.6

History of present illness: A 39-year-old female was admitted to the hospital with signs of restlessness and uncontrollable muscle movements.

Health conditions: History of bipolar, depression, and migraine

Current medications: Aripiprazole (Abilify) 400 mg daily, bupropion (Wellbutrin) 150 mg daily, and Rimegepant (NurtecODT) 75 mg daily as needed.

A PGx test was recommended by the treating clinician at the hospital, which revealed the following:

PGx test results: Gene CYP2D6 PM

Based on aripiprazole's package label, individuals with a CYP2D6 PM status should be given half the usual starting dose due to the risk for increased adverse events.

Explanation: In this case, due to being a PM status, the serum concentration of aripiprazole can increase due to decreased metabolism. The patient's dose was decreased in half from 400 to 200 mg at the hospital and was sent home. The patient was advised to follow up with his treating provider.

Case 14.7

History of present illness: A 43-year-old male was prescribed acetaminophen and codeine (Tylenol #3) for pain associated with his broken leg from a motorcycle accident. He had been using it for 4 days with no pain relief and when he ran out, his provider sent over a refill to his local pharmacy. The pharmacist reviewing the order denied his prescription assuming he is a drug seeker. The pharmacist on duty recommended a PGx test from the treating provider since the patient was keen on being a first-time narcotic user.

Health conditions: History of depression and new onset of pain due to his recent accident

Current medications: Fluoxetine (Prozac) 40 mg daily, acetaminophen and codeine (Tylenol #3) 325 mg every 4–6 h as needed

PGx test results: Gene CYP2D6 EM

Codeine found in Tylenol #3 is an inactive medication or a prodrug. This means it requires activation in the body to morphine by using CYP2D6 enzyme. Since the patient is an extensive or normal metabolizer, he is able to convert efficiently. However, fluoxetine also uses the same CYP2D6 enzyme to metabolize but also inhibits CYP2D6 or its own metabolism at the same time. The co-administration of the two medications can create a phenomenon called phenoconversion, which can block the conversion of codeine to morphine causing inadequate pain relief in this patient.

Explanation: In this case, the patient was switched to morphine and kept on fluoxetine as prescribed.

Critical reflections and practice applications

Emerging therapeutics such as siRNA-based therapy, mRNA-based therapeutics, cell and gene therapy, stem cell therapy, and immunotherapy are rapidly growing. Research and biotechnology advances have led several of these drugs to be approved by FDA and be part of pharmaceutical markets. These therapeutics have shown significant and unique therapeutic potential for the treatment of rare diseases, cancer, metabolic disorder, autoimmune diseases, and genetic disorders. Some of the relevant points about their utility in clinical pharmacy are noted below.

- A pharmacist working in health care settings can provide specific recommendations related to siRNA drugs, mRNA drugs, and immunotherapy drugs
- Understanding of the mechanism of action, structure, and stability of these drugs can better equip a clinical pharmacist to counsel the patient about safety, efficacy, stability, and storage of these molecular therapeutics
- Understanding this specialized medicine in genetic disorders, cancer, and rare disease can also provide knowledge when dispensing personalized or precision medicine.
- Cell and gene therapies have the potential to change the treatment of diseases, especially for those with limited or no treatment options. However, there is a need to study long-term risks to patients.
- Currently there are only a few FDA-approved cell and gene therapy products, but it is anticipated that dozens of new products to be approved in the next 5–10 years.
- While the initial focus has been primarily on oncology and monogenetic disorders, extensive research and development are ongoing to develop CGT products for other therapeutic areas including neurodegenerative diseases, diabetes, cardiovascular diseases, infectious diseases, and ophthalmology.

- It is critical for pharmacists, especially health system pharmacists, to understand the complexity of CGT products and other unique product-specific requirements to ensure therapeutic success and safety of patients and healthcare professionals involved.
- Long-term follow-up studies for 15 years are required for these products due to the long-acting nature of these products.
- Cell and gene therapy products require ultra-cold storage temperatures throughout the shelf life and require special handling to preserve the activity of the cells and gene therapy products to achieve the desired biological effect.
- The use of CGT products requires close collaboration between the pharmacist, physician, and other healthcare professionals to prepare the patient and coordinate the timing of dose preparation because these products are required to be administered within a short period of time after preparation.
- Currently, there is only one FDA-approved stem cell-based product for hematopoietic reconstitution.
- The safety and efficacy of the use of stem cells derived from peripheral or cord blood, or bone marrow for hematopoietic reconstitution are well established.
- Extensive research is going on using stem cells derived from a wide range of sources such as adipose tissue to treat multiple orthopedic, neurologic, and other diseases.
- Stem cells derived from autologous or allogeneic sources are being investigated for potential clinical applications.
- Stem cell therapy is not a miracle cure and needs rigorous scientific investigation before it can be used clinically [64,88].
- Clinical applications of PGx would provide safer medicine in a customized dose as per patient's metabolic profile.

References

[1] M.M. Zhang, R. Bahal, T.P. Rasmussen, J.E. Manautou, X.B. Zhong, The growth of siRNA-based therapeutics: updated clinical studies, Biochem. Pharmacol. 189 (2021) 114432, https://doi.org/10.1016/j.bcp.2021.114432. Epub 2021 Jan 26. PMID: 33513339; PMCID: PMC8187268.

[2] H. Wood, FDA approves patisiran to treat hereditary transthyretin amyloidosis, Nat. Rev. Neurol. 14 (10) (2018) 570.

[3] R.L. Setten, J.J. Rossi, S.P. Han, The current state and future directions of RNAi-based therapeutics, Nat. Rev. Drug Discov. 18 (6) (2019) 421−446 [PubMed: 30846871].

[4] H. Dana, et al., Molecular mechanisms and biological functions of siRNA, Int. J. Biomed. Sci. 13 (2) (2017) 48−57 [PubMed: 28824341].

[5] S.F. Dowdy, Overcoming cellular barriers for RNA therapeutics, Nat. Biotechnol. 35 (3) (2017) 222−229 [PubMed: 28244992].

[6] S. Gao, et al., The effect of chemical modification and nanoparticle formulation on stability and biodistribution of siRNA in mice, Mol. Ther. 17 (7) (2009) 1225−1233.

[7] E. Blanco, H. Shen, M. Ferrari, Principles of nanoparticle design for overcoming biological barriers to drug delivery, Nat. Biotechnol. 33 (9) (2015) 941−951 [PubMed: 26348965].

[8] B. Hu, et al., Therapeutic siRNA: state of the art, Signal Transduct. Targeted Ther. 5 (1) (2020) 101.

[9] Y. Sun, et al., Enhancing the therapeutic delivery of oligonucleotides by chemical modification and nanoparticle encapsulation, Molecules 22 (10) (2017).

[10] P. Guo, O. Coban, N.M. Snead, J. Trebley, S. Hoeprich, S. Guo, et al., Engineering RNA for targeted siRNA delivery and medical application, Adv. Drug Deliv. Rev. 62 (6) (2010) 650−666.

[11] Y. Gao, X.L. Liu, X.R. Li, Research progress on siRNA delivery with nonviral carriers, Int. J. Nanomed. 6 (2011) 1017−1025.

[12] T.S. Zatsepin, Y.V. Kotelevtsev, V. Koteliansky, Lipid nanoparticles for targeted siRNA delivery - going from bench to bedside, Int. J. Nanomed. 11 (2016) 3077−3086, https://doi.org/10.2147/IJN.S106625. PMID: 27462152; PMCID: PMC4939975.

[13] I.S. Padda, A.U. Mahtani, M. Parmar, Small Interfering RNA (siRNA) Based Therapy. [Updated 2022 Jul 12]. in: StatPearls [Internet], StatPearls Publishing, Treasure Island (FL), 2022. Available from: https://www.ncbi.nlm.nih.gov/books/NBK580472/.

[14] K.K.W. To, W.C.S. Cho, An overview of rational design of mRNA-based therapeutics and vaccines, Expet Opin. Drug Discov. 16 (11) (2021) 1307−1317, https://doi.org/10.1080/17460441.2021.1935859.

[15] S. Qin, X. Tang, Y. Chen, K. Chen, N. Fan, W. Xiao, Q. Zheng, G. Li, Y. Teng, M. Wu, X. Song, mRNA-based therapeutics: powerful and versatile tools to combat diseases, Signal Transduct. Targeted Ther. 7 (1) (2022) 166, https://doi.org/10.1038/s41392-022-01007-w. PMID: 35597779; PMCID: PMC9123296.

[16] P.S. Kowalski, A. Rudra, L. Miao, D.G. Anderson, Delivering the messenger: advances in technologies for therapeutic mRNA delivery, Mol. Ther. 27 (4) (2019) 710−728, https://doi.org/10.1016/j.ymthe.2019.02.012. Epub 2019 Feb 19. PMID: 30846391; PMCID: PMC6453548.

[17] B. Bhat, S. Karve, D.G. Anderson, mRNA therapeutics: beyond vaccine applications, Trends Mol. Med. 27 (9) (2021) 923−924, https://doi.org/10.1016/j.molmed.2021.05.004. Epub 2021 Jun 23. PMID: 34172390.

[18] J.D. Beck, D. Reidenbach, N. Salomon, U. Sahin, Ö. Türeci, M. Vormehr, L.M. Kranz, mRNA therapeutics in cancer immunotherapy, Mol. Cancer 20 (1) (2021) 69, https://doi.org/10.1186/s12943-021-01348-0. PMID: 33858437; PMCID: PMC8047518.

[19] U. Sahin, K. Kariko, O. Tureci, mRNA-based therapeutics—developing a new class of drugs, Nat. Rev. Drug Discov. 13 (2014) 759−780.

[20] S. Akkın, G. Varan, E. Bilensoy, A review on cancer immunotherapy and applications of nanotechnology to chemoimmunotherapy of different cancers, Molecules 26 (2021) 3382, https://doi.org/10.3390/molecules26113382.

[21] H. Borghaei, M.R. Smith, K.S. Campbell, Immunotherapy of cancer, Eur. J. Pharmacol. 625 (2009) 41−54.

[22] NCI-Types of Cancer Treatment, (Accessed on 07/31/2022) https://www.cancer.gov/about-cancer/treatment.

[23] M.W. Rohaan, S. Wilgenhof, J.B.A.G. Haanen, Adoptive cellular therapies: the current landscape, Virchows Arch. 474 (2019) 449—461.

[24] C.E. Handy, E.S. Antonarakis, Sipuleucel-T for the treatment of prostate cancer: novel insights and future directions, Future Oncol. 14 (2018) 907—917.

[25] American Society of Gene and Cell Therapy, Gene and Cell Therapy FAQ's, 2022. https://www.asgct.org/education/gene-and-cell-therapy-faqs. (Accessed 28 July 2022).

[26] R. Maldonado, S. Jalil, K. Wartiovaara, Curative gene therapies for rare diseases, J Community Genet 12 (2) (2021) 267—276, https://doi.org/10.1007/s12687-020-00480-6.

[27] C.E. Dunbar, K.A. High, J.K. Joung, D.B. Kohn, K. Ozawa, M. Sadelain, Gene therapy comes of age, Science (6372) (January 12, 2018) 359.

[28] Statement from FDA commissioner Scott Gottlieb, M.D. and Peter Marks, M.D., Ph.D., Director of the Center for Biologics Evaluation and Research on New Policies to Advance Development of Safe and Effective Cell and Gene Therapies Retrieved From, https://www.fda.gov/news-events/press-announcements/statement-fda-commissioner-scott-gottlieb-md-and-peter-marks-md-phd-director-center-biologics.

[29] J. Petrich, D. Marchese, C. Jenkins, M. Storey, J. Blind, Gene replacement therapy: a primer for the health-system pharmacist, J. Pharm. Pract. 33 (6) (2020) 846—855.

[30] C.M. Young, C. Quinn, M.R. Trusheim, Durable cell and gene therapy potential patient and financial impact: US projections of product approvals, patients treated, and product revenues, Drug Discov. Today 27 (1) (2022) 17—30.

[31] Gene therapy needs a long-term approach, Nat. Med. 27 (4) (April 2021) 563.

[32] B. Thorne, R. Takeya, F. Vitelli, X. Swanson, Gene therapy, Adv. Biochem. Eng. Biotechnol. 165 (2018) 351—399.

[33] A.L. Gimpel, G. Katsikis, S. Sha, A.J. Maloney, M.S. Hong, T.N.T. Nguyen, J. Wolfrum, S.L. Springs, A.J. Sinskey, S.R. Manalis, P.W. Barone, R.D. Braatz, Analytical methods for process and product characterization of recombinant adeno-associated virus-based gene therapies, Mol Ther Methods Clin Dev 20 (2021) 740—754.

[34] U.S. Food and Drug Administration, Guidance for Industry, Long-Term Follow-Up after Administration of Human Gene Therapy Products, 2020. https://www.fda.gov/regulatory-information/search-fda-guidance-documents/long-term-follow-after-administration-human-gene-therapy-products.

[35] A. Bazinet, G. Popradi, A general practitioner's guide to hematopoietic stem-cell transplantation, Curr. Oncol. 26 (3) (2019) 187—191.

[36] S. Berglund, I. Magalhaes, A. Gaballa, B. Vanherberghen, M. Uhlin, Advances in umbilical cord blood cell therapy: the present and the future, Expet Opin. Biol. Ther. 17 (6) (2017) 691—699.

[37] R.C. Sterner, R.M. Sterner, CAR-T cell therapy: current limitations and potential strategies, Blood Cancer J. 11 (4) (2021) 69.

[38] B.L. Levine, J. Miskin, K. Wonnacott, C. Keir, Global manufacturing of CAR T cell therapy, Mol Ther Methods Clin Dev 4 (2016) 92—101.

[39] C.H. June, R.S. O'Connor, O.U. Kawalekar, et al., CAR T cell immunotherapy for human cancer, Science 359 (2018) 1361—1365.

[40] K.J. Caldwell, S. Gottschalk, A.C. Talleur, Allogeneic CAR cell therapy-more than a pipe dream, Front. Immunol. 11 (2021) 618427.

[41] J.T. Bulcha, Y. Wang, H. Ma, P.W.L. Tai, G. Gao, Viral vector platforms within the gene therapy landscape, Signal Transduct. Targeted Ther. 6 (1) (2021) 53.

[42] J.R. Mendell, S.A. Al-Zaidy, L.R. Rodino-Klapac, K. Goodspeed, S.J. Gray, C.N. Kay, S.L. Boye, S.E. Boye, L.A. George, S. Salabarria, M. Corti, B.J. Byrne, J.P. Tremblay, Current clinical applications of in vivo gene therapy with AAVs, Mol. Ther. 29 (2) (2021) 464—488.

[43] M. Ramamoorth, A. Narvekar, Non viral vectors in gene therapy-an overview, J. Clin. Diagn. Res. 9 (1) (2015) GE01—GE06.

[44] H. Yin, R. Kanasty, A. Eltoukhy, et al., Non-viral vectors for gene-based therapy, Nat. Rev. Genet. 15 (2014) 541—555.

[45] A. Raguram, S. Banskota, D.R. Liu, Therapeutic in vivo delivery of gene editing agents, Cell 185 (15) (2022) 2806—2827.

[46] C.J. Myers, Preparing pharmacists to manage gene therapies, J. Am. Pharmaceut. Assoc. 61 (3) (2021) e78—e82. Journal of the American Pharmacists Association 61 (2021) e78ee8.

[47] M.B. Marzal-Alfaro, V. Escudero-Vilaplana, J.L. Revuelta-Herrero, R. Collado-Borrell, A. Herranz-Alonso, M. Sanjurjo-Saez, Chimeric antigen receptor T cell therapy management and safety: a practical tool from a multidisciplinary team perspective, Front. Oncol. 11 (2021) 6360680.

[48] K.L. McCance, L.K. Roberts, in: K.L. McCance, S.E. Huether, publisher (Eds.), Biology of Cancer in the Book Titled Pathophysiology: The Biological Basis of Disease in Adults and Children, third ed., Mosby-Year Book, Inc., St. Louis, MO 68146, 1998, ISBN 0-8151-9481-1, p. 308.

[49] Stem Cells: What They Are and what They Do, https://www.mayoclinic.org/tests-procedures/bone-marrow-transplant/in-depth/stem-cells/art-20048117 [Accessed July 25, 2022].

[50] A. Zarepour, A. Bal Öztürk, D. Koyuncu Irmak, G. Yasayan, A. Gökmen, E. Karaöz, A. Zarepour, A. Zarrabi, E. Mostafavi, Combination therapy using nanomaterials and stem cells to treat spinal cord injuries, Eur. J. Pharm. Biopharm. S0939—6411 (22) (2022) 00142—00144, https://doi.org/10.1016/j.ejpb.2022.07.004. Epub ahead of print. PMID: 35850168.

[51] A. Helman, D.A. Melton, A stem cell approach to cure type 1 diabetes, Cold Spring Harbor Perspect. Biol. 13 (1) (2021) a035741, https://doi.org/10.1101/cshperspect.a035741. PMID: 32122884; PMCID: PMC7778150.

[52] T. Stoddard-Bennett, R. Reijo Pera, Treatment of Parkinson's disease through personalized medicine and induced pluripotent stem cells, Cells 8 (1) (2019) 26, https://doi.org/10.3390/cells8010026. PMID: 30621042; PMCID: PMC6357081.

[53] G. Je, K. Keyhanian, M. Ghasemi, Overview of stem cells therapy in amyotrophic lateral sclerosis, Neurol. Res. 43 (8) (2021) 616—632, https://doi.org/10.1080/01616412.2021.1893564. Epub 2021 Feb 25. PMID: 33632084.

[54] F. Han, J. Bi, L. Qiao, O. Arancio, Stem cell therapy for Alzheimer's disease, Adv. Exp. Med. Biol. 1266 (2020) 39—55, https://doi.org/10.1007/978-981-15-4370-8_4. PMID: 33105494.

[55] T. Sano, S. Ishigami, T. Ito, S. Sano, Stem cell therapy in heart disease: limitations and future possibilities, Acta Med. Okayama 74 (3) (2020) 185—190, https://doi.org/10.18926/AMO/59948. PMID: 32577015.

[56] M.R. Chrostek, E.G. Fellows, A.T. Crane, A.W. Grande, W.C. Low, Efficacy of stem cell-based therapies for stroke, Brain Res. 1722 (2019) 146362, https://doi.org/10.1016/j.brainres.2019.146362. Epub 2019 Aug 2. PMID: 31381876; PMCID: PMC6815222.

[57] S. Amini-Nik, R. Dolp, G. Eylert, A.K. Datu, A. Parousis, C. Blakeley, M.G. Jeschke, Stem cells derived from burned skin - the future of burn care, EBioMedicine 37 (2018) 509—520, https://doi.org/10.1016/j.ebiom.2018.10.014. Epub 2018 Nov 5. PMID: 30409728; PMCID: PMC6284415.

[58] T. Lan, M. Luo, X. Wei, Mesenchymal stem/stromal cells in cancer therapy, J. Hematol. Oncol. 14 (1) (2021) 195, https://doi.org/10.1186/s13045-021-01208-w. PMID: 34789315; PMCID: PMC8596342.

[59] W.S. Lee, H.J. Kim, K.I. Kim, G.B. Kim, W. Jin, Intra-articular injection of autologous adipose tissue-derived mesenchymal stem cells for the treatment of knee osteoarthritis: a phase IIb, randomized, placebo-controlled clinical trial, Stem Cells Transl. Med. 8 (6) (2019) 504–511, https://doi.org/10.1002/sctm.18-0122. Epub 2019 Mar 5. PMID: 30835956; PMCID: PMC6525553.

[60] L.L. Rubin, K.M. Haston, Stem cell biology and drug discovery, BMC Biol. 9 (2011) 42, https://doi.org/10.1186/1741-7007-9-42. PMID: 21649940; PMCID: PMC3110139.

[61] L.A. Hook, Stem cell technology for drug discovery and development, Drug Discov. Today 17 (7–8) (2012) 336–342, https://doi.org/10.1016/j.drudis.2011.11.001. Epub 2011 Nov 7. PMID: 22100998.

[62] B. Lo, L. Parham, Ethical issues in stem cell research, Endocr. Rev. 30 (3) (2009) 204–213, https://doi.org/10.1210/er.2008-0031. Epub 2009 Apr 14. PMID: 19366754; PMCID: PMC2726839.

[63] G. Barazzetti, S.A. Hurst, A. Mauron, Adapting preclinical benchmarks for first-in-human trials of human embryonic stem cell-based therapies, Stem Cells Transl Med 5 (8) (2016) 1058–1066, https://doi.org/10.5966/sctm.2015-0222. Epub 2016 Jun 22. PMID: 27334488; PMCID: PMC4954447.

[64] H. Peter, The regeneration promise, The Facts behind Stem Cell Therapies 1–15 (2020) 2, 2020.

[65] Approved Cellular and Gene Therapy Products, Available at: https://www.fda.gov/vaccines-blood-biologics/cellular-gene-therapy-products/approved-cellular-and-gene-therapy-products [Accessed Jlu 26, 2022].

[66] Clevecord, https://www.fda.gov/vaccines-blood-biologics/cellular-gene-therapy-products/clevecord-hpc-cord-blood [Accessed on July 26, 2022].

[67] ALLOCORD, https://www.fda.gov/vaccines-blood-biologics/cellular-gene-therapy-products/allocord-hpc-cord-blood.

[68] Ducord, https://www.fda.gov/vaccines-blood-biologics/cellular-gene-therapy-products/ducord-hpc-cord-blood.

[69] Hemacord, https://www.fda.gov/vaccines-blood-biologics/cellular-gene-therapy-products/hemacord-hpc-cord-blood.

[70] Clinimmune Labs, HPC, Cord Blood, https://www.fda.gov/vaccines-blood-biologics/cellular-gene-therapy-products/hpc-cord-blood.

[71] MD Anderson, HPC, Cord Blood, https://www.fda.gov/vaccines-blood-biologics/cellular-gene-therapy-products/hpc-cord-blood-md-anderson-cord-blood-bank.

[72] LifeSouth, https://www.fda.gov/vaccines-blood-biologics/cellular-gene-therapy-products/hpc-cord-blood-lifesouth.

[73] Bloodworks, https://www.fda.gov/vaccines-blood-biologics/cellular-gene-therapy-products/hpc-cord-blood-bloodworks.

[74] A.O. Fakoya, New delivery systems of stem cells for vascular regeneration in ischemia, Front Cardiovasc Med 4 (2017) 7, https://doi.org/10.3389/fcvm.2017.00007. PMID: 28286751; PMCID: PMC5323391.

[75] M. Yousef, C.M. Schannwell, M. Köstering, T. Zeus, M. Brehm, B.E. Strauer, The BALANCE Study: clinical benefit and long-term outcome after intracoronary autologous bone marrow cell transplantation in patients with acute myocardial infarction, J. Am. Coll. Cardiol. 53 (24) (2009) 2262–2269, https://doi.org/10.1016/j.jacc.2009.02.051. PMID: 19520249.

[76] W. Wang, Q. Jiang, H. Zhang, P. Jin, X. Yuan, Y. Wei, S. Hu, Intravenous administration of bone marrow mesenchymal stromal cells is safe for the lung in a chronic myocardial infarction model, Regen. Med. 6 (2) (2011) 179–190, https://doi.org/10.2217/rme.10.104. PMID: 21391852.

[77] L. Pleva, P. Kukla, K. Vítková, V. Procházka, Rationale and design of a prospective, randomised study of retrograde application of bone marrow aspirate concentrate (BMAC) through coronary sinus in patients with congestive heart failure of ischemic etiology (the RETRO study), BMC Cardiovasc. Disord. 19 (1) (2019) 32, https://doi.org/10.1186/s12872-019-1011-9. PMID: 30704414; PMCID: PMC6357383.

[78] I.M. Barbash, P. Chouraqui, J. Baron, M.S. Feinberg, S. Etzion, A. Tessone, L. Miller, E. Guetta, D. Zipori, L.H. Kedes, R.A. Kloner, J. Leor, Systemic delivery of bone marrow-derived mesenchymal stem cells to the infarcted myocardium: feasibility, cell migration, and body distribution, Circulation 108 (7) (2003) 863–868, https://doi.org/10.1161/01.CIR.0000084828.50310.6A. Epub 2003 Aug 4. PMID: 12900340.

[79] A. Andrzejewska, S. Dabrowska, B. Lukomska, M. Janowski, Mesenchymal stem cells for neurological disorders, Adv. Sci. 8 (7) (2021) 2002944, https://doi.org/10.1002/advs.202002944. PMID: 33854883; PMCID: PMC8024997.

[80] S. Bobis-Wozowicz, K. Kmiotek, K. Kania, E. Karnas, A. Labedz-Maslowska, M. Sekula, S. Kedracka-Krok, J. Kolcz, D. Boruczkowski, Z. Madeja, E.K. Zuba-Surma, Diverse impact of xeno-free conditions on biological and regenerative properties of hUC-MSCs and their extracellular vesicles, J. Mol. Med. (Berl.) 95 (2) (2017) 205–220, https://doi.org/10.1007/s00109-016-1471-7. Epub 2016 Sep 16. PMID: 27638341; PMCID: PMC5239805.

[81] R. Sackstein, J.S. Merzaban, D.W. Cain, N.M. Dagia, J.A. Spencer, C.P. Lin, R. Wohlgemuth, *Ex vivo* glycan engineering of CD44 programs human multipotent mesenchymal stromal cell trafficking to bone, Nat. Med. 14 (2) (2008) 181–187, https://doi.org/10.1038/nm1703. Epub 2008 Jan 13. PMID: 18193058.

[82] S. François, M. Bensidhoum, M. Mouiseddine, C. Mazurier, B. Allenet, A. Semont, J. Frick, A. Saché, S. Bouchet, D. Thierry, P. Gourmelon, N.C. Gorin, A. Chapel, Local irradiation not only induces homing of human mesenchymal stem cells at exposed sites but promotes their widespread engraftment to multiple organs: a study of their quantitative distribution after irradiation damage, Stem Cell. 24 (4) (2006) 1020–1029, https://doi.org/10.1634/stemcells.2005-0260. Epub 2005 Dec 8. PMID: 16339642.

[83] S.Y. Lee, J. Ma, T.S. Khoo, N. Abdullah, Md Nik, N.N.F. Noordin Kahar, Z.A. Abdul Hamid, M. Mustapha, Polysaccharide-based hydrogels for microencapsulation of stem cells in regenerative medicine, Front. Bioeng. Biotechnol. 9 (2021) 735090, https://doi.org/10.3389/fbioe.2021.735090. PMID: 34733829; PMCID: PMC8558675.

[84] P. Khayambashi, J. Iyer, S. Pillai, A. Upadhyay, Y. Zhang, S.D. Tran, Hydrogel encapsulation of mesenchymal stem cells and their derived exosomes for tissue engineering, Int. J. Mol. Sci. 22 (2) (2021) 684, https://doi.org/10.3390/ijms22020684. PMID: 33445616; PMCID: PMC7827932.

[85] S. Saghati, R. Rahbarghazi, A. Baradar Khoshfetrat, K. Moharamzadeh, H. Tayefi Nasrabadi, L. Roshangar, Phenolated alginate-collagen hydrogel induced chondrogenic capacity of human amniotic mesenchymal stem cells, J. Biomater. Appl. 36 (5) (2021) 789–802, https://doi.org/10.1177/08853282211021692. Epub 2021 Jun 1. PMID: 34074175.

[86] S.K. Leslie, R.C. Kinney, Z. Schwartz, B.D. Boyan, Microencapsulation of stem cells for therapy, Methods Mol. Biol. 1479 (2017) 251–259, https://doi.org/10.1007/978-1-4939-6364-5_20. PMID: 27738942.

[87] A Cautionary Tale of 'Stem Cell Tourism', https://www.nytimes.com/2016/06/23/health/a-cautionary-tale-of-stem-cell-tourism.html?searchResultPosition=9.

[88] P.W. Marks, C.M. Witten, R.M. Califf, Clarifying stem-cell therapy's benefits and risks, N Eengl J Med 376 (2017) 11.

[89] The White House, Precision Medicine Initiative, https://obamawhitehousearchivesgov/precision-medicine.

[90] Psychiatryonline Online, What Did STAR*D Teach Us? Results From a Large-Scale, Practical, Clinical Trial for Patients With Depression, https://pspsychiatryonlineorg/doi/101176/ps200960111439.

[91] D.F. Santomauro, A.M.M. Herrera, J. Shadid, P. Zheng, C. Ashbaugh, D.M. Pigott, et al., Global prevalence and burden of depressive and anxiety disorders in 204 countries and territories in 2020 due to the COVID-19 pandemic, Lancet 398 (10312) (2021) 1700–1712.

[92] O. Muhorakeye, E. Biracyaza, Exploring barriers to mental health services utilization at kabutare district hospital of Rwanda: perspectives from patients, Front. Psychol. 12 (2021) 669.

[93] A.F. Leuchter, I.A. Cook, A.M. Hunter, A.S. Korb, A new paradigm for the prediction of antidepressant treatment response, Dialogues Clin. Neurosci. 11 (4) (2022) 435–446.

[94] Mental Health Data Science Scotland (MHDSS), Talking about Stratified Medicine, https://mhdssacuk/news/20/11/20/talking-about-stratified-medicine.

[95] The American Journal of Managed Care (AJMC). Economic Burden Among Patients With Major Depressive Disorder: An Analysis of Healthcare Resource Use, Work Productivity, and Direct and Indirect Costs by Depression Severity, https://wwwajmccom/view/economic-burden-mdd.

[96] U. Gundert-Remy, Age as a factor in dose-response relationship of drugs, Zeitschrift fur Gerontologie und Geriatrie 28 (6) (1995) 408–414.

[97] C. Kyriakopoulos, V. Gupta, Renal Failure Drug Dose Adjustments. [Updated 2021 Aug 9]. in: StatPearls [Internet]. Treasure Island (FL), StatPearls Publishing, 2022. Available from: https://www.ncbi.nlm.nih.gov/books/NBK560512/.

[98] G. Kaur, C. Phillips, K. Wong, B. Saini, Timing is important in medication administration: a timely review of chronotherapy research, Int. J. Clin. Pharm. 35 (3) (2013) 344–358.

[99] FDA, CDER Conversation: Evaluating the Risk of Drug-Drug Interactions, https://wwwfdagov/drugs/news-events-human-drugs/cder-conversation-evaluating-risk-drug-drug-interactions.

[100] D. Primorac, L. Bach-Rojecky, D. Vađunec, A. Juginović, K. Žunić, V. Matišić, et al., Pharmacogenomics at the center of precision medicine: challenges and perspective in an era of Big Data, Pharmacogenomics 21 (2) (2020) 141–156.

[101] M. Rasool, A. Malik, M.I. Naseer, A. Manan, S.A. Ansari, I. Begum, et al., The role of epigenetics in personalized medicine: challenges and opportunities, BMC Med. Genom. 8 (1) (2015) 1–8.

[102] R.R. Shah, R.L. Smith, Addressing phenoconversion: the Achilles' heel of personalized medicine, Br. J. Clin. Pharmacol. 79 (2) (2015) 222–240.

[103] E. Abrahams, M. Silver, The history of personalized medicine, Integr. Neurosci. Personalized Med. (2010) 3–16.

[104] FDA, *In Vitro* Diagnostics; Precision Medicine, https://wwwfdagov/medical-devices/in-vitro-diagnostics/precision-medicine.

[105] P.E. Velmovitsky, T. Bevilacqua, P. Alencar, D. Cowan, P.P. Morita, Convergence of precision medicine and public health into precision public health: toward a big data perspective, Front. Public Health 9 (2021).

[106] J.L. Jameson, D.L. Longo, Precision medicine—personalized, problematic, and promising, Obstet. Gynecol. Surv. 70 (10) (2015) 612–614.

[107] M. Hasanzad, N. Sarhangi, H.R.A. Meybodi, S. Nikfar, F. Khatami, B. Larijani, Precision medicine in non communicable diseases, Int. J. Mol. Cellular Med. 8 (Suppl. 1) (2019) 1.

[108] W.E. Evans, M.V. Relling, Pharmacogenomics: translating functional genomics into rational therapeutics, Science 286 (5439) (1999) 487–491.

[109] J.A. Marcum, P7 medicine: humanizing systems medicine, Teorema: Revista Internacional de Filosofía. 40 (1) (2021) 213–231.

[110] J.A. Johnson, K.W. Weitzel, Advancing pharmacogenomics as a component of precision medicine: how, where, and who? Clin. Pharmacol. Therapeut. 99 (2) (2016) 154–156.

[111] Pharmaceutical, Services, Negotiating, Committee, (PCNC), Essential Facts, Stats and Quotes Relating to Prescriptions, 2021.

[112] International Conference on Harmonisation, Guidance on E15 pharmacogenomics definitions and sample coding, Availability. Notice. Federal Register. 73 (68) (2008) 19074–19076.

[113] K.A. Gray, B. Yates, R.L. Seal, M.W. Wright, E.A. Bruford, Genenames. org: the HGNC resources in 2015, Nucleic Acids Res. 43 (D1) (2015) D1079–D1085.

[114] G. Umamaheswaran, D.K. Kumar, C. Adithan, Distribution of genetic polymorphisms of genes encoding drug metabolizing enzymes & drug transporters-a review with Indian perspective, Indian J. Med. Res. 139 (1) (2014) 27.

[115] R. Cacabelos, N. Cacabelos, J.C. Carril, The role of pharmacogenomics in adverse drug reactions, Expet Rev. Clin. Pharmacol. 12 (5) (2019) 407–442.

[116] R. Cacabelos, J.C. Carril, A. Sanmartín, P. Cacabelos, Pharmacoepigenetic processors: epigenetic drugs, drug resistance, toxicoepigenetics, and nutriepigenetics, in: Pharmacoepigenetics, Elsevier, 2019, pp. 191–424.

[117] F.S. Collins, L. Fink, The human genome project, Alcohol Health Res. World 19 (3) (1995) 190.

[118] L. Weng, L. Zhang, Y. Peng, R.S. Huang, Pharmacogenetics and pharmacogenomics: a bridge to individualized cancer therapy, Pharmacogenomics 14 (3) (2013) 315–324.

[119] Food and Drug Adminstration (FDA), FDA Drug Safety Communication: Revised Recommendations for Celexa (Citalopram Hydrobromide) Related to a Potential Risk of Abnormal Heart Rhythms With High Doses, https://wwwfdagov/drugs/drug-safety-and-availability/fda-drug-safety-communication-revised-recommendations-celexa-citalopram-hydrobromide-related.

[120] National Human Genome Research Institute, Nucleotide, https://wwwgenomegov/genetics-glossary/Nucleotide.

[121] Genetics Generation. SNP's, https://knowgeneticsorg/snps/.

[122] M. Kane, CYP2D6 overview: allele and phenotype frequencies. 2021 oct 15, in: V.M. Pratt, S.A. Scott, M. Pirmohamed, et al. (Eds.), Medical Genetics Summaries [Internet], National Center for Biotechnology Information (US), Bethesda (MD), 2012. Available from, https://www.ncbi.nlm.nih.gov/books/NBK574601/.

[123] N. von Ahsen, V.W. Armstrong, M. Oellerich, Rapid, long-range molecular haplotyping of thiopurine s-methyltransferase (TPMT*)* 3A,* 3B, and* 3C, Clin. Chem. 50 (9) (2004) 1528–1534.

[124] Merck Manuals Consumer Version, Drug Metabolism, https://wwwmerckmanualscom/home/drugs/administration-and-kinetics-of-drugs/drug-metabolism.

[125] A.M. McDonnell, C.H. Dang, Basic review of the cytochrome p450 system, J. Adv. Practitioner Oncol. 4 (4) (2013) 263.

[126] Food and Drug Adminstration (FDA), Precision Medicine, Table of Pharmacogenetic Associations, https://wwwfdagov/medical-devices/precision-medicine/table-pharmacogenetic-associations.

[127] L. Dean, M. Kane, Codeine therapy and CYP2D6 genotype [updated 2021 Mar 30], in: V.M. Pratt, S.A. Scott, M. Pirmohamed, B. Esquivel, M.S. Kane, B.L. Kattman, A.J. Malheiro (Eds.), Medical Genetics Summaries [Internet], National Center for Biotechnology Information (US), Bethesda (MD), 2012, 2012—. PMID: 28520350.

[128] M. Marino, Z. Jamal, P.M. Zito, Pharmacodynamics. StatPearls [Internet], StatPearls Publishing, Treasure Island (FL), 2023. PMID: 29939568.

[129] Centers for Disease Control and Prevention (CDC), What is Epigenetics?, https://wwwcdcgov/genomics/disease/epigeneticshtm.

[130] R.R. Shah, R.L. Smith, Addressing phenoconversion: the Achilles' heel of personalized medicine, Br. J. Clin. Pharmacol. 79 (2) (2015) 222—240.

[131] S. Cho, Y.-R. Yoon, Understanding the pharmacokinetics of prodrug and metabolite, Trans. Clin. Pharmacol. 26 (1) (2018) 1—5.

[132] S.H. Preskorn, Clinically relevant pharmacology of selective serotonin reuptake inhibitors. An overview with emphasis on pharmacokinetics and effects on oxidative drug metabolism, Clin. Pharmacokinet. 32 (Suppl. 1) (1997) 1—21.

[133] S. Zevin, N.L. Benowitz, Drug interactions with tobacco smoking. An update, Clin. Pharmacokinet. 36 (6) (1999) 425—438.

[134] Food and Drug Adminstration (FDA), Grapefruit Juice and Some Drugs Don't Mix, https://wwwfdagov/consumers/consumer-updates/grapefruit-juice-and-some-drugs-dont-mix.

[135] D.L. Murphy, P.R. Moya, Human serotonin transporter gene (SLC6A4) variants: their contributions to understanding pharmacogenomic and other functional G× G and G× E differences in health and disease, Curr. Opin. Pharmacol. 11 (1) (2011) 3—10.

[136] D.M. Lovinger, Communication networks in the brain: neurons, receptors, neurotransmitters, and alcohol, Alcohol Res. Health 31 (3) (2008) 196—214.

[137] Neuroscience News, Compound Enhances SSRI Antidepressant's Effects in Mice, https://neurosciencenewscom/neuropharmacology-decynium-22-ssri-serotonin-248/.

[138] S. Vandghanooni, M. Eskandani, Z. Sanaat, Y. Omidi, Recent advances in the production, reprogramming, and application of CAR-T cells for treating hematological malignancies, Life Sci. 309 (2022), 121016, https://doi.org/10.1016/j.lfs.2022.121016.

[139] S. Ramachandran, S.R. Satapathy, T. Dutta, Delivery Strategies for mRNA Vaccines, Pharmaceut. Med. 36 (1) (2022) 11—20, https://doi.org/10.1007/s40290-021-00417-5.

15

Quality Assurances of Dosage Forms

Alekha K. Dash

Department of Pharmacy Sciences, School of Pharmacy and Health Professions, Creighton University, Omaha, NE, United States

CHAPTER OBJECTIVES

- Understand the difference between FDA-approved drug products and compounded products.
- Describe the differences in quality assurance requirements between FDA-approved drug products and compounded products.
- Appreciate the need of Good Manufacturing Practice (GMP) in drug formulation manufacturing.
- Discuss the importance of quality assurance for both FDA-approved drug products and compounded products.
- Understand the quality assurance aspects of pharmaceutical compounding; United States Pharmacopeia (USP) <1163>.
- Understand different components of analytical instrument qualification; USP <1058>.
- Understand the process of validation as described under USP <1225>.
- Understand the differences between quality assurance and quality control.
- Understand the differences and advantages of quality-by-testing (QbT) and quality-by-design (QbD).
- Appreciate and understand the various quality control tests recommended for pharmaceutical dosage forms.

Keywords: Good manufacturing practices; Quality assurance; Quality control; Quality by design; Quality by testing.

Pharmaceutics, Second Edition
https://doi.org/10.1016/B978-0-323-99796-6.00016-3

15.1 Introduction

As a practicing pharmacist, one must deal with two distinct types of drug products that include FDA-approved brand or generic, and compounded product in a pharmacy. A brand-name drug product is approved by FDA after strict pre- and post-clinical evaluations to make sure the drug product is effective, safe, and reliable. This further assures that the drug product can be made consistently to a high-quality standard. FDA can also grant a generic version of the brand after the expiration of the patent protection period of the drug product. Such approval needs only confirmation that the generic product is bioequivalent to the brand name product without any toxicological and safety evaluations. Both FDA-approved drug products (brand and generic) are manufactured under Good Manufacturing Practice (GMP) guidelines. These federal mandates govern the production and testing of these products. The FDA regulates and regularly inspects pharmaceutical manufacturing facilities to ensure compliance with GMPs. Some of the GMP requirements and considerations for FDA-approved drug products (brand or generics) are listed below [1].

- Organization and personnel used
- Facilities and equipment used to manufacture drugs
- Education and training of personnel engaged in the manufacturing process
- Containers and closers used during manufacturing, storage, and distribution
- Calibration and cleaning processes for equipment used
- Validation of analytical test procedures used (to ensure that drugs conform to FDA-approved specifications for potency, purity, and other requirements such as sterility)
- Retesting of active pharmaceutical ingredients (API) and excipients used upon receipt
- Validation of manufacturing processes to consistently meet quality standards
- Independent quality control unit (to oversee the manufacturing, packaging, labeling, and testing processes)
- Storage and distribution of raw materials, in-process materials, and final product
- Stability studies to support the expiration date of products
- Rejection and documentation of substandard batches
- Records and reports for all activities

Pharmacy compounding of individualized medicines, on the other hand, is an essential component of our health care system today. Its benefit for a patient is well recognized when an FDA-approved drug product is not available or even not appropriate for the patient. In some instances, a dosage form must be altered in some manner, such as strength, excipient, or route of administration.

- According to FDA, compounding is generally a practice in which a licensed pharmacist, a licensed physician, or, in the case of an outsourcing facility, a person under the supervision of a licensed pharmacist, combines, mixes, or alters ingredients of a drug to create a medication tailored to the needs of an individual patient [2].
- The National Association of Boards of Pharmacy (NABP) describes compounding as the result of a practitioner's prescription drug order based on the practitioner/patient/pharmacist/compounder relationship during professional practice [3].

15.2 Comparison between compounded drug products versus FDA-approved drug products

There are significance differences between these two drug products. Some of these differences are listed in Table 15.1 [4].

15.3 Quality assurance

Quality assurance of drug products intended for human and animal use assures that these products meet acceptable standards for quality and safety. Without such assurance, any health benefits rendered by their use will certainly be compromised. Quality assurance is a broad concept that covers all matters that individually or collectively contribute to the quality, safety, and effectiveness of the final product. Therefore, quality assurance covers a wide area in addition to GMP practices and beyond the scope of this chapter to cover all such areas. However, this chapter will only focus on the quality assurance of compounded drug products as described in the USP.

TABLE 15.1 Comparison between compounded drug versus FDA-approved drug products.

Testing and regulatory needs	FDA-approved drug products	Compounded drug products
Toxicity and safety	Clinically tested for toxicity and safety evaluation	Not clinically tested for safety and efficacy
Bioequivalence	Bioequivalence testing is required for generic drugs	Bioequivalence testing is not conducted
The type and extent of quality control testing	Requirement is greater	Requirement is less
Raw material analysis	Retesting of all raw materials are mandatory according to GMP	Rely on certificate of analysis for raw materials
GMP regulation requirement	Obligatory for all approved pharmaceutical manufacturers	Compounding pharmacies are exempt from GMP regulations
Product labeling	Regulated and standardize	Neither regulated nor standardized
Advertising and promotion of approved drugs	Subject to FDA oversight and restriction	Not subject to FDA oversight and restriction
Report of adverse events	Adverse event reporting is mandatory for manufacturers of FDA-approved drugs	Not required to report adverse events to the FDA
Jurisdiction	Manufacturing facilities are regulated and inspected by FDA to ensure compliance with GMPs.	Pharmacies are primarily under the authority of state boards of pharmacy.

15.3.1 Quality assurance in pharmaceutical compounding <USP 1163> [5]

USP clearly describes the need for quality assurance in pharmaceutical compounding in general chapter <1163>. Some of the USP's general chapters also describe quality control under pharmaceutical compounding—Nonsterile preparations <795> and quality assurance (QA) programs under pharmaceutical compounding—Sterile preparations <797>. The quality assurance program is guided by written protocols with quality attributes to meet the need for the patient and other healthcare personnel. Seven separate and independent components as listed below have been identified and recommended to be included in the quality assurance program for compounded drug products as listed below.

- **Training**: Personnel involved in both sterile and non-sterile compounding activities should be well trained and retrained with proper certification and documentation. Training for non-sterile compounders should meet or exceed the standards set forth in <795>. Similarly, personnel training for sterile preparation compounders should meet or exceed the standards set forth in <797>.
- **Standard operating procedure (SOP)**: These are documents describing detailed step-by-step descriptions of any compounding process. The SOP must include beyond-use-date (BUD), stability (physical and chemical), cleaning and disinfecting, quality evaluation of components, method of compounding, dispensing; documentation, environmental quality and maintenance, equipment (calibration, maintenance, and operation), formulation development, labeling; material and final product handling and storage, measuring and weighing, packaging and repackaging, patient monitoring (complaints and adverse events), personal cleanliness and garb, purchasing, quality assurance and continuous quality monitoring, safety, shipping, testing, training, and retraining. SOPs

must be reviewed regularly and updated as necessary. The SOP should also be specific to each instrument and process used in compounding.

- **Documentation**: Documentation should provide a record of all aspects of the compounding operation as described by both chapters <795> and <797>. Compounding records should be entered immediately as soon as the task is completed. It should be reviewed for accuracy and completeness and finally approved by the appropriate personnel.
- **Verification**: This provides signed assurance and documentation that a process, procedure, and equipment is functioning properly. This may include checking a calculation, weighing and measuring, order of mixing, compounding procedure, checking the quality of ingredients (certificate of analysis, manufacture's label, outside laboratory testing), and equipment verification with a standard calibrator.
- **Testing**: Testing must be done on the sample collected during the process and on the final product after compounding as appropriate and described in both chapters <795> and <797>. Testing protocols must include parameters critical for the overall quality of a compounded product such as when to test, what to test, what method and equipment to be used, how to interpret the results, limit of a test, and what specific action to be taken when the test limit fails. USP chapter <1163> Table 1 describes selected quality test methods and procedures and their corresponding USP chapters. However, Table 2 of chapter <1163> describes selected compendial testing methods for bulk substances and various dosage forms.
- **Cleaning, disinfecting, and safety**: This section is applicable to both equipment and facilities as described in USP chapters <795> and <797>. Disinfectants and antiseptics are described in USP chapter <1072>.
- **Containers, packaging, repackaging, labeling, and storage**: For storage, packaging, repackaging, and labeling of compounded preparations and repackaging of manufactured products (when defined as compounding in USP) are provided in various USP general chapters. Some of these general chapters are outlined below.
  - Containers—glass <660>
  - Containers—plastic <661>
  - Good packaging practices <1177>
  - Good repackaging practices <1178>
  - Good storage and shipping practices <1079>
  - Injections <1>
  - Packaging and repackaging—single-unit containers <1136>
  - Pharmaceutical dosage forms <1150>
- **Outsourcing**: This addresses only the purchasing or selling of compounded preparations from pharmacy to pharmacy. Pharmacies that prepare the compounded product must provide the beyond use dating upon request. Documentation of compliance with USP chapters <795> and <797> is required and shall be provided upon request.
- **Responsible personnel**: The responsibility and authority of the quality assurance personnel should be well defined and documented. The responsible personnel should have appropriate education, training, and experiences to perform the assigned tasks. They should assure that documentation, verification, and testing are performed according to the written SOP. It is the responsibility of such individual/s to implement any appropriate corrective actions if deviations occur. They are the responsible personnel in the quality assurance program that assures the safety, identity, strength, quality, and purity of a compounded product.

15.4 Analytical instruments qualification; USP <1058> [6]

Pharmaceutical industry, as well as compounding pharmacies, used varieties of laboratory instruments and equipment to acquire data to help ensure that the tested products are suitable for the intended use. An analyst's main goal is to acquire consistently reliable and valid data from the equipment they use. Analytical instrument qualification (AIQ) currently has no specific guidance and procedures. With more automation and sophistication of many instruments used today, it is more prudent to consider AIQ as one of the major components required for generating reliable and consistent data from analytical instruments.

15.4.1 Validation versus qualification

According to USP chapter <1058>, validation is a term used mostly for manufacturing processes, analytical methods, and software procedures, but qualification is used only for instruments. AIQ is used for the process of ensuring that an instrument is suitable for its intended use. Quality data in analytical procedures mean they are consistent and reliable. Data quality depends on four major components that start with analytical instrument qualification as its base. The other three quality components that contribute to overall data quality are analytical method validation, system suitability test, and quality control check samples.

15.4.2 Analytical instrument qualification

It is the collection of documented evidence that ensures an instrument performs suitably for its intended purpose. Use of a qualified instrument in analytical methods provides confidence in the collected data for the analytical purpose.

15.4.3 Analytical method validation

Analytical method validation is the collection of documented evidence that an analytical procedure is suitable for its intended use. In addition to AIQ, analytical method development adds additional confidence that the procedure will generate reliable and consistent data with acceptable quality. Analytical method validation is presented as a separate USP chapter <1225> and will be described in detail later.

15.4.4 System suitability test

System suitability tests verify that the system used in the analysis performs in accordance with the criteria set forth for the procedure. These tests are performed with the sample analyses to ensure that the systems performance is acceptable at the time of the test.

15.4.5 Quality control check samples

Many analysts routinely test reference materials and/or calibration standards with analytes of interest on the instrument. In some instances, the analysis may require the inclusion of quality control check samples to provide an in-process assurance of the test's performance suitability.

AIQ is not considered as a single continuous process, rather a combination of four discrete phases. These four phases are design qualifications (DQ), installation qualifications (IQ), operational qualifications (OQ), and performance qualifications (PQ).

Design qualification is the collection of documented activities that describes the functional and operational aspect of the instrument and why that instrument and vendor are selected for that intended use. DQ is not only performed by the manufacturer but also should be carried out by the user. The manufacturer is responsible for developing a robust instrument with quality checkpoints and should provide adequate education and training to the end user. They are responsible for testing the instrument before shipment.

IQ is the documented collection of activities that establishes the instrument is installed properly with the environment and that the necessary additional peripherals are available and suitable during installation. IQ is applicable only to new instruments that have not yet been qualified. IQ is also necessary for qualified instruments stored for a long time and if transported from one place to another place. IQ will include activities such as the description of the instrument; proper delivery of the instrument; site verification checklist; assembly and installation; data storage and handling; installation verification.

OQ deals with the documented collection of activities required to demonstrate that the instrument is performing according to its specification in the new environment. Some of the test parameters may include fixed parameters (length, height, electrical input, etc.) that do not change over the life of the instrument, data storage security and backup, and instrument function tests.

PQ is the documented collection of activities necessary to demonstrate that the instrument performs consistently according to specifications and is appropriate for intended use. Some of the PQ parameters may include performance checks, preventive maintenance and repair, and establishment of practices to maintain and calibrate the instrument.

15.4.6 Instrument categories

Pharmaceutical analysis utilizes simple to very sophisticated instruments. USP chapter <1058> provides three categories of instruments depending on their calibration needs. The exact grouping of an instrument must be determined by the user.

Group A: Standard equipment with no measurement capability or requirement for calibration. Examples: magnetic stirrers, evaporators, vortex mixture.

Group B: Standard equipment providing measured values as well as controlling physical parameters (temp, pressure, flow) that need calibration. Examples: Oven, furnaces, refrigerators and freezers, water bath, and pumps.

Group C: This group includes instruments that may need automation and a computer for their operation and data collection. For this category of instruments, all four qualification processes, as outlined earlier, should be applied. Examples: Atomic Absorption Spectrometers, Differential Scanning Calorimeter, Dissolution Apparatus, Electron Microscope, Mass Spectrometer, X-ray Powder Diffractometer, IR Spectrometers, Raman Spectrometers, UV–Vis Spectrometers, etc.

15.5 Validation of compendial procedures <1225> [7,8]

Method validation is an integral part of any analytical method development. This is a systematic evaluation of a method that assures consistency, reliability, and reproducibility. Before an analytical method can be validated, it must be completely developed, and the detailed procedure is documented. Some of the important analytical characteristics used in method validation are described below.

15.5.1 Accuracy

The closeness of a measured value to its true value is called accuracy. In establishing the accuracy of a dosage form assay, one should show that all the analytes are recovered from the matrix without bias. The weight of the analyte mixed in the dosage form is taken as its true value. Theoretical content of analyte, content determined by the assay, and the percent recovery should be reported. Accuracy can be determined by the application of the analytical procedure to an analyte of known purity (reference standard) or by comparison of the results of the procedure with those of a well-established second method whose accuracy has already been established. As an example, in the spiked placebo method, a known amount of the pure API is added to a mixture of excipients (blank). The resulting mixture is assayed, and the results are compared to their theoretical values. Accuracy is calculated as the percentage of recovery by the assay of the known added amount of analyte in the sample or as the difference between the mean and the accepted true value, together with confidence intervals. Assessment of accuracy can be accomplished by evaluating the recovery of the analyte (percent recovery) across the range of the assay or by establishing the linear relationship between estimated and actual concentrations. The statistically preferred criterion is that the confidence interval for the slope be contained in an interval around 1.0, or alternatively, that the slope be close to 1.0. In either case, the interval or the definition of closeness should be specified in the validation protocol.

15.5.2 Precision

The precision of an analytical procedure is the degree of agreement among individual test results when the procedure is applied repeatedly to multiple samplings of a homogeneous sample. It is usually expressed as the standard deviation or relative standard deviation (coefficient of variation) of a series of measurements. Precision may be a measure of either the degree of reproducibility or of repeatability of the analytical procedure. Reproducibility refers to the use of the analytical procedure in different laboratories. Intermediate precision (also known as ruggedness) expresses within-laboratory variation, as on different days (day-to-day or inter-day precision), or with different analysts or equipment within the same laboratory. Repeatability refers to the use of the analytical procedure within a laboratory over a short period of time using the same analyst with the same equipment (within-day or intra-day precision). Precision is expressed as the relative standard deviation (RSD or coefficient of variation) and calculated as shown in Eq. (15.1).

$$\text{Relative Standard Deviation (RSD)} = \frac{\text{SD}}{\text{Mean value}} \times 100 \tag{15.1}$$

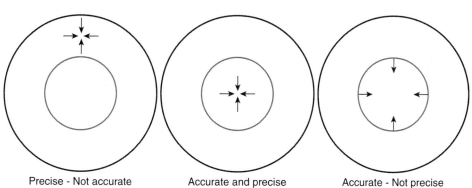

Precise - Not accurate   Accurate and precise   Accurate - Not precise

FIGURE 15.1 Accuracy versus precision.

Differences between accuracy and precision are depicted in Fig. 15.1.

15.5.3 Specificity

Specificity is the ability to assess unequivocally the analyte/s of interest in the presence of other components that may be expected to be present (impurities, degradation products, and matrix components) in a sample. As an example, in a chromatographic system, the separation must show its capability of resolving from the peak of interest all other components that provide a detector signal under the chromatographic condition used. International Union of Pure and Applied Chemistry (IUPAC) and other international authorities used the word "selectivity" and reserved the word specificity to the ones which are highly selective. In the case of an identification test, the ability to select between API and compounds with a closely related structure that is likely to be present should be demonstrated. In the case of a purity test, all impurities present either from samples or from forced degradation should be determined with acceptable accuracy and precision. In the case of the assay, demonstration of specificity requires to show that the presence of impurities or excipients should not affect the assay results.

15.5.4 Sensitivity: limit of detection or detection limit

Limit of detection of an analytical method is the lowest amount of analyte in a sample that can be detected, but not necessarily quantitated, under the stated experimental conditions. It is usually expressed as the concentration of the analyte in the sample. An acceptable signal-to-noise ratio (S/N) of 2:1 or 3:1 is generally accepted as the detection limit.

15.5.5 Sensitivity: limit of quantitation or quantitation limit

It is the lowest amount of analyte in a sample that can be determined with acceptable precision and accuracy under experimental conditions. It is usually expressed as the concentration of the analyte in the sample. The minimum concertation of the analyte, where a signal-to-noise ratio (S/N) of 10:1 is observed, is generally accepted as the quantitation limit.

15.5.6 Linearity and range

The linearity of an analytical procedure is its ability to show whether the test responses are directly or by a mathematical transformation, proportional to the concentration of analyte in samples within a given range. The range of an analytical procedure is the interval between the upper and lower levels of analyte (including these levels) that have been demonstrated to be determined with a suitable level of precision, accuracy, and linearity using the procedure as written. Typically, at least five solutions of analyte or standards are prepared with concentration varied from 50% to 150% of the expected working range, which is considered as a narrow range. The correlation coefficient of the linear regression equation is determined and must vary between 0.98 and 1.00.

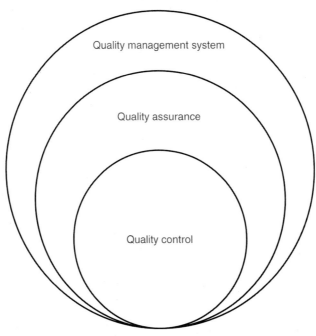

FIGURE 15.2   Quality assurance versus quality control.

15.5.7 Robustness

The robustness of an analytical procedure is a measure of its capacity to remain unaffected by small but deliberate variations in procedural parameters. Robustness may be determined during the development of an analytical procedure.

15.6 Quality assurance versus quality control

Often both the terms quality assurance (QA) and quality control (QC) are used interchangeably. However, QA is not the same as QC. They are distinctly different, but both are a part of the quality management plan. The vain diagram shown in Fig. 15.2 as well as Table 15.2 shows the differences between QA and QC. QA and QC are both required by FDA and other International regulatory organizations to provide safe, effective, and reliable drug products to the patient.

A thorough understanding of these two and their roles in quality management can help to bring the best possible quality product to the market.

15.7 Quality control requirements for pharmaceutical dosage forms

Quality control of various dosage forms, their requirements, and procedure details for each such test has been provided in each individual dosage form chapter. This section will only highlight and list the various quality control test requirements for each of these dosage forms. The quality of these products is achieved by following some strict rules and by testing the final products. In this QbT system, the quality of a product is ensured by raw material testing, fixed drug product manufacturing according to the SOP, and final product analysis. Any failure at any stage needs possible reprocessing of the entire batch. Generally, the root cause of such failure is not well understood because of the poor understanding of the process when QbT is followed. In such quality control programs of the past, the pharmaceutical companies spent an enormous amount of time and money to understand the root cause of the failure, possibly due to a fault in the process itself.

Recently, with the development of the QbD approach, there was a significant development in pharmaceutical quality regulation from an empirical process to a more risked-based approach [10]. In the QbD model, drug quality is ensured by understanding and controlling formulation and processing variables. Analytical tests are applied to

TABLE 15.2 The major differences between quality assurance and quality control [9].

Quality assurance	Quality control
Proactive: aims to prevent defects before they occur through process design and management	*Reactive:* identify defects in the quality of products after they are manufactured
Process: QA is a process-oriented approach that focuses on preventing quality issues by process design	*Product:* QC is product-oriented and focuses on identifying quality issues in manufactured products
Control systems: QA controls systems, methods and procedures that safeguard quality	*Focus on parts:* QC systems focus on parts use to create products
Creation: QA activities creates high-quality products.	*Verification:* QC involves verification of products after they are-manufactured and before distribution confirming their safety and efficacy
Entire team: quality assurance activities involve the entire team.	*Limited personnel:* QC is generally the responsibility of certain personnel or group within the organization

the finished product only to confirm quality. In this model, consistency comes from the planning and control of the production process and drug specification. QbD consists of many elements, and some of the important ones are listed below [11].

- Quality target product profile (QTPP): This includes dosage forms, delivery systems, and dosage strengths. QTTP is a summary of quality characteristics expected to be achieved from the final product.
- Critical quality attributes (CQAs): This includes physical, chemical, biological, or microbiological properties or characteristics of the finished drug products (output material).
- Critical material attributes (CMAs): This includes physical, chemical, biological, or microbiological properties or characteristics of the input material.
- Critical process parameters (CPPs): This includes monitoring of parameters before or during the process that influence the appearance, impurity, and yield of the final product significantly.

During the QbD process, product design and understanding must include the identification of CMAs (for input materials), which are different from CQAs (for output materials).

15.7.1 Pharmaceutical tests to ensure compliance with usp standards [12]

Pharmaceutical tests for dosage form performance fall into one of the following areas: Dose Uniformity, Stability, Bioavailability, Release profile, Manufacturing, Route of Administration, Packaging and Storage, and Labeling. International Council for Harmonization (ICH) also recommends some universally applied tests to ensure safety, efficacy, strength, quality, and purity of drug products. These tests include description, identification, assay, impurities, physicochemical properties, particle size, uniformity of dosage form, water content, microbial limits, preservative contents, antioxidant content, sterility, disintegration, dissolution, breaking force, friability, leachability, alcohol content, particle size distribution, rheological properties, pyrogen test, pH, and osmolarity.

15.7.1.1 QC tests for solid dosage forms

In this category, three important dosage forms such as tablet, capsule, and powder dosage forms are being considered. Some of the quality control tests for this group include:

- Visual appearance, taste, order, texture, hardness, and friability
- Moisture content

- Flow properties (powder and granules)
- Thickness (Tablets)
- Identity test
- Homogeneity of mixing
- Purity
- Assays for the API and degradation products
- Test for content uniformity and weight variation
- Performance evaluation
  - Disintegration (tablets and granules)
  - Dissolution
- Stability indicating tests
- Storage conditions
- Microbial limits

15.7.1.2 QC test for liquid dosage forms

Liquid dosage forms are known to be less stable than their solid counterpart. Some of these liquid formulations may include solutions, suspensions, emulsions, lotions, elixirs, syrups, sprays, irrigations, and injections. Some of the quality control tests for liquid dosage forms are listed below.

- Evaluation for visual appearance, color, taste, odor, and homogeneity
- Assay of active ingredients and degradation products
- Pourability
- Viscosity
- Isotonicity
- Spreadability
- Particle size and size distribution
- Clarity
- Crystallization and precipitation
- pH
- Surface tension
- Surface charge
- Microbial limit tests
- Stability of the active ingredient(s), and identification tests
- Photo-chemical stability
- Container and closure compatibility
- Dispersibility
- Storage condition

15.7.1.3 QC test for aerosol dosage forms [13]

Aerosol dosage forms refer only to those products packaged under pressure that releases a fine mist of particles or droplets when actuated. Some of the required QC tests for such products are listed below.

- Flammability and combustibility tests:
  Flashpoint
  Flame extension
- Physico-chemical characteristics:
  Vapor pressure
  Density
  Moisture content
  Identification of propellant(s)
- Performance:
  Aerosol valve discharge rate
  Spray pattern
  Dosage with metered valves
  Net contents
  Foam stability

Particle size determination

Leakage

- Biologic characteristics:

Therapeutic activities

Toxicity

15.7.1.4 *QC test for semisolid dosage forms*

Some of the semi-solid dosage forms listed in USP general chapter <1151> may include creams, gels, gums, ointments, pastes, and suppositories. Some of the QC tests for semi-solid dosage forms as recommended by USP may include:

- Evaluation for visual appearance, color, odor, and homogeneity
- Loss of water
- Consistency
- Softening range (for suppositories)
- Viscosity
- Particle size distribution
- pH
- Assay of active ingredients and the degradation products
- Identification test for active ingredients and possible contaminants
- Stability of the API in the dosage form
- Release of the API from the dosage form
- Storage conditions.

15.8 Conclusions

Quality assurance is one of the most important aspects of the entire drug manufacturing process. It helps the reputation of the company as well as allows them to avoid hefty penalties from regulatory organizations. However, the major objective of pharmaceutical quality assurance is to produce quality drug products that meet all the quality requirements and relevant regulations that make them effective, safe, and reliable for patients. The same requirements and regulations are also applicable for compounded formulations prepared by a pharmacist/compounder for an individualized patient. Quality assurance of drug products is essential to minimize the risk of marketing or delivering an unsafe product to the patient. Whether it is an FDA-approved drug product or a compounded one, quality assurance is equally important for maintaining the quality of drug products.

Case studies

Case 15.1

A survey was conducted by FDA in 2001 on 37 compounded products from 12 compounding pharmacies throughout the United States [14]. The results of this survey were compared with the analytical testing failure rate for commercially produced samples. The failure rate of compounded products was found to be 17 times more than commercial products. How could you explain this to a pharmacist intern working under your supervision in your compounding pharmacy facility?

Approach: The quality of a finished compounded drug product can be affected by numerous factors, including the quality of the API used and the compounding practices of the pharmacy in which the product is prepared. In this case, FDA collected 3,000 commercial drug products, and the analytical failure was found to be less than 2%. In this survey, out of 37 samples collected, 29 of them were subjected to repeated analytical testing. Ten out of 29 samples (34%) products failed one or more standard quality tests. More importantly, nine out of 10 failed assay or potency. This is a clear indication of quality assurance issues with the compounded drug products and needs to be addressed. The failure rate of 34% versus less than 2% in commercial products explains stricter adherence of quality assurance protocol for commercial products as compared to compounded ones.

Case 15.2

In 2001, a Kansas-based pharmacist was found guilty of adulterating 72 drugs, including some oncological products [15]. During the pharmacist's trial, one of the ovarian cancer patients explained to the judge that the compounded drug product (Taxol) she received from this pharmacist did not show any side effects as compared to some of the previous ones she purchased from another pharmacy. She further added that she had a recurrence of her cancer. As an oncology pharmacist and expert witness working on behalf of the plaintiff (the victim), how can you simply explain this to the judge that the compounding pharmacist is responsible for the recurrence of her cancer?

Approach: This case was covered in the New York Times magazine in 2001 with the title "The toxic Pharmacist" and considered as a dark day to the profession of pharmacy. Again, this is a clear case of unethical, unprofessional, and intentionally motivated victimization of cancer patients for greediness and to make illegal money by taking advantage of their disease condition. This is also a case of adulteration and total failure of the quality assurance program at the compounding pharmacy facility. The cause of no side effects from Taxol could be explained by the dilution effect. The pharmacist was only dispensing 17%–39% of paclitaxel to the patient during dilution and saving 60%–80% of this costly drug for himself for sale and for profit. This was further confirmed by two independent lab tests conducted by FBI and FDA. There was no supervisor or personnel to check the calculation, dilution, and/or report any illegal activities. The sub-therapeutic dose of this life-saving drug might have contributed to the relapse of this victim's cancer.

Case 15.3

A drug received by a compounding pharmacy from a supplier was subjected to analysis. The reported purity of the drug was 90%. A 2.557 g of the drug was dissolved in an aqeous buffer, and the volume was adjusted to 100 mL in a volumetric flask. Four samples were withdrawn individually, and their drug content was determined by using a freshly prepared standard curve using a spectrophotometer. The four determined concentrations were: $X_1 = \mathbf{23.41}$ mg/mL; $X_2 = \mathbf{23.18}$ mg/mL; $X_3 = \mathbf{23.27}$ mg/mL; and $X_4 = \mathbf{23.23}$ mg/mL. If the acceptable error is less than 1% according to the SOP of the compounding pharmacy, is the accuracy of this method of determination satisfactory?

Approach: This is a problem related to accuracy determination using a standard curve and spectrophotometer.

The accuracy of the test procedure is determined as follows:

Step 1. Theoretical concentration of the drug should be calculated first

2.557 g with 90% purity is equivalent to 2.557 g $\times$ 0.9 = 2.301 g

$$\text{Theoretical concentration} = \frac{2.301 \text{ g}}{100 \text{ mL}} = \frac{2.301 \times 1000 \text{ mg}}{100 \text{ mL}} = 23.01 \text{ mg/mL}$$

Step 2. Concentration of the drug in all four samples is determined using the standard curve and the spectrophotometer:

$X_1 = \mathbf{23.41}$ mg/mL
$X_2 = \mathbf{23.18}$ mg/mL
$X_3 = \mathbf{23.27}$ mg/mL
$X_4 = \mathbf{23.23}$ mg/mL

Step 3. Experimentally determined mean concentration is determined next

$$\text{Mean concentration} = \frac{(23.41 + 23.18 + 23.27 + 23.23)}{4} \frac{mg}{mL} = \frac{93.09}{4} \frac{mg}{mL} = 23.27 \text{ mg/mL}$$

Step 4. Percentage error is then calculated

$$\% \text{ Error} = \frac{(23.27 - 23.01) \text{ mg/mL}}{23.01 \text{ mg/mL}} \times 100 = 1.13 \%$$

Therefore, the accuracy of this determination is not satisfactory since the calculated error is more than the allowable limit of 1%. The standard curve preparation as well as method validation needed further review and revisit.

Case 15.4

In a pharmaceutics skills lab, all students follow an SOP for each compounded preparation. A prescription was received from an instructor to prepare five Poly(ethylene glycol) (PEG) suppositories containing 250 mg of aspirin per suppository. As there was no SOP for PEG suppository available to the student and the mold to be used was the same, the students followed an SOP for making cocoa butter suppository instead. During the preparation, the student noticed that the calculated amount of material used for the preparation of suppositories was insufficient to complete five suppositories. How can this situation be explained to this student?

Approach: First, an SOP written for a cocoa butter suppository should not be used in making a PEG suppository. The density difference and the displacement factor are different for both bases. The mold should be calibrated with the PEG base first. The average weight for each blank PEG suppository is to be determined. Suppose its average weight is 2.2 g. The same mold needs to be calibrated with cocoa butter. Suppose the average blank suppository weight of cocoa butter is 1.9 g.

$$\text{Ratio between two weights} = \frac{\text{Weight of a blank PEG suppository}}{\text{Weight of a blank Cocoa butter suppository}} = \frac{2.2}{1.9} = 1.16$$

Density factor of aspirin in cocoa butter is 1.3 *from* Table 12.2
Density of PEG base relative to cocoa butter = 1.16 (the ratio determined from the early calibration)

$$0.250 \text{ g of Aspirin will then replace} = \frac{0.25 \text{ g}}{1.3} \times 1.16 = 0.22 \text{ g of PEG Base}$$

For each PEG suppository, (2.2 − 0.22 = 1.98 g) of PEG base will be mixed with 0.250 g of aspirin. If five suppositories are made, then 1.98 × 5 = 9.9 g PEG base will be added to 0.25 × 5 = 1.25 g of aspirin.

Since density difference and the displacement factor were not taken into account during the preparation of the PEG suppository, the amount of PEG base used was much less. Therefore, the amount of PEG base calculated was not able to fill all five suppositories.

Critical reflections and practice applications

- FDA-approved drugs are manufactured and tested in accordance with GMP regulations
- Compounded drug products are not subjected to FDA GMP guidelines
- Traditional pharmacy compounding offers an important therapeutic option for individualized drug products for patients
- FDA-approved drug products meet higher drug quality standards than the compounded drug product
- For both classes of drug products (FDA approved and compounded), quality assurance is equally important to assure the product is safe, effective, and reliable
- Quality assurance is a broad concept that covers all matters that individually or collectively contribute to the quality, safety, and effectiveness of the final product
- USP general chapter <1163> describes the quality assurance aspects of pharmaceutical compounding
- USP general chapter <1058> describes the different steps of analytical instruments qualification
- USP general chapter <1225> describes the different aspects of validation process that include accuracy, specificity, precision, detection limits, quantification limits, linearity and range, and robustness.
- Quality control requirements for pharmaceutical dosage forms are unique and different from dosage forms to dosage forms.

References

[1] S.A. Hanna, Quality assurance, Drug Dev. Ind. Pharm. 15 (6−7) (1989) 869−894, https://doi.org/10.3109/03639048909043654.
[2] https://www.fda.gov/drugs/guidance-compliance-regulatory-information/human-drug-compounding, Accessed on 6/24/2022.
[3] https://nabp.pharmacy/members/board-resources/model-pharmacy-act-rules/Asssesed on 6/24/2022.
[4] J. Gudeman, M. Jozwiakowski, J. Chollet, M. Randell, Potential risks of pharmacy compounding, Drugs R 13 (1) (2013) 1−8, https://doi.org/10.1007/s40268-013-0005-9.
[5] https://www.in.gov/health/files/USP1163_Quality%20Assurance%20in%20Compounding.pdf, Accessed on 6/26/2022.
[6] http://www.uspbpep.com/usp31/v31261/usp31nf26s1_c1058.asp. Accessed 6/26/2022.
[7] http://www.uspbpep.com/usp29/v29240/usp29nf24s0_c1225.html. Accessed on 6/26/2022.

[8] E.L. Inman, J.K. Frischmann, P.J. Jimenez, G.D. Winkel, M.L. Persinger, B.S. Rutherford, General method validation guidelines for pharmaceutical samples, J. Chromatogr. Sci. 25 (Issue 6) (1987) 252–256, https://doi.org/10.1093/chromsci/25.6.252.

[9] Quality Assurance vs. Quality Control Explained: 5 key differences. https://www.qualio.com/blog/quality-assurance-vs-quality-control, Accessed on 6/26/2022.

[10] L.X. Yu, Pharmaceutical quality by design: product and process development, understanding, and control, Pharm. Res. (N. Y.) 25 (2008) 781–791, https://doi.org/10.1007/s11095-007-9511-1.

[11] L. Zhang, S. Mao, Application of quality by design in the current drug development, Asian J. Pharm. Sci. 12 (2017) 1–8.

[12] http://www.uspbpep.com/usp31/v31261/usp31nf26s1_c1151.asp, Accessed on 6/26/2022.

[13] R.W. Abdo, N. Saadi, N.I. Hijazi, Y.A. Suleiman, Quality control and testing evaluation of pharmaceutical aerosols, Drug Deliv. Syst. (2020) 579–614, https://doi.org/10.1016/B978-0-12-814487-9.00012-0. Epub 2019 Oct 25. PMCID: PMC7155167.

[14] https://www.fda.gov/drugs/human-drug-compounding/report-limited-fda-survey-compounded-drug-products. Assesesd on 6/26/2022.

[15] https://www.nytimes.com/2003/06/08/magazine/the-toxic-pharmacist.html, Assessed on 7/19/2022.

Biological applications of pharmaceutics

16

Membrane Transport and Permeation

Maria P. Lambros[1] and Justin A. Tolman[2]

[1]Department of Pharmaceutical Sciences, College of Pharmacy, Western University of Health Sciences, Pomona, CA, United States [2]Department of Pharmacy Sciences, School of Pharmacy and Health Professions, Creighton University, Omaha, NE, United States

> **CHAPTER OBJECTIVES**
> - Describe the composition of biological membranes.
> - Explain the fluid mosaic model of membranes.
> - Compare and contrast the membrane transport processes of diffusion, carrier-mediated, and vesicular transport.
> - Develop and evaluate clinically relevant scenarios that involve medications that target or interact with membrane transport processes.

Keywords: Active transport; Carrier-mediated transport; Diffusion; Drug transport; Efflux transport; Lipid bilayer; Passive transport; Phospholipid and Vesicle-medicated transport.

16.1 Introduction

Drug movement in biological systems is usually governed by interactions between the drug molecule and cellular membranes. These interactions principally describe drug permeation, or movement, from one side of a membrane to the other. That is, permeation is the ability of a drug molecule to pass through biological membranes and can include both passive and active transport phenomena. Drug transport can often be predominantly affected by one type of membrane permeation and then by perturbations to these systems. This chapter briefly reviews the composition of cell membranes and then describes membrane transport processes.

16.2 Cell membranes

All the cells in our body are surrounded by plasma membranes [1]. The plasma membrane is a semipermeable barrier that functions as a protective shield from the external environment. Although substantial variability exists in cell membrane composition throughout the body, most cell membranes consist of amphiphilic lipids and phospholipids arranged in a lipid bilayer with proteins embedded in or through this bilayer as shown in Fig. 16.1.

Pharmaceutics, Second Edition
https://doi.org/10.1016/B978-0-323-99796-6.00013-8

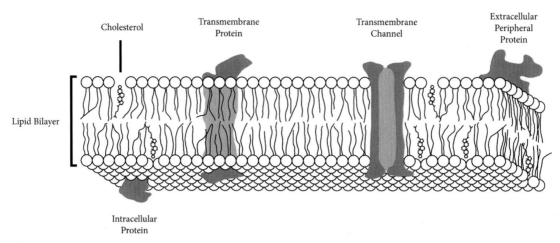

FIGURE 16.1   A schematic representation of a cell membrane. It consists of a lipid bilayer and embedded protein structures.

16.2.1 Membrane composition

Most membrane lipids are phospholipid molecules containing a glycerol backbone, with two of the three —OH groups of glycerol linked to two long acyl chains and the third —OH group is linked to a phosphate group which is further linked to a small polar molecule such as choline, ethanolamine or serine (Fig. 16.2). These acyl chains can be of varying lengths and can be saturated or unsaturated. The two acyl chains represent the non-polar, lipophilic part of the phospholipid molecule, while the glycerol backbone with the phosphate group and its linked molecule represents the polar, hydrophilic part of the phospholipid molecule. Examples of common cell membrane lipids include phosphatidylcholine, phosphatidylserine, phosphatidylinositol, sphingomyelin, glycolipids, and cholesterol.

In physiologic conditions, these lipids form a bilayer with hydrophilic head groups toward the external aqueous environment and hydrophobic fatty acid chains pointed into a lipophilic core region. These membrane bilayers are often stable under normal physiologic conditions to minimize aqueous exposure of lipophilic membrane lipid portions. Despite relative membrane integrity, there is a great deal of flexibility and "fluidity" due to the fatty acid chains in the lipophilic membrane core [2]. Most of the lipid movement in intact membranes is lateral (sideways)

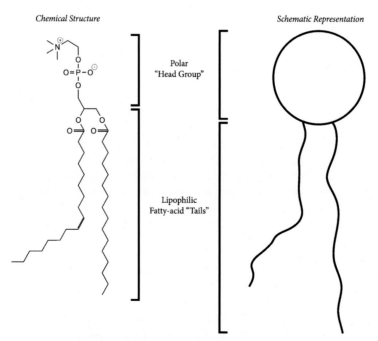

FIGURE 16.2   Chemical structure of phospholipids.

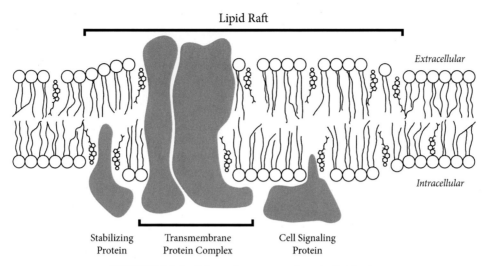

FIGURE 16.3 Schematic representation of a lipid raft.

within one layer of the membrane. Rarely, a lipid in one layer of the bilayer may exchange position with another lipid in the other monolayer. Lipid movement and distribution within biological membranes can be substantially affected by normal cellular functions and changes to cellular shape [2].

Lipid composition is an important factor in determining the properties of biological membranes. Long-chain fatty acids tend to thicken the cell membrane and create a more substantial lipophilic core. The presence of double bonds in the fatty acid chains also prevents the close association of lipophilic tails and induces more membrane fluidity. In contrast, cholesterol can intercalate between fatty acids to induce more close association of lipophilic tails and induce membrane rigidity.

16.2.2 Fluid mosaic model for membranes

In 1972, Singer and Nicolson proposed the "fluid mosaic" model from which our current view of biological membranes has evolved [3]. The fluid portion of this model is derived from the flexible and fluid lipid bilayer, as previously described. The mosaic portion of this model describes heterogeneous globular protein structures either partially or fully embedded in the lipid bilayer (Fig. 16.1). The lipid and protein constituents of the bilayer float freely in the bilayer plane and form a mosaic pattern.

The scientific understanding of the fluid-mosaic model has evolved with scientific advances. Specifically, cell membranes are not freely fluid but have regions of increased order imposed by large-scale structures and complexes (Fig. 16.3). Lipid rafts are heterogeneous membrane domains with clusters of lipids and associated protein complexes in ordered spatial relationships [4]. These organized regions have varied structures and temporal stabilities but exist for the proper functioning of cellular processes. One example of a lipid raft includes a membrane domain containing a cell surface receptor and intracellular machinery communicating extracellular signals to intracellular second messenger systems and functions. Another type of lipid raft includes membrane domains that stabilize protein-mediated transport systems for the physical transfer of substances into or out of the cell.

16.3 Membrane transport

The semi-permeable nature of biological membranes is due to the fluid mosaic nature of membranes. The composition of both lipid bilayers and embedded protein structures can affect the permeation of substances through membranes. That is, a substance must then be able to pass directly through the membrane, be transported through the membrane with the assistance of a protein structure, or be transported through membranes through vesicles that merge with, or are formed from, the cell membrane. These three broad categories of permeation are described as diffusion, carrier-mediated transport, or vesicular transport. Within these categories, some substances can be transported passively without the cellular expenditure of energy, whereas other transport systems require energy to move substances. Most substances are predominantly transported through biological membranes by limited permeation mechanisms based on substance physicochemical properties such as molecular size, polarity, ionization state, aqueous solubility, hydrophilicity/lipophilicity balance, and mimicry of endogenous compounds [5].

16.3.1 Diffusion

Diffusion is the movement of substances from a region of high concentration to a region of low concentration. The process of diffusion can be described by Fick's First Law of Diffusion. When used to describe diffusion through a semipermeable biological membrane, the flux (J) of a substance through the membrane is inversely proportional to the membrane thickness (h) and proportional to the diffusion coefficient (D) of the drug through the membrane and the concentration gradient ($C_1 - C_2$) across the membrane:

$$J = DK(C_1 - C_2)/h \tag{16.1}$$

where K is the partition coefficient of the diffusing molecule in the membrane (K = concentration of the drug in the membrane/concentration of the drug in the donor, C_D or receiver compartment, C_R). In Eq. (16.1), the units for D are in cm^2/s; the thickness, h, in cm; the concentration, C, in g/cm^3, and the flux, J, in $g\ cm^{-2}\ s^{-1}$.

The driving force for diffusion is the concentration gradient, while the resistive force for diffusion is the thickness of the membrane (Fig. 16.4). As a result, diffusion is a passive phenomenon that does not directly require energy for the movement of substances. This passive process will continue with net substance movement occurring from a region of high concentration to low concentration (with a concentration gradient) until an equilibrium is established such that there is no difference in drug concentrations across the membrane. During this equilibrium, drug movement will continue to occur but with no net change in drug concentrations across the membrane.

Because in pharmaceutical applications it is difficult to measure the diffusion coefficient, D, the partition coefficient, K, or the membrane thickness, all these terms are combined in a single term called permeability coefficient, P, which can be measured experimentally and its unit is cm/s.

$$P = \frac{DK}{h} \tag{16.2}$$

Based on the permeability Eq. (16.2), the flux Eq. (16.1) can be written as

$$J = P(C_1 - C_2) \tag{16.3}$$

Not all substances are able to diffuse across biological membranes. Water is able to diffuse through cell membranes. Many nonpolar substances, such as oxygen and carbon dioxide, as well as many drug molecules, are able to passively diffuse directly through membranes. The drug molecule must also be lipophilic enough to pass through the membrane but not so lipophilic as to be retained within the lipid bilayer lipophilic core. The rate of diffusion is

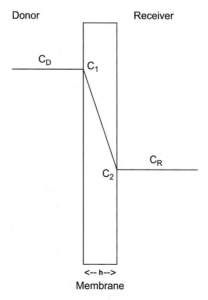

FIGURE 16.4   Steady-state diffusion through a thin membrane.

then limited by the surface area across which diffusion can take place. If a substance is unable to pass directly through the lipid bilayer, protein-mediated phenomena can potentially cause transport across biological membranes.

16.3.1.1 Pharmacologically relevant processes to diffusion

A number of drugs as well as environmental or chemical agents exert their effects by disrupting the lipid bilayer. For example, amphotericin B is a large macrocyclic polyene antifungal agent (Fig. 16.5) that is formulated in a variety of commercially available preparations (Amphotec, Abelcet, and AmBisome) [5b]. The amphiphilic faces of this large molecule are thought to intercalate into the lipid bilayer of fungal cell membranes through association with prevalent lipid sterols in fungal membranes. Clusters of amphotericin B molecules then associate into loose lipid raft structures and form indiscriminate holes [6] or gaps in the fungal cell membrane integrity. The disruption of membrane integrity has catastrophic effects on fungal cell viability and contributes to cell death.

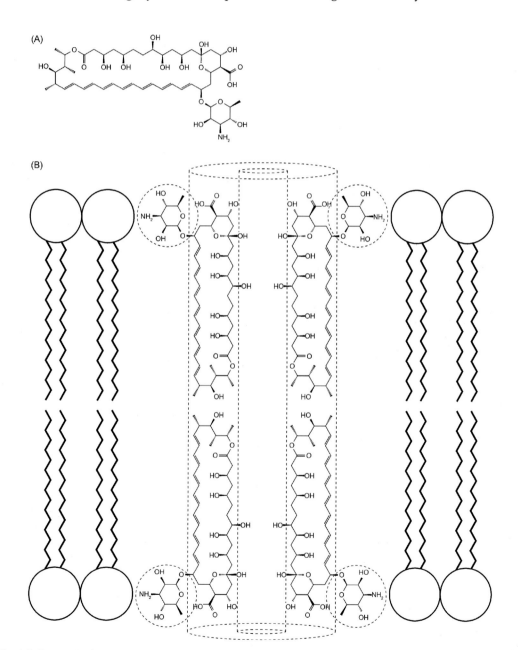

FIGURE 16.5   (A) Chemical structure of amphotericin B, (B) schematic representation of a fungal membrane disrupted by amphotericin B.

Amphotericin B also can cause nephrotoxicity that is thought to be due in part to association with sterols present in renal cell lipid bilayers. Other drugs that affect cell membranes are often cytotoxic and used for cell-killing pharmacologic effects as antibacterial or antifungal agents.

16.3.2 Carrier-mediated transport

Many biologically relevant substances can pass through membranes through specialized pores and channels or protein structures. Many small charged species (e.g., Na^+, K^+, Ca^{2+}, and Cl^- ions) pass via specific channels formed by transmembrane integral proteins that allow dissolved ion movement through membranes in response to electrical or chemical stimuli. Notably, these pores or channels principally allow passive ion movement with a concentration gradient. Other protein transporters can facilitate the passive diffusion of small polar molecules (e.g., glucose) into cells with transport described as facilitated diffusion. Facilitative diffusion does not require energy from ATP hydrolysis directly.

In contrast, using an energy source such as ATP, other embedded protein structures, promote direct substance movement against concentration gradients and are termed primary active transport systems. Some of these systems are specialized protein structures that move ions or small polar molecules against concentration gradients to maintain electrochemical gradients and transport important biological substances. Separate protein systems are efflux pumps or transporters and cause substance movement out of cells for protective purposes. Many primary active systems allow substances to permeate through membranes based on distinct chemical or molecular properties, whereas others are promiscuous and might transport substances based on a broad range of properties such as molecular size, polarity, ionization state (including cations and anions), lipophilicity, and functional groups.

Protein-mediated systems that cause substance movement against gradients but do so through co-transport of other ions with a gradient are designated as secondary active transport systems. These systems simultaneously transport a small polar molecule or ion against an established concentration gradient while a separate ion or molecule is transported with an established ion gradient. Secondary active transport systems then do not directly require energy for the movement of substances but instead rely on ion gradients established by primary active transport systems. Most secondary active transport systems are highly specialized for the movement of specific molecules or ions.

Despite numerous differences in protein function, all carrier-mediated transport systems are dependent on specialized protein structures embedded in biological membranes (Fig. 16.6) [7]. Carrier-mediated systems require some degree of protein conformational change to achieve substance permeation through membranes.

Due to the physical reliance on a distinct protein structure, these carrier-mediated systems can become saturated to demonstrate transport maxima at a maximum rate of transport. The rate of substance transport is then limited by the number of transport proteins available for substance movement.

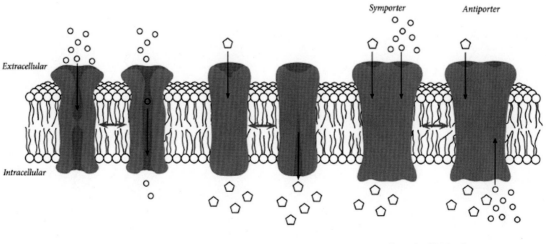

○ = Ion or Small Molecule

⬠ = Small Molecule or Macromolecule

FIGURE 16.6 Schematic representations of various protein structures embedded in biological membranes involved in membrane transport.

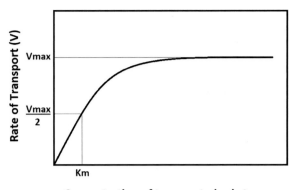

Concentration of transported substance

FIGURE 16.7 Carrier-mediated transport reaches a maximum transport rate, V_{max}, when the carrier protein is saturated. The Michaelis constant, K_m, is numerically equal to the concentration of the transported substance, when the transport rate reaches half of its maximal value.

The rate, V, of active transport of a substance is described by the Michaelis—Menten equation:

$$V = V_{max}C/(K_m + C) \tag{16.4}$$

where C is the concentration of the substrate (substance), V_{max} is the maximum transport rate that can be attained, and K_m is the Michaelis—Menten constant (Fig. 16.7).

16.3.2.1 Pharmacologically relevant processes to carrier-mediated transport

Numerous drugs and agents exert pharmacologic action on protein-mediated membrane transport systems. Many drugs affect the regulation of ion gradients across cell membranes through the inhibition of ion transporters. These ion-regulating drugs are therapeutically used in a variety of disease states, including hypertension, cardiac arrhythmias, seizures, and nerve signal transduction. Nontherapeutic insecticides, chemical warfare agents, and chemical toxins can also affect ion gradients and ion transport systems [8,9]. Other therapeutic and nontherapeutic agents directly affect primary active transport systems that are used for the movement of endogenous biochemical substances and exogenous drug molecules. Secondary active transport systems can also be directly and indirectly affected by drugs.

One example of a drug affecting a primary active transport system is omeprazole (Prilosec) [5b]. It is a small molecule in a drug class that targets a specific ion transporter in the gut (Fig. 16.8). This class is referred to as proton-pump inhibitors (PPIs) and irreversibly inhibits the H^+/K^+ ATPase co-transporter present on the apical surface of gastric parietal cells of the stomach. This primary active co-transport system pumps protons against the pH gradient to concentrate acid in the gastric lumen while also scavenging a potassium ion from the gastric lumen and transporting it against the potassium gradient into the cell. Omeprazole and other PPIs covalently bind to cysteine residues in hydrogen-potassium pumps to irreversibly inhibit their function and result in the inhibition of gastric acid secretion [10].

Several diseases are the result of the dysfunction of iron-transporting proteins that reduce the iron transport through membranes, impeding the iron import into and/or export out of cells. For example, microcytic hypochromic anemia is a common form of anemia in which there is decreased iron absorption, decreased iron in enterocytes, and iron overload in liver. It is caused by the dysfunction of the divalent metal transporter 1 (DMT1), which causes a reduction in the iron uptake into the duodenal enterocytes and prevents the endosomal iron release in progenitor red blood cells [11].

16.3.3 Vesicular transport

Vesicular transport is a cellular mechanism that allows the permeation of large polar substances or large volumes of substances through biological membranes by the formation or fusion of membrane-enclosed vesicles with the cellular membrane (Fig. 16.9) [12]. Endocytosis is the process in which a substance enters the cell because the cell engulfs it [22]. Exocytosis is the process in which a substance inside an intracellular vesicle exits the cell after the fusion of the intracellular vesicle with the cell membrane. Endocytosis and exocytosis rates are regulated to maintain constant cellular membrane surface area and cell volume. Both endocytosis and exocytosis require energy to form and move vesicles within cells.

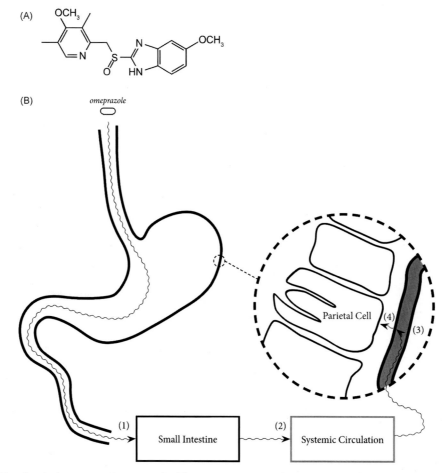

FIGURE 16.8 (A) The chemical structure of omeprazole, (B) representative membrane transport processes for omeprazole. (1) Dissolution of omeprazole in the small intestine and absorption of the drug across the apical membrane of the intestinal epithelium, (2) transport of omeprazole through the basolateral membrane of the intestinal epithelium through the capillary epithelium and into the systemic circulation, (3) transport of omeprazole through the capillary epithelium and to the parietal cell, (4) transport of omeprazole through the parietal cell membrane to exert pharmacologic action on proton pumps located in the apical membrane of parietal cells.

16.3.3.1 Examples of pharmacologically relevant processes to vesicular transport

The gastrointestinal epithelium contains specialized M-cells for the vesicular transport of macromolecules and microorganisms [13]. M-cells internalize antigenic pathogens or particles by engulfing them in vesicles on the apical side of the cell and transporting them to the basolateral side through transcytosis. In this way, appropriate immune responses can be generated against ingested antigens. By adapting oral vaccination strategies, the normally nonspecific vesicle formation can be tailored to provide mucosal vaccination against specific ingested antigens. The live, attenuated oral polio vaccine (OPV) uses M-cell vesicular transport to promote vesicle formation [14]. Specifically, the OPV causes epithelial M-cells to be primed for increased vesicular formation and transport of the attenuated polio virus to provide mucosal immunity to polio which contributed to polio eradication [15].

16.4 Select membrane transport systems as drug interactions

Many drugs utilize carrier-mediated transport systems through facilitated, primary, or secondary systems for drug permeation through membranes. This increases the likelihood that some drug/substance combinations could utilize or affect the same protein system for drug movement processes. These interactions could be competitive or beneficial for therapeutic drug effects but must be considered for appropriate drug therapy evaluation.

One example of membrane transport—based drug interactions involves a promiscuous efflux pump referred to as P-glycoprotein (Pgp) [16]. Pgp belongs to the ATP-binding cassette transporter (ABC) protein superfamily. ABC

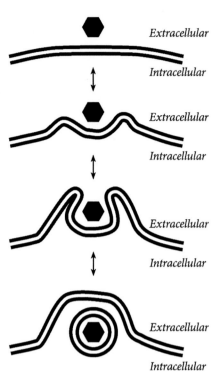

FIGURE 16.9 Schematic representation of vesicular transport.

transporters involved in the translocation of substances through biological membranes are a very diverse group and include numerous protein structures that impart multidrug resistance (MDR) [17]. Pgp is a well-characterized protein that is widely distributed and expressed throughout the body [18]. It actively inhibits net drug permeation across biological membranes. Pgp is a protective efflux pump that can expel exogenous substances that have permeated through a membrane back into the lumen of various organs or tissues. Many hydrophobic drugs are affected by Pgp efflux under normal physiologic conditions, whereas some pathogenic conditions, including cancer, can cause overexpression of Pgp. Pgp primary active transport expression can be a significant cause of MDR for many pathologic conditions.

16.5 Conclusions

Drug permeation through biological membranes is a nontrivial barrier to pharmacologic action. However, permeation is possible through the semipermeable nature of biological membranes. A large diversity of substances is able to pass through membranes based on a surplus of transport mechanisms. These transport mechanisms include passive drug diffusion and carrier-mediated transport, which includes facilitated diffusion, as well as active transport phenomena of primary and secondary active transport and vesicular-mediated transport. In the next chapter (Chapter 17), the process of drug absorption and disposition in biological systems would expand on this understanding of the membrane transport process and drug permeation.

Case studies

Case 16.1

Loperamide is an over-the-counter antidiarrheal drug taken orally. *In vitro* studies have shown that it is a very potent μ-opioid receptor agonist. The expected activity would include analgesia, sedation, drowsiness, constipation, and respiratory depression. However, *in vivo*, it exhibits only antidiarrheal activity. Can you suggest why such central nervous system (CNS) activity is not seen in the case of oral loperamide use? If the drug will be co-administered with quinidine, do you expect any drug–drug interaction problem? Hints: *Quinidine is a potent Pgp inhibitor.*

Approach: We did not see any central nervous activity due to abundant P-gp activity at the blood—brain barrier (BBB). Therefore, the transport of this molecule to the brain is restricted. When Pgp inhibitors such as quinidine are co-administered, things change, and we expect a drug—drug interaction. We see an elevated antidiarrheal activity along with CNS side effects.

Case 16.2

Targeted delivery to a tumor by nanoparticles has gained tremendous attention because of their extra-permeability and retention (EPR) effect. Explain how it works in the case of a solid tumor.

Approach: Nanoparticles in particle sizes at approximately 100 nm can pass through leaky vasculature. Therefore, their tumor uptake is very high. Because of their particle size range, they are not cleared by reticuloendothelial systems (RES) and can be circulated in the blood for a long time. Finally, because solid tumors are devoid of lymphatic drainage, once nanoparticles are taken into tumors, they stay for a longer time in the tumors. This combined phenomenon is called the EPR effect.

Case 16.3

Tetracycline is an antibiotic and is used to treat bacterial infections, including respiratory tract infections, intestinal, skin, urinary, and other infections. Tetracycline should not be taken with products that contain calcium such as milk, yogurt, cheese, and products that contain magnesium, aluminum such as antiacids, please explain why.

Approach: Tetracycline binds to polyvalent cations such as Ca^{2+}, Mg^{2+}, Al^{3+}, Fe^{2+}, Fe^{3+}, and Zn^{2+} and forms chelates with these ions resulting in reduced absorption. It is recommended that patients take tetracycline 2 or 3 h before or after preparations containing calcium, magnesium, aluminum, iron, and zinc ions.

Case 16.4

Calcium supplementation is common in patients who have inadequate dietary calcium consumption or with conditions associated with calcium deficiency. When taken enterally, calcium is absorbed primarily by active transport in the upper small intestine. Explain the calcium supplementation dosing guidelines based on the differences in total calcium intake.

Approach: The recommendations for calcium intake acknowledge that it has dose-limited absorption. Because of saturable calcium absorption, upper dosage limits exist beyond which absorption of calcium becomes negligible. The National Institutes of Health has stated in, *Calcium: Fact Sheet for Health Professionals* [19],

> An inverse relationship exists between calcium intake and absorption. Absorption of calcium from food is about 45% at intakes of 200 mg/day but only 15% when intakes are higher than 2,000 mg/day.

The percentage of calcium absorbed from supplements, as with that from foods, depends not only on the source of calcium but also on the total amount of elemental calcium consumed at one time; as the amount increases, the percentage absorbed decreases. Absorption from supplements is highest, with doses of 500 mg or less. For example, the body absorbs about 36% of a 300 mg calcium dose and 28% of a 1000 mg dose.

Case 16.5

The permeability of sulfasalazine across Caco-2 cell monolayer was studied as a function of concentration and direction of transport [20]. Permeability coefficients of sulfasalazine across Caco-2 cell monolayers were approximately 342-, 261-, and 176-fold higher from basolateral to apical direction (BL→AP) than from apical to basolateral direction (AP→BL) at 100, 200, and 500 mM, respectively. How one can explain the very low permeability of this drug in *in vitro* caco-2 cell monolayer as well as the low *in vivo* absorption?

Approach: This study was carried out to determine whether sulfasalazine is a substrate for the apically polarized efflux systems in Caco-2 cell monolayers. The permeability values at three different concentrations are provided below. The PDR (Permeability directional ratio) was calculated using the equation

$$PDR = \frac{P_{\text{Caco-2}}\,(\text{BL} \rightarrow \text{AP})}{P_{\text{Caco-2}}(\text{AP} \rightarrow \text{BL})}$$

Permeability (cm/sec)	Concentration of sulfasalazine (mM)		
	100	200	500
$P_{\text{Caco-2}}$ (AP-BL)	3.4×10^{-8} cm/s	3.2×10^{-8} cm/s	3.2×10^{-8} cm/s
$P_{\text{Caco-2}}$ (BL-AP)	1.12×10^{-5} cm/s	0.84×10^{-5} cm/s	0.56×10^{-5} cm/s
PDR	342	261	176

AP, apical; *BL*, basolateral.

Sulfasalazine exhibited a high PDR value at all concentrations tested. This indicates a strong interaction with cellular efflux pumps and transporters in Caco-2 cells. This efflux and transporters may partly explain the low absorption of sulfasalazine in the GI tract.

Case 16.6

The effect of molecular weight on skin permeability of compounds with similar lipophilicity was reported by Potts and Guy (1992) [21]. By simple doubling the molecular weight of a penetrant from 400 g/mol to 800 g/mol with similar lipophilicity, the permeability of skin decreased by a factor of almost 2.5 log units or 300-fold. How could you explain this to a pharmacy intern working with you during their clinical rotation?

Approach: Potts and Guy developed a predictive model using a published permeability coefficient for the transport of molecules through mammalian epidermis based on their molecular weight and octanol water partition coefficient, K_{Oct} as follows:

$$Log\ K_P = -6.3 + 0.71 \times\ Log\ K_{Oct} - 0.0061 \times \text{MW}$$

Using the above equation and keeping the K_{Oct} the same for both drugs with molecular weights 400 and 800, one can easily calculate the permeability coefficients for both these drugs. The calculated K_P for a drug with low molecular weight is higher than that of the drug with high molecular weight.

Critical reflections and practice applications

Most drugs must pass through biological membranes when absorbed, distributed throughout the body, elicit their pharmacologic action, metabolized, and/or excreted. The mechanisms by which drugs move through or across membranes directly affect drug therapy. A pharmacist must understand diffusion, carrier-mediated transport, and vesicular transport processes to synthesize the pharmacologic principles of drug action and adverse effects, the pharmacokinetic properties of drugs, and their therapeutic use.

References

[1] L. Sherwood, The plasma membrane and membrane potential (Ch 3), in: L. Sherwood (Ed.), Human Physiology: From Cells to Systems, Brooks/Cole, Belmont, CA, 2013.

[2] D. Marguet, Dynamics in the plasma membrane: how to combine fluidity and order, EMBO J. 25 (15) (2006) 3446–3457.

[3] S.J. Singer, G.L. Nicolson, The fluid mosaic model of the structure of cell membranes, Science (New York, N.Y.). 175 (4023) (1972) 720–731.

[4] A. Catalá, Lipid peroxidation modifies the picture of membranes from the "fluid mosaic model" to the "lipid whisker model", Biochimie 94 (1) (2012) 101–109.

[5] (a) D.E. Golan, Principles of pharmacology: the pathophysiologic basis of drug therapy, In: D.E. Golan, Principles of Pharmacology: The Pathophysiologic Basis of Drug Therapy, Lippincott Williams & Wilkins, Philadelphia, PA2011. (b) G.K. McEvoy, AHFS Drug Information American Hospital Formulary Service, American Society of Health-System Pharmacists, 2013.

[6] K.C. Gray, D.S. Palacios, I. Dailey, Amphotericin primarily kills yeast by simply binding ergosterol, Proc. Natl. Acad. Sci. U.S.A. 109 (7) (2012) 2234–2239.

[7] N. Mizuno, Impact of drug transporter studies on drug discovery and development, Pharmacol. Rev. 55 (3) (2003) 425–461.

[8] J.D. Doherty, Insecticides affecting ion transport, Pharmacol. Ther. 7 (1) (1979) 123–151.

[9] G. Schiavo, M. Matteoli, C. Montecucco, Neurotoxins affecting neuroexocytosis, Physiol. Rev. 80 (2) (2000) 717–766.

[10] J.M. Shin, Pharmacology of proton pump inhibitors, Curr. Gastroenterol. Rep. 10 (6) (2008) 528–534.

[11] A.S. Grillo, A.M. SantaMaria, M.D. Kafina, et al., Restored iron transport by a small molecule promotes absorption and hemoglobinization in animals, Sciences 356 (2017) 608–616.

[12] J.J. Rennick, A.P.R. Johnston, R.G. Parton, Key principles and methods for studying the endocytosis of biological and nanoparticle therapeutics, Nat. Nanotechnol. 16 (2021) 266–276.

[13] L.J. Hathaway, J.P. Kraehenbuhl, The role of M cells in mucosal immunity, Cell. Mol. Life Sci. 57 (2) (2000) 323–332.

[14] A. Gebert, Antigen transport into Peyer's patches: increased uptake by constant numbers of M cells, Am. J. Pathol. 164 (1) (2004) 65–72.

[15] A.N. Donlan, W.A. Petri, Mucosal immunity and the eradication of polio, Science 368 (6489) (2020) 362–363, https://doi.org/10.1126/science.abb8588.

[16] D.K. Yu, The contribution of P-glycoprotein to pharmacokinetic drug-drug interactions, J. Clin. Pharmacol. 39 (12) (1999) 1203–1211.

[17] J. Sun, Multidrug resistance P-glycoprotein: crucial significance in drug disposition and interaction, Med. Sci. Mon. Int. Med. J. Exp. Clin. Res. 10 (1) (2004) RA5–R14.

[18] B.L. Lum, M.P. Gosland, MDR expression in normal tissues. Pharmacologic implications for the clinical use of P-glycoprotein inhibitors, Hematol. Oncol. Clin. N. Am. 9 (2) (1995) 319–336.

[19] National Institutes of Health (NIH), Office of dietary supplements (ODS). Calcium: Fact Sheet for Health Professionals, 2022.

[20] E. Liang, J. Proudfoot, M. Yazdanian, Mechanisms of transport and structure-permeability relationship of sulfasalazine and its analogs in caco-2 cell monolayers, Pharmaceut. Res. 17 (10) (2000).

[21] R.O. Potts, R.H. Guy, Predicting skin permeability, Pharm. Res. (N. Y.) 9 (1992) 663–669, https://doi.org/10.1023/A:1015810312465.

[22] G.J. Doherty, H.T. McMahon, Mechanisms of endocytosis, Ann. Rev. Biochem. 78 (2009) 857–902.

17

Factors Affecting Drug Absorption and Disposition

Chong-Hui Gu[1], Anuj Kuldipkumar[2] and Harsh Chauhan[3]

[1]Foghorn Therapeutics, Cambridge, MA, United States [2]Syner-G BioPharm Group, Southborough, MA, United States [3]Shattuck Labs, Durham, NC, United States

---

CHAPTER OBJECTIVES

- Describe the process of drug absorption from a drug product into the systemic circulation.
- Relate the processes that govern drug dissolution, permeation, and first-pass metabolism to overall drug absorption from the gastrointestinal tract.
- Compare and contrast the factors affecting drug absorption from the gastrointestinal tract.
- Describe the factors that affect drug disposition following absorption.
- Understand the concept of volume of distribution to describe the extent of distribution of drugs in patients.
- Understand the various processes of drug elimination pathways.

Keywords: Absorption; Disposition; Distribution; Elimination; Food effects; Oral absorption and permeation.

17.1 Introduction

To treat a disease with a drug therapy, a sufficient amount of drug should be delivered to the site of action to achieve desirable therapeutic effects with minimal undesirable side effects. As the drug concentration in the action site is influenced by absorption and disposition processes in the body, it is therefore important to study the factors affecting how these processes affect drug action and to select optimal drug products.

After drug administration, except for local treatment, a drug molecule must first enter the systemic circulation to reach the site of action and exert pharmacologic effects. The processes of drug transfer from the extravascular site of administration to systemic circulation are defined as absorption [1]. This chapter describes the general process of absorption and then focuses on the process of oral absorption and the factors affecting oral absorption. Although a drug is absorbed from numerous routes of administration, the specific factors that affect drug absorption from those sites do not necessarily correlate with those that affect oral absorption [2].

The term "drug disposition" is used in this chapter to describe distribution (the processes of drug movement within a patient) and elimination (the removal of a drug from a patient) [1]. Detailed descriptions of drug disposition lie in the field of pharmacokinetics (PK), which is beyond the scope of this textbook. However, this chapter introduces the basic concepts of drug disposition and factors affecting drug disposition.

17.2 Drug absorption

Drug absorption is a heterogeneous process by which a drug travels into a patient. For many drugs, absorption into the patient is preceded by several steps and followed by several others before pharmacologic effects can be detected (Fig. 17.1). First, the drug is incorporated into a specific formulation for the preparation of a drug product. Second, that drug product is administered to the patient. Third, the drug is released from the drug product and becomes potentially available for absorption. Fourth, the drug is absorbed into the systemic circulation. Fifth, the drug travels to the site of action via systemic circulation.

Not all drug products experience these steps for pharmacologic action. For example, there is no absorption process for drugs that are administered directly into the systemic blood circulation by injection or infusion. All other routes of drug administration will have some absorption potential. However, the route of administration is not the only factor influencing drug absorption in patients. The physicochemical properties of the drug molecule, the dosage form, membrane permeation, and physiologic and pathologic processes in the patient are some factors that can affect absorption.

Although the complexities of drug absorption are substantial in the various organs and tissues involved in drug administration, oral absorption provides clear and common explanations and illustrations of these factors. Following this discussion of oral drug absorption, the pharmaceutical expert should be able to synthesize anatomical and physiological understandings of organs and tissues with the pharmaceutics principles for a basic understanding of drug absorption in various organs and tissues. Chapter 19 also provides brief overviews for absorptive processes in common sites of drug administration.

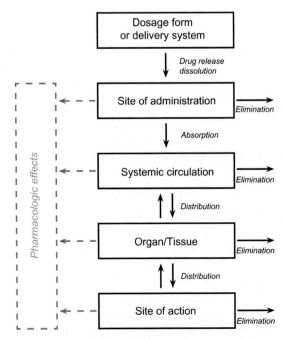

FIGURE 17.1   Schematic diagram illustrating the processes of drug movement preceding pharmacologic effects.

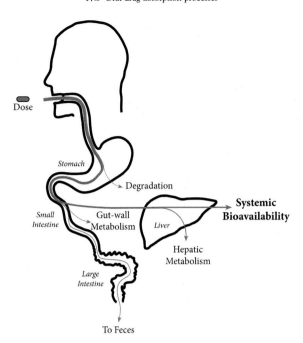

FIGURE 17.2 Oral drug absorption processes. (A) Drug, given as a solid orally, must overcome dissolution, permeation, and metabolism barriers to reach systemic circulation. Incomplete dissolution, incomplete permeation, and removal of drugs by metabolism in the gut and liver are often the causes of poor oral absorption.

17.3 Oral drug absorption processes

Oral drug absorption involves the release of drugs in a dissolved state in the gastrointestinal (GI) tract (dissolution), permeation through the GI membrane, and entrance into the systemic circulation after passing through the portal vein and liver. The absorbed drug molecules must survive gut metabolism and first-pass extraction by the liver before reaching systemic circulation [3]. Fig. 17.2 illustrates the oral absorption processes.

17.3.1 Dissolution

The first step of oral absorption after administration of a solid dosage form is the dissolution of the drug in the GI lumen. The process of drug dissolution is explained in detail in Chapters 6 and 8. In review, drug dissolution consists of two steps: (1) the formation of a loose drug molecule at the solid–liquid interface, similar to a surface reaction, and (2) the diffusion of the loose drug molecule through the solid–liquid interface into the bulk of the solution. Many dissolution profiles can be described by the diffusion rate limited process in the form of the Noyes–Whitney equation, as shown in Eq. (17.1) [4]:

$$\frac{dM}{dt} = \frac{DA(S-c)}{h} \tag{17.1}$$

where M is the amount dissolved, t is time, D is the diffusion coefficient of the drug molecule, h is the diffusion layer thickness, A is the surface area, c is the concentration of drug in the dissolution medium at time t, and S is the solubility of the drug in the dissolution medium. For spherical particles under the sink condition when c is much smaller than S, the Noyes–Whitney equation can be expressed as shown in Eq. (17.2):

$$M_0^{1/3} - M^{1/3} = kt, \quad k = \frac{DS}{h}\left(\frac{4\pi\rho}{3}\right)^{1/3} \tag{17.2}$$

where M_0 is the initial drug mass, M is the remaining undissolved drug mass at time t, and k is the dissolution rate constant determined by the diffusion coefficient, diffusion layer thickness, solubility, and density of the material (ρ) [5]. Eq. 14.2 is well known as Hixson–Crowell's cubic root law of dissolution. However, under different conditions, it is also possible that the dissolution rate is controlled by the formation of loose drug molecules at the solid–liquid interface. For the surface reaction—controlled dissolution, the dissolution rate can be described similar to the equation used to describe chemical reactions [6].

It is clear from the Noyes—Whitney equation that the dissolution rate of diffusion-controlled dissolution is influenced by diffusivity, diffusion layer thickness, surface area, and solubility. These factors are determined by the physicochemical properties of the drug molecule and its formulation as well as the physiological conditions of the GI tract. Among these factors, solubility not only directly influences the dissolution rate, which can then control the absorption rate if the permeation rate is fast enough, but also determines the maximum amount of drug dissolved, which may control the extent of absorption.

The dissolution step as the first step of oral absorption presents both a challenge and an opportunity for drug delivery. Recently, many drugs in development have very poor aqueous solubility, as discussed in Chapters 6 and 8 [7]. The challenge of delivering these drugs is to improve the solubility and dissolution rate to ensure that enough drugs are absorbed to provide a therapeutic effect. New technologies have been developed to improve the oral bioavailability of these drugs. For example, by reducing the drug particle size through micronizing or nano sizing, the surface area of the drug can be increased to improve the dissolution rate [8]. Using either salt or cocrystal forms of a drug substance or by developing amorphous or lipid formulations, one can achieve higher apparent solubility to improve both the rate and extent of dissolution and absorption [7,8]. On the other hand, by altering the dissolution rate to control the absorption rate and the site of absorption in the GI tract, the modified release formulation technology is able to deliver an optimal plasma drug concentration-time profile. Fig. 17.3 shows the dissolution and plasma drug concentration-time profiles of orally administered isosorbide mononitrate immediate- and

FIGURE 17.3 (A) *In vitro* dissolution profile of immediate-release and sustained-release profile of isomorbide nitrate. (B) *In vivo* plasma concentration-time profile of the same immediate-release and sustained-release formulation of isomorbide nitrate. *(Adapted from Ref. [9] with permission).*

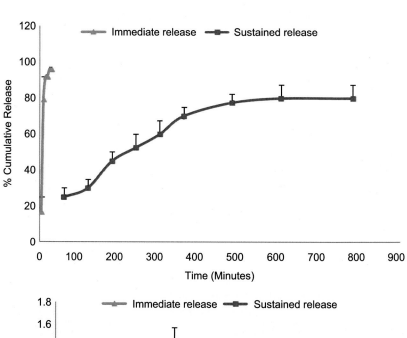

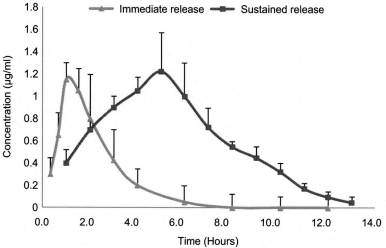

sustained-release formulations [9]. By decreasing the rate of drug dissolution in the GI tract, the sustained-release formulation was able to maintain drug concentrations above the therapeutic effective concentration for a longer duration of time.

The physiological factors that influence the dissolution of drugs in the GI tract include GI anatomy, volume, pH and composition of fluid in the GI, and GI motility. These factors are further influenced by other variables such as age, genetics, disease state, co-medication, and food consumption. It is therefore not surprising that significant inter- and intraindividual variability of factors important for absorption (e.g., solubility) are observed in a population and can contribute to variability in oral drug absorption rates [10]. For weakly acidic or basic drugs with pH-dependent solubility, the gastric pH can significantly affect the dissolution rate and solubility. For example, itraconazole is a poorly soluble weak base that is more soluble under low pH. When 200 mg of itraconazole (Sporanox Capsules) were administered after ranitidine pretreatment, which raised the gastric pH to 6, itraconazole was absorbed to a lesser extent than when Sporanox Capsules were administered alone, with decreases in the total amount of drug absorbed and the maximal drug concentrations [11]. Interestingly, the reduced amount absorbed was mitigated when Sporanox Capsules were administered with a cola beverage, which is acidic, after ranitidine pretreatment [11]. To avoid reduced absorption due to elevated gastric pH, patients are advised on the prescription label of Sporanox that antacids should be administered at least 1 hour before or 2 hours after the administration of Sporanox.

17.3.2 Permeation

After dissolution, the next step in oral absorption is for the drug molecule to permeate through the gastrointestinal membrane. It is generally believed that the vast majority of drug molecules can permeate through the GI barrier only as a single molecule or as small aggregates of molecules. Therefore, drug dissolution must occur before absorption when administering a nondissolved drug dosage form. The GI tract maintains a barrier between the luminal environment and the internal environment of the body through a continuous sheet of polarized columnar epithelial cells, often called an epithelial barrier [12]. When a drug is administered orally, the drug molecules must pass through the epithelial barrier to be absorbed into the gastric vasculature and subsequently into the systemic circulation. Two routes are available for the drug to permeate through this barrier: either transcellularly (through cells) or paracellularly (through spaces between cells). A series of intercellular junctions connect the individual cells, among which the tight junction is the most important for the paracellular barrier. The tight junction is perforated by aqueous pores, with a wide size range of 4—40 Å radius [13]. For the transcellular pathway, a drug can permeate either through passive transcellular diffusion or carrier-mediated uptake or endocytosis. Enterocytes also contain efflux transporters, such as p-glycoprotein, which can pump drugs to the outside of cells [14]. Recent studies have found that transporters are often involved in the permeation of most drugs [15]. Fig. 17.4A provides a list of transporters in the enterocytes [77].

As discussed in Chapter 16, effective drug permeability is the net result of passive diffusion, active transport mechanisms, and vesicular transport. For each process, the permeation rate is influenced by different relationships to the drug concentration at the site of drug transport. For passive diffusion, the rate is proportional to the concentration, whereas carrier-mediated uptake follows a sigmoidal relationship with the concentration as protein and vesicular-mediated transport systems become saturated.

Practically, the overall effective permeability is often used to characterize the rate of drug permeation. Permeability of drugs across human epithelial colorectal adenocarcinoma (Caco-2) cells or Mardin—Darby canine kidney (MDCK) cells grown on a membrane is often studied to characterize *in vitro* drug permeability [16]. Permeability of drugs in the human jejunum has also been measured using in situ intestinal perfusion. A perfusion tube is placed in the human jejunum to allow the passage of a drug through a 10-cm segment. By measuring the drug concentration at the inlet and outlet of the perfusion tube, one determines drug permeability [17]. A correlation between caco-2 permeability and human jejunum permeability has been established using statistical [18] and mechanistic [19] approaches. Attempts have been made to predict drug intestinal permeability based on molecular structure. However, a reliable model is still evasive, partially due to a lack of reliable prediction of the role of membrane transporters in permeability [20].

Absorption of most orally administered compounds occurs in the small intestine. This can be attributed to the significantly larger surface area available for absorption in the small intestine as compared to other parts of GI tract. The absorptive surface area of jejunum and ileum is approximately 120 m^2 in humans as compared to 0.25 m^2 in the colon [21]. The uneven presence of transporters in various segments of the GI tract also contributes to the different absorption rates in different GI segments. Expression levels of the major transporters (uptake and efflux) have been

(A)   (B)

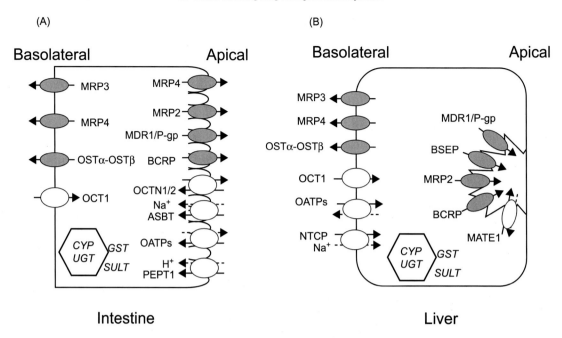

FIGURE 17.4 Schematic diagram of transporters and enzymes in the enterocyte (A) and hepatocyte (B). *ASBT*, Apical sodium dependent bile acid transporter; *BCRP*, Breast cancer resistant protein; *BSEP*, Bile salt export pump; *MATE*, Multidrug and toxin extrusion; *MDR*, Multidrug-resistance; *MRP*, Multidrug-resistance protein; *NTCP*, Sodium-taurocholate cotransporting polypeptide; *OATP*, Organic anion-transporting protein; *OCT*, Organic vation; *OCTN*, Organic zwitterions/cation; *OST*, Organic solute; *PEPT*, Peptide transporter; *SULT*, Sulfotransferases. *Reproduced from Refs. [27,77], respectively with permission.*

shown to vary depending on the region of the GI tract (Table 17.1) [22]. However, there are conflicting reports regarding the distribution of transporters. For instance, P-glycoprotein (P-gp, an efflux transporter) expression was found to be the highest in jejunum in one study [22] but was reported to progressively increase from proximal to distal regions of the intestine in another study [23]. The activity of transporters is unlikely to be important for highly permeable drugs but will play a dominant role for drugs with low passive permeability [24]. Depending on the passive permeability and propensity for active transport of any drug, absorption may occur along the entire GI tract or may be limited to the proximal GI tract. The absorption of lefradafiban (a highly permeable compound) has been shown to occur along the entire GI tract, whereas danoprevir is preferentially absorbed from the upper small intestine and has very low bioavailability upon colonic administration [25,26].

17.3.3 Gut metabolism and first-pass extraction by liver

A drug molecule that permeates into the enterocytes must then survive gut metabolism (also referred to as intestinal first-pass extraction) and first-pass metabolism by the liver before it reaches the systemic circulation [27]. Intestinal epithelial cells and hepatocytes contain a variety of enzymes involved in phase I and II metabolisms (Fig. 17.5) [28]. Phase I metabolism reactions typically affect the drug molecular structure and include oxidation,

TABLE 17.1 Distribution of ATP-binding cassette (ABC) transporters P-gp, MRP1, MRP2, and cytochrome P450 3A4 (CYP3A4) in different segments of the gastrointestinal tract [22].

	Based on mRNA level	Based on protein level
P-gp	Jejunum ~ ileum > colon	Jejunum ~ colon > ileum
MRP1	Jejunum ~ ileum ~ colon	Jejunum ~ ileum ~ colon
MRP2	Jejunum > ileum > colon	Jejunum > ileum > colon
CYP3A4	Jejunum > ileum > colon	Jejunum > ileum ~ colon

Phase I Enzymes

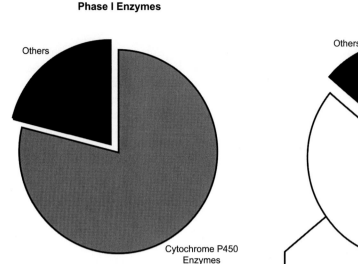

Phase II Enzymes

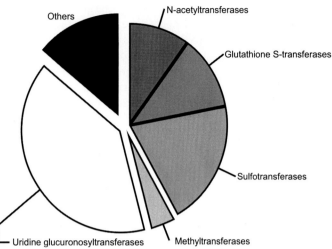

FIGURE 17.5 A chart representing the phase I and phase II drug-metabolizing enzymes. The relative size of each pie section represents the prevalence of that enzyme in overall drug metabolism. *ADH*, alcohol dehydrogenase; *ALDH*, aldehyde dehydrogenase; *COMT*, catechol O-methyltransferase; *CYP*, cytochrome P450; *DPD*, dihydropyrimidine dehydrogenase; *GST*, glutathione S-transferase; *HMT*, histamine methyl-transferase; *NAT*, N-acetyltransferase; *NQO1*, NADPH:quinone oxidoreductase or DT diaphorase; *STs*, sulfotransferases; *TPMT*, thiopurine methyltransferase; *UGTs*, uridine 59-triphosphate glucuronosyltransferases. *Generated using the data from Ref.[28] with permission.*

TABLE 17.2 Distribution of metabolic enzymes in the liver and small intestine [22].

	[a]**Phase I enzymes**	[a]**Phase II enzymes**	**Enzyme P450s**	[b]**SULT**
Liver	Cytochrome P450, Flavin monooxygenases, monoamine oxidase, carbonyl reductase, sulfatase, Glucuronidases, carboxylesterases	SULT, UGT, GST, methyltransferase, N-acetyltransferase, amino acid N-Nacetyltransferase	CYP3A (>40%), CYP2C (25%), CYP1A2 (18%) CYP2E1 (9%), CYP2A6 (6%), CYP2D6 (2%)	SULT1A1 (>50%)SULT2A1, SULT1B1, and SULT1E1 are also present in the liver.
Small intestine	CYP3A (82%), CYP2C9 (14%), CYP2C19 (2%), CYP2D6 (0.7%)	SULT1B1 (36%), SULT1A3 (31%), SULT1A1 (19%), SULT1E1 (8%), SULT2A1 (6%)		

[a]*Liver contains much higher amounts of Phase I and Phase II enzymes than the small intestine.*
[b]*The small intestine contains the largest overall amount of SULT of any of the tissues.*

reduction, and hydrolysis reactions. Phase I drug metabolism is conducted by a variety of enzymes, with Cytochrome P450 enzymes (CYP) being the most prominent class (Fig. 17.5) [29]. Phase II metabolism includes conjugation reactions such as glucuronidation, glycosidation, sulfation, methylation, acetylation, glutathione conjugation, amino acid conjugation, fatty acid conjugation, and condensation. Phase II metabolism enzymes, such as glucuronidating UDP-Glucuronosyltransferases (UGT) [30], sulfotransferases, and glutathione S-transferases, are present in both the small intestine and liver (Fig. 17.5) [31]. Table 17.2 summarizes the relative abundances of enzymes in the intestine and liver as well as the distribution of CYP enzyme types in different segments of the GI tract [22].

It is estimated that the CYP3A enzyme subfamily is involved in the metabolism of a large portion of currently marketed drugs [32]. Both CYP3A4 and CYP3A5 are present in all regions of the GI tract [33]. Among them, CYP3A4 is the most common CYP enzyme found in the human intestine and liver. The level of CYP3A4 expression is lower in the duodenum before rising in the jejunum and subsequently decreasing toward the ileum and colon [33]. Although the liver contains substantially more drug-metabolizing enzymes than the intestine, intestinal first-pass metabolism has been shown to be significant for many drugs. For example, cyclosporine [34], midazolam [35], tacrolimus [36], nifedipine [37], felodipine [38], and verapamil [39] have been identified to undergo substantial intestinal Phase I metabolism, whereas raloxifene undergoes intestinal Phase II metabolism [40].

After the drug molecule permeates the GI membrane, it enters the mesenteric vessels surrounding the intestine. These vessels then drain into the hepatic portal vein system and carry the drug to the liver. In the liver, the blood from the hepatic portal vein system (approximately 75% of total hepatic blood flow) is mixed with those from hepatic arteries [41]. The blood then flows through liver sinusoids and leaves the liver through the central vein. The liver is a major site for the metabolism of many drugs due to prevalent metabolizing enzymes and transporters (Fig. 17.4B) [27]. Some drug molecules entering the liver will not be able to reach the systemic circulation due to hepatic metabolism. This phenomenon is called first-pass metabolism or the first-pass effect. First-pass extraction happens when a drug permeates into hepatocytes and is either metabolized by enzymes or secreted into bile. The portion that is secreted into the bile will drain into the small intestine and can either be reabsorbed through enterohepatic recirculation or eliminated into the feces.

It has been recognized that the interplay between membrane transporters and enzymes in both the intestine and liver plays an important role in the first-pass effect. To explain the significant intestinal metabolism of some drugs, it was proposed that the existence of efflux transporters, such as P-gp, play an important role in increasing the exposure of susceptible drugs to metabolizing enzymes in the intestine through repeated cycling of drug into and out of the gut enterocytes via passive diffusion and active efflux, that is, secretion by P-gp. This process is thought to result in reduced drug concentration in the enterocyte and thereby a reduced saturation of the metabolizing enzymes in terms of concentration and duration above saturated level, a higher exposure of drug to enzymes and an increased mean residence time of the drug in the intestine [42]. In the liver, the degree of first-pass metabolism is also influenced by the rate and extent of uptake mediated through the uptake transporters and excretion mediated through biliary transporters relative to the metabolic rate by liver enzymes [43].

Because first-pass metabolism is influenced by blood flow rate and activity of transporters and enzymes in the intestine and liver, food uptake and co-medication can significantly affect the extent of first-pass extraction. The increase of splenic blood flow rate postprandially leads to a significant decrease in the first-pass metabolism of propranolol and a bioavailability increase of up to 250% [44,45]. The involvement of a drug with membrane transporters and metabolizing enzymes in both the intestine and liver is a major underlying cause of drug—drug interactions that must be evaluated for inappropriate drug utilization reviews. For example, ketoconazole, an antifungal medication, is a known CYP inhibitor that will inhibit the metabolism of many coadministered medications. When ketoconazole was co-dosed with cyclosporine, the oral bioavailability of cyclosporine was more than doubled, with approximately one-third of the increase attributed to the decreased liver first-pass effect and the rest attributed to the decreased gut metabolism by ketoconazole [34].

17.4 Food effects on oral drug absorption

Food intake causes physiological changes in the gastrointestinal tract and exerts complicated effects on the oral absorption of drugs. Postprandial changes in GI physiology include delayed gastric emptying, changes in gastric pH, increased bile flow, and increased splanchnic blood flow [46]. Additionally, food components may change gut metabolism or have a physicochemical interaction with the drug molecule, thereby interfering with its absorption [46]. These changes can alter the drug product GI transit time, drug dissolution, permeability, and first-pass extraction ratio, leading to changes in the rate and extent of drug absorption and subsequently systemic drug concentrations.

The effect of food on drug absorption is generally influenced by drug solubility, membrane permeability, and metabolism. Many drugs with low aqueous solubility and either high membrane permeability or extensive metabolism have increased absorption with food intake, referred to as a "positive food effect." In contrast, many drugs with high aqueous solubility and either low membrane permeability or poor metabolism have reduced absorption with food intake, referred to as a "negative food effect" [47]. No trends in drug absorption with food intake are observed for drugs with high solubility and permeability or for drugs that have low solubility and low permeability [46]. However, drug-specific exceptions to these general relationships can exist for compounds with very high first-pass effects (e.g., the propranolol example earlier in this chapter), extensive drug adsorption or binding to substances, complexation, or chemical instability of the drug substance in the GI tract.

More detailed and drug-specific analyses of food effects are often reported in the pharmaceutical literature. Some studies have revealed that a positive food effect is most likely due to an improved solubility of the poorly soluble drug under fed conditions, whereas a negative food effect is often due to the negative interference on the permeation of poorly permeable drugs in the presence of food [48]. Due to the significant effect of food intake on the absorption of some drugs, the prescription label of these drugs often specifies when to administer the drugs with regard to food intake. For example, Mepron (atovaquone) showed a threefold increase in its bioavailability when taken with a meal, and subsequently, patients are instructed to take Mepron with meals to improve their oral absorption [49,50]. Grapefruit or orange juice was found to reduce the bioavailability of Allegra (fexofenadine HCl) by 36%, likely due to the inhibition of uptake transporters responsible for the permeation of fexofenadine [51]. It is therefore recommended to take Allegra with water only [50].

17.5 Evaluation of oral absorption

It is desirable to understand the influence of these multiple factors on the oral absorption and subsequent systemic drug concentrations for a drug to design a drug product accordingly for optimal efficacy with low propensity for adverse effects. When drug dissolution is the rate-limiting step for oral absorption, it is often possible to correlate the *in vitro* dissolution profile of a drug product with *in vivo* systemic drug concentrations. This correlation is often referred as the *in vitro–in vivo* correlation (IVIVC) [52]. A broader definition of IVIVC may also include correlating other *in vitro* data with *in vivo* parameters [53]. A proper discussion of IVIVC requires an understanding of basic pharmacokinetic principles and is beyond the scope of the present work. However, this chapter provides a brief discussion of IVIVC as it applies to the principles of oral drug absorption.

Generally, IVIVC studies relate data through statistically validated mathematical models. The strongest relationships correlate the entire *in vitro* dissolution profile to the entire *in vivo* drug concentration profile. A slightly less robust correlation can be established using mean *in vitro* dissolution times to either the mean *in vivo* residence time for a drug molecule within the systemic circulation or the mean *in vivo* dissolution time. The least robust IVIVC methods correlate one dissolution time point ($t_{50\%}$, $t_{90\%}$, etc.) to one mean *in vivo* pharmacokinetic parameter. The correlation does not reflect all drug concentrations but selects one datum for comparison.

To build a successful IVIVC, drug dissolution must be the rate-limiting step for oral absorption, and the *in vitro* dissolution method needs to be biorelevant by simulating physiological conditions to the best ability possible. As discussed in Chapter 9, a dissolution test has historically been used as a quality control (QC) tool to release a dosage form for commercial use [54]. The focus of dissolution testing in quality control is to ensure batch-to-batch consistency and to detect manufacturing deviations. A dissolution method developed for quality control may or may not be indicative of *in vivo* dissolution performance. Many modifed dissolution devices, such as the TIM-1 system [55] and a dynamic dissolution setup [56], as well as improved dissolution media, such as simulated intestinal fluid [57], have been proposed to more closely mimic the *in vivo* GI condition. It has been shown in the literature that these modified dissolution tests provide a more realistic prediction of the *in vivo* drug absorption from drug products [58,59].

In general, the IVIVC methods discussed previously use a statistical approach to establish a correlation. Recently, physiology-based oral absorption modeling software has been developed to enable mechanism-based IVIVC through direct simulation of *in vivo* systemic drug concentrations based on *in vitro* properties of a drug, including the dissolution profile [60]. The physiology-based oral absorption model describes the steps of oral absorption mechanistically and incorporates physiological parameters of the GI tract into the model. The most widely used model to describe absorption physiology is called the compartment and transition model, which was originally developed at the University of Michigan [61], and has since been adapted by commercial software packages, including GastroPlus (ACAT model) [62], Simcyp (ADAM model) [63], and PKsim [64]. The compartment and transition model divides the GI tract into theoretical sections or compartments (e.g., nine compartments in the case of GastroPlus), and drugs are transferred into the subsequent compartments in a rate defined by first-order kinetic principles and physiological GI residence time. In each compartment, drug dissolution and absorption are modeled using the corresponding rate equations. Because physiology-based oral absorption models take into consideration physicochemical factors, such as pKa, solubility, particle size, and permeability, as well as GI physiological factors, such as pH in each GI segment, GI absorption surface area, volume of GI fluid, gastric emptying time, intestinal transit rate, and first-pass, the model enables mechanistic understanding and prediction of oral drug absorption [54]. The effects of membrane transporter systems can also be included in these models for even more accurate IVIVC relationships [46]. Applications of physiology-based oral absorption modeling include simulation of the influence of formulation on oral absorption based on *in vitro* dissolution [65], food effect on oral absorption [66], drug–drug interaction [67], and the effect of changes in GI physiology on absorption [63].

17.6 Drug disposition

Following absorption into the systemic circulation, a drug is delivered through the systemic blood flow to all organs and tissues. The drug will eventually leave the body through a process referred to as elimination from a variety of organs, such as the liver, kidney, and lung. Drug concentration can rarely be measured at the site of pharmacologic action. As a result, drug concentrations in the blood or plasma are used to evaluate a drug's bioavailability and are typically evaluated as a function of time after drug administration. The concentration versus time relationship then serves as the basis to understand drug movement in patients and can inform the understanding of pharmacologic or toxicologic effects. Distribution is the process of reversible movement of the drug within the body. Elimination is the irreversible loss of drug from the body and can occur through metabolism as well as excretion. Distribution and elimination are collectively referred to as drug disposition [1]. Pharmacokinetics is the study of drug movement in living systems and uses mathematical models to evaluate the processes of absorption, distribution, metabolism, and excretion [68]. Although a discussion of basic pharmacokinetic concepts is beyond the scope of this textbook, the processes of drug disposition are illustrated to facilitate a conceptual understanding of drug movement following absorption.

17.6.1 Factors affecting distribution

Distribution of a drug between blood and various tissues occurs at different rates and to different extents. Numerous factors affect drug distribution including the physicochemical properties of the drug, hydrophilicity and lipophilicity, blood flow rate to the tissue, membrane transport processes, selective organ/tissue permeability, drug binding within the blood or in an organ/tissue, and partitioning into fat [69]. For some drugs, the rate of distribution into organs and tissues is principally affected by blood perfusion or membrane permeability. For example, some drugs stay in a tissue longer when the perfusion rate is slow, whereas others have prolonged perfusion rates when drug affinity to tissue is high.

One key measure of distribution is the volume of distribution (V_d). The V_d represents a theoretical space or volume in which a drug is distributed following administration and is ultimately affected by all those factors mentioned previously. While some V_d values might have a physiological significance (e.g., some highly water-soluble drugs have a V_d approximately equal to the total body water volume) or might respond to some pathologic process, the volume of distribution is an imaginary space that has no direct relationship to drug or patient parameters. As a result, the V_d varies widely for different drugs and is a key parameter for the evaluation of drug therapy.

For example, quinacrine, a highly lipophilic compound, has a V_d of 40,000 L. In contrast, the V_d of salicylic acid and warfarin, both of which are highly bound to plasma proteins, is approximately 0.1 L/kg and corresponds to the plasma fluid volume. Erythropoietin, a high molecular weight compound, has a large steric volume and has a V_d of only 0.05 L/kg, which may represent the lower limit of a volume that might correspond to the plasma water [68].

The volume of distribution is governed by partition coefficients that quantify the equilibrium drug concentration ratio between a tissue and plasma. Partition coefficient values describe relative drug affinity to tissues. Many factors affect the tissue affinity of a drug, including lipophilicity (often characterized by logP), ionization state of the drug (characterized by pKa and environment pH), binding affinity of the drug to plasma proteins, and membrane transporter systems. Attempts have been made to estimate the tissue affinity based on tissue composition and physicochemical properties of a drug with some success. A study of 18 drugs found that 61% of the drugs had observed V_d values within a twofold difference of the predicted values [69]. In addition to the properties of a drug, individual subject variability, such as weight, body mass index, disease state, and age, can also affect the variability of the V_d in a population [70].

17.6.2 Factors affecting drug elimination

A drug is eliminated from the body through two main processes: excretion and metabolism [1]. Excretion is the irreversible loss of a chemically unchanged drug while metabolism is the conversion of a drug molecule chemically into its metabolites. Although infrequent, metabolites may be converted back into the original drug through enterohepatic recirculation or other processes [33]. Elimination by metabolism refers, then, to only the portion of metabolism that leads to irreversible drug loss. Although a drug can be eliminated by many organs, most drugs are eliminated by the liver and/or kidneys. Elimination is also typically, but not always, a first-order process where the rate of drug elimination is dependent on the drug concentration in the patient at a given time.

A key pharmacokinetic parameter used to describe the process of elimination is total body clearance (Cl). Clearance is defined as the volume that has all drug eliminated from it per unit time (with units of volume/time). Clearance can be used to determine the rate of drug elimination (R_e) from the patient at a given drug concentration (C) [68]. The rate of drug elimination is shown in Eq. (17.3):

$$R_e = Cl \times C \tag{17.3}$$

In the absence of metabolic enzyme saturation, intrinsic clearance may be expressed as the sum of V_{max}/K_m values of all the enzymes involved in the metabolism of a particular compound where V_{max} is the maximum rate of enzymatic reaction and K_m is the Michaelis–Menten constant. The value of V_{max}/K_m is often estimated *in vitro* using liver microsomes or hepatocytes or recombinantly expressed enzymes [53].

Total body clearance is also equal to the sum total of all organ- or tissue-specific elimination processes that affect a drug, as shown in Eq. 14.4. Specifically,

$$Cl_{total} = \sum Cl_{hepatic} + Cl_{renal} + Cl_{pulmonary} + \cdots \tag{17.4}$$

Clearance can then be evaluated for many drugs conveniently, if the process of drug elimination can be assumed to involve primarily one organ. For some drugs, elimination can be assumed to be principally either through hepatic metabolism or renal excretion. The fraction eliminated unchanged in the urine (f_e) is a simple pharmacokinetic parameter used to evaluate the proportion of the total drug dose that is recovered from the urine in an unmetabolized state. Drugs with a low f_e value (<0.1) can be assumed to be hepatically metabolized, whereas drugs with a high f_e value (>0.9) can be assumed to be renally excreted if a clinician can assume no other routes of drug elimination are prevalent. This assumption would then lead to the following equations (Eqs. 17.5 and 17.6):

$$Cl_{renal} = Cl_{total} \times f_e \tag{17.5}$$

$$Cl_{hepatic} = Cl_{total} \times (1 - f_e) \tag{17.6}$$

The rate of hepatic metabolism is influenced by the hepatic blood flow rate, the degree of drug/protein binding in the liver (often represented by measuring plasma protein binding), and the total drug clearance rate. When the liver blood flow is more prevalent than the degree of drug metabolism, hepatic drug clearance will be controlled by the liver blood flow rate and won't change significantly if there is variability in the process of drug metabolism through changes in metabolizing enzyme expression or activity. On the other hand, when the degree of drug metabolism is more prevalent than liver blood flow, the hepatic clearance will be controlled by the metabolizing enzymatic activity and expression, and changes to liver blood flow will not significantly affect drug clearance. Hepatic drug clearance can be influenced by an interplay between both uptake transporters and biliary transporters. It was proposed to include the intrinsic clearance of uptake and efflux across the sinusoidal membrane in the overall description of the intrinsic hepatic clearance [43]. Currently, due to limited knowledge on the abundance of specific transporters in the human liver, it is still difficult to predict the hepatic clearance accurately when the factors involving the transporters need to be considered [53].

The kidney is a major organ for drug excretion [1]. For drugs that are exclusively eliminated by the kidneys without being reabsorbed into the systemic circulation, the rate of renal drug elimination would be equivalent to the glomerular filtration rate. In typical healthy patients, the glomerular filtration rate is the rate at which plasma water is filtered and has an average value of approximately 120 mL/min [1]. However, most drugs with substantial renal elimination cannot be assumed to have an elimination rate equal to the glomerular filtration rate. The kidneys are designed for reabsorption processes with substantial possibilities for drug diffusion and numerous active membrane transport systems. Drug reabsorption is influenced by the urine pH for ionizable drugs because the urine pH affects the ionization state of the drug and subsequently its permeability. More recently, it is reported that urine pH can also affect transporter activities, such as PEP-T2, which then affects the renal clearance in the case of cephalexin [71].

17.6.3 Pharmacokinetics models

This discussion on drug distribution and elimination provides a brief introduction to pharmacokinetic processes that affect drug disposition following absorption. A more thorough analysis of basic pharmacokinetic principles is needed to adequately appreciate the processes of absorption, distribution, metabolism, and excretion. In this more thorough analysis, statistically validated modeling systems are used to describe drug movement in patients. The complexity of human anatomy and physiology would make it appear that it is difficult to describe the plasma drug concentration-time profile with a model. Surprisingly, simple compartmental models are predominantly

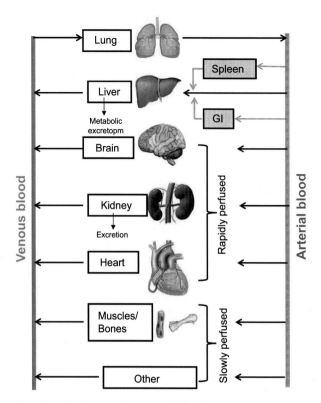

FIGURE 17.6 Illustration of a physiology-based pharmacokinetics model. Elimination is depicted as occurring from only the liver and kidneys, whereas it can occur also at other sites for some drugs. Enterohepatic recirculation can be included in the model but is not depicted in the graph. *Adapted from Ref. [72]*

used for clinical evaluation of drug pharmacokinetic properties and provide an adequate depiction of the concentration versus time profiles for many drugs [68].

Although appropriate and valid pharmacokinetic models are widely used to describe drug movement in patients, these models do not provide detailed mechanistic understandings of the fate of a drug in the body. More complex physiology-based pharmacokinetic (PBPK) models attempt to gain mechanistic insight into how a drug is absorbed, distributed, and eliminated in the body. Fig. 17.6 depicts a typical PBPK model [72]. The physiology-based oral absorption model mentioned previously can be considered a partial PBPK model when simple models are used to depict drug pharmacokinetics postabsorption.

A PBPK model comprises a model structure to describe absorption and disposition processes through the utilization of drug physicochemical properties, such as solubility, permeability, and fraction unbound in plasma; and physiological parameters, such as organ/tissue volume, blood flow rates to each organ/tissue, and partition coefficients for each organ/tissue. The PBPK model provides an integrated framework to mechanistically and quantitatively describe the influence of drug properties and physiology parameters on drug absorption and disposition. A unique feature of PBPK models is to understand the influence of individual physiological variables on drug absorption and disposition. PBPK modeling has been used to predict drug absorption [63], human plasma concentration-time profiles based on *in vitro* data [73], as well as influences of drug—drug interaction, age, gender, and disease states on pharmacokinetics [70]. The accuracy of PBPK is expected to be continuously improved as the understanding of drug absorption and disposition processes is enhanced. A major development of PK modeling is likely to connect PBPK with population pharmacokinetics (POPPK) to understand individual variability in PK [72]. PBPK modeling accuracy will further improve with an increased understanding of the physiology and more powerful computational technology.

17.7 Conclusions

Drug absorption and disposition are influenced by both the physicochemical properties of a drug and individual physiology conditions. The rate and extent of oral absorption are influenced by the dissolution characteristics of dosage forms, physicochemical and biopharmaceutical properties of the active drug ingredient, physiological

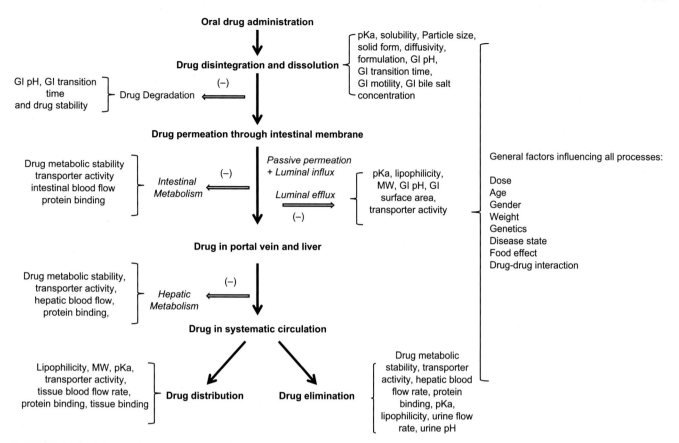

FIGURE 17.7 Scheme of drug oral absorption and disposition processes and major factors that influence the processes. *Adapted from Ref. [72]*

condition of the GI tract, and the extent of first-pass extraction at the gut and liver. Both drug distribution and disposition are also influenced by drug properties, individual physiological conditions, and other factors such as co-medication. Fig. 17.7 summarizes the factors that influence drug absorption and disposition discussed in this chapter [60,72]. Recent advancements in physiology-based absorption and pharmacokinetics modeling offer the opportunity to simulate and predict the influence of multiple factors on absorption and disposition mechanistically. As our knowledge of absorption and disposition processes is enhanced, we will continue to leverage our understanding to provide better pharmaceutical care to patients.

Case studies

Case 17.1

A doctoral student in pharmacy on a clinical rotation is presented with a plasma chloramphenicol concentration time profile from old pharmaceutical literature, as shown in Fig. 17.8, and is asked to explain this graph in the context of the effect of crystal forms of the drug on its bioavailability. What should be the ideal response of the student to his or her preceptor?

Approach: A crystalline drug can exist in different polymorphic forms. Each polymorph can have distinctly different physical properties that can affect its solubility, dissolution, absorption, and bioavailability. This is a classic example in which chloramphenicol palmitate can exist at least in two forms: α and β. The former has lower absorption and bioavailability as compared to the latter form. This is due to differences in solubility and dissolution of these two different forms of the same drug.

Case 17.2

An *in vitro–in vivo* correlation study is presented in a midyear pharmacy meeting. The data are presented in Figs. 17.9 and 17.10. The preceptor at the rotation site asks you to submit a five-line report on this finding. What is your approach to address this case?

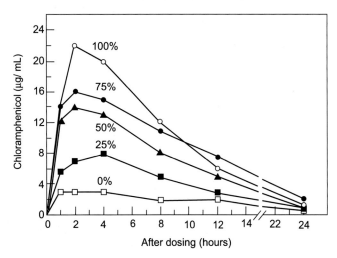

FIGURE 17.8 Comparison of mean blood serum levels obtained with chloramphenicol palmitate suspension containing varying ratios of α and β polymorphs, following a single oral dose equivalent to 1.5 g chloramphenicol. The percentage in the figure represents the percentage of β polymorph in the suspension. *Used from Ref. [75] with permission.*

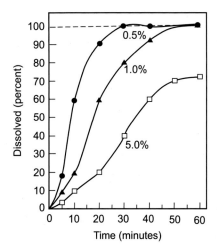

FIGURE 17.9 Effect of lubricant on drug dissolution. The % symbol in the figure represents the percentage of magnesium stearate in the formulation [74].

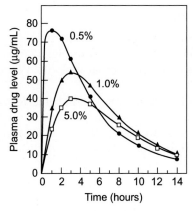

FIGURE 17.10 Effect of lubricant on drug absorption. The % symbol in the figure represents the percentage of magnesium stearate in the formulation. Incomplete drug absorption occurs for formulation with 5% magnesium stearate [74].

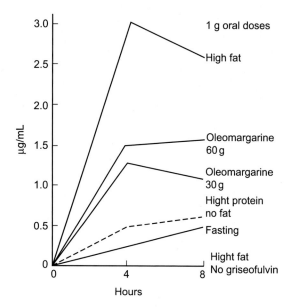

FIGURE 17.11 Comparison of the effects of different types of food intake on the serum griseofulvin levels following the 1.0 g of oral dose. *Used from Ref. [76] with permission.*

Approach: This *in vitro–in vivo* correlation study compares the effect of lubricant (magnesium stearate) in an oral tablet on dissolution and bioavailability. A good correlation between *in vitro* dissolution and *in vivo* exposure was observed. An increase in the percentage of magnesium stearate in the tablet reduces its dissolution and thereby slows down oral absorption. In this case, 0.5% magnesium stearate provides better dissolution and AUC compared to 5% of magnesium stearate in the formulation. Hydrophobicity of this excipient is responsible for this difference.

Case 17.3

Literature data suggest that food can affect the oral absorption of certain drugs. Data showing the absorption of one such drug are illustrated in Fig. 17.11. What are your recommendations for a man on griseofulvin for fungal infection of his nails?

Approach: Griseofulvin is a highly hydrophobic drug and has solubility/dissolution limited oral absorption and bioavailability issues. From the graph in Fig. 17.11, it is clear that taking the drug with food can increase the oral absorption of this drug. A high-fat diet showed the highest absorption compared to any other diets tested. The drug product label should contain guidelines on how to take the drug regarding food intake. The patient should be advised to follow the label carefully regarding the timing of drug administration with food.

Case 17.4

Biopharmaceutical classification system describes molecules into Class I–IV based on their solubility and permeability. Class II/IV molecules represent poorly soluble compounds and require apparent solubility enhancement for optimum absorption. As a pharmacist, you are given a novel compound that requires solubility enhancement. List some approaches that you can use to enhance the overall absorption of Class II/IV compounds.

Approach: As a pharmacist, you will carefully evaluate the physical-chemical properties of the novel molecules and resources available to you. Particle size reductions, salt formation, complexation with cyclodextrins, addition of surfactants, amorphous solid dispersions, lipid-based delivery systems, co-crystals, etc. are some of the approaches that as a pharmacist you can select and utilize to enhance the solubility of various type of poorly soluble compounds.

Critical reflections and practice applications

- The processes of drug transfer from the extravascular site of administration to systemic circulation are defined as absorption.

- The physicochemical properties of the drug molecule, the dosage form, membrane permeation, and physiologic and pathologic processes in the patient are some of the factors that can affect absorption.
- Noyes—Whitney equation relates that the dissolution rate of diffusion-controlled dissolution is influenced by diffusivity, diffusion layer thickness, surface area, and solubility.
- Two routes are available for the drug to permeate through this barrier: either transcellularly (through cells) or paracellularly (through spaces between cells).
- Phase I metabolism reactions typically affect the drug molecular structure and include oxidation, reduction, and hydrolysis reactions. Phase II metabolism includes conjugation reactions such as glucuronidation, glycosylation, sulfation, methylation, acetylation, glutathione conjugation, amino acid conjugation, fatty acid conjugation, and condensation.
- Factors affecting drug distribution include the physicochemical properties of the drug, hydrophilicity and lipophilicity, blood flow rate to the tissue, membrane transport processes, selective organ/tissue permeability, drug binding within the blood or in an organ/tissue, and partitioning between fatty tissues/muscles.
- Excretion is the irreversible loss of a chemically unchanged drug while metabolism is the conversion of a drug molecule chemically into its metabolites.

References

[1] M. Rowland, T.N. Tozer, in: Clinical Pharmacokinetics Concepts and Applications, 3rd ed., Williams and Wilkins, Philadelphia, PA, 1995.

[2] L.V. Allen, N.G. Popovich, H.C. Ansel, in: Ansel's Pharmaceutical Dosage Forms and Drug Delivery Systems, 9th ed., Lippincott Williams and Wilkins, Philadelphia, PA, 2010.

[3] M.N. Martinez, G.L. Amidon, A mechanistic approach to understanding the factors affecting drug absorption: a review of fundamentals, J. Clin. Pharmacol. (2002) 620—643.

[4] A.A. Noyes, W.R. Whitney, The rate of solution of solid substances in their own solutions, J. Am. Chem. Soc. 19 (1897) 930—934.

[5] A. Hixson, J. Crowell, Dependence of reaction velocity upon surface and agitation (I) theoretical consideration, Ind. Eng. Chem. 23 (1931) 923—931.

[6] A. Dokoumetzidis, V. Papadopoulou, G. Valsami, P. Macheras, Development of a reaction-limited model of dissolution: application to official dissolution tests experiments, Int. J. Pharm. 355 (1—2) (2008) 114—125.

[7] J. Brouwers, M.E. Brewster, P. Augustijns, Supersaturating drug delivery systems: the answer to solubility-limited oral bioavailability? J. Pharmaceut. Sci. 98 (8) (2009) 2549—2572.

[8] R. Liu, Water Insoluble Drug Formulation, 2nd ed., CRC Press, 2008.

[9] Z.-Q. Li, X. He, X. Gao, Y.-Y. Xu, Y.-F. Wang, H. Gu, Study on dissolution and absorption of four dosage forms of isosorbide mononitrate: level A in vitro—in vivo correlation, Eur. J. Pharm. Biopharm. 79 (2011) 364—371.

[10] S. Clarysse, D. Psachoulias, J. Brouwers, J. Tack, P. Annaert, G. Duchateau, Postprandial changes in solubilizing capacity of human intestinal fluids for BCS class II drugs, Pharm. Res. 26 (2009) 1456—1466.

[11] D.P. Lange, J. Hardin, J. Wu, M. Klausner, Effect of a cola beverage on the bioavailability of itraconazole in the presence of H2 blockers, J. Clin. Pharmacol. 37 (1997) 535—540.

[12] T.Y. Ma, J.M. Anderson, L.R. Johnson, Tight junctions and the intestinal barrier, in: L.R. Johnson (Ed.), Physiology of Gastrointestinal Tract, Elsevier, Boca Raton, FL, 2006, pp. 1559—1594.

[13] J.A. Firth, Endothelial barriers: from hypothetical pores to membrane proteins, J. Anat. 200 (2002) 541—548.

[14] S.B. Shugarts, Z. Leslie, The role of transporters in the pharmacokinetics of orally administered drugs, Pharm. Res. 26 (2009) 2039—2054.

[15] K.M.H. Giacomini, S.-M. Huang, D.J. Tweedie, L.Z. Benet, K.L.R. Brouwer, X. Chu, Membrane transporters in drug development, Nat. Rev. Drug Discov. 9 (2010) 215—236.

[16] B. Press, K. Turksen, Optimization of the Caco-2 permeability assay to screen drug compounds for intestinal absorption and efflux, in: K. Turksen (Ed.), Methods in Molecular Biology, Springer, New York, NY, 2011, 139—N2011154.

[17] H. Lennernäs, Human intestinal permeability, J. Pharmaceut. Sci. 87 (1998) 403—410.

[18] D. Sun, L.X. Yu, M.A. Hussain, D.A. Wall, R.L. Smith, G.L. Amidon, In vitro testing of drug absorption for drug 'developability' assessment: forming an interface between in vitro preclinical data and clinical outcome, Curr. Opin. Drug Discov. Dev. 7 (2004) 75—85.

[19] A. Avdeef, K.Y. Tam, How well can the Caco-2/Madin—Darby canine kidney models predict effective human jejunal permeability? J. Med. Chem. 53 (9) (2010) 3566—3584.

[20] T.V.H. Geerts, Y.V. Heyden, In silico predictions of ADME-tox properties: drug absorption, Comb. Chem. High Throughput Screen. 14 (2011) 339—361.

[21] T.T. Kararli, Comparison of the gastrointestinal anatomy, physiology, and biochemistry of humans and commonly used laboratory animals, Biopharm. Drug Dispos. 16 (1995) 351—380.

[22] S. Berggren, C. Gall, N. Wollnitz, M. Ekelund, U. Karlbom, J. Hoogstraate, Gene and protein expression of P-glycoprotein, MRP1, MRP2, and CYP3A4 in the small and large human intestine, Mol. Pharm. 4 (2007) 252—257.

[23] S. Mouly, M.F. Paine, P-glycoprotein increases from proximal to distal regions of human small intestine, Pharm. Res. 20 (2003) 1595—1599.

[24] X.Y. Cao, X. Lawrence, C. Barbaciru, C.P. Landowski, H.-C. Shin, S. Gibbs, Permeability dominates in vivo intestinal absorption of P-gp substrate with high solubility and high permeability, Mol. Pharm. 2 (2005) 329—340.

[25] J. Drewe, H. Narjes, G. Heinzel, R.S. Brickl, A. Rohr, C. Begliner, Absorption of lefradafiban from different sites of the gastrointestinal tract, Br. J. Clin. Pharmacol. 50 (2000) 69—72.

[26] M.B. Reddy, A. Connor, B.J. Brennan, P.N. Morcos, A. Zhou, P. McLawhon, Physiological modeling and assessments of regional drug bioavailability of danoprevir to determine whether a controlled release formulation is feasible, Biopharm. Drug Dispos. 32 (2011) 261–275.

[27] A. Jetter, G.A. Kullak-Ublick, Drugs and hepatic transporters: A review. Pharmacol Res. 154 (2020), 104234, https://doi.org/10.1016/j.phrs.2019.04.018.

[28] Q.Y. Zhang, D. Dunbar, A. Ostrowska, S. Zeloft, J. Yang, L.S. Kaminsky, Characterization of human small intestinal cytochromes P450, Drug Metab. Dispos. 27 (1999) 804–809.

[29] T.S. Klose, J. Blaisdell, J.A. Goldstein, Gene structure of CYP2C8 and extrahepatic distribution of the human CYP2Cs, J. Biochem. Mol. Toxicol. 13 (1999) 280–295.

[30] M.M. Doherty, K.S. Pang, First-pass effect: significance of the intestine for absorption and metabolism, Drug Chem. Toxicol. 20 (1997) 329–344.

[31] L. Liu, K.S. Pang, The roles of transporters and enzymes in hepatic drug processing, Drug Metab. Dispos. 33 (2005) 1–9.

[32] I. De Waziers, P. Cugnenc, C.S. Yang, J.P. Leroux, P.H. Beaune, Cytochrome P450 isoenzymes, epoxide hydrolase and glutathione transferases in rat and human hepatic and extrahepatic tissues, J. Pharmacol. Exp. Therapeut. 253 (1990) 387–394.

[33] M.F. Paine, M. Khalighi, J.M. Fisher, D.D. Shen, K.L. Kunze, C.L. Marsh, Characterization of interintestinal and intraintestinal variations in human CYP3A dependent metabolism, J. Pharmacol. Exp. Therapeut. 283 (1997) 1552–1562.

[34] D.Y.W. Gomez, J. Vincent, S.J. Tomlanovich, M.F. Hebert, L.Z. Benet, The effects of ketoconazole on the intestinal metabolism and bioavailability of cyclosporine, Clin. Pharmacol. Therapeut. 58 (1995) 15–19.

[35] M.F. Paine, D.D. Shen, K.L. Kunze, J.D. Perkins, C.L. Marsh, J.P.B. McVicar, First-pass metabolism of midazolam by the human intestine, Clin. Pharmacol. Ther. 60 (1996) 14–24.

[36] A. Lampen, U. Christians, F.P. Guengerich, P.B. Watkins, J.C. Kolars, A. Bader, Metabolism of the immunosuppressant tacrolimus in the small intestine: cytochrome P450, drug interactions, and interindividual variability, Drug Metab. Dispos. 23 (1995) 1315–1324.

[37] N. Holtbecker, M.F. Fromm, H.K. Kroemer, E.E. Ohnhaus, H. Heidemann, The nifedipine-rifampin interaction. Evidence for induction of gut wall metabolism, Drug Metab. Dispos. 24 (1996) 1121–1123.

[38] D.G. Bailey, J.M. Arnold, C. Munoz, J.D. Spence, Grapefruit juice—felodipine interaction: mechanism, predictability, and effect of naringin, Clin. Pharmacol. Therapeut. 53 (1993) 637–642.

[39] D. Darbar, M.F. Fromm, S. Dell'Orto, R.B. Kim, H.K. Kroemer, M.R. Eichelbaum, Modulation by dietary salt of verapamil disposition in humans, Circulation 98 (1998) 2702–2708.

[40] T. Mizuma, Intestinal glucuronidation metabolism may have a greater impact on oral bioavailability than hepatic glucuronidation metabolism in humans: a study with raloxifene, substrate for UGT1A1, 1A8, 1A9, and 1A10, Int. J. Pharm. 378 (2009) 140–141.

[41] H.S. Brown, M. Halliwell, M. Qamar, A.E. Read, J.M. Evans, P.N. Wells, Measurement of normal portal venous blood flow by Doppler ultrasound, Gut 30 (1989) 503–509.

[42] C.Y. Wu, L.Z. Benet, M.F. Hebert, S.K. Gupta, M. Rowland, D.Y. Gomez, Differentiation of absorption and firstpass gut and hepatic metabolism in humans: studies with cyclosporine, Clin. Pharmacol. Ther. 58 (1995) 492–497.

[43] T. Watanabe, H. Kusuhara, Y. Sugiyama, Application of physiologically based pharmacokinetic modeling and clearance concept to drugs showing transporter-mediated distribution and clearance in humans, J. Pharmacokinet. Pharmacodyn. 37 (6) (2010) 575–590.

[44] J.M.M. Power, J. Denis, A.J. McLean, Effects of sensory (teasing) exposure to food on oral propranolol bioavailability, Biopharm. Drug Dispos. 16 (1995) 579–589.

[45] H. Liedholm, E. Wahlin-Boll, A. Melander, Mechanisms and variations in the food effect on propranolol bioavailability, Eur. J. Clin. Pharmacol. 38 (1990) 469–475.

[46] C.L. David Fleisher, Y. Zhou, L.-H. Pao, A. Karim, Drug, meal and formulation interactions influencing drug absorption after oral administration. Clinical implications, Clin. Pharmacokinet. 36 (1999) 233–254.

[47] J.M. Custodio, C.Y. Wu, L.Z. Benet, Predicting drug disposition, absorption/elimination/transporter interplay and the role of food on drug absorption, Adv. Drug Deliv. Rev. 60 (2008) 717–733.

[48] C.-H. Gu, L. Hua, J. Levons, K. Lentz, R.B. Gandhi, K. Raghavan, Predicting effect of food on extent of drug absorption based on physicochemical properties, Pharm. Res. 24 (2007) 1118–1130.

[49] P.E. Rolan, A.J. Mercer, B.C. Weatherley, T. Holdich, H. Meire, R.W. Peck, Examination of some factors responsible for a food-induced increase in absorption of atovaquone, Br. J. Clin. Pharmacol. 37 (1994) 13–20.

[50] Reference PDs. Available from: http://www.pdr.net/drug-summary/allegra-and-children39s-allerga-allergy-tablets?druglabelid=1459&id=3408. (Accessed May 2011).

[51] M. Stoltz, A. Thangam, C. Lippert, D. Yu, V. Bhargava, M. Eller, Effect of food on the bioavailability of fexofenadine hydrochloride, Biopharm. Drug Dispos. 18 (1997) 645–648.

[52] U.S. Pharmacopoeia, In Vitro and in Vivo Evaluations of Dosage Forms, 27th ed., Mack Publishing Co., Revision, Easton, PA, 2004.

[53] A. Rostami-Hodjegan, G.T. Tucker, Simulation and prediction of in vivo drug metabolism in human populations from in vitro data, Nat. Rev. Drug Discov. 6 (2) (2007) 140–148.

[54] W. Jiang, S. Kim, X. Zhang, R.A. Lionberger, B.M. Davit, D.P. Conner, The role of predictive biopharmaceutical modeling and simulation in drug development and regulatory evaluation, Int. J. Pharm. 418 (2) (2011) 151–160.

[55] S. Blanquet, E. Zeijdner, E. Beyssac, J.P. Meunier, S. Denis, R. Havenaar, A dynamic artificial gastrointestinal system for studying the behavior of orally administered drug dosage forms under various physiological conditions, Pharm. Res. 21 (2004) 585–591.

[56] C.H. Gu, D. Rao, R.B. Gandhi, J. Hilden, K. Raghavan, Using a novel multicompartment dissolution system to predict the effect of gastric pH on the oral absorption of weak bases with poor intrinsic solubility, J. Pharmaceut. Sci. 94 (2005) 199–208.

[57] E. Jantratid, N. Janssen, C. Reppas, J.B. Dressman, Dissolution media simulating conditions in the proximal human gastrointestinal tract: an update, Pharm. Res. 25 (7) (2008) 1663–1676.

[58] M. Vertzoni, A. Diakidou, M. Chatzilias, E. Soderlind, B. Abrahamsson, J.B. Dressman, Biorelevant media to simulate fluids in the ascending colon of humans and their usefulness in predicting intracolonic drug solubility, Pharm. Res. 27 (10) (2010) 2187–2196.

[59] J.M. Butler, J.B. Dressman, The developability classification system: application of biopharmaceutics concepts to formulation development, J. Pharmaceut. Sci. 99 (12) (2010) 4940–4954.

[60] W. Huang, S.L. Lee, L.X. Yu, Mechanistic approaches to predicting oral drug absorption, AAPS J. 11 (2) (2009) 217−224.

[61] X. Lawrence, J.R.C. Yu, G.L. Amidon, Compartmental transit and dispersion model analysis of small intestinal transit flow in humans, Int. J. Pharm. 140 (1996) 111−118.

[62] B. Agoram, W.S. Woltosz, M.B. Bolger, Predicting the impact of physiological and biochemical processes on oral drug bioavailability, Adv. Drug Deliv. Rev. 50 (Suppl. 1) (2001) S41−S67.

[63] M. Jamei, D. Turner, J. Yang, S. Neuhoff, S. Polak, A. Rostami-Hodjegan, Population-based mechanistic prediction of oral drug absorption, AAPS J. 11 (2) (2009) 225−237.

[64] K. Thelen, K. Coboeken, S. Willmann, R. Burghaus, J.B. Dressman, J. Lippert, Evolution of a detailed physiological model to simulate the gastrointestinal transit and absorption process in humans, part 1: oral solutions, J. Pharmaceut. Sci. 100 (12) (2011) 5324−5345.

[65] A. Okumu, M. DiMaso, R. Lobenberg, Dynamic dissolution testing to establish in vitro/in vivo correlations for montelukast sodium, a poorly soluble drug, Pharm. Res. 25 (12) (2008) 2778−2785.

[66] M. Hannah, N.P. Jones, G. Ohlenbusch, T. Lavé, Predicting pharmacokinetic food effects using biorelevant solubility media and physiologically based modelling, Clin. Pharmacokinet. 45 (2006) 1213−1226.

[67] L.M. Almond, J. Yang, M. Jamei, G.T. Tucker, A. Rostami-Hodjegan, Towards a quantitative framework for the prediction of DDIs arising from cytochrome P450 induction, Curr. Drug Metabol. 10 (2009) 420−432.

[68] J. Gabrielsson, D. Weiner, Pharmacokinetic and Pharmacodynamic Data Analysis, Swedish Pharmaceutical Press, Stockholm, Sweden, 2006.

[69] R.D. Jones, H.M. Jones, M. Rowland, C.R. Gibson, J.W. Yates, J.Y. Chien, PhRMA CPCDC initiative on predictive models of human pharmacokinetics, part 2: comparative assessment of prediction methods of human volume of distribution, J. Pharmaceut. Sci. 100 (10) (2011) 4074−4089, https://doi.org/10.1002/jps.22553.

[70] M. Jamei, G.L. Dickinson, A. Rostami-Hodjegan, A framework for assessing inter-individual variability in pharmacokinetics using virtual human populations and integrating general knowledge of physical chemistry, biology, anatomy, physiology and genetics: a tale of 'bottom-up' vs 'top-down' recognition of covariates, Drug Metabol. Pharmacokinet. 24 (2009) 53−75.

[71] R. Liu, A.M. Tang, Y.L. Tan, L.M. Limenta, E.J. Lee, Effects of sodium bicarbonate and ammonium chloride pre-treatments on PEPT2 (SLC15A2) mediated renal clearance of cephalexin healthy subjects, Drug Metabol. Pharmacokinet. 26 (2011) 87−93.

[72] M. Rowland, C. Peck, G. Tucker, Physiologically-based pharmacokinetics in drug development and regulatory science, Annu. Rev. Pharmacol. Toxicol. 51 (2011) 45−73.

[73] P. Poulin, R.D. Jones, H.M. Jones, C.R. Gibson, M. Rowland, J.Y. Chien, PHRMA CPCDC initiative on predictive models of human pharmacokinetics, part 5: prediction of plasma concentration-time profiles in human by using the physiologically-based pharmacokinetic modeling approach, J. Pharmaceut. Sci. 100 (10) (2011) 4127−4157, https://doi.org/10.1002/jps.22550.

[74] L. Shargel, S. Wu-Pong, A.B.C. Yu, in: Applied Biopharmaceutics and Pharmacokinetics, 5th ed., McGraw-Hill, New York, USA, 2005.

[75] A.J. Agular, J. Krc, A.W. Kinkel, J.C. Samyn, Effect of polymorphism on the absorption of chloramphenicol from chloramphenicol palmitate, J. Pharmaceut. Sci. 56 (7) (1967) 847−853.

[76] R.G. Crounse, Human pharmacology of griseolfulvin: the effect of fat intake on gastrointestinal absorption, J. Invest. Dermatol. 37 (1961) 529−533.

[77] M. Estudante, J.G. Morais, G. Soveral, L.Z. Benet, Intestinal drug transporters: an overview. Adv Drug Deliv Rev 65 (10) (2013) 1340−1356, https://doi.org/10.1016/j.addr.2012.09.042.

18

Bioavailability and Bioequivalence

Ajit S. Narang[1] and Ram I. Mahato[2]

[1]Department of Pharmaceutical Sciences, ORIC Pharmaceuticals, Inc., South San Francisco, CA, United States

[2]Department of Pharmaceutical Sciences, University of Nebraska Medical Center, Omaha, NE, United States

CHAPTER OBJECTIVES

- Define and differentiate between bioavailability and bioequivalence.
- Differentiate between absolute and relative bioavailability.
- Discuss how bioavailability is determined.
- Discuss different dosage form and drug substance—related factors that affect drug bioavailability.
- Describe the role of physiological variables in oral drug absorption.
- Discuss the statistical basis of bioequivalence analysis.
- Discuss important considerations in study design for bioavailability and bioequivalence assessment.

Keywords: Area under the curve (AUC); Bioavailability (BA); Bioequivalence (BE); Drug absorption; *In vitro—in vivo* correlation (IVIVC).

18.1 Introduction

A non-intravenously administered drug must be absorbed in the body for it to elicit its desired pharmacological action. The amount and rate of drug absorption in the body, quantitated as bioavailability (BA) and bioequivalence (BE) studies against intravenous or comparator administration, play a key role in new drug development as well as in the understanding of certain drug interactions and clinical variation in drug effects. The BA and BE provide essential information that ensures safety and efficacy of new and generic medicines. The BA and BE studies also form the basis of regulation for the introduction of new drug products to the market. BA studies form the cornerstone of approval of new drugs, whereas BE studies are the foundation of generic drug approvals.

This chapter discusses the background, concepts, and methodology for the assessment of BA. In addition, factors affecting BA related to drug substance characteristics, dosage form factors, and physiological parameters are

Pharmaceutics, Second Edition
https://doi.org/10.1016/B978-0-323-99796-6.00004-7

discussed, along with their potential interactions. Finally, the concepts of BE, study design, data interpretation, and the criteria for the assessment of BE are discussed.

18.2 Bioavailability

The rate and extent of the drug entering the systemic circulation or at its site of action, such as a target organ or tissue, is termed BA. Drug availability at its site of action is not readily quantifiable in most cases. Nevertheless, most drugs need to go through systemic circulation to reach their site of action. For drugs that need to be systemically available for their pharmacological action, drug availability in plasma is typically measured and considered indicative of their target tissue availability.

18.2.1 Estimation of area under the curve

Drug availability in the plasma is typically quantified in terms of the total amount of drug in the plasma from the time of drug administration until its complete elimination. Drug plasma concentration is measured at several time points after drug administration and used to construct a plasma concentration–time profile (Fig. 18.1).

The total amount of drug in the plasma is calculated by quantifying the area under the plasma concentration–time profile curve (AUC).

The AUC is utilized for the assessment of BA. Typically, the trapezoidal rule is utilized to calculate the AUC by adding together the results of multiplying the mean of plasma concentrations to the time period for each consequent sampling time point. This method of assessing AUC is highly dependent on the sampling design of the study. While the arithmetic trapezoidal rule may work well for a study with high frequency of sampling time points in the absorption phase and adequate time points in the elimination phase (as exemplified in Fig. 18.1A), it can underestimate the true area if the sampling is not frequent enough in the absorption phase (as exemplified in Fig. 18.1B) or overestimate the true area if the sampling is not frequent enough in the elimination phase (as exemplified in Fig. 18.1C) [1].

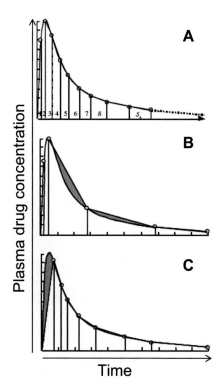

FIGURE 18.1   Plasma concentration–time profile of a drug constructed by measuring drug blood/plasma concentrations (plotted on the *y*-axis) at different points in time after drug administration (plotted on the *x*-axis). This figure further demonstrates the use of trapezoidal rule for measurement of area under the plasma concentration–time curve (AUC). The accuracy of AUC measurement by the arithmetic trapezoidal rule depends on the sampling design of the study. Thus, while the arithmetic trapezoidal rule may work well for a study with high frequency of sampling time points in the absorption phase and adequate time points in the elimination phase (as exemplified in case **A**), it can underestimate the true area if the sampling is not frequent enough in the absorption phase (as exemplified in case **B**) or overestimate the true area if the sampling is not frequent enough in the elimination phase (as exemplified in case **C**) [1].

When the concavity of the plasma concentration–time profile is substantial, the log-linear trapezoidal rule may provide a more accurate measure of AUC. The log-linear rule is based on taking geometric rather than arithmetic mean of the plasma concentration. Thus, for all plasma concentrations c_1 and c_2 at all time points t_1 and t_2, the trapezoidal rule would estimate AUC using Eq. (18.1), whereas the log-linear trapezoidal rule would use Eq. (18.2):

$$AUC_{0-t} = \sum_{0}^{t} \left(\frac{C_1 + C_2}{2} \right) \times (t_2 - t_1) \tag{18.1}$$

$$AUC_{0-t} = \sum_{0}^{t} (\sqrt{C_1 \times C_2}) \times (t_2 - t_1) \tag{18.2}$$

Nonlinear mixed effects modeling can be used for estimating AUC in populations when samples are not taken at fixed time points for plasma concentration determination. It is also useful in cases of sparse sampling, such as in toxicokinetic studies wherein the number of samples per animal is fairly limited, and kinetic analysis often requires the pooling of data from multiple animals. Mixed effects modeling partitions variability in the magnitude of plasma concentration between and within animals based on user-specified models, allowing better estimation of typical drug exposures. However, it requires appropriate structural models for the description of pharmacokinetics.

18.2.2 Absolute bioavailability

By definition, drug administration directly into the systemic circulation by an intravenous injection results in complete (100%) BA. However, when a drug is administered by another route, not all drugs may reach systemic circulation. The percentage of drug available in the systemic circulation after its administration from a given dosage form and through a selected route of administration as compared to the amount of drug available in plasma after direct intravenous injection is termed *absolute* BA and is designated as $F_{absolute}$. For example, $F_{absolute}$ by the oral route can be defined by Eq. (18.3):

$$F_{absolute} = \frac{AUC_{per\ oral}}{AUC_{intravenous}} \times 100 \tag{18.3}$$

Frequently, the drug dose used for oral drug administration is different from that used for intravenous administration. This requires dose normalization to calculate $F_{absolute}$ as in Eq. (18.4):

$$F_{absolute} = \frac{AUC_{per\ oral}}{AUC_{intravenous}} \times \frac{Dose_{intravenous}}{Dose_{peroral}} \times 100 \tag{18.4}$$

18.2.3 Relative bioavailability

When the BA of a drug (from a given dosage form and through a selected route of administration) is measured as a proportion of a drug's systemic availability through any route other than the intravenous administration, it is termed *relative* BA and is designated as $F_{relative}$. The $F_{relative}$ of one formulation (Formulation A) can be compared to another formulation (Formulation B) through the same or another route of administration. Thus, $F_{relative}$ can be defined by Eqs. 18.5 and 18.6:

$$F_{relative} = \frac{AUC_{formulation\ A,\ route\ 1}}{AUC_{formulation\ B,\ route\ 1}} \times 100 \tag{18.5}$$

$$F_{relative} = \frac{AUC_{formulation\ A,\ route\ 1}}{AUC_{formulation\ A,\ route\ 2}} \times 100 \tag{18.6}$$

Drug administration by different routes of administration may require different doses. Also, if formulations with significantly different drug release or $F_{absolute}$ are compared, different doses may need to be administered. These scenarios require dose normalization to calculate $F_{relative}$ as in Eqs. (18.7) and (18.8):

$$F_{relative} = \frac{AUC_{formulation\ A,\ route\ 1}}{AUC_{formulation\ B,\ route\ 1}} \times \frac{Dose_{formulation\ B,\ route\ 1}}{Dose_{formulation\ A,\ route\ 1}} \times 100 \tag{18.7}$$

$$F_{relative} = \frac{AUC_{formulation\ A,\ route\ 1}}{AUC_{formulation\ A,\ route\ 2}} \times \frac{Dose_{formulation\ A,\ route\ 2}}{Dose_{formulation\ A,\ route\ 1}} \times 100 \qquad (18.8)$$

18.2.4 Measurement of bioavailability

Estimation of $F_{absolute}$ from a reference formulation (given dosage form and route of administration) is important to appreciate the clinical significance of changes in BA. For example, if any modification, such as change in the dosage form, route of administration, or food effect, changes the BA by 100%, its significance would be much greater for a reference formulation with $F_{absolute}$ of 50% than for a reference formulation with $F_{absolute}$ of 5%. Thus, the anti-arrhythmic compound felodipine has low and variable oral BA, attributable to metabolism by intestinal CYP3A4 enzymes during absorption. Its BA can significantly increase with the co-ingestion of grapefruit, which inhibits intestinal CYP enzyme activity [2]. In addition, intersubject variability may be linked to the variability in the $F_{absolute}$ of drugs. Thus, drugs with low BA usually tend to show high variability (Fig. 18.2) [3].

$F_{absolute}$ is typically estimated by quantitating the AUC from time of drug administration ($t = 0$) to the last sampling time point (t) to give $AUC_{0 \to t}$. Extrapolation of the curve to infinite time by estimation of terminal elimination rate constant yields $AUC_{0 \to \infty}$. For prodrugs and drugs that are metabolized into active metabolites, BA assessment may be done only for the active moiety. This assumes complete metabolism during administration or by a first-pass effect, which may not be the case. Therefore, either both administered drug or prodrug and the active moiety may be quantitated or a nonspecific assay (such as a radioactive label) may be utilized for the quantitation of $F_{absolute}$.

Special modifications to the measurement of BA are sometimes required depending on the underlying factors. For example:

- If plasma drug concentrations are not measurable, drug concentrations in the urine are utilized for an assessment of $F_{absolute}$ by an extravascular (EV) route of administration—if excretion through kidney is the major route of drug elimination. This assumes that the ratio of renal clearance to total drug clearance is the same for the intravenous (IV) and the EV routes of administration.
- Semisimultaneous drug administration may be utilized for drugs with long terminal half-life [4]. In this case, two doses (IV followed by EV, or vice versa) are administered at a short, optimal interval, and mathematical model fitting of the plasma concentration–time profile is utilized to estimate BA.
- If, for any reason, a drug can not be administered by the IV route, measurement of $F_{absolute}$ is possible by measuring the amount of drug eliminated if a drug is eliminated by one or more experimentally accessible routes, such as urine.

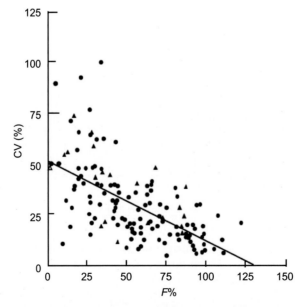

FIGURE 18.2 Plot of absolute bioavailability ($F_{absolute}$, F%) against intersubject variability (% coefficient of variation, CV) for 100 drugs in humans. Drugs with lower $F_{absolute}$ tend to show higher variability [3].

- Measurement of $F_{relative}$ between two formulations or two EV routes of administration may also be done under steady-state conditions since the total AUC over a dosing interval at steady state is equal to $AUC_{0 \to \infty}$. This method requires achieving steady state with one formulation and then shifting the formulation to achieve another steady state. This method is useful for drugs with long terminal half-lives and assumes that drug absorption does not continue beyond the dosing interval.

18.2.5 Underlying assumptions in bioavailability assessment

$F_{absolute}$ of a dosage form is the actual percentage of administered dose that reaches the general circulation. In general, the $F_{absolute}$ of a drug administered by the IV route of administration is considered 100%. Therefore, $F_{absolute}$ is typically estimated by measuring the plasma drug concentration after IV and EV drug administration. The EV route of administration requires the step of drug absorption before it becomes available in systemic circulation. However, the rate of drug absorption may not reflect the rate of drug availability in plasma, such as in cases where drug gets metabolized after absorption. The first-pass effect in the liver or the lung can reduce oral BA of drugs even though they may be well absorbed.

$F_{absolute}$ of drugs administered by the IV route is generally assumed to be 100%, but this may not necessarily be the case. The systemic circulation relevant to the drug concentration at the site of action is the arterial blood concentration. Drugs administered systemically are typically administered intravenously. There could be differences between the venous drug concentration and the drug concentration in the arteries. This difference could be due to, for example, drug metabolism in the lungs since the drugs administered by the IV route must cross the pulmonary circulation before reaching arterial blood. Prostaglandins, for example, are significantly metabolized in the lungs. Also, the BA of a drug after IV administration of its prodrug can sometimes be less than 100%. For example, the BA of methylprednisolone after IV administration of its succinic acid ester prodrug in dogs was about 44% [5].

In addition, the measurement of $F_{absolute}$ involves several assumptions. For example, the clearance of a drug by the IV and the EV routes of administration is assumed to be the same. Also, the utilization of a crossover study design (drug administration by one route followed by a washout period, and then another route) assumes no carryover effect. While the washout period takes care of residual drug concentration from the first period of administration to the next, there could be carryover effects by indirect means such as induction or inhibition of metabolizing enzymes after the first drug administration. These effects could lead to nonlinearity due to time dependency. Also, the determination of $F_{absolute}$ typically requires the estimation of the terminal half-life of a drug beyond the last sampling time point for measured plasma drug concentration. This estimation may not be robust depending on the sampling design of the study and the possible presence of other confounding factors such as continued drug absorption into the elimination phase, which could happen due to, for example, entero-hepatic recycling.

18.3 Factors affecting bioavailability

The BA of a drug from a dosage form is a result of sequential processes of drug dissolution and absorption. Several drugs and drug products or dosage form characteristics can affect either of these processes, thus affecting the rate and extent of drug availability in the systemic circulation. In addition, physiological variables such as GI motility, gastric emptying time, pH of the gastric milieu, window of absorption of the drug, and interindividual variations in the content and/or activity of metabolizing enzymes and transporters can influence drug absorption either directly or by interacting with drug or dosage form properties.

18.3.1 Drug substance characteristics

Drug substance characteristics that affect the rate and extent of drug release include solubility, surface area, polymorphism, and salt form.

18.3.1.1 Solubility

The solubility of a drug in a given medium represents the concentration of the drug in solution when a thermodynamic equilibrium has been reached between the drug in solution and the solid drug in contact with each other at a fixed temperature. The thermodynamic solubility, however, may not be the biorelevant solubility of a drug. In cases in which the drug dissolution rate is so low that the amount of time and agitation needed to reach thermodynamic solubility is higher than the drug residence time at its site of absorption, such as the gastrointestinal tract (GIT). In these cases, kinetic drug solubility within biorelevant time frames (such as a few hours) may be more important. Also, some drugs tend to self-associate in solution to form dimers, trimers, micelles, or continuous self-association structures. The formation of these structures leads to an increase in the perceived solubility of the drug compared to the monomeric form alone.

Most drugs are weak acids or weak bases. Accordingly, they exhibit pH-dependent solubility. For weak acids, the solubility is higher at basic pH and lower at acidic pH. For weak bases, the solubility is higher at acidic pH and lower at basic pH. The extent of difference in the solubility of a weakly acidic/basic drug with the change in pH depends on the solubility of the unionized free acid/free base and the ionized form of a drug. The pH-dependent extent of ionization of a drug can be calculated by the modified Henderson—Hasselbalch equation, as shown in Eqs. (18.9) and (18.10):

$$\frac{[\text{salt of weakly acidic drug}]}{[\text{free acid}]} = 10^{\text{pH}-\text{pKa}} \tag{18.9}$$

$$\frac{[\text{free base}]}{[\text{salt of weakly basic drug}]} = 10^{\text{pH}-\text{pKa}} \tag{18.10}$$

where pKa represents the negative log of the ionization constant of the drug.

The pH-dependent drug solubility differences can lead to drug solubility changes with pH differences across the GIT for orally administered drugs to affect oral drug BA. Thus, a weakly acidic drug would not dissolve substantially in the stomach but would dissolve rapidly when it reaches the intestines. Only the unionized form of the drug rapidly permeates passively through membranes, leading to drug absorption. Thus, although a weakly acidic drug would have a greater proportion of the free acid form of the dissolved drug present in the stomach, the lower surface area of the absorptive surface in the stomach, compared to that of intestines, and lower total amount of dissolved drug is likely to lead to some, but not substantial, drug absorption from the stomach.

For a weakly basic drug, the drug would be predominantly ionized and dissolved in the acidic stomach, while the intestinal pH favors the unionized form. Thus, the higher surface area of the intestines combined with the presence of higher proportion of unionized form of the drug in the solution can lead to higher rate and extent of drug absorption from the intestines. However, the drug dissolved in the stomach may precipitate upon a change in pH as it transitions to the intestine. The precipitated form of the drug may be amorphous or crystalline, or admixed with components from the GI milieu, and would need to undergo dissolution again in the intestinal environment for absorption. This rate of redissolution may be slow and/or erratic, leading to low and variable oral drug BA. In these cases, the rate of drug precipitation and the ability of the drug to sustain supersaturation (such as by self-association) can affect oral drug absorption.

In addition to pH, the solubility of a drug is also affected by temperature and the physical form of the drug. Solubility should always be determined under isothermal conditions, that is, at a fixed temperature. The temperature of biorelevant solubility is 37°C, whereas the temperature at which the dosage form is formulated is typically room temperature.

In addition, the solubility of a drug can be significantly altered by the preparation of its solvate (e.g., hydrate), salt, or prodrug. Salt forms of drugs typically have a higher solubility than the corresponding free acid or the free base form [6]. In terms of the physical form of the drug, the amorphous (noncrystalline) form of a drug typically has a higher solubility than the crystalline form. For drugs that exist in more than one crystalline form (polymorphism), solubility differences between the polymorphic forms are commonly observed in addition to differences in melting point, dissolution rate, and physicochemical stability. Typically, the metastable (physically less stable) form of the drug has higher solubility, which may also translate into a higher dissolution rate and BA. For example, chloramphenicol palmitate exists in three polymorphic forms, which differ in solubility and dissolution rates [7], as well as BA [8].

Highly hydrophobic drugs that may have a functional group for conjugation in a manner that can be cleaved in vivo, such as for the formation of an ester that can release the parent compound by hydrolysis, can be developed into prodrugs. For example, brivanib alaninate is a higher-solubility ester prodrug of the active moiety brivanib [9]. Prodrug strategies are also utilized for in vivo targeting to the site of drug action, such as the targeting of drugs to cancer by developing macromolecular prodrugs that can undergo selective extravasation in the tumor vasculature [10], or delivery to the preferred site of drug action, such as balsalazide for colon-specific delivery of the antiinflammatory aminosalicylic acid [11].

18.3.1.2 Dissolution rate

Dissolution rate represents the rate at which a solid drug dissolves in a given medium. It is a function of the surface area of the drug particles, its solubility, the diffusion coefficient, the amount of drug dissolved, and the hydrodynamic conditions during dissolution—represented by the thickness of an unstirred hydrodynamic layer of the dissolved drug. These interrelationships are given by the Noyes—Whitney equation (Eq. 18.11):

$$\frac{dQ}{dt} = \frac{D}{h} S(C_s - C) \tag{18.11}$$

where Q is the amount of drug dissolved; t is time; D is the diffusion coefficient of the drug in the dissolving medium; h is the thickness of the stationary, saturated layer of solvent on a solid surface; S is the effective surface area of particles; C_s is the saturation solubility of the drug; and C is the drug concentration in solution.

Particle size and surface area of a solid drug are inversely related to each other. The smaller the drug particle size, the greater is its surface area-to-volume ratio. As the surface area increases with decreasing particle size, micronization generally leads to higher dissolution rates. For example, micronization of the poorly water-soluble drugs griseofulvin, chloramphenicol, and tetracycline resulted in higher dissolution rates when compared with their nonmicronized forms [12,13]. Micronization has also been used for the solubility enhancement of griseofulvin [13], aspirin [14], and several other drugs. The dissolution rate of hydrophobic drugs can be further enhanced by the concomitant use of surfactants (e.g., Tween-80) and hydrophilic polymers (e.g., polyvinyl pyrrolidone (PVP) and polyethylene glycol (PEG)) as wetting agents, to decrease the interfacial tension and displace adsorbed air on the surface of solid particles.

Micronization sometimes leads to the unexpected observation of a decrease in surface area and dissolution rate. This effect is often due to the aggregation of micronized particles, due to high surface energy and/or electrostatic charge, during the micronization process. In such cases, the use of excipients during or after micronization is helpful in reducing aggregation. Thus, the deposition of a micronized drug on an excipient surface can also lead to an increase in surface area and dissolution. For example, microparticles of nevirapine, a poorly water-soluble drug, were prepared by the supercritical antisolvent method and deposited on the surface of excipients such as lactose and microcrystalline cellulose. The nevirapine/excipients mixture showed a faster dissolution rate compared to drug microparticles alone or when physically mixed with the excipients [15]. This could be due to the minimization of aggregation in micronized drug particles.

Viscosity-inducing hydrophilic macromolecules such as povidone, carboxymethyl cellulose (CMC), pectin, and gelatin, when incorporated in an intimate mixture with the drug in the dosage form, can minimize the rate of interconversion of one polymorphic form into another. In addition, the conversion of drugs to their salt forms can improve their solubility and dissolution rate, thus impacting BA. Furthermore, prodrug strategies are often utilized to maximize drug absorption. Passive transport of a drug across the biological membrane is governed by the proportion of the unionized form present, which is governed by the drug's dissociation constant (pKa) and pH at the site of absorption, and lipid solubility of the unionized drug. Prodrug strategies that alter the pKa and lipophilicity of drug molecules can impact their absorption.

18.3.1.3 In vitro—in vivo correlation

Predictive mathematical correlations describing the relationship between an *in vitro* property of the dosage form, such as the rate and extent of drug release, and an *in vivo* response, such as the rate and extent of drug absorption, are termed *in vitro—in vivo* correlations (IVIVC). These correlations are based on the central premise that the rate of drug release determines the rate of drug absorption. While drug dissolution from the dosage form must precede drug absorption in all cases, the relative rate of drug release and drug absorption determines the feasibility of establishing IVIVC for drug products. For example, while IVIVC may be established for drugs where dissolution from the dosage form is the rate-limiting factor (i.e., rate of drug release < rate of drug absorption), it may not be meaningful for drugs where the rate of drug absorption is rate limiting (i.e., rate of drug absorption < rate of drug release). In line with these considerations, IVIVC is generally more likely to be established for sustained- or controlled-release dosage forms, but not for immediate-release dosage forms.

The value of establishing IVIVC stems from its potential use in allowing *in vitro* drug-release studies to be used as a surrogate for *in vivo* BE or BA studies. Thus, if an IVIVC is established during drug product development, subsequent changes to the drug product, such as formulation composition or the manufacturing process, which might otherwise necessitate a $F_{relative}$ or BE study can be substituted with an *in vitro* drug-release study. A further advantage of establishing IVIVC is to be able to set up realistic specification controls for *in vitro* drug release that are reflective of *in vivo* performance of the drug product. Any dissolution method may be selected for establishing IVIVC, as long as it meets the validation criteria outlined in the compendia.

As per the United States Food and Drug Administration (US FDA) guidance for industry on the application of IVIVC to extended-release dosage forms (available at http://www.fda.gov/cder/guidance/index.htm), IVIVC has been categorized into following levels:

- *Level A correlation* involves establishing a point-to-point correlation between *in vitro* dissolution and *in vivo* input rate of the drug. The *in vivo* input rate can be interpreted as the fraction of drug dissolved *in vivo* or the fraction of drug absorbed. The latter can be obtained by deconvolution of the plasma concentration—time profile of a drug. Such correlations are usually linear but could also be nonlinear. In the case of linear correlations, the *in vitro* dissolution and *in vivo* absorption curves may be superimposable with or without the use of a scaling or conversion factor. An alternative approach to generate a level A IVIVC is to convolute the *in vitro* dissolution data to obtain a predicted plasma concentration—time profile, which may then be compared with the *in vivo* data obtained with test formulations. Level A correlations are generally the most difficult to establish because the model should predict good correlation of the entire *in vitro* dissolution-time data with the *in vivo* concentration—time profile.
- *Level B correlation* is the correlation of mean *in vitro* dissolution time to the mean *in vivo* dissolution time or the mean residence time of the drug. Level B correlation is based on statistical moment analysis, and while it utilizes all the *in vitro* and *in vivo* data in establishing a correlation, it is not considered a point-to-point correlation. An example of a level B correlation would be a linear regression model between the mean dissolution time and the mean absorption time of a dosage form. This correlation does not predict the exact *in vivo* plasma concentration—time profile of a drug.
- *Level C correlation* establishes a single-point relationship between a dissolution parameter and a pharmacokinetic parameter. The parameters used in this correlation could be the time to 50% drug release during dissolution testing with the total exposure, the time to maximum concentration, or the maximum plasma concentration of the drug from the *in vivo* data. An example of a level C correlation would be the linear regression between the fraction of drug dissolved at a given time point and the maximum drug concentration in plasma. Level C correlation uses a single parameter, which usually does not reflect the complete shape of the plasma concentration—time profile. Sometimes multiple level C correlations can be established using different parameters, such as by relating one or more pharmacokinetic parameters of interest to the amount of drug dissolved at various time points in the *in vitro* dissolution profile.

18.3.1.4 *In vitro—in vivo relationship*

Sometimes only a qualitative relationship can be established between the *in vitro* and the *in vivo* parameters, especially for immediate-release dosage forms. These qualitative relationships can be of the rank-order correlation kind, where, for example, a slow rate of drug release is considered indicative of lower total exposure or a lower rate of drug absorption. Such cases are termed *in vitro—in vivo* relationships (IVIVR) and have sometimes also been called level D IVIVC. Establishing IVIVR can be of value in determining formulation strategies during drug product development.

18.3.1.5 *Dimensionless representation of factors affecting drug absorption*

Establishing IVIVC and the probability of success of delivery strategies in altering the pharmacokinetics of a drug depends largely on the relative rates of drug absorption and dissolution, in the context of drug dose and therapeutic window. These variables are assessed using three dimensionless numbers: the absorption number, the dose number, and the dissolution number.

- *Dissolution number* represents the time required for drug dissolution. It is the ratio of the mean residence time of the drug in the intestines to its mean dissolution time. The mean dissolution time, in turn, is a function of the diameter, density, and diffusivity of particles, in addition to the drug's saturation concentration.
- *Dose number* is indicative of drug solubility. It is the ratio of drug concentration in the administered volume of 250 mL to the saturation solubility of the drug in water.
- *Absorption number* is the ratio of the effective permeability of the drug and the gut radius times the residence time of the drug in the small intestine.

Dose number and absorption number represent the inherent properties of the drug and the physiological system that may not be readily altered by the dosage form, except perhaps by the preparation of a prodrug or a complex to alter permeability and/or solubility, or use of a mucoadhesive or gastro-retentive dosage form. Dissolution number, on the other hand, can be more readily influenced by dosage form—related factors, such as by the preparation of extended- or sustained-release dosage forms.

These numbers can be utilized to calculate the absorbable dose of a drug ($D_{absorbable}$). The absorbable dose is the maximum amount of drug that can be absorbed after oral administration, considering the transit time of the drug ($T_{intestinal}$), effective drug permeability ($P_{effective}$), saturation concentration of the drug ($C_{saturation}$), and the area of small intestine available for absorption (A). It assumes the presence of a saturated concentration of the drug in the solution at the site of absorption. Thus,

$$D_{absorbable} = A \times P_{effective} \times C_{saturation} \times T_{intestinal}$$

18.3.1.6 Biopharmaceutics classification system

The relative importance of solubility and permeability in oral drug absorption is reflected in various aspects of drug development, such as the ability to establish an IVIVC, the need and ability to develop an extended- or controlled-release dosage form, and the variability in drug absorption between and among subjects. For the relative assessment of drugs based on their solubility and permeability parameters, Amidon et al. [16] proposed a Biopharmaceutics Classification System (BCS) that categorizes drugs into four classes:

- BCS Class I drugs are the drugs with high solubility and high permeability.
- BCS Class II drugs are the drugs with low solubility and high permeability.
- BCS Class III drugs are the drugs with high solubility and low permeability.
- BCS Class IV drugs are the drugs with low solubility and low permeability.

The boundary of what may be considered high or low in terms of solubility and permeability for the BCS is defined in the US FDA guidance for industry on the waiver of in vivo BA and BE studies for immediate-release solid oral dosage forms (available at http://www.fda.gov). A highly soluble drug is defined as one whose highest dose is soluble in 250 mL or less of aqueous media across the pH range of 1—7.5. This solubility criterion is based on the administration of eight fluid ounces of water with drug administration in clinical studies, and the pH range criterion ensures lack of pH-induced precipitation of drug in the gastrointestinal milieu.

The permeability category of a drug is defined based on direct measurement of the rate of drug transport across a human intestinal membrane and indirectly by assessing the fraction of dose absorbed after oral administration. A drug that demonstrates 90% or more extent of absorption after oral administration is considered to be highly permeable.

BCS can be utilized in supporting a waiver of in vivo BA or BE study for immediate-release oral solid dosage forms once the BA has been initially established and a change in the formulation composition or manufacturing process is made that would otherwise necessitate a BE study. In addition, generic drug products filing an abbreviated new drug application can utilize BCS classification in support of requests for waiver of BE studies against the then-marketed innovator or brand drug product. Typically, drugs that belong to BCS class I have a low risk of variation in BA based on dosage form—related factors.

18.3.1.7 Biopharmaceutics drug disposition classification system

The biopharmaceutics drug disposition classification system (BDDCS) was proposed in 2005 as a surrogate for determining the permeability of compounds using the elimination criteria to predict overall drug disposition, including the effect of the route of drug administration, transporters (efflux and absorptive), and food effect [17]. BDDCS is useful in predicting the effect of efflux and uptake transporters on drug absorption. This classification proposes the use of extent of drug metabolism (≥90%) to define highly permeable compounds to feed into the BCS classification system. This can provide a robust in vivo approach to overcome the difficulties associated with experimentally determining the permeability of compounds using in vitro cell culture assays using cell lines such as Caco-2 or Pampa, or direct intestinal permeability assessment. The BDDCS proposes that if the major route of elimination of a drug is metabolism, then the drug should be categorized as a highly permeable compound since it must be absorbed to be metabolized.

18.3.1.8 Developability classification system

The Developability Classification System (DCS) builds on the BCS by subcategorizing BCS II drugs into IIa and IIb. Drugs that fall in the DCS IIa are closer to BCS I in solubility and have higher permeability, compared to the drugs that fall in DCS IIb. The DCS provides guidance to formulation scientists on approaches to improve the oral bioavailability of compounds. For compounds that fall in DCS IIa, the absorption is likely to be dissolution rate limited and can be increased with approaches such as reducing the particle size of the drug. For compounds that fall in DCS IIb, the absorption is likely to be solubility rate limited and might require enabling formulations, such as amorphous solid dispersion or lipid/surfactant-based solutions or emulsions, to improve oral BA.

18.3.2 Dosage form factors

A dosage form is utilized more often than not to deliver a drug to its target site of absorption. The dosage form design factors inherently affect the rate and extent of drug release, which can impact BA. The following would exemplify some dosage form—related factors that can affect drug BA:

18.3.2.1 Disintegration and drug release

The rate and extent of drug release from the dosage form can impact the BA of drugs where disintegration and dissolution are the rate-limiting steps for absorption. For example, increased disintegration time led to reduced BA for the antihelmintic agent praziquantel [18]. Therefore, superdisintegrants, such as croscarmellose sodium, crospovidone, and sodium starch glycolate, are frequently added to immediate-release solid dosage forms for rapid disintegration in the aqueous medium.

In addition, coprocessing, such as the preparation of solid—solid dispersions, is utilized to change drug-release characteristics by preparation of a microcrystalline or amorphous drug-containing matrix. Solid dispersions are prepared by combining two solid ingredients, one of which is the poorly soluble drug, and the other is a release-modifying hydrophilic excipient, together in a manner that allows molecular mixing (which leads to solid solutions) or formation of very fine particle size dispersion of one component in the other. These techniques include melt fusion, hot melt extrusion, spray drying, freeze drying, and supercritical fluid precipitation. The hydrophilic excipients typically used are PVP and various derivatives of hydroxypropyl methylcellulose (HPMC) [19—21]. Solid dispersions often lead to improved dissolution rate and BA of drugs [22—25].

Longer duration of drug residence at its site of absorption can help improve the extent of drug absorption. This is typically attempted with the use of mucoadhesive excipients in dosage forms. Thus, coprocessing of a drug with a bioadhesive excipient can lead to longer residence time of the drug at the absorptive surface. For example, freeze-drying of a combination of maize starch and Carbopol 974P, a cross-linked acrylic acid-based polymer, increased the nasal delivery of metoprolol tartrate in rabbits [26].

Sustained-release dosage forms are prepared with an intentional and a controlled rate and/or timing of drug release to produce delayed and/or prolonged plasma drug concentrations. Thus, oral-delayed release dosage forms employ technologies such as enteric coating or colonic delivery that allow the drug to be released only later in the GIT [11]. These drug products are often formulated to release the drug in a bolus when environmental conditions, such as the pH, for drug release are optimum. Other dosage forms, such as drug complexes with ion exchange resins or drugs embedded in an insoluble polymer matrix, can lead to a sustained and/or controlled rate of drug release. The rate of drug release may or may not be pH dependent. This is important since the pH of the GIT varies from acidic in the stomach to increasingly basic in the small intestinal duodenum, jejunum, ileum, and colon.

Also, depending on the site of drug absorption, dosage forms may be designed to be retained longer at a given site, leading to higher BA. For example, gastro-retentive dosage forms can allow higher drug absorption from the duodenum. In addition, a change in the route of administration can lead to significant changes in the rate and extent of drug BA, as well as the duration of drug action. For example, the use of a parenteral depot formulation can allow prolonged drug absorption over several days or weeks, whereas oral sustained-release formulations can typically extend the duration of drug absorption to no longer than a day.

18.3.2.2 Drug—excipient interactions

Drug—excipient interactions may affect the stability, release, and/or BA of drugs from their dosage forms. In certain cases, drug—excipient binding interactions affect drug release but not BA. For example, cyclodextrin complexation increased both drug release and oral BA of griseofulvin [27] and spironolactone [28], but not of naproxen [29] and tolbutamide [30]. This difference in whether changes in *in vitro* drug release correspond to changes in *in vivo* BA is dependent on the selection of dissolution method, in addition to the biopharmaceutical characteristics of the drug (e.g., its absorption window), and the strength and extent of binding.

Drug—excipient binding interactions could be specific or nonspecific. Specific binding interactions involve, for example, complexation through a known mechanism. Drug complexation with cyclodextrins is utilized to affect a drug's solubility, dissolution rate, stability, and/or diffusion coefficient. These complexes are expected to be pharmacologically inert and to dissociate readily at the site of absorption. The use of cyclodextrins has resulted in improved BA of several drugs such as griseofulvin [27], ursodeoxycholic acid [31], cinnarizine [32], acyclovir [33], artemisinin [34], glibenclamide [35], ibuprofen [36], nifedipine [37], and theophylline [38].

Drug—excipient complexes that do not readily dissociate at the site of absorption can lead to altered, or reduced, BA of drugs, due to the altered biopharmaceutical properties of the drug, including reduction in partition coefficient and diffusion coefficient (due to the large molecular size of the drug—excipient complex). These cases are illustrated by the complexation of tetracycline with divalent cations [39] and of phenobarbital with PEG 4000 [40]. In both cases, the formation of insoluble complexes led to a decrease in drug BA.

Nonspecific drug—excipient binding interactions are exemplified by acid—base pairing of drug and a polymeric excipient in the dosage form, such that the exact site of interaction is not well established. These interactions are commonly utilized in the use of ion exchange resins, for example, sulfonated and/or carboxylated polystyrenes, for preparing sustained-release dosage forms of amine drugs such as dextromethorphan [41] and phenylpropanolamine [42].

In general, whether drug—excipient binding interactions affect oral drug BA is not well understood. For ionic interactions, disruption of the interaction *in vitro* by physiological salt concentration is considered an indicator of lack of its impact on a drug's BA.

18.3.3 Physiological factors

GI physiological characteristics often interact with drug substance or dosage form characteristics to impact drug absorption. In addition, interindividual variability in the physiological characteristics can lead to variability in a drug's pharmacokinetic parameters. An understanding of the interaction of physiological variables with drug and dosage form can allow drug product design strategies that may minimize or mitigate variability in drug absorption.

18.3.3.1 Gastrointestinal motility

The peristaltic motion of the stomach and the intestines carry their contained mass forward to the progressing segments of the GI tract. The normal motility of the GI tract is characterized in terms of transit time through different "compartments" of the GI tract, which are utilized in modeling drug absorption. The transit time is defined as the time taken for a dosage form or its components to pass through a compartment. For example, the following parameters are utilized in the GastroPlus software (Simulations Plus, Inc., Lancaster, CA) for the simulation of human drug absorption after oral administration:

- *Stomach*: Gastric emptying time in the fasted state is generally less than half an hour, while a high fat breakfast can increase the gastric emptying time to several hours.
- *Small intestines*: Transit time through different intestinal segments is estimated based on the volume of fluid in each segment. The average small intestinal transit time is considered about 3.3 h.
- *Cecum*: Transit time for human cecum is 4.5 h.
- *Colon*: Human colon transit time is generally considered to be 13.5 h.

The rate of transfer of a drug product from one segment of the GI tract to the next can influence the time period available for drug dissolution or absorption in one particular component. Of all the stages of GI transit, gastric emptying provides the greatest influence on the rate of oral drug absorption because an orally administered dosage form encounters the stomach first. In addition to the emptying of stomach contents, gastric muscles exert mechanical pressure on the dosage form. GI transit times can influence oral drug bioavailability through a multitude of mechanisms, such as the following:

- *Rapid gastric emptying*: Basic drugs that are administered as solid particles or tablets first dissolve in the acidic gastric environment before being transported as drug solutions to the upper intestinal tract, where most of the drug absorption takes place. In some cases, rapid gastric emptying can lead to incomplete drug dissolution in the stomach, leading to the transfer of partially undissolved drug particles into the duodenum. This can not only lead to incomplete drug dissolution and absorption, but the undissolved drug particles can serve as nucleation sites for the precipitation of dissolved drug into the duodenum—which can further reduce the extent of drug absorption and also introduce interindividual variability. This phenomenon is the main reason for the variability in drug absorption in monkey models for many drugs that exhibit pH-based solubility and supersaturation in the duodenum.

- *Increased intestinal transit rate*: A general increase in intestinal motility can increase the rate of drug transport from one intestinal segment to the next. This can impact the total duration of time a drug has for absorption from the proximal segments of the intestine (such as duodenum), which have a higher surface area than latter segments (such as the ileum and colon). Thus, the effect of GI motility on the extent of drug absorption would depend on the rate of drug absorption and the effective permeability of the compound. The impact can be higher for drugs with a specific and short window of absorption.

GI motility can be affected by several factors, including the pharmacological effect of the drug itself. Gastric emptying is affected by a multitude of factors including posture and presence of food.

18.3.3.2 Food and pH effect

Food intake can affect drug absorption either by directly interacting with the dosage form or by affecting GI physiological parameters relevant to drug absorption. For example, GI fluid volumes are different in the fed and the fasted state, as illustrated in Table 18.1 [43].

Food also influences gastric pH. Thus, while the normal gastric pH is one to three in the fasted state, the fed state gastric pH in humans can be 4.3–5.4 [44]. The effect of gastric pH on oral drug absorption can be most predominant for weakly basic compounds that have high solubility at acidic pH and low solubility at the basic pH. The rate and extent of oral bioavailability of these drugs in humans are dependent on their rapid dissolution from an oral solid dosage form in the acidic stomach. Change in gastric pH, due to coadministration of food or other reasons such as the use of antihistaminic drugs, can lead to altered oral drug bioavailability.

In addition to the quantity and type of food (e.g., liquid ingestion vs. solid food), fat content in the food can affect GI motility, the concentration of bile in upper intestines, and drug-release characteristics from the dosage form. Fat and high calorie meals delay gastric emptying. The presence of surfactants in the intestinal milieu (e.g., from the bile) can lead to solubilization of a drug at the site of absorption (small intestine), leading to supersaturation of the drug. This can prevent the precipitation of a weakly basic compound that dissolved in the low gastric pH and was subsequently transported to the high intestinal pH environment, in which it has low solubility. In cases in which the supersaturation phenomenon contributes to oral drug bioavailability, alterations in bile secretion or other physiological changes in the intestinal fluids can become significant determinants of drug absorption.

18.3.3.3 Window of absorption

Passive absorption of orally administered drugs is assumed to follow a uniform rate of permeation across the GI tract. The rate of absorption for these drugs, therefore, is a function of the relative area of a GI segment and the residence time of the drug in that segment. Some drugs, however, display significantly high absorption in some specific region of the GI tract, while the absorption rate may be very low in other segments. The high absorption regions for these drugs are termed the "window of absorption." The phenomenon of the window of absorption of a drug can also be related to differential drug solubility and stability in various regions of the GI tract, or the presence of active transporters in certain regions.

The window of absorption of a drug *in vitro* can be ascertained by measuring drug permeability across different sections of the GI tract mounted in an Ussing chamber. *In vivo* assessment, or confirmation of a window of absorption, is generally deductive based on the plasma concentration–time profile of a drug after administration to different regions of the GI tract. Such studies may be carried out using, for example, a radio-frequency-based remote-controlled delivery capsule coupled with real-time visualization of capsule location in the GI tract using gamma scintigraphy. In addition, direct administration of a drug to different intestinal segments using animals

TABLE 18.1   Gastrointestinal fluid volumes in the fasted and fed state.

Compartment	Fasted state volume (mL, mean ± SD)	Fed state volume (mL, mean ± SD)
Stomach	45 ± 18	686 ± 93
Small intestine	105 ± 72	54 ± 41
Large intestine	13 ± 12	11 ± 26

that are ported for direct drug administration to such regions of the GI tract (e.g., cynomolgus monkeys can be surgically ported for direct drug administration to the duodenum and ileum) can help elucidate relative absorption rates of the drug from different segments. Significant change in the AUC of the drug after administration to different regions is indicative of a window of absorption.

A window of absorption in the proximal regions of the small intestine, such as the duodenum, can potentially limit the oral bioavailability of drugs and also present an obstacle to the development of controlled-release formulations. Drugs that show higher permeability in the upper intestinal regions include ciprofloxacin, levodopa, furosemide, captopril, acyclovir, and gabapentin. Oral drug absorption from these drugs is sensitive to physiological parameters, such as GI motility. This sensitivity is reflected in the inter- and intrasubject variability in their oral drug absorption. In addition, such drugs are also amenable to dosage form strategies that target to maximize and prolong drug concentration in the upper GI tract—such as gastroretentive dosage forms or bioadhesive microspheres. For example, a prolonged-release gastroretentive dosage form of ciprofloxacin prolonged the exposure of the drug in humans [45].

18.3.3.4 Variability in metabolizing enzymes and efflux transporters

Several drugs are substrates of drug-metabolizing enzymes in the GI tract, such as the cytochrome P450 (CYP) enzymes in the intestinal mucosa, and efflux transporters, such as the P-glycoprotein (P-gp) family of transporters. CYP enzymes are membrane-bound heme-containing proteins that are responsible for the metabolism of endogenous compounds such as steroids and fatty acids and are often the metabolizing enzymes of drugs and xenobiotics. Isoform 3A4 of the cytochrome P450—metabolizing enzyme has been recognized as dominant in the gut wall metabolism of drugs. P-gp is the active transporter that secretes drugs back into the GI tract and is located on the mucosal surface of GI epithelial cells. P-gp expression in normal tissues, such as the canalicular side of hepatocytes, the apical surface of renal proximal tubules, and endothelial cells of the blood—brain barrier, serves to minimize physiological exposure to potentially toxic xenobiotics.

Oral absorption of drugs that are substrates of efflux transporters and metabolizing enzymes is affected by the interindividual expression level and intraindividual distribution of these proteins in the GI tract. The distribution of the P-gp transporter and CYP3A4 metabolizing enzymes differs across regions of the GI tract, which can contribute to variability in oral drug absorption. P-gp transport has been linked to the low and variable oral bioavailability of several compounds, such as propranolol and felodipine [46]. Drugs such as itraconazole and cyclosporin are substrates for both CYP3A4 and P-gp. In addition, drugs whose absorption is affected by transporters and metabolizing enzymes can also be sensitive to certain food effects. For example, grapefruit juice is an inhibitor of CYP3A4 [47] and can thus affect the oral absorption of drugs that are CYP3A4 substrates.

18.4 Bioequivalence

The BE refers to the equivalent rate and extent of drug absorption of a drug from two different formulations or dosage forms when administered in the same molar dose. Two drug products with similar rate and extent of drug absorption are termed bioequivalent. Rate of absorption of a drug influences the maximum plasma concentration reached (C_{max}) and the time to maximum plasma concentration (t_{max}). The extent of drug absorption is indicated by $F_{relative}$ of the two formulations or drug products.

BE to the marketed brand-name drug product is a requirement for granting the marketing authorization of generic drug products by regulatory agencies such as the US FDA and the European Medicines Agency (EMEA) in Europe.

18.4.1 Derived pharmacokinetic parameters for bioequivalence assessment

When two drug products are administered for the purpose of single-dose BE assessment, the data collected are typically the plasma concentration—time profile for a fixed duration of time, such as 48 h or 72 h. Direct comparison of the two profiles becomes difficult and subjective given various aspects of the data that are of importance in identifying their similarity or differences. These aspects include the rate of absorption, intersubject variability in the data, total amount of drug absorbed, peak plasma concentration (C_{max}), and the time to reach the peak plasma concentration (T_{max}). Notably, the rate of elimination is an aspect of the plasma concentration—time profile that typically would not depend on the dosage form. Assessing the similarity of the two profiles becomes difficult when several aspects of the profiles need to be taken into consideration. Parameters that are used for BE assessment include C_{max} and the total amount of drug absorbed. The latter can be inferred from AUC from the time of dose administration ($t = 0$) to the last sampling time point (t) or an infinite time point (∞), which estimates drug concentrations in plasma until very low levels by extrapolating the last time point using a parameter derived from the curve (terminal rate of drug elimination). These AUC parameters are termed $AUC_{0 \to t}$ and $AUC_{0 \to \infty}$, respectively.

BE assessment is conducted using the parameters $AUC_{0 \to t}$, $AUC_{0 \to \infty}$, and C_{max}. The first two of these parameters represent the extent of drug absorption, whereas C_{max} is primarily affected by the rate of drug absorption. Notably, the parameter T_{max}, which also represents the rate of drug absorption, is not used in the BE calculations. The reason is that T_{max} is a discrete measured parameter that depends on the design of the study in terms of sampling time points. Further, the shape of the plasma concentration—time profile can influence T_{max}. For example, the presence of two peaks in the plasma concentration—time profile can lead to a perception of significant differences between two formulations in terms of T_{max} if the two peaks have minor differences in their peak concentration. While these limitations also hold true for C_{max}, the assessment of peak plasma concentration is critical to drug safety because many drugs exhibit concentration-dependent toxicity.

18.4.2 Statistical basis of bioequivalence assessment

Statistically, two drug products are considered bioequivalent if the 90% confidence intervals (CI) for the ratio of the population geometric means between the test (T) and the reference (R) drug products for log-transformed values of parameters representing the rate (C_{max}) and the extent (AUC) of drug absorption fall within the 0.80—1.25 range. The 90% CI is based on a two-sided test and is equivalent to two one-sided tests of significance with null hypothesis of bioinequivalence at a significance level (α) of 0.05 [48].

The log-transformed data is analyzed using the analysis of variance (ANOVA), a parametric statistical model, to derive the confidence interval for the difference between formulations. The confidence interval is then back-transformed to obtain the desired confidence interval for the ratio of the two formulations on the original scale. The sources of variation that are usually accounted for in the ANOVA model are sequence, period, and formulation using fixed effects for all terms.

18.4.2.1 Logarithmic transformation

The logarithmic transformation of data is preferred for clinical and pharmacokinetic reasons [49]. The primary comparison of interest in a BE study is the ratio, rather than the difference of the average pharmacokinetic parameters from the two formulations. Therefore, logarithmic transformation allows the use of a linear statistical model (which utilizes differences between the means) to infer differences between the two means (which are transformed on a log scale). The analyzed data can be back-transformed to derive inferences about the ratio of the two averages on the original scale. This allows comparison between the two formulations on the basis of this ratio.

The pharmacokinetic rationale for log transformation of data is to convert the factors responsible for variation in drug plasma levels from a multiplicative to an additive model. This enables the use of linear statistical methods that utilize differences in the comparison of two formulations. For example, the total amount of drug absorbed, $AUC_{0 \to \infty}$, is a function of administered dose (D), fraction absorbed (F), and clearance (CL), as shown in Eq. (18.12):

$$AUC_{0 \to \infty} = \frac{FD}{CL} \tag{18.12}$$

This equation relates the $AUC_{0 \to \infty}$ to subject-factors that influence this parameter using multiplicative terms, which could lead to the effect of the subject not being additive. Logarithmic transformation of data indicates logarithmic transformation of underlying mechanistic terms, which were originally multiplicative, thus allowing their use in additive statistical models. Thus, logarithmic transformation of $AUC_{0 \to \infty}$ yields Eq. (18.13):

$$\ln(AUC_{0 \to \infty}) = \ln(F) + \ln(D) - \ln(CL) \tag{18.13}$$

18.4.2.2 Range of confidence interval

BE study is designed to evaluate differences between two different drug products or formulations made of the same drug substance or active pharmaceutical ingredient (API) at the same dose. The pharmacokinetic parameters and therapeutic window of the API, however, can influence the statistical criteria for BE by affecting variability in the data and the clinical tolerance for such variability. Thus, the recommended range of 90% CI could be different depending on the inherent variability and the therapeutic window of a compound.

The general recommended range of 90% confidence intervals (CIs) for assessing BE is 80%–125% of the ratio of averages for each drug product tested. This ratio represents a multiplicative symmetry for 20% variation since $1.25 = (0.8)^{-1}$. In addition to meeting the BE limit based on these confidence interval boundaries, the point estimate of the geometric mean ratio of pharmacokinetic parameters should fall within this range.

The European Committee for Proprietary Medicinal Products (CPMP) guidance recognizes highly variable drug products as those whose intrasubject variability for a parameter is larger than 30% [50]. For these products, when a wider difference in C_{max} may be considered clinically irrelevant, the C_{max} acceptance criteria may be widened to 69.84%–143.19%. For all other cases (clinically relevant parameters), widening of the acceptable confidence interval range is allowed to different extents based on the intrasubject variability. Thus, the widening of acceptance criteria for the CI requires the study design to involve replicate dosing of the same drug product to demonstrate intrasubject variability. Similarly, for narrow therapeutic index drugs, the acceptance interval for AUC could be tightened to 90.00%–111.11%. These tighter limits could also be applied to C_{max}, where the maximum drug concentration is of particular importance for drug safety.

18.4.3 Bioequivalence study design considerations

The objective of a BE study is to assess variation in mean drug pharmacokinetics based on differences between the two formulations (groups) while separately accounting for intersubject variability (to assess the power of the study). A typical BE study design incorporates several elements, such as the following:

- *Crossover* instead of parallel group design: Crossover design refers to the administration of both formulations to all subjects in the study in a sequential fashion; that is, each subject undergoes two dosings: the subject receives one of the two formulations in the first dose and the other formulation in the second dose. A parallel group design, on the other hand, would involve different subjects receiving the two different formulations. This approach is not preferred because any inherent pharmacokinetic variation in the subjects chosen between the two groups can introduce bias in the study.
- *Random*: Since each subject undergoes two dosings, the formulation administered in each dosing period is not unique but mixed up. For example, if 12 subjects were to be utilized for BE assessment, both formulations must be utilized in both dosing periods, and an equal number of subjects should receive each formulation in each dosing period. Each subject is randomly selected to receive either of the two formulations in each dosing period. These aspects are included to avoid any systematic bias in the study design that can alter the effect of the study.
- *Washout period*: Since each subject must undergo two dosings, the dose periods must be separated by adequate time to allow complete elimination of the drug administered in period one before the drug is readministered in period 2. This period of time between the two dosings when the subjects are "rested" is known as the washout period. The minimum duration of time for the washout is based on the elimination half-life of the drug. A minimum time equivalent to five half-lives is preferred to allow complete drug elimination from the system.
- *Double blinded*: BE studies are designed such that none of the study subjects or other participants (including physicians and analysts) are aware of the identity of the formulation given to the subjects. Blinding is carried out by assigning a code to each drug product, which is not revealed until study completion (including sample analysis and statistical interpretation of data). This aspect is designed to avoid any bias from the patients, physicians, or other study participants toward one of the two products.

The blinding requirement places a further burden on the study directors to ensure that both products being administered are organoleptically similar. In other words, if two tablets are administered, the patient or physicians should not be able to make out differences between the two based on their appearance, odor, or any such perceptible feature. This, therefore, requires that both tablets be of similar size, shape, color, and markings (if any). These requirements can become challenging when one of the products being compared is a marketed drug product, which cannot be altered. Often, these requirements are fulfilled by encapsulating both drug products in hard gelatin capsules.

18.5 Conclusions

The rate and extent of drug absorption into the systemic circulation can be measured by estimation of the C_{max}, T_{max}, and *AUC* after drug administration. These measures of BA are also helpful in determining BE of different formulations or dosage forms. Assessment of $F_{relative}$ is important to new drug product development, while assessment of $F_{absolute}$ is important to understand the clinical impact of changes in a drug's BA.

Oral drug BA is determined by the physicochemical characteristics of the drug and the dosage form, and their interactions with GI physiology. Drug properties important to oral drug absorption include its solubility, stability, lipophilicity, and surface activity. The pH-dependent variation in these drug substance properties can lead to their interactions with physiological variations in GI pH, which may affect drug absorption in different regions of the GI tract. In addition, physiological parameters such as gastric emptying time, intestinal motility, and expression of metabolizing enzymes and transporters can also affect the oral drug BA. Dosage form–related factors that affect drug BA include drug–excipient interactions and drug-release characteristics.

The dosage form design can be tailored in certain ways to achieve the desired targeted oral drug absorption profile. Drug product development, therefore, must take into consideration the interaction of drug substance characteristics with physiological parameters to design optimal drug delivery strategies. Drug product design characteristics, such as controlled-release formulations or regionally targeted dosage forms, can often be helpful in optimizing drug absorption and BA.

Case studies

Case 18.1

A brand and a generic product were compared, and the data are as follows:

	Dose (mg)	AUC (mg*hr/mL)
Brand	250	6392
Generic	350	7992

Advise the FDA panel on the relative bioavailability of this generic product.

Approach: The calculated relative bioavailability of the generic product is 89.3%

$$F_{rel} = \frac{\dfrac{AUC_{Generic}}{Dose_{Generic}}}{\dfrac{AUC_{Brand}}{Dose_{Brand}}} = \frac{\dfrac{7992}{350}}{\dfrac{6392}{250}} = \frac{22.834}{25.568} = 0.893$$

$$F_{rel} = 0.893 \times 100 = 89.3\%$$

Case 18.2

Two dosage forms are available to you. You also have information on their bioavailability and salt factor, as shown here. You have been asked to determine an equivalent dose for the coated tablet in this situation. How will you proceed on this calculation?

Dosage form	Dose	Salt factor S	Bioavailability F
Immediate release (IR) tablet	500 mg	0.87	0.35
Coated tablet (CT)		0.94	0.70

Approach: The equivalent dose for the coated tablet can be determined as follows, where D represents dose, IR represents immediate release, and CT represents coated tablets:

$$S_{IR} \times F_{IR} \times D_{IR} = S_{CT} \times F_{CT} \times D_{CT}$$

$$0.87 \times 0.35 \times 500 = 0.94 \times 0.7 \times D_{CT}$$

$$D_{CT} = 231.4 \approx 230 \text{ mg}$$

Therefore, your recommendation should be for a coated 230 mg tablet. Note that salt factor refers to the ratio of molecular weight of the free acid or free base of the drug with that of the corresponding salt. This example illustrates calculating the relative dose of two different salt forms of a drug (different salt factors).

Case 18.3

You are working as a clinical pharmacist in a startup generic pharmaceutical company. The company wishes to evaluate the absolute bioavailability of new investigation drug products that are available as 250 mg oral tablets and also as a parenteral solution (100 mg/mL). You are asked to design this study in 10 human volunteers and interpret the data to determine the absolute bioavailability of the oral tablet.

Approach.

Step one: Each volunteer will receive a single oral tablet (250 mg) of the drug or a single IV bolus injection containing 100 mg of drug in 1 mL.

Step two: Plasma samples will be collected at predetermined time points over a 48 h period.

Step three: Drug concentration in the plasma sample will be determined by a validated analytical method.

The results of the study are presented below:

Dosage form	Dose (mg)	Average AUC (0−48 h) μg h/mL	Standard deviation
Oral tablet	250	120	17.0
IV bolus injection	100	55.2	6.2

$n = 10$.

Step four: The absolute availability of the tablet formation is determined using the following equation:

$$\text{Absolute Bioavailability } (F) = (\text{AUC peroral} / \text{Dose peroral}) / (\text{AUC IV} / \text{Dose IV})$$

$$F = (120/250)/(55.2/100) = 0.48/0.552 = \mathbf{0.87}$$

Interpretation: Since the fraction of dose absorbed from the tablet, in this case, was less than 1, it indicates that this investigational drug is not completely absorbed systemically.

Case 18.4

A study conducted by Lobenberg et al. [51] suggested that clinicians should avoid assumptions that formulations sold across the globe are therapeutically equivalent, even when labeled to contain the same drug substance and strength. How could you justify their statement in a journal club discussion of this manuscript? This study tested the *in vitro* dissolution characteristics of different amoxicillin, metronidazole, and Zidovudine products purchased in the Americas to comparator pharmaceutical product (CPP) as described by WHO. Results showed all tested Zidovudine products showed *in vitro* equivalence as compared to all other products.

Approach: These three drugs are BCS class I drug. Therefore, there is a possibility that *in vitro* dissolution finding might be used to document bioequivalence. All investigated zidovudine products were found to be *in vitro* equivalent to the CPP. Only 3 of 12 tested amoxicillin products were found to be *in vitro* equivalent to the CPP. None of the tested metronidazole products were *in vitro* equivalent to the CPP. These findings suggest but do not confirm bioinequivalence where *in vitro* comparisons failed, given that an *in vivo* blood level study might have confirmed bioequivalence. At times, identifying a CPP in one of the selected markets proved difficult. The study demonstrates that products sold across national markets may not be bioequivalent.

Critical reflection and practice applications

- Drug product selection and generic product substitution are an important responsibilities of physicians, pharmacists, and other healthcare providers authorized to prescribe
- Bioavailability is the rate and extent to which the active ingredient or active moiety is absorbed from a drug product and becomes available at the site of action
- These studies are used to determine the effect of changes in the physiochemical properties of drug substance and the effect of dosage forms on the pharmacokinetic of the drug
- Bioavailability is measured by using three pharmacokinetic variables: The area under blood drug concentration (AUC), The maximum blood concentration (C_{max}), and the time to reach maximum concentration (T_{max})
- Bioequivalence means the absence of a significant difference in the rate and extent to which the active ingredient or active moiety in pharmaceutical equivalents or pharmaceutical alternatives becomes available at the site of drug action when administered at the same molar dose and under similar conditions in an appropriately designed study
- Bioequivalence studies are used to compare the bioavailability of the same drug from various dosage forms
- Bioequivalence is a surrogate measure of *in vivo* drug product performance and dissolution profile comparisons as a measure of *in vitro* drug product performance
- Bioavailability and bioequivalence studies are considered as the performance measure of the drug product *in vivo*

References

[1] P.L. Toutain, A. Bousquet-Melou, Bioavailability and its assessment, J. Vet. Pharmacol. Therapeut. 27 (6) (2004) 455–466.

[2] D.G. Bailey, G.K. Dresser, J.H. Kreeft, C. Munoz, D.J. Freeman, J.R. Bend, Grapefruit-felodipine interaction: effect of unprocessed fruit and probable active ingredients, Clin. Pharmacol. Ther. 68 (5) (2000) 468–477.

[3] E.T. Hellriegel, T.D. Bjornsson, W.W. Hauck, Interpatient variability in bioavailability is related to the extent of absorption: implications for bioavailability and bioequivalence studies, Clin. Pharmacol. Ther. 60 (6) (1996) 601–607.

[4] M.O. Karlsson, U. Bredberg, Bioavailability estimation by semisimultaneous drug administration: a Monte Carlo simulation study, J. Pharmacokinet. Biopharm. 18 (2) (1990) 103–120.

[5] P.L. Toutain, G.D. Koritz, P.M. Fayolle, M. Alvinerie, Pharmacokinetics of methylprednisolone, methylprednisolone sodium succinate, and methylprednisolone acetate in dogs, J. Pharmaceut. Sci. 75 (3) (1986) 251–255.

[6] A.T. Serajuddin, Salt formation to improve drug solubility, Adv. Drug Deliv. Rev. 59 (7) (2007) 603–616.

[7] A.J. Aguiar, J.E. Zelmer, Dissolution behavior of polymorphs of chloramphenicol palmitate and mefenamic acid, J. Pharmaceut. Sci. 58 (8) (1969) 983–987.

[8] T. Maeda, H. Takenaka, Y. Yamahira, T. Noguchi, Use of rabbits for absorption studies on polymorphs of chloramphenicol palmitate, Chem. Pharm. Bull. 28 (2) (1980) 431–436.

[9] Z.W. Cai, Y. Zhang, R.M. Borzilleri, L. Qian, S. Barbosa, D. Wei, Discovery of brivanib alaninate ((S)-((R)-1-(4-(4-fluoro-2-methyl-1H-indol-5-yloxy)-5-methylpyrrolo[2,1-f] [1,2,4]triazin-6-yloxy)propan-2-yl)2-aminopropanoate), a novel prodrug of dual vascular endothelial growth factor receptor-2 and fibroblast growth factor receptor-1 kinase inhibitor (BMS-540215), J. Med. Chem. 51 (6) (2008) 1976–1980.

[10] A.S. Narang, D.D. Desai, R.I. Mahato, Y. Lu, Anticancer drug development: unique aspects of pharmaceutical developmentPharmaceutical perspectives of cancer therapeutics, in: R.I. Mahato, Y. Lu (Eds.), Pharmaceutical Perspectives of Cancer Therapeutics, AAPS-Springer Publishing Program, New York, NY, 2009.

[11] A.S. Narang, R.I. Mahato, A.S. Narang, R.I. Mahato, Targeting colon and kidney: pathophysiological determinants of design strategyTargeted delivery of small and macromolecular drugs, in: A.S. Narang, R.I. Mahato (Eds.), Targeted Delivery of Small and Macromolecular Drugs, CRC Press, New York, N.Y, 2010, pp. 351–370.

[12] J.C. Chaumeil, Micronization: a method of improving the bioavailability of poorly soluble drugs, Methods Find. Exp. Clin. Pharmacol. 20 (3) (1998) 211–215.

[13] E. Reverchon, G. Della Porta, A. Spada, A. Antonacci, Griseofulvin micronization and dissolution rate improvement by supercritical assisted atomization, J. Pharm. Pharmacol. 56 (11) (2004) 1379–1387.

[14] R.B. Hammond, K. Pencheva, K.J. Roberts, T. Auffret, Quantifying solubility enhancement due to particle size reduction and crystal habit modification: case study of acetyl salicylic acid, J. Pharmaceut. Sci. 96 (8) (2007) 1967–1973.

[15] G.P. Sanganwar, S. Sathigari, R.J. Babu, R.B. Gupta, Simultaneous production and co-mixing of microparticles of nevirapine with excipients by supercritical antisolvent method for dissolution enhancement, Eur. J. Pharmaceut. Sci. 39 (1–3) (2010) 164–174.

[16] G.L. Amidon, H. Lennernas, V.P. Shah, J.R. Crison, A theoretical basis for a biopharmaceutic drug classification: the correlation of *in vitro* drug product dissolution and *in vivo* bioavailability, Pharm. Res. 12 (3) (1995) 413–420.

[17] C.Y. Wu, L.Z. Benet, Predicting drug disposition via application of BCS: transport/absorption/elimination interplay and development of a biopharmaceutics drug disposition classification system, Pharm. Res. 22 (1) (2005) 11–23.

[18] S. Kaojarern, S. Nathakarnkikool, U. Suvanakoot, Comparative bioavailability of praziquantel tablets, Dicp 23 (1) (1989) 29–32.

[19] J.M. Clarke, L.E. Ramsay, J.R. Shelton, M.J. Tidd, S. Murray, R.F. Palmer, Factors influencing comparative bioavailability of spironolactone tablets, J. Pharmaceut. Sci. 66 (10) (1977) 1429–1432.

[20] G. Owusu-Ababio, N.K. Ebube, R. Reams, M. Habib, Comparative dissolution studies for mefenamic acid-polyethylene glycol solid dispersion systems and tablets, Pharmaceut. Dev. Technol. 3 (3) (1998) 405–412.

[21] K.P.R. Chowdary, K.V.V. Suresh Babu, Dissolution, bioavailability and ulcerogenic studies on solid dispersions of indomethacin in water soluble cellulose polymers, Drug Dev. Ind. Pharm. 20 (1994) 799–813.

[22] S. Janssens, A. De Zeure, A. Paudel, J. Van Humbeeck, P. Rombaut, G. Van den Mooter, Influence of preparation methods on solid state supersaturation of amorphous solid dispersions: a case study with itraconazole and eudragit e100, Pharm. Res. 27 (5) (2010) 775–785.

[23] X. Liu, M. Lu, Z. Guo, L. Huang, X. Feng, C. Wu, Improving the chemical stability of amorphous solid dispersion with cocrystal technique by hot melt extrusion, Pharm. Res. 29 (3) (2012) 806–817.

[24] P.J. Marsac, H. Konno, A.C. Rumondor, L.S. Taylor, Recrystallization of nifedipine and felodipine from amorphous molecular level solid dispersions containing poly(vinylpyrrolidone) and sorbed water, Pharm. Res. (N. Y.) 25 (3) (2008) 647–656.

[25] S.L. Shimpi, B. Chauhan, K.R. Mahadik, A. Paradkar, Stabilization and improved in vivo performance of amorphous etoricoxib using Gelucire 50/13, Pharm. Res. 22 (10) (2005) 1727–1734.

[26] D. Coucke, C. Vervaet, P. Foreman, P. Adriaensens, R. Carleer, J.P. Remon, Effect on the nasal bioavailability of co-processing drug and bioadhesive carrier via spray-drying, Int. J. Pharm. 379 (1) (2009) 67–71.

[27] M.D. Dhanaraju, K.S. Kumaran, T. Baskaran, M.S. Moorthy, Enhancement of bioavailability of griseofulvin by its complexation with beta-cyclodextrin, Drug Dev. Ind. Pharm. 24 (6) (1998) 583–587.

[28] A.M. Kaukonen, H. Lennernas, J.P. Mannermaa, Water-soluble beta-cyclodextrins in paediatric oral solutions of spironolactone: preclinical evaluation of spironolactone bioavailability from solutions of beta-cyclodextrin derivatives in rats, J. Pharm. Pharmacol. 50 (6) (1998) 611–619.

[29] F.J. Otero-Espinar, S. Anguiano-Igea, N. GarcÃa-Gonzalez, J.L. Vila-Jato, J. Blanco-MÃndez, Oral bioavailability of naproxen-Î²-cyclodextrin inclusion compound, Int. J. Pharm. 75 (1) (1991) 37–44.

[30] F. Kedzierewicz, C. Zinutti, M. Hoffman, P. Maincent, Bioavailability study of tolbutamide Î²-cyclodextrin inclusion compounds, solid dispersions and bulk powder, Int. J. Pharm. 94 (1–3) (1993) 69–74.

[31] R. Panini, M.A. Vandelli, F. Forni, J.M. Pradelli, G. Salvioli, Improvement of ursodeoxycholic acid bioavailability by 2-hydroxypropyl-beta-cyclodextrin complexation in healthy volunteers, Pharmacol. Res. 31 (3–4) (1995) 205–209.

[32] T. Jarvinen, K. Jarvinen, N. Schwarting, V.J. Stella, Beta-cyclodextrin derivatives, SBE4-beta-CD and HP-beta-CD, increase the oral bioavailability of cinnarizine in beagle dogs, J. Pharmaceut. Sci. 84 (3) (1995) 295–299.

[33] J. Luengo, T. Aranguiz, J. Sepulveda, L. Hernandez, C. Von Plessing, Preliminary pharmacokinetic study of different preparations of acyclovir with beta-cyclodextrin, J. Pharmaceut. Sci. 91 (12) (2002) 2593–2598.

[34] J.W. Wong, K.H. Yuen, Improved oral bioavailability of artemisinin through inclusion complexation with beta- and gamma-cyclodextrins, Int. J. Pharm. 227 (1–2) (2001) 177–185.

[35] J. Savolainen, K. Jarvinen, H. Taipale, P. Jarho, T. Loftsson, T. Jarvinen, Co-administration of a water-soluble polymer increases the usefulness of cyclodextrins in solid oral dosage forms, Pharm. Res. (N. Y.) 15 (11) (1998) 1696–1701.

[36] N. Nambu, M. Shimoda, Y. Takahashi, H. Ueda, T. Nagai, Bioavailability of powdered inclusion compounds of nonsteroidal antiinflammatory drugs with beta-cyclodextrin in rabbits and dogs, Chem. Pharm. Bull. 26 (10) (1978) 2952–2956.

[37] L.H. Emara, R.M. Badr, A.A. Elbary, Improving the dissolution and bioavailability of nifedipine using solid dispersions and solubilizers, Drug Dev. Ind. Pharm. 28 (7) (2002) 795–807.

[38] H.O. Ammar, M. Ghorab, S.A. El-nahhas, S.M. Omar, M.M. Ghorab, Improvement of some pharmaceutical properties of drugs by cyclodextrin complexation. 5, Theophylline. Pharmazie. 51 (1) (1996) 42–46.

[39] L. Shargel, W.-P. Susanna, B.C.Y. Andrew, in: 5th ed. (Ed.), Applied Biopharmaceutics & Pharmacokinetics, Appleton & Lange Reviews/McGraw-Hill, Medical Pub. Division, 2005.

[40] P. Singh, J.K. Guillory, T.D. Sokoloski, L.Z. Benet, V.N. Bhatia, Effect of inert tablet ingredients on drug absorption. I. Effect of polyethylene glycol 4000 on the intestinal absorption of four barbiturates, J. Pharmaceut. Sci. 55 (1) (1966) 63–68.

[41] S.H. Jeong, K. Park, Drug loading and release properties of ion-exchange resin complexes as a drug delivery matrix, Int. J. Pharm. 361 (1–2) (2008) 26–32.

[42] Y. Raghunathan, L. Amsel, O. Hinsvark, W. Bryant, Sustained-release drug delivery system I: coated ion-exchange resin system for phenylpropanolamine and other drugs, J. Pharmaceut. Sci. 70 (4) (1981) 379–384.

[43] C. Schiller, C.-P. Frohlich, T. Giessmann, W. Siegmund, H. Monnikes, N. Hosten, Intestinal fluid volumes and transit of dosage forms as assessed by magnetic resonance imaging, Aliment. Pharmacol. Ther. 22 (10) (2005) 971–979.

[44] W.L. Chiou, P.W. Buehler, Comparison of oral absorption and bioavailablity of drugs between monkey and human, Pharm. Res. 19 (6) (2002) 868–874.

[45] A. Mostafavi, J. Emami, J. Varshosaz, N.M. Davies, M. Rezazadeh, Development of a prolonged-release gastroretentive tablet formulation of ciprofloxacin hydrochloride: pharmacokinetic characterization in healthy human volunteers, Int. J. Pharm. 409 (1–2) (2011) 128–136.

[46] W. Siegmund, K. Ludwig, G. Engel, M. Zschiesche, G. Franke, A. Hoffmann, Variability of intestinal expression of P-glycoprotein in healthy volunteers as described by absorption of talinolol from four bioequivalent tablets, J. Pharmaceut. Sci. 92 (3) (2003) 604–610.

[47] S.M. Kakar, M.F. Paine, P.W. Stewart, P.B. Watkins, 6′7′-Dihydroxybergamottin contributes to the grapefruit juice effect, Clin. Pharmacol. Ther. 75 (6) (2004) 569–579.

[48] R.I. Mahato, A.S. Narang, in: 2nd ed (Ed.), Pharmaceutical Dosage Forms and Drug Delivery, CRC Press, Boca Raton, FL, 2012.

[49] Center for Drug Evaluation and Research, US Food and Drug Administration, Guidance for Industry: Statistical Approaches to Establishing Bioequivalence, 2001. Available from: http://www.fda.gov/cder/guidance/index.htm.

[50] Committee for Medicinal Products for Human Use, European Medical Agency, Guideline on the Investigation of Bioequivalence, Available from: http://www.ema.europa.eu.

[51] R. Löbenberg, N.B. Chacra, E.S. Stippler, et al., Toward global standards for comparator pharmaceutical products: case studies of amoxicillin, metronidazole, and zidovudine in the Americas, AAPS J. 14 (2012) 462–472.

19

Routes of Drug Administration

Mohsen A. Hedaya

Department of Pharmaceutics, Faculty of Pharmacy, Kuwait University, Safat, Kuwait

CHAPTER OBJECTIVES
- Describe the physiologic makeup of common routes of drug administration.
- Identify acceptable dosage forms based on the route of drug administration.
- Compare the common routes of drug administration based on barriers to systemic drug absorption.
- Evaluate the influence of drug physicochemical and formulation properties on systemic drug absorption from various routes of drug administration.

Keywords: Absorption barriers; Nasal drug administration; Ocular drug administration; Oral drug administration; Parenteral drug administration; Physiological barriers; Pulmonary drug administration; Transdermal drug administration.

19.1 Introduction

Drug administration involves the application of a drug on a body surface or the introduction of the drug into a body space to produce systemic or local effects. Drugs intended to produce systemic effects must be absorbed from the site of drug administration to the systemic circulation and then distributed throughout the body to exert pharmacologic effects. Locally acting drugs produce their effect at or near the site of administration without the need to be absorbed into the systemic circulation. Whether used for its local or systemic effects, the drug molecule encounters biological barriers that can impede movement from the site of administration to the site of action. The initial barriers include permeation across biological membranes during the processes of drug absorption and diffusion. As discussed in Chapters 16 and 17, the characteristics of the biological membranes and cell structures vary substantially throughout the body despite the existence of common structural features. As a result, drug administration by different routes results in varied rates and extents of drug absorption and distribution. The United States Food and Drug Administration (FDA) has defined more than a hundred terms to describe the various routes of drug administration (Table 19.1).

However, the commonly used routes of drug administration include intravenous injection or infusion directly to the systemic circulation; intramuscular injection; intradermal or subcutaneous injections; transdermal application to

TABLE 19.1 FDA-approved terms for labeled routes of administration.

Auricular (otic)	Intrabiliary	Intraepidermal	Intrapleural	Iontophoresis	Subarachnoid
Buccal	Intrabronchial	Intraesophageal	Intraprostatic	Irrigation	Subconjunctival
Conjunctival	Intrabursal	Intragastric	Intrapulmonary	Laryngeal	Subcutaneous
Cutaneous	Intracardiac	Intragingival	Intraruminal	Nasal	Subgingival
Dental	Intracartilaginous	Intrahepatic	Intrasinal	Nasogastric	Sublingual
Electro-osmosis	Intracaudal	Intraileal	Intraspinal	Not applicable	Submucosal
Endocervical	Intracavernous	Intralesional	Intrasynovial	Occlusive dressing technique	Subretinal
Endosinusial	Intracavitary	Intralingual	Intratendinous	Ophthalmic	Topical
Endotracheal	Intracerebral	Intraluminal	Intratesticular	Oral	Transdermal
Enteral	Intracisternal	Intralymphatic	Intrathecal	Oropharyngeal	Transendocardial
Epidural	Intracorneal	Intramammary	Intrathoracic	Parenteral	Transmucosal
Extra-amniotic	Intracoronal, dental	Intramedullary	Intratubular	Percutaneous	Transplacental
Extracorporeal	Intracoronary	Intrameningeal	Intratumor	Periarticular	Transtracheal
Hemodialysis	Intracorporus cavernosum	Intramuscular	Intratympanic	Peridural	Transtympanic
Infiltration	Intradermal	Intranodal	Intrauterine	Perineural	Ureteral
Interstitial	Intradiscal	Intraocular	Intravascular	Periodontal	Urethral
Intra-abdominal	Intraductal	Intraomentum	Intravenous	Rectal	Vaginal
Intra-amniotic	Intraduodenal	Intraovarian	Intraventricular	Respiratory (inhalation)	
Intra-arterial	Intradural	Intrapericardial	Intravesical	Retrobulbar	
Intra-articular	Intraepicardial	Intraperitoneal	Intravitreal	Soft tissue	

the skin; ophthalmic instillation or injection to the eye; auricular instillation to the ear; nasal application to the nose; respiratory inhalation to the lungs; oral ingestion; rectal application to the rectum; and vaginal application to the vagina. The choice of the route depends on drug, formulation, and patient factors, in addition to the condition being treated. For example, the pharmaceutical dosage forms should be prepared with specific characteristics that suit the intended route of administration and optimize the drug availability at its site of action. The rate and extent at which the drug becomes available at its site of action depend on the drug properties such as solubility and permeability; dosage form characteristics; and anatomical, physiological, and pathological characteristics of the site of drug administration. This chapter discusses specific characteristics of common routes of drug administration and describes formulation strategies relevant to each route of drug administration.

19.2 Parenteral drug administration

Parenteral drug administration refers to drug administration outside the alimentary canal in the broadest sense but is classically used to describe routes of administration that involve drug injection. These commonly include intravenous (IV), intramuscular (IM), intradermal (ID), and subcutaneous (SC) injections (Fig. 19.1).

Other less commonly used parenteral routes could also include intra-arterial, intrathecal, and intra-articular injections. The common feature of parenteral drug administration is that the drug is introduced to the body using a hypodermic needle or catheter. Since parenteral drug administration delivers the drug directly into the body and bypasses the skin and other defense mechanisms for protecting the body from infections, formulations intended for parenteral administration must be sterile, nonimmunogenic, and pyrogen free. Intravenously administered drugs bypass the absorption process by administration directly to the systemic circulation for subsequent distribution to all parts of the body. However, other parenteral routes necessitate the drug be absorbed from the site of

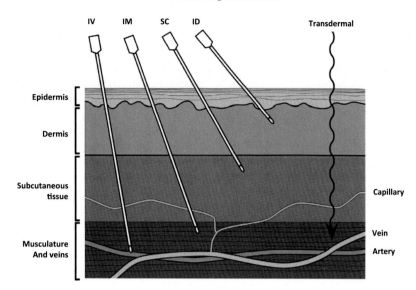

FIGURE 19.1 Schematic representation of parenteral drug delivery routes of drug administration.

administration to be systemically available. The rate and extent of systemic drug availability following parenteral administration is influenced by the anatomical and physiological characteristics at the site of injection, drug physicochemical properties, and drug formulation.

19.2.1 Intravenous injection

Drugs administered into the venous circulation return to the heart, where they are available for distribution to all parts of the body. This route of administration guarantees complete bioavailability, meaning that the entire dose of the drug reaches the systemic circulation (see Chapter 18). In the tissues, the capillary endothelium allows passage of small molecules, such as water and low molecular weight drugs and proteins, to the interstitial fluid, which fills the spaces between the cells based on membrane transport processes described in Chapter 16. The movement of fluids between the capillaries and the interstitial fluids is controlled by the balance between the hydrostatic pressure in the capillaries, which favor moving water from the capillaries to the tissues, and the osmotic pressure of the solutes in the capillaries, which favor water movement from the tissues to the capillaries. Distribution of drugs from the blood in the capillaries to the tissues occurs through membrane transport processes and usually results in initial net drug transfer from the blood to the tissues. Eventually, a distribution equilibrium is established between the drug in the circulation and the drug in tissues. The extent of drug distribution to tissues depends on the affinity of the drug to different tissues and can be different from one tissue to the other (see Chapter 17) [1].

Drugs are administered via the IV route when rapid drug effect is desired, such as in cases of emergency, when the drug has limited or unpredictable absorption, or in patients who cannot receive the drug by other routes. However, IV drug administration must be carried out by trained individuals, and special precautions must be considered. IV drug products must be sterile, nonimmunogenic, and pyrogen free. The formulations should also be generally solutions free of suspended particles that could obstruct small capillaries, have physiologically compatible pH values near 7.4, be isotonic with the blood, and be formulated in physiologically compatible solvents. Large- and small-volume IV drug products are usually formulated to comply with these requirements. However, some IV drug products cause administration site reactions because the formulations are irritating to the vascular epithelium, often due to high or low pH values; hypertonic or hypotonic solutions; or irritating drug, solvents, or excipients. These irritating formulations can cause phlebitis (inflammation of the vascular epithelium) and potentially severe damage in the tissues surrounding the site of administration after a single or repeated injections. It is more common and severe especially when the injection is inadvertently delivered extravascularly or when extravasation of the administered drug occurs. However, these formulations should be administered slowly to allow the drug solution to be diluted in and buffered with the blood to prevent injection-site reactions. For example, vancomycin is an intravenously administered antibiotic that is associated with inflammatory responses if it is administered too quickly. It is usually administered slowly over a period of at least 60 min to avoid these reactions.

Drug administration via the IV route can either be by IV bolus administration or by IV infusion. IV bolus administration involves the delivery of the entire drug dose over a short period of time (usually seconds to minutes), which achieves the highest observed drug concentration immediately following drug administration. IV infusion is the administration of an IV drug solution at a constant rate over a period of time. Usually, the rate of drug administration by IV infusions (i.e., the infusion rate) is controlled by a mechanical pump that delivers a preset constant volume per unit time. The period of infusion can be long (hours to days) or short (minutes to hours) times. Long IV infusions will cause the drug concentration in the plasma to gradually increase until a constant drug concentration is achieved. These long infusions are typically referred to as continuous infusions and usually involve large fluid volumes. Continuous IV infusions are typically used in hospitalized patients, and the infusion rate can be increased or decreased to achieve a desired drug concentration, desired drug effect, or until the patient condition is stabilized.

Some drugs are administered by repeated short infusions of relatively small fluid volumes referred to as intermittent IV infusions. Drugs administered by intermittent IV infusions are infused at a constant rate over a short period of time, usually 30 min to 2 h. Repeated infusions are then administered after a period of time referred to as the dosing interval. Intermittent infusions are used for drugs that might produce injection-site irritation or produce high toxic drug concentrations if administered as a bolus dose. Drug administration by intermittent IV infusion allows the drug to distribute to the tissues during the infusion, and the maximum drug concentration achieved in blood at the end of the infusion is usually lower than the blood concentration achieved if an equivalent dose were administered by IV bolus.

19.2.2 Intramuscular injection

Intramuscular (IM) drug administration involves injecting the drug formulation directly into the muscles. The rate of drug absorption after IM administration is influenced by the formulation properties and the blood perfusion rate of the site of drug injection. The deltoid muscle is a highly perfused muscle of sufficient size for injection in the shoulder and is preferred when rapid absorption after IM administration is needed. Other large muscle groups can also be considered, such as the Vastus lateralis in the thigh, and may be preferred to avoid possible accidental drug injection into a blood vessel. The most important advantage of IM administration as compared to IV injections is the wide variety of formulations that can be administered to the muscles. Formulations such as aqueous solutions and suspensions, emulsions, and oil-based solutions and suspensions can be administered intramuscularly. The choice of formulation usually depends on the desired rate of absorption. After IM drug administration, the drug has to leave the injected formulation and dissolve in the interstitial fluid at the site of injection where it can be absorbed to the systemic circulation. Drugs injected in the form of aqueous solutions rapidly mix with interstitial fluids where they become available to be absorbed. In this case, the rate-limiting step for drug absorption is the perfusion rate of the site of IM injection.

On the other hand, IM administration of aqueous suspensions or oily solutions or suspensions slows the rate of drug release from the formulation to the interstitial fluid. The rate-limiting step for drug absorption after administration of these formulations is the rate of drug release from the formulations. IM administration of some oily solutions and suspensions has been used for sustained-release formulations of drugs that are absorbed very slowly and provide continuous rates of release to the systemic circulation over a prolonged period of time.

19.2.3 Intradermal and subcutaneous injection

Intradermal and subcutaneous injections deliver the drug to specific locations within the skin. The skin consists of multiple layers (Fig. 19.1) with differing properties. The epidermis is composed of a rapidly dividing inner layer, called the stratum germinativum, which grows upward to renew an outer layer of dead keratinized cells, called the stratum corneum. In this layer, the keratinocytes are surrounded by the lipid matrix that prevents direct contact between these cells and forms continuous lipophilic channels or paths through the stratum corneum. The epidermis protects the body from foreign objects and the outer environment, and also prevents the loss of water and electrolytes from the body. The epidermis is not innervated and does not have a direct blood supply. The thickness of epidermal layers varies significantly in different regions of the body. Underneath the epidermis is the dermis. It is a thick connective tissue layer that is innervated and vascularized. The dermis also contains lymph vessels, hair follicles, and sweat and sebum glands. Underneath the dermis is the subcutaneous tissue that is, a loose layer of fat and connective tissue that is also innervated and vascularized. Vascularized muscle tissue can be found underneath the subcutaneous tissue.

ID drug administration is made by injecting a drug formulation into the dermis or between the dermis and epidermis layers. It is a shallow injection that should not penetrate deep into the skin. While SC injections are made by delivering the drug formulation into the connective tissue underneath the dermis layer. SC injections should not penetrate into the underlying muscle. The volume of the interstitial fluid and the blood perfusion are very limited in the dermis which results in a slow rate of drug absorption after ID administration. ID injections are usually used to administer vaccines or to induce inflammatory responses. In contrast, the SC tissue layer has a larger interstitial fluid volume where the drug can dissolve before it is absorbed. Drug absorption after SC administration usually occurs either by absorption to the blood capillaries or to the lymphatic system, which drains slowly in the systemic circulation, resulting in very slow and unpredictable absorption. This variable absorption then produces unpredictable and erratic systemic drug concentrations after SC drug administration. This problem can be avoided by slowing the rate of drug release from the drug formulation to make it the rate-limiting step for drug absorption. Controlled drug delivery can be achieved in this way for some SC drug products (e.g., some insulin formulations).

19.3 Transdermal drug administration

While the ID and SC drug administration inject drug product to specific locations within the skin, the transdermal route of administration is used to deliver the drug through the skin. Transdermal drug delivery requires a drug product to be applied topically to the skin. A wide variety of acceptable dosage forms can be used for transdermal drug delivery including solid, semisolid, and liquid formulations. Under most circumstances, topically applied products will have some degree of drug penetration into the skin and potentially be absorbed into the systemic circulation. The rate and extent of drug permeation through the skin are based on numerous factors, including drug's physicochemical properties, formulation factors, skin integrity, and pathologic conditions. Some products applied to the skin will have negligible drug absorption and are intended for topical use only. However, pathological conditions or interventional strategies can promote systemic drug absorption even when it does not happen under normal circumstances. Therefore, all topically administered drug products must be clinically evaluated for their intentional and unintentional systemic drug absorption.

Drug absorption through the skin after application of transdermal drug product goes through several steps, which starts with the drug release from the dosage form and the drug becoming available to be absorbed. Then the drug must diffuse through the epidermal layer, including the keratin/lipid barrier of the stratum corneum, to the dermis, where the drug can be absorbed by the capillary vasculature. The rate of transdermal drug absorption is slow and highly variable. Most of this variability is due to physiological and pathological differences in skin structure, thickness, hydration, and inflammation as well as dose differences and formulation factors. Despite this variability in systemic drug absorption, transdermal drug delivery has several advantages. Transdermal drug delivery bypasses first-pass hepatic metabolism. It is sometimes considered when oral administration is not possible (e.g., veterinary applications), for potent drugs, and for drugs with a very short half-life.

The site of drug application can affect the rate of drug absorption across the skin, with thick and keratinized skin providing a more substantial barrier to drug permeation. Transdermal drug products intended for systemic delivery are recommended to be applied to the outer upper portions of the arms and shoulders, the upper and lower back, the upper chest, and the lower hips. Pediatric patients and especially neonates have a thinner and more permeable stratum corneum, resulting in higher extent and faster drug absorption compared to adults. Furthermore, skin hydration is influenced by environmental factors and can affect drug permeation. Occlusion at the site of application can substantially increase the permeability of drugs across the skin and might not be clinically advised for products not intended to be occluded. Skin integrity can affect transdermal drug absorption because the barrier function of the skin is compromised if the skin is damaged or broken.

Transdermal drug delivery requires the application of the drug formulation to the skin to maintain direct contact with the skin for a certain length of time. There are several mechanisms by which the drug can be absorbed through the skin. Two principal mechanisms involve the lipid channels in the epidermis, through which lipophilic drugs tend to be absorbed, and the hydrophilic keratinized cells, through which hydrophilic drugs are often absorbed. Lipophilic drugs tend to diffuse more slowly through the epidermis and dermis compared to hydrophilic drugs. Drugs can also be absorbed through the hair follicles and sebaceous glands. Patients with substantial subcutaneous fat deposits will also have altered rates of transdermal drug absorption, particularly for lipophilic drugs. Skin hydration also increases the moisture content of the lipid channel and the keratinized cells, which increases the possibility of drug dissolution and permeation through the skin. A balance in the hydrophilic and lipophilic drug properties is typically favorable for optimal transdermal administration [2].

The conventional dosage forms for the transdermal route of administration include semisolid preparations of ointments, creams, lotions, and gels. Additionally, topically applied powders, aerosols, liquids (aqueous solutions and suspensions as well as oleaginous solutions and suspensions), liniments, collodions, and pastes are used on the skin. Many of these dosage forms are often used for the treatment of topical skin conditions. Topically administered dosage forms also tend to have more erratic rates and extents of systemic drug absorption. Drug absorption after topical administration is dependent on the drug release rate from the formulation and the skin drug penetration rate which is dependent on the area of application and skin characteristics at the site of application.

Specialized transdermal drug delivery systems have been developed as patches to control the rate of systemic drug absorption after topical application. The general principle of controlling the rate of drug absorption after the application of these delivery systems is to control the rate of drug release from a fixed surface area and to make it slower than the rate of drug penetration across the skin. Unidirectional absorption through the skin allows the surface area in contact with the skin to be a key determinant in the rate of drug absorption with larger applied surface areas producing a greater magnitude of drug absorption. Transdermal patches tend to minimize the effect of physiological or pathological differences on the drug absorption rate. Good candidates for transdermal delivery include potent drugs because the amount of drug that can be absorbed after application of these patches is usually very small. Drugs with short half-lives are also suitable for transdermal delivery because the slow drug absorption from these delivery systems can achieve relatively constant blood-drug concentration over an extended period.

Several formulation strategies have been used to improve drug penetration across the skin after the application of these transdermal patches [3]. This includes skin hydration, which can enhance drug permeation through the skin, and can be achieved by using occlusive devices and moisturizing additives. Some formulations may include penetration enhancers as additives, which can transiently enhance the permeability of the drug across the skin. Another strategy is the use of prodrugs with better permeability through the skin. However, topical formulation excipients as well as patch adhesives should not cause irritation or immunological sensitization. Patients starting to use transdermal delivery systems should exercise caution before long-term use is undertaken. The skin should be evaluated after initial and repeated application of these delivery systems for possible allergic reactions or hypersensitivity.

19.4 Ophthalmic drug administration

The eye consists of two spherical pieces joined together with the smaller frontal part known as the cornea and the larger posterior unit known as the sclera. The cornea is curved and completely transparent, and the sclera is white and encloses the ocular structure. The cornea and sclera are connected by a ring known as the limbus. The iris is a circular structure that gives the eye color. Light enters the eye through a central opening in the transparent cornea known as the pupil. The pupil can change in size by contraction or relaxation of the muscles of the iris to regulate the amount of light available for vision. The lens is located toward the rear of the pupil and is connected from above and below to sets of ciliary muscles that are responsible for shaping the lens to focus the light on the retina. The retina is located on the inner surface of the back of the eye and has a pale disk where the optic nerve is attached to the eye. The anterior portion of the eye is filled with aqueous humor that is a clear fluid. The posterior part of the eye is filled with a vitreous body that is clear gelatinous material. The conjunctiva is the inner surface of the eyelids and usually covers the outside surface of the cornea. Fig. 19.2 shows the general structure of the human eye.

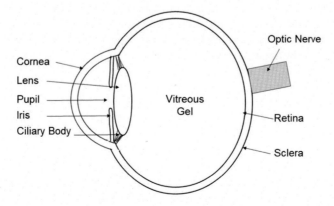

FIGURE 19.2   A diagram showing the general structure of the human eye.

Drug distribution into and out of the eye from systemic circulation is negligible. Therefore, ocular drug administration is typically used for the treatment of eye conditions. Ophthalmic drug administration is typically a topical application of the drug to the external eye or by intraocular injection to the vitreous body. Although some parenteral drug products can be injected directly into the eye, those clinical circumstances are typically chronic and associated with other medical interventions.

Topical application of ophthalmic drug products is a relatively straightforward route of drug administration. The cornea is made up mainly of the stroma, which is covered externally by the epithelium layer and internally by the endothelium layer. The epithelial and endothelial layers are permeable to lipophilic compounds, while the stroma is a cellular layer with a high water content that makes it permeable to hydrophilic compounds. Compounds that can penetrate the cornea should have balanced hydrophilic/lipophilic properties with partition coefficients in the range of 10–100 [4]. Drug ionization is an important factor in determining corneal penetration of drugs because the union-ized form of the drug can penetrate the lipophilic epithelial and endothelial layers of the cornea easier than the ionized form of the drug. When ophthalmic products are administered in the eye, the drug is mixed with tears, and the resulting pH will be influenced by the pH of the formulation for a period of time before the tears return the local pH to the physiological level. Buffering the ophthalmic formulation is an important formulation factor that can be used to optimize ocular drug absorption.

Another important factor in determining corneal penetration of drugs is the drug binding to the proteins such as albumin, globulin, and lysozyme, which are present in tears. Bound drugs cannot penetrate the cornea because of the size of the protein molecule. Drug binding to the protein in the conjunctiva decreases the drug available for corneal absorption, and some inflammatory conditions increase the number of proteins in the tears, which increases the drug protein binding. The sclera is another route through which some drugs can penetrate to reach the inner structure of the eye, especially for drugs with low corneal permeability. In vitro studies have shown that the main mechanism of scleral penetration is by diffusion across the intercellular aqueous space [5].

Conventional drug formulations administered to the eye include liquid solutions and suspension as well as ointments. It is critical that ophthalmic drug products be sterile, non-immunogenic, and pyrogen free to avoid infection, allergic response, or inflammation. Additionally, ophthalmic drug products should be isotonic to avoid eye irritation and stinging.

A major challenge for the ocular route of drug administration is tear production. The tears form a thin layer of fluids that bathe the corneal surface and the conjunctiva to provide nutrition for the cornea, to protect against bacterial infections, and to clear any cell debris and foreign substances. Drugs administered to the eye can be diluted and rapidly cleared from the eye by the tears which shorten the drug contact time with the eye. This may necessitate frequent drug administration to the eye to maintain adequate pharmacologic effects. A limited number of drug products are also formulated as polymeric inserts under the eyelids or as contact lenses for controlled drug delivery for prolonged periods. Several additional approaches have been shown to influence the retention of the drug formulation on the eye to counteract this rapid clearance. These factors include proper administration technique, administration volume, formulation viscosity, and drug release rates [4].

The proper way of administering eye drops should be by gently pulling the lower lid from the eye to form a pocket to receive the drug product. When the eyelid is released, some drug is usually entrapped between the eyelid and the sclera to prolong drug contact time with the sclera. The drug contact time with the eye can be increased further by eyelid closure for a short time and gentle ocular movement. Administration of large volumes also increases the rate of tear formation which rapidly clears the drug from its site of administration. Often, administration of small volumes may require formulation with high drug concentrations that may represent tonicity or solubilization challenges. Ophthalmic formulations usually include preservatives to prevent microbial growth in multiple dose containers. The most commonly used preservative in ophthalmic formulations is benzalkonium chloride at a concentration of 0.01% although other preservatives can also be used. At higher preservative concentrations, irritation and increased tear formation may occur leading to faster drug clearance.

Ophthalmic liquid dosage forms cannot maintain high local drug concentrations because of their short contact times with the eye. The contact time of eye drops can be increased through the addition of polymers that can increase the formulation viscosity, such as methylcellulose and polyvinyl alcohol. Ointments are also used as ophthalmic dosage forms, but they are not as acceptable as eye drops because they may cause blurred vision after application. Ophthalmic ointments are used in pediatric patients, for overnight use, and when the eye is covered by a bandage. Ointments have the advantage of prolonged contact time with the eye. Other topically applied ophthalmic formulations include aqueous drug suspensions. The particle size of these suspensions is an important factor affecting drug retention on the eye since larger particles can cause irritation and increase the rate of drug removal with the tears. Novel sustained-release devices for ocular drug administration have been used to maintain adequate drug concentration for an extended time. Soft contact lenses can be used as a drug reservoir that releases a drug in a controlled manner. The drug can be introduced to the lens by soaking the lens in a drug solution before use or by installing drops of drug solution while using the lens. Polymeric inserts have also been formulated to be inserted under the eyelid, where they can dissolve or disintegrate while gradually releasing the drug. These inserts have been used for the ocular delivery of a drug for an extended period of time.

Treatment of intraocular diseases using topical drug application on the eye or systemic drug administration usually cannot achieve therapeutic drug concentration in the vitreous body. Topically applied drugs are usually removed rapidly by the efficient clearance mechanism of the eye, while systemically administered drugs usually have limited intraocular distribution, which requires the administration of large doses that can increase the drug systemic side effects. Intravitreal injection of drugs is the main route of delivery of drugs for the treatment of ophthalmic conditions that affect the posterior segment of the eye. After intravitreal injection, the drug can diffuse through the vitreous body, where the drug is cleared with aqueous humor drainage or through the retina by active secretion. Drugs that are mainly cleared from the eye with aqueous humor drainage usually have a residence time of about 20 h in the eye, whereas drugs mainly cleared through the transretinal route usually have a residence time of 5–10 h. Since most of intraocular diseases are usually chronic in nature, repeated intravitreal injections may be required to maintain therapeutic drug concentration in the eye. Alternatively, pharmaceutical formulations such as liposomes and nanoparticles have been developed to increase drug residence time in the eye after intravitreal injection. Parenteral liposomal amphotericin B formulations have been shown to have a longer residence time in the eye and less intraocular toxicity compared to the free amphotericin B formulation when administered intravitreally for the treatment of fungal eye infections. Nanoparticles made of erodible polymers provide a potential formulation strategy that can slowly release the drug in the eye, which increases the residence time of the drug in the eye. Intraocular devices or implants that can release the drug at a constant rate over an extended period of time have been developed for the treatment of diseases that require treatment for a long time to avoid the need to repeat intravitreal injections. Vitrasert is a commercially available sustained-release ganciclovir formulation approved for the treatment of cytomegalovirus infections of the eye.

19.5 Auricular (otic) drug administration

Drug administration to the ear is very similar to transdermal drug delivery in that the ears are specialized skin and soft-tissue structures. The ear is composed of three parts: the external ear, the middle ear, and the inner ear. The external ear is a skin-covered cartilaginous structure that collects and funnels sounds down the ear canal. The middle ear includes the tympanic membrane and auditory ossicles that transmit sound to the inner ear. The inner ear contains the structures involved in the transfer of fluid sound waves to nerve signals and for balance and the Eustachian tubes that allow auricular communication with the sinuses.

The ear has poor blood perfusion and is unlikely to promote systemic drug absorption following topical instillation of otic drug products. As a result, most dosage forms intended for auricular administration are for the topical treatment of ear conditions. Common dosage forms include aqueous and oily solutions and suspensions as well as semisolid formulations such as ointments, creams, and lotions. Formulations administered to the ear are unlikely to encounter mucous membranes, which limit the concerns regarding formulation tonicity, sterility, immunogenicity, and pyrogenicity. More variability in drug product formulations and excipients is permissible than for parenteral or ophthalmic preparations. As a result, otic formulations must not be used in the eye. However, ophthalmic drug products may be used in the ear.

19.6 Nasal drug administration

The external openings of the nose are known as nostrils, and the nasal cavity extends backward into the nasopharynx, which then leads to the trachea and esophagus. The nose is the principal entrance of air to the body for respiration. The main functions of the nose are to filter, warm, and moisten the inspired air. The nasal cavity is covered with a layer of mucous membrane with projections that can remove large particles and debris from inspired air. The blood supply of the nasal cavity helps in warming the inspired air while the fluids secreted by the glands and cells covering the nasal cavity humidify the inspired air. The average pH of the fluid lining the nasal cavity ranges from 6.2 to 6.4 [4].

The epithelial layer in the nasal cavity has ciliated microvilli, which increase the surface area available for drug absorption in the nasal cavity. The nasal cavity is also supplied by the lymphatic system, which is also involved in the absorption of drugs after nasal administration. The nasal epithelium is covered with a thin layer of mucus, which is renewed every 10 min by the secretions of the mucosal cells and glands. The ciliated epithelial cells also facilitate the clearance of deposited particles toward the back of the nasal cavity, where they can be swallowed or forwarded to be expelled by sneezing. The action of the ciliated epithelium and mucous layer can significantly limit drug absorption from the nasal cavity due to nasal drug clearance before the drug can be absorbed [4].

Nasal drug administration can be utilized for systemic drug delivery as well as local drug effects. Drug absorption from the nasal cavity is usually rapid and occurs mainly by passive diffusion or through epithelial pores. However, nasal drug absorption can be variable and erratic. Systemic drug concentrations after nasal administration typically increase rapidly and can achieve relatively high values. Nasal administration bypasses hepatic first-pass metabolism. However, drugs removed from the nasal cavity by mucociliary clearance can be ingested and then absorbed from the gastrointestinal tract.

The rate and extent of drug absorption after nasal drug administration are affected by drug retention in the nasal cavity and the significance of nasal drug clearance through mucociliary elimination. Longer drug retention in the nasal cavity can result from appropriate methods of drug administration and specialized formulation design to reduce the rate of mucous clearance. Physicochemical and formulation factors such as the volume of the drug solution per drug dose, drug concentration, particle density, and solution viscosity can also affect the rate and extent of drug absorption after nasal administration.

Different dosage forms can be administered to the nose, including solutions, suspensions, emulsions, and dry powders. The appropriate method of drug administration to the nose is product specific based on the formulation and method of application. Some drug products are instilled as liquid drops and require proper head positioning and dropper positioning within the nostrils. Other nasal products are spray pumps, actuators, or dry powder nasal inhalers that require patient coordination with the device orientation and breathing for proper droplet or particle deposition in the nasal cavity.

Poor nasal administration technique can lead to premature drug deposition in the nasal cavity which could promote rapid mucociliary clearance. Strategies used for improving drug absorption after nasal drug administration include modification of the formulation pH, use of a penetration enhancer, and prolongation of the nasal residence time [6]. The formulation pH can be adjusted to keep the active drug in the unionized form, which can be absorbed better than the ionized form across the nasal mucosa. Penetration enhancers such as bile salts, EDTA, and fatty acids have been utilized to increase the paracellular absorption of drugs from the nasal mucosa. Increasing the formulation viscosity or using bioadhesive formulations can significantly prolong the transit time of the drug administered in the nasal cavity, which can lead to increasing the extent of drug absorption.

19.7 Pulmonary drug administration

Pulmonary drug administration and the anatomical features of the lung were explained in detail in Chapter 11. Briefly, inhaled drugs are administered to the respiratory system through gases, fine liquid droplets, or solid particles. Pulmonary drug administration is also device specific with substantial differences between formulations, devices, and proper administration techniques. The administered drug can deposit in different parts of the respiratory tract, where the drug may exert local effects, or be absorbed into the circulation to produce systemic effects. Formulation and physiological factors can significantly influence the drug deposition patterns. For solid and liquid inhaled particles, the aerosol particle size distribution is an important parameter in determining pulmonary drug deposition. Typically, particles with an average aerodynamic particle size of 1–5 μm have optimal drug deposition in the deep lung. Pulmonary pathological conditions can also affect the deposition patterns.

Pulmonary drug deposition in the deep lungs can lead to very rapid rates of drug absorption due to the extremely large alveolar surface area, thin alveolar epithelial membranes, and high blood perfusion rate. Drugs absorbed from the lungs bypass the hepatic first-pass metabolism. Although systemic drug absorption will likely take place following inhalation, pulmonary administration can be used for local drug effect in the respiratory system to minimize systemic drug exposure. For example, inhaled corticosteroids have been used to avoid the side effects of systemically administered corticosteroids. During the administration of formulations intended for pulmonary drug delivery, a fraction of the administered dose is often deposited in the mouth and the upper part of the respiratory tract, where it can be swallowed for further systemic absorption from the gastrointestinal system [7].

19.8 Oral drug administration

The process of oral absorption was discussed in Chapter 18. Briefly, the oral route of drug administration is a very convenient route of administration, with the majority of all marketed drugs administered by this route. Most orally administered drugs are intended to produce systemic effects following their absorption to the systemic circulation. Drugs can be absorbed from several locations within the gastrointestinal tract, such as the buccal cavity, stomach, small intestine, large intestine (colon), and rectum. These segments of the gastrointestinal tract have different anatomical and physiological characteristics that can affect drug absorption. Formulation strategies can also be used to design orally administered dosage forms that can target specific segments and optimize the rate and extent of drug absorption as described in Chapter 17.

19.8.1 The buccal cavity

The buccal cavity includes the spaces or gaps in the cheek adjacent to the mouth and extends from the lips to the oropharynx. The oral mucosa lines the buccal cavity and consists of a multilayered epithelial lining that includes the basement membrane, the lamina propria, and a layer of connective tissues supplied by blood vessels and nerves. Saliva is continuously secreted in the mouth at a slow rate that increases in the presence or smelling of food. The pH of the saliva ranges from 6.2 to 7.4, and it consists of water, mucus, protein, minerals, and the enzyme amylase. The buccal cavity is a good site for drug absorption due to its rich blood supply and substantial lymphatic drainage, which can lead to fast absorption and rapid drug effect [8]. Drugs absorbed into buccal capillaries drain into the jugular vein and escape hepatic first-pass metabolism. For a drug to be absorbed in the buccal cavity, it must dissolve in the saliva and then diffuse through the buccal mucosa. Dissolved or undissolved drugs that are not buccally absorbed will pass into the esophagus for possible absorption from other parts of the gastrointestinal tract.

Several factors can limit the buccal absorption of drugs. Drug absorption through the buccal mucosa is mainly by passive diffusion with little paracellular absorption, active transport, and endocytosis, which is favorable for absorbing lipophilic drugs that are not ionized in the buccal pH. Polar drugs usually have limited buccal absorption, whereas highly lipophilic drugs usually have limited solubility in the saliva and will not be absorbed from the buccal cavity. Also, the small surface area of the buccal cavity and the short transit time through the mouth usually limit drug absorption from the buccal cavity. Furthermore, there are differences in drug absorption from the different areas in the oral cavity. For example, drug absorption from the sublingual area is usually better than drug absorption from the mucous membrane lining the cheeks and the periodontal area. Drug formulations intended for buccal drug delivery should be designed to be retained in the buccal cavity for optimal drug absorption.

Sublingual tablets are rapidly dissolving tablets placed under the tongue to achieve a fast rate of drug absorption. This fast rate of drug absorption makes sublingual tablets suitable for the treatment of acute conditions when fast onset of drug effect is required. Sublingual nitrate tablets have been used for many decades in the treatment of acute ischemic heart events. Also, medicated chewable formulations can be used to prolong the drug transit time in the buccal cavity and increase drug absorption. The rate of drug release from chewable tablets is dependent on the drug-water solubility, with water-soluble drugs released faster than poorly soluble drugs. Slowly released drugs usually have a better chance of absorption from the buccal cavity. Chewable formulations can also be used to produce a local effect as in the treatment of dental conditions and for antifungal therapy. Mucoadhesive dosage forms have been used to retain the formulation in the buccal cavity for a prolonged time to increase the extent of drug absorption. These formulations usually utilize polymers that can adhere to the mucosal surface of the buccal cavity and slowly release the drug over an extended period of time. Bioadhesive formulations have been used for nitroglycerin and also for the local anesthetic drug lidocaine [9].

19.8.2 Esophagus

The esophagus is the gastrointestinal tract segment connecting the pharynx to the stomach. It is a muscular tube, approximately 25 cm in length in adults, and has a pH value of approximately 6–7. The typical transit time for most pharmaceutical dosage forms in the esophagus is about 15 s. Any drug administered orally must pass through the esophagus when it is swallowed. However, drugs are not absorbed from the esophagus because of the short transit time, thick mucosal lining, and limited surface area.

19.8.3 Stomach

The stomach is located in the left upper part of the abdominal cavity and is attached to the esophagus by the cardiac sphincter and the duodenum by the pyloric sphincter. The inner surface of the stomach is a thick, vascular, and glandular mucosa that is covered by a layer of mucus secreted by the epithelial lining. The gastric mucus is principally composed of glycoproteins that lubricate and facilitate the movement of food through the stomach. The gastric epithelium produces approximately 1.5 L of secretions per day that are rich in hydrochloric acid and enzymes. The mucous layer also protects the gastric epithelium from the low pH (approximately 1−3) and proteolytic enzymes present in the stomach [10]. The gastric pH depends on many factors including acid secretion, gastric contents, gender, and age. After eating, the gastric pH usually increases due to the buffering and neutralizing effects of food. Generally, women have slightly higher gastric pH compared to men [11]. Furthermore, older individuals have been shown to have more gastric secretions and lower gastric pH compared to younger individuals [12].

The stomach usually has a limited role in the absorption of orally administered conventional dosage forms because of the small surface area and the relatively short transit time. The gastric transit time is especially short if the dosage form is administered on an empty stomach. The low gastric pH can affect the absorption of acid-labile drugs and ionizable drug molecules. The rate of drug dissolution is also affected by the pH of the gastric contents with basic drugs dissolving faster in the acidic pH of the stomach and getting ready to be absorbed once they leave the stomach and reach the small intestine. Furthermore, the gastric pH affects the ionization of drugs with weak acids usually present in the unionized form that can be absorbed better in the acidic pH of the stomach.

The gastric emptying rate is the rate at which stomach contents move from the stomach into the small intestine. It is an important factor in determining the rate of drug absorption because the small intestine is the main site of absorption for orally administered drugs. In general, the stomach undergoes multiphase cycles, which cause gradual emptying of the gastric contents into the duodenum. When a drug is administered on an empty stomach, the gastric emptying rate is rapid, and the drug reaches the small intestine faster. However, when the drug is taken with food, it is usually mixed with the gastric contents and then emptied from the stomach at the same rate as the gastric contents.

Typically, food slows the gastric emptying rate which is influenced by the meal consistency, composition, and size [13]. Liquids and low-viscosity food are emptied from the stomach faster than solid and high-viscosity food [14]. Furthermore, meals with higher calories per volume and fat-rich meals slow the rate of gastric emptying. The gastric emptying rate is also affected by drugs and diseases. Narcotic analgesics and drugs with anticholinergic effects can significantly slow the gastric emptying rate, whereas prokinetic drugs can speed the gastric emptying rate. Diseases such as pyloric stenosis, gastroenteritis, and gastroesophageal reflux can slow the gastric emptying rate resulting in slower drug absorption. Modifying the gastric emptying rate of the dosage form is one of the strategies that can be used to affect the rate of drug absorption after oral administration.

The rate and extent of drug absorption after oral administration are affected by the acidic environment of the stomach and the gastric contents. Specialized dosage forms can be used to optimize drug absorption, either by protecting the drug from the effect of the acidic gastric secretions or controlling the drug release from the dosage form and hence the rate of drug absorption. Enteric-coated tablets are usually used to protect acid labile drugs from the acidic environment of the stomach and deliver the drug to the small intestine. These tablets are usually coated with an acid-resistant material that keeps the tablet intact while going through the stomach. The tablet coat dissolves in the alkaline medium of the small intestine, and drug absorption starts once the tablet reaches the small intestine. In this case, the onset of drug absorption will be dependent on the gastric emptying rate, which differs depending on whether the drug is administered on an empty stomach or after a meal.

Other dosage forms can be designed to remain in the stomach and gradually release the drug over a prolonged period of time. This approach can be useful when the drug is intended for the treatment of a stomach condition, such as in the treatment of *Helicobacter pylori* infections. Gastric retention of dosage forms can also be used to formulate controlled-release formulations for drugs with site-specific absorption in the upper segment of the small intestine to improve the extent of their absorption. The retention of the dosage forms in the stomach can be achieved through several approaches, including mucoadhesion through the incorporation of polymers that adhere to the mucous lining. Mucoadhesion protects the dosage form from emptying with the gastric content into the small intestine, and the drug is slowly released from the dosage form [15]. Floating tablets are low-density formulations that can absorb water and swell once they come in contact with the gastric contents. Because of the low density of the floating formulations, these tablets remain floating on top of the gastric contents and slowly release the drug over a prolonged period of time [16]. Formulations that expand or unfold when they reach the stomach and become too large to exit through the pylorus have been used to prolong the formulation retention in the stomach. The effect of gastric retention of dosage forms in the stomach on the rate and extent of drug absorption depends on the drug's physicochemical characteristics, stability, and the mechanism of drug absorption.

19.8.4 Small intestine

The small intestine is approximately 6 m long, and it is abruptly divided into three segments that have different absorption capacities. The first segment that follows the stomach is the duodenum, and it is about 20–30 cm; the following 2.5 m is called the jejunum; and the last 3.5-m segment represents the ileum. The small intestine wall is formed of several layers: the outermost layer is the serosa, followed by a layer of longitudinal muscles, and a layer of circular muscles that play an important role in the peristaltic movement of the intestine. These muscular layers are followed by a layer of connective tissues forming the submucosa and then the mucosa, which consists of several layers of cells that end with the epithelium. The epithelium layer consists mainly of a single layer of columnar cells, or the enterocytes, which cover all the inner surface of the small intestine. Other cells in the epithelial layer can secrete mucus and a variety of enzymes, hormones, and peptides. The small intestine has the folds of Kerckring, which extend most of the way into the lumen. The inner surface of the small intestine is covered with finger-like structures known as the villi, and the microvilli, which are small projections on the apical surface of the epithelial cells that are directed to the lumen of the intestine as presented in Fig. 19.3.

The folds of Kerckring, villi, and microvilli increase the absorptive surface area of the small intestine to about 600 times that of a cylinder with the same diameter. This large surface area makes the small intestine the major site of absorption for most orally administered drugs. During the absorption process, the drug is transferred to the blood supply of the small intestine, which drains into the portal vein that passes the blood to the liver. Highly lipophilic compounds and fats can be absorbed from the small intestine by the lymphatic system [4].

The epithelial permeability to small ions and water-soluble molecules is greater in the duodenum and jejunum compared to the ileum. The reason is due to the presence of numerous larger aqueous pores in the upper segment of the small intestine compared to the lower segment. Also, the surface area per unit length in the proximal segment of the small intestine is much higher than that of the distal segment, and the proximal segment has more carrier-mediated transport systems [4]. Moreover, more commensal bacteria are present in the ileum compared to the duodenum and jejunum. The pH in the lumen of the different intestinal segments ranges from 6 to 6.5 in the duodenum, and 7 to 8 in the other parts of the small intestine [17]. The microenvironment of the mucosal fluid adjacent to the intestinal epithelium has a pH of 4.5–6.0 which allows the absorption of weak acids in the small intestine. This pH causes the ionization of weak bases and suggests poor absorption of weak bases in the small intestine, which is not the case.

A fraction of the drug dose may be lost in the gastrointestinal tract lumen during the absorption process by degradation, metabolism, or excretion in the feces, which reduces the amount of the drug available to be absorbed. The gut wall contains a variety of drug-metabolizing enzymes and transporters that allow only a fraction of the drug in the

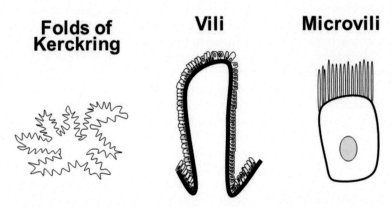

FIGURE 19.3   Intestinal structures that increases the absorption surface area.

gastrointestinal tract lumen to be absorbed into the portal vein. The drugs in the portal vein are delivered to the liver, where they can be metabolized or excreted in bile, thus allowing only a fraction of the drug absorbed to reach the systemic circulation [18]. The bioavailability of the drug after oral administration is the fraction of the administered dose that escapes degradation or metabolism during the absorption process and reaches the systemic circulation. All orally administered drugs are exposed to the previously mentioned conditions that can cause drug loss during the absorption process before they reach the systemic circulation, which is known as presystemic elimination. The extent of presystemic elimination of different drugs is different depending on the susceptibility of the drugs to the degradation and metabolism before reaching the systemic circulation. It can be minimal, causing a large fraction of the drug dose to reach the systemic circulation, or it can be large, allowing only a small fraction of the administered dose to reach the systemic circulation. Some drugs are not administered orally due to their extensive presystemic elimination after oral administration.

The enterocytes of the small intestine contain several transport systems that play an important role in drug absorption, such as the p-glycoprotein (P-gp) transport system. The P-gp transport is an efflux transporter localized on the apical side of the epithelial cells, which can transport a wide variety of drugs outside the epithelial cell back to the intestinal lumen. The extent of absorption of the drugs that are substrates for the P-gp can be low because this transport system acts as a barrier for their absorption. Since drugs that are substrates for the P-gp can compete for this transporter, drug interaction can result from the administration of multiple drugs that are substrates for the same transport system. The small intestine also contains a variety of metabolizing enzymes that can metabolize many drugs, reducing the extent of their absorption. Since the drug-metabolizing enzymes can be inhibited and induced, drug interaction that affects the extent of drug absorption can result from the administration of enzyme inhibitors or inducers with drugs that undergo extensive presystemic metabolism [19].

The time the drug spends in the small intestine before it reaches the colon, known as the intestinal transit time, is an important factor affecting drug absorption. The average time from drug administration until it reaches the colon is between 6 and 8 h, and can vary depending on the presence of food, diseases, administration of other drugs, and dosage form characteristics [20]. Dosage forms administered on an empty stomach pass through the small intestine much faster than when administered with food.

Conditions such as constipation and intestinal obstruction usually prolong the intestinal transit time, whereas diarrhea and irritable bowel syndrome can shorten the transit time. Drugs such as narcotic analgesics and drugs with anticholinergic activity prolong the intestinal transit time, whereas prokinetic drugs such as metoclopramide shorten the intestinal transit time. Dosage forms designed to release the drug over a period of more than 8 h have to be retained in the small intestine during the period of drug release, or the drug has to be absorbed in the large intestine to ensure complete absorption.

In general, the absorption of most drugs after administration of conventional dosage forms, including solutions, suspensions, capsules, and tablets, occurs in the small intestine. The drug in solution dosage forms is ready to be absorbed once it reaches the site of its absorption, whereas suspended drugs have to dissolve first before they can be absorbed. Immediate-release solid dosage forms such as capsules and tablets have to disintegrate and then dissolve in the gastrointestinal tract before the drug can be absorbed. This makes the general order of drug absorption rate solution > suspension > capsule > tablets. Modified-release formulations are formulations with a slow rate of drug release, which slows the rate of drug absorption and maintains therapeutic drug concentrations for an extended period of time during multiple drug administration of these formulations. The transit time of the dosage forms in the gastrointestinal tract is an important factor affecting the time over which the drug can be absorbed, indicating that the dosage form characteristics are important in determining the rate and extent of drug absorption.

19.8.5 Large intestine

The large intestine is the section of the gastrointestinal tract that follows the small intestine, and it consists of the cecum; ascending, transverse, descending, and sigmoid colon; rectum; and anus. It is about 130 cm long and has a larger diameter than that of the small intestine. The mucosa of the large intestine has the same structural features of the small intestine, but it does not have villi and microvilli, which result in a much smaller surface area compared with that of the small intestine. The pH of the large intestine contents is approximately 6.5 [21]. The metabolic activity in the wall of the large intestine is very low, but the lumen of the large intestine has many aerobic and anaerobic bacteria that have digestive and metabolic functions and can cause drug degradation. The blood supply to the large intestine, except for the lower part of the rectum, drains into the portal circulation that takes the blood to the liver. Most of the drug absorption from the large intestine is through transmucosal passive diffusion and paracellular absorption because there is no documented active transport system in the large intestine. The transit time through the large intestine is very long, which compensates for the small surface area and allows more drug absorption. The average transit time in the large intestine is approximately 14 h, which can be prolonged by high dietary fiber intake [22].

Other factors that can prolong the large intestine transit time include drugs such as narcotic analgesics and anticholinergic drugs. Drug absorption in the large intestine mainly occurs in the cecum and ascending colon, where the contents are less viscous and contain more water compared to the other parts of the large intestine. The gradual absorption of water makes the contents of the distal sections of the large intestine more viscous, which slows drug solubility and decreases the chance of the drug coming into contact with the absorption surface. Dosage forms intended for colonic drug delivery have to target the proximal part of the colon.

Drug delivery to the colon can be to treat local colon disease, such as in the case of treating inflammatory diseases and infections, or to treat systemic disease when the drug can be absorbed from the colon into the systemic circulation. Formulations designed for colonic drug delivery have to be protected from the effect of the acidic and alkaline secretions and the digestive enzymes in the stomach and small intestine, and then release the drug in the ascending colon. Several strategies have been utilized to deliver the drug to the colon, including the use of an acid-resistant coating that keeps the formulation intact in the acidic contents of the stomach. Then, controlling the drug release to start about 4 h after leaving the stomach can allow the release of the drug at approximately the time when the formulation reaches the base of the ascending colon [23]. Other formulations take advantage of the colonic bacteria by including prodrugs that can be hydrolyzed by the colonic bacteria and liberate the active drug in the colon, such as the use of salicylazosulfapyridine for the treatment of inflammatory bowel disease [24]. Additionally, formulations have been coated with polymers that can be hydrolyzed by the colonic bacteria and release the drug when the formulation reaches the colon. The onset of drug absorption after administration of colonic delivery systems is usually delayed and depends on the gastric and intestinal transit times.

19.9 Rectal drug administration

The rectum is the final segment of the large intestine and can be utilized for drug administration in the form of suppositories or enemas. Suppositories are solid dosage forms that usually melt or dissolve in the rectum to release the drug, whereas enemas are liquid dosage forms in which the drug is dissolved or suspended in the vehicle. Rectal drug administration is a convenient route of administration for elderly, young, and unconscious patients, especially when oral drug administration is not possible and parenteral formulations are not available. Because of the limited fluids available in the rectum, the drug is not diluted after rectal administration, and drug absorption is usually transcellular by passive diffusion or paracellular through the aqueous pores. After rectal administration, the absorbed drug can escape the first-pass hepatic metabolism if the drug is administered to the lower part of the rectum because the venous return from this part of the rectum does not go through the portal circulation [25].

The rate of drug absorption after rectal drug administration is usually dependent on the rate of drug release from the dosage form. Because of the small area of the absorptive surface of the rectum, the relatively short rectal transit time, and the limited spreading of the rectally administered drugs to the colon, rapid drug release from the rectal formulation is preferred. The high concentration of the drug produced in the rectum, due to the rapid drug release from the dosage form and the limited dilution with the rectal contents, produces the driving force of drug absorption after rectal administration because most of the drug absorption in the rectum is by passive diffusion. When the drug is formulated in the form of suppositories, the base that provides faster release is usually selected. Hydrophilic drugs are released faster from lipophilic bases and slower from hydrophilic bases, whereas lipophilic drugs are released faster from hydrophilic bases and slower from lipophilic bases. This is because the solubility of hydrophilic drugs in hydrophilic bases and the solubility of lipophilic drugs in lipophilic bases usually slow the rate of drug release from the dosage forms [26].

The physicochemical properties of the drug are important in determining the drug solubility in the contents of the rectum, and hence the drug absorption. Highly lipophilic drugs have poor solubility in the limited volume of aqueous fluids in the rectum, whereas highly hydrophilic drugs have very limited diffusivity across biological membranes. So, balanced lipophilic and hydrophilic drug properties are necessary for optimal drug absorption after rectal drug administration. Other factors that can affect rectal drug absorption include the drug particle size, which affects the rate of drug dissolution. Also, the surface properties of the drug particles and the drug load per unit dose can cause particle agglomeration, leading to a slower drug dissolution rate and causing unequal drug distribution in the dosage forms. The *in vitro* release of the drug from the dosage forms is useful for quality control purposes, but they have limited predictive value for *in vivo* formulation performance, and the human *in vivo* studies are still the most reliable method for evaluating the rate and extent of drug absorption after rectal administration of dosage forms.

19.10 Vaginal drug administration

The vagina is a fibromuscular tube that is part of the birth canal in females. The vaginal mucosa is a stratified squamous epithelium with several layers of epithelial cells that are attached together with desmosomes and tight junctions. The mucosa is followed by two layers of longitudinal and circular muscles that are covered with connective tissues supplied by blood vessels, lymph ducts, and nerves. Vaginal secretions vary in viscosity during different phases of the menstrual cycle.

Vaginal drug administration has been used mainly for the treatment of local conditions such as inflammation and infections and also for the administration of contraceptive agents. The vagina can be a route for systemic drug delivery due to a permeable and highly vascularized epithelium. However, drug absorption following vaginal administration can be highly variable due to variable epithelial and musculature thicknesses during the different stages of the menstrual cycle. The permeability of steroid hormones through the vaginal mucosa has been shown to be widely variable during the different stages of the menstrual cycle in experimental animals [27]. Other factors that can affect the absorption after vaginal drug administration include secretions, personal hygiene, and the nature of the dosage forms.

Solutions, suspensions, and foams can spread much better than tablets or capsules when administered to the vagina. Creams, foams, and jellies are the most commonly used formulations for the delivery of topical drug products for local effects but are less appealing due to leakage of the dosage form after application. Tablets and suppositories for vaginal insertion are usually formulated to dissolve or melt after application, thereby releasing the drug. Medicated sponges made of polyester resins have also been used for vaginal drug administration. Polymeric rings have also been formulated for controlled drug delivery to the systemic circulation following vaginal administration. Mucoadhesive tablets and particles have also been used for the sustained delivery of drugs for the treatment of local vaginal disorders. Some intrauterine implants and devices have been used for controlled drug delivery.

19.11 Conclusions

Drugs are administered by different routes with each route having different characteristics that can affect the absorption of drugs. The specific characteristics of the different routes of administration are used in conjunction with the drug physicochemical properties and stability information to design dosage forms that are suitable for each route. When the drugs are used, the choice of the route of administration is dependent on many factors including the physiological conditions for each route including the local pH, presence of enzymes, the absorption surface characteristics, and if the absorption involves presystemic metabolism. Also, the physicochemical properties of the drug including solubility, dissolution rate, and stability. Furthermore, the drug release rate form the dosage form, the mechanism of drug absorption, and the rate of absorption from the site of administration. This is in addition to the condition being treated whether acute or chronic, and the patient age and health status that are important in selecting the dosage forms and the route of drug administration.

Case studies

Case 19.1

Dobutamine is an inotropic agent used by IV infusion in emergency cases. When administered as IV infusions, the range of doses is usually 2.5–10 ug/kg/min. You were asked to calculate the infusion rate of dobutamine 2.5 ug/kg/min in a patient whose weight is 70 kg.

Approach: Dobutamine is supplied as 50 mL vials with concentration of 5 mg/mL.

Dobutamine administration rate in 70 kg patient = 2.5 ug/kg/min × 70 kg = 175 ug/min

Dobutamine administration rate = 175 ug/min × 60 min/h = 10.5 mg/h

The infusion rate of the infusion solution = 10.5 mg/h/5 mg/mL = 2.1 mL/h
The infusion rate can be increased or decreased to change dobutamine administration rate.

Case 19.2

Nitroglycerin is a vasodilator used for the management of ischemic heart disease. It is formulated as sublingual tablets for the treatment of acute ischemic attacks and as transdermal patches for the management of chronic ischemic heart diseases. Please discuss the rationale for using the two formulations by the different routes of administration.

Approach: Nitroglycerin is a vasodilator that has a short half-life and undergoes extensive presystemic metabolism. Also, repeated administration of nitroglycerin can result in the development of tolerance and decrease in the vasodilatation effect of nitroglycerin. If nitroglycerin is administered as conventional oral tablet, most of the administered dose undergoes presystemic metabolism. The small fraction of dose that reaches the systemic circulation will be eliminated rapidly due to nitroglycerin short half-life leading to short duration of effect.

In acute ischemic heart attack administration of sublingual nitroglycerin tablets results in rapid absorption of nitroglycerin. The absorbed nitroglycerin escapes the presystemic metabolism and produces its vasodilatation effect to relieve the ischemic attack symptoms.

Transdermal nitroglycerin patches are designed to release nitroglycerin at a very slow rate over a long time. The released nitroglycerin is absorbed into the systemic circulation and achieves steady nitroglycerin systemic concentration as long as the transdermal patch is applied on the skin which produces a vasodilatation effect. The patients are usually instructed to remove the transdermal patch at night before sleeping to allow a nitroglycerin-free period. This is important to prevent the development of tolerance to the effect of nitroglycerin.

Case 19.3

Treatment of diseases of the eye posterior segment has not been successful using topical and systematic drug delivery. This is due to the limited drug delivery to the eye posterior segment after these routes of administration. This led to the development of other strategies for the delivery of drugs to the posterior eye segments. Discuss some of these strategies.

Approach: Several strategies have been developed to increase drug delivery to the posterior segment of the eye. This includes:

- **Intravitreal injections** are formulated in small volumes (25–100 μL) of the sterile drug by an experienced physician. These injections have good efficacy and safety, but in chronic diseases upon repeated administration, they may cause intraocular side effects.
- **Intravitreal implants** are used to avoid multiple injections and their associated complications and patient's discomfort. Intraocular implantable drug delivery system is developed to provide an extended and controlled drug release over prolong time. These implants are inserted into the vitreous chamber surgically through a minor incision, so it is still considered as an invasive technique. However, due to its advantage of providing sustained release over a prolonged time, the frequency of inserting the implants is less as compared to injections.

Case 19.4

Discuss the rationale for using enteric-coated tablets, and give examples of drugs that are suitable for formulation as enteric-coated tablets.

Approach: Acid labile drugs can be degraded by the acidic environment of the stomach when administered orally in the form of conventional formulations. Enteric coating has been used to deliver acid labile drugs to the small intestine by coating the formulation with an acid-resistant coat that can protect the formulation from the acidic pH of the stomach. Once in the alkaline environment of the small intestine, the coat dissolves releasing the drug in the small intestine. Same principle applies for highly gastic irritant drugs.

Examples of drugs formulated as enteric-coated tablets are omeprazole, diclofenac, erythromycin sulfasalazine, and bisacodyl.

Critical reflections and practice applications

There are many ways to administer a drug to a patient. A pharmacist is expected to make a recommendation for the route and site of drug administration so that the drug can reach its site of action in an appropriate time and concentration for optimal therapeutic outcomes as reflected below:

- Drugs are administered to produce local effects at the site of administration or to produce systemic effects after absorption into the systemic circulation.
- Factors that affect the absorption of drugs from their site of administration including the physiological and anatomical characteristics of the site of administration, the drug physicochemical properties, and the formulation characteristics can affect the rate and extent of drug absorption, and hence the onset and intensity of drug effects.
- Intravenous drug administration is the only route that guarantees 100% bioavailability, while drug administration by all other routes requires drug absorption to the systemic circulation which may or may not be complete.
- The rate of drug absorption after IM administration can be controlled by changing the formulation characteristics with the general rank of drug absorption rate after administration of aqueous solution > aqueous suspension > oily solution and emulsion > oily suspension > solid/semisolid implants.
- Transdermal delivery systems are designed to deliver potent drugs at a specific rate over an extended period of time to produce systemic effects such as nitrates in the management of ischemic heart diseases, scopolamine for motion sickness, and nicotine for smoking cessation.
- Ophthalmic drug administration is used to treat eye conditions by applying the drug solution, suspension, ointment, or polymeric inserts to the external eye. Also, by intraocular injection to the vitreous body or insertion of implants or drug-releasing devices used to treat diseases of the posterior segment of the eye.
- Drug absorption after intranasal administration is very rapid, escapes the first-pass effect, and achieves high systemic drug concentration providing that the drug is properly administered and the dosage form is retained in the nasal cavity and contains ingredients that can promote drug absorption.
- Pulmonary drug administration is mainly used for local drug effects on the respiratory system to avoid systemic side effects, with very few examples of drugs that can be administered for systemic effects.
- The oral route is the most commonly used route for the administration of drugs used for their systemic effects. Orally administered drugs pass through the different segments of the gastrointestinal tract that have different characteristics that can affect drug absorption from the different segments.
- Drug absorption from the buccal cavity is rapid and escapes the first-pass metabolism when the drugs are administered as sublingual tables that are retained under the tongue or chewable tablets that release the drug over a period of time.
- The small intestine is the main site for the absorption of most drugs after oral drug administration because of its massive surface area available for drug absorption.
- The gastric emptying rate is a major factor in determining the rate of drug absorption and is affected by food composition and consistency, diseases, and drugs.
- Colonic drug delivery is used to treat local colon conditions such as ulcerative colitis or inflammatory bowel diseases and can be achieved by controlling the rate of drug release, protecting the drug by a polymeric coating that can be hydrolyzed by the colonic bacteria, or prodrugs that can liberate the active drug after hydrolysis by the colonic bacteria.
- Rectal drug administration is useful for the administration of drugs in patients in which administration of other routes is not possible and the absence of parenteral drug dosage forms, such as in very young age, unconscious patients, and elderly.

References

[1] M.A. Hedaya, in: Basic Pharmacokinetics, second ed., CRC Press, Boca Raton, 2012.

[2] M. Katz, B.J. Poulsen, B.B. Brodie, J.R. Gilette, Absorption of drugs through the skinHandbook of experimental pharmacology, in: B.B. Brodie, J.R. Gilette (Eds.), Handbook of Experimental Pharmacology, Springer-Verlag, Berlin, 1971.

[3] V.V. Ranade, Drug delivery systems: 6. Transdermal drug delivery, J. Clin. Pharmacol. 31 (1991) 401—418.

[4] N. Washington, C. Washington, C.G. Wilson, Physiological Pharmaceutics, Barriers to Drug Absorption, second ed., Taylor&Francis, New York, 2001.

[5] I. Ahmed, R.D. Gokhale, M.V. Shah, T.F. Patton, Physicochemical determinations of drug diffusion across the conjunctiva, sclera and cornea, J. Pharmaceut. Sci. 76 (1987) 583—586.

[6] Y.W. Chien, K.S.E. Su, S. Chang, Y.W. Chien, Nasal systemic drug deliveryDrugs and the pharmaceutical sciences, in: Y.W. Chien (Ed.), Drugs and the Pharmaceutical Sciences, Marcel Dekker, New York, 1989.

[7] S.R. Walker, M.E. Evans, A.J. Richards, J.W. Paterson, The clinical pharmacology of oral and inhaled salbutamol, Clin. Pharmacol. Ther. 13 (1972) 861—867.

[8] C.A. Squier, N.W. Johnson, Permeability of the oral mucosa, Br. Med. Bull. 31 (1975) 169—175.

[9] T. Nagai, R. Konishi, Buccal/gingival drug delivery systems, J. Contr. Release 6 (1987) 353—360.

[10] G. McLaughlan, G.M. Fullarton, G.P. Crean, K.E.L. McColl, Comparison of gastric body and antral pH: a 24 hour ambulatory study in healthy volunteers, Gut 30 (1989) 573—578.

[11] M. Feldman, C. Barnett, Fasting gastric pH and its relationship to true hypochlorhydria in humans, Dig. Dis. Sci. 36 (1991) 866—869.

[12] M. Goldschmiedt, C. Barnett, B.E. Schwartz, Effect of age on gastric acid secretion and serum gastric concentration in healthy men and women, Gastroenterol. 101 (1991) 977—990.

[13] M. Feldman, H.J. Smith, T.R. Simon, Gastric emptying of solid radiopaque markers: studies in healthy subjects and diabetes patients, Gastroenterol. 87 (1984) 895—902.

[14] N.J. Hunt, M.T. Knox, A relation between the chain length of fatty acids and the slowing of gastric emptying, J. Physiol. 194 (1968) 327—336.

[15] S. Burton, N. Washington, R.J.C. Steele, R. Musson, L. Feely, Intragastric distribution of ion-exchange resins: a drug delivery system for the topical treatment of the gastric mucosa, J. Pharm. Pharmacol. 47 (1995) 901—906.

[16] H.M. Ingani, J. Timmermans, A.J. Moes, Concept and in vivo investigation of peroral sustained release floating dosage forms with enhanced gastrointestinal transit, Int. J. Pharm. (Amst.) 35 (1987) 157—164.

[17] J.G. Hardy, D.F. Evans, I. Zaki, A.G. Clark, H.H. Tennesen, O.N. Gamst, Evaluation of an enteric-coated naproxen tablet using gamma scintigraphy and pH monitoring, Int. J. Pharm. (Amst.) 37 (1987) 245—250.

[18] M. Rowland, L.Z. Benet, G.G. Graham, Clearance concepts in pharmacokinetics, J. Pharmacokinet. Biopharm. 1 (1973) 123—136.

[19] P. Watkins, The barrier function of CYP3A4 and P-glycoprotein in the small bowel, Adv. Drug Deliv. Rev. 27 (1997) 161—170.

[20] S.S. Davis, J.G. Hardy, J.W. Fara, Transit of pharmaceutical dosage forms through the small intestine, Gut 27 (1986) 886—892.

[21] D.F. Evans, G. Pye, R. Bramley, A.G. Clark, T.J. Dyson, J.D. Hardcastle, Measurement of gastrointestinal pH profiles in normal ambulant human subjects, Gut 29 (1988) 1035—1041.

[22] A.M. Metcalf, S.F. Phillips, A.R. Zinsmeister, R.L. MacCarty, R.W. Beart, B.G. Wolff, Simplified assessment of segmental colonic transit, Gastroenterol. 92 (1987) 40—47.

[23] M.J. Dew, P.J. Hughes, M.G. Lee, B.K. Evans, J. Rhodes, An oral preparation to release drugs in the human colon, Br. J. Clin. Pharmacol. 14 (1982) 405—408.

[24] A. Rubinstein, Microbially controlled drug delivery to the colon, Biopharm. Drug Dispos. 11 (1990) 465—487.

[25] A.G. DeBoer, D.D. Breimer, F.J. Pronk, J.M. Gubbens-Stibbe, Rectal bioavailability of lidocaine in rats: absence of significant first-pass elimination, J. Pharmaceut. Sci. 69 (1980) 804—807.

[26] A.G. DeBoer, F. Moolenaar, L.G.J. deLeede, D.D. Breimer, Rectal drug administration: clinical pharmacokinetic considerations, Clin. Pharmacokinet. 7 (1982) 285—311.

[27] J.L. Richardson, L. Illum, The vaginal route of peptide and protein drug delivery, Adv. Drug Deliv. Rev. 8 (1992) 341—366.

Index

Printed in the United States
by Baker & Taylor Publisher Services